ESSAYS IN CONTEXT

ESSAYS IN CONTEXT

❖

Sandra Fehl Tropp
Boston University

Ann Pierson D'Angelo
Boston University

New York   Oxford
Oxford University Press
2001

Oxford University Press

Oxford   New York
Athens   Auckland   Bangkok   Bagotá   Buenos Aires   Calcutta
Cape Town   Chennai   Dar es Salaam   Delhi   Florence   Hong Kong   Istanbul
Karachi   Kuala Lumpur   Madrid   Melbourne   Mexico City   Mumbai
Nairobi   Paris   São Paulo   Singapore   Taipei   Tokyo   Toronto   Warsaw

and associated companies in
Berlin   Ibadan

Copyright © 2001 by Oxford University Press, Inc.
Published by Oxford University Press, Inc.,
198 Madison Avenue, New York, New York 10016
http://www.oup-usa.org

Library of Congress Cataloging-in-Publication Data

Essays in context / edited by Sandra Fehl Tropp & Ann Pierson D'Angelo.
    p. cm.
  ISBN 0-19-511836-7 (alk. paper)
    1. College readers. 2. English language—Rhetoric—Problems, exercises, etc. 3. Report
writing—Problems, exercises, etc. I. Tropp, Sandra Fehl, 1944– II. Pierson-D'Angelo,
Ann, 1971–

  PE1417.E89 1000
  808′.0427-dc21   99-086330

Printing (last digit): 9 8 7 6 5 4 3 2 1
Printed in the United States of America
on acid-free paper

CONTENTS

THEMATIC TABLE OF CONTENTS

CONTROVERSY IN ACADEMIA

FAMILY

HUMAN NATURE

HUMOR

LANGUAGE: THEORY AND USAGE

LEARNING

LITERARY ESSAYS

LITERATURE

LITERATURE AND SCIENCE

SCIENTIFIC ESSAYS

WAR

PREFACE

Although many people contributed to the development of this text, its initial impetus came from senior Oxford editor, D. Anthony English. His knowledge of composition texts and his enthusiasm about this project reminded me of the pleasure and the pain of selecting a limited number of essays to create an anthology. I had truly enjoyed putting together *Shaping Tradition*, my first chronological collection by essayists from Montaigne to Tan. This time my goal was to select from a century's worth of essays pieces that fit together to complete a chronological reader of the twentieth century. Tony and I agreed that the text must present the essays as unique works in themselves but also as responses to the times and voices around them. Nearly two years into the project, I had read hundreds of essays, selected all but the last few choices, and written biographies, footnotes, and questions to accompany twenty-five of the essays selected. Clearly I needed help.

Tony hired Amy Kelly, pregnant with her first child, to complete the footnotes, and I convinced Ann Pierson D'Angelo, a graduate student on leave and about to get married, to become the second editor and write the remaining sixty biographies. She is also responsible for the inclusion in this text of Malcolm X's "Message to the Grassroots" and bell hooks's "Malcolm X: The Longed-for Feminist Manhood."

With three of us working steadily, and Tony tirelessly attentive to our every email, we still needed Ann's husband, Jason, and my husband, Marty, to finish the project. Jason and Marty both scoured the libraries for extra information on the authors and essays. Both helped with the photocopying. And, at the last minute, Marty added details to some of the earlier biographies.

In addition to selecting the essays, I wrote the introduction, the chapter on reading the essays, the questions, the themes and sequences, the timeline, and twenty-five of the biographies. I also reviewed Ann's biographies. Without Amy's footnotes and Ann's biographies, this anthology could not have been produced. As always, my greatest debt is to Marty, whose most important contribution is his encouragement and his confidence in me and in this project. No book is the work of one person alone. This one is truly a joint effort.

Sandra Fehl Tropp

When Sandy invited me to co-edit this anthology, she refused to hear any answer until I came to her house to see the library books, the photocopies, the Tables of Contents, the drafts of questions—in short, the project in all its magnitude. Since then, my own house has been overrun with source materials, and I have developed, for the first time in my life, a filing system. This book has been with Jason and me through some major moments, the stuff of our lives: getting married, leaving graduate school for good, losing loved ones, learning that we were going to have a child. It has also been a frankly inspirational experience, showing us the value of whims, the necessity of coincidence and inconvenience, and several other life lessons we dare not confess in public for fear of losing our reputations as seasoned cynics. Although I have not used life lessons to structure my biographies, I have made life itself, and all of the strange and interesting and daring ways in which people lead it, my central structuring principle. Authors are not always admirable; they are not even reliably likable. They are, however, human, and in their humanity they are fascinating. My experience in the classroom tells me that while fascination may not be essential to intellectual growth, it sure does help.

Many thanks to Sandy for her unflagging support. Thanks also to Nomi Sofer, Eric and Melanie Johnson-Debaufre, and Rob Hockberg. Jason knows the depth of my gratitude already; upon him, I bestow an honorary Master of Library Science.

Ann Pierson D'Angelo

ACKNOWLEDGMENTS

Thanks go to Harcourt, Brace, Jovanovich for allowing me to reprint from *Shaping Tradition* all or parts of the biographies of Mark Twain, George Orwell, Virginia Woolf, E. B. White, Zora Neale Hurston, James Baldwin, Joan Didion, Stephen Jay Gould, Richard Rodriguez, Annie Dillard, Cynthia Ozick, and Amy Tan.

Thanks also go to Susan Jackson for interpreting a phrase in French, Harald Grote for translating a word from the German, Ross Wollin for tracking down Eliot's Greek, Rachel Tropp for reading drafts of the introduction and first chapter, Jonathan Rubel for investigating Early's involvement with *Baseball,* Katherine Emery for finding hooks's graduation date, and Production Editor Benjamin Clark for overseeing this project with a scrupulous eye.

We also thank the following libraries: the Boston Public Library, the Mugar Library at Boston University, the Newton Public Library, and the Widner Library at Harvard University.

What is good in this text is owed to all who helped; what isn't is the sole responsibility of the editors.

CREDITS

INTRODUCTION

To the Student and the Teacher

Like all such texts, this one is based on a theory about how we learn to write. Thirty years of experience, both in the classroom and at my own desk, have convinced me that most of us learn to write by reading carefully, understanding accurately what we have read, analyzing that material, criticizing it, questioning it, imitating what we admire in it, comparing it to other things we've read, and then writing and rewriting to discover and to communicate what we ourselves think. Writing is always a process, a constant conversation with the self, other texts, and readers.

For many reasons, then, essays are an essential part of the curriculum in a writing course. Short, and varied in content, style, and purpose, essays allow writers to read closely, question, and compare before they write. Book-length works allow us to pursue in the classroom a close reading of only a few pages from selected chapters. Essays, on the other hand, offer us needed practice in the close reading of nearly every page. As readers we can see how an essay works as a whole, and as writers we can apply our new knowledge to our own writing of essays. The close reading of an entire essay also teaches us to read and reread every page we ourselves write. We learn to find our own mistakes. Moreover, essays offer us a range of styles. As writers, we need a range of styles for different audiences and different purposes. Essays also cover a variety of subjects. Writers in college and beyond must write on many subjects and for many audiences.

It is no wonder, then, that composition courses throughout the twentieth century have included essays as a major part of the curriculum. Of course, the emphasis on the type of essay assigned and the approach the teacher recommends have changed from decade to decade. Early in the century, essays were prized for their whimsy. A good essay of this type examined a familiar object or topic from a unique and entertaining perspective, often drawing from it some "universal" principle. Students were expected to imitate the style or, better yet, use the techniques to invent their own. Another traditional approach, the modes, also emphasized imitation; students read essays that offer the best models of a number of modes—narration, description, definition, classification, comparison, and argument or persuasion. By the mid-sixties, most essays were selected because they raised our consciousness about specific issues or hotly argued a position. Students were taught to argue using logic and other rhetorical techniques.

Beginning in the late sixties and in the seventies, the narrative and descriptive essays students read became increasingly autobiographical and multicultural. In the eighties, questioning received ideas and the motives of writers put more emphasis on what the writer said than on the techniques used to say it. At the same time, students were encouraged to read across the curriculum to prepare themselves for the thinking and writing required of them in college and beyond. Later still, the subject of the essay canon itself became an issue to read and write about, both for the students and for specialists in composition.

Despite these shifts in emphasis over the years, new editors of composition texts offering one or another of these styles and pedagogical approaches are published every year. All types of essays, incorporating all sorts of styles, appear every year as well. The competing ways of reading and writing all flourish because each appeals to large groups of students and teachers. In fact, most of us benefit from all these ways of reading and writing. Each approach offers a useful way to join the ongoing conversation. This text is therefore designed to encourage us, both students and instructors, to make use of all these approaches to reading and writing as we think about, discuss, and write about a given essay.

ESSAYS IN THIS TEXT

Each essay has been selected because it is excellent or popular or important. Some essays fit one of these categories. Some fit two categories. Some fit all three. Like Francis Bacon's types of books (those to be tasted, those to be swallowed, and those to be chewed and digested), some of these essays can be gulped while others require rumination. Some are short and whimsical; some are long and complex; some are journalistic; some are academic; some are printed speeches; some are excerpts from longer works; some are polemical; some are introspective; some are optimistic; some are bitter. In this artful diversity lies the enduring vitality of the essay, a prose form that allows us to listen to living voices from the past.

One way this text differs from most of the others is that it is arranged chronologically. This organization emphasizes both the historical context and the variety and enduring appeal of the essay. Another benefit of the chronological order is that it allows us as students and teachers to make use of all the ways of reading and writing that have appeared over the century. We can decide for ourselves to what extent the various pedagogical approaches are "fads," as Mencken calls them in "Bearers of the Torch." We can examine an essay, E. B. White's "Once More to the Lake," for example, for its technical flourishes—its complex sentences, alliteration, and evocative prose. And we can see it as a model of comparison and contrast. But we can also see how the events of each decade affect a writer's choice of subject and style. White's classic account of his trip to the lake, for example, is not only an excellent essay of the whimsical variety but also a poignant voicing of the nation's nostalgia during a time of disruption, uncertainty, and war.

Moreover, in comparing it to Ellison's "The Way It Is," written one year later, we can also ask questions about the kind of past White describes and the privileged people who could remember such a past. And when we compare White's essay to Woolf's "The Death of the Moth," written in the same year that Ellison wrote his essay, and to Hughes's "Salvation" written one year before White's essay, we can see Hughes and Woolf and White as practitioners of the literary essay, as opposed to others in the text who write about such fields as science, anthropology, economics, or politics. In other words, the chronological arrangement invites us as students to examine an essay from all the approaches to reading and writing that work for us.

Another benefit of the chronological order is that it helps us as readers to discover developing patterns of thought and feeling. In the first thirty years we see the themes that came to occupy us throughout the century: Twain analyzes the sources of our opinions, why we think in the ways we do. With humor, irony, and a duplicitous honesty, he examines nature and nurture, money and status, prejudices and ethics. Chesterton and Parker each look at issues of class, one to see how they work to create a culture of the elite and a culture of the masses and the other to offer a comic perspective on class and behavior. Du Bois reviews the paths African-Americans have chosen in their fight against prejudice. Beerbohm and Eliot each imagine the past and connect it to the future, Beerbohm through nostalgia and whimsy and Eliot through thinking about thinking.

Mencken and Lippmann also think about thinking, the one with comic disdain, the other with academic tools still relevant today. Graves writes with grace and honesty about a brutal war; Mencken writes about revenge. Lawrence offers suggestions for womankind; Mead examines nature and nurture on an island remote from western thought. By 1929 most of the issues of the text and the century have been introduced: racial prejudice, class prejudice, high art and low art, nature versus nurture, aggression and war, the feminist movement, education—all issues that pertain to our understanding of who we are and what we want to be.

The second thirty years concentrate on war and its repercussions. We can examine war as it affects civilians (Panter-Downes and Ellison), journalists (Hemingway and Pyle), a prescient social analyst (Lewisohn), and a prescient statesman (Churchill). We can see its effects on literature in Forster's "What I Believe," in Faulkner's Nobel Prize speech, and in Orwell's "Politics and the English Language."

This period also introduces a new intellectual issue, the battles between literature and science. We can compare Frost's borrowing from science to make his statements about metaphor in 1930 with Lewisohn's analysis of the role of literature in Nazi Germany four years later and Orwell's analysis of the role of literature in 1945. We will see that both Lewisohn and Orwell are early participants in a controversy that led to the vituperative arguments of Snow and Leavis in mid-century.

Some of the essays from the last forty years extend themes introduced in the first sixty years, and some intensify the quest for the twin ideals of freedom and individual rights. X. J. Kennedy, for example, applies the cultural criticism Chesterton uses in his analysis of popular literature to an analysis of a popular film. Carr and Kuhn examine theories of history and science and help us see the importance of what is missing and misunderstood. Clifford Geertz interprets the Balinese cockfight, and Martin Gardner assesses the pitfalls of anthropological interpretation in the controversy over Mead. Martin Luther King, Jr., and Malcolm X demand racial equality; Judy Brady and Germaine Greer argue against limited roles for women. Rachel Carson urges us to protect the environment; Jessica Mitford alerts us to consumer fraud. Vidal proposes the legalization of drugs; Gellhorn and Hoagland oppose the war in Vietnam. Sontag examines our response to AIDS; Reich and Coontz look at our economic future. Many writers describe what it is like to hold a dual identity in America, among them Momaday, Kingston, Rodriguez, Rich, Cofer, Preston, and Tan.

FOOTNOTES AND TIMELINE

The footnotes identify pertinent references that may be unfamiliar, and the timeline allows readers to see the writers and the essays in relation to the major events of the century. For example, a footnote in Twain's "Corn-Pone Opinions" identifies Amelia Jenks Bloomer as the women's rights activist who made bloomers fashionable, and the timeline allows readers to see at a glance that women gained the right to vote in the United States in 1920, a full nine years after Twain's essay was published.

THE QUESTIONS

The questions in this text are intended to direct all of us to examine an essay first as a single entity and then as the focus within an increasingly complex context. Answering them may require a second or even third reading. And our answers may change as we read and reread. For each essay, some questions prepare readers for writing assignments by encouraging us to count paragraphs, note transitions, keep track of repeated images or ideas, underline the important passages, and take brief or extensive notes to trace our own critical responses to the argument and the style. Other questions are designed to serve as writing assignments leading to a close analysis of a specific essay or to a comparison of techniques and ideas in two or more essays. Answering these questions may require a paper of two or three or even five or ten pages.

Because the essays in this text vary widely in length and complexity, the number and length of the questions accompanying them vary also. Moreover, no one pattern of inquiry or way of reading can adequately account for every essay. Some essays repay close attention to diction and style. Some invite many levels of interpretation. Some are especially well argued. And some are not. The questions, therefore, are shaped in large part by the nature of the individual essay.

Three types of question do not appear in this text. One asks students to imitate the style of a particular essay. Another asks students to find connections between an essay and the life of the author as presented in the accompanying biography. The third type asks students to examine their own lives in relation to the issues raised in a particular essay. All three are useful types of question and are encouraged. The actual questions are missing only because they are generic. It is assumed that as instructors and students we will pose them at appropriate times. Moreover, because no set of questions can explore all relevant topics for an essay, each of us will no doubt omit, revise, and add to certain questions in this text. Reading and rereading will provoke our own questions and our own responses.

Questions under UNDERSTANDING AND ANALYSIS emphasize structure, audience, technical devices, and matters of content and argument. Often extensive, particularly for the early essays, which may be less immediately accessible than the later ones, these questions encourage us as readers to summarize accurately and to make clear distinctions between the author's ideas and our own. Once the entire essay is clear and the argument, however clear or confusing, is laid open, we are encouraged to analyze its effectiveness on all relevant levels. What is excellent will stand up to such scrutiny and will reward the reader with the pleasure of the text and with a model to imitate. In discovering for ourselves what is faulty, we will see why and will learn from others' mistakes. Moreover, what is faulty to some readers may be excellent to others. As students and instructors, we will likely change our minds about our preferences. Sometimes we will disagree with each other; sometimes we will surprise and teach each other. In either case, we are sure to discover more and more about the written word and our reactions to it as we continue to read and reread.

Questions under COMPARISON are designed to sharpen analytical skills in two ways. First, they help us as writers to discover general principles of style and rhetoric and recurring patterns of thought and feeling throughout the century. We can discover, for example, what comic techniques are shared by many authors and how the intended audience shapes a writer's style. We can also discover prevailing patterns of thought and feeling that emerge on such issues as the origin of stereotypes, the relationships between science and literature, and the role of aggression in human nature. Second, these questions prepare us as writers to take a stand on these important issues. Examining from a variety of perspectives a topic such as the role of language in determining one's identity allows us as readers and writers to develop thoughtful, informed responses. We can see that most issues cannot be settled by simply accepting or rejecting whatever an author writes. Instead, we learn to position ourselves along a continuum, accepting some elements, rejecting others, and contributing our own perspectives.

THEMATIC CONTEXT

A list of eighteen themes is offered at the end of the text to supplement the questions under COMPARISON. The thematic organization encourages both the discovery of general principles and the evaluation of argument and style. For example, under the theme PREJUDICE, we can trace changes in theories about national identity and race by comparing Eliot's sense of the "European mind" and Lippmann's use of the "melting pot" in the twenties with Hurston's museum of stereotypes in "What White Publishers Won't Print" and Baldwin's assertion that "[t]his world is white no longer" in "Stranger in the Village" in the early fifties. These in turn can be compared to the views presented in essays by Podhoretz, King, Malcolm X, Rodriguez, Staples, Early, Gates, hooks, and others during the last fifty years. At the same time, we can evaluate these changing theories. We can, for example, see the importance of both reading and experience in Baldwin, Hurston, and Podhoretz and apply these perceptions to the assessments of Malcolm X supplied by Early and hooks. Comparing how Early and hooks evaluate Malcolm X gives us models to use in our own evaluations and helps us decide for ourselves which rhetorical tools work best.

SUGGESTED WRITING SEQUENCES

Within selected themes, some essays appear under subheadings that highlight productive sequences of reading and writing. Under the theme of *War*, for example, are subsections covering reports to the homefront, the responses of civilians, retrospective analyses of war, and the role of violence in human nature. Each section further complicates the contexts. We can read and compare all the essays under each subsection, or we can read one from two or more groups. For example, in a short sequence teachers and students could examine Pyle's "The Death of Captain Waskow" from as many perspectives as possible, seeing how audience shapes Pyle's description and what has made this report one of the most widely read in the century. Next we could read Graves's description of his experiences in World War I, learning how the soldier in combat actually feels and how he keeps himself going from day to day. In Graves's memoir, some of the observations in Pyle's report are confirmed and some are questioned.

After finding connections between these two, we could read Fussell, who describes in even more graphic detail what the regular soldier endures. Finally we could read Carr on theories of history. There readers will see that the experiences of individuals and even of groups cannot alone provide an accurate description of an ever-elusive truth. Objective scholars and thinkers need to assemble and assess all the evidence available from as many points of view as possible to arrive at a fair and reasonable understanding of our past.

Each additional essay widens the perspective. As new essays are added to the conversation, we will see new patterns emerge and begin to respond with ideas and complex questions of our own.

BIOGRAPHICAL CONTEXT

The biographies in this text differ from those in most readers in length and content. Most texts provide either a short statement listing the dates of the author's birth, death, and major publications or a longer intellectual biography illustrated with apt quotations from the major works. Over the last few years, I have presented my students with these two types and a third, a two- or three-page biography offering salient details about the writer's early life, the way she or he became involved in writing, the major events in terms of career and relationships, the works produced, and a few quotations from these works. In literally every case, my students have preferred biography number three. I think we all find the details of early life fascinating. We can see each writer as a potential role model whose career we can trace from its beginnings, usually in the high-school years, to its zenith in later life. Knowing what has happened to a particular writer, how chance and determination interact, and how both personal and historical events can shape a writer's perspective provides us with a context for reading and interpreting the writer's words. Thus the biographies are designed to make the writers come alive for us and so spark in us a lively interest in their works.

HOW TO READ THESE ESSAYS

To the Student

Most instructors agree that in order to write well you need to learn to read critically. What does "reading critically" mean? First of all it means reading attentively, that is, with great care. And it means reading appreciatively, that is, with eye and ear alert for the logic and clarity of a persuasive argument and for the deliberate patterns of diction and syntax the artful essayist employs. It also means reading skeptically, that is, with eye and ear alert for areas of disagreement, infelicities, opportunities to extend the author's points or to include your own ideas. How, then, do you teach yourself to read critically? What exactly should you direct your attention to? How can you translate that attentiveness, appreciation, and skepticism into improved writing skills?

HOW TO PAY ATTENTION

When most of us read a paragraph, or even a sentence, we not only see the words on the page but also hear the words in our heads. Fortunately for us, however, our brains are so well adapted for reading and thinking that while we are actually hearing and seeing these words, we can also be thinking about an itch near the elbow, what we want for lunch, and one or two other things as well. Then, having read that sentence or paragraph, we move on to the next one. We have retained some of what's in the sentence or paragraph, but not nearly as much as we could. This method works well for much of the reading we do (magazines, newspapers, and entertainment reading of all sorts).

Another kind of reading, skimming, allows us to catch the gist of a piece of writing, often without actually hearing all the words in our heads or even reading every word on the page. We are likely to read this way whenever we look over a familiar recipe or set of directions or check an article to find a specific idea or word. In this sort of reading, any given word or sentence is not all that important.

These two types of reading work well in many situations; we are quite good at them because we practice them every day. Unfortunately, however, they won't work well in a composition course or in most college courses. These situations require critical, that is, attentive, appreciative, skeptical reading.

To read critically, you have to hear and see ONLY the words on the page. Like any other skill, such concentration requires practice; the more often you read attentively the more likely you will do it automatically the next time you settle down to read. The rule here is this: whenever your mind wanders as you read, even for a tiny bit, you must force yourself to reread that sentence or that paragraph. You may not notice your lack of attention until you've read several lines or even paragraphs beyond the initial lapse. That's fine. Be pleased that you have noticed. In fact, you should mark your text whenever you do notice that you have not been paying attention. (See tips one and two below.)

Some distractions may not be relevant to the work at hand, but some may indicate that you are already reading attentively, appreciatively, and skeptically. For example, if you stopped paying attention because of events happening around you, the loss of attention is probably not significant to your understanding of the essay. But if you stopped paying attention because you were truly bored or lost or annoyed or because the writer's words impressed you or reminded you of something that once happened to you, the lapse in attention may be useful in understanding the essay and in responding to it in class or in writing.

At this point, you should mark the passage and jot down the cause of the lapse, using any shorthand marks that you know you will recognize later. Then, force yourself to reread what you just read without full attention. In the beginning, you may have to reread, as part of the "first reading," a particular sentence or passage two or even three or more times. If on the first or second rereading of this passage you notice an apt transition, a memorable metaphor, persuasive logic or flaws in the argument, confused or confusing passages, or opportunities for you to expand or rebut the author's argument, make sure you jot these down in the margins or in a notebook. The point here is to understand what the writer is saying without losing your own responses to those words.

HERE ARE SOME OTHER TIPS:

1. Read with a pencil or pen in hand. Mark up the text with underlining, question marks, exclamation points, circles, etc.
2. Keep a reading and writing notebook in which you take notes. (See below for what to note.)
3. Practice reading attentively in many different locations so that you can concentrate on the bus or subway, in the park, in the library, in your room, at a café.

Remember, concentrated critical reading is a skill developed through repetition. Repetition will make it a habit. You will soon be able to turn it off and on at will. Remember that the purpose of this skill is to help you understand what someone else thinks and how someone else expresses his or her thoughts. Your understanding of the text will help you to shape your own responses to it. What you read will supply you with the evidence you need to support your own interpretations. Concentrated, appreciative, skeptical reading gives you mastery, which means it gives you control over the text and what you want to say about it.

WHAT SHOULD YOU PAY ATTENTION TO FIRST?

The obvious answer to that question is the words on the first page of the essay you are reading. Different openings will attract or repel you in different ways. Some will leave you indifferent. Once you are actually concentrating with pen in hand, you should note whatever strikes you. Anything you notice will be useful. Just react and note and keep reading. When you have finished a concentrated reading of an entire short essay or a large chunk of a longer one, tell yourself, or better yet jot down in your notebook, your overall emotional reaction. Be honest. You are reading at this point for yourself and no one else. Note how many times your attention wandered. Decide what these lapses indicate to you about the work as a whole.

Now look over the questions at the end of the essay, and read the essay a second time. This time, concentrate on reading appreciatively and skeptically. Notice what exactly makes you feel the way you do. You may, for example, find the essay boring (because of words you don't understand, an obvious argument you've heard a million times, a stuffy tone, etc.) Or you may notice a particularly apt use of alliteration that sticks in your head long after you have closed your book. At this point, you are beginning to analyze the essay as you read. Your analysis will lead to questions and answers in class, extensive notes, and possibly preparations for writing the first draft of an essay of your own. Analytic rereading is hard, messy work, but it gets easier each time you do it, just as concentrating gets easier each time you concentrate.

Don't expect yourself to understand completely any essay after the first or second reading. Assume that other members of the class, as well as the instructor, will have things to say that you may not have thought of and that you will notice things others have missed. The list below offers some of the elements that will help you support or shift your understanding of the essay as you work on it. Your instructor will also guide you in finding these elements and explaining their relevance to the work. Bear in mind that although each one contributes to the effect of the essay, some elements may be more important than others, depending on the essay.

1. Author's biography, historical context of essay, original audience

2. Matters of craft such as attitude toward reader (tone), sentence length and variety, choice of diction (level of complexity and formality, alliteration, repetition, figurative language), structure of paragraphs, transitions, topic sentences, placement of thesis, examples

3. Matters of argument such as thesis, logic, understanding of an opponent's point of view, missed opportunities to make a point, confusions that can be seen as either deliberate invitations to multiple interpretations or just muddled thinking

4. Connections to your own experience, things you've read or seen in other contexts, ideas or styles you've found in this text

Note any of these elements in any order during this second reading of the essay. If, in the process or reading and note-taking, you come up with some ideas of your own on the subject, make sure you write them down legibly enough so that you can retrieve them later. You may then want to reread a complex passage or the whole essay even a third time. By the time of the second or third reading, you are ready to think about answers to the questions at the end of the essay.

These questions follow the order of the essay so that you can find the answers as you read through the text. They are not meant to cover every aspect you may notice, or even every important aspect, but simply to direct you to useful approaches to each particular essay. Even if you simply skim the questions before a second reading, the elements you retain will help to guide your responses as you reread. Then you can jot down specific answers. Reading the questions over and trying to answer them for each essay will make it easier and easier for you to answer other questions in this text as well as questions your instructor and other students pose. Again, practice actually works. You don't have to write out complete answers, unless your instructor tells you to, but it will surely help to jot down some notes in the margins of the essay or in your reading journal so you'll remember your ideas when you are in the classroom and when you are ready to write.

Remember once again, attentive, appreciative, skeptical reading is a skill that can be practiced and perfected. Your peers and your instructors, and indeed all readers, are always in the process of improving these skills every time they read with concentration.

SAMPLE READING ASSIGNMENT

Suppose you have been assigned a short essay, such as "Mrs. Post Enlarges on Etiquette" by Dorothy Parker, reproduced below. Because this essay is not easy, it is a good one to use as a sample assignment. It presents problems you are likely to encounter in any of the essays in this text. For example, the essay was written in the early part of this century, and you may not have heard of this author before. Moreover, she is writing satire, a particularly difficult genre to analyze.

From reading the biography, you discover among other things that Parker is known for her wit and mordant poetry. In other words, she is supposed to be a funny writer who made her original audience laugh. You see that the essay is a book review that appeared in *The New Yorker* dated December 31, 1927. A quick glance at the timeline shows you that the essay was written during Prohibition and that women had been voting for seven years. The stock market crash is two years in the future.

Mrs. Post Enlarges on Etiquette

Emily Post's *Etiquette* is out again, this time in a new and an enlarged edition, and so the question of what to do with my evenings has been all fixed up for me. There will be an empty chair at the deal table at Tony's, when the youngsters gather to discuss life, sex, literature, the drama, what is a gentleman, and whether or not to go on to Helen Morgan's Club when the place closes; for I shall be at home among my book. I am going in for a course of study at the knee of Mrs. Post. Maybe, some time in the misty future, I shall be Asked Out, and I shall be ready. You won't catch me being intentionally haughty to subordinates or refusing to be a pallbearer for any reason except serious ill health. I shall live down the old days, and with the help of Mrs. Post and God (always mention a lady's name first) there will come a time when you will be perfectly safe in inviting me to your house, which should never be called a residence except in printing or engraving.

It will not be a grueling study, for the sprightliness of Mrs. Post's style makes the textbook as fascinating as it is instructive. Her characters, introduced for the sake of example, are called by no such unimaginative titles as Mrs. A., or Miss Z., or Mr. X.; they are Mrs. Worldly, Mr. Bachelor, the Gildings, Mrs. Oldname, Mrs. Neighbor, Mrs. Stranger, Mrs. Kindhart, and Mr. and Mrs. Nono Better. This gives the work all the force and the application of a morality play.

It is true that occasionally the author's invention plucks at the coverlet, and she can do no better by her brain-children than to name them Mr. Jones and Mrs. Smith. But it must be said, in fairness, that the Joneses and the Smiths are the horrible examples, the confirmed pullers of social boners. They deserve no more. They go about saying "Shake hands with Mr. Smith" or "I want to make you acquainted with Mrs. Smith" or "Will you permit me to recall myself to you?" or "Pardon me!" or "Permit me to assist you" or even "Pleased to meet you!" One pictures them as small people, darting about the outskirts of parties, fetching plates of salad and glasses of punch, applauding a little too enthusiastically at the end of a song, laughing a little too long at the point of an anecdote. If you could allow yourself any sympathy for such white trash, you might find something pathetic in their eagerness to please, their desperate readiness to be friendly. But one must, after all, draw that line somewhere, and Mr. Jones, no matter how expensively he is dressed, always gives the effect of being in his shirt-sleeves, while Mrs. Smith is so unmistakably the daughter of a hundred Elks. Let them be dismissed by somebody's phrase (I wish to heaven it were mine)—"the sort of people who buy their silver."

These people in Mrs. Post's book live and breathe; as Heywood Broun once said of the characters in a play, "they have souls and elbows." Take Mrs. Worldly, for instance, Mrs. Post's heroine. The woman will live in American letters. I know of no character in the literature of the last quarter-century who is such a complete pain in the neck.

See her at that moment when a younger woman seeks to introduce herself. Says the young woman: " 'Aren't you Mrs. Worldly?' Mrs. Worldly, with rather freezing politeness, says 'Yes,' and waits." And the young woman, who is evidently a glutton for punishment, neither lets her wait from then on nor replies, "Well, Mrs. Worldly, and how would you like a good sock in the nose, you old meat-axe?" Instead she flounders along with some cock-and-bull story about being a sister of Millicent Manners, at which Mrs. Worldly says, "I want very much to hear you sing some time," which marks her peak of enthusiasm throughout the entire book.

See Mrs. Worldly, too, in her intimate moments at home. "Mrs. Worldly seemingly pays no attention, but nothing escapes her. She can walk through a room without appearing to look either to the right or left, yet if the slightest detail is amiss, an ornament out of place, or there is one dull button on a footman's livery, her house telephone is rung at once!" Or watch her on that awful night when she attends the dinner where everything goes wrong. "In removing the plates, Delia, the assistant, takes them up by piling one on top of the other, clashing them together as she does so. You can feel Mrs. Worldly looking with almost hypnotized fascination—as her attention might be drawn to a street accident against her will."

There is also the practical-joker side to Mrs. W. Thus does Mrs. Post tell us about that: "For example, Mrs. Worldly writes:

> " 'Dear Mrs. Neighbor:
>
> "'Will you and your husband dine with us very informally on Tuesday, the tenth, etc.'
>
> "Whereupon, the Neighbors arrive, he in a dinner coat, she in her simplest evening dress, and find a dinner of fourteen people and every detail as formal as it is possible to make it. . . . In certain houses—such as the Worldlys' for instance—formality is inevitable, no matter how informal may be her 'will you dine informally' intention."

One of Mrs. Post's minor characters, a certain young Struthers, also stands sharply out of her pages. She has caught him perfectly in that scene which she entitles "Informal Visiting Often Arranged by Telephone" (and a darn good name for it, too). We find him at the moment when he is calling up Millicent Gilding, and saying, " 'Are you going to be in this afternoon?' She says, 'Yes, but not until a quarter of six.' He says, 'Fine, I'll come then.' Or she says, 'I'm so sorry, I'm playing bridge with Pauline—but I'll be in tomorrow!' He says, 'All right, I'll come tomorrow.' " Who, ah, who among us does not know a young Struthers?

As one delves deeper and deeper into Etiquette, disquieting thoughts come. That old Is-It-Worth-It Blues starts up again, softly, perhaps, but plainly. Those who have mastered etiquette, who are entirely, impeccably right, would seem to arrive at a point of exquisite dullness. The letters and the conversations of the correct, as quoted by Mrs. Post, seem scarcely worth the striving for. The rules for the finding of topics of conversation fall damply on the spirit. "You talk of something you have been doing or thinking about—planting a garden, planning a journey, contemplating a journey, or similar safe topics. Not at all a bad plan is to ask advice: "We want to motor through the South. Do you know about the roads?' Or, 'I'm thinking of buying a radio. Which make do you think is best?' "

I may not dispute Mrs. Post. If she says that is the way you should talk, then, indubitably, that is the way you should talk. But though it be at the cost of that future social success I am counting on, there is no force great enough ever to make me say, "I'm thinking of buying a radio."

It is restful, always, in a book of many rules—and Etiquette has six hundred and eighty-four pages of things you must and mustn't do—to find something that can never touch you, some law that will never affect your ways. . . .

And in Etiquette, too, I had the sweetly restful moment of chancing on a law which I need not bother to memorize, let come no matter what. It is in that section called "The Retort Courteous to One You Have Forgotten," although it took a deal of dragging to get it in under that head. "If," it runs, "after being introduced to you, Mr. Jones" (of course, it would be Mr. Jones that would do it) "calls you by a wrong name, you let it pass, at first, but if he persists you may say: 'If you please, my name is Stimson.' "

No, Mrs. Post; persistent though Mr. Smith be, I may not say, "If you please, my name is Stimson." The most a lady may do is give him the wrong telephone number.

December 31, 1927

After reading the essay through once, you have an emotional reaction. You may find the essay mildly amusing, totally boring, pointless, rather funny, or distressing. Any of these reactions is plausible and fair. In any case, you note your reaction, jot down some ideas from the margins of your text, and turn to the questions as you reread:

UNDERSTANDING AND ANALYSIS

1. *Parker's voice is especially striking. What are some of her techniques for humor?*

In the first question you encounter the voice of another reader of Parker's essay, one whose opinion may well differ from yours. This reader obviously thinks Parker is funny. If you disagree with the questioner, you can note some failed attempts at humor. If you agree, you can note some of the better lines. Either way you can try to figure out the techniques.

For example, the last phrase of the second sentence, "for I shall be at home among my book," is odd, certainly. What is odd about it? Since the expected plural is missing in the word "book," Parker implies that Post's book is a very big book indeed, the equivalent of many. The effect is subtle, and the technique is to subvert expectations.

Although you may or may not notice this particular example, you do note that the questioner asks specifically about the voice. As an attentive reader, one who concentrates, you listen for the tone of the voice. It is clearly self-deprecatory, in that Parker claims a need to "study" the book of manners so that she'll be ready for a date and won't make blunders. But hers is also the voice of a quick learner. Her demonstrations of her new knowledge offer other opportunities for the subversion of expectations, even as she plays the role of good student: Mrs. Post comes before God—"(always mention a lady's name first.)" This is the voice of one who pretends to be learning from the book, while she is really mocking it.

You can find other examples of Parker's comic voice in the first paragraph, such as her use of capital letters in "Asked Out" or her "going in for a course of study at the knee of Mrs. Post," but you may not be aware of the techniques. Whenever you are uncertain about something, make sure you ask about it in class. There, you may discover that in the first example, the capital letters imitate or parody Post's own categories. The second example illustrates a comic use of synecdoche, that is the substitution of a part (the knee) for the whole (Mrs. Post). It also plays on a cliché about learning that implies a great teacher and a humble student, but in this case a book is given the knee and the humble student is making fun of the great teacher.

2. *Parker lets us know that in her opinion the subject of manners is essentially frivolous. How does she convey that point?*

In this question, you have to look at the content as well as the comic tone of the first paragraph or so. What specific manners does Parker select to offer the reading public? Are they in fact, as the questioner assumes, frivolous? You could point to serious issues of class or to matters of life and death, as for example, in the following sentence: "You won't catch me being intentionally haughty to subordinates or refusing to be a pallbearer for any reason except serious ill health." But then you still have to deal with the phrase "You won't catch me" at the beginning of the sentence, which subversively suggests that it's all a matter of not being caught out rather than being kind and thoughtful to others. At the end of the paragraph, Parker claims that eventually it will be "safe" to invite her to your house because she will know better than to call it a "residence." You could claim frivolity here, but maybe not, especially if you think distinctions in diction can lead to unfair treatment of others.

3. *What connection, if any, do you think exists between manners and morals? Does Parker imply a connection?*

Here the questioner appears to recognize that all is not frivolity in this essay. Since the questions follow the order of the essay, the focus is probably on the words "morality play," which are glossed in a footnote. At this point, you may have been appalled once again (a second reading, remember) by Parker's use of the phrase "white trash," which leads you to that whole sentence once again, in which you discover that Post refuses to allow her readers to feel sympathy for those who lack upper class manners. You wonder if "white trash" is Parker's phrase and figure that it is unlikely to be Post's, but may well represent Post's real opinion, at least according to Parker. By now, you may agree with the implicit assumption of the questioner that manners can slide into morals. The implication is that elitism based on inheritance, not merely wealth, leads to social and racial intolerance. "White trash" hurts not only those it labels but also those who are not white. Parker herself becomes a bit harder to pinpoint. She seems to envy those who are rich and have inherited their wealth: "Let them be dismissed by somebody's phrase (I wish to heaven it were mine)—'the sort of people who buy their silver.'" And she may well find the Smiths of the world "pathetic." You wonder if Parker is being ironic here, or if she in fact subscribes to this view herself, making fun of the Smiths' desperate attempts to please. You carry on with the questions.

4. *Parker introduces some of her own observations about poor manners in this essay. What does she especially dislike? What values can you ascribe to her on the basis of her dislikes?*

Here the questioner asks for specific examples again. You could pick out the obvious Mrs. Worldly, whom Parker cannot bear because, contrary to Mrs. Post's values as suggested in Parker's first paragraph, her heroine, Mrs. Worldly, is in fact quite haughty to her supposed inferiors—"when a younger woman seeks to introduce herself," Mrs. Worldly replies with what Parker calls "freezing politeness." Even worse from Parker's point of view is the quotation from Post in which the "clashing" of plates is compared to "a street accident" in its ability to fascinate Mrs. Worldly. This comparison brings us back to the issue of morals. In a "street accident" someone may be physically injured. Sympathy is clearly missing in both instances. Obviously good manners do not guarantee kindness.

5. *Why do you suppose Parker thinks good manners are boring? Are there any further indications in this essay that good manners can be not merely boring but pernicious?*

This question requires supposition on your part. Parker gives examples of boring conversations about journeys and gardens, but she does not say outright what the problem is until she reminds us about the point of this book in the first place: to help the reader climb the social ladder. The implication is that you memorize rules to become something you are not so that you can reap the rewards of hobnobbing with the rich and possibly even marrying into a rich society family. Here all the themes come together: issues of class, complications of motives, subversions of the status seekers combined with a desire to move among them, confusion of kindness and sympathy with coldness and selfishness. You may decide that nothing "pernicious" is going on here. Or you may decide that whether or not Parker intends the point or the original audience was interested, you think books about good manners lead to cruel class distinctions and ominous suggestions equating accidents with undue noise caused by clumsy servants.

6. *What does Parker tell her readers about the style and quality of Post's book?*

Throughout the essay, and especially in the third paragraph from the end, Parker alludes to the size of the book, implying that it is too big. In the second paragraph, Parker draws attention to the "sprightliness of Mrs. Post's style" and the personality of the characters Post uses as examples. But the praise is faint because the well-mannered people are so dull and annoying. A much less obvious example can be found in the last two paragraphs of the essay, where Parker subtly draws attention to an editorial error in the text: "The Retort Courteous to One You Have Forgotten" is supposed to be to One Who Has Forgotten YOU, as the example that follows shows. Post has a Mr. Jones call you the wrong name, not the other way round as the title of the section suggests. Parker emphasizes this mistake in her switch of the name Jones for that of Smith in the last paragraph.

7. *From the examples Parker offers, can you tell why Post's book was so popular and why Parker's column was so popular too?*

Here the questioner is directing you back to the original audience. Readers of *The New Yorker* in 1927 were probably fairly well off, enjoying the prosperity of Wall Street, and readers of Emily Post's book were probably not quite as well off or at least they were uncertain of themselves. By positioning herself between these two audiences in terms of class, claiming to be uncertain of all the rules, finding them funny, and wanting to be rich, Parker presents herself as being above the middle classes Post is deigning to teach in her book. The examples, the haughty Mrs. Worldly and all the Smiths and Joneses, are examples of what to do and not do. But they are likely to appeal to those who do not live in that world rather than to those who do. And whether or not the readers of either the magazine or the book are actually in the upper or middle classes, the readers of the magazine can, at least as they read Parker, believe themselves to be already above it all. Like Martha Stewart's publications, Post's book presents a world readers can both aspire to and make fun of at the same time.

By this time, you've read all the questions under the first heading, formulated some answers, jotted down some ideas, and perhaps thought of some questions about Parker and class issues to ask in class. In any case, your answering of the questions has focused your attention on tone, humor, and Parker's point of view. There's still much you could examine in this essay, including Parker's actual thesis, the role of a victim in humor, and many other points. Some of these are raised in the questions under the heading COMPARISON.

Look these questions over now, but don't feel compelled to answer them until after your first class discussion of the essay. Your instructor will tell you which, if any, questions to answer for further discussion or for a later writing assignment.

COMPARISON

1. Parker calls Post's book a "textbook" and emphasizes its burdensome rules. What, aside from manners, can you learn from reading such books? Read FitzGerald's essay on history textbooks and apply some of her techniques to a column by Miss Manners, our current specialist on the topic of good manners.

2. Compare the style and tone of Miss Manners with that of both Post herself and of Parker. What values does each writer appear to espouse? Have the rules changed much for introducing people or inviting them to informal evenings at home?

3. What can you deduce about the roles of women in the twenties from reading Parker on Post? Do women play these roles today as well?

4. Do you think the adoption of good manners as determined by Emily Post or Miss Manners can actually help a person move up in American society? If so, how? If not, why not?

5. Read Jamaica Kincaid's selection from *A Small Place*. What role do manners play in setting boundaries between groups?

6. Compare the techniques for humor in the essays by Parker and Allen. Does humor always require a victim? Who are the victims in the essays by Parker and Allen? What about the humor in Baker's essay? Is there a victim there?

7. Compare the issues of class found in the book review with the reports on the war some ten years later, also written for *The New Yorker*, by Mollie Panter-Downes. Are the assumptions about the audience similar? What aspects of class do both writers note?

8. Read the essays by Twain and Staples. To what degree do these authors also imply connections between manners and morals?

Many other questions will be raised in class as readers other than you and the questioner examine the essay together. Moreover you and other members of your class may well find connections other than the ones suggested in the comparison questions between Parker's essay and works in this text. All of these questions and connections should help stimulate your thinking about the essay and lead, ultimately, to your written response.

HOW TO CONNECT YOUR CRITICAL
READING TO YOUR WRITING

You can write only as well as you can read. The truth of this statement becomes clear when you realize that your revision depends on your ability to read your own work. When you can perceive the techniques and arguments of another writer and decide for yourself which please you and which do not, you can apply these insights to your own writing. What does not please you can be revised.

In other words, reading well translates into writing well in three specific ways: first, you learn what to imitate and what to avoid; second, you discover ideas to use, modify, or reject; third, you learn to read your own work as attentively as you read the work of others. These skills translate directly into revised and improved drafts.

One way to translate reading skills into writing skills is to imitate what you like in someone else's writing and avoid what you don't like. If you like Parker's wry, inflated style, try to imitate her tone in an essay on another subject. If you don't like it, be aware of how one can fall into that tone. If you like her humor, analyze her techniques for humor and try adapting them to your own purposes. For example, we have already seen that Parker uses self-deprecation, reversal of expectations, and parodic imitation for comic effect. She also uses personification (as in "the author's invention plucks at the coverlet"), exaggeration ("that awful night when everything goes wrong"), and colloquial diction ("you old meat-axe"). Whether or not you think each instance is successful, you can apply her techniques in a comic piece of your own. Other techniques you can imitate include ways of appealing to a specific audience, sentence length and style, structure of the essay, types of examples, appropriate quotations from other sources, and so on.

Another way to translate reading skills into writing skills is to use the argument as a starting point for an argument of your own. Rare indeed is the writer who can convince you of every point proffered and leave you satisfied that no more can possibly be said on that topic. Whatever disagreement, modification, alternative viewpoint, or added piece of evidence you can come up with will lead you to an essay of your own. Writers stimulate one another; each examined assertion offers a way in to the ongoing conversation.

Moreover, such a close examination of argument leads you back to the other two ways to translate careful reading into careful writing: imitation or avoidance and astute revision. Whatever pleases you in a writer's argument can be adapted to suit your own. Whatever displeases you alerts you to a tactic to avoid. The more carefully you scrutinize another's argument, the more carefully you will be able to scrutinize your own.

Imitation, amplification, modification, disagreement, avoidance—each requires the ability to see another's argument clearly and to distinguish it from your own ideas and preconceptions. In other words, to respond to an author's work in any meaningful way, you must be able to summarize the work accurately.

Summary is tricky because it veers close to interpretation every step of the way. Misreading an essay is usually caused by not reading carefully. If you write a summary based on such a misreading, you may lose your reader's trust in whatever you have to say. But misreading can also be an unfair label for a plausible interpretation of a complex and obscure passage. And misreading can even be deliberate, that is, a ploy to allow the author space for a different argument.

Parker, for example, is representing Post's text for the public. In other words, she is summarizing it for a book review. However, she is not trying to offer an impartial and absolutely accurate picture of Post's text. She may even be deliberately selecting damaging passages to suit her purpose of making fun of Post and of manners and the upper classes in general. In other words, Post may have compared something rather trivial, such as a loud noise, to something potentially serious, such as an accident in the street, only once in the whole book. We don't know. On the other hand, Parker may be quoting perfectly fairly, offering representative passages throughout her review.

What we can assume as readers, however, is that Parker is quoting accurately. We also know, because we are close readers of Parker by now, that she is quoting to make a point. And we know that her point is not Post's point. Although Post may accuse her of misreading, we know that Parker is simply adept at making Post's own language and examples undercut the ostensible purpose of good manners in the first place—to ease social interactions and make everyone feel comfortable. In Parker's capable hands, good manners appear at best designed to dull all feeling and sympathy for our fellows and at worst to encourage their public mortification.

In other words, Parker's essay offers a model of how to quote accurately to serve the purpose of irony and parody. Other essays in this text offer models of how to quote to support opinions held in all seriousness, how to quote to disagree with a writer, and how to quote another's words as a way of enlarging upon or moving in a slightly different direction from the ideas of another author.

Paying attention to how the writers in this text write will help you pay attention to how you write. You can use these essays as models to imitate, examples of what to avoid, and starting points for arguments of your own. Moreover, the more closely you read the work of others, the more closely will you read your own writing. Such attentive reading will lead to careful revision. The apparatus in this text and your teacher's and peers' comments will also help. But the hardest and most exciting part of the task is yours alone. In reading these essays and writing essays of your own, you are joining a century's worth of conversation on subjects that still matter.

CONTEXTUAL TIMELINE

1901   First long-distance radio transmission from England to Newfoundland; Queen Victoria dies; President McKinley assassinated

1905   Einstein publishes papers on the special theory of relativity

1914   Archduke Franz Ferdinand, heir to Austro-Hungarian throne, assassinated June 28; Germany declares war on Russia, August 1 and on France, August 3; Britain declares war on Germany, August 4 and World War I begins

1917   United States enters the war

1918   War ends November 11; Spanish flu epidemic; Great Britain grants women over 30 the right to vote

1919   Treat of Versailles establishes the League of Nations; Mussolini founds fascism; 18th Amendment prohibits manufacture, sale, and transportation of alcoholic beverages.

1920   United States is first nation to grant all women voting rights equal to those of men (age 21 and over) in the nineteenth Amendment

1927   Werner Heisenberg publishes his paper on the uncertainty principle

1928   Alexander Fleming discovers penicillin

1929   Thursday, October 24, the stock market crashes

1930   The Great Depression causes widespread unemployment; Nazis become second strongest party in Germany

1933   Franklin Delano Roosevelt inaugurated as 32nd President of US; Prohibition repealed in twenty-first amendment; first concentration camps established in Germany

1935   The Nuremberg Laws remove the civil rights of Jews in Germany; Nazis reject the Versaille Treat and institute compulsory military service

1936   Spanish Civil War begins

1938   Kristallnacht, November 9, when Nazis of all ages break store windows, burn synagogues, and attack Jews, murdering 90 people. Three hundred thousand Jews are sent to concentration camps.

1939   Hitler invades Poland, September 1; Britain and France declare war on Germany, September 3, and World War II begins; Spanish Civil War ends in fascist victory

1941   Japanese attack Pearl Harbor on December 7; United States and Great Britain declare war on Japan, December 8

1942   The United States confines Japanese-Americans in detention camps

1944   D-Day, June 6, Allied forces invade Normandy; Paris liberated from Nazis

1945   August 6, American bomber drops atomic bomb on Hiroshima, killing 80,000 people instantly; on August 10 another atomic bomb is dropped on Nagasaki, killing 40,000 people instantly; Japan surrenders on August 14; World War II ends; Allied forces liberate death camps

1946   Conclusion of Nuremberg Trials begun in 1945 against Nazi war criminals; last Japanese-Americans released from detention camps

1947   House Committee on Un-American Activities begins hearings, asking each witness, "Are you now or have you ever been a member of the Communist Party?"

1948   State of Israel created

1949   Germany divided into two states, democratic West Germany and communist East Germany

1950   Korean War; Senator Joseph McCarthy claims State Department harbors Communists

1953   Coronation of Queen Elizabeth II; Watson and Crick discover the double helix structure of DNA; Korean War ends

1954   Supreme Court declares segregation in public schools unconstitutional; Army-McCarthy hearings and end of "the witch hunt" on national television

1955   Rosa Parks refuses to give up seat on Montgomery, Alabama, bus; her arrest leads to year-long boycott

1957   Soviet Union launches Sputnik I and II and tests first intercontinental ballistic missile; US Vanguard carrying satellite explodes on launchpad; Explorer I launches first US satellite

1959   Fidel Castro takes over Cuba

1960   Sit-in at all-white lunch counter in Greensboro, NC; U. S. Food and Drug Administration approves first birth control pills

1961   East Germany builds Berlin Wall; Castro defeats C.I.A.-trained army of Cuban exiles in Bay of Pigs invasion; Freedom Riders protesting segregation are stoned and beaten on their way from Washington, D.C. to New Orleans

1962   Cuban missile crisis

1963   Civil rights march on Washington, August 28; President Kennedy assassinated November 22

1964   Chaney, Goodman, and Schwerner, in Mississippi to register voters, are murdered; Civil Rights Act outlawing discrimination in public buildings passed; Gulf of Tonkin Resolution in August allows escalation of military efforts in Vietnam without a declaration of war; Palestine Liberation Organization established

1965   Malcolm X assassinated in February; King heads march of civil rights demonstrators from Selma to Montgomery, Alabama; Voting Rights Act passed; US sends troops to Vietnam

1967   Israel defeats Egypt in punitive war against Palestinian guerilla attacks

1968   Martin Luther King, Jr., assassinated, April 4; Robert Kennedy assassinated, June 5; student strikes and riots in Paris; peaceful and unruly demonstrators at Democratic National Convention in Chicago beaten by police; Fair Housing Act passed

1969 Gay Liberation emerges from Stonewall Inn raid in June; July 21, Neil Armstrong and Buzz Aldrin walk on the moon; US and USSR begin nuclear disarmament negotiations

1970 First Earth Day; April invasion of Cambodia; sporadic student strikes; Members of National Guard kill four unarmed students at Kent State; three student revolutionaries killed in bomb explosion in New York City

1972 Christmas bombing of Hanoi and Haiphong

1973 January treaty ends US military involvement in Vietnam; Arabs attack Israel on Yom Kippur; June break-in at headquarters of Democratic party in Watergate complex

1974 In televised hearings John Dean implicates Nixon in Watergate scandal; President Nixon resigns August 9

1975 Spain's dictator, General Franco, dies; Saigon becomes Ho Chi Minh City and Vietnam becomes one nation under Communist rule

1978 Anwar Sadat of Egypt and Menachim Begin of Israel sign Camp David Peace Accord

1980 John Lennon murdered

1981 Illnesses later determined to be caused by AIDS first appear

1986 Challenger explodes in January; Chernobyl nuclear power plant meltdown in April; US bombs Libya; Iran-Contra scandal

1989 June 3, soldiers drive tanks into protesting students and kill hundreds or more in Tianammen Square, China; Berlin Wall demolished; cold war ends, eastern Europe throws off Communist rule; the Exxon Valdez tanker dumps millions of gallons of crude oil into coastalwaters near Alaska

1990 Nelson Mandela, sentenced to life imprisonment in 1963 for opposing segregation in South Africa, is finally released

1991 International force headed by US attacks Iraq for invading Kuwait in Operation Desert Storm; collapse of Communism leads to ethnic battles in Yugoslavia

1992 Serbia attacks Bosnia; NATO force sent to enforce peace; white police officers are acquitted in Rodney King beating; riots in L. A.

1993 Internet expands to allow people across the country and the world to communicate through their home computers; Yassir Arafat, head of the PLO, and Yitzak Rabin of Israel sign peace accord after 45 years of sporadic fighting

1994 South African blacks gain the right to vote and elect Nelson Mandela as president; Balkan war continues despite UN peacekeeping forces and NATO bombing of Serbian airbase

1995 Bombing of federal building in Oklahoma City

1999 President Clinton impeached and acquitted; Serbians agree to peacekeeping force in Kosovo after NATO bombing

Essays in Context

Mark Twain
(1835–1910)

Samuel Langhorne Clemens was born in Florida, Missouri, where the family had moved at the suggestion of his maternal uncle, John Quarles, who owned a successful farm and hoped that his sister's family could also prosper there. Sam was the fifth of six children of John Marshall Clemens, a sober lawyer and shopkeeper perpetually in search of better fortune, and his wife, Jane Lampton Clemens, a cheerful, plucky woman who loved stories. When Sam was four, John Clemens moved the family to Hannibal, Missouri, but Sam returned to his uncle's farm in Florida every summer until he was twelve.

Pleasure, piety, and peril shaped Twain's early life. On the farm in Florida he ate well, played hard with his many cousins, and listened to the stories and songs of the slaves his uncle owned. In Hannibal, he swam, fished, skated, spelunked, and watched the riverboats on the Mississippi. For piety, he was sent to three grammar schools, each devoted to the development of good manners and morals, and to Methodist and later Presbyterian Sunday schools and church services, which, with his mother's help, created in Twain a tender and stinging conscience. For peril, Sam had only to look about him. His nine-year-old sister Margaret died of fever when he was not quite four, and his ten-year-old brother Ben sickened and died within a week when Sam was eight. Before he was twelve Sam had seen slaves chained and beaten on their way south and had witnessed three murders. In his chaotic autobiography, written near the end of his life, Twain says that he drew on his memories from these early years to write *The Adventures of Tom Sawyer* and *The Adventures of Huckleberry Finn*.

In 1847, after a series of financial disasters forced him to sell all he could to pay his debts, John Clemens died of pneumonia, leaving his wife and children (Orion, twenty-one; Pamela, nineteen; Sam, twelve; and Henry, ten) with a house and little else. A year later Sam quit school to work as a printer, first for the *Missouri Courier* and then at sixteen for his brother Orion, who had started a paper in 1850. Finding it hard to work for his older brother, Sam left Hannibal when he was eighteen and for the next four years worked as a printer in St. Louis, New York, Philadelphia, Keokuk (Iowa), and Cincinnati, learning the printing business and developing an ear for regional idiosyncrasies.

In 1857, Sam took a steamboat to New Orleans. He had planned to go to South America but instead became apprenticed to Horace Bixby, senior pilot on a Mississippi steamboat. He earned his license in two years, saw his brother Henry, then about twenty, die from injuries suffered in a steamboat explosion, and piloted more than twenty-one ships before the Civil War ended all steamboat traffic in 1861.

After a two-week stint in the Confederate Army, Twain set off in a stagecoach with his remaining brother, Orion, for Carson City, Nevada. For the next five years, Twain wrote articles, essays, and comic pieces for various newspapers, particularly the Virginia *City Territorial Enterprise*, where the name Mark Twain first appeared in 1863, and for three papers in San Francisco. In 1865, he wrote a story based on a tale he'd heard in a mining camp, "Jim Smiley and His Jumping Frog," which was printed in New York and then picked up by papers around the country. Suddenly Mark Twain was a famous name. The next year, Twain sailed to the Sandwich Islands (now Hawaii) as a correspondent for the *Sacramento Union*, and by 1866 he was lecturing on his travels. In 1867, he published his first book, The *Celebrated Jumping Frog of Calaveras County, and Other Sketches*, and arrived in New York to lecture and to sail on the Quaker *City* to the Holy Land as correspondent for the San Francisco *Alta Californian*.

This voyage proved pivotal for Twain, both personally and professionally. Among his fellow passengers was Charles Langdon, the eighteen-year-old son of a coal merchant in Elmira, New York, who one day showed Twain a picture of his sister Olivia. From that day on, Twain told his friend and biographer Albert Bigelow Paine, he was in love. He met Olivia shortly after the voyage ended and became engaged to her in 1869. Meanwhile Twain collected the letters he'd sent to the paper in San Francisco and devised from them his second publication, *Innocents Abroad*, which confirmed his national reputation as an American humorist.

With a loan from Olivia's father, Twain bought a partnership in the *Buffalo Express*, and in 1870 he and Olivia were married. Despite the death from diphtheria of their two-year-old son Langdon and the delicate health of his wife, the family was a happy one, Olivia bearing three daughters, Susy in 1872, Clara in 1874, and Jean in 1880. Twain continued to lecture in both America and England and to publish, drawing on his travels and later on his early life for his materials. *Roughing It*, based on the stagecoach trip with Orion, came out in 1872, The *Adventures of Tom Sawyer* in 1876, *A Tramp Abroad* in 1880, *The Prince and the Pauper* in 1882, and *Life on the Mississippi* in 1883. From 1876 to 1883 he worked on his masterpiece, *The Adventures of Huckleberry Finn*, which was published in 1885.

During these years, the family prospered, moved to a twenty-eight-room house in Hartford, Connecticut, employed six servants, and entertained guests with warmth and splendor. But this happiness did not last. In 1890, at age ten, their daughter Jean was diagnosed as epileptic. In the early 1890s, Twain took his family to Europe for a prolonged visit, but by 1894 he was bankrupt, plunged into debt because of investments in the Paige typesetting machine. Like his father before him, Twain was determined to pay off all his debts, which he did in 1895–1896 by performing a grueling lecture trip around the world to raise the necessary funds. While he and his wife were away, Susy died of meningitis. By 1898, Twain had paid off the last of his debts, and by 1903, having published prodigiously and recouped his fortunes, he was able to travel with his wife to Italy in hopes of improving her failing health. She died the following year.

Throughout his changing fortunes, Twain continued in his private life and in his writing to deflate pretension and pomposity with humor and honesty. In the 1930s, Van Wyck Brooks and others attributed the increasingly sardonic and bitter tone of Twain's later works, such as *The Man That Corrupted Hadleyburg and Other Stories and Essays* (1900) and *What Is Man?* (published privately in 1906), to a release of feelings he had suppressed to please his conventional wife. However, research has turned up no evidence to support this view. His bitterness has also been attributed to a mechanistic philosophy adopted as a result of private misfortunes. Yet Twain's last years, like his first ones, were marked by pleasures as well as by pangs of conscience and sensitivity to the perils of life. He was pleased by the popular acclaim he received on his return to America in 1900 and by his honorary degrees from Yale (1901), the University of Missouri (1902), and Oxford (1907). He continued to enjoy good food, good company, and travel, visiting Bermuda and England in 1907 and Bermuda again in 1909. That year his daughter Clara married a concert pianist, and his daughter Jean, who had suffered periodic attacks from epilepsy, died. After Jean's death, he returned to Bermuda but came home again in April 1910, suffering from bronchitis and ready to fulfill the prediction he had made to Albert Bigelow Paine: "I came in with Halley's comet in 1835. It is coming again next year, and I expect to go out with it." He did.

Despite the fact that he produced most of his fiction and non-fiction in the nineteenth century, Twain is truly the first modern essayist. His personal experiences growing up in Hannibal, Missouri, his extensive travels through Europe, the Middle East, and South Africa, and his knowledge of science, literature, and world events provided him with plenty of raw material on which to focus his sharp eye and satiric wit. The result is a deflation of all human pretensions, a cosmic, comic cynicism that has become an identifying mark of our time.

CORN–PONE OPINIONS (1901)

FIFTY YEARS AGO, when I was a boy of fifteen and helping to inhabit a Missourian village on the banks of the Mississippi, I had a friend whose society was very dear to me because I was forbidden by my mother to partake of it. He was a gay and impudent and satirical and delightful young black man—a slave—who daily preached sermons from the top of his master's woodpile, with me for sole audience. He imitated the pulpit style of the several clergymen of the village, and did it well, and with fine passion and energy. To me he was a wonder. I believed he was the greatest orator in the United States and would some day be heard from. But it did not happen; in the distibution of rewards he was overlooked. It is the way, in this world.

He interrupted his preaching, now and then, to saw a stick of wood; but the sawing was a pretense—he did it with his mouth; exactly imitating the sound the bucksaw makes in shrieking its way through the wood. But it served its purpose; it kept his master from coming out to see how the work was getting along. I listened to the sermons from the open window of a lumber room at the back of the house. One of his texts was this:

"You tell me whar a man gits his corn pone,[1] en I'll tell you what his 'pinions is."

I can never forget it. It was deeply impressed upon me. By my mother. Not upon my memory, but elsewhere. She had slipped in upon me while I was absorbed and not watching. The black philosopher's idea was that a man is not independent, and cannot afford views which might interfere with his bread and butter. If he would prosper, he must train with the majority; in matters of large moment, like politics and religion, he must think and feel with the bulk of his neighbors, or suffer damage in his social standing and in his business prosperities. He must restrict himself to corn-pone opinions—at least on the surface. He must get his opinions from other people; he must reason out none for himself; he must have no first-hand views.

I think Jerry was right, in the main, but I think he did not go far enough.

1. It was his idea that a man conforms to the majority view of his locality by calculation and intention.

This happens, but I think it is not the rule.

2. It was his idea that there is such a thing as a first-hand opinion; an original opinion; an opinion which is coldly reasoned out in a man's head, by a searching analysis of the facts involved, with the heart unconsulted, and the jury room closed against outside influences. It may be that such an opinion has been born somewhere, at some time or other, but I suppose it got away before they could catch it and stuff it and put it in the museum.

I am persuaded that a coldly-thought-out and independent verdict upon a fashion in clothes, or manners, or literature, or politics, or religion, or any other matter that is projected into the field of our notice and interest, is a most rare thing—if it has indeed ever existed.

A new thing in costume appears—the flaring hoopskirt, for example—and the passersby are shocked, and the irreverent laugh. Six months later everybody is reconciled; the fashion has established itself; it is admired, now, and no one laughs. Public opinion resented it before, public opinion accepts it now, and is happy in it. Why? Was the resentment reasoned out? Was the acceptance reasoned out? No. The instinct that

---

[1]*corn pone* bread made with corn but without eggs or milk.

moves to conformity did the work. It is our nature to conform; it is a force which not many can successfully resist. What is its seat? The inborn requirement of self-approval. We all have to bow to that; there are no exceptions. Even the woman who refuses from first to last to wear the hoopskirt comes under that law and is its slave; she could not wear the skirt and have her own approval; and that she must have, she cannot help herself. But as a rule our self-approval has its source in but one place and not elsewhere— the approval of other people. A person of vast consequences can introduce any kind of novelty in dress and the general world will presently adopt it—moved to do it, in the first place, by the natural instinct to passively yield to that vague something recognized as authority, and in the second place by the human instinct to train with the multitude and have its approval. An empress introduced the hoopskirt, and we know the result. A nobody introduced the bloomer,[2] and we know the result. If Eve should come again, in her ripe renown, and reintroduce her quaint styles—well, we know what would happen. And we should be cruelly embarrassed, along at first.

The hoopskirt runs its course and disappears. Nobody reasons about it. One woman abandons the fashion; her neighbor notices this and follows her lead; this influences the next woman; and so on and so on, and presently the skirt has vanished out of the world, no one knows how nor why, nor cares, for that matter. It will come again, by and by and in due course will go again.

Twenty-five years ago, in England, six or eight wine glasses stood grouped by each person's plate at a dinner party, and they were used, not left idle and empty; to-day there are but three or four in the group, and the average guest sparingly uses about two of them. We have not adopted this new fashion yet, but we shall do it presently. We shall not think it out; we shall merely conform, and let it go at that. We get our notions and habits and opinions from outside influences; we do not have to study them out.

Our table manners, and company manners, and street manners change from time to time, but the changes are not reasoned out; we merely notice and conform. We are creatures of outside influences; as a rule we do not think, we only imitate. We cannot invent standards that will stick; what we mistake for standards are only fashions, and perishable. We may continue to admire them, but we drop the use of them. We notice this in literature. Shakespeare is a standard, and fifty years ago we used to write tragedies which we couldn't tell from—from somebody else's; but we don't do it any more, now. Our prose standard, three quarters of a century ago, was ornate and diffuse; some authority or other changed it in the direction of compactness and simplicity, and conformity followed, without argument. The historical novel starts up suddenly, and sweeps the land. Everybody writes one, and the nation is glad. We had historical novels before, but nobody read them, and the rest of us conformed—without reasoning it out. We are conforming in the other way, now, because it is another case of everybody.

The outside influences are always pouring in upon us, and we are always obeying their orders and accepting their verdicts. The Smiths like the new play; the Joneses go to see it, and they copy the Smith verdict. Morals, religions, politics, get their following from

[2]*bloomer* In 1851, an advocate for temperance and women's rights, Amelia Jenks Bloomer (1818–1894), recommended the adoption of calf-length skirts and dresses worn over ankle-length trousers for women. Although first introduced by Elizabeth Smith Miller, it was Bloomer who wore the outfit whenever she lectured and advertised it in the newspaper she edited, *Lily,* that made it fashionable.

surrounding influences and atmospheres, almost entirely; not from study, not from think-ing. A man must and will have his own approval first of all, in each and every moment and circumstance of his life—even if he must repent of a self-approved act the moment after its commission, in order to get his self-approval *again:* but, speaking in general terms, a man's self-approval in the large concerns of life has its source in the approval of the peoples about him, and not in a searching personal examination of the matter. Mohammedans are Mohammedans because they are born and reared among that sect, not because they have thought it out and can furnish sound reasons for being Mohammedans; we know why Catholics are Catholics; why Presbyterians are Presbyterians; why Bap-tists are Baptists; why Mormons are Mormons; why thieves are thieves; why monarchists are monarchists; why Republicans are Republicans and Democrats, Democrats. We know it is a matter of association and sympathy, not reasoning and examination; that hardly a man in the world has an opinion upon morals, politics, or religion which he got other-wise than through his associations and sympathies. Broadly speaking, there are none but corn-pone opinions. And broadly speaking, corn-pone stands for self-approval. Self-approval is acquired mainly from the approval of other people. The result is conformity. Sometimes conformity has a sordid business interest—the bread-and-butter interest—but not in most cases, I think. I think that in the majority of cases it is unconscious and not calculated; that it is born of the human being's natural yearning to stand well with his fellows and have their inspiring approval and praise—a yearning which is commonly so strong and so insistent that it cannot be effectually resisted, and must have its way.

A political emergency brings out the corn-pone opinion in fine force in its two chief varieties—the pocketbook variety, which has its origin in self-interest, and the bigger variety, the sentimental variety—the one which can't bear to be outside the pale;[3] can't bear to be in disfavor; can't endure the averted face and the cold shoulder; wants to stand well with his friends, wants to be smiled upon, wants to be welcome, wants to hear the precious words, *"He's* on the right track!" Uttered, perhaps by an ass, but still an ass of high degree, an ass whose approval is gold and diamonds to a smaller ass, and confers glory and honor and happiness, and membership in the herd. For these gauds many a man will dump his life-long principles into the street, and his conscience along with them. We have seen it happen. In some millions of instances.

Men think they think upon great political questions, and they do; but they think with their party, not independently; they read its literature, but not that of the other side; they arrive at convictions, but they are drawn from a partial view of the matter in hand and are of no particular value. They swarm with their party, they feel with their party, they are happy in their party's approval; and where the party leads they will follow, whether for right and honor, or through blood and dirt and a mush of mutilated morals.

In our late canvass half of the nation passionately believed that in silver lay salvation,[4] the other half as passionately believed that that way lay destruction. Do you believe that a tenth part of the people, on either side, had any rational excuse for having an opinion about the matter at all? I studied that mighty question to the bottom—and came out empty. Half of our people passionately believe in high tariff, the other half believe otherwise.

[3]*outside the pale* the fence marking a boundary.

[4]*in silver lay salvation* In 1896, William Jennings Bryan had electrified the Democratic convention with his famous Cross of Gold speech; with the election of the Republican president, William McKinley, the nation went on the gold standard in 1900.

Does this mean study and examination, or only feeling? The latter, I think. I have deeply studied that question, too—and didn't arrive. We all do no end of feeling, and we mistake it for thinking. And out of it we get an aggregation which we consider a Boon. Its name is Public Opinion. It is held in reverence. It settles everything. Some think it the Voice of God. Pr'aps.

I suppose that in more cases than we should like to admit, we have two sets of opinions: one private, the other public; one secret and sincere, the other corn-pone, and more or less tainted.

Understanding and Analysis

1. Twain gives us two definitions of corn-pone opinions, Jerry's and his own. What are they and how do they differ?

2. Twain provides a fairly straightforward sentence early in the essay that appears to serve as his thesis: "I am persuaded that a coldly-thought-out and independent verdict upon a fashion in clothes, or manners, or literature, or politics, or religion, or any other matter that is projected into the field of our notice and interest, is a most rare thing—if it has indeed ever existed." Note that Twain does not follow the order he implies he will follow in that sentence. Where does the change occur?

3. Twain claims that conformity is an "instinct," that an "inborn requirement of self-approval" motivates us to conform. Where does Twain say we find our self-approval? How does he account for a person who changes his mind?

4. When Twain talks about religion, how does he define corn pone? How does this section compare to Twain's two earlier definitions?

5. When Twain talks about politics, he again defines two types of corn pone. What are they?

6. Why does Twain claim that he "came out empty" in the controversy over silver or gold currency?

7. Twain seems to change his mind at the end of the essay, siding with Jerry and defining his terms for yet a third (or fourth) time. Why? What are the definitions now? Does Twain change his mind? Explain your opinion.

8. What is the rhetorical effect, that is, the effect on the audience, of pursuing two opinions at once? Do you agree that "we have two sets of opinions"?

9. What are some of the methods Twain uses to entertain his audience, to get us to smile or even laugh? List all the comic devices you can think of, for example, exaggeration, unexpected reversal, incongruous levels of diction, from any source with which you are familiar. Then look for these devices in Twain's essay.

Comparison

1. In "Stereotypes" Walter Lippmann addresses similar issues. On what points do Lippmann and Twain agree? Where do they differ?

2. Read Parker's essay. Both Twain and Parker address manners and morals to some degree. What similarities and differences do you see in their attitudes toward these subjects? Do both see a connection between manners and morals?

3. Synthesize the ideas in five or six essays, beginning with "Corn-Pone Opinions," to help you form your own opinion about how we formulate opinions. How do we as a culture create change? Read, for example, Eliot, Lippmann, Hurston, Orwell ("Politics and the English Language"), and Postman. How does Woolf or Greer or hooks fit in this discussion?

4. Compare the humor in Twain with that in Mencken, Parker, Thurber, Baker, and Allen. What devices do all employ? What, if any, elements are unique to one writer?

G. K. Chesterton
(1874–1936)

Gilbert Keith Chesterton was born in London, the son of Edward, a real estate agent, and Mary Louise, who was an invalid and, according to Gilbert's younger brother Cecil, the "cleverest woman in London." The only two siblings, Cecil kept cockroaches as pets, while Gilbert was addicted to reading and drawing. Tall, awkward, and nearsighted, Gilbert was badly treated at St. Paul's school, although he did make a lifelong friend, Edmund Bentley, whom he met in a schoolyard fight. By the time he was seventeen, Chesterton was writing articles and poems for *The Debator*, a magazine founded by another school friend, who also founded the Junior Debating Club, where Gilbert honed his rhetorical skills. Although some considered him a slow learner, when his mother met his schoolmaster to discuss his erratic progress, he described Gilbert as "Six foot of genius. Cherish him, Mrs. Chesterton, cherish him."

After attending art school and University College, London, Chesterton left without a degree in 1895. He had decided on a career as a writer and journalist. In 1898, as a poorly paid reviewer and editor at a publishing house, Chesterton proposed to Frances Blogg, realizing he'd have to supplement his income with freelance writing. He soon discovered that he could be exceptionally prolific. Chesterton wrote poetry, *The Wild Knight* (1900); books of criticism on Browning and Dickens; fiction, *The Napoleon of Notting Hill* (1904), which made his reputation; a bestselling spy novel, *The Man Who Was Thursday* (1908); a popular series of detective novels about a priest, Father Brown; and even plays, *Magic* (1913), which ran for three weeks, and *The Judgement of Dr. Johnson* (1927), which lasted only six performances. He also published a variety of religious works (*Heretics* in 1905, *Orthodoxy* in 1908, and *The Book of*

Job in 1929, for instance) and finally converted to the Roman Catholic faith in 1922. But he remains best known for his collections of essays, such as *All Things Considered* (1908), *Tremendous Trifles* (1909), *The Uses of Diversity* (1921), *Come to Think of It* (1931), *All Is Grist* (1932), and *On Running After One's Hat and Other Whimsies* (1933).

He loved children, but never had any, although he and his wife were popular with the children in the small town to which they moved in 1909. Chesterton's choice of town seems as capricious as some of his beloved essays. Deciding to leave London, he and Francis boarded a random bus, took it to a random train station, took the very next train to a random spot in the country, and walked until they reached a town, Beconsfield, as it turns out, where they lived for the rest of their lives.

During the First World War, too overweight to be accepted for military service, Chesterton contributed to the war effort by writing propaganda. In 1929, he met Benito Mussolini in Italy, and admired him. Much of the next year was spent in an exhausting lecture tour of the United States and Canada. He returned an ill man, still overweight and suffering from heart trouble, which sapped his strength and led to his death five years later.

Chesterton was an extremely popular essayist, known as "The Prince of Paradox" because he habitually started an essay on a whimsical, airy topic and ended by finding in it a surprising yet significant truth, a "tremendous trifle." His subjects, such as his hat, a piece of chalk, the contents of his pockets, came to be accepted as the ideal topics for the genre. While many found his essays to be brilliant displays of wit, others saw in his work a conservative or even reactionary dogmatism. Moreover, Chesterton's attitude toward Jews was problematical; although he always denied the anti-Semitism that was attributed to him, he did include insulting stereotypes of Jews in his writing.

In later years one admirer of his prose, W. H. Auden, admitted a reluctance to reread Chesterton because of his reputation as both an anti-Semite and a journalist engaged in writing about what is merely "amusing." In 1970, however, Auden published *G. K. Chesterton: A Selection from his Non-Fiction Prose*, in which he presents excerpts primarily from Chesterton's literary criticism. In the Foreward, Auden notes the contradictions in Chesterton's beliefs, his reactionary "distrust" of business, technology, and all things modern, and his "unreliable" political assessments, but claims for his criticism "observations which, once they have been made, seem so obviously true that one cannot understand why one had not seen them for oneself."

More cultural criticism than literary criticism, Chesterton's "A Defence of Penny Dreadfuls," written in 1901, does not appear in Auden's collection. The first popular essay of cultural analysis produced in the twentieth century, it precedes by forty years Orwell's classic description of postcards, "The Art of Donald McGill." Both essays use classification, comparison, and analysis to assess and appreciate what the elite would see as low art. Chesterton's reflections on "Penny Dreadfuls" initiated a field of study that expanded tremendously later in the century.

A DEFENCE OF PENNY DREADFULS (1901)

ONE OF THE strangest examples of the degree to which ordinary life is undervalued is the example of popular literature, the vast mass of which we contentedly describe as vulgar. The boy's novelette may be ignorant in a literary sense, which is only like saying that a modern novel is ignorant in the chemical sense, or the economic sense, or the astronomical sense; but it is not vulgar intrinsically—it is the actual centre of a million flaming imaginations.

In former centuries the educated class ignored the ruck[1] of vulgar literature. They ignored, and therefore did not, properly speaking, despise it. Simple ignorance and indifference does not inflate the character with pride. A man does not walk down the street giving a haughty twirl to his moustaches at the thought of his superiority to some variety of deep-sea fishes. The old scholars left the whole under-world of popular compositions in a similar darkness.

Today, however, we have reversed this principle. We do despise vulgar compositions, and we do not ignore them. We are in some danger of becoming petty in our study of pettiness; there is a terrible Circean[2] law in the background that if the soul stoops too ostentatiously to examine anything it never gets up again. There is no class of vulgar publications about which there is, to my mind, more utterly ridiculous exaggeration and misconception than the current boys' literature of the lowest stratum. This class of composition has presumably always existed, and must exist. It has no more claim to be good literature than the daily conversation of its readers to be fine oratory, or the lodging-houses and tenements they inhabit to be sublime architecture. But people must have conversation, they must have houses, and they must have stories. The simple need for some kind of ideal world in which fictitious persons play an unhampered part is infinitely deeper and older than the rules of good art, and much more important. Every one of us in childhood has constructed such an invisible *dramatis personae;* but it never occurred to our nurses to correct the composition by careful comparison with Balzac.[3] In the East the professional story-teller goes from village to village with a small carpet; and I wish sincerely that any one had the moral courage to spread that carpet and sit on it in Ludgate Circus.[4] But it is not probable that all the tales of the carpet-bearer are little gems of orig-

---

[1]*ruck* jumble.

[2]*Circean* refers to Circe, enchantress in Greek mythology who lures sailors to her island. In Homer's *Odyssey* she turned Odysseus' companions into swine.

[3]*Balzac* Honore de Balzac (1799–1850), French novelist best known for his huge work *La Comédie humaine,* wherein he depicts in vivid detail characters from all classes of French society.

[4]*Ludgate Circus* name of a circle or range of houses situated near the gate to London, where a debtor's prison was once located; a poor area of London.

inal artistic workmanship. Literature and fiction are two entirely different things. Literature is a luxury; fiction is a necessity. A work of art can hardly be too short, for its climax is its merit. A story can never be too long, for its conclusion is merely to be deplored, like the last halfpenny or the last pipelight. And so, while the increase of the artistic conscience tends in more ambitious works to brevity and impressionism,[5] voluminous industry still marks the producer of the true romantic trash. There was no end to the ballads of Robin Hood; there is no end to the volumes about Dick Deadshot and the Avenging Nine. These two heroes are deliberately conceived as immortal.

But instead of basing all discussion of the problem upon the common-sense recognition of this fact—that the youth of the lower orders always has had and always must have formless and endless romantic reading of some kind, and then going on to make provision for its wholesomeness—we begin, generally speaking, by fantastic abuse of this reading as a whole and indignant surprise that the errand-boys under discussion do not read *The Egoist* and *The Master Builder*.[6] It is the custom, particularly among magistrates, to attribute half the crimes of the Metropolis to cheap novelettes. If some grimy urchin runs away with an apple, the magistrate shrewdly points out that the child's knowledge that apples appease hunger is traceable to some curious literary researches. The boys themselves, when penitent, frequently accuse the novelettes with great bitterness, which is only to be expected from young people possessed of no little native humour. If I had forged a will, and could obtain sympathy by tracing the incident to the influence of Mr George Moore's novels, I should find the greatest entertainment in the diversion. At any rate, it is firmly fixed in the minds of most people that gutter-boys, unlike everybody else in the community, find their principal motives for conduct in printed books.

Now it is quite clear that this objection, the objection brought by magistrates, has nothing to do with literary merit. Bad story writing is not a crime. Mr. Hall Cain[7] walks the streets openly, and cannot be put in prison for an anti-climax. The objection rests upon the theory that the tone of the mass of boys' novelettes is criminal and degraded, appealing to low cupidity and low cruelty. This is the magisterial theory, and this is rubbish.

So far as I have seen them, in connexion with the dirtiest bookstalls in the poorest districts, the facts are simply these: The whole bewildering mass of vulgar juvenile literature is concerned with adventures, rambling, disconnected, and endless. It does not express any passion of any sort, for there is no human character of any sort. It runs eternally in certain grooves of local and historical type: the medieval knight, the eighteenth-century duellist, and the modern cowboy recur with the same stiff simplicity as the conventional human figures in an Oriental pattern. I can quite as easily imagine a human being kindling wild appetites by the contemplation of his Turkey carpet as by such dehumanized and naked narrative as this.

Among these stories there are a certain number which deal sympathetically with the adventures of robbers, outlaws, and pirates, which present in a dignified and romantic

[5]*impressionism* Impressionism in art was introduced in the 1870s and '80s, but was not admired by critics until the 1920s and '30s, after which it became increasingly popular. The impressionists as a group—Monet, Renoir, Sisley, for example—had broken with the academic style of the past to concentrate on capturing the fleeting beauty of nature.

[6]*The Egoist* (1879), novel by George Meredith (1828–1909) and the *Masterbuilder* (1892), play by Henrik Ibsen (1828–1906)

[7]*Mr. Hall Caine* (1853–1931) friend and secretary to Dante Gabriel Rosetti and author of popular novels such as *The Shadow of a Crime,* (1885), *The Deemster* (1887), *The Manxman* (1894), and *The Prodigal Son* (1904). Manx is an extinct language of the Celtic subfamily.

light thieves and murderers like Dick Turpin[8] and Claude Duval. That is to say, they do precisely the same thing as Scott's[9] *Ivanhoe,* Scott's *Rob Roy,* Scott's *Lady of the Lake,* Byron's *Corsair, Wordsworth's Rob Roy's Grave,* Stevenson's *Macaire,* Mr Max Pemberton's *Iron Pirate,* and a thousand more works distributed systematically as prizes and Christmas presents. Nobody imagines that an admiration of Locksley in *Ivanhoe* will lead a boy to shoot Japanese arrows at the deer in Richmond Park; no one thinks that the incautious opening of Wordsworth at the poem on Rob Roy will set him up for life as a blackmailer. In the case of our own class, we recognize that this wild life is contemplated with pleasure by the young, not because it is like their own life, but because it is different from it. It might at least cross our minds that, for whatever other reason the errand-boy reads *The Red Revenge,* it really is not because he is dripping with the gore of his own friends and relatives.

In this matter, as in all such matters, we lose our bearings entirely by speaking of the 'lower classes' when we mean humanity minus ourselves. This trivial romantic literature is not specially plebeian: it is simply human. The philanthropist can never forget classes and callings. He says, with a modest swagger, 'I have invited twenty-five factory hands to tea.' If he said, 'I have invited twenty-five chartered accountants to tea', every one would see the humour of so simple a classification. But this is what we have done with this lumberland[10] of foolish writing: we have probed, as if it were some monstrous new disease, what is, in fact, nothing but the foolish and valiant heart of man. Ordinary men will always be sentimentalists: for a sentimentalist is simply a man who has feelings and does not trouble to invent a new way of expressing them. These common and current publications have nothing essentially evil about them. They express the sanguine and heroic truisms on which civilization is built; for it is clear that unless civilization is built on truisms, it is not built at all. Clearly, there could be no safety for a society in which the remark by the Chief Justice that murder was wrong was regarded as an original and dazzling epigram.

If the authors and publishers of *Dick Deadshot,* and such remarkable works, were suddenly to make a raid upon the educated class, were to take down the name of every man, however distinguished, who was caught at a University Extension Lecture, were to confiscate all our novels and warn us all to correct our lives, we should be seriously annoyed. Yet they have far more right to do so than we; for they, with all their idiocy, are normal and we are abnormal. It is the modern literature of the educated, not of the uneducated, which is avowedly and aggressively criminal. Books recommending profligacy and pessimism, at which the high-souled errand-boy would shudder, lie upon all our drawing-room tables. If the dirtiest old owner of the dirtiest old bookstall in Whitechapel dared to display works really recommending polygamy or suicide, his stock would be seized by the police. These things are our luxuries. And with a hypocrisy so ludicrous as to be almost unparalleled in history, we rate the gutter-boys for their immorality at the very time that we are discussing (with equivocal German professors) whether morality is valid

---

[8]*Dick Turpin* (1706–1739) English criminal hanged at York after a career of theft and brutality.

[9]*Scott's* Sir Walter Scott (1771–1832), Scottish novelist and poet; George Gordon Byron (1788–1824), English poet; William Wordsworth (1770–1850), English poet; Robert Louis Stevenson (1850–1894), Scottish novelist, poet, and essayist; Max Pemberton (1863–1950), English editor and novelist.

[10]*lumberland* storage area for useless furniture or ideas; see Nicholson Baker's humorous and exhaustive study of the term in "Lumber" in *The Size of Thoughts* 1996.

at all. At the very instant that we curse the Penny Dreadful for encouraging thefts upon property, we canvass the proposition that all property is theft.[11] At the very instant we accuse it (quite unjustly) of lubricity and indecency, we are cheerfully reading philosophies which glory in lubricity and indecency. At the very instant that we charge it with encouraging the young to destroy life, we are placidly discussing whether life is worth preserving.

But it is we who are the morbid exceptions; it is we who are the criminal class. This should be our great comfort. The vast mass of humanity, with their vast mass of idle books and idle words, have never doubted and never will doubt that courage is splendid, that fidelity is noble, that distressed ladies should be rescued, and vanquished enemies spared. There are a large number of cultivated persons who doubt these maxims of daily life, just as there are a large number of persons who believe they are the Prince of Wales; and I am told that both classes of people are entertaining conversationalists. But the average man or boy writes daily in these great gaudy diaries of his soul, which we call Penny Dreadfuls, a plainer and better gospel than any of those iridescent ethical paradoxes that the fashionable change as often as their bonnets. It may be a very limited aim in morality to shoot a 'many-faced and fickle traitor', but at least it is a better aim than to be a many-faced and fickle traitor, which is a simple summary of a good many modern systems from Mr d'Annunzio's[12] downwards. So long as the coarse and thin texture of mere current popular romance is not touched by a paltry culture it will never be vitally immoral. It is always on the side of life. The poor—the slaves who really stoop under the burden of life—have often been mad, scatter-brained, and cruel, but never hopeless. That is a class privilege, like cigars. Their drivelling literature will always be a 'blood and thunder' literature, as simple as the thunder of heaven and the blood of men.

Understanding and Analysis

1. Who does Chesterton imagine his audience to be?

2. What is the proposition Chesterton is arguing against?

3. What evidence does he marshal to refute the magistrates?

4. According to Chesterton, why do the upper classes "despise vulgar compositions"?

5. Chesterton is known for his paradoxes or reversals of the readers' expectations. Where does he use reversal in this essay?

6. Chesterton is also known for his epigrammatic style, which becomes a force in his argument. Readers are more likely to believe an assertion if it is expressed in memorable language. Find as many epigrammatic sentences as you can in this essay. What stylistic devices make these sentences memorable?

[11]*all property is theft* famous line from Pierre-Joseph Proudhon (1809–1865), French political theorist who wrote *What Is Property?* (1840).

[12]*Mr d'Annunzio's* Gabriele D'Annunzio (1863–1938), Italian poet, novelist, dramatist, and soldier who supported Mussolini (and in 1921 introduced the black shirt, which became the uniform of the Fascists). In 1900, the year before Chesterton wrote his essay, D'Annunzio had published a novel in which he depicted florid details of his love affair with Italian actress Elenora Duse. Influenced by the German philosophers Arthur Schopenhauer and Freidrich Nietzsche, D'Annunzio aspired to be a modern Renaissance man.

7. What evidence does Chesterton offer to support his belief that "the modern literature of the educated . . . is avowedly and aggressively criminal"?

8. What does Chesterton mean by the words "a paltry culture" in his last paragraph? Does Chesterton believe that the content of a person's reading material affects a person's ethics or behavior? Do you?

9. Choose one of Chesterton's epigrams. Write an essay of your own, using modern examples, either supporting or undermining the assertion.

Comparison

1. Do Twain and Chesterton agree on why certain classes prefer certain types of literature?

2. Chesterton claims that people "must have stories." Read essays by Virginia Woolf, Zora Neale Hurston, E. B. White, X. J. Kennedy, Barry Lopez, Neil Postman, Judith Ortiz Cofer, and others to see if they agree and why. How do their ideas connect to those of Chesterton?

3. Recently, critics and parents have complained about the violence depicted in the movies and on TV. Criminals have even pointed to specific films that they say motivated their behavior. How might Chesterton respond to concerned parents? Are Chesterton's ideas about books relevant to films? Why or why not? Do you think X. J. Kennedy would agree with Chesterton?

W. E. B. Du Bois
(1868–1963)

William Edward Burghardt Du Bois was born in Great Barrington, Massachusetts, the son of Alfred, a barber who had served in the Union Army, and Mary Silvina. Two years after his birth, his father left, and William and his half-brother, Adelbert, then eight, were raised by their mother and their uncle Jim. Although he remembered his childhood fondly, the family was poor, and among the few African-American families in the area. According to biographer David Levering Lewis, Du Bois later recalled being more aware of class differences than race. At his mother's insistence, William stayed in school, where he excelled, and was encouraged by the principal of Great Barrington High School, Frank Hosmer, to prepare for college. Hosmer also arranged to get him the textbooks his family could not afford. When he graduated from high school at sixteen, he was asked to deliver one of the speeches, following those by the valedictorian and others. The local paper reported that

"William Dubois, a colored lad who has had good standing...provoked repeated applause" with his speech. Many thought his was the best of the lot.

Du Bois had put off his dreams of Harvard to help support the family, when, in March 1885, the year after his graduation, his mother suddenly died. He was taken in by his aunt Minerva and, supported by four Congregational churches, was sent to a college for blacks, Fisk University in Nashville. As an African-American in the South, Du Bois began to experience the racial hatred that he had largely avoided in Massachusetts. Once he accidentally brushed against a white woman in town, apologized, and was stunned by a string of curses from the red-faced woman. In the summer after his sophomore year, he decided to walk through rural Tennessee, where he discovered how rural blacks lived less than fifty years after Emancipation. Du Bois later said that at Fisk he accepted his racial identity: "Henceforward I was a Negro."

In 1888, Du Bois finally headed for Harvard, where he earned his Ph.D. in social science, writing his dissertation on the slave trade. His Harvard years were interrupted in 1892 when he traveled to Europe on a fellowship, studying at the University of Berlin. His first teaching job, in 1895, was as classics professor at Wilberforce University in Ohio, where he met and married Nina Gomer, one of his students. The following year he worked in Philadelphia on a sociological study called *The Philadelphia Negro*, which was published in 1899. By then Du Bois was a professor of economics and history at Atlanta University, and the father of a son, Burghardt.

In that same year an incident occurred that changed his life. A black farmer, Sam Hose, had been lynched and burned after killing a white farmer, and pieces of his body distributed as souvenirs. Heading to the offices of the *Atlanta Constitution* with a restrained letter to the editor on the lynching, Du Bois passed a white storeowner's window, where he saw the burned knuckles of Sam Hose on display. Returning to the university, he decided that "one could not be a calm, cool, detached scientist while Negroes were lynched, murdered, and starved." Soon after, his son died of diphtheria and Nina, who hated the racism of Atlanta, begged him to leave. The next year, 1900, Du Bois lectured in Europe, while his wife, back in Great Barrington, gave birth to a daughter, Nina Yolande. Also during this time, Du Bois developed deep disagreement with Booker T. Washington over the way to combat racism, which saw its expression in Du Bois's writings, including *Souls of Black Folk* (1903).

In 1910, Du Bois and his family left Atlanta so that he could take a position as editor of *Crisis*, the journal of the National Association for the Advancement of Colored People (NAACP), where he remained until 1934, when he returned to Atlanta University for ten more years. In addition to *The Souls of Black Folk*, Du Bois is the author of such works as *The Negro* (1915), *Black Reconstruction in America* (1935), *Color and Democracy* (1945), *The World and Africa* (1947), and *In Battle for Peace: The Story of My 83rd Birthday* (1952). In 1961, he joined the Communist party, renounced his American citizenship, and moved to Ghana, where he died two years later.

In 1903, Du Bois saw education as the key to African–American equality. The "Talented Tenth," the educated elite of African–Americans and whites together, he believed, would lead the masses to a new society of freedom and equality. By 1932, however, as Alvin F. Poussaint writes in his introduction to the 1969 reprinting of *Souls of Black Folk*, Du Bois no longer believed in the power of this joint elite nor in the power of the vote to achieve equality; instead he called for African–Americans to take control themselves. Poussaint traces the black power movement of the sixties directly to W. E. B. Du Bois:

> The current programs for black economic independence, political control by blacks of their own communities, the sudden outgrowth of courses in Afro-American history, art, etc., taught by blacks for blacks in centers of learning across the country, the heavy emphasis on the psychological uplifting of the black masses by concentrating on the positive aspects of blackness—all were part of Du Bois's message, and all are part of the current movement in black America today. Indeed the whole concept of what is today known as black consciousness found its beginnings in the mind of Du Bois.

OF MR. BOOKER T. WASHINGTON AND OTHERS (1903)

From birth till death enslaved; in word, in deed, unmanned!

·

Hereditary bondsmen! Know ye not
Who would be free themselves must strike the blow?
—BYRON[1]

EASILY THE MOST striking thing in the history of the American Negro since 1876[2] is the ascendancy of Mr. Booker T. Washington.[3] It began at the time when war memories and ideals were rapidly passing; a day of astonishing commercial development was dawning;

---

[1]*Byron* from *Childe Harold's Pilgrimage* Part 2 lxxvi.

[2]*1876* Du Bois is referring to the year that Rutherford B. Hayes became president. Hayes withdrew all federal troops from the south, thereby ending Reconstruction and allowing the restoration of white rule. As a result, African-Americans lost many civil and political rights.

[3]*Mr. Booker T. Washington* (1856–1915) American educator whose mother had been a slave on a plantation. He worked as a janitor to pay for his board at Hampton Institute in Virginia, where a friend of the principal paid his tuition. Before his schooling, he had worked in a coal mine. After he graduated, he taught at Hampton and later developed a night school. In 1881, he organized Tuskegee Institute, an industrial school for African-Americans located in Alabama.

a sense of doubt and hesitation overtook the freedmen's sons,—then it was that his leading began. Mr. Washington came, with a single definite programme, at the psychological moment when the nation was a little ashamed of having bestowed so much sentiment on Negroes, and was concentrating its energies on Dollars. His programme of industrial education, conciliation of the South, and submission and silence as to civil and political rights, was not wholly original; the Free Negroes from 1830 up to war-time had striven to build industrial schools, and the American Missionary Association had from the first taught various trades; and Price[4] and others had sought a way of honorable alliance with the best of the Southerners. But Mr. Washington first indissolubly linked these things; he put enthusiasm, unlimited energy, and perfect faith into his programme, and changed it from a by-path into a veritable Way of Life. And the tale of the methods by which he did this is a fascinating study of human life.

It startled the nation to hear a Negro advocating such a programme after many decades of bitter complaint; it startled and won the applause of the South, it interested and won the admiration of the North; and after a confused murmur of protest, it silenced if it did not convert the Negroes themselves.

To gain the sympathy and coöperation of the various elements comprising the white South was Mr. Washington's first task; and this, at the time Tuskegee was founded, seemed, for a black man, well-nigh impossible. And yet ten years later it was done in the word spoken at Atlanta: "In all things purely social we can be as separate as the five fingers, and yet one as the hand in all things essential to mutual progress." This "Atlanta Compromise" is by all odds the most notable thing in Mr. Washington's career. The South interpreted it in different ways: the radicals received it as a complete surrender of the demand for civil and political equality; the conservatives, as a generously conceived working basis for mutual understanding. So both approved it, and to-day its author is certainly the most distinguished Southerner since Jefferson Davis,[5] and the one with the largest personal following.

Next to this achievement comes Mr. Washington's work in gaining place and consideration in the North. Others less shrewd and tactful had formerly essayed to sit on these two stools and had fallen between them; but as Mr. Washington knew the heart of the South from birth and training, so by singular insight he intuitively grasped the spirit of the age which was dominating the North. And so thoroughly did he learn the speech and thought of triumphant commercialism, and the ideals of material prosperity, that the picture of a lone black boy poring over a French grammar amid the weeds and dirt of a neglected home soon seemed to him the acme of absurdities. One wonders what Socrates[6] and St. Francis of Assisi[7] would say to this.

[4]*Price* Joseph C. (1854–1893) educator and writer.

[5]*Jefferson Davis* (1808–1889) elected President of the Confederacy in February 1861.

[6]*Socrates* (469–399 B.C.) Greek philosopher of Athens whose belief in the identity of virtue and knowledge compelled him to seek out virtue through discussions with fellow citizens on the streets. Charged with corrupting youth, he was condemned to death by drinking hemlock. His questioning of statements by examining their implications through dialogue is called the Socratic method of teaching. Most of our information about Socrates comes from Plato, his most famous pupil, who described the trial and death of Socrates in the *Apology,* the *Crito,* and the *Phaedo.*

[7]*St. Francis of Assisi* (1182?–1286) Although born in Italy, the saint's wealthy father often visited France and was fond of its culture. He was therefore nicknamed Francesco, Italian for "Frenchman." The son, who took his father's nickname, converted after imprisonment and an illness, began preaching in rags, and founded the Franciscans, an order of monks devoted to humility, poverty,

And yet this very singleness of vision and thorough oneness with his age is a mark of the successful man. It is as though Nature must needs make men narrow in order to give them force. So Mr. Washington's cult has gained unquestioning followers, his work has wonderfully prospered, his friends are legion, and his enemies are confounded. To-day he stands as the one recognized spokesman of his ten million fellows, and one of the most notable figures in a nation of seventy millions. One hesitates, therefore, to criticise a life which, beginning with so little, has done so much. And yet the time is come when one may speak in all sincerity and utter courtesy of the mistakes and shortcomings of Mr. Washington's career, as well as of his triumphs, without being thought captious or envious, and without forgetting that it is easier to do ill than well in the world.

The criticism that has hitherto met Mr. Washington has not always been of this broad character. In the South especially has he had to walk warily to avoid the harshest judgments,—and naturally so, for he is dealing with the one subject of deepest sensitiveness to that section. Twice—once when at the Chicago celebration of the Spanish-American War[8] he alluded to the color-prejudice that is "eating away the vitals of the South," and once when he dined with President Roosevelt[9] has the resulting Southern criticism been violent enough to threaten seriously his popularity. In the North the feeling has several times forced itself into words, that Mr. Washington's counsels of submission overlooked certain elements of true manhood, and that his educational programme was unnecessarily narrow. Usually, however, such criticism has not found open expression, although, too, the spiritual sons of the Abolitionists have not been prepared to acknowledge that the schools founded before Tuskegee, by men of broad ideals and self-sacrificing spirit, were wholly failures or worthy of ridicule. While, then, criticism has not failed to follow Mr. Washington, yet the prevailing public opinion of the land has been but too willing to deliver the solution of a wearisome problem into his hands, and say, "If that is all you and your race ask, take it."

Among his own people, however, Mr. Washington has encountered the strongest and most lasting opposition, amounting at times to bitterness, and even today continuing strong and insistent even though largely silenced in outward expression by the public opinion of the nation. Some of this opposition is, of course, mere envy; the disappointment of displaced demagogues and the spite of narrow minds. But aside from this, there is among educated and thoughtful colored men in all parts of the land a feeling of deep regret, sorrow, and apprehension at the wide currency and ascendancy which some of Mr. Washington's theories have gained. These same men admire his sincerity of purpose, and are willing to forgive much to honest endeavor which is doing something worth the doing. They coöperate with Mr. Washington as far as they conscientiously can; and, indeed, it is no ordinary tribute to this man's tact and power that, steering as he must between so many diverse interests and opinions, he so largely retains the respect of all.

and the Roman Catholic Church. He had a vision two years before his death in which he was afflicted with the wounds Jesus suffered during the crucifixion (stigmata). Known for his love of nature and humanity, St. Francis was said to have preached to the sparrows.

[8]*Spanish-American War* (1898) expansionist war fought in support of rebels in Cuba, who were seeking independence from Spain. The Treaty of Paris was ratified by Congress in 1899, freeing Cuba and ceding to the United States Puerto Rico and Guam. Spain also sold the Philippines to the U.S. for $20 million.

[9]*President Roosevelt* Theodore Roosevelt (1858–1919) He became President of the United States (1901–1909) when McKinley was assassinated. Roosevelt was a champion for the common man and as president broke up huge corporate trusts. Among many other achievements, he was a Rough Rider in the Spanish-American War.

But the hushing of the criticism of honest opponents is a dangerous thing. It leads some of the best of the critics to unfortunate silence and paralysis of effort, and others to burst into speech so passionately and intemperately as to lose listeners. Honest and earnest criticism from those whose interests are most nearly touched,—criticism of writers by readers, of government by those governed, of leaders by those led,—this is the soul of democracy and the safeguard of modern society. If the best of the American Negroes receive by outer pressure a leader whom they had not recognized before, manifestly there is here a certain palpable gain. Yet there is also irreparable loss,—a loss of that peculiarly valuable education which a group receives when by search and criticism it finds and commissions its own leaders. The way in which this is done is at once the most elementary and the nicest[10] problem of social growth. History is but the record of such group-leadership; and yet how infinitely changeful is its type and character! And of all types and kinds, what can be more instructive than the leadership of a group within a group?—that curious double movement where real progress may be negative and actual advance be relative retrogression. All this is the social student's inspiration and despair.

Now in the past the American Negro has had instructive experience in the choosing of group leaders, founding thus a peculiar dynasty which in the light of present conditions is worth while studying. When sticks and stones and beasts form the sole environment of a people, their attitude is largely one of determined opposition to and conquest of natural forces. But when to earth and brute is added an environment of men and ideas, then the attitude of the imprisoned group may take three main forms,—a feeling of revolt and revenge; an attempt to adjust all thought and action to the will of the greater group; or, finally, a determined effort at self-realization and self-development despite environing opinion. The influence of all of these attitudes at various times can be traced in the history of the American Negro, and in the evolution of his successive leaders.

Before 1750, while the fire of African freedom still burned in the veins of the slaves, there was in all leadership or attempted leadership but the one motive of revolt and revenge,—typified in the terrible Maroons,[11] the Danish blacks,[12] and Cato of Stono,[13] and veiling all the Americas in fear of insurrection. The liberalizing tendencies of the latter half of the eighteenth century brought, along with kindlier relations between black and white, thoughts of ultimate adjustment and assimilation. Such aspiration was especially voiced in the earnest songs of Phyllis,[14] in the martyrdom of Attucks,[15] the fight-

---

[10]*nicest* most subtle or precise.

[11]*Maroons* term for fugitive slaves in the 17th and 18th centuries in Guiana and the West Indies.

[12]*Danish blacks* descendants of slaves. What are now called the American Virgin Islands became a royal colony of Denmark in 1784. The Danes had claimed the islands as early as 1683 and had purchased St. Croix from France in 1733. The United States bought the islands from Denmark in 1917.

[13]*Cato of Stono* In 1739, slaves in Stono, South Carolina, robbed a store for arms and headed for Florida, collecting more runaways and killing whites as they moved along. The rebellion resulted in the deaths of forty-four blacks and thirty whites, and was known as the Cato Conspiracy at Stono.

[14]*Phyllis* Wheatley (1753?–1784), poet brought from Africa in 1761 and purchased by Boston merchant John Wheatley, who educated her and encouraged her talent. She published *Poems on Various Subjects* in 1773. Although she later gained her freedom and visited England, she died in poverty.

[15]*Attucks* Crispus (1723?–1770) One of five people killed by British troops in the Boston Massacre, Attucks, believed to be of African descent, was an active agitator for independence.

ing of Salem and Poor,[16] the intellectual accomplishments of Banneker and Derham,[17] and the political demands of the Cuffes.[18]

Stern financial and social stress after the war cooled much of the previous humanitarian ardor. The disappointment and impatience of the Negroes at the persistence of slavery and serfdom voiced itself in two movements. The slaves in the South, aroused undoubtedly by vague rumors of the Haytian revolt,[19] made three fierce attempts at insurrection,—in 1800 under Gabriel in Virginia, in 1822 under Vesey[20] in Carolina, and in 1831 again in Virginia under the terrible Nat Turner.[21] In the Free States, on the other hand, a new and curious attempt at self-development was made. In Philadelphia and New York color-prescription led to a withdrawal of Negro communicants from white churches and the formation of a peculiar socio-religious institution among the Negroes known as the African Church,—an organization still living and controlling in its various branches over a million of men.

Walker's[22] wild appeal against the trend of the times showed how the world was changing after the coming of the cotton-gin. By 1830 slavery seemed hopelessly fastened on the South, and the slaves thoroughly cowed into submission. The free Negroes of the North, inspired by the mulatto immigrants from the West Indies, began to change the basis of their demands; they recognized the slavery of slaves, but insisted that they themselves were freemen, and sought assimilation and amalgamation with the nation on the same terms with other men. Thus, Forten[23] and Purvis[24] of Philadelphia, Shad of Wilmington, Du Bois[25] of New Haven, Barbadoes of Boston, and others, strove singly and together as men, they said, not as slaves; as "people of color," not as "Negroes." The trend of the times, however, refused them recognition save in individual and exceptional cases, considered them as one with all the despised blacks, and they soon found themselves striving to keep even the rights they formerly had of voting and working and moving as freemen. Schemes of migration and colonization arose among them; but these they refused to entertain, and they eventually turned to the Abolition movement as a final refuge.

[16]*Salem and Poor* Peter Salem (1750–1816), black soldier in the American revolution.

[17]*Banneker and Derham* Benjamin Banneker (1731–1806) was a black inventor, mathematician, and astronomer who helped to survey the land and devise the plan for Washington, D.C. James Derham (1762–18??), African-American physician.

[18]*the Cuffes* Paul (1759–1817), a mariner and merchant.

[19]*Haytain revolt* The 1791 uprising of Creoles against the French led by Vincent Oge; this revolt led to sporadic rebellions of bands of blacks led by Toussaint L'Overature, a French officer who had once been a slave.

[20]*Vesey,* Denmark (1767–1822) He bought his freedom from slavery in 1800 after winning a lottery. In 1822, he planned a rebellion of slaves in South Carolina, but he and thirty-four others were hanged when an informer gave away their plans.

[21]*Nat Turner* (1800–1831), leader of the insurrection of slaves in 1831 in Southhampton, Virginia. His band of slaves killed Turner's owners and perhaps fifty-five others before thirteen slaves and freed blacks were hanged. Turner ran off into the woods, but was captured and hanged six weeks later.

[22]*Walker's* David Walker (1785–1830), African-American abolitionist.

[23]*Forten,* James (1766–1842), African-American inventor and abolitionist.

[24]*Purvis,* Robert (1810–1898), African-American abolitionist.

[25]*Du Bois* Probably Alexander Du Bois, who was W. E. B.'s grandfather.

Here, led by Remond,[26] Nell,[27] Wells-Brown,[28] and Douglass,[29] a new period of self-assertion and self-development dawned. To be sure, ultimate freedom and assimilation was the ideal before the leaders, but the assertion of the manhood rights of the Negro by himself was the main reliance, and John Brown's[30] raid was the extreme of its logic. After the war and emancipation, the great form of Frederick Douglass, the greatest of American Negro leaders, still led the host. Self-assertion, especially in political lines, was the main programme, and behind Douglass came Elliot,[31] Bruce,[32] and Langston,[33] and the Reconstruction politicians, and, less conspicuous but of greater social significance, Alexander Crummell[34] and Bishop Daniel Payne.[35]

Then came the Revolution of 1876,[36] the suppression of the Negro votes, the changing and shifting of ideals, and the seeking of new lights in the great night. Douglass, in his old age, still bravely stood for the ideals of his early manhood,—ultimate assimilation *through* self-assertion, and on no other terms. For a time Price[37] arose as a new leader, destined, it seemed, not to give up, but to re-state the old ideals in a form less repugnant to the white South. But he passed away in his prime. Then came the new leader. Nearly all the former ones had become leaders by the silent suffrage of their fellows, had sought to lead their own people alone, and were usually, save Douglass, little known outside their race. But Booker T. Washington arose as essentially the leader not of one race but of two,—a compromiser between the South, the North, and the Negro. Naturally the Negroes resented, at first bitterly, signs of compromise which surrendered their civil and political rights, even though this was to be exchanged for larger chances of economic development. The rich and dominating North, however, was not only weary of the race

[26]*Remond,* Charles L. (1810–1873), African-American abolitionist.

[27]*Nell,* William C. Nell (1816–1874), African-American writer and abolitionist.

[28]*Wells-Brown,* William (1814–1884), African-American abolitionist.

[29]*Douglass,* Frederick (1817?–1895), escaped from slavery in 1838, worked in Massachusetts and delivered a famous speech before the Massachusetts Anti-Slavery Society in 1841. In 1845, he published *Narrative of the Life of Frederick Douglass.* In New York State he edited the abolitionist paper *North Star* for seventeen years, and became a strong voice for the civil rights of blacks during Reconstruction, serving as marshal to the District of Columbia (1877–1881) and minister to Haiti (1889–1891).

[30]*John Brown* (1800–1859) was a white abolitionist who, with four sons and two others, killed five proslavery men claiming he was an instrument of God. In 1859, he and his followers, hoping to arm slaves, incite rebellions, and establish a refuge for blacks, took over Harpers Ferry in West Virginia, holding the people there as prisoners. The U.S. Marines, led by Robert E. Lee, attacked and killed ten of Brown's men. Brown was hanged, but his calm confidence in the cause made him appear to be a martyr to many in the North.

[31]*Elliot,* Robert Brown (1842–1884), United States Congressman from South Carolina.

[32]*Bruce,* Blanche Kelso (1841–1898), United States Senator from Mississippi.

[33]*Langston,* John Mercer (1829–1897), United States Congressman.

[34]*Alexander Crummell* (1819–1898), African-American minister and abolitionist (see essay by Gates).

[35]*Bishop Daniel Payne* founded Wilberforce University, a co-educational African Methodist Episcopal institution, in 1856.

[36]*Revolution of 1876* See footnote 2.

[37]*Price,* See footnote 4.

problem, but was investing largely in Southern enterprises, and welcomed any method of peaceful coöperation. Thus, by national opinion, the Negroes began to recognize Mr. Washington's leadership; and the voice of criticism was hushed.

Mr. Washington represents in Negro thought the old attitude of adjustment and submission; but adjustment at such a peculiar time as to make his programme unique. This is an age of unusual economic development, and Mr. Washington's programme naturally takes an economic cast, becoming a gospel of Work and Money to such an extent as apparently almost completely to overshadow the higher aims of life. Moreover, this is an age when the more advanced races are coming in closer contact with the less developed races, and the race-feeling is therefore intensified; and Mr. Washington's programme practically accepts the alleged inferiority of the Negro races. Again, in our own land, the reaction from the sentiment of war time has given impetus to race-prejudice against Negroes, and Mr. Washington withdraws many of the high demands of Negroes as men and American citizens. In other periods of intensified prejudice all the Negro's tendency to self-assertion has been called forth; at this period a policy of submission is advocated. In the history of nearly all other races and peoples the doctrine preached at such crises has been that manly self-respect is worth more than lands and houses, and that a people who voluntarily surrender such respect, or cease striving for it, are not worth civilizing.

In answer to this, it has been claimed that the Negro can survive only through submission. Mr. Washington distinctly asks that black people give up at least for the present, three things,—

First, political power,

Second, insistence on civil rights,

Third, higher education of Negro youth,—and concentrate all their energies on industrial education, and accumulation of wealth, and the conciliation of the South. This policy has been courageously and insistently advocated for over fifteen years, and has been triumphant for perhaps ten years. As a result of this tender of the palm-branch, what has been the return? In these years there have occurred:

1. The disfranchisement of the Negro.
2. The legal creation of a distinct status of civil inferiority for the Negro.
3. The steady withdrawal of aid from institutions for the higher training of the Negro.

These movements are not, to be sure, direct results of Mr. Washington's teachings; but his propaganda has, without a shadow of doubt, helped their speedier accomplishment. The question then comes: Is it possible, and probable, that nine millions of men can make effective progress in economic lines if they are deprived of political rights, made a servile caste, and allowed only the most meagre chance for developing their exceptional men? If history and reason give any distinct answer to these questions, it is an emphatic *No*. And Mr. Washington thus faces the triple paradox of his career:

1. He is striving nobly to make Negro artisans business men and property-owners; but it is utterly impossible, under modern competitive methods, for workingmen and property-owners to defend their rights and exist without the right of suffrage.
2. He insists on thrift and self-respect, but at the same time counsels a silent submission to civic inferiority such as is bound to sap the manhood of any race in the long run.
3. He advocates common-school and industrial training, and depreciates institutions of higher learning; but neither the Negro common-schools, nor Tuskegee itself, could

remain open a day were it not for teachers trained in Negro colleges, or trained by their graduates.

This triple paradox in Mr. Washington's position is the object of criticism by two classes of colored Americans. One class is spiritually descended from Toussaint the Savior,[38] through Gabriel, Vesey, and Turner, and they represent the attitude of revolt and revenge; they hate the white South blindly and distrust the white race generally, and so far as they agree on definite action, think that the Negro's only hope lies in emigration beyond the borders of the United States. And yet, by the irony of fate, nothing has more effectually made this programme seem hopeless than the recent course of the United States toward weaker and darker peoples in the West Indies, Hawaii, and the Philippines,—for where in the world may we go and be safe from lying and brute force?[39]

The other class of Negroes who cannot agree with Mr. Washington has hitherto said little aloud. They deprecate the sight of scattered counsels, of internal disagreement; and especially they dislike making their just criticism of a useful and earnest man an excuse for a general discharge of venom from small-minded opponents. Nevertheless, the questions involved are so fundamental and serious that it is difficult to see how men like the Grimkes,[40] Kelly Miller,[41] J. W. E. Bowen, and other representatives of this group, can much longer be silent. Such men feel in conscience bound to ask of this nation three things:

1. The right to vote.
2. Civic equality.
3. The education of youth according to ability.

They acknowledge Mr. Washington's invaluable service in counselling patience and courtesy in such demands; they do not ask that ignorant black men vote when ignorant whites are debarred, or that any reasonable restrictions in the suffrage should not be applied; they know that the low social level of the mass of the race is responsible for much discrimination against it, but they also know, and the nation knows, that relentless color-prejudice is more often a cause than a result of the Negro's degradation; they seek the abatement of this relic of barbarism, and not its systematic encouragement and pampering by all agencies of social power from the Associated Press to the Church of Christ. They advocate, with Mr. Washington, a broad system of Negro common schools supplemented by thorough industrial training; but they are surprised that a man of Mr. Washington's insight cannot see that no such educational system ever has rested or can rest on any other basis than that of the well-equipped college and university, and they insist that

---

[38]*Toussaint the Savior.* See footnote 19.

[39]*brute force* Du Bois is referring to the imperialistic occupation of the West Indies, first by Europeans and later by the United States. European colonists obliterated most of the indigenous populations of the West Indies and imported Africans to supply labor for sugar cane plantations. The U.S. purchased the Virgin Islands from Denmark in 1917 (see also footnote 13). The U.S. claimed Hawaii as a protectorate in 1893, having already established a long-time commercial interest in its sugar industry. For Puerto Rico and the Philippines, see footnote 8.

[40]*the Grimkes,* Archibald Henry (1849–1930), U. S. consul and writer; Charlotte Forten Grimke (1837–1914), writer and abolitionist, and Francis James Grimke (1850–1937), writer and scholar.

[41]*Kelly Miller* (1863–1939), educator.

there is a demand for a few such institutions throughout the South to train the best of the Negro youth as teachers, professional men, and leaders.

This group of men honor Mr. Washington for his attitude of conciliation toward the white South; they accept the "Atlanta Compromise" in its broadest interpretation; they recognize, with him, many signs of promise, many men of high purpose and fair judgment, in this section; they know that no easy task has been laid upon a region already tottering under heavy burdens. But, nevertheless, they insist that the way to truth and right lies in straightforward honesty, not in indiscriminate flattery; in praising those of the South who do well and criticising uncompromisingly those who do ill; in taking advantage of the opportunities at hand and urging their fellows to do the same, but at the same time in remembering that only a firm adherence to their higher ideals and aspirations will ever keep those ideals within the realm of possibility. They do not expect that the free right to vote, to enjoy civic rights, and to be educated, will come in a moment; they do not expect to see the bias and prejudices of years disappear at the blast of a trumpet; but they are absolutely certain that the way for a people to gain their reasonable rights is not by voluntarily throwing them away and insisting that they do not want them; that the way for a people to gain respect is not by continually belittling and ridiculing themselves; that, on the contrary, Negroes must insist continually, in season and out of season, that voting is necessary to modern manhood, that color discrimination is barbarism, and that black boys need education as well as white boys.

In failing thus to state plainly and unequivocally the legitimate demands of their people, even at the cost of opposing an honored leader, the thinking classes of American Negroes would shirk a heavy responsibility,—a responsibility to themselves, a responsibility to the struggling masses, a responsibility to the darker races of men whose future depends so largely on this American experiment, but especially a responsibility to this nation,—this common Fatherland. It is wrong to encourage a man or a people in evildoing; it is wrong to aid and abet a national crime simply because it is unpopular not to do so. The growing spirit of kindliness and reconciliation between the North and South after the frightful difference of a generation ago ought to be a source of deep congratulation to all, and especially to those whose mistreatment caused the war; but if that reconciliation is to be marked by the industrial slavery and civic death of those same black men, with permanent legislation into a position of inferiority, then those black men, if they are really men, are called upon by every consideration of patriotism and loyalty to oppose such a course by all civilized methods, even though such opposition involves disagreement with Mr. Booker T. Washington. We have no right to sit silently by while the inevitable seeds are sown for a harvest of disaster to our children, black and white.

First, it is the duty of black men to judge the South discriminatingly. The present generation of Southerners are not responsible for the past, and they should not be blindly hated or blamed for it. Furthermore, to no class is the indiscriminate endorsement of the recent course of the South toward Negroes more nauseating than to the best thought of the South. The South is not "solid"; it is a land in the ferment of social change, wherein forces of all kinds are fighting for supremacy; and to praise the ill the South is today perpetrating is just as wrong as to condemn the good. Discriminating and broad-minded criticism is what the South needs,—needs it for the sake of her own white sons and daughters, and for the insurance of robust, healthy mental and moral development.

To-day even the attitude of the Southern whites toward the blacks is not, as so many assume, in all cases the same; the ignorant Southerner hates the Negro, the workingmen fear his competition, the money-makers wish to use him as a laborer, some of the educated see a menace in his upward development, while others—usually the sons of the masters—

wish to help him to rise. National opinion has enabled this last class to maintain the Negro common schools, and to protect the Negro partially in property, life, and limb. Through the pressure of the money-makers, the Negro is in danger of being reduced to semi-slavery, especially in the country districts; the workingmen, and those of the educated who fear the Negro, have united to disfranchise him, and some have urged his deportation; while the passions of the ignorant are easily aroused to lynch and abuse any black man. To praise this intricate whirl of thought and prejudice is nonsense; to inveigh indiscriminately against "the South" is unjust; but to use the same breath in praising Governor Aycock, exposing Senator Morgan, arguing with Mr. Thomas Nelson Page,[42] and denouncing Senator Ben Tillman,[43] is not only sane, but the imperative duty of thinking black men.

It would be unjust to Mr. Washington not to acknowledge that in several instances he has opposed movements in the South which were unjust to the Negro; he sent memorials to the Louisiana and Alabama constitutional conventions, he has spoken against lynching, and in other ways has openly or silently set his influence against sinister schemes and unfortunate happenings. Notwithstanding this, it is equally true to assert that on the whole the distinct impression left by Mr. Washington's propaganda is, first, that the South is justified in its present attitude toward the Negro because of the Negro's degradation; secondly, that the prime cause of the Negro's failure to rise more quickly is his wrong education in the past; and, thirdly, that his future rise depends primarily on his own efforts. Each of these propositions is a dangerous half-truth. The supplementary truths must never be lost sight of: first, slavery and race-prejudice are potent if not sufficient causes of the Negro's position; second, industrial and common-school training were necessarily slow in planting because they had to await the black teachers trained by higher institutions,— it being extremely doubtful if any essentially different development was possible, and certainly a Tuskegee was unthinkable before 1880; and, third, while it is a great truth to say that the Negro must strive and strive mightily to help himself, it is equally true that unless his striving be not simply seconded, but rather aroused and encouraged, by the initiative of the richer and wiser environing group, he cannot hope for great success.

In his failure to realize and impress this last point, Mr. Washington is especially to be criticised. His doctrine has tended to make the whites, North and South, shift the burden of the Negro problem to the Negro's shoulders and stand aside as critical and rather pessimistic spectators; when in fact the burden belongs to the nation, and the hands of none of us are clean if we bend not our energies to righting these great wrongs.

The South ought to be led, by candid and honest criticism, to assert her better self and do her full duty to the race she has cruelly wronged and is still wronging. The North— her co-partner in guilt—cannot salve her conscience by plastering it with gold. We cannot settle this problem by diplomacy and suaveness, by "policy" alone. If worse come to worst, can the moral fibre of this country survive the slow throttling and murder of nine millions of men?

The black men of America have a duty to perform, a duty stern and delicate,—a forward movement to oppose a part of the work of their greatest leader. So far as Mr. Wash-

---

[42]*Mr. Thomas Nelson Page* (1853–1922) diplomat and author of sentimental novels and stories of the old South, such as *Red Rock* (1898) and *Ole Virginia* (1887). Page was ambassador to Italy from 1913–1919.

[43]*Senator Ben Tillman* (1847–1918) Senator from South Carolina from 1895–1918, he served two terms as governor (1890–1894) and led the state constitutional convention in 1890, in which rules were adopted that prevented African-Americans from voting in his state. He supported Bryan and free silver at the Democratic National convention of 1896.

ington preaches Thrift, Patience, and Industrial Training for the masses, we must hold up his hands and strive with him, rejoicing in his honors and glorying in the strength of this Joshua called of God and of man to lead the headless host. But so far as Mr. Washington apologizes for injustice, North or South, does not rightly value the privilege and duty of voting, belittles the emasculating effects of caste distinctions, and opposes the higher training and ambition of our brighter minds,—so far as he, the South, or the Nation, does this,—we must unceasingly and firmly oppose them. By every civilized and peaceful method we must strive for the rights which the world accords to men, clinging unwaveringly to those great words which the sons of the Fathers would fain forget: "We hold these truths to be self-evident: That all men are created equal; that they are endowed by their Creator with certain unalienable rights; that among these are life, liberty, and the pursuit of happiness."

Understanding and Analysis

1. This third chapter is carefully structured. What are the main sections of the chapter?

2. When do you as a reader first sense that Du Bois does not agree with Washington's ideas? Select some specific words that indicate the tone Du Bois takes in his description of Washington's success.

3. When constructing an argument, it is good practice to grant to your opponent as much ground as possible early on, so that you can gain his or her trust before you present your position. What good qualities does Du Bois grant to Washington?

4. Why does Du Bois hesitate to criticize Washington?

5. Who before Du Bois has criticized Washington? Why have they been "hushed"?

6. Du Bois defines three attitudes an "imprisoned group may take." What are they? Which of the three attitudes does Washington take? Which attitude do Du Bois and other "Negroes who cannot agree with Mr. Washington" take?

7. What are some of the reasons that Du Bois spends so much of the chapter tracing "the evolution of [the American Negro's] successive leaders"?

8. What kind of audience does Du Bois appear to be addressing in this section of the chapter?

9. What are some of the evils that Du Bois says Washington has committed?

10. Why does Du Bois again grant Washington some ground near the end of the chapter? How do you react to such praise this time?

11. Find some sentences in the chapter that particularly appeal to you. What are some of the characteristics of Du Bois's style that contribute to the force of his argument?

Comparison

1. Chesterton and Du Bois make good use of the epigram. Examine three or four examples from each essayist to discover similarities and differences in the style of each. Does one seem more effective to you than the other? Why?

2. Compare Twain's claims about the ways we form opinions with Du Bois's presentation of his opinion of Washington. How important is the audience to the views of each essayist? Do you think Du Bois would agree with Twain's final statement? What is your evidence?

3. Du Bois and Washington are two early and significant leaders of African-Americans in America. Can you find traces of their attitudes in the attitudes of later African-American leaders and writers such as Zora Neale Hurston, Martin Luther King, Jr., Malcolm X, James Baldwin, Gerald Early, or Jamaica Kincaid?

Max Beerbohm
(1872–1956)

Max Beerbohm was born in London, the youngest child of a middle-class merchant who had four children by his first wife, married her sister after his first wife died, and had four more. Max's half-brother, Herbert, a successful actor and theater manager, introduced the young Max to many celebrities and helped kindle a love for the arts, sketching, and dressing theatrically. Early on, Max became, as biographer Bruce McElderry notes "a young dandy." Educated at the Charterhouse and Merton College, Oxford, Beerbohm left in 1894 before earning a degree. His career was already underway. While still at Oxford, he sold thirty-six drawings, entitled "Club Types," to a magazine called the *Strand* and at least twenty other caricatures to other magazines before 1896. When he was only twenty-two, his comic essays were accepted by the famous turn-of-the-century quarterly *The Yellow Book* (1894), which also published the work of Aubrey Beardsley and Henry James. After returning from a trip to America with his half brother's theatrical troupe, he published the ironic *Works of Max Beerbohm* (1895), and in 1898 he succeeded George Bernard Shaw as drama critic for the *Saturday Review*.

By 1910, when he married Florence Kahn, he had published two more collections of essays, *More* in 1899 and *Yet Again* in 1909, and held four exhibitions of his drawings, in 1901, 1904 (published as *The Poets' Corner*), 1907, and 1908 (published as *A Book of Caricatures*). After his marriage, he gave up his position at the *Saturday Review* and moved with his wife to Italy. He continued nonetheless to exhibit his drawings and publish his prose in England—in 1911 *Zuleika Dobson*, a deliciously satiric novel about life at Oxford, in 1912 *A Christmas Garland*, a parody of the prose styles of such famous authors such as Henry James, Rudyard Kipling, Thomas Hardy, and Joseph Conrad. In 1920, he published a series of essays entitled *And Even Now*, from which "A Clergyman" is taken.

Beerbohm was perhaps most popular in the 1920s, when he published numerous collections of drawings, including those of poets (*Rosetti and his Circle*, 1922), politicians, members of the royal family, and a hundred and nine people (*Ghosts*, 1928). Also between 1922 and 1928 he again published his *Works*, this time in ten volumes. For the duration of the two world wars, he returned to England and was knighted in 1939. During the Second World War he delivered highly popular radio talks that were published in 1947 as *Mainly on the Air*. In 1944, his cottage south of London was destroyed by a German bomb, and he and his wife had to live with friends. Three years later the Beerbohms returned to Italy where, in 1950, his wife died after a long illness. In his final years, Max Beerbohm lived quietly in Italy, visited by friends, whom he entertained with amusing stories from his life. In 1958, at age 83, he married his nurse and housekeeper, Elizabeth Jungmann; a month later he died.

Beerbohm gained early popularity because of his wit, charm, and brilliance. Although both Twain and Beerbohm delighted in pricking pretension, Beerbohm derived humor not from regional dialects but from his classical background, peppering his pages with Latin phrases, literary allusions, satirical jabs at the snobs of his day. But his was not a biting satire. What he says of caricatures may also be said of his prose—they present "exaggeration for the mere sake of exaggeration" to make us laugh, not to impose a moral judgment:

> "The most perfect caricature is that which, on a small surface, with the simplest means, most accurately exaggerates, to the highest point, the peculiarities of a human being, at his most characteristic moment, in the most beautiful manner" ("The Spirit of Caricature" from *A Variety of Things*, 1928).

Throughout his life, he held in mind the image of the future, but, like Chesterton, he was at heart opposed to the new technologies. In "London Revisited" from *Mainly on the Air* he writes:

> I ought to keep my pity for the young people who never saw what I have seen, who will live to see what I shall not see—future great vistas of more and more commercialism, more machinery, more standardization, more nullity.

A Clergyman (*1918*)

FRAGMENTARY, PALE, MOMENTARY; almost nothing; glimpsed and gone; as it were, a faint human hand thrust up, never to reappear, from beneath the rolling waters of Time, he forever haunts my memory and solicits my weak imagination. Nothing is told of him but that once, abruptly, he asked a question, and received an answer.

This was on the afternoon of April 7th, 1778, at Streatham, in the well-appointed house of Mr Thrale.[1] Johnson,[2] on the morning of that day, had entertained Bos-

---

[1]*Mr. Thrale* Beginning in about 1765, the Thrales, Henry and Hester, often entertained Samuel Johnson.

[2]*Johnson,* Samuel (1709–1784). Dr. Johnson was one of the most important literary figures in the eighteenth century. His works include poetry, a play, essays, biographies, criticism, and a diction-

well[3] at breakfast in Bolt Court, and invited him to dine at Thrale Hall. The two took coach and arrived early. It seems that Sir John Pringle had asked Boswell to ask Johnson 'what were the best English sermons for style.' In the interval before dinner, accordingly, Boswell reeled off the names of several divines whose prose might or might not win commendation. 'Atterbury?' he suggested. 'JOHNSON: Yes, Sir, one of the best. BOSWELL: Tillotson? JOHNSON: Why, not now. I should not advise any one to imitate Tillotson's style; though I don't know; I should be cautious of censuring anything that has been applauded by so many suffrages.[4]—South is one of the best, if you except his peculiarities, and his violence, and sometimes coarseness of language.—Seed has a very fine style; but he is not very theological. Jortin's sermons are very elegant. Sherlock's style, too, is very elegant, though he has not made it his principal study.—And you may add Smalridge. BOSWELL: I like Ogden's Sermons on Prayer very much, both for neatness of style and subtility of reasoning. JOHNSON: I should like to read all that Ogden has written. BOSWELL: What I want to know is, what sermons afford the best specimen of English pulpit eloquence. JOHNSON: We have no sermons addressed to the passions, that are good for anything; if you mean that kind of eloquence. A CLERGYMAN, whose name I do not recollect: Were not Dodd's sermons addressed to the passions? JOHNSON: They were nothing, Sir, be they addressed to what they may.'

The suddenness of it! Bang!—and the rabbit that had popped from its burrow was no more.

I know not which is the more startling—the début of the unfortunate clergyman, or the instantaneousness of his end. Why hadn't Boswell told us there was a clergyman present? Well, we may be sure that so careful and acute an artist had some good reason. And I suppose the clergyman was left to take us unawares because just so did he take the company. Had we been told he was there, we might have expected that sooner or later he would join in the conversation. He would have had a place in our minds. We may assume that in the minds of the company around Johnson he had no place. He sat forgotten, overlooked; so that his self-assertion startled every one just as on Boswell's page it startles us. In Johnson's massive and magnetic presence only some very remarkable man, such as Mr Burke,[5] was sharply distinguishable from the rest. Others might, if they had something in them, stand out slightly. This unfortunate clergyman may have had something in him, but I judge that he lacked the gift of seeming as if he had. That deficiency, however, does not account for the horrid fate that befell him. One of Johnson's strongest and most inveterate feelings was his veneration for the Cloth. To any one in Holy Orders he habitually listened with a grave and charming deference. To-day moreover, he was in

ary. Among the most famous of his works are *The Vanity of Human Wishes* (1749), *The Rambler*, essays published twice weekly from 1750–1752, *Dictionary of the English Language* (1755), *History of Rasselas* (1759), *Preface to Shakespeare* (1765), and *Lives of the Poets* (1781). Johnson established the Literary Club in 1764, where he met with important men of his time, such as the portrait artist Sir Joshua Reynolds, the writer and statesman Edmund Burke, writer and dramatist Oliver Goldsmith, and others.

[3]*Boswell,* James (1740–1795) The famous Scottish biographer of Samuel Johnson met the Doctor in 1763 and joined the Literary Club ten years later. Boswell published *The Life of Samuel Johnson* in 1791; he recorded the conversations of Johnson and his friends so carefully and minutely that Dr. Johnson has been remembered for his talk as much as, if not more than, for his works.

[4]*suffrages* opinions.

[5]*Mr. Burke* see footnote 2.

excellent good humour. He was at the Thrales', where he so loved to be; the day was fine; a fine dinner was in close prospect; and he had had what he always declared to be the sum of human felicity—a ride in a coach. Nor was there in the question put by the clergyman anything likely to enrage him. Dodd was one whom Johnson had befriended in adversity; and it had always been agreed that Dodd in his pulpit was very emotional. What drew the blasting flash must have been not the question itself, but the manner in which it was asked. And I think we can guess what that manner was.

Say the words aloud: 'Were not Dodd's sermons addressed to the passions?' They are words which, if you have any dramatic and histrionic sense, *cannot* be said except in a high, thin voice.

You may, from sheer perversity, utter them in a rich and sonorous baritone or bass. But if you do so, they sound utterly unnatural. To make them carry the conviction of human utterance, you have no choice: you must pipe them.

Remember, now, Johnson was very deaf. Even the people whom he knew well, the people to whose voices he was accustomed, had to address him very loudly. It is probable that this unregarded, young, shy clergyman, when at length he suddenly mustered courage to 'cut in,' let his high, thin voice soar *too* high, insomuch that it was a kind of scream. On no other hypothesis can we account for the ferocity with which Johnson turned and rended him. Johnson didn't, we may be sure, mean to be cruel. The old lion, startled, just struck out blindly. But the force of paw and claws was not the less lethal. We have endless testimony to the strength of Johnson's voice; and the very cadence of those words, 'They were nothing, Sir, be they addressed to what they may,' convinces me that the old lion's jaws never gave forth a louder roar. Boswell does not record that there was any further conversation before the announcement of dinner. Perhaps the whole company had been temporarily deafened. But I am not bothering about *them*. My heart goes out to the poor dear clergyman exclusively.

I said a moment ago that he was young and shy; and I admit that I slipped those epithets in without having justified them to you by due process of induction. Your quick mind will have already supplied what I omitted. A man with a high, thin voice, and without power to impress any one with a sense of his importance, a man so null in effect that even the retentive mind of Boswell did not retain his very name, would assuredly not be a self-confident man. Even if he were not naturally shy, social courage would soon have been sapped in him, and would in time have been destroyed, by experience. That he had not yet given himself up as a bad job, that he still had faint wild hopes, is proved by the fact that he did snatch the opportunity for asking that question. He must, accordingly, have been young. Was he the curate[6] of the neighbouring church? I think so. It would account for his having been invited. I see him as he sits there listening to the great Doctor's pronouncement on Atterbury and those others. He sits on the edge of a chair in the background. He has colourless eyes, fixed earnestly, and a face almost as pale as the clerical bands beneath his somewhat receding chin. His forehead is high and narrow, his hair mouse-coloured. His hands are clasped tight before him, the knuckles standing out sharply. This constriction does not mean that he is steeling himself to speak. He has no positive intention of speaking. Very much, nevertheless, is he wishing in the back of his mind that he *could* say something—something whereat the great Doctor would turn on him and say, after a pause for thought, 'Why yes, Sir. That is most justly observed' or 'Sir, this has never occurred to me. I thank you'—thereby fixing the observer for ever high in the esteem of all. And now in a flash the chance presents itself. 'We have,' shouts Johnson, 'no sermons addressed to the passions, that are

[6]*curate* spiritual pastor in charge of local parish.

good for anything.' I see the curate's frame quiver with sudden impulse, and his mouth fly open, and—no, I can't bear it, I shut my eyes and ears. But audible, even so, is something shrill, followed by something thunderous.

Presently I re-open my eyes. The crimson has not yet faded from that young face yonder, and slowly down either cheek falls a glistening tear. Shades of Atterbury and Tillotson! Such weakness shames the Established Church. What would Jortin and Smalridge have said?—what Seed and South? And, by the way, who *were* they, these worthies? It is a solemn thought that so little is conveyed to us by names which to the palaeo-Georgians[7] conveyed so much. We discern a dim, composite picture of a big man in a big wig and a billowing black gown, with a big congregation beneath him. But we are not anxious to hear what he is saying. We know it is all very elegant. We know it will be printed and be bound in finely-tooled full calf,[8] and no palaeo Georgian gentleman's library will be complete without it. Literate people in those days were comparatively few; but, bating that, one may say that sermons were as much in request as novels are to-day. I wonder, will mankind continue to be capricious? It is a very solemn thought indeed that no more than a hundred-and-fifty years hence the novelists of our time, with all their moral and political and sociological outlook and influence, will perhaps shine as indistinctly as do those old preachers, with all their elegance, now. 'Yes, Sir,' some great pundit may be telling a disciple at this moment, 'Wells[9] is one of the best. Galsworthy[10] is one of the best, if you except his concern for delicacy of style. Mrs Ward[11] has a very firm grasp of problems, but is not very creational.—Caine's[12] books are very edifying. I should like to read all that Caine has written. Miss Corelli,[13] too, is very edifying.—And you may add Upton Sinclair.'[14] 'What I want to know,' says the disciple, 'is, what English novels may be selected as specially enthralling.' The pundit answers: 'We have no novels addressed to the passions that are good for anything, if you mean that kind of enthralment.' And here some poor wretch (whose name the disciple will not remember) inquires: 'Are not Mrs Glyn's[15] novels addressed to the passions?' and is in due form annihilated. Can it be that a time will come

---

[7]*palaeo-Georgians* the British populace living in the early 1700s. "Paleo" means "ancient" and "Georgians" refers to the period in England ruled by the four Georges, that is, from 1714–1830.

[8]*full calf* Calf skin was considered a superior kind of leather.

[9]*Wells,* Herbert George (1866–1946), English science fiction writer best known for *The Time Machine* (1895), *The War of the Worlds* (1898), and *The Shape of Things to Come* (1933).

[10]*Galsworthy,* John (1867–1933), English novelist best known for his set of three trilogies, the *Forsyth Saga* (1922) [the first of which, *A Man of Property,* appeared in 1906], *A Modern Comedy* (1928), and *End of the Chapter* (1934).

[11]*Mrs. Ward* (1850–1920) English novelist known for works that applied religious principles to social situations, such as *Fenwick's Career* (1906) and *The Case of Richard Meynell* (1911).

[12]*Caine* Mr. Hall Caine (1853–1931) friend and secretary to Dante Gabriel Rosetti and author of popular novels such as *The Shadow of a Crime* (1885), *The Deemster* (1887), *The Manxman* (1894), and *The Prodigal Son* (1904). See essay by Chesterton.

[13]*Miss Corelli* pseudonym for Mary Mackay (1855–1924), popular, moralistic English novelist, said to be Queen Victoria's favorite, who wrote *Barabbas* (1893) and *The Sorrows of Satan* (1895).

[14]*Upton Sinclair* (1878–1968) American writer and muckraker, who promoted social and industrial reform through such novels as *The Jungle,* about the Chicago stockyards (1906), *King Coal* (1917), and *Oil!* (1927).

[15]*Mrs. Glyn's* Elinor Glyn (1864–1943) British author of popular romantic novels such as *Three Weeks, One Day, Sequel to Three Weeks, The Point of View,* and her autobiography, *Romantic Adventure.*

when readers of this passage in our pundit's Life will take more interest in the poor name-less wretch than in all the bearers of those great names put together, being no more able or anxious to discriminate between (say) Mrs Ward and Mr Sinclair than we are to set Ogden above Sherlock, or Sherlock above Ogden? It seems impossible. But we must remember that things are not always what they seem.

Every man illustrious in his day, however much he may be gratified by his fame, looks with an eager eye to posterity for a continuance of past favours, and would even live the remainder of his life in obscurity if by so doing he could insure that future generations would preserve a correct attitude towards him forever. This is very natural and human, but, like so many very natural and human things, very silly. Tillotson and the rest need not, after all, be pitied for our neglect of them. They either know nothing about it, or are above such terrene[16] trifles. Let us keep our pity for the seething mass of divines who were *not* elegantly verbose, and had no fun or glory while they lasted. And let us keep a specially large portion for one whose lot was so much worse than merely undistinguished. If that nameless curate had not been at the Thrales' that day, or, being there, had kept the silence that so well became him, his life would have been drab enough, in all con-science. But at any rate an unpromising career would not have been nipped in the bud. And that is what in fact happened, I'm sure of it. A robust man might have rallied under the blow. Not so our friend. Those who knew him in infancy had not expected that he would be reared. Better for him had they been right. It is well to grow up and be ordained, but not if you are delicate and very sensitive, and shall happen to annoy the greatest, the most stentorian and roughest of contemporary personages. 'A Clergyman' never held up his head or smiled again after the brief encounter recorded for us by Boswell. He sank into a rapid decline. Before the next blossoming of Thrale Hall's almond trees he was no more. I like to think that he died forgiving Dr Johnson.

Understanding and Analysis

1. What is the tone of the opening lines of this essay? What effect does the sudden shift in the second paragraph have on your re-evaluation of the first paragraph?

2. The second paragraph is a summary from a passage in Boswell's biography. The rest of the essay is an imaginative analysis of the anecdote, almost what we now call a "close reading" of the story. What deductions does Beerbohm make and upon what evidence? What seems to you to be purely imaginary?

3. Beerbohm addresses the reader directly in this essay and frequently refers to himself as "I." Find and examine all of these instances to determine Beerbohm's attitude toward you, his reader. Who does the author assume is reading his essay?

4. After providing a summary and analysis of an anecdote, Beerbohm provides an imita-tion, recreating the event in what was for him modern times. Although the names and figures change, the structure of the incident remains intact. What is it about the incident that so captures Beerbohm's "weak imagination"? What, in other words, does Beerbohm think is likely to endure throughout time?

5. The author feels pity for the "seething mass" who are not eloquent, not admired during their lives or afterwards. Why is the clergyman's "lot so much worse than merely undis-tinguished"?

[16]*terrene* earthly.

6. Beerbohm seems preoccupied with time in this essay and with things that "are not always what they seem." What are some of the metaphors and comparisons that emphasize his sense of time?

7. What, according to Beerbohm, had already changed in terms of people's preferences between "paleo-Georgian" times and 1918, when this essay was written?

8. Where, if anywhere, is the humor in this essay?

Comparison

1. Despite the fact that one-sentence paragraphs are rare, most of the early authors in this text use them well. Find every instance that you can and compare how they are used. Can you draw some general principles about the effective use of one-sentence paragraphs? Some later essayists also use the one-sentence paragraph. Look, for example, at Dillard's essay. How does her use of that rarity compare with earlier versions of the technique?

2. In this essay Beerbohm skirts a serious question: How can we tell what will be of lasting value in our literature? Does he offer any hints toward an answer? Compare these hints with Eliot's claims in "Tradition and the Individual Talent."

3. Can you think of other circumstances in which a structure similar to that in the anecdote of the clergyman applies? Use your imagination to re-create the structure in a current setting. Include direct addresses to your readers and an analysis of the incident. Try to provide the kind of reasoning and imaginative speculation that Beerbohm uses in your own analysis of your incident. Try also to turn some of your observations into aphoristic claims.

4. Of the men and women mentioned in the essay, probably only two, Johnson and Boswell, will be remembered into the next century. According to Beerbohm, a man who is famous in his own day wants "future generations" to "preserve a correct attitude towards him forever." Beerbohm calls such a wish "silly." Read Eliot's "Tradition and the Individual Talent." Does Eliot care about reputation? Does he believe there to be a "correct attitude" toward an artist or his work? What do you think Beerbohm's fate will be?

5. Read the essays by Carr and FitzGerald. How do their ideas about history affect your reading of Beerbohm?

T. S. Eliot
(1888–1965)

Among the most respected and influential poets and critics of the modern period, Thomas Stearns Eliot was born in St. Louis, Missouri, the youngest of seven children of Henry, president of the Hydraulic-Press Brick Company, and Charlotte, a teacher. As members of a distinguished family (Eliot's grandfather had founded a church, two private schools, and what became Washington University), the Eliots kept to themselves. Tom grew up in an atmosphere of isolation (when he was born, his mother was forty-five, his father forty-seven, and his closest sibling nine years old), and strict control (the family forbade not only drinking and smoking for themselves, but also candy or books such as *Tom Sawyer* and *Huckleberry Finn* for Tom). At Smith Academy, he excelled, both in the classroom and as a writer of stories and verse for the school newspaper. In 1906, he left St. Louis for Harvard, was graduated in three years, then studied at the Sorbonne and at Merton College, Oxford. At Oxford he met Vivienne Haigh-Wood, whom he married in 1915, without the attendance or approval of his family. Deciding to stay in England, Eliot taught for one year at Wycombe Grammar School before taking a post at Lloyds Bank in 1917, where he worked for the next five years. At the same time, he was hired as assistant editor at the *Egoist*, a journal run by Harriet Shaw Weaver.

Meanwhile, Eliot had developed friendships with writers and thinkers such as Bertrand Russell, Ezra Pound, and Virginia Woolf; in June of 1917 the Egoist Press published five hundred copies of *The Lovesong of J. Alfred Prufrock*. The poem caused a sensation among its readers. Also in 1917, at the age of 29, he published his first collection of poems, *Prufrock and Other Observations;* the next year he published his first book of literary criticism, *The Sacred Wood* (from which "Tradition and the Individual Talent" is taken), one of the most important works of criticism of the modern period. Eliot also continued his career in publishing, as founder and editor of the *Criterion* (1922–1939), and editor and director of the publishing company Faber and Faber (1925–1965).

Just as Eliot was establishing his literary and critical reputation, his personal life was becoming strained. On the recommendation of a nerve specialist, he took a three-month leave of absence in 1921. While in Switzerland, he wrote perhaps his most influential poem, *The Waste Land*. At the same time, Vivienne was suffering from insomnia, migraines, and mental instability. According to biographer T. S. Matthews, in 1926, when visiting St. Peter's in Rome, Eliot embarrassed his companions by kneeling "right at the front entrance." Soon after, at the age of thirty-eight, he joined the Anglican Church, later declaring that without religion he could not have survived. Eliot found in his faith a respite from both his personal pain and what he saw as the isolation and tawdry emptiness of modern life. That same year, he renounced his American citizenship and became a British subject. In 1932, he separated from Vivienne, who then spent years calling and writing him in the hope that he would return. She once reportedly sent an advertisement to the Personal column of the *Times* (mercifully never printed) asking, "Will T. S. Eliot please return to his home . . . which he abandoned Sept. 17th 1932 . . . ?"

From his Harvard days to the end of his life, Eliot maintained a close friendship with Emily Hale, to whom he wrote more than a thousand letters.

There has been much speculation on the nature of that friendship; the letters are under seal at the University Library at Princeton until 2020. In 1956, at age sixty-eight, Eliot married his secretary, Valerie Fletcher, this time, by all accounts, happily. Nine years later he died; his *Times* obituary was titled "The Most Influential English Poet of His Time."

Among his best works of poetry are *The Waste Land* (1922), *The Hollow Men* (1925), *Collected Poems 1909–1935* (1936), and *Four Quartets* (1943). His criticism includes *For Lancelot Andrewes* (1928), *The Use of Poetry and the Use of Criticism* (1933), *Elizabethan Essays* (1934), *Essays Ancient and Modern* (1936), and *Notes Toward a Definition of Culture* (1949). He also wrote plays in verse, *Murder in the Cathedral* (1935) and *The Cocktail Party* (1949), as well as *Old Possum's Book of Practical Cats*, on which the musical *Cats!* is based. Influenced by French symbolist poetry, the classical western tradition, eastern philosophy, and the British metaphysical poets, Eliot documented, particularly in his early poetry, the fragmentation and spiritual aridity that has come to be associated with the modern period. In his criticism, Eliot established a new, impersonal theory of literature, which he describes in detail in "Tradition and the Individual Talent." Like Chesterton, T. S. Eliot presented in both his private papers and his public poems views that are anti-Semitic. The most charitable approach to these views is to apply to them Eliot's own prescription: "the past should be altered by the present as much as the present is directed by the past." What he means here is not that we should censor the writers of the past but that we should see them more clearly and objectively than they could see themselves.

TRADITION AND THE INDIVIDUAL TALENT *(1920)*

I

IN ENGLISH WRITING we seldom speak of tradition, though we occasionally apply its name in deploring its absence. We cannot refer to "the tradition" or to "a tradition"; at most, we employ the adjective in saying that the poetry of So-and-so is "traditional" or even "too traditional." Seldom, perhaps, does the word appear except in a phrase of censure. If otherwise, it is vaguely approbative,[1] with the implication, as to the work approved, of some pleasing archæological reconstruction. You can hardly make the word agreeable to English ears without this comfortable reference to the reassuring science of archæology.

Certainly the word is not likely to appear in our appreciations of living or dead writers. Every nation, every race, has not only its own creative, but its own critical turn of mind; and is even more oblivious of the shortcomings and limitations of its critical habits than of those of its creative genius. We know, or think we know, from the enormous mass

---

[1]*approbative* approving or positive.

of critical writing that has appeared in the French language the critical method or habit of the French; we only conclude (we are such unconscious people) that the French are "more critical" than we, and sometimes even plume ourselves a little with the fact, as if the French were the less spontaneous. Perhaps they are; but we might remind ourselves that criticism is as inevitable as breathing, and that we should be none the worse for articulating what passes in our minds when we read a book and feel an emotion about it, for criticizing our own minds in their work of criticism. One of the facts that might come to light in this process is our tendency to insist, when we praise a poet, upon those aspects of his work in which he least resembles anyone else. In these aspects or parts of his work we pretend to find what is individual, what is the peculiar essence of the man. We dwell with satisfaction upon the poet's difference from his predecessors, especially his immediate predecessors; we endeavour to find something that can be isolated in order to be enjoyed. Whereas if we approach a poet without his prejudice[2] we shall often find that not only the best, but the most individual parts of his work may be those in which the dead poets, his ancestors, assert their immortality most vigorously. And I do not mean the impressionable period of adolescence, but the period of full maturity.

Yet if the only form of tradition, of handing down, consisted in following the ways of the immediate generation before us in a blind or timid adherence to its successes, "tradition" should positively be discouraged. We have seen many such simple currents soon lost in the sand; and novelty is better than repetition. Tradition is a matter of much wider significance. It cannot be inherited, and if you want it you must obtain it by great labour. It involves, in the first place, the historical sense, which we may call nearly indispensable to anyone who would continue to be a poet beyond his twenty-fifth year; and the historical sense involves a perception, not only of the pastness of the past, but of its presence; the historical sense compels a man to write not merely with his own generation in his bones, but with a feeling that the whole of the literature of Europe from Homer and within it the whole of the literature of his own country has a simultaneous existence and composes a simultaneous order. This historical sense, which is a sense of the timeless as well as of the temporal and of the timeless and of the temporal together, is what makes a writer traditional. And it is at the same time what makes a writer most acutely conscious of his place in time, of his contemporaneity.

No poet, no artist of any art, has his complete meaning alone. His significance, his appreciation is the appreciation of his relation to the dead poets and artists. You cannot value him alone; you must set him, for contrast and comparison, among the dead. I mean this as a principle of æsthetic, not merely historical, criticism. The necessity that he shall conform, that he shall cohere, is not one-sided; what happens when a new work of art is created is something that happens simultaneously to all the works of art which preceded it. The existing monuments form an ideal order among themselves, which is modified by the introduction of the new (the really new) work of art among them. The existing order is complete before the new work arrives; for order to persist after the supervention[3] of novelty, the *whole* existing order must be, if ever so slightly, altered; and so the relations, proportions, values of each work of art toward the whole are readjusted; and this is conformity between the old and the new. Whoever has approved this idea of order, of the form of European, of English literature, will not find it preposterous that the past should be altered by the pres-

---

[2]*prejudice* Eliot here means the poet's individual characteristics, although the usual meaning of the word applies as well.

[3]*supervention* addition.

ent as much as the present is directed by the past. And the poet who is aware of this will be aware of great difficulties and responsibilities.

In a peculiar sense he will be aware also that he must inevitably be judged by the standards of the past. I say judged, not amputated, by them; not judged to be as good as, or worse or better than, the dead; and certainly not judged by the canons of dead critics. It is a judgment, a comparison, in which two things are measured by each other. To conform merely would be for the new work not really to conform at all; it would not be new, and would therefore not be a work of art. And we do not quite say that the new is more valuable because it fits in; but its fitting in is a test of its value—a test, it is true, which can only be slowly and cautiously applied, for we are none of us infallible judges of conformity. We say: it appears to conform, and is perhaps individual, or it appears individual, and may conform; but we are hardly likely to find that it is one and not the other.

To proceed to a more intelligible exposition of the relation of the poet to the past: he can neither take the past as a lump, an indiscriminate bolus, nor can he form himself wholly on one or two private admirations, nor can he form himself wholly upon one preferred period. The first course is inadmissible, the second is an important experience of youth, and the third is a pleasant and highly desirable supplement. The poet must be very conscious of the main current, which does not at all flow invariably through the most distinguished reputations. He must be quite aware of the obvious fact that art never improves, but that the material of art is never quite the same. He must be aware that the mind of Europe—the mind of his own country—a mind which he learns in time to be much more important than his own private mind—is a mind which changes, and that this change is a development which abandons nothing *en route,* which does not superannuate[4] either Shakespeare, or Homer, or the rock drawing of the Magdalenian draughtsmen.[5] That this development, refinement perhaps, complication certainly, is not, from the point of view of the artist, any improvement. Perhaps not even an improvement from the point of view of the psychologist or not to the extent which we imagine; perhaps only in the end based upon a complication in economics and machinery. But the difference between the present and the past is that the conscious present is an awareness of the past in a way and to an extent which the past's awareness of itself cannot show.

Some one said: "The dead writers are remote from us because we *know* so much more than they did." Precisely, and they are that which we know.

I am alive to a usual objection to what is clearly part of my programme for the *métier*[6] of poetry. The objection is that the doctrine requires a ridiculous amount of erudition (pedantry), a claim which can be rejected by appeal to the lives of poets in any pantheon.[7] It will even be affirmed that much learning deadens or perverts poetic sensibility. While, however, we persist in believing that a poet ought to know as much as will not encroach upon his necessary receptivity and necessary laziness, it is not desirable to confine knowl-

---

[4]*superannuate* To set aside or discard as obsolete; in this passage Eliot is arguing against Plato's position in *The Republic* concerning the value of the past to the present. For Plato, the past must be viewed in terms of the present so that the errors of the past can be discarded. For Eliot, the "conscious present" leads to an understanding of the past beyond its own knowledge of itself, but not to a discarding of errors.

[5]*rock drawing of the Magdalenian draughtsmen* artists belonging to the last upper Paleolithic culture of Europe, from *La Madeleine,* a village in Dordogne, France, where such cave art was found.

[6]*metier* craftsmanship or art.

[7]*pantheon* group of the most eminent figures in a field, in this case the field of poetry.

edge to whatever can be put into a useful shape for examinations, drawing-rooms, or the still more pretentious modes of publicity. Some can absorb knowledge, the more tardy must sweat for it. Shakespeare acquired more essential history from Plutarch[8] than most men could from the whole British Museum. What is to be insisted upon is that the poet must develop or procure the consciousness of the past and that he should continue to develop this consciousness throughout his career.

What happens is a continual surrender of himself as he is at the moment to something which is more valuable. The progress of an artist is a continual self-sacrifice, a continual extinction of personality.

There remains to define this process of depersonalization and its relation to the sense of tradition. It is in this depersonalization that art may be said to approach the condition of science. I shall, therefore, invite you to consider, as a suggestive analogy, the action which takes place when a bit of finely filiated platinum is introduced into a chamber containing oxygen and sulphur dioxide.

II

Honest criticism and sensitive appreciation is directed not upon the poet but upon the poetry. If we attend to the confused cries of the newspaper critics and the susurrus[9] of popular repetition that follows, we shall hear the names of poets in great numbers; if we seek not Blue-book knowledge[10] but the enjoyment of poetry, and ask for a poem, we shall seldom find it. In the last article I tried to point out the importance of the relation of the poem to other poems by other authors, and suggested the conception of poetry as a living whole of all the poetry that has ever been written. The other aspect of this Impersonal theory of poetry is the relation of the poem to its author. And I hinted, by an analogy, that the mind of the mature poet differs from that of the immature one not precisely in any valuation of "personality," not being necessarily more interesting, or having "more to say," but rather by being a more finely perfected medium in which special, or very varied, feelings are at liberty to enter into new combinations.

The analogy was that of the catalyst. When the two gases previously mentioned are mixed in the presence of a filament of platinum, they form sulphurous acid. This combination takes place only if the platinum is present; nevertheless the newly formed acid contains no trace of platinum, and the platinum itself is apparently unaffected; has remained inert, neutral, and unchanged. The mind of the poet is the shred of platinum. It may partly or exclusively operate upon the experience of the man himself; but, the more perfect the artist, the more completely separate in him will be the man who suffers and the mind which creates; the more perfectly will the mind digest and transmute the passions which are its material.

The experience, you will notice, the elements which enter the presence of the transforming catalyst, are of two kinds: emotions and feelings. The effect of a work of art upon the person who enjoys it is an experience different in kind from any experience not

---

[8]*Plutarch* (A.D. 46?–c. 120) Greek biographer whose great work is *Parallel Lives,* a collection of biographies of Greek and Roman heroes set in parallel form to reveal the moral character of each pair. Shakespeare used Sir Thomas North's translation of Plutarch for his Roman plays.

[9]*susurrus* a soft, whispering or rustling sound.

[10]*Blue-book knowledge* the kind solicited in examinations.

of art. It may be formed out of one emotion, or may be a combination of several; and various feelings, inhering for the writer in particular words or phrases or images, may be added to compose the final result. Or great poetry may be made without the direct use of any emotion whatever: composed out of feelings solely. Canto XV of the *Inferno* (Brunetto Latini)[11] is a working up of the emotion evident in the situation; but the effect, though single as that of any work of art, is obtained by considerable complexity of detail. The last quatrain gives an image, a feeling attaching to an image, which "came," which did not develop simply out of what precedes, but which was probably in suspension in the poet's mind until the proper combination arrived for it to add itself to. The poet's mind is in fact a receptacle for seizing and storing up numberless feelings, phrases, images, which remain there until all the particles which can unite to form a new compound are present together.

If you compare several representative passages of the greatest poetry you see how great is the variety of types of combination, and also how completely any semi-ethical criterion of "sublimity" misses the mark. For it is not the "greatness," the intensity, of the emotions, the components, but the intensity of the artistic process, the pressure, so to speak, under which the fusion takes place, that counts. The episode of Paolo and Francesca[12] employs a definite emotion, but the intensity of the poetry is something quite different from whatever intensity in the supposed experience it may give the impression of. It is no more intense, furthermore, than Canto XXVI, the voyage of Ulysses,[13] which has not the direct dependence upon an emotion. Great variety is possible in the process of transmutation of emotion: the murder of Agamemnon,[14] or the agony of Othello, gives an artistic effect apparently closer to a possible original than the scenes from Dante. In the *Agamemnon*, the artistic emotion approximates to the emotion of an actual spectator; in *Othello* to the emotion of the protagonist himself. But the difference between art and the event is always absolute; the combination which is the murder of Agamemnon is probably as complex as that which is the voyage of Ulysses. In either case there has been a fusion of elements. The ode of Keats[15] contains a number of feelings which have noth-

---

[11]*(Brunetto Latini) The Inferno* is the first part of *The Divine Comedy* (the other two are *The Purgatorio* and *Paradisio*), an epic poem by the Italian poet Dante Aligheri (1265–1321). Canto XV takes place in the Seventh Circle and depicts the Sodomites. Brunetto Latini (1220–1294) was a famous political figure in Florence whose allegorical books Dante admired. The image to which Eliot refers in the last quatrain depicts Latini's return to his band of sinners in hell; he is compared to a winning runner for the cloth in a traditional race in Verona, not as one might expect, to one who lost.

[12]*Paolo and Francesca* In Canto V the Second Circle of *The Inferno,* these two lovers tell the story of how, seduced by romantic literature, they allowed their lust to overcome their reason.

[13]*Ulysses* In Canto XXVI, the Eighth Circle Dante sees among the fraudulent counselors Ulysses (hero of Homer's *Odyssey*), who describes his last voyage, the encouragement he gave his old companions, and their drowning in the sea.

[14]*Agamemnon* Greek play by Aeschylus (525–456 B.C.). Part of a trilogy called *The Oresteia*, it dramatizes the return and death of the Greek mythological king of Mycenae, son of Atreus and brother to Menelaus. He sacrificed his daughter Iphigenia to Artemis to get the winds needed to sail to Troy. After the war, when the play takes place, Agamemnon was murdered by his wife, Clytemnestra, and her lover, Aegisthus. His children, Orestes and Electra, killed their mother to avenge his death.

[15]*Keats* "Ode to a Nightingale," 1819.

ing particular to do with the nightingale, but which the nightingale, partly, perhaps, because of its attractive name, and partly because of its reputation, served to bring together.

The point of view which I am struggling to attack is perhaps related to the metaphysical theory of the substantial unity of the soul: for my meaning is, that the poet has, not a "personality" to express, but a particular medium, which is only a medium and not a personality, in which impressions and experiences combine in peculiar and unexpected ways. Impressions and experiences which are important for the man may take no place in the poetry, and those which become important in the poetry may play quite a negligible part in the man, the personality.

I will quote a passage which is unfamiliar enough to be regarded with fresh attention in the light—or darkness—of these observations:

> And now methinks I could e'en chide myself
> For doating on her beauty, though her death
> Shall be revenged after no common action.
> Does the silkworm expend her yellow labours
> For thee? For thee does she undo herself?
> Are lordships sold to maintain ladyships
> For the poor benefit of a bewildering minute?
> Why does yon fellow falsify highways,
> And put his life between the judge's lips,
> To refine such a thing—keeps horse and men
> To beat their valours for her? . . . [16]

In this passage (as is evident if it is taken in its context) there is a combination of positive and negative emotions: an intensely strong attraction toward beauty and an equally intense fascination by the ugliness which is contrasted with it and which destroys it. This balance of contrasted emotion is in the dramatic situation to which the speech is pertinent, but that situation alone is inadequate to it. This is, so to speak, the structural emotion, provided by the drama. But the whole effect, the dominant tone, is due to the fact that a number of floating feelings, having an affinity to this emotion by no means superficially evident, have combined with it to give us a new art emotion.

It is not in his personal emotions, the emotions provoked by particular events in his life, that the poet is in any way remarkable or interesting. His particular emotions may be simple, or crude, or flat. The emotion in his poetry will be a very complex thing, but not with the complexity of the emotions of people who have very complex or unusual emotions in life. One error, in fact, of eccentricity in poetry is to seek for new human emotions to express; and in this search for novelty in the wrong place it discovers the perverse. The business of the poet is not to find new emotions, but to use the ordinary ones and, in working them up into poetry, to express feelings which are not in actual emotions at all. And emotions which he has never experienced will serve his turn as well as those familiar to him. Consequently, we must believe that "emotion recollected in tranquillity"[17] is an inexact formula. For it is neither emotion, nor recollection, nor, without

[16]*for her? . . .* from *The Revenger's Tragedy,* 1607, Act 3, Scene iv by British dramatist Cyril Tourneur (1575–1626).

[17]*in tranquillity* famous description of poetry by William Wordsworth (1770–1850) found in the Preface to the second edition of *Lyrical Ballads,* published in 1800—"Poetry is the spontaneous overflow of powerful feelings; it takes its origin from emotion recollected in tranquility."

distortion of meaning, tranquillity. It is a concentration, and a new thing resulting from the concentration, of a very great number of experiences which to the practical and active person would not seem to be experiences at all; it is a concentration which does not happen consciously or of deliberation. These experiences are not "recollected," and they finally unite in an atmosphere which is "tranquil" only in that it is a passive attending upon the event. Of course this is not quite the whole story. There is a great deal, in the writing of poetry, which must be conscious and deliberate. In fact, the bad poet is usually unconscious where he ought to be conscious, and conscious where he ought to be unconscious. Both errors tend to make him "personal." Poetry is not a turning loose of emotion, but an escape from emotion; it is not the expression of personality, but an escape from personality. But, of course, only those who have personality and emotions know what it means to want to escape from these things.

III

δ δὲ νοῦς ἴσως θειότερόν τι χαὶ ἀπαθές ἐστιν[18]

This essay proposes to halt at the frontier of metaphysics or mysticism, and confine itself to such practical conclusions as can be applied by the responsible person interested in poetry. To divert interest from the poet to the poetry is a laudable aim: for it would conduce to a juster estimation of actual poetry, good and bad. There are many people who appreciate the expression of sincere emotion in verse, and there is a smaller number of people who can appreciate technical excellence. But very few know when there is expression of *significant* emotion, emotion which has its life in the poem and not in the history of the poet. The emotion of art is impersonal. And the poet cannot reach this impersonality without surrendering himself wholly to the work to be done. And he is not likely to know what is to be done unless he lives in what is not merely the present, but the present moment of the past, unless he is conscious, not of what is dead, but of what is already living.

Understanding and Analysis

1. This essay has been one of the most influential critical essays of the century. Look through the essay for clues about the audience Eliot is addressing. In the first paragraph, for instance, Eliot uses "we" to include himself and his readers. From other clues in the paragraph, can you tell more specifically whom "we" includes? Note also Eliot's use of "you." Why does he switch from "we" to "you" here?

2. When Eliot claims that "criticism is as inevitable as breathing," he immediately defines what he means by "criticism": "articulating what passes in our minds when we read a book and feel an emotion about it." Do you agree that "criticism" is as inevitable as breathing?

3. What Eliot is encouraging us to do here, however, is one step more complicated than criticism: he wants us to "criticize our own minds in their work of criticism." Eliot directs

[18]From Aristotle's *On the Soul*, 1:4: "The mind is no doubt something more divine and not subject to pain or suffering."

his attention to the field of English literature, but his comments may apply to other fields as well. What, is he claiming, is most important to readers in 1920? Do we still admire that quality?

4. Eliot writes, "we shall often find that not only the best, but the most individual parts of [a poet's] work may be those in which the dead poets, his ancestors, assert their immortality most vigorously. And I do not mean the impressionable period of adolescence." What kind of influence on the adolescent poet is he alluding to? See also question 8.

5. Eliot expends several paragraphs defining what he means by "tradition" and why he believes it is essential to artists in any field. Explain his position in your own words.

6. What difference does Eliot see between originality and novelty?

7. What does Eliot mean by "judgment"? How does what is original in the poet affect the tradition?

8. Eliot offers three paths that the mature poet cannot take in relation to the poetic tradition. What are they? How does the second one illuminate Eliot's earlier reference to "adolescence"? According to Eliot in part two, in what ways does the adolescent poet differ from the mature poet?

9. What does he mean by "the mind of Europe"?

10. What does Eliot claim is "the difference between the present and the past"?

11. What is Eliot's attitude toward knowledge gained in school? Where else in the essay do you find this attitude?

12. In part one of his essay, Eliot explains the importance of tradition; in part two, Eliot explains the insignificance of the poet's "personality" by presenting his "Impersonal theory of poetry." What is this theory?

13. Explain in your own words how Eliot's analogy of the catalyst works.

14. Eliot is making a distinction between "emotions" and "feelings," a distinction most of us do not make. Earlier he had defined criticism as the "emotion" we "feel." Which does he take to be the more comprehensive term?

15. Eliot appears to reject "semi-ethical criterion" in his judgment of poetry. How does this rejection connect to his "Impersonal theory of poetry"?

16. In putting forth his own ideas, Eliot is attacking an earlier view of the "metier of poetry." What can you infer about the earlier view?

17. Do you agree with Eliot that "new human emotions" are not the subject of poetry but of the "perverse"?

18. According to Eliot, "Poetry is not a turning loose of emotion, but an escape from emotion; it is not the expression of personality, but an escape from personality." What does he mean?

19. Part three of Eliot's essay serves to summarize his main points. Restate them in your own words.

Comparison

1. Think about Eliot's comments about tradition, the "timid adherence to its successes," and its larger historical sense. Do these ideas ring true for you in other areas with which you may be familiar? To what degree do you agree or disagree with these ideas as they

connect to the traditions of another field (history, philosophy, architecture, business, etc.) or your religious traditions or your family's traditions?

2. Passion or "the passions," which Eliot claims are the "material" of poetry, appear in Beer-bohm's essay on the clergyman. Compare each author's use of the word and come to some definition of what it means to you.

3. Both Eliot and Frost make use of science in their essays on poetry. Compare their analogies and draw some conclusions about how and why they use scientific analogies.

4. Read essays by Leavis, Snow, Orwell, Frost, and Eiseley. Based on these essays and your own experience, what do you think is the relationship between science and art?

5. Read Walter Lippmann's "Stereotypes." Compare his discussion of "Group Minds and National Souls" with Eliot's understanding of "the European mind."

6. T. S. Eliot has been accused of anti-Semitism. To what degree, if at all, do prejudices affect the validity of his or anyone's arguments?

7. Read the essays by Carr, Kuhn, and FitzGerald. Compare Eliot's ideas about tradition and innovation with the ideas you discover in these essays.

Walter Lippmann
(1889–1974)

Born into a wealthy family, the only child of Jacob and Daisy Lippmann, the young Walter traveled in exclusive circles in New York City and Saratoga, meeting such famous people as President McKinley, Admiral Dewey, and Justice Oliver Wendell Holmes. His family belonged to the prestigious Temple Emanu-El, one of the earliest temples of Reform Judaism, described by *The New York Times* in 1870 as "the first to stand forward before the world and proclaim the dominion of reason over blind and bigoted faith." Like T. S. Eliot, despite the advantages of private school, private lessons, and a doting family, Lippmann was restricted to the world inside his social circle. When, at 18, he entered Harvard University, his parents expected him to study law, but he was unsure. Becoming part of a group of would-be writers and poets and crusaders for social justice, Lippmann began writing for college magazines; in his first article he attacked one of his professors for elitism, which led to a congratulatory visit from the philosopher William James. Lippmann was soon writing and acting against the social structure, helping to form an undergraduate Socialist Club in 1908 and working to reform both Harvard and local Cambridge politics through political action and a stream of articles. After his graduation from Harvard in 1910, Lippmann got a job as a reporter for a weekly paper, the *Boston Common*, and started corresponding with the famous reformer Lincoln Steffins, who was writing a series of muckraking articles for *Everybody's* magazine. After accepting a position as Steffin's assistant, he became a subeditor at the magazine.

Also like T. S. Eliot, Lippmann forged a career as both writer and editor. He published his first book, *A Preface to Politics*, in 1913 and took a post as associate editor at *The New Republic* the following year (1914–1917). His second book, *Drift and Mastery*, appeared in 1914, followed by *The Stakes of Diplomacy* in 1915. Meanwhile, he courted and, in 1917, married Faye Albertson, daughter of the socialist minister who had founded the *Boston Common*. During the First World War, Lippmann served as Assistant Secretary of War. In the twenties, he became assistant editor, and later senior editor, for the New York *World*, as well as a prolific writer on politics and social criticism and a columnist for *Vanity Fair*. *Public Opinion* appeared in 1922, *The Phantom Public* in 1925, *Men of Destiny* in 1927, *American Inquisitors* in 1928, and *A Preface to Morals* in 1929. During these years Lippmann was a strong advocate of liberalism and, after the stock market crash, an outspoken supporter of Franklin D. Roosevelt's New Deal. In 1931, he left the *World* to write a widely syndicated column for the *New York Herald Tribune*, which he produced for thirty-one years before taking the column to the Washington *Post* in 1962 for five more years. He continued to publish books and articles in the 1930s, including *The United States in World Affairs* (1931), *Preface to Politics* (1933), *Methods of Freedom* (1934), *The New Imperative* (1935), but had broken with the New Dealers by 1937, when he published *The Good Society*.

In 1937, Lippmann began an affair with Helen Armstrong, who was socially prominent, married to Hamilton Fish Armstrong, and the mother of a thirteen-year-old daughter. After a public scandal that accompanied their mutual divorces, they were married the following year. Her first husband was so bitter that, as editor of *Foreign Affairs* magazine, he never allowed Lippmann's name to appear in its pages, even though Lippmann was one of the most prominent writers on foreign affairs in America.

During the rest of his career, Lippmann maintained a moderate political stance. In the forties and fifties, he produced books on the Second World War (*U.S. Foreign Policy: Shield of the Republic*, 1943, *U.S. War Aims*, 1944); the cold war and communism (*The Cold War*, 1947, and *The Communist World*, 1959); and public policy (*Essays on the Public Philosophy*, 1955); winning a Pulitzer Prize in 1958 for his astute analysis of national and international politics. His last books, published in the early sixties, concern communism (*The Coming Tests with Russia*, 1961), and the world market (*Western Unity and the Common Market*, 1962).

In the 1960s, Lippmann strongly supported civil rights and Lyndon Johnson, until Lippmann split with the president over Vietnam. Lippmann's growing anti-war stance helped to fortify opposition to the war, but it cut him off from access to a president and administration that worked to discredit him.

This alienation, the assassination of Robert Kennedy, and the election of Richard Nixon in 1968, led Lippmann to withdraw from public life. By the 1970s, Lippmann was in failing health and confined to a nursing home. He died in 1974, shortly after an eighty-fifth birthday celebration that included telegrams from President Ford and German Chancellor Helmut Schmidt, as well as a ceremony at Yale Library opening an exhibit of his life's work.

Although Lippmann is reputed to have become a moderate only after the New Deal, his stance in "Stereotypes," taken from *Public Opinion* (1922), shows that from the beginning Lippmann was able to examine a subject he held dear, the swaying of public opinion and the nature of democracy, from the vantage point of informed skepticism and detachment. According to one biographer, Ronald Steele, Lippmann developed a view of democracy in *Public Opinion*, elaborated more fully in *The Phantom Public*, that he retained all his life. Because the average person cannot know all the facts needed to make informed political decisions, one must rely on the "insiders" to make those decisions; the regular voter has only one power: to vote the old group out and let a new group try to do better.

STEREOTYPES (1922)

1

EACH OF US lives and works on a small part of the earth's surface, moves in a small circle, and of these acquaintances knows only a few intimately. Of any public event that has wide effects we see at best only a phase and an aspect. This is as true of the eminent insiders who draft treaties, make laws, and issue orders, as it is of those who have treaties framed for them, laws promulgated to them, orders given at them. Inevitably our opinions cover a bigger space, a longer reach of time, a greater number of things, than we can directly observe. They have, therefore, to be pieced together out of what others have reported and what we can imagine.

Yet even the eyewitness does not bring back a naïve picture of the scene.[1] For experience seems to show that he himself brings something to the scene which later he takes away from it, that oftener than not what he imagines to be the account of an event is

---

[1] *picture of the scene E.G. cf.* Edmund Locard, *L'Enquête Criminelle et les Methodes Scientifiques.* A great deal of interesting material has been gathered in late years on the credibility of the witness, which shows, as an able reviewer of Dr. Locard's book says in *The Times* (London) *Literary Supplement* (August 18, 1922), that credibility varies as to classes of witnesses and classes of events, and also as to type of perception. Thus, perceptions of touch, odor, and taste have low evidential value. Our hearing is defective and arbitrary when it judges the source and direction of sound, and in listening to the talk of other people "words which are not heard will be supplied by the witness in all good faith. He will have a theory of the purport of the conversation, and will arrange the

really a transfiguration of it. Few facts in consciousness seem to be merely given. Most facts in consciousness seem to be partly made. A report is the joint product of the knower and known, in which the rôle of the observer is always selective and usually creative. The facts we see depend on where we are placed, and the habits of our eyes.

An unfamiliar scene is like the baby's world, "one great, blooming, buzzing confusion."[2] This is the way, says Mr. John Dewey,[3] that any new thing strikes an adult, so far as the thing is really new and strange. "Foreign languages that we do not understand always seem jibberings, babblings, in which it is impossible to fix a definite, clear-cut, individualized group of sounds. The countryman in the crowded street, the landlubber at sea, the ignoramus in sport at a contest between experts in a complicated game, are further instances. Put an inexperienced man in a factory, and at first the work seems to him a meaningless medley. All strangers of another race proverbially look alike to the visiting stranger. Only gross differences of size or color are perceived by an outsider in a flock of sheep, each of which is perfectly individualized to the shepherd. A diffusive blur and an indiscriminately shifting suction characterize what we do not understand. The problem of the acquisition of meaning by things, or (stated in another way) of forming habits of simple apprehension, is thus the problem of introducing (a) *definiteness* and *distinction* and (2) *consistency* or *stability* of meaning into what is otherwise vague and wavering."

But the kind of definiteness and consistency introduced depends upon who introduces them. In a later passage[4] Dewey gives an example of how differently an experienced layman and a chemist might define the word metal. "Smoothness, hardness, glossiness, and brilliancy, heavy weight for its size . . . the serviceable properties of capacity for being hammered and pulled without breaking, or being softened by heat and hardened by cold, of retaining the shape and form given, of resistance to pressure and decay, would probably be included" in the layman's definition. But the chemist would likely as not ignore these esthetic and utilitarian qualities, and define a metal as "any chemical element that enters into combination with oxygen so as to form a base."

For the most part we do not first see, and then define, we define first and then see. In the great blooming, buzzing confusion of the outer world we pick out what our culture has already defined for us, and we tend to perceive that which we have picked out in the form stereotyped for us by our culture. Of the great men who assembled at Paris to settle the affairs of mankind, how many were there who were able to see much of the Europe

---

sounds he heard to fit it." Even visual perceptions are liable to great error, as in identification, recognition, judgment of distance, estimates of numbers, for example, the size of a crowd. In the untrained observer, the sense of time is highly variable. All these original weaknesses are complicated by tricks of memory, and the incessant creative quality of the imagination. *CF.* also Sherrington, *The Integrative Action of the Nervous System,* pp. 318–327.

The late Professor Hugo Munsterberg wrote a popular book on this subject called *On the Witness Stand.* [Lippmann's footnote]

[2]*buzzing confusion* Wm. James, *Principles of Psychology* Vol. I, [1890] p. 488 [Lippmann's note] William James (1842–1910) was Harvard professor of psychology and philosophy and brother of novelist Henry James.

[3]*Mr. John Dewey* John Dewey, *How We Think,* p. 122. [Lippmann's note] Dewey (1859–1952) was an American philosopher and educator known for his progressive ideas, which include teaching by means of experiment and experience rather than by rote memory. *How We Think* was published in 1910.

[4]*In a later passage Op. cit.,* p. 133 [Lippmann's note]

about them, rather than their commitments about Europe? Could anyone have penetrated the mind of M. Clemenceau,[5] would he have found there images of the Europe of 1919, or a great sediment of stereotyped ideas accumulated and hardened in a long and pugnacious existence? Did he see the Germans of 1919, or the German type as he had learned to see it since 1871.[6] He saw the type, and among the reports that came to him from Germany, he took to heart those reports, and, it seems, those only, which fitted the type that was in his mind. If a junker[7] blustered, that was an authentic German; if a labor leader confessed the guilt of the empire, he was not an authentic German.

At a Congress of Psychology in Göttingen an interesting experiment was made with a crowd of presumably trained observers.[8]

> Not far from the hall in which the Congress was sitting there was a public fête with a masked ball. Suddenly the door of the hall was thrown open and a clown rushed in madly pursued by a negro, revolver in hand. They stopped in the middle of the room fighting; the clown fell, the negro leapt upon him, fired, and then both rushed out of the hall. The whole incident hardly lasted twenty seconds.
>
> The President asked those present to write immediately a report since there was sure to be a judicial inquiry. Forty reports were sent in. Only one had less than 20% of mistakes in regard to the principal facts; fourteen had 20% to 40% of mistakes; twelve from 40% to 50%; thirteen more than 50%. Moreover in twenty-four accounts 10% of the details were pure inventions and this proportion was exceeded in ten accounts and diminished in six. Briefly a quarter of the accounts were false.
>
> It goes without saying that the whole scene had been arranged and even photographed in advance. The ten false reports may then be relegated to the category of tales and legends; twenty-four accounts are half legendary, and six have a value approximating to exact evidence.

Thus out of forty trained observers writing a responsible account of a scene that had just happened before their eyes, more than a majority saw a scene that had not taken place. What then did they see? One would suppose it was easier to tell what had occurred, than to invent something which had not occurred. They saw their stereotype of such a brawl. All of them had in the course of their lives acquired a series of images of brawls, and these images flickered before their eyes. In one man these images displaced less than 20% of the actual scene, in thirteen men more than half. In thirty-four out of the forty observers the stereotypes preëmpted at least one-tenth of the scene.

A distinguished art critic[9] has said that "what with the almost numberless shapes assumed by an object. . . . What with our insensitiveness and inattention, things scarcely

[5]*Clemenceau,* George (1841–1929) French politician and premier from 1906–1909 and 1917–1920. He led the French delegation to the Paris Peace Conference in 1919 and insisted on the disarmament of Germany.

[6]*1871* As a result of the Franco-Prussian War (1870–1871), William I was proclaimed emperor of Germany; the treaty awarded the contested lands of Alsace-Lorraine to Germany.

[7]*junker* an ultra-reactionary member of the Prussian landed aristocracy.

[8]*trained observers* A. von Gennep, *La formation des legendes*, pp. 158–159. Cited by F. van Langenhove, *The Growth of a Legend*, pp. 120–122. [Lippmann's note]

[9]*art critic* Bernard Berenson, *The Central Italian Painters of the Renaissance*, pp. 60, *et seq.* [Lippmann's note] Berenson (1865–1959) was a distinguished American art critic who published a number of books on art and selected paintings for many art collectors, as, for example, Isabella Gard-

would have for us features and outlines so determined and clear that we could recall them at will, but for the stereotyped shapes art has lent them." The truth is even broader than that, for the stereotyped shapes lent to the world come not merely from art, in the sense of painting and sculpture and literature, but from our moral codes and our social philosophies and our political agitations as well. Substitute in the following passage of Mr. Berenson's the words 'politics,' 'business,' and 'society,' for the word 'art' and the sentences will be no less true: " . . . unless years devoted to the study of all schools of art have taught us also to see with our own eyes, we soon fall into the habit of moulding whatever we look at into the forms borrowed from the one art with which we are acquainted. There is our standard of artistic reality. Let anyone give us shapes and colors which we cannot instantly match in our paltry stock of hackneyed forms and tints, and we shake our heads at his failure to reproduce things as we know they certainly are, or we accuse him of insincerity."

Mr. Berenson speaks of our displeasure when a painter "does not visualize objects exactly as we do," and of the difficulty of appreciating the art of the Middle Ages because since then "our manner of visualizing forms has changed in a thousand ways." He goes on to show how in regard to the human figure we have been taught to see what we do see. "Created by Donatello[10] and Masaccio,[11] and sanctioned by the Humanists,[12] the new canon of the human figure, the new cast of features . . . presented to the ruling classes of that time the type of human being most likely to win the day in the combat of human forces . . . Who had the power to break through this new standard of vision and, out of the chaos of things, to select shapes more definitely expressive of reality than those fixed by men of genius? No one had such power. People had perforce to see things in that way and in no other, and to see only the shapes depicted, to love only the ideals presented. . . . "[13]

2

If we cannot fully understand the acts of other people, until we know what they think they know, then in order to do justice we have to appraise not only the information which has been at their disposal, but the minds through which they have filtered it. For the accepted types, the current patterns, the standard versions, intercept information on its way to consciousness. Americanization, for example, is superficially at least the substitution of American for European stereotypes. Thus the peasant who might see his landlord as if he were the lord of the manor, his employer as he saw the local magnate, is taught by Americanization to see the landlord and employer according to American standards. This constitutes a change of mind, which is, in effect, when the inoculation succeeds, a change of vision. His eye sees differently. One kindly gentlewoman has confessed that the stereotypes are of such overweening importance, that when hers are not indulged, she at least is unable to

---

ner whose collection is in Boston's Gardner Museum. *The Central Italian Painters of the Renaissance* was published in 1897.

[10]*Donatello* (c. 1386–1466) Italian Renaissance sculptor.

[11]*Masaccio* (1401–1428?) Italian Renaissance painter.

[12]*Humanists* those Renaissance philosophers and literary figures who posited man and his capabilities as their central concern. They emphasized a return to classical studies and the humanities.

[13]*The Central Italian Painters,* pp. 6–67. [Lippmann's note]

accept the brotherhood of man and the fatherhood of God. "We are strangely affected by the clothes we wear. Garments create a mental and social atmosphere. What can be hoped for the Americanism of a man who insists on employing a London tailor? One's very food affects his Americanism. What kind of American consciousness can grow in the atmosphere of sauerkraut and Limburger cheese? Or what can you expect of the Americanism of the man whose breath always reeks of garlic?"[14]

This lady might well have been the patron of a pageant which a friend of mine once attended. It was called the Melting Pot, and it was given on the Fourth of July in an automobile town where many foreign-born workers are employed. In the center of the baseball park at second base stood a huge wooden and canvas pot. There were flights of steps up to the rim on two sides. After the audience had settled itself, and the band had played, a procession came through an opening at one side of the field. It was made up of men of all the foreign nationalities employed in the factories. They wore their native costumes, they were singing their national songs; they danced their folk dances, and carried the banners of all Europe. The master of ceremonies was the principal of the grade school dressed as Uncle Sam. He led them to the pot. He directed them up the steps to the rim, and inside. He called them out again on the other side. They came, dressed in derby hats, coats, pants, vest, stiff collar and polka dot tie, undoubtedly, said my friend, each with an Eversharp pencil in his pocket, and all singing the Star-Spangled Banner.

To the promoters of this pageant, and probably to most of the actors, it seemed as if they had managed to express the most intimate difficulty to friendly association between the older peoples of America and the newer. The contradiction of their stereotypes interfered with the full recognition of their common humanity. The people who change their names know this. They mean to change themselves, and the attitude of strangers toward them.

There is, of course, some connection between the scene outside and the mind through which we watch it, just as there are some long-haired men and short-haired women in radical gatherings. But to the hurried observer a slight connection is enough. If there are two bobbed heads and four beards in the audience, it will be a bobbed and bearded audience to the reporter who knows beforehand that such gatherings are composed of people with these tastes in the management of their hair. There is a connection between our vision and the facts, but it is often a strange connection. A man has rarely looked at a landscape, let us say, except to examine its possibilities for division into building lots, but he has seen a number of landscapes hanging in the parlor. And from them he has learned to think of a landscape as a rosy sunset, or as a country road with a church steeple and a silver moon. One day he goes to the country, and for hours he does not see a single landscape. Then the sun goes down looking rosy. At once he recognizes a landscape and exclaims that it is beautiful. But two days later, when he tries to recall what he saw, the odds are that he will remember chiefly some landscape in a parlor.

Unless he has been drunk or dreaming or insane he did see a sunset but he saw in it, and above all remembers from it, more of what the oil painting taught him to observe, than what an impressionist painter, for example, or a cultivated Japanese would have seen and taken away with him. And the Japanese and the painter in turn will have seen and remembered more of the form they had learned, unless they happen to be the very rare people who find fresh sight for mankind. In untrained observation we pick recognizable

[14]*garlic?"* Cited by Mr. Edward Hale Bierstadt, *New Republic,* June 1, 1921, p. 21. [Lippmann's note]

signs out of the environment. The signs stand for ideas, and these ideas we fill out with our stock of images. We do not so much see this man and that sunset; rather we notice that the thing is man or sunset, and then see chiefly what our mind is already full of on those subjects.

3

There is economy in this. For the attempt to see all things freshly and in detail, rather than as types and generalities, is exhausting, and among busy affairs practically out of the question. In a circle of friends, and in relation to close associates or competitors, there is no shortcut through, and no substitute for, an individualized understanding. Those whom we love and admire most are the men and women whose consciousness is peopled thickly with persons rather than with types, who know us rather than the classification into which we might fit. For even without phrasing it to ourselves, we feel intuitively that all classification is in relation to some purpose not necessarily our own; that between two human beings no association has final dignity in which each does not take the other as an end in himself. There is a taint on any contact between two people which does not affirm as an axiom the personal inviolability of both.

But modern life is hurried and multifarious, above all physical distance separates men who are often in vital contact with each other, such as employer and employee, official and voter. There is neither time nor opportunity for intimate acquaintance. Instead we notice a trait which marks a well known type, and fill in the rest of the picture by means of the stereotypes we carry about in our heads. He is an agitator. That much we notice, or are told. Well, an agitator is this sort of person, and so he is this sort of person. He is an intellectual. He is a plutocrat. He is a foreigner. He is a "South European." He is from Back Bay. He is a Harvard Man. How different from the statement: he is a Yale Man. He is a regular fellow. He is a West Pointer. He is an old army sergeant. He is a Greenwich Villager: what don't we know about him then, and about her? He is an international banker. He is from Main Street.

The subtlest and most pervasive of all influences are those which create and maintain the repertory of stereotypes. We are told about the world before we see it. We imagine most things before we experience them. And those preconceptions, unless education has made us acutely aware, govern deeply the whole process of perception. They mark out certain objects as familiar or strange, emphasizing the difference, so that the slightly familiar is seen as very familiar, and the somewhat strange as sharply alien. They are aroused by small signs, which may vary from a true index to a vague analogy. Aroused, they flood fresh vision with older images, and project into the world what has been resurrected in memory. Were there no practical uniformities in the environment, there would be no economy and only error in the human habit of accepting foresight for sight. But there are uniformities sufficiently accurate, and the need of economizing attention is so inevitable, that the abandonment of all stereotypes for a wholly innocent approach to experience would impoverish human life.

What matters is the character of the stereotypes, and the gullibility with which we employ them. And these in the end depend upon those inclusive patterns which constitute our philosophy of life. If in that philosophy we assume that the world is codified according to a code which we possess, we are likely to make our reports of what is going on describe a world run by our code. But if our philosophy tells us that each man is only a small part of the world, that his intelligence catches at best only phases and aspects in a coarse net of ideas, then, when we use our stereotypes, we tend to know that they are only stereotypes, to hold them lightly, to modify them gladly. We tend, also, to realize more and more clearly when our ideas started, where they started, how they came to us, why we accepted them. All useful history is antiseptic in this fashion. It enables us to know what fairy tale, what school book, what tradition, what novel, play, picture, phrase, planted one preconception in this mind, another in that mind.

4

Those who wish to censor art do not at least underestimate this influence. They generally misunderstand it, and almost always they are absurdly bent on preventing other people from discovering anything not sanctioned by them. But at any rate, like Plato[15] in his argument about the poets, they feel vaguely that the types acquired through fiction tend to be imposed on reality. Thus there can be little doubt that the moving picture is steadily building up imagery which is then evoked by the words people read in their newspapers. In the whole experience of the race there has been no aid to visualization comparable to the cinema. If a Florentine wished to visualize the saints, he could go to the frescoes in his church, where he might see a vision of saints standardized for his time by Giotto.[16] If an Athenian wished to visualize the gods he went to the temples. But the number of objects which were pictured was not great. And in the East, where the spirit of the second commandment was widely accepted, the portraiture of concrete things was even more meager, and for that reason perhaps the faculty of practical decision was by so much reduced. In the western world, however, during the last few centuries there has been an enormous increase in the volume and scope of secular description, the word picture, the narrative, the illustrated narrative, and finally the moving picture and, perhaps, the talking picture.

Photographs have the kind of authority over imagination today, which the printed word had yesterday, and the spoken word before that. They seem utterly real. They come, we imagine, directly to us without human meddling and they are the most effortless food for the mind conceivable. Any description in words, or even any inert picture, requires an effort of memory before a picture exists in the mind. But on the screen the whole process of observing, describing, reporting, and then imagining, has been accomplished for you. Without more trouble than is needed to stay awake the result which your imagination is always aiming at is reeled off on the screen. The shadowy idea becomes vivid; your hazy notion, let us say, of the Ku Klux Klan, thanks to Mr. Griffiths, takes vivid shape when you see the Birth of a Nation.[17] Historically it may be the wrong shape, morally it may be a pernicious shape, but it is a shape, and I doubt whether anyone who has seen the

---

[15]*Plato* (427?–347 B.C.) Greek philosopher and pupil of Socrates. In Part Three of *The Republic* Plato objects to poetry and literary fiction in general because he believes they misrepresent truth.

[16]*Giotto* (c. 1266–1337) Florentine painter and architect.

[17]*Birth of a Nation* D. W. Griffith [no "s"] (1880–1948) was the first major American film director. *Birth of a Nation* (1915), his second film, used close-ups and other new cinematic techniques to present an overtly positive view of white supremacy and the Ku Klux Klan. Although Griffith experimented with sound in 1921, the first all-talk motion picture, *Lights of New York,* did not appear until 1928.

film and does not know more about the Ku Klux Klan than Mr. Griffiths, will ever hear the name again without seeing those white horsemen.

5

And so when we speak of the mind of a group of people, of the French mind, the militarist mind, the bolshevik mind, we are liable to serious confusion unless we agree to separate the instinctive equipment from the stereotypes, the patterns, and the formulae which play so decisive a part in building up the mental world to which the native character is adapted and responds. Failure to make this distinction accounts for oceans of loose talk about collective minds, national souls, and race psychology. To be sure a stereotype may be so consistently and authoritatively transmitted in each generation from parent to child that it seems almost like a biological fact. In some respects, we may indeed have become, as Mr. Wallas[18] says, biologically parasitic upon our social heritage. But certainly there is not the least scientific evidence which would enable anyone to argue that men are born with the political habits of the country in which they are born. In so far as political habits are alike in a nation, the first places to look for an explanation are the nursery, the school, the church, not in that limbo inhabited by Group Minds and National Souls. Until you have thoroughly failed to see tradition being handed on from parents, teachers, priests, and uncles, it is a solecism[19] of the worst order to ascribe political differences to the germ plasm.[20]

It is possible to generalize tentatively and with a decent humility about comparative differences within the same category of education and experience. Yet even this is a tricky enterprise. For almost no two experiences are exactly alike, not even of two children in the same household. The older son never does have the experience of being the younger. And therefore, until we are able to discount the difference in nurture, we must withhold judgment about differences of nature. As well judge the productivity of two soils by comparing their yield before you know which is in Labrador and which in Iowa, whether they have been cultivated and enriched, exhausted, or allowed to run wild.

Understanding and Analysis

1. This essay is an excellent example of the synthesis of sources in support of an argument. How many sources does Lippmann use in making his own points? What fields does he draw upon? What types of footnote does he use?

2. Reread the first paragraph. What does Lippmann mean by "a phase" and an "aspect"? What is the referent of the word "They" in the last sentence? In some ways, this short first paragraph lays out nearly all that Lippmann wants to argue—that is, the opinions of the insiders as well as of the common man must be "pieced together out of what others have reported and what we can imagine." Each part of this thesis must be illu-

[18]*Wallas,* Graham Wallas, *Our Social Heritage*, p. 17. [Lippmann's note] Wallas (1858–1932) was an English political scientist and psychologist.

[19]*solecism* impropriety or incongruity.

[20]*germ plasm* in biology, a cell that produces growth and development.

minated before the whole passage is clear. Which part from the first paragraph does Lippmann begin to examine in the second paragraph?

3. List the fields from which Lippmann draws examples to support his first point: "The facts we see depend on where we are placed, and the habits of our eyes."

4. Lippmann begins part two by claiming that we can understand people's behavior only if "we know what they think they know" and if we examine "not only the information which has been at their disposal, but the minds through which they have filtered it." What examples does he offer?

5. How does this point connect to Lippmann's assertion in the first paragraph about our need to rely on "what others have reported"?

6. In part three, Lippmann explains the value of our reliance on "recognizable signs out of the environment." Why is it helpful to us to rely on "our stock of images"?

7. How do the ideas in part three connect to the thesis in the first paragraph: our opinions "have, therefore, to be pieced together out of what others have reported and what we can imagine"?

8. What is Lippmann's point in part four?

9. In part five, Lippmann makes a distinction between "the instinctive equipment" and "the stereotypes, the patterns, and the formulae." What does he mean here?

Comparison

1. Beerbohm's essay is an example of an opinion that is made from another's report (Boswell's) and Beerbohm's own imagination. Apply Lippmann's ideas to help you discover stereotypes in Beerbohm's essay. What are they?

2. T. S. Eliot, in "Tradition and the Individual Talent," encourages us as readers to examine "our own minds in their work of criticism." This thinking about thinking is exactly what Lippmann is doing in his essay. Twain also examines the source of our opinions. Compare the views of these three authors on the sources of our opinions. Where do they agree and where do they disagree?

3. Lippmann was born into a highly assimilated Jewish family. Eliot has been accused of anti-Semitism. Based on the ideas in their essays, do you think either of these authors would find such personal information about them relevant? Why or why not?

4. We have heard in the last few years a good deal about "recovered memory" of adults who claim to have only recently remembered that they had witnessed crimes or themselves been abused. We have also heard conflicting ideas about the reliability of the testimony of children in child abuse cases. What reservations would Lippmann raise if he were confronted with allegations based on recovered memory or the testimony of children? What do you think would constitute believable testimony?

5. Compare Lippmann's description of the Melting Pot analogy with FitzGerald's description of the changes in American history textbooks of the seventies. What does each author convey about the analogy he or she describes? Examine your own neighborhood or your college community. Create an analogy that best describes the relationship between individual Americans and their ethnic traditions in your experience and in your limited locale.

6. Examine essays by Mead, Orwell, Podhoretz, and Geertz, for example, to see in what ways these writers may be influenced by cultural stereotypes of the sort Lippmann describes.

7. Compare Lippmann's ideas about art to those of Ozick.

8. Lippmann expresses some concern about the effect of movies on our habits of mind. Read Chesterton's "In Defense of Penny Dreadfuls" and X. J. Kennedy's "Who Killed King Kong?" Compare the reservations expressed by Lippmann and present-day educators concerned about the influence of television on the minds of the populace with the views of Chesterton and Kennedy. Have these concerns changed over time? Do you think they are valid? Why or why not?

9. Compare Lippmann and Podhoretz in terms of the importance of authority and personal experience in forming our opinions.

10. Compare the ideas in Lippmann with those in the essay by Carr. To what extent do these writers agree?

H. L. Mencken
(1880–1956)

Journalist, literary critic, and editor, Henry Louis Mencken was also a satirist whose target was the middle class, which he called the "booboisie." Born into a family of German tobacconists in Baltimore, as a child he was a voracious reader, later declaring, "I doubt that any human being in this world has ever read more than I did between my twelfth and eighteenth years." Loving both literature and science, Henry graduated as valedictorian of his high school, Baltimore Polytechnic Institute, which emphasized science and mechanics. He then announced to his family that he was through with school and wished to become a newspaperman. Given a choice by his parents of going to college to study law or entering the family cigar business, Henry worked for his father, hating every minute.

When his father died in 1899, Henry immediately quit the business and began his career as a journalist for the Baltimore *Morning Herald*; five years later he became city editor of the Baltimore *Evening Herald*. But he spent most of his career working for the Baltimore *Sun* papers (1906–1948). At twenty, he published his first book, an edition of the plays of George Bernard Shaw. In 1911, he began a signed column, "The Free Lance," that became the talk of Baltimore. From 1911 to 1923, he was co-editor with George Jean Nathan of *Smart Set*, a popular literary journal that published and reviewed the latest in short stories, books, drama, and ideas (1914–1923). In 1915, Mencken's *Sun* column was suspended because of his obvious pro-German sympathies. He soon left the *Sun* to work in New York for the *Evening Mail*, but when the publisher was arrested for publishing German propaganda, Mencken temporarily left the newspaper business and took up writing books: *In Defense of Women* and *A Book of Prefaces* in 1917, six volumes of *Prejudices*, from 1919–1927, and the first of four editions of a huge philological study, *The American Language* (first edition 1919).

By 1920, Mencken was back on the staff of the *Sun* papers, contributing weekly articles and daily reports. In 1924, he began a four-year stint as a columnist for the Chicago *Sunday Tribune* as well, and, with co-editor Nathan, he created a new journal, *The American Mercury*, for which Mencken became the sole editor from 1925 to 1933. While working as editor and columnist, he also found time to write books of literary and cultural criticism, *Criticism in America, Its Function and Status* (1924), *Treatise on the Gods* (1930), *Treatise on Right and Wrong* (1934), and *A New Dictionary of Quotations* (1942), as well as three books of autobiographical essays, *Happy Days* (1940), *Newspaper Days* (1941), and *Heathen Days* (1943). In 1948, Mencken suffered a stroke that left him unable to read or write for the remaining eight years until his death.

Mencken was known for his pungent criticism of all humanity. Whereas Walter Lippmann believed that most people do not have the time to learn what it takes to run a country, Mencken believed that most people are idiots, particularly those who are running our country. His biting, ironic humor would probably not be tolerated in our politically correct times. Moreover, like T. S. Eliot and G. K. Chesterton before him, H. L. Mencken is known for his prejudice. Nonetheless, Lippmann spoke for many when he proclaimed the "Holy Terror from Baltimore" to be "splendidly and exultantly and contagiously alive. He calls you a swine, and an imbecile, and increases your will to live."

BEARERS OF THE TORCH (1923)

THE GREAT PROBLEMS of human society are plainly too vexatious and difficult to be set before college undergraduates or pupils yet lower down the scale. The best that the teacher can hope to do, considering the short time at his disposal and the small attention that he can engage, is to fill his students with certain broad generalizations and conclusions. But precisely *what* generalizations and conclusions? Obviously, the safest are those that happen to be official at the moment, not only because they are most apt to slip into the minds of the pupils with least resistance, but also and more importantly because they are most apt to coincide with the prejudices, superstitions and ways of thought of the pedagogue himself, an ignorant and ninth-rate man.

In brief, the teaching process, as commonly observed, has nothing to do with the investigation and establishment of facts, assuming that actual facts may ever be determined. Its sole purpose is to cram the pupils, as rapidly and as painlessly as possible, with the largest conceivable outfit of current axioms, in all departments of human thought—to make the pupil a good citizen, which is to say, a citizen differing as little as possible, in positive knowledge and habits of mind, from all other citizens. In other words, it is the mission of the pedagogue, not to make his pupils think, but to make them think *right,* and the more nearly his own mind pulsates with the great ebbs and flows of popular delusion and emotion, the more admirably he performs his function. He may be an ass, but that is surely no demerit in a man paid to make asses of his customers.

This central aim of the teacher is often obscured by pedagogical pretension and bombast. The pedagogue, discussing himself, tries to make it appear that he is a sort of scientist. He is actually a sort of barber, and just as responsive to changing fashions. That this is his actual character is now, indeed, a part of the official doctrine that he must inculcate. On all hands, he is told plainly by his masters that his fundamental function in America is to manufacture an endless corps of sound Americans. A sound American is simply one who has put out of his mind all doubts and questionings, and who accepts instantly, and as incontrovertible gospel, the whole body of official doctrine of his day, whatever it may be and no matter how often it may change. The instant he challenges it, no matter how timorously and academically, he ceases by that much to be a loyal and creditable citizen of the Republic.

Understanding and Analysis

1. Where in this essay do you find the first loaded word, that is, the first indication of Mencken's tone or attitude toward his subject? From whose point of view does he at first appear to be writing? How does this point of view work to draw you into his essay? What, if anything, do you find amusing about the first paragraph?

2. Do you find wit or humor in either of the other two paragraphs?

3. What metaphors does Mencken use? How do they propel his argument?

4. What does Mencken present to support his assertions?

5. What role does money play in the relationship between teacher and pupil? Who are the "masters" of the teacher? How is the teacher different from the pupil?

6. What are Mencken's attitudes toward science, as implied in this essay?

Comparison

1. Twain and Mencken both believe that the common man reveals little real thinking in his opinions. What explanation does each provide for this view? Do they agree?

2. Compare the melting pot analogy in Lippmann's essay with Mencken's assertions about the "endless corps of sound Americans." What metaphor is Mencken using? What are the implications of each analogy?

3. Do you think you have been taught to think in high school or college? Based on your own experience, do you agree with Mencken's assessment? Give specific examples.

4. To what degree does FitzGerald's essay on history textbooks confirm or undermine Mencken's assertions?

5. Mencken says the teacher "is actually a sort of barber, and just as responsive to changing fashions." Several other essayists in this collection refer to hairstyles. Collect as many instances as you can find (look in Lippmann and Panter-Downes, for starters). What generalizations about the significance of hair and politics or fashion can you ascertain?

6. A number of essayists in this collection examine various aspects of education. Read, for example, Eliot, Thurber, Frost, Woolf, Orwell, and Mairs. How do these authors view the quality of education they received in school? What general conclusions can you draw?

H. L. Mencken

The Penalty of Death (1926)

OF THE ARGUMENTS against capital punishment that issue from uplifters, two are commonly heard most often, to wit:

1. That hanging a man (or frying him or gassing him) is a dreadful business, degrading to those who have to do it and revolting to those who have to witness it.

2. That it is useless, for it does not deter others from the same crime.

The first of these arguments, it seems to me, is plainly too weak to need serious refutation. All it says, in brief, is that the work of the hangman is unpleasant. Granted. But suppose it is? It may be quite necessary to society for all that. There are, indeed, many other jobs that are unpleasant, and yet no one thinks of abolishing them—that of the plumber, that of the soldier, that of the garbage-man, that of the priest hearing confessions, that of the sand-hog, and so on. Moreover, what evidence is there that any actual hangman complains of his work? I have heard none. On the contrary, I have known many who delighted in their ancient art, and practiced it proudly.

In the second argument of the abolitionists there is rather more force, but even here, I believe, the ground under them is shaky. Their fundamental error consists in assuming that the whole aim of punishing criminals is to deter other (potential) criminals—that we hang or electrocute A simply in order to so alarm B that he will not kill C. This, I believe, is an assumption which confuses a part with the whole. Deterrence, obviously, is one of the aims of punishment, but it is surely not the only one. On the contrary, there are at least a half dozen, and some are probably quite as important. At least one of them, practically considered, is *more* important. Commonly, it is described as revenge, but revenge is really not the word for it. I borrow a better term from the late Aristotle: *katharsis.* *Katharsis,* so used, means a salubrious discharge of emotions, a healthy letting off of steam. A school-boy, disliking his teacher, deposits a tack upon the pedagogical chair;

the teacher jumps and the boy laughs. This is *katharsis*. What I contend is that one of the prime objects of all judicial punishments is to afford the same grateful relief (*a*) to the immediate victims of the criminal punished, and (*b*) to the general body of moral and timorous men.

These persons, and particularly the first group, are concerned only indirectly with deterring other criminals. The thing they crave primarily is the satisfaction of seeing the criminal actually before them suffer as he made them suffer. What they want is the peace of mind that goes with the feeling that accounts are squared. Until they get that satisfaction they are in a state of emotional tension, and hence unhappy. The instant they get it they are comfortable. I do not argue that this yearning is noble; I simply argue that it is almost universal among human beings. In the face of injuries that are unimportant and can be borne without damage it may yield to higher impulses; that is to say, it may yield to what is called Christian charity. But when the injury is serious Christianity is adjourned, and even saints reach for their sidearms. It is plainly asking too much of human nature to expect it to conquer so natural an impulse. A keeps a store and has a bookkeeper, B. B steals $700, employs it in playing at dice or bingo, and is cleaned out. What is A to do? Let B go? If he does so he will be unable to sleep at night. The sense of injury, of injustice, of frustration will haunt him like pruritus. So he turns B over to the police, and they hustle B to prison. Thereafter A can sleep. More, he has pleasant dreams. He pictures B chained to the wall of a dungeon a hundred feet underground, devoured by rats and scorpions. It is so agreeable that it makes him forget his $700. He has got his *katharsis*.

The same thing precisely takes place on a larger scale when there is a crime which destroys a whole community's sense of security. Every law-abiding citizen feels menaced and frustrated until the criminals have been struck down—until the communal capacity to get even with them, and more than even, has been dramatically demonstrated. Here, manifestly, the business of deterring others is no more than an afterthought. The main thing is to destroy the concrete scoundrels whose act has alarmed everyone, and thus made everyone unhappy. Until they are brought to book that unhappiness continues; when the law has been executed upon them there is a sigh of relief. In other words, there is *katharsis*.

I know of no public demand for the death penalty for ordinary crimes, even for ordinary homicides. Its infliction would shock all men of normal decency of feeling. But for crimes involving the deliberate and inexcusable taking of human life, by men openly defiant of all civilized order—for such crimes it seems, to nine men out of ten, a just and proper punishment. Any lesser penalty leaves them feeling that the criminal has got the better of society—that he is free to add insult to injury by laughing. That feeling can be dissipated only by a recourse to *katharsis,* the invention of the aforesaid Aristotle. It is more effectively and economically achieved, as human nature now is, by wafting the criminal to realms of bliss.

The real objection to capital punishment doesn't lie against the actual extermination of the condemned, but against our brutal American habit of putting it off so long. After all, every one of us must die soon or late, and a murderer, it must be assumed, is one who makes that sad fact the cornerstone of his metaphysic. But it is one thing to die, and quite another thing to lie for long months and even years under the shadow of death. No sane man would choose such a finish. All of us, despite the Prayer Book, long for a swift and unexpected end. Unhappily, a murderer, under the irrational American system, is tortured for what, to him, must seem a whole series of eternities. For months on end he sits in prison while his lawyers carry on their idiotic buffoonery with writs, injunctions, mandamuses, and appeals. In order to get his money (or that of his friends) they have to feed him with hope. Now and then, by the imbecility of a judge or some trick of juridic science, they actually justify it. But let us say that, his money all gone, they finally throw up their hands. Their client is now ready for the rope or the chair. But he must still wait for months before it fetches him.

That wait, I believe, is horribly cruel. I have seen more than one man sitting in the death-house, and I don't want to see any more. Worse, it is wholly useless. Why should he wait at all? Why not hang him the day after the last court dissipates his last hope? Why torture him as not even cannibals would torture their victims? The common answer is that he must have time to make his peace with God. But how long does that take? It may be accomplished, I believe, in two hours quite as comfortably as in two years. There are, indeed, no temporal limitations upon God. He could forgive a whole herd of murderers in a millionth of a second. More, it has been done.

Understanding and Analysis

1. Mencken lists the two most frequent arguments against the death penalty. What arguments has he left out? After rereading the essay, can you think of other missing arguments for the other side?

2. What evidence can you find in the first four paragraphs that he is aware of at least one of the missing arguments?

3. What are Mencken's reasons for supporting the death penalty?

4. Mencken infuses his essay with humor. Where do you first see signs of his playfulness with language? List as many comic instances as you can. What comic techniques does he use? (For example, does he exaggerate, mix slang with erudite diction, and so on?) What effect do these comic techniques have on Mencken's argument?

5. Note the structure of this essay. Mencken examines the feelings of the hangman, of the victim's family, of society, and of the murderer. Why does he follow this particular order?

6. What is the effect of the last sentence in the essay?

Comparison

1. Read Orwell's "A Hanging." Where do the two authors seems to agree? What arguments does Orwell implicitly present to oppose the death penalty? Does Mencken address these arguments?

2. Compare the uses and effects of laughter in the two essays.

3. Read other essays of persuasion, such as those by Brady and Vidal. What characteristics, if any, do these essays share?

Dorothy Parker
(1893–1967)

Dorothy Parker was the last of four children born to Henry Rothschild, a successful businessman, and Eliza Marston Rothschild, a former schoolteacher. When Dorothy was five, her mother died. Two years later her father married Eleanor Lewis, a retired schoolteacher, whom Dorothy despised. When Dorothy was ten, Eleanor died of a brain hemorrage. According to one biographer, Marion Meade, Dorothy felt somehow responsible for the deaths of both her mothers, the one she loved and the one she hated. She spent much of the rest of her childhood miserable, finding consolation only in her dogs, her reading, and her own talent for writing. When she was away from her father, visiting her sister at the seashore, Dorothy and her father exchanged rhymed verse extolling the virtues and day-to-day doings of the dogs. Such letters and verses, as well as her attendance at a private Catholic school and, briefly, a boarding school, constitute her only formal education. At fourteen, she left school for good. Three years later her father retired, and he and Dorothy formed a family of two, her older siblings having left home to start their own lives. From then on, Dorothy undertook the care of her increasingly ailing father. After his brother's sudden death on the *Titanic*, Dorothy's father grew melancholy, as well as ill. When Henry died in 1913, Dorothy discovered little money left to support her. She was twenty years old and in need of a job.

At first she turned to her talent for playing the piano to help pay the bills. She played at a dance studio and later also worked as a dance instructor. Meanwhile, she published her first poem in *Vanity Fair* when she was twenty-one. Two years later, in 1917, she was made a staff writer for the journal, taking over as drama critic from P. G. Wodehouse in 1920. Also in 1917, she married Edwin Pond Parker II, a stockbroker on Wall Street, just before he left to serve in the ambulance corps in the war. In 1919, with humorist Robert Benchley, who became her best friend, and playwright Robert Sherwood, she founded the Round Table at the Algonquin Hotel, a group that met regularly over lunch to exchange witty repartee, which invariably ended up in the newspapers. In 1920, she was fired from *Vanity Fair*; in protest, Benchley also quit. The two rented a small office together where they did their writing and supported each other through the ups and downs of both their private lives.

When Edwin returned from the war, he was an alcoholic and a drug addict. Although he and Dorothy lived together on and off for several years (finally divorcing in 1928), it was clear to her early on that the marriage would never work. Gradually Dorothy herself became addicted to alcohol. She attempted suicide in 1923, 1926, and 1932. But between bouts of misery, she produced her best work. In the twenties, she published her poetry and stories in magazines such as *Smart Set, Saturday Evening Post, Ladies Home Journal,* and *Life.*

Her first volume of poetry, *Enough Rope,* came out in 1926, winning her an admiring public because of her mordant humor. From 1927 to 1931, she reviewed books for the *New Yorker* and in 1928 began a column for *McCalls.* Also during this period, she continued to produce volumes of verse, *Sunset Gun* in 1928, *Death and Taxes* in 1931, and *Not So Deep* in 1936. *After Such Pleasures,* her first collection of short stories, was published in 1933, followed by *Here Lies* in 1939, and *Collected Stories* in 1942.

In 1933, after many unsuccessful love affairs, Parker married Alan Campbell, good-looking man, eleven years younger than she, who was willing to look after her despite her disordered life and problems with alchohol and melancholy. The two traveled by car across the country to Los Angeles to write, and moved to Beverly Hills in 1935. In Hollywood during the thirties and forties, Parker collaborated with Campbell and others on numerous film scripts, and in 1934 she helped organize the Screen Writers Guild. In 1946, she and Campbell divorced. In 1950 they remarried. Parker was made a member of the American Academy of Arts and Letters in 1959, while she was still producing book reviews for *Esquire* (1957–1963). In 1963, when Alan Campbell died of an overdose of barbituates, Dorothy mourned by drinking. She spent her last years in New York, recording some of her works on tape and coediting an anthology of short stories. She died of a heart attack at the age of seventy-three.

Famous for the sardonic wit of her short stories, poems, and book reviews, Dorothy Parker was one of the few women of her time to succeed in the popular literary world. She shared with Mencken a love of language and a biting wit, although Mencken's politics were to the right of center, whereas Parker's were to the left. She marched against the execution of Sacco and Vanzetti in 1927, helped create the Anti-Nazi League in 1936, and was a target of the House Un-American Activities Committee in the fifties. Politics, however, are not the subject of her essays, stories, and poetry. Instead she skewers the pretensions of the elite and rubs raw the idealized loves once lost and won. In her first collection of poetry, for example, she captures in classic form the elegiac tones of *A Shropshire Lad* by A. E. Houseman—and upends them with a twist. Compare, for example, his well-known "To An Athlete Dying Young," in which the poet ironically celebrates early death ("Smart lad, to slip betimes away/From fields where glory does not stay,/And early though the laurel grows/It withers quicker than the rose."), to her "Epitaph For A Darling Lady," in which Parker makes fun of early death, callow lovers, and the tradition of feminine beauty all at once: "Leave for her a red young rose,/Go your way, and save your pity;/She is happy, for she knows/That her dust is very pretty." It was Dorothy Parker who wrote, "Men seldom make passes/At girls who wear glasses" and had the wit to title the epigram "News Item." Although her poetry and stories are perhaps better known, her essays too employ both a sly irony and an unexpected twist.

MRS. POST ENLARGES ON ETIQUETTE (1927)

EMILY POST'S[1] *ETIQUETTE* is out again, this time in a new and an enlarged edition, and so the question of what to do with my evenings has been all fixed up for me. There will be an empty chair at the deal table at Tony's, when the youngsters gather to discuss life, sex, literature, the drama, what is a gentleman, and whether or not to go on to Helen Morgan's Club[2] when the place closes; for I shall be at home among my book. I am going in for a course of study at the knee of Mrs. Post. Maybe, some time in the misty future, I shall be Asked Out, and I shall be ready. You won't catch me being intentionally haughty to subordinates or refusing to be a pallbearer for any reason except serious ill health. I shall live down the old days, and with the help of Mrs. Post and God (always mention a lady's name first) there will come a time when you will be perfectly safe in inviting me to your house, which should never be called a residence except in printing or engraving.

It will not be a grueling study, for the sprightliness of Mrs. Post's style makes the text-book as fascinating as it is instructive. Her characters, introduced for the sake of example, are called by no such unimaginative titles as Mrs. A., or Miss Z., or Mr. X.; they are Mrs. Worldly, Mr. Bachelor, the Gildings, Mrs. Oldname, Mrs. Neighbor, Mrs. Stranger, Mrs. Kindhart, and Mr. and Mrs. Nono Better. This gives the work all the force and the application of a morality play.[3]

It is true that occasionally the author's invention plucks at the coverlet, and she can do no better by her brain-children than to name them Mr. Jones and Mrs. Smith. But it must be said, in fairness, that the Joneses and the Smiths are the horrible examples, the confirmed pullers of social boners. They deserve no more. They go about saying "Shake hands with Mr. Smith" or "I want to make you acquainted with Mrs. Smith" or "Will you permit me to recall myself to you?" or "Pardon *me!*" or "Permit me to assist you" or even "Pleased to meet you!" One pictures them as small people, darting about the outskirts of parties, fetching plates of salad and glasses of punch, applauding a little too enthusiastically at the end of a song, laughing a little too long at the point of an anecdote. If you could allow yourself any sympathy for such white trash, you might find some-

---

[1]*Post,* Emily (1873–1960). *Etiquette,* first published in 1922, sold over a million copies; Post later had her own radio show and a syndicated column in over 200 newspapers.

[2]*Helen Morgan's Club* Morgan (1900–1941) was a popular torch singer in the twenties and early thirties. She played Julie in the Broadway musical *Show Boat,* which opened at Ziegfeld Theatre Dec. 27, 1927. She was also owner of a nightclub called the House of Morgan in New York City.

[3]*morality play* Characters in medieval dramas had such names as Fellowship, Kindred, Good-Deeds, and Death (*Everyman*).

thing pathetic in their eagerness to please, their desperate readiness to be friendly. But one must, after all, draw that line somewhere, and Mr. Jones, no matter how expensively he is dressed, always gives the effect of being in his shirt-sleeves, while Mrs. Smith is so unmistakably the daughter of a hundred Elks.[4] Let them be dismissed by somebody's phrase (I wish to heaven it were mine)—"the sort of people who buy their silver."

These people in Mrs. Post's book live and breathe; as Heywood Broun[5] once said of the characters in a play, "they have souls and elbows." Take Mrs. Worldly, for instance, Mrs. Post's heroine. The woman will live in American letters. I know of no character in the literature of the last quarter-century who is such a complete pain in the neck.

See her at that moment when a younger woman seeks to introduce herself. Says the young woman: "'Aren't you Mrs. Worldly?' Mrs. Worldly, with rather freezing polite-ness, says 'Yes,' and waits." And the young woman, who is evidently a glutton for pun-ishment, neither lets her wait from then on nor replies, "Well, Mrs. Worldly, and how would you like a good sock in the nose, you old meat-axe?" Instead she flounders along with some cock-and-bull story about being a sister of Millicent Manners, at which Mrs. Worldly says, "I want very much to hear you sing some time," which marks her peak of enthusiasm throughout the entire book.

See Mrs. Worldly, too, in her intimate moments at home. "Mrs. Worldly seemingly pays no attention, but nothing escapes her. She can walk through a room without appear-ing to look either to the right or left, yet if the slightest detail is amiss, an ornament out of place, or there is one dull button on a footman's livery, her house telephone is rung at once!" Or watch her on that awful night when she attends the dinner where everything goes wrong. "In removing the plates, Delia, the assistant, takes them up by piling one on top of the other, clashing them together as she does so. You can feel Mrs. Worldly look-ing with almost hypnotized fascination—as her attention might be drawn to a street acci-dent against her will."

There is also the practical-joker side to Mrs. W. Thus does Mrs. Post tell us about that: "For example, Mrs. Worldly writes:

" 'Dear Mrs. Neighbor:

" 'Will you and your husband dine with us very informally on Tuesday, the tenth, etc.'

"Whereupon, the Neighbors arrive, he in a dinner coat, she in her simplest evening dress, and find a dinner of fourteen people and every detail as formal as it is possible to make it. . . . In certain houses—such as the Worldlys' for instance—formality is inevitable, no matter how informal may be her 'will you dine informally' intention."

One of Mrs. Post's minor characters, a certain young Struthers, also stands sharply out of her pages. She has caught him perfectly in that scene which she entitles "Informal Vis-iting Often Arranged by Telephone" (and a darn good name for it, too). We find him at the moment when he is calling up Millicent Gilding, and saying, "'Are you going to be in this afternoon?' She says, 'Yes, but not until a quarter of six.' He says, 'Fine, I'll come then.' Or she says, 'I'm so sorry, I'm playing bridge with Pauline—but I'll be in tomor-row!' He says, 'All right, I'll come tomorrow.'" Who, ah, who among us does not know a young Struthers?

---

[4]*Elks,* Benevolent and Protective Order of. Established in 1868, this fraternal and charitable organ-ization has lodges all over the United States.

[5]*Heywood Broun* (1888–1939) Columnist for *The New York World* from 1921–1928, Broun was a popular champion of social justice.

As one delves deeper and deeper into *Etiquette,* disquieting thoughts come. That old Is-It-Worth-It Blues starts up again, softly, perhaps, but plainly. Those who have mastered etiquette, who are entirely, impeccably right, would seem to arrive at a point of exquisite dullness. The letters and the conversations of the correct, as quoted by Mrs. Post, seem scarcely worth the striving for. The rules for the finding of topics of conversation fall damply on the spirit. "You talk of something you have been doing or thinking about—planting a garden, planning a journey, contemplating a journey, or similar safe topics. Not at all a bad plan is to ask advice: "We want to motor through the South. Do you know about the roads?' Or, 'I'm thinking of buying a radio. Which make do you think is best?' "

I may not dispute Mrs. Post. If she says that is the way you should talk, then, indubitably, that is the way you should talk. But though it be at the cost of that future social success I am counting on, there is no force great enough ever to make me say, "I'm thinking of buying a radio."

It is restful, always, in a book of many rules—and *Etiquette* has six hundred and eighty-four pages of things you must and mustn't do—to find something that can never touch you, some law that will never affect your ways. . . .

And in *Etiquette,* too, I had the sweetly restful moment of chancing on a law which I need not bother to memorize, let come no matter what. It is in that section called "The Retort Courteous to One You Have Forgotten," although it took a deal of dragging to get it in under that head. "If," it runs, "after being introduced to you, Mr. Jones" (of course, it would be Mr. Jones that would do it) "calls you by a wrong name, you let it pass, at first, but if he persists you may say: 'If you please, my name is Stimson.'"

No, Mrs. Post; persistent though Mr. Smith be, I may not say, "If you please, my name is Stimson." The most a lady may do is give him the wrong telephone number.

Understanding and Analysis

1. Parker's voice is especially striking. What are some of her techniques for humor?

2. Parker lets us know that in her opinion the subject of manners is essentially frivolous. How does she convey that point?

3. What connection, if any, do you think exists between manners and morals? Does Parker imply a connection?

4. Parker introduces some of her own observations about poor manners in this essay. What does she especially dislike? What values can you ascribe to her on the basis of her dislikes?

5. Why do you suppose Parker thinks good manners are boring? Are there any further indications in this essay that good manners can be not merely boring but pernicious?

6. What does Parker tell her readers about the style and quality of Post's book?

7. From the examples Parker offers, can you tell why Post's book was so popular and why Parker's column was so popular too?

Comparison

1. Parker calls Post's book a "textbook" and emphasizes its burdensome rules. What, aside from manners, can you learn from reading such books? Read FitzGerald's essay on his-

tory textbooks and apply some of her techniques to a column by Miss Manners, our current specialist on the topic of good manners.

2. Compare the style and tone of Miss Manners with that of both Post herself and of Parker. What values does each writer appear to espouse? Have the rules changed much for introducing people or inviting them to informal evenings at home?

3. What can you deduce about the roles of women in the twenties from reading Parker on Post? Do women play these roles today as well?

4. Do you think the adoption of good manners as determined by Emily Post or Miss Manners can actually help a person move up in American society? If so, how? If not, why not?

5. Read Jamaica Kincaid's selection from "A Small Place." What role do manners play in setting boundaries between groups?

6. Compare the techniques for humor in the essays by Parker and Allen. Does humor always require a victim? Who are the victims in the essays by Parker and Allen? What about the humor in Baker's essay? Is there a victim there?

7. Compare the issues of class found in this book review with the reports on the war some ten or more years later, also written for the *New Yorker*, by Mollie Panter-Downes. Are the assumptions about the audience similar? What aspects of class do both writers note?

8. Read the essays by Twain and Staples. To what degree do these authors also imply connections between manners and morals?

Margaret Mead
(1901–1978)

Margaret Mead was the first-born child of two academic parents, Edward, a professor at the Wharton School in Philadelphia, and Emily, who continued her research into the families of Italian immigrants as she brought up Margaret and her five siblings (one of whom, Katherine, died at the age of nine months). Luther Cressman, Margaret's first husband, knew the family well, commenting that despite the intellectual atmosphere and the many intervals spent in the country, Margaret's life seemed to lack a sense of fun. He concluded, "I don't think Margaret ever had an honest-to-god childhood." Although she wanted to go to Wellesley College, she enrolled at DePauw University in 1919, her father's choice. She was already engaged to Luther. After a year she transferred to Barnard, where she became the center of a group of intense intellectual and fun-loving women, rebels who called themselves the "Ash Can Cats," after the Ashcan School of painting that focused on drunks and other seedy subjects. Many of these women remained Mead's lifelong friends. On November 7, 1922, they caused a scandal when they appeared in the dining hall in red dresses, with red flags and flowers, and sang the "Internationale" to celebrate the fifth anniversary of the Bolshevik revolution.

As a psychology major during her senior year, she took courses in anthropology with Franz Boas. Excited by the opportunities to make substantial contributions in the field and encouraged by Boas's teaching assistant, Ruth Benedict (with whom Margaret formed an intense friendship), Mead began her graduate studies in anthropology at Columbia in 1923. At that time, Boas, Benedict, and other anthropologists were investigating the relationship between nature and nurture in the behavior of human beings. Boas was certain that those who favored nature and assumed that whites, especially Europeans, were biologically superior to peoples of color were dead wrong. Boas believed that all human beings are biologically equal. Culture, he believed, determines nearly all of human behavior.

In 1925, after working for two years on literature involving cultural stability in five Polynesian cultures, (and two years after her marriage to Luther Cressman), Mead undertook a field study in Samoa, but not on cultural stability. Instead, she agreed to investigate a question Boas helped her pose: "Are the disturbances which vex our adolescents due to the nature of adolescence itself or to civilization? Under different circumstances does adolescence present a different picture?" The result of her nine months of field work, *Coming of Age in Samoa*, published in 1928, confirmed the primacy of culture and became a bestseller in both the popular press and in academic circles. H. L. Mencken, in the *American Mercury*, praised its scientific accuracy. The reading public was fascinated by its claim that a typical Samoan female adolescent hopes to "live as a girl with many lovers as long as possible and then to marry in one's own village, near one's own relatives and to have many children."

Meanwhile, Mead's own marriage ended in divorce after she met Reo Fortune, a fellow anthropologist, while sailing to Europe with her husband. The day they disembarked, Margaret reminded Luther that he had once claimed to have "no objection to my living with someone else if I loved someone who loved me, and it was possible, and that I might go with him and marry him if his love gave me more than yours." "Well," she concluded, "I have found him."

On her return from Samoa, Mead was offered a position as assistant curator of the American Museum of Natural History. (She was made an associate curator in 1942 and chief curator from 1964–1969). She completed her Ph.D. in 1929. During the next ten years she divorced her second husband and married Gregory Bateson, with whom she undertook two more field trips, to New Guinea and Bali. She also began a career of publishing and lecturing. Her works include *Growing Up in New Guinea* (1930), *The Changing Culture of an Indian Tribe* (1932), *Sex and Temperament in Three Primitive Societies* (1935), *Male and Female* (1949), *New Lives for Old: Cultural Transformation in Manu 1928–1953* (1956), *People and Places* (1959), *Continuities in Cultural Evolution* (1964), *Culture and Commitment* (1970), and an autobiography, *Blackberry Winter: My Earlier Years* (1972). In addition to her full-time position as curator and her lecturing and publishing, Mead taught part-time at Columbia and wrote a column for *Redbook* magazine.

In 1939, Gregory and Margaret's only child, Mary Catherine, was born, witnessed by still and movie photographers and the pediatrician Dr. Benjamin Spock. Many of these people, at Mead's request, had seen the Bateson-Mead documentary, "First Days in the Life of a New Guinea Baby." By this time, Mead and Bateson had become among the most famous social scientists of their day. When they attended a conference at Smith College in 1941, a sociology student (later the feminist Betty Friedan) recalled that they were irreverently referred to as "God the Mother and Jesus Christ." Margaret Mead's phenomenal energy sustained a long and distinguished reputation as writer, lecturer, and public figure, even after she began to weaken with what was later diagnosed as pancreatic cancer. After a long decline, she finally succumbed on November 15, 1978. According to her Episcopalian priest, Austin Ford, on one of her last nights, she told her nurse she was dying. "'Yes,' the nurse said gently. 'We all will, someday.'" Mead supposedly replied, "But this is different."

Although later field work and scholarship have questioned the validity of Mead's work in Samoa (see Gardner "The Great Samoan Hoax"), Mead is nonetheless credited with developing important methods for observing and analyzing data in the field. Moreover, the question that she and Franz Boas and Ruth Benedict were asking in the 1920s continued to be of major concern throughout the century: How much of our behavior is determined by our genes and how much is socially constructed?

A DAY IN SAMOA (1928)

THE LIFE OF the day begins at dawn, or if the moon has shown until daylight, the shouts of the young men may be heard before dawn from the hillside. Uneasy in the night, populous with ghosts, they shout lustily to one another as they hasten with their work. As the dawn begins to fall among the soft brown roofs and the slender palm trees stand out against a colourless, gleaming sea, lovers slip home from trysts beneath the palm trees or in the shadow of beached canoes, that the light may find each sleeper in his appointed place. Cocks crow, negligently, and a shrill-voiced bird cries from the breadfruit trees. The insistent roar of the reef seems muted to an undertone for the sounds of a waking village. Babies cry, a few short wails before sleepy mothers give them the breast. Restless little children roll out of their sheets and wander drowsily down to the beach to freshen their faces in the sea. Boys, bent upon an early fishing, start collecting their tackle and go to rouse their more laggard companions. Fires are lit, here and there, the white smoke hardly visible against the paleness of the dawn. The whole village, sheeted and frowsy, stirs, rubs its eyes, and stumbles towards the beach. "Talofa!"[1] "Talofa!" "Will the journey start to-day?" "Is it bonito[2] fishing your lordship is going?" Girls stop to giggle over some young ne'er-do-well who escaped during the night from an angry father's pursuit and to venture a shrewd guess that the daughter knew more about his presence than she told. The boy who is taunted by another, who has succeeded him in his sweetheart's favour, grapples with his rival, his foot slipping in the wet sand. From the other end of the village comes a long drawn-out, piercing wail. A messenger has just brought word of the death of some relative in another village. Half-clad unhurried women, with babies at their breasts, or astride their hips, pause in their tale of Losa's outraged departure from her father's house to the greater kindness in the home of her uncle, to wonder who is dead. Poor relatives whisper their requests to rich relatives, men make plans to set a fish trap together, a woman begs a bit of yellow dye from a kinswoman, and through the village sounds the rhythmic tattoo which calls the young men together. They gather from all parts of the village, digging sticks in hand, ready to start inland to the plantation. The older men set off upon their more lonely occupations, and each household, reassembled under its peaked roof, settles down to the routine of the morning. Little children, too hungry to wait for the late breakfast, beg lumps of cold taro which they munch greedily. Women carry piles of washing to the sea or to the spring at the far end of the village, or set off inland after weaving materials. The older girls go fishing on the reef, or perhaps set themselves to weaving a new set of Venetian blinds.

In the houses, where the pebbly floors have been swept bare with a stiff long-handled broom, the women great with child and the nursing mothers, sit and gossip with one another. Old men sit apart, unceasingly twisting palm husk on their bare thighs and muttering old tales under their breath. The carpenters begin work on the new house, while the owner bustles about trying to keep them in a good humor. Families who will cook to-day are hard at work; the taro, yams and bananas have already been brought from inland; the children are scuttling back and forth, fetching sea water, or leaves to stuff the pig. As the sun rises higher in the sky, the shadows deepen under the thatched roofs, the sand is burning to the touch, the hibiscus flowers wilt on the hedges, and little children bid the smaller ones, "Come out of the sun." Those whose excursions have been short return to the village, the women with strings of crimson jelly fish, or baskets of shell fish, the men with cocoanuts, carried in baskets slung on a shoulder pole. The women and children eat their breakfast, just hot from the oven, if this is cook day, and the young men work swiftly in the mid-day heat, preparing the noon feast for their elders.

It is high noon. The sand burns the feet of the little children, who leave their palm leaf balls and their pinwheels of frangipani blossoms to wither in the sun, as they creep into the shade of the houses. The women who must go abroad carry great banana leaves as sun-shades or wind wet cloths about their heads. Lowering a few blinds against the slanting sun, all who are left in the village wrap their heads in sheets and go to sleep. Only a few adventurous children may slip away for a swim in the shadow of a high rock, some industrious woman continues with her weaving, or a close little group of women bend anxiously over a woman in labour. The village is dazzling and dead; any sound seems

---

[1]*Talofa!* Samoan greeting.

[2]*bonito* fish related to and similar to tuna.

oddly loud and out of place. Words have to cut through the solid heat slowly. And then the sun gradually sinks over the sea.

A second time, the sleeping people stir, roused perhaps by the cry of "a boat," resounding through the village. The fishermen beach their canoes, weary and spent from the heat, in spite of the slaked lime on their heads, with which they have sought to cool their brains and redden their hair. The brightly coloured fishes are spread out on the floor, or piled in front of the houses until the women pour water over them to free them from taboo. Regretfully, the young fishermen separate out the "Taboo fish," which must be sent to the chief, or proudly they pack the little palm leaf baskets with offerings of fish to take to their sweethearts. Men come home from the bush, grimy and heavy laden, shouting as they come, greeted in a sonorous rising cadence by those who have remained at home. They gather in the guest house for their evening kava[3] drinking. The soft clapping of hands, the high-pitched intoning of the talking chief who serves the kava echoes through the village. Girls gather flowers to weave into necklaces; children, lusty from their naps and bound to no particular task, play circular games in the half shade of the late afternoon. Finally the sun sets, in a flame which stretches from the mountain behind to the horizon on the sea, the last bather comes up from the beach, children straggle home, dark little figures etched against the sky; lights shine in the houses, and each household gathers for its evening meal. The suitor humbly presents his offering, the children have been summoned from their noisy play, perhaps there is an honoured guest who must be served first, after the soft, barbaric singing of Christian hymns and the brief and graceful evening prayer. In front of a house at the end of the village, a father cries out the birth of a son. In some family circles a face is missing, in others little runaways have found a haven! Again quiet settles upon the village, as first the head of the household, then the women and children, and last of all the patient boys, eat their supper.

After supper the old people and the little children are bundled off to bed. If the young people have guests the front of the house is yielded to them. For day is the time for the councils of old men and the labours of youth, and night is the time for lighter things. Two kinsmen, or a chief and his councillor, sit and gossip over the day's events or make plans for the morrow. Outside a crier goes through the village announcing that the communal breadfruit pit will be opened in the morning, or that the village will make a great fish trap. If it is moonlight, groups of young men, women by twos and threes, wander through the village, and crowds of children hunt for land crabs or chase each other among the breadfruit trees. Half the village may go fishing by torchlight and the curving reef will gleam with wavering lights and echo with shouts of triumph or disappointment, teasing words or smothered cries of outraged modesty. Or a group of youths may dance for the pleasure of some visiting maiden. Many of those who have retired to sleep, drawn by the merry music, will wrap their sheets around them and set out to find the dancing. A white-clad, ghostly throng will gather in a circle about the gaily lit house, a circle from which every now and then a few will detach themselves and wander away among the trees. Sometimes sleep will not descend upon the village until long past midnight; then at last there is only the mellow thunder of the reef and the whisper of lovers, as the village rests until dawn.[4]

[3]*kava* intoxicating drink made from the powdered root of the shrub *Piper methysticum.*

[4]In *Quest for the Real Samoa,* Bergin & Garvey Publishers, Inc. (1987) Lowell D. Holmes, who, with his wife, studied Samoa in 1954, provides a different view: "Mead's picture of a noisy, busy village with young men shouting to one another as they go to and from the plantations was not observed by me, nor do such actions on the part of young men seem characteristic of a Samoan

Understanding and Analysis

1. Mead divides her description into five paragraphs. What is her organizing principle?

2. Many readers in 1928 saw in Mead's description an idyllic and peaceful island existence. What indications can you find of stress or discomfort in her description?

3. What are the main activities in the Samoan day? What activities do you find surprising, if any? What activities seem most different from your own? What seem most similar? What activities do you think are motivated by biological necessities?

Comparison

1. What, if any, do you think are the implications of Holmes's critique of Mead's description? (See footnote 4.)

2. Lippmann notes that "even the eyewitness does not bring back a naive picture of the scene . . . A report is the joint product of the knower and the known, in which the role of observer is always selective and usually creative." What creative elements do you see in Mead's description?

3. Lippmann cites studies that show that even trained observers misrepresent a scene: "In thirty-four out of the forty observers the stereotypes preempted at least one-tenth of the scene." What scientific data would you require in order to determine the reliability of either Mead or Holmes?

4. Lippmann presents the views of many of his generation, including Mead and Boas, when he claims that "until we are able to discount the difference in nurture, we must withhold judgment about differences of nature." In other words, Lippmann also was prepared to accept what Mead saw and the conclusions she drew about the effect of culture on the adolescent personality. Read Martin Gardner's essay, "The Great Samoan Hoax." Does Gardner offer any ways to overcome the influence of theory on our ability to see and

village, where part of the respect shown to chiefs includes not disturbing them with undue noise. Prohibitions against such noise in the village are well documented by Kramer (1941:101–102). Nor were Mead's descriptions of the awakening village muting the sound of the breaking surf confirmed by this research. In the morning, the village was deathly quiet, and people moved about like shadows, performing their morning tasks. Many times on awakening, the Samoan members of our household were found to have completed many of their chores.

While nearly all of the activities described in Mead's 'A Day in Samoa' were witnessed during my five-month stay in Manu'a, not all of them are typical of a single day. Although the compression of typical activities into a typical day is an accepted literary device, it tends to distort perspective on the tempo of village life. After having been immersed in Mead's account, it came as a surprise to find Ta'u not a bustling village, but one almost deserted during the daytime. People went off one by one to their occupations by way of the rear path of the village. One or two girls were observed fishing on the reef, unless the tide was very low, when perhaps a dozen women engaged in the task. Only one house was begun during five months of this research; the bonito boats did not go out a single time; the society of untitled men (*aumaga*) danced for visiting maidens only two or three times; and pigs were cooked only on infrequent ceremonial occasions. Mead's typical day, therefore, presents a composite picture, but one which is not representative of actual conditions to be encountered on any given day" (109).

interpret data? Compare his evidence and conclusions with the evidence you said you would require in your answer to question 3.

Robert Graves
(1895–1985)

When he was fourteen, Robert Graves was sent to Charterhouse, the same private school Max Beerbohm had attended, where he spent four miserable years. Even after he joined the Poetry Society, he had trouble making friends. His excessive righteousness led him to snitch on fellow students, further undermining his popularity, until another poetically inclined youth, a few years older, convinced him to learn boxing. Although he dislocated his thumbs (and later broke his nose) in boxing matches, Graves did briefly gain the respect of his fellow students. He had hoped that the high point of his Charterhouse days would be the confirmation service in his junior year, but, as he writes in his autobiography *Good-bye to All That*, "the Holy Ghost failed to descend." The anticlimax contributed to his gradual loss of faith.

After Charterhouse, his parents wanted him to earn a scholarship to Oxford, where he was to become a professor of classical studies. His parents considered poetry to be "a hobby." But in 1914, when he was eighteen years old, war was declared; he enlisted in the Royal Welsh Fusiliers. The war proved the decisive event of his life. In 1916, he was so badly wounded that he was assumed dead; his mother received a letter informing her of her loss, and his death was reported in the *Times*. After a long convalescence, Graves returned to the front, but when he contracted bronchitis two days later, he was sent home for good.

In his life and his poetry, Graves brought together the themes of his childhood—his admiration for strong women like his mother, his love of folk tales, mythology, and classical poetics first learned from his father, and his dependence on an ordered world that could protect him from the horror of his experiences at the front. Throughout his life, he found inspiration for his poetry and safety from his fears in women whom he eventually characterized as earthly muses, incarnations of the eternal goddess.

His first source of inspiration was Nancy Nicholson, whom he married in 1918. According to one of Graves's biographers, Miranda Seymour, Nancy was an artist and early feminist who refused to give up her maiden name or wear a wedding ring. In 1920, increasingly short of money, Graves entered

St. John's College, Oxford, and completed his degree, but he managed to avoid teaching. The couple tried to make money by opening a village shop, which Nancy designed, but it failed; they lost all the money they had invested in it. Over the next eight years, the couple lived in various rented houses and cottages with financial help from relatives and friends. Graves wrote poems, tended the garden, cooked the dinner, and watched over their four children, while Nancy, increasingly ill and depressed, lay in bed or painted and sewed. In 1926, needing mental stimulation, Graves and Nancy invited the poet Laura Riding to visit. They took her with them when Graves accepted a post as Professor of English Literature in Egypt, but the family was not happy there and returned after one year.

In 1929, Graves published his best-selling autobiography, *Good-bye to All That*, from which "Triste La Guerre" is taken. Also in 1929, his marriage over, Graves left England for Majorca with Laura Riding, who was to become his major source of security and the woman he idealized and trusted absolutely for the next thirteen years. Riding was even more certain than Graves, if possible, about her importance to the world of poetry and even politics. While in Majorca Graves and Riding wrote *A Survey of Modernist Poetry* and published their own poems as well as the work of other poets on their press, Seizin. To earn needed money, Graves also wrote his two most famous novels, *I, Claudius* and *Claudius the King* (1934). Despite his protestations, Graves's work was highly praised, whereas Riding's work was all but ignored.

Forced to leave Majorca in 1936 at the start of the Spanish Civil War, Graves and Riding returned to England. Soon after, Riding went back to America and Graves married Beryl Hodge, the former wife of a member the Graves and Riding literary circle. Like Nancy and Laura, Beryl was at first for Graves a strong and beautiful mythic muse. Beryl's husband, Alan Hodge, remained a friend and was the author with Graves of *The Long Weekend* (1940), a history of Britain between the two world wars.

With Beryl, Graves created a life similar to the one he had established with Nancy, consisting of many friends, four more children, much reading and writing, gardening, and cooking. He and Beryl continued that life in Majorca, to which they returned in 1946. Here he wrote his most famous work of criticism, *The White Goddess* (1948), which explains in detail his theories about poetry and the muse. T. S. Eliot published it with Faber and Faber and called it "a prodigious, monstrous, stupefying, indescribable book" in the publisher's catalog.

Once Beryl ceased to inspire Graves, he took on at least three younger women, each of whom became, for a while, his muse. In later years, he traveled to America to lecture, accepted awards for his poetry, and experimented with hallucinogenic mushrooms well before the popularity of such drugs in the sixties. From 1961 until 1966 he was Professor of Poetry at Oxford. Graves died in 1985 at the age of 90, having outlived both his mental acuity and his poetic sensibility. But he left a prodigious legacy of poetry and prose—fifty-five books of poetry, one play, twenty books of fiction, as well as numerous translations and works of criticism.

TRISTE LA GUERRE (*1929*)

IN MARCH I rejoined the First Battalion on the Somme. It was the primrose season. We went in and out of the Fricourt trenches, with billets at Morlancourt, a country village still untouched by shell-fire. (Later it got knocked to pieces; the Australians and the Germans captured and recaptured it from each other several times, until only the site remained.) 'A' Company Headquarters were a farmhouse kitchen, where we slept in our valises on the red-brick floor. An old lady and her daughter stayed to safeguard their possessions. The old lady was senile and paralyzed; almost all she could do was to shake her head and say: '*Triste, la guerre!*'[1] We called her 'Triste la Guerre'. The daughter used to carry her about in her arms.

At Fricourt, the trenches were cut in chalk, which we found more tolerable in wet weather than La Bassée clay. The Division gave us a brigade frontage where the lines came closer to each other than at any other point for miles. The British had only recently extended their line down to the Somme, and the French had been content, as they usually were, unless definitely contemplating a battle, to be at peace with the Germans and not dig in too near. But here a slight ridge occurred, and neither side could afford to let the other hold the crest, so they shared it, after a prolonged dispute. This area was used by both the Germans and ourselves as an experimental station for new types of bombs and grenades. The trenches were wide and tumbledown, too shallow in many places, and without sufficient traverses. The French had left relics both of their nonchalance—corpses buried too near the surface; and of their love of security—a number of deep though lousy dug-outs. We busied ourselves raising the front-line parapet and building traverses to limit the damage of the trench-mortar shells that fell continually. Every night not only the companies in the front line, but both support companies, kept hard at work all the time. It was an even worse place than Cuinchy for rats; they scuttled about 'A' Company Mess at meal-time. We always ate with revolvers beside our plates, and punctuated our conversation with sudden volleys at a rat rummaging at somebody's valise or crawling along the timber support of the roof above our heads. 'A' Company officers were gay. We had all been in our school choirs (except Edmund Dadd, who sang like a crow) and used to chant anthems and bits of cantatas whenever things went well. Edmund insisted on taking his part.

At dinner one day a Welsh boy came rushing in, hysterical from terror. He shouted to Richardson: 'Sirr, Sirr, there is a trenss-mortar in my dug-out!'

His sing-song Welsh made us all hoot with laughter. 'Cheer up, 33 Williams,' Richardson said, 'how did a big thing like a trench-mortar happen to occur in your dugout?'

But 33 Williams could not explain. He went on again and again: 'Sirr, Sirr, there is a trenss-mortar in my dug-out!'

---

[1]*Triste, la guerre* sad, the war.

Edmund Dadd went off to investigate. He reported that a mortar shell had fallen into the trench, bounced down the dug-out steps, exploded and killed five men. 33 Williams, the only survivor, had been lying asleep, protected by the body of another man.

Our greatest trial was the German canister—a two-gallon drum with a cylinder inside containing about two pounds of an explosive called ammonal that looked like salmon paste, smelled like marzipan and, when it went off, sounded like the Day of Judgement. The hollow around the cylinder contained scrap metal, apparently collected by French villagers behind the German lines: rusty nails, fragments of British and French shells, spent bullets, and the screws, nuts and bolts that heavy lorries leave behind on the road. We dissected one unexploded canister, and found in it, among other things, the cog-wheels of a clock and half a set of false teeth. The canister could easily be heard approaching and looked harmless in the air, but its shock was as shattering as the very heaviest shell. It would blow in any but the very deepest dug-outs; and the false teeth, rusty nails, cog-wheels, and so on, went flying all over the place. We could not agree how the Germans fired a weapon of that size. The problem remained unsolved until July 1st, when the Battalion attacked from these same trenches and found a long wooden cannon buried in the earth and discharged with a time-fuse. The crew offered to surrender, but our men had sworn for months to get them.

One evening (near 'Trafalgar Square', should any of my readers remember that trench-junction), Richardson, David Thomas and I met Pritchard and the Adjutant. We stopped to talk. Richardson complained what a devil of a place this was for trench-mortars.

'That's where I come in,' said Pritchard. As Battalion Trench-Mortar Officer he had just been given two Stokes mortar-guns. 'They're beauties,' Pritchard went on. 'I've been trying them out, and tomorrow I'm going to get some of my own back. I can put four or five shells in the air at once.'

'About time, too,' the Adjutant said. 'We've had three hundred casualties in the last month here. It doesn't seem so many as that because, curiously enough, none of them have been officers. In fact, we've had about five hundred casualties in the ranks since Loos, and not a single officer.'

Then he suddenly realized that his words were unlucky.

'Touch wood!' David cried. Everybody jumped to touch wood, but it was a French trench and unriveted. I pulled a pencil out of my pocket; that was wood enough for me.

Richardson said: 'I'm not superstitious, anyway.'

The following evening I led 'A'. Company forward as a working-party. 'B' and 'D' Companies were in the line, and we overtook 'C' also going to work. David, bringing up the rear of 'C', looked worried about something. 'What's wrong?' I asked.

'Oh, I'm fed up,' he answered, 'and I've got a cold.'

'C' Company filed along to the right of the Battalion frontage; and we went to the left. It was a weird kind of night, with a bright moon. Germans occupied a sap only forty or fifty yards away. We stood on the parapet piling the sandbags, with the moon at our backs, but the German sentries ignored us—probably because they had work on hand themselves. It happened at times when both sides were busy putting up needful defences that they turned a blind eye to each other's work. Occasionally, it was said, the rival wiring-parties 'as good as used the same mallets' for hammering in the pickets. The Germans seemed much more ready than we were to live and let live. (Only once, so far as I know, apart from Christmas 1914, did both sides show themselves in daylight without firing at each other: one February at Ypres, when the trenches got so flooded that everyone had to crawl out on top to avoid drowning.) Nevertheless, a continuous exchange of grenades and trench-mortars had begun. Several canisters went over, and the men found it difficult to get out of their way in the dark; but for the first time we were giving the enemy as good as they gave us. Pritchard had been using his Stokes mortars all day, and sent over hundreds of rounds; twice the Germans located his emplacement and forced him to shift hurriedly.

'A' Company worked from seven in the evening until midnight. We must have put three thousand sandbags into position, and fifty yards of front trench were already looking presentable. About half-past ten, rifle-fire broke out on the right, and the sentries passed along the news: 'Officer hit.'

Richardson hurried away to investigate. He came back to say: 'It's young Thomas. A bullet through the neck; but I think he's all right. It can't have hit his spine or an artery, because he's walking to the dressing-station.'

I was delighted: David should now be out of it long enough to escape the coming offensive, and perhaps even the rest of the War.

At twelve o'clock we finished for the night. Richardson said: 'Von Ranke,' (only he pronounced it 'Von Runicke'—which was my Regimental nickname) 'take the Company down for their rum and tea, will you? They've certainly earned it tonight. I'll be back in a few minutes. I'm going out with Corporal Chamberlen to see what the wiring-party's been at.'

As I took the men back, I heard a couple of shells fall somewhere behind us. I noticed them, because they were the only shells fired that night: five-nines, by the noise. We had hardly reached the support line on the reverse side of the hill, when we heard the cry: 'Stretcher-bearers!' and presently a man ran up to say: 'Captain Graves is hit!'

That raised a general laugh, and we walked on; but all the same I sent a stretcher-party to investigate. It was Richardson: the shells had caught him and Corporal Chamberlen among the wire. Chamberlen lost his leg and died of wounds a day or two later. Richardson, blown into a shell-hole full of water, lay there stunned for some minutes before the sentries heard the corporal's cries and realized what had happened. The stretcher-bearers brought him down semi-conscious; he recognized us, said he wouldn't be long away from the Company, and gave me instructions about it. The doctor found no wound in any vital spot, though the skin of his left side had been riddled, as we saw, with the chalky soil blown against it. We felt the same relief in his case as in David's: that he would be out of it for a while.

Then news came that David was dead. The Regimental doctor, a throat specialist in civil life, had told him at the dressing-station: 'You'll be all right, only don't raise your head for a bit.' David then took a letter from his pocket, gave it to an orderly, and said: 'Post this!' It had been written to a girl in Glamorgan, for delivery if he got killed. The doctor saw that he was choking and tried tracheotomy; but too late.

Edmund and I were talking together in 'A' Company Headquarters at about one o'clock when the Adjutant entered. He looked ghastly. Richardson was dead: the explosion and the cold water had overstrained his heart, weakened by rowing in the Eight at Radley. The Adjutant said nervously: 'You know, somehow I feel—I feel responsible in a way for this; what I said yesterday at Trafalgar Square. Of course, really, I don't believe in superstition, but . . .

Just at that moment three or four whizz-bang shells burst about twenty yards off. A cry of alarm went up, followed by: 'Stretcher-bearers!'

The Adjutant turned white, and we did not have to be told what had happened. Pritchard, having fought his duel all night, and finally silenced the enemy, was coming off duty. A whizz-bang had caught him at the point where the communication trench reached Maple Redoubt—a direct hit. The total casualties were three officers and one corporal.

It seemed ridiculous, when we returned without Richardson to 'A' Company billets at Morlancourt to find the old lady still alive, and to hear her once more quaver: '*Triste, la guerre!*', when her daughter explained that *le jeune capitaine*[2] had been killed. The old woman had taken a fancy to *le jeune capitaine;* we used to chaff him about it.

I felt David's death worse than any other since I had been in France, but it did not anger me as it did Siegfried. He was Acting Transport Officer and every evening now, when he came up with the rations, went out on patrol looking for Germans to kill. I just felt empty and lost.

One of the anthems that we used to sing in the Mess was: 'He that shall endure to the end, shall be savèd.' The words repeated themselves in my head, like a charm, whenever things went wrong. 'Though thousands languish and fall beside thee, And tens of thousands around thee perish. Yet still it shall not come nigh thee.' And there was another bit: 'To an inheritance incorruptible . . . Through faith unto salvation, Ready to be revealèd at the last trump.' For 'trump' we always used to sing 'crump'. A crump was German five-point-nine shell, and 'the last crump' would be the end of the War. Should we ever live to hear it burst safely behind us? I wondered whether I could endure to the end with faith unto salvation . . . My breaking-point was near now, unless something happened to stave it off. Not that I felt frightened. I had never yet lost my head and turned tail through fright, and knew that I never would. Nor would the break-down come as insanity; I did not have it in me. It would be a general nervous collapse, with tears and twitchings and dirtied trousers; I had seen cases like that.

We were issued with a new gas-helmet, popularly known as 'the goggle-eyed booger with the tit'. It differed from the previous models. One breathed in through the nose from inside the helmet, and breathed out through a special valve held in the mouth; but I could not manage this. Boxing with an already broken nose had recently displaced the septum, which forced me to breathe through my mouth. In a gas-attack, I would be unable to use the helmet—the only type claimed to be proof against the newest German gas. The Battalion doctor advised a nose-operation as soon as possible.

I took his advice, and missed being with the First Battalion when the expected offensive started. Sixty per cent of my fellow-officers were killed in it. Scatter's dream of open warfare failed to materialize. He himself got very badly wounded. Of 'A' Company choir, there is one survivor besides myself: C. D. Morgan, who had his thigh smashed, and was still in hospital some months after the War ended.

Understanding and Analysis

1. Although it is an excerpt from his autobiography, this chapter takes the shape of a short story. What are the elements that contribute to that shape? Who are the characters? What is the plot? What, if any, elements mark this piece as nonfiction?

2. What purpose does the second sentence serve?

3. Graves interweaves past, present, and future in this chapter. Where does the first allusion to the future occur? Where does the first allusion to the past occur? Keep track of

---

[2]*le jeune capitaine* the young captain.

these references to past and future. How do they support Graves's view of the war? How does the description of the occupants of the farmhouse contribute to this theme?

4. The following several paragraphs describe life in the trenches. What were the soldiers doing?

5. The soldiers laugh frequently. Locate each instance and explain what is funny. What purpose does this laughter serve?

6. The soldiers are also superstitious. What purpose do their superstitions serve? What previous experience had all but one of the "A" company officers shared? What can you surmise is Graves's attitude toward superstition and religion? Can you offer an alternate explanation for what happens in this excerpt from Graves's book?

7. What do the soldiers appear to hope for in this chapter? Why?

Comparison

1. Apply Lippmann's comments about selectivity and creativity in a viewer's first-hand description of an event to Graves's description of his time in the trenches of World War I. How trustworthy an eyewitness do you think Graves is?

2. Can you find instances of stereotyping as defined by Lippmann or class issues as depicted by Chesterton in Graves's description of the soldiers?

3. Read Orwell's "A Hanging." Compare the narrative elements in each essay. Does one report seem more believable than the other? How are these two narratives different from short stories?

4. Read Hemingway, Ellison, Pyle, and Fussell. In what ways do the authors and audiences differ in each work? How do audience and point of view affect the purpose and degree of detail in each essay?

D. H. Lawrence
(1885–1930)

D. H. Lawrence was the fourth of five children born to Arthur Lawrence, a hard working and fairly prosperous coal miner in England, and Lydia Lawrence, an unhappily married woman who set her hopes on the academic success of her two middle sons, William Ernest and David Herbert. When David Herbert was sixteen, William died, forcing the mother to place all her hopes on the younger brother. Although less studious than William, in 1898, Lawrence had won a scholarship to the Nottingham Boys' High School. From 1902 to 1906, Lawrence was an apprentice teacher in Eastwood and Ilkeston. Despite his lack of enthusiasm for the profession, he enrolled in 1926 at University College, Nottingham, for a two-year teacher-training course. He hated the program. And the school magazine rejected his poetry.

Like Robert Graves, who also felt compelled to please an overbearing mother, Lawrence found support for his literary aspirations in strong women, primarily Jessie Chambers, whom he fictionalized as Miriam in *Sons and Lovers*, and Frieda Weekley, the wife of the one professor he admired at University College. With the encouragement of Jessie Chambers, Lawrence published his early poetry in the *English Review*, edited by Ford Maddox Ford. Ford, in turn, helped him publish his first novel, *The White Peacock* (1911). His relationship with Jessie lasted through college but was entangled emotionally with his relationship with his mother, who disapproved of Jessie and saw her as a rival for her son's affections. Even after his mother's death in 1910, Lawrence could not betray his mother by marrying Jessie. According to biographer Jeffrey Meyers, at about the same time that Lawrence became certain he did not want to teach, he met Frieda Weekley, a strikingly beautiful and energetic woman who was bored in her marriage. In 1912, the two ran off together to Italy, leaving behind Frieda's distraught husband and their three young children. In 1914, Frieda was given a divorce and the couple married in July. During World War I, they were confined in England, suspected of being German spies because Frieda was the daughter of a German baron and Lawrence was outspoken in his disapproval of war.

Over the next eleven years, the couple lived in Sicily, Ceylon, Australia, the United States, and Mexico, while Lawrence wrote and sought relief from the illnesses that plagued him all his life—pneumonia, severe influenza, and tuberculosis. Despite his recurring illness and worries about money, Frieda's occasional affairs, and her guilt over leaving her children, Lawrence became a prolific writer, publishing poetry, short stories, novels, essays, plays, and travel books. His works reveal his belief in the importance of the physical as opposed to the intellectual side of life and his assumption that industrialization had destroyed the natural impulses of mankind. His most famous works are his trilogy of autobiographical novels, *Sons and Lovers* (1913), *The Rainbow* (1915), and *Women in Love* (1921), his novel of sexual emancipation, *Lady Chatterley's Lover* (1928), and his collected poetry (1977). Lawrence died of tuberculosis at the age of forty-five in France. Like his novels, "The Real Trouble About Women," first published in 1929, reflects the fashions of the times, patriarchial notions, his own vexed emotions, and his conviction that women "aren't fools."

THE REAL TROUBLE ABOUT WOMEN (1929)

THE REAL TROUBLE about women is that they must always go on trying to adapt themselves to men's theories of women, as they always have done. When a woman is thoroughly herself, she is being what her type of man wants her to be. When a woman is hysterical it's because she doesn't quite know what to be, which pattern to follow, which man's picture of woman to live up to.

For, of course, just as there are many men in the world, there are many masculine theories of what women should be. But men run to type, and it is the type, not the individual, that produces the theory, or "ideal" of woman. Those very grasping gentry, the Romans, produced a theory or ideal of the matron, which fitted in very nicely with the Roman property lust. "Cæsar's wife should be above suspicion."—So Cæsar's wife kindly proceeded to be above it, no matter how far below it the Cæsar fell. Later gentlemen like Nero[1] produced the "fast" theory of woman, and later ladies were fast enough for everybody. Dante[2] arrived with a chaste and untouched Beatrice, and chaste and untouched Beatrices began to march self-importantly through the centuries. The Renaissance discovered the learned woman, and learned women buzzed mildly into verse and prose. Dickens invented the child-wife, so child-wives have swarmed ever since. He also fished out his version of the chaste Beatrice, a chaste but marriageable Agnes. George Eliot imitated this pattern, and it became confirmed. The noble woman, the pure spouse, the devoted mother took the field, and was simply worked to death. Our own poor mothers were this sort. So we younger men, having been a bit frightened of our noble mothers, tended to revert to the child-wife. We weren't very inventive. Only the child-wife must be a boyish little thing—that was the new touch we added. Because young men are definitely frightened of the real female. She's too risky a quantity. She is too untidy, like David's Dora.[3] No, let her be a boyish little thing, it's safer. So a boyish little thing she is.

There are, of course, other types. Capable men produce the capable woman ideal. Doctors produce the capable nurse. Business men produce the capable secretary. And so you get all sorts. You can produce the masculine sense of honour (whatever that highly mysterious quantity may be) in women, if you want to.

There is, also, the eternal secret ideal of men—the prostitute. Lots of women live up to this idea: just because men want them to.

And so, poor woman, destiny makes away with her. It isn't that she hasn't got a mind—she has. She's got everything that man has. The only difference is that she asks for a pattern. Give me a pattern to follow! That will always be woman's cry. Unless of course she has already chosen her pattern quite young, then she will declare she is herself absolutely, and no man's idea of women has any influence over her.

Now the real tragedy is not that women ask and must ask for a pattern of womanhood. The tragedy is not, even, that men give them such abominable patterns, child-wives, little-boy-baby-face girls, perfect secretaries, noble spouses, self-sacrificing mothers, pure women who bring forth children in virgin coldness, prostitutes who just make themselves low, to please the men; all the atrocious patterns of womanhood that men have supplied to woman; patterns all perverted from any real natural fulness of a human being. Man is willing to accept woman as an equal, as a man in skirts, as an angel, a devil, a baby-face, a machine, an instrument, a bosom, a womb, a pair of legs, a servant, an encyclopædia, an ideal or an obscenity; the one thing he won't accept her as is a human being, a real human being of the feminine sex.

[1]*Nero* Nero Claudius Caesar, emperor of Rome from 54–68 A.D.

[2]*Dante, Beatrice* Dante Alighieri, author of *The Divine Comedy;* Beatrice is the hero's beloved.

[3]*David's Dora* from Charles Dickens's novel *David Copperfield.*

And, of course, women love living up to strange patterns, weird patterns—the more uncanny the better. What could be more uncanny than the present pattern of the Eton-boy girl with flower-like artificial complexion? It is just weird. And for its very weird-ness women like living up to it. What can be more gruesome than the little-boy-baby-face pattern? Yet the girls take it on with avidity.

But even that isn't the real root of the tragedy. The absurdity, and often, as in the Dante-Beatrice business, the inhuman nastiness of the pattern—for Beatrice had to go on being chaste and untouched all her life, according to Dante's pattern, while Dante had a cosy wife and kids at home—even that isn't the worst of it. The worst of it is, as soon as a woman has really lived up to the man's pattern, the man dislikes her for it. There is intense secret dislike for the Eton-young-man girl, among the boys, now that she is actu-ally produced. Of course, she's very nice to show in public, absolutely the thing. But the very young men who have brought about her production detest her in private and in their private hearts are appalled by her.

When it comes to marrying, the pattern goes all to pieces. The boy marries the Eton-boy girl, and instantly he hates the *type*. Instantly his mind begins to play hysterically with all the other types, noble Agneses, chaste Beatrices, clinging Doras and lurid *filles de joie*. He is in a wild welter of confusion. Whatever pattern the poor woman tries to live up to; he'll want another. And that's the condition of modern marriage.

Modern woman isn't really a fool. But modern man is. That seems to me the only plain way of putting it. The modern man is a fool, and the modern young man a prize fool. He makes a greater mess of his women than men have ever made. Because he absolutely doesn't know what he wants her to be. We shall see the changes in the woman-pattern follow one another fast and furious now, because the young men hysterically don't know what they want. Two years hence women may be in crinolines—there was a pat-tern for you!—or a bead flap, like naked negresses in mid-Africa—or they may be wear-ing brass armour, or the uniform of the Horse Guards. They may be anything. Because the young men are off their heads, and don't know what they want.

The women aren't fools, but they must live up to some pattern or other. They *know* the men are fools. They don't really respect the pattern. Yet a pattern they must have, or they can't exist.

Women are not fools. They have their own logic, even if it's not the masculine sort. Women have the logic of emotion, men have the logic of reason. The two are comple-mentary and mostly in opposition. But the woman's logic of emotion is no less real and inexorable than the man's logic of reason. It only works differently.

And the woman never really loses it. She may spend years living up to a masculine pat-tern. But in the end, the strange and terrible logic of emotion will work out the smashing of that pattern, if it has not been emotionally satisfactory. This is the partial explanation of the astonishing changes in women. For years they go on being chaste Beatrices or child-wives. Then on a sudden—bash! The chaste Beatrice becomes something quite different, the child-wife becomes a roaring lioness! The pattern didn't suffice, emotionally.

Whereas men are fools. They are based on a logic of reason, or are supposed to be. And then they go and behave, especially with regard to women, in a more-than-feminine unreasonableness. They spend years training up the little-boy-baby-face type, till they've got her perfect. Then the moment they marry her, they want something else. Oh, beware, young women, of the young men who adore you! The moment they've got you they'll want something utterly different. The moment they marry the little-boy-baby face, instantly they begin to pine for the noble Agnes, pure and majestic, or the infinite mother with deep bosom of consolation, or the perfect business woman, or the lurid prostitute on black silk sheets: or, most idiotic of all, a combination of all the lot of them at once. And that is the logic of reason! When it comes to women, modern men are idiots. They don't know what they want, and so they never want, permanently, what they get. They want a cream cake that is at the same time ham and eggs and at the same time porridge. They are fools. If only women weren't bound by fate to play up to them!

For the fact of life is that women *must* play up to man's pattern. And she only gives her best to a man when he gives her a satisfactory pattern to play up to. But today, with a stock of ready-made, worn-out idiotic patterns to live up to, what can women give to men but the trashy side of their emotions? What could a woman possibly give to a man who wanted her to be a boy-baby face? What could she possibly give him but the drib-blings of an idiot?—And, because women aren't fools, and aren't fooled even for very long at a time, she gives him some nasty cruel digs with her claws, and makes him cry for mother dear!—abruptly changing his pattern.

Bah! men are fools. If they want anything from women, let them give women a decent, satisfying idea of womanhood—not these trick patterns of washed-out idiots.

Understanding and Analysis

1. Reread the first sentence of the essay. Based on this sentence alone, what does Lawrence appear to mean here? In the first paragraph, does Lawrence allow women any power over who they are?

2. What style is Lawrence referring to when he describes the current pattern for women in 1929 as "boyish"?

3. In the third paragraph Lawrence says a woman does have a mind. What does he mean? How does he account for the woman who asserts that she knows who she is before she has met her man?

4. Does Lawrence explain why a woman "must ask for a pattern"? If so, why? If not, why not?

5. What does Lawrence believe is the nature of women? He offers two points about women that he claims are givens? What are they? What characteristics of women does Lawrence believe are not natural to women?

6. Why is modern man a fool according to Lawrence? Why is he not satisfied with any of his patterns for women?

7. Why, according to Lawrence, does a modern woman change her pattern mid-marriage?

8. Lawrence uses repetition to assert his message. Where do these repetitions occur? He also uses several exclamation marks. Locate them. What is the effect of repetition and exclamation marks on the reader?

9. What characteristics do men and women share, according to Lawrence?

10. Examine Lawrence's logic in this essay. Is there any way, given his premises, that his theory about the problem with women could be proven wrong?

Comparison

1. To what degree would Twain agree with Lawrence about the various styles or patterns women follow?

2. Compare Lawrence's views of women with those of Woolf, Brady, and Greer. Do you detect similarities among the patterns or stereotypes each discusses?

3. Compare the lives and ideas of some of the women writers in this text with Lawrence's idea that women need a pattern to follow. Do *they* appear to follow a pattern?

James Thurber
(1894–1961)

James Thurber was born in Columbus, Ohio, the second of three sons. When Thurber was six years old, his seven-year-old brother accidentally shot him in the left eye with an arrow, and, because the eye was not immediately removed, his other eye became inflamed, a reaction of the immune system called sympathetic ophthalmia. Despite his glass eye and his weak vision, Thurber developed an early flair for writing. He published short stories in his high school magazine and hoped to become its editor. According to one biographer, Neil A. Grauer, Thurber later found out that he lost the position because his mother had intervened out of concern for his weak vision. He was nonetheless elected senior class president and gave the President's Address at graduation.

In 1913, he enrolled at Ohio State University. During his second year, he cut so many classes that he failed every course. Although he registered again the following year and did much better, by the time Thurber was twenty-three he had spent five years at college and was still a junior. He never graduated. Declared 4-F during World War I because of his glass eye, Thurber studied cryptology in Washington and arrived in Paris as a code clerk on November 13, 1918, two days after the armistice. After sixteen months in Paris, he returned to Columbus and worked at a variety of odd jobs until he was hired as a reporter for the *Columbus Dispatch*. During this period he also contributed articles to the *Christian Science Monitor* and the *Cleveland New Leader*; in 1923, he began a column, "Credos and Curios" for the Sunday *Dispatch*. In addition, he was writing comic essays, short stories, and a musical comedy with a friend, actor Elliot Nugent. Because only one of these projects was actually published, Thurber also began working as a press agent, a position that paid more than any of his other jobs.

After another desultory year in Paris, Thurber moved to Greenwich Village, determined to earn his living as a writer. When his first pieces were rejected by *The New Yorker*, he worked for the *Evening Post* while continuing to send in pieces to *The New Yorker* and elsewhere. Finally, in 1927, Thurber sold a story to *The New Yorker*. Soon after, he met E. B. White, who Thurber later claimed, taught him "discipline" and "how to write." Whatever other help he may have offered, E. B. White encouraged Thurber to draw as well as write, introduced him to Harold Ross, the editor of *The New Yorker*, and helped Thurber to land a job with the magazine, writing regular pieces for the "Talk of the Town" section. White and Thurber together wrote a popular send-up of the self-help books of the time, called *Is Sex Necessary?* (1929), with illustrations by Thurber. Soon Thurber was drawing cartoons for *The New Yorker*, as well as writing short stories and essays.

Among his works are *The Owl in the Attic and Other Perplexities* (1931), *The Seal in the Bedroom and Other Predicaments* (1932), *My Life and Hard Times* (1933), *The Middle-Aged Man on the Flying Trapeze* (1935), *The Last Flower* (1939), *Fables for Our Time and Famous Poems Illustrated* (1940), *Many Moons* (1943), *Men, Women, and Dogs* (1943), *The Thurber Carnival* (1945), *The Beast in Me and Other Animals* (1948), *The 13 Clocks* (1950), *Thurber Country* (1953), *Thurber's Dogs* (1955), and *The Wonderful O* (1957). His most famous story, "The Secret Life of Walter Mitty," (1940) has been widely anthologized and even made into a movie (1947).

By the forties, Thurber had become nearly blind; he was able to draw only by using a device called the Zeiss Loop Helmet, used by defense workers in World War II to magnify precision equipment. He produced his final drawing for the July 9, 1951, issue of *Time* magazine, which presented tributes to Thurber from, among others, T. S. Eliot (who is said to have been a greater admirer of Thurber than Thurber was of Eliot). Eliot saw in Thurber's work "a criticism of life": "his writings and illustrations are capable of surviving the immediate environment and time out of which they spring. To some extent, they will be a document of the age they belong to."

Although Thurber admired Mencken and indulged in word-play even more than his predecessor, he was, like his fellow cartoonist Max Beerbohm, more subtle and gentle in his satire. In both his prose and his drawings, he details with wit, irony, and sympathy the quandaries of the beleaguered common man, the Walter Mitty in us all.

WHICH *(1929)*

THE RELATIVE PRONOUN "which" can cause more trouble than any other word, if recklessly used. Foolhardy persons sometimes get lost in which-clauses and are never heard of again. My distinguished contemporary, Fowler,[1] cites several tragic cases, of which the following is one: "It was rumoured that Beaconsfield intended opening the Conference with

---

[1]*Fowler* (1858–1933) lexicographer, grammarian, essayist, and poet, Henry Watson Fowler is famous for his thorough, clear, and feisty prescriptions in *A Dictionary of Modern Usage*, first published in 1926 and widely consulted ever since.

a speech in French, his pronounciation of which language leaving everything to be desired . . ." That's as much as Mr. Fowler quotes because, at his age, he was afraid to go any farther. The young man who originally got into that sentence was never found. His fate, however, was not as terrible as that of another adventurer who became involved in a remarkable which-mire. Fowler has followed his devious course as far as he safely could on foot: "Surely what applies to games should also apply to racing, the leaders of which being the very people from whom an example might well be looked for . . ." Not even Henry James could have successfully emerged from a sentence with "which," "whom," and "being" in it. The safest way to avoid such things is to follow in the path of the American author, Ernest Hemingway. In his youth he was trapped in a which-clause one time and barely escaped with his mind. He was going along on solid ground until he got into this: "It was the one thing of which, being very much afraid—for whom has not been warned to fear such things—he . . ." Being a young and powerfully built man, Hemingway was able to fight his way back to where he had started, and begin again. This time he skirted the treacherous morass in this way: "He was afraid of one thing. This was the one thing. He had been warned to fear such things: Everybody has been warned to fear such things." Today Hemingway is alive and well, and many happy writers are following along the trail he blazed.

What most people don't realize is that one "which" leads to another. Trying to cross a paragraph by leaping from "which" to "which" is like Eliza crossing the ice. The danger is in missing a "which" and falling in. A case in point is this: "He went up to a pew which was in the gallery, which brought him under a colored window which he loved and always quieted his spirit." The writer, worn out, missed the last "which"—the one that should come just before "always" in that sentence. But supposing he had got it in! We would have: "He went up to a pew which was in the gallery, which brought him under a colored window which he loved and which always quieted his spirit." Your inveterate whicher in this way gives the effect of tweeting like a bird or walking with a crutch, and is not welcome in the best company.

It is well to remember that one "which" leads to two and that two "whiches" multiply like rabbits. You should never start out with the idea that you can get by with one "which." Suddenly they are all around you. Take a sentence like this: "It imposes a problem which we either solve, or perish." On a hot night, or after a hard day's work, a man often lets himself get by with a monstrosity like that, but suppose he dictates that sentence bright and early in the morning. It comes to him typed out by his stenographer and he instantly senses that something is the matter with it. He tries to reconstruct the sentence, still clinging to the "which," and gets something like this: "It imposes a problem which we either solve, or which, failing to solve, we must perish on account of." He goes to the water-cooler, gets a drink, sharpens his pencil, and grimly tries again. "It imposes a problem which we either solve or which we don't solve . . ." He begins once more: "It imposes a problem which we either solve, or which we do not solve, and from which . . ." The more times he does it the more "whiches" he gets. The way out is simple: "We must either solve this problem, or perish." Never monkey with "which." Nothing except getting tangled up in a typewriter ribbon is worse.

Understanding and Analysis

1. How many examples does Thurber use to make his point? What is his point?

2. List the metaphors and similes Thurber uses. How do they contribute to the humor and to the point of the essay?

3. What are some of the other humorous devices Thurber uses in this essay? Find several examples of each type.

4. Why does Thurber refer specifically to Ernest Hemingway and Henry James?

5. What are the other relative pronouns? Does Thurber use them to good effect?

Comparison

1. Read the other essay by Thurber in this collection. Do you see similarities in the techniques of humor in the two essays?

2. In "Education by Poetry" Frost describes enthusiasm as "taken through the prism of intellect and spread on the screen in a color, all the way from hyperbole at one end–or overstatement, at one end–to understatement at the other end." According to Frost's description, is Thurber enthusiastic about good style?

3. As you read other essays in this text and your own writing, note the appearance of "which" and decide in each instance if the word helps or hinders clarity and style. Write a modern version of Thurber's essay, using approximately the same number of examples, types of humor, and metaphorical language, to support or refute Thurber's point.

Robert Frost
(1874–1963)

Robert Frost was born in San Francisco, the first of two children and the only son of William Prescott Frost, Jr., and Isabelle Moodie Frost. His parents had been schoolteachers when they met in Pennsylvania, but when they moved to California, William Frost began a career in journalism. His rebellious nature, drunkenness, and tuberculosis led to his death in 1885, when Robert was eleven and his sister Jeanie was nine. Left virtually penniless, Isabelle moved to her husband's hometown, Lawrence, Massachusetts, where she hoped her in-laws would help raise the children of their only son. But Will's family did not approve of his wife because of her lower-class background; she spent the rest of her life scraping together a meager living by teaching in various small schools in Salem, New Hampshire, Methuen, and Lawrence. When Robert Frost and his sister entered their mother's fifth-grade class, they began the first year of their formal education.

In high school in Lawrence, his father's old school, Robert studied classics, earned excellent grades, and was the top student in a class of thirty-six—his future wife, Elinor White, provided his best competition and shared the podium as valedictorian at commencement. Like many a poet before and since, Frost's first publication was in his school paper, where Elinor had also published a few poems. In his senior year he became editor of the *Bulletin*. Committed to poetry, education, and a romantic, intellectual life together, he and Elinor exchanged rings and promises after graduation, though they did not actually marry until four years later. Robert had completed the requirements for entrance into Harvard, again his father's alma mater, but his grandparents, who were paying all expenses not covered by a scholarship, chose Dartmouth instead. Elinor went to St. Lawrence College. Just before midterms in his first year, Frost left Dartmouth, disappointed by the conformity at school and longing for his beloved Elinor. It is also possible, according to biographer Jeffrey Meyers, that Frost was expelled because of a cruel college trick played on a fellow student.

Hoping that Elinor would leave college and join him, Frost spent the next few years doing odd jobs, helping his mother in her school, working in a mill, tutoring students, reporting for the local paper. When he visited Elinor at school and she refused to spend time with him, even after he had presented her with a book of poems he had privately printed, Frost punished her by running off to the Dismal Swamp in Virginia, where he toyed with suicide. Impressed by the passion of his love for her, Elinor completed her education in three years and finally agreed to marry Frost, despite her father's objections and Frost's apparent inability to support a family. After the wedding, the couple moved in with Frost's mother and sister in the two rented rooms Isabelle had converted into a school in downtown Lawrence. Like his parents, he and Elinor started life together as teachers.

Over the next sixteen years, Frost wrote poetry, taught at various schools, took up a course of study at Harvard (but left after two years), and tried his hand at chicken farming, settling on a farm in Derry, New Hampshire, bought for him by his grandfather. Meanwhile, he and Elinor had six children. The first, Elliot, died at age three of cholera, before the family moved to Derry. The sixth died two days after birth. In all this time, Frost had published only a few poems. To further his career, he decided to move his family to England in 1912. He was thirty-eight years old and still unknown as a poet. In England, a London publisher accepted his first book of poetry, *A Boy's Will*, and Ezra Pound reviewed it. Then followed a second, *North of Boston*. When he returned to the U.S. in 1915, Holt agreed to publish the two books Frost had already published in England. Many volumes followed, including *New Hampshire* (1923), *West-running Brook* (1928), *Collected Poems* (1930), *A Further Range* (1936), *A Witness Tree* (1942), *Steeple Bush* (1947), and *In the Clearing* (1962). He also wrote two plays in verse, *A Mask of Reason* (1945) and *A Mask of Mercy* (1947).

Until his death in 1963, Frost continued to write, teach, and lecture on the subject he loved best. He lived primarily on a farm near Franconia, New Hampshire, and taught at various times at Amherst, University of Michigan,

Dartmouth, and Harvard. Later he spent time in Florida as well. He was awarded the Pulitzer Prize for poetry four times. Like another of America's beloved lecturers, Mark Twain, Frost suffered much pain in his family life, despite his eventual success as a poet and his long, active professional life. His sister Jeanie had to be committed to an insane asylum when she was forty. His fourth child, Marjorie, died in childbirth. Elinor died of a heart attack at sixty-four, having survived breast cancer a year before. Two years later his son Carol committed suicide. His second daughter, Irma, suffered several mental crises and, in 1947, Frost had to commit her to an institution to keep her from harming herself and others.

Frost's poetry records in detail ordinary people struggling to understand each other and to accept the complexities of life in a natural world at once beautiful, cruel, and devoid of sympathy.

EDUCATION BY POETRY (1930)

I AM GOING to urge nothing in my talk. I am not an advocate. I am going to consider a matter, and commit a description. And I am going to describe other colleges than Amherst. Or, rather say all that is good can be taken as about Amherst; all that is bad will be about other colleges.

I know whole colleges where all American poetry is barred—whole colleges. I know whole colleges where all contemporary poetry is barred.

I once heard of a minister who turned his daughter—his poetry-writing daughter—out on the street to earn a living, because he said there should be no more books written; God wrote one book, and that was enough. (My friend George Russell "Æ" has read no literature, he protests, since just before Chaucer.)

That all seems sufficiently safe, and you can say one thing for it. It takes the onus off the poetry of having to be used to teach children anything. It comes pretty hard on poetry, I sometimes think—what it has to bear in the teaching process.

Then I know whole colleges where, though they let in older poetry, they manage to bar all that is poetical in it by treating it as something other than poetry. It is not so hard to do that. Their reason I have often hunted for. It may be that these people act from a kind of modesty. Who are professors that they should attempt to deal with a thing as high and as fine as poetry? Who are *they*? There is a certain manly modesty in that.

That is the best general way of settling the problem; treat all poetry as if it were something else than poetry, as if it were syntax, language, science. Then you can even come down into the American and into the contemporary without any special risk.

There is another reason they have, and that is that they are, first and foremost in life, markers. They have the marking problem to consider. Now, I stand here a teacher of many years' experience and I have never complained of having had to mark. I had rather mark anyone for anything—for his looks, carriage, his ideas, his correctness, his exactness, anything you please,—I would rather give him a mark in terms of letters, A, B, C, D, than have to use adjectives on him. We are all being marked by each other all the time, classified, ranked, put in our place, and I see no escape from that. I am no sentimentalist. You have got to mark, and you have got to mark, first of all, for accuracy, for correctness. But if I am going to give a mark, that is the least part of my marking. The hard part is the part beyond that, the part where the adventure begins.

One other way to rid the curriculum of the poetry nuisance has been considered. More merciful than the others it would neither abolish nor denature the poetry, but only turn it out to disport itself, with the plays and games—in no wise discredited, though given no credit for. Any one who liked to teach poetically could take his subject, whether English, Latin, Greek or French, out into the nowhere along with the poetry. One side of a sharp line would be left to the rigorous and righteous; the other side would be assigned to the flowery where they would know what could be expected of them. Grade marks where more easily given, of course, in the courses concentrating on correctness and exactness as the only forms of honesty recognized by plain people; a general indefinite mark of X in the courses that scatter brains over taste and opinion. On inquiry I have found no teacher willing to take position on either side of the line, either among the rigors or among the flowers. No one is willing to admit that his discipline is not partly in exactness. No one is willing to admit that his discipline is not partly in taste and enthusiasm.

How shall a man go through college without having been marked for taste and judgment? What will become of him? What will his end be? He will have to take continuation courses for college graduates. He will have to go to night schools. They are having night schools now, you know, for college graduates. Why? Because they have not been educated enough to find their way around in contemporary literature. They don't know what they may safely like in the libraries and galleries. They don't know how to judge an editorial when they see one. They don't know how to judge a political campaign. They don't know when they are being fooled by a metaphor, an analogy, a parable. And metaphor is, of course, what we are talking about. Education by poetry is education by metaphor.

Suppose we stop short of imagination, initiative, enthusiasm, inspiration and originality—dread words. Suppose we don't mark in such things at all. There are still two minimal things, that we have got to take care of, taste and judgment. Americans are supposed to have more judgment than taste, but taste is there to be dealt with. That is what poetry, the only art in the colleges of arts, is there for. I for my part would not be afraid to go in for enthusiasm. There is the enthusiasm like a blinding light, or the enthusiasm of the deafening shout, the crude enthusiasm that you get uneducated by poetry, outside of poetry. It is exemplified in what I might call "sunset raving." You look westward toward the sunset, or if you get up early enough, eastward toward the sunrise, and you rave. It is oh's and ah's with you and no more.

But the enthusiasm I mean is taken through the prism of the intellect and spread on the screen in a color, all the way from hyperbole at one end—or overstatement, at one end—to understatement at the other end. It is a long strip of dark lines and many colors. Such enthusiasm is one object of all teaching in poetry. I heard wonderful things said about Virgil[1] yesterday, and many of them seemed to me crude enthusiasm, more like a deafening shout, many of them. But one speech had range, something of overstatement, something of statement, and something of understatement. It had all the colors of an enthusiasm passed through an idea.

I would be willing to throw away everything else but that: enthusiasm tamed by metaphor. Let me rest the case there. Enthusiasm tamed to metaphor, tamed to that much

---

[1]*Virgil* Publius Vergilius Maro, 70–19 B.C., a Latin poet most famous for the *Aenied,* a legend about the founding of the Roman nation.

of it. I do not think anybody ever knows the discreet use of metaphor, his own and other people's, the discreet handling of metaphor, unless he has been properly educated in poetry.

Poetry begins in trivial metaphors, pretty metaphors, "grace" metaphors, and goes on to the profoundest thinking that we have. Poetry provides the one permissible way of saying one thing and meaning another. People say, "Why don't you say what you mean?" We never do that, do we, being all of us too much poets. We like to talk in parables and in hints and in indirections—whether from diffidence or some other instinct.

I have wanted in late years to go further and further in making metaphor the whole of thinking. I find some one now and then to agree with me that all thinking, except mathematical thinking, is metaphorical, or all thinking except scientific thinking. The mathematical might be difficult for me to bring in, but the scientific is easy enough.

Once on a time all the Greeks were busy telling each other what the All was—or was like unto. All was three elements, air, earth, and water (we once thought it was ninety elements; now we think it is only one). All was substance, said another. All was change, said a third. But best and most fruitful was Pythagoras' comparison of the universe with number. Number of what? Number of feet, pounds, and seconds was the answer, and we had science and all that has followed in science. The metaphor has held and held, breaking down only when it came to the spiritual and psychological or the out of the way places of the physical.

The other day we had a visitor here, a noted scientist, whose latest word to the world has been that the more accurately you know where a thing is, the less accurately you are able to state how fast it is moving. You can see why that would be so, without going back to Zeno's problem of the arrow's flight. In carrying numbers into the realm of space and at the same time into the realm of time you are mixing metaphors, that is all, and you are in trouble. They won't mix. The two don't go together.

Let's take two or three more of the metaphors now in use to live by. I have just spoken of one of the new ones, a charming mixed metaphor right in the realm of higher mathematics and higher physics: that the more accurately you state where a thing is, the less accurately you will be able to tell how fast it is moving. And, of course, everything is moving. Everything is an event now. Another metaphor. A thing, they say, is an event. Do you believe it is? Not quite. I believe it is almost an event. But I like the comparison of a thing with an event.

I notice another from the same quarter. "In the neighborhood of matter space is something like curved." Isn't that a good one! It seems to me that that is simply and utterly charming—to say that space is something like curved in the neighborhood of matter. "Something like."

Another amusing one is from—what is the book?—I can't say it now; but here is the metaphor. Its aim is to restore you to your ideas of free will. It wants to give you back your freedom of will. All right, here it is on a platter. You know that you can't tell by name what persons in a certain place will be dead ten years after graduation, but you can tell actuarially how many will be dead. Now, just so this scientist says of the particles of matter flying at a screen, striking a screen; you can't tell what individual particles will come, but you can say in general that a certain number will strike in a given time. It shows, you see, that the individual particle can come freely. I asked Bohr about that particularly, and he said, "Yes, it is so. It can come when it wills and as it wills; and the action of the individual particle is unpredictable. But it is not so of the action of the mass. There you can predict." He says, "That gives the individual atom its freedom, but the mass its necessity."

Another metaphor that has interested us in our time and has done all our thinking for us is the metaphor of evolution. Never mind going into the Latin word. The metaphor is simply the metaphor of the growing plant or of the growing thing. And somebody very brilliantly, quite a while ago, said that the whole universe, the whole of everything, was like unto a growing thing. That is all. I know the metaphor will break down at some point, but it has not failed everywhere. It is a very brilliant metaphor, I acknowledge, though I myself get too tired of the kind of essay that talks about the evolution of candy, we will say, or the evolution of elevators—the evolution of this, that, and the other. Everything is evolution. I emancipate myself by simply saying that I didn't get up the metaphor and so am not much interested in it.

What I am pointing out is that unless you are at home in the metaphor, unless you have had your proper poetical education in the metaphor, you are not safe anywhere. Because you are not at ease with figurative values: you don't know the metaphor in its strength and its weakness. You don't know how far you may expect to ride it and when it may break down with you. You are not safe in science; you are not safe in history. In history, for instance—to show that [it] is the same in history as elsewhere—I heard somebody say yesterday that Aeneas[2] was to be likened unto (those words, "likened unto"!) George Washington. He was that type of national hero, the middle-class man, not thinking of being a hero at all, bent on building the future, bent on his children, his descendants. A good metaphor, as far as it goes, and you must know how far. And then he added that Odysseus[3] should be likened unto Theodore Roosevelt. I don't think that is so good. Someone visiting Gibbon[4] at the point of death, said he was the same Gibbon as of old, still at his parallels.

Take the way we have been led into our present position morally, the world over. It is by a sort of metaphorical gradient. There is a kind of thinking—to speak metaphorically—there is a kind of thinking you might say was endemic in the brothel. It is always there. And every now and then in some mysterious way it becomes epidemic in the world. And how does it do so? By using all the good words that virtue has invented to maintain virtue. It uses honesty, first,—frankness, sincerity—those words; picks them up, uses them. "In the name of honesty, let us see what we are." You know. And then it picks up the word joy. "Let us in the name of joy, which is the enemy of our ancestors, the Puritans . . . Let us in the name of joy, which is the enemy of the kill-joy Puritan . . ." You see. "Let us," and so on. And then, "In the name of health . . ." Health is another good word. And that is the metaphor Freudianism trades on, mental health. And the first thing we know, it has us all in up to the top knot. I suppose we may blame the artists a good deal, because they are great people to spread by metaphor. The stage too—the stage is always a good intermediary between the two worlds, the under and the upper—if I may say so without personal prejudice to the stage.

In all this I have only been saying that the devil can quote Scripture, which simply means that the good words you have lying around the devil can use for his purposes as well as anybody else. Never mind about my morality. I am not here to urge anything. I don't care whether the world is good or bad—not on any particular day.

Let me ask you to watch a metaphor breaking down here before you.

Somebody said to me a little while ago, "It is easy enough for me to think of the universe as a machine, as a mechanism."

[2]*Aeneas* a Trojan hero who escaped the sack of Troy, wandered for years, and settled in Italy.

[3]*Odysseus* a Greek hero in the Trojan war, whose journey home took ten years.

[4]*Gibbon* Edward Gibbon, 1734–1797; a British historian whose best-known work is *The History of the Decline and Fall of the Roman Empire.*

I said, "You mean the universe is like a machine?"

He said, "No, I think it is one . . . Well, it is like . . ."

"I think you mean the universe is like a machine."

"All right. Let it go at that."

I asked him, "Did you ever see a machine without a pedal for the foot, or a lever for the hand, or a button for the finger?"

He said, "No—no."

I said, "All right. Is the universe like that?"

And he said, "No. I mean it is like a machine, only . . ."

". . . it is different from a machine," I said.

He wanted to go just that far with that metaphor and no further. And so do we all. All metaphor breaks down somewhere. That is the beauty of it. It is touch and go with the metaphor, and until you have lived with it long enough you don't know when it is going. You don't know how much you can get out of it and when it will cease to yield. It is a very living thing. It is as life itself.

I have heard this ever since I can remember, and ever since I have taught: the teacher must teach the pupil to think. I saw a teacher once going around in a great school and snapping pupils' heads with thumb and finger and saying, "Think." That was when thinking was becoming the fashion. The fashion hasn't yet quite gone out.

We still ask boys in college to think, as in the nineties, but we seldom tell them what thinking means; we seldom tell them it is just putting this and that together; it is just saying one thing in terms of another. To tell them is to set their feet on the first rung of a ladder the top of which sticks through the sky.

Greatest of all attempts to say one thing in terms of another is the philosophical attempt to say matter in terms of spirit, or spirit in terms of matter, to make the final unity. That is the greatest attempt that ever failed. We stop just short there. But it is the height of poetry, the height of all thinking, the height of all poetic thinking, that attempt to say matter in terms of spirit and spirit in terms of matter. It is wrong to call anybody a materialist simply because he tries to say spirit in terms of matter, as if that were a sin. Materialism is not the attempt to say all in terms of matter. The only materialist—be he poet, teacher, scientist, politician, or statesman—is the man who gets lost in his material without a gathering metaphor to throw it into shape and order. He is the lost soul.

We ask people to think, and we don't show them what thinking is. Somebody says we don't need to show them how to think; bye and bye they will think. We will give them the forms of sentences and, if they have any ideas, then they will know how to write them. But that is preposterous. All there is to writing is having ideas. To learn to write is to learn to have ideas.

The first little metaphor . . . Take some of the trivial ones. I would rather have trivial ones of my own to live by than the big ones of other people.

I remember a boy saying, "He is the kind of person that wounds with his shield." That may be a slender one, of course. It goes a good way in character description. It has poetic grace. "He is the kind that wounds with his shield."

The shield reminds me—just to linger a minute—the shield reminds me of the inverted shield spoken of in one of the books of the "Odyssey," the book that tells about the longest swim on record. I forget how long it lasted—several days, was it?—but at last as Odysseus came near the coast of Phaeacia, he saw it on the horizon "like an inverted shield."

There is a better metaphor in the same book. In the end Odysseus comes ashore and crawls up the beach to spend the night under a double olive tree, and it says, as in a lonely farmhouse where it is hard to get fire—I am not quoting exactly—where it is hard to start the fire again if it goes out, they cover the seeds of fire with ashes to preserve it for the night, so Odysseus covered himself with the leaves around him and went to sleep. There you have something that gives you character, something of Odysseus himself. "Seeds of fire." So Odysseus covered the seeds of fire in himself. You get the greatness of his nature.

But these are slighter metaphors than the ones we live by. They have their charm, their passing charm. They are as it were the first steps toward the great thoughts, grave thoughts, thoughts lasting to the end.

The metaphor whose manage we are best taught in poetry—that is all there is of thinking. It may not seem far for the mind to go but it is the mind's furthest. The richest accumulation of the ages is the noble metaphors we have rolled up.

I want to add one thing more that the experience of poetry is to anyone who comes close to poetry. There are two ways of coming close to poetry. One is by writing poetry. And some people think I want people to write poetry, but I don't; that is, I don't necessarily. I only want people to write poetry if they want to write poetry. I have never encouraged anybody to write poetry that did not want to write it, and I have not always encouraged those who did want to write it. That ought to be one's own funeral. It is a hard, hard life, as they say.

(I have just been to a city in the West, a city full of poets, a city they have made safe for poets. The whole city is so lovely that you do not have to write it up to make it poetry; it is ready-made for you. But, I don't know—the poetry written in that city might not seem like poetry if read outside of the city. It would be like the jokes made when you were drunk; you have to get drunk again to appreciate them.)

But as I say, there is another way to come close to poetry, fortunately, and that is in the reading of it, not as linguistics, not as history, not as anything but poetry. It is one of the hard things for a teacher to know how close a man has come in reading poetry. How do I know whether a man has come close to Keats in reading Keats? It is hard for me to know. I have lived with some boys a whole year over some of the poets and I have not felt sure whether they have come near what it was all about. One remark sometimes told me. One remark was their mark for the year; had to be—it was all I got that told me what I wanted to know. And that is enough, if it was the right remark, if it came close enough. I think a man might make twenty fool remarks if he made one good one some time in the year. His mark would depend on that good remark.

The closeness—everything depends on the closeness with which you come, and you ought to be marked for the closeness, for nothing else. And that will have to be estimated by chance remarks, not by question and answer. It is only by accident that you know some day how near a person has come.

The person who gets close enough to poetry, he is going to know more about the word *belief* than anybody else knows, even in religion nowadays. There are two or three places where we know belief outside of religion. One of them is at the age of fifteen to twenty, in our self-belief. A young man knows more about himself than he is able to prove to anyone. He has no knowledge that anybody else will accept as knowledge. In his foreknowledge he has something that is going to believe itself into fulfillment, into acceptance.

There is another belief like that, the belief in someone else, a relationship of two that is going to be believed into fulfillment. That is what we are talking about in our novels, the belief of love. And the disillusionment that the novels are full of is simply the disillusionment from disappointment in that belief. That belief can fail, of course.

Then there is a literary belief. Every time a poem is written, every time a short story is written, it is written not by cunning, but by belief. The beauty, the something, the little charm of the thing to be, is more felt than known. There is a common jest, one that always annoys me, on the writers, that they write the last end first, and then work up to it; that they lay a train toward one sentence that they think is pretty nice and have all fixed up to set like a trap to close with. No, it should not be that way at all. No one who has ever come close to the arts has failed to see the difference between things written that way, with cunning and device, and the kind that are believed into existence, that begin in something more felt than known. This you can realize quite as well—not quite as well, perhaps, but nearly as well—in reading as you can in writing. I would undertake to separate short stories on that principle; stories that have been believed into existence and stories that have been cunningly devised. And I could separate the poems still more easily.

Now I think—I happen to think—that those three beliefs that I speak of, the self-belief, the love-belief, and the art-belief, are all closely related to the God-belief, that the belief in God is a relationship you enter into with Him to bring about the future.

There is a national belief like that, too. One feels it. I have been where I came near getting up and walking out on the people who thought that they had to talk against nations, against nationalism, in order to curry favor with internationalism. Their metaphors are all mixed up. They think that because a Frenchman and an American and an Englishman can all sit down on the same platform and receive honors together, it must be that there is no such thing as nations. That kind of bad thinking springs from a source we all know. I should want to say to anyone like that: "Look! First I want to be a person. And I want you to be a person, and then we can be as interpersonal as you please. We can pull each other's noses—do all sorts of things. But, first of all, you have got to have the personality. First of all, you have got to have the nations and then they can be as international as they please with each other."

I should like to use another metaphor on them. I want my palette, if I am a painter, I want my palette on my thumb or on my chair, all clean, pure, separate colors. Then I will do the mixing on the canvas. The canvas is where the work of art is, where we make the conquest. But we want the nations all separate, pure, distinct, things as separate as we can make them; and then in our thoughts, in our arts, and so on, we can do what we please about it.

But I go back. There are four beliefs that I know more about from having lived with poetry. One is the personal belief, which is a knowledge that you don't want to tell other people about because you cannot prove that you know. You are saying nothing about it till you see. The love belief, just the same, has that same shyness. It knows it cannot tell; only the outcome can tell. And the national belief we enter into socially with each other, all together, party of the first part, party of the second part, we enter into that to bring the future of the country. We cannot tell some people what it is we believe, partly, because they are too stupid to understand and partly because we are too proudly vague to explain. And anyway it has got to be fulfilled, and we are not talking until we know more, until we have something to show. And then the literary one in every work of art, not of cunning and craft, mind you, but of real art, that believing the thing into existence, saying as you go more than you even hoped you were going to be able to say, and coming with surprise to an end that you foreknew only with some sort of emotion. And then finally the relationship we enter into with God to believe the future in—to believe the hereafter in.

Understanding and Analysis

1. What are the ways some colleges (other than Amherst) have dealt with poetry?
2. What are the general characteristics of all disciplines, according to Frost?

3. Does he approve of grades? How do you know?

4. How does poetry teach?

5. What does Frost mean by "enthusiasm tamed by metaphor"? Later he revises this phrase as "enthusiasm tamed to metaphor." What is the difference? How, if at all, does this difference connect to his longer description of enthusiasm—"taken through the prism of intellect and spread on the screen in a color, all the way from hyperbole at one end—or overstatement, at one end—to understatement at the other end"?

6. How does Frost describe metaphor and our motives for it?

7. What metaphors from science does Frost point out?

8. What examples does Frost offer of the limits of metaphor?

9. What does thinking mean according to Frost?

10. Near the end of his talk, Frost returns to the subject of marking. How does he mark the student of poetry?

11. What are the beliefs that Frost describes? How many are there in total?

12. What connection do you see in this essay between Frost's discussion of science and his discussion of beliefs?

13. Does Frost's own essay cover the territory from hyperbole to understatement?

Comparison

1. Frost says he wants to claim that metaphor "is the whole of thinking." Recent discoveries in linguistics and in research on how the brain works support this claim. Examine your everyday speech about subjects such as the pursuit of knowledge. What metaphor is implicit in the previous sentence, for example? Can you think of ideas you are studying in biology or other fields that also help to make sense of Frost's assertion?

2. Read Mencken on teaching. Compare his ideas with those of Frost. Both men establish a special tone or relationship with the reader. Compare and contrast their tones in these essays.

3. Both Eliot and Frost make use of science in their essays on poetry. Compare their analogies and draw some conclusions about how and why they use scientific analogies.

4. Read essays by Eliot, Leavis, Snow, Orwell, Bronowski, and Eiseley. Based on these essays and your own experience, what relationships do you see between science and art?

5. Lippmann and Frost both use metaphor when talking about nationalities. How does metaphor clarify their points? What connections between the two essays can you find?

George Orwell
(1903–1950)

George Orwell was born Eric Arthur Blair in Motihari, Bengal. His father, Richard Walmesley Blair, forty-six, was an opium agent in the Indian Civil Service; his mother, Ida Mabel Limouzin Blair, twenty-eight, had lived outside of England most of her life, first in Burma, where her father had sold teak, and later in India with her husband. The Blairs were thus members of what Orwell called the "lower-upper-middle class," their position secured by imperialism and maintained by proper education. When Eric was nearly two, his mother brought him and his seven-year-old sister Marjorie to England to live in Henley, Oxforshire, where, in 1908, his younger sister Avril was born. Because Marjorie was five years older and Avril five years younger than he, Orwell lived a somewhat lonely childhood. Moreover, aside from occasional brief leaves, his father did not live with the family until he retired from the Indian Civil Service in 1912, too late to develop a close relationship with his son.

The year before his father returned, Eric had been sent, at age eight, to a private boarding school, St. Cyprian's, in Sussex. For the next five years, as he describes the experience in "Such, Such Were the Joys...," he inhabited a cruel world where the rules were impossible to obey and where the rich were treated with respect and the poor with ridicule. Moreover, the school encouraged a conformity that Orwell felt himself unable to achieve. Although he knew he was supposed to love God and his father, he felt he could not. According to the standards of St. Cyprian's, he saw himself as "damned." He relates, "I had no money, I was weak, I was ugly, I was unpopular, I had a chronic cough, I was cowardly, I smelt." Yet it was his scholarship to this school that maintained his social status and kept him from becoming in his own eyes, and in the eyes of all he knew, a total failure.

Despite his misery, the schooling achieved its goal: in 1917, after a term at Wellington College, Eric entered Eton, again on scholarship, to complete his indoctrination in the values of the British upper middle class. His position as both an outsider and an insider, a believer who cannot believe, served Orwell all his life and provided him with the courage and perhaps the compulsion to tell the truth or say nothing at all. His writings show that loyalty to abstract virtues such as honor, duty, courage, and patriotism (as opposed to nationalism) persisted side by side with prejudices against birth control advocates and the "smells" of the poor, even when he had become the passionate champion of socialism and the working class.

After Eton, where he ranked in the bottom third among the scholarship boys, Eric followed in his father's footsteps, taking a post not in India but in Burma, as an assistant administrator of police. He worked there for five years, again both an insider and an outsider: "I was stuck between my hatred of the empire I served and my rage against the evil-spirited little beasts who tried to make my job impossible." When he returned to England on leave in 1927, he informed his family that he'd decided to resign to pursue a career as a writer.

For the next five years, like Twain, White, and others, Eric Blair foundered in a pattern typical of the developing writer practicing his craft. While living with his parents in Southwold, Suffolk, a community popular with retired servants of the empire in India, he began his forays into the underside of British life, walking the roads in dirty, torn clothes and staying at run-down lodging houses, but reappearing among his friends periodically to discuss his ideas and take long walks in the country. His behavior mystified his friends, some attributing it to guilt caused by serving the empire, some to his need for material to write about. Blair acknowledged both motives; he also knew that his parents were disappointed in his behavior. In the spring of 1928, he left for a working-class area in Paris (near his mother's sister Nellie) to write. Although some of his essays were accepted by *Le Monde* and *Le Progrès civique*, the two novels and numerous short stories he composed were rejected and no longer survive. In 1929 he caught pneumonia and spent time in the Hôpital Cochin, which he describes in detail in his essay "How the Poor Die." After working as a dishwasher and a kitchen helper, Blair returned to England and began writing *Down and Out in Paris and London* and articles for *Adelphi*, a leftist literary journal. By 1933 he had taught school in London, suffered another bout of pneumonia, lived at home, worked at a bookstore in Hampstead, and written three novels: *Burmese Days*, about the unpleasant behavior of both the rulers and the ruled, and *A Clergyman's Daughter* and *Keep the Aspidistra Flying*, both about the struggling middle class to which he clearly belonged.

In 1933 Blair finally found a publisher, leftist Victor Gollancz, for *Down and Out in Paris and London*, which was published under the pseudonym that gradually became Blair's public self. Later, rejecting *Burmese Days* (first published in America) for fear of political repercussions, Gollancz accepted Orwell's two middle-class novels under the name Eric Blair. This dual perspective, a part of Orwell since his days at St. Cyprian's, was perpetuated, his older friends knowing him as Blair and his newer friends as Orwell. Taken from the river Orwell in his parents' community of Southwold, his pseudonym, like the man it represents, retains a muted connection with the lower upper middle class.

By 1935 Gollancz had agreed to publish *Burmese Days* and Orwell had met his future wife, Eileen O'Shaughnessy, a graduate of Oxford with a degree in English who was studying psychology at University College, London. In his relationships with women, as in most other aspects of his life, Orwell "had a power of facing unpleasant facts." According to several women he courted in those days, he clearly wanted a woman who would admire him, listen to him, and recognize that his writing would always come first in their lives. And in 1935 his prospects for earning money seemed dim. Knowing all this, Eileen O'Shaughnessy still married George Orwell in June of 1936 in Wallington, Hertfordshire, a small village where Orwell had bought a country store with the advance he had been paid by Victor Gollancz and the Left Book Club to study the lives of the poor and unemployed miners in northern England. While Orwell wrote *The Road to Wigan Pier* and tended his garden and his goats and chickens, Eileen tended the store.

In 1937 the book was published, with an introductory disclaimer by Gollancz provoked by Orwell's irritating prejudice against feminists, vegetarians, and other "cranks" that Orwell believed gave socialists a bad name. As soon as he had finished writing the book, Orwell had gone to Spain to fight for the Republicans in the Spanish Civil War. He enlisted in the poum (*Partido Obrero de Unificacion Marxista,* or Workers' Party of Marxist Unification) in Barcelona, where the workers were in fact running the city and class distinctions seemed to have disappeared. In February, when his wife arrived to be near him and to work as a secretary for the Independent Labour Party, Orwell was serving as a corporal in the front lines. The democracy he experienced at the front made a socialist of him, but he never lost his ability to see the "unpleasant facts." In Spain the facts that the leftists in Britain shunned infuriated Orwell: Stalin and the Communists, Orwell saw, were not interested in the POUM and the workers' revolution but in suppressing them as traitors: the Communists were as totalitarian as the Fascists. In May, during the fighting, Orwell was shot through the neck by a sniper and nearly died. In June he and his wife left for France and then Wallington, where Orwell wrote *Homage to Catalonia,* which Gollancz refused to publish because it contradicted the established leftist view of the Communist Party. (Like *Animal Farm* and *Nineteen Eighty-Four, Homage to Catalonia* was published by Secker & Warburg.)

For the last twelve years of his life Orwell was committed to a political ideal, the kind of democratic classless socialism he had seen at the front in the Spanish Civil War. He was also increasingly ill with tuberculosis. When he was first diagnosed as having the disease in March of 1938, he was sent to a sanatorium in Kent and later, through financial support from another writer, to Morocco with Eileen for rest. There he wrote *Coming Up for Air,* the last novel by Eric Blair. Rejected by the army as physically unfit, Orwell spent the war years in London as a sergeant in the Home Guard, a producer for the BBC, literary editor and writer of a weekly column for the *Tribune,* and frequent contributor to such journals as *Horizon* and *Partisan Review.* He published a collection of essays, *Inside the Whale*, in 1940 and a book urging revolution, *The Lion and the Unicorn*, in 1941. Meanwhile Eileen worked for the Censorship Department and later for the Ministry of Food, but she quit her job in 1944, while Orwell was finishing *Animal Farm*, because Orwell wanted very much to have a child. They adopted a baby, Richard Horatio Blair, in June.

Eight months later Orwell left for France as a reporter for the *Observer*, leaving Eileen behind with the baby. She had been feeling ill and was scheduled for what Orwell had called a minor operation but was in fact a hysterectomy for a cancerous tumor. When he was in Cologne, he learned that his wife had died under the anesthetic. He had lost a true companion who had shared his struggles—economic, political, physical, and literary. Nonetheless, he was devoted to Richard and determined to raise him, alone if necessary.

In September of 1945 Orwell rented a cottage for himself and Richard on the island of Jura off the coast of Scotland. He liked it so well that he later rented a farmhouse, where, after the death of his older sister Margaret, his younger sister Avril came to live with him. During the winter of 1946 he returned to London and began *Nineteen Eighty-Four*. He proposed to more than one woman, again offering the "unpleasant truth" of his situation, but no one accepted, and Orwell went back to Jura in April of 1947, increasingly ill but committed to his son and his novel. Some of his friends believed that the move to Jura was suicidal, but others were convinced that the island appealed to some central need for beauty and peace. Orwell spent his time there writing, working on his garden, fishing, caring for his animals, and doing unremarkable carpentry. He and his son were clearly happy, though Orwell was torn between his fear of infecting Richard and his fear of the emotional distance that a greater physical distance between them could produce. By 1949 Orwell was placed in a sanatorium; *Nineteen Eighty-Four* was published that June.

In October, from his hospital bed, Orwell married Sonia Brownell, a literary editor at *Horizon* who, according to Stephen Wadhams (*Remembering Orwell*, Penguin, 1984), had been one of those who had rejected Orwell's earlier proposals. After the wedding, he was looking forward to a trip to Switzerland and to writing a short book, but he never left his bed. He died on January 26, 1950.

Orwell's reputation rests on his ability to focus on the unpleasant complexities that prejudice engenders and to describe "unpleasant facts" in vivid detail; he records for us the irony of being important enough to be hated when shooting an elephant and the collaborative shame in the "impulse . . . to snigger" after a hanging. Even in his book reviews, Orwell manages to find a moral crux: Mark Twain, he says, did not write the books he should have written "because of that flaw in his own nature, his inability to despise success." He sees in Twain's art only the recording of "social history," because Orwell's rigid standards require a writer to limit his income to "reasonable proportions," whatever those may be. Thus Orwell tells the truth as he sees it, even when that "truth" reveals Orwell's own lack of logic or awareness, or, even sometimes, style. Always, however, his truth makes us think about our own.

A HANGING (1931)

IT WAS IN Burma, a sodden morning of the rains. A sickly light, like yellow tinfoil, was slanting over the high walls into the jail yard. We were waiting outside the condemned cells, a row of sheds fronted with double bars, like small animal cages. Each cell measured about ten feet by ten and was quite bare within except for a plank bed and a pot of drinking water. In some of them brown silent men were squatting at the inner bars, with their blankets draped round them. These were the condemned men, due to be hanged within the next week or two.

One prisoner had been brought out of his cell. He was a Hindu, a puny wisp of a man, with a shaven head and vague liquid eyes. He had a thick, sprouting moustache, absurdly too big for his body, rather like the moustache of a comic man on the films. Six tall Indian warders were guarding him and getting him ready for the gallows. Two of them stood by with rifles and fixed bayonets, while the others handcuffed him, passed a chain through his handcuffs and fixed it to their belts, and lashed his arms tight to his sides. They crowded very close about him, with their hands always on him in a careful, caressing grip, as though all the while feeling him to make sure he was there. It was like men handling a fish which is still alive and may jump back into the water. But he stood quite unresisting, yielding his arms limply to the ropes, as though he hardly noticed what was happening.

Eight o'clock struck and a bugle call, desolately thin in the wet air, floated from the distant barracks. The superintendent of the jail, who was standing apart from the rest of us, moodily prodding the gravel with his stick, raised his head at the sound. He was an army doctor, with a grey toothbrush moustache and a gruff voice. "For God's sake hurry up, Francis," he said irritably. "The man ought to have been dead by this time. Aren't you ready yet?"

Francis, the head jailer, a fat Dravidian[1] in a white drill suit and gold spectacles, waved his black hand. "Yes sir, yes sir," he bubbled. "All iss satisfactorily prepared. The hangman iss waiting. We shall proceed."

"Well, quick march, then. The prisoners can't get their breakfast till this job's over."

We set out for the gallows. Two warders marched on either side of the prisoner, with their rifles at the slope; two others marched close against him, gripping him by arm and shoulder, as though at once pushing and supporting him. The rest of us, magistrates and the like, followed behind. Suddenly, when we had gone ten yards, the procession stopped short without any order or warning. A dreadful thing had happened—a dog, come goodness knows whence, had appeared in the yard. It came bounding among us with a loud volley of barks, and leapt round us wagging its whole body, wild with glee at finding so

---

[1]*Dravidian* native of southern India.

many human beings together. It was a large woolly dog, half Airedale, half pariah.[2] For a moment it pranced round us, and then, before anyone could stop it, it had made a dash for the prisoner, and jumping up tried to lick his face. Everyone stood aghast, too taken aback even to grab at the dog.

"Who let that bloody brute in here?" said the superintendent angrily. "Catch it, someone!"

A warder, detached from the escort, charged clumsily after the dog, but it danced and gambolled just out of his reach, taking everything as part of the game. A young Eurasian jailer picked up a handful of gravel and tried to stone the dog away, but it dodged the stones and came after us again. Its yaps echoed from the jail walls. The prisoner, in the grasp of the two warders, looked on incuriously, as though this was another formality of the hanging. It was several minutes before someone managed to catch the dog. Then we put my handkerchief through its collar and moved off once more, with the dog still straining and whimpering.

It was about forty yards to the gallows. I watched the bare brown back of the prisoner marching in front of me. He walked clumsily with his bound arms, but quite steadily, with that bobbing gait of the Indian who never straightens his knees. At each step his muscles slid neatly into place, the lock of hair on his scalp danced up and down, his feet printed themselves on the wet gravel. And once, in spite of the men who gripped him by each shoulder, he stepped slightly aside to avoid a puddle on the path.

It is curious, but till that moment I had never realised what it means to destroy a healthy, conscious man. When I saw the prisoner step aside to avoid the puddle, I saw the mystery, the unspeakable wrongness, of cutting a life short when it is in full tide. This man was not dying, he was alive just as we were alive. All the organs of his body were working—bowels digesting food, skin renewing itself, nails growing, tissues forming—all toiling away in solemn foolery. His nails would still be growing when he stood on the drop, when he was falling through the air with a tenth of a second to live. His eyes saw the yellow gravel and the grey walls, and his brain still remembered, foresaw, reasoned—reasoned even about puddles. He and we were a party of men walking together, seeing, hearing, feeling, understanding the same world; and in two minutes, with a sudden snap, one of us would be gone—one mind less, one world less.

The gallows stood in a small yard, separate from the main grounds of the prison, and overgrown with tall prickly weeds. It was a brick erection like three sides of a shed, with planking on top, and above that two beams and a crossbar with the rope dangling. The hangman, a grey-haired convict in the white uniform of the prison, was waiting beside his machine. He greeted us with a servile crouch as we entered. At a word from Francis the two warders, gripping the prisoner more closely than ever, half led, half pushed him to the gallows and helped him clumsily up the ladder. Then the hangman climbed up and fixed the rope round the prisoner's neck.

We stood waiting, five yards away. The warders had formed in a rough circle round the gallows. And then, when the noose was fixed, the prisoner began crying out on his god. It was a high, reiterated cry of "Ram! Ram! Ram! Ram!",[3] not urgent and fearful like a prayer or a cry for help, but steady, rhythmical, almost like the tolling of a bell. The dog answered the sound with a whine. The hangman, still standing on the gallows, produced a small cotton bag like a flour bag and drew it down over the prisoner's face.

---

[2]*pariah* Hindi for 'outsider', "mutt" in this case.

[3]*Ram* from Rama, a term for the three incarnations of Vishnu, a Hindu god.

But the sound, muffled by the cloth, still persisted, over and over again: "Ram! Ram! Ram! Ram! Ram!"

The hangman climbed down and stood ready, holding the lever. Minutes seemed to pass. The steady, muffled crying from the prisoner went on and on, "Ram! Ram! Ram!" never faltering for an instant. The superintendent, his head on his chest, was slowly poking the ground with his stick; perhaps he was counting the cries, allowing the prisoner a fixed number—fifty, perhaps, or a hundred. Everyone had changed colour. The Indians had gone grey like bad coffee, and one or two of the bayonets were wavering. We looked at the lashed, hooded man on the drop, and listened to his cries—each cry another second of life; the same thought was in all our minds: oh, kill him quickly, get it over, stop that abominable noise!

Suddenly the superintendent made up his mind. Throwing up his head he made a swift motion with his stick. "Chalo!" he shouted almost fiercely.

There was a clanking noise, and then dead silence. The prisoner had vanished, and the rope was twisting on itself. I let go of the dog, and it galloped immediately to the back of the gallows; but when it got there it stopped short, barked, and then retreated into a corner of the yard, where it stood among the weeds, looking timorously out at us. We went round the gallows to inspect the prisoner's body. He was dangling with his toes pointed straight downwards, very slowly revolving, as dead as a stone.

The superintendent reached out with his stick and poked the bare body; it oscillated, slightly. "He's all right," said the superintendent. He backed out from under the gallows, and blew out a deep breath. The moody look had gone out of his face quite suddenly. He glanced at his wrist-watch. "Eight minutes past eight. Well, that's all for this morning, thank God."

The warders unfixed bayonets and marched away. The dog, sobered and conscious of having misbehaved itself, slipped after them. We walked out of the gallows yard, past the condemned cells with their waiting prisoners, into the big central yard of the prison. The convicts, under the command of warders armed with lathis,[4] were already receiving their breakfast. They squatted in long rows, each man holding a tin pannikin,[5] while two warders with buckets marched round ladling out rice; it seemed quite a homely, jolly scene, after the hanging. An enormous relief had come upon us now that the job was done. One felt an impulse to sing, to break into a run, to snigger. All at once everyone began chattering gaily.

The Eurasian boy walking beside me nodded towards the way we had come, with a knowing smile: "Do you know, sir, our friend (he meant the dead man), when he heard his appeal had been dismissed, he pissed on the floor of his cell. From fright.—Kindly take one of my cigarettes, sir. Do you not admire my new silver case, sir? From the boxwallah,[6] two rupees eight annas.[7] Classy European style."

Several people laughed—at what, nobody seemed certain.

Francis was walking by the superintendent, talking garrulously: "Well sir, all hass passed off with the utmost satisfactoriness. It wass all finished—flick! like that. It iss not always so—oah, no! I have known cases where the doctor wass obliged to go beneath the gallows and pull the prisoner's legs to ensure decease. Most disagreeable!"

---

[4]*lathis* heavy bamboo sticks bound with iron.

[5]*pannikin* small container for drinks.

[6]*boxwallah* peddler.

[7]*rupees, annas* Indian currency.

"Wriggling about, eh? That's bad," said the superintendent.

"Ach, sir, it iss worse when they become refractory! One man, I recall, clung to the bars of hiss cage when we went to take him out. You will scarcely credit, sir, that it took six warders to dislodge him, three pulling at each leg. We reasoned with him. 'My dear fellow,' we said, 'think of all the pain and trouble you are causing to us!' But no, he would not listen! Ach, he wass very troublesome!"

I found that I was laughing quite loudly. Everyone was laughing. Even the superintendent grinned in a tolerant way. "You'd better all come out and have a drink" he said quite genially. "I've got a bottle of whiskey in the car. We could do with it."

We went through the big double gates of the prison, into the road. "Pulling at his legs!" exclaimed a Burmese magistrate suddenly, and burst into a loud chuckling. We all began laughing again. At that moment Francis's anecdote seemed extraordinarily funny. We all had a drink together, native and European alike, quite amicably. The dead man was a hundred yards away.

Understanding and Analysis

1. Orwell is known for his vivid description. What details in the opening paragraphs, and throughout the essay, are striking to you?

2. This essay is like a short story. Who are the characters? Describe the physical characteristics of each one. What else do we know about each one? In what ways are they alike and in what ways different? Try to distinguish the degree of power each has in the prison hierarchy.

3. What effect does the dog have on each of the different characters?

4. Orwell provides exact measurements in this essay. Where are they? What effect do they have on the narrative?

5. How do the anecdotes Francis relates contribute to the argument against the death penalty?

6. Orwell injects references to humor and laughter early on. Locate as many as you can. Why is humor connected to the hanging?

7. What differentiates this essay from a short story?

8. Timothy Garton Ash, reviewing *The Complete Works of George Orwell* in the October 22, 1998, issue of *The New York Review of Books* states that Orwell "told three separate people that this was 'only a story' (10). Does this information change your view of the piece?

Comparison

1. In "Education by Poetry," Frost claims that we need metaphor to think. What metaphors does Orwell use in "A Hanging"?

2. Reread Mencken's "The Penalty of Death." Which of Mencken's arguments does Orwell address, however obliquely, in his essay?

3. In his essay favoring the death penalty, Mencken leaves out certain arguments an opponent would undoubtedly dwell on. Does Orwell also leave out points his opponent would emphasize?

4. Compare the laughter described in "A Hanging" with the laughter described by Graves. How does this laughter compare with Mencken's humor in "The Penalty of Death"?

Virginia Woolf
(1882–1941)

Virginia Stephen was born into the comfortable middle class, the daughter of Leslie Stephen, a prominent British philosopher, and his second wife, Julia Prinsep. Virginia's mother had seven children, George (1868–1934), Stella (1869–1897), and Gerald (1870–1937) from her first marriage, and Vanessa (1879–1961), Thoby (1880–1906), Virginia, and Adrian (1883–1948) from her second. Also living at the house where Virginia was born was her insane half-sister Laura (1870–1945), the only child of Leslie Stephen's first marriage to a daughter of William Thackeray.

The household was ideal for the development of the intellect. The year Virginia was born her father, already editor of the *Cornhill Magazine*, became editor of *A Dictionary of National Biography*. Many famous Victorians, such as Thomas Hardy, Henry James, and George Meredith, visited the Stephens regularly, both at their London home and at their summer house, St. Ives, in Cornwall. While the boys were sent to preparatory school, the girls were taught Greek, Latin, mathematics, drawing, dancing, and music at home. All were allowed to browse at will in Leslie Stephen's marvelous library.

It was a heady world for the development of both emotions and perceptions. The four younger children, all quite close in age, formed a special group of their own, Virginia excelling in words and her sister in the visual arts. Both sisters admired their brother Thoby, the leader of most of their adventures. At St. Ives they climbed rocks, picnicked, collected butterflies and moths, went wading and boating, bowled and played cricket. Back in London, when Virginia was nine, the children started a weekly family newspaper, the *Hyde Park Gate News*, full of comic character sketches and imitations of the literary styles the children had come to know through their own reading and through their father's regular sessions of reading aloud.

But Virginia's early life was also scarred, like Twain's, by suffering and loss. She was subjected to incestuous sexual advances, at age six from Gerald and later from George, who indulged in improper fondling off and on for more than five years. These episodes, along with her recognition of the special education accorded her brothers, awakened in her a distaste for male domination and aggression and no doubt contributed significantly to her emotional fragility. Between the ages of thirteen and twenty-four she suffered the loss of four close family members. The death in 1895 of her mother, when Virginia was thirteen, precipitated her first emotional breakdown. Stella took charge of the children after their mother's death, but two years later, just after her marriage, Stella also died, of peritonitis.

During the next few years Virginia practiced her writing, imitating novelists, and according to her nephew and biographer Quentin Bell, composing a history of women and an imitation of Sir Thomas Browne called *Religio Laici*; neither work remains. Meanwhile her brother Thoby entered Trinity College, and in 1900 her father completed his editorship of the sixty-three volumes of *A Dictionary of National Biography*. The following year her sister Vanessa entered art school and Virginia took private lessons in Greek and learned to bind books. In 1902 she developed her first intense friendship with a woman, Violet Dickinson, her younger brother Adrian entered Trinity College, and her father became ill with cancer. When her father died in 1904, Virginia suffered her second major breakdown.

Following their father's death, the Stephen siblings moved to 46 Gordon Square, Bloomsbury, where Thoby's friends from Cambridge, particularly the biographer Lytton Strachey and the art critic Clive Bell, began meeting for Thursday evening discussions of literature, art, love, and religion. Here too, encouraged by Violet Dickinson, Virginia began writing reviews for publication in the *Guardian* and a memoir of her father for his biographer, F. W. Maitland. For three years, she taught literature and writing at Morley College, an institute for working men and women. In the early fall of 1906 Virginia, Violet, Vanessa, Thoby, and Adrian left Bloomsbury for a tour of Greece. But first Vanessa and then Thoby became ill. In November, the trip concluded, both were in bed with fever. On November 20 Thoby died of typhoid fever; two days later Vanessa announced her decision to marry Clive Bell.

By 1907 Vanessa had married, and Virginia and Adrian had moved to 29 Fitzroy Square. Despite her fragile emotional health, Virginia began working on a novel. Over the next few years she and Adrian shocked their more conventional friends and the members of the Duckworth side of the family by including nonfamily members in their household, now located in Brunswick Square: the economist John Maynard Keynes, the artist Duncan Grant, and, when he returned from Ceylon, the Jewish socialist and political activist Leonard Woolf. These men and others, such as the art critic Roger Fry and occasionally the novelist E. M. Forster, became part of what is called the Bloomsbury Group, whose members were brilliant, creative, and radical in their ideas and in their personal relationships. In 1911 Virginia suffered a mild breakdown and consulted a psychologist. She felt at this time that she ought to marry. Although she had considered marrying several men, particularly her old friend Lytton Strachey, she did not feel she could love any of them. Finally, in 1912, after much thought, she married Leonard Woolf, a man who lacked the financial resources of many of the Bloomsbury Group but who loved her faithfully and provided the stability she required during her creative years as novelist and critic.

In 1913, after completing her first novel, *The Voyage Out*, Virginia broke down and attempted suicide. For the next two years, her health was uncertain; just after her novel was published in 1915, she suffered a terrible relapse. By 1917, however, she had recovered and was writing regularly for the *Times Literary Supplement*. That July she and Leonard each published a short story on their own printing press set up in the dining room and named, after their house in Richmond, the Hogarth Press. The press proved to be of value in several ways. The physical work of reading manuscripts, setting type, and binding and stacking books provided a relief from emotional preoccupations. Moreover, the press provided a necessary addition to their income and served as a means of introducing some of the best literature of the period, including works by Katherine Mansfield, T. S. Eliot and Virginia Woolf herself. Their one major mistake was to reject Joyce's *Ulysses*.

In 1919 the Woolfs bought Monks House, a cottage in Rodmell on the river Ouse in Sussex, as a retreat from the sometimes stressful social life of Hogarth House in Richmond. In these two houses, between bouts of mania and depression, Virginia Woolf wrote her best novels and essays. *Jacob's Room* (1922), *Mrs Dalloway* (1925), *The Common Reader* (1925), *To the Lighthouse* (1927), *Orlando* (1928), *A Room of One's Own* (1929), *The Waves* (1931), *The Common Reader: Second Series* (1932), *The Years* (1937), and *Three Guineas* (1938).

By 1941 Virginia Woolf had completed the biography of her friend Roger Fry and had written a draft of an eighth novel, *Between the Acts*, when she felt another period of insanity descending on her. On the morning of March 28, after writing three letters, one to her sister Vanessa and two to Leonard, she drowned herself in the river Ouse. In the note addressed to Leonard that she left on the mantle she explained that she no longer wanted to burden him with her illness. This note, which Quentin Bell reproduces in his biography, also reveals the gratitude she felt for Leonard's constant solicitude and support. "If anybody could have saved me it would have been you," she wrote. Despite the several close relationships Virginia had developed over the years with women like Violet Dickinson, Katherine Mansfield, Lady Ottoline Morrell, and especially Vita Sackville-West, her relationship with her husband had given her "the greatest possible happiness."

In her novels, Virginia Woolf turned away from the description of external reality so well depicted by the Victorians; instead, like the painters of the modern period, she concentrated on the individual impressions of her characters, on life as it feels when lived. Many of her best-known essays examine the difficulties women face as writers and other professionals in a society whose laws and customs discourage them from full participation in the affairs of humankind. Many other essays convey her sense of the rapture of thought and feeling through precise, declarative sentences. "The Death of the Moth," for instance, is packed with the detail and allusive precision of poetry. Both types of essay are represented here and serve as stellar examples of that rare category: excellent writing that has remained popular and influential throughout the century.

PROFESSIONS FOR WOMEN[1] *(1931)*

WHEN YOUR SECRETARY invited me to come here, she told me that your Society[2] is concerned with the employment of women and she suggested that I might tell you something about my own professional experiences. It is true I am a woman; it is true I am employed; but what professional experiences have I had? It is difficult to say. My profession is literature; and in that profession there are fewer experiences for women than in any other, with the exception of the stage—fewer, I mean, that are peculiar to women. For the road was cut many years ago—by Fanny Burney,[3] by Aphra Behn,[4] by Harriet Martineau,[5] by Jane Austen,[6] by George Eliot[7]—many famous women, and many more unknown and forgotten, have been before me, making the path smooth, and regulating my steps. Thus, when I came to write, there were very few material obstacles in my way. Writing was a reputable and harmless occupation. The family peace was not broken by the scratching of a pen. No demand was made upon the family purse. For ten and sixpence one can buy paper enough to write all the plays of Shakespeare—if one has a mind that way. Pianos and models, Paris, Vienna and Berlin, masters and mistresses, are not needed by a writer. The cheapness of writing paper is, of course, the reason why women have succeeded as writers before they have succeeded in the other professions.

But to tell you my story—it is a simple one. You have only got to figure to yourselves a girl in a bedroom with a pen in her hand. She had only to move that pen from left to

---

[1]*Women* first published in *The Death of the Moth* (1942) but written and delivered as a speech in 1931.

[2]*Society* the Women's Service League.

[3]*Burney* Madame D'Arblay (1752–1840). English novelist who was well read but lacked a formal education; she was a member of Samuel Johnson's circle. Her novels include *Evelina* (1778), *Cecilia* (1782), *Camilla* (1796), and *The Wanderer* (1814).

[4]*Behn* Known as the first English woman to write professionally, Behn (1640–1689) was an English spy in the Dutch wars and an inmate in debtors' prison before she wrote a successful play, *The Rover*, and her famous novel *Oroanoko* (1688), a philosophical love story.

[5]*Martineau* English author and journalist (1802–1876), deaf from childhood, who wrote on a variety of subjects, including religion, the economy, the abolition of slavery, and philosophy. She also wrote a novel, *Deerbrook* (1839), and *Letters on Mesmerism* (1845).

[6]*Austen* Jane (1775–1817) English novelist, daughter of a clergyman, she lived in Hampshire and Bath and wrote comedies of manners: *Sense and Sensibility* (1811), *Pride and Prejudice* (1813), *Mansfield Park* (1814), *Emma* (1816), and *Persuasion* and *Northanger Abbey* (1818).

[7]*Eliot* (1819–1880) Mary Ann Evans, clergyman's daughter and English novelist. Her best known works are *Mill on the Floss* (1860), *Silas Marner* (1861), *Middlemarch* (1872) and *Daniel Deronda* (1876).

right—from ten o'clock to one. Then it occurred to her to do what is simple and cheap enough after all—to slip a few of those pages into an envelope, fix a penny stamp in the corner, and drop the envelope into the red box at the corner. It was thus that I became a journalist; and my effort was rewarded on the first day of the following month—a very glorious day it was for me—by a letter from an editor containing a cheque for one pound ten shillings and sixpence. But to show you how little I deserve to be called a professional woman, how little I know of the struggles and difficulties of such lives, I have to admit that instead of spending that sum upon bread and butter, rent, shoes and stockings, or butcher's bills, I went out and bought a cat—a beautiful cat, a Persian cat, which very soon involved me in bitter disputes with my neighbours.

What could be easier than to write articles and to buy Persian cats with the profits? But wait a moment. Articles have to be about something. Mine, I seem to remember, was about a novel by a famous man. And while I was writing this review, I discovered that if I were going to review books I should need to do battle with a certain phantom. And the phantom was a woman, and when I came to know her better I called her after the heroine of a famous poem, The Angel in the House.[8] It was she who used to come between me and my paper when I was writing reviews. It was she who bothered me and wasted my time and so tormented me that at last I killed her. You who come of a younger and happier generation may not have heard of her—you may not know what I mean by the Angel in the House. I will describe her as shortly as I can. She was intensely sympathetic. She was immensely charming. She was utterly unselfish. She excelled in the difficult arts of family life. She sacrificed herself daily. If there was chicken, she took the leg; if there was a draught she sat in it—in short she was so constituted that she never had a mind or a wish of her own, but preferred to sympathize always with the minds and wishes of others. Above all—I need not say it—she was pure. Her purity was supposed to be her chief beauty—her blushes, her great grace. In those days—the last of Queen Victoria—every house had its Angel. And when I came to write I encountered her with the very first words. The shadow of her wings fell on my page; I heard the rustling of her skirts in the room. Directly, that is to say, I took my pen in hand to review that novel by a famous man, she slipped behind me and whispered: "My dear, you are a young woman. You are writing about a book that has been written by a man. Be sympathetic; be tender; flatter; deceive; use all the arts and wiles of our sex. Never let anybody guess that you have a mind of your own. Above all, be pure." And she made as if to guide my pen. I now record the one act for which I take some credit to myself, though the credit rightly belongs to some excellent ancestors of mine who left me a certain sum of money— shall we say five hundred pounds a year?—so that it was not necessary for me to depend solely on charm for my living. I turned upon her and caught her by the throat. I did my best to kill her. My excuse, if I were to be had up in a court of law, would be that I acted in self-defence. Had I not killed her she would have killed me. She would have plucked the heart out of my writing. For, as I found, directly I put pen to paper, you cannot review even a novel without having a mind of your own, without expressing what you think to be the truth about human relations, morality, sex. And all these questions, according to the Angel in the House, cannot be dealt with freely and openly by women; they must charm, they must conciliate, they must—to put it bluntly—tell lies if they are to succeed. Thus, whenever I felt the shadow of her wing or the radiance of her halo upon my page, I took up the inkpot and flung it at her. She died hard. Her fictitious nature was of great

[8]*Angel in the House* title of a poem in four books praising the joys of married life by Coventry Patmore (1823–1896), English poet and librarian at the British Museum.

assistance to her. It is far harder to kill a phantom than a reality. She was always creeping back when I thought I had despatched her. Though I flatter myself that I killed her in the end, the struggle was severe; it took much time that had better have been spent upon learning Greek grammar; or in roaming the world in search of adventures. But it was a real experience; it was an experience that was bound to befall all women writers at that time. Killing the Angel in the House was part of the occupation of a woman writer.

But to continue my story. The Angel was dead; what then remained? You may say that what remained was a simple and common object—a young woman in a bedroom with an inkpot. In other words, now that she had rid herself of falsehood, that young woman had only to be herself. Ah, but what is "herself"? I mean, what is a woman? I assure you, I do not know. I do not believe that you know. I do not believe that anybody can know until she has expressed herself in all the arts and professions open to human skill. That indeed is one of the reasons why I have come here—out of respect for you, who are in process of showing us by your experiments what a woman is, who are in process of providing us, by your failures and successes, with that extremely important piece of information.

But to continue the story of my professional experiences. I made one pound ten and six by my first review; and I bought a Persian cat with the proceeds. Then I grew ambitious. A Persian cat is all very well, I said; but a Persian cat is not enough. I must have a motor car. And it was thus that I became a novelist—for it is a very strange thing that people will give you a motor car if you will tell them a story. It is a still stranger thing that there is nothing so delightful in the world as telling stories. It is far pleasanter than writing reviews of famous novels. And yet, if I am to obey your secretary and tell you my professional experiences as a novelist, I must tell you about a very strange experience that befell me as a novelist. And to understand it you must try first to imagine a novelist's state of mind. I hope I am not giving away professional secrets if I say that a novelist's chief desire is to be as unconscious as possible. He has to induce in himself a state of perpetual lethargy. He wants life to proceed with the utmost quiet and regularity. He wants to see the same faces, to read the same books, to do the same things day after day, month after month, while he is writing, so that nothing may break the illusion in which he is living—so that nothing may disturb or disquiet the mysterious nosings about, feelings round, darts, dashes and sudden discoveries of that very shy and illusive spirit, the imagination. I suspect that this state is the same both for men and women. Be that as it may, I want you to imagine me writing a novel in a state of trance. I want you to figure to yourselves a girl sitting with a pen in her hand, which for minutes, and indeed for hours, she never dips into the inkpot. The image that comes to my mind when I think of this girl is the image of a fisherman lying sunk in dreams on the verge of a deep lake with a rod held out over the water. She was letting her imagination sweep unchecked round every rock and cranny of the world that lies submerged in the depths of our unconscious being. Now came the experience, the experience that I believe to be far commoner with women writers than with men. The line raced through the girl's fingers. Her imagination had rushed away. It had sought the pools, the depths, the dark places where the largest fish slumber. And then there was a smash. There was an explosion. There was foam and confusion. The imagination had dashed itself against something hard. The girl was roused from her dream. She was indeed in a state of the most acute and difficult distress. To speak without figure she had thought of something, something about the body, about the passions which it was unfitting for her as a woman to say. Men, her reason told her, would be shocked. The consciousness of what men will say of a woman who speaks the truth about her passions had roused her from her artist's state of unconsciousness. She could write no more. The trance was over. Her imagination could work no longer. This I believe to be a very common experience with women writers—they are impeded by the extreme conventionality of the other sex. For though men sensibly allow themselves great freedom in these respects, I doubt that they realize or can control the extreme severity with which they condemn such freedom in women.

These then were two very genuine experiences of my own. These were two of the adventures of my professional life. The first—killing the Angel in the House—I think I solved. She died. But the second, telling the truth about my own experiences as a body, I do not think I solved. I doubt that any woman has solved it yet. The obstacles against her are still immensely powerful—and yet they are very difficult to define. Outwardly, what is simpler than to write books? Outwardly, what obstacles are there for a woman rather than for a man? Inwardly, I think, the case is very different; she has still many ghosts to fight, many prejudices to overcome. Indeed it will be a long time still, I think, before a woman can sit down to write a book without finding a phantom to be slain, a rock to be dashed against. And if this is so in literature, the freest of all professions for women, how is it in the new professions which you are now for the first time entering?

Those are the questions that I should like, had I time, to ask you. And indeed, if I have laid stress upon these professional experiences of mine, it is because I believe that they are, though in different forms, yours also. Even when the path is nominally open—when there is nothing to prevent a woman from being a doctor, a lawyer, a civil servant—there are many phantoms and obstacles, as I believe, looming in her way. To discuss and define them is I think of great value and importance; for thus only can the labour be shared, the difficulties be solved. But besides this, it is necessary also to discuss the ends and the aims for which we are fighting, for which we are doing battle with these formidable obstacles. Those aims cannot be taken for granted; they must be perpetually questioned and examined. The whole position, as I see it—here in this hall surrounded by women practising for the first time in history I know not how many different professions—is one of extraordinary interest and importance. You have won rooms of your own in the house hitherto exclusively owned by men. You are able, though not without great labour and effort, to pay the rent. You are earning your five hundred pounds a year. But this freedom is only a beginning; the room is your own, but it is still bare. It has to be furnished; it has to be decorated; it has to be shared. How are you going to furnish it, how are you going to decorate it? With whom are you going to share it, and upon what terms? These, I think, are questions of the utmost importance and interest. For the first time in history you are able to ask them; for the first time you are able to decide for yourselves what the answers should be. Willingly would I stay and discuss those questions and answers—but not tonight. My time is up; and I must cease.

Understanding and Analysis

1. What are the characteristics of the Angel in the House?

2. Woolf claims that "all women writers" must kill the Angel. Do women in other professions need to perform the same murder? Why or why not?

3. What motive does Woolf give for becoming a novelist? In this essay, what do you think is the significance to Woolf of earning money? What does she assume may be its significance for many others? What is its significance for the original audience?

4. Woolf says she has not yet "solved" the problem of "telling the truth about [her] own experiences as a body." What does she mean? What truths "about the passions" might be "unfitting for her as a woman to say"?

5. According to Woolf how may her experiences be of help to her original audience?

6. What does Woolf imply when she says that the rooms women have won must be furnished and decorated?

Comparison

1. Both of the problems Woolf encounters stem from the fear of telling men the truth. How do the two points differ? Do men also fear to tell women the truth?

2. Read the essays by Dorothy Parker, Germaine Greer, Annie Dillard, and bell hooks. Do you think they have killed the Angel and solved the problem of the body? Why or why not?

3. Read Judy Brady, Germaine Greer, Cynthia Ozick, Annie Dillard, and bell hooks. How does Woolf anticipate some of their questions and answers? What are the areas of agreement and disagreement among these writers?

James Thurber

UNIVERSITY DAYS (1933)

I PASSED ALL the other courses that I took at my University, but I could never pass botany. This was because all botany students had to spend several hours a week in a laboratory looking through a microscope at plant cells, and I could never see through a microscope. I never once saw a cell through a microscope. This used to enrage my instructor. He would wander around the laboratory pleased with the progress all the students were making in drawing the involved and, so I am told, interesting structure of flower cells, until he came to me. I would just be standing there. "I can't see anything," I would say. He would begin patiently enough, explaining how anybody can see through a microscope, but he would always end up in a fury, claiming that I could *too* see through a microscope but just pretended that I couldn't. "It takes away from the beauty of flowers anyway," I used to tell him. "We are not concerned with beauty in this course," he would say. "We are concerned solely with what I may call the *mechanics* of flars." "Well," I'd say, "I can't see anything." "Try it just once again," he'd say, and I would put my eye to the microscope and see nothing at all, except now and again a nebulous milky substance— a phenomenon of maladjustment. You were supposed to see *a* vivid, restless clockwork of sharply defined plant cells. "I see what looks like a lot of milk," I would tell him. This, he claimed, was the result of my not having adjusted the microscope properly, so he would readjust it for me, or rather, for himself. And I would look again and see milk.

I finally took a deferred pass, as they called it, and waited a year and tried again. (You had to pass one of the biological sciences or you couldn't graduate.) The professor had come back from vacation brown as a berry, bright-eyed, and eager to explain cell-structure again to his classes. "Well," he said to me, cheerily, when we met in the first laboratory hour of the semester, "we're going to see cells this time, aren't we?" "Yes, sir," I said. Students to right of me and to left of me and in front of me were seeing cells; what's more, they were quietly drawing pictures of them in their notebooks. Of course, I didn't see anything.

"We'll try it," the professor said to me, grimly, "with every adjustment of the microscope known to man. As God is my witness, I'll arrange this glass so that you see cells through it or I'll give up teaching. In twenty-two years of botany, I—" He cut off abruptly for he was beginning to quiver all over, like Lionel Barrymore,[1] and he genuinely wished to hold onto his temper; his scenes with me had taken a great deal out of him.

So we tried it with every adjustment of the microscope known to man. With only one of them did I see anything but blackness or the familiar lacteal opacity, and that time I saw, to my pleasure and amazement, a variegated constellation of flecks, specks, and dots. These I hastily drew. The instructor, noting my activity, came back from an adjoining desk, a smile on his lips and his eyebrows high in hope. He looked at my cell drawing. "What's that?" he demanded, with a hint of a squeal in his voice. "That's what I saw," I said. "You didn't, you didn't, you *did*n't!" he screamed, losing control of his temper instantly, and he bent over and squinted into the microscope. His head snapped up. "That's your eye!" he shouted. "You've fixed the lens so that it reflects! You've drawn your eye!"

Another course that I didn't like, but somehow managed to pass, was economics. I went to that class straight from the botany class, which didn't help me any in understanding either subject. I used to get them mixed up. But not as mixed up as another student in my economics class who came there direct from a physics laboratory. He was a tackle on the football team, named Bolenciecwcz. At that time Ohio State University had one of the best football teams in the country, and Bolenciecwcz was one of its outstanding stars. In order to be eligible to play it was necessary for him to keep up in his studies, a very difficult matter, for while he was not dumber than an ox he was not any smarter. Most of his professors were lenient and helped him along. None gave him more hints, in answering questions, or asked him simpler ones than the economics professor, a thin, timid man named Bassum. One day when we were on the subject of transportation and distribution, it came Bolenciecwcz's turn to answer a question. "Name one means of transportation," the profession said to him. No light came into the big tackle's eyes. "Just any means of transportation," said the professor. Bolenciecwcz sat staring at him. "That is," pursued the professor, "any medium, agency, or method of going from one place to another." Bolenciecwcz had the look of a man who is being led into a trap. "You may choose among steam, horse-drawn, or electrically propelled vehicles," said the instructor. "I might suggest the one which we commonly take in making long journeys across land." There was a profound silence in which everybody stirred uneasily, including Bolenciecwcz and Mr. Bassum. Mr. Bassum abruptly broke this silence in an amazing manner. "Choo-choo-choo," he said, in a low voice, and turned instantly scarlet. He glanced appealingly around the room. All of us, of course, shared Mr. Bassum's desire that Bolenciecwcz should stay abreast of the class in economics, for the Illinois game, one of the hardest and most important of the season, was only a week off. "Toot, toot, too-

---

[1]*Lionel Barrymore* 1878–1954, a well-known actor.

tooooooot!" some student with a deep voice moaned, and we all looked encouragingly at Bolenciecwcz. Somebody else gave a fine imitation of a locomotive letting off steam. Mr. Bassum himself rounded off the little show. "Ding, dong, ding, dong," he said, hopefully. Bolenciecwcz was staring at the floor now, trying to think, his great brow furrowed, his huge hands rubbing together, his face red.

"How did you come to college this year, Mr. Bolenciecwcz?" asked the professor. "*Chuf*fa chuffa, *chuf*fa chuffa."

"M'father sent me," said the football player.

"What on?" asked Bassum.

"I git an 'lowance," said the tackle, in a low, husky voice, obviously embarrassed.

"No, no," said Bassum. "Name a means of transportation. What did you *ride* here on?"

"Train," said Bolenciecwcz.

"Quite right," said the professor. "Now, Mr. Nugent, will you tell us—"

If I went through anguish in botany and economics—for different reasons—gymnasium work was even worse. I don't even like to think about it. They wouldn't let you play games or join in the exercises with your glasses on and I couldn't see with mine off. I bumped into professors, horizontal bars, agricultural students, and swinging iron rings. Not being able to see, I could take it but I couldn't dish it out. Also, in order to pass gymnasium (and you had to pass it to graduate) you had to learn to swim if you didn't know how. I didn't like the swimming pool, I didn't like swimming, and I didn't like the swimming instructor, and after all these years I still don't. I never swam but I passed my gym work anyway, by having another student give my gymnasium number (978) and swim across the pool in my place. He was a quiet, amiable blonde youth, number 473, and he would have seen through a microscope for me if we could have got away with it, but we couldn't get away with it. Another thing I didn't like about gymnasium work was that they made you strip the day you registered. It is impossible for me to be happy when I am stripped and being asked a lot of questions. Still, I did better than a lanky agricultural student who was cross-examined just before I was. They asked each student what college he was in—that is, whether Arts, Engineering, Commerce, or Agriculture. "What college are you in?" the instructor snapped at the youth in front of me. "Ohio State University," he said promptly.

It wasn't that agricultural student but it was another a whole lot like him who decided to take up journalism, possibly on the ground that when farming went to hell he could fall back on newspaper work. He didn't realize, of course, that that would be very much like falling back full-length on a kit of carpenter's tools. Haskins didn't seem cut out for journalism, being too embarrassed to talk to anybody and unable to use a typewriter, but the editor of the college paper assigned him to the cow barns, the sheep house, the horse pavilion, and the animal husbandry department generally. This was a genuinely big "beat," for it took up five times as much ground and got ten times as great a legislative appropriation as the College of Liberal Arts. The agricultural student knew animals, but nevertheless his stories were dull and colorlessly written. He took all afternoon on each of them, on account of having to hunt for each letter on the typewriter. Once in a while he had to ask somebody to help him hunt. "C" and "L," in particular, were hard letters for him to find. His editor finally got pretty much annoyed at the farmer-journalist because his pieces were so uninteresting. "See here, Haskins," he snapped at him one day, "Why is it we never have anything hot from you on the horse pavilion? Here we have two hundred head of horses on this campus—more than any other university in the Western Conference except Purdue—and yet you never get any real low down on them. Now shoot over to the horse barns and dig up something lively." Haskins shambled out and came back in about an hour; he said he had something. "Well, start it off snappily," said the editor. "Something people will read." Haskins set to work and in a couple of hours brought a sheet of typewritten paper to the desk; it was a two-hundred-word story about some disease that had broken out among the horses. Its opening sentence was simple but arresting. It read: "Who has noticed the sores on the tops of the horses in the animal husbandry building?"

Ohio State was a land grant university and therefore two years of military drill was compulsory. We drilled with old Springfield rifles and studied the tactics of the Civil War even though the World War was going on at the time. At 11 o'clock each morning thousands of freshmen and sophomores used to deploy over the campus, moodily creeping up on the old chemistry building. It was good training for the kind of warfare that was waged at Shiloh but it had no connection with what was going on in Europe. Some people used to think there was German money behind it, but they didn't dare say so or they would have been thrown in jail as German spies. It was a period of muddy thought and marked, I believe, the decline of higher education in the Middle West.

As a soldier I was never any good at all. Most of the cadets were glumly indifferent soldiers, but I was no good at all. Once General Littlefield, who was commandant of the cadet corps, popped up in front of me during regimental drill and snapped, "You are the main trouble with this university!" I think he meant that my type was the main trouble with the university but he may have meant me individually. I was mediocre at drill, certainly—that is, until my senior year. By that time I had drilled longer than anybody else in the Western Conference, having failed at military at the end of each preceding year so that I had to do it all over again. I was the only senior still in uniform. The uniform which, when new, had made me look like an interurban railway conductor, now that it had become faded and too tight made me look like Bert Williams in his bellboy act. This had a definitely bad effect on my morale. Even so, I had become by sheer practise little short of wonderful at squad manoeuvres.

One day General Littlefield picked our company out of the whole regiment and tried to get it mixed up by putting it through one movement after another as fast as we could execute them: squads right, squads left, squads on right into line, squads right about, squads left front into line, etc. In about three minutes one hundred and nine men were marching in one direction and I was marching away from them at an angle of forty degrees, all alone. "Company, halt!" shouted General Littlefield, "That man is the only man who has it right!" I was made a corporal for my achievement.

The next day General Littlefield summoned me to his office. He was swatting flies when I went in. I was silent and he was silent too, for a long time. I don't think he remembered me or why he had sent for me, but he didn't want to admit it. He swatted some more flies, keeping his eyes on them narrowly before he let go with the swatter. "Button up your coat!" he snapped. Looking back on it now I can see that he meant me although he was looking at a fly, but I just stood there. Another fly came to rest on a paper in front of the general and began rubbing its hind legs together. The general lifted the swatter cautiously. I moved restlessly and the fly flew away. "You startled him!" barked General Littlefield, looking at me severely. I said I was sorry. "That won't help the situation!" snapped the general, with cold military logic. I didn't see what I could do except offer to chase some more flies toward his desk, but I didn't say anything. He stared out the window at the faraway figures of co-eds crossing the campus toward the library. Finally, he told me I could go. So I went. He either didn't know which cadet I was or else he forgot what he wanted to see me about. It may have been that he wished to apologize for having called me the main trouble with the university; or maybe he had decided to compliment me on my brilliant drilling of the day before and then at the last minute decided not to. I don't know. I don't think about it much any more.

Understanding and Analysis

1. How many areas of study does Thurber cover in this essay?
2. Reread the first anecdote. What are the comic devices Thurber uses to describe his experiences with botany?
3. Look for figurative language in this essay, for example, the words, "his scenes with me had taken a great deal out of him," in paragraph three. How does figurative language add to the humor?
4. Is Thurber's portrait of Bolenciecwcz a stereotype? If so, what other stereotypes does Thurber draw on? How, for example, does Thurber portray himself? What about the faculty?
5. What was wrong with the "simple but arresting" headline Haskins created?
6. Reread the opening sentences for each story and the last sentences of the essay. What is Thurber's point in writing this essay, other than that of pure entertainment?

Comparison

1. Read Nancy Mairs's essay "On Being a Scientific Booby." What differences do you see between the two authors' views of themselves and of science and education?
2. Does Thurber's essay add a helpful perspective to the controversy set up in the essays by Orwell, Snow, and Leavis? Explain your opinion.
3. Write a comic analysis of your experiences in some of the classes you are now taking in college. Try to adapt Thurber's comic techniques and structure to serve your own interests in your essay.

Ludwig Lewisohn
(1882–1955)

Ludwig Lewisohn was born in Berlin to a Jewish couple of modest affluence. Disaster struck in 1889 when Lewisohn's father, Jacques, made a bad investment and lost both his inheritance and his mental stability. Convinced that family friends had turned against him, Jacques readily agreed when his wife suggested moving to South Carolina, where her brother lived. Starting over in America improved Jacques's mental health, but as Lewisohn explains in his first autobiography, *Up Stream,* it started the family on its social and financial "descent."

Living in America also put an increasing strain on Ludwig Lewisohn's sense of ethnic and cultural identity. Even in Germany, he writes, "all the members of my family seemed to feel that they were Germans first and Jews afterwards." Once the family emigrated, Lewisohn's parents became Americans first and Jews principally in name. At the suggestion of a new family friend, Lewisohn began attending Sunday school to sharpen his English, but English was not the only thing he learned there. By the age of 15, when he graduated from high school, Lewisohn perceived himself to be "an American, a Southerner and a Christian."

Having already impressed his high-school Latin teacher with his aptitude for literature, Lewisohn developed a relationship with a college English professor who recognized his talents by giving him the individual instruction he needed to perform undergraduate and graduate work simultaneously. Writing articles and reviews for the local newspaper in his spare time, Lewisohn was awarded both a B.A. and M.A. in English when he graduated from the College of Charleston at the age of 19. Community leaders proposed him for a teaching position at a nearby Methodist institution, but he was rejected, apparently on the grounds that he was Jewish. Lewisohn resolved to dismiss this rejection as atypical and "un-American" and decided to go forward with his graduate work.

Enrolled at Columbia University at the age of 20, Lewisohn rediscovered German literature while working on his second M.A. in English. He was denied a doctoral fellowship at the end of his first year, and he took a loan to finance a second year of study, only to be told at the end of that year that a Jew was unlikely to find work as a professor. He felt himself an exile, and "for the first time in my life my heart turned with grief and remorse to the thought of my brethren in exile all over the world." After he left the program, a member of the faculty found him a position as an editor.

In 1904, while he was still in New York, Lewisohn met a playwright named Mary Arnold Crocker. The couple parted when Lewisohn returned home to South Carolina in the same year. Unable to work as an academic, Lewisohn decided to write; he had published four stories and completed the manuscript of a novel by the time he married Mary in 1906. The two soon returned to New York, where, with the assistance of Theodore Dreiser, Lewisohn published his novel, *The Broken Snare,* in 1908. Despite enthusiastic reviews, it sold poorly. In need of money, Lewisohn determined to seek a position as a professor of German, which he found at the University of Wisconsin in 1910. The following year, he joined the faculty at Ohio State University, where he taught until 1917. Lewisohn's years at Ohio State were among his most productive as a translator and a critic. He published *The Modern Drama* (1915) and *The Spirit of Modern German Literature* (1916), and he translated, among other works, several volumes of plays by Gerhart Hauptmann. After America entered World War I, Lewisohn's commitment to German literature came under suspicion, as did his refusal to condone the war. He was ultimately asked to leave the university.

In 1919, Lewisohn became a drama critic for *The Nation*. Several of his reviews were reprinted in a collection called *The Drama and the Stage* in 1922; in the same year, he published *Up Stream*, in which he expressed his mounting frustration with a culture he perceived as repressive and puritanical. As his reputation increased, his marriage grew unbearable, but he could not secure a divorce. In 1924, he fled to Europe with a woman named Thelma Spear, travelling extensively before settling in Paris. There he wrote *The Case of Mr. Crump* (1926), a partly autobiographical novel about a difficult marriage that eventually drives the protagonist to murder his wife with a poker. In 1932, he released another critical work, a Freudian history of American literature called *Expression in America*.

Before returning to America in 1934, Lewisohn published several works of fiction concerned with Jewish exile and identity, including *The Island Within* (1928), *The Last Days of Shylock* (1931), and *This People* (1933). He also published essays criticizing the Nazis, whose influence was already at work in Germany, and became active in the Zionist movement. As World War II approached, his relationship with Thelma disintegrated; after he finally obtained a divorce from Mary, he married Edna Manley in 1940. This marriage likewise ended in divorce, and Lewisohn married Louise Wolk in 1944. Although his reputation suffered during the minor media scandals generated by his romantic choices, he regained enough footing to become the editor of the Zionist magazine *New Palestine*, maintaining the position until 1948. In his remaining years, Lewisohn worked as a professor and a librarian at Brandeis University. He died in 1955 at the age of 73.

Lewisohn made significant contributions to the literature of Jewish life in America, questioning assimilation and showing the value of solidarity. "Considered heretical, possibly un-American," critic Evelyn Avery argues, "Lewisohn's life and works actually anticipated the cultural pluralism of the 1960s and 1970s and the renaissance of ethnic literature." In the Prologue to *Up Stream*, Ludwig Lewisohn celebrates his willingness to speak his own mind, casting himself in the quasi-heroic role of the writer who removes the "mask" of polite decorum in order to provide his "judgment on this civilization in which we are ensnared." This bold stance is characteristic of other works as well. In *The Case of Mr. Crump*, which Evelyn Avery describes as "a misogynist's dream, a bitter portrait of woman as predator," Lewisohn's frankness about his frustrations proves disturbing. But in many cases, his boldness posed an important challenge—to the prevailing silence about anti-Semitism in America, to the demonization of Eastern Europeans during World War I, and to the spread of Nazism in the years leading up to World War II.

THE REVOLT AGAINST CIVILIZATION (1934)

MY FRIEND, A blond and blue-eyed specimen of the Nordic race, had come back from a three-weeks visit to his native Hamburg.[1] He walked up and down clasping his head. "The frontier of Europe and of civilization," he said in a voice hoarse with horror and grief, "has been shifted from the Vistula[2] to the Rhine.[3] My people is possessed by a demon." He did not know how aptly, using a common phrase, he had chosen his symbol. For a good many years now vast numbers of Germans have been possessed by a demon. We shall come to the psychological, to the more or less scientific background by and by. What justly horrifies the world today is that demon, whose character is ill understood; it is what Thomas Mann,[4] in a great warning addressed to his people three years ago, called the "St. Vitus dance[5] of fanaticism," which since he spoke has raged and ravaged—as such spiritual infections have done before in history—like a forest fire or a pestilence.

The demon by which the German people is possessed is no night fear of the Middle Ages. To say, as has been done, that National-Socialism[6] is a throw-back to medievalism is to misunderstand the movement. The demon is the old pagan demon which the Christian Middle Ages sought to exorcise and to drive out forever. German nationalism today is a revolt against Christianity in its broadest as well as in its deepest sense; it is a pagan revolt against the whole of Christian civilization; it dreams, spinning like a dervish of Nordic armies overrunning the earth, of berserker rage in battle, of the ecstasy of death and blood. To think of the Nazis merely as hoodlums and fools stung into action by hunger and demagogues is gravely to under-estimate both the force and the menace of the movement, which has its mad but highly articulate prophets, which has at the core of its inner circle as its ultimate leader (*Führer*), of whom the Hitlers and Goebbels[7] are only vulgar echoes, that extraordinarily gifted poet, Stefan George. Many years ago George prayed for Sicilian Vespers; in 1922 he called to his disciples that it was too late, according to the decree of heaven, for "patience or potion." No,

> Ten thousand must the holy madness seize,
> Ten thousand must the sacred pestilence slay
> And tens of thousands more the holy war.

---

[1]*Hamburg* a German city.

[2]*Vistula* a Polish river.

[3]*Rhine* a German river.

[4]*Thomas Mann* (1875–1955), a German author and Nobel Laureate who was also known for his opposition to Nazism.

[5]*St. Vitus' Dance* Some 16th-century Germans believed they could obtain a year's good health by dancing before the statue of Saint Vitus on his feast day. This dancing developed almost into a mania, and was confused with chorea, the nervous condition later known as Saint Vitus' dance.

[6]*National-Socialism* the Nazi party's doctrine.

[7]*Goebbels* Joseph Geobbels, (1897–1945) master propagandist of the Nazi regime and dictator of its cultural life from 1929 to 1941.

Well, we are witnessing the "holy madness" and the "sacred pestilence," are we not? Let us beware of the "holy war."

I am not one of those who blankly assert that there was no Jewish problem in Germany. Both Jews and Gentiles had made mistakes. But there was no problem that decent and intelligent co-operation could not have gradually solved. The "holy madness," however, the demon of pagan revolt, had to wreak itself upon an immediate and accessible object. And that object had to be, however unconsciously, a symbol of all that was to be destroyed; it had to be the symbol of peace and forgiveness; it had to be the symbol of the free personality alone with its God; it had to be the symbol of the critical intelligence, which the "holy madness" holds in especial abhorrence; it had to be non-pagan, anti-pagan, non-Germanic. It had to be the Jews. It had to be Jesus, the Jew. They could not crucify Jesus. They crucified the Jews. And that is the reason why Jews are not permitted freely to leave the hell that is made for them. If the Jews were not there to be tortured, upon what symbolical object could the "holy madness" wreak it self-justificatory pagan rage? Let no one say that I am being fantastic. The Catholic Church is profoundly aware of the pagan character of the German revolution and of its symbolical re-crucifixion of Christ. It was not for nothing that the Prince Bishop of Cologne pleaded for the Jews up to the last possible moment; it was not for nothing that the Cardinal-Archbishop of Paris commended the persecuted Jews of Germany to the prayers of the faithful of his diocese. These prelates were motivated by no shallow humanitarianism. They protested in the name of the human catholicity of the Church against the pagan-racist particularism of the Nazis; they protested against the symbolical pagan attack upon the very roots of the Judæo-Christian ethical and humane tradition.

Now let us examine the specific content of the "holy madness" of this pagan revolt. The chief article of its creed is the fanatical belief in the superiority of the Aryan-Germanic racial strain. All of the ills of Germany are due to the biological and spiritual contamination of this race by alien, specifically Mediterranean races, and their slavishness of soul. According to certain extremists of the neo-Nationalist movement, such as Hielscher, author of "Das Reich," the Mediterranean Judæo-Christian contamination and corruption of this Germany of today have gone so far and are so hopeless that it were best to plunge the land into war after war to make it the battleground of the world, so that in "nine times one hundred thousand years" the pure German "substance," preserved in a few specimens, may come into its ultimate triumph and apotheosis. (Please understand: I am not caricaturing, but soberly reporting and translating.) The most serious philosopher of the movement, the late Professor Friedrich Wolters, who taught at the universities of Marburg, Frankfurt, and Kiel, who was the personally appointed chief disciple of George and who wrote two enormously influential books, "*Herrschaft und Dienst*"[8] and "*Vier Reden über das Vaterland*,"[9] stopped short of Hielscher's epileptic contortions. He was the more dangerous in that he proposed definite aims: "We are and shall be forced again to engage in a combat for life or death, survival or annihilation, with those barbarian Gauls, whom Cæsar described and overthrew, that people which for some centuries has eaten away the Roman and Germanic racial substances, has wasted it in its revolutions and now seeks to hurl itself upon its flourishing neighbor with all the vengefulness of subject and inferior races, with all the bloodthirstiness of re-barbarized Celts." This

---

[8]*Herrschaft und Dienst* leadership and duty.

[9]*Vier Reden uber das Vaterland* four speeches about the fatherland.

insane racial arrogance, it will be observed, is directed not only against the Semitic or the colored peoples, but against Latin and Celt as well.

Now the first step toward these wars and tumults and conquests must be the re-purification of the German race from foreign blood and foreign faith, specifically, from the Jews and from Christianity. The churches, keeping the superficial traditional nomenclature, are re-organizing from this point of view as Aryan, as Germanic churches. This is inevitable, since the Nazis openly repudiate the ethics of Jesus in favor of the virtues of their pagan ancestors. Thus the speech that Franz von Papen[10] made at Münster the other day, and which rather horrified readers of newspapers everywhere, was nothing but a frank popularization of current Nazi doctrine: "Pacifist literature . . . does not understand the ancient Germanic horror of death in bed. . . . The representatives of the national revolution are men and soldiers who are physically and morally warriors." In so far as perhaps they are not yet all "morally" warriors, it will be seen to it that they become so by racial purification, by re-paganization, by conditioning their reflexes through blind obedience into the militarization of a whole people until the Germanic ecstasy of death in battle is the highest ideal of every German.

Again readers may think that I exaggerate. Luckily for our knowledge and for our being warned, Germany has professors. And one of these, Professor Alfred Bäumler, who holds the newly created chair of Political Pedagogics (!)[11] at Berlin, has left no doubt concerning the aims of the Third Reich. "To the type of the educated man, which philosophy has hitherto sought to create, is to be opposed the type of the soldier. The soldier used to be considered as unintellectual (*ungeistig*), and it was not recognized that the army was an integral part of the education of our people. It was no idealistic and humanistic philosophy that won the battles of the World War; it was the inarticulate philosophy of the army. The aim of our new philosophy is to be the transcendence of the false antithesis Spirit—Force." The treacherous misuse of philosophical terms can go no farther. The plain meaning of "the transcendence of the false antithesis: Spirit—Force" is the worship of naked brutality, when exercised by pure Nordic Germans, the repudiation of every moral scruple, of compassion, of shame, of humility. The universal goose-step of a slavishly obedient soldiery, psychically and physically taught to regard murder and rapine as the highest good, is the frankly avowed ideal of the Third Reich.

How very deep this pagan revolt with its worship of brutality goes is illustrated by the fact that the universities of Germany, once the strongholds of research and intellectual freedom, have been swept by a new theory of knowledge which justifies all the outrages of the Nazi student organizations and automatically eliminates all that has hitherto been known as either thought or science. According to this theory, there are no objective criteria of truth. Truth is arrived at by feeling, specifically by the feeling of uncontaminated Germans. Reason is to be "strictly in the service" of these Germanic institutions. Woe to him who sets up his reason against the Germanic intuition of his "leaders." And indeed, it is a fundamental principle of the redoubtable Wolters and his disciples that the new Germanic relation of absolute obedience to absolute command excludes independence of thinking. "The utter self-subjection of him who serves to the hero"—such was Wolters' definition of the spirit of the new Germany. That spirit, be it observed, is now leaving the studies of Nazi professors and is being embodied in every institution, in every organization in the Reich. The entire structure of German society is being recast with an aston-

---

[10]*Franz von Papen* (1879–1969) a German politician who helped bring Hitler to power.

[11]*Political Pedagogics* political teachings.

ishing rapidity. Everywhere parliamentary forms and technics of self-government have been abandoned. The nation has constituted itself into a mass of robots who roar and foam at the mouth and reel with berserker rage as the leaders, the *Führer,* the "heroes," press the emotional Germanic button. All non-Germans as well as all German political opponents are simply to be excluded, save as objects of just destruction, from the field of the true German consciousness. It is the duty of the German from now on, according to Hitler, the great popularizer himself, "not to seek out objective truth in so far as it may be favorable to others, but uninterruptedly to serve one's own truth."

Among the various consequences of this return of an entire society to a pagan, pre-Christian level, let me select one of very profound significance—the resubjection of women. The principle of the slavish obedience of all males to their leaders evidently eliminates woman as a spiritual and intellectual factor in society. That she is to be so eliminated is the practical tendency of the Third Reich. This, like all the other fundamental traits and principles, was also announced long ago by the poet Stefan George:

> Woman
> Bears but the beast: man creates man and woman,
> She being cursed or kind as his rib.
> Leave her the mystery of inner order
> Who on the marketplace is lawless outrage.
> As in the book of books speaks the anointed
> At very crisis of the world: "I am come
> Utterly to destroy the woman's work."

"Woman bears but the beast—*Das Weib gebiert das Tier*"—that announces not only the lower merely physically generative function of woman; it announces equally the repudiation of Christian romantic love with its mutual respect and faithfulness. In actual practice many, many thousands of the younger National-Socialists are in fact substituting love and loyalty toward male-comrades and toward their leaders for the love of woman, who is limited to breeding and caring for the very young. As in Greece (note again the return to paganism) and as among certain very primitive peoples with their "men's houses," this society of heroes and henchmen, of leaders and blindly obedient warriors is to be an exclusively male society. After that it is scarcely necessary to add the notorious fact that the entire neonationalist movement has been from the start both deeply and broadly tainted by sexual perversity and its accompanying sadism.

That completes the picture of the results of the "holy madness" by which Germany is to be delivered and the world to be redeemed. Germans are, in quite the sense of the old-fashioned British colonizer, the only really "white men;" Germany is the land, according to George again,

> Where the all-blossoming Mother first revealed
> To the white race (corrupt since and grown wild)
> Her genuine countenance.

Well, the Christian-Mediterranean corruption is to be "cleaned out." The Germans, the "white men," the conquerors, welded together into an indistinguishable mass of heroes with but one impulse and but one will glorying in the death of battle, ruthless to others by the divine right of their Germanic purity, will set out sooner or later to conquer and to save the world.

How, the reader may ask in our pleasant American phrase—how did they get that way? How did it come to pass that a good half of one of the very great and spiritually productive contemporary peoples could fall into a group-madness so brutal, so stupid, and so menacing to the rest of the world? No answer and no explanation can be complete. For we are back to the old conundrum: which came first, the egg or the hen? So we ask and have no answer: Does a people's character shape its history or does its history shape its character? Was it untoward circumstance or that character which *is* fate that kept the German people from uniting as the French and the English did and entering two centuries earlier the competition for world-trade and colonial expansion? The fact remains that, especially since the founding of the Empire in 1870, the German people have had the sense of having been unjustly and to their detriment left out of the great game of the conquering powers and of having been somehow wronged and disinherited. But always they had the suspicion, whether conscious or not, that the facts they deplored were rooted in some weakness of the national character, some failure in the ability to unite, to show a common front to the world, to concentrate their energies. The Nazi Government of today emphasizes and condemns these old inner divisions and their consequences; it proposes, as I have shown, to weld all Germans into an indistinguishable mass; from the same point of view it is hectically eliminating all traces of Federalism from the structure of the German state, and has reduced even Bavaria to the status of a Prussian Province.

Bet let us go back to that inner doubt which the Germans harbored, to their deep suspicion that it was something in their own character that had caused them to fall short when compared with the French, with the English. They have been for a long time a nation unsure of itself, infirm in self-esteem, harboring within the core of consciousness a profound self-distrust. But even as the individual will not admit a conviction of inferiority either to himself or to his fellows, but seeks to make up for it, to compensate and to over-compensate for it, and answers every doubt of his own worth by declaring that he is much better than the next man, so did the Germans from 1870 on seek—and in a thousand ways worthily and brilliantly—to compensate by achievement, by power, even by waving plumes and glittering arms for that rankling suspicion of inadequacy in their own breasts. But, again like a neurotic individual, they had no fortitude, which is the fruit of a calm self-esteem. Whenever things went a little wrong, whenever the compensatory mechanism did not work perfectly, they lost their heads. Thus when the so-called *Gründerjahre* after the Franco-Prussian War—the fat years, in a word—were followed by lean ones and depression succeeded boom, there arose an anti-Semitic agitation which sought to fasten on the Jews (who lost—as I happen to know from the history of my immediate ancestors—their fortunes as quickly and thoroughly as anyone) the responsibility both for the crash on the exchanges and for the growth of Socialism among the masses. This agitation increased in fire and fury for a number of years, years which also included Bismarck's notorious proscription of the Socialist Party in 1878. Returning prosperity brought a calmer and more reasonable state of mind. But the whole situation, a miniature counterpart of today's, made it clear enough that these modern Germans were afflicted with a neurosis that made it impossible for them to shoulder the responsibility for their own errors and misfortunes. They had to have a goat, a scapegoat, someone to whom to impute guilt and an evil eye. The Jews were handy and convenient, then as today.

Now it is a matter of common observation as well as of scientific fact that individuals who harbor a deep and wounded suspicion of their own inferiority cannot bear to assume responsibility for their own errors or sins, and hence are incapable of either humility or expiation. Desperately afraid that they will whine and creep, they clamor and strut; in their agonized practice of over-compensation they will be madly arrogant. But since they must hide the nature of this process from themselves, they must assign apparently rational causes and motives. Hence they must believe themselves to have been outrageously maltreated, especially in view of their extraordinary superiority to their fellows. The real superiority, which they often possess, does not suffice them. They must invent unheard-of virtues and merits for themselves; they must at the same time invent a mystic and malevolent author of their ills to serve them as enemy and scapegoat. Unable to bear the hard world of reality within which they are, like everyone else, a mixture of virtues and vices, of strength and feebleness, of good sense and folly, and in which it would behoove them to accept with a measure of serenity and good sportsmanship the consequences of their errors and their sins, they withdrew into a fictive world in which *they* alone are well-born and virtuous and handsome and clever but in which the conspiracies of evil and inferior forces corrupt their wills and render vain their virtues. Into this neurotic world of their escape they will often incorporate details from reality, a fact which makes it especially difficult to clarify them concerning their delusions. It is the structural and moral *pattern* of this fictive world of theirs which so hopelessly falsifies and caricatures the fact and patterns of reality. Who has not met such individuals—so-called arrogant Jews, very often, into whose soul has crept the universal disesteem of their race, sensitive women unable to recover from some early slight or moral mishap that has disturbed their psychical equilibrium?

The reader who has followed me so far already sees, of course, the analogy and the lesson. What happens to individuals can evidently happen to groups of individuals. And it is well understood by psychologists from Gustave Le Bon on that in groups all psychical mechanisms or technics are intolerably intensified and coarsened at the same time. Many, many years ago, leaning upon the absurd theories of the Frenchman Gobineau,[12] the Germans invented the defensive myth of their racial superiority which dark and corrupt races were seeking to destroy. They invented this myth as a safeguard for the future. Nor is it without the greatest significance that precisely toward the year 1914, as though out of a deep inner distrust and presage of its necessity for them, large numbers of Germans embraced this myth with a new intensity. The War came, and the confidence in victory was, at least in the upper strata of consciousness, sincere and universal, and William II declared that he knew neither races nor parties nor religious groups—only Germans. The Jews rose as one man to that apparently generous declaration; thousands volunteered before being called to the colors; before the War was over twelve thousand of them had laid down their lives in Poland and in Flanders. But 1916 came, and it was evident now that no easy victory was to be achieved. In anticipation of defeat and guilt the scapegoat was selected. An anti-Semitic member of the Reichstag named Werner demanded that the Jews be counted, to find out where these "slackers" were. The humiliating and discriminatory census was carried out. Its results were, from a militaristic point of view, supremely honorable to the Jews. Half of the more than sixty thousand Jewish soldiers were in front-line trenches. That made no difference. It was from now on at least subconsciously determined who was to bear the burden of Germany's defeat and shame, who was to be scapegoat and crucified one; to whom, in our good popular phrases, the buck was to be passed in order that the Germans might let themselves out. The thing clicks like a typical case-history out of the records of a psychiatrist.

[12]*Gobineau* Joseph Arthur Gobineau, (1816–82) French diplomat and man of letters. The chief early French proponent of Nordic supremacy, he was antidemocratic and anti-Semitic.

The rest of the story unrolls itself easily. Defeat approached. A Jew, the late Albert Ballin, implored the Emperor to make peace on reasonable terms and committed suicide when his council was harshly rejected. Hunger came on account of the blockade and the cries that the Jews be crucified rose higher and higher. And the humiliating peace came with its nefarious war-guilt clause and its stupid and inhuman reparation clauses and its inexcusable tearing asunder of the eastern provinces of the Reich. Now the Germans had, as all the world was ready to acknowledge in recent years, genuine grievances. But alas the neurotic, individual or group, responds to real grievances not otherwise than to fancied ones. He will not deal with them directly and honorably. This is what the leaders of the German Republic from Ebert and Rathenau to Stresemann and even Brüning sought to do. And for that they were hated more and more bitterly by the increasingly soul-sick masses of the National-Socialist movement, who in ever-intensified frenzies finally persuaded themselves that Germany had been in actual fact not defeated at all, that neither the hunger blockade nor America's troops had had anything to do with the case, but that the gleaming unsullied warriors of the North had been betrayed and "stabbed in the back" in their homeland by these Republicans and Jews who alone were responsible for the otherwise impossible defeat of the Empire.

Incredible as it may appear to sane people elsewhere in the world, this myth is *believed.* On April 1, the Association of Nationalist-Socialist Women issued an announcement to its membership: "It is your duty to enlighten German women concerning the fact that Jewish propaganda was responsible for the outcome of the World War, for the two millions of our dead, for the old people, the women and the children who died of hunger, for Versailles[13] and Dawes and Young.[14]" Not German mismanagement of the War nor a world in arms against them, but Jewish propaganda and the Republican-Socialist "stab in the back" were responsible. This myth is believed because it is fanatically believed that the superior Aryan German *could* not have been defeated except by treachery, and that even this treachery served to undo him only because he had consorted with Latins and with Jews and had permitted his lordly virtues to be tarnished by the slavish morals of Christianity (a vile Jewish invention) and by the republican and libertarian fallacies of the West, introduced into Germany by international Jewry and unworthy of the noble descendants of the Nibelungen.[15] The whole thing would be more like a ghastly farce if it did not constitute so grave a danger for human civilization, if it were not corrupting the souls and hopelessly addling the brains of a whole generation of the German people. For it is clear today that they will act according to their myths. They have begun. The scapegoat is being slain; the Jew is crucified.

The repercussion of Germany's pagan revolt against civilization in the sphere of practical politics and world-peace is already very clear. Those who were most profoundly convinced of the utter stupidity and wickedness of the provisions of Versailles are now afraid to propose or support revision. Who would dare to place one additional Pole or Jew under the

---

[13]*Versailles* the Treaty of Versailles was signed in 1919, ending the bitter Paris Peace talks and World War I. It formally placed the responsibility for the war on Germany and its allies and imposed on Germany the burden of the reparations payments.

[14]*Dawes and Young* the Dawes and Young plans were set up to regulate German reparations after World War I; the Young plan was adopted after it became apparent that Germany could not meet the huge annual payments called for by the Dawes plan.

[15]*Nibelungen* the true race.

Nazi heel? Who would dare to favor equality of armaments for a nation fanatically convinced that it would be helping to save the world for the savior race of the Germans to "gas in" (*einzugasen*) foreign provinces and exterminate life where inferior races live and then replace them? German politicians, even Hitler, will not use such language. They will repudiate with a certain superficial sincerity the extremes to which their own mad myths lead them. They will even play the game of international political decency when it suits their purposes. But it will be a game. Nor will the cool heads of the party—and there must be such—be able to restrain the terrible forces of fanaticism which they have first fed and next unleashed. It is possible, of course, that the whole regime will crash through economic catastrophes. Meanwhile we are dealing with a people which has indeed (this was *not* true in 1914) made both philosophical doctrine and a religious duty of ruthlessness.

It is this fact that constitutes the revolt against civilization. Take quite dispassionately the economic aspect of the Jewish question. Five hundred thousand German citizens are being gradually but mercilessly forced out of the economic life and structure of the country. Nakedness and hunger are already very close to thousands of them. The question was raised: "But what, even on your own ground, do you expect these people do do?" The *Völkischer Beobachter*[16] of Munich, the official organ of the Nazis, replied blankly that it was nobody's business, and that these accursed "Nomads" would manage, as they always did. But what is actually happening is this, that Paris and Amsterdam and Zürich are flooded with penniless fugitives, men, women, and children, and that Jews in all these countries, as well as in England and America—Jews who are integrated with the economic systems in which they live—are forced in this poverty-stricken time to give and give again and give more than they can afford to help their stricken brethren both within Germany and without. In brief, the Nazis are forcing the other economic systems of the world to pay for their jamboree. For since help is brought by civilized people to earthquake sufferers in Japan and famine-stricken coolies in China, it is clear that we cannot let a group so highly civilized, so close to us in habit, speech, sensitiveness, taste, and culture as the German Jews simply die of hunger.

But it is precisely this order of sentiment, it is precisely this great classical tradition of the Christian world that the neo-Nationalists of Germany are theoretically and practically repudiating. In a hundred manifestoes one hears again and again the summons to be "hard"! "We must once more learn to punish!" is the slogan of the new ministry of justice. So one can well imagine the fate of those thousands of Republicans and Liberals and Socialists who are crowded in the concentration camps. To be hard on principle in the name of one's own madly and neurotically conceived superiority, to take delight in punishment, to be unashamed of insane pride and the cruelty that it engenders—is that not a pagan revolt against the whole inner meaning of Western civilization, however, imperfectly, however haltingly that meaning has been wrought out by us in practice? Is it not an unbearable repudiation of all that constitutes the one faint hope of humanity? For that hope may be said to have arisen when the unknown scribe recorded in Leviticus the words: "Thou shalt bear love unto thy neighbor (I translate the dative of the Hebrew text) as to thyself." And this became the groundwork of the prophets from Amos of Tekoa to Jesus of Nazareth. And all the sages of the Talmud and all the doctors of the Catholic Church and all leaders of Protestant revolts and all republicans and liberals and humanitarians and whosoever in all our Western civilization had any vision of goodness and the good life, any hope of better things for mankind—all, all, whatever differences divided them, united on this fundamental prin-

---

[16]*Volkisher Beobachter* People's Observer.

ciple of the duty of love, of mercy, of forgiveness between man and his brother. It is this foundation that the German neo nationalists repudiate and seek to destroy. They must meet an unbroken front of moral resistance in which all civilized men, irrespective of nation, race, or creed wholeheartedly unite.

Understanding and Analysis

1. Lewisohn's first paragraphs set up his definition of National-Socialism, the Nazi Party, as a "demon." A "night fear of the Middle Ages" was a nightmare caused by an incubus, masculine spirit, or a succubus, feminine spirit, that was believed to descend at night to rape its sleeping victim or to sit on the chest and suffocate its victim. Why, according to Lewisohn, is the Nazi demon not like the medieval night terror?

2. A "beserker" was an ancient Norse warrior who fought with fanatic frenzy. What other allusions to frenzy do you recognize in these paragraphs? How do these allusions help to describe the Nazi party?

3. Who was the "ultimate leader" of the Nazi party according to Lewisohn?

4. What reasons does Lewisohn give for the Jews being made the object of destruction in the Nazi holy war?

5. Lewisohn first published this essay in *Harper's Magazine.* His readers were the American public. What evidence does Lewisohn offer in the opening pages and throughout the essay to persuade his fellow Americans that he is an objective observer and analyzer of the Nazi movement? Where does he first indicate that he is Jewish?

6. After defining what he means by "demon," Lewisohn describes the creed of the "pagan revolt." What is the "chief article"? Who in Germany were the theorists for this article? What were the "definite aims"? What for the Nazis was the "highest ideal of every German"?

7. What steps were to be accomplished to achieve these aims?

8. What was the new Nazi "theory of knowledge"?

9. Stefan George (1868–1933) was considered a major poet of the classical style in Germany and was known for his revolt against realism. What was Stefan George's attitude toward women? What effect did his attitudes have on the Nazi youth?

10. After defining and describing, Lewisohn asks how a people could come to believe that they must conquer the world by means of this demonic creed. What are some of the specific factual explanations offered? What analogy does Lewisohn develop to explain the German character? What evidence does he present to support the analogy?

11. After a brief review of the history of Germany, Lewisohn shifts from setting up the analogy to asserting that his understanding of the neurotic individual is based on "common observation" and "scientific fact." How does he then use this analogy to surprise the reader when he applies it to a group other than the Germans? What is the effect of this strategy?

12. When Lewisohn returns to his analysis of German history, how does he account for World War I?

13. How does the neurotic individual treat real grievances? What does Lewisohn predict will happen in Germany? What will Hitler say and what will he do? Was Lewisohn correct in his predictions?

14. What was already happening to the Jews when this essay was written?

15. Lewisohn saves his appeal to emotion for the last few sentences of the essay. What, in this appeal, is based on reason, and what does he want Americans to do?

16. Reread the opening paragraph of the essay. Note details of diction, structure, tone. In what ways does this paragraph serve as an introduction to the subject? Where in the essay does Lewisohn first state his thesis?

17. Why do you think most readers did not believe Lewisohn?

Comparison

1. Read Forster's "What I Believe." Compare Forster's views of Christianity with those of Lewisohn. Where do the two authors agree and disagree on this topic? Does Lewisohn believe in "Love the Beloved Republic"?

2. How do you think Lewisohn would respond to Orwell's arguments about the effects of an education in the arts in "What Is Science"?

3. Where, if anywhere, in Lewisohn's essay do you see evidence for the validity of Orwell's claims in "Politics and the English Language"?

4. Read Tuchman's essay. Compare the attitudes toward and treatment of the Jews during the epidemic of the Black Death with the attitude toward and treatment of the Jews as described in Lewisohn's essay. What explanations offered, if any, are the same in both essays?

Ernest Hemingway
(1899–1961)

Ernest Hemingway was born in Oak Park, Illinois, the first son and second child in a family of six children. His mother was a religious woman who doted on her first son; his father was a country doctor who introduced Ernest to the pleasures of nature, hunting, and fishing, pleasures that became for Hemingway the lifelong passions that motivated both his joy in living and his writing. His mother, Grace, took pride in his outdoor exploits, but also his indoor ones: "Ernest Miller at 5 1/2 years old is a little man....He likes to build cannons and forts with building blocks. Collects cartoons of the Russo-Japanese War." In her letters, Grace also reported on her son's love of sewing; that youthful interest was one of the few that Hemingway did not carry with him into adulthood.

In high school, Hemingway took up football and boxing; he also boasted that he could write "better stuff" than Cicero "with both hands tied behind me." Like many young writers, he began his literary career by writing short stories and articles for school publications. After he graduated, he traveled to Kansas City to work for the *Star*, where he trained himself as a reporter. Eager as he was to hone his writing style, Hemingway was still more eager to go to war. Although he was unable to join the armed forces because of a vision deficit in his left eye, he signed on with the Red Cross in 1918 to become an ambulance driver. This duty took him first to France and then to Italy, where he received more than 200 wounds in his leg during an explosion. He returned to America a hero.

Soon, however, Hemingway grew restless. He travelled to Toronto, became a reporter for the Toronto *Star*, and then moved to Chicago to write for a local magazine. Through friends, he met the author Sherwood Anderson; he also met his first wife, Hadley Richardson, whom he married in September of 1921. Anderson had urged Hemingway to travel to Paris; in December, Ernest and Hadley sailed for France, where he earned money by writing pieces for the Toronto *Star*, and where warm letters from Anderson gave him the means to meet Gertrude Stein and other famous expatriates. Soon Hemingway's literary circle expanded to include Ezra Pound, Max Beerbohm, James Joyce, John Dos Passos, and F. Scott Fitzgerald.

In Europe, Hemingway published short stories, as well as his first book, *Three Stories and Ten Poems* (1923). After a brief return to Toronto, where Hadley gave birth to a son, he began a novel, but he abandoned the manuscript in 1925. A trip to Spain inspired him to start another novel, which became his first triumph. Beginning with the title FIESTA, and almost becoming THE LOST GENERATION, Hemingway's novel appeared in print in 1926 as *The Sun Also Rises*. During and after his divorce from Hadley, precipitated by his affair with Pauline Pfeiffer, an editor with *Vogue*, Hemingway experienced suicidal impulses, followed by a renewed sense of religious faith.

In 1927, Hemingway married Pauline, published his second novel, *Men Without Women*, and moved to Key West, Florida. There, he worked on his third novel, *A Farewell to Arms*. During the early 1930s, he travelled, fished, hunted, and wrote. Aware of the problems in Spain, he nonetheless did not pursue politics in his writing, which caused liberal critics to attack him for being a sportsman rather than an activist.

When the Spanish Civil War broke out in 1936, Hemingway was invited to serve as a war correspondent for the North American Newspaper Alliance. Before leaving for Spain, he assisted with an anti-Fascist documentary entitled *Spain in Flames*, and, once he arrived, he worked on a second documentary entitled *The Spanish Earth*. He brought the film back to America and screened it for President Roosevelt and the First Lady before taking it out West, where he hoped to raise money that could be spent on ambulances for the Loyalists.

Hemingway's experiences in Spain led to the publication of three works: a miscellany, *To Have and Have Not*; a play, *The Fifth Column*; and a novel, *For Whom the Bell Tolls* (1940). While in Spain, he met the writer Martha Gellhorn, and, once again smitten, left his second wife. In 1940, he married Gellhorn, bought a house in Cuba, wrote an introduction to an anthology called *Men at War* (1942), and became almost entirely preoccupied with fishing. Having turned his friends and acquaintances into his characters, sometimes satirizing them in the process, Hemingway became involved in numerous literary feuds that led him to snub his friends as a way of avenging perceived insults to his courage as a man and to his integrity as a writer.

Impatient with his growing isolation and misogyny and his refusal to become involved with World War II, Gellhorn left for England but soon returned to insist that Hemingway cover the war as well. Through the London Air Ministry, he flew to Europe and became a correspondent for *Colliers*. In 1944, he met his fourth and final wife, Mary Welsh.

In 1952, Hemingway published the novel that won him a Pulitzer and eventually led to a Nobel Prize: *The Old Man and the Sea*. He continued to travel in the final decade of his life, returning both to Spain and to Africa, but he also battled with his weight and his blood pressure and feared that he might have cancer. He committed suicide in Ketchum, Idaho, in 1961.

Like his contemporary William Faulkner, Hemingway expressed the disillusionment of a post-war generation, or, as Gertrude Stein called it, the lost generation. Both men drew much of their subject matter from the events of their own lives and the worlds they knew well. Unlike Faulkner, however, Hemingway defined his world in deceptively simple prose, stark nouns and verbs that convey the grace under pressure Hemingway demanded of his heroes in the bull-ring, on the battlefield, and in their private lives. In diammetrically opposite prose styles, Hemingway and Faulkner both document the struggle for life and dignity in a time and a place no longer our own.

A Brush with Death (1937)

MADRID.—THEY SAY you never hear the one that hits you. That's true of bullets, because, if you hear them, they are already past. But your correspondent heard the last shell that hit this hotel. He heard it start from the battery, then come with a whistling incoming roar like a subway train to crash against the cornice and shower the room with broken glass and plaster. And while the glass still tinkled down and you listened for the next one to start, you realized that now finally you were back in Madrid.

Madrid is quiet now. Aragon is the active front. There's little fighting around Madrid except mining, counter-mining, trench raiding, trench mortar strafing and sniping, in a stalemate of constant siege warfare going on in Carabanchel, Usera and University City.

These cities are shelled very little. Some days there is no shelling and the weather is beautiful and the streets are crowded. The shops are full of clothing, jewelry stores, camera shops, picture dealers and antiquarians are all open and the bars are crowded.

Beer is scarce and whisky is almost unobtainable. Store windows are full of Spanish imitations of all cordials, whiskies and vermouths. These are not recommended for internal use, although I am employing something called Milords Ecosses Whisky on my face after shaving. It smarts a little, but I feel very hygenic. I believe it would be possible to cure athlete's foot with it, but one must be very careful not to spill it on one's clothes because it eats wool.

The crowds are cheerful and the sandbag-fronted cinemas are crowded every afternoon. The nearer one gets to the front, the more cheerful and optimistic the people are. At the front itself, optimism reaches such a point that your correspondent, very much against his good judgment, was induced to go swimming in a small river forming a no-man's land on the Cuenca front the day before yesterday.

The river was a fast-flowing stream, very chilly and completely dominated by Fascist positions, which made me even chillier. I became so chilly at the idea of swimming in the river at all under the circumstances that, when I actually entered the water, it felt rather pleasant. But it felt even pleasanter when I got out of the water and behind a tree.

At that moment, a government officer who was a member of the optimistic swimming party shot a water snake with his pistol, hitting it on the third shot. This brought a reprimand from another not so completely optimistic officer member who asked what he wanted to do with that shooting—get machine guns turned on us?

We shot no more snakes that day, but I saw three trout in the stream which would weigh over four pounds apiece; heavy, solid, deep-sided ones that rolled up to take the grasshoppers I threw them, making swirls in the water as deep as though you had dropped a paving stone into the stream. All along the stream, where no road ever led until the war, you see trout; small ones in the shallows and the biggest kind in the pools and in the shadow of the bank. It's a river worth fighting for, but just a little cold for swimming.

At this moment, a shell has just alighted on a house up the street from the hotel where I am typing this. A little boy is crying in the street. A militiaman has picked him up and is comforting him. There was no one killed on our street, and the people who started to run slow down and grin nervously. The one who never started to run at all looks at the others in a very superior way, and the town we are living in now is called Madrid.

Understanding and Analysis

1. What are the meanings of the word "you" in the first sentence, the second sentence, and the third sentence? How does each one differ from the others? Is Hemingway being sloppy here?

2. What war is Hemingway observing? From whose perspective is he observing this war?

3. What punctuation in the second sentence of the third paragraph would help you to understand the meaning more easily?

4. Why does Hemingway include the description of the shops, the weather, the river, the fish, and the snake?

5. Hemingway is known for his tough-guy persona, his love of guns and sport, his code of grace under pressure. What examples of this persona do you see in this report?

6. Why are people optimistic at the front? Where is the front?

7. Trace Hemingway's movements in the essay. Where is he at the opening and closing of the essay? Where does the tense shift? Why?

8. What does the last sentence mean? Where do you think Hemingway was when he experienced his "brush with death"?

9. What is his purpose in writing this report?

Comparison

1. Read the reports written by Mollie Panter-Downes. What similarities do you see? Why do you think these similarities exist?

2. Read Pyle's description of the death of a captain in World War II. Although Pyle and Hemingway are describing two very different events in two very different wars, what characteristics do both reporters share?

3. How do the reports by Hemingway and Pyle differ from the descriptions of war offered by Robert Graves and Martha Gellhorn?

Mollie Panter-Downes
(1906–1997)

Mollie Panter-Downes spent her early childhood in London. At the age of six, she moved in with friends of the family in Brighton, while her father served as a Colonel in an Irish army unit. When the First World War began, her father journeyed to France to join in the fighting and was killed within a month. Her mother stayed with her in Brighton for a time before they moved to a rural village, where Panter-Downes attended school. A good deal of her early reading consisted of the "romantic novels" that her mother checked out of the library, but she also "dug into the public library on my own account, and came up with quantities of poetry and lives of poets."

Panter-Downes followed an early exposure to books with an early debut as a writer. When she was a teenager, she published a novel called *The Shoreless Sea*, which sold well and was praised by *The London Times* for its "maturity of style." From this novel, she turned to short stories, many of which appeared in *Cosmopolitan;* she also branched out into journalism. At the age of 20, she was introduced to Clare Robinson, whom she soon married. Through Robinson's job as an inspector for British Celanese, the couple traveled extensively during the early years of the marriage, returning to England in the early 1930s and settling down in Surrey around 1935.

Continuing to write short stories, Panter-Downes also submitted a poem—
or "a bit of verse, you couldn't call it poetry at all"—to *The New Yorker*. Its publication represented her first success with the elite magazine, but by no means
her greatest. She later submitted an article on Jewish refugees in England, and
it was this article that the editor remembered when he found himself without a European correspondent on the brink of World War II. Thus it was
that Mollie Panter-Downes became, in September of 1939, the eyes and ears
of *The New Yorker* in England; thus was born her highly successful "Letter from
London." The date of her first "Letter" was September 3, the same day that
England declared war on Germany. To gather material for the letters she continued to write throughout the war, she traveled back and forth between her
rural home and the urban scenes of evacuations and air raids, sending the
results to America through Western Union.

In 1940, her letters were republished in a volume entitled *Letter from England*.
With additions, they were published again in 1972, under the title *London War
Notes*. She also published, among other things, a post-war novel called *One
Fine Day* (1947). Her "Letter from London" remained a regular feature of *The
New Yorker* until 1984. She died on January 22, 1997, at the age of 90.

In the Introduction to *One Fine Day*, Nicola Beauman maintains that "Mollie Panter-Downes's first loyalty in 'Letters from London' was to the resolution and cheerfulness of the British people." Although Panter-Downes also
reported on the disruptions, the destruction, and the anger of the people rendered homeless, she did indeed emphasize the will of the citizenry to carry
on: "The courage, humor, and kindliness of ordinary people continue to be
astonishing under conditions which possess many of the merry features of a
nightmare." With a densely descriptive and captivating prose, Panter-Downes
focused her attention not only on the common sort of people, but also on
the common sort of details, details about sandbags on the ground and daily
routines forged against the larger political chaos of bombings and sirens. Her
coverage of World War II contributes an important chapter to its history, one
rarely recorded in histories of war.

SEPTEMBER 3 (1939)

[*September 1, 1939, Germany invades Poland. September 3, Great Britain declares war
on Germany.*]

FOR A WEEK, everybody in London had been saying every day that if there wasn't a war
tomorrow there wouldn't be a war. Yesterday, people were saying that if there wasn't a
war today it would be a bloody shame. Now that there is a war, the English, slow to start,
have already in spirit started and are comfortably two laps ahead of the official war

machine, which had to await the drop of somebody's handkerchief. In the general opinion, Hitler has got it coming to him.

The London crowds are cool—cooler than they were in 1914—in spite of thundery weather which does its best to scare everybody by staging unofficial rehearsals for air raids at the end of breathlessly humid days. On the stretch of green turf by Knightsbridge Barracks, which used to be the scampering ground for the smartest terriers in London, has appeared a row of steam shovels that bite out mouthfuls of earth, hoist it aloft, and dump it into lorries; it is then carted away to fill sandbags. The eye has now become accustomed to sandbags everywhere and to the balloon barrage, the trap for enemy planes, which one morning spread over the sky like some form of silvery dermatitis. Posting a letter has acquired a new interest, too, since His Majesty's tubby, scarlet pillar boxes have been done up in squares of yellow detector paint, which changes color if there is poison gas in the air and is said to be as sensitive as a chameleon.

Gas masks have suddenly become part of everyday civilian equipment, and everybody is carrying the square cardboard cartons that look as though they might contain a pound of grapes for a sick friend. Bowlegged admirals stump jauntily up Whitehall with their gas masks slung neatly in knapsacks over their shoulders. Last night, London was completely blacked out. A few cars crawled through the streets with one headlight out and the other hooded while Londoners, suddenly become homebodies, sat under their shaded lights listening to a Beethoven Promenade concert interspersed with the calm and cultured tones of the B.B.C. telling motorists what to do during air raids and giving instructions to what the B.B.C. referred to coyly as expectant mothers with pink cards, meaning mothers who are a good deal more than expectant.

The evacuation of London, which is to be spaced over three days, began yesterday and was apparently a triumph for all concerned. At seven o'clock in the morning, all inward traffic was stopped and A.A. scouts raced through the suburbs whisking shrouds of sacking off imposing bulletin boards which informed motorists that all the principal routes out of town were one-way streets for three days. Cars poured out pretty steadily all day yesterday and today, packed with people, luggage, children's perambulators, and domestic pets, but the congestion at busy points was no worse than it is at any other time in the holiday season. The railways, whose workers had been on the verge of going out on strike when the crisis came, played their part nobly, and the London stations, accustomed to receiving trainloads of child refugees from the Third Reich, got down to the job of dispatching trainload after trainload of children the other way—this time, cheerful little cockneys who ordinarily get to the country perhaps once a year on the local church outing and could hardly believe the luck that was sending them now. Left behind, the mothers stood around rather listlessly at street corners waiting for the telegrams that were to be posted up at the various schools to tell them where their children were.

All over the country, the declaration of war has brought a new lease of life to retired army officers, who suddenly find themselves the commanders of battalions of willing ladies who have emerged from the herbaceous borders to answer the call of duty. Morris 10s, their windshields plastered with notices that they are engaged on business of the A.R.P. or W.V.S. (both volunteer services), rock down quiet country lanes propelled by firm-lipped spinsters who yesterday could hardly have said "Boo!" to an aster.

Although the summer holiday is still on, village schools have reopened as centres where the evacuated hordes from London can be rested, sorted out, medically examined, refreshed with tea and biscuits, and distributed to their new homes. The war has brought the great unwashed right into the bosoms of the great washed; while determined ladies in white V.A.D. overalls search the mothers' heads with a knitting needle for unwelcome signs of life, the babies are dandled and patted on their often grimy diapers by other ladies, who have been told off to act as hostesses and keep the guests from pining for Shoreditch. Guest rooms have been cleared of Crown Derby knickknacks and the best guest towels, and the big houses and cottages alike are trying to overcome the traditional British dislike of strangers, who may, for all they know, be parked with them for a matter of years, not weeks.

Everybody is so busy that no one has time to look up at the airplanes that pass overhead all day. Today was a day of unprecedented activity in the air. Squadrons of bombers bustled in all directions, and at midday an enormous number of vast planes, to which the knowing pointed as troop-carriers, droned overhead toward an unknown destination that was said by two sections of opinion to be (a) France and (b) Poland. On the ground, motor buses full of troops in bursting good humor tore through the villages, the men waving at the girls and howling "Tipperary" and other ominously dated ditties, which everybody has suddenly remembered and found to be as good for a war in 1939 as they were in 1914.

London and the country are buzzing with rumors, a favorite one being that Hitler carries a gun in his pocket and means to shoot himself if things don't go too well; another school of thought favors the version that he is now insane and Göring has taken over. It is felt that Mussolini was up to no good with his scheme for holding a peace conference and spoiling what has become everybody's war. The English were a peace-loving nation up to two days ago, but now it is pretty widely felt that the sooner we really get down to the job, the better.

Understanding and Analysis

1. What does Panter-Downes mean by "the drop of somebody's handkerchief"?

2. What is the structure of this essay?

3. What figurative language does Panter-Downes use?

4. What indicators of social class do you see? What role does class play in this essay?

5. What is the effect of the word "we" in the last paragraph?

6. This essay first appeared in the *New Yorker*. In what ways do you think Panter-Downes shaped her essay to appeal to her audience?

Comparison

1. Compare this essay with the one Panter-Downes wrote in 1940. What differences do you see, if any, in the attitudes of the people she describes or in her own attitude?

2. What similarities or differences do you see between Panter-Downes's report on civilians and Hemingway's or Pyle's report on the military?

E. M. Forster
(1879–1970)

Henry Morgan Forster was born on January 1, 1879, becoming Edward Morgan Forster the following month, thanks to a mistake at his christening. He learned to read at the age of four and liked to be alone with his books, saying to his aunt's nurse, "Can't you tell the people I am busy reading?" In grammar school, he was still a rather solitary boy, unpopular among his classmates; it was not until he matriculated to King's College at Cambridge that he gained a lasting group of friends. During his final year, he was elected to the "Apostles," a selective club with connections to the Bloomsbury group.

In 1901, Forster left England with his mother for an extended tour of Italy. He had started dreaming up stories when he was a young child, but during this trip, ideas for serious stories started to flow, resulting in early drafts of a novel. By 1904, he had the ideas, at least, for his first three novels: *Where Angels Fear to Tread*, on which he was then working; *The Longest Journey*, for which he had drafted a plot; and *A Room with a View*, which he had started in Italy. Critics responded warmly to *Where Angels Fear to Tread* (1905); the reception of *The Longest Journey* (1907) was cooler. One reviewer took the time to calculate the percentage of adult characters who died suddenly. Unruffled by negative responses to his writing, Forster continued working on *A Room with a View* (1908). Although it met with success, *Howards End* (1910) was the work that earned Forster a lasting literary reputation and an increased role in the Bloomsbury group. At one of the Bloomsbury gatherings, he gave a talk on "The Feminine Note in Literature" that was highly praised. He also sat for the painter Roger Fry.

Having developed a close friendship with an Indian man named Syed Masood, Forster planned a voyage to India in 1912. Like his trip to Italy, this trip inspired a novel, his first extended treatment of love and relationships between men. Forster entitled the novel *Maurice* and circulated it among friends, but he did not endeavor to have it published. (According to Forster biographer P. N. Furbank, Forster said it "could not be published 'until my death or England's.'" It was indeed published posthumously in 1971.)

Following the eruption of World War I, Forster went to Egypt to work with the Red Cross. There he began a relationship with a man named Mohammed, which made him long to be writing *Maurice* all over again. Instead, he made plans for a work of non-fiction entitled *Alexandria: a History and a*

Guide and wrote pieces for the *Egyptian Mail*. Returning to England in 1919, Forster followed stories about resistance to imperialism in both Egypt and India with great interest. In 1921, he traveled back to India to work for the Maharaja of Dewas. When he returned, he took up a manuscript that he had begun before the war; this manuscript was to become the novel *A Passage to India*.

In 1922, as Forster worked on *A Passage to India*, Mohammed died. With his publishers stalling on the release of *Alexandria: a History and a Guide*, Forster conceived of another work of non-fiction, *Pharos and Pharillon*, which Furbank describes as a "kind of tribute to Mohammed." This work contained some of the essays that Forster had written for the *Eyptian Mail*, as well as an essay on the Greek poet Constantine Cavafy. Before the Woolfs published *Pharos and Pharillon* in 1923, *Alexandria: a History and a Guide* was at last in print, but most copies were destroyed in a fire, and the book was not widely available until it was reprinted in 1938.

A Passage to India appeared in 1924. Although it was his last novel, Forster remained active as a writer. In 1926, he delivered a literary lecture series at Cambridge, and in 1928, in the midst of controversy over the lesbian novel *The Well of Loneliness*, he began speaking out against censorship. Over the decade that followed, Forster worked with various writing groups and wrote the now-famous "What I Believe" in 1939. His reputation was cemented— particularly in America—with the release of Lionel Trilling's book on his works. Until his death in 1970, he continued to write, publishing reviews, essays, and two biographies.

In his fiction, E. M. Forster was preoccupied with questions of culture; in his non-fiction, he contributed both to culture and to cultural debates. The publication of *Pharos and Pharillon* brought the work of Constantine Cavafy to the attention of such prominent figures as T. S. Eliot and Arnold Toynbee. After the death of D. H. Lawrence, Forster tangled with Eliot, who doubted Lawrence's literary contributions, while Forster defended them. In his non-fiction, Forster also addressed a variety of literary and political issues, opposing not only censorship, but also anti-Semitism. Despite his bold articulation of often unpopular positions on literary, cultural, and political issues, even those with personal significance, Forster was chary of subscribing to a single party or position. Above all he cherished his liberty to think as he wished. His agnosticism was one of the few positions he maintained in both his private life and his public writing. D. H. Lawrence once planned a critical essay on Forster's books but found that he could not make the books match with the man. Forster's prose style, like the man, is often humorous, often sharp, even cruel, and always passionate.

WHAT I BELIEVE (1939)

I DO NOT believe in Belief. But this is an age of faith, and there are so many militant creeds that, in self-defence, one has to formulate a creed of one's own. Tolerance, good temper and sympathy are no longer enough in a world which is rent by religious and racial persecution, in a world where ignorance rules, and science, who ought to have ruled, plays the subservient pimp. Tolerance, good temper and sympathy—they are what matter really, and if the human race is not to collapse they must come to the front before long. But for the moment they are not enough, their action is no stronger than a flower, battered beneath a military jack-boot. They want stiffening, even if the process coarsens them. Faith, to my mind, is a stiffening process, a sort of mental starch, which ought to be applied as sparingly as possible. I dislike the stuff. I do not believe in it, for its own sake, at all. Herein I probably differ from most people, who believe in Belief, and are only sorry they cannot swallow even more than they do. My law-givers are Erasmus and Montaigne, not Moses and St. Paul. My temple stands not upon Mount Moriah but in that Elysian Field where even the immoral are admitted. My motto is: "Lord, I disbelieve—help thou my unbelief."

I have, however, to live in an Age of Faith—the sort of epoch I used to hear praised when I was a boy. It is extremely unpleasant really. It is bloody in every sense of the word. And I have to keep my end up in it. Where do I start?

With personal relationships. Here is something comparatively solid in a world full of violence and cruelty. Not absolutely solid, for Psychology has split and shattered the idea of a "Person," and has shown that there is something incalculable in each of us, which may at any moment rise to the surface and destroy our normal balance. We don't know what we are like. We can't know what other people are like. How, then, can we put any trust in personal relationships, or cling to them in the gathering political storm? In theory we cannot. But in practice we can and do. Though A is not unchangeably A or B unchangeably B, there can still be love and loyalty between the two. For the purpose of living one has to assume that the personality is solid, and the "self" is an entity, and to ignore all contrary evidence. And since to ignore evidence is one of the characteristics of faith, I certainly can proclaim that I believe in personal relationships.

Starting from them, I get a little order into the contemporary chaos. One must be fond of people and trust them if one is not to make a mess of life, and it is therefore essential that they should not let one down. They often do. The moral of which is that I must, myself, be as reliable as possible, and this I try to be. But reliability is not a matter of contract—that is the main difference between the world of personal relationships and the world of business relationships. It is a matter for the heart, which signs no documents. In other words, reliability is impossible unless there is a natural warmth. Most men possess this warmth, though they often have bad luck and get chilled. Most of them, even when they are politicians, *want* to keep faith. And one can, at all events, show one's own little light here, one's own poor little trembling flame, with the knowledge that it is not the only light that is shining in the darkness, and not the only one which the darkness does not comprehend. Personal relations are despised today. They are regarded as bourgeois luxuries, as products of a time of fair weather which is now past, and we are urged to get rid of them, and to dedicate ourselves to some movement or cause instead. I hate the idea of causes, and if I had to choose between betraying my country and betraying my friend, I hope I should have the guts to betray my country. Such a choice may scandalize the modern reader, and he may stretch out his patriotic hand to the telephone at once and ring up the police. It would not have shocked Dante, though. Dante places Brutus and Cassius[1] in the lowest circle of Hell because they had chosen to betray their friend Julius Caesar rather than their country Rome. Probably one will not be asked to make such an agonizing choice. Still, there lies at the back of every creed something terrible and hard for which the worshipper may one day be required to suffer, and there is even terror and a hardness in this creed of personal relationships, urbane and mild though it sounds. Love and loyalty to an individual can run counter to the claims of the State. When they do—down with the State, say I, which means that the State would down me.

This brings me along to Democracy, "even Love, the Beloved Republic, which feeds upon Freedom and lives." Democracy is not a Beloved Republic really, and never will be. But it is less hateful than other contemporary forms of government, and to that extent it deserves our support. It does start from the assumption that the individual is important, and that all types are needed to make a civilization. It does not divide its citizens into the bossers and the bossed—as an efficiency-regime tends to do. The people I admire most are those who are sensitive and want to create something or discover something, and do not see life in terms of power, and such people get more of a chance under a democracy than elsewhere. They found religions, great or small, or they produce literature and art, or they do disinterested scientific research, or they may be what is called "ordinary people," who are creative in their private lives, bring up their children decently, for instance, or help their neighbors. All these people need to express themselves; they cannot do so unless society allows them liberty to do so, and the society which allows them most liberty is a democracy.

Democracy has another merit. It allows criticism, and if there is not public criticism there are bound to be hushed-up scandals. That is why I believe in the Press, despite all its lies and vulgarity, and why I believe in Parliament. Parliament is often sneered at because it is a Talking Shop. I believe in it *because* it is a talking shop. I believe in the Private Member who makes himself a nuisance. He gets snubbed and is told that he is cranky or ill-informed, but he does expose abuses which would otherwise never have been mentioned, and very often an abuse gets put right just by being mentioned. Occasionally, too, a well-meaning public official starts losing his head in the cause of efficiency, and thinks himself God Almighty. Such officials are particularly frequent in the Home Office. Well, there will be questions about them in Parliament sooner or later, and then they will have to mind their steps. Whether Parliament is either a representative body or an efficient one is questionable, but I value it because it criticizes and talks, and because its chatter gets widely reported.

So Two Cheers for Democracy: one because it admits variety and two because it permits criticism. Two cheers are quite enough: there is no occasion to give three. Only Love the Beloved Republic deserves that.

What about Force, though? While we are trying to be sensitive and advanced and affectionate and tolerant, an unpleasant question pops up: does not all society rest upon force? If a government cannot count upon the police and the army, how can it hope to rule? And if an individual gets knocked on the head or sent to a labor camp, of what significance are his opinions?

This dilemma does not worry me as much as it does some. I realize that all society rests upon force. But all the great creative actions, all the decent human relations, occur

---

[1]*Dante, Brutus, Cassius* in the Inferno, part of Dante Alighieri's *Divine Comedy,* hell is made up of descending circles.

during the intervals when force has not managed to come to the front. These intervals are what matter. I want them to be as frequent and as lengthy as possible, and I call them "civilization." Some people idealize force and pull it into the foreground and worship it, instead of keeping it in the background as long as possible. I think they make a mistake, and I think that their opposites, the mystics, err even more when they declare that force does not exist. I believe that it exists, and that one of our jobs is to prevent it from getting out of its box. It gets out sooner or later, and then it destroys us and all the lovely things which we have made. But it is not out all the time, for the fortunate reason that the strong are so stupid. Consider their conduct for a moment in the Niebelung's Ring.[2] The giants there have the guns, or in other words the gold; but they do nothing with it, they do not realize that they are all-powerful, with the result that the catastrophe is delayed and the castle of Walhalla, insecure but glorious, fronts the storms. Fafnir, coiled round his hoard, grumbles and grunts; we can hear him under Europe today; the leaves of the wood already tremble, and the Bird calls its warnings uselessly. Fafnir will destroy us, but by a blessed dispensation he is stupid and slow, and creation goes on just outside the poisonous blast of his breath. The Nietzschean[3] would hurry the monster up, the mystic would say he did not exist, but Wotan,[4] wiser than either, hastens to create warriors before doom declares itself. The Valkyries[5] are symbols not only of courage but of intelligence; they represent the human spirit snatching its opportunity while the going is good, and one of them even finds time to love. Brünnhilde's[6] last song hymns the recurrence of love, and since it is the privilege of art to exaggerate, she goes even further, and proclaims the love which is eternally triumphant and feeds upon freedom, and lives.

So that is what I feel about force and violence. It is, alas! the ultimate reality on this earth, but it does not always get to the front. Some people call its absences "decadence"; I call them "civilization" and find in such interludes the chief justification for the human experiment. I look the other way until fate strikes me. Whether this is due to courage or to cowardice in my own case I cannot be sure. But I know that if men had not looked the other way in the past, nothing of any value would survive. The people I respect most behave as if they were immortal and as if society was eternal. Both assumptions are false; both of them must be accepted as true if we are to go on eating and working and loving, and are to keep open a few breathing holes for the human spirit. No millennium seems likely to descend upon humanity; no better and stronger League of Nations will be instituted; no form of Christianity and no alternative to Christianity will bring peace to the world or integrity to the individual; no "change of heart" will occur. And yet we need not despair, indeed, we cannot despair; the evidence of history shows us that men have always insisted on behaving creatively under the shadow of the sword; that they have done their artistic and scientific and domestic stuff for the sake of doing it, and that we had better follow their example under the shadow of the aeroplanes. Others, with more vision or courage than myself, see the salvation as paltry, a sort of top-and-run game. Certainly it is presumptuous to say that we *cannot* improve, and that Man, who has only been in power for a few thousand years, will never learn to make use of his power. All I mean is that, if people continue to kill one another as they do, the world cannot get bet-

[2]*Niebelung's Ring* an opera by the German composer Richard Wagner.

[3]*Nietzschean* Friedrich Nietzsche (1844–1900) was an influential German philosopher.

[4]*Wotan* also known as Woden, the chief of the early Germanic-Celtic gods.

[5]*Valkyries* mythical handmaidens of Wotan, who chose the victors and casualties during battles.

[6]*Brunnhilde* a Valkyrie in Niebelung's Ring.

ter than it is, and that since there are more people than formerly, and their means for destroying one another superior, the world may well get worse. What is good in people— and consequently in the world—is their insistence on creation, their belief in friendship and loyalty for their own sakes; and though Violence remains and is, indeed, the major partner in this muddled establishment, I believe that creativeness remains too, and will always assume direction when violence sleeps. So, though I am not an optimist, I cannot agree with Sophocles[7] that it were better never to have been born. And although, like Horace,[8] I see no evidence that each batch of births is superior to the last, I leave the field open for the more complacent view. This is such a difficult moment to live in, one cannot help getting gloomy and also a bit rattled, and perhaps short-sighted.

In search of a refuge, we may perhaps turn to hero-worship. But here we shall get no help, in my opinion. Hero-worship is a dangerous vice, and one of the minor merits of a democracy is that it does not encourage it, or produce that unmanageable type of citizen known as the Great Man. It produces instead different kinds of small men—a much finer achievement. But people who cannot get interested in the variety of life, and cannot make up their own minds, get discontented over this, and they long for a hero to bow down before and to follow blindly. It is significant that a hero is an integral part of the authoritarian stock-in-trade today. An efficiency-regime cannot be run without a few heroes stuck about it to carry off the dullness—much as plums have to be put into a bad pudding to make it palatable. One hero at the top and a smaller one each side of him is a favorite arrangement, and the timid and the bored are comforted by the trinity, and, bowing down, feel exalted and strengthened.

No, I distrust Great Men. They produce a desert of uniformity around them and often a pool of blood too, and I always feel a little man's pleasure when they come a cropper. Every now and then one reads in the newspapers some such statement as: "The coup d'état appears to have failed, and Admiral Toma's whereabouts is at present unknown." Admiral Toma had probably every qualification for being a Great Man—an iron will, personal magnetism, dash, flair, sexlessness—but fate was against him, so he retires to unknown whereabouts instead of parading history with his peers. He fails with a completeness which no artist and no lover can experience, because with them the process of creation is itself an achievement, whereas with him the only possible achievement is success.

I believe in aristocracy, though—if that is the right word, and if a democrat may use it. Not an aristocracy of power, based upon rank and influence, but an aristocracy of the sensitive, the considerate and the plucky. Its members are to be found in all nations and classes, and all through the ages, and there is a secret understanding between them when they meet. They represent the true human tradition, the one permanent victory of our queer race over cruelty and chaos. Thousands of them perish in obscurity, a few are great names. They are sensitive for others as well as for themselves, they are considerate without being fussy, their pluck is not swankiness but the power to endure, and they can take a joke. I give no examples—it is risky to do that—but the reader may as well consider whether this is the type of person he would like to meet and to be, and whether (going farther with me) he would prefer that this type should *not* be an ascetic one. I am against asceticism myself. I am with the old Scotsman who wanted less chastity and more delicacy. I do not feel that my aristocrats are a real aristocracy if they thwart their bodies, since bodies are the instruments through which we register and enjoy the world. Still, I

---

[7]*Sophocles* (496(?)–406 B.C.) a Greek tragedian.

[8]*Horace* (65–8 B.C.) a Latin poet.

do not insist. This is not a major point. It is clearly possible to be sensitive, considerate and plucky and yet be an ascetic too; if anyone possesses the first three qualities, I will let him in! On they go—an invincible army, yet not a victorious one. The aristocrats, the elect, the chosen, the Best People—all the words that describe them are false, and all attempts to organize them fail. Again and again Authority, seeing their value, has tried to net them and to utilize them as the Egyptian Priesthood or the Christian Church or the Chinese Civil Service or the Group Movement, or some other worthy stunt. But they slip through the net and are gone; when the door is shut, they are no longer in the room; their temple, as one of them remarked, is the Holiness of the Heart's Affection, and their kingdom, though they never possess it, is the wide-open world.

With this type of person knocking about, and constantly crossing one's path if one has eyes to see or hands to feel, the experiment of earthly life cannot be dismissed as a failure. But it may well be hailed as a tragedy, the tragedy being that no device has been found by which these private decencies can be transmitted to public affairs. As soon as people have power they go crooked and sometimes dotty as well, because the possession of power lifts them into a region where normal honesty never pays. For instance, the man who is selling newspapers outside the Houses of Parliament can safely leave his papers to go for a drink and his cap beside them: anyone who takes a paper is sure to drop a copper into the cap. But the men who are inside the Houses of Parliament—they cannot trust one another like that, still less can the Government they compose trust other governments. No caps upon the pavement here, but suspicion, treachery and armaments. The more highly public life is organized the lower does its morality sink; the nations of today behave to each other worse than they ever did in the past, they cheat, rob, bully and bluff, make war without notice, and kill as many women and children as possible; whereas primitive tribes were at all events restrained by taboos. It is a humiliating outlook—though the greater the darkness, the brighter shine the little lights, reassuring one another, signalling: "Well, at all events, I'm still here. I don't like it very much, but how are you?" Unquenchable lights of my aristocracy! Signals of the invincible army! "Come along—anyway, let's have a good time while we can." I think they signal that too.

The Saviour of the future—if ever he comes—will not preach a new Gospel. He will merely utilize my aristocracy, he will make effective the good will and the good temper which are already existing. In other words, he will introduce a new technique. In economics, we are told that if there was a new technique of distribution, there need be no poverty, and people would not starve in one place while crops were being ploughed under in another. A similar change is needed in the sphere of morals and politics. The desire for it is by no means new; it was expressed, for example, in theological terms by Jacopone da Todi[9] over six hundred years ago. "Ordina questo amore, O tu che m'ami," he said; "O thou who lovest me—set this love in order." His prayer was not granted, and I do not myself believe that it ever will be, but here, and not through a change of heart, is our probable route. Not by becoming better, but by ordering and distributing his native goodness, will Man shut up Force into its box, and so gain time to explore the universe and to set his mark upon it worthily. At present he only explores it at odd moments, when Force is looking the other way, and his divine creativeness appears as a trivial by-product, to be scrapped as soon as the drums beat and the bombers hum.

Such a change, claim the orthodox, can only be made by Christianity, and will be made by it in God's good time: man always has failed and always will fail to organize his own

---

[9]*Jacopone da Todi* (1230(?)–1306) Italian religious poet.

goodness, and it is presumptuous of him to try. This claim—solemn as it is—leaves me cold. I cannot believe that Christianity will ever cope with the present world-wide mess, and I think that such influence as it retains in modern society is due to the money behind it, rather than to its spiritual appeal. It was a spiritual force once, but the indwelling spirit will have to be restated if it is to calm the waters again, and probably restated in a non-Christian form. Naturally a lot of people, and people who are not only good but able and intelligent, will disagree here; they will vehemently deny that Christianity has failed, or they will argue that its failure proceeds from the wickedness of men, and really proves its ultimate success. They have Faith, with a large F. My faith has a very small one, and I only intrude it because these are strenuous and serious days, and one likes to say what one thinks while speech is comparatively free: it may not be free much longer.

The above are the reflections of an individualist and a liberal who has found liberalism crumbling beneath him and at first felt ashamed. Then, looking around, he decided there was no special reason for shame, since other people, whatever they felt, were equally insecure. And as for individualism—there seems no way of getting off this, even if one wanted to. The dictator-hero can grind down his citizens till they are all alike, but he cannot melt them into a single man. That is beyond his power. He can order them to merge, he can incite them to mass-antics, but they are obliged to be born separately, and to die separately, and, owing to these unavoidable termini, will always be running off the totalitarian rails. The memory of birth and the expectation of death always lurk within the human being, making him separate from his fellows and consequently capable of intercourse with them. Naked I came into the world, naked I shall go out of it! And a very good thing too, for it reminds me that I am naked under my shirt, whatever its color.

Understanding and Analysis

1. We call those who do not "believe in Belief" skeptics. Think about Forster's claim that in this period just before the Second World War "ignorance rules, and science, who ought to have ruled, plays the subservient pimp." What was going on in Germany that turned science into a "pimp"?

2. What values does Forster support in the first paragraph? What metaphor does he use to explain what was happening to these values at that time?

3. What distinction, if any, do you see between "Faith" and "Belief" in Forster's first paragraph? Does Forster think faith is necessary in these times?

4. Forster uses a sentence fragment to begin his third paragraph. How does it connect to the previous paragraph? Do you think the fragment is effective? Why or why not? Can you find other sentence fragments in the essay? If so, are they effective?

5. This essay is an attempt to "get a little order into the contemporary chaos." What are the basic requirements, as Forster explains them, for order in these times?

6. Forster's most quoted and controversial statement occurs in this essay: "I hate the idea of causes, and if I had to choose between betraying my country and betraying my friend, I hope I should have the guts to betray my country." Think about this statement from the point of view of someone living in England and of someone living in Germany. Under what conditions would you agree with Forster?

7. Why does Forster support democracy? How many "merits" does Forster find in democracy, and what are they?

8. What is "Love the Beloved Republic"?

9. List all the characteristics Forster is willing to attribute to force. What does he "believe" about force? What do his two opponents, those who "idealize force" and those who are "mystics," believe?

10. Does Forster believe in a coming utopia? Why or why not?

11. What does Forster think of hero worship? Why?

12. Forster says he believes in "an aristocracy of the sensitive, the considerate, and the plucky." How do these terms connect to his points in the first paragraph of this essay? Why does he deliberately use the word "believe" when he writes, "I believe in aristocracy"?

13. What attitude does Forster reject because "bodies are the instruments through which we register and enjoy the world"?

14. Why do words fail to "describe" and "Authority" fail to "organize" the members of Forster's aristocracy?

15. Do you believe, with Forster, that the people of the past behaved better toward one another than the people of this century?

16. Near the end of his essay Forster returns again to define his sort of faith. What is it?

17. How has Forster prepared the reader for the last sentences of the essay?

Comparison

1. Read "The Revolt Against Civilization" and compare Lewisohn's understanding of "civilization" with that of Forster. To what extent do these writers agree and disagree?

2. Compare Forster's view of war and force with that of Graves, Fussell, and other writers in this text who have witnessed or experienced battle. What evidence can you find to show similarities and differences in their attitudes?

3. Would Forster consider the people Panter-Downes describes in her two essays as fit members of his aristocracy? Why or why not?

4. Read Tuchman's account of the Black Death. Does her analysis of the behavior of people under stress change your opinion of Forster's essay?

Mollie Panter-Downes

SEPTEMBER 21 (1940)

AFTER A FORTNIGHT of savage nocturnal bombardments, Londoners are settling down with courage and resource to live by a completely new timetable. The big stores and many of the offices now close an hour earlier in order to give workers a chance to get home and have a meal before the uncomfortable evening program begins, which it does with unfailing regularity. Getting home is a tricky business for those who live in the suburbs, for bomb damage and rush hours at unexpected times of day have put a strain on the transport services. Lucky commuters have been cadging lifts from passing motorists and lorry-drivers; the not-so-lucky have been doggedly hiking rather than risk being caught out in the night air, which definitely isn't healthy just now, as much because of the terrific anti-aircraft barrages as because of bombs.

Families of modest means who have no cellars in their homes and perhaps don't care to trust to their Anderson shelters start queuing up outside the public shelters as early as six in the evening, with their bundles of bedding and their baskets of food. Thousands more turn the tube stations into vast dormitories every night—a kind of lie-down strike which at first perplexed the authorities, who could not think what to do with passengers who paid their three-hapence and then proceeded to encamp quietly on the platforms. Since these folk have given no trouble and haven't, as was feared, cluttered up the corridors to the inconvenience of passengers with a genuine urge to get somewhere, the latest semi-official ruling is that the practice can be continued. The Ministries of Transport and Home Security, however, have appealed to the public not to use the tube as a shelter except in cases of urgent necessity. The urgent necessity of many of the sleepers who doss down on the platforms nightly is that they no longer have homes to go to; each morning, more are leaving their underground sanctuary to go back and find a heap of rubble and splinters where their houses used to be. The bravery of these people has to be seen to be believed. They would be heart-rending to look at if they didn't so conspicuously refuse to appear heart-rending. Their reaction has taken the form of anger, and there is a good deal of hopeful talk about smashing reprisals on Berlin. Anger has probably been responsible for a recent rise in munitions production. Hundreds of men and women are working a bit faster as they think of those heaps of rubble.

Bombs of heavy calibre were dropped in some of this week's raids, and time bombs were also extensively used. A new headache for householders is the possibility of being evacuated with only a few minutes warning, as they must be when a time bomb falls anywhere near. The most heroic among the millions of heroic workers in London these days are the Royal Engineers, who deal in squads with time bombs, going down into the craters and working with mathematical nicety. The squad which saved St. Paul's naturally came in for much deserved publicity, but there are plenty of equally courageous groups risking their lives daily with the same coolness, if under less spectacular circumstances. The auxilary fire services, too, have done magnificent work, and an announcement of civilian-service decorations which will be the equivalent of military honors is expected shortly. Firemen, wardens, Home Guards, and nurses alike were killed while on duty during this week's raids. Nurses have been under fire constantly, for several hospitals have been hit more than once. St. Thomas's, on the river opposite the Houses of Parliament (which presumably were the target), is a tragic sight, its wards ripped open by bombs.

The bombers have turned their attention to the West End for the last few nights and the big stores have suffered heavily. John Lewis & Co. and others were badly damaged, but one gutted building looks much like another, and Londoners, after a brief glance, go briskly on to work. Taxi-drivers grumble about the broken glass, which is hard on their tires, and about the difficulty of navigating in neighborhoods which they know like the backs of their hands but which may overnight become unrecognizable. All the same, their grumbles have the usual cockney pithiness and gaiety, and taxis get you home in spite of anything short of a raid right overhead. Gaiety does turn up even in such grim days.

It was funny to see raw sirloins of beef being carried from one stately club, which was temporarily cut off from its gas supply, to another equally stately establishment, which had offered the hospitality of its old-fashioned coal ranges; it was funny to see a florist's beautifully arranged hot-house blossoms waving in a stiff breeze that blew through the shattered windows of his shop.

There are now more people who appear to believe that the invasion is imminent and that the increasing fury of the air attacks is the first stage of the German plan for it. A story has been widely circulated that some sort of attempt at invasion was made and failed a few weeks back. It's certain that the bulk of the population (and, one hears, of the Army, too) is now yearning for the invasion to be tried. With the land forces praying daily that the Germans will start, the R.A.F. goes over nightly and stops them from starting.

Understanding and Analysis

1. In the second sentence, what comparison is implicit in the words "evening program"?

2. What did unhealthy "night air" used to mean before the war?

3. What is the meaning of "terrific" at the end of the first paragraph? Note also her use of "smashing" and "funny." What do these words have in common? What effect do they have on the reader?

4. What groups of civilians does Panter-Downes describe in this essay?

Comparison

1. What changes do you see in Panter-Downes's description of civilians between September, 1939, and September, 1940?

2. Would Forster consider the people Panter-Downes describes in her two essays as fit members of his aristocracy? Why or why not?

Langston Hughes
(1902–1967)

Born February 1, 1902, in Joplin, Missouri, Langston Hughes rarely stayed in one place for more than a few years at a time. After his father left the family for Mexico, where he became a successful businessman, Hughes lived on the edge of poverty in Topeka, Kansas, with his mother, who introduced him to theater and literature. Hughes writes in his autobiography, *Big Sea*, "even before I was six, books began to happen to me, so that after a while, there came a time when I believed in books more than in people—which, of course, was wrong." By the time he entered eighth grade in Illinois, Hughes had moved five times, once to Mexico with his mother in hopes of reconciling with his father, once to Topeka, where his mother had found work, and three times to Lawrence, Kansas, to live with his grandmother. While living in Illinois, Hughes was named class poet, and his mother remarried; soon after, the family moved once again, this time to Cleveland, Ohio, where Hughes started high school.

Like many writers, Hughes began his career by publishing short stories and poems in his high-school newspaper, the *Central High Monthly*. After spending a summer with his father in Mexico, Hughes returned to high school in Ohio, convinced that his father was too materialistic. During his senior year, he was again named class poet. Despite growing disagreements with his father, after graduation in June of 1920, Hughes returned to Mexico, where he read novels in Spanish, learned German from his father's housekeeper, rode horses on his father's ranch, wrote poetry, and continued to argue with his father, who wanted him to study engineering. In 1921, he enrolled in Columbia, his father footing the bill. That year he published his first poem in *The Crisis*, the journal edited by W. E. B. Du Bois.

By 1922, he had published thirteen poems in *The Crisis*. He decided he had to leave Columbia because he knew he would never become an engineer. And he refused to return to Mexico, even after his father's stroke and requests for help. Instead, he took up various odd jobs in New York before working in 1923 on a steamship bound for the west coast of Africa; in 1924, he jumped ship on another voyage to spend time in France and Italy. Through connections he made in New York while accepting a poetry prize, Hughes published his first volume of poetry, *The Weary Blues*, in 1926. In the late twenties, while living in Washington, D.C., with his mother, Hughes met important figures in the Harlem Renaissance who encouraged him to study at Lincoln University in Pennsylvania, where he was graduated in 1929. Following the failure of a magazine called *Fire*, which Hughes founded with Zora Neale Hurston and other writers, he published his second volume of poetry, and, during his senior year of college, he worked on his first play, *Mulatto*, and revised his first novel, *Not Without Laughter*, which won the Harmon Gold Prize for Literature. Like Hurston, Hughes was supported for a number of years by Mrs. Charlotte Mason, a white socialite who required her African-American artists to call her "Godmother" and who tried to control their artistic development. Her restrictions led Hughes to break with "Godmother" in 1931.

Without secure funding, Hughes spent the rest of his life traveling from place to place, living with friends for short periods, lecturing around the country, writing poetry, short stories, and drama whenever and wherever he could find a quiet place to live and write. With grant money from the government and private foundations, Hughes made trips to the Soviet Union to do a film on race relations, to China and Japan to expand his cultural knowledge, to

Spain to cover the Spanish Civil War for black newspapers, to Paris to attend leftist writers' conferences, to Los Angeles to write scripts. (Because of his trip to Russia, he was called to testify before Senator Joseph McCarthy in 1953.) He lived in Carmel (CA), Chicago, New York, Atlanta, and Washington, D.C., and met with writers in Ghana, Nigeria, Senegal, and Ethiopia. Among his many works are collected stories about a character named Simple, a variety of plays, novels, children's books, and, most notably, his volumes of poetry (*The Weary Blues*, 1926, *Shakespeare in Harlem*, 1942, *One-Way Ticket*, 1949, and *The Collected Poems* 1994). The essay reproduced here is from the first of his two volumes of autobiography, *The Big Sea*, 1940, and *I Wonder as I Wander*, 1956.

During the final decade of his life, according to biographer James. S. Haskins, Hughes became increasingly "militant" on questions of race. He died on May 22, 1967. Throughout his life Hughes resisted what he saw as the elitism of many black intellectuals. In his works, he shows a consistent interest in the experiences of working-class African-Americans, sometimes using dialect and non-standard grammar to give voice to the common man. His works also reveal the influence of his grandmother's early stories of suffering and perservering without crying. Indeed, Hughes often approached his subject matter with a spirit of humor—an "ironic humor" or a "plain, gentle kind of humor"—because he believed that too much of what had been written about blacks focused on "the tragedies of frustration and weakness" and because he found that blacks could laugh even as they sang the blues. Of course, Hughes did not shy away from representing weariness and anguish: he initiated his painful separation from Charlotte Mason, who wanted him to write "beautiful poetry," in order to write poems that were frank and harsh.

In the poem called "Justice" Hughes cuts away centuries of complacency to help us review the wisdom of "blind justice":

> That justice is a blind goddess
> Is a thing to which we black are wise.
> Her bandage hides two festering sores
> That once perhaps were eyes.

SALVATION (1940)

I WAS SAVED from sin when I was going on thirteen. But not really saved. It happened like this. There was a big revival at my Auntie Reed's church. Every night for weeks there had been much preaching, singing, praying, and shouting, and some very hardened sinners had been brought to Christ, and the membership of the church had grown by leaps and bounds. Then just before the revival ended, they held a special meeting for children, "to bring the young lambs to the fold." My aunt spoke of it for days ahead. That night I was escorted to the front row and placed on the mourners' bench with all the other young sinners, who had not yet been brought to Jesus.

My aunt told me that when you were saved you saw a light, and something happened to you inside! And Jesus came into your life! And God was with you from then on! She said you could see and hear and feel Jesus in your soul. I believed her. I have heard a great many old people say the same thing and it seemed to me they ought to know. So I sat there calmly in the hot, crowded church, waiting for Jesus to come to me.

The preacher preached a wonderful rhythmical sermon, all moans and shouts and lonely cries and dire pictures of hell, and then he sang a song about the ninety and nine safe in the fold, but one little lamb was left out in the cold. Then he said: "Won't you come? Won't you come to Jesus? Young lambs, won't you come?" And he held out his arms to all us young sinners there on the mourners' bench. And the little girls cried. And some of them jumped up and went to Jesus right away. But most of us just sat there.

A great many old people came and knelt around us and prayed, old women with jet-black faces and braided hair, old men with work-gnarled hands. And the church sang a song about the lower lights are burning, some poor sinners to be saved. And the whole building rocked with prayer and song.

Still I kept waiting to *see* Jesus.

Finally all the young people had gone to the altar and were saved, but one boy and me. He was a rounder's son named Westley. Westley and I were surrounded by sisters and deacons praying. It was very hot in the church, and getting late now. Finally Westley said to me in a whisper: "God damn! I'm tired o' sitting here. Let's get up and be saved." So he got up and was saved.

Then I was left all alone on the mourners' bench. My aunt came and knelt at my knees and cried, while prayers and songs swirled all around me in the little church. The whole congregation prayed for me alone, in a mighty wail of moans and voices. And I kept waiting serenely for Jesus, waiting, waiting—but he didn't come. I wanted to see him, but nothing happened to me. Nothing! I wanted something to happen to me, but nothing happened.

I heard the songs and the minister saying: "Why don't you come? My dear child, why don't you come to Jesus? Jesus is waiting for you. He wants you. Why don't you come? Sister Reed, what is this child's name?"

"Langston," my aunt sobbed.

"Langston, why don't you come? Why don't you come and be saved? Oh, Lamb of God! Why don't you come?"

Now it was really getting late. I began to be ashamed of myself, holding everything up so long. I began to wonder what God thought about Westley, who certainly hadn't seen Jesus either, but who was now sitting proudly on the platform, swinging his knickerbockered legs and grinning down at me, surrounded by deacons and old women on their knees praying. God had not struck Westley dead for taking his name in vain or for lying in the temple. So I decided that maybe to save further trouble, I'd better lie, too, and say that Jesus had come, and get up and be saved.

So I got up.

Suddenly the whole room broke into a sea of shouting, as they saw me rise. Waves of rejoicing swept the place. Women leaped in the air. My aunt threw her arms around me. The minister took me by the hand and led me to the platform.

When things quieted down, in a hushed silence, punctuated by a few ecstatic "Amens," all the new young lambs were blessed in the name of God. Then joyous singing filled the room.

That night, for the last time in my life but one—for I was a big boy twelve years old— I cried. I cried, in bed alone, and couldn't stop. I buried my head under the quilts, but my aunt heard me. She woke up and told my uncle I was crying because the Holy Ghost had come into my life, and because I had seen Jesus. But I was really crying because I couldn't bear to tell her that I had lied, that I had deceived everybody in the church, that I hadn't seen Jesus, and that now I didn't believe there was a Jesus any more, since he didn't come to help me.

Understanding and Analysis

1. Examine the alliteration, word choice, biblical allusions, and sentence length in the first paragraph. How do these elements work together to create a sense of expectation but also a sense of doom?

2. What is the effect of the exclamation marks in the second paragraph?

3. What is the effect of the last sentence in the third paragraph?

4. Why was Westley saved?

5. What other motivations do the young members of the congregation have for being saved? List as many as you can find evidence for in the essay.

6. What do you think the older Hughes has learned that the twelve-year-old Hughes did not understand the night he cried in bed?

Comparison

1. Several pieces of expository prose in this anthology are narratives. Like short stories, they are carefully shaped with plots and characters. Compare this narrative with one by Orwell or Graves or Angelou.

2. Can you find connections between Forster's descriptions of "belief" and "faith" and Hughes's narrative?

3. In light of Frost's definition of "enthusiasm," what kind of enthusiasm is revealed in Hughes's narrative and by whom?

E. B. White

(1899–1985)

Elwyn Brooks White was born in Mt. Vernon, New York, the last child of Samuel Tilly White, vice president and secretary of the Waters Piano Company, and his wife, Jesse Hart White. At the time of his birth, July 11, 1899, the household consisted of a maid, a cook, his parents, and five siblings—Marion, 18, Clara, 15, Albert, 11, Stanley, 8, and Lillian, 5. Elwyn's position in the family was particularly advantageous because, having attained a comfortable income, his father was finally able to spend time with his family and to provide his youngest child with such luxuries as the first bicycle on the block and later a canoe of his own to use during summer vacations on Great Pond, North Belgrade, Maine. From his brother Stanley, Elwyn learned how to paddle a canoe, cut with a jackknife, and read both books and nature. From Lillian he learned to laugh at the old-fashioned ways of their parents and to develop some social graces. But by the time Elwyn was twelve all his brothers and sisters had left home.

Like many writers whose work appears in this text, E. B. White drew on his childhood for the materials in his fiction, *Stuart Little* (1945), *Charlotte's Web* (1952), and *Trumpet of the Swan* (1970), but White's experiences were unusual in that they included few of life's perils. All his siblings prospered, the older girls marrying at 18 and 20, and producing numerous healthy children, the boys going off to Cornell and, finally, Lillian leaving for boarding school and later for Vassar. White spent these lonely years skiing and playing hockey in the winter; biking, roller skating, climbing trees, swimming, and boating in the summer. He made trips to New York City to visit the circus and the zoo and sported with his dogs, Mac and Beppo. He watched eggs hatch, observed the activities of salamanders, caterpillars, snakes, frogs, pigeons, geese, turkeys, ducks, rabbits, and horses, and once, when he was sick, he kept a pet mouse.

Despite this apparently idyllic environment, White was a fearful child and became subject to attacks of panic and hypochondria in his teenage years, a condition that plagued him all his life. Some of his fear probably derived from his persistent hay fever and from the effects of elderly, solicitous parents and a circumscribed social life, consisting primarily of Sunday visits to the homes of his married sisters. Although disasters never happened to him or his family, he knew that they could, that they had happened to neighbors and other people he read about in the newspaper. And he saw death regularly in the world of nature. His biographer, Scott Elledge, argues that writing became for White a way of escaping and controlling his loneliness and fears.

He began writing early, winning a prize for a poem about a mouse from the *Women's Home Companion* in 1909 and two prizes for pieces about nature from *St. Nicholas Magazine*, when he was eleven and fourteen. In high school he was assistant editor of the literary magazine, and he kept a journal of poems, both comic and serious, as well as reflections about the war, his desire for independence, and his uncertainty about the future. His concerns about the war led him to register for the draft in September of his sophomore year of college—two months before the armistice.

At Cornell he kept up his journal and his poetry, was a reporter for and later editor-in-chief of the student newspaper, the *Cornell Daily Sun*, and joined two literary groups. But his interests lay more in journalism and the practical requirements of what he called a "material world" than in the pursuit of literary criticism. Although exempted from Freshman Composition, he earned a D in second-semester English.

After graduation, White worked for a while in Manhattan as a reporter and writer of press releases until, in March of 1922, restless and uncertain, he set off in his Model-T Ford for parts west. He and a friend, Howard Cushman, drove through Ohio, Kentucky, Indiana, Illinois, Wisconsin, North Dakota, and Montana, washing dishes, playing the piano, picking fruit, and sand-papering floors to pay their way. They reached Seattle in September; White stayed on for nine months, working as a reporter and writer of light verse for the *Seattle Times*. In June of 1923 he spent most of his money on a ticket to Skagway, Alaska, aboard the S. S. Buford, bound for Siberia and back again. At Skagway, the ship's captain gave him a job as saloon boy so that he could remain aboard through the return trip. After the boat docked, he took a train home to New York, still discouraged, still uncertain of his future.

Though unaware of the pattern himself, like Twain and Hughes, E. B. White was enacting the typical apprenticeship of the writer. And like them, he eventually made use of his travels in his writing, publishing "Farewell my Lovely" (based on a suggestion from Richard L. Strout) about the Model T in 1936 and "The Years of Wonder" about the trip to Alaska in 1961. Back in Manhattan, White worked for an advertising agency, while keeping up his journal and publishing a few poems in *The New York World*. Meanwhile, Harold Ross began publishing a new weekly magazine, *The New Yorker*; E. B. White bought the first issue the day it appeared, February 19, 1925. By 1927, *The New Yorker* was an established enterprise and E. B. White one of its main contributors; he wrote the newsbreaks that appear at the bottom of selected pages (that is, the witty responses to comic headlines and mistakes which he compiled from newspapers across the country), as well as Notes and Comments, essays, and light verse. That year also, he met and fell in love with Katherine Sergeant Angell, seven years older than he and the literary editor of *The New Yorker*. After a long and complicated courtship, they married in November of 1929. Katherine had been increasingly unhappy in her marriage to Ernest Angell, a lawyer, but she had two children, Nancy, who was 12 when her mother remarried, and Roger, who was nine. In the end, custody was given to their father. The marriage was a success, marred only by Katherine's illnesses and White's attacks of panic and hypochondria. In December, 1930, their son, Joel, was born.

With both partners working, the family prospered, despite the depression. By 1933, they were able to buy a water front farm in Maine where White could indulge his three favorite passions—sailing, writing, and farming. That purchase set up an enduring conflict for White between the weekly deadlines of *The New Yorker* in the city and his longing for unlimited time to write in the country. Moreover, he felt confined by Ross's requirement that he use the editorial "we" in his unsigned essays in Notes and Comments. Finally, in 1938, he agreed to write a signed monthly column for *Harper's Magazine* and moved the family to the farm. Katherine continued to work for *The New Yorker*, reading manuscripts in Maine, but she missed the staff and the activity of the city. Nonetheless, both were productive; by 1944, when the two edited *A Subtreasury of American Humor*, White had published twelve books, including *Is Sex Necessary?* with Thurber (1929) and *One Man's Meat* (1942), a collection of the essays from *Harper's*. While writing for *Harper's*, White developed the themes and the introspective tone, both wry and poetic, that have made him famous.

In 1943, the Whites moved back to New York City to help Ross with *The New Yorker*. White had become interested in the war effort and hoped to communicate his ideas about internationalism and a world government through his pieces in *The New Yorker*. One result was a book of his political writing, *The Wild Flag*, published in 1946. During the next eleven years, frequently troubled by Katherine's illnesses and White's depression and hypochondria, the couple traveled back and forth from city to country, but kept their primary residence in New York. In addition to his regular contributions to *The New Yorker*, White wrote *Charlotte's Web* and, in 1954, published *Second Tree from the Corner*, a collection of his essays from *The New Yorker*.

In 1957, when Katherine gave up her full-time work at *The New Yorker*, the Whites moved permanently to Maine. While Katherine worked part-time, White revised a "little book" written by his former English teacher at Cornell and published it as *The Elements of Style* (1959). By this time the family had a combined total of nine grandchildren and a handsome income from White's best-selling children's books. In 1961, poor health forced Katherine to retire from her editorial work; though increasingly ill, she continued to help her husband and work on her garden until her death in 1977.

From his farmhouse, enlarged over the years to 11 rooms on 40 acres of land, White continued to write his *New Yorker* essays, collected in *The Points of My Compass* (1962), *An E. B. White Reader* (1966), *Essays of E. B. White* (1977), *Poems and Sketches* (1981), and a reissue of *One Man's Meat* with an introduction (1982).

Although he received honorary degrees from the University of Maine, Dartmouth, Yale, Bowdoin, Harvard, and Colby, his highest recognition was a Pulitzer citation in 1978 for excellence in writing. White spent his last years enjoying visits with his family, writing letters to friends, doing his farm chores, sailing, and watching the sea.

Despite his success as an essayist, E. B. White is probably most famous for his children's books and for his revision of the "little book" known by all as "Strunk and White." Both the children's books and the essays are written in an informal, intimate, and humorous style; both convey his love of the details of nature and his preoccupation with the passage of time. White's wry comedy balances the disarray of his emotions with the ordered cycles of nature to create poignant reminders of the brevity and joy of life.

ONCE MORE TO THE LAKE (1941)

ONE SUMMER, ALONG about 1904, my father rented a camp on a lake in Maine and took us all there for the month of August. We all got ringworm from some kittens and had to rub Pond's Extract on our arms and legs night and morning, and my father rolled over in a canoe with all his clothes on; but outside of that the vacation was a success and from then on none of us ever thought there was any place in the world like that lake in Maine. We returned summer after summer—always on August 1 for one month. I have since become a salt-water man, but sometimes in summer there are days when the restlessness of the tides and the fearful cold of the sea water and the incessant wind that blows across the afternoon and into the evening make me wish for the placidity of a lake in the woods. A few weeks ago this feeling got so strong I bought myself a couple of bass hooks and a spinner and returned to the lake where we used to go, for a week's fishing and to revisit old haunts.

I took along my son, who had never had any fresh water up his nose and who had seen lily pads only from train windows. On the journey over to the lake I began to wonder what it would be like. I wondered how time would have marred this unique, this holy spot—the coves and streams, the hills that the sun set behind, the camps and the paths behind the camps. I was sure that the tarred road would have found it out, and I wondered in what other ways it would be desolated. It is strange how much you can remember about places like that once you allow your mind to return into the grooves that lead back. You remember one thing, and that suddenly reminds you of another thing. I guess I remembered clearest of all the early mornings, when the lake was cool and motionless, remembered how the bedroom smelled of the lumber it was made of and of the wet woods whose scent entered through the screen. The partitions in the camp were thin and did not extend clear to the top of the rooms, and as I was always the first up I would dress softly so as not to wake the others, and sneak out into the sweet outdoors and start out in the canoe, keeping close along the shore in the long shadows of the pines. I remembered being very careful never to rub my paddle against the gunwale for fear of disturbing the stillness of the cathedral.

The lake had never been what you would call a wild lake. There were cottages sprinkled around the shores, and it was in farming country although the shores of the lake were quite heavily wooded. Some of the cottages were owned by nearby farmers, and you would live at the shore and eat your meals at the farmhouse. That's what our family did. But although it wasn't wild, it was a fairly large and undisturbed lake and there were places in it that, to a child at least, seemed infinitely remote and primeval.

I was right about the tar: it led to within half a mile of the shore. But when I got back there, with my boy, and we settled into a camp near a farmhouse and into the kind of summertime I had known, I could tell that it was going to be pretty much the same as it had been before—I knew it, lying in bed the first morning, smelling the bedroom and hearing the boy sneak quietly out and go off along the shore in a boat. I began to sustain the illusion that he was I, and therefore, by simple transposition, that I was my father. This sensation persisted, kept cropping up all the time we were there. It was not an entirely new feeling, but in this setting it grew much stronger. I seemed to be living a dual existence. I would be in the middle of some simple act, I would be picking up a bait box or laying down a table fork, or I would be saying something, and suddenly it would be not I but my father who was saying the words or making the gesture. It gave me a creepy sensation.

We went fishing the first morning. I felt the same damp moss covering the worms in the bait can, and saw the dragonfly alight on the tip of my rod as it hovered a few inches from the surface of the water. It was the arrival of this fly that convinced me beyond any doubt that everything was as it always had been, that the years were a mirage and that there had been no years. The small waves were the same, chucking the rowboat under the chin as we fished at anchor, and the boat was the same boat, the same color green and the ribs broken in the same places, and under the floorboards the same fresh-water leavings and débris—the dead helgramite,[1] the wisps of moss, the rusty discarded fishhook, the dried blood from yesterday's catch. We stared silently at the tips of our rods, at the dragonflies that came and went. I lowered the tip of mine into the water, tentatively, pensively dislodging the fly, which darted two feet away, poised, darted two feet back, and came to rest again a little farther up the rod. There had been no years between the ducking of this dragonfly and the other one—the one that was part of memory. I looked at the boy, who was silently watching his fly, and it was my hands that held his rod, my eyes watching. I felt dizzy and didn't know which rod I was at the end of.

We caught two bass, hauling them in briskly as though they were mackerel, pulling them over the side of the boat in a businesslike manner without any landing net, and stunning them with a blow on the back of the head. When we got back for a swim before lunch, the lake was exactly where we had left it, the same number of inches from the dock, and there was only the merest suggestion of a breeze. This seemed an utterly enchanted sea, this lake you could leave to its own devices for a few hours and come back to, and find that it had not stirred, this constant and trustworthy body of water. In the shallows, the dark, water-soaked sticks and twigs, smooth and old, were undulating in clusters on the bottom against the clean ribbed sand, and the track of the mussel was plain. A school of minnows swam by, each minnow with its small individual shadow, doubling the attendance, so clear and sharp in the sunlight. Some of the other campers were in swimming, along the shore, one of them with a cake of soap, and the water felt thin and clear and unsubstantial. Over the years there had been this person with the cake of soap, this cultist, and here he was. There had been no years.

Up to the farmhouse to dinner through the teeming, dusty field, the road under our sneakers was only a two-track road. The middle track was missing, the one with the marks of the

---

[1]*helgramite* large brown insect (dobson fly) larva used as bait for bass.

hooves and the splotches of dried, flaky manure. There had always been three tracks to choose from in choosing which track to walk in; now the choice was narrowed down to two. For a moment I missed terribly the middle alternative. But the way led past the tennis court, and something about the way it lay there in the sun reassured me; the tape had loosened along the backline, the alleys were green with plantains and other weeds, and the net (installed in June and removed in September) sagged in the dry noon, and the whole place steamed with midday heat and hunger and emptiness. There was a choice of pie for dessert, and one was blueberry and one was apple, and the waitresses were the same country girls, there having been no passage of time, only the illusion of it as in a dropped curtain—the waitresses were still fifteen; their hair had been washed, that was the only difference—they had been to the movies and seen the pretty girls with the clean hair.

Summertime, oh summertime, pattern of life indelible, the fadeproof lake, the woods unshatterable, the pasture with the sweetfern and the juniper forever and ever, summer without end; this was the background, and the life along the shore was the design, the cottagers with their innocent and tranquil design, their tiny docks with the flagpole and the American flag floating against the white clouds in the blue sky, the little paths over the roots of the trees leading from camp to camp and the paths leading back to the out-houses and the can of lime for sprinkling, and at the souvenir counters at the store the miniature birch-bark canoes and the postcards that showed things looking a little better than they looked. This was the American family at play, escaping from the city heat, wondering whether the newcomers in the camp at the head of the cove were "common" or "nice," wondering whether it was true that the people who drove up for Sunday dinner at the farmhouse were turned away because there wasn't enough chicken.

It seemed to me, as I kept remembering all this, that those times and those summers had been infinitely precious and worth saving. There had been jollity and peace and goodness. The arriving (at the beginning of August) had been so big a business in itself, at the railway station the farm wagon drawn up, the first smell of the pine-laden air, the first glimpse of the smiling farmer, and the great importance of the trunks and your father's enormous authority in such matters, and the feel of the wagon under you for the long ten-mile haul, and at the top of the last long hill catching the first view of the lake after eleven months of not seeing this cherished body of water. The shouts and cries of the other campers when they saw you, and the trunks to be unpacked, to give up their rich burden. (Arriving was less exciting nowadays, when you sneaked up in your car and parked it under a tree near the camp and took out the bags and in five minutes it was all over, no fuss, no loud wonderful fuss about trunks.)

Peace and goodness and jollity. The only thing that was wrong now, really, was the sound of the place, an unfamiliar nervous sound of the outboard motors. This was the note that jarred, the one thing that would sometimes break the illusion and set the years moving. In those other summertimes all motors were inboard; and when they were at a little distance, the noise they made was a sedative, an ingredient of summer sleep. They were one-cylinder and two-cylinder engines, and some were make-and-break and some were jump-spark, but they all made a sleepy sound across the lake. The one-lungers throbbed and fluttered, and the twin-cylinder ones purred and purred, and that was a quiet sound, too. But now the campers all had outboards. In the daytime, in the hot mornings, these motors made a petulant, irritable sound; at night, in the still evening when the after-glow lit the water, they whined about one's ears like mosquitoes. My boy loved our rented outboard, and his great desire was to achieve single-handed mastery over it, and authority, and he soon learned the trick of choking it a little (but not too much), and the adjustment of the needle valve. Watching him I would remember the things you could do with the old one-cylinder engine with the heavy flywheel, how you could have it eating out of your hand if you got really close to it spiritually. Motorboats in those days didn't have clutches, and you would make a landing by shutting off the motor at the proper time and coasting in with a dead rudder. But there was a way of reversing them, if you learned the trick, by cutting the switch and putting it on again exactly on the final dying revolution of the flywheel, so that it would kick back against compression and begin reversing. Approaching a dock in a strong following breeze, it was difficult to slow up sufficiently by the ordinary coasting method, and if a boy felt he had complete mastery over his motor, he was tempted to keep it running beyond its time and then reverse it a few feet from the dock. It took a cool nerve, because if you threw the switch a twentieth of a second too soon you would catch the flywheel when it still had speed enough to go up past center, and the boat would leap ahead, charging bull-fashion at the dock.

We had a good week at the camp. The bass were biting well and the sun shone endlessly, day after day. We would be tired at night and lie down in the accumulated heat of the little bedrooms after the long hot day and the breeze would stir almost imperceptibly outside and the smell of the swamp drift in through the rusty screens. Sleep would come easily and in the morning the red squirrel would be on the roof, tapping out his gay routine. I kept remembering everything, lying in bed in the mornings—the small steamboat that had a long rounded stern like the lip of a Ubangi,[2] and how quietly she ran on the moonlight sails, when the older boys played their mandolins and the girls sang and we ate doughnuts dipped in sugar, and how sweet the music was on the water in the shining night, and what it had felt like to think about girls then. After breakfast we would go up to the store and the things were in the same place—the minnows in a bottle, the plugs and spinners disarranged and pawed over by the youngsters from the boys' camp, the Fig Newtons and the Beeman's gum. Outside, the road was tarred and cars stood in front of the store. Inside, all was just as it had always been, except there was more Coca-Cola and not so much Moxie and root beer and birch beer and sarsaparilla. We would walk out with a bottle of pop apiece and sometimes the pop would backfire up our noses and hurt. We explored the streams, quietly, where the turtles slid off the sunny logs and dug their way into the soft bottom; and we lay on the town wharf and fed worms to the tame bass. Everywhere we went I had trouble making out which was I, the one walking at my side, the one walking in my pants.

One afternoon while we were there at that lake a thunderstorm came up. It was like the revival of an old melodrama that I had seen long ago with childish awe. The second-act climax of the drama of the electrical disturbance over a lake in America had not changed in any important respect. This was the big scene, still the big scene. The whole thing was so familiar, the first feeling of oppression and heat and a general air around camp of not wanting to go very far away. In midafternoon (it was all the same) a curious darkening of the sky, and a lull in everything that had made life rich; and then the way the boats suddenly swung the other way at their moorings with the coming of a breeze out of the new quarter, and the premonitory rumble. Then the kettle drum, then the snare, then the bass drum and cymbals, then crackling light against the dark, and the gods grinning and licking their chops in the hills. Afterward the calm, the rain steadily rustling in the calm lake, the return of light and hope and spirits, and the campers run-

[2]*Ubangi* member of a group of people living in the Central African Republic. The women were known for using disks to extend their lips.

ning out in joy and relief to go swimming in the rain, their bright cries perpetuating the deathless joke about how they were getting simply drenched, and the children screaming with delight at the new sensation of bathing in the rain, and the joke about getting drenched linking the generations in a strong indestructible chain. And the comedian who waded in carrying an umbrella.

When the others went swimming, my son said he was going in, too. He pulled his dripping trunks from the line where they had hung all through the shower and wrung them out. Languidly, and with no thought of going in, I watched him, his hard little body, skinny and bare, saw him wince slightly as he pulled up around his vitals the small, soggy, icy garment. As he buckled the swollen belt, suddenly my groin felt the chill of death.

Understanding and Analysis

1. After you have read this essay once, explain why White chooses to end the first paragraph with the word "haunts." What are the several implications of this word? White says that the "dual existence" makes him feel "creepy" and "dizzy." How does White's sensation of a dual existence manifest itself? Have you ever experienced this sensation in relation to one or both of your parents?

2. Given the year that this essay was written, what might be one of the reasons White yearns for the "placidity" of the lake?

3. Contrast the pleasures of the lake with those of the sea as White describes them.

4. In the second paragraph, White notices that one thing "suddenly reminds you of another thing." Note the length and types of sentences White uses in this essay. How does the sentence structure contribute to the emphasis on memory?

5. List the changes White finds between 1904 when he first began going to Maine with his father and siblings and 1941 when he visits Maine again with his son. What kinds of change take place? Are any of them appealing to White?

6. Where is the first appearance of the word "illusion"? How does the difference between what is imagined and what is real compare to the difference between what is remembered and what exists when White returns? In other words, what are the roles of the imagination in this essay?

7. What is the purpose of the paragraph beginning "Summertime, oh summertime, pattern of life indelible"? Where in this paragraph can you find evidence of the extended metaphor to come?

8. What evidence do you find in the essay of "jollity and peace and goodness"? What kinds of discord or trouble does White remember from his earlier trips to Maine?

9. What is the extended metaphor White develops to make his point?

10. What is the role of nature in this essay? What is the role of comedy? The last sentence is one of White's best known. What do you think makes it effective?

Comparison

1. This essay is one of the most popular of the century. Read some of the essays written in the late thirties and early forties. Why do you think readers have found this essay so appealing?

2. Both Woolf, in "Death of the Moth," and White each depict death amid a background of the natural world. Compare and contrast their versions of death and nature.

3. Read other biographical essays in this collection. What characteristics, if any, do these essays share? What makes them work as essays?

4. Read Hughes's "Salvation." What connections, if any, do you see between these two essays?

5. Read "Landscape and Narrative" by Barry Lopez. Do you see any characteristics described by Lopez in the essays by Hughes and White?

6. Read Ellison's "The Way It Is." What privileges does White enjoy during these years? Does he have anything in common with the people Ellison describes?

Virginia Woolf

THE DEATH OF THE MOTH (1942)

MOTHS THAT FLY by day are not properly to be called moths; they do not excite that pleasant sense of dark autumn nights and ivy-blossom which the commonest yellow-underwing asleep in the shadow of the curtain never fails to rouse in us. They are hybrid creatures, neither gay like butterflies nor sombre like their own species. Nevertheless the present specimen, with his narrow hay-coloured wings, fringed with a tassel of the same colour, seemed to be content with life. It was a pleasant morning, mid-September, mild, benignant, yet with a keener breath than that of the summer months. The plough was already scoring the field opposite the window, and where the share had been, the earth was pressed flat and gleamed with moisture. Such vigour came rolling in from the fields and the down beyond that it was difficult to keep the eyes strictly turned upon the book. The rooks too were keeping one of their annual festivities; soaring round the tree tops until it looked as if a vast net with thousands of black knots in it had been cast up into the air; which, after a few moments sank slowly down upon the trees until every twig seemed to have a knot at the end of it. Then, suddenly, the net would be thrown into the air again in a wider circle this time, with the utmost clamour and vociferation, as though to be thrown into the air and settle slowly down upon the tree tops were a tremendously exciting experience.

The same energy which inspired the rooks, the ploughmen, the horses, and even, it seemed, the lean bare-backed downs, sent the moth fluttering from side to side of his square of the window-pane. One could not help watching him. One was, indeed, conscious of a queer feeling of pity for him. The possibilities of pleasure seemed that morning so enormous and so various that to have only a moth's part in life, and a day moth's at that, appeared a hard fate, and his zest in enjoying his meagre opportunities to the full, pathetic. He flew vigorously to one corner of his compartment, and, after waiting there a second, flew across to the other. What remained for him but to fly to a third corner and then to a fourth? That was all he could do, in spite of the size of the downs, the width of the sky, the far-off smoke of houses, and the romantic voice, now and then, of a steamer out at sea. What he could do he did. Watching him, it seemed as if a fibre, very thin but pure, of the enormous energy of the world had been thrust into his frail and diminutive body. As often as he crossed the pane, I could fancy that a thread of vital light became visible. He was little or nothing but life.

Yet, because he was so small, and so simple a form of the energy that was rolling in at the open window and driving its way through so many narrow and intricate corridors in my own brain and in those of other human beings, there was something marvellous as well as pathetic about him. It was as if someone had taken a tiny bead of pure life and decking it as lightly as possible with down and feathers, had set it dancing and zigzagging to show us the true nature of life. Thus displayed one could not get over the strangeness of it. One is apt to forget all about life, seeing it humped and bossed and garnished and cumbered so that it has to move with the greatest circumspection and dignity. Again, the thought of all that life might have been had he been born in any other shape caused one to view his simple activities with a kind of pity.

After a time, tired by his dancing apparently, he settled on the window ledge in the sun, and, the queer spectacle being at an end, I forgot about him. Then, looking up, my eye was caught by him. He was trying to resume his dancing, but seemed either so stiff or so awkward that he could only flutter to the bottom of the window-pane; and when he tried to fly across it he failed. Being intent on other matters I watched these futile attempts for a time without thinking, unconsciously waiting for him to resume his flight, as one waits for a machine, that has stopped momentarily, to start again without considering the reason of its failure. After perhaps a seventh attempt he slipped from the wooden ledge and fell, fluttering his wings, on to his back on the window sill. The helplessness of his attitude roused me. It flashed upon me that he was in difficulties; he could no longer raise himself; his legs struggled vainly. But, as I stretched out a pencil, meaning to help him to right himself, it came over me that the failure and awkwardness were the approach of death. I laid the pencil down again.

The legs agitated themselves once more. I looked as if for the enemy against which he struggled. I looked out of doors. What had happened there? Presumably it was midday, and work in the fields had stopped. Stillness and quiet had replaced the previous animation. The birds had taken themselves off to feed in the brooks. The horses stood still. Yet the power was there all the same, massed outside indifferent, impersonal, not attending to anything in particular. Somehow it was opposed to the little hay-coloured moth. It was useless to try to do anything. One could only watch the extraordinary efforts made by those tiny legs against an oncoming doom which could, had it chosen, have submerged an entire city, not merely a city, but masses of human beings; nothing, I knew had any chance against death. Nevertheless after a pause of exhaustion the legs fluttered again. It was superb this last protest, and so frantic that he succeeded at last in righting himself. One's sympathies, of course, were all on the side of life. Also, when there was nobody to care or to know, this gigantic effort on the part of an insignificant little moth, against a power of such magnitude, to retain what no one else valued or desired to keep, moved one strangely. Again, somehow, one saw life, a pure bead. I lifted the pencil again, useless though I knew it to be. But even as I did so, the unmistakable tokens of death showed themselves. The body relaxed, and instantly grew stiff. The struggle was over. The insignificant little creature now knew death. As I looked at the dead moth, this minute wayside triumph of so great a force over so mean an antagonist filled me with wonder.

Just as life had been strange a few minutes before, so death was now as strange. The moth having righted himself now lay most decently and uncomplainingly composed. O yes, he seemed to say, death is stronger than I am.

Understanding and Analysis

1. How does Woolf classify and describe the moth in the first three sentences? What words suggest a scientific analysis of the moth and what words suggest an emotional reaction to the moth?

2. What metaphors can you find in the first two paragraphs?

3. Why does Woolf pity the moth in the first three paragraphs?

4. What details from the first two paragraphs does Woolf return to in her description of the scene outside her window in the last paragraph?

5. In this essay Woolf depicts nature as seen from behind a barrier, a window. In what ways does this barrier frame or shape the vision of nature she presents?

6. Woolf's prose is often called poetic. What characteristics usually found in poetry can you find here?

7. Does Woolf pity the moth at the end of the essay?

Comparison

1. Read Dillard's essay. Compare Dillard's depiction of the struggles of the deer with Woolf's description of the struggles of the moth. Compare also the reactions of the two women. How do they differ? In what ways, if at all, are the reactions similar?

2. Compare and contrast E. B. White's description of nature with that of Woolf and Dillard.

3. Read the essay by Lopez. Does his understanding of the relationship between landscape and story help you to interpret Woolf's essay? If so, how? If not, why not?

Ralph Ellison
(1914–1994)

Born in Oklahoma City on March 1, 1914, Ralph Waldo Ellison spent the early part of his life concentrating not on writing literature, but on making music. Although his father, who played the drums and named him after Ralph Waldo Emerson, died when his son was three, Ellison remembered attending a musical rehearsal with him. Ralph himself began to play music at the age of eight, when he joined the school band and took up the mellophone, an instrument similar to the French horn. Later his instrument of choice was the trumpet.

Aspiring to be a Renaissance man, Ellison also read, and he took great interest in *Esquire* magazine, which featured pieces by Ernest Hemingway, and in *Vanity Fair*, which he credited with exposing him to the "avant garde." Ellison's interest in literature was intensified by the experience of reading T. S. Eliot's *The Waste Land* at the Tuskegee Institute, where he enrolled on scholarship in 1933 to major in music. In a 1965 interview with Richard Kostelanetz, Ellison remarked that one of the things that particularly excited him about *The Waste Land* was Eliot's "style of improvisation—that quality of improvising which is very close to jazz." He elaborated on the importance of Eliot's poem in a 1974 interview with John Hersey, explaining that "it was Eliot's *Waste Land*, with its footnotes, that made me become fascinated with how writing was written."

In the summer of 1936, he traveled to New York to study sculpture, and in 1937, he went to Dayton, Ohio, for his mother's funeral and remained there for several months with his brother, hunting to earn money, and sometimes sleeping in a car. On his first day back in New York, he met Langston Hughes, who in turn served as his connection to Richard Wright, then a poet. "At that time," Ellison told Hersey, "I had no thought of becoming a writer myself— my world was music." Nevertheless, at the behest of Richard Wright, Ellison did write, first a book review and then a short story, both for the magazine *New Challenge*, which Wright edited. Only the review was published, because the magazine fell apart, but once Ellison had gotten a taste of writing, he wanted to continue.

Although he never returned to Tuskegee, Ellison had learned much about artistic labor from the time he spent there. Talking with Hersey, he recalled that he would get up "early in the morning—and this was required of brass instrument players—and I'd blow sustained tones for an hour. I knew the other students used to hate it, but this developed embouchure, breath control, and so on. And I approached writing in the same way." Engrossed with "how writing was written," he worked on the Federal Writers' Project, and he returned to the novels of Mark Twain, also studying the prefaces of Henry James and reading essays about writing by Joseph Conrad and others. He published his first short story, "Slick Gonna Learn," in 1939, and he became the editor of *Negro Quarterly* in 1942.

Denied admission to the Navy's band, Ellison joined the Merchant Marine in 1943, serving as a cook. In 1944, while preparing to go to sea, he married. Upon his return in 1945, he began work on *Invisible Man* (1952), which won the National Book Award in 1953 and earned him lasting renown. He delivered lectures in Germany and Austria in 1954 and at Bard College in 1958. A visiting professor at the University of Chicago in 1961, he also accepted visiting positions from Rutgers and Yale. In 1964 he published *Shadow and Act*, a collection of essays, and he took a permanent position at New York University in 1970. Over the next ten years, he was awarded honorary doctoral degrees from numerous universities. He died on April 16, 1994.

Critical assessments of *Invisible Man* have varied over the years. Many have noted the influences of music, literature, symbolism, and surrealism on Ellison's remarkable prose, but the subject of critical debate has been the status of *Invisible Man* as a "black" novel. During the 1960s, many critics charged that the novel was insufficiently radical and written by an Uncle Tom. Ellison deeply resented the insistence that African-American artists produce militant treatises on race. In an article that appeared in the *New York Times Magazine* in 1966, John Corry quotes Ellison on this issue:

> Ellison accused [Irving] Howe of trying to 'designate the role which Negro writers are to play more rigidly than any Southern politician—and for the best of reasons. We must express "black anger" and "clenched militancy"; most of all we should not become too interested in the problems of the art of literature, even though it is through these that we seek our individual identities. And between writing well and being ideologically militant, we must choose militancy. Well, it all sounds quite familiar and I fear the social order which it forecasts more than I do that of Mississippi.'

Despite objections to his racial politics, Ralph Ellison and *Invisible Man* hold an enduring place in American literature.

In 1999, Ellison's literary executor, John F. Callahan, published *Juneteenth*, a novel based on notes, pages, and chapters Ellison had written over the last twenty years of his life. The book is not Ellison's as he would have wanted it, but novelist and critic Robert Stone believes that "[a]ll in all, the work will sustain and enlarge Ellison's artistic reputation." Stone writes, "for the sum of his work and the grandeur and generosity of his vision, I believe his country and the literary community of which he was so important a part owe him more than has been acknowledged."

THE WAY IT IS (1942)

THE BOY LOOKED at me through the cracked door and stood staring with his large eyes until his mother came and invited me in. It was an average Harlem apartment, cool now with the shift in the fall weather. The room was clean and furnished with the old-fashioned furniture found so often up our way, two old upholstered chairs and a divan upon a faded blue and red rug. It was painfully clean, and the furniture crowded the narrow room.

"Sit right there, sir," the woman said. "It's where Wilbur use to sit before he went to camp, it's pretty comfortable."

I watched her ease herself tiredly upon the divan, the light from the large red lamp reflected upon her face from the top of a mirrored side table.

She must have been fifty, her hair slightly graying. The portrait of a young soldier smiled back from the top of a radio cabinet beside her.

She pointed. "That's my boy Wilbur right there," she said proudly. "He's a sergeant."

"Wilbur's got a medal for shooting so good," the boy said.

"You just be quiet and go eat your supper," she said. "All you can think about is guns and shooting." She spoke with the harsh tenderness so often used by Negro mothers.

The boy went, reluctantly opening the door. The odor of peas and rice and pork chops drifted through.

"Who was it, Tommy?" shrilled a voice on the other side.

"You two be quiet in there and eat your supper now," Mrs. Jackson called. "Them two just keeps my hands full. They just get into something *all* the time. I was coming up the street the other day and like to got the fright of my life. There was Tommy hanging on the back of a streetcar! But didn't I tan his bottom! I bet he won't even *look* at a street-car for a long, long time. It ain't really that he's a *bad* child, it's just that he tries to do what he sees the other boys do. I wanted to send both him and his sister away to camp for the summer, but things was so tight this year that I couldn't do it. Raising kids in Harlem nowadays is more than a notion."

As is true so often in Negro American life, Mrs. Jackson, the mother, is the head of her family. Her husband had died several years ago; the smaller children were babies. She had kept going by doing domestic work and had kept the family together with the help of the older boy.

There is a quiet courage about Mrs. Jackson. And yet now and then the clenching and unclenching of her work-hardened fingers betray an anxiety that does not register in her face. I offer to wait until after she has eaten, but she says no, that she is too tired right now and she would rather talk than eat.

"You finding the writing business any better since the war?" she asked.

"I'm afraid not," I said.

"Is that so? Well, I don't know nothing about the writing business. I just know that don't many colored go in for it. But I guess like everything else, some folks is doing good while others ain't. The other day I was over on 126th Street and saw them dispos-sessing a lawyer! Yes, sir, it was like back in the thirties. Things piled all over the side-walk, the Negroes a-hanging out of the windows, and the poor man rushing around try-ing to get his stuff off the streets before it got dark, and everything."

I remembered the incident myself, having passed through the street that afternoon. Files, chest of drawers, bedsteads, tables and barrels had been piled along the sidewalk; with pink, blue and white mattresses and bundles of table linen and bedclothing piled on top. And the crowd had been as she described: some indignant, some curious, and all talking in subdued tones so as not to offend the evicted family. Law books had been piled upon the sidewalk near where a black and white kitten—and these are no writer's details—played games with itself in the coils of an upright bedspring. I told her I had seen the incident.

"Lord," she said. "And did you see all those law books he had? Looks like to me that anybody with all those books of law oughtn't to never get dispossessed.

"I was dispossessed, myself, back in thirty-seven, when we were all out of work. And they threatened me once since Wilbur's been in the Army. But I stood up for my rights and when the government sent the check we pulled through. Anybody's liable to get dis-possessed though." She said it defensively.

"Just how do you find it otherwise?" I asked.

"Things is mighty tight, son . . . You'll have to excuse me for calling you 'son,' because I suspect you must be just about Wilbur's age."

She sat back abruptly. "How come you not in the Army?" she asked.

"I've a wife and dependents," I said.

"I see," She pondered. "Wilbur would have got married too, but he was helping me with the kids."

"That's the way it goes," I said.

"Things is tight," she said again. "With food so high and everything I sometimes don't know what's going to happen. Then, too, with Wilbur in the Army we naturally misses the money he use to bring in."

She regarded me shrewdly. "So you want to know about how we're doing? Don't you live in Harlem?"

"Oh, yes, but I want to know what *you* think about it."

"So's you can write it up?"

"Some of it, sure. But I won't use your name."

"Oh I don't care 'bout that. I *want* them to know how I feel."

She became silent. Then, "You didn't tell me where you live, you know," she said cagily. I had to laugh and she laughed too.

"I live up near Amsterdam Avenue," I said.

"You telling me the truth?"

"Honest."

"And is your place a nice one?"

"Just average. You know how they go," I said.

"I bet you live up there on Sugar Hill."

"Not me," I said.

"And you're sure you're not one of these investigators?"

"Of course not."

"I bet you are too." She smiled.

I shook my head and she laughed.

"They always starting something new," she said. "You can't keep up with them."

But now she seemed reassured and settled down to talk, her hands clasped loosely in her lap against the checkered design of her dress.

"Well, we're carrying on somehow. I'm still working and I manage to keep the young uns in school, and I pays the rent too. I guess maybe it would be a little better if the government would send the checks on time . . ."

She paused and pointed across the room to the picture of a young woman. "And it would be even better if Mary, that's my next oldest after Wilbur—if she could get some of that defense training so she could get a job what pays decent money. But don't look like she's going to get anything. She was out to the Western Electric plant in Kearney, New Jersey, the other day and they give her some kind of test, but that was the end of that."

"Did she pass the test?" I asked.

"Sure she passed. But they just put her name down on a card and told her they would keep her in mind. They always do that. They ask her a lot of questions, then they want to know if she ever had any experience in running machines, and when she says she ain't, they just take down her name. Now where is a colored girl going to get any experience in running all these kinds of machines they never even seen before?"

When I could not answer she threw up her hands.

"Well, there you have it, they got you any which way you turn. A few gets jobs, but most don't."

"Things are much better outside of New York," I said.

"So I hear," she said. "Guess if I was younger I'd take the kids and move to Jersey or up to Connecticut, where I hear there's some jobs for colored. Or even down South. Only I keep hearing about the trouble they're having down there. And I don't want the kids to grow up down there no-how. Had enough of that when I was a kid . . ."

"Have any of your friends gotten work through the F.E.P.C.?"

She thought for a moment.

"No, son. It seems to me that that committee is doing something everywhere but here in New York. Maybe that's why it's so bad for us—and you know it's bad 'cause you're colored yourself."

As I heard the clatter of dishes coming from the kitchen, her face suddenly assumed an outraged expression.

"Now you take my sister's boy, William. God bless his poor soul. William went to the trade schools and learned all about machines. He got so he could take any kind of machine apart and fix it and put it together again. He was machine-crazy! But he was a smart boy and a good boy. He got good marks in school too. But when he went to get a job in one of those factories where they make war machines of some kind, they wouldn't take him 'cause he was colored—*and they told him so!*"

She paused for breath, a red flush dyeing her skin. The tinted portrait of a brown mother holding a brown, shiny-haired baby posed madonna-like from a calendar above her head.

"Well, when they wouldn't take him some of the folks over to the church told him to take his case to the F.E.P.C., and he did. But they had so many cases and it took so long that William got discouraged and joined up in the Merchant Marine. That poor boy was just so disgusted that he said that he would have enlisted in the Army, only that his mamma's got two little ones like I have. So he went out on that boat 'cause it paid good money and a good bonus. It was real good money and he helped his mamma a heap. But it didn't last long before one of those submarines sunk the boat."

Her eyes strayed to the window, where a line of potted plants crowded the sill; a profusion of green things, slowly becoming silhouettes in the fading light. Snake plants, English ivy, and others, a potato plant in a glass jar, its vines twining around a cross of wood and its thousand thread-fine roots pushing hungrily against the wall of glass. A single red bloom pushed above the rest, and in one corner a corn plant threatened to touch the ceiling from the floor with its blade-like leaves.

The light was fading and her voice had slipped into the intense detachment of recent grief. "It was just about four months yesterday," she said, "He was such a fine boy. Every body liked William."

She shook her head silently, her fingers gripping her folded arms as she swallowed tensely.

"It hurts to think about it," she said, getting up and snapping on another light, revealing a child's airplane model beneath the table. "Well, the folks from his union is being very nice to my sister, the whites as well as the colored. And you know," she added, leaning toward me, "it really makes you feel a little better when they come round—the white ones, I mean—and really tries to help. Like some of these ole relief investigators who come in wanting to run your life for you, but really like they interested in you. Something like colored folks in a way. We used to get after William for being with white folks so much, but these sure have shown themselves to be real friends."

She stared at me as though it was a fact which she deeply feared to accept.

"Some of them is going to try and see that my sister gets some sort of defense work. But what I'm trying to tell you is that it's a sin and a shame that a fine boy like William had to go fooling round on them ships when ever since he was a little ole boy he'd been crazy about machines."

"But don't you think that the Merchant Marine is helping to win the war?" I said. "It takes brave men to go out there, and they've done a lot."

"Sure they have," she said. "Sure they have. But I'm not talking about that. Anybody could do what they had him doing on that boat. Anybody can wait tables who's got sense enough to keep his fingernails clean! Waiting tables, when he could *make* things on a machine!

"You see that radio there? Well, William made that radio. It ain't no store set, no, sir, even though it looks like one. William made it for the kids. Made everything but the cabinet, and you can hear way down to Cuba and Mexico with it. And to think of that boy! Oh, it makes me so mad I don't know what to do! He ought to be here right now helping his mamma and lil brother and sister. But what can you do? You educated, son, you one of our educated Negroes that's been to college and everything. Now you tell me, *what can we do?*" She paused. "I'm a colored woman, and colored women can take it. I can hit the chillies to the subway every morning and stand in the white folks' kitchen all day long, but so much is happening in the world that I don't know which way to turn. First it's my sister's boy and then they sends my own boy down to Fort Bragg. I tells you I'm even afraid to open Wilbur's letters, some of the things he tells is so awful. I'm even afraid to open letters that the *government* sends sometimes about his insurance or something like that, 'cause I'm afraid it might be a message that Wilbur's been beaten up or killed by some of those white folks down there. Then I gets so mad I don't know what to do. I use to pray, but praying don't do no good. And too, like the union folks was telling us when we was so broken up about William, we got to fight the big Hitler over yonder even with all the little Hitlers over here. I wish they'd hurry up and send Wilbur on out of the country 'cause then maybe my mind would know some ease. Lord!" she sighed. "If it wasn't so serious I'd break down and laugh at my ownself."

She smiled now and the tension eased from her face and she leaned back against the divan and laughed. Then she became serious again.

"But, son, you really can't laugh about it. Not honestly laugh like you can about some things. It reminds me of that crazy man what's always running up and down the streets up here. You know, the one who's always hollering at the cars and making out like he's throwing bombs?"

"Of course, I've seen him often," I said.

"Sure you have. Well, I use to laugh at that poor man when he'd start acting the fool—you know how it is, you feel sorry for him but you can't help but laugh. They say he got that way in the last war. Well, I can understand him better now. Course I ain't had no bombs bursting in my ears like he had. But yet and still, with things pulling me thisaway and thataway, I sometimes feel that I'm going to go screaming up and down the streets just like that poor fellow does."

"He's shell-shocked," I said. "Sometimes I've seen him talking and acting just as normal as anyone."

"Is that so?" she said. "I always thought it was funny he never got hit by a car. I've seen them almost hit him, but he goes right back. One day I heard a man say, Lord, if that crazy fellow really had some bombs he'd get rid of every car in Harlem!"

We laughed and I prepared to go.

"Sorry you found me so gloomy today, son. But you know, things have a way of just piling up these days and I just had to talk about them. Anyway, you asked for me to tell you what I thought."

She walked with me to the door. Street lamps glowed on the avenue, lighting the early dark. The after-school cries of children drifted dimly in from the sidewalk.

She shivered close beside me.

"It's getting chilly already," she said. "I'm wondering what's going to happen this winter about the oil and coal situation. These ole holes we have to live in can get mighty cold. Now can't they though?"

I agreed.

"A friend of mine that moved up on Amsterdam Avenue about a month ago wanted to know why I don't move out of Harlem. So I told her it wouldn't do no good to move 'cause anywhere they let us go gets to be Harlem right on. I done moved round too much not to know that. Oh yes!"

She shook her head knowingly.

"Harlem's like that old song says:

> It's so high you can't get over it
> So low, you can't get under it,
> And so wide, you can't get round it . . .

"That's the way it really is," she said. "Well, good-bye, son."

And as I went down the dimmed-out street the verse completed itself in my mind, *You must come through by the living gate . . .*

So there you have Mrs. Jackson. And that's the way "it really is" for her and many like her who are searching for that gate of freedom. In the very texture of their lives there is confusion, war-made confusion. And the problem is to get around, over, under and through this confusion. They do not ask for a lighter share of necessary war sacrifices than other Americans have to bear. But they do ask for equal reasons to believe that their sacrifices are worth-while, and they *do* want to be rid of the heavy resentment and bitterness which has been theirs for long before the war.

Forced in normal times to live at standards much lower than those the war has brought to the United States generally, they find it emotionally difficult to give their attention to the war. The struggle for existence constitutes a war in itself. The Mrs. Jacksons of Harlem offer one of the best arguments for the stabilization of prices and the freezing of rents. For twenty-five percent of those still on relief come from our five percent of New York's population. Mrs. Jackson finds it increasingly difficult to feed her children. She must pay six cents more on the dollar for food than do the mothers of similar-income sections of the city. And with the prospect of a heatless winter, Harlem, with its poor housing and high tuberculosis death rate, will know an increase of hardship.

It is an old story. Touch any phase of urban living in our democracy and its worst aspects are to be found in Harlem. Our housing is the poorest, and our rents the highest. Our people are the sickest, and Harlem Hospital the most over-crowded and understaffed. Our unemployment is the greatest, and our cost of food the most exorbitant. Our crime the most understandable and easily corrected, but the policemen sent among us the most brutal. Our desire to rid the world of fascism the most burning, and the obstacles placed in our way the most frustrating. Our need to see the war as a struggle between democracy and fascism the most intense and our temptation to interpret it as a "color" war the most compelling. Our need to believe in the age of the "common man" the most hope-inspiring, and our reasons to doubt that it will include us the most disheartening (this is no Whitmanesque catalogue of democratic exultations, while more than anything else we wish that it could be). And that's the way it is.

Many of Mrs. Jackson's neighbors are joining in the fight to freeze rents and for the broadening of the F.E.P.C., for Negroes and all other Americans. Their very lives demand that they back the President's stabilization program. That they must be victorious is one of the necessities upon which our democratic freedom rests. The Mrs. Jacksons cannot make the sacrifices necessary to participate in a total war if the conditions under which they live, the very ground on which they must fight, continues its offensive against them. Nor is this something to be solved by propaganda. Morale grows out of realities, not out of words alone. Only concrete action will be effective—lest irritation and confusion turn into exasperation, and exasperation change to disgust and finally into anti-war sentiment (and there is such a danger). Mrs. Jackson's reality must be democratized so that she may clarify her thinking and her emotions. And that's the way it really is.

Understanding and Analysis

1. In the first paragraph, Ellison repeats the fact that Mrs. Jackson's home was clean. Why do you think he does that? Who do you suppose was his audience of readers when this essay was first published in *New Masses*, a paper of the extreme left, in October of 1942?

2. How does Ellison show the reader that there are variations of status within the Harlem community?

3. Describe Mrs. Jackson's character, based on her own words and those of the interviewer.

4. Who are the other members of the family? What was each doing at the time of the interview?

5. What are some of the problems that these people faced in October, 1942? Which are directly connected to the war and which are not?

6. Find all references to white people in the essay. What is Mrs. Jackson's attitude toward white people?

7. Ellison alternates between long passages directly quoting the words of Mrs. Jackson, shorter passages of dialogue between her and the interviewer, and passages of description and analysis. What details do we learn about the interviewer from his side of the conversation? How does his voice differ from that of Mrs. Jackson? What can you tell about him from his description of specific items in the house? What do these descriptive details reveal about Mrs. Jackson and her family?

8. What is the reason the interviewer gives for not being in the army himself? Read the biography of Ellison in this text to find out what Ellison did during the war. Does this information change your attitude toward the interviewer and if so how?

Comparison

1. What similarities do you see between this essay and the two by Panter-Downes? What goals do the two authors share? How are their goals different? What is your evidence?

2. Compare Ellison's essay to Orwell's "A Hanging." Does anything in either essay strike you as fictional? What evidence can you find to support your opinions?

3. Read Angelou's "Graduation." What issues do both essays address?

4. Compare the views presented by Angelou and Ellison to those found in the essay by Du Bois. What similarities and differences do you see?

5. Read the essay by Podhoretz. What, if anything, do these two authors have in common?

Ernie Pyle
(1900–1945)

Born August 3, 1900, Ernest Taylor Pyle grew up on a farm in rural Indiana, where he developed the speech patterns that later characterized his "homey" journalistic style. When he was a teenager, his father took him to see the Indianapolis 500, an event that inspired a lasting interest not only in racing, but in heroes. After the United States entered World War I, Pyle wanted to leave high school to join the fighting; his parents forbade him, so he waited until graduation and then joined the Naval Reserve. The war ended before he finished training.

In 1919, Pyle enrolled at Indiana University, taking up journalism after a friend suggested, "Well, why not . . . ? At least you don't have to add and subtract." By the summer after his junior year, Pyle was the editor-in-chief of the *Indiana Daily Student*, but he did not finish college. In 1923, he took a job with a paper in La Porte, soon moving on to a paper in Washington, D.C. There he met his friend and future biographer, Lee Miller, as well as his future wife, Jerry Siebolds. Ernie and Jerry married in 1925, and a year later, they quit their jobs to drive around the country. At Miller's invitation, Pyle returned to Washington to serve as telegraph editor for the *Washington News*. In 1928, he started writing a column on aviators. For his subject matter, he prowled local airports and military air stations, scooping several stories and gaining a reputation among the likes of Amelia Earhart. Pyle reluctantly ended his aviation column when he was offered the position of managing editor.

After several exhausting years of editing, Pyle requested an assignment as a roving reporter, and, in 1935, Ernie and Jerry headed out across the country again. According to Miller, Pyle's "instructions were to drive wherever he liked, [and] write six columns a week about anything that interested him." In his columns, he covered topics ranging from his childhood in Indiana to a leper colony in Hawaii. He asked Miller to stop editing the "little" mid-western phrases out of his writing, the "homey touch" that gave his prose a "swing and an ease for reading." The columns came to be very successful, marking the beginning of Pyle's national following and his fame.

By the time World War II broke out, Jerry was suffering from serious psychological and physical problems; nevertheless, she agreed that Ernie should go overseas to cover the war. He left in 1940, and his coverage of the bombing of London generated great interest. He returned to the U.S. in 1941, shortly after his mother's death, and plans were soon underway for a book called *Ernie Pyle in England*. Pyle took a leave of absence to spend time in New Mexico with Jerry. In 1942, they agreed to try a divorce, with a promise of remarriage if she triumphed over her depression.

Pyle went back to Europe a veritable celebrity among the troops. Interested as he was in the famous heroes, the race car drivers and the aviators, he was also devoted to the common heroes in the infantry: "I love the infantry because they are the underdogs. They are the mud-rain-frost-and-wind boys. They have no comforts, and they even learn to live without the necessities. And in the end they are the guys that wars can't be won without." In the spring of 1943, while Pyle was still abroad, he and Jerry remarried; a friend stood in for him at the ceremony. Pyle returned to the States in the fall, finding himself in popular demand with interviewers and even the First Lady, who was so impressed with his second book, *Here Is Your War*, that she invited him to tea. He returned to the field in the winter, but he worried that he had "lost his touch." Reading the piece on Captain Waskow included in this anthology, an AP reporter remarked, "If this is a sample from a guy who has lost his touch, then the rest of us had better go home."

In 1944, Lee Miller nominated Ernie Pyle for a Pullitzer Prize, which he won. Plans were underway for his third book, *Brave Men*, as well as for a movie, and he appeared on the cover of *Time*. His personal life seemed to run in parallel opposition to his professional life; Jerry attempted suicide and began shock treatment in a hospital where Pyle was not allowed to visit her. He was awarded two honorary doctorates before he left the States for the last time. On April 18, 1945, he was killed while riding in a jeep in Okinawa, shot in the temple by an enemy gunner.

A few months before his death, Pyle received a letter from General Dwight Eisenhower, asking to join in Pyle's efforts to spread the word about the common soldier. "I have come to the conclusion," Eisenhower wrote, "that education along this one simple line might do a lot toward promoting future reluctance to engage in war." If Eisenhower's theory had been correct, Pyle might indeed have prevented future wars with his devotion to the infantrymen who fought in World War II. Soldiers respected him, and officers said that unlike other journalists, he didn't try to direct conversations in order to get material for his columns; he sat back and listened, drawing his materials from the stories traded among the men. His prose style, like his subject matter, has its own unaffected elegance and power, which is simple but never simplistic. With his columns, Ernie Pyle moved an entire generation of readers and writers, prompting John Steinbeck to write, "There are really two wars and they haven't much to do with each other. There is the war of maps and logistics, of campaigns...and that is General Marshall's war. Then there is the war of homesick, weary, funny, violent, common men, who wash their socks in their helmets...and that is Ernie Pyle's war."

THE DEATH OF CAPTAIN WASKOW (1944)

AT THE FRONT lines in Italy, *January 10, 1944*—In this war I have known a lot of officers who were loved and respected by the soldiers under them. But never have I crossed the trail of any man as beloved as Capt. Henry T. Waskow of Belton, Texas.

Capt. Waskow was a company commander in the 36th Division. He had led his company since long before it left the States. He was very young, only in his middle twenties, but he carried in him a sincerity and gentleness that made people want to be guided by him.

"After my own father, he came next," a sergeant told me.

"He always looked after us," a soldier said. "He'd go to bat for us every time."

"I've never knowed him to do anything unfair," another one said.

I was at the foot of the mule trail the night they brought Capt. Waskow's body down. The moon was nearly full at the time, and you could see far up the trail, and even part way across the valley below. Soldiers made shadows in the moonlight as they walked.

Dead men had been coming down the mountain all evening, lashed onto the backs of mules. They came lying belly-down across the wooden pack-saddles, their heads hanging down on the left side of the mule, their stiffened legs sticking out awkwardly from the other side, bobbing up and down as the mule walked.

The Italian mule-skinners were afraid to walk beside dead men, so Americans had to lead the mules down that night. Even the Americans were reluctant to unlash and lift off the bodies at the bottom, so an officer had to do it himself, and ask others to help.

The first one came early in the morning. They slid him down from the mule and stood him on his feet for a moment, while they got a new grip. In the half light he might have been merely a sick man standing there, leaning on the others. Then they laid him on the ground in the shadow of the low stone wall alongside the road.

I don't know who that first one was. You feel small in the presence of dead men, and ashamed at being alive, and you don't ask silly questions.

We left him there beside the road, that first one, and we all went back into the cowshed and sat on water cans or lay on the straw, waiting for the next batch of mules.

Somebody said the dead soldier had been dead for four days, and then nobody said anything more about it. We talked soldier talk for an hour or more. The dead man lay all alone outside in the shadow of the low stone wall.

Then a soldier came into the cowshed and said there were some more bodies outside. We went out into the road. Four mules stood there, in the moonlight, in the road where the trail came down off the mountain. The soldiers who led them stood there waiting. "This one is Captain Waskow," one of them said quietly.

Two men unlashed his body from the mule and lifted it off and laid it in the shadow beside the low stone wall. Other men took the other bodies off. Finally there were five lying end to end in a long row, alongside the road. You don't cover up dead men in the combat zone. They just lie there in the shadows until somebody else comes after them.

The unburdened mules moved off to their olive orchard. The men in the road seemed reluctant to leave. They stood around, and gradually one by one I could sense them moving close to Capt. Waskow's body. Not so much to look, I think, as to say something in finality to him, and to themselves. I stood close by and I could hear.

One soldier came and looked down, and he said out loud, "God damn it." That's all he said, and then he walked away. Another one came. He said, "God damn it to hell anyway." He looked down for a few last moments, and then he turned and left.

Another man came; I think he was an officer. It was hard to tell officers from men in the half light, for all were bearded and grimy dirty. The man looked down into the dead captain's face, and then he spoke directly to him, as though he were alive. He said: "I'm sorry, old man."

Then a soldier came and stood beside the officer, and bent over, and he too spoke to his dead captain, not in a whisper but awfully tenderly, and he said:

"I sure am sorry, sir."

Then the first man squatted down, and he reached down and took the dead hand, and he sat there for a full five minutes, holding the dead hand in his own and looking intently into the dead face, and he never uttered a sound all the time he sat there.

And finally he put the hand down, and then reached up and gently straightened the points of the captain's shirt collar, and then he sort of rearranged the tattered edges of his uniform around the wound. And then he got up and walked away down the road in the moonlight, all alone.

After that the rest of us went back into the cowshed, leaving the five dead men lying in a line, end to end, in the shadow of the low stone wall. We lay down on the straw in the cowshed, and pretty soon we were all asleep.

Understanding and Analysis

1. Pyle was reporting from the front lines of the Sicilian campaign in 1944 when he wrote this essay. Like all his reports, it appeared in over 200 newspapers across the United States. From the opening sentence, what is the thesis of this report? How is it shaped for his readers back home?

2. What evidence does Pyle assemble to support his thesis?

3. What is the effect of words such as "never" and "every time" in the first few paragraphs?

4. Look for alliteration in this essay. What words recur? Why?

5. Look at the sentence structure. Which sentences are the longest? Which are the shortest? How do they contribute to the stark beauty Pyle evokes?

6. What is the effect of using "you" instead of "I" in some of the sentences? Why does "you" appear in these particular sentences?

7. What indications of class do you see in this essay? Look at the dialogue and at the military hierarchy. Look also at the description of the Italian mule-skinners.

8. Why does Captain Waskow's age matter? What relationships does Pyle depict between the dead soldiers and the living ones?

9. What details does Pyle omit? Why?

10. Does the fact that Pyle was killed in the spring of 1945 affect your opinion of his work? In what way?

11. The line between sentiment and sentimentality is fine. Do you think Pyle crosses that line? Explain your opinion.

Comparison

1. Read the reports on war written by Hemingway and Panter-Downes. What characteristics do these reports have in common with Pyle's report? Why?

2. Read Graves's description of the front lines. What are the similarities and differences in these two descriptions? Compare these views with war as depicted by Fussell. How is each one shaped for the original audience?

3. Read Gellhorn's description of civilians in the Vietnam War. Does she rely on any of the techniques Pyle uses? Compare their motives in reporting on their respective wars.

George Orwell

What Is Science? (1945)

IN LAST WEEK'S *Tribune,* there was an interesting letter from Mr J. Stewart Cook, in which he suggested that the best way of avoiding the danger of a "scientific hierarchy" would be to see to it that every member of the general public was, as far as possible, scientifically educated. At the same time, scientists should be brought out of their isolation and encouraged to take a greater part in politics and administration.

As a general statement, I think most of us would agree with this, but I notice that, as usual, Mr Cook does not define science, and merely implies in passing that it means certain exact sciences whose experiments can be made under laboratory conditions. Thus, adult education tends "to neglect scientific studies in favour of literary, economic and social subjects", economics and sociology not being regarded as branches of science, apparently. This point is of great importance. For the word science is at present used in at least two meanings, and the whole question of scientific education is obscured by the current tendency to dodge from one meaning to the other.

Science is generally taken as meaning either (a) the exact sciences, such as chemistry, physics, etc, or (b) a method of thought which obtains verifiable results by reasoning logically from observed fact.

If you ask any scientist, or indeed almost any educated person, "What is science?" you are likely to get an answer approximating to (b). In everyday life, however, both in speaking and in writing, when people say "science" they mean (a). Science means something that happens in a laboratory: the very word calls up a picture of graphs, test-tubes, balances, Bunsen burners, microscopes. A biologist, an astronomer, perhaps a psychologist or a mathematician, is described as a "man of science": no one would think of applying this term to a statesman, a poet, a journalist or even a philosopher. And those who tell us that the young must be scientifically educated mean, almost invariably, that they should be taught more about radioactivity, or the stars, or the physiology of their own bodies, rather than that they should be taught to think more exactly.

This confusion of meaning, which is partly deliberate, has in it a great danger. Implied in the demand for more scientific education is the claim that if one has been scientifically trained one's approach to *all* subjects will be more intelligent than if one had had no such training. A scientist's political opinions, it is assumed, his opinions on sociological questions, on morals, on philosophy, perhaps even on the arts, will be more valuable than those of a layman. The world, in other words, would be a better place if the scientists were in control of it. But a "scientist", as we have just seen, means in practice a specialist in one of the exact sciences. It follows that a chemist or a physicist, as such, is politically more intelligent than a poet or a lawyer, as such. And, in fact, there are already millions of people who do believe this.

But is it really true that a "scientist", in this narrower sense, is any likelier than other people to approach non-scientific problems in an objective way? There is not much reason for thinking so. Take one simple test—the ability to withstand nationalism. It is often loosely said that "Science is international", but in practice the scientific workers of all countries line up behind their own governments with fewer scruples than are felt by the writers and the artists. The German scientific community, as a whole, made no resistance to Hitler. Hitler may have ruined the long-term prospects of German science, but there were still plenty of gifted men to do the necessary research on such things as synthetic oil, jet planes, rocket projectiles and the atomic bomb. Without them the German war machine could never have been built up.

On the other hand, what happened to German literature when the Nazis came to power? I believe no exhaustive lists have been published, but I imagine that the number of German scientists—Jews apart—who voluntarily exiled themselves or were persecuted by the regime was much smaller than the number of writers and journalists. More sinister than this, a number of German scientists swallowed the monstrosity of "racial science". You can find some of the statements to which they set their names in Professor Brady's *The Spirit and Structure of German Fascism.*

But, in slightly different forms, it is the same picture everywhere. In England, a large proportion of our leading scientists accept the structure of capitalist society, as can be seen from the comparative freedom with which they are given knighthoods, baronetcies and even peerages. Since Tennyson, no English writer worth reading—one might, perhaps, make an exception of Sir Max Beerbohm—has been given a title. And those English scientists who do not simply accept the *status quo* are frequently Communists, which means that, however intellectually scrupulous they may be in their own line of work, they are ready to be uncritical and even dishonest on certain subjects. The fact is that a mere training in one or more of the exact sciences, even combined with very high gifts, is no guarantee of a humane or sceptical outlook. The physicists of half a dozen great nations, all feverishly and secretly working away at the atomic bomb, are a demonstration of this.

But does all this mean that the general public should *not* be more scientifically educated? On the contrary! All it means is that scientific education for the masses will do little good, and probably a lot of harm, if it simply boils down to more physics, more chemistry, more biology, etc to the detriment of literature and history. Its probable effect on the average human being would be to narrow the range of his thoughts and make him more than ever contemptuous of such knowledge as he did not possess: and his political reactions would probably be somewhat less intelligent than those of an illiterate peasant who retained a few historical memories and a fairly sound aesthetic sense.

Clearly, scientific education ought to mean the implanting of a rational, sceptical, experimental habit of mind. It ought to mean acquiring a *method*—a method that can be used on any problem that one meets—and not simply piling up a lot of facts. Put it in those words, and the apologist of scientific education will usually agree. Press him further, ask him to particularise, and somehow it always turns out that scientific education means more attention to the exact sciences, in others words—more *facts*. The idea that science means a way of looking at the world, and not simply a body of knowledge, is in practice strongly resisted. I think sheer professional jealousy is part of the reason for this. For if science is simply a method or an attitude, so that anyone whose thought-processes are sufficiently rational can in some sense be described as a scientist—what then becomes of the enormous prestige now enjoyed by the chemist, the physicist, etc. and his claim to be somehow wiser than the rest of us?

A hundred years ago, Charles Kingsley[1] described science as "making nasty smells in a laboratory." A year or two ago a young industrial chemist informed me, smugly, that he "could not see what was the use of poetry." So the pendulum swings to and fro, but it does not seem to me that one attitude is any better than the other. At the moment, science is on the upgrade, and so we hear, quite rightly, the claim that the masses should be scientifically educated: we do not hear, as we ought, the counterclaim that the scientists themselves would benefit by a little education. Just before writing this, I saw in an American magazine the statement that a number of British and American physicists refused from the start to do research on the atomic bomb, well knowing what use would be made of it. Here you have a group of sane men in the middle of a world of lunatics. And though no names were published, I think it would be a safe guess that all of them were people with some kind of general cultural background, some acquaintance with history or literature or the arts—in short, people whose interests were not, in the current sense of the word, purely scientific.

Understanding and Analysis

1. What, in your own words, are the two definitions of "science" that Orwell puts forth?

2. Orwell rightly claims that an expert in, let's say, chemistry is not necessarily better able than others "to approach non-scientific problems in an objective way." Why not?

---

[1]*Charles Kingsley* (1819–1875) English clergyman and novelist. An advocate of Christian socialism, he is best known for his children's book *The Water Babies* (1863). In 1859, he was made chaplain to Queen Victoria; the next year he was appointed professor of modern history at Cambridge, and in 1873 he was made canon of Westminster.

3. What does Orwell mean by "nationalism?"

4. Orwell makes a number of claims in this essay, for example that scientists are more likely than writers and artists to succumb to nationalism, that more writers than scientists "exiled themselves" from Germany, and that scientists are more willing than writers to accept capitalism. What evidence does he offer in each case?

5. Orwell clearly reveals his position in favor of socialism and against capitalism in this essay. Does Orwell here reveal "a humane or skeptical outlook"?

6. What prejudices is Orwell revealing?

7. What attitude does Orwell appear to have toward "facts"?

8. What is his evidence for his final claim about those scientists who refused to work on the bomb? What assumptions does Orwell make about the use of the bomb?

9. What is the effect on his argument of the quality of evidence Orwell presents?

10. Orwell takes a strong stand in this essay on several issues, including his preference for socialism over capitalism or communism, his preference for literature and the humanities over the sciences, and his certainty that dropping the bomb was an immoral and insane act. What role do facts play in his or your understanding of these issues? Can reasonable and skeptical people disagree? Why?

Comparison

1. Orwell writes about "professional jealousy" between scientists and others in the humanities. Do you think Forster exhibits such jealousy? Have you ever encountered that kind of jealousy?

2. Read the essays by Snow and Leavis. What evidence do they present to support their claims? Are any of Orwell's observations supported in their essays?

3. Read the essays by Thurber, Mairs, Eiseley, and Bronowski, in addition to those by Snow and Leavis. What are the problems each group has in seeing the other's point of view? Do any of these writers apply Orwell's second definition of science in the development of their arguments?

4. Read the essay by Ludwig Lewisohn. Do Lewisohn and Orwell agree about the political proclivities of writers and artists?

Winston Churchill
(1874–1965)

Born November 30, 1874, Winston Leonard Spencer Churchill was the elder son of Jennie Jerome, an American, and Lord Randolph Churchill, an Englishman and a member of the House of Commons. At the age of seven, two years after the birth of his brother, Jack, Churchill entered a boarding school called St. George's. Receiving visits from his governess, Mrs. Everest, Churchill longed for visits from his mother. ("My mother made a brilliant impression upon my childhood's life," he later wrote. "She shone for me like the evening star—I loved her dearly, but at a distance.") His performance in school, meanwhile, displeased his parents immensely. According to biographer Martin Gilbert, instructors for the first term deemed his composition skills "very feeble" and his spelling "about as bad as it well can be." For the second term, one wrote, "Began term well...but latterly has been *very* naughty!" After he entered the prestigious boarding school called Harrow in 1888, he became a more dedicated student, but he still inspired one of his masters to send a note home: "his forgetfulness, carelessness, unpunctuality, and irregularity in every way, have really been so serious, that I write to ask you, when he is at home to speak very gravely to him on the subject."

Around the age of fourteen, Churchill began to express an interest in politics. He remarked to an aunt, "If I had two lives I would be a soldier and a politician. But as there will be no war in my time I shall have to be a politician." Despite this resolution, he made great efforts to become a soldier, twice failing entrance exams to Sandhurst, the preeminent English military academy, before finally gaining admission at the age of 18. After his father's death in 1895, he became a Second Lieutenant in the Royal Army and left England within the year to go to Cuba ("Spanish forces were trying to crush a rebellion" there, according to Gilbert). Before Churchill departed, he arranged to send reports back to the *Daily Graphic*, a newspaper for which his father had once written, and thus began his twin career as soldier and journalist. In 1898, he published his first book, a collection of writings from India called *The Story of the Malakind Field Force: An Episode of Frontier War*. Receiving good reviews, he published *The River War* in 1899, and in 1900, *London to Ladysmith via Pretoria*, reports from the Boer War in which he recounts the assault on his armored train that led to his capture, as well as his escape from the Pretoria POW camp. After Churchill returned to England in 1900, he published *London to Ladysmith's* companion volume, *Ian Hamilton's March* (1900); got himself elected to Parliament; and embarked on a lecture tour of England, the United States, and Canada. In New York, Churchill was given an introduction by Mark Twain. Over the course of his tour, he also met President William McKinley and Vice President Theodore Roosevelt.

Queen Victoria died little more than a week before Winston Churchill took office for the first time in 1901. In 1905, he was appointed Under-Secretary of State for the colonies, and in 1906, he was re-elected to Parliament. Moving through the ranks, he became president of the board of trade in 1908, the year he married Clementine Hozier. By 1910, he occupied the office of home secretary, and in 1911, he became first lord of the admiralty and prepared the

English navy, as it turned out, for the First World War. Stepping down near the beginning of the war—he fell into disfavor over the handling of an early campaign—Churchill soon joined the battle in France but was summoned home to serve as the Minister of Munitions in 1916. Named Secretary of State for War and for Air in 1918, he became the Secretary of State for the Colonies in 1921. In 1923, when he was preparing to publish a multi-volume history eventually entitled, to his chagrin, *The World Crisis,* he became so enthusiastic about his work and so "persuasive" that publisher Charles Scribner III found him "difficult" to manage. Still, Churchill finally accepted the title *The World Crisis,* "bewailing," as Scribner wrote in a letter, "that he had never yet had his way in anything so he was schooled in accepting other's [sic] judgement." Churchill published three volumes of *The World Crisis* in 1923, and by the time he concluded his service as Chancellor of the Exchequer in 1929, he had published the remaining two. In 1930, he published the autobiographical *My Early Life: A Roving Commission.*

Over the course of the 1930s, as Churchill published six volumes of the biography of his ancestor, *Marlborough: His Life and Times,* the Nazis gained increasing power in Germany. According to the *Dictionary of Literary Biography,* "Churchill's stand on the Nazi threat, though perhaps not as consistent as he later presented it in *The Gathering Storm* (1948), was sufficient to ensure his reintroduction to government as first lord of the Admirality with the outbreak of war in 1939." The following year, he became prime minister, a position he lost during the election of 1945. "Early in 1946," David Cannadine explains, "Churchill decided to absent himself from Parliament for a few months." Traveling to the United States, he delivered his famous "Iron Curtain" speech on March 5, 1946, at Westminster College in Fulton, Missouri. During the remainder of the year, Cannadine continues, he toured Europe "receiving honorary degrees, medals, and gifts, and widespread public homage." He regained the position of prime minister shortly before the death of King George VI and the coronation of Queen Elizabeth II in February of 1952. In 1953, the year he was both knighted and awarded a Nobel Prize for Literature, he suffered a severe stroke, yet he still published volumes of *A History of the English-speaking Peoples* (1956–1958) and *The Second World War* (1948–1954), of which *The Gathering Storm* was the first. He retired from public life in 1955 at the age of 80. He suffered a fatal stroke in January of 1965, at the age of 89.

At the time of Churchill's death, former Prime Minister Clement Attlee characterized him as "the greatest Englishman of our time—I think the greatest citizen of the world of our time." While assessments of his governance vary, he will always live on in world history as part of the triumvirate that defeated Hitler. Churchill also lives on through his famous humor and eloquence, through quotations preserved for their general wit and wisdom—"Politics are almost as exciting as war, and quite as dangerous. In war you can only be killed once, but in politics many times"—and through quotations preserved for their historical importance—"I have nothing to offer but blood, toil, tears, and sweat." A forceful orator, he also impressed Colin Coote, who collected his *Maxims and Reflections* (1949), with the force of his personality: "It was like strychnine. You were not very sure whether it was a tonic or a poison, but you were very sure it was very powerful." Churchill's politics, like his personality, did not agree with everyone, and there are those who maintain that his importance is exaggerated. Still, it can be no exaggeration to say that Churchill remains one of the greatest citizens of the twentieth century.

THE IRON CURTAIN (1946)

I AM GLAD TO come to Westminster College this afternoon, and am complimented that you should give me a degree. The name 'Westminster' is somehow familiar to me. I seem to have heard of it before. Indeed, it was at Westminster that I received a very large part of my education in politics, dialectic, rhetoric, and one or two other things. In fact we have both been educated at the same, or similar, or, at any rate, kindred establishments.

It is also an honour, perhaps almost unique, for a private visitor to be introduced to an academic audience by the President of the United States. Amid his heavy burdens, duties, and responsibilities—unsought but not recoiled from—the President has travelled a thousand miles to dignify and magnify our meeting here today and to give me an opportunity of addressing this kindred nation, as well as my own countrymen across the ocean, and perhaps some other countries too. The President has told you that it is his wish, as I am sure it is yours, that I should have full liberty to give my true and faithful counsel in these anxious and baffling times. I shall certainly avail myself of this freedom, and feel the more right to do so because any private ambitions I may have cherished in my younger days have been satisfied beyond my wildest dreams. Let me, however, make it clear that I have no official mission or status of any kind, and that I speak only for myself. There is nothing here but what you see.

I can therefore allow my mind, with the experience of a lifetime, to play over the problems which beset us on the morrow of our absolute victory in arms, and to try to make sure with what strength I have that what has been gained with so much sacrifice and suffering shall be preserved for the future glory and safety of mankind.

The United States stands at this time at the pinnacle of world power. It is a solemn moment for the American Democracy. For with primacy in power is also joined an awe-inspiring accountability to the future. If you look around you, you must feel not only the sense of duty done but also you must feel anxiety lest you fall below the level of achievement. Opportunity is here now, clear and shining for both our countries. To reject it or ignore it or fritter it away will bring upon us all the long reproaches of the after-time. It is necessary that constancy of mind, persistency of purpose and the grand simplicity of decision shall guide and rule the conduct of the English-speaking peoples in peace as they did in war. We must, and I believe we shall, prove ourselves equal to this severe requirement.

When American military men approach some serious situation they are wont to write at the head of their directive the words 'overall strategic concept'. There is wisdom in this, as it leads to clarity of thought. What then is the overall strategic concept which we should inscribe today? It is nothing less than the safety and welfare, the freedom and progress, of all the homes and families of all the men and women in all the lands. And here I speak particularly of the myriad cottage or apartment homes where the wage-earner strives amid the accidents and difficulties of life to guard his wife and children from privation and bring the family up in the fear of the Lord, or upon ethical conceptions which often play their potent part.

To give security to these countless homes, they must be shielded from the two giant marauders, war and tyranny. We all know the frightful disturbances in which the ordinary family is plunged when the curse of war swoops down upon the breadwinner and those for whom he works and contrives. The awful ruin of Europe, with all its vanished glories, and of large parts of Asia glares us in the eyes. When the designs of wicked men or the aggressive urge of mighty States dissolve over large areas the frame of civilized society, humble folk are confronted with difficulties with which they cannot cope. For them all is distorted, all is broken, even ground to pulp.

When I stand here this quiet afternoon I shudder to visualize what is actually happening to millions now and what is going to happen in this period when famine stalks the earth. None can compute what has been called 'the unestimated sum of human pain'. Our supreme task and duty is to guard the homes of the common people from the horrors and miseries of another war. We are all agreed on that.

Our American military colleagues, after having proclaimed their 'over-all strategic concept' and computed available resources, always proceed to the next step—namely, the method. Here again there is widespread agreement. A world organization has already been erected for the prime purpose of preventing war. UNO, the successor of the League of Nations, with the decisive addition of the United States and all that that means, is already at work. We must make sure that its work is fruitful, that it is a reality and not a sham, that it is a force for action, and not merely a frothing of words, that it is a true temple of peace in which the shields of many nations can some day be hung up, and not merely a cockpit in a Tower of Babel.[1] Before we cast away the solid assurances of national armaments for self-preservation we must be certain that our temple is built, not upon shifting sands or quagmires, but upon the rock. Anyone can see with his eyes open that our path will be difficult and also long, but if we persevere together as we did in the two world wars—though not, alas, in the interval between them—I cannot doubt that we shall achieve our common purpose in the end.

I have, however, a definite and practical purpose to make for action. Courts and magistrates may be set up but they cannot function without sheriffs and constables. The United Nations Organization must immediately begin to be equipped with an international armed force. In such a matter we can only go step by step, but we must begin now. I propose that each of the Powers and States should be invited to delegate a certain number of air squadrons to the service of the world organization. These squadrons would be trained and prepared in their own countries, but would move around in rotation from one country to another. They would wear the uniform of their own countries but with different badges. They would not be required to act against their own nation, but in other respects they

---

[1]*Tower of Babel* in the Bible, place where Noah's descendants (who spoke one language) tried to build a tower reaching up to heaven to make a name for themselves. For this presumption, the speech of the builders was confused, thus ending the project.

would be modest in scale and would grow as confidence grew. I wished to see this done after the First World War, and I devoutly trust it may be done forthwith.

It would nevertheless be wrong and imprudent to entrust the secret knowledge or experience of the atomic bomb, which the United States, Great Britain and Canada now share, to the world organization, while it is still in its infancy. It would be criminal madness to cast it adrift in this still agitated and un-united world. No one in any country has slept less well in their beds because this knowledge and the method and the raw materials to apply it, are at present largely retained in American hands. I do not believe we should all have slept so soundly had the positions been reversed and if some Communist or neo-Fascist State monopolized for the time being these dread agencies. The fear of them alone might easily have been used to enforce totalitarian systems upon the free democratic world, with consequences appalling to human imagination. God has willed that this shall not be and we have at least a breathing space to set our house in order before this peril has to be encountered: and even then, if no effort is spared, we should still possess so formidable a superiority as to impose effective deterrents upon its employment, or threat of employment by others. Ultimately, when the essential brotherhood of man is truly embodied and expressed in a world organization with all the necessary practical safeguards to make it effective, these powers would naturally be confided to that world organization.

Now I come to the second danger of these two marauders which threatens the cottage, the home, and the ordinary people—namely, tyranny. We cannot be blind to the fact that the liberties enjoyed by individual citizens throughout the British Empire are not valid in a considerable number of countries, some of which are very powerful. In these States control is enforced upon the common people by various kinds of all-embracing police governments. The power of the State is exercised without restraint, either by dictators or by compact oligarchies operating through a privileged party and a political police. It is not our duty at this time when difficulties are so numerous to interfere forcibly in the internal affairs of countries which we have not conquered in war. But we must never cease to proclaim in fearless tones the great principles of freedom and the rights of man which are the joint inheritance of the English-speaking world and which through Magna Carta,[2] the Bill of Rights, the *Habeas Corpus*,[3] trial by jury, and the English common law find their most famous expression in the American Declaration of Independence.

All this means that the people of any country have the right, and should have the power by constitutional action, by free unfettered elections, with secret ballot, to choose or change the character or form of government under which they dwell; that freedom of speech and thought should reign; that courts of justice, independent of the executive, unbiased by any party, should administer laws which have received the broad assent of large majorities or are consecrated by time and custom. Here are the title deeds of freedom which should lie in every cottage home. Here is the message of the British and American peoples to mankind. Let us preach what we practise—let us practise what we preach.

I have now stated the two great dangers which menace the homes of the people: War and Tyranny. I have not yet spoken of poverty and privation which are in many cases the

---

[2]*Magna Carta* literally, Latin for "great charter"; the most famous document of British constitutional history, issued by King John at Runnymede in June, 1215, under compulsion from the barons and the church, protected the rights of subjects.

[3]*Habeas Corpus* literally, Latin for "you shall have the body," a legal writ whose function is to release an individual from unlawful imprisonment, and which is considered a key part of the English and American constitutional law.

prevailing anxiety. But if the dangers of war and tyranny are removed, there is no doubt that science and co-operation can bring in the next few years to the world, certainly in the next few decades newly taught in the sharpening school of war, an expansion of material well-being beyond anything that has yet occurred in human experience. Now, at this sad and breathless moment, we are plunged in the hunger and distress which are the aftermath of our stupendous struggle: but this will pass and may pass quickly, and there is no reason except human folly or sub-human crime which should deny to all the nations the inauguration and enjoyment of an age of plenty. I have often used words which I learned fifty years ago from a great Irish-American orator, a friend of mine, Mr. Bourke Cockran. 'There is enough for all. The earth is a generous mother; she will provide in plentiful abundance food for all her children if they will but cultivate her soil in justice and in peace.' So far I feel that we are in full agreement.

Now, while still pursuing the method of realizing our overall strategic concept, I come to the crux of what I have travelled here to say. Neither the sure prevention of war, nor the continuous rise of world organization will be gained without what I have called the fraternal association of the English-speaking peoples. This means a special relationship between the British Commonwealth and Empire and the United States. This is no time for generalities, and I will venture to be precise. Fraternal association requires not only the growing friendship and mutual understanding between our two vast but kindred systems of society, but the continuance of the intimate relationship between our military advisers, leading to common study of potential dangers, the similarity of weapons and manuals of instructions, and to the interchange of officers and cadets at technical colleges. It should carry with it the continuance of the present facilities for mutual security by the joint use of all Naval and Air Force bases in the possession of either country all over the world. This would perhaps double the mobility of the American Navy and Air Force. It would greatly expand that of the British Empire Forces and it might well lead, if and as the world calms down, to important financial savings. Already we use together a large number of islands; more may well be entrusted to our joint care in the near future.

The United States has already a Permanent Defence Agreement with the Dominion of Canada, which is so devotedly attached to the British Commonwealth and Empire. This Agreement is more effective than many of those which have often been made under formal alliances. This principle should be extended to all British Commonwealths with full reciprocity. Thus, whatever happens, and thus only, shall we be secure ourselves and able to work together for the high and simple causes that are dear to us and bode no ill to any. Eventually there may come—I feel eventually there will come—the principle of common citizenship, but that we may be content to leave to destiny, whose outstretched arm many of us can already clearly see.

There is however an important question we must ask ourselves. Would a special relationship between the United States and the British Commonwealth be inconsistent with our overriding loyalties to the World Organization? I reply that, on the contrary, it is probably the only means by which that organization will achieve its full stature and strength. There are already the special United States relations with Canada which I have just mentioned, and there are the special relations between the United States and the South American Republics. We British have our twenty years Treaty of Collaboration and Mutual Assistance with Soviet Russia. I agree with Mr Bevin, the Foreign Secretary of Great Britain, that it might well be a fifty years Treaty so far as we are concerned. We aim at nothing but mutual assistance and collaboration. The British have an alliance with Portugal unbroken since 1384, and which produced fruitful results at critical moments in the late war. None of these clash with the general interest of a world agreement, or a world organization; on the contrary they help it. 'In my father's house are many mansions.' Special associations between members of the United Nations which have no aggressive point against any other country, which harbour no design incompatible with the Charter of the United Nations, far from being harmful, are beneficial and, as I believe, indispensable.

I spoke earlier of the Temple of Peace. Workmen from all countries must build that temple. If two of the workmen know each other particularly well and are old friends, if their families are intermingled, and if they have 'faith in each other's purpose, hope in each other's future and charity towards each other's shortcomings'—to quote some good words I read here the other day—why cannot they work together at the common task as friends and partners? Why cannot they share their tools and thus increase each other's working powers? Indeed they must do so or else the temple may not be built, or, being built, it may collapse, and we shall all be proved again unteachable and have to go and try to learn again for a third time in a school of war, incomparably more rigorous than that from which we have just been released. The dark ages may return, the Stone Age may return on the gleaming wings of science, and what might now shower immeasurable material blessings upon mankind, may even bring about its total destruction. Beware, I say; time may be short. Do not let us take the course of allowing events to drift along until it is too late. If there is to be a fraternal association of the kind I have described, with all the extra strength and security which both our countries can derive from it, let us make sure that that great fact is known to the world, and that it plays its part in steadying and stabilizing the foundations of peace. There is the path of wisdom. Prevention is better than cure.

A shadow has fallen upon the scenes so lately lighted by the Allied victory. Nobody knows what Soviet Russia and its Communist international organization intends to do in the immediate future, or what are the limits, if any, to their expansive and proselytizing tendencies. I have a strong admiration and regard for the valiant Russian people and for my wartime comrade, Marshal Stalin. There is deep sympathy and goodwill in Britain—and I doubt not here also—towards the peoples of all the Russias and a resolve to persevere through many differences and rebuffs in establishing lasting friendships. We understand the Russian need to be secure on her western frontiers by the removal of all possibility of German aggression. We welcome Russia to her rightful place among the leading nations of the world. We welcome her flag upon the seas. Above all, we welcome constant, frequent and growing contacts between the Russian people and our own people on both sides of the Atlantic. It is my duty, however, for I am sure you would wish me to state the facts as I see them to you, to place before you certain facts about the present position in Europe.

From Stettin in the Baltic to Trieste in the Adriatic, an iron curtain has descended across the Continent. Behind that line lie all the capitals of the ancient states of Central and Eastern Europe. Warsaw, Berlin, Prague, Vienna, Budapest, Belgrade, Bucharest and Sofia, all these famous cities and the populations around them lie in what I must call the Soviet sphere, and all are subject in one form or another, not only to Soviet influence but to a very high and, in many cases, increasing measure of control from Moscow. Athens alone—Greece with its immortal glories—is free to decide its future at an election under British American and French observation. The Russian-dominated Polish Government has been encouraged to make enormous and wrongful inroads upon Germany, and mass expulsions of millions of Germans on a scale grievous and undreamed-of are now taking place. The Communist parties, which were very small in all these Eastern States of Europe, have been raised to pre-eminence and power far beyond their numbers and are seeking everywhere to obtain totalitarian control. Police governments are prevailing in nearly every case, and so far, except in Czechoslovakia, there is no true democracy.

Turkey and Persia [Iran] are both profoundly alarmed and disturbed at the claims which are being made upon them and at the pressure being exerted by the Moscow Government. An attempt is being made by the Russians in Berlin to build up a quasi-Communist party in their zone of Occupied Germany by showing special favours to groups of left-wing German leaders. At the end of the fighting last June, the American and British Armies withdrew westwards, in accordance with an earlier agreement, to a depth at some points of 150 miles upon a front of nearly four hundred miles, in order to allow our Russian allies to occupy this vast expanse of territory which the Western Democracies had conquered.

If now the Soviet Government tries, by separate action, to build up a pro-Communist Germany in their areas, this will cause new serious difficulties in the British and American zones, and will give the defeated Germans the power of putting themselves up to auction between the Soviets and the Western Democracies. Whatever conclusions may be drawn from these facts—and facts they are—this is certainly not the Liberated Europe we fought to build up. Nor is it one which contains the essentials of permanent peace.

The safety of the world requires a new unity in Europe, from which no nation should be permanently outcast. It is from the quarrels of the strong parent races in Europe that the world wars we have witnessed, or which occurred in former times, have sprung. Twice in our own lifetime we have seen the United States, against their wishes and their traditions, against arguments, the force of which it is impossible not to comprehend, drawn by irresistible forces, into these wars in time to secure the victory of the good cause, but only after frightful slaughter and devastation had occurred. Twice the United States has had to send several millions of its young men across the Atlantic to find the war; but now war can find any nation, wherever it may dwell between dusk and dawn. Surely we should work with conscious purpose for a grand pacification of Europe, within the structure of the United Nations and in accordance with its Charter. That I feel is an open cause of policy of very great importance.

In front of the iron curtain which lies across Europe are other causes for anxiety. In Italy the Communist Party is seriously hampered by having to support the Communist-trained Marshal Tito's claims to former Italian territory at the head of the Adriatic. Nevertheless, the future of Italy hangs in the balance. Again one cannot imagine a regenerated Europe without a strong France. All my public life I have worked for a strong France and I never lost faith in her destiny, even in the darkest hours. I will not lose faith now. However, in a great number of countries, far from the Russian frontiers and throughout the world, Communist fifth columns are established and work in complete unity and absolute obedience to the directions they receive from the Communist centre. Except in the British Commonwealth and in the United States where Communism is in its infancy, the Communist parties or fifth columns constitute a growing challenge and peril to Christian civilization. These are sombre facts for anyone to have to recite on the morrow of a victory gained by so much splendid comradeship in arms and in the cause of freedom and democracy; but we should be most unwise not to face them squarely while time remains.

The outlook is also anxious in the Far East and especially in Manchuria. The Agreement which was made at Yalta,[4] to which I was a party, was extremely favourable to

[4]*the agreement . . . at Yalta* The conference took place in February of 1945. Three months later, Berlin fell. At Yalta, Churchill, Stalin, and Roosevelt agreed to divide Germany. Stalin was also

Soviet Russia, but it was made at a time when no one could say that the German war might not extend all through the summer and autumn of 1945 and when the Japanese war was expected to last for a further eighteen months from the end of the German war. In this country you are all so well informed about the Far East, and such devoted friends of China, that I do not need to expatiate on the situation there.

I have felt bound to portray the shadow which, alike in the west and in the east, falls upon the world. I was a high minister at the time of the Versailles Treaty[5] and a close friend of Mr Lloyd George, who was the head of the British delegation at Versailles. I did not myself agree with many things that were done, but I have a very strong impression in my mind of that situation, and I find it painful to contrast it with that which prevails now. In those days there were high hopes and unbounded confidence that the wars were over, and that the League of Nations would become all-powerful. I do not see or feel that same confidence or even the same hopes in the haggard world at the present time.

On the other hand I repulse the idea that a new war is inevitable; still more that it is imminent. It is because I am sure that our fortunes are still in our own hands and that we hold the power to save the future, that I feel the duty to speak out now that I have the occasion and the opportunity to do so. I do not believe that Soviet Russia desires war. What they desire is the fruits of war and the indefinite expansion of their power and doctrines. But what we have to consider here today while time remains, is the permanent prevention of war and the establishment of conditions of freedom and democracy as rapidly as possible in all countries. Our difficulties and dangers will not be removed by closing our eyes to them. They will not be removed by mere waiting to see what happens; nor will they be removed by a policy of appeasement. What is needed is a settlement, and the longer this is delayed, the more difficult it will be and the greater our dangers will become.

From what I have seen of our Russian friends and Allies during the war, I am convinced that there is nothing they admire so much as strength, and there is nothing for which they have less respect than for weakness, especially military weakness. For that reason the old doctrine of a balance of power is unsound. We cannot afford, if we can help it, to work on narrow margins, offering temptations to a trial of strength. If the Western Democracies stand together in strict adherence to the principles of the United Nations Charter, their influence for furthering those principles will be immense and no one is likely to molest them. If, however, they become divided or falter in their duty and if these all-important years are allowed to slip away then indeed catastrophe may overwhelm us all.

Last time I saw it all coming and cried aloud to my own fellow-countrymen and to the world, but no one paid any attention. Up till the year 1933 or even 1935, Germany might have been saved from the awful fate which has overtaken her and we might all have been spared the miseries Hitler let loose upon mankind. There never was a war in all history easier to prevent by timely action than the one which has just desolated such great areas of the globe. It could have been prevented in my belief without the firing of a single shot, and Germany might be powerful, prosperous and honoured today; but no one would listen and one by one we were all sucked into the awful whirlpool. We surely

promised the return of Russian territory from Japan as a reward for joining the war against Japan after Germany's defeat.

[5]*Versailles Treaty* the Treaty of Versailles was signed in 1919, ending the bitter Paris Peace talks and World War I. It formally placed the responsibility for the war on Germany and its allies and imposed on Germany the burden of the reparations payments.

must not let that happen again. This can only be achieved by reaching now, in 1946, a good understanding on all points with Russia under the general authority of the United Nations Organization and by the maintenance of that good understanding through many peaceful years, by the world instrument, supported by the whole strength of the English-speaking world and all its connections. There is the solution which I respectfully offer to you in this Address to which I have given the title 'The Sinews of Peace'.

Let no man underrate the abiding power of the British Empire and Commonwealth. Because you see the forty-six millions in our island harassed about their food supply, of which they only grow one-half, even in wartime, or because we have difficulty in restarting our industries and export trade after six years of passionate war effort, do not suppose that we shall not come through these dark years of privation as we have come through the glorious years of agony, or that half a century from now, you will not see seventy or eighty millions of Britons spread about the world and united in defence of our traditions, our way of life, and of the world causes which you and we espouse. If the population of the English-speaking Commonwealths be added to that of the United States with all that such co-operation implies in the air, on the sea, all over the globe and in science and in industry, and in moral force, there will be no quivering, precarious balance of power to offer its temptation to ambition or adventure. On the contrary, there will be an overwhelming assurance of security. If we adhere faithfully to the Charter of the United Nations and walk forward in sedate and sober strength seeking no one's land or treasure, seeking to lay no arbitrary control upon the thoughts of men; if all British moral and material forces and convictions are joined with your own in fraternal association, the highroads of the future will be clear, not only for us but for all, not only for our time, but for a century to come.

Understanding and Analysis

1. In the second paragraph of this speech, Churchill calls the period just after the war "these anxious and baffling times." The phrase is telling not only because of its content but also because of its form: the balanced pair is characteristic of Churchill's rhetorical style. The balanced pair is effective only if the two terms are different yet equally compelling. Does "anxious" differ from "baffling"? Note other appearances of the balanced pair. Are they effective?

2. Why has Churchill come to Westminster College to speak? What does he offer as his authority for doing so? What is his subject?

3. Churchill uses the methods of the American military to help structure his speech. How would this method appeal to his audience? The first is the "over-all strategic concept." What are the other parts he delineates? Find some sentences marking other transitions in the essay. How do these sentences guide the listener and reader through the essay?

4. What is the goal or "over-all strategic concept" that Churchill lays out for the American democracy? What are the "two giant marauders" from which the world must be protected?

5. What role does Churchill describe for the UNO? How should it work?

6. Why does Churchill believe the secrets of the bomb should at first be kept from the UNO?

7. The major portion of Churchill's speech consists of a description of the second marauder, tyranny. How does he hope to prevent tyranny?

8. What is the purpose of his metaphor of the Temple of Peace?

9. Beginning with the words "A shadow has fallen," Churchill describes the conditions he perceives in Soviet Russia. Where does he first use the phrase "the iron curtain"?

10. Why do you think that the iron curtain metaphor was so powerful during the Cold War?

11. What activities does Churchill predict will occur in the next few years?

12. What basis does he offer his listeners for believing that his present warnings should be heeded?

Comparison

1. Examine the newspaper accounts of the reception of Churchill's speech in the United States, Great Britain, and Soviet Russia. What was the popular reaction to the speech?

2. Compare the actions of NATO in the Balkans in 1999 with the recommendations of Churchill in 1946.

3. Read Orwell's "Politics and the English Language." Do you detect in Churchill's speech any of the faults Orwell finds in the speeches of politicians?

4. Read the essays by Frost and Sontag to see what they say about metaphor. Analyze Churchill's metaphors in light of the theoretical perspectives of Frost and/or Sontag.

George Orwell

POLITICS AND THE ENGLISH LANGUAGE (1946)

MOST PEOPLE WHO bother with the matter at all would admit that the English language is in a bad way, but it is generally assumed that we cannot by conscious action do anything about it. Our civilization is decadent and our language—so the argument runs—must inevitably share in the general collapse. It follows that any struggle against the abuse of language is a sentimental archaism, like preferring candles to electric light or hansom cabs to aeroplanes. Underneath this lies the half-conscious belief that language is a natural growth and not an instrument which we shape for our own purposes.

Now, it is clear that the decline of a language must ultimately have political and economic causes: it is not due simply to the bad influence of this or that individual writer. But an effect can become a cause, reinforcing the original cause and producing the same effect in an intensified form, and so on indefinitely. A man may take to drink because he feels himself to be a failure, and then fail all the more completely because he drinks. It is rather the same thing that is happening to the English language. It becomes ugly and inaccurate because our thoughts are foolish, but the slovenliness of our language makes it easier for us to have foolish thoughts. The point is that the process is reversible. Modern English, especially written English, is full of bad habits which spread by imitation and which can be avoided if one is willing to take the necessary trouble. If one gets rid of these habits one can think more clearly, and to think clearly is a necessary first step towards political regeneration: so that the fight against bad English is not frivolous and is not the exclusive concern of professional writers. I will come back to this presently, and I hope that by that time the meaning of what I have said here will have become clearer. Meanwhile, here are five specimens of the English language as it is now habitually written.

These five passages have not been picked out because they are especially bad—I could have quoted far worse if I had chosen—but because they illustrate various of the mental vices from which we now suffer. They are a little below the average, but are fairly representative samples. I number them so that I can refer back to them when necessary:

(1) I am not, indeed, sure whether it is not true to say that the Milton who once seemed not unlike a seventeenth-century Shelley had not become, out of an experience ever more bitter in each year, more alien [*sic*] to the founder of that Jesuit sect which nothing could induce him to tolerate.

—Professor Harold Laski
(*Essay in Freedom of Expression*).

(2) Above all, we cannot play ducks and drakes[1] with a native battery[2] of idioms which prescribes such egregious[3] collocations of vocables as the Basic *put up with* for *tolerate* or *put at a loss* for *bewilder*.

—Professor Lancelot Hogben (*Interglossa*)

(3) On the one side we have the free personality: by definition it is not neurotic, for it has neither conflict nor dream. Its desires, such as they are, are transparent, for they are just what institutional approval keeps in the forefront of consciousness; another institutional pattern would alter their number and intensity; there is little in them that is natural, irreducible, or culturally dangerous. But *on the other side*, the social bond itself is nothing but the mutual reflection of these self-secure integrities. Recall the definition of love. Is not this the very picture of a small academic? Where is there a place in this hall of mirrors for either personality or fraternity?

—Essay on psychology in *Politics* (New York)

(4) All the "best people" from the gentlemen's clubs, and all the frantic fascist captains, united in common hatred of Socialism and bestial horror of the rising tide of the mass revolutionary movement, have turned to acts of provocation, to foul incendiarism, to medieval legends of poisoned wells, to legalize their own destruction of proletarian organizations, and rouse the agitated petty-bourgeoisie to chauvinistic fervor on behalf of the fight against the revolutionary way out of the crisis.

—Communist pamphlet

(5) If a new spirit *is* to be infused into this old country, there is one thorny and contentious reform which must be tackled, and that is the humanization and galvanization of the B.B.C. Timidity here will bespeak canker and atrophy of the soul. The heart of Britain may be sound and of strong beat, for instance, but the British lion's roar at present is like that of Bottom

---

[1]*ducks and drakes* to squander or waste, from the game of skimming flat stones along the surface of the water so that they bounce as many times as possible. The stone "ducks" in the water as it skips along.

[2]*battery* an array or group of like things to be used together.

[3]*egregious* outstandingly bad.

in Shakespeare's *Midsummer Night's Dream*—as gentle as any sucking dove. A virile new Britain cannot continue indefinitely to be traduced in the eyes, or rather ears, of the world by the effete languors of Langham Place, brazenly masquerading as "standard English." When the Voice of Britain is heard at nine o'clock, better far and infinitely less ludicrous to hear aitches honestly dropped than the present priggish, inflated, inhibited, school-ma'amish arch braying of blameless bashful mewing maidens!

—Letter in *Tribune*

Each of these passages has faults of its own, but, quite apart from avoidable ugliness, two qualities are common to all of them. The first is staleness of imagery; the other is lack of precision. The writer either had a meaning and cannot express it, or he inadvertently says something else, or he is almost indifferent as to whether his words mean anything or not. This mixture of vagueness and sheer incompetence is the most marked characteristic of modern English prose, and especially of any kind of political writing. As soon as certain topics are raised, the concrete melts into the abstract and no one seems able to think of terms of speech that are not hackneyed: prose consists less and less of *words* chosen for the sake of their meaning, and more and more of *phrases* tacked together like the sections of a prefabricated hen-house. I list below, with notes and examples, various of the tricks by means of which the work of prose-construction is habitually dodged:

DYING METAPHORS. A newly invented metaphor assists thought by evoking a visual image, while on the other hand a metaphor which is technically "dead" (e.g., *iron resolution*) has in effect reverted to being an ordinary word and can generally be used without loss of vividness. But in between these two classes there is a huge dump of worn-out metaphors which have lost all evocative power and are merely used because they save people the trouble of inventing phrases for themselves. Examples are: *Ring the changes on, take up the cudgels for, toe the line, ride roughshod over, stand shoulder to shoulder with, play into the hands of, no axe to grind, grist to the mill, fishing in troubled waters, on the order of the day, Achilles' heel, swan song, hotbed.* Many of these are used without knowledge of their meaning (what is a "rift," for instance?), and incompatible metaphors are frequently mixed, a sure sign that the writer is not interested in what he is saying. Some metaphors now current have been twisted out of their original meaning without those who use them even being aware of the fact. For example, *toe the line* is sometimes written *tow the line*. Another example is *the hammer and the anvil*, now always used with the implication that the anvil gets the worst of it. In real life it is always the anvil that breaks the hammer, never the other way about: a writer who stopped to think what he was saying would be aware of this, and would avoid perverting the original phrase.

OPERATORS OR VERBAL FALSE LIMBS. These save the trouble of picking out appropriate verbs and nouns, and at the same time pad each sentence with extra syllables which give it an appearance of symmetry. Characteristic phrases are *render inoperative, militate against, make contact with, be subjected to, give rise to, give grounds for, have the effect of, play a leading part (role) in, make itself felt, take effect, exhibit a tendency to, serve the purpose of, etc., etc.* The keynote is the elimination of simple verbs. Instead of being a single word, such as *break, stop, spoil, mend, kill*, a verb becomes a *phrase*, made up of a noun or adjective tacked on to some general-purposes verb such as *prove, serve, form, play, render*. In addition, the passive voice is wherever possible used in preference to the active, and noun constructions are used instead of gerunds (*by examination of* instead of *by examining*). The range of verbs is further cut down by means of the *-ize* and *de-* formations, and the banal statements are given an appearance of profundity by means of the *not un*formation. Simple conjunctions and prepositions are replaced by such phrases as *with respect to, having regard to, the fact that, by dint of, in view of, in the interests of, on the hypothesis that;* and the ends of sentences are saved from anticlimax by such resounding commonplaces as *greatly to be desired, cannot be left out of account, a development to be expected in the near future, deserving of serious consideration, brought to a satisfactory conclusion,* and so on and so forth.

PRETENTIOUS DICTION. Words like *phenomenon, element, individual* (as noun), *objective, categorical, effective, virtual, basic, primary, promote, constitute, exhibit, exploit, utilize, eliminate, liquidate* are used to dress up simple statement and give an air of scientific impartiality to biased judgments. Adjectives like *epoch-making, epic, historic, unforgettable, triumphant, age-old, inevitable, inexorable, veritable,* are used to dignify the sordid processes of international politics, while writing that aims at glorifying war usually takes on an archaic color, its characteristic words being: *realm, throne, chariot, mailed fist,*[4] *trident,*[5] *sword, shield, buckler,*[6] *banner, jackboot,*[7] *clarion.*[8] Foreign words and expressions such as *cul de sac,*[9] *ancien régime, deus ex machina,*[10] *mutatis mutandis,*[11] *status quo, gleichschaltung,*[12] *weltanschauung,*[13] are used to give an air of culture and elegance. Except for the useful abbreviations *i.e., e.g.,* and *etc.,* there is no real need for any of the hundreds of foreign phrases now current in English. Bad writers, and especially scientific, political and sociological writers, are nearly always haunted by the notion that Latin or Greek words are grander than Saxon ones, and unnecessary words like *expedite, ameliorate, predict, extraneous, deracinated,*[14] *clandestine, subaqueous* and hundreds of others constantly gain ground from their Anglo-Saxon opposite numbers.[15] The jargon peculiar to Marxist writing (*hyena, hangman, cannibal, petty bourgeois, these gentry, lacquey, flunkey, mad dog, White Guard,*[16] etc.) consists largely of words and phrases translated from Russian, German or French; but the normal way of coining a new word

[4]*mailed fist* one covered with flexible body armor.

[5]*trident* a three-pronged spear.

[6]*buckler* a small round shield carried or worn on the arm.

[7]*jackboot* a stout military boot that rises above the knee.

[8]*clarion* medieval trumpet with a shrill, clear tone.

[9]*cul de sac* French for "dead-end."

[10]*deus ex machina* Latin for "a god out of a machine." In Greek drama, a god that descends from a crane to solve the problem at the end of the play.

[11]*mutatis mutandis* Latin for "the necessary changes having been made."

[12]*gleichschaltung* German for "keeping things equitable."

[13]*weltanschauung* German for "ideology" or "worldview."

[14]*deracinated* uprooted.

[15]An interesting illustration of this is the way in which the English flower names which were in use till very recently are being ousted by Greek ones, *snapdragon* becoming *antirrhinum, forget-me-not* becoming *myosotis,* etc. It is hard to see any practical reason for this change of fashion: it is probably due to an instinctive turning-away from the more homely word and a vague feeling that the Greek word is scientific. [Orwell's note]

[16]*White Guard* Organized by Carl Mannerheim in Finland, the White Guards fought against the Bolsheviks in the civil war following the Russian Revolution and were responsible for pogroms in the Ukraine.

is to use a Latin or Greek root with the appropriate affix and, where necessary, the *-ize* formation. It is often easier to make up words of this kind (*deregionalize, impermissible, extramarital, nonfragmentary* and so forth) than to think up the English words that will cover one's meaning. The result, in general, is an increase in slovenliness and vagueness.

MEANINGLESS WORDS. In certain kinds of writing, particularly in art criticism and literary criticism, it is normal to come across long passages which are almost completely lacking in meaning.[17] Words like *romantic, plastic, values, human, dead, sentimental, natural, vitality,* as used in art criticism, are strictly meaningless, in the sense that they not only do not point to any discoverable object, but are hardly ever expected to do so by the reader. When one critic writes, "The outstanding feature of Mr. X's work is its living quality," while another writes, "The immediately striking thing about Mr. X's work is its peculiar deadness," the reader accepts this as a simple difference of opinion. If words like *black* and *white* were involved, instead of the jargon words *dead* and *living,* he would see at once that language was being used in an improper way. Many political words are similarly abused. The word *Fascism* has now no meaning except in so far as it signifies "something not desirable." The words *democracy, socialism, freedom, patriotic, realistic, justice,* have each of them several different meanings which cannot be reconciled with one another. In the case of a word like *democracy,* not only is there no agreed definition, but the attempt to make one is resisted from all sides. It is almost universally felt that when we call a country democratic we are praising it: consequently the defenders of every kind of régime claim that it is a democracy, and fear that they might have to stop using the word if it were tied down to any one meaning. Words of this kind are often used in a consciously dishonest way. That is, the person who uses them has his own private definition, but allows his hearer to think he means something quite different. Statements like *Marshal Pétain*[18] *was a true patriot, The Soviet Press is the freest in the world, The Catholic Church is opposed to persecution,* are almost always made with intent to deceive. Other words used in variable meanings, in most cases more or less dishonestly, are: *class, totalitarian, science, progressive, reactionary, bourgeois, equality.*

Now that I have made this catalogue of swindles and perversions, let me give another example of the kind of writing that they lead to. This time it must of its nature be an imaginary one. I am going to translate a passage of good English into modern English of the worst sort. Here is a well-known verse from *Ecclesiastes:*

> I returned and saw under the sun, that the race is not to the swift, nor the battle to the strong, neither yet bread to the wise, nor yet riches to men of understanding, nor yet favour to men of skill; but time and chance happeneth to them all.

[17]Example: "Comfort's catholicity of perception and image, strangely Whitmanesque in range, almost the exact opposite in aesthetic compulsion, continues to evoke that trembling atmospheric accumulative hinting at a cruel, an inexorably serene timelessness . . . Wrey Gardiner scores by aiming at simple bull's-eyes with precision. Only they are not so simple, and through this contented sadness runs more than the surface bitter-sweet of resignation." (*Poetry Quarterly*) [Orwell's note]

[18]*Marshal Petain* Henri Petain (1856–1951) French army officer who became a hero in World War I and head of the fascistic Vichy government in France in World War II. He collaborated with the Germans and was sentenced to death for treason after the war. General De Gaulle commuted the sentence to life in prison.

Here it is in modern English:

Objective consideration of contemporary phenomena compels the conclusion that success or failure in competitive activities exhibits no tendency to be commensurate with innate capacity, but that a considerable element of the unpredictable must invariably be taken into account.

This is a parody, but not a very gross one. Exhibit (3), above, for instance, contains several patches of the same kind of English. It will be seen that I have not made a full translation. The beginning and ending of the sentence follow the original meaning fairly closely, but in the middle the concrete illustrations—race, battle, bread—dissolve into the vague phrase "success or failure in competitive activities." This had to be so, because no modern writer of the kind I am discussing—no one capable of using phrases like "objective consideration of contemporary phenomena"—would ever tabulate his thoughts in that precise and detailed way. The whole tendency of modern prose is away from concreteness. Now analyse these two sentences a little more closely. The first contains forty-nine words but only sixty syllables, and all its words are those of everyday life. The second contains thirty-eight words of ninety syllables: eighteen of its words are from Latin roots, and one from Greek. The first sentence contains six vivid images, and only one phrase ("time and chance") that could be called vague. The second contains not a single fresh, arresting phrase, and in spite of its ninety syllables it gives only a shortened version of the meaning contained in the first. Yet without a doubt it is the second kind of sentence that is gaining ground in modern English. I do not want to exaggerate. This kind of writing is not yet universal, and outcrops of simplicity will occur here and there in the worst written page. Still, if you or I were to write a few lines on the uncertainty of human fortunes, we should probably come much nearer to my imaginary sentence than to the one from *Ecclesiastes*.

As I have tried to show, modern writing at its worst does not consist in picking out words for the sake of their meaning and inventing images in order to make the meaning clearer. It consists in gumming together long strips of words which have already been set in order by someone else, and making the results presentable by sheer humbug. The attraction of this way of writing is that it is easy. It is easier—even quicker, once you have the habit—to say *In my opinion it is not an unjustifiable assumption that* than to say *I think*. If you use readymade phrases, you not only don't have to hunt about for words; you also don't have to bother with the rhythms of your sentences, since these phrases are generally so arranged as to be more or less euphonious. When you are composing in a hurry—when you are dictating to a stenographer, for instance, or making a public speech—it is natural to fall into a pretentious, Latinized style. Tags like *a consideration which we should do well to bear in mind* or *a conclusion to which all of us would readily assent* will save many a sentence from coming down with a bump. By using stale metaphors, similes and idioms, you save much mental effort, at the cost of leaving your meaning vague, not only for your reader but for yourself. This is the significance of mixed metaphors. The sole aim of a metaphor is to call up a visual image. When these images clash—as in *The Fascist octopus has sung its swan song, the jackboot is thrown into the melting pot*—it can be taken as certain that the writer is not seeing a mental image of the objects he is naming; in other words he is not really thinking. Look again at the examples I gave at the beginning of this essay. Professor Laski (1) uses five negatives in fifty-three words. One of these is superfluous, making nonsense of the whole passage, and in addition there is the slip *alien* for akin, making further nonsense, and several avoidable pieces of clumsiness which increase the general vagueness. Professor Hogben (2) plays ducks and drakes with a battery which is able to write prescriptions, and, while disapproving of the everyday phrase *put up with,* is unwilling to look *egregious* up in the dictionary and see what it means; (3), if one takes an uncharitable attitude towards it, is simply meaningless: probably one could work out its intended meaning by reading the whole of the article in which it occurs. In (4), the writer knows more or less what he wants to say, but an accumulation of stale phrases chokes him like tea leaves blocking a sink. In (5), words and meaning have almost parted company. People who write in this manner usually have a general emotional meaning—they dislike one thing and want to express solidarity with another—but they are not interested in the detail of what they are saying. A scrupulous writer, in every sentence that he writes, will ask himself at least four questions, thus: What am I trying to say? What words will express it? What image or idiom will make it clearer? Is this image fresh enough to have an effect? And he will probably ask himself two more: Could I put it more shortly? Have I said anything that is avoidably ugly? But you are not obliged to go to all this trouble. You can shirk it by simply throwing your mind open and letting the ready-made phrases come crowding in. They will construct your sentences for you—even think your thoughts for you, to a certain extent—and at need they will perform the important service of partially concealing your meaning even from yourself. It is at this point that the special connection between politics and the debasement of language becomes clear.

In our time it is broadly true that political writing is bad writing. Where it is not true, it will generally be found that the writer is some kind of rebel, expressing his private opinions and not a "party line." Orthodoxy, of whatever color, seems to demand a lifeless, imitative style. The political dialects to be found in pamphlets, leading articles, manifestos, White Papers[19] and the speeches of under-secretaries do, of course, vary from party to party, but they are all alike in that one almost never finds in them a fresh, vivid, home-made turn of speech. When one watches some tired hack on the platform mechanically repeating the familiar phrases—*bestial atrocities, iron heel, bloodstained tyranny, free peoples of the world, stand shoulder to shoulder*—one often has a curious feeling that one is not watching a live human being but some kind of dummy: a feeling which suddenly becomes stronger at moments when the light catches the speaker's spectacles and turns them into blank discs which seem to have no eyes behind them. And this is not altogether fanciful. A speaker who uses that kind of phraseology has gone some distance towards turning himself into a machine. The appropriate noises are coming out of his larynx, but his brain is not involved as it would be if he were choosing his words for himself. If the speech he is making is one that he is accustomed to make over and over again, he may be almost unconscious of what he is saying, as one is when one utters the responses in church. And this reduced state of consciousness, if not indispensable, is at any rate favorable to political conformity.

In our time, political speech and writing are largely the defence of the indefensible. Things like the continuance of British rule in India, the Russian purges and deportations, the dropping of the atom bombs on Japan, can indeed be defended, but only by arguments which are too brutal for most people to face, and which do not square with the professed aims of political parties. Thus political language has to consist largely of euphemism, question-begging and sheer cloudy vagueness. Defenceless villages are bombarded from the air, the inhabitants driven out into the countryside, the cattle machine-gunned,

---

[19]*White Paper* official statement or publication by a government stating its policies.

the huts set on fire with incendiary bullets: this is called *pacification*. Millions of peasants are robbed of their farms and sent trudging along the roads with no more than they can carry: this is called *transfer of population* or *rectification of frontiers*. People are imprisoned for years without trial, or shot in the back of the neck or sent to die of scurvy in Arctic lumber camps: this is called *elimination of unreliable elements*. Such phraseology is needed if one wants to name things without calling up mental pictures of them. Consider for instance some comfortable English professor defending Russian totalitarianism. He cannot say outright, "I believe in killing off your opponents when you can get good results by doing so." Probably, therefore, he will say something like this:

> While freely conceding that the Soviet régime exhibits certain features which the humanitarian may be inclined to deplore, we must, I think, agree that a certain curtailment of the right to political opposition is an unavoidable concomitant of transitional periods, and that the rigors which the Russian people have been called upon to undergo have been amply justified in the sphere of concrete achievement.

The inflated style is itself a kind of euphemism. A mass of Latin words falls upon the facts like soft snow, blurring the outlines and covering up all the details. The great enemy of clear language is insincerity. When there is a gap between one's real and one's declared aims, one turns as it were instinctively to long words and exhausted idioms, like a cuttlefish squirting out ink. In our age there is no such thing as "keeping out of politics." All issues are political issues, and politics itself is a mass of lies, evasions, folly, hatred and schizophrenia. When the general atmosphere is bad, language must suffer. I should expect to find—this is a guess which I have not sufficient knowledge to verify—that the German, Russian and Italian languages have all deteriorated in the last ten or fifteen years, as a result of dictatorship.

But if thought corrupts language, language can also corrupt thought. A bad usage can spread by tradition and imitation, even among people who should and do know better. The debased language that I have been discussing is in some ways very convenient. Phrases like *a not unjustifiable assumption, leaves much to be desired, would serve no good purpose, a consideration which we should do well to bear in mind,* are a continuous temptation, a packet of aspirins always at one's elbow. Look back through this essay, and for certain you will find that I have again and again committed the very faults I am protesting against. By this morning's post I have received a pamphlet dealing with conditions in Germany. The author tells me that he "felt impelled" to write it. I open it at random, and here is almost the first sentence that I see: "[The Allies] have an opportunity not only of achieving a radical transformation of Germany's social and political structure in such a way as to avoid a nationalistic reaction in Germany itself, but at the same time of laying the foundations of a cooperative and unified Europe." You see, he "feels impelled" to write—feels, presumably, that he has something new to say—and yet his words, like cavalry horses answering the bugle, group themselves automatically into the familiar dreary pattern. This invasion of one's mind by ready-made phrases (*lay the foundations, achieve a radical transformation*) can only be prevented if one is constantly on guard against them, and every such phrase anaesthetizes a portion of one's brain.

I said earlier that the decadence of our language is probably curable. Those who deny this would argue, if they produced an argument at all, that language merely reflects existing social conditions, and that we cannot influence its development by any direct tinkering with words and constructions. So far as the general tone or spirit of a language goes, this may be true, but it is not true in detail. Silly words and expressions have often disappeared, not through any evolutionary process but owing to the conscious action of a minority. Two recent examples were *explore every avenue* and *leave no stone unturned,* which were killed by the jeers of a few journalists. There is a long list of flyblown metaphors which could similarly be got rid of if enough people would interest themselves in the job; and it should also be possible to laugh the *not un-* formation out of existence,[20] to reduce the amount of Latin and Greek in the average sentence, to drive out foreign phrases and strayed scientific words, and, in general, to make pretentiousness unfashionable. But all these are minor points. The defence of the English language implies more than this, and perhaps it is best to start by saying what it does *not* imply.

To begin with it has nothing to do with archaism, with the salvaging of obsolete words and turns of speech, or with the setting up of a "standard English" which must never be departed from. On the contrary, it is especially concerned with the scrapping of every word or idiom which has outworn its usefulness. It has nothing to do with correct grammar and syntax, which are of no importance so long as one makes one's meaning clear, or with the avoidance of Americanisms, or with having what is called a "good prose style." On the other hand it is not concerned with fake simplicity and the attempt to make written English colloquial. Nor does it even imply in every case preferring the Saxon word to the Latin one, though it does imply using the fewest and shortest words that will cover one's meaning. What is above all needed is to let the meaning choose the word, and not the other way about. In prose, the worst thing one can do with words is to surrender to them. When you think of a concrete object, you think wordlessly, and then, if you want to describe the thing you have been visualizing you probably hunt about till you find the exact words that seem to fit it. When you think of something abstract you are more inclined to use words from the start, and unless you make a conscious effort to prevent it, the existing dialect will come rushing in and do the job for you, at the expense of blurring or even changing your meaning. Probably it is better to put off using words as long as possible and get one's meaning as clear as one can through pictures or sensations. Afterwards one can choose—not simply *accept*—the phrases that will best cover the meaning, and then switch round and decide what impression one's words are likely to make on another person. This last effort of the mind cuts out all stale or mixed images, all prefabricated phrases, needless repetitions, and humbug and vagueness generally. But one can often be in doubt about the effect of a word or a phrase, and one needs rules that one can rely on when instinct fails. I think the following rules will cover most cases:

i. Never use a metaphor, simile or other figure of speech which you are used to seeing in print.

ii. Never use a long word where a short one will do.

iii. If it is possible to cut a word out, always cut it out.

iv. Never use the passive where you can use the active.

v. Never use a foreign phrase, a scientific word or a jargon word if you can think of an everyday English equivalent.

vi. Break any of these rules sooner than say anything outright barbarous.

---

[20]One can cure oneself of the *not un-* formation by memorizing this sentence; *A not unblack dog was chasing a not unsmall rabbit across a not ungreen field.* [Orwell's note]

These rules sound elementary, and so they are, but they demand a deep change in attitude in anyone who has grown used to writing in the style now fashionable. One could keep all of them and still write bad English, but one could not write the kind of stuff that I quoted in those five specimens at the beginning of this article.

I have not here been considering the literary use of language, but merely language as an instrument for expressing and not for concealing or preventing thought. Stuart Chase[21] and others have come near to claiming that all abstract words are meaningless, and have used this as a pretext for advocating a kind of political quietism. Since you don't know what Fascism is, how can you struggle against Fascism? One need not swallow such absurdities as this, but one ought to recognize that the present political chaos is connected with the decay of language, and that one can probably bring about some improvement by starting at the verbal end. If you simplify your English, you are freed from the worst follies of orthodoxy. You cannot speak any of the necessary dialects, and when you make a stupid remark its stupidity will be obvious, even to yourself. Political language—and with variations this is true of all political parties, from Conservatives to Anarchists—is designed to make lies sound truthful and murder respectable, and to give an appearance of solidity to pure wind. One cannot change this all in a moment, but one can at least change one's own habits, and from time to time one can even, if one jeers loudly enough, send some worn-out and useless phrase—some *jackboot, Achilles' heel, hotbed, melting pot, acid test, veritable inferno* or other lump of verbal refuse—into the dustbin where it belongs.

Understanding and Analysis

1. This essay has been criticized for poor organization. Do you agree that it is poorly organized? Explain your position. If you think it is poorly organized, offer some alternative structures that you think would improve the organization of the essay.

2. What are the two qualities Orwell claims each of the examples illustrates? List as many as you can of the negative qualities that Orwell finds in modern English prose.

3. List the images and analogies that Orwell uses to make his points clear. Orwell's first rule for good writing is "Never use a metaphor, simile or other figure of speech which you are used to seeing in print." Have you seen his figures of speech before?

4. Examine the modifying phrases in Orwell's rules, as for example the words "where a short one will do" in number 2. What effect do they have on the rules they modify? How would the rules change without them?

5. Orwell provides an excellent analysis of both the passage from *Ecclesiastes* and his "modern" translation. What steps does he take to perform this analysis? What makes his analysis convincing?

6. In the beginning of the essay, Orwell promises "to come back to this presently," meaning that he will return to the point that "the fight against bad English is not frivolous and is not the exclusive concern of professional writers." Where does he return to this point?

7. Orwell claims that "political writing is bad writing" because it must follow the party line. Do you agree?

[21]*Stuart Chase* (1888–1985) American economist.

8. Do you agree with Orwell that we can change the language?

9. Orwell claims that you may well find the problems he details in his own essay because they are so pervasive. Can you find any?

Comparison

1. Can you find examples of the flaws you list in question 2 in prose you are reading in your textbooks or in newspapers? Find as many examples as you can, and classify them according to Orwell's categories.

2. Do you think the language has improved since Orwell wrote his essay? Compare the examples you collect from your own reading with the examples Orwell offers. Have you found new categories? Are some of Orwell's categories missing in your survey of recent prose?

3. Orwell says that he sees no reason for using the Greek names for flowers. Can you think of any good reasons? Do you think jargon is ever justifiable? Examine the special terms you may be using in a science, engineering, business, art, or history course. Do these terms help or hinder your understanding of the material?

4. Read bell hook's essay on Malcolm X, Gates's essay on language, Kuhn's essay on science, and Carr's essay on history. Do these authors use jargon? If so, does it help or hinder your understanding of the material? Can you draw some general conclusions about the use of jargon in special fields?

5. Go through your own prose from this course or another that requires extensive writing. Look for the problems Orwell lists, and correct any you find in your own work.

6. Read essays by Thurber, Baldwin, Gates, and Tan. Compare Orwell's view of language with the views expressed in these essays. Where do these writers agree and where do they disagree?

Zora Neale Hurston
(1895?–1960)

Zora Neale Hurston was born in Eatonville, Florida, the sixth of eight children of Lucy Ann Potts and John Hurston, a Baptist preacher, carpenter, and three-term mayor of the all African-American town. In her autobiography, *Dust Tracks on a Road* (1942), she describes herself as an exceptionally strong, confident, and imaginative child, unafraid of snakes, who believed that the moon followed only her. She was also curious. On her errands to Joe Clarke's store, "the heart and spring of the town," Zora overheard men talking about women in language not intended for children's ears, and she lingered on to hear their "lying" sessions, when they outdid each other swapping folk tales about God, the Devil, and animals that talked. She read voraciously—fairy tales, Greek and Roman myths, stories of the Norse, books like *The Swiss Family Robinson*, and, of course, the Bible. Immersed in this wealth of material, Hurston began making up her own tall tales; her mother approved, but her maternal grandmother called her a liar; her father had always complained that she "had too much spirit." When Hurston was nine, her mother died, the family dispersed, and Hurston was sent off to school in Jacksonville. Nevertheless, sheltered from the racism outside Eatonville and nourished by the local folk tales, the poetry of her father's Baptist services, and her mother's challenge to "jump at de sun," Hurston had developed a pride in herself and her race that remained undiminished all her life.

Lack of funds soon forced Hurston to leave the Jacksonville school. For the next ten years, she worked sporadically as a maid, receptionist, dishwasher, and wardrobe girl with a traveling Gilbert and Sullivan repertory company, all the time hoping to save enough money to return to school. After the Gilbert and Sullivan tour, she enrolled in night school in Maryland, working days as a waitress, and graduated from high school in 1918. That summer she worked in Washington as a manicurist before entering Howard University where she studied with Alain Locke, philosophy professor and editor of *Stylus*, the literary magazine in which, in 1921, Hurston published her first story, "John Redding Goes to Sea."

In 1925, Hurston left Howard for New York City, finances again keeping her from finishing school. But by then she had published several short stories based on life in Eatonville ("Drenched in Light" in 1924, "Spunk" and "Magnolia Flower" in 1925) and, with the backing of Locke and other intellectuals of the Harlem Renaissance, Hurston was soon in the center of that society, entertaining friends with her flamboyance and her tales from Eatonville. When she won second place at an awards dinner for her short story "Spunk," one of the founders of Barnard College, impressed with Hurston's talent, offered her a scholarship to Barnard beginning in the fall of 1925.

At Barnard, Hurston studied anthropology under Dr. Franz Boas and shifted her interests from that of creative artist to that of recorder and collector of folk tales and black culture. Her new enthusiasm led her to measure heads on the streets of Harlem to supply evidence for Boas's refutation of nineteenth-century assertions about racial differences in brain size. In 1927, just before her graduation from Barnard, she was given a fellowship to study folklore in the South. While in Florida, Hurston married Herbert Sheen, a man she had met at Howard in 1920. He had worked his way through school as a waiter and pianist and then moved to Chicago to enter medical school. Unfortunately, both the fieldwork and the marriage proved unsuccessful. Alienated by her Barnard education, her informants refused to cooperate.

Commitment to their separate careers, one in Chicago and the other in New York and the South, eroded the marriage (they divorced four years later), and Hurston drove back from her fieldwork with the poet Langston Hughes.

Hurston arrived to report to Boas miserable and nearly empty-handed. The one article she did manage to produce was found, years later, (by William Stewart in 1972) to have been plagiarized. Her biographer, Robert Hemenway, argues that plagiarism "may be an unconscious attempt at academic suicide." He explains that Hurston was torn between her love of art and her respect for science, for neither alone could convey the power and integrity of black folk culture to a nation dominated by racial prejudice. As an artist, she felt she lacked credibility, yet as an anthropologist, she was forced to suppress her imagination and to publish in scholarly journals read only by those knowledgeable in the field. Moreover, she was afraid of failure as a scientist. She knew that, if discovered, the plagiarism would destroy her career, but the discovery would also have solved her dilemma. As it was, she was left to solve the dilemma herself.

By December of 1927, Hurston had found another sponsor for her fieldwork, Mrs. Charlotte Osgood Mason, rich, white, and the patron of Langston Hughes and other African-American artists. In return for her funding, Mason required absolute loyalty and a contract that gave her ownership of all material collected and control over all publishing of this material. In fact, Mason refused to let Hurston publish anything; she was to collect only. Mason's strict control and her preference for science over art eventually led first Hughes and then Hurston to reject her money. But without this money, Hurston would not have been able to regain her confidence as an anthropologist. On this second venture Hurston was quite successful; masquerading as a runaway from a bootlegging husband, she lived for a time with the workers of the Everglades Cypress Lumber Company and later worked as an apprentice hoo-doo doctor in New Orleans. In 1929, she went to the Bahamas to collect Afro-Caribbean folklore, songs, and hoo-doo material. Although Mason funded Hurston's fieldwork for three years, the money was barely enough to keep Hurston in gas and shoes, and she longed to publish some of her findings, particularly the songs and dances, in the form of drama, which Mason absolutely forbade. While she was writing up her notes, she was also, behind Mason's back, conspiring with Hughes on a play to be called "Mule Bone." Never produced in her lifetime, the play caused the break-up of Hurston's friendship with Hughes (they argued over who had written what and over the addition of a third party to the project), but it also pointed up Hurston's own struggles between what she saw as sterile reporting and imaginative art. Worse, when Mason was finally ready for Hurston to publish her findings, no one was willing to publish her material without extensive revisions. Mason now wanted a return for her investment. Based on some of the material from her notes, Hurston created a musical show, *The Great Day*, which was an artistic success, but not a financial one. It was largely underwritten, again, by Mason. Finally, when Hurston returned to Eatonville in 1932 she was able to write the manuscript that became *Mules and Men*, a combination of the folk material collected and a first-person narrative that was neither fiction nor pure research.

For the next ten years, Hurston supported herself through odd jobs and her writing, both fiction and non-fiction. She was drama instructor at Bethune Cookman College in Daytona in 1933, and producer of another *Great Day* in Chicago in 1934. When the publisher Lippincott read her short story "The Gilded Six-Bits" (1933) and asked if she had a novel to submit, Hurston said yes and quickly produced her first novel, *Jonah's Gourd Vine* (1934). After that, her publisher was willing, finally, to publish *Mules and Men* (1935) as well. She worked for the Federal Theatre Project in New York, went to the West Indies on a Guggenheim Fellowship in 1936, and wrote *Their Eyes Were Watching God* in Haiti in 1937, infusing the story with the passion she had felt for a young man, a member of the cast of *The Great Day*, whom after much soul-searching she had forsaken, again because of her career. Unlike that novel, her next book, *Tell My Horse* (1938), based on her collections of material in the West Indies, did not sell well, and Hurston joined the writers' project in Florida in 1938. In 1939, she published her third novel, *Moses, Man of the Mountain*, married Albert Price III, whom she divorced four years later, and took a job as manager of a drama program at the North Carolina College for Negroes at Durham. In 1941, she was in New York and, in 1942, living in California with a wealthy friend. There Hurston wrote her autobiography *Dust Tracks on a Road*, 1942, and consulted at Paramount Studios. The autobiography was so successful that she was asked to write numerous articles for magazines during the forties. But she was still living hand to mouth, even in 1944 when she received an award from Howard University. In the mid-forties, she worked for the Republicans in political campaigns in New York, and in 1948 she published *Seraph on the Sewanee*, a novel about white people in the South.

Her writing during the forties has perplexed and annoyed many of Hurston's admires, who see this work, particularly the autobiography and the last novel, as rejections of the goals she had pursued in the twenties and thirties. The manuscript for the autobiography shows that her publisher had cut out Hurston's criticism of the United States' racist policies, but even so, her writing seems to be patriotic in time of war and shaped to please a white audience. Hurston became even more conservative after she was arrested and falsely accused of child molestation in 1948. Although she proved that she had been out of the country at the time of the supposed incidents and although the case against her was dropped, an African-American newspaper picked up the story in lurid headlines and Hurston was deeply hurt.

Depressed but not beaten, Hurston returned to Florida, wrote articles for magazines, and lived for a while in a houseboat. During the fifties, she shocked many African-Americans by her anti-communism, her support for Republicans, and particularly by her rejection of the 1954 Supreme Court decision forbidding separate but equal public education. But it was Hurston's pride in the all-African-American community of Eatonville that had led her to this position. She spent much of her last years researching, reading the works of Flavius Josephus (A.D. 37–95), a Jewish historian and soldier, in order to write a novel about Herod the Great, which found merit in the eyes of the author only. It was rejected for publication in 1955. Nonetheless, Hurston continued to believe in her book and supported herself while rewriting by working as a maid, librarian, reporter, and part-time teacher. She had suffered much of her life from periodic stomach ailments, including appendicitis, gall bladder attacks, and gastroenteritis picked up on her trips to the Bahamas and the West Indies. In later years she had become obese and finally suffered a stroke. In 1959, when she could no longer care for herself, she entered the Saint Lucie County welfare home, where she died a year later. She was buried in the segregated cemetery of Fort Pierce, Florida.

Like Twain, Hurston was adept at juxtaposing levels of diction. Like Mencken and Parker, she loved the sound of words, and she loved to shock her readers. And, like Du Bois, she believed in the beauty of African-American culture and the importance of the inner lives of African-American people and white people in America. But unlike both Twain and Du Bois, she remained optimistic, even when the public, both African-American and white, had turned against her. Hurston insisted that the internal life of African-American men and women is as important as the external barriers against them, and though she railed against those barriers, she also wrote with pride about African-American people living in America.

WHAT WHITE PUBLISHERS WON'T PRINT (1950)

I HAVE BEEN amazed by the Anglo-Saxon's lack of curiosity about the internal lives and emotions of the Negroes, and for that matter, any non-Anglo-Saxon peoples within our borders, above the class of unskilled labor.

This lack of interest is much more important than it seems at first glance. It is even more important at this time than it was in the past. The internal affairs of the nation have bearings on the international stress and strain, and this gap in the national literature now has tremendous weight in world affairs. National coherence and solidarity is implicit in a thorough understanding of the various groups within a nation, and this lack of knowledge about the internal emotions and behavior of the minorities cannot fail to bar out understanding. Man, like all the other animals, fears and is repelled by that which he does not understand, and mere difference is apt to connote something malign.

The fact that there is no demand for incisive and full-dress stories around Negroes above the servant class is indicative of something of vast importance to this nation. This blank is NOT filled by the fiction built around upper-class Negroes exploiting the race problem. Rather, it tends to point it up. A college-bred Negro still is not a person like other folks, but an interesting problem, more or less. It calls to mind a story of slavery time. In this story, a master with more intellectual curiosity than usual, set out to see how much he could teach a particularly bright slave of his. When he had gotten him up to higher mathematics and to be a fluent reader of Latin, he called in a neighbor to show off his brilliant slave, and to argue that Negroes had brains just like the slave-owners had, and given the same opportunities, would turn out the same.

The visiting master of slaves looked and listened, tried to trap the literate slave in Algebra and Latin, and failing to do so in both, turned to his neighbor and said:

"Yes, he certainly knows his higher mathematics, and he can read Latin better than many white men I know, but I cannot bring myself to believe that he understands a thing that he is doing. It is all an aping of our culture. All on the outside. You are crazy if you think that it has changed him inside in the least. Turn him loose, and he will revert at once to the jungle. He is still a savage, and no amount of translating Virgil and Ovid is going to change him. In fact, all you have done is to turn a useful savage into a dangerous beast."

That was in slavery time, yes, and we have come a long, long way since then, but the troubling thing is that there are still too many who refuse to believe in the ingestion and digestion of western culture as yet. Hence the lack of literature about the higher emotions and love life of upper-class Negroes and the minorities in general.

Publishers and producers are cool to the idea. Now, do not leap to the conclusion that editors and producers constitute a special class of unbelievers. That is far from true. Publishing houses and theatrical promoters are in business to make money. They will sponsor anything that they believe will sell. They shy away from romantic stories about Negroes and Jews because they feel that they know the public indifference to such works, unless the story or play involves racial tension. It can then be offered as a study in Sociology, with the romantic side subdued. They know the scepticism in general about the complicated emotions in the minorities. The average American just cannot conceive of it, and would be apt to reject the notion, and publishers and producers take the stand that they are not in business to educate, but to make money. Sympathetic as they might be, they cannot afford to be crusaders.

In proof of this, you can note various publishers and producers edging forward a little, and ready to go even further when the trial balloons show that the public is ready for it. This public lack of interest is the nut of the matter.

The question naturally arises as to the why of this indifference, not to say scepticism, to the internal life of educated minorities.

The answer lies in what we may call THE AMERICAN MUSEUM OF UNNATURAL HISTORY. This is an intangible built on folk belief. It is assumed that all non-Anglo-Saxons are uncomplicated stereotypes. Everybody knows all about them. They are lay figures mounted in the museum where all may take them in at a glance. They are made of bent wires without insides at all. So how could anybody write a book about the nonexistent?

The American Indian is a contraption of copper wires in an eternal war bonnet, with no equipment for laughter, expressionless face and that says "How" when spoken to. His only activity is treachery leading us to massacres. Who is so dumb as not to know all about Indians, even if they have never seen one, not talked with anyone who ever knew one?

The American Negro exhibit is a group of two. Both of these mechanical toys are built so that their feet eternally shuffle, and their eyes pop and roll. Shuffling feet and those popping, rolling eyes denote the Negro and no characterization is genuine without this monotony. One is seated on a stump picking away on his banjo and singing and laughing. The other is a most amoral character before a share-cropper's shack mumbling about injustice. Doing this makes him out to be a Negro "intellectual." It is as simple as all that.

The whole museum is dedicated to the convenient "typical." In there is the "typical" Oriental, Jew, Yankee, Westerner, Southerner, Latin, and ever out-of-favor Nordics like the German. The Englishman "I say old chappie," and the gesticulating Frenchman. The least observant American can know all at a glance. However, the public willingly accepts the untypical in Nordics, but feels cheated if the untypical is portrayed in others. The author of *Scarlet Sister Mary*[1] complained to me that her neighbors objected to her book on the grounds that she had the characters thinking, "and everybody know that Nigras don't think."

But for the national welfare, it is urgent to realize that the minorities do think, and think about something other than the race problem. That they are very human and internally, according to natural endowment, are just like everybody else. So long as this is not conceived, there must remain that feeling of unsurmountable difference, and difference to the average man means something bad. If people were made right, they would be just like him.

The trouble with the purely problem arguments is that they leave too much unknown. Argue all you will or may about injustice, but as long as the majority cannot conceive of a Negro or a Jew feeling and reacting inside just as they do, the majority will keep right on believing that people who do not feel like them cannot possibly feel as they do, and conform to the established pattern. It is well known that there must be a body of waived matter, let us say, things accepted and taken for granted by all in a community before there can be that commonality of feeling. The usual phrase is having things in common. Until this is thoroughly established in respect to Negroes in America, as well as of other minorities, it will remain impossible for the majority to conceive of a Negro experiencing a deep and abiding love and not just the passion of sex. That a great mass of Negroes can be stirred by the pageants of Spring and Fall; the extravaganza of summer, and the majesty of winter. That they can and do experience discovery of the numerous subtle faces as a foundation for a great and selfless love, and the diverse nuances that go to destroy that love as with others. As it is now, this capacity, this evidence of high and complicated emotions, is ruled out. Hence the lack of interest in a romance uncomplicated by the race struggle has so little appeal.

This insistence on defeat in a story where upperclass Negroes are portrayed, perhaps says something from the subconscious of the majority. Involved in western culture, the hero or the heroine, or both, must appear frustrated and go down to defeat, somehow. Our literature reeks with it. Is it the same as saying, "You can translate Virgil, and fumble with the differential calculus, but can you really comprehend it? Can you cope with our subtleties?"

That brings us to the folklore of "reversion to type." This curious doctrine has such wide acceptance that it is tragic. One has only to examine the huge literature on it to be convinced. No matter how high we may *seem* to climb, put us under strain and we revert to type, that is, to the bush. Under a superficial layer of western culture, the jungle drums throb in our veins.

This ridiculous notion makes it possible for that majority who accept it to conceive of even a man like the suave and scholarly Dr. Charles S. Johnson[2] to hide a black cat's

[1]*Scarlet Sister Mary* (1928), by Julia Mood (1880–1961), who also published *Black April* (1927) and *Roll, Jordan, Roll* (1933).

[2]*Johnson* (1893–1956) an author and social scientist at Fisk University.

bone on his person, and indulge in a midnight voodoo ceremony, complete with leopard skin and drums if threatened with the loss of the presidency of Fisk University, or the love of his wife. "Under the skin . . . better to deal with them in business, etc., but otherwise keep them at a safe distance and under control. I tell you, Carl Van Vechten[3], think as you like, but they are just not like us."

The extent and extravagance of this notion reaches the ultimate in nonsense in the widespread belief that the Chinese have bizarre genitals, because of that eye-fold that makes their eyes seem to slant. In spite of the fact that no biology has ever mentioned any such difference in reproductive organs makes no matter. Millions of people believe it. "Did you know that a Chinese has . . ." Consequently, their quiet contemplative manner is interpreted as a sign of slyness and a treacherous inclination.

But the opening wedge for better understanding has been thrust into the crack. Though many Negroes denounced Carl Van Vechten's *Nigger Heaven* because of the title, and without ever reading it, the book, written in the deepest sincerity, revealed Negroes of wealth and culture to the white public. It created curiosity even when it aroused scepticism. It made folks want to know. Worth Tuttle Hedden's *The Other Room*[4] has definitely widened the opening. Neither of these well-written works take a romance of upperclass Negro life as the central theme, but the atmosphere and the background is there. These works should be followed up by some incisive and intimate stories from the inside.

The realistic story around a Negro insurance official, dentist, general practitioner, undertaker and the like would be most revealing. Thinly disguised fiction around the well known Negro names is not the answer, either. The "exceptional" as well as the Ol' Man Rivers has been exploited all out of context already. Everybody is already resigned to the "exceptional" Negro, and willing to be entertained by the "quaint." To grasp the penetration of western civilization in a minority, it is necessary to know how the average behaves and lives. Books that deal with people like in Sinclair Lewis' *Main Street*[5] is the necessary metier. For various reasons, the average, struggling, non-morbid Negro is the best-kept secret in America. His revelation to the public is the thing needed to do away with that feeling of difference which inspires fear and which ever expresses itself in dislike.

It is inevitable that this knowledge will destroy many illusions and romantic traditions which America probably likes to have around. But then, we have no record of anybody sinking into a lingering death on finding out that there was no Santa Claus. The old world will take it in its stride. The realization that Negroes are no better nor no worse, and at times just as boring as everybody else, will hardly kill off the population of the nation.

Outside of racial attitudes, there is still another reason why this literature should exist. Literature and other arts are supposed to hold up the mirror to nature. With only the fractional "exceptional" and the "quaint" portrayed, a true picture of Negro life in America cannot be. A great principle of national art has been violated.

These are the things that publishers and producers, as the accredited representatives of the American people, have not as yet taken into consideration sufficiently. Let there be light!

---

[3]*Van Vechten* (1880–1964) music critic and novelist who encouraged positive interactions between blacks and whites.

[4]*The Other Room* Hurston here seems to have confused Hedden with Lyman Abbott (1835–1922), who wrote *The Other Room* (1915).

[5]*Main Street* (1920); Sinclair Lewis (1885–1951) was an American novelist whose satires of middle-class life and hypocrisy helped Americans reassess their views of conformity and success.

Understanding and Analysis

1. Hurston soon makes clear what white publishers won't print. Where do you first find the answer to that question? What is the answer?

2. What is the point of the "story from slavery time"?

3. What question is Hurston answering in the rest of her essay?

4. Hurston relies on an extended metaphor to answer this second question. What is it? Why do you think Hurston chooses this particular metaphor to display these stereotypes?

5. Why does Hurston believe that "it is urgent to realize that the minorities do think"?

6. What is the problem with the depiction of upper-class African-Americans in 1950, according to Hurston?

7. What is the role of class in this essay?

8. What is the other reason literature about the middle-class African-American should exist, according to Hurston in 1950?

Comparison

1. Do you think that any of the stereotypes Hurston describes have survived to this day? If so, which ones?

2. Read "Stranger in the Village." Compare the attitudes of Baldwin and Hurston toward the achievements of western civilization as expressed in these two essays.

3. Read the essay by Gates. What connections do you see between these essays?

4. Read the essay by Ellison. Does his essay offer the picture of African-Americans that Hurston finds missing in 1950? Why or why not?

5. Read the essays by Twain, Lippmann, and Postman. What connections can you make between their arguments and Hurston's arguments?

William Faulkner
(1897–1962)

William Faulkner was born in New Albany, Mississippi, on September 25, 1897. In his early years in Oxford, Mississippi, where his parents moved when he was five, he was a precocious, artistic child. His mother taught him to read before he entered school at the age of eight, and he declared his ambition to become a writer at the age of nine. Around the age of ten, according to biographer David Minter, Faulkner began to withdraw into his imagination, writing and drawing instead of listening to his teachers. He did not finish high school; after repeating his junior year, he took a job at his grandfather's bank, where he was first exposed to drinking alcohol.

Although he spent much of his time with high-school sweetheart Estelle Oldham, Faulkner resisted marrying her without their parents' permission. When she became engaged to another man, Faulkner tried to become a pilot to serve in World War I, but he was rejected because he was too short. Soon after he finagled his way into the English Royal Air Force by falsifying his identity, the war ended. He never did learn to fly.

Now drinking regularly, Faulkner turned back to the poetry that had attracted him as a teenager. His first poem was published in 1919 in *The New Republic*. His first volume of poetry, *The Marble Faun*, appeared in 1924, and he wrote his first novel, *Soldier's Pay*, while living in New Orleans. After he returned to Oxford, Faulkner began working on the novel that most regard as his first masterpiece, *The Sound and the Fury*, published in 1929. He also planned to write another novel, a sensational, violent, popular novel that would ease his financial difficulties, later published as *Sanctuary*. This twinning of very different literary efforts—the creation of deliberate, high art and the production of popular fiction—characterized Faulkner's early literary career; he wanted to write serious fiction, but he needed to make money, which he often did, as he said, by "whoring" himself out to magazines with short stories.

Faulkner's return to Oxford also brought him in contact with Estelle, who was now seeking a divorce from her husband of ten years. Although he and Estelle both had serious misgivings about the prospect of getting together, they married in 1929. Soon, problems with alcohol, money, and his marriage plagued Faulkner steadily. He published another of his greatest novels, *As I Lay Dying*, in 1930, and *Light in August* in 1932. The sensational *Sanctuary* appeared between the two, in 1931, bringing money for the publishers, but little for Faulkner himself. In need of steady pay, Faulkner felt compelled to turn—first in 1932, and then several more times over the next decade—to Hollywood, an unattractive alternative to the literary whoredom of popular periodicals. He meanwhile published the novel *Absalom, Absalom!* (1936), among others.

Interest in Faulkner as a literary figure grew in the 1940s with the publication of the *Portable Faulkner*, edited by Malcolm Cowley, one of Faulkner's earliest critical champions. Faulkner received the Nobel Prize for Literature in 1949. During the 1950s, as his reputation grew, he traveled to Japan and served as a writer-in-residence at the University of Virginia. Faulkner died near Oxford, in Byhalia, on July 6, 1962.

Like James Joyce, Virginia Woolf, and T. S. Eliot, William Faulkner worked at the forefront of modernism, expressing in rich, new literary forms the disillusionment and alienation produced by a modernized, mechanized, postwar world. Faulkner's radical techniques of narration focus on the interior life of characters caught in the complex web of history, justice, tradition, and time. His fictional Yoknapatawpha County serves as a microcosm of the South, a world where everyone, rich and poor, black and white, is subject to the horror, tragedy, comedy, and farce of a decaying way of life.

Poetry and the Human Spirit (1950)

I FEEL THAT this award was not made to me as a man, but to my work—a life's work in the agony and sweat of the human spirit, not for glory and least of all for profit, but to create out of the materials of the human spirit something which did not exist before. So this award is only mine in trust. It will not be difficult to find a dedication for the money part of it commensurate with the purpose and significance of its origin. But I would like to do the same with the acclaim too, by using this moment as a pinnacle from which I might be listened to by the young men and women already dedicated to the same anguish and travail, among whom is already that one who will some day stand here where I am standing.

Our tragedy today is a general and universal physical fear so long sustained by now that we can even bear it. There are no longer problems of the spirit. There is only the question: When will I be blown up? Because of this, the young man or woman writing today has forgotten the problems of the human heart in conflict with itself which alone can make good writing because only that is worth writing about, worth the agony and the sweat.

He must learn them again. He must teach himself that the basest of all things is to be afraid; and, teaching himself that, forget it forever, leaving no room in his workshop for anything but the old verities and truths of the heart, the old universal truths lacking which any story is ephemeral and doomed—love and honor and pity and pride and compassion and sacrifice. Until he does so, he labors under a curse. He writes not of love but of lust, of defeats in which nobody loses anything of value, of victories without hope and, worst of all, without pity or compassion. His griefs grieve on no universal bones, leaving no scars. He writes not of the heart but of the glands.

Until he relearns these things, he will write as though he stood among and watched the end of man. I decline to accept the end of man. It is easy enough to say that man is immortal simply because he will endure: that when the last ding-dong of doom has clanged and faded from the last worthless rock hanging tideless in the last red and dying evening, that even then there will still be one more sound: that of his puny inexhaustible voice, still talking. I refuse to accept this. I believe that man will not merely endure: he will prevail. He is immortal, not because he alone among creatures has an inexhaustible voice, but because he has a soul, a spirit capable of compassion and sacrifice and endurance. The poet's, the writer's, duty is to write about these things. It is his privilege to help man endure by lifting his heart, by reminding him of the courage and honor and hope and pride and compassion and pity and sacrifice which have been the glory of his past. The poet's voice need not merely be the record of man, it can be one of the props, the pillars to help him endure and prevail.

Understanding and Analysis

1. To whom is Faulkner specifically addressing his speech? What metaphor does he employ to situate himself before his audience?

2. How does Faulkner characterize his "life's work"?

3. What does Faulkner believe is worth writing about? Find all the references to this subject in the speech.

4. Why does he believe that in 1950 writers no longer write about that subject?

5. What does Faulkner mean by the words "His griefs grieve on no universal bones, leaving no scars." Note the language of that sentence and the one that follows it. What metaphor is Faulkner developing? How does he contrast the physical with the spiritual?

6. Reread the description of the end of man that Faulkner imagines. What is poetic in that description? Why does Faulkner reject it?

7. What good does the writer do for mankind, according to Faulkner?

Comparison

1. Faulkner says that the award was given to him not "as a man" but given to his "work." Do you think we as readers can separate the man from the work? Read T. S. Eliot's "Tradition and the Individual Talent." Do Eliot and Faulkner agree on this point?

2. Read Frost's "Education by Poetry." Compare Frost's "God belief" to Faulkner's belief that man will prevail.

3. Read the biography of Faulkner in this text. Do you believe that he wrote not for profit in light of the facts? Why or why not?

4. Read the essay by Hurston. To what degree, if at all, do Hurston and Faulkner agree?

James Baldwin
(1924–1987)

When James Arthur Baldwin was born in Harlem Hospital in August of 1924, the surname on his birth certificate was that of his mother, Emma Berdis Jones, for she never revealed the name of his father. The man who became Baldwin's father, gave him his name, and shaped his reality was David Baldwin, a preacher from New Orleans. He arrived in Harlem with his aging mother, a former slave, and a son, Samuel, age twelve, to marry Emma Jones when James was three. David Baldwin was a man of strong beliefs—hatred of whites, commitment to religion, rejection of street life, theater, and movies. James knew that his father favored Samuel despite the older boy's fierce rebellion against his strict upbringing. Even after Samuel left home, James felt rejected by David Baldwin. Yet it was this same home that also supplied James with a sense of his own worth and helped him to withstand the degradations of prejudice. Through his mother's love and her reliance on James to help her with the growing family—

eight more children, three boys and five girls—James developed a sense of responsibility, an understanding of the meaning of family, of the need for discipline and affection and the saving grace of love.

While his mother worked, cleaning the houses of white people, James tended the children, read (Charles Dickens, Harriet Beecher Stowe, Horatio Alger), ran errands, worked odd jobs, attended school. Reading led to writing. By the time he was graduated from Public School 24 at age eleven he had already written a history of Harlem based on library research and had won a prize for a short story he'd sent to a church newspaper. At Frederick Douglass Junior High School he continued to write, contributing stories and editorials to the school magazine. When he was fourteen, entrapped by his hatred of his stepfather as well as his fear of succumbing to the lure of the racketeers and the drug addicts of the street, Baldwin underwent an anguished religious conversion at the hands of the Pentecostals. Soon he became an immensely popular preacher, succeeding to his great satisfaction in his stepfather's own profession. At this time, he entered De Witt Clinton High School where he again took up writing, editing *The Magpie*, the school's literary magazine.

Three years after his conversion, James Baldwin gave up preaching, drawn away not only by his love of the literary life and the movies and plays forbidden by the church but also by his sexual experiences, with girls but also and especially with his first male lover. After high school, Baldwin left home, got a job laying railroad track for the army in New Jersey, and began writing what became, eleven years later, his first novel, *Go Tell It On the Mountain*. The following year, 1943, he was fired from his job, David Baldwin was dying, and James returned home. According to his friend and biographer, W. J. Weatherby, after his stepfather's funeral, James found and lost job after job. Although his brothers were now old enough to work and contribute to the household finances, Baldwin knew the family depended on him; he believed his best hope of supporting them was through his writing. Suffering from insomnia, he read Milton, Shakespeare, Chaucer, and the African-American writer Richard Wright, searching for techniques that would help him tell his own story about his life in Harlem. He realized finally that to become a writer he had to write the truth as he saw it, and to do that he had to accept his homosexuality and he had to leave his home.

He moved to the gay community of Greenwich Village where he seemed to be the only African-American. Now twenty, Baldwin arranged through a friend to meet Wright, who at thirty-six provided for Baldwin the role model he needed. In 1945, with Wright's help, Baldwin was awarded the Eugene Saxton Fellowship, a grant of $500 from *Harper's* with the possibility of publishing the work with them when it was finished. But *Harper's* turned him down. The next year, Richard Wright moved to France. Dejected and humiliated over his failure to publish his novel, Baldwin turned to drink. But the pride that had kept him from asking Wright for more help also spurred him to try again. In bars and through connections made during a brief flirtation with social-ism, he met editors and writers, eventually landing work writing a book review for *The Nation* and, later, steady work as a reviewer for *The New Leader*. For *Commentary* he wrote his first essay, "The Harlem Ghetto," which took him six months of rewriting because the topics, especially anti-Semitism in Harlem, were painful for him to face and work out.

Although the essay was widely admired, Baldwin was nearly broke when it was finally published in February of 1948. Comparing himself, Weatherby says, to Orwell in *Down and Out in Paris and London*, Baldwin joined with a photographer to write a book on storefront churches; the book remained unpublished but earned him the Rosenwald Fellowship, money he hoped to use to write a different novel, about Greenwich Village and the gay community. When he was told of the suicide of a good friend, who at twenty-four had jumped off the George Washington Bridge, Baldwin felt more and more hopeless and anxious. Finally he decided to spend all but forty dollars of the money from his fellow-ship on air fare to Paris. He left his mother and his brothers and sisters behind, believing that only by leaving America could he be free to write about it.

In Paris, friends met him at the airport and took him to Les Deux Magots, where Richard Wright introduced him to the editor of a new magazine called *Zero* and recommended a cheap hotel. Baldwin soon became part of a group of American writers who were linked through Wright and others to Sartre and the French intelligentsia. But his money was running out, forcing him to borrow money and clothes to get by. In 1949, *Zero* published his essay "Every-body's Protest Novel," in which Baldwin compares *Uncle Tom's Cabin* with Wright's *Native Son*, concluding that though opposite, "Bigger is Uncle Tom's descendant" because neither figure conveys the full humanity of an individ-ual African-American man. Each character accepts the burden of a stultify-ing stereotype; each claims "that it is his categorization alone which is real and which cannot be transcended." These words caused a permanent rift between the two writers; when Wright died in 1960 Baldwin called him "the man I fought so hard and who meant so much to me."

Baldwin remained in France and later in Switzerland for the next eight years, returning briefly to America in 1952 and 1956. In Europe he read Henry James, developed a close friendship with a young Swiss named Lucien, and found the quiet and the determination to write about his life in Europe as well as about life in Harlem and in Greenwich Village. Essays such as "Stranger in the Village" and "Equal in Paris" were later collected in *Notes of a Native Son* (1955). His novels about Harlem and Greenwich Village, *Go Tell It On the Moun-tain* and *Giovanni's Room*, were published in 1953 and 1956. He also wrote a play, *The Amen Corner*, which was performed at Howard University in 1954–1955. By this time Baldwin had become famous, his books had brought him large royalties, and his self-confidence had increased.

He returned to New York in 1957 and soon after flew south. In Georgia he met Martin Luther King in a hotel room, followed him to Alabama to hear him preach, and came away committed to the civil rights movement, despite the artist's traditional shunning of politics. Throughout the 1960s, Baldwin drove himself to speak, protest, and witness for the movement. He spent all the money he earned traveling between the South and New York City, help-ing his family and friends, throwing and attending parties, drinking, and, miraculously, writing. Involved with the theatrical community in New York, he hoped to see a play develop from his novel about the homosexual world of Greenwich Village.

In these days he moved among celebrities from various fields—Harry Bela-fonte, Roy Innis of the Congress of Racial Equality (CORE), Norman Mailer, Marlon Brando, Lorraine Hansberry, William Styron, Eli Kazan, Sidney Poitier. Although *Giovanni* was never produced as a play, Baldwin did publish a sec-ond collection of essays, *Nobody Knows My Name*, in 1961, including in it "Fifth Avenue, Uptown," a look at Harlem twelve years after his first essay was pub-lished, and "Alas, Poor Richard," his essay on the death of Richard Wright. In 1962, he published a third novel, *Another Country*, met with Malcolm X, and trav-eled to Africa. In 1963, he published *The Fire Next Time*, a long essay describing the rage and inhumanity produced by racism. By 1970, he had published two plays, *Blues for Mister Charlie* (1964) and *The Amen Corner* (1965), each of which had been produced in New York City, as well as a collaboration with photographer Richard Avedon, *Nothing Personal* (1964), a collection of short stories *Going To Meet the Man* (1965), and another novel *Tell Me How Long the Train's Been Gone* (1968).

According to his biographer, Baldwin believed that the death of Martin Luther King in 1968 marked the death of the civil rights movement. Exhausted, he returned to Paris, but fame and misery drove him to Istanbul, London, and Italy before he collapsed and was hospitalized. Friends brought him to St. Paul-de-Vence, near Nice, where he settled permanently, making periodic visits to the United States.

In the 1970s, finding it increasingly difficult to write, Baldwin published a number of minor works, including transcripts of conversations, several ex-tended essays, a children's book, and two more novels (*If Beale Street Could Talk*, 1974, and *Just Above My Head*, 1979). The reviews of these works were not favorable. Although he was often ill, depressed, and restless, he continued to produce short essays such as "If Black English Isn't a Language, Then Tell Me What Is?" (1979) for the *New York Times* and "Dark Days" (1980) for *Esquire*.

In 1983 and 1984, as a professor for Five Colleges, Inc. (University of Mass-achusetts, Hampshire College, Mount Holyoke, Smith, and Amherst), Baldwin taught at the University of Massachusetts at Amherst in the W. E. B. DuBois Department of African Studies, lecturing on the controversial subjects he had always met head on. One time, according to Weatherby, he lectured on "Blacks and Jews," reiterating his view that to many African-Americans, Jews are simply "white Christians," and accepting with no comment the blatantly anti-Semitic responses his African-American students contributed during the question period. Transient emotional attachments as well as drinking, smoking, and working too hard had left him vulnerable to exhaustion and depression. On his way to a writing class he was teaching at Hampshire College, he suffered a heart attack.

The following year, 1985, despite the publication of three books, his reputation hit its lowest point. *Evidence of Things Not Seen*, an essay about a series of child murders in Atlanta, received uniformly negative reviews; his book of poems, *Jimmy's Blues: Selected Poems*, was ignored; and the collection of fifty-one essays, none new, in one large volume entitled *The Price of the Ticket: Collected Non-Fiction 1948-85* showed, the critics said, that over the years his writing had traded power for bombast. In 1987 he was diagnosed as having cancer of the esophagus; his brother David kept the news from him as long as he could, allowing James to rest comfortably in his home outside Nice. When James Baldwin died in early December, his body was flown home to Harlem, where his funeral was attended by his mother, his brothers and sisters, his friends, his admirers, the famous and the unknown, homosexuals and heterosexuals, African-Americans and whites, a mixture of the humanity about which Baldwin had written and in whom, despite all odds, he had never failed to believe.

In "Autobiographical Notes," Baldwin says that his writing was influenced by "the King James Bible, the rhetoric of the store-front church, something ironic and violent and perpetually understated in Negro speech—and something of Dickens' love for bravura." His style also reflects Orwell's unflinching honesty, an honesty Baldwin worked hard to discover for himself and to reveal to others, an honesty that survived the increasingly bitter and disappointing struggle for the acceptance of all men and women on the basis of their merits, not their religion or their skin color or their sexual preferences.

STRANGER IN THE VILLAGE (1953)

FROM ALL AVAILABLE evidence no black man had ever set foot in this tiny Swiss village before I came. I was told before arriving that I would probably be a "sight" for the village; I took this to mean that people of my complexion were rarely seen in Switzerland, and also that city people are always something of a "sight" outside of the city. It did not occur to me—possibly because I am an American—that there could be people anywhere who had never seen a Negro.

It is a fact that cannot be explained on the basis of the inaccessibility of the village. The village is very high, but it is only four hours from Milan and three hours from Lausanne. It is true that it is virtually unknown. Few people making plans for a holiday would elect to come here. On the other hand, the villagers are able, presumably, to come and go as they please—which they do: to another town at the foot of the mountain, with a population of approximately five thousand, the nearest place to see a movie or go to the bank. In the village there is no movie house, no bank, no library, no theater; very few radios, one jeep, one station wagon; and at the moment, one typewriter, mine, an invention which the woman next door to me here had never seen. There are about six hundred people living here, all Catholic—I conclude this from the fact that the Catholic church is open all year round, whereas the Protestant chapel, set off on a hill a little removed from the village, is open only in the summertime when the tourists arrive. There are four or five hotels, all closed now, and four or five *bistros*, of which, however, only two do any business during the winter. These two do not do a great deal, for life in the village seems to end around nine or ten o'clock. There are a few stores, butcher, baker, épicerie, a hardware store, and a money-changer—who cannot change travelers' checks, but must send them down to the bank, an operation which takes two or three days. There is something called the *Ballet Haus,* closed in the winter and used for God knows what, certainly not ballet, during the summer. There seems to be only one schoolhouse in the village, and this for the quite young children; I suppose this to mean that their older brothers and sisters at some point descend from these mountains in order to complete their education—possibly, again, to the town just below. The landscape is absolutely forbidding, mountains towering on all four sides, ice and snow as far as the eye can reach. In this white wilderness, men and women and children move all day, carrying washing, wood, buckets of milk or water, sometimes skiing on Sunday afternoons. All week long boys and young men are to be seen shoveling snow off the rooftops, or dragging wood down from the forest in sleds.

The village's only real attraction, which explains the tourist season, is the hot spring water. A disquietingly high proportion of these tourists are cripples, or semi-cripples, who come year after year—from other parts of Switzerland, usually—to take the waters. This lends the village, at the height of the season, a rather terrifying air of sanctity, as though it were a lesser Lourdes. There is often something beautiful, there is always something awful, in the spectacle of a person who has lost one of his faculties, a faculty he never questioned until it was gone, and who struggles to recover it. Yet people remain people, on crutches or indeed on deathbeds; and wherever I passed, the first summer I was here, among the native villagers or among the lame, a wind passed with me—of astonishment, curiosity, amusement, and outrage. That first summer I stayed two weeks and never intended to return. But I did return in the winter, to work; the village offers, obviously, no distractions whatever and has the further advantage of being extremely cheap. Now it is winter again, a year later, and I am here again. Everyone in the village knows my name, though they scarcely ever use it, knows that I come from America—though, this, apparently, they will never really believe: black men come from Africa—and everyone knows that I am the friend of the son of a woman who was born here, and that I am staying in their chalet. But I remain as much a stranger today as I was the first day I arrived, and the children shout *Neger! Neger!* as I walk along the streets.

It must be admitted that in the beginning I was far too shocked to have any real reaction. In so far as I reacted at all, I reacted by trying to be pleasant—it being a great part of the American Negro's education (long before he goes to school) that he must make people "like" him. This smile-and-the-world-smiles-with-you routine worked about as well in this situation as it had in the situation for which it was designed, which is to say that it did not work at all. No one, after all, can be liked whose human weight and complexity cannot be, or has not been, admitted. My smile was simply another unheard-of phenomenon which allowed them to see my teeth—they did not, really, see my smile and I began to think that, should I take to snarling, no one would notice any difference. All of the physical characteristics of the Negro which had caused me, in America, a very different and almost forgotten pain were nothing less than miraculous—or infernal—in the eyes of the village people. Some thought my hair was the color of tar, that it had the texture of wire, or the texture of cotton. It was jocularly suggested that I might let it all grow long and make myself a winter coat. If I sat in the sun for more than five minutes some daring creature was certain to come along and gingerly put his fingers on my hair, as though he were afraid of an electric shock, or put his hand on my hand, astonished that the color did not rub off. In all of this, in which it must be conceded there was the charm of genuine wonder and in which there were certainly no elements of intentional unkindness, there was yet no suggestion that I was human: I was simply a living wonder.

I knew that they did not mean to be unkind, and I know it now; it is necessary, nevertheless, for me to repeat this to myself each time that I walk out of the chalet. The children who shout *Neger!* have no way of knowing the echoes this sound raises in me. They are brimming with good humor and the more daring swell with pride when I stop to speak with them. Just the same, there are days when I cannot pause and smile, when I have no heart to play with them; when, indeed, I mutter sourly to myself, exactly as I muttered on the streets of a city these children have never seen, when I was no bigger than these children are now: *Your* mother was a *nigger*. Joyce is right about history being a nightmare—but it may be the nightmare from which no one *can* awaken. People are trapped in history and history is trapped in them.

There is a custom in the village—I am told it is repeated in many villages—of "buying" African natives for the purpose of converting them to Christianity. There stands in the church all year round a small box with a slot for money, decorated with a black figurine, and into this box the villagers drop their francs. During the *carnaval* which precedes Lent, two village children have their faces blackened—out of which bloodless darkness their blue eyes shine like ice—and fantastic horsehair wigs are placed on their blond heads; thus disguised, they solicit among the villagers for money for the missionaries in Africa. Between the box in the church and the blackened children, the village "bought" last year six or eight African natives. This was reported to me with pride by the wife of one of the *bistro* owners and I was careful to express astonishment and pleasure at the solicitude shown by the village for the souls of black folks. The *bistro* owner's wife beamed with a pleasure far more genuine than my own and seemed to feel that I might now breathe more easily concerning the souls of at least six of my kinsmen.

I tried not to think of these so lately baptized kinsmen, of the price paid for them, or the peculiar price they themselves would pay, and said nothing about my father, who having taken his own conversion too literally never, at bottom, forgave the white world (which he described as heathen) for having saddled him with a Christ in whom, to judge at least from their treatment of him, they themselves no longer believed. I thought of white men arriving for the first time in an African village, strangers there, as I am a stranger here, and tried to imagine the astounded populace touching their hair and marveling at the color of their skin. But there is a great difference between being the first white man to be seen by Africans and being the first black man to be seen by whites. The white man takes the astonishment as tribute, for he arrives to conquer and to convert the natives, whose inferiority in relation to himself is not even to be questioned; whereas I, without a thought of conquest, find myself among a people whose culture controls me, has even, in a sense, created me, people who have cost me more in anguish and rage than they will ever know, who yet do not even know of my existence. The astonishment with which I might have greeted them, should they have stumbled into my African village a few hundred years ago, might have rejoiced their hearts. But the astonishment with which they greet me today can only poison mine.

And this is so despite everything I may do to feel differently, despite my friendly conversations with the *bistro* owner's wife, despite their three-year-old son who has at last become my friend, despite the *saluts and bonsoirs*[1] which I exchange with people as I walk, despite the fact that I know that no individual can be taken to task for what history is doing, or has done. I say that the culture of these people controls me—but they can scarcely be held responsible for European culture. America comes out of Europe, but these people have never seen America, nor have most of them seen more of Europe than the hamlet at the foot of their mountain. Yet they move with an authority which I shall never have; and they regard me, quite rightly, not only as a stranger in their village but as a suspect latecomer, bearing no credentials, to everything they have—however unconsciously—inherited.

For this village, even were it incomparably more remote and incredibly more primitive, is the West, the West onto which I have been so strangely grafted. These people cannot be, from the point of view of power, strangers anywhere in the world; they have made the modern world, in effect, even if they do not know it. The most illiterate among them is related, in a way that I am not, to Dante, Shakespeare, Michelangelo, Aeschylus, Da Vinci, Rembrandt, and Racine; the cathedral at Chartres says something to them which it cannot say to me, as indeed would New York's Empire State Building, should anyone here ever see it. Out of their hymns and dances come Beethoven and Bach. Go back a few centuries and they are in their full glory—but I am in Africa, watching the conquerors arrive.

The rage of the disesteemed is personally fruitless, but it is also absolutely inevitable; this rage, so generally discounted, so little understood even among the people whose daily bread it is, is one of the things that makes history. Rage can only with difficulty, and never entirely, be brought under the domination of the intelligence and is therefore not susceptible to any arguments whatever. This is a fact which ordinary representatives of the *Herrenvolk*,[2] having never felt this rage and being unable to imagine, quite fail to understand. Also, rage cannot be hidden, it can only be dissembled. This dissembling deludes the thoughtless, and strenthens rage and adds, to rage, contempt. There are, no doubt, as many ways of coping with the resulting complex of tensions as there are black men in the world, but no black man can hope ever to be entirely liberated from this internal warfare—rage, dissembling, and contempt having inevitably accompanied his first realization of the power of white men. What is crucial here is that, since white men represent in the black man's world so heavy a weight, white men have for black men a reality which is far from being reciprocal; and hence all black men have toward all white men an attitude which is designed, really, either to rob the white man of the jewel of his naïveté, or else to make it cost him dear.

The black man insists, by whatever means he finds at his disposal, that the white man cease to regard him as an exotic rarity and recognize him as a human being. This is a

[1]*Saluts* and *Bonsoirs* hellos and good evenings.
[2]*Herrenvolk* master race.

very charged and difficult moment, for there is a great deal of will power involved in the white man's naïveté. Most people are not naturally reflective any more than they are naturally malicious, and the white man prefers to keep the black man at a certain human remove because it is easier for him thus to preserve his simplicity and avoid being called to account for crimes committed by his forefathers, or his neighbors. He is inescapably aware, nevertheless, that he is in a better position in the world than black men are, nor can he quite put to death the suspicion that he is hated by black men therefor. He does not wish to be hated, neither does he wish to change places, and at this point in his uneasiness he can scarcely avoid having recourse to those legends which white men have created about black men, the most usual effect of which is that the white man finds himself enmeshed, so to speak, in his own language which describes hell, as well as the attributes which lead one to hell, as being as black as night.

Every legend, moreover, contains its residuum of truth, and the root function of language is to control the universe by describing it. It is of quite considerable significance that black men remain, in the imagination, and in overwhelming numbers in fact, beyond the disciplines of salvation; and this despite the fact that the West has been "buying" African natives for centuries. There is, I should hazard, an instantaneous necessity to be divorced from this so visibly unsaved stranger, in whose heart, moreover, one cannot guess what dreams of vengeance are being nourished; and, at the same time, there are few things on earth more attractive than the idea of the unspeakable liberty which is allowed the unredeemed. When, beneath the black mask, a human being begins to make himself felt one cannot escape a certain awful wonder as to what kind of human being it is. What one's imagination makes of other people is dictated, of course, by the laws of one's own personality and it is one of the ironies of black-white relations that, by means of what the white man imagines the black man to be, the black man is enabled to know who the white man is.

I have said, for example, that I am as much a stranger in this village today as I was the first summer I arrived, but this is not quite true. The villagers wonder less about the texture of my hair than they did then, and wonder rather more about me. And the fact that their wonder now exists on another level is reflected in their attitudes and in their eyes. There are the children who make those delightful, hilarious, sometimes astonishingly grave overtures of friendship in the unpredictable fashion of children; other children, having been taught that the devil is a black man, scream in genuine anguish as I approach. Some of the older women never pass without a friendly greeting, never pass, indeed, if it seems that they will be able to engage me in conversation; other women look down or look away or rather contemptuously smirk. Some of the men drink with me and suggest that I learn how to ski—partly, I gather, because they cannot imagine what I would look like on skis—and want to know if I am married, and ask questions about my *métier*.[3] But some of the men have accused *le sale nègre*[4]—behind my back—of stealing wood and there is already in the eyes of some of them that peculiar, intent, paranoiac malevolence which one sometimes surprises in the eyes of American white men when, out walking with their Sunday girl, they see a Negro male approach.

There is a dreadful abyss between the streets of this village and the streets of the city in which I was born, between the children who shout *Neger!* today and those who shouted *Nigger!* yesterday—the abyss is experience, the American experience. The syllable hurled

[3]*Metier* job, profession.

[4]*Le sale negre* the dirty Negro.

behind me today expresses, above all, wonder: I am a stranger here. But I am not a stranger in America and the same syllable riding on the American air expresses the war my presence has occasioned in the American soul.

For this village brings home to me this fact: that there was a day, and not really a very distant day, when Americans were scarcely Americans at all but discontented Europeans, facing a great unconquered continent and strolling, say, into a marketplace and seeing black men for the first time. The shock this spectacle afforded is suggested, surely, by the promptness with which they decided that these black men were not really men but cattle. It is true that the necessity on the part of the settlers of the New World of reconciling their moral assumptions with the fact—and the necessity—of slavery enhanced immensely the charm of this idea, and it is also true that this idea expresses, with a truly American bluntness, the attitude which to varying extents all masters have had toward all slaves.

But between all former slaves and slave-owners and the drama which begins for Americans over three hundred years ago at Jamestown, there are at least two differences to be observed. The American Negro slave could not suppose, for one thing, as slaves in past epochs had supposed and often done, that he would ever be able to wrest the power from his master's hands. This was a supposition which the modern era, which was to bring about such vast changes in the aims and dimensions of power, put to death; it only begins, in unprecedented fashion, and with dreadful implications, to be resurrected today. But even had this supposition persisted with undiminished force, the American Negro slave could not have used it to lend his condition dignity, for the reason that this supposition rests on another: that the slave in exile yet remains related to his past, has some means— if only in memory—of revering and sustaining the forms of his former life, is able, in short, to maintain his identity.

This was not the case with the American Negro slave. He is unique among the black men of the world in that his past was taken from him, almost literally, at one blow. One wonders what on earth the first slave found to say to the first dark child he bore. I am told that there are Haitians able to trace their ancestry back to African kings, but any American Negro wishing to go back so far will find his journey through time abruptly arrested by the signature on the bill of sale which served as the entrance paper for his ancestor. At the time—to say nothing of the circumstances—of the enslavement of the captive black man who was to become the American Negro, there was not the remotest possibility that he would ever take power from his master's hands. There was no reason to suppose that his situation would ever change, nor was there, shortly, anything to indicate that his situation had ever been different. It was his necessity, in the words of E. Franklin Frazier,[5] to find a "motive for living under American culture or die." The identity of the American Negro comes out of this extreme situation, and the evolution of this identity was a source of the most intolerable anxiety in the minds and the lives of his masters.

For the history of the American Negro is unique also in this: that the question of his humanity, and of his rights therefore as a human being, became a burning one for several generations of Americans, so burning a question that it ultimately became one of those used to divide the nation. It is out of this argument that the venom of the epithet *Nigger!* is derived. It is an argument which Europe has never had, and hence Europe quite sincerely fails to understand how or why the argument arose in the first place, why its

[5]*E. Franklin Frazier* (1894–1962) African-American sociologist and author who became head of the sociology department at Howard University.

effects are frequently disastrous and always so unpredictable, why it refuses until today to be entirely settled. Europe's black possessions remained—and do remain—in Europe's colonies, at which remove they represented no threat whatever to European identity. If they posed any problem at all for the European conscience it was a problem which remained comfortingly abstract: in effect, the black man, as a *man* did not exist for Europe. But in America, even as a slave, he was an inescapable part of the general social fabric and no American could escape having an attitude toward him. Americans attempt until today to make an abstraction of the Negro, but the very nature of these abstractions reveals the tremendous effects the presence of the Negro has had on the American character.

When one considers the history of the Negro in America it is of the greatest importance to recognize that the moral beliefs of a person, or a people, are never really as tenuous as life—which is not moral—very often causes them to appear; these create for them a frame of reference and a necessary hope, the hope being that when life has done its worst they will be enabled to rise above themselves and to triumph over life. Life would scarcely be bearable if this hope did not exist. Again, even when the worst has been said, to betray a belief is not by any means to have put oneself beyond its power; the betrayal of a belief is not the same thing as ceasing to believe. If this were not so there would be no moral standards in the world at all. Yet one must also recognize that morality is based on ideas and that all ideas are dangerous—dangerous because ideas can only lead to action and where the action leads no man can say. And dangerous in this respect: that confronted with the impossibility of remaining faithful to one's beliefs, and the equal impossibility of becoming free of them, one can be driven to the most inhuman excesses. The ideas on which American beliefs are based are not, though Americans often seem to think so, ideas which originated in America. They came out of Europe. And the establishment of democracy on the American continent was scarcely as radical a break with the past as was the necessity, which Americans faced, of broadening this concept to include black men.

This was, literally, a hard necessity. It was impossible, for one thing, for Americans to abandon their beliefs, not only because these beliefs alone seemed able to justify the sacrifices they had endured and the blood that they had spilled, but also because these beliefs afforded them their only bulwark against a moral chaos as absolute as the physical chaos of the continent it was their destiny to conquer. But in the situation in which Americans found themselves, these beliefs threatened an idea which, whether or not one likes to think so, is the very warp and woof of the heritage of the West, the idea of white supremacy.

Americans have made themselves notorious by the shrillness and the brutality with which they have insisted on this idea, but they did not invent it; and it has escaped the world's notice that those very excesses of which Americans have been guilty imply a certain, unprecedented uneasiness over the idea's life and power, if not, indeed, the idea's validity. The idea of white supremacy rests simply on the fact that white men are the creators of civilization (the present civilization, which is the only one that matters; all previous civilizations are simply "contributions" to our own) and are therefore civilization's guardians and defenders. Thus it was impossible for Americans to accept the black man as one of themselves, for to do so was to jeopardize their status as white men. But not so to accept him was to deny his human reality, his human weight and complexity, and the strain of denying the overwhelmingly undeniable forced Americans into rationalizations so fantastic that they approached the pathological.

At the root of the American Negro problem is the necessity of the American white man to find a way of living with the Negro in order to be able to live with himself. And the history of this problem can be reduced to the means used by Americans—lynch law and law, segregation and legal acceptance, terrorization and concession—either to come to terms with this necessity, or to find a way around it, or (most usually) to find a way of doing both these things at once. The resulting spectacle, at once foolish and dreadful, led someone to make the quite accurate observation that "the Negro-in-America is a form of insanity which overtakes white men."

In this long battle, a battle by no means finished, the unforeseeable effects of which will be felt by many future generations, the white man's motive was the protection of his identity; the black man was motivated by the need to establish an identity. And despite the terrorization which the Negro in America endured and endures sporadically until today, despite the cruel and totally inescapable ambivalence of his status in his country, the battle for his identity has long ago been won. He is not a visitor to the West, but a citizen there, an American; as American as the Americans who despise him, the Americans who fear him, the Americans who love him—the Americans who became less than themselves, or rose to be greater than themselves by virtue of the fact that the challenge he represented was inescapable. He is perhaps the only black man in the world whose relationship to white men is more terrible, more subtle, and more meaningful than the relationship of bitter possessed to uncertain possessors. His survival depended, and his development depends, on his ability to turn his peculiar status in the Western world to his own advantage and, it may be, to the very great advantage of that world. It remains for him to fashion out of his experience that which will give him sustenance, and a voice.

The cathedral at Chartres, I have said, says something to the people of this village which it cannot say to me; but it is important to understand that this cathedral says something to me which it cannot say to them. Perhaps they are struck by the power of the spires, the glory of the windows; but they have known God, after all, longer than I have known him, and in a different way, and I am terrified by the slippery bottomless well to be found in the crypt, down which heretics were hurled to death, and by the obscene, inescapable gargoyles jutting out of the stone and seeming to say that God and the devil can never be divorced. I doubt that the villagers think of the devil when they face a cathedral because they have never been identified with the devil. But I must accept the status which myth, if nothing else, gives me in the West before I can hope to change the myth.

Yet, if the American Negro has arrived at his identity by virtue of the absoluteness of his estrangement from his past, American white men still nourish the illusion that there is some means of recovering the European innocence, of returning to a state in which black men do not exist. This is one of the greatest errors Americans can make. The identity they fought so hard to protect has, by virtue of that battle, undergone a change: Americans are as unlike any other white people in the world as it is possible to be. I do not think, for example, that it is too much to suggest that the American vision of the world—which allows so little reality, generally speaking, for any of the darker forces in human life, which tends until today to paint moral issues in glaring black and white—owes a great deal to the battle waged by Americans to maintain between themselves and black men a human separation which could not be bridged. It is only now beginning to be borne in on us—very faintly, it must be admitted, very slowly, and very much against our will—that this vision of the world is dangerously inaccurate, and perfectly useless. For it protects our moral high-mindedness at the terrible expense of weakening our grasp of reality. People who shut their eyes to reality simply invite their own destruction, and anyone who insists on remaining in a state of innocence long after that innocence is dead turns himself into a monster.

The time has come to realize that the interracial drama acted out on the American continent has not only created a new black man, it has created a new white man, too. No road whatever will lead Americans back to the simplicity of this European village where white men still have the luxury of looking on me as a stranger. I am not, really, a stranger any longer for any American alive. One of the things that distinguishes Americans from other people is that no other people has ever been so deeply involved in the lives of black men, and vice versa. This fact faced, with all its implications, it can be seen that the history of the American Negro problem is not merely shameful, it is also something of an achievement. For even when the worst has been said, it must also be added that the perpetual challenge posed by this problem was always, somehow, perpetually met. It is precisely this black-white experience which may prove of indispensable value to us in the world we face today. This world is white no longer, and it will never be white again.

Understanding and Analysis

1. Why, according to Baldwin, did his smile not work when he walked along the streets in the village? Why did it not work in America? What, in fact, was the result in each case? What other attempts does Baldwin make to appear pleasant to the villagers? How effective do you think this behavior is in each instance? What is the effect of this "dissembling" on Baldwin?

2. What behavior on the part of the villagers indicated to Baldwin that he was to them inhuman? What caused their reaction to him? How does their collection of missionary money contribute to this implication that Baldwin is inhuman?

3. In this essay, Baldwin is setting up an explicit comparison between the reactions of white people in the small Swiss village and in a large American city. Reread the essay. Find as many comparisons as you can. What exactly are the differences and similarities?

4. Why, according to Baldwin, do the people of this village "move with an authority [Baldwin] shall never have"?

5. Why does naivete or innocence not exonerate white people, according to Baldwin? What is its ultimate effect?

6. What is the function of language, according to Baldwin? What words does Baldwin use to explain his point? Where do these words recur? Note the instances and contexts of Baldwin's use of the word "charm." What associations does this word carry? How is it connected to the themes of the essay?

7. How does the black man "know who the white man is"? What versions of Baldwin have the villagers developed? What does Baldwin learn about the villagers?

8. Baldwin has described several internal wars and battles in this essay. What are they?

9. What determines a person's identity, according to Baldwin?

10. How was Europe different from America in its perspective on the Negro?

11. What is "the heritage of the West," according to Baldwin? What was the difference between the American slaves and those who had been enslaved in the past?

12. What does the cathedral at Chartres say to Baldwin? What does it say to you? Why?

13. What is the tone and meaning of the last sentence?

14. According to Baldwin, "People are trapped in history and history is trapped in them." Does Baldwin believe that individuals can overcome or escape that trap? What is your evidence?

Comparison

1. Read Baldwin's "If Black English Isn't a Language, Then Tell Me, What Is?" Compare Baldwin's definitions and descriptions of language in the two essays.

2. Read the essay by Hurston in this text. Compare Hurston's attitudes toward Western culture with those of Baldwin.

3. Compare Baldwin's views on Western culture with those of Martin Luther King, Jr., and Henry Louis Gates, Jr.

Jacob Bronowski
(1908–1974)

Jacob Bronowski was born in Poland on January 18, 1908. His family made two major moves during his childhood, the first to Germany, when he was three, and the second to England, when he was 12. On the boat that took the family over the English Channel, Bronowski picked up only two English words. Of course, he could not read English at all. With two or three years of "self-education" and regular schooling, however, he read well and voraciously, consuming the works of Charles Dickens, Aphra Behn, and Bernard Shaw, as well as the Renaissance and Romantic poets. This wide exposure to literature may seem an unusual preparation for a career as a scientist, but Bronowski explains, "I grew up to be indifferent to the distinction between literature and science, which in my teens were simply two languages for experience that I learned together."

When he enrolled at Cambridge in 1927, Bronowski was preparing for a career in mathematics, although science and literature interested him deeply. With friends, he started a literary publication called *Experiment*, and he found himself stimulated by developments in physics, by surrealism in literature, and by the increasing artistic sophistication of film. After spending six years in the scintillating intellectual scene of Cambridge, Bronowski took a position at University College in Hull, lecturing on mathematics. He remained there through the early years of World War II, publishing his first book, *The Poet's Defence*, in 1939, and beginning a book on William Blake entitled *The Man Without a Mask*.

By the time this book appeared in 1943, Bronowski had married and changed jobs, leaving Hull for the Ministry of Home Security. He explained the move by saying, "naturally (if that is the right word) my official business as a scientist in war time was with the work of destruction." His work with the ministry, more specifically, involved bombs. At the end of the war, the ministry sent him to Japan "to assess how well we had done our dread ful work." This trip had a profound impact on him, prompting a career change, a philosophical and intellectual shift, and a new ambition. "From that time," Bronowski said, "my ambition has been to create a philosophy of the twentieth century which shall be all of one piece. One part of that is to teach people to command science—to have command of the basic ideas of modern science, so that they can take command of its use."

Bronowski worked for several years as a statistical researcher before taking a job with the National Coal Board, overseeing research on new fuel. After publishing a book called *The Common Sense of Science*, he served as a visiting professor at MIT in 1953, delivering lectures on "the human content of science." He then returned to the National Coal Board and remained there until 1964, when he took a position at the Salk Institute for Biological Studies. The following year, he delivered a lecture series entitled "Man and Nature" at the American Museum of Natural History, which served as the basis for a book called *The Identity of Man*.

In the early 1970s, Bronowski worked on a television series for the BBC called *The Ascent of Man*. It was first broadcast in 1973, a year before his death, and it aired again in the winter and spring of 1975. Writing during the time of this airing, Malachi Martin of the *National Review* explains, "The television series qualifies as a credit course for an estimated 25,000 students in two hundred colleges. . . . The premiere on January 7 of this year beat the *Merv Griffin Show* in the ratings, and reached an estimated 700,000 viewers in the New York metropolitan area alone."

In *The Common Sense of Science*, Bronowski explains the perceived split between science and literature, even between science and feeling: "Much of this quarrel between science and soul was trumped up by the religious apologists of Queen Victoria's day, who were anxious to find science materialistic and unspiritual." Bronowski consistently worked to mend "this quarrel"; he forged connections between science and the arts not only through the content of his writings, but through his form, quoting poetry in the midst of explaining scientific principle, creating analogies between science and language, and borrowing metaphors from a wealth of disciplines in the humanities.

Apprehending a second split between science and daily social existence, Bronowski faulted scientists who "have enjoyed acting the mysterious stranger, the powerful voice without emotion," "fail[ing] to make themselves comfortable in the talk of people on the street." Yet he also argued that the needs of "people on the street" have dictated the direction of scientific research since the Renaissance, and that however great the destructive capacity of science, it is also a powerfully creative force at work in society, improving life expectancy, as well as developing technologies and markets that benefit all. As a champion of science, Bronowski dedicated himself to bringing science to bear on fundamental questions of human identity, and above all, on education.

The essay below is excerpted from the first chapter of *Science and Human Values* (1956). In the opening paragraphs of the chapter, he describes his arrival in Nagasaki in November, 1945. That first moment of recognition Bronowski calls "a universal moment" when he confronted "the experience of mankind" and was moved to write the book. In it he refutes two main misunderstandings of science: that it is a wonderful dream for the good or a modern evil: "our subject [science] and our fears are as old as the tool-making civilizations." Science, like art, is a natural tool of mankind and has always had the potential for both good and evil. In the closing paragraph of the chapter he claims both as human interpretations of nature: "We remake nature by the act of discovery, in the poem or in the theorem. And the great poem and the deep theorem are new to every reader, and yet are his own experiences, because he himself recreates them. They are marks of unity in variety; and in the instant when the mind seizes this for itself, in art or in science, the heart misses a beat."

THE NATURE OF SCIENTIFIC REASONING (1956)

WHAT IS THE insight in which the scientist tries to see into nature? Can it indeed be called either imaginative or creative? To the literary man the question may seem merely silly. He has been taught that science is a large collection of facts; and if this is true, then the only seeing which scientists need to do is, he supposes, seeing the facts. He pictures them, the colorless professionals of science, going off to work in the morning into the universe in a neutral, unexposed state. They then expose themselves like a photographic plate. And then in the darkroom or laboratory they develop the image, so that suddenly and startlingly it appears, printed in capital letters, as a new formula for atomic energy.

Men who have read Balzac and Zola[1] are not deceived by the claims of these writers that they do no more than record the facts. The readers of Christopher Isherwood[2] do not take him literally when he writes "I am a camera." Yet the same readers solemnly carry with them from their schooldays this foolish picture of the scientist fixing by some mechanical process the facts of nature. I have had of all people a historian tell me that science is a collection of facts, and his voice had not even the ironic rasp of one filing cabinet reproving another.

It seems impossible that this historian had ever studied the beginnings of a scientific discovery. The Scientific Revolution can be held to begin in the year 1543 when there was brought to Copernicus,[3] perhaps on his deathbed, the first printed copy of the book

[1]*Honore de Balzac and Emile Zola* 19th-century French novelists.

[2]*Christopher Isherwood* modern English novelist and playwright.

[3]*Nicolas Copernicus* (1473–1543) a Polish astronomer who is said to be the founder of modern astronomy and who suggested that the sun did not revolve around the Earth.

he had finished about a dozen years earlier. The thesis of this book is that the earth moves around the sun. When did Copernicus go out and record this fact with his camera? What appearance in nature prompted his outrageous guess? And in what odd sense is this guess to be called a neutral record of fact?

Less than a hundred years after Copernicus, Kepler[4] published (between 1609 and 1619) the three laws which describe the paths of the planets. The work of Newton and with it most of our mechanics spring from these laws. They have a solid, matter-of-fact sound. For example, Kepler says that if one squares the year of a planet, one gets a number which is proportional to the cube of its average distance from the sun. Does anyone think that such a law is found by taking enough readings and then squaring and cubing everything in sight? If he does, then, as a scientist, he is doomed to a wasted life; he has as little prospect of making a scientific discovery as an electronic brain has.

It was not this way that Copernicus and Kepler thought, or that scientists think today. Copernicus found that the orbits of the planets would look simpler if they were looked at from the sun and not from the earth. But he did not in the first place find this by routine calculation. His first step was a leap of imagination—to lift himself from the earth, and put himself wildly, speculatively into the sun. "The earth conceives from the sun," he wrote; and "the sun rules the family of stars." We catch in his mind an image, the gesture of the virile man standing in the sun, with arms outstretched, overlooking the planets. Perhaps Copernicus took the picture from the drawings of the youth with outstretched arms which the Renaissance teachers put into their books on the proportions of the body. Perhaps he had seen Leonardo's[5] drawings of his loved pupil Salai. I do not know. To me, the gesture of Copernicus, the shining youth looking outward from the sun, is still vivid in a drawing which William Blake[6] in 1780 based on all these: the drawing which is usually called *Glad Day*.

Kepler's mind, we know, was filled with just such fanciful analogies; and we know what they were. Kepler wanted to relate the speeds of the planets to the musical intervals. He tried to fit the five regular solids into their orbits. None of these likenesses worked, and they have been forgotten; yet they have been and they remain the stepping stones of every creative mind. Kepler felt for his laws by way of metaphors, he searched mystically for likenesses with what he knew in every strange corner of nature. And when among these guesses he hit upon his laws, he did not think of their numbers as the balancing of a cosmic bank account, but as a revelation of the unity in all nature. To us, the analogies by which Kepler listened for the movement of the planets in the music of the spheres are farfetched. Yet are they more so than the wild leap by which Rutherford and Bohr[7] in our own century found a model for the atom in, of all places, the planetary system?

No scientific theory is a collection of facts. It will not even do to call a theory true or false in the simple sense in which every fact is either so or not so. The Epicureans[8] held that matter is made of atoms two thousand years ago and we are now tempted to say that

---

[4]*Kepler* Johannes Kepler (1571–1630) a German astronomer.

[5]*Leonardo* Leonardo Da Vinci.

[6]*William Blake* (1857–1927) a British poet.

[7]*Rutherford and Bohr* Ernest Rutherford (1871–1937) and Neils Bohr (1885–1962), were prominent nuclear physicists.

[8]*Epicureans* 3rd-century BC followers of Epicurus who sought freedom from pain and emotional disturbances.

their theory was true. But if we do so we confuse their notion of matter with our own. John Dalton[9] in 1808 first saw the structure of matter as we do today, and what he took from the ancients was not their theory but something richer, their image: the atom. Much of what was in Dalton's mind was as vague as the Greek notion, and quite as mistaken. But he suddenly gave life to the new facts of chemistry and the ancient theory together, by fusing them to give what neither had: a coherent picture of how matter is linked and built up from different kinds of atoms. The act of fusion is the creative act.

All science is the search for unity in hidden likenesses. The search may be on a grand scale, as in the modern theories which try to link the fields of gravitation and electromagnetism. But we do not need to be brow-beaten by the scale of science. There are discoveries to be made by snatching a small likeness from the air too, if it is bold enough. In 1935 the Japanese physicist Hideki Yukawa wrote a paper which can still give heart to a young scientist. He took as his starting point the known fact that waves of light can sometimes behave as if they were separate pellets. From this he reasoned that the forces which hold the nucleus of an atom together might sometimes also be observed as if they were solid pellets. A schoolboy can see how thin Yukawa's analogy is, and his teacher would be severe with it. Yet Yukawa without a blush calculated the mass of the pellet he expected to see, and waited. He was right; his meson was found, and a range of other mesons, neither the existence nor the nature of which had been suspected before. The likeness had borne fruit.

The scientist looks for order in the appearances of nature by exploring such likenesses. For order does not display itself of itself; if it can be said to be there at all, it is not there for the mere looking. There is no way of pointing a finger or camera at it; order must be discovered and, in a deep sense, it must be created. What we see, as we see it, is mere disorder.

This point has been put trenchantly in a fable by Karl Popper.[10] Suppose that someone wished to give his whole life to science. Suppose that he therefore sat down, pencil in hand, and for the next twenty, thirty, forty years recorded in notebook after notebook everything that he could observe. He may be supposed to leave out nothing: today's humidity, the racing results, the level of cosmic radiation and the stockmarket prices and the look of Mars, all would be there. He would have compiled the most careful record of nature that has ever been made; and, dying in the calm certainty of a life well spent, he would of course leave his notebooks to the Royal Society. Would the Royal Society thank him for the treasure of a lifetime of observation? It would not. The Royal Society would treat his notebooks exactly as the English bishops have treated Joanna Southcott's[11] box. It would refuse to open them at all, because it would know without looking that the notebooks contain only a jumble of disorderly and meaningless items.

Science finds order and meaning in our experience, and sets about this in quite a different way. It sets about it as Newton did in the story which he himself told in his old age, and of which the schoolbooks give only a caricature. In the year 1665, when Newton was

---

[9]*John Dalton* (1766–1844) a British chemist.

[10]*Karl Popper* (1902–1994) an Anglo-Austrian philosopher.

[11]*Joanna Southcott* a 19th-century English farm servant who claimed to be a prophetess. She left behind a box to be opened in a time of national emergency in the presence of all the English bishops. In 1927, a bishop agreed to officiate; when the box was opened, it was found to contain only some odds and ends.

twenty-two, the plague broke out in southern England, and the University of Cambridge was closed. Newton therefore spent the next eighteen months at home, removed from traditional learning, at a time when he was impatient for knowledge and, in his own phrase, "I was in the prime of my age for invention." In this eager, boyish mood, sitting one day in the garden of his widowed mother, he saw an apple fall. So far the books have the story right; we think we even know the kind of apple; tradition has it that it was a Flower of Kent. But now they miss the crux of the story. For what struck the young Newton at the sight was not the thought that the apple must be drawn to the earth by gravity; that conception was older than Newton. What struck him was the conjecture that the same force of gravity, which reaches to the top of the tree, might go on reaching out beyond the earth and its air, endlessly into space. Gravity might reach the moon: this was Newton's new thought; and it might be gravity which holds the moon in her orbit. There and then he calculated what force from the earth (falling off as the square of the distance) would hold the moon, and compared it with the known force of gravity at tree height. The forces agreed; Newton says laconically, "I found them answer pretty nearly." Yet they agreed only nearly: the likeness and the approximation go together, for no likeness is exact. In Newton's science modern science is full grown.

It grows from a comparison. It has seized a likeness between two unlike appearances; for the apple in the summer garden and the grave moon overhead are surely as unlike in their movements as two things can be. Newton traced in them two expressions of a single concept, gravitation: and the concept (and the unity) are in that sense his free creation. The progress of science is the discovery at each step of a new order which gives unity to what had long seemed unlike.

Understanding and Analysis

1. This essay was first presented as a speech before the faculty and students of the Massachusetts Institute of Technology in 1953. What words in the opening two paragraphs seem specifically directed to an audience of scientists? Study the pronouns Bronowski uses in the first six paragraphs. How does he distinguish between his audience and those with whom he disagrees?

2. What indications do you see in the first two paragraphs of Bronowski's "imaginative or creative" powers?

3. In the first three paragraphs, what attitude does Bronowski hold toward the unenlightened historian or "literary man"? What is your evidence? Reread the entire essay. How does Bronowski make particular use of literature and history in this essay?

4. What is the point of the third and fourth paragraphs?

5. In the fifth paragraph, why does Bronowski find connections between Copernicus, Da Vinci, and Blake?

6. How does Bronowski tie together the fifth and sixth paragraphs? Note topic sentences and transitions and repetitions of words and ideas.

7. The topic sentences of the next two paragraphs are short, almost epigrammatic. Explain what each one means. What methods does Bronowski employ to clarify their meaning?

8. The ninth paragraph is very short. How does it connect the earlier paragraphs of the essay with the later ones?

9. Explain the fable in light of the topic sentence in paragraph seven. What progression do
   you see in the topic sentences of paragraphs seven through nine (skipping ten) and including paragraph eleven? How does paragraph ten fit in this progression?

10. What comparison or metaphor is Bronowski using when he writes, "It [modern science]
    grows from a comparison"?

11. State as succinctly as you can the thesis of Bronowski's essay.

Comparison

1. Read Frost's "Education by Poetry." How many connections can you find between the
   two essays?

2. Read Orwell's "What is Science?" To what degree do Bronowski and Orwell agree or
   disagree? What is your evidence?

3. Read the essays by Snow and Leavis and the two by Gould. What is your evaluation
   of this controversy?

4. Read the essay by Carr. What connections do you see?

C. P. Snow
(1905–1980)

Charles Percy Snow grew up in an area of Leicester, England, that he characterized as a "peculiar kind of petty bourgeois-cum-proletarian suburb." The
descendant of working-class families, Snow received early intellectual encouragement from his grandfather, William Snow, a "striking example of the superior Victorian working man." He began his formal education in a local private school at the age of five, matriculating to a larger school called Alderman
Newton's at the age of eleven. When he was 16, he started serving as a lab
assistant at Alderman Newton's, and he kept this position over the next several years as he prepared for university examinations.

Snow took a bachelor's in chemistry in 1927 and an M. A. in physics in 1928,
both from University College, Leicester. At Leicester, he also wrote his first novel,
but he destroyed his own copy of the manuscript and asked his girlfriend to
do the same with hers. Once he had finished his master's, he entered Christ's
College at Cambridge, completing a doctorate in physics in 1930.

Over the next decade, Snow remained at Cambridge, serving as a Fellow. His
first published book, a detective novel called *Death Under Sail*, appeared in 1932,
and two publishers deemed it so successful that they offered Snow a "little for-

tune" to continue in the genre. He declined. He published his next book, *New Lives for Old*, in 1933; this was the same year that he wrote *The Search*, a characteristically personal novel concerned with the protagonist's decision to pursue writing rather than science. In one of his later interviews with John Halperin, the author of *C. P. Snow: An Oral Biography*, Snow said, "Science deliberately cuts out from its purview those things which interfere with its particular line of truth. That is the nature of science. Obviously humane letters don't, which is on the whole why I wanted to devote my life to them." Halperin answered, "Precisely. That's the impression one gets at the end of *The Search*."

During the late 1930s, as he edited a scientific journal, Snow made plans for a series of novels. The first of these, published in 1940 under the title *Strangers and Brothers*, caught the attention of the novelist Pamela Hansford Johnson, who was writing literary reviews for the *Liverpool Post*. She "praised it up to the skies" for its "personality" and originality, and after Snow wrote to thank her for the review, they began a correspondence that led eventually, though not directly, to their marriage.

Following England's entrance into World War II, Snow went to work for the Ministry of Labour. One of his tasks was to locate scientists, some of whom were then trained as spies and sent out to determine whether the Germans had the bomb. Snow later confirmed that his name had appeared on Hitler's "blacklist" of Allied individuals singled out for immediate placement in concentration camps. Through most of the war he carried in his pocket a lethal dose of cyanide in the event of a German victory.

After the war, Snow accepted various administrative positions and produced two more in his series of novels, *The Light and the Dark* (1947) and *Time of Hope* (1949). In July of 1950, he married Pamela. The following year, he published *The Masters*, which many regard as his master work; both *The Masters* and *The New Men* (1954) earned him literary honors. When he received a knighthood in 1957, he and Pamela became Lord and Lady Snow.

The biggest controversy of Snow's career broke out in 1959 after he returned to Cambridge to give the Rede Lectures, subsequently published both in *Encounter* magazine and in the form of a book called *The Two Cultures and the Scientific Revolution*. Inspired by his earlier essay "The Two Cultures" (1956), these lectures elaborated on his initial description of a split between science and literature with explosive results, sparking extended epistolary debate among *Encounter*'s readers. The debate intensified in 1962 when F. R. Leavis delivered a lecture later published under the title *Two Cultures? The Significance of C. P. Snow*. Snow scholar David Shusterman calls Leavis's lecture "the most savage attack by one writer upon another in our time." The controversy apparently had little effect on his reputation; throughout the 1960s Snow accepted numerous honorary degrees from English and American universities.

In 1964, the year Snow published *The Two Cultures and a Second Look,* he also accepted a government position in the Ministry of Technology that inspired future novels such as *Corridors of Power* (1966). The novel originally entitled *Strangers and Brothers* was republished in 1970 under the title *George Passant;* in the same year, Snow published the final volume of the series, *Last Things.* Despite serious difficulties with his eyes, he remained active as a writer, producing two more novels, *The Malcontents* (1972) and *A Coat of Varnish* (1979), and two works of literary criticism, *Trollope: His Life and Art* (1975) and *The Realists* (1978). He died on July 1, 1980.

Reflecting on his career with John Halperin, C. P. Snow said that by his own standards, "I should never have made a *good* scientist, but I should have made a perfectly adequate one." Some critics—Leavis especially—have charged that he did not make a good novelist, either. By and large, however, Snow enjoyed literary renown during his lifetime. Many critics contend that he contributed important novels about the work of science and the nature of power. "All my novels," Snow said, "are part of one complicated theme, which is power in the modern state." Modern culture, of course, was of great interest to him as well, and whatever posterity's opinion of his novels, his contribution to one of the defining cultural debates of the twentieth century will surely be remembered.

THE TWO CULTURES *(1956)*

'IT'S RATHER ODD,' said G. H. Hardy,[1] one afternoon in the early Thirties, 'but when we hear about "intellectuals" nowadays, it doesn't include people like me and J. J. Thomson and Rutherford.'[2] Hardy was the first mathematician of his generation, J. J. Thomson the first physicist of his; as for Rutherford, he was one of the greatest scientists who have ever lived. Some bright young literary person (I forget the exact context) putting them outside the enclosure reserved for intellectuals seemed to Hardy the best joke for some time. It does not seem quite such a good joke now. The separation between the two cultures has been getting deeper under our eyes; there is now precious little communication between them, little but different kinds of incomprehension and dislike.

The traditional culture, which is, of course, mainly literary, is behaving like a state whose power is rapidly declining—standing on its precarious dignity, spending far too much energy on Alexandrian[3] intricacies, occasionally letting fly in fits of aggressive pique quite beyond its means, too much on the defensive to show any generous imagi-

---

[1]*G. H. Hardy* G(odfrey) H(arold) Hardy (1877–1947) a British mathematician who held professorships at both Cambridge and Oxford, Hardy is well-known for developing the Hardy-Weinberg law of population genetics.

[2]*J. J. Thomson and Rutherford* Sir J(oseph) J(ohn) Thomson (1856–1940) and Ernest Rutherford (1871–1937) were eminent physicists.

[3]*Alexandrian* concerned with the study, imitation, and explication of earlier forms and masterpieces.

nation to the forces which must inevitably reshape it. Whereas the scientific culture is expansive, not restrictive, confident at the roots, the more confident after its bout of Oppenheimerian[4] self-criticism, certain that history is on its side, impatient, intolerant, creative rather than critical, good-natured and brash. Neither culture knows the virtues of the other; often it seems they deliberately do not want to know. The resentment which the traditional culture feels for the scientific is shaded with fear; from the other side, the resentment is not shaded so much as brimming with irritation. When scientists are faced with an expression of the traditional culture, it tends (to borrow Mr William Cooper's eloquent phrase) to make their feet ache.

It does not need saying that generalizations of this kind are bound to look silly at the edges. There are a good many scientists indistinguishable from literary persons, and vice versa. Even the stereotype generalizations about scientists are misleading without some sort of detail—e.g. the generalizations that scientists as a group stand on the political Left. This is only partly true. A very high proportion of engineers is almost as conservative as doctors; of pure scientists, the same would apply to chemists. It is only among physicists and biologists that one finds the Left in strength. If one compared the whole body of scientists with their opposite numbers of the traditional culture (writers, academics, and so on), the total result might be a few per cent more towards the Left wing, but not more than that. Nevertheless, as a first approximation, the scientific culture is real enough, and so is its difference from the traditional. For anyone like myself, by education a scientist, by calling a writer, at one time moving between groups of scientists and writers in the same evening, the difference has seemed dramatic.

The first thing, impossible to miss, is that scientists are on the up and up; they have the strength of a social force behind them. If they are English, they share the experience common to us all—of being in a country sliding economically downhill—but in addition (and to many of them it seems psychologically more important) they belong to something more than a profession, to something more like a directing class of a new society. In a sense oddly divorced from politics, they are the new men. Even the staidest and most politically conservative of scientific veterans, lurking in dignity in their colleges, have some kind of link with the world to come. They do not hate it as their colleagues do; part of their mind is open to it; almost against their will, there is a residual glimmer of kinship there. The young English scientists may and do curse their luck; increasingly they fret about the rigidities of their universities, about the ossification of the traditional culture which, to the scientists, makes the universities cold and dead; they violently envy their Russian counterparts who have money and equipment without discernible limit, who have the whole field wide open. But still they stay pretty resilient: they are swept on by the same social force. Harwell and Winscale have just as much spirit as Los Alamos and Chalk River:[5] the neat petty bourgeois houses, the tough and clever young, the crowds of children: they are symbols, frontier towns.

There is a touch of the frontier qualities, in fact, about the whole scientific culture. Its tone is, for example, steadily heterosexual. The difference in social manners between Harwell and Hampstead, or as far as that goes between Los Alamos and Greenwich Village,[6]

[4]*Oppenheimerian* J. Robert Oppenheimer (1904–1967) was known as the "father of the atomic bomb."

[5]*Los Alamos and Chalk River* Cites in New Mexico and Ontario, Canada, respectively, that are home to national nuclear laboratories.

[6]*Greenwich Village* an area of New York City known for its flamboyant art culture.

would make an anthropologist blink. About the whole scientific culture, there is an absence—surprising to outsiders—of the feline and oblique. Sometimes it seems that scientists relish speaking the truth, especially when it is unpleasant. The climate of personal relations is singularly bracing, not to say harsh: it strikes bleakly on those unused to it, who suddenly find that the scientists' way of deciding on action is by a full-dress argument, with no regard for sensibilities and no holds barred. No body of people ever believed more in dialectic as the primary method of attaining sense; and if you want a picture of scientists in their off-moments it could be just one of a knock-about argument. Under the argument there glitter egotisms as rapacious as any of ours: but, unlike ours, the egotisms are driven by a common purpose.

How much of the traditional culture gets through to them? The answer is not simple. A good many scientists, including some of the most gifted, have the tastes of literary persons, read the same things, and read as much. Broadly, though, the infiltration is much less. History gets across to a certain extent, in particular social history: the sheer mechanics of living, how men ate, built, travelled, worked, touches a good many scientific imaginations, and so they have fastened on such works as Trevelyan's[7] *Social History,* and Professor Gordon Childe's[8] books. Philosophy the scientific culture views with indifference, especially metaphysics. As Rutherford said cheerfully to Samuel Alexander:[9] 'When you think of all the years you've been talking about those things, Alexander, and what does it all add up to? *Hot air,* nothing but *hot air.*' A bit less exuberantly, that is what contemporary scientists would say. They regard it as a major intellectual virtue, to know what not to think about. They might touch their hats to linguistic analysis, as a relatively honourable way of wasting time; not so to existentialism.

The arts? The only one which is cultivated among scientists is music. It goes both wide and deep; there may possibly be a greater density of musical appreciation than in the traditional culture. In comparison, the graphic arts (except architecture) score little, and poetry not at all. Some novels work their way through, but not as a rule the novels which literary persons set most value on. The two cultures have so few points of contact that the diffusion of novels shows the same sort of delay, and exhibits the same oddities, as though they were getting into translation in a foreign country. It is only fairly recently, for instance, that Graham Greene and Evelyn Waugh[10] have become more than names. And, just as it is rather startling to find that in Italy Bruce Marshall is by a long shot the best-known British novelist, so it jolts one to hear scientists talking with attention of the works of Nevil Shute.[11] In fact, there is a good reason for that: Mr Shute was himself a high-class engineer, and a book like *No Highway* is packed with technical stuff that is not only accurate but often original. Incidentally, there are benefits to be gained from listening to intelligent men, utterly removed from the literary scene and unconcerned as to

[7]*Trevelyan* George Macaulay Trevelyan (1876–1962) an English historian and professor of modern history at Cambridge who was a master of the so-called "literary" school of historical writing.

[8]*Gordon Childe* (1892–1957) Australian archaeologist who became a professor of archaeology at Edinburgh and later director of the University of London Institute of Archaeology.

[9]*Samuel Alexander* (1859–1938) Australian philosopher and Jewish social activist.

[10]*Graham Greene and Evelyn Waugh* Greene (1904–1991) and Waugh (1903–1966) were both popular English writers.

[11]*Nevil Shute* Nevil Shute Norway (1899–1960), he studied aeronautical engineering at Oxford and later wrote novels.

who's in and who's out. One can pick up such a comment as a scientist once made, that it looked to him as though the current preoccupations of the New Criticism,[12] the extreme concentration on a tiny passage, had made us curiously insensitive to the total flavour of a work, to its cumulative effects, to the epic qualities in literature. But, on the other side of the coin, one is just as likely to listen to three of the most massive intellects in Europe happily discussing the merits of *The Wallet of Kai-Lung*.[13]

When you meet the younger rank-and-file of scientists, it often seems that they do not read at all. The prestige of the traditional culture is high enough for some of them to make a gallant shot at it. Oddly enough, the novelist whose name to them has become a token of esoteric literary excellence is that difficult highbrow Dickens. They approach him in a grim and dutiful spirit as though tackling *Finnegan's Wake*,[14] and feel a sense of achievement if they manage to read a book through. But most young technicians do not fly so high. When you ask them what they read—'As a married man,' one says, 'I prefer the garden.' Another says: 'I always like just to use my books as tools.' (Difficult to resist speculating what kind of tool a book would make. A sort of hammer? A crude digging instrument?)

That, or something like it, is a measure of the incommunicability of the two cultures. On their side the scientists are losing a great deal. Some of that loss is inevitable: it must and would happen in any society at our technical level. But in this country we make it quite unnecessarily worse by our educational patterns. On the other side, how much does the traditional culture lose by the separation?

I am inclined to think, even more. Not only practically—we are familiar with those arguments by now—but also intellectually and morally. The intellectual loss is a little difficult to appraise. Most scientists would claim that you cannot comprehend the world unless you know the structure of science, in particular of physical science. In a sense, and a perfectly genuine sense, that is true. Not to have read *War and Peace* and *La Cousine Bette* and *La Chartreuse de Parme* is not to be educated; but so is not to have a glimmer of the Second Law of Thermodynamics. Yet that case ought not to be pressed too far. It is more justifiable to say that those without any scientific understanding miss a whole body of experience: they are rather like the tone deaf, from whom all musical experience is cut off and who have to get on without it. The intellectual invasions of science are, however, penetrating deeper. Psycho-analysis once looked like a deep invasion, but that was a false alarm; cybernetics may turn out to be the real thing, driving down into the problems of will and cause and motive. If so, those who do not understand the method will not understand the depths of their own cultures.

But the greatest enrichment the scientific culture could give us is—though it does not originate like that—a moral one. Among scientists, deep-natured men know, as starkly as any men have known, that the individual human condition is tragic; for all its triumphs and joys, the essence of it is loneliness and the end death. But what they will not admit

---

[12]*New Criticism* a theory and practice that held sway in literary scholarship from the 1940s to the 1960s, New Criticism argued that a literary work could best be understood by a detailed examination of the work itself, rather than by studying its historical or social context.

[13]*The Wallet of Kai-Lung* one of a series of Kai Lung books by British writer Ernest Brahmah which were popular in the 1920s and 30s.

[14]*Finnegans Wake* a complicated and experimental novel published by Irish writer James Joyce in 1939. Snow adds to the title an apostrophe that Joyce deliberately omits.

is that, because the individual condition is tragic, therefore the social condition must be tragic, too. Because a man must die, that is no excuse for his dying before his time and after a servile life. The impulse behind the scientists drives them to limit the area of tragedy, to take nothing as tragic that can conceivably lie within men's will. They have nothing but contempt for those representatives of the traditional culture who use a deep insight into man's fate to obscure the social truth—or to do something pettier than obscure the truth, just to hang on to a few perks. Dostoevski sucking up to the Chancellor Pobedonostsev, who thought the only thing wrong with slavery was that there was not enough of it; the political decadence of the *avant garde* of 1914, with Ezra Pound finishing up broadcasting for the Fascists; Claudel agreeing sanctimoniously with the Marshal about the virtue in others' suffering; Faulkner[15] giving sentimental reasons for treating Negroes as a different species. They are all symptoms of the deepest temptation of the clerks—which is to say: 'Because man's condition is tragic, everyone ought to stay in their place, with mine as it happens somewhere near the top.' From that particular temptation, made up of defeat, self-indulgence, and moral vanity, the scientific culture is almost totally immune. It is that kind of moral health of the scientists which, in the last few years, the rest of us have needed most; and of which, because the two cultures scarcely touch, we have been most deprived.

Understanding and Analysis

1. In the second paragraph, Snow begins by comparing the literary or traditional culture of 1956 to a waning political power and, by implication, the scientific culture to a robust conquering country. What are the characteristics of each side, according to Snow?

2. What is the point of the third paragraph? What purpose does it serve in the presentation of Snow's argument?

3. Snow compares the general attitudes of the two cultures toward politics in the third paragraph. What areas does he compare in the following two paragraphs? Find as many as you can.

4. Snow claims to be part of both cultures. What evidence of this joint membership does he offer his readers? Note tone and pronouns as well as direct statements. Do you believe that Snow is neutral? Why or why not?

5. Snow writes, "those who do not understand the method will not understand the depths of their own cultures." What does he mean by this statement?

6. What does Snow believe is the greatest benefit of science?

Comparison

1. Read Orwell's "What Is Science?" Where do these two authors agree and where do they disagree?

2. Do you think the literary culture is alienated from the scientific culture today? If so, what are the suspicions each holds about the other?

---

[15]*Dostoevski; Ezra Pound; Claudel; Faulkner* Fyodor Dostoevsky (1821–1881) was a Russian writer, Ezra Pound (1885–1972) and William Faulkner (1897–1962) were both American writers; Paul Claudel (1868–1955) was a French diplomat, poet, and dramatist.

5. Read Bronowski's "The Nature of Scientific Reasoning." Does Snow's characterization of the scientific culture fit Bronowski and his views?

4. Jacob Bronowski offers a way of mediating between the two cultures. What does he offer and how would Snow and Orwell respond?

5. What stereotypes do you see exhibited in the essays in this collection that address the literary and scientific culture clashes? Which authors seem to you to be the most fair in their treatment of the subject? What position do you take?

John Kenneth Galbraith
(1908–)

John Kenneth Galbraith was born in Ontario, Canada. He entered high school at age ten, graduated at 18, having attended sporadically, and spent the next five years at Ontario Agricultural College, where he studied animal, field, poultry, and dairy husbandry, butchering, meat-cutting, farm management, and many other subjects. According to his autobiography, *A Life In Our Times* (1981), the two subjects he found most useful were freshman composition and plumbing. Like many destined to write, Galbraith was the editor of the college paper. He graduated with distinction in 1931 and went on to the University of California at Berkeley. There, while earning his Ph.D., he worked as a research assistant, taught farm management and agricultural economics at U. C. Davis, and wrote articles for the *Journal of Farm Economics.*

An ardent Democrat and strong supporter of Franklin D. Roosevelt, Galbraith (though not yet a citizen), decided to visit Washington in the summer of 1934 before taking up a post as instructor at Harvard. He was immediately offered employment at the Department of Agriculture. At the end of the summer, it became clear that the report he and others were working on would need to be revised, and, because Galbraith had been an apt pupil in his college composition course, he was called away from Harvard to Washington nearly every weekend to help with the revision. In 1936, he married the former Catherine Atwater; he also worked to reelect FDR. In 1937, Galbraith became a U.S. citizen. That year, too, he studied the economic theories of John Maynard Keynes in Cambridge, England, and began a life-long commitment to travel, teaching, writing, and politics.

During the late thirties, Galbraith studied agricultural and economic practices in Italy, Germany, Prussia, and Czechoslovakia, taught at Harvard and, for a year, at Princeton. During the forties, he worked for the American Farm

Bureau Federation, enlisted once again because of his writing talents and wide knowledge of economic affairs to work on price control. When he volunteered for the draft, he was told that, at 6' 8 1/2", he was too tall. Instead, he worked for *Fortune* as a writer and editor and in 1944 served on the United States Strategic Bombing Survey, traveling to Washington, London, and Japan. During the fifties, he wrote and taught, again at Harvard, returning to Washington to become a speechwriter for Adlai Stevenson and to serve on the Democratic Advisory Council of the Democratic National Committee. In 1953, he was made the Paul M. Warburg Professor of Economics at Harvard, a position he held until his retirement in 1975. In addition to teaching and writing, Galbraith campaigned on behalf of JFK, LBJ, Eugene McCarthy, and George McGovern. He also served as ambassador to India from 1961–1963 and as national chairman of Americans for Democratic Action from 1967–1969. He is well known for voicing early, strong, and consistent opposition to the Vietnam War.

Among his works are *Toward Full Employment* (1938), *A Theory of Price Control* (1952), *American Capitalism: The Concept of Countervailing Power* (1952), *The Great Crash* (1955), *The Affluent Society* (1958), *Journey to Poland and Yugoslavia* (1958), *The Scotch* (1964), *How To Get Out of Viet Nam* (1967), *The New Industrial State* (1967), *Ambassador's Journal 1969*, *Economics and the Public Purpose* (1973), *The Age of Uncertainty* (1977), *The Nature of Mass Poverty* (1979), *The Voice of the Poor* (1983), *The Culture of Contentment* (1992), *The Good Society* (1996), and *Name Dropping* (1999). He has also written several successful novels and an autobiography.

He and his wife live in Cambridge, Massachusetts, and spend summers in Newfane, Vermont. They have three grown sons. A popular lecturer and recipient of many honors and awards, Galbraith is known for his wit, wisdom, and willingness to speak his mind. One persistent thread in his autobiography is his love of and respect for the work of the writer—"To write adequately one must know, above all, how bad are one's first drafts. They are bad because the need to combine composition with thought, both in their own way taxing, leads initially to a questionable, even execrable, result. With each revision the task eases, the product improves. Eventually there can be clarity and perhaps even grace."

LABOR, LEISURE AND THE NEW CLASS (1958)

IN A SOCIETY of high and increasing affluence, there are three plausible tendencies as regards toil. As the production of goods comes to seem less urgent, and as individuals are less urgently in need of income for the purchase of goods, they will work fewer hours or days in the week. Or they will work less hard. Or, as a final possibility, it may be that fewer people will work all the time.

In the last century, a drastic decline has occurred in the work week. In 1850, it is estimated to have averaged just under seventy hours, the equivalent of seven ten-hour days a week or roughly six days at from six in the morning to six at night. A hundred years later, the average was 40.0 hours or five eight-hour days.[1]

This decline reflects a tacit but unmistakable acceptance of the declining marginal urgency of goods. There is no other explanation. However, such is the hold of production on our minds that this explanation is rarely offered. The importance and rewards of leisure are urged, almost never the unimportance of goods. Or, since production per hour has been increasing as the work week has declined, it is said that we are able to reduce the work because more is produced in less time. No mention is made of the fact that even more would be produced in more time. Or, finally, the decline is related to the feeling that steps must be taken to share the available work as productivity per worker rises. This also implies that the marginal urgency of production is low or negligible, but again the point remains unmade.

A reduction in the work week is an exceedingly plausible reaction to the declining marginal urgency of product. Over the span of man's history, although a phenomenal amount of education, persuasion, indoctrination and incantation have been devoted to the effort, ordinary people have never been quite persuaded that toil is as agreeable as its alternatives. Thus, to take increased well-being partly in the form of more goods and partly in the form of more leisure is unquestionably rational. In addition, the institution of overtime enables the worker to go far to adjust work and income to his own taste and requirements. It breaks with the barbarous uniformity of the weekly wage with its assumption that all families have the same tastes, needs and requirements. Few things enlarge the liberty of the individual more substantially than to grant him a measure of control over the amount of his income.

Unfortunately, in the conventional wisdom the reduction in hours has emerged as the only legitimate response to increasing affluence. This is at least partly because the issue has never been faced in terms of the increasing unimportance of goods. Accordingly, though we have attributed value to leisure, a ban still lies on other courses which seem to be more directly in conflict with established attitudes on productive efficiency. In a society rationally concerned with its own happiness, these alternatives have a strong claim to consideration.

II

The first of these is that work can be made easier and more pleasant.

The present-day industrial establishment is a great distance removed from that of the last century or even of twenty-five years ago. This improvement has been the result of a variety of forces—government standards and factory inspection; general technological and architectural advance; the fact that productivity could be often increased by substituting machine power for heavy or repetitive manual labor; the need to compete for a labor force; and union intervention to improve working conditions in addition to wages and hours.

[1]J. Frederic Dewhurst and Associates, *America's Needs and Resources, A New Survey* (New York: Twentieth Century Fund, 1955), p. 1053. These figures are the weighted average of agricultural and nonagricultural workers. The average work week in nonagricultural enterprise in 1950 was estimated to be 38.8 hours. [Galbraith's note]

However, except where the improvement contributed to increased productivity, the effort to make work more pleasant has had to support a large burden of proof. It was permissible to seek the elimination of hazardous, unsanitary, unhealthful or otherwise objectionable conditions of work. The speed-up might be resisted—to a point. But the test was not what was agreeable but what was unhealthful or, at a minimum, excessively fatiguing. The trend toward increased leisure is not reprehensible, but we resist vigorously the notion that a man should work less hard while on the job. Here, older attitudes are involved. We are gravely suspicious of any tendency to expend less than the maximum effort, for this has long been a prime economic virtue.

In strict logic, there is as much to be said for making work pleasant and agreeable as for shortening hours. On the whole, it is probably as important for a wage earner to have pleasant working conditions as a pleasant home. To a degree, he can escape the latter but not the former—though no doubt the line between an agreeable tempo and what is flagrant feather-bedding is difficult to draw. Moreover, it is a commonplace of the industrial scene that the dreariest and most burdensome tasks, requiring as they do a minimum of thought and skill, frequently have the largest numbers of takers. The solution to this problem lies, as we shall see presently, in drying up the supply of crude manpower at the bottom of the ladder. Nonetheless the basic point remains: the case for more leisure is not stronger on purely *prima facie* grounds than the case for making labor-time itself more agreeable. The test, it is worth repeating, is not the effect on productivity. It is not seriously argued that the shorter work week increases productivity—that men produce more in fewer hours than they would in more. Rather, it is whether fewer hours are always to be preferred to more but more pleasant ones.

III

The third of the obvious possibilities with increasing affluence is for fewer people to work. This tendency has also been operating for many years although in a remarkably diverse form. Since 1890, when one boy in four and one girl in ten between the ages of ten and fifteen were gainfully employed, large numbers of juveniles have been retired from the labor force and their number now is negligible. At the same time, a large number of women have been added. In 1890, 19.5 percent of the female population ten years and over was in the labor force and by 1953, this proportion had risen to 29.7 percent.[2] However, this change reflects in considerable measure the shift of tasks—food preparation, clothing manufacture, even child-rearing—out of the home. Women who previously performed them have gone along to other work. The woman who takes charge of a day nursery has joined the labor force, as have the women whose children she cares for.

For seventy-five years, the proportion of the male population in the labor force has been constant at around 75 percent of those over ten years of age. There are a smaller percentage of the very young and of those over sixty-five, but this has been offset by the increase in population in the ages between twenty and sixty-five where the proportion of workers to the total is very high.[3]

With diminishing marginal urgency of goods, it is logical that the first to be spared should be old and young. We have yet, however, to view this tendency consistently and

[2]*Ibid.*, pp. 726–727. [Galbraith's note]
[3]*Ibid.*, pp. 725–726. [Galbraith's note]

comprehensively. We are able to dispense with the labor of those who have reached retiring age because the goods they add are a low order of urgency, whereas a poor society must extract the last ounce of labor effort from all. But we have ordinarily subjected those who retire to a drastic reduction in income and living standards. Obviously, if the retirement can be afforded because the product is no longer urgent, a satisfactory—meaning, for most purposes, the customary—living standard can be accorded to the retired employee for the same reason. Similarly, we have excluded youngsters from the labor market, partly on the ground that labor at too early an age is unduly painful and injurious to health, and partly to make way for educational opportunity. But while we have felt it possible to dispense with the goods that the youngsters produce, we have yet to provide them, at least in full and satisfactory measure, with the education that their exemption from labor was designed to make possible. If we are affluent enough to dispense with the product of juvenile labor, it again follows that we are affluent enough to provide the education that takes its place.

In addition to releasing the old and young, it may be that we need not use all of the labor force at all times. This possibility was explored in Chapter XX. If the marginal urgency of goods is low, then so is the urgency of employing the last man or the last million men in the labor force. By allowing ourselves such a margin, in turn, we reduce the standards of economic performance to a level more nearly consonant with the controls available for its management. And in so widening the band of what is deemed tolerable performance lies our best hope of minimizing the threat of inflation with its further and persistent threat to social balance.

Such a step requires that there be a substitute for production as a source of income— and that it be ample. But this accords wholly with the logic of the situation. It is also a point which even conservatives, in effect, accept. They are always open to the suggestion that unemployment is better than inflation. This means that they do not worry about the output so lost. So they cannot be too seriously perturbed by providing people who do not produce with income. If we do not miss what these non-producers do not make when they are unemployed, we will not miss what they eat and wear and otherwise need for something approximating their accustomed standard of living.

IV

However, the greatest prospect that we face—indeed what must now be counted one of the central economic goals of our society—is to eliminate toil as a required economic institution. This is not a utopian vision. We are already well on the way. Only an extraordinarily elaborate exercise in social camouflage has kept us from seeing what has been happening.

Nearly all societies at nearly all times have had a leisure class—a class of persons who were exempt from toil. In modern times and especially in the United States, the leisure class, at least in any identifiable phenomenon, has disappeared. To be idle is no longer considered rewarding or even entirely respectable.

But we have barely noticed that the leisure class has been replaced by another and much larger class to which work has none of the older connotation of pain, fatigue or other mental or physical discomfort. We have failed to appreciate the emergence of this New Class, as it may be called, largely as the result of one of the oldest and most effective obfuscations in the field of social science. This is the effort to assert that all work— physical, mental, artistic or managerial—is essentially the same.

This effort to proclaim the grand homogeneity of work has commanded, for different reasons, the support of remarkably numerous and diverse groups. To economists, it has seemed a harmless and, indeed, an indispensable simplification. It has enabled them to deal homogeneously with all of the different kinds of productive effort and to elaborate a general theory of wages applying to all who receive an income for services. Doubts have arisen from time to time, but they have been suppressed or considered to concern special cases.[4] The identity of all classes of labor is one thing on which capitalist and communist doctrine wholly agree. The president of the corporation is pleased to think that his handsomely appointed office is the scene of the same kind of toil as the assembly line and that only the greater demands in talent and intensity justify his wage differential. The communist office-holder cannot afford to have it supposed that his labor differs in any significant respect from that of the comrade at the lathe or on the collective farm with whom he is ideologically one. In both societies, it serves the democratic conscience of the more favored groups to identify themselves with those who do hard physical labor. A lurking sense of guilt over a more pleasant, agreeable and remunerative life can often be assuaged by the observation, "I am a worker too," or, more audaciously, by the statement that "mental labor is far more taxing than physical labor." Since the man who does physical labor is intellectually disqualified from comparing his toil with that of the brainworker, the proposition, though outrageous, is uniquely unassailable.

For, in fact, the differences in what labor means to different people could not be greater. For some, and probably a majority, it remains a stint to be performed. It may be preferable, especially in the context of social attitudes toward production, to doing nothing. Nevertheless, it is fatiguing or monotonous or, at a minimum, a source of no particular pleasure. The reward rests not in the task but in the pay.

For others, work, as it continues to be called, is an entirely different matter. It is taken for granted that it will be enjoyable. If it is not, this is a legitimate source of dissatisfaction, even frustration. No one regards it as remarkable that the advertising man, tycoon, poet or professor who suddenly finds his work unrewarding should seek the counsel of a psychiatrist. One insults the business executive or the scientist by suggesting that his principal motivation in life is the pay he receives. Pay is not unimportant. Among other things, it is a prime index of prestige. Prestige—the respect, regard and esteem of others—is in turn one of the more important sources of satisfaction associated with this kind of work. But, in general, those who do this kind of work expect to contribute their best regardless of compensation. They would be disturbed by any suggestion to the contrary.[5]

---

[4]Marshall defined labor as "any exertion of mind or body undergone partly or wholly with a view to some good other than the pleasure derived directly from the work." *Principles of Economics* (8th ed.; London: Macmillan, 1927), p. 65. This definition obviously recognizes a category of individuals for whom work is a reward in itself. However, this group, having been introduced, plays little or no further part in Marshall's analysis. It has played almost no formal role in economic theory since. [Galbraith's note]

[5]We have here an important reason why the income tax, despite high marginal rates and frequent warnings of the damage these may do in impairing incentives, has so far had no visibly deleterious effect. The surtax rates fall almost entirely on members of the New Class. These are people who, by their own claim except when they are talking about the effect of income taxes, are not primarily motivated by money. Hence the tax, which also does not disturb the prestige structure—people are rated by before-tax income—touches no vital incentive. Were high marginal rates to be placed on (say) the overtime income of automobile workers, we would expect a substantial withdrawal of effort. Here pay, as an incentive, remains important. [Galbraith's note]

Such is the labor of the New Class. No aristocrat ever contemplated the loss of feudal privileges with more sorrow than a member of this class would regard his descent into ordinary labor where the reward was only the pay. From time to time, grade school teachers leave their posts for substantially higher paid factory work. The action makes headlines because it represents an unprecedented desertion of an occupation which is assumed to confer the dignity of the New Class. The college professor, who is more securely a member of the New Class than the schoolteacher, would never contemplate such a change even as an exercise in eccentricity and no matter how inadequate he may consider his income.

In keeping with all past class behavior, the New Class seeks energetically to perpetuate itself. Offspring are not expected to plan their lives in order to make a large amount of money. (Those who go into business are something of an exception at least partly because income, in business, is uniquely an index of prestige.) From their earliest years, the children of the New Class are carefully indoctrinated in the importance of finding an occupation from which they will derive satisfaction—one which will involve not toil but enjoyment. One of the principal sources of sorrow and frustration in the New Class is the son who fails to make the grade—who drops down into some tedious and unrewarding occupation. The individual who meets with this misfortune—the son of the surgeon who becomes a garage hand—is regarded by the community with pity not unmixed with horror. But the New Class has considerable protective powers. The son of the surgeon rarely does become a garage hand. However inadequate, he can usually manage to survive, perhaps somewhat exiguously, on the edge of his caste. And even if, as a salesman or an investment counselor, he finds little pleasure in his work, he will be expected to assert the contrary in order to affirm his membership in the New Class.

V

The New Class is not exclusive. While virtually no one leaves it, thousands join it every year. Overwhelmingly, the qualification is education.[6] Any individual whose adolescent situation is such that sufficient time and money is invested in his preparation, and who has at least the talents to carry him through the formal academic routine, can be a member. There is a hierarchy within the class. The son of the factory worker who becomes an electrical engineer is on the lower edge; his son who does graduate work and becomes a university physicist moves to the higher echelons; but opportunity for education is, in either case, the open sesame.

There can be little question that in the last hundred years, and even in the last few decades, the New Class has increased enormously in size. In early nineteenth-century

---

[6] Political capacity is another qualification, and it is of especial importance to those who seek to make their escape after reaching their adult years. The intensity of the campaigns for local political offices—city councilors, school committeemen, and county supervisors—is to be explained by this fact as also the enduring interest in appointive political office. Those who are already members of the New Class often fail to see how such posts are valued as an entrée. They look askance at the competition for such posts between the less well educated members of the community. They fail to realize that such posts provide the greatest opportunity for such individuals and that it is upon such people that we depend for much good (as well as some bad) civic enterprise. The union is another important opportunity for the individual of political capacity. Cf. the interesting sketches by Harvey Swados in *On the Line* (Boston: Atlantic-Little, Brown, 1957). [Galbraith's note]

England or the United States, excluding the leisure class and considering the New Class as a group that lived on what it has carefully called earned income, it consisted only of a handful of educators and clerics, with, in addition, a trifling number of writers, journalists and artists. In the United States of the eighteen-fifties, it could not have numbered more than a few thousand individuals. Now the number whose primary identification is with their job, rather than the income it returns, is in the millions.

Some of the attractiveness of membership in the New Class, to be sure, derives from a vicarious feeling of superiority—another manifestation of class attitudes. However, membership in the class unquestionably has other and more important rewards. Exemption from manual toil; escape from boredom and confining and severe routine; the chance to spend one's life in clean and physically comfortable surroundings; and some opportunity for applying one's thoughts to the day's work, are regarded as unimportant only by those who take them completely for granted. For these reasons, it has been possible to expand the New Class greatly without visibly reducing its attractiveness.

This being so, there is every reason to conclude that the further and rapid expansion of this class should be a major, and perhaps next to peaceful survival itself, *the* major social goal of the society. Since education is the operative factor in expanding the class, investment in education, assessed qualitatively as well as quantitatively, becomes very close to being the basic index of social progress. It enables people to realize a dominant aspiration. It is an internally consistent course of development.

Recent experience has shown that the demand for individuals in the occupations generally identified with the New Class increases much more proportionately with increased income and well-being. Were the expansion of the New Class a deliberate objective of the society, this, with its emphasis on education and its ultimate effect on intellectual, literary, cultural and artistic demands, would greatly broaden the opportunities for membership. At the same time, the shrinking in the number of those who engage in work *qua* work is something to be regarded not alone with equanimity but with positive approval. One of the inevitable outlets for the intellectual energies and inventiveness of the New Class is, in fact, in finding substitutes for routine and repetitive manual labor. To the extent that such labor is made scarce and more expensive, this tendency will, of course, be accelerated. This is a highly plausible social goal.

It is a measure of how little we need worry about the danger from reducing the number of people engaged in work *qua* work that, as matters now stand, our concern is not that we will have too few available for toil but too many. We worry lest such technical advances as automation, an already realized dividend of the expansion of the New Class, will proceed so rapidly as to leave a surplus of those who still work. This, indeed, is probably the greater danger.

VI

I venture to suggest that the unprofessional reader will find rather reasonable and rational the ideas here offered. Why should men struggle to maximize income when the price is many dull and dark hours of labor? Why especially should they do so as goods become more plentiful and less urgent? Why should they not seek instead to maximize the rewards of all the hours of their days? And since this is the plain and obvious aspiration of a great and growing number of the most perceptive people, why should it not be the central goal of the society? And now to complete the case, we have a design for progress. It is education or, more broadly, investment in human as distinct from material capital.

But in the more sophisticated levels of the conventional wisdom, including, regrettably, some professional economists, any such goal will seem exceedingly undesirable. The production of material goods, urgent or otherwise, is the accepted measure of our progress. Investment in material capital is our basic engine of progress. Both this product and the means for increasing it are measurable and tangible. What is measurable is better. To talk of transferring increasing numbers of people from lives spent mostly in classical toil to lives which, for the most part, are spent pleasantly has less quantitative precision. Since investment in individuals, unlike investment in a blast furnace, provides a product that can be neither seen nor valued, it is inferior. And here the conventional wisdom unleashes its epithet of last resort. Since these achievements are not easily measured, as a goal, they are "fuzzy." What economics finds inconvenient, it invariably so attacks and it is widely deemed to be a fatal condemnation. The precise, to be sure, is usually the old and familiar. Because it is old and familiar, it has been defined and measured. Thus does insistence on precision become another of the tautological devices by which the conventional wisdom protects itself. Nor should one doubt its power.

Yet anyone who finds this analysis and these proposals sensible should not be entirely discouraged. We are here in one of the contexts where circumstance has marched far beyond the conventional wisdom. We have seen how general are the efforts to join the New Class and how rapid is its expansion. We are not here establishing a new economic and social goal but identifying one that is already widely if but tacitly accepted. In this situation, the conventional wisdom cannot resist indefinitely. The economist of impeccable credentials in the conventional wisdom, who believes that there is no goal in life of comparable urgency with the maximization of total and individual real income, would never think of applying such a standard to himself. In his own life, he is an exponent of all the aspirations of the New Class. He educates and indoctrinates his own children with but one thing in mind. It is not that they should maximize their income. This is abhorrent. He wants above all that they will have an occupation that is interesting and rewarding. On this, he hopes, indeed, that they will take their learned parent as their model.

Understanding and Analysis

1. What is Galbraith's explanation for the reduction in the length of the work week? What explanations do others offer? Locate other statements in the essay of those opposed to Galbraith's view. What are the characteristics of Galbraith's imagined opponent?

2. What are the two elements of "increased well-being" that Galbraith says people want?

3. What does Galbraith see as the benefit of overtime?

4. What, according to Galbraith, are the alternatives to leisure that we as a society can choose to make ourselves happier? Where are they first articulated in the essay?

5. When you reread, count the number of sections in this essay. How many are there? What is the basic structure of the essay?

6. What are the connotations of the word "toil" as opposed to the word "work"? Where, if anywhere, do you find humor in this essay? What is Galbraith's tone?

7. If fewer people work, who should be laid off first, according to Galbraith?

8. Galbraith is clearly a liberal. What is his tone when he speaks in the last paragraph of section three about conservatives?

9. What is Galbraith's definition of the leisure class?

10. What view do communists, capitalists, and economists all share, according to Galbraith?

11. What, on the other hand, is the truth, according to Galbraith? What are some of the definitions of work according to different groups?

12. Define the characteristics of labor according to members of the New Class. Why was it growing when Galbraith wrote this chapter of his book? Do you think the New Class is still growing?

13. What is Galbraith's "design for progress"?

Comparison

1. What changes in the work force do you think have taken place since Galbraith wrote this essay? Do you agree with Galbraith that the "greater danger" is that we will have a surplus of those who are "available for toil"?

2. Read Russell Baker's "Work in Corporate America." Where do Galbraith and Baker agree and disagree?

3. Read Richard Rodriguez's "Labor." What ideas do Galbraith and Rodriguez share?

4. Read the essay by Reich. Is Galbraith right, according to Reich?

X. J. Kennedy
(1929–)

Born August 21, 1929, roughly two months before Black Thursday, Joseph Charles Kennedy remembers many people stopping by his childhood home in Dover, New Jersey, trying to sell homemade cookies and doughnuts to survive the Depression. His own family, though by no means wealthy, managed to make ends meet with occasional assistance from his Aunt Effie, who wanted her nephew to be a "child movie star like Shirley Temple. And so I was obligated to spend hours by the piano, belting out hit songs, 'On the Good Ship Lollipop' and 'Animal Crackers in My Soup.'" Left to his own devices, Kennedy enjoyed making comic books and listening to his father recite poetry; he also stayed close to the radio, tuning in for programs like *Dick Tracy* and *The Shadow.* When *War of the Worlds* was broadcast (1938), Kennedy recalls, "it had immediate local interest, for it claimed that Martians had landed not far from Dover." One of Kennedy's neighbors packed up and left town to escape the Martian invasion; his own family stayed put, but science fiction had a lasting hold on Kennedy's imagination. After writing plays and poems in elementary school, he created two fanzines as an adolescent, *Terrifying Test-tube Tales* and *Vampire.*

At the age of 15, he almost became a published sci-fi writer; *Planet Stories* accepted one of his works, but he could not bear to comply with the editor's mandate that he supply a happy ending.

When he graduated from high school in 1946, Kennedy discovered that his father "expected" him to go to college. "I didn't know my father had that kind of money," Kennedy says, "and indeed he didn't." Kennedy enrolled at Seton Hall, commuting from his home in Dover to save money. He edited the college paper, and at 21, he published two stories in *Other Worlds* and *Science Fiction Quarterly*. Turning his interest to education during his senior year, he became a student teacher. Once he graduated from Seton Hall, however, he had difficulty "compet[ing] for a teaching job with all the returning veterans." He commuted to Columbia University in New York, spending five hours a day in transit to earn his M.A. in English in 1951. By this time, he had "run out of draft deferments," so he joined the Navy during the "Korean Emergency," serving as a journalist. While at sea, he published a paper for his shipmates and wrote poetry in his spare time. His first break as a poet came in his final year of naval service, when *The New Yorker* accepted two submissions; these appeared in print under Kennedy's new pseudonym. "To distinguish myself from the better-known Joe Kennedys," he explains, "I had stuck a fictitious X on my byline, and ever since, have been stuck with it."

In 1956, Kennedy entered the University of Michigan, planning to earn a doctorate in English. After he won a university poetry contest, his manuscript was published in 1961 under the title *Nude Descending a Staircase*. The following year, Kennedy married Dorothy Mintzlaff, who had also been pursuing her doctorate in English. Both of them left the program, and Kennedy took a job as a "teaching poet" at the Woman's College of the University of North Carolina. Still, money was scarce. After the couple's first child was born in 1963, Kennedy submitted a Christmas poem to *Glamour* magazine in order to earn money to pay the delivering physician. Later that same year, he accepted "a better-paying job at Tufts University," where he remained on the faculty until 1979. In 1971, Kennedy and his wife started a poetry magazine called *Counter/Measures*, and Kennedy produced several volumes of poetry while teaching at Tufts, including *Growing into Love* (1969), *Bulsh* (1970), and *Emily Dickinson in Southern California* (1974). These books attracted largely favorable reviews, but by his own account, Kennedy "was feeling downcast" about his work. After one of his children's poems from *Nude Descending a Staircase* was included in a children's anthology, he brightened at the prospect of writing a complete book of children's verse. His first work for children, *One Winter Night in August*, appeared in 1975; over the next 20 years, he published almost a dozen more. Kennedy estimates that "more than one and a half million students" have learned about poetry from *An Introduction to Poetry* (1966), his most famous textbook.

Although X. J. Kennedy is not a major poet, he is nevertheless a gifted writer. Critics over the years have been nearly unanimous in their praise of his technical skill, and those reviewers who mix praise and criticism, like Loxley Nichols, still express admiration for Kennedy's "allegiance to [the] traditional verse forms" eschewed by so many other poets of his generation. Kennedy can use strict meter and rhyme to a comical effect, as in "Epitaph for a Postal Clerk":

> Here lies wrapped up tight in sod
> Henry Harkins c/o God.
> On the day of Resurrection
> May be opened for inspection.

His humor, however, is not always light, nor are his themes. Indeed, his refusal of the happy ending at the age of 15 may have been an early mark of burgeoning writerly character. In his writings, Kennedy confronts dark features of the human condition, as well as the literal and spiritual environments in which human beings live, and even when he does this with humor, he does it with a sobriety of purpose. Kennedy liked to think of his works as "seriously funny"; in both senses, they are just that.

Who Killed King Kong? (1960)

The ordeal and spectacular death of King Kong, the giant ape, undoubtedly have been witnessed by more Americans than have ever seen a performance of *Hamlet, Iphigenia at Aulis,* or even *Tobacco Road.* Since RKO-Radio Pictures first released *King Kong,* a quarter-century has gone by; yet year after year, from prints that grow more rain-beaten, from sound tracks that grow more tinny, ticket-buyers by thousands still pursue Kong's luckless fight against the forces of technology, tabloid journalism, and the DAR. They see him chloroformed to sleep, see him whisked from his jungle isle to New York and placed on show, see him burst his chains to roam the city (lugging a frightened blonde), at last to plunge from the spire of the Empire State Building, machine-gunned by model airplanes.

Though Kong may die, one begins to think his legend unkillable. No clearer proof of his hold upon the popular imagination may be seen than what emerged one catastrophic week in March 1955, when New York WOR-TV programmed *Kong* for seven evenings in a row (a total of sixteen showings). Many a rival network vice-president must have scowled when surveys showed that *Kong*—the 1933 B-picture—had lured away fat segments of the viewing populace from such powerful competitors as Ed Sullivan, Groucho Marx and Bishop Sheen.

But even television has failed to run *King Kong* into oblivion. Coffee-in-the-lobby cinemas still show the old hunk of hokum, with the apology that in its use of composite shots and animated models the film remains technically interesting. And no other monster in movie history has won so devoted a popular audience. None of the plodding mummies, the stultified draculas, the whitecoated Lugosis with their shiny pinball-machine laboratories, none of the invisible stranglers, berserk robots, or menaces from Mars has ever enjoyed so many resurrections.

Why does the American public refuse to let King Kong rest in peace? It is true, I'll admit, that *Kong* outdid every monster movie before or since in sheer carnage. Producers Cooper and Schoedsack crammed into it dinosaurs, headhunters, riots, aerial battles, bullets, bombs, bloodletting. Heroine Fay Wray, whose function is mainly to scream, shuts her mouth for hardly one uninterrupted minute from first reel to last. It is also true that *Kong* is larded with good healthy sadism, for those whose joy it is to see the frantic girl dangled from cliffs and harried by pterodactyls. But it seems to me that the abiding appeal of the giant ape rests on other foundations.

Kong has, first of all, the attraction of being manlike. His simian nature gives him one huge advantage over giant ants and walking vegetables in that an audience may conceivably identify with him. Kong's appeal has the quality that established the Tarzan series as American myth—for what man doesn't secretly image himself a huge hairy howler against whom no other monster has a chance? If Tarzan recalls the ape in us, then Kong may well appeal to that great-granddaddy primordial brute from whose tribe we have all deteriorated.

Intentionally or not, the producers of *King Kong* encourage this identification by etching the character of Kong with keen sympathy. For the ape is a figure in a tradition familiar to moviegoers: the tradition of the pitiable monster. We think of Lon Chaney in the role of Quasimodo, of Karloff in the original *Frankenstein*. As we watch the Frankenstein monster's fumbling and disastrous attempts to befriend a flower-picking child, our sympathies are enlisted with the monster in his impenetrable loneliness. And so with Kong. As he roars in his chains, while barkers sell tickets to boobs who gape at him, we perhaps feel something more deep than pathos. We begin to sense something of the problem that engaged Eugene O'Neill in *The Hairy Ape:* the dilemma of a displaced animal spirit forced to live in a jungle built by machines.

King Kong, it is true, had special relevance in 1933. Landscapes of the depression are glimpsed early in the film when an impresario, seeking some desperate pretty girl to play the lead in a jungle movie, visits souplines and a Woman's Home Mission. In Fay Wray—who's been caught snitching an apple from a fruitstand—his search is ended. When he gives her a big feed and a movie contract, the girl is magic-carpeted out of the world of the National Recovery Act. And when, in the film's climax, Kong smashes that very Third Avenue landscape in which Fay had wandered hungry, audiences of 1933 may well have felt a personal satisfaction.

What is curious is that audiences of 1960 remain hooked. For in the heart of urban man, one suspects, lurks the impulse to fling a bomb. Though machines speed him to the scene of his daily grind, though IBM comptometers ("freeing the human mind from drudgery") enable him to drudge more efficiently once he arrives, there comes a moment when he wishes to turn upon his machines and kick hell out of them. He wants to hurl his combination radioalarmclock out the bedroom window and listen to its smash. What subway commuter wouldn't love—just for once—to see the downtown express smack head-on into the uptown local? Such a wish is gratified in that memorable scene in *Kong* that opens with a wideangle shot: interior of a railway car on the Third Avenue El. Straphangers are nodding, the literate refold their newspapers. Unknown to them, Kong has torn away a section of trestle toward which the train now speeds. The motorman spies Kong up ahead, jams on the brakes. Passengers hurtle together like so many peas in a pail. In a window of the car appear Kong's bloodshot eyes. Women shriek. Kong picks up the railway car as if it were a rat, flips it to the street and ties knots in it, or something. To any commuter the scene must appear one of the most satisfactory pieces of celluloid ever exposed.

Yet however violent his acts, Kong remains a gentleman. Remarkable is his sense of chivalry. Whenever a fresh boa constrictor threatens Fay, Kong first sees that the lady is safely parked, then manfully thrashes her attacker. (And she, the ingrate, runs away every time his back is turned.) Atop the Empire State Building, ignoring his pursuers, Kong places Fay on a ledge as tenderly as if she were a dozen eggs. He fondles her, then turns to face the Army Air Force. And Kong is perhaps the most disinterested lover since Cyrano: his attentions to the lady are utterly without hope of reward. After all, between a five-foot blonde and a fifty-foot ape, love can hardly be more than an intellectual flirtation. In his simian way King Kong is the hopelessly yearning lover of Petrarchan convention. His forced exit from his jungle, in chains, results directly from his single-minded pursuit of Fay. He smashes a Broadway theater when the notion enters his dull brain that the flash-bulbs of photographers somehow endanger the lady. His perilous shinnying up a skyscraper to pluck Fay from her boudoir is an act of the kindliest of hearts. He's impossible to discourage even though the love of his life can't lay eyes on him without shrieking murder.

The tragedy of King Kong then, is to be the beast who at the end of the fable fails to turn into the handsome prince. This is the conviction that the scriptwriters would leave with us in the film's closing line. As Kong's corpse lies blocking traffic in the street, the enterpreneur who brought Kong to New York turns to the assembled reporters and proclaims: "That's your story, boys—it was Beauty killed the Beast!" But greater forces than those of the screaming Lady have combined to lay Kong low, if you ask me. Kong lives for a time as one of those persecuted near-animal souls bewildered in the middle of an industrial order, whose simple desires are thwarted at every turn. He climbs the Empire State Building because in all New York it's the closest thing he can find to the clifftop of his jungle isle. He dies, a pitiful dolt, and the army brass and publicity-men cackle over him. His death is the only possible outcome to as neat a tragic dilemma as you can ask for. The machine-guns do him in, while the manicured human hero (a nice clean Dartmouth boy) carries away Kong's sweetheart to the altar. O, the misery of it all. There's far more truth about upper-middle-class American life in *King Kong* than in the last seven dozen novels of John P. Marquand.

A Negro friend from Atlanta tells me that in movie houses in colored neighborhoods throughout the South, *Kong* does a constant business. They show the thing in Atlanta at least every year, presumably to the same audiences. Perhaps this popularity may simply be due to the fact that Kong is one of the most watchable movies ever constructed, but I wonder whether Negro audiences may not find some archetypical appeal in this serio-comic tale of a huge black powerful free spirit whom all the hardworking white police-men are out to kill.

Every day in the week on a screen somewhere in the world, King Kong relives his agony. Again and again he expires on the Empire State Building, as audiences of the devout assist his sacrifice. We watch him die, and by extension kill the ape within our bones, but these little deaths of ours occur in prosaic surroundings. We do not die on a tower, New York before our feet, nor do we give our lives to smash a few flying machines. It is not for us to bring to a momentary standstill the civilization in which we move. King Kong does this for us. And so we kill him again and again, in much-spliced celluloid, while the ape in us expires from day to day, obscure, in desperation.

Understanding and Analysis

1. What does Kennedy accomplish for his readers in the first paragraph?

2. What is the topic sentence of the second paragraph? What evidence does Kennedy use to support the point?

3. What question does this essay try to answer?

4. What are the reasons Kennedy proposes? How many different ones can you find? What reason does he immediately reject? Do you agree with Kennedy's rejection of his first reason? Which reasons are based on the appeal to the public in 1933 and which on an enduring appeal? Which reasons depend on a desire for violence?

5. What, according to Kennedy, is Kong's tragedy?

6. According to Kennedy, what role does human evolution play in the enduring fascination of the movie? What role does class play? What role does race play? Do you agree with Kennedy?

7. What other forms of entertainment and literature does Kennedy refer to in making his argument? How many genres does he name? What does he gain through all these allusions?

Comparison

1. Read Chesterton's "A Defense of Penny Dreadfuls." To what extent do Chesterton and Kennedy agree?

2. Have you seen this movie? Do you think it continues to appeal to viewers today? Why or why not?

3. What other movies have you seen that you believe have an enduring appeal? Write an essay about one and explain your reasons.

4. What, if any, attitudes do you think Galbraith and Kennedy may share about definitions of labor and leisure?

Bruno Bettelheim
(1903–1990)

Born in Vienna, Austria, on August 28, 1903, Bruno Bettelheim began his education at the age of eleven. By the time he was ready to apply to college, his father was slowly dying of syphilis, so Bettelheim prepared to assume control of his father's lumber business by enrolling simultaneously in a business program and at the University of Vienna. After he completed the business program, he worked with his father part-time while pursuing his university studies in art history. He left school in 1926, after his father's death.

During the 1920s, Bettelheim courted an educator named Gina Altstadt, and the couple married in March of 1930. The marriage was not a successful one. By 1936, Bettelheim was seeing another educator named Gertrude (Trude) Weinfeld, and at Trude's urging, he returned to the University of Vienna, taking a doctorate in philosophy in February of 1938. A little more than a month later, Hitler invaded Austria. Gina obtained a visa to travel to America, but Bettelheim stayed behind, as did his mother and his sister. In June, Bettelheim was picked up and sent to Dachau; in September, he was transferred to Buchenwald. While he was in the camps, many people worked to get him a visa, and after his release on April 14, 1939, Bettelheim sailed for America. According to biographer Richard Pollack, "All the details of how Bettelheim's release came about may never be known."

In America, Bettelheim searched for work and ultimately took a position as a research associate at the University of Chicago. After he filed for divorce from Gina, he married Trude in 1941, and, the following year, he became an Associate Professor of Psychology at Rockford College. Inside the classroom, Bettelheim was a charismatic and dominating teacher; outside of the classroom, he took his first steps toward fame by writing "Individual and Mass Behavior in Extreme Situations," a psychological study of prisoners in the camps. Many skeptical editors rejected the essay, but it finally found publication in *The Journal of Abnormal and Social Psychology* in 1943.

In 1944, Bettelheim returned to the University of Chicago, becoming the principal of the Orthogenic School, which housed and treated children with a variety of mental illnesses. Along with Emmy Sylvester, a fellow Austrian and a trained analyst, he worked to develop a "therapeutic milieu," a total environment of healing. Bettelheim maintained that the conditions of the children were analogous to the conditions of the prisoners in the camps; both reacted to "extreme situations." The milieu that Bettelheim wanted to develop, then, was the very antithesis of the camps, offering absolute security, a host of choices, and even the freedom to leave. Parents, however, were not permitted either to tour the school or to visit their children, and these were only some of Bettelheim's controversial practices. Although Bettelheim maintained repeatedly that he did not believe in spanking or physical punishment, after his death, several former students came forward with allegations of abuse.

While he was overseeing the Orthogenic School, Bettelheim published three books about his experiences there: *Love Is Not Enough* (1950), *Truants from Life* (1955), and *The Empty Fortress: Infantile Autism and the Birth of the Self* (1967). He earned considerable renown for his work with the school, and he was named the Stella M. Rowley Professor of Education on February 19, 1963. Yet Bettelheim also had his critics. Members of the academic community did not embrace his work, nor did many parents. Indeed, his theory that autism results from poor parenting prompted one mother and more than one researcher to dispute his beliefs in books of their own.

Deeply embittered, Bettelheim took time out from his work with the school to write *The Informed Heart* (1960). In this book, Bettelheim adopted a position that might now be called blaming the victim: he charged Anne Frank's family in particular, and Jews in general, with abetting their own persecution and extermination through their failures to resist the Nazis. When Bettelheim traveled to Israel in 1964 to study the communal child-rearing practices of the kibbutzim, he experienced something of a religious awakening, but he never radically altered his views on the Holocaust. His work in Israel appeared in *Children of the Dream* (1969).

After serving for decades at the Orthogenic School, Bettelheim moved to California in 1973. While teaching at Stanford, he finished another book about the school, *A Home for the Heart* (1974), and published a book on fairy tales, *The Uses of Enchantment* (1976). In 1979, Trude's health began to fail. She died five years later, after a long battle with cancer. Although Bettelheim continued to work, finishing a book called *A Good Enough Parent* (1987), he was permanently devastated by Trude's death and often talked of suicide. Suffering from health problems of his own, he decided to move to a home in Maryland to be close to his daughter Naomi. It was there, on March 12, 1990, that Bettelheim took his own life.

During his lifetime, Bruno Bettelheim enjoyed a reputation as one of the world's foremost authorities on subjects ranging from autism to the Holocaust. Since his death, his reputation has taken a serious turn, not only because of the allegations of abuse, but also because of the research undertaken by his most recent biographers, Nina Sutton and Richard Pollak. Sutton and Pollak both maintain that Bettelheim never had any formal training as a psychoanalyst. While the two biographers do not always agree on the validity of the stories Bettelheim told about prisoners in the camps and students in the classroom, both note his tendency toward prevarication. Pollak also provides evidence that Bettelheim fabricated many of his professional credentials. Given the weight of this information, it is difficult to assess Bettelheim's contribution to twentieth-century thought. That he was a significant writer, of course, cannot be disputed; "Individual and Mass Behavior" was a staple of college courses for decades, and his books influenced millions. His book on fairy tales continues to be taught in colleges across the country. New evaluations of Bettelheim are sure to continue well into the twenty-first century, as students and scholars attempt to sort out the meaning and the value of his life's work.

A Victim   (1960)

Many students of discrimination are aware that the victim often reacts in ways as undesirable as the action of the aggressor. Less attention is paid to this because it is easier to excuse a defendant than an offender, and because they assume that once the aggression stops the victim's reactions will stop too. But I doubt if this is of real service to the persecuted. His main interest is that the persecution cease. But that is less apt to happen if he lacks a real understanding of the phenomenon of persecution, in which victim and persecutor are inseparably interlocked.

Let me illustrate with the following example: in the winter of 1938 a Polish Jew murdered the German attaché in Paris, vom Rath. The Gestapo used the event to step up anti-Semitic actions, and in the camp new hardships were inflicted on Jewish prisoners. One of these was an order barring them from the medical clinic unless the need for treatment had originated in work accident.

Nearly all prisoners suffered from frostbite which often led to gangrene and then amputation. Whether or not a Jewish prisoner was admitted to the clinic to prevent such a fate depended on the whim of an SS private. On reaching the clinic entrance, the prisoner explained the nature of his ailment to the SS man, who then decided if he should get treatment or not.

I too suffered from frostbite. At first I was discouraged from trying to get medical care by the fate of Jewish prisoners whose attempts had ended up in no treatment, only abuse. Finally things got worse and I was afraid that waiting longer would mean amputation. So I decided to make the effort.

When I got to the clinic, there were many prisoners lined up as usual, a score of them Jews suffering from severe frostbite. The main topic of discussion was one's chances of being admitted to the clinic. Most Jews had planned their procedure in detail. Some thought it best to stress their service in the German army during World War I: wounds received or decorations won. Others planned to stress the severity of their frostbite. A few decided it was best to tell some "tall story," such as that an SS officer had ordered them to report at the clinic.

Most of them seemed convinced that the SS man on duty would not see through their schemes. Eventually they asked me about my plans. Having no definite ones, I said I would go by the way the SS man dealt with other Jewish prisoners who had frostbite like me, and proceed accordingly. I doubted how wise it was to follow a preconceived plan, because it was hard to anticipate the reactions of a person you didn't know.

The prisoners reacted as they had at other times when I had voiced similar ideas on how to deal with the SS. They insisted that one SS man was like another, all equally vicious and stupid. As usual, any frustration was immediately discharged against the person who caused it, or was nearest at hand. So in abusive terms they accused me of not wanting to share my plan with them, or of intending to use one of theirs; it angered them that I was ready to meet the enemy unprepared.

No Jewish prisoner ahead of me in the line was admitted to the clinic. The more a prisoner pleaded, the more annoyed and violent the SS became. Expressions of pain amused him; stories of previous services rendered to Germany outraged him. He proudly remarked that *he* could not be taken in by Jews, that fortunately the time had passed when Jews could reach their goal by lamentations.

When my turn came he asked me in a screeching voice if I knew that work accidents were the only reason for admitting Jews to the clinic, and if I came because of such an accident. I replied that I knew the rules, but that I couldn't work unless my hands were freed of the dead flesh. Since prisoners were not allowed to have knives, I asked to have the dead flesh cut away. I tried to be matter-of-fact, avoiding pleading, deference, or arrogance. He replied: "If that's all you want, I'll tear the flesh off myself." And he started to pull at the festering skin. Because it did not come off as easily as he may have expected, or for some other reason, he waved me into the clinic.

Inside, he gave me a malevolent look and pushed me into the treatment room. There he told the prisoner orderly to attend to the wound. While this was being done, the guard watched me closely for signs of pain but I was able to suppress them. As soon as the cutting was over, I started to leave. He showed surprise and asked why I didn't wait for further treatment. I said I had gotten the service I asked for, at which he told the orderly to make an exception and treat my hand. After I had left the room, he called me back and gave me a card entitling me to further treatment, and admittance to the clinic without inspection at the entrance.

* * *

Because my behavior did not correspond to what he expected of Jewish prisoners on the basis of his projection, he could not use his prepared defenses against being touched by the prisoner's plight. Since I did not act as the dangerous Jew was expected to, I did not activate the anxieties that went with his stereotype. Still he did not altogether trust me, so he continued to watch while I received treatment.

Throughout these dealings, the SS felt uneasy with me, though he did not unload on me the annoyance his uneasiness aroused. Perhaps he watched me closely because he expected that sooner or later I would slip up and behave the way his projected image of the Jew was expected to act. This would have meant that his delusional creation had become real.

Understanding and Analysis

1. What is Bettelheim's main assertion in the first paragraph?
2. What is the source of his evidence to back up his assertion?
3. What were Bettelheim's reasons for not making a definite plan while he was in line for treatment at the clinic?
4. How did the other prisoners characterize the SS?
5. How does Bettelheim characterize the other Jewish prisoners?
6. What did Bettelheim observe about the behavior of the SS toward the Jewish prisoners as they presented their cases?
7. How did the SS man characterize the other Jewish prisoners?
8. How does Bettelheim's behavior evade the SS man's stereotype of the Jews?
9. What do you think would have happened if all the Jewish prisoners had behaved as Bettelheim says he did?

Comparison

1. One of Bettelheim's biographers, Richard Pollak, notes that Bruno Bettelheim published three versions of this episode, one in 1947 in the *Journal of Abnormal and Social Psychology,*

the next in 1948 in *Commentary*, and the third in 1960 in *The Informed Heart*, from which this version is taken. In the second version the hero of the tale is called simply "N." Also according to Pollak, another prisoner at Buchenwald claims that Bettelheim did not work outdoors but only indoors, "mending socks." If it were proven that Bettelheim was reporting the experience of another prisoner rather than his own, would that fact undermine Bettelheim's argument? What would the effect on his argument be if it were proven that the incident never took place at all?

2. Read Lippmann's "Stereotypes." How does Lippmann's essay help you to reinterpret Bettelheim's "A Victim?"

3. Read other short essays of persuasion in this collection, such as Mencken's "The Penalty of Death," Vidal's "Drugs," and Brady's "I Want a Wife." How do essays of persuasion differ from complex arguments? What characteristics, if any, do they share?

Edward Hallet Carr
(1892–1982)

Born in London on June 28, 1892, Edward Hallet Carr studied at Trinity College, with a concentration in Classics. In 1916, he began working for the British Foreign Office, serving as a clerk until 1919, when he transferred to the British Embassy in Paris. Named Commander of the Order of the British Empire in 1920, Carr transferred again in 1925, this time to Riga, Lithuania, where he moved up to the position of second secretary. After returning to London in 1929, he became an adviser to the League of Nations, and he published his first book, *Dostoyevsky, 1821–1881: A New Biography* (1931), while serving in this position.

Carr published two more books, *The Romantic Exiles: A Nineteenth-Century Portrait Gallery* (1993) and *Karl Marx: A Study in Fanaticism* (1934), before taking a job at the University College of Wales. As a Professor of International Politics, he taught at the College for over a decade. During World War II, he also acted as the director of foreign publicity for the Ministry of Information and became an assistant editor for *The Times*. Scholar Chimen Abramsky notes that Carr used many of his editorials to convince his readers of "the need for a better understanding of Russia and its rightful place in the council of nations after the war."

Carr published numerous studies of international relations and foreign policy during the 1930s and the 1940s, but it was the work that he began publishing in the 1950s that cemented his reputation as a Soviet historian. The first three volumes of his *A History of Soviet Russia* appeared between 1950 and 1953; he published 14 volumes and some 6,000 pages in all. According to the *Los Angeles Times*, Carr's "history of the Soviet Union from 1917–1929 is considered the most comprehensive political study of the Bolshevik's consolidation of power." As part of the extensive research he undertook to complete this *History*, Abramsky notes, "Carr 'questioned and cross-examined' all the leaders and chief participants of the Russian Revolution, 'asked them for their motives' for various actions they had done." Carr's near romanticizing of Stalin, in particular, prompted criticism, but reviewer Alex Nove maintains that "the overriding impression of any reader of Carr's great study must be one of ungrudging admiration: what a colossal scholarly achievement!"

In 1953, as Carr worked on the fourth volume of his *History*, he took a position at Balliol College, and in 1955, he returned to Trinity College, serving as a fellow there until the time of his death. For the remainder of his career, he delivered lectures and published works such as *What Is History?* (1961), which became a best-seller; *The October Revolution: Before and After* (1969); and *From Napoleon to Stalin and Other Essays* (1980). He died on November 3, 1982.

E. H. Carr had his fair share of critics over the years, some of them concerned not only by his approach to Stalin, but also by his fundamental approach to history. William Pfaff, a critic for *The New Yorker*, claims that Carr sought "to demonstrate by his history, tautologically, that those who were successful were right, as is proved by their success." Despite their quarrels with Carr's methodology, however, critics tend to agree that his *History* will remain an essential work of reference for students of Russian history. Roger Morgan also maintains that while some of Carr's work on international relations is dated, the argument that Carr sets forward in *The Twenty Years' Crisis, 1919–1939* "retains an enduring value." His popular book defining history, from which the chapter below is taken, has influenced more than a generation of readers to see the relationship between fact and theory in the development of what historians of various schools and political prejudices have deemed historical and worthy of preservation.

The Historian and His Facts (1961)

WHAT IS HISTORY? Lest anyone think the question meaningless or superfluous, I will take as my text two passages relating respectively to the first and second incarnations of *The Cambridge Modern History*. Here is Acton in his report of October 1896 to the Syndics of the Cambridge Press on the work which he had undertaken to edit:

It is a unique opportunity of recording, in the way most useful to the greatest number, the fullness of the knowledge which the nineteenth century is about to bequeath. . . . By the judicious division of labor we should be able to do it, and to bring home to every man the last document, and the ripest conclusions of international research.

Ultimate history we cannot have in this generation; but we can dispose of conventional history, and show the point we have reached on the road from one to the other, now that all information is within reach, and every problem has become capable of solution.

And almost exactly sixty years later Professor Sir George Clark, in his general introduction to the second Cambridge *Modern History,* commented on this belief of Acton and his collaborators that it would one day be possible to produce "ultimate history," and went on:

> Historians of a later generation do not look forward to any such prospect. They expect their work to be superseded again and again. They consider that knowledge of the past has come down through one or more human minds, has been "processed" by them, and therefore cannot consist of elemental and impersonal atoms which nothing can alter. . . . The exploration seems to be endless, and some impatient scholars take refuge in scepticism, or at least in the doctrine that, since all historical judgments involve persons and points of view, one is as good as another and there is no "objective" historical truth.

Where the pundits contradict each other so flagrantly the field is open to enquiry. I hope that I am sufficiently up-to-date to recognize that anything written in the 1890's must be nonsense. But I am not yet advanced enough to be committed to the view that anything written in the 1950's necessarily makes sense. Indeed, it may already have occurred to you that this enquiry is liable to stray into something even broader than the nature of history. The clash between Acton and Sir George Clark is a reflection of the change in our total outlook on society over the interval between these two pronouncements. Acton speaks out of the positive belief, the clear-eyed self-confidence of the later *Victorian age;*[1] Sir George Clark echoes the bewilderment and distracted scepticism of the *beat generation.*[2] When we attempt to answer the question, What is history?, our answer, consciously or unconsciously, reflects our own position in time, and forms part of our answer to the broader question, what view we take of the society in which we live. I have no fear that my subject may, on closer inspection, seem trivial. I am afraid only that I may seem presumptuous to have broached a question so vast and so important.

The nineteenth century was a great age for facts. "What I want," said Mr. Gradgrind *in Hard Times,*[3] "is Facts. . . . Facts alone are wanted in life." Nineteenth-century historians on the whole agreed with him. When *Ranke*[4] in the 1830's, in legitimate protest against moralizing history, remarked that the task of the historian was "simply to show how it really was [wie es eigentlich gewesen]" this not very profound aphorism had an astonishing success. Three generations of German, British, and even French historians marched into bat-

---

[1]*Victorian age* the era during which Queen Victoria was ruler of England, from 1837–1901.

[2]*beat generation* in the 1950s, a group of American artists and writers who were influenced by Eastern religions and the rhythms of progressive jazz, and who rejected traditional forms and sought expression in intense experiences and beatific illumination.

[3]*Hard Times* an 1854 novel by Charles Dickens, in which he assaults the industrial greed and political economy that exploited the working classes.

[4]*Ranke* Leopold von Ranke (1795–1886) prominent German historian who believed that historians should not teach or direct, but simply reflect reality.

tle intoning the magic words, "Wie es eigentlich gewesen" like an incantation—designed, like most incantations, to save them from the tiresome obligation to think for themselves. The *Positivists,* anxious to stake out their claim for history as a science, contributed the weight of their influence to this cult of facts. First ascertain the facts, said the positivists, then draw your conclusions from them. In Great Britain, this view of history fitted in perfectly with the empiricist tradition which was the dominant strain in British philosophy from *Locke to Bertrand Russell.*[5] The empirical theory of knowledge presupposes a complete separation between subject and object. Facts, like sense-impressions, impinge on the observer from outside, and are independent of his consciousness. The process of reception is passive: having received the data, he then acts on them. *The Shorter Oxford English Dictionary,* a useful but tendentious work of the empirical school, clearly marks the separateness of the two processes by defining a fact as "a datum of experience as distinct from conclusions." This is what may be called the common-sense view of history. History consists of a corpus of ascertained facts. The facts are available to the historian in documents, inscriptions, and so on, like fish on the fishmonger's slab. The historian collects them, takes them home, and cooks and serves them in whatever style appeals to him. Acton, whose culinary tastes were austere, wanted them served plain. In his letter of instructions to contributors to the first *Cambridge Modern History* he announced the requirement "that our Waterloo[6] must be one that satisfies French and English, German and Dutch alike; that nobody can tell, without examining the list of authors where the Bishop of Oxford[7] laid down the pen, and whether Fairbairn or Gasquet, Liebermann or Harrison took it up." Even Sir George Clark, critical as he was of Acton's attitude, himself contrasted the "hard core of facts" in history with the "surrounding pulp of disputable interpretation"—forgetting perhaps that the pulpy part of the fruit is more rewarding than the hard core. First get your facts straight, then plunge at your peril into the shifting sands of interpretation—that is the ultimate wisdom of the empirical, common-sense school of history. It recalls the favorite dictum of the great liberal journalist C. P. Scott: "Facts are sacred, opinion is free."

Now this clearly will not do. I shall not embark on a philosophical discussion of the nature of our knowledge of the past. Let us assume for present purposes that the fact that Caesar crossed the Rubicon and the fact that there is a table in the middle of the room are facts of the same or of a comparable order, that both these facts enter our consciousness in the same or in a comparable manner, and that both have the same objective character in relation to the person who knows them. But, even on this bold and not very plausible assumption, our argument at once runs into the difficulty that not all facts about the past are historical facts, or are treated as such by the historian. What is the criterion which distinguishes the facts of history from other facts about the past?

What is a historical fact? This is a crucial question into which we must look a little more closely. According to the common-sense view, there are certain basic facts which are the same for all historians and which form, so to speak, the backbone of history—the fact, for example, that the Battle of Hastings was fought in 1066. But this view calls for two observations. In the first place, it is not with facts like these that the historian is primarily con-

[5]*Locke to Bertrand Russell* John Locke (1632–1704) was an English philosopher; *Bertrand Russell* (1872–1970) was a British philosopher, mathematician, and social reformer. Both Locke and Russell believed in logic and rationalism as a way of explaining the world.

[6]*Waterloo* The Battle of Waterloo in 1815 in which the Duke of Wellington defeated the French army led by Napoleon.

[7]*Bishop of Oxford . . . Harrison* contributors to the *Cambridge Modern History.*

cerned. It is no doubt important to know that the great battle was fought in 1066 and not in 1065 or 1067, and that it was fought at Hastings and not at Eastbourne or Brighton. The historian must not get these things wrong. But when points of this kind are raised, I am reminded of *Housman's*[8] *remark*[9] that "accuracy is a duty, not a virtue." To praise a historian for his accuracy is like praising an architect for using well-seasoned timber or properly mixed concrete in his building. It is a necessary condition of his work, but not his essential function. It is precisely for matters of this kind that the historian is entitled to rely on what have been called the "auxiliary sciences" of history—archaeology, epigraphy, numismatics, chronology, and so forth. The historian is not required to have the special skills which enable the expert to determine the origin and period of a fragment of pottery or marble, or decipher an obscure inscription, or to make the elaborate astronomical calculations necessary to establish a precise date. These so-called basic facts which are the same for all historians commonly belong to the category of the raw materials of the historian rather than of history itself. The second observation is that the necessity to establish these basic facts rests not on any quality in the facts themselves, but on an *a priori* decision of the historian. In spite of C. P. Scott's motto, every journalist knows today that the most effective way to influence opinion is by the selection and arrangement of the appropriate facts. It used to be said that facts speak for themselves. This is, of course, untrue. The facts speak only when the historian calls on them: It is he who decides to which facts to give the floor, and in what order or context. It was, I think, one of *Pirandello's*[10] characters who said that a fact is like a sack—it won't stand up till you've put something in it. The only reason why we are interested to know that the battle was fought at Hastings in 1066 is that historians regard it as a major historical event. It is the historian who has decided for his own reasons that Caesar's crossing of that petty stream, the Rubicon, is a fact of history, whereas the crossing of the Rubicon by millions of other people before or since interests nobody at all. The fact that you arrived in this building half an hour ago on foot, or on a bicycle, or in a car, is just as much a fact about the past as the fact that Caesar crossed the Rubicon. But it will probably be ignored by historians. Professor Talcott Parsons once called science "a selective system of cognitive orientations to reality." It might perhaps have been put more simply. But history is, among other things, that. The historian is necessarily selective. The belief in a hard core of historical facts existing objectively and independently of the interpretation of the historian is a preposterous fallacy, but one which it is very hard to eradicate.

Let us take a look at the process by which a mere fact about the past is transformed into a fact of history. At Stalybridge Wakes in 1850, a vendor of gingerbread, as the result of some petty dispute, was deliberately kicked to death by an angry mob. Is this a fact of history? A year ago I should unhesitatingly have said "no." It was recorded by an eyewitness in some little-known memoirs;[11] but I had never seen it judged worthy of mention by any historian. A year ago Dr. Kitson Clark cited it in his Ford lectures in Oxford. Does this make it into a historical fact? Not, I think, yet. Its present status, I suggest, is

---

[8]*Housman* Alfred Edward Housman (1859–1936) an English poet and professor of Latin at Cambridge University.

[9]In the preface to his critical edition of Manilius, *Astronomicon,* an obscure Latin work. [Carr's note]

[10]*Pirandello* Luigi Pirandello (1867–1936) Italian author; a major figure in twentieth-century theater, he was awarded the 1934 Nobel Prize in literature.

[11]Lord George Sanger: *Seventy Years a Showman* (London: J. M. Dent & Sons, 1926), pp. 188–9 [Carr's note]

that it has been proposed for membership of the select club of historical facts. It now awaits a seconder and sponsors. It may be that in the course of the next few years we shall see this fact appearing first in footnotes, then in the text, of articles and books about nineteenth-century England, and that in twenty or thirty years' time it may be a well established historical fact. Alternatively, nobody may take it up, in which case it will relapse into the limbo of unhistorical facts about the past from which Dr. Kitson Clark has gallantly attempted to rescue it. What will decide which of these two things will happen? It will depend, I think, on whether the thesis or interpretation in support of which Dr. Kitson Clark cited this incident is accepted by other historians as valid and significant. Its status as a historical fact will turn on a question of interpretation. This element of interpretation enters into every fact of history.

May I be allowed a personal reminiscence? When I studied ancient history in this university many years ago, I had as a special subject "Greece in the period of the Persian Wars." I collected fifteen or twenty volumes on my shelves and took it for granted that there, recorded in these volumes, I had all the facts relating to my subject. Let us assume—it was very nearly true—that those volumes contained all the facts about it that were then known, or could be known. It never occurred to me to enquire by what accident or process of attrition that minute selection of facts, out of all the myriad facts that must have once been known to somebody, had survived to become *the* facts of history. I suspect that even today one of the fascinations of ancient and medieval history is that it gives us the illusion of having all the facts at our disposal within a manageable compass: the nagging distinction between the facts of history and other facts about the past vanishes because the few known facts are all facts of history. As Bury, who had worked in both periods, said, "the records of ancient and medieval history are starred with lacunae." History has been called an enormous jig-saw with a lot of missing parts. But the main trouble does not consist of the lacunae. Our picture of Greece in the fifth century *b.c.* is defective not primarily because so many of the bits have been accidentally lost, but because it is, by and large, the picture formed by a tiny group of people in the city of Athens. We know a lot about what fifth-century Greece looked like to an Athenian citizen; but hardly anything about what it looked like to a Spartan, a Corinthian, or a Theban—not to mention a Persian, or a slave or other non-citizen resident in Athens. Our picture has been preselected and predetermined for us, not so much by accident as by people who were consciously or unconsciously imbued with a particular view and thought the facts which supported that view worth preserving. In the same way, when I read in a modern history of the Middle Ages that the people of the Middle Ages were deeply concerned with religion, I wonder how we know this, and whether it is true. What we know as the facts of medieval history have almost all been selected for us by generations of chroniclers who were professionally occupied in the theory and practice of religion, and who therefore thought it supremely important, and recorded everything relating to it, and not much else. The picture of the Russian peasant as devoutly religious was destroyed by the revolution of 1917. The picture of medieval man as devoutly religious, whether true or not, is indestructible, because nearly all the known facts about him were preselected for us by people who believed it, and wanted others to believe it, and a mass of other facts, in which we might possibly have found evidence to the contrary, has been lost beyond recall. The dead hand of vanished generations of historians, scribes, and chroniclers has determined beyond the possibility of appeal the pattern of the past. "The history we read," writes Professor Barraclough, himself trained as a mediaevalist, "though based on facts, is, strictly speaking, not factual at all, but a series of accepted judgments."

But let us turn to the different, but equally grave, plight of the modern historian. The ancient or medieval historian may be grateful for the vast winnowing process which, over the years, has put at his disposal a manageable corpus of historical facts. As Lytton Strachey said in his mischievous way, "ignorance is the first requisite of the historian, ignorance which simplifies and clarifies, which selects and omits." When I am tempted, as I sometimes am, to envy the extreme competence of colleagues engaged in writing ancient or mediaeval history, I find consolation in the reflection that they are so competent mainly because they are so ignorant of their subject. The modern historian enjoys none of the advantages of this built-in ignorance. He must cultivate this necessary ignorance for himself—the more so the nearer he comes to his own times. He has the dual task of discovering the few significant facts and turning them into facts of history, and of discarding the many insignificant facts are unhistorical. But this is the very converse of the nineteenth-century heresy that history consists of the compilation of a maximum number of irrefutable and objective facts. Anyone who succumbs to this heresy will either have to give up history as a bad job, and take to stamp-collecting or some other form of antiquarianism, or end in a madhouse. It is this heresy, which during the past hundred years has had such devastating effects on the modern historian, producing in Germany, in Great Britain, and in the United States a vast and growing mass of dry-as-dust factual histories, of minutely specialized monographs, of would-be historians knowing more and more about less and less, sunk without trace in an ocean of facts. It was, I suspect, this heresy—rather than the alleged conflict between liberal and Catholic loyalties—which frustrated Acton as a historian. In an early essay he said of his teacher Döllinger: "He would not write with imperfect materials, and to him the materials were always imperfect."[12] Acton was surely here pronouncing an anticipatory verdict on himself, on that strange phenomenon of a historian whom many would regard as the most distinguished occupant the Regius Chair of Modern History this university has ever had—but who wrote no history. And Acton wrote his own epitaph in the introductory note to the first volume of the *Cambridge Modern History,* published just after his death, when he lamented that the requirements pressing on the historian "threaten to turn him from a man of letters into the compiler of an encyclopedia." Something had gone wrong. What had gone wrong was the belief in this untiring and unending accumulation of hard facts as the foundation of history, the belief that facts speak for themselves and that we cannot have too many facts, a belief at that time so unquestioning that few historians then thought it necessary—and some still think it unnecessary today—to ask themselves the question: What is history?

The nineteenth-century fetishism of facts was completed and justified by a fetishism of documents. The documents were the *Ark of the Covenant*[13] in the temple of facts. The reverent historian approached them with bowed head and spoke of them in awed tones. If you find it in the documents, it is so. But what, when we get down to it, do these documents—the decrees, the treaties, the rent-rolls, the blue books, the official correspondence, the private letters and diaries—tell us? No document can tell us more than what the author of the document thought—what he thought had happened, what he thought ought to happen or would happen, or perhaps only what he wanted others to think he thought, or even only what he himself thought he thought. None of this means anything

---

[12]Later Acton said of Döllinger that "it was given to him to form his philosophy of history on the largest induction ever available to man." [Carr's note]

[13]*Ark of the Covenant* from the Old Testament; a holy chest containing scripture, which the people of Israel carried with them on their wanderings.

until the historian has got to work on it and deciphered it. The facts, whether found in documents or not, have still to be processed by the historian before he can make any use of them: the use he makes of them is, if I may put it that way, the processing process. . . .[14]

In the first place, the facts of history never come to us "pure," since they do not and cannot exist in a pure form: they are always refracted through the mind of the recorder. It follows that when we take up a work of history, our first concern should be not with the facts which it contains but with the historian who wrote it. Let me take as an example the great historian in whose honor and in whose name these lectures were founded. Trevelyan,[15] as he tells us in his autobiography, was "brought up at home on a somewhat exuberantly Whig tradition"; and he would not, I hope, disclaim the title if I described him as the last and not the least of the great English liberal historians of the Whig tradition.[16] It is not for nothing that he traces back his family tree, through the great Whig historian George Otto Trevelyan, to Macaulay,[17] incomparably the greatest of the Whig historians. Dr. Trevelyan's finest and maturest work *England under Queen Anne* was written against that background, and will yield its full meaning and significance to the reader only when read against that background. The author, indeed, leaves the reader with no excuse for failing to do so. For if, following the technique of connoisseurs of detective novels, you read the end first, you will find on the last few pages of the third volume the best summary known to me of what is nowadays called the Whig interpretation of history; and you will see that what Trevelyan is trying to do is to investigate the origin and development of the Whig tradition, and to root it fairly and squarely in the years after the death of its founder, William III. Though this is not, perhaps, the only conceivable interpretation of the events of Queen Anne's reign, it is a valid and, in Trevelyan's hands, a fruitful interpretation. But, in order to appreciate it at its full value, you have to understand what the historian is doing. For if, as Collingwood[18] says, the historian must re-enact in thought what has gone on in the mind of his *dramatis personae,* so the reader in his turn must re-enact what goes on in the mind of the historian. Study the historian before you begin to study the facts. This is, after all, not very abstruse. It is what is already done by the intelligent undergraduate who, when recommended to read a work by that great scholar Jones of St. Jude's, goes round to a friend at St. Jude's to ask what sort of chap Jones is, and what bees he has in his bonnet. When you read a work of history, always listen out for the buzzing. If you can detect none, either you are tone deaf or your historian is a dull dog. The facts are really not at all like fish on the fishmonger's slab.

---

[14]A Long illustration of Carr's point has been deleted. The next paragraph introduces three "neglected truths" of Collingwood's history.

[15]*Trevelyan* George Macaulay Trevelyan (1876–1962), an English historian and professor of modern history at Cambridge who was a master of the so-called "literary" school of historical writing.

[16]*Whig tradition* the Whigs were a political party in England from the seventeenth to the nineteenth century. They were advocates of personal freedom, maintaining that the king governed at the people's consent; they were also the party of financial and mercantile interests (vs. the landed nobility); and were later identified with the Evangelical faction of the Church of England. After 1841, the term Whig was gradually replaced by the term Liberal.

[17]*Macaulay* Thomas Babington Macaulay (1800–1859) an English historian and statesman.

[18]*Collingwood* Robin George Collingwood (1889–1943) an archeologist and an Oxford professor of philosophy. He believed history to be made up of the interaction between the past and the historian's thoughts about that past.

They are like fish swimming about in a vast and sometimes inaccessible ocean; and what the historian catches will depend partly on chance, but mainly on what part of the ocean he chooses to fish in and what tackle he chooses to use—these two factors being, of course, determined by the kind of fish he wants to catch. By and large, the historian will get the kind of facts he wants. History means interpretation. Indeed, if, standing Sir George Clark on his head, I were to call history "a hard core of interpretation surrounded by a pulp of disputable facts," my statement would, no doubt, be one-sided and misleading, but no more so, I venture to think, than the original dictum.

The second point is the more familiar one of the historian's need of imaginative understanding for the minds of the people with whom he is dealing, for the thought behind their acts: I say "imaginative understanding," not "sympathy," lest sympathy should be supposed to imply agreement. The nineteenth century was weak in mediaeval history, because it was too much repelled by the superstitious beliefs of the Middle Ages and by the barbarities which they inspired, to have any imaginative understanding of mediaeval people. Or take Burckhardt's censorious remark about the *Thirty Years' War:*[19] "It is scandalous for a creed, no matter whether it is Catholic or Protestant, to place its salvation above the integrity of the nation." It was extremely difficult for a nineteenth-century liberal historian, brought up to believe that it is right and praiseworthy to kill in defense of one's country, but wicked and wrong-headed to kill in defense of one's religion, to enter into the state of mind of those who fought the Thirty Years' War. This difficulty is particularly acute in the field in which I am now working. Much of what has been written in English-speaking countries in the last ten years about the Soviet Union, and in the Soviet Union about the English-speaking countries, has been vitiated by this inability to achieve even the most elementary measure of imaginative understanding of what goes on in the mind of the other party, so that the words and actions of the other are always made to appear malign, senseless, or hypocritical. History cannot be written unless the historian can achieve some kind of contact with the mind of those about whom he is writing.

The third point is that we can view the past, and achieve our understanding of the past, only through the eyes of the present. The historian is of his own age, and is bound to it by the conditions of human existence. The very words which he uses—words like democracy, empire, war, revolution—have current connotations from which he cannot divorce them. Ancient historians have taken to using words like *polis* and *plebs* in the original, just in order to show that they have not fallen into this trap. This does not help them. They, too, live in the present, and cannot cheat themselves into the past by using unfamiliar or obsolete words, any more than they would become better Greek or Roman historians if they delivered their lectures in a *chlamys* or a *toga*. The names by which successive French historians have described the Parisian crowds which played so prominent a role in the French Revolution—*les sansculottes, le peuple, la canaille, les bras-nus*—are all, for those who know the rules of the game, manifestos of a political affiliation and of a particular interpretation. Yet the historian is obliged to choose: the use of language forbids him to be neutral. Nor is it a matter of words alone. Over the past hundred years the changed balance of power in Europe has reversed the attitude of British historians to Frederick the Great. The changed balance of power within the Christian churches between Catholicism and Protestantism has profoundly altered their attitude to such figures as Loyola, Luther, and Cromwell. It requires only a superficial knowledge of the work of French

[19]*Thirty Years' War* a long and complex religious and political war from 1618–1648 which pitted Catholics against Lutherans and Calvinists in Europe.

historians of the last forty years on the French revolution to recognize how deeply it has been affected by the Russian revolution of 1917. The historian belongs not to the past but to the present. Professor Trevor-Roper tells us that the historian "ought to love the past." This is a dubious injunction. To love the past may easily be an expression of the nostalgic romanticism of old men and old societies, a symptom of loss of faith and interest in the present or future.[20] *Cliché* for *cliché,* I should prefer the one about freeing oneself from "the dead hand of the past." The function of the historian is neither to love the past nor to emancipate himself from the past, but to master and understand it as the key to the understanding of the present.

If, however, these are some of the sights of what I may call the Collingwood view of history, it is time to consider some of the dangers. The emphasis on the role of the historian in the making of history tends, if pressed to its logical conclusion, to rule out any objective history at all: history is what the historian makes. Collingwood seems indeed, at one moment, in an unpublished note quoted by his editor, to have reached this conclusion:

> St. Augustine looked at history from the point of view of the early Christian; Tillemont, from that of a seventeenth-century Frenchman; Gibbon, from that of an eighteenth-century Englishman; Mommsen, from that of a nineteenth-century German. There is no point in asking which was the right point of view. Each was the only one possible for the man who adopted it.

This amounts to total scepticism, like Froude's remark that history is "a child's box of letters with which we can spell any word we please." Collingwood, in his reaction against "scissors-and-paste history," against the view of history as a mere compilation of facts, comes perilously near to treating history as something spun out of the human brain, and leads back to the conclusion referred to by Sir George Clark in the passage which I quoted earlier, that "there is no 'objective' historical truth." In place of the theory that history has no meaning, we are offered here the theory of an infinity of meanings, none any more right than any other—which comes to much the same thing. The second theory is surely as untenable as the first. It does not follow that, because a mountain appears to take on different shapes from different angles of vision, it has objectively either no shape at all or an infinity of shapes. It does not follow that, because interpretation plays a necessary part in establishing the facts of history, and because no existing interpretation is wholly objective, one interpretation is as good as another, and the facts of history are in principle not amenable to objective interpretation. I shall have to consider at a later stage what exactly is meant by objectivity in history.

But a still greater danger lurks in the Collingwood hypothesis. If the historian necessarily looks at his period of history through the eyes of his own time, and studies the problems of the past as a key to those of the present, will he not fall into a purely pragmatic view of the facts, and maintain that the criterion of a right interpretation is its suitability to some present purpose? On this hypothesis, the facts of history are nothing, interpretation is everything. Nietzsche had already enunciated the principle: "The falseness of an opinion is not for us any objection to it. . . . The question is how far it is life-

---

[20]Compare Nietzsche's view of history: "To old age belongs the old man's business of looking back and casting up his accounts, of seeking consolation in the memories of the past, in historical culture." [Carr's note]

furthering, life-preserving, species-preserving, perhaps species-creating." The American pragmatists moved, less explicitly and less wholeheartedly, along the same line. Knowledge is knowledge for some purpose. The validity of the knowledge depends on the validity of the purpose. But, even where no such theory has been professed, the practice has often been no less disquieting. In my own field of study, I have seen too many examples of extravagant interpretation riding roughshod over facts, not to be impressed with the reality of this danger. It is not surprising that perusal of some of the more extreme products of Soviet and anti-Soviet schools of historiography should sometimes breed a certain nostalgia for that illusory nineteenth-century heaven of purely factual history.

How then, in the middle of the twentieth century, are we to define the obligation of the historian to his facts? I trust that I have spent a sufficient number of hours in recent years chasing and perusing documents, and stuffing my historical narrative with properly footnoted facts, to escape the imputation of treating facts and documents too cavalierly. The duty of the historian to respect his facts is not exhausted by the obligation to see that his facts are accurate. He must seek to bring into the picture all known or knowable facts relevant, in one sense or another, to the theme on which he is engaged and to the interpretation proposed. If he seeks to depict the Victorian Englishman as a moral and rational being, he must not forget what happened at Stalybridge Wakes in 1850. But this, in turn, does not mean that he can eliminate interpretation, which is the life-blood of history. Laymen—that is to say, non-academic friends or friends from other academic disciplines—sometimes ask me how the historian goes to work when he writes history. The commonest assumption appears to be that the historian divides his work into two sharply distinguishable phases or periods. First, he spends a long preliminary period reading his source and filling his notebooks with facts: then, when this is over, he puts away his sources, takes out his notebooks, and writes his book from beginning to end. This is to me an unconvincing and unplausible picture. For myself, as soon as I have got going on a few of what I take to be the capital sources, the itch becomes too strong and I begin to write—not necessarily at the beginning, but somewhere, anywhere. Thereafter, reading and writing go on simultaneously. The writing is added to, subtracted from, re-shaped, cancelled, as I go on reading. The reading is guided and directed and made fruitful by the writing: the more I write, the more I know what I am looking for, the better I understand the significance and relevance of what I find. Some historians probably do all this preliminary writing in their head without using pen, paper, or typewriter, just as some people play chess in their heads without recourse to board and chess-men: this is a talent which I envy, but cannot emulate. But I am convinced that, for any historian worth the name, the two processes of what economists call "input" and "output" go on simultaneously and are, in practice, parts of a single process. If you try to separate them, or to give one priority over the other, you fall into one of two heresies. Either you write scissors-and-paste history without meaning or significance; or you write propaganda or historical fiction, and merely use facts of the past to embroider a kind of writing which has nothing to do with history.

Our examination of the relation of the historian to the facts of history finds us, therefore, in an apparently precarious situation, navigating delicately between the Scylla of an untenable theory of history as an objective compilation of facts, of the unqualified primacy of fact over interpretation, and the Charybdis of an equally untenable theory of history as the subjective product of the mind of the historian who establishes the facts of history and masters them through the process of interpretation, between a view of history having the center of gravity in the past and the view having the center of gravity in the present. But our situation is less precarious than it seems. We shall encounter the same dichotomy of fact and interpretation again in these lectures in other guises—the particular and the general, the empirical and the theoretical, the objective and the subjective. The predicament of the historian is a reflection of the nature of man. Man, except perhaps in earliest infancy and in extreme old age, is not totally involved in his environment and unconditionally subject to it. On the other hand, he is never totally independent of it and its unconditional master. The relation of man to his environment is the relation of the historian to his theme. The historian is neither the humble slave, nor the tyrannical master, of his facts. The relation between the historian and his facts is one of equality, of give-and-take. As any working historian knows, if he stops to reflect what he is doing as he thinks and writes, the historian is engaged on a continuous process of moulding his facts to his interpretation and his interpretation to his facts. It is impossible to assign primacy to one over the other.

The historian starts with the provisional selection of facts and a provisional interpretation in the light of which that selection has been made—by others as well as by himself. As he works, both the interpretation and the selection and ordering of facts undergo subtle and perhaps partly unconscious changes through the reciprocal action of one or the other. And this reciprocal action also involves reciprocity between present and past, since the historian is part of the present and the facts belong to the past. The historian and the facts of history are necessary to one another. The historian without his facts is rootless and futile; the facts without their historian are dead and meaningless. My first answer therefore to the question, What is history?, is that it is a continuous process of interaction between the historian and his facts, an unending dialogue between the present and the past.

Understanding and Analysis

1. Describe in your own words the difference in the attitude toward history found in the two editions of *The Cambridge Modern History*.

2. What is the "broader question" that Carr is raising?

3. Describe the "empirical theory of knowledge." What view of history emerges from this theory?

4. What role does accuracy play in the work of the historian?

5. What is the difference between "a mere fact" and a "fact of history"?

6. What is the main cause of the "defective" picture of fifth-century Greece?

7. Who wrote the history of the Middle Ages? Why is the source of the history important?

8. What makes the study of ancient history somewhat easier than the study of modern history?

9. What exactly do documents tell us, according to Carr?

10. Carr lists three "neglected truths" of Collingwood's view of history. What are they? How do these points clarify Carr's earlier assertions?

11. Answer again the question posed in number 5.

12. What are the dangers Carr sees in Collingwood's view of history?

13. What, according to Carr, is the pragmatists' philosophy of history?

14. What are the two extreme views of history and how does Carr reconcile them?

15. How does the historian write?

16. What is Carr's answer to his question, 'What is history?'

17. What does Carr mean by "moulding his facts to his interpretation"? Is he saying in this penultimate paragraph that the historian can deliberately misrepresent or distort facts to suit the preferred interpretation? What evidence from his essay can you assemble to support an answer of "yes" and an answer of "no" to this question?

18. Carr relies on metaphor and analogy to clarify his points. Find as many figures as you can. Do these figures help to enliven his prose?

Comparison

1. Read Lippmann's "Stereotypes." Where do Carr and Lippmann agree?

2. Read the essays on war in this collection. In what sense are they documents of history?

3. Read the essays on science in this collection. In what ways are scientists and historians alike?

4. Carr's ideas about history have been widely influential. Read the essays by Kuhn, Podhoretz, Tuchman, FitzGerald, and Postman. What, if anything, connects these essays to Carr's? Read the essay by Bronowski. What connections do you see?

Rachel Carson
(1907–1964)

As a child, Rachel Carson was likely to be in one of two places: in the woods behind her house or behind the pages of a book. Her passion for reading soon convinced her that she wanted to become a writer. "I have no idea why," Carson reflected later. "There were no writers in the family. I read a great deal almost from infancy, and I suppose I must have realized someone wrote the books and thought it would be fun to make up stories, too." Carson's ambition found early satisfaction: *St. Nicholas* magazine purchased one of her essays when she was just 11 years old. After she enrolled at the Pennsylvania College for Women, however, she put her writing on hold. Starting out as an English major, she became an aspiring zoologist in her junior year. Biographer Paul Brooks explains, "At the time, she believed that she had abandoned her dream of a literary career; only later did she realize that, on the contrary, she had discovered what she wanted to write about." In 1928, after graduating from college, she went on to Johns Hopkins, earning an M.A. in zoology that allowed her to teach the subject part-time.

During the 1930s, Carson took two positions at the Bureau of Fisheries in Washington, D. C., the first as a script writer for the bureau's radio program, and the second as a junior aquatic biologist. When the program ended, Carson's boss requested a "general" script about the ocean. Carson complied, recalling later, "My chief read it and handed it back with a twinkle in his eye. 'I don't think it will do,' he said.... But send this one to the *Atlantic*.'" Carson's piece appeared in *The Atlantic Monthly* in 1937, attracting the attention of an editor at Simon and Schuster who encouraged her to undertake a full-length book about the sea. Thus was born *Under the Sea-Wind* (1941). With the nation on the brink of World War II, the book generated wonderful reviews but terrible sales. The war itself required Carson to devote most of her time to writing government pamphlets designed to introduce untapped food resources into the American diet.

Promoted to Information Specialist after the war, Carson attained the rank of Chief Editor in 1949. By this point, she had begun work on her second book, *The Sea Around Us* (1951). Thanks to serialization in magazines like *The New Yorker* and *Vogue*, the book aroused enormous public interest, even before it appeared. After publication, it hit the best-seller list, where it remained for 86 weeks. It also won the National Book Award. With the money she earned from *The Sea Around Us*, Carson bought land on the coast of Maine near the home of Dorothy Murdoch Freeman. Carson and Freeman became intimate friends, exchanging hundreds of handwritten letters in which they describe their lives and their love for each other.

Although Carson regarded writing as a "lonely" and laborious business, she started planning her third book before she had even finished her second. Retiring in 1952, she devoted three years to *The Edge of the Sea* (1955), voted "outstanding book of the year" by the National Council of Women of the United States. Carson planned to write her next book about "the origins of Life," but those plans changed after she received a letter from a woman named Olga Owens Huckins. Originally written to the editor of *The Boston Herald*, the letter protested the spraying of DDT; Huckins had forwarded it to Carson to ask for help in preventing future sprayings. Carson remembered, "I began to ask around for the information she wanted, and the more I learned about the use of pesticides the more appalled I became." By February, Carson had started her fourth book, *Silent Spring* (1962), a reference to the birds killed by sprayings. Intent on showing that her "concerns" about pesticides were "well founded," she undertook intensive research that often overwhelmed her, not only because of its vastness, but also because of its grim subject matter. Dorothy Freeman's objections likewise made the labor difficult. In June of 1958, Carson wrote to her, "I know you dread the unpleasantness that will inevitably be associated with its publication. That I can understand, darling. But it is something I have taken into account; it will not surprise me!...Knowing what I do, there would be no future peace for me if I kept silent!...I wish you could feel, as I do, that it is, in the deepest sense, a privilege as well as a duty to have the opportunity to speak out—to many thousands of people—on something so important." Diagnosed with cancer in 1960, Carson nevertheless persisted in the writing of "the poison book."

Freeman and Carson were right to anticipate serious "unpleasantness" surrounding its release. Chemical companies reacted swiftly and forcefully, threatening a lawsuit, releasing parodies, even characterizing Carson as an hysteric with no real credentials. *Silent Spring* generated so much controversy, in fact, that President John F. Kennedy called for a formal study of pesticides. That study, Brooks states, "amounted to an official scientific endorsement of Rachel Carson's position"; one day after its release, on May 16, 1963, the Senate began hearings to consider ways to deal with the problem. Carson herself appeared before the Senate committee in June.

As she was receiving public acclaim, Carson was suffering privately; her battle with cancer, complicated by other health problems, left her too weak to accept many of her honors. She died on April 14, 1964, leaving behind this letter to Freeman: "I think that you must have no regrets in my behalf. I have had a rich life, full of rewards and satisfactions that come to few, and if it must end now, I can feel that I have achieved most of what I wished to do." Eight years after her death, the U.S. Environmental Protection Agency banned DDT.

One of the earliest conservationists to achieve international fame, Rachel Carson was fiercely committed both to the environment and to her writing. While she earned a reputation in the scientific community for the breadth of her knowledge and the soundness of her research, she won over the public with her remarkable ability to bring the natural world to life in her prose. In writing about the seas and shores, Carson asked of her readers an "active exercise of the imagination and the temporary abandonment of many human concepts and human yardsticks." In return, she deliberately departed from "formal scientific writing," sometimes endowing sea creatures with apparently human emotions in order to make sea life "understandable to us." The result is something truly extraordinary: a set of scientific and informative books with all of the drama and the interest of good novels. Carson herself thought in literary terms when approaching her material, speaking of the "central character" in her first book as "the sea itself." The "central character" of *Silent Spring,* which differs from Carson's other books in its clear and consistent advancement of an environmental argument, is very nearly life itself. And in spite of her health problems, as Paul Brooks says, "she managed to make this book about death a celebration of life."

THE OBLIGATION TO ENDURE (1962)

THE HISTORY OF LIFE on earth has been a history of interaction between living things and their surroundings. To a large extent, the physical form and the habits of the earth's vegetation and its animal life have been molded by the environment. Considering the whole span of earthly time, the opposite effect, in which life actually modifies its surroundings, has been relatively slight. Only within the moment of time represented by the present century has one species—man—acquired significant power to alter the nature of his world.

During the past quarter century this power has not only increased to one of disturbing magnitude but it has changed in character. The most alarming of all man's assaults upon the environment is the contamination of air, earth, rivers, and sea with dangerous and even lethal materials. This pollution is for the most part irrecoverable; the chain of evil it initiates not only in the world that must support life but in living tissues is for the most part irreversible. In this now universal contamination of the environment, chemicals are the sinister and little-recognized partners of radiation in changing the very nature of the world—the very nature of its life. Strontium 90, released through nuclear explosions into the air, comes to earth in rain or drifts down as fallout, lodges in soil, enters into the grass or corn or wheat grown there, and in time takes up its abode in the bones of a human being, there to remain until his death. Similarly, chemicals sprayed on croplands or forests or gardens lie long in soil, entering into living organisms, passing from one to another in a chain of poisoning and death. Or they pass mysteriously by underground streams until they emerge and, through the alchemy of air and sunlight, combine into new forms that kill vegetation, sicken cattle, and work unknown harm on those who drink from once pure wells. As *Albert Schweitzer*[1] has said, "Man can hardly even recognize the devils of his own creation."

It took hundreds of millions of years to produce the life that now inhabits the earth— eons of time in which that developing and evolving and diversifying life reached a state of adjustment and balance with its surroundings. The environment, rigorously shaping and directing the life it supported, contained elements that were hostile as well as supporting. Certain rocks gave out dangerous radiation; even within the light of the sun, from which all life draws its energy, there were short-wave radiations with power to injure. Given time—time not in years but in millennia—life adjusts, and a balance has been reached. For time is the essential ingredient; but in the modern world there is no time.

The rapidity of change and the speed with which new situations are created follow the impetuous and heedless pace of man rather than the deliberate pace of nature. Radiation is no longer merely the background radiation of rocks, the bombardment of cosmic rays, the ultraviolet of the sun that have existed before there was any life on earth; radiation is now the unnatural creation of man's tampering with the atom. The chemicals to which life is asked to make its adjustment are no longer merely the calcium and silica and copper and all the rest of the minerals washed out of the rocks and carried in rivers to the sea; they are the synthetic creations of man's inventive mind, brewed in his laboratories, and having no counterparts in nature.

---

[1]*Albert Schweitzer* (1875–1965) French theologian, musician, and medical missionary who won the Nobel Peace Prize in 1952.

To adjust to these chemicals would require time on the scale that is nature's; it would require not merely the years of a man's life but the life of generations. And even this, were it by some miracle possible, would be futile, for the new chemicals come from our laboratories in an endless stream; almost five hundred annually find their way into actual use in the United States alone. The figure is staggering and its implications are not easily grasped—500 new chemicals to which the bodies of men and animals are required somehow to adapt each year, chemicals totally outside the limits of biologic experience.

Among them are many that are used in man's war against nature. Since the mid-1940s over 200 basic chemicals have been created for use in killing insects, weeds, rodents, and other organisms described in the modern vernacular as "pests"; and they are sold under several thousand different brand names.

These sprays, dusts, and aerosols are now applied almost universally to farms, gardens, forests, and homes—nonselective chemicals that have the power to kill every insect, the "good" and the "bad," to still the song of birds and the leaping of fish in the streams, to coat the leaves with a deadly film, and to linger on in soil—all this though the intended target may be only a few weeds or insects. Can anyone believe it is possible to lay down such a barrage of poisons on the surface of the earth without making it unfit for all life? They should not be called "insecticides," but "biocides."

The whole process of spraying seems caught up in an endless spiral. Since DDT[2] was released for civilian use, a process of escalation has been going on in which ever more toxic materials must be found. This has happened because insects, in a triumphant vindication of Darwin's principle of the survival of the fittest, have evolved super races immune to the particular insecticide used, hence a deadlier one has always to be developed—and then a deadlier one than that. It has happened also because, for reasons to be described later, destructive insects often undergo a "flareback," or resurgence, after spraying, in numbers greater than before. Thus the chemical war is never won, and all life is caught in its violent crossfire.

Along with the possibility of the extinction of mankind by nuclear war, the central problem of our age has therefore become the contamination of man's total environment with such substances of incredible potential for harm—substances that accumulate in the tissues of plants and animals and even penetrate the germ cells to shatter or alter the very material of heredity upon which the shape of the future depends . . . All this is not to say there is no insect problem and no need of control. I am saying, rather, that control must be geared to realities, not to mythical situations, and that the methods employed must be such that they do not destroy us along with the insects . . .

It is not my contention that chemical insecticides must never be used. I do contend that we have put poisonous and biologically potent chemicals indiscriminately into the hands of persons largely or wholly ignorant of their potentials for harm. We have subjected enormous numbers of people to contact with these poisons, without their consent and often without their knowledge. If the Bill of Rights contains no guarantee that a citizen shall be secure against lethal poisons distributed either by private individuals or by public officials, it is surely only because our forefathers, despite their considerable wisdom and foresight, could conceive of no such problem.

I contend, furthermore, that we have allowed these chemicals to be used with little or no advance investigation of their effect on soil, water, wildlife, and man himself. Future

---

[2]*DDT* the abbreviation for dichlorodiphenyltrichlorethane, a toxic insecticide.

generations are unlikely to condone our lack of prudent concern for the integrity of the natural world that supports all life.

There is still very limited awareness of the nature of the threat. This is an era of specialists, each of whom sees his own problem and is unaware of or intolerant of the larger frame into which it fits. It is also an era dominated by industry, in which the right to make a dollar at whatever cost is seldom challenged. When the public protests, confronted with some obvious evidence of damaging results of pesticide applications, it is fed little tranquilizing pills of half truth. We urgently need an end to these false assurances, to the sugar coating of unpalatable facts. It is the public that is being asked to assume the risks that the insect controllers calculate. The public must decide whether it wishes to continue on the present road, and it can do so only when in full possession of the facts. In the words of Jean Rostand,[3] "The obligation to endure gives us the right to know."

Understanding and Analysis

1. According to Carson, how much of the environment is contaminated? To what degree does she believe that pollution can be reversed?

2. What causes this contamination?

3. In the third paragraph, Carson says that the present "state of adjustment and balance with its [life's] surroundings" developed over "hundreds of millions of years." What exactly does she mean here, and is her assertion correct?

4. What words does she use to reveal her attitudes toward nature and toward man? How long does she claim it will take life to adjust to man-made chemicals?

5. Why has the "process of spraying" escalated?

6. What does Carson see as the two central problems of our age?

7. To what degree does Carson oppose the battle against pests? What limits does she advocate?

8. What exactly does she want us to do to preserve the environment?

9. Why, according to Carson, were so many people in the early sixties ignorant of the problems of pollution?

10. What does the last sentence mean?

11. Compare the first section of this essay with the last. Does Carson ever deliberately exaggerate? Does she modify her position in the second half? What does her attitude toward science appear to be in the two halves of the essay?

Comparison

1. What, if any, of the problems Carson enumerates have been addressed since the publication of her book *Silent Spring*?

2. What do you think needs to be addressed now?

---

[3]*Jean Rostand* (1894–1977) a French biologist and writer who specialized in genetics, evolutionary theory, and entomology.

3. Read C. P. Snow's description of the "scientific culture." How do you think Carson would respond to Snow's characterization of the scientists?

4. Read some of the other scientific essays in this text. Compare Carson's prose style to that of Eiseley and Gould. How do these authors address the reader? What characteristics, if any, do they have in common?

5. Read the essays by Jessica Mitford and Martha Gellhorn. Both of these writers share with Carson the desire to persuade the reader to take action. What techniques of persuasion, if any, do all three use?

F. R. Leavis
(1895–1978)

Born in Cambridge, England, Frank Raymond Leavis attended the Perse School during his youth. One of his teachers later remembered him as "a very quiet boy" with "an introspective look in his eye"; the school paper celebrated him as an athlete. After World War I, however, Leavis lost some of his physical vigor. Although he refused to fight, conscientiously objecting to the proposition of killing enemy soldiers, Leavis served on the front lines, carrying stretchers to the ambulances. Exposure to gas, combined with the trauma of watching "innumerable" boys "mown down" by "machine guns," left him with an assortment of problems. According to biographer Ronald Hayman, Leavis had difficulty sleeping and eating for the rest of his life.

After the war, Leavis matriculated to Emmanuel College. Initially focusing on history, he turned to English in his second year, taking his bachelor's degree in 1921 and his doctoral degree in 1924. Remaining at Cambridge, Leavis attended lectures given by the influential literary critic I. A. Richards; he also delivered lectures of his own, working, Hayman says, "on a freelance basis" with the university between 1925 and 1926. Controversy surrounded Leavis even in these early years of his academic career. In one of his courses, he taught what Hayman describes only as "a passage of [James] Joyce's prose." Thanks to the reigning opinion that Joyce's works were obscene, that passage was enough to attract the attention of the police, who kept a close eye on Leavis's lectures for the public prosecutor. Never charged with a crime, Leavis earned a reputation at the university that sparked talk of a "Leavis Prize for Pornography." Such talk did not prevent his appointment as a probationary lecturer in 1927, but it did damage his career. Passed over for promotion to the position of university lecturer—a rank he did not attain until 1936—Leavis found consolation and intellectual companionship in Queenie Dorothy Roth, whom he married in 1929. In 1930, Leavis published his first works, two pamphlets called *Mass Civilization and Minority Culture* and *D. H. Lawrence.* A year later, when the terms of the probationary lectureship ran out, he was out of work.

Leavis had two defining interests over the course of his career: evaluating literature and educating students. In 1932, the year Leavis found work as the director of studies at Downing College, he released two books born of these interests: *New Bearings in English Poetry,* his first major work of literary criticism, and *How to Teach Reading: A Primer for Ezra Pound,* his response to Pound's *How to Read* (1931). Leavis encouraged his new students at Downing to read *New Bearings in English Poetry,* as well as *Fiction and the Reading Public,* published by his wife. Although Q. D. Leavis focused principally on the novel and F. R. Leavis principally on poetry, husband and wife shared many of the same ideas about literature, and they both became important contributors to the literary quarterly *Scrutiny,* founded in 1932. While he was unofficially collaborating with his wife, Leavis officially collaborated with a former student, Denys Thompson, for another book on education: *Culture and Environment* (1933). Hayman explains that the role of Thompson, by then an English teacher, "was to advise on school conditions and possibilities," but "that the book was essentially Leavis's in conception and method. . . . It wielded a tremendous influence, penetrating into classrooms and encouraging sixth-formers to examine their environment as critically as they were learning to examine literature."

Over the next ten years, Leavis divided his interests equally between criticism and education, publishing *Revaluation: Tradition and Development in English Poetry* (1936) and *Education and the University: a Sketch for an English School* (1943). By the late 1940s, however, he was directing most of his energies into criticism. He was also broadening his critical horizons, showing a new interest in the novel that critics suggest was inspired by the work of his wife. In 1948, he released *The Great Tradition: George Eliot, Henry James, and Joseph Conrad,* and in 1955, *D. H. Lawrence: Novelist.*

During the 1960s, Leavis became, in the words of biographer Michael Bell, "a figure of national notoriety" when he entered into the debate about the "two cultures" set off by C. P. Snow's 1959 Rede Lectures at Cambridge. Asked to deliver the Richmond Lecture at Downing three years later, Leavis weighed in with "Two Cultures? The Significance of C. P. Snow," on February 28, 1962. After seeing his ideas publicly misrepresented by members of the press who were not present for the lecture, Leavis determined to have his lecture published. It appeared in *The Spectator* on March 9, prompting numerous letters, a story in *The Times Literary Supplement,* and charges that Leavis was attempting character assassination. Hayman speculates that while Leavis "must have expected a controversy," he "must have been surprised by the quantity of animosity he had aroused." Still, Leavis kept the debate alive. Following a lecture tour of the United States in 1966, F. R. and Q. D. Leavis co-authored *Lectures in America* (1969), a collection that contained "Luddites? or There Is Only One Culture." This work appeared again in Leavis's *Nor Shall My Sword: Discourses on Pluralism, Compassion and Social Hope* (1972), along with the re-printed and re-titled "Two Cultures? The Significance of Lord Snow." Leavis published several other works before his death, including *The Living Principle: 'English' as a Discipline of Thought* (1975) and *Thought, Words and Creativity* (1976). He died April 14, 1978, in Cambridge.

Admirers of F. R. Leavis eagerly claim for him an essential place in the intellectual history of the twentieth century. Christopher Norris, the general editor of the series *Critics of the Twentieth Century*, maintains that "F. R. Leavis was undoubtedly the single most influential figure in twentieth-century English literary criticism." Even scholars who do not particularly admire Leavis's brand of literary criticism characterize him as a kind of secular savior for the discipline of English. Crediting the work of F. R. Leavis, Q. D. Leavis, and I. A. Richards, Terry Eagleton argues: "In the early 1920s it was desperately unclear why English was worth studying at all; by the early 1930s it had become a question of why it was worth wasting your time on anything else. English was not only a subject worth studying, but *the* supremely civilizing pursuit." As Eagleton suggests, it was Leavis's emphasis on morality in literary criticism that helped to transform the discipline, making it into "an arena in which the most fundamental questions of human existence—what it meant to be a person, to engage in significant relationship with others, to live from the vital centre of the most essential values—were thrown into vivid relief."

While there is certainly nothing immoral about Leavis's "Two Cultures? The Significance of C. P. Snow," these glowing descriptions of Leavis as a noble champion of literature and morality may seem to jar with the tone of Leavis's infamous lecture. In the lecture, Leavis protests that he is "not enjoying" the process of attacking Snow; Leavis's defenders even insist that given Snow's status, the degree of vitriol Leavis used was necessary to make his point. Nevertheless, Leavis's tone often tends toward cruelty, suggesting that if he was not enjoying the attack, he was at least relishing his position as the attacker. For this reason, the debate between C. P. Snow and F. R. Leavis is a fascinating study not only of cultural issues, but also of personality and personae, and of rhetoric.

Two Cultures?
The Significance of C. P. Snow *(1962)*

IF CONFIDENCE IN oneself as a master-mind, qualified by capacity, insight and knowledge to pronounce authoritatively on the frightening problems of our civilisation, is genius, then there can be no doubt about Sir Charles Snow's. He has no hesitations. Of course, anyone who offers to speak with inwardness and authority on both science and literature will be conscious of more than ordinary powers, but one can imagine such consciousness going with a certain modesty—with a strong sense, indeed, of a limited range and a limited warrant. The peculiar quality of Snow's assurance expresses itself in a pervasive tone; a tone of which one can say that, while only genius could justify it, one cannot readily think of genius adopting it. It is the tone we have (in so far as it can be given in an isolated sentence) here:

> The only writer of world-class who seems to have had an understanding of the industrial revolution was IBSEN[1] in his old age: and there wasn't much that old man didn't understand.

Clearly, there is still less Sir Charles Snow doesn't understand: he pays the tribute with authority. We take the implication and take it the more surely at its full value because it carries the *élan,* the essential inspiration, of the whole self-assured performance. Yet Snow is in fact portentously ignorant. No doubt he could himself pass with ease the tests he proposes for his literary friends with the intimation that *they* would fail them, and so expose themselves as deplorably less well educated in respect of science than he, though a scientist, can claim to be in respect of literature. I have no doubt that *he* can define a machine-tool and state the second law of thermodynamics. It is even possible, I suppose (though I am obliged to say that the evidence seems to me to be against it), that he could make a plausible show of being inward with the Contradiction of Parity, that esoteric upshot of highly subtle experiment which, he suggests, if things were well with our education, would have been a major topic at our High Tables. But of history, of the nature of civilisation and the history of its recent developments, of the human history of the Industrial Revolution, of the human significances entailed in that revolution, of literature, of the nature of that kind of collaborative human creativity of which literature is the type, it is hardly an exaggeration to say that Snow exposes complacently a complete ignorance.

The judgment I have to come out with is that not only is he not a genius; he is intellectually as undistinguished as it is possible to be. If that were all, and Snow were merely negligible, there would be no need to say so in any insistent public way, and one wouldn't choose to do it. But I used the adverb 'portentously' just now with full intention: Snow is a portent. He is a portent in that, being in himself negligible, he has become for a vast public on both sides of the Atlantic a master-mind and a sage. His significance is that he has been accepted—or perhaps the point is better made by saying 'created': he has been created as authoritative intellect by the cultural conditions manifested in his acceptance. Really distinguished minds are themselves, of course, *of* their age; they are responsive at the deepest level to its peculiar strains and challenges: that is why they are able to be truly illuminating and prophetic and to influence the world positively and creatively. Snow's relation to the age is of a different kind; it is characterised not by insight and spiritual energy, but by blindness, unconsciousness and automatism. He doesn't know what he means, and doesn't know he doesn't know. That is what his intoxicating sense of a message and a public function, his inspiration, amounts to. It is not any challenge he thinks of himself as uttering, but the challenge he *is,* that demands our attention. The

---

[1]*Ibsen* Henrik Ibsen (1828–1906) a Norwegian playwright and poet famous for such works as *A Doll's House* and *When We Dead Awaken.*

commentary I have to make on him is necessarily drastic and dismissive; but don't, I beg, suppose that I am enjoying a slaughterous field-day. Snow, I repeat, is in himself negligible. My preoccupation is positive in spirit. Snow points to its nature when he turns his wisdom upon education and the university.

I have not been quick to propose for myself the duty of dealing with him: that will, I hope, be granted. *The Two Cultures and the Scientific Revolution,* the Rede Lecture which established him as an Intellect and a Sage, was given at this ancient university in 1959. I turned over the pages of the printed lecture in the show-room of the Cambridge University Press, was struck by the mode of expression Snow found proper and natural, perceived plainly enough what kind of performance the lecture was, and had no inclination to lay down three and sixpence. To my surprise, however, it rapidly took on the standing of a classic. It was continually being referred to—and not only in the Sunday papers— as if Snow, that rarely qualified and profoundly original mind, had given trenchant formulation to a key contemporary truth. What brought me to see that I must overcome the inner protest, and pay my three and sixpence, was the realising, from marking scholarship scripts, that sixth-form masters were making their bright boys read Snow as doctrinal, definitive and formative—and a good examination investment.

Well, I bought the lecture last summer, and, having noted that it had reached the sixth printing, read it through. I was then for the first time in a position to know how mild a statement it is to say that *The Two Cultures* exhibits an utter lack of intellectual distinction and an embarrassing vulgarity of style. The lecture, in fact, with its show of giving us the easily controlled spontaneity of the great man's talk, exemplifies kinds of bad writing in such richness and so significant a way that there would, I grant, be some point in the schoolmaster's using it as a text for elementary criticism; criticism of the style, here, becomes, as it follows down into analysis, criticism of the thought, the essence, the pretensions.

The intellectual nullity is what constitutes any difficulty there may be in dealing with Snow's panoptic pseudo-cogencies, his parade of a thesis: a mind to be argued with— that is not there; what we have is something other. Take that crucial term 'culture,' without which and the work he relies on it to do for him Snow would be deprived of his seer's profundity and his show of a message. His use of it focuses for us (if I may be permitted what seems to me an apt paradox) the intellectual nullity; it confronts us unmistakably with the absence of the thought that is capable of posing problems (let alone answering them). The general nature of his position and his claim to authority are well known: there are the two uncommunicating and mutually indifferent cultures, there is the need to bring them together, and there is C. P. Snow, whose place in history is that he has them both, so that we have in him the paradigm of the desired and necessary union.

Snow is, of course, a—no, I can't say that; he isn't: Snow thinks of himself as a novelist. I don't want to discuss that aspect of him, but I can't avoid saying something. The widespread belief that he is a distinguished novelist (and that it should be widespread is significant of the conditions that produced him) has certainly its part in the success with which he has got himself accepted as a mind. The seriousness with which he takes himself as a novelist is complete—if seriousness can be so ineffably blank, so unaware. Explaining why he should have cut short a brilliant career (we are to understand) as a scientist, he tells us that it had always been his vocation to be a writer. And he assumes with a happy and undoubting matter-of-factness—the signs are unmistakable—that his sense of vocation has been triumphantly vindicated and that he is beyond question a novelist of a high order (of 'world-class' even, to adopt his own idiom). Confidence so astonishingly enjoyed might politely be called memorable—if one could imagine the memory of Snow the novelist long persisting; but it won't, it can't, in spite of the British Council's brochure on him (he is a British Council classic). I say 'astonishingly enjoyed,' for as a novelist he doesn't exist; he doesn't begin to exist. He can't be said to know what a novel is. . . .[2]

The significance of his blankness in the face of literature is immense. It is a significance the more damning (in relation to his pretensions) because of the conviction with which he offers himself as an authority on the literature of the present and the past. I didn't exaggerate when I said that he doesn't know what literature is. Every pronouncement he makes about it—and he makes a great many—enforces that truth. Illustrating his notion of the important kind of relation between art and life, the writer and the contemporary world, he tells us that the Russians (he knows all about Russian literature) 'are as ready to cope in art with the processes of production as *Balzac*[3] was with the processes of craft manufacture.' But, for those preoccupied with the problems Snow confronts us with, unintentionally, literature has its immediate and crucial relevance because of the kind of writer who asks, who lives in his art and makes *us* live, kinds of question that, except as conventional profundities to which one should sometimes lift one's hat, seem never to have come within Snow's cognisance (an effect only emphasised by his 'tragic' and 'we die alone'—which belong, of course, to the most abject journalism). What for—what ultimately for? What, ultimately, do men live by? These questions are in and of the creative drive that produces great art in *Conrad* and *Lawrence*[4] (to instance two very different novelists of the century who haven't, one gathers, impressed Snow).

Take, as a simple illustration, Conrad's *The Shadow Line,* and note—well, note everything, but note particularly the evocation of the young master's inner response when he first sets eyes on his ship, his first command. The urgent creative exploring represented by the questions is immeasurably more complex in *Women in Love,* a comprehensive and intensely 'engaged' study of modern civilisation. Of course, to such questions there can't be, in any ordinary sense of the word, 'answers,' and the effect as of total 'answer' differs as between Conrad and Lawrence, or as between any two great writers. But life in the civilisation of an age for which such creative questioning is not done and is not influential on general sensibility tends characteristically to lack a dimension: it tends to have no depth—no depth against which it doesn't tacitly protect itself by the habit of unawareness (so Snow enjoins us to do our living in the dimension of 'social hope'). In coming to terms with great literature we discover what at bottom we really believe. What for—what ultimately for? what do men live by—the questions work and tell at what I can only call a religious depth of thought and feeling. Perhaps, with my eye on the adjective, I may just recall for you Tom Brangwen, in *The Rainbow,*[5] watching by the fold in lambing-time under the night-sky: 'He knew he did not belong to himself.'

---

[2] This essay has been abridged. In the missing parts, Leavis points out flaws in Snow's understanding of literature, asserts that there is very little of science or literature in Snow's lecture, and draws the reader's attention to cliche's in Snow's writing.

[3] *Balzac* Honore de Balzac (1799–1850) a French realist novelist.

[4] *Conrad and Lawrence* Joseph Conrad (1857–1942) and D(avid) H(erbert) Lawrence (1885–1930), both British writers.

[5] *The Rainbow* one of Lawrence's best-known novels.

It is characteristic of Snow that 'believe' for him should be a very simple word. 'Statistically,' he says, 'I suppose slightly more scientists are in religious terms unbelievers, compared with the rest of the intellectual world.' There are believers and unbelievers; we all know what 'religious terms' are; and everything relevant in relation to the adjective has been said. Snow goes on at once: 'Statistically, I suppose slightly more scientists are on the Left in open politics.' The *naïveté* is complete; it is a *naïveté* indistinguishable from the portentous ignorance. The ignorance is that which appears as historical ignorance in his account of the Industrial Revolution, and its consequences, in the nineteenth century. It manifests itself as a terrifying confidence of simplification—terrifying because of the distortions and falsifications it entails, and the part it plays in that spirit of practical wisdom about the human future of which Snow's Rede Lecture might be called a classic. Disposing with noble scorn of a wholly imaginary kind of opposition to his crass Wellsianism,[6] he says (and *this* is his history—and his logic): 'For, with singular unanimity, in any country where they have had the chance, the poor have walked off the land into the factories as fast as the factories could take them.' This, of course, is mere brute assertion, callous in its irresponsibility. But it is essential to Snow's wisdom. If one points out that the actual history has been, with significance for one's apprehension of the full human problem, incomparably and poignantly more complex than that, Snow dismisses one as a 'natural *Luddite.*'[7] He dismisses so—sees no further significance in—Dickens and Ruskin,[8] and all the writers leading down to Lawrence. Yet—to confine myself to the noncreative writer, about whom the challenged comment is most easily made—it was Ruskin who put into currency the distinction between wealth and well-being, which runs down through Morris[9] and the British Socialist movement to the Welfare State.

But for Ruskin 'well-being' or 'welfare' could not conceivably be matters of merely material standard of living, with the advantages of technology and scientific hygiene. And there we have the gap—the gap that is the emptiness beneath Snow's ignorance—between Snow and not only Ruskin, but the great creative writers of the century before Snow: they don't exist for him; nor does civilisation. Pressing on this ancient university his sense of the urgency of the effort to which we must give ourselves, he says: 'Yet'—in spite, that is, of the 'horror' which, he says, is 'hard to look at straight'—'yet they've proved that common men can show astonishing fortitude in chasing jam tomorrow. Jam today, and men aren't at their most exciting: jam tomorrow, and one often sees them at their noblest. The transformations have also proved something which only the scientific culture can take in its stride. Yet, when we don't take it in our stride, it makes us look silly.'

The callously ugly insensitiveness of the mode of expression is wholly significant. It gives us Snow, who is wholly representative of the world, or culture, to which it belongs. It is the world in which Mr. Macmillan said—or might, taking a tip from Snow, have

---

[6]*Wellsianism* referring to H(erbert) G(eorge) Wells, a nineteenth century British science-fiction writer who was also known for his socio-philosophical work.

[7]*Luddite* originally one of a group of British textile workers who staged demonstrations and broke machinery they felt was stealing their jobs, the term has come to signify someone who resists change and technology.

[8]*Ruskin* John Ruskin (1819–1900) an artist, scientist, poet, environmentalist, philosopher, and a pre-eminent art critic who particularly supported a group of artists known as the Pre-Raphaelites.

[9]*Morris* William Morris (1834–1896) a British craftsman, designer, writer, typographer, and Socialist.

varied his phrase by saying—'You never had so much jam'; and in which, if you are enlightened, you see that the sum of wisdom lies in expediting the processes which will ensure the Congolese, the Indonesians, and Bushmen (no, not the Bushmen—there aren't enough of them), the Chinese, the Indians, *their* increasing supplies of jam. It is the world in which the vital inspiration, the creative drive, is 'Jam tomorrow' (if you haven't any today) or (if you have it today) '*More* jam tomorrow.' It is the world in which, even at the level of the intellectual weeklies, 'standard of living' is an ultimate criterion, its raising an ultimate aim, a matter of wages and salaries and what you can buy with them, reduced hours of work, and the technological resources that make your increasing leisure worth having, so that productivity—the supremely important thing—must be kept on the rise, at whatever cost to protesting conservative habit.

Don't mistake me. I am not preaching that we should defy, or try to reverse, the accelerating movement of external civilisation (the phrase sufficiently explains itself, I hope) that is determined by advancing technology. Nor am I suggesting that Snow, in so far as he is advocating improvements in scientific education, is wrong (I suspect he isn't very original). What I *am* saying is that such a concern is not enough—disastrously not enough. Snow himself is proof of that, product as he is of the initial cultural consequences of the kind of rapid change he wants to see accelerated to the utmost and assimilating all the world, bringing (he is convinced), provided we are foresighted enough to perceive that no one now will long consent to be without abundant jam, salvation and lasting felicity to all mankind.

It must be recognised, though, that he doesn't *say* 'salvation' or 'felicity,' but 'jam.' And if 'jam' means (as it does) the prosperity and leisure enjoyed by our well-to-do working class, then the significant fact not noticed by Snow is that the felicity it represents cannot be regarded by a fully human mind as a matter for happy contemplation. Nor is it felt by the beneficiaries to be satisfying. I haven't time to enlarge on this last point. I will only remark that the observation is not confined to 'natural Luddites': I recently read in the *Economist* a disturbed review of a book by a French sociologist of which the theme is (not a new idea to us) the incapacity of the industrial worker, who—inevitably—looks on real living as reserved for his leisure, to use his leisure in any but essentially passive ways. And this, for me, evokes that total vision which makes Snow's 'social hope' unintoxicating to many of us—the vision of our imminent tomorrow in today's America: the energy, the triumphant technology, the productivity, the high standard of living and the life-impoverishment—the human emptiness; emptiness and boredom craving alcohol—of one kind or another. Who will assert that the average member of a modern society is more fully human, or more alive, than a Bushman, an Indian peasant, or a member of one of those poignantly surviving primitive peoples, with their marvellous art and skills and vital intelligence?

But I will come to the explicit positive note that has all along been my goal (for I am not a Luddite) in this way: the advance of science and technology means a human future of change so rapid and of such kinds, of tests and challenges so unprecedented, of decisions and possible non-decisions so momentous and insidious in their consequences, that mankind—this is surely clear—will need to be in full intelligent possession of its full humanity (and 'possession' here means, not confident ownership of that which belongs to *us*—our property, but a basic living deference towards that to which, opening as it does into the unknown and itself unmeasurable, we know we belong). I haven't chosen to say that mankind will need all its traditional wisdom; that might suggest a kind of conservatism that, so far as I am concerned, is the enemy. What we need, and shall continue to need not less, is something with the livingness of the deepest vital instinct; as intelligence, a power—rooted, strong in experience, and supremely human—of creative response to the new challenges of time; something that is alien to either of Snow's cultures.

His blankness comes out when, intimating (he supposes) that his concern for university reform envisages the total educational function, he tells us how shocking it is that educated people should not be able to appreciate the Shakespeare of science. It simply hasn't occurred to him that to call the master scientific mind (say Rutherford) a Shakespeare is nothing but a cheap journalistic infelicity. He enforces his intention by telling us, after reporting the failure of his literary friends to describe the second law of thermodynamics: 'yet I was asking something which is about the equivalent of *Have you read a work of Shakespeare's?*' There *is* no scientific equivalent of that question; equations between orders so disparate are meaningless—which is not to say that the Neo-Wellsian assurance that proposes them hasn't *its* significance. More largely, Snow exclaims: 'As though the scientific edifice of the physical world were not, in its intellectual depth, complexity and articulation, the most beautiful and wonderful collective work of the mind of man.'

It is pleasant to think of Snow contemplating, daily perhaps, the intellectual depth, complexity and articulation in all their beauty. But there is a prior human achievement of collaborative creation, a more basic work of the mind of man (and more than the mind), one without which the triumphant erection of the scientific edifice would not have been possible: that is, the creation of the human world, including language. It is one we cannot rest on as on something done in the past. It lives in the living creative response to change in the present. I mentioned language because it is in terms of literature that I can most easily make my meaning plain, and because of the answer that seems to me called for by Snow's designs on the university. It is in the study of literature, the literature of one's own language in the first place, that one comes to recognise the nature and priority of the third realm (as, unphilosophically, no doubt, I call it, talking with my pupils), the realm of that which is neither merely private and personal nor public in the sense that it can be brought into the laboratory or pointed to. You cannot point to the poem; it is 'there' only in the re-creative response of individual minds to the black marks on the page. But—a necessary faith—it is something in which minds can meet. The process in which this faith is justified is given fairly enough in an account of the nature of criticism. A judgment is personal or it is nothing; you cannot take over someone else's. The implicit form of a judgment is: This is so, isn't it? The question is an appeal for confirmation that the thing *is* so; implicitly that, though expecting, characteristically, an answer in the form, 'yes, but———,' the 'but' standing for qualifications, reserves, corrections. Here we have a diagram of the collaborative-creative process in which the poem comes to be established as something 'out there,' of common access in what is in some sense a public world. It gives us, too, the nature of the existence of English literature, a living whole that can have its life only in the living present, in the creative response of individuals, who collaboratively renew and perpetuate what they participate in—a cultural community or consciousness. More, it gives us the nature in general of what I have called the 'third realm' to which all that makes us human belongs.

Perhaps I need say no more by way of enforcing my conviction that, for the sake of our humanity—our humanness, for the sake of a human future, we must do, with intelligent resolution and with faith, all we can to maintain the full life in the present—and life is growth—of our transmitted culture. Like Snow I look to the university. Unlike Snow, I am concerned to make it really a university, something (that is) more than a collocation of specialist departments—to make it a centre of human consciousness: perception, knowledge, judgment and responsibility. And perhaps I have sufficiently indicated on what lines I would justify my seeing the centre of a university in a vital English School. I mustn't say more now about what I mean by that, I will only say that the academic is the enemy and that the academic *can* be beaten, as we who ran *Scrutiny* for twenty years proved. We were, and knew we were, Cambridge—the essential Cambridge in spite of Cambridge: that gives you the spirit of what I have in mind. Snow gets on with what he calls 'the traditional culture' better than I do. To impress us with his anti-academic astringency, he tells us of the old Master of Jesus[10] who said about trains running into Cambridge on Sunday: 'It is equally displeasing to God and to myself.' More to the point is that *that*, I remember, was very much the attitude of the academic powers when, thirty years ago, I wrote a pioneering book on modern poetry that made *Eliot*[11] a key figure and proposed a new chart, and again when I backed Lawrence as a great writer.

It is assumed, I believe, that work in the scientific departments must be in close touch with the experimental-creative front. In the same way, for the university English School there is a creative front with which, of its function and nature, the School must be in the closest relation. I am not thinking of the fashionable idea that the right qualification for a teaching post is to be a poet—or a commercially successful novelist. I am thinking again of what *Scrutiny* stood—and stands—for: of the creative work it did on the contemporary intellectual-cultural frontier in maintaining the critical function. I must not try now to say more about the way in which such a school would generate in the university a centre of consciousness (and conscience) for our civilisation. I will merely insist that it is not inconceivable that Cambridge might become a place where the culture of the Sunday papers was not taken to represent the best that is thought and known in our time.

If so, it is conceivable, perhaps, that the journalistic addiction of our academic intellectuals—and journalism (in one form or another) is now the menacing disease of university 'English'—might, at Cambridge, be pretty generally recognised for the thing it is. In such a Cambridge the attention I have paid to a Snow would be unnecessary.

Understanding and Analysis

1. At what point in the first paragraph do you realize what Leavis's attitude is toward Snow?

2. What areas does Leavis believe Snow to be ignorant in? How does Leavis characterize Snow?

3. Why does Leavis believe that he must address the ideas of such a man?

4. What is Snow a "portent" of, according to Leavis?

5. What, according to Leavis, characterizes Snow's "relation to the age"?

6. How does Leavis prepare the reader to accept his attacks on the character of Snow? What excuses does he give for having to make these accusations?

[10]*Master of Jesus* Jesus is one of the colleges which comprise Cambridge University.

[11]*Eliot* T(homas) S(tearns) Eliot (1888–1965) an Anglo-American modernist poet, critic, dramatist, and editor who won the 1948 Nobel Prize for literature.

7. What impression did Leavis get of the lecture by Snow when he bought it and read it for the first time?

8. What is Leavis's attitude toward Snow as a novelist?

9. What does Leavis mean when he says that Snow "doesn't know what literature is"?

10. What, according to Leavis, are the important questions that writers of literature ask?

11. In what way is Snow's understanding of the word "believe" a simplification, according to Leavis?

12. What other words of Snow's that Leavis cites seem to be glossed over or simplified?

13. What is "the emptiness beneath Snow's ignorance"?

14. Does Leavis claim to oppose technical advances?

15. Why does Leavis not have time to "enlarge on" the reason that "prosperity and leisure" are not "satisfying" to the working class?

16. What exactly is Leavis's argument?

17. Why does Leavis introduce a discussion of human language in his assessment of the relationship between science and literature?

18. How does Leavis define the literary community?

19. How does he believe the university should change?

Comparison

1. Does Leavis fairly represent Snow's argument in the following summary: "there are two uncommunicating and mutually indifferent cultures, there is the need to bring them together, and there is C. P. Snow, whose place in history is that he has them both, so that we have in him the paradigm of the desired and necessary union"?

2. What qualities, if any, do Snow and Leavis share?

3. Do you agree with any of Snow's assertions? Do you agree with any of Leavis's assertions about Snow or his ideas? If so, why?

4. What do Carson and Leavis have in common, regarding their concern for the future of humanity?

5. Do you think Leavis would approve of Bronowski's essay? Why or why not?

6. Leavis apparently admired T. S. Eliot. What differences in tone and style do you see between the two critics?

7. Read the other essays in this text that directly address the Snow and Leavis controversy. Why do you suppose the exchange between Snow and Leavis stimulated so much discussion of the relationship between science and literature? What makes this controversy still relevant, if you think it is? If you do not think so, why do you think the issue is finally dead?

8. Find out what the reactions on both sides of the Atlantic were to this controversy at the time. What attitudes did American scientists and literary critics take toward each man and his ideas?

Thomas S. Kuhn
(1922–1996)

Born July 18, 1922, in Cincinnati, Ohio, Thomas Samuel Kuhn began his academic career at Harvard University, earning a B.A. in Physics in 1943. Fresh out of college, he took a job with the U.S. Office of Scientific Research and Development, working in Cambridge, Massachusetts, for a year before transferring to a post in Europe. After returning to America and his alma mater, he was awarded an M.A. in 1946, and he became a junior fellow in 1948, while working toward his doctorate in theoretical physics. "[A]lready within sight of the end of [his] dissertation," Kuhn later wrote, he became involved "with an experimental college course treating physical science for the non-scientist." This course ignited Kuhn's lifelong interest in the history of science; it also inaugurated, as he said, a "dramatic shift in my career plans." Those plans notwithstanding, Kuhn completed his dissertation in physics, receiving his doctorate in 1949. His junior fellowship lasted until 1951, when he delivered a series of lectures in Boston called "The Quest for Physical Theory."

In 1952, Kuhn was promoted to assistant professor, specializing in the history of science. Since he "had never systematically studied" the subject he was now teaching, he found it necessary to devote much of his time to class preparation, and he had "little" left over for his own writing and research. In 1956, roughly 17 years after he first arrived at Harvard, he moved to the West Coast with his wife, Kathryn Louise Muhs, to teach history and philosophy at UC Berkeley.

Kuhn published his first book, *The Copernican Revolution: Planetary Astronomy in the Development of Western Thought*, in 1957. A year later, after he attained the rank of associate professor, he accepted "an invitation" to become a Fellow at the Center for Advanced Studies in the Behavioral Sciences. This fellowship gave him time to pursue the work that he had begun to envision as a graduate student thinking about the history of science. The result, published in 1962, was *The Structure of Scientific Revolutions*, the book that made his career. Mounting what scholar Dudley Shapere describes as "a sustained attack on the prevailing image of scientific change as a linear process of ever-increasing knowledge," Kuhn earned a reputation in scientific circles across the county. According to the *Los Angeles Times Book Review*, the book "changed" the way that experts thought about science "almost overnight."

In 1964, Kuhn left Berkeley to teach the history of science at Princeton, where he remained for the next 15 years. During this time, he published *The Essential Tension: Selected Studies in Scientific Tradition and Change* (1977), which was nominated for an American Book Award, and *Black-Body Theory and the Quantum Discontinuity, 1894–1912* (1978). Following his divorce in 1978, he returned to Cambridge in 1979 to take a position at MIT, teaching there as a professor emeritus for the remainder of his career. He died in Cambridge on June 17, 1996.

In *The Structure of Scientific Revolutions*, Kuhn contends that scientific research is governed by paradigms, which he defines in his Preface as "universally recognized scientific achievements that for a time provide model problems and solutions to a community of practitioners." Data that "will not fit" into the "preformed and relatively inflexible box that the paradigm supplies," meanwhile, are temporarily ignored. Eventually, however, such data generate a crisis. Kuhn argues: "Confronted with anomaly or with crisis, scientists take a different attitude toward existing paradigms, and the nature of their research changes accordingly. The proliferation of competing articulations, the willingness to try anything, the expression of explicit discontent, the recourse to philosophy and to debate over fundamentals, all these are symptoms of a transition from normal to extraordinary research." At the end of this process of transition, a new paradigm is born, one that is "incompatible" with the old. In this sense, the history of science is not simply a narrative of knowledge smoothly accumulating to "replace ignorance," but of knowledge rising up, with the force of a revolution, to "displace" what is presumably already known.

Since the time of its original publication, Kuhn's second book has met with considerable criticism, particularly over his methods of defining a paradigm. (In a 1970 article called "The Nature of a Paradigm," Margaret Masterman maintains that he uses the term in more than twenty different senses over the course of the book.) Kuhn himself recognized problems with his argument; in a "Postscript" for the second edition, according to Alan Musgrave, he "worried about the circularity involved in defining a paradigm as that which the members of a scientific group share, and then defining the group by its shared paradigm." Even with its flaws, however, Kuhn's theory about paradigms has proven enormously influential, sparking scholarly discussion not only in the field of science, but also in the fields of sociology, psychology, theology, literature, and economics. Kuhn's prose may seem occasionally daunting, as when he characterizes revolutions as "non–cumulative developmental episodes," but his work rewards diligent readers of any specialty with ideas as rich in their expression as in their intellectual sophistication. New critiques may ensue, but *The Structure of Scientific Revolutions* will remain, as Musgrave describes it, a "classic."

ANOMALY AND THE EMERGENCE
OF SCIENTIFIC DISCOVERIES (1962)

NORMAL SCIENCE, THE puzzle-solving activity we have just examined, is a highly cumulative enterprise, eminently successful in its aim, the steady extension of the scope and precision of scientific knowledge. In all these respects it fits with great precision the most usual image of scientific work. Yet one standard product of the scientific enterprise is missing. Normal science does not aim at novelties of fact or theory and, when successful finds none. New and unsuspected phenomena are, however, repeatedly uncovered by scientific research, and radical new theories have again and again been invented by scientists. History even suggests that the scientific enterprise has developed a uniquely powerful technique for producing surprises of this sort. If this characteristic of science is to be reconciled with what has already been said, then research under a paradigm must be a particularly effective way of inducing paradigm change. That is what fundamental novelties of fact and theory do. Produced inadvertently by a game played under one set of rules, their assimilation requires the elaboration of another set. After they have become parts of science, the enterprise, at least of those specialists in whose particular field the novelties lie, is never quite the same again.

We must now ask how changes of this sort can come about, considering first discoveries, or novelties of fact, and then inventions, or novelties of theory. That distinction between discovery and invention or between fact and theory will, however, immediately prove to be exceedingly artificial. Its artificiality is an important clue to several of this essay's main theses. Examining selected discoveries in the rest of this section, we shall quickly find that they are not isolated events but extended episodes with a regularly recurrent structure. Discovery commences with the awareness of anomaly, i.e., with the recognition that nature has somehow violated the paradigm-induced expectations that govern normal science. It then continues with a more or less extended exploration of the area of anomaly. And it closes only when the paradigm theory has been adjusted so that the anomalous has become the expected. Assimilating a new sort of fact demands a more than additive adjustment of theory, and until that adjustment is completed—until the scientist has learned to see nature in a different way—the new fact is not quite a scientific fact at all.

To see how closely factual and theoretical novelty are intertwined in scientific discovery examine a particularly famous example, the discovery of oxygen. At least three different men have a legitimate claim to it, and several other chemists must, in the early 1770's, have had enriched air in a laboratory vessel without knowing it. The progress of normal science, in this case of pneumatic chemistry, prepared the way to a breakthrough quite thoroughly. The earliest of the claimants to prepare a relatively pure sample of the gas was the Swedish apothecary, C. W. Scheele. We may, however, ignore his work since it was not published until oxygen's discovery had repeatedly been announced elsewhere and thus had no effect upon the historical pattern that most concerns us here. The second in time to establish a claim was the British scientist and divine, Joseph Priestley, who collected the gas released by heated red oxide of mercury as one item in a prolonged normal investigation of the "airs" evolved by a large number of solid substances. In 1774 he identified the gas thus produced as nitrous oxide and in 1775, led by further tests, as common air with less than its usual quantity of phlogiston.[1] The third claimant, Lavoisier,

---

[1]*phlogiston* a hypothetical substance formerly thought to be released as part of all flames in combustion.

started the work that led him to oxygen after Priestley's experiments of 1774 and possibly as the result of a hint from Priestley. Early in 1775 Lavoisier reported that the gas obtained by heating the red oxide of mercury was "air itself entire without alteration [except that] . . . it comes out more pure, more respirable." By 1777, probably with the assistance of a second hint from Priestley, Lavoisier had concluded that the gas was a distinct species, one of the two main constituents of the atmosphere, a conclusion that Priestley was never able to accept.

This pattern of discovery raises a question that can be asked about every novel phenomenon that has ever entered the consciousness of scientists. Was it Priestley or Lavoisier, if either, who first discovered oxygen? In any case, when was oxygen discovered? In that form the question could be asked even if only one claimant had existed. As a ruling about priority and date, an answer does not at all concern us. Nevertheless, an attempt to produce one will illuminate the nature of discovery, because there is no answer of the kind that is sought. Discovery is not the sort of process about which the question is appropriately asked. The fact that it is asked—the priority for oxygen has repeatedly been contested since the 1780's—is a symptom of something askew in the image of science that gives discovery so fundamental a role. Look once more at our example. Priestley's claim to the discovery of oxygen is based upon his priority in isolating a gas that was later recognized as a distinct species. But Priestley's sample was not pure, and, if holding impure oxygen in one's hands is to discover it, that had been done by everyone who ever bottled atmospheric air. Besides, if Priestley was the discoverer, when was the discovery made? In 1774 he thought he had obtained nitrous oxide, a species he already knew; in 1775 he saw the gas as dephlogisticated air, which is still not oxygen or even, for phlogistic chemists, a quite unexpected sort of gas. Lavoisier's claim may be stronger, but it presents the same problems. If we refuse the palm to Priestley, we cannot award it to Lavoisier for the work of 1775 which led him to identify the gas as the "air itself entire." Presumably we wait for the work of 1776 and 1777 which led Lavoisier to see not merely the gas but what the gas was. Yet even this award could be questioned, for in 1777 and to the end of his life Lavoisier insisted that oxygen was an atomic "principle of acidity" and that oxygen gas was formed only when that "principle" united with caloric, the matter of heat. Shall we therefore say that oxygen had not yet been discovered in 1777? Some may be tempted to do so. But the principle of acidity was not banished from chemistry until after 1810, and caloric lingered until the 1860's. Oxygen had become a standard chemical substance before either of those dates.

Clearly we need a new vocabulary and concepts for analyzing events like the discovery of oxygen. Though undoubtedly correct, the sentence, "Oxygen was discovered," misleads by suggesting that discovering something is a single simple act assimilable to our usual (and also questionable) concept of seeing. That is why we so readily assume that discovering, like seeing or touching, should be unequivocally attributable to an individual and to a moment in time. But the latter attribution is always impossible, and the former often is as well. Ignoring Scheele, we can safely say that oxygen had not been discovered before 1774, and we would probably also say that it had been discovered by 1777 or shortly thereafter. But within those limits or others like them, any attempt to date the discovery must inevitably be arbitrary because discovering a new sort of phenomenon is necessarily a complex event, one which involves recognizing both *that* something is and what it is. Note, for example, that if oxygen were dephlogisticated air for us, we should insist without hesitation that Priestley had discovered it, though we would still not know quite when. But if both observation and conceptualization, fact and assimilation to theory, are inseparably linked in discovery, then discovery is a process and must take time. Only when all the relevant conceptual categories are prepared in advance, in which case the phenomenon would not be of a new sort, can discovering *that* and discovering *what* occur effortlessly, together, and in an instant.

Grant now that discovery involves an extended, though not necessarily long, process of conceptual assimilation. Can we also say that it involves a change in paradigm? To that question, no general answer can yet be given, but in this case at least, the answer must be yes. What Lavoisier announced in his papers from 1777 on was not so much the discovery of oxygen as the oxygen theory of combustion. That theory was the keystone for a reformulation of chemistry so vast that it is usually called the chemical revolution. Indeed, if the discovery of oxygen had not been an intimate part of the emergence of a new paradigm for chemistry, the question of priority from which we began would never have seemed so important. In this case as in others, the value placed upon a new phenomenon and thus upon its discoverer varies with our estimate of the extent to which the phenomenon violated paradigm-induced anticipations. Notice, however, since it will be important later, that the discovery of oxygen was not by itself the cause of the change in chemical theory. Long before he played any part in the discovery of the new gas, Lavoisier was convinced both that something was wrong with the phlogiston theory and that burning bodies absorbed some part of the atmosphere. That much he had recorded in a sealed note deposited with the Secretary of the French Academy in 1772. What the work on oxygen did was to give much additional form and structure to Lavoisier's earlier sense that something was amiss. It told him a thing he was already prepared to discover—the nature of the substance that combustion removes from the atmosphere. That advance awareness of difficulties must be a significant part of what enabled Lavoisier to see in experiments like Priestley's gas that Priestley had been unable to see there himself. Conversely, the fact that a major paradigm revision was needed to see what Lavoisier saw must be the principal reason why Priestley was, to the end of his long life, unable to see it.

Two other and far briefer examples will reinforce much that has just been said and simultaneously carry us from an elucidation of the nature of discoveries toward an understanding of the circumstances under which they emerge in science. In an effort to represent the main ways in which discoveries can come about, these examples are chosen to be different both from each other and from the discovery of oxygen. The first, X-rays, is a classic case of discovery through accident, a type that occurs more frequently than the impersonal standards of scientific reporting allow us easily to realize. Its story opens on the day that the physicist *Roentgen*[2] interrupted a normal investigation of cathode rays because he had noticed that a barium platinocyanide screen at some distance from his shielded apparatus glowed when the discharge was in process. Further investigations— they required seven hectic weeks during which Roentgen rarely left the laboratory—indicated that the cause of the glow came in straight lines from the cathode ray tube, that the radiation cast shadows, could not be deflected by a magnet, and much else besides. Before announcing his discovery, Roentgen had convinced himself that his effect was not due to cathode rays but to an agent with at least some similarity to light.

Even so brief an epitome reveals striking resemblances to the discovery of oxygen: before experimenting with red oxide of mercury, Lavoisier had performed experiments that did not produce the results anticipated under the phlogiston paradigm; Roentgen's discovery commenced with the recognition that his screen glowed when it should not. In

[2]*Roentgen* Wilhelm Roentgen (1845–1923) a German scientist who discovered the X-ray.

both cases the perception of anomaly—of a phenomenon, that is, for which his paradigm had not readied the investigator—played an essential role in preparing the way for perception of novelty. But, again in both cases, the perception that something had gone wrong was only the prelude to discovery. Neither oxygen nor X-rays emerged without a further process of experimentation and assimilation. At what point in Roentgen's investigation, for example, ought we say that X-rays had actually been discovered? Not, in any case, at the first instant, when all that had been noted was a glowing screen. At least one other investigator had seen that glow and, to his subsequent chagrin, discovered nothing at all. Nor, it is almost as clear, can the moment of discovery be pushed forward to a point during the last week of investigation, by which time Roentgen was exploring the properties of the new radiation he had *already* discovered. We can only say that X-rays emerged in Würzburg between November 8 and December 28, 1895.

In a third area, however, the existence of significant parallels between the discoveries of oxygen and of X-rays is far less apparent. Unlike the discovery of oxygen, that of X-rays was not, at least for a decade after the event, implicated in any obvious upheaval in scientific theory. In what sense, then, can the assimilation of that discovery be said to have necessitated paradigm change? The case for denying such a change is very strong. To be sure, the paradigms subscribed to by Roentgen and his contemporaries could not have been used to predict X-rays. (Maxwell's electromagnetic theory[3] had not yet been accepted everywhere, and the particulate theory of cathode rays was only one of several current speculations.) But neither did those paradigms, at least in any obvious sense, prohibit the existence of X-rays as the phlogiston theory had prohibited Lavoisier's interpretation of Priestley's gas. On the contrary, in 1895 accepted scientific theory and practice admitted a number of forms of radiation—visible, infrared, and ultraviolet. Why could not X-rays have been accepted as just one more form of a well-known class of natural phenomena? Why were they not, for example, received in the same way as the discovery of an additional chemical element? New elements to fill empty places in the periodic table were still being sought and found in Roentgen's day. Their pursuit was a standard project for normal science, and success was an occasion only for congratulations, not for surprise.

X-rays, however, were greeted not only with surprise but with shock. Lord Kelvin[4] at first pronounced them an elaborate hoax. Others, though they could not doubt the evidence, were clearly staggered by it. Though X-rays were not prohibited by established theory, they violated deeply entrenched expectations. Those expectations, I suggest, were implicit in the design and interpretation of established laboratory procedures. By the 1890's cathode ray equipment was widely deployed in numerous European laboratories. If Roentgen's apparatus had produced X-rays, then a number of other experimentalists must for some time have been producing those rays without knowing it. Perhaps those rays, which might well have other unacknowledged sources too, were implicated in behavior previously explained without reference to them. At the very least, several sorts of long familiar apparatus would in the future have to be shielded with lead. Previously completed work on normal projects would now have to be done again because earlier scientists had failed to recognize and control a relevant variable. X-rays, to be sure, opened up a new field and thus added to the potential domain of normal science. But they also, and this is now the more

---

[3]*Maxwell's electromagnetic theory* named after James Clerk Maxwell (1831–1879) a Scottish physicist.

[4]*Lord Kelvin* Baron William Thomson Kelvin (1824–1907) a British physicist, mathematician, and inventor, after whom the "kelvin," a unit of thermodnamic temperature measurement, was named.

important point, changed fields that had already existed. In the process they denied previously paradigmatic types of instrumentation their right to that title.

In short, consciously or not, the decision to employ a particular piece of apparatus and to use it in a particular way carries an assumption that only certain sorts of circumstances will arise. There are instrumental as well as theoretical expectations, and they have often played a decisive role in scientific development. One such expectation is, for example, part of the story of oxygen's belated discovery. Using a standard test for "the goodness of air," both Priestley and Lavoisier mixed two volumes of their gas with one volume of nitric oxide, shook the mixture over water, and measured the volume of the gaseous residue. The previous experience from which this standard procedure had evolved assured them that with atmospheric air the residue would be one volume and that for any other gas (or for polluted air) it would be greater. In the oxygen experiments both found a residue close to one volume and identified the gas accordingly. Only much later and in part through an accident did Priestley renounce the standard procedure and try mixing nitric oxide with his gas in other proportions. He then found that with quadruple the volume of nitric oxide there was almost no residue at all. His commitment to the original test procedure—a procedure sanctioned by much previous experience—had been simultaneously a commitment to the non-existence of gases that could behave as oxygen did.

Illustrations of this sort could be multiplied by reference, for example, to the belated identification of uranium fission. One reason why that nuclear reaction proved especially difficult to recognize was that men who knew what to expect when bombarding uranium chose chemical tests aimed mainly at elements from the upper end of the periodic table. Ought we conclude from the frequency with which such instrumental commitments prove misleading that science should abandon standard tests and standard instruments? That would result in an inconceivable method of research. Paradigm procedures and applications are as necessary to science as paradigm laws and theories, and they have the same effects. Inevitably they restrict the phenomenological field accessible for scientific investigation at any given time. Recognizing that much, we may simultaneously see an essential sense in which a discovery like X-rays necessitates paradigm change—and therefore change in both procedures and expectations—for a special segment of the scientific community. As a result, we may also understand how the discovery of X-rays could seem to open a strange new world to many scientists and could thus participate so effectively in the crisis that led to twentieth-century physics.

Our final example of scientific discovery, that of the *Leyden jar,*[5] belongs to a class that may be described as theory-induced. Initially, the term may seem paradoxical. Much that has been said so far suggests that discoveries predicted by theory in advance are parts of normal science and result in no *new sort* of fact. I have, for example, previously referred to the discoveries of new chemical elements during the second half of the nineteenth century as proceeding from normal science in that way. But not all theories are paradigm theories. Both during preparadigm periods and during the crises that lead to large-scale changes of paradigm, scientists usually develop many speculative and unarticulated theories that can themselves point the way to discovery. Often, however, that discovery is not quite the one anticipated by the speculative and tentative hypothesis. Only as experiment and tentative theory are together articulated to a match does the discovery emerge and the theory become a paradigm.

[5]*Leyden jar* a glass jar lined with foil used to store and conduct electricity.

The discovery of the Leyden jar displays all these features as well as the others we have observed before. When it began, there was no single paradigm for electrical research. Instead, a number of theories, all derived from relatively accessible phenomena, were in competition. None of them succeeded in ordering the whole variety of electrical phenomena very well. That failure is the source of several of the anomalies that provide background for the discovery of the Leyden jar. One of the competing schools of electricians took electricity to be a fluid, and that conception led a number of men to attempt bottling the fluid by holding a water-filled glass vial in their hands and touching the water to a conductor suspended from an active electrostatic generator. On removing the jar from the machine and touching the water (or a conductor connected to it) with his free hand, each of these investigators experienced a severe shock. Those first experiments did not, however, provide electricians with the Leyden jar. That device emerged more slowly, and it is again impossible to say just when its discovery was completed. The initial attempts to store electrical fluid worked only because investigators held the vial in their hands while standing upon the ground. Electricians had still to learn that the jar required an outer as well as an inner conducting coating and that the fluid is not really stored in the jar at all. Somewhere in the course of the investigations that showed them this, and which introduced them to several other anomalous effects, the device that we call the Leyden jar emerged. Furthermore, the experiments that led to its emergence, many of them performed by Franklin, were also the ones that necessitated the drastic revision of the fluid theory and thus provided the first full paradigm for electricity.

To a greater or lesser extent (corresponding to the continuum from the shocking to the anticipated result), the characteristics common to the three examples above are characteristic of all discoveries from which new sorts of phenomena emerge. Those characteristics include: the previous awareness of anomaly, the gradual and simultaneous emergence of both observational and conceptual recognition, and the consequent change of paradigm categories and procedures often accompanied by resistance. There is even evidence that these same characteristics are built into the nature of the perceptual process itself. In a psychological experiment that deserves to be far better known outside the trade, Bruner and Postman asked experimental subjects to identify on short and controlled exposure a series of playing cards. Many of the cards were normal, but some were made anomalous, e.g., a red six of spades and a black four of hearts. Each experimental run was constituted by the display of a single card to a single subject in a series of gradually increased exposures. After each exposure the subject was asked what he had seen, and the run was terminated by two successive correct identifications.

Even on the shortest exposures many subjects identified most of the cards, and after a small increase all the subjects identified them all. For the normal cards these identifications were usually correct, but the anomalous cards were almost always identified, without apparent hesitation or puzzlement, as normal. The black four of hearts might, for example, be identified as the four of either spades or hearts. Without any awareness of trouble, it was immediately fitted to one of the conceptual categories prepared by prior experience. One would not even like to say that the subjects had seen something different from what they identified. With a further increase of exposure to the anomalous cards, subjects did begin to hesitate and to display awareness of anomaly. Exposed, for example, to the red six of spades, some would say: That's the six of spades, but there's something wrong with it—the black has a red border. Further increase of exposure resulted in still more hesitation and confusion until finally, and sometimes quite suddenly, most subjects would produce the correct identification without hesitation. Moreover, after doing this with two or three of the anomalous cards, they would have little further difficulty with the others. A few subjects, however, were never able to make the requisite adjustment of their categories. Even at forty times the average exposure required to recognize normal cards for what they were, more than 10 per cent of the anomalous cards were not correctly identified. And the subjects who then failed often experienced acute personal distress. One of them exclaimed: "I can't make the suit out, whatever it is. It didn't even look like a card that time. I don't know what color it is now or whether it's a spade or a heart. I'm not even sure now what a spade looks like. My God!" In the next section we shall occasionally see scientists behaving this way too.

Either as a metaphor or because it reflects the nature of the mind, that psychological experiment provides a wonderfully simple and cogent schema for the process of scientific discovery. In science, as in the playing card experiment, novelty emerges only with difficulty, manifested by resistance, against a background provided by expectation. Initially, only the anticipated and usual are experienced even under circumstances where anomaly is later to be observed. Further acquaintance, however, does result in awareness of something wrong or does relate the effect to something that has gone wrong before. That awareness of anomaly opens a period in which conceptual categories are adjusted until the initially anomalous has become the anticipated. At this point the discovery has been completed. I have already urged that that process or one very much like it is involved in the emergence of all fundamental scientific novelties. Let me now point out that, recognizing the process, we can at last begin to see why normal science, a pursuit not directed to novelties and tending at first to suppress them, should nevertheless be so effective in causing them to arise.

In the development of any science, the first received paradigm is usually felt to account quite successfully for most of the observations and experiments easily accessible to that science's practitioners. Further development, therefore, ordinarily calls for the construction of elaborate equipment, the development of an esoteric vocabulary and skills, and a refinement of concepts that increasingly lessens their resemblance to their usual commonsense prototypes. That professionalization leads, on the one hand, to an immense restriction of the scientist's vision and to a considerable resistance to paradigm change. The science has become increasingly rigid. On the other hand, within those areas to which the paradigm directs the attention of the group, normal science leads to a detail of information and to a precision of the observation-theory match that could be achieved in no other way. Furthermore, that detail and precision-of-match have a value that transcends their not always very high intrinsic interest. Without the special apparatus that is constructed mainly for anticipated functions, the results that lead ultimately to novelty could not occur. And even when the apparatus exists, novelty ordinarily emerges only for the man who, knowing *with precision* what he should expect, is able to recognize that something has gone wrong. Anomaly appears only against the background provided by the paradigm. The more precise and far reaching that paradigm is, the more sensitive an indicator it provides of anomaly and hence of an occasion for paradigm change. In the normal mode of discovery, even resistance to change has a use that will be explored more fully in the next section. By ensuring that the paradigm will not be too easily surrendered, resistance guarantees that scientists will not be lightly distracted and that the anomalies that lead to paradigm change will penetrate existing knowledge to the core. The very fact that a significant scientific novelty so often emerges simultaneously from several laboratories is an index both to the strongly traditional nature of normal science and to the completeness with which that traditional pursuit prepares the way for its own change.

Understanding and Analysis

1. In the opening paragraph of this essay, the sixth chapter of *The Structure of Scientific Revolutions*, Kuhn reminds his readers of the nature of standard or "normal" scientific activity and prepares the reader for the question to be investigated in this chapter. How do "novelties" appear, and what must happen to them?

2. In the second paragraph, what two types of novelty does Kuhn tell the reader he will discuss?

3. What does Kuhn tell readers they will discover as they read the rest of the chapter? Why does Kuhn tell us what he is going to tell us?

4. What examples does Kuhn use to illustrate his view that paradigm shifts take place as "extended episodes with a regularly recurrent structure"?

5. In the example of oxygen, why according to Kuhn is the statement "Oxygen was discovered" misleading?

6. How were X-rays discovered? What parallels does Kuhn draw between the discovery of X-rays and the discovery of oxygen?

7. According to Kuhn, in the assimilation of X-rays what makes the case against a paradigm shift strong? What expectations were upset in this case?

8. If "normal science" leads to discoveries predicted by theory, what role does theory play in the third example of the pattern of a paradigm shift?

9. Following his description of the discovery of the Leyden jar, Kuhn reviews the characteristics all three of his examples share. What are these characteristics?

10. Kuhn believes that this pattern may be part of the way humans perceive the external world. What evidence does he offer for this belief?

11. If the pattern is not part of the way the mind works, why does Kuhn still think it is so striking? How can the card experiment act as a metaphor?

12. What role does specialization or division of labor play in the development of science?

Comparison

1. Read Carr's essay on history. Compare Carr's ideas with Kuhn's, paying particular attention to the following statement from Kuhn: "Assimilating a new sort of fact demands a more than additive adjustment of theory, and until that adjustment is completed—until the scientist has learned to see nature in a different way—the new fact is not quite a scientific fact at all."

2. Read Bronowski's essay on scientific reasoning. In what ways are these two versions of how scientists work compatible?

3. Read the essays by Margaret Mead and Clifford Geertz. What relationship do you see between theory and fact in these works?

4. Read the essay by T. S. Eliot. Compare Eliot's ideas about novelty and change within a tradition with Kuhn's ideas about these issues in science.

5. Read Lippmann's essay. What connections do you see?

Martin Luther King, Jr.
(1929–1968)

When Martin Luther King, Jr., was born in January of 1929, one of America's great ills—the depression—was just around the corner, and one of its greatest—segregation—was already firmly in place. Thanks to the affluence of his family, King was able to observe the ravages of the depression from a distance. Segregation was a different story. According to biographer Adam Fairclough, King's father "tried to shield his family from the more humiliating aspects of segregation," but Reverend Martin Luther King could not, perforce, truly protect his children.

Martin Luther King, Jr., saw the racist signs posted on restaurants and businesses; he also lost a close friend, a white boy whose parents forbade the friendship after the children entered different schools in 1935. Deeply distressed, King decided, as he later said, "to hate every white person." Even more powerful in King's memory than this early incident was one that took place during his junior year in high school. Returning to Atlanta from a speech contest in another town, King was forced to give up his seat on the bus for a white passenger. Standing up for the remainder of the trip—90 miles, by one biographer's estimate—King said, made him "the angriest" he'd ever been in his life.

King performed well in school, and, though not a straight-A student, he skipped his freshman year of high school. Ultimately, he was able to skip his senior year as well. As biographer Stephen B. Oates explains, Morehouse College found its enrollment suffering during World War II and opened its doors to "exceptional high school juniors to fill its depleted ranks." Thus it was that King graduated from high school and entered college in 1944, at the age of 15. He chose a major in sociology and a minor in English; after three years of college, he also chose a career. Deciding to follow in the footsteps of his father, he graduated from Morehouse and entered Crozer Theological Seminary, where he was exposed to Gandhi's philosophy of nonviolence. Upon graduation in 1951, King earned a scholarship, and at the age of 22, equipped with two bachelor's degrees, he matriculated to Boston University to attain his Ph.D. Marrying Coretta Scott in 1953, King completed the preliminary work for his dissertation in 1954 and determined to seek a job. He accepted a pastorate in Montgomery, Alabama, and he finished his dissertation in June of 1955, roughly five months before the birth of his first child and roughly six months before Rosa Parks refused to give up her seat on the bus.

Although King became a civil rights leader of national stature in the months that followed, he did not initiate the protest. After Parks's arrest on December 1, 1955, local women called for a bus boycott, and ministers and community leaders quickly joined them. They planned the boycott for December 5; that day, despite the immense inconvenience, nearly every African-American in Montgomery stayed off the buses. When black leaders met again, they formed the Montgomery Improvement Association (MIA), a group designed to oversee an extended boycott. Choosing King as president, the MIA orchestrated a vast transportation network of cars and drivers, which police attempted to break by arresting drivers for petty traffic offenses. Already receiving threatening letters and phone calls, King, too, was arrested, and several days later, his house was bombed. In mid–February, the city of Montgomery formalized efforts to end the boycott by convening a grand jury, which indicted King and scores of others for staging a boycott "without legal excuse or just cause." Members of the media flocked to King's trial in March and reported the guilty verdict all over the world, but still the boycott continued. King and the MIA achieved an important legal victory in June when federal judges ruled on a lawsuit contesting the Alabama law that required buses to be segregated. That law, the judges pronounced, was unconstitutional, and the Supreme Court agreed. On December 21, 1956, King rode on Montgomery's first integrated bus. White racist groups were quick to protest the new system, sometimes with guns. Churches were bombed, and shots were fired into King's house.

In January of 1957, King asked black leaders around the South to meet with him in Atlanta, and together, they founded the group later known as the Southern Christian Leadership Council (SCLC). The SCLC twice called upon President Eisenhower and Vice President Nixon to travel to the South to encourage respect for the Supreme Court's ruling, eventually pledging that if government officials did not act, then the Council would be "compelled to initiate a mighty Prayer Pilgrimage to Washington." In late March, King met with Asa Philip Randolph and Roy Wilkins to plan the Pilgrimage, setting the date for May 17. One of the goals of the march was to "mobiliz[e] support for pending Civil Rights legislation"; this legislation, in the words of Oates, included provisions that "would have given the U.S. Attorney General injunctive power to enforce school desegregation" and "voting rights" for blacks. King's speech to the crowd on May 17 stressed voting rights, as King repeated, in a characteristic use of anaphora (deliberate repetition), "Give us the ballot." The ballot was, in the end, virtually the only thing the Senate was willing to grant. King finally gained an audience with President Eisenhower roughly a year after the Pilgrimage, holding a meeting whose value lay not in any presidential action, but in the attention it received in the press. A few months later, in September of 1958, King publicized his cause himself, publishing *Stride Toward Freedom: The Montgomery Story.*

In 1959, King made a pilgrimage of his own, journeying to India. At the end of the year, he decided to move from Montgomery back to Atlanta, and in February of 1960, he assumed partial leadership of his father's church. Around the same time, in North Carolina, African-American college students staged a sit-in at a "whites only" lunch counter. King praised their efforts at an SCLC convention in April, but concentrated his own efforts on the upcoming presidential election and on voter registration. After Atlanta, college students convinced King to join their sit-ins, and King was arrested and sentenced to time in prison; only through the intervention of the Kennedy family was he released. John F. Kennedy won the election, with much support from black voters, but his administration did not provide the support King had hoped for. In the first years of his term, Kennedy repeatedly stalled on proposing new civil rights legislation, and in 1962, after white officials stymied King's every effort to help desegregate Albany, Georgia, Attorney General Robert Kennedy praised Albany's mayor for keeping the town peaceful. Drawing from FBI records, biographer Adam Fairclough quotes in his biography a telephone conversation between King and Kennedy in which King declared, "This can't go on.... I'm tired. We're sick of it." In the fall, several black churches in Albany were bombed. Discouraged almost to the point of quitting, King nevertheless persisted.

Early in 1963, King turned his attention to Birmingham, Alabama. He waited out the mayoral election between the notoriously racist police commissioner Eugene "Bull" Connor and the supposedly benign Albert Boutwell, and then he put forward the "Birmingham Manifesto," calling for desegregation of local businesses and new jobs for blacks. With the election just decided, King was criticized for acting before the new mayor, Boutwell, had a chance to prove himself. He rallied support, slowly recruiting protesters for his "nonviolent army," but trouble arose when leaders learned that the SCLC had no more money to bail marching protesters out of jail. After prayer and reflection, King determined to march anyway, and on Good Friday, he and others were arrested. Locked away in solitary confinement, King obtained a newspaper from attorneys, and read a condemnatory piece signed by eight Southern clergymen. He wrote his famous response, "Letter from Birmingham Jail," on the sides of the newspaper and on bits of toilet paper until he could obtain writing paper from his lawyers, who took finished sections of the "Letter" out of the jail in bits and pieces, unnoticed by police. More than a week after his arrest, King left the jail to find that protests were falling apart. Young children begged to join in the movement, and King, though criticized, finally consented. Bull Connor arrested young and old alike; he also turned dogs and hoses on the crowds. The photographs of the violence inflicted upon the nonviolent protesters horrified members of the government and the public alike. Under scrutiny, with jails literally filled to capacity, Birmingham business owners finally sat down to deal.

King's demonstrations in Birmingham inspired protests across the South. On June 11, 1963, President Kennedy at last addressed the nation on the subject of civil rights, promising a new Civil Rights Bill. Prompted by A. Philip Randolph, leaders began to plan a march scheduled for August 28, ultimately called the March on Washington for Jobs and Freedom. The march was an enormous success, and King delivered his "I Have a Dream" speech to an exhilarated audience of nearly a quarter of a million. With triumph, however, came tragedy, as happened so often during the civil rights movement. After Kennedy's address, civil rights activist Medgar Evers was assassinated; after the March on Washington, a bomb exploded in a Birmingham church, killing four children, Denise McNair, Cynthia Wesley, Carol Robertson, and Addie Mae Collins.

In 1964, the year King received the Nobel Peace Prize, the Civil Rights Act became federal law, marking a victory for the movement, but not a complete one, since city officials still used various underhanded methods to block registration. In 1964, King and the SCLC planned a voter registration drive in Selma, Alabama, for 1965. Selma had its own Bull Conner in the form of local sheriff James Clark, a man who had, as biographer L.G. Davis explains, "herded more than 100 Negroes off to jail with sticks and cattle prods, when they tried to register to vote." Over the course of King's voter registration drive, Clark jailed hundreds more, responding to the singing of "We Shall Overcome" by producing a button that said "Never." King planned marches to dramatize the problem, and marchers were brutally beaten. After the death of a white minister assaulted by Selma locals, ostensibly for eating in a restaurant with blacks, President Lyndon Johnson made a public statement and promised legislation. The Voting Rights Act was approved in August 1965.

The Watts riot in California drew King's attention to the problem of urban poverty. In the final years of his life, King divided his efforts between poverty and the war in Viet Nam, maintaining that as an advocate of nonviolence, he had an obligation to condemn mass bloodshed in the name of colonialism. Critics were quick to condemn his involvement with anti-war protests— Barry Goldwater all but accused King of treason—but King persisted in both his causes. He planned another march on Washington in 1968, this time with an "army" of the poor, and throughout the month of March, he traveled the country to arouse support. A sanitation strike in Memphis, however, altered King's plans. Nearly 1,500 workers, the majority of them African-American, were demanding better wages from the city. A march on City Hall turned violent, a teenager named Larry Payne was shot, and a riot broke out, prompting King to plan a Memphis demonstration himself—one without violence. He arrived in Memphis on the night of April 3, 1968, giving a speech and then spending the night in the Lorraine Motel. On April 4, on the balcony overlooking the parking lot, just outside his room, Martin Luther King, Jr., was shot.

A devoted crusader, a commanding orator, and an enormously gifted writer, King lived a life that has become a central part of America's history. His life's work has influenced millions of people, as well as an impressive array of institutions and traditions, legal, political, religious, and literary. During his life, he battled accusations that he was a communist and an Uncle Tom; he also battled a government that, at its most sympathetic, still gave little or no ground. Although he made a commitment to nonviolent protest, he was frequently frustrated with the system and with his wide array of critics, and his frustration appears in his writings and in his speeches, even in the most beautiful of his metaphors. This frustration is a part of the complexity of King as a person, rather than a legend, a person posthumously charged with plagiarizing portions of his dissertation, and a person critiqued for conservative sexual politics. His words deserve to be remembered and to be quoted, but they also deserve to be considered in the context of a human life, one lived in a constant struggle with defeat, one carried out by force of will, and of conviction.

LETTER FROM BIRMINGHAM JAIL (1963)

MY DEAR FELLOW CLERGYMEN:

While confined here in the Birmingham city jail, I came across your recent statement calling my present activities "unwise and untimely." Seldom do I pause to answer criticism of my work and ideas. If I sought to answer all the criticisms that cross my desk, my secretaries would have little time for anything other than such correspondence in the course of the day, and I would have no time for constructive work. But since I feel that you are men of genuine good will and that your criticisms are sincerely set forth, I want to try to answer your statement in what I hope will be patient and reasonable terms.

I think I should indicate why I am here in Birmingham, since you have been influenced by the view which argues against "outsiders coming in." I have the honor of serving as president of the Southern Christian Leadership Conference, an organization operating in every southern state, with headquarters in Atlanta, Georgia. We have some eighty-five affiliated organizations across the South, and one of them is the Alabama Christian Movement for Human Rights. Frequently we share staff, educational, and financial resources with our affiliates. Several months ago the affiliate here in Birmingham asked us to be on call to engage in a nonviolent direct-action program if such were deemed necessary. We readily consented, and when the hour came we lived up to our promise.

So I, along with several members of my staff, am here because I was invited here. I am here because I have organizational ties here.

But more basically, I am in Birmingham because injustice is here. Just as the prophets of the eighth century B.C. left their villages and carried their "thus saith the Lord" far beyond the boundaries of their home towns, and just as the Apostle Paul left his village of Tarsus and carried the gospel of Jesus Christ to the far corners of the Greco-Roman world, so am I compelled to carry the gospel of freedom beyond my own home town. Like Paul, I must constantly respond to the Macedonian call for aid.

Moreover, I am cognizant of the interrelatedness of all communities and states. I cannot sit idly by in Atlanta and not be concerned about what happens in Birmingham. Injustice anywhere is a threat to justice everywhere. We are caught in an inescapable network of mutuality, tied in a single garment of destiny. Whatever affects one directly, affects all indirectly. Never again can we afford to live with the narrow, provincial "outside agitator" idea. Anyone who lives inside the United States can never be considered an outsider anywhere within its bounds.

You deplore the demonstrations taking place in Birmingham. But your statement, I am sorry to say, fails to express a similar concern for the conditions that brought about the demonstrations. I am sure that none of you would want to rest content with the superficial kind of social analysis that deals merely with effects and does not grapple with underlying causes. It is unfortunate that demonstrations are taking place in Birmingham, but it is even more unfortunate that the city's white power structure left the Negro community with no alternative.

In any nonviolent campaign there are four basic steps: collection of the facts to determine whether injustices exist; negotiation; self-purification; and direct action. We have gone through all these steps in Birmingham. There can be no gainsaying the fact that racial injustice engulfs this community. Birmingham is probably the most thoroughly segregated city in the United States. Its ugly record of brutality is widely known. Negroes have experienced grossly unjust treatment in the courts. There have been more unsolved bombings of Negro homes and churches in Birmingham than in any other city in the nation. These are the hard, brutal facts of the case. On the basis of these conditions, Negro leaders sought to negotiate with the city fathers. But the latter consistently refused to engage in good-faith negotiation.

Then, last September, came the opportunity to talk with leaders of Birmingham's economic community. In the course of the negotiations, certain promises were made by the merchants—for example, to remove the stores' humiliating racial signs. On the basis of these promises, the Reverend Fred Shuttlesworth and the leaders of the Alabama Christian Movement for Human Rights agreed to a moratorium on all demonstrations. As the weeks and months went by, we realized that we were the victims of a broken promise. A few signs, briefly removed, returned; the others remained.

As in so many past experiences, our hopes had been blasted, and the shadow of deep disappointment settled upon us. We had no alternative except to prepare for direct action, whereby we would present our very bodies as a means of laying our case before the conscience of the local and the national community. Mindful of the difficulties involved, we decided to undertake a process of self-purification. We began a series of workshops on nonviolence, and we repeatedly asked ourselves: "Are you able to accept blows without retaliating?" "Are you able to endure the ordeal of jail?" We decided to schedule our direct-action program for the Easter season, realizing that except for Christmas, this is the main shopping period of the year. Knowing that a strong economic-withdrawal program would be the by-product of direct action, we felt that this would be the best time to bring pressure to bear on the merchants for the needed change.

Then it occurred to us that Birmingham's mayoral election was coming up in March, and we speedily decided to postpone action until after election day. When we discovered that the Commissioner of Public Safety, Eugene "Bull" Connor, had piled up enough votes to be in the run-off, we decided again to postpone action until the day after the runoff so that the demonstrations could not be used to cloud the issues. Like many others, we wanted to see Mr. Connor defeated, and to this end we endured postponement after postponement. Having aided in this community need, we felt that our direct-action program could be delayed no longer.

You may well ask, "Why direct action? Why sit-ins, marches, and so forth? Isn't negotiation a better path?" You are quite right in calling for negotiation. Indeed, this is the very purpose of direct action. Nonviolent direct action seeks to create such a crisis and foster such a tension that a community which has constantly refused to negotiate is forced to confront the issue. It seeks so to dramatize the issue that it can no longer be ignored. My citing the creation of tension as part of the work of the nonviolent-resister may sound rather shocking. But I must confess that I am not afraid of the word "tension." I have earnestly opposed violent tension, but there is a type of constructive, nonviolent tension which is necessary for growth. Just as Socrates[1] felt that it was necessary to create a tension in the mind so that individuals could rise from the bondage of myths and half-truths to the unfettered realm of creative analysis and objective appraisal, so must we see the need for nonviolent gadflies to create the kind of tension in society that will help men rise from the dark depths of prejudice and racism to the majestic heights of understanding and brotherhood.

The purpose of our direct-action program is to create a situation so crisis-packed that it will inevitably open the door to negotiation. I therefore concur with you in your call for negotiation. Too long has our beloved Southland been bogged down in a tragic effort to live in monologue rather than dialogue.

One of the basic points in your statement is that the action that I and my associates have taken in Birmingham is untimely. Some have asked: "Why didn't you give the new city administration time to act?" The only answer that I can give to this query is that the new Birmingham administration must be prodded about as much as the outgoing one, before it will act. We are sadly mistaken if we feel that the election of Albert Boutwell as mayor will bring the millennium to Birmingham. While Mr. Boutwell is a much more gentle person than Mr. Connor, they are both segregationists, dedicated to maintenance of the status quo. I have hoped that Mr. Boutwell will be reasonable enough to see the futility of massive resistance to desegregation. But he will not see this without pressure from devotees of civil rights. My friends, I must say to you that we have not made a single gain in civil rights without determined legal and nonviolent pressure. Lamentably, it is an historical fact that privileged groups seldom give up their privileges voluntarily. Individuals may see the moral light and voluntarily give up their unjust posture; but, as Reinhold Niebuhr[2] has reminded us, groups tend to be more immoral than individuals.

We know through painful experience that freedom is never voluntarily given by the oppressor; it must be demanded by the oppressed. Frankly, I have yet to engage in a

---

[1]*Socrates* (469–399 BC,) a Greek philosopher who was convicted of corrupting the morals of his students and sentenced to die by drinking a cup of poisonous hemlock.

[2]*Reinhold Niebuhr* (1892–1971), an American religious and social activist.

direct-action campaign that was "well timed" in the view of those who have not suffered unduly from the disease of segregation. For years now I have heard the word "Wait!" It rings in the ear of every Negro with piercing familiarity. This "Wait" has almost always meant "Never." We must come to see, with one of our distinguished jurists, that "justice too long delayed is justice denied."

We have waited for more than 340 years for our constitutional and God-given rights. The nations of Asia and Africa are moving with jetlike speed toward gaining political independence, but we still creep at horse-and-buggy pace toward gaining a cup of coffee at a lunch counter. Perhaps it is easy for those who have never felt the stinging darts of segregation to say, "Wait." But when you have seen vicious mobs lynch your mothers and fathers at will and drown your sisters and brothers at whim; when you have seen hate-filled policemen curse, kick, and even kill your black brothers and sisters; when you see the vast majority of your twenty million Negro brothers smothering in an airtight cage of poverty in the midst of an affluent society; when you suddenly find your tongue twisted and your speech stammering as you seek to explain to your six-year-old daughter why she can't go to the public amusement park that has just been advertised on television, and see tears welling up in her eyes when she is told that Funtown is closed to colored children, and see ominous clouds of inferiority beginning to form in her little mental sky, and see her beginning to distort her personality by developing an unconscious bitterness toward white people; when you have to concoct an answer for a five-year-old son who is asking, "Daddy, why do white people treat colored people so mean?"; when you take a cross-country drive and find it necessary to sleep night after night in the uncomfortable corners of your automobile because no motel will accept you; when you are humiliated day in and day out by nagging signs reading "white" and "colored"; when your first name becomes "nigger," your middle name becomes "boy" (however old you are) and your last name becomes "John," and your wife and mother are never given the respected title "Mrs."; when you are harried by day and haunted by night by the fact that you are a Negro, living constantly at tiptoe stance, never quite knowing what to expect next, and are plagued with inner fears and outer resentments; when you are forever fighting a degenerating sense of "nobodiness"—then you will understand why we find it difficult to wait. There comes a time when the cup of endurance runs over, and men are no longer willing to be plunged into the abyss of despair. I hope, sirs, you can understand our legitimate and unavoidable impatience.

You express a great deal of anxiety over our willingness to break laws. This is certainly a legitimate concern. Since we so diligently urge people to obey the Supreme Court's decision of 1954 outlawing segregation in the public schools, at first glance it may seem rather paradoxical for us consciously to break laws. One may well ask: "How can you advocate breaking some laws and obeying others?" The answer lies in the fact that there are two types of laws: just and unjust. I would be the first to advocate obeying just laws. One has not only a legal but a moral responsibility to obey just laws. Conversely, one has a moral responsibility to disobey unjust laws. I would agree with St. Augustine[3] that "an unjust law is no law at all."

Now, what is the difference between the two? How does one determine whether a law is just or unjust? A just law is a man-made code that squares with the moral law or the law of God. An unjust law is a code that is out of harmony with the moral law. To put

---

[3]*St. Augustine* (354–430), an Algerian scholar who converted to Christianity and whose works deeply influenced the Church during the Middle Ages.

it in the terms of St. Thomas Aquinas:[4] An unjust law is a human law that is not rooted in eternal law and natural law. Any law that uplifts human personality is just. Any law that degrades human personality is unjust. All segregation statutes are unjust because segregation distorts the soul and damages the personality. It gives the segregator a false sense of superiority and the segregated a false sense of inferiority. Segregation, to use the terminology of the Jewish philosopher Martin Buber[5] substitutes an "I-it" relationship for an "I-thou" relationship and ends up relegating persons to the status of things. Hence segregation is not only politically, economically, and sociologically unsound, it is morally wrong and sinful. Paul Tillich[6] has said that sin is separation. Is not segregation an existential expression of man's tragic separation, his awful estrangement, his terrible sinfulness? Thus it is that I can urge men to obey the 1954 decision of the Supreme Court, for it is morally right; and I can urge them to disobey segregation ordinances, for they are morally wrong.

Let us consider a more concrete example of just and unjust laws. An unjust law is a code that a numerical or power majority group compels a minority group to obey but does not make binding on itself. This is difference made legal. By the same token, a just law is a code that a majority compels a minority to follow and that it is willing to follow itself. This is sameness made legal.

Let me give another explanation. A law is unjust if it is inflicted on a minority that, as a result of being denied the right to vote, had no part in enacting or devising the law. Who can say that the legislature of Alabama which set up that state's segregation laws was democratically elected? Throughout Alabama all sorts of devious methods are used to prevent Negroes from becoming registered voters, and there are some counties in which, even though Negroes constitute a majority of the population, not a single Negro is registered. Can any law enacted under such circumstances be considered democratically structured?

Sometimes a law is just on its face and unjust in its application. For instance, I have been arrested on a charge of parading without a permit. Now, there is nothing wrong in having an ordinance which requires a permit for a parade. But such an ordinance becomes unjust when it is used to maintain segregation and to deny citizens the First-Amendment privilege of peaceful assembly and protest.

I hope you are able to see the distinction I am trying to point out. In no sense do I advocate evading or defying the law, as would the rabid segregationist. That would lead to anarchy. One who breaks an unjust law must do so openly, lovingly, and with a willingness to accept the penalty. I submit that an individual who breaks a law that conscience tells him is unjust, and who willingly accepts the penalty of imprisonment in order to arouse the conscience of the community over its injustice, is in reality expressing the highest respect for law.

Of course, there is nothing new about this kind of civil disobedience. It was evidenced sublimely in the refusal of Shadrach, Meshach, and Abednego to obey the laws of Ne-

---

[4]*St. Thomas Aquinas* (1227(?)–1274), a philosopher and theologian known for his extensive writings and sacred life.

[5]*Martin Buber* (1878–1965), a philosopher and theologian who organized a spiritual resistance to Nazism. His work has had a profound impact on Christian as well as Jewish thinkers.

[6]*Paul Tillich* (1886–1965), a German philosopher and Christian theologian who emigrated to America when the Nazis came to power.

buchadnezzar,[7] on the ground that a higher moral law was at stake. It was practiced superbly by the early Christians, who were willing to face hungry lions and the excruciating pain of chopping blocks rather than submit to certain unjust laws of the Roman Empire. To a degree, academic freedom is a reality today because Socrates practiced civil disobedience. In our own nation, the Boston Tea Party represented a massive act of civil disobedience.

We should never forget that everything Adolf Hitler did in Germany was "legal" and everything the Hungarian freedom fighters[8] did in Hungary was "illegal." It was "illegal" to aid and comfort a Jew in Hitler's Germany. Even so, I am sure that, had I lived in Germany at the time, I would have aided and comforted my Jewish brothers. If today I lived in a Communist country where certain principles dear to the Christian faith are suppressed, I would openly advocate disobeying that country's antireligious laws.

I must make two honest confessions to you, my Christian and Jewish brothers. First, I must confess that over the past few years I have been gravely disappointed with the white moderate. I have almost reached the regrettable conclusion that the Negro's great stumbling block in his stride toward freedom is not the White Citizen's Counciler or the Ku Klux Klanner, but the white moderate, who is more devoted to "order" than to justice; who prefers a negative peace which is the absence of tension to a positive peace which is the presence of justice; who constantly says, "I agree with you in the goal you seek, but I cannot agree with your methods of direct action"; who paternalistically believes he can set the timetable for another man's freedom; who lives by a mythical concept of time and who constantly advises the Negro to wait for a "more convenient season." Shallow understanding from people of good will is more frustrating than absolute misunderstanding from people of ill will. Lukewarm acceptance is much more bewildering than outright rejection.

I had hoped that the white moderate would understand that law and order exist for the purpose of establishing justice and that when they fail in this purpose they become the dangerously structured dams that block the flow of social progress. I had hoped that the white moderate would understand that the present tension in the South is a necessary phase of the transition from an obnoxious negative peace, in which the Negro passively accepted his unjust plight, to a substantive and positive peace, in which all men will respect the dignity and worth of human personality. Actually, we who engage in nonviolent direct action are not the creators of tension. We merely bring to the surface the hidden tension that is already alive. We bring it out in the open, where it can be seen and dealt with. Like a boil that can never be cured so long as it is covered up but must be opened with all its ugliness to the natural medicines of air and light, injustice must be exposed, with all the tension its exposure creates, to the light of human conscience and the air of national opinion, before it can be cured.

In your statement you assert that our actions, even though peaceful, must be condemned because they precipitate violence. But is this a logical assertion? Isn't this like condemning a robbed man because his possession of money precipitated the evil act of

---

[7]*Shadrach, Meshach, Abednego, Nebuchadnezzar* a reference to the seventh-century biblical story of King Nebuchadnezzar who threw Shadrach, Meshach, and Abednego into a furnace to punish them for refusing to worship a giant statue of himself. God protected the three men, who emerged unscathed.

[8]*Hungarian freedom fighters* in the anti-Communist revolution of 1956, which the Russian army quickly suppressed.

robbery? Isn't this like condemning Socrates because his unswerving commitment to truth and his philosophical inquiries precipitated the act by the misguided populace in which they made him drink hemlock? Isn't this like condemning Jesus because his unique God-consciousness and never-ceasing devotion to God's will precipitated the evil act of crucifixion? We must come to see that, as the federal courts have consistently affirmed, it is wrong to urge an individual to cease his efforts to gain his basic constitutional rights because the quest may precipitate violence. Society must protect the robbed and punish the robber.

I had also hoped that the white moderate would reject the myth concerning time in relation to the struggle for freedom. I have just received a letter from a white brother in Texas. He writes: "All Christians know that the colored people will receive equal rights eventually, but it is possible that you are in too great a religious hurry. It has taken Christianity almost two thousand years to accomplish what it has. The teachings of Christ take time to come to earth." Such an attitude stems from a tragic misconception of time, from the strangely irrational notion that there is something in the very flow of time that will inevitably cure all ills. Actually, time itself is neutral; it can be used either destructively or constructively. More and more I feel that the people of ill will have used time much more effectively than have the people of good will. We will have to repent in this generation not merely for the hateful words and actions of the bad people, but for the appalling silence of the good people. Human progress never rolls in on wheels of inevitability; it comes through the tireless efforts of men willing to be co-workers with God, and without this hard work, time itself becomes an ally of the forces of social stagnation. We must use time creatively, in the knowledge that the time is always ripe to do right. Now is the time to make real the promise of democracy and transform our pending national elegy into a creative psalm of brotherhood. Now is the time to lift our national policy from the quicksand of racial injustice to the solid rock of human dignity.

You speak of our activity in Birmingham as extreme. At first I was rather disappointed that fellow clergymen would see my nonviolent efforts as those of an extremist. I began thinking about the fact that I stand in the middle of two opposing forces in the Negro community. One is a force of complacency, made up in part of Negroes who, as a result of long years of oppression, are so drained of self-respect and a sense of "somebodiness" that they have adjusted to segregation; and in part of a few middle-class Negroes who, because of a degree of academic and economic security and because in some ways they profit by segregation, have become insensitive to the problems of the masses. The other force is one of bitterness and hatred, and it comes perilously close to advocating violence. It is expressed in the various black nationalist groups that are springing up across the nation, the largest and best-known being Elijah Muhammad's Muslim movement. Nourished by the Negro's frustration over the continued existence of racial discrimination, this movement is made up of people who have lost faith in America, who have absolutely repudiated Christianity, and who have concluded that the white man is an incorrigible "devil."

I have tried to stand between these two forces, saying that we need emulate neither the "do-nothingism" of the complacent nor the hatred and despair of the black nationalist. For there is the more excellent way of love and nonviolent protest. I am grateful to God that, through the influence of the Negro church, the way of nonviolence became an integral part of our struggle.

If this philosophy had not emerged, by now many streets of the South would, I am convinced, be flowing with blood. And I am further convinced that if our white brothers dismiss as " rabblerousers" and "outside agitators" those of use who employ nonviolent direct action, and if they refuse to support our nonviolent efforts, millions of Negroes will, out of frustration and despair, seek solace and security in black-nationalist ideologies—a development that would inevitably lead to a frightening racial nightmare.

Oppressed people cannot remain oppressed forever. The yearning for freedom eventually manifests itself, and that is what has happened to the American Negro. Something within has reminded him of his birthright of freedom, and something without has reminded him that it can be gained. Consciously or unconsciously, he has been caught up by the *Zeitgeist*[9] and with his black brothers of Africa and his brown and yellow brothers of Asia, South America, and the Caribbean, the United States Negro is moving with a sense of great urgency toward the promised land of racial justice. If one recognizes this vital urge that has engulfed the Negro community, one should readily understand why public demonstrations are taking place. The Negro has many pent-up resentments and latent frustrations, and he must release them. So let him march; let him make prayer pilgrimages to the city hall; let him go on freedom rides—and try to understand why he must do so. If his repressed emotions are not released in nonviolent ways, they will seek expression through violence; this is not a threat but a fact of history. So I have not said to my people, "Get rid of your discontent." Rather, I have tried to say that this normal and healthy discontent can be channeled into the creative outlet of nonviolent direct action. And now this approach is being termed extremist.

But though I was initially disappointed at being categorized as an extremist, as I continued to think about the matter I gradually gained a measure of satisfaction from the label. Was not Jesus an extremist for love: "Love your enemies, bless them that curse you, do good to them that hate you, and pray for them which despitefully use you, and persecute you." Was not Amos an extremist for justice: "Let justice roll down like waters and righteousness like an ever-flowing stream." Was not Paul an extremist for the Christian gospel: "I bear in my body the marks of the Lord Jesus." Was not Martin Luther an extremist: "Here I stand; I cannot do otherwise, so help me God." And John Bunyan: "I will stay in jail to the end of my days before I make a butchery of my conscience." And Abraham Lincoln: "This nation cannot survive half slave and half free." And Thomas Jefferson: "We hold these truths to be self-evident, that all men are created equal. . . ." So the question is not whether we will be extremists, but what kind of extremists we will be. Will we be extremists for hate or for love? Will we be extremists for the preservation of injustice or for the extension of justice? In that dramatic scene on Calvary's hill three men were crucified. We must never forget that all three were crucified for the same crime—the crime of extremism. Two were extremists for immorality, and thus fell below their environment. The other, Jesus Christ, was an extremist for love, truth, and goodness, and thereby rose above his environment. Perhaps the South, the nation, and the world are in dire need of creative extremists.

I had hoped that the white moderate would see this need. Perhaps I was too optimistic; perhaps I expected too much. I suppose I should have realized that few members of the oppressor race can understand the deep groans and passionate yearnings of the oppressed race, and still fewer have the vision to see that injustice must be rooted out by strong, persistent, and determined action. I am thankful, however, that some of our white brothers in the South have grasped the meaning of this social revolution and committed themselves to it. They are still all too few in quantity, but they are big in quality. Some—such as Ralph McGill, Lillian Smith, Harry Golden, James McBridge Dabbs, Ann Braden, and Sarah Patton Boyle—have written about our struggle in eloquent and prophetic terms.

[9]*Zeitgeist* the spirit of the times.

Others have marched with us down nameless streets of the South. They have languished in filthy, roach-infested jails, suffering the abuse and brutality of policemen who view them as "dirty nigger-lovers." Unlike so many of their moderate brothers and sisters, they have recognized the urgency of the moment and sensed the need for powerful "action" antidotes to combat the disease of segregation.

Let me take note of my other major disappointment. I have been so greatly disappointed with the white church and its leadership. Of course, there are some notable exceptions. I am not unmindful of the fact that each of you has taken some significant stands on this issue. I commend you, Reverend Stallings, for your Christian stand on this past Sunday, in welcoming Negroes to your worship service on a nonsegregated basis. I commend the Catholic leaders of this state for integrating Spring Hill College several years ago.

But despite these notable exceptions, I must honestly reiterate that I have been disappointed with the church. I do not say this as one of those negative critics who can always find something wrong with the church. I say this as a minister of the gospel, who loves the church; who was nurtured in its bosom; who has been sustained by its spiritual blessings and who will remain true to it as long as the cord of life shall lengthen.

When I was suddenly catapulted into the leadership of the bus protest in Montgomery, Alabama, a few years ago, I felt we would be supported by the white church. I felt that the white ministers, priests, and rabbis of the South would be among our strongest allies. Instead, some have been outright opponents, refusing to understand the freedom movement and misrepresenting its leaders; all too many others have been more cautious than courageous and have remained silent behind the anesthetizing security of stainedglass windows.

In spite of my shattered dreams, I came to Birmingham with the hope that the white religious leadership of this community would see the justice of our cause and, with deep moral concern, would serve as the channel through which our just grievances could reach the power structure. I had hoped that each of you would understand. But again I have been disappointed.

I have heard numerous southern religious leaders admonish their worshipers to comply with a desegregation decision because it is the law, but I have longed to hear white ministers declare: "Follow this decree because integration is morally right and because the Negro is your brother." In the midst of blatant injustices inflicted upon the Negro, I have watched white churchmen stand on the sideline and mouth pious irrelevancies and sanctimonious trivialities. In the midst of a mighty struggle to rid our nation of racial and economic injustice, I have heard many ministers say: "Those are social issues, with which the gospel has no real concern." And I have watched many churches commit themselves to a completely otherworldly religion which makes a strange, un-Biblical distinction between body and soul, between the sacred and the secular.

I have traveled the length and breadth of Alabama, Mississippi, and all the other southern states. On sweltering summer days and crisp autumn mornings I have looked at the South's beautiful churches with their lofty spires pointing heavenward. I have beheld the impressive outlines of her massive religious-education buildings. Over and over I have found myself asking: "What kind of people worship here? Who is their God? Where were their voices when the lips of Governor Barnett dripped with words of interposition and nullification? Where were they when Governor Wallace[10] gave a clarion call for defiance

---

[10]*Governor Wallace* George Wallace (1919–1998), as Governor of Alabama, Wallace tried unsuccessfully to prevent the desegregation of the state's public schools in the early 1960s. He later renounced his segregationist views.

and hatred? Where were their voices of support when bruised and weary Negro men and women decided to rise from the dark dungeons of complacency to the bright hills of creative protest?"

Yes, these questions are still in my mind. In deep disappointment I have wept over the laxity of the church. But be assured that my tears have been tears of love. There can be no deep disappointment where there is not deep love. Yes, I love the church. How could I do otherwise? I am in the rather unique position of being the son, the grandson, and the great-grandson of preachers. Yes, I see the church as the body of Christ. But, oh! How we have blemished and scarred that body through social neglect and through fear of being nonconformists.

There was a time when the church was very powerful—in the time when the early Christians rejoiced at being deemed worthy to suffer for what they believed. In those days the church was not merely a thermometer that recorded the ideas and principles of popular opinion; it was a thermostat that transformed the mores of society. Whenever the early Christians entered a town, the people in power became disturbed and immediately sought to convict the Christians for being "disturbers of the peace" and "outside agitators."But the Christians pressed on, in the conviction that they were "a colony of heaven," called to obey God rather than man. Small in number, they were big in commitment. They were too God-intoxicated to be "astronomically intimidated." By their effort and example they brought an end to such ancient evils as infanticide and gladiatorial contests.

Things are different now. So often the contemporary church is a weak, ineffectual voice with an uncertain sound. So often it is an archdefender of the status quo. Far from being disturbed by the presence of the church, the power structure of the average community is consoled by the church's silent—and often even vocal—sanction of things as they are.

But the judgment of God is upon the church as never before. If today's church does not recapture the sacrificial spirit of the early church, it will lose its authenticity, forfeit the loyalty of millions, and be dismissed as an irrelevant social club with no meaning for the twentieth century. Every day I meet young people whose disappointment with the church has turned into outright disgust.

Perhaps I have once again been too optimistic. Is organized religion too inextricably bound to the status quo to save our nation and the world? Perhaps I must turn my faith to the inner spiritual church, the church within the church, as the true *ekklesia,*[11] and the hope of the world. But again I am thankful to God that some noble souls from the ranks of organized religion have broken loose from the paralyzing chains of conformity and joined us as active partners in the struggle for freedom. They have left their secure congregations and walked the streets of Albany, Georgia, with us. They have gone down the highways of the South on tortuous rides for freedom. Yes, they have gone to jail with us. Some have been dismissed from their churches, have lost the support of their bishops and fellow ministers. But they have acted in the faith that right defeated is stronger than evil triumphant. Their witness has been the spiritual salt that has preserved the true meaning of the gospel in these troubled times. They have carved a tunnel of hope through the dark mountain of disappointment.

I hope the church as a whole will meet the challenge of this decisive hour. But even if the church does not come to the aid of justice, I have no despair about the future. I have no fear about the outcome of our struggle in Birmingham, even if our motives are

---

[11]*ekklesia* the Greek New Testament word for the early Christian church.

at present misunderstood. We will reach the goal of freedom in Birmingham and all over the nation, because the goal of America is freedom. Abused and scorned though we may be, our destiny is tied up with America's destiny. Before the pilgrims landed at Plymouth, we were here. Before the pen of Jefferson etched the majestic words of the Declaration of Independence across the pages of history, we were here. For more than two centuries our forebears labored in this country without wages; they made cotton king; they built the homes of their masters while suffering gross injustice and shameful humiliation—and yet out of a bottomless vitality they continued to thrive and develop. If the inexpressible cruelties of slavery could not stop us, the opposition we now face will surely fail. We will win our freedom because the sacred heritage of our nation and the eternal will of God are embodied in our echoing demands.

Before closing I feel impelled to mention one other point in your statement that has troubled me profoundly. You warmly commended the Birmingham police force for keeping "order" and "preventing violence." I doubt that you would have so warmly commended the police force if you had seen its dogs sinking their teenth into unarmed, nonviolent Negroes. I doubt that you would so quickly commend the policemen if you were to observe their ugly and inhumane treatment of Negroes here in the city jail; if you were to watch them push and curse old Negro women and young Negro girls; if you were to see them slap and kick old Negro men and young boys; if you were to observe them, as they did on two occasions, refuse to give us food because we wanted to sing our grace together. I cannot join you in your praise of the Birmingham police department.

It is true that the police have exercised a degree of discipline in handling the demonstrators. In this sense they have conducted themselves rather "nonviolently" in public. But for what purpose? To preserve the evil system of segregation. Over the past few years I have consistently preached that nonviolence demands that the means we use must be as pure as the ends we seek. I have tried to make clear that it is wrong to use immoral means to attain moral ends. But now I must affirm that it is just as wrong, or perhaps even more so, to use moral means to preserve immoral ends. Perhaps Mr. Connor and his policemen have been rather nonviolent in public, as was Chief Pritchett in Albany, Georgia, but they have used the moral means of nonviolence to maintain the immoral end of racial injustice. As T. S. Eliot[12] has said, "The last temptation is the greatest treason: To do the right deed for the wrong reason."

I wish you had commended the Negro sit-inners and demonstrators of Birmingham for their sublime courage, their willingness to suffer, and their amazing discipline in the midst of great provocation. One day the South will recognize its real heroes. They will be the James Merediths,[13] with the noble sense of purpose that enables them to face jeering and hostile mobs, and with the agonizing loneliness that characterizes the life of the pioneer. They will be old, oppressed, battered Negro women, symbolized in a seventy-two-year-old woman in Montgomery, Alabama, who rose up with a sense of dignity and with her people decided not to ride segregated buses, and who responded with ungrammatical profundity to one who inquired about her weariness: "My feets is tired, but my soul is at rest." They will be the young high school and college students, the young ministers of the gospel and a host of their elders, courageously and nonviolently sitting in at lunch counters and willingly going to jail for conscience' sake. One day the South will

---

[12]*T. S. Eliot* T(homas) S(tearns) Eilot (1888–1965), an Anglo-American modernist poet, critic, dramatist, and editor who won the 1948 Nobel Prize for literature.

[13]*James Meredith* the first African-American to enroll at the University of Mississippi.

know that when these disinherited children of God sat down at lunch counters, they were in reality standing up for what is best in the American dream and for the most sacred values in our Judaeo-Christian heritage, thereby bringing our nation back to those great wells of democracy which were dug deep by the founding fathers in their formulation of the Constitution and the Declaration of Independence.

Never before have I written so long a letter. I'm afraid it is much too long to take your precious time. I can assure you that it would have been much shorter if I had been writing from a comfortable desk, but what else can one do when he is alone in a narrow jail cell, other than write long letters, think long thoughts, and pray long prayers?

If I have said anything in this letter that overstates the truth and indicates an unreasonable impatience, I beg you to forgive me. If I have said anything that understates the truth and indicates my having a patience that allows me to settle for anything less than brotherhood, I beg God to forgive me.

I hope this letter finds you strong in the faith. I also hope that circumstances will soon make it possible for me to meet each of you, not as an integrationist or a civil-rights leader but as a fellow clergyman and a Christian brother. Let us all hope that the dark clouds of racial prejudice will soon pass away and the deep fog of misunderstanding will be lifted from our fear-drenched communities, and in some not too distant tomorrow the radiant stars of love and brotherhood will shine over our great nation with all their scintillating beauty.

Yours for the cause of Peace and Brotherhood,
MARTIN LUTHER KING, JR.

Understanding and Analysis

1. What contrasts does King establish in the first paragraph? How does he position himself in relationship to the clergymen who were to be the original readers of his letter?

2. After reading the essay once through, reconstruct the criticisms the clergy must have made in the statement to which this letter is a response. How many do you find? Where do you find them? How does King use these criticisms to structure his argument? In addition to his paraphrasing of the clergymen's criticisms, King also anticipates possible reactions and questions from them. Locate some of these anticipatory comments in the essay.

3. How many reasons does King offer for his presence in Birmingham? What are the reasons?

4. What are the "four basic steps" in a "nonviolent campaign"?

5. King builds much of the letter around the criticism that his actions were "untimely." As you reread the letter, underline all references to time, speed, and postponement. What are some of the ways that King answers that charge?

6. What, according to King, is the difference between a just and an unjust law?

7. What has made King "disappointed" with the white moderates and with the white church? In what ways would King define himself as a moderate?

8. In the course of the letter, King refers to numerous figures, both contemporary and historical, to support his ideas. Categorize these figures, and explain how King uses them to persuade his audience.

9. What is the tone of the last few paragraphs of the letter?

10. King is known for his linguistic skill in both speeches and writing. Analyze his use of language in one or two paragraphs selected at random. Look for metaphors, alliteration, repetition, and so on. Compare the literary devices in your selected paragraphs with

those you find in the long sentence in the fourteenth paragraph. Why is this particular sentence so carefully constructed?

Comparison

1. Read King's "I Have a Dream" speech. What linguistic characteristics do the two pieces share?

2. Read Baldwin's "Stranger in the Village." To what extent do you think King would agree with the views presented by Baldwin?

3. Read the essay by Gerald Early. Given Early's position on Malcolm X, what do you think his attitude is toward King? What is your evidence?

I HAVE A DREAM (1963)

I AM HAPPY to join with you today in what will go down in history as the greatest demonstration for freedom in the history of our nation.

Five score years ago, a great American, in whose symbolic shadow we stand today, signed the Emancipation Proclamation. This momentous decree came as a great beacon light of hope to millions of Negro slaves who had been seared in the flames of withering injustice. It came as a joyous daybreak to end the long night of their captivity.

But one hundred years later, the Negro still is not free; one hundred years later, the life of the Negro is still sadly crippled by the manacles of segregation and the chains of discrimination; one hundred years later, the Negro lives on a lonely island of poverty in the midst of a vast ocean of material prosperity; one hundred years later, the Negro is still languished in the corners of American society and finds himself in exile in his own land.

So we've come here today to dramatize a shameful condition. In a sense we've come to our nation's capital to cash a check. When the architects of our republic wrote the magnificent words of the Constitution and the Declaration of Independence, they were signing a promissory note to which every American was to fall heir. This note was the promise that all men, yes, black men as well as white men, would be guaranteed the unalienable rights of life, liberty, and the pursuit of happiness.

It is obvious today that American has defaulted on this promissory note in so far as her citizens of color are concerned. Instead of honoring this sacred obligation, America has given the Negro people a bad check, a check which has come back marked "insufficient funds." But we refuse to believe that the bank of justice is bankrupt. We refuse to believe that there are insufficient funds in the great vaults of opportunity of this nation. And so we've come to cash this check, a check that will give us upon demand the riches of freedom and the security of justice.

We have also come to this hallowed spot to remind America of the fierce urgency of now. This is no time to engage in the luxury of cooling off or to take the tranquilizing drug of gradualism. Now is the time to make real the promises of democracy; now is the time to rise from the dark and desolate valley of segregation to the sunlit path of racial justice; now is the time to lift our nation from the quicksands of racial injustice to the solid rock of brotherhood; now is the time to make justice a reality for all of God's children. It would be fatal for the nation to overlook the urgency of the moment. This sweltering summer of the Negro's legitimate discontent will not pass until there is an invigorating autumn of freedom and equality.

Nineteen sixty-three is not an end, but a beginning. And those who hope that the Negro needed to blow off steam and will now be content, will have a rude awakening if the nation returns to business as usual. There will be neither rest nor tranquility in America until the Negro is granted his citizenship rights. The whirlwinds of revolt will continue to shake the foundations of our nation until the bright day of justice emerges.

But there is something that I must say to my people, who stand on the worn threshold which leads into the palace of justice. In the process of gaining our rightful place, we must not be guilty of wrongful deeds. Let us not seek to satisfy our thirst for freedom by drinking from the cup of bitterness and hatred. We must forever conduct our struggle on the high plain of dignity and discipline. We must not allow our creative protests to degenerate into physical violence. Again and again we must rise to the majestic heights of meeting physical force with soul force. The marvelous new militancy, which has engulfed the Negro community, must not lead us to a distrust of all white people. For many of our white brothers, as evidenced by their presence here today, have come to realize that their destiny is tied up with our destiny. And they have come to realize that their freedom is inextricably bound to our freedom. We cannot walk alone. And as we walk, we must make the pledge that we shall always march ahead. We cannot turn back.

There are those who are asking the devotees of Civil Rights, "When will you be satisfied?" We can never be satisfied as long as the Negro is the victim of the unspeakable horrors of police brutality; we can never be satisfied as long as our bodies, heavy with the fatigue of travel, cannot gain lodging in the motels of the highways and the hotels of the cities; we cannot be satisfied as long as the Negro's basic mobility is from a smaller ghetto to a larger one; we can never be satisfied as long as our children are stripped of their selfhood and robbed of their dignity by signs stating "For Whites Only"; we cannot be satisfied as long as the Negro in Mississippi cannot vote and a Negro in New York believes he has nothing for which to vote. No! No, we are not satisfied, and we will not be satisfied until "justice rolls down like waters and righteousness like a mighty stream."

I am not unmindful that some of you have come here out of great trials and tribulations. Some of you have come fresh from narrow jail cells. Some of you have come from areas where your quest for freedom left you battered by the storms of persecution and staggered by the winds of police brutality. You have been the veterans of creative suffering. Continue to work with the faith that unearned suffering is redemptive. Go back to Mississippi. Go back to Alabama. Go back to South Carolina. Go back to Georgia. Go back to Louisiana. Go back to the slums and ghettos of our Northern cities, knowing that somehow this situation can and will be changed. Let us not wallow in the valley of despair.

I say to you today, my friends, so even though we face the difficulties of today and tomorrow, I still have a dream. It is a dream deeply rooted in the American dream. I have a dream that one day this nation will rise up and live out the true meaning of its creed, "We hold these truths to be self-evident, that all men are created equal." I have a dream that one day on the red hills of Georgia, sons of former slaves and the sons of former slave owners will be able to sit down together at the table of brotherhood. I have a dream that one day even the state of Mississippi, a state sweltering with the heat of injustice, sweltering with the heat of oppression, will be transformed into an oasis of freedom and justice. I have a dream that my four little children will one day live in a nation where they will not be judged by the color of their skin, but by the content of their character.

I HAVE A DREAM TODAY!

I have a dream that one day down in Alabama—with its vicious racists, with its Governor having his lips dripping with the words of interposition and nullification—one day right there in Alabama, little black boys and black girls will be able to join hands with little white boys and white girls as sisters and brothers.

I HAVE A DREAM TODAY!

I have a dream that one day every valley shall be exalted, and every hill and mountain shall be made low. The rough places will be plain and the crooked places will be made straight, "and the glory of the Lord shall be revealed, and all flesh shall see it together."

This is our hope. This is the faith that I go back to the South with. With this faith we will be able to hew out of the mountain of despair a stone of hope. With this faith we will be able to transform the jangling discords of our nation into a beautiful symphony of brotherhood. With this faith we will be able to work together, to pray together, to struggle together, to go to jail together, to stand up for freedom together, knowing that we will be free one day. And this will be the day. This will be the day when all of God's children will be able to sing with new meaning, "My country 'tis of thee, sweet land of liberty, of thee I sing. Land where my father died, land of the pilgrim's pride, from every mountainside, let freedom ring." And if America is to be a great nation, this must become true.

So let freedom ring from the prodigious hilltops of New Hampshire; let freedom ring from the mighty mountains of New York; let freedom ring from the heightening Alleghenies of Pennsylvania; let freedom ring from the snow-capped Rockies of Colorado; let freedom ring from the curvaceous slopes of California. But not only that. Let freedom ring from Stone Mountain of Georgia; let freedom ring from Lookout Mountain of Tennessee; let freedom ring from every hill and mole hill of Mississippi. "From every mountainside, let freedom ring."

And when this happens, and when we allow freedom to ring, when we let it ring from every village and every hamlet, from every state and every city, we will be able to speed up that day when all of God's children, black men and white men, Jews and Gentiles, Protestants and Catholics, will be able to join hands and sing in the words of the old Negro spiritual: "Free at last. Free at last. Thank God Almighty, we are free at last."

Understanding and Analysis

1. What are the characteristics of this piece that mark it as a speech?

2. What is the goal of this speech?

3. What lines do you find to be especially striking or moving? How are these lines different from others you find less striking?

4. Although usually speeches do not allow for the subtlety of thought that essays can provide, this speech does make an argument. What is it? How does King incorporate the views of an opponent, even in this short speech?

Comparison

1. Read the speech by Malcolm X, also delivered in 1963. What characteristics does King's speech share with that of Malcolm X? Compare and contrast both ideas and rhetorical techniques.

2. Read other speeches collected in this anthology, for example those by Churchill and Bronowski. What, if any, characteristics do these speeches share?

Malcolm X
(1925–1965)

Malcolm Little was born on May 19, 1925, the fourth of eight children. Despite a difficult childhood, during which his father died, his mother was institutionalized, and he himself was almost sent to reform school, Malcolm earned high grades in junior high school. He expressed interest in becoming a lawyer, but when his English teacher told him that this was "no realistic goal for a nigger," he grew disturbed and withdrawn. At the age of 15 (?), he went to live with his half-sister Ella in Boston, where he first became involved with gambling and drugs. After spending several years in Harlem, selling drugs and growing further involved with crime, he returned to Boston and was arrested in 1946 for burglary.

While Malcolm was in prison, his brother Reginald introduced him to the religion of Islam as practiced by Elijah Muhammad. Malcolm then began to educate himself. Paroled in 1952, he soon abandoned his "white slavemaster name of 'Little.'" As Malcolm X, he became a minister for the Nation of Islam, preaching black separatism and describing the atrocities committed by "the white devil" under the guise of Christianity. While traveling the East Coast to start temples, he met his future wife, Sister Betty.

In 1959, Elijah Muhammad gave permission for a documentary on the Nation to be filmed and shown on TV. It was that documentary, entitled "The Hate That Hate Produced," that put the Nation—and Malcolm X—in the national spotlight. The media immediately began referring to members of the Nation as "black supremacists" and "black racists," and Malcolm X became a regular part of the news, critiquing nonviolence and advancing a militant black nationalism. By the spring of 1963, he was one of the most widely sought speakers on college campuses. Malcolm X was suspended from the Nation in November of 1963, apparently for claiming that the assassination of John F. Kennedy was an instance of the "chickens coming home to roost." Following his split with the Nation in March of 1964, in a speech on "Black Revolution," Malcolm X argued that the United States should be brought before the United Nations for violating the human rights of 22 million African-Americans. Malcolm X's ideas continued to evolve during his subsequent journey to Mecca, where he encountered white Muslims whose kindness prompted him to reconsider his position on "the white devil." After returning to America, he stated, "I no longer subscribe to sweeping indictments of one race. My pilgrimage...served to convince me that perhaps American whites can be cured of the rampant racism which is consuming them and about to destroy this country."

While abroad, Malcolm X had also traveled to Africa, and he was impressed with possibilities for international solidarity that he recognized both there and in Mecca. He discussed with various leaders the need for "the type of Pan-African unity that would also include the Afro-Americans," for just as he believed that blacks in America would profit from a greater attention to the world, he believed that the world, in turn, needed to be more mindful of blacks in America. In a speech before members of the Ghanian Parliament, he asked how they could "condemn Portugal and South Africa while our black people in America are being bitten by dogs and beaten with clubs." This was a question that he also posed to Americans, charging that America could not purport to be a true democracy, a free country, while African-Americans were denied fundamental human rights and freedoms. Malcolm X was assassinated on February 25, 1965.

A powerful and controversial force in American culture during the 1960s, Malcolm X rightly argued that he aided the civil rights movement by offering an alternative that made Martin Luther King and the NAACP appear less radical—and more attractive—to a racist white establishment. Indeed, King and Malcolm X proved mutually beneficial, each invoking the other as the unwelcome alternative to his own views. The controversy that surrounded Malcolm X was not restricted to matters of race; he was also charged with sexism and anti-Semitism. For all of the controversy that he generated, however, Malcolm X also delivered important messages of empowerment for African-Americans.

Now remembered principally for his *Autobiography of Malcolm X*, written by Alex Haley from years of interviews, Malcolm X was known during his lifetime for his speeches. Refusing the polished, stylized rhetoric of speakers like King, he also refused elevated diction and the appearance of expertise. In the same speech in which he insisted that he was politically unlearned, he cited statistics about the government. In the same breath with which he protested his ignorance of a term, he then defined that term. Unfortunately, he was not always completely accurate in his speeches. But Malcolm X chose for himself a speaking persona of rough, untutored, almost spontaneous anger; he chose a persona of anger to deliver a message of anger.

MESSAGE TO THE GRASS ROOTS (1963)

WE WANT TO have just an off-the-cuff chat between you and me, us. We want to talk right down to earth in a language that everybody here can easily understand. We all agree tonight, all of the speakers have agreed, that America has a very serious problem. Not only does America have a very serious problem, but our people have a very serious problem. America's problem is us. We're her problem. The only reason she has a problem is she doesn't want us here. And every time you look at yourself, be you black, brown, red or yellow, a so-called Negro, you represent a person who poses such a serious problem for America because you're not wanted. Once you face this as a fact, then you can start plotting a course that will make you appear intelligent, instead of unintelligent.

What you and I need to do is learn to forget our differences. When we come together, we don't come together as Baptists or Methodists. You don't catch hell because you're a Baptist, and you don't catch hell because you're a Methodist. You don't catch hell because you're a Methodist or Baptist, you don't catch hell because you're a Democrat or a Republican, you don't catch hell because you're a Mason or an Elk, and you sure don't catch hell because you're an American; because if you were an American, you wouldn't catch hell. You catch hell because you're a black man. You catch hell, all of us catch hell, for the same reason.

So we're all black people, so-called Negroes, second-class citizens, ex-slaves. You're nothing but an ex-slave. You don't like to be told that. But what else are you? You are ex-slaves. You didn't come here on the "Mayflower." You came here on a slave ship. In chains, like a horse, or a cow, or a chicken. And you were brought here by the people who came here on the "Mayflower," you were brought here by the so-called Pilgrims, or Founding Fathers. They were the ones who brought you here.

We have a common enemy. We have this in common: We have a common oppressor, a common exploiter, and a common discriminator. But once we all realize that we have a common enemy, then we unite—on the basis of what we have in common. And what we have foremost in common is that enemy—the white man. He's an enemy to all of us. I know some of you all think that some of them aren't enemies. Time will tell.

In Bandung back in, I think, 1954, was the first unity meeting in centuries of black people. And once you study what happened at the Bandung conference, and the results of the Bandung conference, it actually serves as a model for the same procedure you and I can use to get our problems solved. At Bandung all the nations came together, the dark nations from Africa and Asia. Some of them were Buddhists, some of them were Muslims, some of them were Christians, some were Confucianists, some were atheists. Despite their religious differences, they came together. Some were communists, some were socialists, some were capitalists—despite their economic and political differences, they came together. All of them were black, brown, red or yellow.

The number-one thing that was not allowed to attend the Bandung conference was the white man. He couldn't come. Once they excluded the white man, they found that they could get together. Once they kept him out, everybody else fell right in and fell in line. This is the thing that you and I have to understand. And these people who came together didn't have nuclear weapons, they didn't have jet planes, they didn't have all of the heavy armaments that the white man has. But they had unity.

They were able to submerge their little petty differences and agree on one thing: That there one African came from Kenya and was being colonized by the Englishman, and another African came from the Congo and was being colonized by the Belgian, and another African came from Guinea and was being colonized by the French, and another came from Angola and was being colonized by the Portuguese. When they came to the Bandung conference, they looked at the Portuguese, and at the Frenchman, and at the Englishman, and at the Dutchman, and learned or realized the one thing that all of them had in common—they were all from Europe, they were all Europeans, blond, blue-eyed and white skins. They began to recognize who their enemy was. The same man that was colonizing our people in Kenya was colonizing our people in the Congo. The same one in the Congo was colonizing our people in South Africa, and in Southern Rhodesia, and in Burma, and in India, and in Afghanistan, and in Pakistan. They realized all over the world where the dark man was being oppressed, he was being oppressed by the white man; where the dark man was being exploited, he was being exploited by the white man. So they got together on this basis—that they had a common enemy.

And when you and I here in Detroit and in Michigan and in America who have been awakened today look around us, we too realize here in America we all have a common enemy, whether he's in Georgia or Michigan, whether he's in California or New York. He's the same man—blue eyes and blond hair and pale skin—the same man. So what we have to do is what they did. They agreed to stop quarreling among themselves. Any little spat that they had, they'd settle it among themselves, go into a huddle—don't let the enemy know that you've got a disagreement.

Instead of airing our differences in public, we have to realize we're all the same family. And when you have a family squabble, you don't get out on the sidewalk. If you do, everybody calls you uncouth, unrefined, uncivilized, savage. If you don't make it at home, you settle it at home; you get in the closet, argue it out behind closed doors, and then when you come out on the street, you pose a common front, a united front. And this is what we need to do in the community, and in the city, and in the state. We need to stop airing our differences in front of the white man, put the white man out of our meetings, and then sit down and talk shop with each other. That's what we've got to do.

I would like to make a few comments concerning the difference between the black revolution and the Negro revolution. Are they both the same? And if they're not, what is the difference? What is the difference between a black revolution and a Negro revolution? First, what is a revolution? Sometimes I'm inclined to believe that many of our people are using this word "revolution" loosely, without taking careful consideration of what this word actually means, and what its historic characteristics are. When you study the historic nature of revolutions, the motive of a revolution, the objective of a revolution, the result of a revolution, and the methods used in a revolution, you may change words. You may devise another program, you may change your goal and you may change your mind.

Look at the American Revolution in 1776. That revolution was for what? For land. Why did they want land? Independence. How was it carried out? Bloodshed. Number one, it was based on land, the basis of independence. And the only way they could get it was bloodshed. The French Revolution—what was it based on? The landless against the landlord. What was it for? Land. How did they get it? Bloodshed. Was no love lost, was no compromise, was no negotiation. I'm telling you—you don't know what a revolution is. Because when you find out what it is, you'll get back in the alley, you'll get out of the way.

The Russian Revolution—what was it based on? Land; the landless against the landlord. How did they bring it about? Bloodshed. You haven't got a revolution that doesn't involve bloodshed. And you're afraid to bleed. I said, you're afraid to bleed.

As long as the white man sent you to Korea, you bled. He sent you to Germany, you bled. He sent you to the South Pacific to fight the Japanese, you bled. You bleed for white people, but when it comes to seeing your own churches being bombed and little black girls murdered, you haven't got any blood. You bleed when the white man says bleed; you bite when the white man says bite; and you bark when the white man says bark. I hate to say this about us, but it's true. How are you going to be nonviolent in Mississippi, as violent as you were in Korea? How can you justify being nonviolent in Mississippi and Alabama, when your churches are being bombed, and your little girls are being murdered, and at the same time you are going to get violent with Hitler, and Tojo,[1] and somebody else you don't even know?

If violence is wrong in America, violence is wrong abroad. If it is wrong to be violent defending black women and black children and black babies and black men, then it is wrong for America to draft us and make us violent abroad in defense of her. And if it is right for America to draft us, and teach us how to be violent in defense of her, then it is right for you and me to do whatever is necessary to defend our own people right here in this country.

The Chinese Revolution—they wanted land. They threw the British out, along with the Uncle Tom[2] Chinese. Yes, they did. They set a good example. When I was in prison, I read an article—don't be shocked when I say that I was in prison. You're still in prison. That's what America means: prison. When I was in prison, I read an article in *Life* magazine showing a little Chinese girl, nine years old; her father was on his hands and knees and she was pulling the trigger because he was an Uncle Tom Chinaman. When they had the revolution over there, they took a whole generation of Uncle Toms and just wiped them out. And within ten years that little girl became a full-grown woman. No more Toms in China. And today it's one of the toughest, roughest, most feared countries on this earth—by the white man. Because there are no Uncle Toms over there.

Of all our studies, history is best qualified to reward our research. And when you see that you've got problems, all you have to do is examine the historic method used all over the world by others who have problems similar to yours. Once you see how they got theirs straight, then you know how you can get yours straight. There's been a revolution, a black revolution, going on in Africa. In Kenya, the Mau Mau were revolutionary; they were the ones who brought the word "Uhuru"[3] to the fore. The Mau Mau, they were revolutionary, they believed in scorched earth, they knocked everything aside that got in their way, and their revolution also was based on land, a desire for land. In Algeria, the northern part of Africa, a revolution took place. The Algerians were revolutionists, they wanted land. France offered to let them be integrated into France. They told France, to hell with France, they wanted some land, not some France. And they engaged in a bloody battle.

So I cite these various revolutions, brothers and sisters, to show you that you don't have a peaceful revolution. You don't have a turn-the-other-cheek revolution. There's no such thing as a nonviolent revolution. The only kind of revolution that is nonviolent is the Negro revolution. The only revolution in which the goal is loving your enemy is the Negro revolution. It's the only revolution in which the goal is a desegregated lunch counter, a desegregated theater, a desegregated park, and a desegregated public toilet; you can sit down next to white folks—on the toilet. That's no revolution. Revolution is based on land. Land is the basis of all independence. Land is the basis of freedom, justice, and equality.

The white man knows what a revolution is. He knows that the black revolution is world-wide in scope and in nature. The black revolution is sweeping Asia, is sweeping Africa, is rearing its head in Latin America. The Cuban Revolution—that's a revolution.

---

[1]*Tojo* Hideki Tojo (1884–1948) the Japanese prime minister who initiated the bombing of Pearl Harbor and directed Japan's involvement in World War II until 1944.

[2]*Uncle Tom* a slave in Harriet Beecher Stowe's novel, *Uncle Tom's Cabin.* The term has come to mean anyone who capitulates to his or her oppressors.

[3]*Uhuru* the Swahili word for "freedom."

They overturned the system. Revolution is in Asia, revolution is in Africa, and the white man is screaming because he sees revolution in Latin America. How do you think he'll react to you when you learn what a real revolution is? You don't know what a revolution is. If you did, you wouldn't use that word.

Revolution is bloody, revolution is hostile, revolution knows no compromise, revolution overturns and destroys everything that gets in its way. And you, sitting around here like a knot on the wall, saying, "I'm going to love these folks no matter how much they hate me." No, you need a revolution. Whoever heard of a revolution where they lock arms, as Rev. Cleage[4] was pointing out beautifully, singing "We Shall Overcome"? You don't do that in a revolution. You don't do any singing, you're too busy swinging. It's based on land. A revolutionary wants land so he can set up his own nation, an independent nation. These Negroes aren't asking for any nation—they're trying to crawl back on the plantation.

When you want a nation, that's called nationalism. When the white man became involved in a revolution in this country against England, what was it for? He wanted this land so he could set up another white nation. That's white nationalism. The American Revolution was white nationalism. The French Revolution was white nationalism. The Russian Revolution too—yes, it was—white nationalism. You don't think so? Why do you think Khrushchev and Mao[5] can't get their heads together? White nationalism. All the revolutions that are going on in Asia and Africa today are based on what?—black nationalism. A revolutionary is a black nationalist. He wants a nation. I was reading some beautiful words by Rev. Cleage, pointing out why he couldn't get together with someone else in the city because all of them were afraid of being identified with black nationalism. If you're afraid of black nationalism, you're afraid of revolution. And if you love revolution, you love black nationalism.

To understand this, you have to go back to what the young brother here referred to as the house Negro and the field Negro back during slavery. There were two kinds of slaves, the house Negro and the field Negro. The house Negroes—they lived in the house with master, they dressed pretty good, they ate good because they ate his food—what he left. They lived in the attic or the basement, but still they lived near the master; and they loved the master more than the master loved himself. They would give their life to save the master's house—quicker than the master would. If the master said, "We got a good house here," the house Negro would say, "Yeah, we got a good house here." Whenever the master said "we," he said "we." That's how you can tell a house Negro.

If the master's house caught on fire, the house Negro would fight harder to put the blaze out than the master would. If the master got sick, the house Negro would say, "What's the matter, boss, *we* sick?" We sick! He identified himself with his master, more than his master identified with himself. And if you came to the house Negro and said, "Let's run away, let's escape, let's separate," the house Negro would look at you and say, "Man, you crazy. What you mean, separate? Where is there a better house than this? Where can I wear better clothes than this? Where can I eat better food than this?" That was that house Negro. In those days he was called a "house nigger." And that's what we call them today, because we've still got some house niggers running around here.

---

[4]*Reverend Cleage* Albert B. Cleage is a civil rights activist, writer, and theologian.

[5]*Khrushchev and Mao* Nikita Khrushchev (1894–1971), and Mao Tse-Tung (1893–1976) Khrushchev was a leader of the communist party in the Soviet Union, and Mao Tse-Tung launched the 1966 Cultural Revolution in China.

This modern house Negro loves his master. He wants to live near him. He'll pay three times as much as the house is worth just to live near his master, and then brag about "I'm the only Negro out here." "I'm the only one on my job." "I'm the only one in this school." You're nothing but a house Negro. And if someone comes to you right now and says, "Let's separate," you say the same thing that the house Negro said on the plantation. "What you mean, separate? From America, this good white man? Where you going to get a better job than you get here?" I mean, this is what you say. "I ain't left nothing in Africa," that's what you say. Why, you left your mind in Africa.

On that same plantation, there was the field Negro. The field Negroes—those were the masses. There were always more Negroes in the field than there were Negroes in the house. The Negro in the field caught hell. He ate leftovers. In the house they ate high up on the hog. The Negro in the field didn't get anything but what was left of the insides of the hog. They call it "chitt'lings" nowadays. In those days they called them what they were—guts. That's what you were—gut-eaters. And some of you are still gut-eaters.

The field Negro was beaten from morning to night; he lived in a shack, in a hut; he wore old, castoff clothes. He hated his master. I say he hated his master. He was intelligent. That house Negro loved his master, but that field Negro—remember, they were in the majority, and they hated the master. When the house caught on fire, he didn't try to put it out; that field Negro prayed for a wind, for a breeze. When the master got sick, the field Negro prayed that he'd die. If someone came to the field Negro and said, "Let's separate, let's run," he didn't say "Where we going?" He'd say, "Any place is better than here." You've got field Negroes in America today. I'm a field Negro. The masses are the field Negroes. When they see this man's house on fire, you don't hear the little Negroes talking about "*our* government is in trouble." They say, "*The* government is in trouble." Imagine a Negro: "*Our* government"! I even heard one say "*our* astronauts." They won't even let him near the plant—and "*our* astronauts"! "*Our* Navy"—that's a Negro that is out of his mind, a Negro that is out of his mind.

Just as the slavemaster of that day used Tom, the house Negro, to keep the field Negroes in check, the same old slavemaster today has Negroes who are nothing but modern Uncle Toms, twentieth-century Uncle Toms, to keep you and me in check, to keep us under control, keep us passive and peaceful and nonviolent. That's Tom making you nonviolent. It's like when you go to the dentist, and the man's going to take your tooth. You're going to fight him when he starts pulling. So he squirts some stuff in your jaw called novocaine, to make you think they're not doing anything to you. So you sit there and because you've got all of that novocaine in your jaw, you suffer—peacefully. Blood running all down you jaw, and you don't know what's happening. Because someone has taught you to suffer—peacefully.

The white man does the same thing to you in the street, when he wants to put knots on your head and take advantage of you and not have to be afraid of your fighting back. To keep you from fighting back, he gets these old religious Uncle Toms to teach you and me, just like novocaine, to suffer peacefully. Don't stop suffering—just suffer peacefully. As Rev. Cleage pointed out, they say you should let your blood flow in the streets. This is a shame. You know he's a Christian preacher. If it's a shame to him, you know what it is to me.

There is nothing in our book, the Koran,[6] that teaches us to suffer peacefully. Our religion teaches us to be intelligent. Be peaceful, be courteous, obey the law, respect every-

---

[6]*Koran* the holy book of the Islamic faith.

one; but if someone puts his hand on you, send him to the cemetery. That's a good religion. In fact, that's that old-time religion. That's the one that Ma and Pa used to talk about: an eye for an eye, and a tooth for a tooth, and a head for a head, and a life for a life. That's a good religion. And nobody resents that kind of religion being taught but a wolf, who intends to make you his meal.

This is the way it is with the white man in America. He's a wolf—and you're sheep. Any time a shepherd, a pastor, teaches you and me not to run from the white man and, at the same time, teaches us not to fight the white man, he's a traitor to you and me. Don't lay down a life all by itself. No, preserve your life, it's the best thing you've got. And if you've got to give it up, let it be even-steven.

The slavemaster took Tom and dressed him well, fed him well and even gave him a little education—a *little* education; gave him a long coat and a top hat and made all the other slaves look up to him. Then he used Tom to control them. The same strategy that was used in those days is used today, by the same white man. He takes a Negro, a so-called Negro, and makes him prominent, builds him up, publicizes him, makes him a celebrity. And then he becomes a spokesman for Negroes—and a Negro leader.

I would like to mention just one other thing quickly, and that is the method that the white man uses, how the white man uses the "big guns," or Negro leaders, against the Negro revolution. They are not a part of the Negro revolution. They are used against the Negro revolution.

When Martin Luther King failed to desegregate Albany, Georgia, the civil-rights struggle in America reached its low point. King became bankrupt almost, as a leader. The Southern Christian Leadership Conference was in financial trouble; and it was in trouble, period, with the people when they failed to desegregate Albany, Georgia. Other Negro civil-rights leaders of so-called national stature became fallen idols. As they became fallen idols, began to lose their prestige and influence, local Negro leaders began to stir up the masses. In Cambridge, Maryland, Gloria Richardson; in Danville, Virginia, and other parts of the country, local leaders began to stir up our people at the grass-roots level. This was never done by these Negroes of national stature. They control you, but they have never incited you or excited you. They control you, they contain you, they have kept you on the plantation.

As soon as King failed in Birmingham, Negroes took to the streets. King went out to California to a big rally and raised I don't know how many thousands of dollars. He came to Detroit and had a march and raised some more thousands of dollars. And recall, right after that Roy Wilkins[7] attacked King. He accused King and CORE [Congress Of Racial Equality] of starting trouble everywhere and then making the NAACP [National Association for the Advancement of Colored People] get them out of jail and spend a lot of money; they accused King and CORE of raising all the money and not paying it back. This happened; I've got it in documented evidence in the newspaper. Roy started attacking King, and King started attacking Roy, and Farmer[8] started attacking both of them. And as these Negroes of national stature began to attack each other, they began to lose their control of the Negro masses.

[7]*Roy Wilkins* (1901–1981) an African-American civil rights activist who headed the NAACP from 1931–1977 and played a significant role in writing the 1964 Civil Rights Act.

[8]*Farmer* James Leonard Farmer (1920–1999) a civil rights activist, author, and scholar, Farmer was a founding member of the Congress of Racial Equality (CORE) in 1942, who led student sit-ins and Freedom Bus rides during the 1960s.

The Negroes were out there in the streets. They were talking about how they were going to march on Washington. Right at that time Birmingham had exploded, and the Negroes in Birmingham—remember, they also exploded. They began to stab the crackers in the back and bust them up 'side their head—yes, they did. That's when Kennedy sent in the troops, down in Birmingham. After that, Kennedy got on the television and said "this is a moral issue." That's when he said he was going to put out a civil-rights bill. And when he mentioned civil-rights bill and the Southern crackers started talking about how they were going to boycott or filibuster it, then the Negroes started talking—about what? That they were going to march on Washington, march on the Senate, march on the White House, march on the Congress, and tie it up, bring it to a halt, not let the government proceed. They even said they were going out to the airport and lay down on the runway and not let any airplanes land. I'm telling you what they said. That was revolution. That was revolution. That was the black revolution.

It was the grass roots out there in the street. It scared the white man to death, scared the white power structure in Washington, D.C., to death; I was there. When they found out that this black steamroller was going to come down on the capital, they called in *Wilkins,* they called in Randolph,[9] they called in these national Negro leaders that you respect and told them, "Call it off." Kennedy said, "Look, you all are letting this thing go too far." And Old Tom said, "Boss, I can't stop it, because I didn't start it." I'm telling you what they said. They said, "I'm not even in it, much less at the head of it." They said, "These Negroes are doing things on their own. They're running ahead of us." And that old shrewd fox, he said, "If you all aren't in it, I'll put you in it. I'll put you at the head of it. I'll endorse it. I'll welcome it. I'll help it. I'll join it."

A matter of hours went by. They had a meeting at the Carlyle Hotel in New York City. The Carlyle Hotel is owned by the Kennedy family; that's the hotel Kennedy spent the night at, two nights ago; it belongs to his family. A philanthropic society headed by a white man named Stephen Currier called all the top civil-rights leaders together at the Carlyle Hotel. And he told them, "By you all fighting each other, you are destroying the civil-rights movement. And since you're fighting over money from white liberals, let us set up what is known as the Council for United Civil Rights Leadership. Let's form this council, and all the civil-rights organizations will belong to it, and we'll use it for fund-raising purposes." Let me show you how tricky the white man is. As soon as they got it formed, they elected Whitney Young as its chairman, and who do you think became the co-chairman? Stephen Currier, the white man, a millionaire. Powell[10] was talking about it down at Cobo Hall today. This is what he was talking about. Powell knows it happened. Randolph knows it happened. Wilkins knows it happened. King knows it happened. Every one of that Big Six—they know it happened.

Once they formed it, with the white man over it, he promised them and gave them $800,000 to split up among the Big Six; and told them that after the march was over they'd give them $700,000 more. A million and a half dollars—split up between leaders

[9]*Randolph* A(sa) Philip Randolph (1889–1979) as a labor leader and social activist, Randolph dedicated his life to unionizing African-American workers; he is also credited with convincing President Truman to integrate the armed forces in 1948 and helping to organize the 1963 March on Washington.

[10]*Powell* Adam Clayton Powell (1865–1953) a preacher and leader of the African-American community who helped found the Urban League and was a member of the NAACP's first board of directors. He was elected several times to the House of Representatives.

that you have been following, going to jail for, crying crocodile tears for. And they're nothing but Frank James and Jesse James and the what-do-you-call-'em brothers.

As soon as they got the setup organized, the white man made available to them top public-relations experts; opened the news media across the country at their disposal, which then began to project these Big Six as the leaders of the march. Originally they weren't even in the march. You were talking this march talk on Hastings Street, you were talking march talk on Lenox Avenue, and on Fillmore Street, and on Central Avenue, and 32nd Street and 63rd Street. That's where the march talk was being talked. But the white man put the Big Six at the head of it; made them the march. They became the march. They took it over. And the first move they made after they took it over, they invited Walter Reuther,[11] a white man; they invited a priest, a rabbi, and an old white preacher, yes, an old white preacher. The same white element that put Kennedy into power—labor, the Catholics, the Jews, and liberal Protestants; the same clique that put Kennedy in power, joined the march on Washington.

It's just like when you've got some coffee that's too black, which means it's too strong. What do you do? You integrate it with cream, you make it weak. But if you pour too much cream in it, you won't even know you ever had coffee. It used to be hot, it becomes cool. It used to be strong, it becomes weak. It used to wake you up, now it puts you to sleep. This is what they did with the march on Washington. They joined it. They didn't integrate it, they infiltrated it. They joined it, became a part of it, took it over. And as they took it over, it lost its militancy. It ceased to be angry, it ceased to be hot, it ceased to be uncompromising. Why, it even ceased to be a march. It became a picnic, a circus. Nothing but a circus, with clowns and all. You had one right here in Detroit—I saw it on television—with clowns leading it, white clowns and black clowns. I know you don't like what I'm saying, but I'm going to tell you anyway. Because I can prove what I'm saying. If you think I'm telling you wrong, you bring me Martin Luther King and A. Philip Randolph and James Farmer and those other three, and see if they'll deny it over a microphone.

No, it was a sellout. It was a takeover. When James Baldwin[12] came in from Paris, they wouldn't let him talk, because they couldn't make him go by the script. Burt Lancaster[13] read the speech that Baldwin was supposed to make; they wouldn't let Baldwin get up there, because they know Baldwin is liable to say anything. They controlled it so tight, they told those Negroes what time to hit town, how to come, where to stop, what signs to carry, what song to sing, what speech they could make, and what speech they couldn't make; and then told them to get out of town by sundown. And every one of those Toms was out of town by sundown. Now I know you don't like my saying this. But I can back it up. It was a circus, a performance that beat anything Hollywood could ever do, the performance of the year. Reuther and those other three devils should get an Academy Award for the best actors because they acted like they really loved Negroes and fooled a whole lot of Negroes. And the Six Negro leaders should get an award too, for the best supporting cast.

---

[11]*Walter Reuther* (1907–1970) an outspoken labor leader who helped to found the powerful United Auto Workers' Union.

[12]*James Baldwin* (1924–1987) an African-American preacher, writer, and civil rights activist.

[13]*Burt Lancaster* (1913–1994) a Hollywood movie actor and producer.

Understanding and Analysis

1. How does Malcolm X establish his relationship to the audience? Who is the "we" Malcolm X refers to in the first line?

2. Why does Malcolm X want to minimize individual differences among the people in his audience?

3. Who is the enemy? Why does Malcolm X want to minimize differences among those designated as the enemy?

4. What effect did the exclusion of the white man have on the Bandung conference, according to Malcolm X? How are these people connected to those in Malcolm X's audience?

5. What methods does Malcolm X use to define the word "revolution?" What is his definition?

6. Why does he tell his audience that they are "afraid to bleed?"

7. What is the difference between the Negro revolution and the black revolution?

8. What is nationalism, according to Malcolm X?

9. Describe briefly the house Negro and the field Negro. How do these types connect to the two revolutions? How do they connect to Malcolm X's desire to minimize differences among groups of people?

10. How does the novocaine metaphor work?

11. What are the two types of religion that Malcolm X contrasts? How are they connected to the house and field Negro?

12. According to Malcolm X, who made Martin Luther King a leader? Why?

13. What is Malcolm X's version of the March on Washington?

14. What does Malcolm X claim the "Big Six" gained from their connection with the white man?

15. How does the coffee metaphor work?

16. Why, according to Malcolm X, did Baldwin not speak at the March on Washington?

17. What rhetorical techniques does Malcolm X use in his speech? Does his relationship toward his audience change during the course of the speech?

Comparison

1. What rhetorical techniques do Malcolm X and King both use in their speeches?

2. On what do the two men agree?

3. Read the essays by James Baldwin. In what ways do Baldwin and Malcolm X agree? Where do they differ?

4. Compare Malcolm X's version of the March on Washington with Hoagland's brief description of his experience of the march in "The Draft Card Gesture."

5. Read four or five of the essays in this text that are written by African-Americans and four or five that are written by whites. How significant do you think individual differences are among African-Americans and whites and between African-American and white groups in this text? Can valid conclusions be drawn from such a study? Why or why not?

6. Before Malcolm X was murdered, he had begun to change his mind about the uniformity of the white enemy. Does this information change your opinion of the validity of any of Malcolm X's claims? Why or why not?

7. Read Early's "Their Malcolm, My Problem." Compare Early's reactions to this speech with your own. Do you agree with Early's assessment of Malcolm X? Why or why not?

8. Read Orwell's essay "What Is Science?" and compare Orwell's definition of nationalism with Malcolm X's definition. How would you define the term?

Flannery O'Connor
(1925–1964)

Born March 25, 1925, in Savannah, Georgia, Mary Flannery O'Connor was an only child, peculiar, creative, and, by her own report, fiercely solitary. One creature whose company she did not disdain was her pet chicken, a Cochin Bantam who "had the distinction of being able to walk either forward or backward." In 1930, the two were filmed together for a newsreel, and, after that experience, she became a passionate collector: "I favored those with one green eye and one orange or with over-long necks and crooked combs. I wanted one with three legs or three wings but nothing in that line turned up. I pondered over the picture in Robert Ripley's book, *Believe It or Not*, of a rooster that had survived thirty days without his head." Chickens dominated her drawings as well, or rather, "the same chicken," which she drew repeatedly. Her father "toted about" these drawings, as well as her poems; he was inclined to write himself, except that he "had not the time or money or training." In the late 1930s, he developed lupus. "At the time," O'Connor wrote in a 1956 letter, "there was nothing for it but the undertaker." He died in 1941, three years after the family moved to Milledgeville, Georgia.

Having started her education in a Catholic school in Savannah, Mary Flannery had to enter the public school system in Milledgeville for lack of any other option. Though she received little guidance from her teachers, she developed her artistic skills during high school, drawing skillful satiric cartoons and writing. Following graduation, she enrolled immediately at the Georgia State College for Women, where she edited *The Corinthian*, the school's literary magazine, and served as the art editor for *The Colonnade*, the student newspaper. She also submitted cartoons to *The New Yorker*. After one of her college professors sent a writing sample to the Writing Workshop at the State University of Iowa, winning her a fellowship for a Master of Fine Arts, O'Connor made the choice to become a writer, rather than a visual artist, even changing her name for her vocation. Biographer Lorine Getz explains, "Reasoning that her double name, Mary Flannery, would be an anomaly outside the South and 'Mary O'Connor' on a dust jacket would be a sure way to obscurity, she legally dropped the 'Mary' before her name, becoming now for the first time 'Flannery O'Connor.'" In 1945, following her graduation from college, Flannery O'Connor left the South.

She performed well at the University of Iowa, studying under visiting professor Robert Penn Warren and publishing her first short story, "The Geranium," in 1946. In 1947, she took her MFA and set to work developing some of her short stories into a full-fledged novel, eventually called *Wise Blood*. To work on this novel, she moved to Yaddo, a 500-acre writers' colony in New York, or as a writer for *Time* magazine put it, a "swank monastery" where visiting authors received free room and board but followed a strict schedule of meal times and work times, remaining in solitude, enforced and uninterrupted, for hours during the day. O'Connor flourished at Yaddo, adopting a similar schedule for herself after she accepted poet Robert Fitzgerald's invitation to live with his family on their Connecticut farm in 1949. By this time, she had secured an agent and seen her work published in *Mademoiselle* and *Partisan Review*. Just as her reputation blossomed, O'Connor developed lupus herself in 1950. Weakened, she returned to Milledgeville to live with her mother on a farm inherited from her uncle. When interviewers came to visit her there, in later years, she was insistent that they not represent her as a "farm girl," telling one of them, "All I know about the land is, it's underneath me."

After five years of writing and revising, O'Connor finished *Wise Blood*, published in 1952 to widespread acclaim. Over the next three years, she published short stories, winning the Kenyon Review Fellowship in 1953 and 1954, and O. Henry prizes for "The Life You Save May Be Your Own" and "A Circle in the Fire" in 1954 and 1955. In 1955, she published her first collection of short stories, *A Good Man Is Hard to Find*. By this time, she had expanded her childhood fascination with chickens into a farmyard full of birds, including peacocks. She also found herself on crutches, feeling "like a large stiff anthropoid ape." In 1956, when she learned that she would be using them permanently, she remained in good spirits, writing to a friend, "I will henceforth be a structure with flying buttresses." She and her mother traveled to Rome in 1958, and O'Connor met with the Pope, buttresses and all.

In 1960, O'Connor published her second and final novel, *The Violent Bear It Away*. Already a prolific writer of short stories and book reviews, she took to writing essays in late 1950s and early 1960s, publishing, among other titles, "Fiction Is a Subject with a History" and "The Role of the Catholic Novelist." In 1962, she received her first honorary doctorate from St. Mary's College;

her second came from Smith in 1963. In 1964, her lupus reactivated. She died August 3 in Milledgeville at the age of 39.

Like the chickens she wanted to collect as a child, Flannery O'Connor's characters tend to be maimed, malformed, and maladjusted, the human equivalents of birds with three wings. Rendered through the sensibility of the cartoonist, their distortions are also savagely comic. Distortion was, for O'Connor, a deliberate strategy; she had "certain preoccupations" as a writer, "preoccupations with belief and with death and grace and the devil" that she attributed to her Catholicism, and to communicate with readers in a "modern secular world," she chose distortion as her method. She explained in a 1963 interview: "When I write a novel in which the central action is baptism, I have to assume that for a general reader, or the general run of readers, baptism is a meaningless rite, and I have to arrange the action so that this baptism carries enough awe and terror to jar the reader into some kind of emotional recognition of its significance... Distortion is an instrument in this case; exaggeration has a purpose."

Although O'Connor's "purpose" is often the transmission of a religious message, she is also praised for avoiding didacticism, for subordinating her message to the process of telling a story and creating a world. Exaggerated and distorted as that world may be, it is still grounded in the rural South, based in the realism of a hot sun, beat-up cars, dusty roads. "As a fiction writer who is a Southerner," O'Connor said, "I use the idiom and the manners of the country I know, but I don't consider that I write about the South." What O'Connor did write about—escaped convicts, itinerant preachers, salvation, sin, even the devil—she committed to beautiful, haunting prose, creating stories that reverberate in the reader long after the book is closed.

THE TOTAL EFFECT AND THE EIGHTH GRADE (1963)

IN TWO RECENT instances in Georgia, parents have objected to their eighth- and ninth-grade children's reading assignments in modern fiction. This seems to happen with some regularity in cases throughout the country. The unwitting parent picks up his child's book, glances through it, comes upon passages of erotic detail or profanity, and takes off at once to complain to the school board. Sometimes, as in one of the Georgia cases, the teacher is dismissed and hackles rise in liberal circles everywhere.

The two cases in Georgia, which involved Steinbeck's *East of Eden* and John Hersey's *A Bell for Adano*, provoked considerable newspaper comment. One columnist, in commending the enterprise of the teachers, announced that students do not like to read the fusty works of the nineteenth century, that their attention can best be held by novels dealing with the realities of our own time, and that the Bible, too, is full of racy stories.

Mr. Hersey himself addressed a letter to the State School Superintendent in behalf of the teacher who had been dismissed. He pointed out that his book is not scandalous, that it attempts to convey an earnest message about the nature of democracy, and that it falls well within the limits of the principle of "total effect," that principle followed in legal cases by which a book is judged not for isolated parts but by the final effect of the whole book upon the general reader.

I do not want to comment on the merits of these particular cases. What concerns me is what novels ought to be assigned in the eighth and ninth grades as a matter of course, for if these cases indicate anything, they indicate the haphazard way in which fiction is approached in our high schools. Presumably there is a state reading list which contains "safe" books for teachers to assign; after that it is up to the teacher.

English teachers come in Good, Bad, and Indifferent, but too frequently in high schools anyone who can speak English is allowed to teach it. Since several novels can't easily be gathered into one textbook, the fiction that students are assigned depends upon their teacher's knowledge, ability, and taste: variable factors at best. More often than not, the teacher assigns what he thinks will hold the attention and interest of the students. Modern fiction will certainly hold it.

Ours is the first age in history which has asked the child what he would tolerate learning, but that is a part of the problem with which I am not equipped to deal. The devil of Educationism that possesses us is the kind that can be "cast out only by prayer and fasting." No one has yet come along strong enough to do it. In other ages the attention of children was held by Homer and Virgil, among others, but, by the reverse evolutionary process, that is no longer possible; our children are too stupid now to enter the past imaginatively. No one asks the student if algebra pleases him or if he finds it satisfactory that some French verbs are irregular, but if he prefers Hersey to Hawthorne,[1] his taste must prevail.

I would like to put forward the proposition, repugnant to most English teachers, that fiction, if it is going to be taught in the high schools, should be taught as a subject and as a subject with a history. The total effect of a novel depends not only on its innate impact, but upon the experience, literary and otherwise, with which it is approached. No child needs to be assigned Hersey or Steinbeck until he is familiar with a certain amount of the best work of Cooper, Hawthorne, Melville, the early James, and Crane,[2] and he does not need to be assigned these until he has been introduced to some of the better English novelists of the eighteenth and nineteenth centuries.

The fact that these works do not present him with the realities of his own time is all to the good. He is surrounded by the realities of his own time, and he has no perspective whatever from which to view them. Like the college student who wrote in her paper on Lincoln that he went to the movies and got shot, many students go to college unaware that the world was not made yesterday; their studies began with the present and dipped backward occasionally when it seemed necessary or unavoidable.

There is much to be enjoyed in the great British novels of the nineteenth century, much that a good teacher can open up in them for the young student. There is no reason why these novels should be either too simple or too difficult for the eighth grade. For the simple, they offer simple pleasures; for the more precocious, they can be made to yield subtler ones if the teacher is up to it. Let the student discover, after reading the nineteenth-century British novel, that the nineteenth-century American novel is quite different as to its literary char-

---

[1]*Hawthorne* Nathaniel Hawthorne (1804–1864) a New England transcendentalist and writer whose works include *The Scarlet Letter* and *The House of the Seven Gables.*

[2]*Cooper, Melville, James, and Crane* James Fennimore Cooper, Herman Melville, Henry James, and Stephen Crane; well-known and much-studied nineteenth-century American authors.

acteristics, and he will thereby learn something not only about these individual works but about the sea-change which a new historical situation can effect in a literary form. Let him come to modern fiction with this experience behind him, and he will be better able to see and to deal with the more complicated demands of the best twentieth-century fiction.

Modern fiction often looks simpler than the fiction that preceded it, but in reality is more complex. A natural evolution has taken place. The author has for the most part absented himself from direct participation in the work and has left the reader to make his own way amid experiences dramatically rendered and symbolically ordered. The modern novelist merges the reader in experience; he tends to raise the passions he touches upon. If he is a good novelist, he raises them to effect by their order and clarity a new experience—the total effect—which is not in itself sensuous or simply of the moment. Unless the child has had some literary experience before, he is not going to be able to resolve the immediate passions the book arouses into any true, total picture.

It is here the moral problem will arise. It is one thing for a child to read about adultery in the Bible or in *Anna Karenina*,[3] and quite another for him to read about it in most modern fiction. This is not only because in both the former instances adultery is considered a sin, and in the latter, at most, an inconvenience, but because modern writing involves the reader in the action with a new degree of intensity, and literary mores now permit him to be involved in any action a human being can perform.

In our fractured culture, we cannot agree on morals; we cannot even agree that moral matters should come before literary ones when there is a conflict between them. All this is another reason why the high schools would do well to return to their proper business of preparing foundations. Whether in the senior year students should be assigned modern novelists should depend both on their parents' consent and on what they have already read and understood.

The high-school English teacher will be fulfilling his responsibility if he furnishes the student a guided opportunity, through the best writing of the past, to come, in time, to an understanding of the best writing of the present. He will teach literature, not social studies or little lessons in democracy or the customs of many lands.

And if the student finds that this is not to his taste? Well, that is regrettable. Most regrettable. His taste should not be consulted; it is being formed.

Understanding and Analysis

1. What is the point of the first three paragraphs? Where does O'Connor clearly state her particular topic?

2. What is her "proposition" or thesis? Where is it located?

3. How does O'Connor describe modern fiction?

4. According to O'Connor, in what way do modern parents and educators treat children differently than they did in the past? Do you agree?

5. What are the benefits, according to O'Connor, of studying novels written in the eighteenth and nineteenth centuries?

6. Compare the moral problem as perceived by the parents in Georgia in 1963, when this essay was first published in the *Georgia Bulletin*, with the moral problem as described by

---

[3]*Anna Karenina* a tragic novel published in 1877 by Russian author Leo Tolstoy.

O'Connor in paragraph 11. To what extent, if at all, does O'Connor agree with these parents on the subject of modern fiction and morality?

7. What is the "proper business" of high schools, according to O'Connor? What is the implication of the penultimate sentence?

8. Where does the phrase "total effect" first appear within the essay? Locate all uses of the word "total." What does the title mean?

Comparison

1. Read the essay by Angelou. Compare the kind of literature that Angelou read with the kind of literature that O'Connor recommends. What kind of literature were you offered in high school?

2. Read the essay by T. S. Eliot. What connections do you see between these two very different essays?

3. Read H. L. Mencken's "Bearers of the Torch." What connections do you see with O'Connor's essay?

4. Read Chesterton's "A Defence of Penny Dreadfuls." To what extent do you think Chesterton and O'Connor agree or disagree about the effect of literature on readers?

Jessica Mitford
(1917–1996)

Born into an aristocratic, English family, Jessica Mitford and her siblings, Nancy, Pamela, Tom, Diana, Unity, and Deborah, grew up in virtual isolation from the rest of society, owing in large part to their father's xenophobia. Like a "lost tribe, separated from its fellow men," Mitford writes in her first autobiography, the Mitford children developed a new language, "unintelligible to any but ourselves, into which we translated various dirty songs…and large chunks of the *Oxford Book of English Verse*." With Deborah, Jessica also created a society known as the Hons, the principal purpose of which was to harass Tom. Soon enough, however, Tom left home for Eton. The Mitford girls studied at home.

As adolescents, Unity and Jessica became fervently political. Jessica flirted briefly with pacifism, but ultimately embraced communism; Unity, from the beginning, was a fascist. After Unity fulfilled her goal of traveling to Germany to meet Hitler, she persuaded her parents to do the same, and Diana eventually married in Germany, with Hitler in attendance. Somewhat at sea in this conservative family, Jessica eagerly followed news of her second cousin, Esmond Romilly, a fellow radical. When Mitford and Romilly finally met, they quickly fell in love, and despite intense familial opposition, they married in June of 1937, when Mitford was 19. Still committed to communism, the newlyweds did not join the party because they disagreed with its direction.

In the early years of their marriage, Romilly and Mitford were in perpetual financial trouble, even trying to start a "gambling den" to make money. Following the death of their infant daughter, they moved to America in 1939, settling briefly in New York and then moving about the country. With the coming of World War II, Esmond left America to train for combat. Staying behind in Washington, D.C., Jessica gave birth to their daughter, Constancia. Esmond died in combat in November of 1941.

Aspiring not merely to join the party, once it had given full support to the war effort, but to become a "secretary to a party leader," Mitford sought training as a typist. Foundering in her classes, she gained employment as a "sub-eligible," or incredibly slow, typist at the Office of Price Administration, but her boss soon promoted her to the rank of inspector. In her time at the OPA, she developed feelings for an attorney named Bob Treuhaft. Uncomfortable with the idea of a second marriage, Mitford moved to San Francisco in 1943. Not long afterward, Treuhaft followed, and the couple married in June. They joined the party together, and, in 1949, while they were living in Oakland, the party asked Mitford to go to work for the East Bay Civil Rights Congress. In her work there, she documented and publicized police brutality, while Treuhaft handled the related lawsuits from his firm.

Over the next decade, Mitford experienced McCarthyism as a very real part of her private existence. Summoned before the California Committee on Un-American Activities in 1951, she had to appear before the House Committee in 1953. In 1955, Mitford lost her job in a classified ad department after the FBI contacted the paper. It was not until this point, when she was almost 40 years old, that Jessica Mitford began to write. Her first published work was a leftist pamphlet; soon after it appeared in print, she and Treuhaft left the party, finding it too disorganized to remain effective.

Mitford's first full-length book, the autobiography eventually entitled *Hons and Rebels* (1960), did not find a publisher until after the genesis of her second book. Treuhaft, a founding member of a society designed "to fight the high cost of dying," suggested that she explore the funeral industry. Thinking that there were greater social injustices to expose than expensive funerals, Mitford remained skeptical until she read the "trade magazines" of the industry. Her foray into the subject, an article called "St. Peter Don't You Call Me," received little attention. Once *Hons and Rebels* appeared, however, Mitford's reputation as an author earned her a seat in a televised "debate," which caught the attention of a writer for the *Saturday Evening Post*. Borrowing research materials from Mitford, Roul Tunley published "Can You Afford to Die?" in June of 1961. Public response was overwhelming. Seeing the opportunity for a book, Mitford wrote *The American Way of Death* (1963), a controversial and wildly popular exposé. Supporters of the funeral industry attempted to discredit her with cries of communism, but they may have only lengthened the book's reign on the best-seller list. Over the next two decades, Mitford published several more books, including *Kind and Usual Punishment: The Prison Business* (1973); *A Fine Old Conflict* (1977), her second autobiography; and *The American Way of Birth* (1992). Committed to exposing public injustices, she also wrote numerous articles for magazines, collected in *Poison Penmanship: The Gentle Art of Muckraking* (1979). She died July 23, 1996.

Dubbed "Queen of the Muckrakers" by *Time* magazine, Jessica Mitford was a relentless researcher and, by most accounts, an excellent reporter. Chided by *The New York Times* for "stepping in the muck" herself, Mitford certainly had critics, many of whom maintained that she demonized the institutions and the individuals she sought to expose. Even so, Mitford's writing style usually won the grudging admiration of her detractors, as it roused the enthusiasm of her champions. Satiric, but rarely caustic, Mitford argues her points with conviction and humor, equally strong, and equally felt.

Behind the Formaldehyde Curtain (1963)

THE DRAMA BEGINS to unfold with the arrival of the corpse at the mortuary.

Alas, poor Yorick![1] How surprised he would be to see how his counterpart of today is whisked off to a funeral parlor and is in short order sprayed, sliced, pierced, pickled, trussed, trimmed, creamed, waxed, painted, rouged and neatly dressed—transformed from a common corpse into a Beautiful Memory Picture. This process is known in the trade as embalming and restorative art, and is so universally employed in the United States and Canada that the funeral director does it routinely, without consulting corpse or kin. He regards as eccentric those few who are hardy enough to suggest that it might be dispensed with. Yet no law requires embalming, no religious doctrine commends it, nor is it dictated by considerations of health, sanitation, or even of personal daintiness. In no part of the world but in Northern America is it widely used. The purpose of embalming is to make the corpse presentable for viewing in a suitably costly container; and here too the funeral director routinely, without first consulting the family, prepares the body for public display.

Is all this legal? The processes to which a dead body may be subjected are after all to some extent circumscribed by law. In most states, for instance, the signature of next of kin must be obtained before an autopsy may be performed, before the deceased may be cremated, before the body may be turned over to a medical school for research purposes;

---

[1]*Alas, poor Yorick* a famous line addressed to a skull by a gravedigger in William Shakespeare's play *Hamlet.*

or such provision must be made in the decedent's will. In the case of embalming, no such permission is required nor is it ever sought. A textbook, *The Principles and Practices of Embalming,* comments on this: "There is some question regarding the legality of much that is done within the preparation room." The author points out that it would be most unusual for a responsible member of a bereaved family to instruct the mortician, in so many words, to "*embalm*" the body of a deceased relative. The very term "embalming" is so seldom used that the mortician must rely upon custom in the matter. The author concludes that unless the family specifies otherwise, the act of entrusting the body to the care of a funeral establishment carries with it an implied permission to go ahead and embalm.

Embalming is indeed a most extraordinary procedure, and one must wonder at the docility of Americans who each year pay hundreds of millions of dollars for its perpetuation, blissfully ignorant of what it is all about, what is done, how it is done. Not one in ten thousand has any idea of what actually takes place. Books on the subject are extremely hard to come by. They are not to be found in most libraries or bookshops.

In an era when huge television audiences watch surgical operations in the comfort of their living rooms, when, thanks to the animated cartoon, the geography of the digestive system has become familiar territory even to the nursery school set, in a land where the satisfaction of curiosity about almost all matters is a national pastime, the secrecy surrounding embalming can, surely, hardly be attributed to the inherent gruesomeness of the subject. Custom in this regard has within this century suffered a complete reversal. In the early days of American embalming, when it was performed in the home of the deceased, it was almost mandatory for some relative to stay by the embalmer's side and witness the procedure. Today, family members who might wish to be in attendance would certainly be dissuaded by the funeral director. All others, except apprentices, are excluded by law from the preparation room.

A close look at what does actually take place may explain in large measure the undertaker's intractable reticence concerning a procedure that has become his major *raison d'être.*[2] Is it possible he fears that public information about embalming might lead patrons to wonder if they really want this service? If the funeral men are loath to discuss the subject outside the trade, the reader may, understandably, be equally loath to go on reading at this point. For those who have the stomach for it, let us part the formaldehyde curtain. . . .

The body is first laid out in the undertaker's morgue—or rather, Mr. Jones is reposing in the preparation room—to be readied to bid the world farewell.

The preparation room in any of the better funeral establishments has the tiled and sterile look of a surgery, and indeed the embalmer-restorative artist who does his chores there is beginning to adopt the term "dermasurgeon" (appropriately corrupted by some mortician-writers as "demi-surgeon") to describe his calling. His equipment, consisting of scalpels, scissors, augers, forceps, clamps, needles, pumps, tubes, bowls and basins, is crudely imitative of the surgeon's, as is his technique, acquired in a nine- or twelve-month post-high-school course in an embalming school. He is supplied by an advanced chemical industry with a bewildering array of fluids, sprays, pastes, oils, powders, creams, to fix or soften tissue, shrink or distend it as needed, dry it here, restore the moisture there. There are cosmetics, waxes and paints to fill and cover features, even plaster of Paris to

[2]*raison d'etre* reason for existence.

replace entire limbs. There are ingenious aids to prop and stabilize the cadaver: a Vari-Pose Head Rest, the Edwards Arm and Hand Positioner, the Repose Block (to support the shoulders during the embalming), and the Throop Foot Positioner, which resembles an old-fashioned stocks.

Mr. John H. Eckels, president of the Eckels College of Mortuary Science, thus describes the first part of the embalming procedure: "In the hands of a skilled practitioner, this work may be done in a comparatively short time and without mutilating the body other than by slight incision—so slight that it scarcely would cause serious inconvenience if made upon a living person. It is necessary to remove the blood, and doing this not only helps in the disinfecting, but removes the principal cause of disfigurements due to discoloration."

Another textbook discusses the all-important time element: "The earlier this is done, the better, for every hour that elapses between death and embalming will add to the problems and complications encountered. . . ." Just how soon should one get going on the embalming? The author tells us, "On the basis of such scanty information made available to this profession through its rudimentary and haphazard system of technical research, we must conclude that the best results are to be obtained if the subject is embalmed before life is completely extinct—that is, before cellular death has occurred. In the average case, this would mean within an hour after somatic death." For those who feel that there is something a little rudimentary, not to say haphazard, about this advice, a comforting thought is offered by another writer. Speaking of fears entertained in early days of premature burial, he points out, "One of the effects of embalming by chemical injection, however, has been to dispel fears of live burial." How true; once the blood is removed, chances of live burial are indeed remote.

To return to Mr. Jones, the blood is drained out through the veins and replaced by embalming fluid pumped in through the arteries. As noted in *The Principles and Practices of Embalming,* "every operator has a favorite injection and drainage point—a fact which becomes a handicap only if he fails or refuses to forsake his favorites when conditions demand it." Typical favorites are the carotid artery, femoral artery, jugular vein, subclavian vein. There are various choices of embalming fluid. If Flextone is used, it will produce a "mild, flexible rigidity. The skin retains a velvety softness, the tissues are rubbery and pliable. Ideal for women and children." It may be blended with B. and G. Products Company's Lyf-Lyk tint, which is guaranteed to reproduce "nature's own skin texture . . . the velvety appearance of living tissue." Suntone comes in three separate tints: Suntan; Special Cosmetic Tint, a pink shade "especially indicated for young female subjects"; and Regular Cosmetic Tint, moderately pink.

About three to six gallons of a dyed and perfumed solution of formaldehyde, glycerin, borax, phenol, alcohol and water is soon circulating through Mr. Jones, whose mouth has been sewn together with a "needle directed upward between the upper lip and gum and brought out through the left nostril," with the corners raised slightly "for a more pleasant expression." If he should be bucktoothed, his teeth are cleaned with Bon Ami and coated with colorless nail polish. His eyes, meanwhile, are closed with flesh-tinted eye caps and eye cement.

The next step is to have at Mr. Jones with a thing called a trocar. This is a long, hollow needle attached to a tube. It is jabbed into the abdomen, poked around the entrails and chest cavity, the contents of which are pumped out and replaced with "cavity fluid." This done, and the hole in the abdomen sewn up, Mr. Jones's face is heavily creamed (to protect the skin from burns which may be caused by leakage of the chemicals), and he is covered with a sheet and left unmolested for a while. But not for long—there is more, much more, in store for him. He has been embalmed, but not yet restored, and the best time to start the restorative work is eight to ten hours after embalming, when the tissues have become firm and dry.

The object of all this attention to the corpse, it must be remembered, is to make it presentable for viewing in an attitude of healthy repose. "Our customs require the presentation of our dead in the semblance of normality . . . unmarred by the ravages of illness, disease or mutilation," says Mr. J. Sheridan Mayer in his *Restorative Art.* This is rather a large order since few people die in the full bloom of health, unravaged by illness and unmarked by some disfigurement. The funeral industry is equal to the challenge: "In some cases the gruesome appearance of a mutilated or disease-ridden subject may be quite discouraging. The task of restoration may seem impossible and shake the confidence of the embalmer. This is the time for intestinal fortitude and determination. Once the formative work is begun and affected tissues are cleaned or removed, all doubts of success vanish. It is surprising and gratifying to discover the results which may be obtained."

The embalmer, having allowed an appropriate interval to elapse, returns to the attack, but now he brings into play the skill and equipment of sculptor and cosmetician. Is a hand missing? Casting one in plaster of Paris is a simple matter. "For replacement purposes, only a cast of the back of the hand is necessary; this is within the ability of the average operator and is quite adequate." If a lip or two, a nose or an ear should be missing, the embalmer has at hand a variety of restorative waxes with which to model replacements. Pores and skin texture are simulated by stippling with a little brush, and over this cosmetics are laid on. Head off? Decapitation cases are rather routinely handled. Ragged edges are trimmed, and head joined to torso with a series of splints, wires and sutures. It is a good idea to have a little something at the neck—a scarf or a high collar—when time for viewing comes. Swollen mouth? Cut out tissue as needed from inside the lips. If too much is removed, the surface contour can easily be restored by padding with cotton. Swollen necks and cheeks are reduced by removing tissue through vertical incisions made down each side of the neck. "When the deceased is casketed, the pillow will hide the suture incisions . . . as an extra precaution against leakage, the suture may be painted with liquid sealer."

The opposite condition is more likely to present itself—that of emaciation. His hypodermic syringe now loaded with massage cream, the embalmer seeks out and fills the hollowed and sunken areas by injection. In this procedure the backs of the hands and fingers and the under-chin area should not be neglected.

Positioning the lips is a problem that recurrently challenges the ingenuity of the embalmer. Closed too tightly, they tend to give a stern, even disapproving expression. Ideally, embalmers feel, the lips should give the impression of being ever so slightly parted, the upper lip protruding slightly for a more youthful appearance. This takes some engineering, however, as the lips tend to drift apart. Lip drift can sometimes be remedied by pushing one or two straight pins through the inner margin of the lower lip and then inserting them between the two front upper teeth. If Mr. Jones happens to have no teeth, the pins can just as easily be anchored in his Armstrong Face Former and Denture Replacer. Another method to maintain lip closure is to dislocate the lower jaw, which is then held in its new position by a wire run through holes which have been drilled through the upper and lower jaws at the midline. As the French are fond of saying, *il faut souffrir pour être belle.*[3]

---

[3]*il faut souffrir pour etre belle* you have to suffer to be beautiful.

If Mr. Jones has died of jaundice, the embalming fluid will very likely turn him green. Does this deter the embalmer? Not if he has intestinal fortitude. Masking pastes and cosmetics are heavily laid on, burial garments and casket interiors are color-correlated with particular care, and Jones is displayed beneath rose-colored lights. Friends will say "How well he looks." Death by carbon monoxide, on the other hand, can be rather a good thing from the embalmer's viewpoint: "One advantage is the fact that this type of discoloration is an exaggerated form of a natural pink coloration." This is nice because the healthy glow is already present and needs but little attention.

The patching and filling completed, Mr. Jones is now shaved, washed and dressed. Cream-based cosmetic, available in pink, flesh, suntan, brunette and blond, is applied to his hands and face, his hair is shampooed and combed (and, in the case of Mrs. Jones, set), his hands manicured. For the horny-handed son of toil special care must be taken; cream should be applied to remove ingrained grime, and the nails cleaned. "If he were not in the habit of having them manicured in life, trimming and shaping is advised for better appearance—never questioned by kin."

Jones is now ready for casketing (this is the present participle of the verb "to casket"). In this operation his right shoulder should be depressed slightly "to turn the body a bit to the right and soften the appearance of lying flat on the back." Positioning the hands is a matter of importance, and special rubber positioning blocks may be used. The hands should be cupped slightly for a more lifelike, relaxed appearance. Proper placement of the body requires a delicate sense of balance. It should lie as high as possible in the casket, yet not so high that the lid, when lowered, will hit the nose. On the other hand, we are cautioned, placing the body too low "creates the impression that the body is in a box."

Jones is next wheeled into the appointed slumber room where a few last touches may be added—his favorite pipe placed in his hand or, if he was a great reader, a book propped into position. (In the case of little Master Jones a Teddy bear may be clutched.) Here he will hold open house for a few days, visiting hours 10 A.M. to 9 P.M.

All now being in readiness, the funeral director calls a staff conference to make sure that each assistant knows his precise duties. Mr. Wilber Kriege writes: "This makes your staff feel that they are a part of the team, with a definite assignment that must be properly carried out if the whole plan is to succeed. You never heard of a football coach who failed to talk to his entire team before they go on the field. They have drilled on the plays they are to execute for hours and days, and yet the successful coach knows the importance of making even the bench-warming third-string substitute feel that he is important if the game is to be won." The winning of this game is predicated upon glass-smooth handling of the logistics. The funeral director has notified the pallbearers whose names were furnished by the family, has arranged for the presence of clergyman, organist, and soloist, has provided transportation for everybody, has organized and listed the flowers sent by friends. In *Psychology of Funeral Service* Mr. Edward A. Martin points out: "He may not always do as much as the family thinks he is doing, but it is his helpful guidance that they appreciate in knowing they are proceeding as they should. . . . The important thing is how well his services can be used to make the family believe they are giving unlimited expression to their own sentiment."

The religious service may be held in a church or in the chapel of the funeral home; the funeral director vastly prefers the latter arrangement, for not only is it more convenient for him but it affords him the opportunity to show off his beautiful facilities to the gathered mourners. After the clergyman has had his say, the mourners queue up to file past the casket for a last look at the deceased. The family is never asked whether they want an open-casket ceremony; in the absence of their instruction to the contrary, this is taken for granted. Consequently well over 90 per cent of all American funerals feature the open casket—a custom unknown in other parts of the world. Foreigners are astonished by it. An English woman living in San Francisco described her reaction in a letter to the writer:

> I myself have attended only one funeral here—that of an elderly fellow worker of mine. After the service I could not understand why everyone was walking towards the coffin (sorry, I mean casket), but thought I had better follow the crowd. It shook me rigid to get there and find the casket open and poor old Oscar lying there in his brown tweed suit, wearing a suntan makeup and just the wrong shade of lipstick. If I had not been extremely fond of the old boy, I have a horrible feeling that I might have giggled. Then and there I decided that I could never face another American funeral—even dead.

The casket (which has been resting throughout the service on a Classic Beauty Ultra Metal Casket Bier) is now transferred by a hydraulically operated device called Porto-Lift to a balloon-tired, Glide Easy casket carriage which will wheel it to yet another conveyance, the Cadillac Funeral Coach. This may be lavender, cream, light green—anything but black. Interiors, of course, are color-correlated, "for the man who cannot stop short of perfection."

At graveside, the casket is lowered into the earth. This office, once the prerogative of friends of the deceased, is now performed by a patented mechanical lowering device. A "Lifetime Green" artificial grass mat is at the ready to conceal the sere earth, and overhead, to conceal the sky, is a portable Steril Chapel Tent ("resists the intense heat and humidity of summer and the terrific storms of winter . . . available in Silver Grey, Rose or Evergreen"). Now is the time for the ritual scattering of earth over the coffin, as the solemn words "earth to earth, ashes to ashes, dust to dust" are pronounced by the officiating cleric. This can today be accomplished "with a mere flick of the wrist with the Gordon Leak-Proof Earth Dispenser. No grasping of a handful of dirt, no soiled fingers. Simple, dignified, beautiful, reverent! The modern way!" The Gordon Earth Dispenser (at $5) is of nickel-plated brass construction. It is not only "attractive to the eye and long wearing"; it is also "one of the 'tools' for building better public relations" if presented as "an appropriate non-commercial gift" to the clergyman. It is shaped something like a saltshaker.

Untouched by human hand, the coffin and the earth are now united.

It is in the function of directing the participants through this maze of gadgetry that the funeral director has assigned to himself his relatively new role of "grief therapist." He has relieved the family of every detail, he has revamped the corpse to look like a living doll, he has arranged for it to nap for a few days in a slumber room, he has put on a well-oiled performance in which the concept of death has played no part whatsoever—unless it was inconsiderately mentioned by the clergyman who conducted the religious service. He has done everything in his power to make the funeral a real pleasure for everybody concerned. He and his team have given their all to score an upset victory over death.

Understanding and Analysis

1. What tone does Mitford adopt to address the subject of embalming? How does the opening line help to establish that tone? How does the metaphor help to establish the tone?

2. Reread the second paragraph. Locate linguistic devices other than metaphor that also work to establish the tone and style of the piece. What are they and how many do you find?

3. What is the purpose of embalming, according to Mitford?

4. Describe the customs associated with care of the corpse at the beginning of the twentieth century.

5. What has changed? What cause for this change does Mitford offer?

6. What are Mitford's sources for her information about the process of embalming? How accessible were these sources in 1963?

7. If you agree that the essay is humorous, analyze the comic techniques Mitford uses.

8. What exactly is the effect the embalmers hope to achieve?

9. Why does Mitford compare the funeral director and his associates to a coach and his football team?

10. What is the meaning of the one-sentence, penultimate paragraph? Examine the diction in the last paragraph. How does Mitford build to the climatic finish in her last sentence?

11. What underlying assumptions does she make about the nature of death and the nature of American culture?

12. What arguments could be presented from the point of view of someone who approves of the activities of the funeral director and his staff?

13. Select one of the paragraphs describing in detail the process of embalming and rewrite it from the point of view of someone who approves of the process. What changes would you make?

Comparison

1. If you have attended a funeral or a viewing, compare your impressions of the event with Mitford's description of a typical viewing and funeral. Have the practices of funeral parlors changed since Mitford wrote this essay?

2. Read Churchill's "The Iron Curtain." Why does Mitford borrow Churchill's metaphor? Do you think that reading Churchill's speech helps to clarify the metaphor? Why or Why not?

3. Examine as many one-sentence paragraphs as you can find in this text. Look for examples in Twain, Beerbohm, Dillard, and Rich. What makes a good one-sentence paragraph?

4. Read other essays in this collection that incorporate humor, such as those by Twain, Mencken, Parker, Thurber, Baker, and Allen. What techniques, if any, do these authors share? Are some techniques more effective than others?

Martin Gansberg
(1920–)

Born in Brooklyn, New York, in 1920, Martin Gansberg worked as a copy editor for *The New York Times* after graduating from St. John's University. Although he had many years of experience with the paper, he had only recently started working as a reporter when he received the assignment that captured the attention of the entire nation: the murder of Kitty Genovese. According to A. M. Rosenthal, then the Metropolitan Editor for the *Times*, Genovese's death on March 13, 1964, originally appeared in the four-paragraph story "Queens Woman Is Stabbed to Death in Front of Home."

It was only after the arrest of Winston Moseley on March 19 that the story began to develop. Following Moseley's arrest, the *Times* reported, he confessed to the murder not only of Kitty Genovese but also of Annie May Johnson. After the New York *Daily News* reported "that Moseley had also confessed to the murder of a fifteen-year-old girl, Barbara Kralik, in July 1963, and that the police were holding another man from whom they had [already] had a confession," Rosenthal made an appointment to speak with the police commissioner about the double confession. About that confession the commissioner denied any knowledge, but he did tell Rosenthal that 38 people had watched Kitty Genovese die "and not one of them had called the police to save her life." Certain the commissioner was "exaggerating," Rosenthal nevertheless saw the makings of a story.

In the weeks that followed, as Rosenthal details in *Thirty-Eight Witnesses*, he had to explain to many an experienced reporter why he chose the relatively inexperienced Martin Gansberg to pursue the story: "The reasons were: (a) Gansberg has a sense of enthusiasm, and I knew I wouldn't have to sell him on the story; (b) he is new enough not to resent dogged difficult work that might turn to nothing, as this story might have turned out; and (c) he was within my line of vision." Once assigned, Gansberg questioned the district attorney, the detectives on the case, and finally the witnesses themselves, whom "[h]e began to hate." Some readers of *The New York Times* felt exactly the same way after reading Gansberg's March 27 article. According to Rosenthal, two demanded that the paper publish the names of the witnesses in order to subject them to "public ridicule."

More common, however, was a near-hysterical impulse to explain, to figure out why 38 "respectable, law-abiding citizens" took no steps to prevent the death of another human being. In *Letters to the Times*, readers faulted "the sad state of our values and morals," violence on television, "restrictive firearms legislation" that armed criminals and jeopardized citizens, and the police themselves. Although some experts also faulted TV, as Rosenthal recounts, they more often cited psychological syndromes—massive denial, according to a sociologist, and vicarious sadistic fulfillment, according to one psychiatrist— and the "depersonalizing" effect of urban living. These explanations did not truly explain, of course. The murder of Kitty Genovese has become emblematic of that which cannot be explained, the worst in human nature: apathy, as Gansberg called it in the *Times*, or in the words of Henry Louis Gates, Jr., "moral indifference."

Gansberg, married to Agatha Miller, went on to a long and distinguished career as a reporter and an editor of the *Times*, and is now retired, but he never wrote another article with the impact of "38 Who Saw Murder Didn't Call the Police."

38 Who Saw Murder Didn't Call the Police (1964)

FOR MORE THAN half an hour thirty-eight respectable, law-abiding citizens in Queens watched a killer stalk and stab a woman in three separate attacks in Kew Gardens.

Twice the sound of their voices and the sudden glow of their bedroom lights interrupted him and frightened him off. Each time he returned, sought her out and stabbed her again. Not one person telephoned the police during the assault; one witness called after the woman was dead.

That was two weeks ago today. But Assistant Chief Inspector Frederick M. Lussen, in charge of the borough's detectives and a veteran of twenty-five years of homicide investigations, is still shocked.

He can give a matter-of-fact recitation of many murders. But the Kew Gardens slaying baffles him—not because it is a murder, but because the "good people" failed to call the police.

"As we have reconstructed the crime," he said, "the assailant had three chances to kill this woman during a thirty-five-minute period. He returned twice to complete the job. If we had been called when he first attacked, the woman might not be dead now."

This is what the police say happened beginning at 3:20 A.M. in the staid, middle-class, tree-lined Austin Street area:

Twenty-eight-year-old Catherine Genovese, who was called Kitty by almost everyone in the neighborhood, was returning home from her job as manager of a bar in Hollis. She parked her red Fiat in a lot adjacent to the Kew Gardens Long Island Rail Road Station, facing Mowbray Place. Like many residents of the neighborhood, she had parked there day after day since her arrival from Connecticut a year ago, although the railroad frowns on the practice.

She turned off the lights of her car, locked the door and started to walk the 100 feet to the entrance of her apartment at 82-70 Austin Street, which is in a Tudor building, with stores on the first floor and apartments on the second.

The entrance to the apartment is in the rear of the building because the front is rented to retail stores. At night the quiet neighborhood is shrouded in the slumbering darkness that marks most residential areas.

Miss Genovese noticed a man at the far end of the lot, near a seven-story apartment house at 82-40 Austin Street. She halted. Then, nervously, she headed up Austin Street toward Lefferts Boulevard, where there is a call box to the 102d Police Precinct in nearby Richmond Hill.

She got as far as a street light in front of a bookstore before the man grabbed her. She screamed. Lights went on in the ten-story apartment house at 82-67 Austin Street, which faces the bookstore. Windows slid open and voices punctured the early-morning stillness.

Miss Genovese screamed: "Oh, my God, he stabbed me! Please help me! Please help me!"

From one of the upper windows in the apartment house, a man called down: "Let that girl alone!"

The assailant looked up at him, shrugged and walked down Austin Street toward a white sedan parked a short distance away. Miss Genovese struggled to her feet.

Lights went out. The killer returned to Miss Genovese, now trying to make her way around the side of the building by the parking lot to get to her apartment. The assailant stabbed her again.

"I'm dying!" she shrieked. "I'm dying!"

Windows were opened again, and lights went on in many apartments. The assailant got into his car and drove away. Miss Genovese staggered to her feet. A city bus, Q-10, the Lefferts Boulevard line to Kennedy International Airport, passed. It was 3:35 A.M.

The assailant returned. By then, Miss Genovese had crawled to the back of the building, where the freshly painted brown doors to the apartment house held out hope of safety. The killer tried the first door; she wasn't there. At the second door, 82-62 Austin Street, he saw her slumped on the floor at the foot of the stairs. He stabbed her a third time—fatally.

It was 3:50 by the time the police received their first call from a man who was a neighbor of Miss Genovese. In two minutes they were at the scene. The neighbor, a seventy-year-old woman and another woman were the only persons on the street. Nobody else came forward.

The man explained that he had called the police after much deliberation. He had phoned a friend in Nassau Country for advice and then he had crossed the roof of the building to the apartment of the elderly woman to get her to make the call.

"I didn't want to get involved," he sheepishly told the police.

Six days later, the police arrested Winston Moseley, a twenty-nine-year-old business-machine operator, and charged him with the homicide. Moseley had no previous record. He is married, has two children and owns a home at 133-19 Sutter Avenue, South Ozone Park, Queens. On Wednesday, a court committed him to Kings County Hospital for psychiatric observation.

When questioned by the police, Moseley also said that he had slain Mrs. Annie May Johnson, twenty-four, of 146-12 133d Avenue, Jamaica, on February 29 and Barbara Kralik, fifteen, of 174-17 140th Avenue, Springfield Gardens, last July. In the Kralik case, the police are holding Alvin L. Mitchell, who is said to have confessed that slaying.

The police stressed how simple it would have been to have gotten in touch with them. "A phone call," said one of the detectives, "would have done it." The police may be reached by dialing "O" for operator or SPring 7-3100.

The question of whether the witnesses can be held legally responsible in any way for failure to report the crime was put to the Police Department's legal bureau. There, a spokesman said:

"There is no legal responsibility, with few exceptions, for any citizen to report a crime."

Under the statutes of the city, he said, a witness to a suspicious or violent death must report it to the medical examiner. Under state law, a witness cannot withhold information in a kidnapping.

Today witnesses from the neighborhood, which is made up of one-family homes in the $35,000 to $60,000 range with the exception of the two apartment houses near the railroad station, find it difficult to explain why they didn't call the police.

Lieut. Bernard Jacobs, who handled the investigation by the detectives, said:

"It is one of the better neighborhoods. There are few reports of crimes. You only get the usual complaints about boys playing or garbage cans being turned over."

The police said most persons had told them they had been afraid to call, but had given meaningless answers when asked what they had feared.

"We can understand the reticence of people to become involved in an area of violence," Lieutenant Jacobs said, "but where they are in their homes, near phones, why should they be afraid to call the police?"

He said his men were able to piece together what happened—and capture the suspect—because the residents furnished all the information when detectives rang doorbells during the days following the slaying.

"But why didn't someone call us that night?" he asked unbelievingly.

Witnesses—some of them unable to believe what they had allowed to happen—told a reporter why.

A housewife, knowingly if quite casually, said, "We thought it was a lover's quarrel." A husband and wife both said, "Frankly, we were afraid." They seemed aware of the fact that events might have been different. A distraught woman, wiping her hands in her apron, said, "I didn't want my husband to get involved."

One couple, now willing to talk about that night, said they heard the first screams. The husband looked thoughtfully at the bookstore where the killer first grabbed Miss Genovese.

"We went to the window to see what was happening," he said, "but the light from our bedroom made it difficult to see the street." The wife, still apprehensive, added: "I put out the light and we were able to see better."

Asked why they hadn't called the police, she shrugged and replied: "I don't know."

A man peeked out from a slight opening in the doorway to his apartment and rattled off an account of the killer's second attack. Why hadn't he called the police at the time? "I was tired," he said without emotion. "I went back to bed."

It was 4:25 A.M. when the ambulance arrived for the body of Miss Genovese. It drove off. "Then," a solemn police detective said, "the people came out."

Understanding and Analysis

1. What does Gansberg cover in the first two paragraphs?

2. Whose reaction does Gansberg first record? Why do you think he chooses this person?

3. In the fifth paragraph, Gansberg quotes the assistant chief inspector. What new information do we receive? What information is repeated?

4. The sixth paragraph consists of one sentence ending with a colon. What does the colon achieve?

5. The following fifteen paragraphs recount the story again, this time in detail. How is the story organized? What sources does Gansberg use? Are there details here that only Miss Genovese could know?

6. How long did it take for the police to arrive after the call was finally made?

7. In paragraph 22, why does Gansberg provide personal details about the confessed killer? Why does Gansberg list the addresses of the other victims Moseley claims to have killed?

8. What is the main point of the essay? How does Gansberg's tone help to convey that point? What effect does he hope to have on his readers?

9. What were some of the reasons that people gave for not calling the police?

10. How many people does Gansberg quote in the essay? Who are they?

11. Chronologically, information in the last paragraph belongs at the end of the narrative, after the police arrive (paragraph 19). Why does Gansberg save it for last?

12. What is the difference between the legal and the moral obligations of witnesses to a crime? How does Gansberg convey his position on this question?

Comparison

1. Read other essays in this text that were originally published as articles in newspapers, for instance, Hemingway's "A Brush with Death," Pyle's "The Death of Captain Waskow," and Mencken's "Bearers of the Torch." What attributes do they have in common?

2. What, if anything, do the essays by Gansberg and Martha Gellhorn have in common?

3. What characteristics, if any, does Gansberg's essay share with that by Jessica Mitford? Consider the purpose each author has in writing the piece, as well as the two subjects and some of the techniques involved.

4. Compare Gansberg's essay with Milgram's and others listed under the theme of Human Nature. What conclusions, if any, can you draw based on some of these essays, as well as your own experience?

Norman Podhoretz
(1930–)

Born in Brooklyn, New York, in 1930, Norman Podhoretz grew up in a lower-class neighborhood known as Brownsville, which he loved so much that he "dreaded the thought of living anywhere else." To the immense delight of his mother, he excelled in school, earning top grades and numerous awards. When he entered high school, he began two battles, one with his father, who wanted him to enter a Jewish seminary school, and one with his English teacher, who wanted him to reject his identity as a lower-class Jew in favor of an assimilated, cultured, middle-class existence and an Ivy League education. Although Podhoretz resisted, both his father and his English teacher more or less got their way. Starting at the Jewish Theological Seminary immediately after high school, Podhoretz also matriculated to Columbia, soon finding himself alienated from his origins. "To wean me away from Brownsville," Podhoretz writes, "all Columbia had to do was give me the superior education it did: in giving me such an education it was working a radical change in my tastes, and in changing my tastes it was ensuring that I would no longer be comfortable in the world from which I had come." Graduating from both the Seminary and Columbia in 1950, Podhoretz received a fellowship that paid his way to enter Clare College at Cambridge.

At Columbia, Podhoretz studied under the renowned literary critic Lionel Trilling and exchanged his childhood dream of becoming a poet for a dream of becoming a "critic-teacher." At Cambridge, he pursued this new dream under the direction of F. R. Leavis. Earning yet another bachelor's in 1952, he returned to America for the summer with thoughts of taking his doctorate at Harvard. While he was home, the editor of *Commentary* invited him to do a book review; this invitation was the highlight of an otherwise "bad summer back in Brooklyn." Podhoretz returned to Cambridge, "my heart lusting for publication and little else." After Leavis lambasted one of Podhoretz's scholarly essays, the desire for a doctorate died altogether. Podhoretz determined to leave Cambridge, despite the inevitability of being drafted. (The Korean War had "recently ended," he explains in his first autobiography, but the draft was still going.) He appeared for duty in December of 1953.

Following his release in December of 1955, he started as an assistant editor at *Commentary*. In 1956, he married Midge Rosenthal Decter, a fellow editor and writer, and by 1960, he was serving as *Commentary's* editor-in-chief, hoping to "turn" the magazine, "as I myself had been turning, in the same leftward direction that I was confident the best energies of the sixties were also preparing to move." He solicited contributions from numerous liberal writers, and he pursued James Baldwin, in particular, for an article on black Muslims. Baldwin agreed to a write a piece—ultimately entitled "The Fire Next Time"—but instead of giving it to *Commentary*, he sold it to *The New Yorker*. Podhoretz was incensed. Over drinks, he told Baldwin "several stories about my childhood relations with Negroes . . . and as I talked, Baldwin's eyes blazed even more fiercely than usual. 'You ought,' he whispered when I had finished, 'to write all that down.'" In "three hot, blissful sessions at the typewriter," Podhoretz did. "My Negro Problem—and Ours" appeared in *Commentary* in February of 1964, eliciting hundreds of letters "calling me everything from a racist to a moral hero."

Having worked as a writer for many years, Podhoretz experienced both an internal desire and an external pressure to produce a book. He published *Doings and Undoings: The Fifties and After in American Writing* (1964) and then edited *The Commentary Reader* (1966). During the writing of his first autobiography, *Making It* (1967), Podhoretz was feeling concerned about "the direction" of radicalism. He swung right not long afterward, describing himself as "an enemy of radicalism in all its forms and varieties" in the prologue to his second autobiography, *Breaking Ranks* (1979). Labeled a neo-conservative for changing camps, Podhoretz wrote *The Present Danger* (1980), *Why We Were in Vietnam* (1982), and *The Bloody Crossroads* (1986) while continuing to edit *Commentary*. At his retirement dinner, held on May 2, 1995, speakers included William J. Bennett, William F. Buckley, Jr., and Henry Kissinger. Since then, Podhoretz has published *Ex-Friends: Falling Out with Allen Ginsberg, Lionel & Diana Trilling, Lillian Hellman, Hannah Arendt, and Norman Mailer* (1999).

A prominent and controversial figure in the intellectual history of the twentieth century, Norman Podhoretz has created a stir by criticizing some of the same liberal thinkers who trained and influenced him in his early years. In *Making It*, he uses his life story as a "concrete setting" for an analysis of the dual role of ambition in American culture, maintaining that Americans are required, at one and the same time, to "lust" after success and to feel "ashamed" for their lust. In an effort to circumvent this "contradiction," Podhoretz cheerfully avows his own desire for fame and fortune, but, in the process, he also suggests that he is not alone, that other scholars and writers quietly strive for power, too, that—in the words of Mark Royden Winchell—"literary intellectuals cherish a dream of success that in its own way is not all that different from the bourgeois ambitions of a used-car salesman." *Making It* had its defenders, but it also provoked intense anger in many intellectual circles. *Breaking Ranks* did the same. Despite the major change in his politics documented there and in *Ex-Friends*, Podhoretz stands by what he regards as his most "radical" moment: the publication of "My Negro Problem—and Ours." "I wouldn't repudiate any of it," he told *Contemporary Authors* in 1981, "not even the end."

My Negro Problem—and Ours (1964)

If we—and…I mean the relatively conscious whites and the relatively conscious blacks, who must, like lovers, insist on, or create, the consciousness of the others—do not falter in our duty now, we may be able, handful that we are, to end the racial nightmare, and achieve our country, and change the history of the world.

—James Baldwin

TWO IDEAS PUZZLED me deeply as a child growing up in Brooklyn during the 1930's in what today would be called an integrated neighborhood. One of them was that all Jews were rich; the other was that all Negroes were persecuted. These ideas have appeared in print; therefore they must be true. My own experience and the evidence of my senses told they were not true, but that only confirmed what a day-dreaming boy in the provinces—for the lower-class neighborhoods of New York belong as surely to the provinces as any rural town in North Dakota—discovers very early: *his* experience is unreal and the evidence of his senses is not to be trusted. Yet even a boy with a head full of fantasies incongruously synthesized out of Hollywood movies and English novels cannot altogether deny the reality of his own experience—especially when there is so much deprivation in that experience. Nor can he altogether gainsay the evidence of his own senses—especially such evidence of the senses as comes from being repeatedly beaten up, robbed, and in general hated, terrorized, and humiliated.

And so for a long time I was puzzled to think that Jews were supposed to be rich when the only Jews I knew were poor, and that Negroes were supposed to be persecuted when it was the Negroes who were doing the only persecuting I knew about—and doing it, moreover, to me. During the early years of the war, when my older sister joined a left-wing youth organization, I remember my astonishment at hearing her passionately denounce my father for thinking that Jews were worse off than Negroes. To me, at the age of twelve, it seemed very clear that Negroes were better off than Jews—indeed, than *all* whites. A city boy's world is contained within three or four square blocks, and in my world it was the whites, the Italians and Jews, who feared the Negroes, not the other way around. The Negroes were tougher than we were, more ruthless, and on the whole they were better athletes. What could it mean, then, to say that they were badly off and that we were more fortunate? Yet my sister's opinions, like print, were sacred, and when she told me about exploitation and economic forces I believed her. I believed her, but I was still afraid of Negroes. And I still hated them with all my heart.

It had not always been so—that much I can recall from early childhood. When did it start, this fear and this hatred? There was a kindergarten in the local public school, and given the character of the neighborhood, at least half of the children in my class must have been Negroes. Yet I have no memory of being aware of color differences at that age, and I know from observing my own children that they attribute no significance to such differences even when they begin noticing them. I think there was a day—first grade? second grade?—when my best friend Carl hit me on the way home from school and announced that he wouldn't play with me any more because I had killed Jesus. When I ran home to my mother crying for an explanation, she told me not to pay any attention to such foolishness, and then in Yiddish she cursed the *goyim* and the *schwartzes,*[1] the *schwartzes* and the *goyim.* Carl, it turned out, was a *schwartze,* and so was added a third to the categories into which people were mysteriously divided.

Sometimes I wonder whether this is a true memory at all. It is blazingly vivid, but perhaps it never happened: can anyone really remember back to the age of six? There is no uncertainty in my mind, however, about the years that followed. Carl and I hardly ever spoke, though we met in school every day up through the eighth or ninth grade. There would be embarrassed moments of catching his eye or of his catching mine—for whatever it was that had attracted us to one another as very small children remained alive

---

[1]*goyim and schwartzes* Yiddish words for non-Jews and African-Americans; both terms are somewhat derogatory.

in spite of the fantastic barrier of hostility that had grown up between us, suddenly and out of nowhere. Nevertheless, friendship would have been impossible, and even if it had been possible, it would have been unthinkable. About that, there was nothing anyone could do by the time we were eight years old.

Item: The orphanage across the street is torn down, a city housing project begins to rise in its place, and on the marvelous vacant lot next to the old orphanage they are building a playground. Much excitement and anticipation as Opening Day draws near. Mayor LaGuardia himself comes to dedicate this great gesture of public benevolence. He speaks of neighborliness and borrowing cups of sugar, and of the playground he says that children of all races, colors, and creeds will learn to live together in harmony. A week later, some of us are swatting flies on the playground's inadequate little ball field. A gang of Negro kids, pretty much our own age, enter from the other side and order us out of the park. We refuse, proudly and indignantly, with superb masculine fervor. There is a fight, they win, and we retreat, half whimpering, half with bravado. My first nauseating experience of cowardice. And my first appalled realization that there are people in the world who do not seem to be afraid of anything, who act as though they have nothing to lose. Thereafter the playground becomes a battleground, sometimes quiet, sometimes the scene of athletic competition between Them and Us. But rocks are thrown as often as baseballs. Gradually we abandon the place and use the streets instead. The streets are safer, though we do not admit this to ourselves. We are not, after all, sissies—that most dreaded epithet of an American boyhood.

Item: I am standing alone in front of the building in which I live. It is late afternoon and getting dark. That day in school the teacher had asked a surly Negro boy named Quentin a question he was unable to answer. As usual I had waved my arm eagerly ("Be a good boy, get good marks, be smart, go to college, become a doctor") and, the right answer bursting from my lips, I was held up lovingly by the teacher as an example to the class. I had seen Quentin's face—a very dark, very cruel, very Oriental-looking face— harden, and there had been enough threat in his eyes to make me run all the way home for fear that he might catch me outside.

Now, standing idly in front of my own house, I see him approaching from the project accompanied by his little brother who is carrying a baseball bat and wearing a grin of malicious anticipation. As in a nightmare, I am trapped. The surroundings are secure and familiar, but terror is suddenly present and there is no one around to help. I am locked to the spot. I will not cry out or run away like a sissy, and I stand there, my heart wild, my throat clogged. He walks up, hurls the familiar epithet ("Hey, mo'f—r"), and to my surprise only pushes me. It is a violent push, but not a punch. Maybe I can still back out without entirely losing my dignity. Maybe I can still say, "Hey, c'mon Quentin, whaddya wanna do *that* for? I dint do nothin' to *you*," and walk away, not too rapidly. Instead, before I can stop myself, I push him back—a token gesture—and I say, "Cut that out, I don't wanna fight, I ain't got nothin' to fight about." As I turn to walk back into the building, the corner of my eye catches the motion of the bat his little brother has handed him. I try to duck, but the bat crashes colored lights into my head.

The next thing I know, my mother and sister are standing over me, both of them hysterical. My sister—she who was later to join the "progressive" youth organization—is shouting for the police and screaming imprecations at those dirty little black bastards. They take me upstairs, the doctor comes, the police come. I tell them that the boy who did it was a stranger, that he had been trying to get money from me. They do not believe me, but I am too scared to give them Quentin's name. When I return to school a few days later, Quentin avoids my eyes. He knows that I have not squealed, and he is ashamed. I try to feel proud, but in my heart I know that it was fear of what his friends might do to me that had kept me silent, and not the code of the street.

Item: There is an athletic meet in which the whole of our junior high school is participating. I am in one of the seventh-grade rapid-advance classes, and "segregation" has now set in with a vengeance. In the last three or four years of the elementary school from which we have just graduated, each grade had been divided into three classes, according to "intelligence." (In the earlier grades the divisions had either been arbitrary or else unrecognized by us as having anything to do with brains.) These divisions by IQ, or however it was arranged, had resulted in a preponderance of Jews in the "1" classes and a corresponding preponderance of Negroes in the "3's," with the Italians split unevenly along the spectrum. At least a few Negroes had always made the "1's," just as there had always been a few Jewish kids among the "3's," and more among the "2's" (where Italians dominated). But the junior high's rapid-advance class of which I am now a member is overwhelmingly Jewish and entirely white—except for a shy lonely Negro girl with light skin and reddish hair.

The athletic meet takes place in a city-owned stadium far from the school. It is an important event to which a whole day is given over. The winners are to get those precious little medallions stamped with the New York City emblem that can be screwed into a belt and that prove the wearer to be a distinguished personage. I am a fast runner, and so I am assigned the position of anchor man on my class's team in the relay race. There are three other seventh-grade teams in the race, two of them all Negro, as ours is all white. One of the all-Negro teams is very tall—their anchor man waiting silently next to me on the line looks years older than I am, and I do not recognize him. He is the first to get the baton and crosses the finishing line in a walk. Our team comes in second, but a few minutes later we are declared the winners, for it has been discovered that the anchor man on the first-place team is not a member of the class. We are awarded the medallions, and the following day our homeroom teacher makes a speech about how proud she is of us for being superior athletes as well as superior students. We want to believe that we deserve the praise, but we know that we could not have won even if the other class had not cheated.

That afternoon, walking home, I am waylaid and surrounded by five Negroes, among whom is the anchor man of the disqualified team. "Gimme my medal, mo'f—r," he grunts. I do not have it with me and I tell him so. "Anyway, it ain't yours," I say foolishly. He calls me a liar on both counts and pushes me up against the wall on which we sometimes play handball. "Gimme my mo'f—n' medal," he says again. I repeat that I have left it home. "Le's search the li'l mo'f—r," one of them suggests, "he prolly got it *hid* in his mo'f—n' *pants*." My panic is now unmanageable. (How many times had I been surrounded like this and asked in soft tones, "Len' me a nickel, boy." How many times had I been called a liar for pleading poverty and pushed around, or searched, or beaten up, unless there happened to be someone in the marauding gang like Carl who liked me across that enormous divide of hatred and who would therefore say, "Aaah, c'mon, le's git someone else, this boy ain't got no money on 'im.") I scream at them through tears of rage and self-contempt, "Keep your f—n' filthy lousy black hands offa me! I swear I'll get the cops." This is all they need to hear, and the five of them set upon me. They bang me around, mostly in the stomach and on the arms and shoulders, and when several adults loitering near the candy store down the block notice what is going on and begin to shout, they run off and away.

I do not tell my parents about the incident. My team-mates, who have also been way-laid, each by a gang led by his opposite number from the disqualified team, have had their medallions taken from them, and they never squeal either. For days, I walk home in terror, expecting to be caught again, but nothing happens. The medallion is put away into a drawer, never to be worn by anyone.

Obviously experiences like these have always been a common feature of childhood life in working-class and immigrant neighborhoods, and Negroes do not necessarily figure in them. Wherever, and in whatever combination, they have lived together in the cities, kids of different groups have been at war, beating up and being beaten up: micks against kikes against wops against spicks against polacks. And even relatively homogeneous areas have not been spared the warring of the young: one block against another, one gang (called in my day, in a pathetic effort at gentility, an "S.A.C.," or social-athletic club) against another. But the Negro-white conflict had—and do doubt still has—a special intensity and was conducted with a ferocity unmatched by intramural white battling.

In my own neighborhood, a good deal of animosity existed between the Italian kids (most of whose parents were immigrants from Sicily) and the Jewish kids (who came largely from East European immigrant families). Yet everyone had friends, sometimes close friends, in the other "camp," and we often visited one another's strange-smelling houses, if not for meals, then for glasses of milk, and occasionally for some special event like a wedding or a wake. If it happened that we divided into warring factions and did battle, it would invariably be half-hearted and soon patched up. Our parents, to be sure, had nothing to do with one another and were mutually suspicious and hostile. But we, the kids, who all spoke Yiddish or Italian at home, were Americans, or New Yorkers, or Brooklyn boys: we shared a culture, the culture of the street, and at least for a while this culture proved to be more powerful than the opposing cultures of the home.

Why, why should it have been so different as between the Negroes and us? How was it borne in upon us so early, white and black alike, that we were enemies beyond any possibility of reconciliation? Why did we hate one another so?

I suppose if I tried, I could answer those questions more or less adequately from the perspective of what I have since learned. I could draw upon James Baldwin—what better witness is there?—to describe the sense of entrapment that poisons the soul of the Negro with hatred for the white man whom he knows to be his jailer. On the other side, if I wanted to understand how the white man comes to hate the Negro, I could call upon the psychologists who have spoken of the guilt that white Americans feel toward Negroes and that turns into hatred for lack of acknowledging itself as guilt. These are plausible answers and certainly there is truth in them. Yet when I think back upon my own experience of the Negro and his of me, I find myself troubled and puzzled, much as I was as a child when I heard that all Jews were rich and all Negroes persecuted. How could the Negroes in my neighborhood have regarded the whites across the street and around the corner as jailers? On the whole, the whites were not so poor as the Negroes, but they were quite poor enough, and the years were years of Depression. As for white hatred of the Negro, how could guilt have had anything to do with it? What share had these Italian and Jewish immigrants in the enslavement of the Negro? What share had they—down-trodden people themselves breaking their own necks to eke out a living—in the exploitation of the Negro?

No, I cannot believe that we hated each other back there in Brooklyn because they thought of us as jailers and we felt guilty toward them. But does it matter, given the fact that we all went through an unrepresentative confrontation? I think it matters profoundly, for if we managed the job of hating each other so well without benefit of the aids to hatred that are supposedly at the root of this madness everywhere else, it must mean that the madness is not yet properly understood. I am far from pretending that I understand it, but I would insist that no view of the problem will begin to approach the truth unless it can account for a case like the one I have been trying to describe. Are the elements of any such view available to us?

At least two, I would say, are. One of them is a point we frequently come upon in the work of James Baldwin, and the other is a related point always stressed by psychologists who have studied the mechanisms of prejudice. Baldwin tells us that one of the reasons Negroes hate the white man is that the white man refuses to look at him: the Negro knows that in white eyes all Negroes are alike; they are faceless and therefore not altogether human. The psychologists, in their turn, tell us that the white man hates the Negro because he tends to project those wild impulses that he fears in himself onto an alien group which he then punishes with his contempt. What Baldwin does *not* tell us, however, is that the principle of facelessness is a two-way street and can operate in both directions with no difficulty at all. Thus, in my neighborhood in Brooklyn, *I* was as faceless to the Negroes as they were to me, and if they hated me because I never looked at them, I must also have hated them for never looking at *me*. To the Negroes, my white skin was enough to define me as the enemy, and in a war it is only the uniform that counts and not the person.

So with the mechanism of projection that the psychologists talk about: it too works in both directions at once. There is no question that the psychologists are right about what the Negro represents symbolically to the white man. For me as a child the life lived on the other side of the playground and down the block on Ralph Avenue seemed the very embodiment of the values of the street—free, independent, reckless, brave, masculine, erotic. I put the word "erotic" last, though it is usually stressed above all others, because in fact it came last, in consciousness as in importance. What mainly counted for me about Negro kids of my own age was that they were "bad boys." There were plenty of bad boys among the whites—this was, after all, a neighborhood with a long tradition of crime as a career open to aspiring talents—but the Negroes were *really* bad, bad in a way that beckoned to one, and made one feel inadequate. We all went home every day for a lunch of spinach-and-potatoes; *they* roamed around during lunch hour, munching on candy bars. In winter we had to wear itchy woolen hats and mittens and cumbersome galoshes; they were bareheaded and loose as they pleased. We rarely played hookey, or got into serious trouble in school, for all our street-corner bravado; *they* were defiant, forever staying out (to do what delicious things?), forever making disturbances in class and in the halls, forever being sent to the principal and returning uncowed. But most important of all, they were *tough;* beautifully, enviably tough, not giving a damn for anyone or anything. To hell with the teacher, the truant officer, the cop; to hell with the whole of the adult world that held *us* in its grip and that we never had the courage to rebel against except sporadically and in petty ways.

This is what I saw and envied and feared in the Negro: this is what finally made him faceless to me, though some of it, of course, was actually there. (The psychologists also tell us that the alien group which becomes the object of a projection will tend to respond by trying to live up to what is expected of them.) But what, on his side, did the Negro see in me that made me faceless to *him?* Did he envy me my lunches of spinach-and-potatoes and my itchy woolen caps and my prudent behavior in the face of authority, as I envied him his noon-time candy bars and his bare head in winter and his magnificent rebelliousness? Did those lunches and caps spell for him the prospect of power and riches in the future? Did they mean that there were possibilities open to me that were denied to him? Very likely they did. But if so, one also supposes that he feared the impulses within himself toward submission to authority no less powerfully than I feared the impulses in myself toward defiance. If I represented the jailer to him, it was not because I was oppressing him or keeping him down: it was because I symbolized for him the dangerous and probably pointless temptation toward greater repression, just as he symbolized for me the equally perilous tug toward greater freedom. I personally was to be rewarded for this repression with a new and better life in the future, but how many of my friends paid an even higher price and were given only gall in return.

We have it on the authority of James Baldwin that all Negroes hate whites. I am trying to suggest that on their side all whites—all American whites, that is—are sick in their feelings about Negroes. There are Negroes, no doubt, who would say that Baldwin is wrong, but I suspect them of being less honest than he is, just as I suspect whites of self-deception who tell me they have no special feeling toward Negroes. Special feelings about color are a contagion to which white Americans seem susceptible even when there is nothing in their background to account for the susceptibility. Thus everywhere we look today in the North we find the curious phenomenon of white middle-class liberals with no previous personal experience of Negroes—people to whom Negroes have always been faceless in virtue rather than faceless in vice—discovering that their abstract commitment to the cause of Negro rights will not stand the test of a direct confrontation. We find such people fleeing in droves to the suburbs as the Negro population in the inner city grows; and when they stay in the city we find them sending their children to private school rather than to the "integrated" public school in the neighborhood. We find them resisting the demand that gerrymandered school districts be re-zoned for the purpose of overcoming de facto segregation; we find them judiciously considering whether the Negroes (for their own good, of course) are not perhaps pushing too hard; we find them clucking their tongues over Negro militancy; we find them speculating on the question of whether there may not, after all, be something in the theory that the races are biologically different; we find them saying that it will take a very long time for Negroes to achieve full equality, no matter what anyone does; we find them deploring the rise of black nationalism and expressing the solemn hope that the leaders of the Negro community will discover ways of containing the impatience and incipient violence within the Negro ghettos.

But that is by no means the whole story; there is also the phenomenon of what Kenneth Rexroth[2] once called "crow-jimism."[3] There are the broken-down white boys like Vivaldo Moore in Baldwin's *Another Country* who go to Harlem in search of sex or simply to brush up against something that looks like primitive vitality, and who are so often punished by the Negroes they meet for crimes that they would have been the last ever to

[2]*Kenneth Rexroth* (1905–1982) a poet, writer, and painter best known for his critical essays and his naturalistic erotic poetry.

[3]*crow-jimism* a play on the term "Jim Crow Laws," which were in effect in the United States, particularly in the South, from the 1880s to the 1960s. The Jim Crow laws prohibited interracial marriages, schools, and public institutions, and were used primarily to oppress African-Americans.

commit and of which they themselves have been as sorry victims as any of the Negroes who take it out on them. There are the writers and intellectuals and artists who romanticize Negroes and pander to them, assuming a guilt that is not properly theirs. And there are all the white liberals who permit Negroes to blackmail them into adopting a double standard of moral judgment, and who lend themselves—again assuming the responsibility for crimes they never committed—to cunning and contemptuous exploitation by Negroes they employ or try to befriend.

And what about me? What kind of feelings do I have about Negroes today? What happened to me, from Brooklyn, who grew up fearing and envying and hating Negroes? Now that Brooklyn is behind me, do I fear them and envy them and hate them still? The answer is yes, but not in the same proportions and certainly not in the same way. I now live on the upper west side of Manhattan, where there are many Negroes and many Puerto Ricans, and there are nights when I experience the old apprehensiveness again, and there are streets that I avoid when I am walking in the dark, as there were streets that I avoided when I was a child. I find that I am not afraid of Puerto Ricans, but I cannot restrain my nervousness whenever I pass a group of Negroes standing in front of a bar or sauntering down the street. I know now, as I did not know when I was a child, that power is on my side, that the police are working for me and not for them. And knowing this I feel ashamed and guilty, like the good liberal I have grown up to be. Yet the twinges of fear and the resentment they bring and the self-contempt they arouse are not to be gainsaid.

But envy? Why envy? And hatred? Why hatred? Here again the intensities have lessened and everything has been complicated and qualified by the guilts and the resulting over-compensations that are the heritage of the enlightened middle-class world of which I am now a member. Yet just as in childhood I envied Negroes for what seemd to me their superior masculinity, so I envy them today for what seems to me their superior physical grace and beauty. I have come to value physical grace very highly, and I am now capable of aching with all my being when I watch a Negro couple on the dance floor, or a Negro playing baseball or basketball. They are on the kind of terms with their own bodies that I should like to be on with mine, and for that precious quality they seemed blessed to me.

The hatred I still feel for Negroes is the hardest of all the old feelings to face or admit, and it is the most hidden and the most overlarded by the conscious attitudes into which I have succeeded in willing myself. It no longer has, as for me it once did, any cause or justification (except, perhaps, that I am constantly being denied my right to an honest expression of the things I earned the right as a child to feel). How, then, do I know that this hatred has never entirely disappeared? I know it from the insane rage that can stir in me at the thought of Negro anti-Semitism; I know it from the disgusting prurience that can stir in me at the sight of a mixed couple; and I know it from the violence that can stir in me whenever I encounter that special brand of paranoid touchiness to which many Negroes are prone.

This, then, is where I am; it is not exactly where I think all other white liberals are, but it cannot be so very far away either. And it is because I am convinced that we white Americans are—for whatever reason, it no longer matters—so twisted and sick in our feelings about Negroes that I despair of the present push toward integration. If the pace of progress were not a factor here, there would perhaps be no cause for despair: time and the law and even the international political situation are on the side of the Negroes, and ultimately, therefore, victory—of a sort, anyway—must come. But from everything we have learned from observers who ought to know, pace has become as important to the Negroes as substance. They want equality and they want it now, and the white world is yielding to their demand only as much and as fast as it is absolutely being compelled to do. The Negroes know this in the most concrete terms imaginable, and it is thus becoming increasingly difficult to buy them off with rhetoric and promises and pious assurances of support. And so within the Negro community we find more and more people declaring—as Harold R. Isaacs recently put it in an article in *Commentary*—that they want *out:* people who say that integration will never come, or that it will take a hundred or a thousand years to come, or that it will come at too high a price in suffering and struggle for the pallid and sodden life of the American middle class that at the very best it may bring.

The most numerous, influential, and dangerous movement that has grown out of Negro despair with the goal of integration is, of course, the Black Muslims.[4] This movement, whatever else we may say about it, must be credited with one enduring achievement: it inspired James Baldwin to write an essay which deserves to be placed among the classics of our language. Everything Baldwin has ever been trying to tell us is distilled in *The Fire Next Time* into a statement of overwhelming persuasiveness and prophetic magnificence. Baldwin's message is and always has been simple. It is this: "Color is not a human or personal reality; it is a political reality." And Baldwin's demand is correspondingly simple; color must be forgotten, lest we all be smited with a vengeance "that does not really depend on, and cannot really be executed by, any person or organization, and that cannot be prevented by any police force or army: historical vengeance, a cosmic vengeance based on the law that we recognize when we say, 'Whatever goes up must come down.'" The Black Muslims Baldwin portrays as a sign and a warning to the intransigent white world. They come to proclaim how deep is the Negro's disaffection with the white world and all its works, and Baldwin implies that no American Negro can fail to respond somewhere in his being to their message: that the white man is the devil, that Allah has doomed him to destruction, and that the black man is about to inherit the earth. Baldwin of course knows that this nightmare inversion of the racism from which the black man has suffered can neither win nor even point to the neighborhood in which victory might be located. For in his view the neighborhood of victory lies in exactly the opposite direction: the transcendence of color through love.

Yet the tragic fact is that love is not the answer to hate—not in the world of politics, at any rate. Color is indeed a political rather than a human or a personal reality and if politics (which is to say power) has made it into a human and personal reality, then only politics (which is to say power) can unmake it once again. But the way of politics is slow and bitter, and as impatience on the one side is matched by a setting of the jaw on the other, we move closer and closer to an explosion and blood may yet run in the streets.

Will this madness in which we are all caught never find a resting-place? Is there never to be an end to it? In thinking about the Jews I have often wondered whether their survival as a distinct group was worth one hair on the head of a single infant. Did the Jews have to survive so that six million innocent people should one day be burned in the ovens of Auschwitz? It is a terrible question and no one, not God himself, could ever answer it to my satisfaction. And when I think about the Negroes in America and about the image

[4]*Black Muslims* followers of a predominantly black religious movement in the United States, who profess Islam as their faith and whose leaders have included Elijah Muhammed, Malcom X, and Louis Farrakhan.

of integration as a state in which the Negroes would take their rightful place as another of the protected minorities in a pluralistic society, I wonder whether they really believe in their hearts that such a state can actually be attained, and if so why they should wish to survive as a distinct group. I think I know why the Jews once wished to survive (though I am less certain as to why we still do): they not only believed that God had given them no choice, but they were tied to a memory of past glory and a dream of imminent redemption. What does the American Negro have that might correspond to this? His past is a stigma, his color is a stigma, and his vision of the future is the hope of erasing the stigma by making color irrelevant, by making it disappear as a fact of consciousness.

I share this hope, but I cannot see how it will ever be realized unless color does *in fact* disappear: and that means not integration, it means assimilation, it means—let the brutal word come out—miscegenation.[5] The Black Muslims, like their racist counterparts in the white world, accuse the "so-called Negro leaders" of secretly pursuing miscegenation as a goal. The racists are wrong, but I wish they were right, for I believe that the wholesale merger of the two races is the most desirable alternative for everyone concerned. I am not claiming that this alternative can be pursued programmatically or that it is immediately feasible as a solution; obviously there are even greater barriers to its achievement than to the achievement of integration. What I am saying, however, is that in my opinion the Negro problem can be solved in this country in no other way.

I have told the story of my own twisted feelings about Negroes here, and of how they conflict with the moral convictions I have since developed, in order to assert that such feelings must be acknowledged as honestly as possible so that they can be controlled and ultimately disregarded in favor of the convictions. It is *wrong* for a man to suffer because of the color of his skin. Beside that clichéd proposition of liberal thought, what argument can stand and be respected? If the arguments are the arguments of feeling, they must be made to yield; and one's own soul is not the worst place to begin working a huge social transformation. Not so long ago, it used to be asked of white liberals, "Would you like your sister to marry one?" When I was a boy and my sister was still unmarried I would certainly have said no to that question. But now I am a man, my sister is already married, and I have daughters. If I were to be asked today whether I would like a daughter of mine "to marry one." I would have to answer: "No, I wouldn't *like* it at all. I would rail and rave and rant and tear my hair. And then I hope I would have the courage to curse myself for raving and ranting, and to give her my blessing. How dare I withhold it at the behest of the child I once was and against the man I now have a duty to be?"

Understanding and Analysis

1. What were Podhoretz's sources of information about Jews and African-Americans when he was growing up in Brooklyn? In what ways did the information from those sources conflict?

2. When does Podhoretz believe his feelings of hatred for African-Americans first began?

3. Characterize both the young Podhoretz as he describes himself in the two sections marked "Item" and the African-American children he grew up with.

[5]*miscegenation* interbreeding of races.

4. In the section beginning "Obviously experiences like these have always been a common feature of childhood life in working-class and immigrant neighborhoods," Podhoretz is putting his memories into a wider context. What is it?

5. What, according to Podhoretz, are the answers given by psychologists and by the writings of James Baldwin to explain why the black and white children that Podhoretz grew up with hated each other so much?

6. Why does Podhoretz reject these explanations? Do you think that children are aware of subtle distinctions in the levels of poverty?

7. What is it about his experiences that Podhoretz believes to be "unrepresentative"?

8. What are the two further explanations of the hatred between African-American and white children that Podhoretz explores?

9. What, according to Podhoretz, created the stereotypes that each side saw in the other?

10. What new information about the relationships between the black and white children emerges in the paragraph on projection? Why does Podhoretz use so many rhetorical questions to convey his ideas in the following paragraph? How do these ideas compare to the two original explanations offered for the hatred between African-Americans and whites?

11. What is Podhoretz's attitude toward James Baldwin?

12. What is Podhoretz's attitude toward the "white middle-class liberals"? To what degree would he label himself as one of them?

13. Podhoretz's views toward African-Americans in 1964 are complex. What contradictory feelings does he hold? Does he agree with Baldwin?

14. How does Podhoretz believe the political problem of color will be overcome?

15. How has Podhoretz matured in his thinking since his childhood, when he compared what he read to what he had experienced?

16. How important do you think religion and class are in this analysis of race relations in 1964?

Comparison

1. Read King's "Letter from Birmingham Jail." In what specific areas do Podhoretz and King agree?

2. Read Lippmann's "Stereotypes." Does this essay help to explain some of Podhoretz's reactions?

3. Read the essays by Baldwin in this collection. Do you see any similarities in the ideas or techniques of Baldwin and Podhoretz?

Loren Eiseley
(1907–1977)

For Loren Eiseley, childhood was not an especially pleasant experience. Growing up in a lower-class home in Lincoln, Nebraska, Eiseley served as a reluctant witness to the daily tensions between his father and his "savage and stone-deaf mother," whom he detested as much for her violent tendencies as for the sound of her voice. He sought mental escape from the family's unhappiness in the books he read, the insects he studied, and, eventually, the things he created. According to biographer Gale Christianson, Eiseley spent hours in "a tall red-brick building on the University of Nebraska campus simply known as the Museum," which housed "extensive exhibits on anthropology, zoology, geology, and archaeology." Captivated by the skulls he saw in the exhibits, Eiseley began to fashion his own skulls out of clay, baking them in the oven with the assistance of his grandmother. Almost all of these skulls, Eiseley later recalled, were "slope-browed and primitive"; they had what his grandmother called "that Darwin look." Loren displayed his skulls in an old, empty barn near his home, creating as his biographers observe, a museum of his own.

During high school, Eiseley developed another defining interest: writing. He entered the University of Nebraska in 1925, and in 1927, he became an associate editor for the school's literary magazine, *The Prairie Schooner*, which published his first poem a year later. While he clearly excelled at writing, publishing nearly 70 poems between the late 1920s and the mid-1930s, Eiseley was not interested in a career in the field of English. Beset with uncertainty about what his career would be and plagued by illness, he phased in and out of college. In the early 1930s, he struck upon a job that ultimately led him to his life's work: he hunted for fossils for the museum. During the summers, he participated in challenging expeditions, battling bad roads, floods, heat, even the bones he was supposed to be excavating: "There was an eroding hill in the vicinity, and on top of that hill, just below sod cover, were the foot bones, hundreds of them, of some lost Tertiary species of American rhinocerous.... [W]e dug carpals and metacarpals till we cursed like an army platoon that headquarters has forgotten." Despite these passing frustrations, Eiseley loved the work of excavation. After eight years of undergraduate work, he took his degree in 1933 and decided to study anthropology at the graduate level. He earned his Ph.D. from the University of Pennsylvania in 1937, and quickly found work teaching sociology and anthropology at the University of Kansas. In 1938, he married Mabel Langdon, a curator to whom he had become engaged during college.

According to biographer E. Fred Carlisle, Eiseley remained at the University of Kansas into the 1940s, "teaching enlisted reservists in the premedical program" during the war. By the time he returned to the University of Pennsylvania to become the chairman of the anthropology department in 1947, he had published more than two dozen pieces, many of them professional, scientific articles, and some of them personal essays. In his first year as chair, as he suffered through a prolonged ear infection that rendered him temporarily deaf, he hit upon a kind of realization about fusing these two kinds of writing. He explains in his autobiography, "While I floundered in utter silence, a scientifically oriented magazine which had requested an article from me upon human evolution reneged in favor of a more distinguished visitor to America....I had done a lot of work on this article, but since my market was gone, why not attempt a more literary venture?...I shifted away from the article as originally intended. A personal anecdote introduced it, personal material lay scattered through it, personal philosophy concluded it, and yet I had done no harm to the scientific data." This realization yielded what Eiseley referred to as the "concealed" anecdotal essay, simultaneously scientific and personal; it also freed Eiseley to write about scientific matters in elaborate literary language. Publishing essays in several magazines, Eiseley then collected and revised them for his first book, *The Immense Journey*, in 1957. It received excellent reviews and hardly a word of criticism, demonstrating the power of Eiseley's new style.

In 1959, a year after he published his first book about the history of science, *Darwin's Century*, Eiseley accepted an appointment as provost. He published the award-winning *Firmament of Time* (1960) while serving in this position, but he did not serve in administration long, refusing several offers for college presidencies in order to remain at Penn teaching anthropology and the history of science. In 1962, he published *The Mind as Nature*, and in 1963, *Francis Bacon and the Modern Dilemma*. While these books did nothing to hurt his national celebrity, they surely did not promote it, as did "Animal Secrets," the television program he hosted between 1966 and 1968. He ushered in the 1970s with *The Invisible Pyramid* (1970) and *The Night Country* (1971), and then he turned to still more purely personal writing, publishing volumes of poetry called *Notes of an Alchemist* (1972) and *The Innocent Assassins* (1973), as well as his autobiography, *All the Strange Hours* (1975). In 1976, he received the Bradford Washburn Award for "outstanding contribution to the public understanding of science." He died of cancer the following July.

For his poetry, Loren Eiseley often received terrible reviews. For the poetry in his prose, however, he often received glorious praise. The passage of time, the reproductive strategies of plants, the silence of sea creatures—all these, in Eiseley's descriptions, take on epic, mystic dimensions, for he casts even spores in a spiritual and evolutionary drama that gives meaning to the smallest thing. In Eiseley's cosmos, indeed, mice and birds and wasps share futile dreams with human beings. While this style makes fascinating reading, it has also brought Eiseley under fire for a lack of strict scientific rigor. Writing for the *Nation*, critic Harold Fruchtbaum faults Eiseley with oversimplification and intellectual irresponsibility, yet as Fruchtbaum himself admits, "He is a stimulating teacher for the layman, and that is by no means a small accomplishment." One of Eiseley's greatest accomplishments, in the final analysis, is the "concealed" essay, the form that allowed him to fuse not only two writing styles, but two parts of himself, the poet and the scientist, the trained anthropologist and the curious man. With the concealed essay, Eiseley captured the interest of his contemporaries and may capture the interest of future generations as well. As Ray Bradbury said of *The Night Country*, Eiseley's works "will have more substance, warm breath and good blood" thirty years into the future "than 99 out of 100 writers who say they are alive today."

THE ILLUSION OF THE TWO CULTURES (1964)

NOT LONG AGO an English scientist, Sir Eric Ashby, remarked that "To train young people in the dialectic between orthodoxy and dissent is the unique contribution which universities make to society." I am sure that Sir Eric meant by this remark that nowhere but in universities are the young given the opportunity to absorb past tradition and at the same time to experience the impact of new ideas—in the sense of a constant dialogue between past and present—lived in every hour of the students' existence. This dialogue, ideally, should lead to a great winnowing and sifting of experience and to a heightened consciousness of self which, in turn, should lead on to greater sensitivity and perception on the part of the individual.

Our lives are the creation of memory and the accompanying power to extend ourselves outward into ideas and relive them. The finest intellect is that which employs an invisible web of gossamer running into the past as well as across the minds of living men, and which constantly responds to the vibrations transmitted through these tenuous lines of sympathy. It would be contrary to fact, however, to assume that our universities always perform this unique function of which Sir Eric speaks, with either grace or perfection; in fact our investment in man, it has been justly remarked, is deteriorating even as the financial investment in science grows.

Over thirty years ago, George Santayana had already sensed this trend. He commented, in a now forgotten essay, that one of the strangest consequences of modern science was that as the visible wealth of nature was more and more transferred and abstracted, the mind seemed to lose courage and to become ashamed of its own fertility. "The hardpressed natural man will not indulge his imagination," continued Santayana, "unless it poses for truth; and being half-aware of this imposition, he is more troubled at the thought of being deceived than at the fact of being mechanized or being bored; and he would wish to escape imagination altogether."

"Man would wish to escape imagination altogether." I repeat that last phrase, for it defines a peculiar aberration of the human mind found on both sides of that bipolar division between the humanities and the sciences, which C. P. Snow has popularized under the title of the two cultures. The idea is not solely a product of this age. It was already emerging with the science of the seventeenth century; one finds it in Bacon. One finds the fear of it faintly foreshadowed in Thoreau. Thomas Huxley lent it weight when he referred contemptuously to the "caterwauling of poets."

Ironically, professional scientists berated the early evolutionists such as Lamarck and Chambers for overindulgence in the imagination. Almost eighty years ago John Burroughs observed that some of the animus once directed by science toward dogmatic theology seemed in his day increasingly to be vented upon the literary naturalist. In the early 1900's a quarrel over "nature faking" raised a confused din in America and aroused W. H. Hudson to some dry and pungent comment upon the failure to distinguish the purposes of science from those of literature. I know of at least one scholar who, venturing to develop some personal ideas in an essay for the layman, was characterized by a reviewer in a leading professional journal as a worthless writer, although, as it chanced, the work under discussion had received several awards in literature, one of them international in scope. More recently, some scholars not indifferent to humanistic values have exhorted poets to leave their personal songs in order to portray the beauty and symmetry of molecular structures.

Now some very fine verse has been written on scientific subjects, but, I fear, very little under the dictate of scientists as such. Rather there is evident here, precisely that restriction of imagination against which Santayana inveighed; namely, an attempt to constrain literature itself to the delineation of objective or empiric truth, and to dismiss the whole domain of value, which after all constitutes the very nature of man, as without significance and beneath contempt.

Unconsciously, the human realm is denied in favor of the world of pure technics. Man, the tool user, grows convinced that he is himself only useful as a tool, that fertility except in the use of the scientific imagination is wasteful and without purpose, even, in some indefinable way, sinful. I was reading J. R. R. Tolkien's great symbolic trilogy, *The Fellowship of the Ring,* a few months ago, when a young scientist of my acquaintance paused and looked over my shoulder. After a little casual interchange the man departed leaving an accusing remark hovering in the air between us. "I wouldn't waste my time with a man who writes fairy stories." He might as well have added, "or with a man who reads them."

As I went back to my book I wondered vaguely in what leafless landscape one grew up without Hans Christian Andersen, or Dunsany, or even Jules Verne. There lingered about the young man's words a puritanism which seemed the more remarkable because, as nearly as I could discover, it was unmotivated by any sectarian religiosity unless a total dedication to science brings to some minds a similar authoritarian desire to shackle the human imagination. After all, it is this impossible, fertile world of our imagination which gave birth to liberty in the midst of oppression, and which persists in seeking until what is sought is seen. Against such invisible and fearful powers, there can be found in all ages and in all institutions—even the institutions of professional learning the humorless man with the sneer, or if the sneer does not suffice, then the torch, for the bright unperishing letters of the human dream.

One can contrast this recalcitrant attitude with an 1890 reminiscence from that great Egyptologist, Sir Flinders Petrie, which steals over into the realm of pure literature. It was written, in unconscious symbolism, from a tomb:

> I here live, and do not scramble to fit myself to the requirements of others. In a narrow tomb, with the figure of Néfermaat standing on each side of me—as he has stood through all that we know as human history—I have just room for my bed, and a row of good reading in

which I can take pleasure after dinner. Behind me is that Great Peace, the Desert. It is an entity—a power—just as much as the sea is. No wonder men fled to it from the turmoil of the ancient world.

It may now reasonably be asked why one who has similarly, if less dramatically, spent his life among the stones and broken shards of the remote past should be writing here about matters involving literature and science. It was while considering this with humility and trepidation that my eye fell upon a stone in my office. I am sure that professional journalists must recall times when an approaching deadline has keyed all their senses and led them to glance wildly around in the hope that something might leap out at them from the most prosaic surroundings. At all events my eyes fell upon this stone.

Now the stone antedated anything that the historians would call art; it had been shaped many hundreds of thousands of years ago by men whose faces would frighten us if they sat among us today. Out of old habit, since I like the feel of worked flint, I picked it up and hefted it as I groped for words over this difficult matter of the growing rift between science and art. Certainly the stone was of no help to me; it was a utilitarian thing which had cracked marrow bones, if not heads, in the remote dim morning of the human species. It was nothing if not practical. It was, in fact, an extremely early example of the empirical tradition which has led on to modern science.

The mind which had shaped this artifact knew its precise purpose. It had found out by experimental observation, that the stone was tougher, sharper, more enduring than the hand which wielded it. The creature's mind had solved the question of the best form of the implement and how it could be manipulated most effectively. In its day and time this hand ax was as grand an intellectual achievement as a rocket.

As a scientist my admiration went out to that unidentified workman. How he must have labored to understand the forces involved in the fracturing of flint, and all that involved practical survival in his world. My uncalloused twentieth-century hand caressed the yellow stone lovingly. It was then that I made a remarkable discovery.

In the mind of this gross-featured, early exponent of the practical approach to nature— the technician, the no-nonsense practitioner of survival—two forces had met and merged. There had not been room in his short and desperate life for the delicate and supercilious separation of the arts from the sciences. There did not exist then the refined distinctions set up between the scholarly precipience of reality and what has sometimes been called the vaporings of the artistic imagination.

As I clasped and unclasped the stone, running my fingers down its edges, I began to perceive the ghostly emanations from a long-vanished mind, the kind of mind which, once having shaped an object of any sort, leaves an individual trace behind it which speaks to others across the barriers of time and language. It was not the practical experimental aspect of this mind that startled me, but rather that the fellow had wasted time.

In an incalculably brutish and dangerous world he had both shaped an instrument of practical application and then, with a virtuoso's elegance, proceeded to embellish his product. He had not been content to produce a plain, utilitarian implement. In some wistful, inarticulate way, in the grip of the dim aesthetic feelings which are one of the marks of man—or perhaps I should say, some men—this archaic creature had lingered over his handiwork.

One could still feel him crouching among the stones on a long-vanished river bar, turning the thing over in his hands, feeling its polished surface, striking, here and there, just one more blow that no longer had usefulness as its criterion. He had, like myself, enjoyed the texture of the stone. With skills lost to me, he had gone on flaking the implement with an eye to beauty until it had become a kind of rough jewel, equivalent in its day, to the carved and gold inlaid pommel of the iron dagger placed in Tutankhamen's tomb.

All the later history of man contains these impractical exertions expended upon a great diversity of objects, and, with literacy, breaking even into printed dreams. Today's secular disruption between the creative aspect of art and that of science is a barbarism that would have brought lifted eyebrows in a Cro-Magnon cave. It is a product of high technical specialization, the deliberate blunting of wonder, and the equally deliberate suppression of a phase of our humanity in the name of an authoritarian institution: science, which has taken on, in our time, curious puritanical overtones. Many scientists seem unaware of the historical reasons for this development, or the fact that the creative aspect of art is not so remote from that of science as may seem, at first glance, to be the case.

I am not so foolish as to categorize individual scholars or scientists. I am, however, about to remark on the nature of science as an institution. Like all such structures it is apt to reveal certain behavioral rigidities and conformities which increase with age. It is no longer the domain of the amateur, though some of its greatest discoverers could be so defined. It is now a professional body, and with professionalism there tends to emerge a greater emphasis upon a coherent system of regulations. The deviant is more sharply treated, and the young tend to imitate their successful elders. In short, an "Establishment"—a trade union—has appeared.

Similar tendencies can be observed among those of the humanities concerned with the professional analysis and interpretation of the works of the creative artist. Here too, a similar rigidity and exclusiveness make their appearance. It is not that in the case of both the sciences and the humanities standards are out of place. What I am briefly cautioning against is that too frequently they afford an excuse for stifling original thought, or constricting much latent creativity within traditional molds.

Such molds are always useful to the mediocre conformist who instinctively castigates and rejects what he cannot imitate. Tradition, the continuity of learning, are, it is true, enormously important to the learned disciplines. What we must realize as scientists is that the particular institution we inhabit has its own irrational accretions and authoritarian dogmas which can be as unpleasant as some of those encountered in sectarian circles—particularly so since they are frequently unconsciously held and surrounded by an impenetrable wall of self-righteousness brought about because science is regarded as totally empiric and open-minded by tradition.

This type of professionalism, as I shall label it, in order to distinguish it from what is best in both the sciences and humanities, is characterized by two assumptions: that the accretions of fact are cumulative and lead to progress, whereas the insights of art are, at best, singular, and lead nowhere, or, when introduced into the realm of science, produce obscurity and confusion. The convenient label "mystic" is, in our day, readily applied to men who pause for simple wonder, or who encounter along the borders of the known, that "awful power" which Wordsworth characterized as the human imagination. It can, he says, rise suddenly from the mind's abyss and enwrap the solitary traveler like a mist.

We do not like mists in this era, and the word *imagination* is less and less used. We like, instead, a clear road, and we abhor solitary traveling. Indeed one of our great scientific historians remarked not long ago that the literary naturalist was obsolescent if not completely outmoded. I suppose he meant that with our penetration into the biophysical realm, life, like matter, would become increasingly represented by abstract symbols. To many it must appear that the more we can dissect life into its elements, the closer we are getting to its ultimate resolution. While I have some reservations on this score, they are not important. Rather, I should like to look at the symbols which in the one case, denote science and, in the other constitute those vaporings and cloud wraiths that are the abomination, so it is said, of the true scientist, but are the delight of the poet and literary artist.

Creation in science demands a high level of imaginative insight and intuitive perception. I believe no one would deny this, even though it exists in varying degrees, just as it does, similarly, among writers, musicians, or artists. The scientist's achievement, however, is quantitatively transmissible. From a single point his discovery is verifiable by other men who may then, on the basis of corresponding data, accept the innovation and elaborate upon it in the cumulative fashion which is one of the great triumphs of science.

Artistic creation, on the other hand, is unique. It cannot be twice discovered as, say, natural selection was discovered. It may be imitated stylistically, in a genre, a school, but, save for a few items of technique, it is not cumulative. A successful work of art may set up reverberations and is, in this, just as transmissible as science, but there is a qualitative character about it. Each reverberation in another mind is unique. As the French novelist François Mauriac has remarked, each great novel is a separate and distinct world operating under its own laws with a flora and fauna totally its own. There is communication, or the work is a failure, but the communication releases our own visions, touches some highly personal chord in our own experience.

The symbols used by the great artist are a key releasing our humanity from the solitary tower of the self. "Man," says Lewis Mumford, "is first and foremost the self-fabricating animal." I will merely add that the artist plays an enormous role in this act of self-creation. It is he who touches the hidden strings of pity, who searches our hearts, who makes us sensitive to beauty, who asks questions about fate and destiny. Such questions, though they lurk always around the corners of the external universe which is the peculiar province of science, the rigors of the scientific method do not enable us to pursue directly.

And yet I wonder.

It is surely possible to observe that it is the successful analogy or symbol which frequently allows the scientist to leap from a generalization in one field of thought to a triumphant achievement in another. For example, Progressionism in a spiritual sense later became the model contributing to the discovery of organic evolution. Such analogies genuinely resemble the figures and enchantments of great literature, whose meanings similarly can never be totally grasped because of their endless power to ramify in the individual mind.

John Donne, in the seventeenth century, gave powerful expression to a feeling applicable as much to science as to literature when he said devoutly of certain Biblical passages: "The literall sense is always to be preserved; but the literall sense is not always to be discerned; for the literall sense is not always that which the very letter and grammar of the place presents."—A figurative sense, he argues cogently, can sometimes be the most "literall intention of the Holy Ghost."

It is here that the scientist and artist sometimes meet in uneasy opposition, or at least along lines of tension. The scientist's attitude is sometimes, I suspect, that embodied in Samuel Johnson's remark that, wherever there is mystery, roguery is not far off.

Yet surely it was not roguery when Sir Charles Lyell glimpsed in a few fossil prints of raindrops the persistence of the world's natural forces through the incredible, mysterious aeons of geologic time. The fossils were a symbol of a vast hitherto unglimpsed order. They are, in Donne's sense, both literal and symbolic. As fossils they merely denote evidence of rain in a past era. Figuratively they are more. To the perceptive intelligence they afford the hint of lengthened natural order, just as the eyes of ancient trilobites tell us similarly of the unchanging laws of light. Equally, the educated mind may discern in a scratched pebble the retreating shadow of vast ages of ice and gloom. In Donne's archaic phraseology these objects would bespeak the principal intention of the Divine Being, that is, of order beyond our power to grasp.

Such images drawn from the world of science are every bit as powerful as great literary symbolism and equally as demanding upon the individual imagination of the scientist who would fully grasp the extension of meaning which is involved. It is, in fact, one and the same creative act in both domains.

Indeed evolution itself has become such a figurative symbol, as has also the hypothesis of the expanding universe. The laboratory worker may think of these concepts in a totally empirical fashion as subject to proof or disproof by the experimental method. Like Freud's doctrine of the subconscious, however, such ideas frequently escape from the professional scientist into the public domain. There they may undergo further individual transformation and embellishment. Whether the scholar approves or not, such hypotheses are now as free to evolve as the creations of art in the mind of the individual. All the resulting enrichment and confusion will bear about it something suggestive of the world of artistic endeavor.

As figurative insights into the nature of things, such embracing conceptions may become grotesquely distorted or glow with added philosophical wisdom. As in the case of the trilobite eye or the fossil raindrop, there lurks behind the visible evidence vast shadows no longer quite of that world which we term natural. Like the words in Donne's Bible enormous implications have transcended the literal expression of the thought. Reality itself has been superseded by a greater reality. As Donne himself asserted, "The substance of the truth is in the great images which lie behind."

It is because these two types of creation—the artistic and the scientific—have sprung from the same being and have their points of contact even in division, that I have the temerity to assert that, in a sense, the two cultures are an illusion, that they are a product of unreasoning fear, professionalism, and misunderstanding. Because of the emphasis upon science in our society, much has been said about the necessity of educating the layman and even the professional student of the humanities upon the ways and the achievements of science. I admit that a barrier exists, but I am also concerned to express the view that there persists in the domain of science itself, an occasional marked intolerance of those of its own membership who venture to pursue the way of letters. As I have previously remarked, this intolerance can the more successfully clothe itself in seeming objectivity because of the supposed open nature of the scientific society. It is not remarkable that this trait is sometimes more manifest in the younger and less secure disciplines.

There was a time, not too many centuries ago, when to be active in scientific investigation was to invite suspicion. Thus it may be that there now lingers among us, even in the triumph of the experimental method, a kind of vague fear of that other artistic world of deep emotion, of strange symbols, lest it seize upon us or distort the hard-won objectivity of our thinking—lest it corrupt, in other words, that crystalline and icy objectivity which, in our scientific guise, we erect as a model of conduct. This model, incidentally, if pursued to its absurd conclusion, would lead to a world in which the computer would determine all aspects of our existence; one in which the bomb would be as welcome as the discoveries of the physician.

Happily, the very great in science, or even those unique scientist-artists such as Leonardo, who foreran the emergence of science as an institution, have been singularly free from this folly. Darwin decried it even as he recognized that he had paid a certain price in concentrated specialization for his achievement. Einstein, it is well known, retained a simple sense of wonder; Newton felt like a child playing with pretty shells on a beach. All show a deep humility and an emotional hunger which is the prerogative of the artist. It is with the lesser men, with the institutionalization of method, with the appearance of dogma and mapped-out territories that an unpleasant suggestion of fenced preserves begins to dominate the university atmosphere.

As a scientist, I can say that I have observed it in my own and others' specialties. I have had occasion, also, to observe its effects in the humanities. It is not science *per se;* it is, instead, in both regions of thought, the narrow professionalism which is also plainly evident in the trade union. There can be small men in science just as there are small men in government, or business. In fact it is one of the disadvantages of big science, just as it is of big government, that the availability of huge sums attracts a swarm of elbowing and contentious men to whom great dreams are less than protected hunting preserves.

The sociology of science deserves at least equal consideration with the biographies of the great scientists, for powerful and changing forces are at work upon science, the institution, as contrasted with science as a dream and an ideal of the individual. Like other aspects of society, it is a construct of men, and is subject, like other social structures, to human pressures and inescapable distortions.

Let me give you an illustration. Even in learned journals, clashes occasionally occur between those who would regard biology as a separate and distinct domain of inquiry and the reductionists who, by contrast, perceive in the living organism only a vaster and more random chemistry. Understandably, the concern of the reductionists is with the immediate. Thomas Hobbes was expressing a similar point of view when he castigated poets as "working on mean minds with words and distinctions that of themselves signifie nothing, but betray (by their obscurity) that there walketh . . . another kingdome, as it were a kingdome of fayries in the dark." I myself have been similarly criticized for speaking of a nature "beyond the nature that we know."

Yet consider for a moment this dark, impossible realm of Fayrie. Man is not totally compounded of the nature we profess to understand. He contains, instead, a lurking unknown future, just as the man-apes of the Pliocene contained in embryo the future that surrounds us now. The world of human culture itself was an unpredictable fairy world until, in some Pre-Ice-Age meadow, the first meaningful sounds in all the world broke through the jungle babble of the past, the nature, until that moment, "known."

It is fascinating to observe that, in the very dawn of science, Bacon, the spokesman for the empirical approach to nature, shared with Shakespeare, the poet, a recognition of the creativeness which adds to nature, and which emerges from nature as "an art which nature makes." Neither the great scholar nor the great poet had renounced the kingdome of Fayrie. They had realized what Bergson was later to express so effectively, that life inserts a vast "indetermination into matter." It is, in a sense, an intrusion from a realm which can never be completely subject to prophetic analysis by science. The novelties of evolution emerge; they cannot be predicted. They haunt, until their arrival, a world of unimaginable possibilities behind the living screen of events, as these last exist to the observer confined to a single point on the time scale.

Oddly enough, much of the confusion that surrounded my phrase, "a nature beyond the nature that we know," resolves itself into pure semantics. I might have pointed out what must be obvious even to the most dedicated scientific mind that the nature which we know has been many times reinterpreted in human thinking, and that the hard, substantial matter of the nineteenth century has already vanished into a dark, bodiless void, a web of "events" in space-time. This is a realm, I venture to assert, as weird as any we have tried, in the past, to exorcise by the brave use of seeming solid words. Yet some minds exhibit an almost instinctive hostility toward the mere attempt to wonder, or to ask what lies below that microcosmic world out of which emerge the particles which compose our bodies, and which now take on this wraith-like quality.

Is there something here we fear to face, except when clothed in safely sterilized professional speech? Have we grown reluctant in this age of power to admit mystery and beauty into our thoughts, or to learn where power ceases? I referred a few moments ago to one of our own forebears on a gravel bar, thumbing a pebble. If, after the ages of building and destroying, if after the measuring of light-years, and the powers probed at the atom's heart, if after the last iron is rust-eaten and the last glass lies shattered in the streets, a man, some savage, some remnant of what once we were, pauses on his way to the tribal drinking place and feels rising from within his soul the inexplicable mist of terror and beauty that is evoked from old ruins—even the ruins of the greatest city in the world—then, I say, all will still be well with man.

And if that savage can pluck a stone from the gravel because it shone like crystal when the water rushed over it, and hold it against the sunset, he will be as we were in the beginning, whole—as we were when we were children, before we began to split the knowledge from the dream. All talk of the two cultures is an illusion; it is the pebble which tells man's story. Upon it is written man's two faces, the artistic and the practical. They are expressed upon one stone over which a hand once closed, no less firm because the mind behind it was submerged in light and shadow and deep wonder.

Today we hold a stone, the heavy stone of power. We must perceive beyond it, however, by the aid of the artistic imagination, those humane insights and understandings which alone can lighten our burden and enable us to shape ourselves, rather than the stone, into the forms which great art has anticipated.

Understanding and Analysis

1. In the first sentence, Eiseley quotes Sir Eric Ashby and then interprets that quotation. What do both men claim the special task of the university to be? What elements from Ashby's comment does Eiseley emphasize, and what does he appear to ignore in his interpretation? As you read the rest of the essay, note instances of "orthodoxy and dissent."

2. What does Eiseley believe to be the ideal result of the "constant dialogue between past and present"?

3. In what way does Eiseley believe the universities may be failing in this function? How does the quotation from Santayana help to explain what Eiseley means?

4. What is the point of the next paragraphs describing past attitudes toward the imagination within the scientific community?

5. What does Eiseley claim was happening to literature at the time of the writing of this essay? What is his evidence? What is the purpose of the extended quotation from Sir Flinders Petrie?

6. How does Eiseley guide the reader's attention to the stone?

7. Describe the character who Eiseley imagines made this stone tool.

8. What does Eiseley say about science as an institution?

9. In what ways are the humanities similar, according to Eiseley?

10. What are the assumptions of "professionalism"?

11. Describe the distinctions between science and art, according to Eiseley. Do you agree?

12. How does analogy work in science, according to Eiseley?

13. What does the quotation from John Donne mean?

14. What elements does Eiseley use to create symbols in this essay?

15. How are the two cultures an illusion?

16. What does Eiseley say he has been accused of, and what is his defense?

17. What has the stone become by the end of the essay?

18. Locate all the sections dealing with history. How can you categorize these histories? How does Eiseley use history to make his point? In what ways does he try to accomplish the goals of the university as stated in his opening paragraphs?

Comparison

1. Read Bronowski's "The Nature of Scientific Reasoning." Compare the ideas and styles of the two essays. Which do you prefer and why?

2. Read the essay by Thomas Kuhn. To what degree does Kuhn's essay bear out Eiseley's assertion that the institution of science "is a construct of men, and is subject, like other social structures, to human pressures and inescapable distortions."

3. After reading the other essays in this collection on the "two cultures" controversy, explain why Eiseley writes, "I am not so foolish as to categorize individual scholars or scientists."

Tom Wolfe
(1931–)

Born March 2, 1931, Thomas Kennerly Wolfe, Jr., grew up in a wealthy, Southern family in Richmond, Virginia. As quoted by Richard Kallan, Wolfe remarked of his early years: "I was lucky, I guess, in my family in that they had a very firm idea of roles: Father, Mother, Child. Nothing was ever allowed to bog down into those morass-like personal hangups. And there was no rebellion. The main thing about childhood was to get out of it." Before he did get out of it, according to Barbara Lounsberry, Wolfe formed a vivid impression of his father, editor of *Southern Planter*, "writing at a desk" and decided that he wanted to become a writer as well. He also became a talented baseball pitcher. Enrolling at Washington and Lee University in 1947, he graduated in 1951 with a major in English and a budding interest in American Studies. In 1952, critic William McKeen writes, Wolfe "earned a tryout with the New York Giants . . . but he was cut after three days in spring training." Vastly disappointed, he entered Yale University to work toward a Ph.D. in American Studies.

By 1956, Wolfe writes in *The New Journalism*, "I was in the twisted grip of a disease of our times in which the sufferer experiences an overwhelming urge to join the 'real world.' So I started working for newspapers." (Wolfe makes his circumstances sound a bit easier than they were: he sought employment from some one hundred papers before he found it at the *Springfield Union* in Massachusetts.) In 1957, he submitted his dissertation, *The League of American Writers: Communist Activity among American Writers, 1929–1942*, and in 1959, he took a job with the *Washington Post and Times Herald*. Remaining there for three years, he moved next to New York to write for the *New York Herald Tribune*. During a strike at the *Tribune*, Wolfe freelanced with *Esquire* and traveled to California to research a piece on custom cars. Because of the extreme strangeness of the world he encountered there, however, he found that an orthodox journalistic approach left him unable to write. Kallan explains, "Byron Dobell, managing editor of *Esquire*, told Wolfe just to submit his notes, and another writer would finish the story." Writing his notes in the form of a "memorandum," Wolfe "started typing away, starting right with the first time I saw any custom cars in California. I just started recording it all." When he finished working shortly after six o'clock the next morning, the memo was nearly 50 pages long. And *Esquire* published it. Wolfe's title is a good indication of his new style: "There Goes (Varoom! Varoom!) That Kandy-Kolored (Thphhhhhh!) Tangerine-Flake Streamline Baby (Rahghhh!) around the Bend (Brummmmmmmmmmmmmmm)."

With the strike over and his article a success, Wolfe returned to the *Herald Tribune* but continued to write for *Esquire*, developing "the feeling, rightly or wrongly, that I was doing things no one had ever done before in journalism." In 1965, he published his first book, *The Kandy-Kolored Tangerine-Flake Streamline Baby*, a collection of his writings, which he also illustrated. His next collection of essays was *The Pump House Gang* (1968), published in the same year as *The Electric Kool-Aid Acid Test*, Wolfe's well-known account of the exploits of Ken Kesey and his Merry Pranksters. At the turn of the next decade, he published one of his most controversial works, a collection of two essays under the title *Radical Chic and Mau Mauing the Flak Catchers* (1970). In "Radical Chic," a phrase he popularized with this article, Wolfe chronicles a party hosted by wealthy white liberals in order to show how they acquire "status" by supporting the Black Panthers. With the release of this book, according to Kallan, "Wolfe unexpectedly found himself politicized: conservatives applauded the truth and courage of his reporting; liberals scoffed at his inaccuracy and insensitivity."

Three years later, Wolfe avoided the political question and emphasized his use of narration when he included excerpts from *Radical Chic* in *The New Journalism* (1973). A two-part work, *The Next Journalism* contains in its first half Wolfe's long essay on journalism and the death of the novel and in its second half an anthology of pieces by Hunter S. Thompson, Truman Capote, Gay Talese, and others. Although Wolfe did not coin the phrase "the New Journalism"—"I have no idea who coined [it] or even when it was coined"—he helped to codify the movement by establishing the four main features of the New Journalism: 1) "scene-by-scene construction"; 2) "realistic dialogue"; 3) "third-person point of view," used to enter the psyches of people other than the journalist; and 4) signs of "status life," or "the entire pattern of behavior and possessions through which people express their position in the world or what they think it is or what they hope it to be."

In the mid-1970s, Wolfe published *The Painted Word* (1975) and *Mauve Gloves & Madmen, Clutter & Vine, and Other Short Stories.* In 1979, a year after he married Sheila Berger, he had his greatest triumph of the decade with *The Right Stuff* (1979), which created another phrase and received almost universal praise as a chronicle of pilots and astronauts. Although *The Right Stuff* differs in style from Wolfe's previous works, seeming sometimes almost traditional by comparison, Wolfe maintains that he "wasn't changing. I was just dealing with different material." In 1982, he published *The Purple Decades: A Reader* and began working on a novel, despite being for years one of the novel's most vocal critics. (According to Lounsberry, he had two goals in writing a novel: proving that he was capable of creating the thing he criticized and "trying to show that 'the future of the fictional novel would be in a highly detailed realism based on reporting.'") First serialized in *Rolling Stone, The Bonfire of the Vanities* (1987) was the result. An impressive and highly acclaimed novel, it was made into a spectacularly bad film. More than a decade later, Wolfe published his second novel, *A Man in Full.*

During the 1960s, Tom Wolfe helped to create a revolution in journalism. He says of his subject matter, "I've completely relished this *terra incognita*, these subcultures, these areas of life that nobody wanted to write about—because they thought either they didn't know about them or they were beneath serious consideration." The pilots and astronauts covered in *The Right Stuff* in the 1970s were not "beneath serious consideration" in the same way as Ken Kesey, yet Wolfe found in their milieu a practice as strange as creating custom cars, a practice of daring death every single day—which he seemed in some ways to admire. Although critics noted a stylistic change in *The Right Stuff*, Wolfe did at a basic level what he had always done: work hard to make it appear as though he hadn't particularly worked at all. "Creating the effect of spontaneity in writing," he said to *Contemporary Authors*, "is one of the most difficult and artificial things you can do." Wolfe applied many of the spontaneous journalistic techniques to his novels, too, and while some critics maintain that they do not approach the realism to which he aspires, no one denies that in both fiction and non-fiction, Wolfe knows how to tell a vivid, gripping story.

THE PEPPERMINT LOUNGE REVISITED *(1965)*

ALL RIGHT, GIRLS, into your stretch nylon denims! You know the ones—the ones that look like they were designed by some leering, knuckle-rubbing old tailor with a case of workbench back who spent five years, like Da Vinci, studying nothing but the ischia, the gemelli and the glutei maximi. Next, hoist up those bras, up to the angle of a Nike missile launcher. Then get into the cable-knit mohair sweaters, the ones that fluff out like a cat by a project heating duct. And then unroll the rollers and explode the hair a couple of feet up in the air into bouffants, beehives and Passaic pompadours. Stroke in the black makeup all around the eyelids, so that the eyes look as though Chester Gould,[1] who does Dick Tracy, drew them on. And then put those patient curls in your lips and tell Mother— you have to spell it out for her like a kid—that yes, you're going out with some of your girlfriends, and no, you don't know where you're going, and yes, you won't be out late, and for God's sake, like don't panic all the time, and then, with an I-give-up groan, tell her that "for God's sake" is *not* cursing.

At least that is the way it always seemed, as if some invisible force were out there. It was as though all these girls, all these flaming little Jersey Teen-agers, had their transistors plugged into their skulls and were taking orders, simultaneously, from somebody like the Ringleader Deejay.

Simultaneously, all over Plainfield, Scotch Plains, Ridgefield, Union City, Weehawken, Elizabeth, Hoboken and all the stretches of the Jersey asphalt, there they went, the Jersey Teenagers, out of the house, off to New York, every week, for the ongoing Jersey Teen-agers' weekend rebellion.

They headed off up Front Street if it was, say, Plainfield, and caught the Somerset Line bus at the stop across the street from the Public Service building around 7:30 P.M. Their bouffant heads would be bouncing up and down like dandelions until the bus hit the Turnpike and those crazy blue lights out there on the toothpaste factories started streaming by. They went through the Lincoln Tunnel, up the spiral ramps into the Port Authority Terminal and disembarked at some platform with an incredible number like 155. One hundred and fifty-five bus platforms; this was New York.

The first time people in Manhattan noticed the Jersey Teenagers was when they would come bobbing out of the Port Authority and move into Times Square. No one ever really figured out what they were up to. They were generally written off as Times Square punks. Besides the bouffant babies in their stretch pants, furry sweaters and Dick Tracy eyes,

---

[1]*Chester Gould* Gould (1900–1985) drew a popular comic strip about a detective known as Dick Tracy that ran from 1931 to 1977.

there would be the boys in Presley, Big Bopper, Tony Curtis and Chicago boxcar hairdos. They would be steadying their hairdos in the reflections in the plate glass of clothing stores on 42nd Street that featured Nehru coats, Stingy-Brim hats, tab-collar shirts and winkle-picker elf boots. No one ever seemed to notice how maniacally serious they were about their hairdos, their flesh-tight pants, puffy sweaters, about the way they walked, idled, ogled or acted cool; in short, how serious they were about anything that had to do with form and each other. They had a Jersey Teen-age nether world going in the middle of Manhattan. Their presence may not have been understood, but it was not ignored. There were nightspots that catered to them with rock and roll music. And when the Jersey Teen-agers started dancing in Times Square nightspots, they were serious about that, too. The Lindy, which was the name the kids had for what an older generation called jitterbugging, was already out. The kids were doing a dance called the Mashed Potatoes and another called the Puppet. Curiously, they were like the dances at a Lebanese maharajan. There was a lot of hip movement, but the boy and girl never touched. Then a new variation caught on, the Twist. There would be the Jersey Teen-agers, every weekend, doing the Mashed Potatoes, the Puppet and the Twist, studying each other's legs and feet through the entire number, never smiling, serious as always about form. One of these places was the Wagon Wheel. Another one was the Peppermint Lounge, 128 West 45th Street, half a block east of Times Square.

The Peppermint Lounge! You know about the Peppermint Lounge. One week in October, 1961, a few socialites, riding hard under the crop of a couple of New York columnists, discovered the Peppermint Lounge and by the next week all of Jet Set New York was discovering the Twist, after the manner of the first 900 decorators who ever laid hands on an African mask. Greta Garbo, Elsa Maxwell, Countess Bernadotte, Noel Coward, Tennessee Williams and the Duke of Bedford—everybody was there, and the hindmost were laying fives, tens and twenty-dollar bills on cops, doormen and a couple of sets of maître d's to get within sight of the bandstand and a dance floor the size of somebody's kitchen. By November, Joey Dee, twenty-two, the band leader at the Peppermint Lounge, was playing the Twist at the $100-a-plate Party of the Year at the Metropolitan Museum of Art.

That, of course, was two years ago. Everybody knows what has happened to the Jet Set in that time, for the Jet Set is always with us. But whatever became of the Jersey Teen-agers and the Peppermint Lounge?

Marlene Klaire, leader of the club's Twist chorus line, is standing in the hall off the dressing rooms in back, talking about the kind of fall it has been for her. Marlene is a short, lithe, gorgeous brunette. It is right after the second show, and she has on her Twist chorus satin, a pair of net stockings, Cleopatra eye makeup and a Passaic pompadour that brings her up to about six feet four. Yes, there is an institution now called the Twist chorus line, tended by a couple of choreographers named Wakefield Poole and Tom Roba. Marlene arrived at the Peppermint Lounge two years ago via the Jersey Teen-age route, but now her life is full of institutions.

"The Waddle," Marlene is saying, "is one of the dances we were demonstrating the other night over at Sacred Heart. You get in two straight lines sort of like, you know, the Hully Gully."

"Sacred Heart?"

"The Catholic Church. We weren't *in* the church, really, it was the auditorium. They let us wear our costumes. They were all adults there. We were teaching them the Waddle, the Dog, the Monkey—the Monkey is probably the most popular right now."

Well, all that was with the young adults at Sacred Heart. And then there was the night the educational program took her and the girls over to the Plaza Hotel for the Bourbon Ball, where they showed the Society people the Waddle, the Dog, the Monkey, the Mashed Potatoes and the Slop.

"The Society people loved it," Marlene is saying, "but the Mashed Potatoes is hard for some of them, and—"

Marlene came to New York over the Jersey Teen-age route way back in 1961 when the Peppermint Lounge was first getting hot. She was from Trenton, and then she had a job as a secretary in Newark, but then one night she came rolling into the Port Authority like everybody else and headed for the Peppermint Lounge. She worked her way up fast. First she got a job as a waitress, then she got one of the jobs dancing between shows, in street clothes, which is to say, something like stretch pants and a mohair sweater, to encourage customers to come up and dance. Marlene could really dance, and she got a job in the first Twist chorus line.

Now, two years later, the Jet Set has moved on from the Peppermint Lounge, but the Jersey Teen-age cycle is continuing. Inside the club the Younger Brothers and the Epics are on the bandstand, and Janet Gail and Misty More and Louis and Ronnie are in street clothes, dancing between shows, and customers are packed in around them, bouncing. A few leggy kids in red satin shorts, waitresses, are standing around the sides miming the Monkey with their hips, shuffling to themselves. And out in the center nine girls from Jersey, all with exploding hair and Dick Tracy eyes, have a table and watch the dancing with that same old dead-serious look. Nobody is doing the Twist anymore. Everybody is doing something like the Monkey, in which you make some motions with your arms like you're climbing the bars of your cage, or the T-Bird, in which there is some complicated business with the hands about opening the front door and going inside and mixing a cocktail. Every now and then Larry Cope, who is one of the Younger Brothers, will introduce a pure Twist number, but he has to use a historical preface, sort of like they do at Roseland or some place when they say, well, now we're going to have a good old-fashioned waltz.

The Jersey Teen-age set has no trouble getting into the place now, although there are always a lot of tourists, especially on the weekends, who have heard of the Twist and the Peppermint Lounge.

"—and we had a lot of little kids in here Saturday, showing them the dances. They were, you know, little kids, four to ten years old, something like that. They catch on pretty fast, or at least they see us, you know, shaking around, and they do that. And then sometimes we get women's groups. They're going to a show or something, and they then drop in here."

On the one hand Marlene sees a limitless future for the Twist as an institution. She figures the tourists coming to the World's Fair will add years to its life, and already she and the dancers are working on an act for the Fair called "Twisting Around the World," in which they will start off doing a native dance from some country when somebody shouts out "Twist!" in the native tongue, which usually comes out "Tweest!" and then the native dance becomes the native twist. Marlene had another idea, which was "Twisting Into Outer Space," but it looks like it will be "Around the World."

In another sense, however, Marlene does not associate the Twist with the future at all. Marlene's goal! Marlene's goal is . . . Marlene's answer should reassure a whole generation of Jersey mothers about where the Jersey Teen-age rebellion is heading, it and all its bouffant babies, nylon stretch denims, Dick Tracy eyes, Nehru coats and Monkey dancers.

Out in the club the Epics, with four electric instruments going, are playing "Doing the Dog," and Misty is doing the Dog, and Janet is doing the Mashed Potatoes, and Jerri Miller is doing the Monkey, with a few baroque emendations, but Marlene reflects a moment, as if upon her busy round of work with the churches, the benefit balls, the women's groups and the youth.

"Well," she says, "I'd like to teach dancing, in my own house, you know, the way it was when I took lessons from my teacher. Or maybe be a psychologist. I used to want to, and I may still do that. Anyway, I don't want to live in New York. I want some place more like where we used to live in New Jersey. I don't like living here. There aren't any trees."

Understanding and Analysis

1. Note the use of the imperative in the first sentence. What other techniques does Wolfe use in the first paragraph to describe the teenage girl?

2. In the second paragraph, Wolfe tells us whom he has been impersonating in the first paragraph. Who is that? How does the tone shift in this paragraph?

3. What role does class play in this essay? Where do you first find indications of the importance of class, as well as the fleeting nature of style?

4. Where are the teenagers going? Why does Wolfe name the cities and towns they come from and the routes they take?

5. What is the attitude the teens display toward their clothes and their dances?

6. In the fourth paragraph, the reader is addressed directly: "You know about the Peppermint Lounge." Who was Wolfe's original audience? Why did they know? How does this sentence work to separate the reader from the teens? What is the point of this paragraph?

7. The following paragraph sets up the main focus of the essay. What is it?

8. Since the Peppermint Lounge craze, what has happened to the New Jersey teenagers, according to Wolfe? Who frequented the lounge at the time Wolfe was writing?

9. How does Wolfe show us that the "Jersey Teen-age cycle is continuing"?

10. What is Marlene's goal?

11. Wolfe focuses on the girls. What, if anything, can you discover about the teenage boys?

12. What is Wolfe's attitude toward the Jersey teenagers?

Comparison

1. Read the essays by Germaine Greer and Russell Baker. What do you see, if anything, that connects these two essays with Wolfe's essay about teenagers?

2. Read the essay by Clifford Geertz. How would you analyze the activities of the teens that Wolfe describes in terms from Geertz's essay?

3. Read Mead's essay. Both Mead and Wolfe describe activities in a cycle. What characteristics do these essays share? What stylistic differences do you see?

4. Read the essays by Lawrence, Brady, and Greer. What connections do you see in terms of attitudes and style between these essays and Wolfe's essay? Read Virginia Woolf's "Professions for Women." How do these essays inform your reading of Wolfe's essay?

Joan Didion
(1934–)

Joan Didion was born and raised in Sacramento, California, on land that her great-great-grandfather had farmed. Her great-great-grandmother, Nancy Hardin Cornwall had been one of the original eighty-seven members of the Donner-Reed party that had set out from Illinois for California in 1846. Luckily, Cornwall had turned north in Nevada, before the rest of the group became trapped by a blizzard in the Sierras. Rather than starve, the forty survivors cannibalized their dead. This unique family history shaped Didion's sense of self from her earliest years. The land in the Sacramento Valley seems to her holy by virtue of the frontier mentality, but its present inhabitants have inherited an "implacable insularity" that renders them "paralyzed by a past no longer relevant." All that Didion had been taught to revere–the understated courage of her forbears, the character developed from "good upbringing"–eventually came to be, in one of her recurring phrases, "beside the point."

In "On Keeping a Notebook" Didion says that she began writing at age five; her first story, of a woman who thinks she is freezing in the Arctic but is really about to die of the heat in the Sahara, records the frightening extremes that, for Didion, articulate her dread. When she was seven, the Japanese attacked Pearl Harbor, and her father, an Army Air Corps finance officer, was shifted, with his family, from California to Washington, North Carolina, and finally Colorado, before returning to Sacramento near the end of the war. For Didion, the war meant a sudden loss of the regular flow of daily life, an abrupt disjuncture that confirmed her sense of the world as a frightening place. Thus, like Woolf, Hoagland, and White, Didion was a nervous, fearful child despite her family's wealth.

In an interview with Didion in the late seventies, Michiko Kakutani unearthed an incident that encapsulates Didion's admittedly "theatrical temperament" and her fascination with fear: one summer evening following eighth grade, Didion told her parents she was taking her brother to a square dance but instead left Jimmy at the bus terminal while she went off to the ocean, notebook in hand, to see what it would be like to drown. Soaked but satisfied, she went back for her brother and both crept unnoticed into the house.

In high school, Didion typed out sentences from Hemingway, Conrad, and James, joined a sorority called the Mañana Club that met in the governor's mansion, drank vodka and orange juice by the river, and was rejected by Stanford University. Again she toyed with suicide, as described in "On Being

Unchosen by the College of One's Choicye." Instead she went, in 1953, to the University of California at Berkeley, joined Tri Delt, majored in English, and won first prize in *Vogue's* Prix de Paris contest for writers.

In "Goodbye to All That," an eponymous allusion to Robert Graves's book about his experiences in World War I, Didion describes her experiences in New York City from 1956 to 1964. She had arrived young, already out-of-love with the boy back home she had promised to marry, sick with fever, intending to stay only six months, and eager for "new faces," new experiences; she left no longer young, newly married but in a state of acute despair, homesick for Sacramento, and hunted by the press of time. During those eight years, she worked for *Vogue, National Review,* and *Mademoiselle,* for "so little money that some weeks I had to charge food at Bloomingdale's gourmet shop in order to eat." She lived in nearly empty apartments, furnished only with a bed and two borrowed "French garden chairs" or "fifty yards of yellow theatrical silk" billowing unweighted from her bedroom windows. For Didion, New York was Xanadu, a never-ending party of late nights oozing into early mornings, famous people, chiffon scarves, Bloody Marys and cheap red wine, Henri Bendel jasmine soap, and women at Gristede's with Yorkshire terriers that, finally, provoked Didion's contempt. During this time she had written her first novel, *River Run,* set in the Sacramento Valley and published in 1963 to only a few mixed reviews. Soon after, a major battle with depression made it impossible for her to go anywhere without crying: "One day I could not go into a Schrafft's; the next day it would be Bonwit Teller."

In January of 1964, Didion married John Gregory Dunne, a fellow writer and friend of seven years who had helped her edit the galleys for her novel; in June, when Didion was no longer able to "get dinner with any degree of certainty," the couple left their jobs and moved to Los Angeles, California. Despite a heartbreaking miscarriage, Didion was able to work in California, publishing essays for *National Review,* a regular film column for *Vogue,* and a variety of pieces for *Holiday, The New York Times Magazine,* the *Saturday Evening Post,* and the *American Scholar.* Nevertheless, in 1965, as Didion records from Hawaii in "Letter From Paradise, 21° 19′N., 157° 52′W," she "had been tired too long and quarrelsome too much and too often frightened of migraine and failure." This sojourn led, if not to happiness, at least to the publication of another essay that helped her come to terms with the major event of her generation, the bombing of Pearl Harbor.

The following year, 1966, the couple adopted a baby daughter, Quintana Roo. In "Los Angeles Notebook," written shortly after the baby's arrival, Didion describes the hot wind called a Santa Ana that epitomizes for her the unpredictable violence of modern life, especially as it was played out in the late sixties. The period before the onset of a Santa Ana is a time of uneasy dread: "The baby frets. The maid sulks. I rekindle a waning argument with the telephone company, then cut my losses and lie down, given over to whatever it is in the air. To live with the Santa Ana is to accept, consciously or unconsciously, a deeply mechanistic view of human behavior." Clearly, despite the pleasures Quintana brought to both her parents, Didion remained the victim of periodic bouts of misery.

Struggling in their marriage, Didion and Dunne nonetheless collaborated on a column called "Points West" for the *Saturday Evening Post*, taking turns each issue, a venture which lasted until the demise of the magazine in 1969. *Slouching Towards Bethlehem*, published in 1968, is a collection of some of these and other essays that Didion had written in New York and in California. That summer, Dunne moved out of their rented house in Hollywood to work out problems with his writing and escape their faltering relationship. That summer also, Didion confesses in the title essay of *The White Album*, she was tested and treated at St. John's Hospital, Santa Monica, for "an attack of vertigo and nausea," prompted, Didion implies, by social and political events as much as by private ones. By December of 1969, their personal lives had not significantly improved: Didion began her first essay for *Life* by acknowledging that she, her husband, and her three-year-old daughter were in Honolulu "in lieu of filing for divorce."

Her second novel, *Play It As It Lays* (1970) was a not only a best seller but also nominated for a National Book Award. She continued writing for *Life* until June of 1970, while publishing essays in *The New York Times Book Review* and *The New York Review of Books* as well. In 1971, she and Dunne again collaborated, this time on a screenplay, *Panic in Needle Park*, for Twentieth Century-Fox. Their marriage improving, they moved to a beach house in Malibu, forty miles up the coast from Los Angeles, with room enough to display a quilt made by Didion's great-great grandmother and a rosewood piano that had belonged to the Didions since 1848. Here Didion and Dunne wrote film scripts of *Play It As It Lays* (1972) and a *A Star Is Born* (1976) and shared a column called "The Coast" for *Esquire* (1976–1977). Here too Didion wrote her third novel, *A Book of Common Prayer* (1977).

The community they found on the Pacific Coast Highway, described in "On the Morning After the Sixties," was "one of shared isolation and adversity," reinforcing Didion's vision of a world of dangerous extremes: snakes lurked in the driveway, fires and floods periodically cut off access to the highway. They lived in this house from the time Quintana was five until she was twelve, when "it rained until the highway collapsed, and one of her friends drowned at Zuma Beach, a casualty of Quaaludes." A few months after the family had moved to a two-story colonial in Brentwood Park, Los Angeles, a Santa Ana blew a fire up the coast which stopped just before it reached their former house.

The next year, 1979, Didion published *The White Album*, her second collection of essays. Since then both she and Dunne have continued to work successfully, moving with ease among celebrities from the film industry as well as fellow writers and artists. Kakutani's article on Didion, written shortly after the publication of *The White Album*, describes Didion's life in Los Angeles as possessing "the soothing order and elegance of a *Vogue* photo spread." In this house Didion exerted control over her small and recurrently painful body through pills, pain killers, and the pleasing rituals of housekeeping: sewing curtains, cooking gourmet meals, polishing silver. But even in this comfortable, secure world, she admitted to her interviewer that she felt afraid.

In 1981, Didion and Dunne produced another screen play, *True Confessions*, based on a novel by Dunne. In 1983, Didion published a work of non-fiction, *Salvador*, and another novel, *Democracy*, the following year. Her most recent books of non-fiction are *Miami* (1987) and *After Henry* (1992). Didion continues to publish essays, more outward-looking than inward these days, in *The New York Review of Books* and elsewhere, which precisely document the disintegration and despair she sees in contemporary American life. Her exact details and unflagging sensitivity to the ironies and absurdities of modern life have made her one of the most anthologized modern essayists. Such popularity suggests that her oppression by "some nameless anxiety," her longing to "go home again" is not, as she speculates in "On Going Home," confined to her generation alone.

Like her contemporary Edward Hoagland, Didion's essays astonish the reader with their vivid, telling details of the author's personal life. Yet neither author tells all, and each finds in private suffering an etching of the public woe. Didion's recognition in *The White Album* that severe depression was a natural response to the events of the sixties articulates her stance as a writer. Another example of this congruence of the private and the public is the opening sentence of that essay: "We tell ourselves stories in order to live." The stories form a shape in the void, help her to forget that outside them lies nothing. Without their control, their limits, their narrative continuity and focus, Didion cannot perceive meaning, cannot find the point. Her essays, as much as her novels, are rituals of avoidance, ways to keep going. That first sentence is typical of Didion in its stark assertion of this fact and in its direct assumption that she speaks for all of us, whether we like it or not, whether or not we always agree.

On Going Home (1967)

I AM HOME for my daughter's first birthday. By "home" I do not mean the house in Los Angeles where my husband and I and the baby live, but the place where my family is, in the Central Valley of California. It is a vital although troublesome distinction. My husband likes my family but is uneasy in their house, because once there I fall into their ways, which are difficult, oblique, deliberately inarticulate, not my husband's ways. We live in dusty houses ("D-U-S-T," he once wrote with his finger on surfaces all over the house, but no one noticed it) filled with mementos quite without value to him (what could the Canton dessert plates mean to him? how could he have known about the assay scales, why should he care if he did know?), and we appear to talk exclusively about people we know who have been committed to mental hospitals, about people we know who have been booked on drunk-driving charges, and about property, particularly about property, land, price per acre and C-2 zoning[1] and assessments and freeway access. My brother does not understand my husband's inability to perceive the advantage in the rather common real-estate transaction known as "sale-leaseback,"[2] and my husband in turn does not understand why so many of the people he hears about in my father's house have recently been committed to mental hospitals or booked on drunk-driving charges. Nor does he understand that when we talk about sale-leasebacks and right-of-way condemnations we are talking in code about things we like best, the yellow fields and the cottonwoods and the rivers rising and falling and the mountain roads closing when the heavy snow comes in. We miss each other's points, have another drink and regard the fire. My brother refers to my husband, in his presence, as "Joan's husband." Marriage is the classic betrayal.

Or perhaps it is not any more. Sometimes I think that those of us who are now in our thirties were born into the last generation to carry the burden of "home," to find in family life the source of all tension and drama. I had by all objective accounts a "normal" and a "happy" family situation, and yet I was almost thirty years old before I could talk to my family on the telephone without crying after I had hung up. We did not fight. Nothing was wrong. And yet some nameless anxiety colored the emotional charges between me and the place that I came from. The question of whether or not you could go home again[3] was a very real part of the sentimental and largely literary baggage with which we left home in the fifties; I suspect that it is irrelevant to the children born of the fragmentation after World War II. A few weeks ago in a San Francisco bar I saw a pretty young girl on crystal[4] take off her clothes and dance for the cash prize in an "amateur-topless" contest. There was no particular sense of moment about this, none of the effect of romantic degradation, of "dark journey," for which my generation strived so assiduously. What sense could that girl possibly make of, say, *Long Day's Journey into Night?*[5] Who is beside the point?

That I am trapped in this particular irrelevancy is never more apparent to me than when I am home. Paralyzed by the neurotic lassitude engendered by meeting one's past at every turn, around every corner, inside every cupboard, I go aimlessly from room to room. I decide to meet it head-on and clean out a drawer, and I spread the contents on the bed. A bathing suit I wore the summer I was seventeen. A letter of rejection from *The Nation*, an aerial photograph of the site for a shopping center my father did not build in 1954. Three teacups hand-painted with cabbage roses and signed "E. M.," my grandmother's initials. There is no final solution for letters of rejection from *The Nation* and teacups hand-painted in 1900. Nor is there any answer to snapshots of one's grandfather as a young man on skis, surveying around Donner Pass in the year 1910. I smooth out

[1]*C-2 zoning* zoning for neighborhood businesses such as small markets and other shops.

[2]*sale-leaseback* the leasing of property by the new owner back to the previous owner.

[3]*whether or not you could go home again* reference to a novel by Thomas Wolfe (1900–1938) titled *You Can't Go Home Again.*

[4]*crystal* an illegal methamphetamine, speed.

[5]*Long Day's Journey into Night* Autobiographical play by Eugene O'Neill about the conflicts and loves within his family.

the snapshot and look into his face, and do and do not see my own. I close the drawer, and have another cup of coffee with my mother. We get along very well, veterans of a guerrilla war we never understood.

Days pass. I see no one. I come to dread my husband's evening call, not only because he is full of news of what by now seems to me our remote life in Los Angeles, people he has seen, letters which require attention, but because he asks what I have been doing, suggests uneasily that I get out, drive to San Francisco or Berkeley. Instead I drive across the river to a family graveyard. It has been vandalized since my last visit and the monuments are broken, overturned in the dry grass. Because I once saw a rattlesnake in the grass I stay in the car and listen to a country-and-Western station. Later I drive with my father to a ranch he has in the foothills. The man who runs his cattle on it asks us to the round-up, a week from Sunday, and although I know that I will be in Los Angeles I say, in the oblique way my family talks, that I will come. Once home I mention the broken monuments in the graveyard. My mother shrugs.

I go to visit my great-aunts. A few of them think now that I am my cousin, or their daughter who died young. We recall an anecdote about a relative last seen in 1948, and they ask if I still like living in New York City. I have lived in Los Angeles for three years, but I say that I do. The baby is offered a horehound drop, and I am slipped a dollar bill "to buy a treat." Questions trail off, answers are abandoned, the baby plays with the dust motes in a shaft of afternoon sun.

It is time for the baby's birthday party: a white cake, strawberry-marshmallow ice cream, a bottle of champagne saved from another party. In the evening, after she has gone to sleep, I kneel beside the crib and touch her face, where it is pressed against the slats, with mine. She is an open and trusting child, unprepared for and unaccustomed to the ambushes of family life, and perhaps it is just as well that I can offer her little of that life. I would like to give her more. I would like to promise her that she will grow up with a sense of her cousins and of rivers and of her great-grandmother's teacups, would like to pledge her a picnic on a river with fried chicken and her hair uncombed, would like to give her *home* for her birthday, but we live differently now and I can promise her nothing like that. I give her a xylophone and a sundress from Madeira[6] and promise to tell her a funny story.

Understanding and Analysis

1. In the second sentence, Didion sets up an assertion that she supports in the rest of the essay—that her parents' ways are not the ways of her own new family and that when she goes back to her first home she falls "into their ways." What exactly does she claim about those ways in that sentence? What proof does she offer for each of the characteristics she names?

2. Note the variety of sentence lengths and patterns in the first paragraph. Which sentence is the most important? Why?

3. What is Didion's evidence for thinking, sometimes at least, that her generation is the last "to find in family life the source of all tension and drama"? Do you agree?

4. Do you think that opportunities to see oneself as mired in "romantic degradation" no longer exist for the young?

[6]*Madeira* a Portuguese island.

5. What does the last sentence of the second paragraph mean?

6. What does Didion mean by the description of her and her mother as "veterans of a guerilla war we never understood"? Where else does Didion pick up that figure of war?

7. How do the details in the last line, describing what she gives her daughter for her birthday, underline the differences between her original home and her present one?

Comparison

1. Read "Salvation" by Langston Hughes. Do you see any similarities in these two very different narratives about growing up?

2. Read the essays by Kingston, Ozick, Mairs, Rich, Cofer, and Tan. Compare the descriptions of family life you see in these essays. Is there any suggestion of "a guerilla war" or the kind of "tension and drama" Didion describes in these essays as well? In what ways, if at all, are these families similar?

3. Read Momaday's "The Way to Rainy Mountain." How does a sense of place help to establish the narrator's identity in the essays by Didion and Momaday?

Martha Gellhorn
(1908–1998)

Born November 8, 1908, in St. Louis, Missouri, Martha Gellhorn was the daughter of George Gellhorn, a physician and a professor, and Edna Fischel Gellhorn, a crusader for women's rights who "almost invented," by her daughter's report, the League of Women Voters. When the time came to choose a college, Gellhorn selected her mother's alma mater, Bryn Mawr. As Gellhorn scholar Jacqueline Orsagh explains, however, Gellhorn dropped out after her third year "to become a cub reporter with the *Albany Times-Union*." Once she earned enough money, she traveled to France in 1929, joining up with a group of "young French pacifists" united by their "poverty" and their "passion." Again Gellhorn earned money through her journalism, this time writing for *Vogue* magazine and the United Press International. In 1934, she returned to the United States and took a job as an investigator for the Federal Emergency Relief Administration; in 1936, she published *The Trouble I've Seen*, a collection of novellas based on her experiences with the unfortunate. (Orsagh characterizes the book as "a vivid collection of case studies of the unemployed.") Following the book's release, Gellhorn returned to Europe. Her career as a war correspondent began a year later, in 1937, during the Spanish Civil War.

Gellhorn first heard about turmoil in Spain while she was staying in Germany, doing research for a novel. In *The Face of War*, she explains: "The Nazi newspapers began to speak of fighting in Spain. They did not talk of war; the impression I got was of a bloodthirsty rabble, attacking the forces of decency and order. This Spanish rabble, which was the duly elected Republic of Spain, was always referred to as 'Red Swine-dogs.' The Nazi papers had one solid value: Whatever they were against, you could be for." Exchanging pacifism for anti-fascism, Gellhorn went to Spain with $50 and a backpack, believing that "all one did about a war was go to it, as a gesture of solidarity, and get killed, or survive." After "a journalist friend" suggested that Gellhorn might help the Loyalists by writing, she sent an article to *Collier's*. The magazine listed her as a staff member after accepting her second piece, and then, Gellhorn writes, "I was evidently a war correspondent. It began like that."

Nothing in Gellhorn's five decades of war reporting was ever again so haphazard. Writing for *Collier's*, she traveled to England, France, and Czechoslovakia before the start of World War II, and to Finland after. In 1940, she published another novel, *A Stricken Field*, and married the writer Ernest Hemingway, with whom she had worked in Spain. Following the Japanese attack on Pearl Harbor, Gellhorn returned to England. When she got word of the Allied invasion at Normandy, she snuck onto a hospital ship sailing to the aid of the wounded. In *Women War Correspondents of World War II*, Lily Wagner reports that for stowing away, Gellhorn was reprimanded and "ordered to an American nurses training camp in England. She could cross France with the nurses, she was told. She tolerated this for a day, then climbed a fence and hitch-hiked to the nearest military airfield. On the pretext of wanting to see her fiance in Italy, she got a lift to Naples." She reported from Italy and Holland in 1944, and in 1945, she covered the Battle of the Bulge. Prolific in her journalism, she also published a novel called *Liana* (1944).

After the war, divorced from Hemingway, Gellhorn bought a house in London, but she found herself uneasy with peace, uncertain how to behave in a post-war atmosphere of forced happiness. In 1946, she covered the war in Java, as well as the Nuremberg trials and the Paris Peace Conference, and, in 1948, she released her most highly-acclaimed novel, a war story called *The Wine of Astonishment*. When the Korean War broke out in 1950, Gellhorn did not go. "As for me," she writes, "I had seen enough dead bodies, and enough refugees, and enough destroyed villages and could not bear to see any more. It was useless to go on telling people what war was like since they went on obediently accepting war." In 1953, she published a collection of stories called *The Honeyed Peace*, and in 1954, she married T. S. Matthews.

Divorcing almost a decade later, Gellhorn was soon on her way to cover the war in Vietnam, deploring the war reporting she was finding in the papers:

"Finally I went to South Vietnam because I had to learn for myself, since I could not learn from anyone else, what was happening to the voiceless Vietnamese people." Approaching 60 when she covered the Six Day War, she was 74 when she traveled to El Salvador and Nicaragua to report on death squads, contras, sandinistas, and routine tortures. In 1986, she published *The View from the Ground*, a collection of articles written in times of peace, and re-released *The Face of War*, a collection of her war reporting originally published in 1959. She died February 16, 1998, in London.

Although she did not like to have it said, Gellhorn was a much better writer of non-fiction than of novels. Then again, it would be difficult for anyone to do two things as well as Martha Gellhorn covered wars. Reviewing *The Face of War* for *New Statesman*, Allen Brien writes: "About Martha Gellhorn's *The Face of War* I find it difficult to write with any restraint. This anthology contains the best prose on its subject written by anybody, from Madrid in 1936 to Managua in 1985." Confronted with sexism and constrained by rules that permitted only one official correspondent per publication (Hemingway took her spot with *Collier's* after Pearl Harbor, for example), Gellhorn often had to work on her own, finding her own means of transportation, gaining access to people and places without proper papers. Nevertheless, as the pieces in *The Face of War* show, Gellhorn consistently managed to be at the scene, riding in a jeep through the middle of a battleground, walking past bombed and shattered buildings to interview civilians.

Early in her career, Gellhorn found strength in her idealism: "When I was young I believed in the perfectibility of man, and in progress, and thought of journalism as a guiding light. If people were told the truth, if dishonor and injustice were clearly shown to them, they would at once demand the saving action, punishment of wrong-doers, and care for the innocent." But repeated exposure to war brought disillusionment. Gellhorn wrote in 1959 that she no longer believed in "the benign power of the press," expressing special bitterness that no one seemed to listen to the "Federation of Cassandras," the "foreign correspondents" who reported on the threat of fascism for years before World War II. Despite her disillusionment and frustration, Gellhorn nevertheless covered wars for another 25 years, finding that "the act of keeping the record straight is valuable in itself." In her own work, she did mind the record, but she also gave the details, describing the wounds and the hospital wards, the dogfights overhead, the piles of the dead at Dachau. She did not flinch from the most disturbing revelations, and she urged action in her readers. Some of her contemporaries thought that she was obsessed with war. If she was obsessed at all, it was rather with the willful forgetting and the savage indifference required to wage war after war in the twentieth century, with full knowledge of the price.

CIVILIAN CASUALTIES IN SOUTH VIETNAM
August–September 1966 (1967)

WE LOVE OUR children. We are famous for loving our children, and many foreigners believe that we love them unwisely and too well. We plan, work and dream for our children; we are tirelessly determined to give them the best of life. "Security" is one of our favorite words; children, we agree, must have security—by which we mean devoted parents, a pleasant, settled home, health, gaiety, education; a climate of hope and peace. Perhaps we are too busy, loving our own children, to think of children 10,000 miles away, or to understand that distant, small, brown-skinned people, who do not look or live like us, love their children just as deeply, but with anguish now and heartbreak and fear.

American families know the awful emptiness left by the young man who goes off to war and does not come home; but American families have been spared knowledge of the destroyed home, with the children dead in it. War happens someplace else, far away. Farther away than ever before, in South Vietnam, a war is being waged in our name, the collective, anonymous name of the American people. And American weapons are killing and wounding uncounted Vietnamese children. Not 10 or 20 children, which would be tragedy enough, but hundreds killed and many more hundreds wounded every month. This terrible fact is officially ignored; no Government agency keeps statistics on the civilians of all ages, from babies to the very old, killed and wounded in South Vietnam. I have witnessed modern war in nine countries, but I have never seen a war like the one in South Vietnam.

My Tho is a charming small town in the Mekong Delta, the green rice bowl of South Vietnam. A wide, brown river flows past it and cools the air. Unlike Saigon, the town is quiet because it is off-limits to troops and not yet flooded with a pitiful horde of refugees. Despite three wars, one after the other, the Delta peasants have stayed in their hamlets and produced food for the nation. Governments and armies come and go, but for 2,000 years peasants of this race have been working this land. The land and their families are what they love. Bombs and machine-gun bullets are changing the ancient pattern. The Delta is considered a Viet Cong stronghold, so death rains from the sky, fast and indiscriminate. Fifteen million South Vietnamese live on the ground; no one ever suggested that there were more than 279,000 Viet Cong and North Vietnamese in all of South Vietnam.

The My Tho children's hospital is a gray cement box surrounded by high grass and weeds overgrowing the peacetime garden. Its 35 cots are generally filled by 55 little patients. One tall, sorrowing nun is the trained nurse; one Vietnamese woman doctor is the medical staff. Relatives bring their wounded children to this hospital however they can, walking for miles with the children in their arms, bumping in carts or the local buses. Organized transport for wounded civilians does not exist anywhere in South Vietnam. Once the relatives have managed to get their small war victims to the hospital, they stay to look after them. Someone must. The corridors and wards are crowded; the children are silent, as are the grown-ups. Yet shock and pain, in this still place, make a sound like screaming.

A man leaned against the wall in the corridor; his face was frozen and his eyes looked half-mad. He held, carefully, a six-month-old baby girl, his first child. At night, four bombs had been dropped without warning on his hamlet. Bomb fragments killed his young wife, sleeping next to her daughter; they tore the arm of the baby. As wounds go, in this war, it was mild—just deep cuts from shoulder to wrist, caked in blood. Yesterday he had a home, a wife, and a healthy, laughing daughter; today he had nothing left except a child dazed with pain and a tiny mutilated arm.

In the grimy wards, only plaster on child legs and arms, bandages on heads and thin bodies were fresh and clean. The children have learned not to move, because moving hurts them more, but their eyes, large and dark, follow you. We have not had to see, in our own children's eyes, this tragic resignation.

Apparently children are classified as adults nowadays if they are over 12 years old. During a short, appalled visit to the big My Tho provincial hospital, among hundreds of wounded peasants, men and women, I noted a 13-year-old girl who had lost her left foot (bomb), sharing a bed with an old woman whose knee was shattered; a 14-year-old girl with a head wound (mortar shell); a 15-year-old girl with bandages over a chest wound (machine-gun bullet). If you stop to ask questions, you discover frequently that someone nearby and loved was killed at the same time, and here is the survivor, mourning a mother or a little brother: loneliness added to pain. All these people suffer in silence. When the hurt is unbearable, they groan very softly, as if ashamed to disturb others. But their eyes talk for them. I take the anguish, grief, bewilderment in their eyes, rightly, as accusation.

The Red Cross Amputee Center in Saigon is a corrugated tin shed, crowded to capacity and as comfortable in that heavy, airless heat as an oven. Two hundred amputees, in relays, have lived here. Now 40 Vietnamese peasants, male and female, ranging in age from six to 60, sit on chromium wheelchairs or their board beds or hobble about on crutches and, though you might not guess it, they are lucky. They did not die from their wounds, they are past the phase of physical agony, and in due course they will get artificial arms or legs.

The demand for artificial arms and legs in South Vietnam may be the greatest in the world, but the supply is limited; for civilians it had run out completely when I was there. These maimed people are content to wait; Saigon is safe from bombs, and they are fed by the Red Cross. To be certain of food is wonderful good luck in a country where hunger haunts most of the people.

A girl of six had received a new arm, ending in a small steel hook to replace her hand. Bomb fragments took off the lower half of her arm and also wounded her face. She has a lovely smile, and a sweet little body and she is pitifully ugly, with that dented, twisted skin and a lopsided eye. She was too young to be distressed about her face, though she cannot have felt easy with her strange arm; she only wore it to have her picture taken.

An older girl, also a bomb victim, perhaps aged 12, had lost an eye, a leg and still had a raw wound on her shoulder. She understood what had happened to her. Since the Vietnamese are a beautiful people, it is natural that they should understand beauty. She hid her damaged face with her hand.

A cocky, merry small boy hopped around on miniature crutches, but could not move so easily when he strapped on his false, pink-tinted leg. Hopefully he will learn to walk with it, and meanwhile he is the luckiest person in that stifling shed, because the American soldiers who found him have not forgotten him. With their gifts of money he buys food from street vendors and is becoming a butterball. I remember no other plump child in South Vietnam.

A young Red Cross orderly spoke some French and served as interpreter while I asked these people how they were hurt. Six had been wounded by Viet Cong mines. One had been caught in machine-gun cross fire between Viet Cong and American soldiers, while working in the fields. One, a sad reminder of the endless misery and futility of war, had lost a leg from Japanese bombing in World War II. One, the most completely ruined of them all, with both legs cut off just below the hip, an arm gone, and two fingers lopped from the remaining hand, had been struck down by a hit-and-run U.S. military car. Thirty-one were crippled for life by bombs or artillery shells or bullets. I discussed these fig-

ures with doctors who operate on wounded civilians all day, and day after day. The percentage seems above* average. "Most of the bits and pieces I take out of people," a doctor said, "are identified as American."

In part, it is almost impossible to keep up with the facts in this escalating war. In part,
the facts about this war are buried under propaganda. I report statistics I have heard or
read, but I regard them as indications of truth rather than absolute accuracy. So: there are
77 orphanages in South Vietnam and 80,000 registered orphans. (Another figure is
110,000.) No one can guess how many orphaned children have been adopted by relatives.
They will need to build new orphanages or enlarge the old ones, because the estimated
increase in orphans is 2,000 a month. This consequence of war is seldom mentioned. A
child, orphaned by war, is a war victim, wounded forever.

The Group orphanage, in the miserable rickety outskirts of Saigon, is splendid by local
standards. Foreign charities have helped the gentle Vietnamese nuns to construct an extra
wing and to provide medical care such as intravenous feeding for shriveled babies, nearly
dead from starvation. They also are war victims. "All the little ones come to us sick from
hunger," a nun said, in another orphanage. "What can you expect? The people are too
poor." The children sit on the floor of two big, open rooms. Here they are again, the tiny
war wounded, hobbling on crutches, hiding the stump of an arm (because already they
know they are odd): doubly wounded, crippled and alone. Some babble with awful mer-
riment. Their bodies seem sound, but the shock of war was too much for their minds;
they are the infant insane.

Each of the 43 provinces in South Vietnam has a free hospital for civilians, built long
ago by the French when they ruled the country. The hospitals might have been adequate
in peacetime; now they are all desperately overcrowded. The wounded lie on bare board
beds, frequently two to a bed, on stretchers, in the corridors, anywhere. Three hundred
major operations a month were the regular quota in the hospitals I saw; they were typical hospitals. Sometimes food is supplied for the patients; sometimes one meal; sometimes none. Their relatives, often by now homeless, must provide everything from the
little cushion that eases pain to a change of tattered clothing. They nurse and cook and
do the laundry and at night sleep on the floor beside their own wounded. The hospitals
are littered with rubbish; there is no money to spend on keeping civilian hospitals clean.
Yet the people who reach these dreadful places are fortunate; they did not die on the way.

In the children's ward of the Qui Nhon provincial hospital I saw for the first time what
napalm does. A child of seven, the size of our four-year-olds, lay in the cot by the door.
Napalm had burned his face and back and one hand. The burned skin looked like swollen,
raw meat: the fingers of his hand were stretched out, burned rigid. A scrap of cheesecloth
covered him, for weight is intolerable, but so is air. His grandfather, an emaciated old
man half blind with cataract, was tending the child. A week ago, napalm bombs were
dropped on their hamlet. The old man carried his grandson to the nearest town; from there
they were flown by helicopter to the hospital. All week, the little boy cried with pain, but
now he was better. He had stopped crying. He was only twisting his body, as if trying to
dodge his incomprehensible torture.

Farther down the ward, another child, also seven years old, moaned like a mourning
dove; he was still crying. He had been burned by napalm, too, in the same village. His

*Editorial cowardice: the word was "about" as the next sentence shows—and is the truth. [Gell-
horn's note]

mother stood over his cot, fanning the little body, in a helpless effort to cool that wet, red skin. Whatever she said, in Vietnamese, I did not understand, but her eyes and her voice revealed how gladly she would have taken for herself the child's suffering.

My interpreter questioned the old man, who said that many had been killed by the fire and many more burned, as well as their houses and orchards and livestock and the few possessions they had worked all their lives to collect. Destitute, homeless, sick with weariness and despair, he watched every move of the small, racked body of his grandson. Viet Cong guerrillas had passed through their hamlet in April the old man said, but were long since gone. Late in August, napalm bombs fell from the sky.

Napalm is jellied gasoline, contained in bombs about six feet long. The bomb, exploding on contact, hurls out gobs of this flaming stuff, and fierce fire consumes everything in its path. We alone possess and freely use this weapon in South Vietnam. Burns are deadly in relation to their depth and extent. If upwards of 30 percent of the entire thickness of the skin is burned, the victim will die within 24 to 48 hours, unless he receives skilled constant care. Tetanus and other infections are a longtime danger, until the big, open-wound surface has healed. Since transport for civilian wounded is pure chance and since the hospitals have neither staff nor facilities for special burn treatment, we can assume that the children who survive napalm and live to show the scars are those who were least burned and lucky enough to reach a hospital in time.

Children are killed or wounded by napalm because of the nature of the bombings. Close air support for infantry in combat zones is one thing. The day and night bombing of hamlets, filled with women, children and the old, is another. Bombs are mass destroyers. The military targets among the peasants—the Viet Cong—are small, fast-moving individuals. Bombs cannot identify them. Impartially, they mangle children, who are numerous, and guerrilla fighters, who are few. The use of fire and steel on South Vietnamese hamlets, because Viet Cong are reported to be in them (and often are not), can sometimes be like destroying your friend's home and family because you have heard there is a snake in the cellar.

South Vietnam is somewhat smaller than the state of Missouri. The disaster now sweeping over its people is so enormous that no single person has seen it all. But everyone in South Vietnam, native and foreign, including American soldiers, knows something of the harm done to Vietnamese peasants who never harmed us. We cannot all cross the Pacific to judge for ourselves what most affects our present and future, and America's honor in the world; but we can listen to eyewitnesses. Here is testimony from a few private citizens like you and me.

An American surgeon, who worked in the provincial hospital at Danang, a northern town now swollen with refugees and the personnel of an American port-base: "The children over there are undernourished, poorly clothed, poorly housed and being hit every day by weapons that should have been aimed at somebody else. . . . Many children died from war injuries because there was nobody around to take care of them. Many died of terrible burns. Many of shell fragments." Since the young men are all drafted in the Vietnam Army or are part of the Viet Cong, "when a village is bombed, you get an abnormal picture of civilian casualties. If you were to bomb New York, you'd hit a lot of men, women and children, but in Vietnam you hit women and children almost exclusively, and a few old men. . . . The United States is grossly careless. It bombs villages, shoots up civilians for no recognizable military objective, and it's terrible."

An American photographer flew on a night mission in a "dragon ship"—an armed DC$_{-3}$ plane—when Viet Cong were attacking a fortified government post in the southern Delta. The post was right next to a hamlet; 1,000 is the usual number of peasants in a hamlet. The dragon ship's three guns poured out 18,000 bullets a minute. This photographer said: "When you shoot so many thousand rounds of ammo, you know you're gonna hit somebody with that stuff . . . you're hitting anybody when you shoot that way . . . a one-second burst puts down enough lead to cover a football field. . . . I was there in the hospital for many days and nights. . . . One night there were so many wounded I couldn't even walk across the room because they were so thick on the floor. . . . The main wounds came from bombs and bullets and indiscriminate machine-gunning."

A housewife from New Jersey, the mother of six, had adopted three Vietnamese children under the Foster Parents Plan, and visited South Vietnam to learn how Vietnamese children were living. Why? "I am a Christian. . . . These kids don't ask to come into the world—and what a world we give them. . . . Before I went to Saigon, I had heard and read that napalm melts the flesh, and I thought that's nonsense, because I can put a roast in the oven and the fat will melt but the meat stays there. Well; I went and saw these children burned by napalm, and it is absolutely true. The chemical reaction of this napalm does melt the flesh, and the flesh runs right down their faces onto their chests and it sits there and it grows there. . . . These children can't turn their heads, they were so thick with flesh. . . . And when gangrene sets in, they cut off their hands or fingers or their feet; the only thing they cannot cut off is their head. . ."

An American physician, now serving as a health adviser to the Vietnamese Government: "The great problem in Vietnam is the shortage of doctors and the lack of minimum medical facilities. . . . We figure that there is about one Vietnamese doctor per 100,000 population, and in the Delta this figure goes up to one per 140,000. In the U.S., we think we have a doctor shortage with a ratio of one doctor to 685 persons."

The Vietnamese director of a southern provincial hospital: "We have had staffing problems because of the draft. We have a military hospital next door with 500 beds and 12 doctors. Some of them have nothing to do right now, while we in the civilian hospital need all the doctors we can get." (Compared to civilian hospitals, the military hospitals in Vietnam are havens of order and comfort. Those I saw in central Vietnam were nearly empty, wasting the invaluable time of frustrated doctors.) "We need better facilities to get people to the hospital. American wounded are treated within a matter of minutes or hours. With civilian casualties it is sometimes a matter of days—if at all. Patients come here by cart, bus, taxi, cycle, sampan, or perhaps on their relatives' backs. The longer it takes to get here, the more danger the patient will die."

There is no shortage of bureaucrats in South Vietnam, both Vietnamese and American. The U.S. Agency for International Development (A.I.D.) alone accounts for 922 of them. In the last 10 years, around a billion dollars have been allotted as direct aid to the people of South Vietnam. The results of all this bureaucracy and all this money are not impressive, though one is grateful that part of the money has bought modern surgical equipment for the civilian hospitals. But South Vietnam is gripped in a lunatic nightmare: the same official hand (white) that seeks to heal wounds inflicts more wounds. Civilian casualties far outweigh military casualties.

Foreign doctors and nurses who work as surgical teams in some provincial hospitals merit warm praise and admiration. So does anyone who serves these tormented people with compassion. Many foreign charitable organizations try to lighten misery. I mention only two because they concentrate on children. Both are volunteer organizations.

Terre des Hommes, a respected Swiss group, uses three different approaches to rescue Vietnamese children from the cruelties of this war: by sending sick and wounded children to Holland, Britain, France and Italy for long-term surgical and medical treatment; by arranging for the adoption of orphans; and by helping to support a children's hospital in Vietnam—220 beds for 660 children. This hospital might better be called an emergency medical center, since its sole purpose is to save children immediately from shock, infection and other traumas.

In England, the Oxford Committee for Famine Relief (OXFAM) has merged all its previous first-aid efforts into one: an OXFAM representative, a trained English nurse, is in Vietnam with the sole mission of channeling money, medicine, food, clothing and eventually toys (an unknown luxury) to the thousands of children in 10 Saigon orphanages.

Everything is needed for the wounded children of Vietnam, but everything cannot possibly be provided there. I believe that the least we can do—as citizens of Western Europe have done before us—is to bring badly burned children here. These children require months, perhaps years, of superior medical and surgical care in clean hospitals.

Here in America there are hopeful signs of alliance between various groups who feel a grave responsibility for wounded Vietnamese children. The U.S. branch of Terre des Hommes and a physician's group called The Committee of Responsibility for Treatment in the U.S. of War-Burned Vietnamese Children are planning ways and means of caring for some of these hurt children in the United States. Three hundred doctors have offered their skills to repair what napalm and high explosives have ruined. American hospitals have promised free beds, American families are eager to share their homes during the children's convalescence, money has been pledged. U.S. military planes, which daily transport our young men to South Vietnam, could carry wounded Vietnamese children back to America—and a chance of recovery.

The American Government is curiously unresponsive to such proposals. A State Department spokesman explains the official U.S. position this way: "Let's say we evacuate 50 children to Europe or the United States. We do not question that they would receive a higher degree of medical care, but it would really not make that much difference. On the other hand, the money spent getting those 50 children out could be better used to help 1,500 similarly wounded children in Vietnam. It seems more practical to put our energies and where-withal into treating them on the scene in Vietnam." The spokesman did not explain why we have not made more "energies and wherewithal" available to treat the wounded children, whether here or in Vietnam. Officially, it is said that children can best be cured in their familiar home environment. True; except when the home environment has been destroyed and there is no place or personnel to do the curing.

We cannot give back life to the dead Vietnamese children. But we cannot fail to help the wounded children as we would help our own. More and more dead and wounded children will cry out to the conscience of the world unless we heal the children who survive the wounds. Someday our children, whom we love, may blame us for dishonoring America because we did not care enough about children 10,000 miles away.

Understanding and Analysis

1. This essay was first published in January of 1967 in the *Ladies Home Journal.* What techniques does Gellhorn use in the first paragraph to attract the attention of her audience? What is her tone? How does she characterize her readers in this paragraph?

2. In the second paragraph, how does Gellhorn establish her readers' confidence in her report? What is the effect of the last line of the second paragraph?

3. Gellhorn's essay divides neatly into seven sections. What does Gellhorn accomplish in the second section describing My Tho and the My Tho children's hospital? What is the purpose of the last sentence in this section?

4. What places does Gellhorn describe in the third section of her essay? Again note the last sentence of the section. What is its purpose?

5. The fourth section opens with a discussion of facts. What point is Gellhorn making here?

6. What is the relationship between the paragraph about facts and the rest this section?

7. How does the final sentence of this fourth section compare to the final sentences of the other sections? Does it serve the purpose served by the other final sentences?

8. In the fifth section, where does Gellhorn describe what napalm is? Why were children victims of napalm? Where does Gellhorn get her information about the devastating effects of napalm? Who are her sources? If they are convincing, what makes them so?

9. What is the purpose of the last two sections of the essay? What actions were available at the time to help these children? What was the official response of the government? What does Gellhorn want her readers to do?

10. Reread the essay. Gellhorn uses description, statistics, analysis, and both paraphrased and quoted evidence from her sources. Do you think her treatment of the children of war is sentimental or justified? Explain your position.

Comparison

1. Read other reports about the effects of war, such as the essays by Graves, Hemingway, Panter-Downes, Pyle, and Fussell. Compare Gellhorn's tone and diction with the tone and diction found in two of the others.

2. Panter-Downes describes people in London during the blitz. Compare her description of civilians being bombed to Gellhorn's. How does audience and purpose shape each essay?

3. Read other essays that attempt to persuade the audience to take action, such as those by Carson, Mitford, Vidal, and Churchill. Do these essays share certain characteristics? If so, what are they? What about each is especially distinctive?

Edward Hoagland
(1932–)

Born in New York City on December 21, 1932, Edward Hoagland can trace his family on his father's side to farmers who settled in America before the Revolution. His paternal grandfather was an obstetrician in Kansas; his father earned a scholarship to Yale and became a financial attorney for an oil company. The Morleys, his mother's side of the family, were businessmen, arriving in America somewhat later than the Hoaglands and making their money in saddles, hardware, department store merchandise, and banking.

Like E. B. White, Hoagland grew up in financial security, loving animals and the outdoors. During the Depression the family remained in the city, where they were able to employ a maid and send their son to "an English-type school called St. Bernard's and to birthday parties at the St. Regis Hotel." By the time Hoagland was ready for the Country Day School, the family had moved to a wealthy community in Fairfield County, Connecticut, to a house with maids, "a series of Negro and old Polish ladies," and "twenty rooms, artesian water, a shady lawn, a little orchard and many majestic maples and spruce . . ." He prowled the woods and brooks on his neighbor's estate, kept dogs and chickens and alligators, and learned about falconry from the local veterinarian. Also like White, Hoagland suffered as a child, primarily from his stutter which he developed at the age of six but also from his allergy to fur and, later, from excessive nervousness.

In "Home Is Two Places," Hoagland attributes some of his adolescent fury toward his parents to "a bunch of nerves," but he also recognizes that his Connecticut community, wealthy and prejudiced, probably produced most of this anger. In "On Not Being a Jew," Hoagland records the cruelty of the townspeople who dug a huge ditch around the house of a Jewish family "to keep their children penned in," who voted in an open town meeting to reject the offer of an estate for the new high school, choosing instead to build it in a swamp near a highway because most of their children attended private school. He also records his own taunting of two Jewish store owners, as well as his enforced golf lessons at the country club, and his education at Deerfield Academy and Harvard College. His rebellion led him to spend summers fighting forest fires, traveling with the circus, tending retired MGM lions in California, sleeping in flophouses, "seeing," as he says in "Home Is Two Places," "what was foreign and maybe wretched, having experiences which were not strictly necessary in my case, and *caring*, however uselessly . . ."

385

In "The Threshold and the Jolt of Pain," Hoagland describes his stutter as "vocal handcuffs" that made him "a desperate, devoted writer at twenty." By 1954, when he graduated from Harvard, Hoagland had had his first novel accepted for publication (*Cat Man*, 1956) and had hitch-hiked through forty-three states. The next year, suffering from both asthma and his stutter, he convinced the doctor at his physical for the draft that he was fine because he knew that either guilt or doubt would plague him if he became 4-F.

After the Army, in 1957, Hoagland returned to New York City, living at times on the Upper West Side, the Lower East Side, and in Greenwich Village, writing and learning, as he describes in "The Threshhold and the Jolt of Pain" and "The Lapping, Itchy Edge of Love," about women and love. In 1960, he married his first wife, Amy, an idealistic mathematician, and published two short stories, as well as his second novel, *The Circle Home*, which received only three reviews and thus caused him "stomach trouble and neck and back cramps." He and Amy lived in Sicily, Spain, and the poorer sections of New York, both caught up in the powerful emotions of their twenties. He blames their troubles primarily on his refusal to have a child. Too late, after the divorce, Hoagland says, he realized that he loved her deeply, cried in anguish, and finally left for Europe and a "wild-oats bachelorhood."

During the sixties, Hoagland taught at the New School for Social Research (1963–1964), Rutgers University (1966), Sarah Lawrence College (1967, 1971), and City College of the City University of New York (1967–1968). He published his third novel, *The Peacock's Tail*, in 1965, after receiving a Longfellow Foundation award in 1961 and an American Academy of Arts and Letters traveling fellow award and a Guggenheim award in 1964. By the time of his second marriage, to Marion Magid, in 1968, Hoagland had finished his fourth book, *Notes From the Century Before: A Journal from British Columbia* (1969), his first non-fiction book, and was ready to commit himself to wife, child, (Molly), and the writing of essays, activities he has thoroughly enjoyed ever since. "The Draft Card Gesture," written for *Commentary* in 1968, is one of his earliest essays.

From the late sixties on, Hoagland combined teaching with writing. He has taught at the University of Iowa (1978) and Columbia (1980), and his essays have appeared in *Commentary*, *Harper's*, the *Village Voice*, the *Atlantic*, and elsewhere. Among his collections of essays are *The Courage of Turtles* (1971), *Walking the Dead Diamond River* (1973), *Red Wolves and Black Bears* (1976), *The Hoagland Reader* (1979), *Tugman's Passage* (1982), and *Balancing Acts* (1992). He has also written a second book of non-fiction, *African Calliope: A Journey to the Sudan* (1979), another novel *Seven Rivers West* (1986), and two collections of short stories, *City Tales* (1986) and *The Final Fate of Alligators* (1992). His latest collections of essays are *Balancing Acts* (1992) and *Elevating Ourselves: Thoreau on Mountains* (1999). He lives in Vermont, where he teaches part-time at Bennington College and continues to write both fiction and non-fiction.

Edward Hoagland is known for his close observation and analysis of a variety of subjects: life in the United States and elsewhere, urban and rural, among human beings and the rest of the animal kingdom. Whatever his topic, his essays often startle his readers because of his direct, personal honesty. Unlike Chesterton, who surprises by finding a significant truth in a trifle, or Mencken, who surprises by telling us forcefully what he thinks of the "boo-boisie," Hoagland surprises by revealing with sometimes painful accuracy details of his personal life that help us understand our own lives as well.

THE DRAFT CARD GESTURE (1968)

A MONTH HAS gone by since I sent my draft card to President Johnson,[1] "symbolically torn in half," as I put it to him. I had written him a more fully reasoned letter ten months before that, and I wanted to transfer myself from one category of dissenters to another one, since the war had gone on. I have no spare card to look at to see what penalties I am liable for. In theory they are fearsome enough, but probably I won't be liable for any, being already thirty-five and a veteran besides. Nobody has visited me. If I had really thought the FBI would become energetically concerned I might not have made the gesture. The last year or so of my two Army years was nearly as stultified in routine as prison must be and I wouldn't want to repeat the experience. I lead a more codified life now, whereas when I was a boy everything was grist to me.

Like many people, I had been looking for a gesture, some concise, limited act which suited me in some way and whose consequences would not be unboundedly grave. One laconic dove I am acquainted with calls this sort of thing therapy, like the professors who shout at recruiters for *Dow*.[2] Admittedly it is; many of us are losing our cool. The Frenchman who watched the drawn-out, appalling Algerian War at least had a flux of developments to contend with and a change of personae, not *Secretary Rusk*[3] for seven years. Nevertheless, although I would do it again for lack of a better idea, I'm not very comfortable with my gesture. It's a glove thrown down that won't be picked up, and it seems falsely, deliberately youthful. I might instead have signed the statement which is available for people who are withholding their income taxes, but I didn't do that because the nit-picking tangle of red tape that would result seemed more distressing to contemplate than even a possible FBI visit. I have no accountant to help me and I decided the tax protest wasn't my style.

Of course I've marched several times, accepting the anomalies of those occasions—the Workers distributed, the teenagers begging for trouble, the simplistic slogans ("Hell, no, we won't go!"). My first march was the great March on Washington in 1963 which crested so much civil-rights accomplishment. I rode down to that in an ancient school bus full of white youngsters who sang *Old Black Joe*. And yet they were not merely gauche. They converted the driver, who had started the day like a typical union man driv-

---

[1]*President Johnson* Lyndon Baines Johnson (1908–1973) United States president from 1963–1969, during a large part of the Vietnam War.

[2]*Dow* Dow Corning, a chemical company.

[3]*Secretary Rusk* Dean Rusk (1909–1994) Secretary of State for Lyndon Johnson, who played a significant role in shaping the administration's policy on the Vietnam War.

ing a busload of kooks, and they sang *We Shall Overcome* so fervently that the maids in the motels stopped working as we went by. When we pulled into the parking lot at the Washington Monument, reporters surrounded us. "Free-dom," chanted our group, which sounded like "We've come," which would have been equally good. The Mississippi contingent marched the length of the mall more than once because they felt they had earned it and because it was a thrill. The police captains beamed as at a fish fry for kids, the city people sneezed with hay fever, the Monument stood gleaming and tall, and happy-looking clergymen stood about everywhere, more happy clergy than had ever gathered before anywhere. The wit of *Wilkins*,[4] the shivering exhortations of *King* were enhanced fantastically by the fact that two hundred thousand people had collected here for the sake of an urgent dream that in some of its practical, easier aspects was on the brink of being achieved. We had a flexible President, we had a national consensus that the time for this change had come due. It was a day of lavish, exhilarating courtesy—of the Golden Rule. Our cheeks felt pouchy with backed-up tears; our throats throbbed the whole afternoon. The crowd carried the day—the speakers took the crowd's cue. Afterwards I flew home. In the airport washroom there was a wretched moment when I tried to persuade a Negro traveler to break a dollar bill for me, assuming that he was the bootblack because he was black. I had no change because I had tipped the cab driver well, and I'd tipped him well because he had undercharged me. He'd undercharged me because, on impulse, I had sat in the front seat with him; and so the day ended appropriately complicatedly. But, just as these exercises would seem like playing games in the context of Black Power, the very idea of trekking to Washington in that hopeful and peaceful mood, believing that as Americans we could evoke a government response, was part of the year 1963.

In October that fall there was a March on City Hall which I joined when it passed my street. It was a ragtag, provocative bunch of angry young militants and painfully fired-up older Negroes, in some cases drunk. "Wagner[5] must go!" was the yell. We avoided looking at one another as we walked, and the police mocked us. None of the featured speakers showed up. The reporters for the *Daily News* grinned. Then, the summer of 1964 was the first summer of riots, the worst in New York since the Second World War. An eerie, gingerly city noticed the line-up of blacks to whites on each subway car. The radio broadcast a Roman roar from 125th Street, and even downtown I saw considerable violence and was almost arrested a couple of times for sticking my nose in, when the Negroes would dodge out from under the policemen's clubs and get away. I saw police beaten up too: much sad courage.

Civil rights splintered confusingly as a cause, and the tiny, vestigial ear for suffering that might be remedied which many of us possess became more attuned to the Vietnam war. The bulky march in April 1967 to the UN was a pleasant stroll, but the memorable exuberance of the '63 march was gone. We knew we were shouting to a deaf ear, and few of us had seen Vietnam, nobody was Vietnamese, so that even the imagery in our minds was thwarted and inaccurate. At the end of the year, the one draft demonstration at Whitehall which I sampled was still harder for me to unite myself with. "*If the horses are charging you, move in a zigzag pattern. If the horses are standing still, put your hands on their noses and they will not charge you.*" (At the Washington March in 1963 we'd been instructed to eat our mayonnaise sandwiches before noon so that they wouldn't spoil

[4]*Wilkins* Roy Wilkins (1901–1981) an African-American civil rights activist who headed the NAACP from 1931–1977 and played a significant role in writing the 1964 Civil Rights Act.

[5]*Wagner* Robert F. Wagner, Jr., (1910–1991) three-time mayor of New York City.

and make us ill.) It was a predawn army with hectoring marshals, a hurry-up-wait atmosphere, and a certain hysteric camaraderie. Plain-clothes detectives with pinprick green buttons in their lapels were everywhere. Dawn arrived, sunrise came. Police and students acted equally belligerently. The police herded us continually, as if enjoying it, rapping their clubs on the wooden barriers. The setting was an attractive, elderly area faced in old stone, and the massed shouts echoed up out of unison like the shouts of the Civil War draft riots there. By eight in the morning the office workers began pouring through, perturbed and scolding, because this wasn't a matter of challenging racial prejudices which they already quite recognized were outdated and contradictory—this was dissent; this was calling an American war an unjust war, a phenomenon unknown to the national experience for a hundred years. I was dressed conventionally but wearing a flower, and on the subway going home I met hundreds of questioning stares.

I wrote my covering letter to the President, saying that one could not forever protest a ferocious war by what are called peaceful means, and attaching the two scraps of the draft card with a paper clip, dropped the letter into the mail chute of my building, listening to its descent. I had been carrying the card since 1950, when Edith Moriarty of Norwalk, Connecticut, signed it for me. To an extent, I had shared the bewilderment of many of the policemen at Whitehall and the starers on the subway because, like them, I was a veteran. I knew that the experience of military service was usually a useful one and, looking around, I could see whom it might have been particularly useful to. Although I live differently now than I did in 1955 when I was waiting to be drafted, even taking me as I was then, there would have been some dissimilarities between my attitude and that of a lot of the kids on the March. I was a direct patriot, a peppy, idealistic fellow living off Union Square. I had hitchhiked all over America, dragging my suitcase through forty-three states. I'd seen the Snake and the Rio Grande, and San Diego and Aberdeen, Wash.; in fact I'd turned down a trip to Europe in order to go out and see more. And so in the evenings I often went to the Square to hear the accents of the soapbox speakers, scanning the wheat-belt and Kentucky faces. It seemed that the entire country was represented there, old men of every occupation, scallop boatmen and soybean farmers. The Communists spoke under an equestrian statue—"under the horse's ass," as they said. Early birds saved the platform for them and they scheduled themselves: first a small dedicated Jewish bookkeeper who spoke seriously from notes; after him, a rangy Dos Passos Communist with Idaho still in his voice and the vocal cords of a labor organizer; and lastly a Khrushchev Communist, an emotive, fair-minded Russian, a family man with an earthy, demonstrative face who rode up from Catherine Street on his bicycle with a white terrier running alongside. They were assigned by the party—even the early birds—to the task, they told us. The other speakers hadn't the training or the podium, but they did their best: a prototype black nationalist, a hollering atheist, a thin Catholic proselytizer who was a retired businessman living on West 72nd Street—he was the odd man out and he tore his voice shouting at all of them. They brought up the Inquisition so many times that at last he started defending it. There were also a couple of opera singers, a vaudeville comedian, and a pacifist who knelt on the pavement after every pugnacious remark that he made. One man, a turkey-necked, pasty-cheeked fellow of fifty, couldn't speak at all; apparently his throat had been operated on. His opponents would give him the floor anyway. Bending down next to his mouth to catch his whisper, they repeated it to the crowd and then answered it.

I loved Dos Passos and Steinbeck, and though my blood beat at the stories of injustice the crowd was told, mainly I came to the square because of the faces I saw, constituting a map of the continent, from the tunafish cannery where I'd worked one July to the Platte River that I'd hitchhiked along. As a matter of fact, I didn't have to be drafted. I chose to be drafted for a number of reasons, one of which was this heated enthusiasm of mine for America as a whole—I loved the pink deserts; I could distinguish a Milwaukee accent from a Cincinnati drawl. But since I was subject to asthma during the summer and stuttered, both ailments which offered me a legitimate out, for more than a year I'd been debating whether to become 4-F or 1-A. When I leaned toward the first choice, however, my asthma reared up and almost asphyxiated me and I stuttered so badly I became mute. I did want to go into the Army for the loving, elated reasons that Steinbeck might have felt, but quite beyond them I realized I *had* to go in. Whether from a sense of guilt or from doubt of my competence as a man otherwise, if I didn't I would be troubled for years afterwards.

The day of the physical came at last. The doctor already had records that would have let me out, but talking as smoothly as Simon Peter, I asked him please to ignore them; I told him I was all right. In basic training I gained twenty pounds and completely stopped stuttering for a while. The jammed early months were a sort of bazaar of cornpone youngsters, sturdy black sergeants, close-order instruction and capsuled war games. At Fort Sam Houston I slept underneath an undertaker. I had porky best friends and skinny best friends, who were perfume chemists and lathe operators. Then I was sent to Pennsylvania, where I stayed twenty months, engrossed in writing a novel whenever I could. The supercharged excitement petered out; I became my accustomed neurotic self.

As long as I actually remained in the Army I wasn't too smug or moralistic about serving because I wasn't entirely glad about it. But when the period was over I grew raucous and difficult for those of my friends who had chosen to huddle in graduate school or had painted their toenails red for the draft exam. I thought they'd denied themselves one of the core experiences. I still think they did, and I'm sorry that so many boys nowadays find it necessary to avoid that first salubrious shock of a training camp—the self-discoveries, the fortuitous friendships, the vaccinal dip in the stewpan of war. But it seems necessary that they do so. This war is too atrociously twisted in its rationale to have been declared. It has become as meaningful now to tear one's draft card in half as it once was to insist upon being drafted. Strong patriots are going to jail, and if I remain anonymous as a number in a file at the Justice Department, at least I have dramatized my dissent by removing myself from a prosaic list to a red-letter list.

Understanding and Analysis

1. What is the significance of the word "gesture" in the title and in the first and second paragraphs?

2. What is the meaning of the "glove thrown down"?

3. Why does Hoagland describe in some detail the marches he has participated in?

4. Describe the salient qualities of the 1963 March on Washington, as Hoagland experienced them.

5. Compare that march to the March on City Hall. What other demonstrations did Hoagland participate in? Does Hoagland present a discernable pattern in his descriptions of these demonstrations?

6. Find the sentence in which Hoagland offers a reason for the shift in interest of many to the cause of the Vietnam War. How does the metaphor of the ear work in that sentence and in the lines following it?

7. The torn draft card appears three times in the essay. How does it contribute to the structure of the essay?

8. Why does Hoagland describe in such detail the speakers he listened to in Washington Square?

9. What reasons does Hoagland give for deciding to become 1–A?

10. What attitudes does Hoagland take toward his experiences in the Army? Why does he believe it is "one of the core experiences"?

11. Does the significance of "the draft card gesture" change by the end of the essay? If so, in what way?

Comparison

1. What qualities does Hoagland share, if any, with writers such as Orwell and Podhoretz?

2. Read the essay by Fussell. Compare the attitudes toward the experience of serving in the army as expressed by the two writers.

3. Compare Hoagland's description of the March on Washington with the speech delivered by Martin Luther King, Jr., and with his "Letter from Birmingham Jail." What perspectives do these essays offer on the civil rights movement? Read Malcolm X's interpretation of the March on Washington. How does his analysis add to the perspectives offered by Hoagland and King?

4. Read Gellhorn's essay on Vietnam. Compare Hoagland's attitude toward the war with that of Gellhorn.

Maya Angelou
(1928–)

Born in St. Louis, Missouri, Marguerite Johnson traveled by rail to Stamps, Arkansas, when she was three years old, jettisoned to her grandmother, along with her four-year-old brother, Bailey, in the wake of her parents' divorce. Living in her grandmother's store, she spent every Sunday in church and the rest of the week working and listening: to the cotton pickers who came in each morning and evening, to her grandmother's admonitions about hard work and Christian living, and to neighborhood gossip about whites and sex.

(Not allowed to remain in the room for such talk, she and her brother devised a system of tag-team eavesdropping.) When she was seven, her father arrived for the first time and took her and Bailey to live with their mother in St. Louis. Roughly a year after they arrived, Angelou was raped by her mother's boyfriend, Mr. Freeman. He was convicted of the crime, but later freed; a few days later, he was found beaten to death. After the murder, Angelou stopped speaking and started writing poetry.

Sent back to Stamps, Angelou found her voice and graduated from the eighth grade in 1940, joining her mother in Oakland, California, at the age of 13. Shortly after she arrived, she writes, "I was on my way to the movies. People in the streets shouted, 'We're at war. We've declared war on Japan.' I ran all the way home. Not too sure I wouldn't be bombed before I reached Bailey and Mother." When the family moved to San Francisco with her mother's new husband, Angelou skipped a grade and won a scholarship—"I never knew why"—to study "dance and drama" at the California Labor School. Disenchanted with high school, Angelou determined that she wanted to become a streetcar conductor, and through sheer persistence became the first African-American conductor in San Francisco. After a few months, she returned to school, and following a one-night encounter with an acquaintance, found herself pregnant with her son, Guy. She graduated from high school in 1945, "[t]wo days after V-Day."

Following Guy's birth, as she recounts in her second autobiography, *Gather Together in My Name* (1974), Angelou worked as a Creole cook, a short-order cook, the Madam of a small whorehouse, and ultimately, a prostitute. Vowing never again to lose her "innocence," she accepted a position in a record store, where she met her first husband, a Greek man named Tosh Angelos, who insisted that she become a housewife. The marriage did not last, and once again in need of work, Angelou started dancing at a club called The Garden of Allah. There she made connections that led her to The Purple Onion, a cabaret club that agreed to feature her as their singer. In collaboration with a drama coach, she chose Maya Angelou as her stage name and began her rise to fame, as recounted in her third autobiography, *Singin' and Swingin' and Gettin' Merry Like Christmas* (1976). When her contract ended, she joined the European tour of *Porgy and Bess*. Leaving Guy in the care of her mother, she traveled to Italy, France, Serbo-Croatia, and Egypt, and for each new country, she bought dictionaries or hired language coaches, doing what she could to learn the language before returning to the United States.

In her twenties, she explains in her fourth autobiography, *The Heart of a Woman* (1981), she really "began to write. At first I limited myself to short sketches, then to song lyrics, then I dared short stories." The writer John Gillens reviewed her work and encouraged her to move to New York to join the

Harlem Writer's Guild. Settling into her new city, she went with Godfrey Cambridge to hear Martin Luther King, Jr. Awed and inspired, the two determined to produce a show and donate all proceeds to King's Southern Christian Leadership Council (SCLC), which asked her to become its northern coordinator in 1959. Two months later, she met King himself.

Leaving the SCLC in 1960, Angelou unofficially married the South African freedom fighter Vus Make, organized an extremely disorganized demonstration of Harlem residents at the UN, and sought advice from Malcolm X (not approving of demonstrations, he had little). No less committed to radical politics, she returned to the theater and acted with Cambridge, James Earl Jones, and Cicely Tyson in the cast of Jean Genet's *The Blacks*. It was her last American run in the theater for some time, as she and her son joined Make in Cairo. With Make's grudging approval, she became an associate editor for the *Arab Observer* and wrote copy for Radio Egypt. When her marriage disintegrated, she decided to enroll Guy at the University of Ghana, and fell in love with the Ghanian nation. Among the group that received Malcolm X when he returned from Mecca, she anticipated working with him when she "came back to the states," but as she told interviewer Stephanie Caruana in 1974, "I got back on a Friday and Malcolm was killed on a Sunday. After that, I decided to have nothing to do with politics, directly."

Working as a lecturer at UCLA in 1966, Angelou "wrote ten one-hour television programs called *Blacks, Blues, Blacks*, which highlighted Africanisms still current in American life." In 1970, two years after they aired, she served as writer in residence at the University of Kansas and published *I Know Why the Caged Bird Sings*, which grew out of conversations with James Baldwin, among others, and was nominated for a National Book Award. When she was not writing autobiographies, Angelou was writing poetry, collected in works such as *Just Give Me a Cool Drink of Water 'fore I Diiie* (1971), nominated for a Pulitzer Prize; *And Still I Rise* (1978), which she later directed for the stage; and *Shaker, Why Don't You Sing?* (1981). In 1973, the year she debuted on Broadway in *Look Away*, she married Paul du Feu, ex-husband of Germaine Greer. Although it was "a great marriage," Angelou told Tricia Crane in 1987, "we wore it out." The couple divorced in 1981, after she had appeared in the movie *Roots* and agreed to teach at Wake Forest University.

In the 1990s, Angelou published additional collections of poetry, a volume of short essays called *Wouldn't Take Nothing for My Journey Now* (1993), and children's books such as *My Painted House, My Friendly Chicken, and Me* (1994). "In 1993," according to *Contemporary Authors*, "Angelou gave a moving reading of her poem 'On the Pulse of the Morning' at Bill Clinton's presidential inauguration, an occasion that brought her wide recognition." For the recording of "On the Pulse of the Morning," Angelou received a Grammy.

Unlike some less fortunate poets, Maya Angelou is an excellent reader of her own work. Indeed, she recorded her first poetry with GWP Records in 1969, two years before she first published it. The United Negro College Fund featured Angelou reading "And Still I Rise" in a late-1990s television commercial, and her voice has been celebrated as "smooth" and "lyrical," "[v]ibrant and deep-toned." The poetry itself, on the other hand, is far more popular than critically acclaimed. Literary critics reserve their praise almost exclusively for her autobiographies. According to *The New York Times*, "Maya Angelou is one of the geniuses of Afro-American serial autobiography." And according to just about everyone, *I Know Why the Caged Bird Sings* is a revelation.

GRADUATION (1969)

THE CHILDREN IN Stamps[1] trembled visibly with anticipation. Some adults were excited too, but to be certain the whole young population had come down with graduation epidemic. Large classes were graduating from both the grammar school and the high school. Even those who were years removed from their own day of glorious release were anxious to help with preparations as a kind of dry run. The junior students who were moving into the vacating classes' chairs were tradition-bound to show their talents for leadership and management. They strutted through the school and around the campus exerting pressure on the lower grades. Their authority was so new that occasionally if they pressed a little too hard it had to be overlooked. After all, next term was coming, and it never hurt a sixth grader to have a play sister in the eighth grade, or a tenth-year student to be able to call a twelfth grader Bubba. So all was endured in a spirit of shared understanding. But the graduating classes themselves were the nobility. Like travelers with exotic destinations on their minds, the graduates were remarkably forgetful. They came to school without their books, or tablets or even pencils. Volunteers fell over themselves to secure replacements for the missing equipment. When accepted, the willing workers might or might not be thanked, and it was of no importance to the pregraduation rites. Even teachers were respectful of the now quiet and aging seniors, and tended to speak to them, if not as equals, as beings only slightly lower than themselves. After tests were returned and grades given, the student body, which acted like an extended family, knew who did well, who excelled, and what piteous ones had failed.

Unlike the white high school, Lafayette County Training School distinguished itself by having neither lawn, nor hedges, nor tennis court, nor climbing ivy. Its two buildings (main classrooms, the grade school and home economics) were set on a dirt hill with no fence to limit either its boundaries or those of bordering farms. There was a large expanse to the left of the school which was used alternately as a baseball diamond or basketball court. Rusty hoops on swaying poles represented the permanent recreational equipment, although bats and balls could be borrowed from the P.E. teacher if the borrower was qualified and if the diamond wasn't occupied.

Over this rocky area relieved by a few shady tall persimmon trees the graduating class walked. The girls often held hands and no longer bothered to speak to the lower students.

---

[1]*Stamps* a town in Arkansas.

There was a sadness about them, as if this old world was not their home and they were bound for higher ground. The boys, on the other hand, had become more friendly, more outgoing. A decided change from the closed attitude they projected while studying for finals. Now they seemed not ready to give up the old school, the familiar paths and classrooms. Only a small percentage would be continuing on to college—one of the South's A & M (agricultural and mechanical) schools, which trained Negro youths to be carpenters, farmers, handymen, masons, maids, cooks and baby nurses. Their future rode heavily on their shoulders, and blinded them to the collective joy that had pervaded the lives of the boys and girls in the grammar school graduating class.

Parents who could afford it had ordered new shoes and readymade clothes for themselves from Sears and Roebuck or Montgomery Ward. They also engaged the best seamstresses to make the floating graduating dresses and to cut down secondhand pants which would be pressed to a military slickness for the important event.

Oh, it was important, all right. Whitefolks would attend the ceremony, and two or three would speak of God and home, and the Southern way of life, and Mrs. Parsons, the principal's wife, would play the graduation march while the lower-grade graduates paraded down the aisles and took their seats below the platform. The high school seniors would wait in empty classrooms to make their dramatic entrance.

In the Store I was the person of the moment. The birthday girl. The center. Bailey[2] had graduated the year before, although to do so he had had to forfeit all pleasures to make up for his time lost in Baton Rouge.

My class was wearing butter-yellow piqué dresses, and Momma launched out on mine. She smocked the yoke into tiny crisscrossing puckers, then shirred the rest of the bodice. Her dark fingers ducked in and out of the lemony cloth as she embroidered raised daisies around the hem. Before she considered herself finished she had added a crocheted cuff on the puff sleeves, and a pointy crocheted collar.

I was going to be lovely. A walking model of all the various styles of fine hand sewing and it didn't worry me that I was only twelve years old and merely graduating from the eighth grade. Besides, many teachers in Arkansas Negro schools had only that diploma and were licensed to impart wisdom.

The days had become longer and more noticeable. The faded beige of former times had been replaced with strong and sure colors. I began to see my classmates' clothes, their skin tones, and the dust that waved off pussy willows. Clouds that lazed across the sky were objects of great concern to me. Their shiftier shapes might have held a message that in my new happiness and with a little bit of time I'd soon decipher. During that period I looked at the arch of heaven so religiously my neck kept a steady ache. I had taken to smiling more often, and my jaws hurt from the unaccustomed activity. Between the two physical sore spots, I suppose I could have been uncomfortable, but that was not the case. As a member of the winning team (the graduating class of 1940) I had outdistanced unpleasant sensations by miles. I was headed for the freedom of open fields.

Youth and social approval allied themselves with me and we trammeled memories of slights and insults. The wind of our swift passage remodeled my features. Lost tears were pounded to mud and then to dust. Years of withdrawal were brushed aside and left behind, as hanging ropes of parasitic moss.

My work alone had awarded me a top place and I was going to be one of the first called in the graduating ceremonies. On the classroom blackboard, as well as on the bul-

[2]*Bailey* the author's brother.

letin board in the auditorium, there were blue stars and white stars and red stars. No absences, no tardinesses, and my academic work was among the best of the year. I could say the preamble to the Constitution even faster than Bailey. We timed ourselves often: "We the people of the United States in order to form a more perfect union . . ." I had memorized the Presidents of the United States from Washington to Roosevelt in chronological as well as alphabetical order.

My hair pleased me too. Gradually the black mass had lengthened and thickened, so that it kept at last to its braided pattern, and I didn't have to yank my scalp off when I tried to comb it.

Louise and I had rehearsed the exercises until we tired out ourselves. Henry Reed was class valedictorian. He was a small, very black boy with hooded eyes, a long, broad nose and an oddly shaped head. I had admired him for years because each term he and I vied for the best grades in our class. Most often he bested me, but instead of being disappointed I was pleased that we shared top places between us. Like many Southern Black children, he lived with his grandmother, who was as strict as Momma and as kind as she knew how to be. He was courteous, respectful and soft-spoken to elders, but on the playground he chose to play the roughest games. I admired him. Anyone, I reckoned, sufficiently afraid or sufficiently dull could be polite. But to be able to operate at a top level with both adults and children was admirable.

His valedictory speech was entitled "To Be or Not to Be." The rigid tenth-grade teacher had helped him write it. He'd been working on the dramatic stresses for months.

The weeks until graduation were filled with heady activities. A group of small children were to be presented in a play about buttercups and daisies and bunny rabbits. They could be heard throughout the building practicing their hops and their little songs that sounded like silver bells. The older girls (nongraduates, of course) were assigned the task of making refreshments for the night's festivities. A tangy scent of ginger, cinnamon, nutmeg and chocolate wafted around the home economics building as the budding cooks made samples for themselves and their teachers.

In every corner of the workshop, axes and saws split fresh timber as the woodshop boys made sets and stage scenery. Only the graduates were left out of the general bustle. We were free to sit in the library at the back of the building or look in quite detachedly, naturally, on the measures being taken for our event.

Even the minister preached on graduation the Sunday before. His subject was, "Let your light so shine that men will see your good works and praise your Father, Who is in Heaven." Although the sermon was purported to be addressed to us, he used the occasion to speak to backsliders, gamblers and general ne'er-do-wells. But since he had called our names at the beginning of the service we were mollified.

Among Negroes the tradition was to give presents to children going only from one grade to another. How much more important this was when the person was graduating at the top of the class. Uncle Willie and Momma had sent away for a Mickey Mouse watch like Bailey's. Louise gave me four embroidered handkerchiefs. (I gave her crocheted doilies.) Mrs. Sneed, the minister's wife, made me an undershirt to wear for graduation, and nearly every customer gave me a nickel or maybe even a dime with the instruction "Keep on moving to higher ground," or some such encouragement.

Amazingly the great day finally dawned and I was out of bed before I knew it. I threw open the back door to see it more clearly, but Momma said, "Sister, come away from that door and put your robe on."

I hoped the memory of that morning would never leave me. Sunlight was itself young, and the day had none of the insistence maturity would bring it in a few hours. In my robe and barefoot in the backyard, under cover of going to see about my new beans, I gave myself up to the gentle warmth and thanked God that no matter what evil I had done in my life He had allowed me to live to see this day. Somewhere in my fatalism I had expected to die, accidentally, and never have the chance to walk up the stairs in the auditorium and gracefully receive my hard-earned diploma. Out of God's merciful bosom I had won reprieve.

Bailey came out in his robe and gave me a box wrapped in Christmas paper. He said he had saved his money for months to pay for it. It felt like a box of chocolates, but I knew Bailey wouldn't save money to buy candy when we had all we could want under our noses.

He was as proud of the gift as I. It was a soft-leather-bound copy of a collection of poems by Edgar Allan Poe, or, as Bailey and I called him, "Eap." I turned to "Annabel Lee" and we walked up and down the garden rows, the cool dirt between our toes, reciting the beautifully sad lines.

Momma made a Sunday breakfast although it was only Friday. After we finished the blessing, I opened my eyes to find the watch on my plate. It was a dream of a day. Everything went smoothly and to my credit, I didn't have to be reminded or scolded for anything. Near evening I was too jittery to attend to chores, so Bailey volunteered to do all before his bath.

Days before, we had made a sign for the Store, and as we turned out the lights Momma hung the cardboard over the doorknob. It read clearly: CLOSED. GRADUATION.

My dress fitted perfectly and everyone said that I looked like a sunbeam in it. On the hill, going toward the school, Bailey walked behind with Uncle Willie, who muttered, "Go on, Ju." He wanted him to walk ahead with us because it embarrassed him to have to walk so slowly. Bailey said he'd let the ladies walk together, and the men would bring up the rear. We all laughed, nicely.

Little children dashed by out of the dark like fireflies. Their crepe-paper dresses and butterfly wings were not made for running and we heard more than one rip, dryly, and the regretful "uh uh" that followed.

The school blazed without gaiety. The windows seemed cold and unfriendly from the lower hill. A sense of ill-fated timing crept over me, and if Momma hadn't reached for my hand I would have drifted back to Bailey and Uncle Willie, and possibly beyond. She made a few slow jokes about my feet getting cold, and tugged me along to the now-strange building.

Around the front steps, assurance came back. There were my fellow "greats," the graduating class. Hair brushed back, legs oiled, new dresses and pressed pleats, fresh pocket handkerchiefs and little handbags, all homesewn. Oh, we were up to snuff, all right. I joined my comrades and didn't even see my family go in to find seats in the crowded auditorium.

The school band struck up a march and all classes filed in as had been rehearsed. We stood in front of our seats, as assigned, and on a signal from the choir director, we sat. No sooner had this been accomplished than the band started to play the national anthem. We rose again and sang the song, after which we recited the pledge of allegiance. We remained standing for a brief minute before the choir director and the principal signaled to us, rather desperately I thought, to take our seats. The command was so unusual that our carefully rehearsed and smooth-running machine was thrown off. For a full minute we fumbled for our chairs and bumped into each other awkwardly. Habits change or solidify under pressure, so in our state of nervous tension we had been ready to follow our usual assembly pattern: the American national anthem, then the pledge of allegiance, then the song every Black person I knew called the Negro National Anthem. All done in the same key, with the same passion and most often standing on the same foot.

Finding my seat at last, I was overcome with a presentiment of worse things to come. Something unrehearsed, unplanned, was going to happen, and we were going to be made to look bad. I distinctly remember being explicit in the choice of pronoun. It was "we," the graduating class, the unit, that concerned me then.

The principal welcomed "parents and friends" and asked the Baptist minister to lead us in prayer. His invocation was brief and punchy, and for a second I thought we were getting on the high road to right action. When the principal came back to the dais, however, his voice had changed. Sounds always affected me profoundly and the principal's voice was one of my favorites. During assembly it melted and lowed weakly into the audience. It had not been in my plan to listen to him, but my curiosity was piqued and I straightened up to give him my attention.

He was talking about Booker T. Washington, our "late great leader," who said we can be as close as the fingers on the hand, etc. . . . Then he said a few vague things about friendship and the friendship of kindly people to those less fortunate than themselves. With that his voice nearly faded, thin, away. Like a river diminishing to a stream and then to a trickle. But he cleared his throat and said, "Our speaker tonight, who is also our friend, came from Texarkana to deliver the commencement address, but due to the irregularity of the train schedule, he's going to, as they say, 'speak and run.' " He said that we understood and wanted the man to know that we were most grateful for the time he was able to give us and then something about how we were willing always to adjust to another's program, and without more ado—"I give you Mr. Edward Donleavy."

Not one but two white men came through the door off-stage. The shorter one walked to the speaker's platform, and the tall one moved to the center seat and sat down. But that was our principal's seat, and already occupied. The dislodged gentleman bounced around for a long breath or two before the Baptist minister gave him his chair, then with more dignity than the situation deserved, the minister walked off the stage.

Donleavy looked at the audience once (on reflection, I'm sure that he wanted only to reassure himself that we were really there), adjusted his glasses and began to read from a sheaf of papers.

He was glad "to be here and to see the work going on just as it was in the other schools."

At the first "Amen" from the audience I willed the offender to immediate death by choking on the word. But Amens and Yes, sir's began to fall around the room like rain through a ragged umbrella.

He told us of the wonderful changes we children in Stamps had in store. The Central School (naturally, the white school was Central) had already been granted improvements that would be in use in the fall. A well-known artist was coming from Little Rock to teach art to them. They were going to have the newest microscopes and chemistry equipment for their laboratory. Mr. Donleavy didn't leave us long in the dark over who made these improvements available to Central High. Nor were we to be ignored in the general betterment scheme he had in mind.

He said that he had pointed out to people at a very high level that one of the first-line football tacklers at Arkansas Agricultural and Mechanical College had graduated from good old Lafayette County Training School. Here fewer Amen's were heard. Those few that did break through lay dully in the air with the heaviness of habit.

He went on to praise us. He went on to say how he had bragged that "one of the best basketball players at Fisk sank his first ball right here at Lafayette County Training School."

The white kids were going to have a chance to become Galileos and Madame Curies and Edisons and Gauguins, and our boys (the girls weren't even in on it) would try to be Jesse Owenses and Joe Louises.

Owens and the Brown Bomber were great heroes in our world, but what school official in the white-goddom of Little Rock had the right to decide that those two men must be our only heroes? Who decided that for Henry Reed to become a scientist he had to work like George Washington Carver, as a bootblack, to buy a lousy microscope? Bailey was obviously always going to be too small to be an athlete, so which concrete angel glued to what country seat had decided that if my brother wanted to become a lawyer he had to first pay penance for his skin by picking cotton and hoeing corn and studying correspondence books at night for twenty years?

The man's dead words fell like bricks around the auditorium and too many settled in my belly. Constrained by hard-learned manners I couldn't look behind me, but to my left and right the proud graduating class of 1940 had dropped their heads. Every girl in my row had found something new to do with her handkerchief. Some folded the tiny squares into love knots, some into triangles, but most were wadding them, then pressing them flat on their yellow laps.

On the dais, the ancient tragedy was being replayed. Professor Parsons sat, a sculptor's reject, rigid. His large, heavy body seemed devoid of will or willingness, and his eyes said he was no longer with us. The other teachers examined the flag (which was draped stage right) or their notes, or the windows which opened on our now-famous playing diamond.

Graduation, the hush-hush magic time of frills and gifts and congratulations and diplomas, was finished for me before my name was called. The accomplishment was nothing. The meticulous maps, drawn in three colors of ink, learning and spelling decasyllabic words, memorizing the whole of *The Rape of Lucrece*[3]—it was for nothing. Donleavy had exposed us.

We were maids and farmers, handymen and washerwomen, and anything higher that we aspired to was farcical and presumptuous.

Then I wished that Gabriel Prosser and Nat Turner[4] had killed all whitefolks in their beds and that Abraham Lincoln had been assassinated before the signing of the Emancipation Proclamation, and that Harriet Tubman[5] had been killed by that blow on her head and Christopher Columbus had drowned in the *Santa Maria*.

It was awful to be a Negro and have no control over my life. It was brutal to be young and already trained to sit quietly and listen to charges brought against my color with no chance of defense. We should all be dead. I thought I should like to see us all dead, one on top of the other. A pyramid of flesh with the whitefolks on the bottom, as the broad base, then the Indians with their silly tomahawks and tepees and wigwams and treaties, the Negroes with their mops and recipes and cotton sacks and spirituals sticking out of their

[3]*The Rape of Lucrece* a long narrative poem by Shakespeare in which the daughter of a Roman official kills herself after she is raped.

[4]*Gabriel Prosser and Nat Turner* Prosser (1776–1800) and Turner (1800–1831) were executed after leading unsuccessful slave rebellions.

[5]*Harriet Tubman* (1820–1913) a black abolitionist known for her work as a "conductor" on the Underground Railroad.

mouths. The Dutch children should all stumble in their wooden shoes and break their necks. The French should choke to death on the Louisiana Purchase (1803) while silkworms ate all the Chinese with their stupid pigtails. As a species, we were an abomination. All of us.

Donleavy was running for election, and assured our parents that if he won we could count on having the only colored paved playing field in that part of Arkansas. Also—he never looked up to acknowledge the grunts of acceptance—also, we were bound to get some new equipment for the home economics building and the workshop.

He finished, and since there was no need to give any more than the most perfunctory thank-you's, he nodded to the men on the stage, and the tall white man who was never introduced joined him at the door. They left with the attitude that now they were off to something really important. (The graduation ceremonies at Lafayette County Training School had been a mere preliminary.)

The ugliness they left was palpable. An uninvited guest who wouldn't leave. The choir was summoned and sang a modern arrangement of "Onward, Christian Soldiers," with new words pertaining to graduates seeking their place in the world. But it didn't work. Elouise, the daughter of the Baptist minister, recited "Invictus,"[6] and I could have cried at the impertinence of "I am the master of my fate, I am the captain of my soul."

My name had lost its ring of familiarity and I had to be nudged to go and receive my diploma. All my preparations had fled. I neither marched up to the stage like a conquering Amazon, nor did I look in the audience for Bailey's nod of approval. Marguerite Johnson, I heard the name again, my honors were read, there were noises in the audience of appreciation, and I took my place on the stage as rehearsed.

I thought about colors I hated: ecru, puce, lavender, beige and black.

There was shuffling and rustling around me, then Henry Reed was giving his valedictory address, "To Be or Not to Be." Hadn't he heard the whitefolks? We couldn't *be,* so the question was a waste of time. Henry's voice came out clear and strong. I feared to look at him. Hadn't he got the message? There was no "nobler in the mind" for Negroes because the world didn't think we had minds, and they let us know it. "Outrageous fortune"? Now, that was a joke. When the ceremony was over I had to tell Henry Reed some things. That is, if I still cared. Not "rub," Henry, "erase." "Ah, there's the erase." Us.

Henry had been a good student in elocution. His voice rose on tides of promise and fell on waves of warnings. The English teacher had helped him to create a sermon winging through Hamlet's soliloquy. To be a man, a doer, a builder, a leader, or to be a tool, an unfunny joke, a crusher of funky toadstools. I marveled that Henry could go through with the speech as if we had a choice.

I had been listening and silently rebutting each sentence with my eyes closed; then there was a hush, which in an audience warns that something unplanned is happening. I looked up and saw Henry Reed, the conservative, the proper, the A student, turn his back to the audience and turn to us (the proud graduating class of 1940) and sing, nearly speaking,

> "Lift ev'ry voice and sing
> Till earth and heaven ring
> Ring with the harmonies of Liberty . . ."

It was the poem written by James Weldon Johnson. It was the music composed by J. Rosamond Johnson. It was the Negro national anthem. Out of habit we were singing it.

---

[6]*Invictus* An inspirational poem by William Ernest Henley.

Our mothers and fathers stood in the dark hall and joined the hymn of encouragement. A kindergarten teacher led the small children onto the stage and the buttercups and daisies and bunny rabbits marked time and tried to follow:

> "Stony the road we trod
> Bitter the chastening rod
> Felt in the days when hope, unborn, had died.
> Yet with a steady beat
> Have not our weary feet
> Come to the place for which our fathers sighed?"

Each child I knew had learned that song with his ABC's and along with "Jesus Loves Me This I Know." But I personally had never heard it before. Never heard the words, despite the thousands of times I had sung them. Never thought they had anything to do with me.

On the other hand, the words of Patrick Henry[7] had made such an impression on me that I had been able to stretch myself tall and trembling and say, "I know not what course others may take, but as for me, give me liberty or give me death."

And now I heard, really for the first time:

> "We have come over a way that with tears
> has been watered,
> We have come, treading our path through
> the blood of the slaughtered."

While echoes of the song shivered in the air, Henry Reed bowed his head, said "Thank you," and returned to his place in the line. The tears that slipped down many faces were not wiped away in shame.

We were on top again. As always, again. We survived. The depths had been icy and dark, but now a bright sun spoke to our souls. I was no longer simply a member of the proud graduating class of 1940; I was a proud member of the wonderful, beautiful Negro race.

Oh, Black known and unknown poets, how often have your auctioned pains sustained us? Who will compute the lonely nights made less lonely by your songs, or the empty pots made less tragic by your tales?

If we were a people much given to revealing secrets, we might raise monuments and sacrifice to the memories of our poets, but slavery cured us of that weakness. It may be enough, however, to have it said that we survive in exact relationship to the dedication of our poets (include preachers, musicians and blues singers).

Understanding and Analysis

1. What details does Angelou offer to support her opening sentence?

2. What details in the second and third paragraphs indicate the distinctions between the white school and the African-American school in Stamps?

---

[7]*Patrick Henry* (1736–1799) an orator and political leader who helped build support for the American Revolution.

3. What expectations do the members of the graduating classes have of the white people who will attend the ceremony?

4. List and categorize the things that made Angelou happy and proud at the time of her graduation from eighth grade.

5. Why did Angelou admire Henry Reed?

6. Why does Angelou provide so many details about the activities of the students, the presents exchanged, the minister's sermon, and so on?

7. What caused the principal to signal "rather desperately"?

8. Why does Angelou emphasize the "we" of the graduating class in her "presentiment of worse things to come"?

9. Describe the tone and content of the principal's speech.

10. Describe the tone and content of Donleavy's speech.

11. What motivates the audience to offer "Amen" to such a speech? Trace the reactions of the audience and the graduating class to Donleavy's speech.

12. Angelou says that sounds had always affected her. What sounds does she record on graduation day?

13. As she listens, Angelou offers a running commentary on the speeches and her responses to them. Out of these reactions she builds a crescendo of bitterness and hate and then another of hope and love. What does she learn from this experience?

14. Angelou was twelve when she graduated from eighth grade. Reread the essay looking for behaviors and reactions characteristic of a pre-teen. How does her age affect her perceptions? Can you distinguish between the older narrator and her younger self?

Comparison

1. Read Du Bois's essay. How has Booker T. Washington's views affected the lives of the African-American students in Stamps? Apply the two views of the education of African-Americans to the details of Angelou's story.

2. Read Hurston's "What White Publishers Won't Print." What connections do you see between Hurston's essay and Angelou's essay?

3. Read the essay by Podhoretz. Compare Podhoretz's views with those of Donleavy in Angelou's essay. Compare as well the types of student Angelou and Podhoretz each describe. What, if anything, do these students have in common?

4. Compare Angelou's attitudes toward whites and toward the shared culture of African-Americans and whites with Baldwin's attitudes as expressed in "Stranger in the Village."

5. Read O'Connor's "The Total Effect and the Eighth Grade." Compare Angelou's education to that advocated by O'Connor.

N. Scott Momaday
(1934–)

By the time that Navarre Scott Momaday was born on February 27, 1934, in Lawton, Oklahoma, his mother, Natachee, had been in the hospital for six weeks, imprisoned there by a nurse who feared for her safety. According to her husband's Kiowa family, Natachee—born Mayme Natachee Scott and named after her only Indian ancestor, her Cherokee great-grandmother—was an outsider, not to be tolerated. (Indeed, as Momaday recounts in his auto-biography, his Uncle James, in a fit of drunkenness, "placed the muzzle of [a] gun against me in my mother's womb and threatened to shoot.") In spite of the tension, Momaday's immediate family did not move away from his extended family for another two years; as he recounted in a 1996 interview with the Academy of Achievement, they all lived in "dire poverty," surviving the depression without "electricity or plumbing."

Once his parents found jobs with the Indian Service, a division of the government's Bureau of Indian Affairs, Momaday moved with them to a Navajo reservation in Shiprock, New Mexico. In 1943, the family moved again to Hobbs, New Mexico, to take advantage of the booming job market created by World War II. In Hobbs, Momaday and his friends "sang...'Let's remember Pearl Harbor, as we do the Alamo'" and "dug trenches and slithered like vipers through the brittle brush, dragging our toy rifles across the minefields." To his new schoolmates, however, he did not appear Indian, but Asian: "Nearly ever day on the playground someone would greet me with 'Hiya Jap,' and the fight was on."

After the war ended, Natachee, who was by vocation a writer, and Alfred, who was by vocation a painter, sought teaching positions. In September of 1946, they received an offer from the "two-teacher day school" in Jemez Pueblo, where they remained for more than 25 years. Traveling great distances in an attempt to find a high school that delivered "sound preparation for college," Momaday spent his sophomore year in Albuquerque living with "an old German couple" and his senior year at Augusta Military Academy in Virginia. For his undergraduate degree, he attended the University of New Mexico, sometimes returning home for the weekend and writing his "first published poem...at one of the second graders' desks" at Jemez. In 1956, he traveled back to Virginia to study at UVA for a year, meeting William Faulkner during his residence there. Graduating from the University of New Mexico in 1958, Momaday got a job teaching at the Dulce School on the Jicarilla Apache

Reservation, and he married Gaye Mangold in 1959. "While at Dulce," Alan R. Velie reports, "Momaday won a creative-writing scholarship to Stanford University, matriculating in fall 1959." Earning an M.A. in 1960, he found a teaching position at UC Santa Barbara in 1963, almost immediately after finishing his Ph.D.

During his first two years at Santa Barbara, when he held the position of assistant professor, he prepared his dissertation for publication under the title *The Complete Poems of Frederick Goddard Tuckerman* (1965). (It appeared the same year his mother published her *Owl in the Cedar Tree.*) During his next four years, after he became an associate professor of English, he published *The Journey of Tai-me* (1967) and *House Made of Dawn* (1968), his first novel, which to his surprise won him a Pulitzer. In 1969, he followed this tremendous triumph with *The Way to Rainy Mountain,* a kind of mythical and familial Kiowa history illustrated by his father and created through the telling of Kiowa stories (some re-told from *The Journey of Tai-me*) mixed with personal reflections. Momaday explains in one of his interviews with Charles L. Woodard, "I can take credit for setting down those Kiowa stories in English, in *The Way to Rainy Mountain,* but I didn't invent them. The imagination that informs those stories is really not mine, though it exists, I think, in my blood. It's an ancestral imagination."

Taking a job at UC Berkeley in 1969, Momaday next published *Colorado: Summer/Fall/Winter/Spring* (1973), which appeared in print the year he left Berkeley for Stanford. Over the next decade, teaching English at Stanford as a full professor, he published two volumes of poetry, *Angle of Geese and Other Poems* (1974) and *The Gourd Dancer* (1976), which he also illustrated. He published his autobiography, *The Names* (1976), as well. At this point, Momaday took a hiatus from publication and concentrated on his painting. Having divorced his wife, with whom he had three daughters, he married Regina Heitzer in 1978 and had one daughter, Lore. When he returned to the literary world in 1989 with his second novel, *The Ancient Child,* he was teaching at the University of Arizona and living in Tucson. Winning the Native American Literature Prize that year, he combined his talents for fiction and poetry with *In the Presence of the Sun: Stories and Poems, 1961–1991* (1992) and soon created his first play, *The Indolent Boys.* After publishing *Circle of Wonder: A Native American Christmas Story* (1994), he published *The Man Made of Words: Essays, Stories, Passages* (1997).

N. Scott Momaday seems to delight in re-telling pieces of stories and myths in his work. "In a sense," Momaday remarked in an interview with Joseph Bruchac, "I'm not concerned to change my subject from book to book. Rather, I'm concerned to keep the story going. I mean to keep the same subject, to carry it farther with each telling." Most critics are not eager to see Momaday change his subject either. Although some object that he has not devoted enough time to what he calls "the dark side of the American Indian experience" and others claim that he has not sufficiently analyzed the American

Indian experience, many critics, like Vernon E. Lattin, rejoice in his "transcendent optimism" and his "reverence for the land." The poetic qualities of Momaday's prose have elicited almost universal praise; his talent for poetry is prodigious, and his experiments with style show his sensitivity to the way that form creates meaning. Adept at bringing out the poetry in every genre, Momaday still prefers poetry itself above all others: "A poem, if it succeeds, brings together the best of your intelligence, the best of your articulation, the best of your emotion. And that is the highest goal of literature."

THE WAY TO RAINY MOUNTAIN (1969)

A SINGLE KNOLL rises out of the plain in Oklahoma, north and west of the Wichita Range. For my people, the Kiowas, it is an old landmark, and they gave it the name Rainy Mountain. The hardest weather in the world is there. Winter brings blizzards, hot tornadic winds arise in the spring, and in summer the prairie is an anvil's edge. The grass turns brittle and brown, and it cracks beneath your feet. There are green belts along the rivers and creeks, linear groves of hickory and pecan, willow and witch hazel. At a distance in July or August the steaming foliage seems almost to writhe in fire. Great green and yellow grasshoppers are everywhere in the tall grass, popping up like corn to sting the flesh, and tortoises crawl about on the red earth, going nowhere in the plenty of time. Loneliness is an aspect of the land. All things in the plain are isolate; there is no confusion of objects in the eye, but one hill or *one* tree or *one* man. To look upon that landscape in the early morning, with the sun at your back, is to lose the sense of proportion. Your imagination comes to life, and this, you think, is where Creation was begun.

I returned to Rainy Mountain in July. My grandmother had died in the spring, and I wanted to be at her grave. She had lived to be very old and at last infirm. Her only living daughter was with her when she died, and I was told that in death her face was that of a child.

I like to think of her as a child. When she was born, the Kiowas were living the last great moment of their history. For more than a hundred years they had controlled the open range from the Smoky Hill River to the Red, from the headwaters of the Canadian to the fork of the Arkansas and Cimarron. In alliance with the Comanches, they had ruled the whole of the southern Plains. War was their sacred business, and they were among the finest horsemen the world has ever known. But warfare for the Kiowas was preeminently a matter of disposition rather than of survival, and they never understood the grim, unrelenting advance of the U.S. Cavalry. When at last, divided and ill-provisioned, they were driven onto the Staked Plains in the cold rains of autumn, they fell into panic. In Palo Duro Canyon they abandoned their crucial stores to pillage and had nothing then but their lives. In order to save themselves, they surrendered to the soldiers at Fort Sill and were imprisoned in the old stone corral that now stands as a military museum. My grandmother was spared the humiliation of those high gray walls by eight or ten years, but she must have known from birth the affliction of defeat, the dark brooding of old warriors.

Her name was Aho, and she belonged to the last culture to evolve in North America. Her forebears came down from the high country in western Montana nearly three centuries ago. They were a mountain people, a mysterious tribe of hunters whose language has never been positively classified in any major group. In the late seventeenth century they began a long migration to the south and east. It was a journey toward the dawn, and it led to a golden age. Along the way the Kiowas were befriended by the Crows, who gave them the culture and religion of the Plains. They acquired horses, and their ancient nomadic spirit was suddenly free of the ground. They acquired Tai-me, the sacred Sun Dance doll, from that moment the object and symbol of their worship, and so shared in the divinity of the sun. Not least, they acquired the sense of destiny, therefore courage and pride. When they entered upon the southern Plains they had been transformed. No longer were they slaves to the simple necessity of survival; they were a lordly and dangerous society of fighters and thieves, hunters and priests of the sun. According to their origin myth, they entered the world through a hollow log. From one point of view, their migration was the fruit of an old prophecy, for indeed they emerged from a sunless world.

Although my grandmother lived out her long life in the shadow of Rainy Mountain, the immense landscape of the continental interior lay like memory in her blood. She could tell of the Crows, whom she had never seen, and of the Black Hills, where she had never been. I wanted to see in reality what she had seen more perfectly in the mind's eye, and traveled fifteen hundred miles to begin my pilgrimage.

Yellowstone, it seemed to me, was the top of the world, a region of deep lakes and dark timber, canyons and waterfalls. But, beautiful as it is, one might have the sense of confinement there. The skyline in all directions is close at hand, the high wall of the woods and deep cleavages of shade. There is a perfect freedom in the mountains, but it belongs to the eagle and the elk, the badger and the bear. The Kiowas reckoned their stature by the distance they could see, and they were bent and blind in the wilderness.

Descending eastward, the highland meadows are a stairway to the plain. In July the inland slope of the Rockies is luxuriant with flax and buckwheat, stonecrop and larkspur. The earth unfolds and the limit of the land recedes. Clusters of trees, and animals grazing far in the distance, cause the vision to reach away and wonder to build upon the mind. The sun follows a longer course in the day, and the sky is immense beyond all comparison. The great billowing clouds that sail upon it are the shadows that move upon the grain like water, dividing light. Farther down, in the land of the Crows and Blackfeet, the plain is yellow. Sweet clover takes hold of the hills and bends upon itself to cover and seal the soil. There the Kiowas paused on their way; they had come to the place where they must change their lives. The sun is at home on the plains. Precisely there does it have the certain character of a god. When the Kiowas came to the land of the Crows, they could see the dark lees of the hills at dawn across the Bighorn River, the profusion of light on the grain shelves, the oldest deity ranging after the solstices. Not yet would they veer southward to the caldron of the land that lay below; they must wean their blood from the northern winter and hold the mountains a while longer in their view. They bore Tai-me in procession to the east.

A dark mist lay over the Black Hills, and the land was like iron. At the top of a ridge I caught sight of Devil's Tower upthrust against the gray sky as if in the birth of time the core of the earth had broken through its crust and the motion of the world was begun. There are things in nature that engender an awful quiet in the heart of man; Devil's Tower is one of them. Two centuries ago, because they could not do otherwise, the Kiowas made a legend at the base of the rock. My grandmother said:

> Eight children were there at play, seven sisters and their brother. Suddenly the boy was struck dumb; he trembled and began to run upon his hands and feet. His fingers became claws, and his body was covered with fur. Directly there was a bear where the boy had been. The sis-

ters were terrified; they ran, and the bear after them. They came to the stump of a great tree, and the tree spoke to them. It bade them climb upon it, and as they did so it began to rise into the air. The bear came to kill them, but they were just beyond its reach. It reared against the tree and scored the bark all around with its claws. The seven sisters were borne into the sky, and they became the stars of the Big Dipper.

From that moment, and so long as the legend lives, the Kiowas have kinsmen in the night sky. Whatever they were in the mountains, they could be no more. However tenuous their well-being, however much they had suffered and would suffer again, they had found a way out of the wilderness.

My grandmother had a reverence for the sun, a holy regard that now is all but gone out of mankind. There was a wariness in her, and an ancient awe. She was a Christian in her later years, but she had come a long way about, and she never forgot her birthright. As a child she had been to the Sun Dances; she had taken part in those annual rites, and by them she had learned the restoration of her people in the presence of Tai-me. She was about seven when the last Kiowa Sun Dance was held in 1887 on the Washita River above Rainy Mountain Creek. The buffalo were gone. In order to consummate the ancient sacrifice—to impale the head of a buffalo bull upon the medicine tree—a delegation of old men journeyed into Texas, there to beg and barter for an animal from the Goodnight herd. She was ten when the Kiowas came together for the last time as a living Sun Dance culture. They could find no buffalo; they had to hang an old hide from the sacred tree. Before the dance could begin, a company of soldiers rode out from Fort Sill under orders to disperse the tribe. Forbidden without cause the essential act of their faith, having seen the wild herds slaughtered and left to rot upon the ground, the Kiowas backed away forever from the medicine tree. That was July 20, 1890, at the great bend of the Washita. My grandmother was there. Without bitterness, and for as long as she lived, she bore a vision of deicide.

Now that I can have her only in memory, I see my grandmother in the several postures that were peculiar to her: standing at the wood stove on a winter morning and turning meat in a great iron skillet; sitting at the south window, bent above her beadwork, and afterwards, when her vision failed, looking down for a long time into the fold of her hands; going out upon a cane, very slowly as she did when the weight of age came upon her; praying. I remember her most often at prayer. She made long, rambling prayers out of suffering and hope, having seen many things. I was never sure that I had the right to hear, so exclusive where they of all mere custom and company. The last time I saw her she prayed standing by the side of her bed at night, naked to the waist, the light of a kerosene lamp moving upon her dark skin. Her long, black hair, always drawn and braided in the day, lay upon her shoulders and against her breasts like a shawl. I do not speak Kiowa, and I never understood her prayers, but there was something inherently sad in the sound, some merest hesitation upon the syllables of sorrow. She began in a high and descending pitch, exhausting her breath to silence; then again and again—and always the same intensity of effort, of something that is, and is not, like urgency in the human voice. Transported so in the dancing light among the shadows of her room, she seemed beyond the reach of time. But that was illusion; I think I knew then that I should not see her again.

Houses are like sentinels in the plain, old keepers of the weather watch. There, in a very little while, wood takes on the appearance of great age. All colors wear soon away in the wind and rain, and then the wood is burned gray and the grain appears and the nails turn red with rust. The windowpanes are black and opaque; you imagine there is nothing within, and indeed there are many ghosts, bones given up to the land. They stand here and there against the sky, and you approach them for a longer time than you expect. They belong in the distance; it is their domain.

Once there was a lot of sound in my grandmother's house, a lot of coming and going, feasting and talk. The summers there were full of excitement and reunion. The Kiowas are a summer people; they abide the cold and keep to themselves, but when the season turns and the land becomes warm and vital they cannot hold still; an old love of going returns upon them. The aged visitors who came to my grand-mother's house when I was a child were made of lean and leather, and they bore themselves upright. They wore great black hats and bright ample shirts that shook in the wind. They rubbed fat upon their hair and wound their braids with strips of colored cloth. Some of them painted their faces and carried the scars of old and cherished enmities. They were an old council of warlords, come to remind and be reminded of who they were. Their wives and daughters served them well. The women might indulge themselves; gossip was at once the mark and compensation of their servitude. They made loud and elaborate talk among themselves, full of jest and gesture, fright and false alarm. They went abroad in fringed and flowered shawls, bright beadwork and German silver. They were at home in the kitchen, and they prepared meals that were banquets.

There were frequent prayer meetings, and great nocturnal feasts. When I was a child I played with my cousins outside, where the lamp light fell upon the ground and the singing of the old people rose up around us and carried away into the darkness. There were a lot of good things to eat, a lot of laughter and surprise. And afterwards, when the quiet returned, I lay down with my grandmother and could hear the frogs away by the river and feel the motion of the air.

Now there is a funeral silence in the rooms, the endless wake of some final word. The walls have closed in upon my grandmother's house. When I returned to it in mourning, I saw for the first time in my life how small it was. It was late at night, and there was a white moon, nearly full. I sat for a long time on the stone steps by the kitchen door. From there I could see out across the land; I could see the long row of trees by the creek, the low light upon the rolling plains, and the stars of the Big Dipper. Once I looked at the moon and caught sight of a strange thing. A cricket had perched upon the handrail, only a few inches away from me. My line of vision was such that the creature filled the moon like a fossil. It had gone there, I thought, to live and die, for there, of all places, was its small definition made whole and eternal. A warm wind rose up and purled like the longing within me.

The next morning I awoke at dawn and went out on the dirt road to Rainy Mountain. It was already hot, and the grasshoppers began to fill the air. Still, it was early in the morning, and the birds sang out of the shadows. The long yellow grass on the mountain shone in the bright light, and a scissortail hied above the land. There, where it ought to be, at the end of a long and legendary way, was my grandmother's grave. Here and there on the dark stones were ancestral names. Looking back once, I saw the mountain and came away.

Understanding and Analysis

1. The opening paragraph describes Rainy Mountain. How does Momaday go about describing it?

2. What pattern does Momaday establish in the second paragraph?

3. Where did the Kiowas come from and what is their history? What changes did they undergo? What role does Momaday say war played in the lives of the Kiowas?

4. How does Momaday learn about the history of his people?

5. What did the Kiowas see in the mountains and in the plains?

6. In 1887, what event took place and how old was his grandmother at the time?

7. What do we learn about his grandmother from his specific memories of her?

8. Contrast Momaday's memory of the house of his grandmother as it once was and as he now sees it.

9. Momaday says he returns to Rainy Mountain to see his grandmother's grave—"There, where it ought to be, at the end of a long and legendary way, was my grandmother's grave." What are some of the journeys or "ways" that Momaday delineates when he describes "The Way to Rainy Mountain"?

Comparison

1. Read Carr on history. What theory about the history of the Kiowas could be drawn from the facts that Momaday presents?

2. Read Margaret Mead and Clifford Geertz. What distinguishes Momaday's essay from the work of these anthropologists?

3. Read Barry Lopez's "Landscape and Narrative." In what ways does the landscape in Momaday's essay shape its narrative? What similarities do you see between these two essays?

4. Read Didion's "On Going Home." What connections, if any, can you see between Didion's essay and Momaday's?

Gore Vidal
(1925–)

Eugene Luther Gore Vidal was born on October 3, 1925, in the Cadet Hospital at West Point, where his father served as the football coach and the first instructor in aeronautics. "It was my father's dream," Vidal writes in his vast memoir, "to be the Henry Ford of aviation." Hoping to sell the idea of affordable airplanes for the masses, Gene Vidal asked his 10-year-old son to fly a "Hammond flivver plane" for a Pathe News crew. Vidal recalls: "I flew the plane; made a bumpy landing; then, overcome by stage fright, I froze before the camera just as I was supposed to say (against my will) that the flight had been just as easy as riding a bicycle." By this time, Vidal and his parents had moved to Washington, D. C., to live at the home of his maternal grandfather, the blind Senator Thomas P. Gore, who inspired Vidal's love of politics. In

1935, after his parents divorced, Vidal's mother, Nina, married Hugh Dudley Auchincloss, and the Auchincloss estate served as Vidal's home base over the next several years as he attended various boarding schools. Starting high school in Los Alamos, Vidal transferred to Exeter after his freshman year and developed an interest in debate: "I took up public speaking partly because I intended to be a politician and partly because I had a stammer, which I gradually lost." Having renamed himself Gore at the age of 14, Vidal graduated from Exeter in 1943.

By June, Vidal was in the army and on his way to Lexington, Virginia, "to be trained as an engineer, for which I had no aptitude. After three months, I flunked out, more or less deliberately." He studied navigation, but found it easier in theory than in practice, becoming "the first mate of an army freight-supply ship in the Aleutians, more in danger of being killed by my own inadequacies...than from enemy fire." In 1944, he began his first novel, *Williwaw,* and finished it a year later. On a trip through the Bering Sea, he developed a case of hypothermia that led to rheumatoid arthritis, and he was transferred to Long Island, a "semi-invalid." Leaving the base to visit his father in New York, he "met a woman who was interviewing Gene for a biography of Amelia Earhart." (Vidal knew Earhart as well. In an essay called "On Flying," he explains that she "was very much a part of my life. She wrote poetry and encouraged me to write, too.") Through this interviewer, Vidal found, in one and the same place, a publisher for *Williwaw* (1946) and a job as an editor, which he started upon his release from the army in 1946. Having already completed his second novel, *In a Yellow Wood,* he "had planned to move to Santa Fe, not far from Los Alamos; go to work at the local newspaper; and begin a political career. Fortunately—or unfortunately?—by 1946 I was writing *The City and the Pillar,* which I knew would make a political career impossible; also, it made a conventional literary career impossible, a lucky break as that turned out, too."

For *Williwaw* (1946), Vidal earned widespread praise among reviewers, who quickly grouped him with post-war writers like Truman Capote. *In a Yellow Wood* (1947) did not receive as much notice, but *The City and the Pillar* (1948), the story of a gay protagonist who seems like the boy next door, turned Vidal into an overnight sensation. According to *Contemporary Authors, The New York Times* gave the book a scathing review, "refused to accept any advertising for it, and then either did not review or published extremely harsh reviews of Vidal's next five novels and books of short stories." In 1950, Vidal bought a home near his birthplace after traveling in Europe and living for a time in Guatemala. With home ownership increasing his need for income, he developed a "five-year plan: an all-out raid on television, which could make me enough money to live the rest of my life." In the first half of the decade, he wrote original teleplays such as the satiric *Visit to a Small Planet* (1955), and adapted works such as Ernest Hemingway's *A Farewell to Arms* (1955); in the second half, he turned to the big screen and wrote *The Catered Affair* (1956), which starred Bette Davis and Debbie Reynolds, and *The Scapegoat*, which starred Alec Guiness. In 1960, to the surprise of many, he mounted his first political campaign, bitterly opposed by the *Times*. Following his loss, he published his first collection of essays, *Rocking the Boat*, in 1962. He had already triumphed on the stage with *The Best Man: A Play of Politics*.

In 1964, the year he became the host of a television program called *Hot Line*, Vidal published *Julian*, a work of historical fiction and politics. He also adapted *The Best Man* for the screen and won a Cannes Critics Prize. Establishing a residence in Italy in 1967, Vidal turned his attention to contemporary politics in the novel *Washington, D. C.* (1967). He also wrote the well-known *Myra Breckinridge* (1968), the story of a woman in Hollywood who has had a sex-change operation. Scholar Robert F. Kiernan characterizes *Myra Breckinridge* as Vidal's "masterpiece of camp." In the 1970s, Vidal wrote novels, a screenplay, and additional collections of essays; in the 1980s, after contributing to the screenplay for *Caligula*, he published *The Second American Revolution and Other Essays* (1982) and *Armageddon? Essays, 1983–1987* (1987), as well the novels *Creation* (1981), *Lincoln* (1984), and *Empire* (1987). No less prolific in the 1990s, Vidal published the controversial, iconoclastic *Live from Golgotha: The Gospel According to Gore Vidal* (1992); the sizeable collection *United States: Essays, 1952–1992* (1992), which won him a National Book Award; and his memoir, *Palimpsest* (1995). Filled with memories of a remarkable life, *Palimpsest* contains a veritable "Who's Who" of the twentieth century, connecting Gore Vidal to everyone from First Lady Jackie Kennedy to author James Baldwin to actress Joanne Woodward.

One of the few literary celebrities of late twentieth-century America, Gore Vidal has become an institution unto himself. As a writer of satiric novels, he has garnered as much animosity as he has admiration. ("For thirty years," *Time* magazine once said, "he has been a cinder in the public eye.") Although he has written numerous best sellers, he has also earned a reputation for being uneven, especially across the works of historical fiction—*Julian*, *Lincoln*, *Burr* (1973), and *1876* (1976), among others—for which he is widely known. As an essayist, Vidal has achieved greater critical success than he has as a novelist. Gerald Clarke writes in *The Atlantic Monthly*: "the qualities that limit him as a novelist are precisely those a good essayist needs: a forceful intelligence, a cool detachment, an unpretentious graceful style, and a sense of perspective that distinguishe[s] the big from the little." The award-winning collection *United States* shows Vidal's command of language and style; it also creates a history of the country during his career. While some of his novels may fade away, Vidal's expository prose is likely to endure, attracting not only those who are interested in his ideas, but also anyone who is interested in the sexual, intellectual, political, literary, and cultural life of the late twentieth century.

DRUGS (1970)

IT IS POSSIBLE to stop most drug addiction in the United States within a very short time. Simply make all drugs available and sell them at cost. Label each drug with a precise description of what effect—good and bad—the drug will have on the taker. This will require heroic honesty. Don't say that marijuana is addictive or dangerous when it is neither, as millions of people know—unlike "speed," which kills most unpleasantly, or heroin, which is addictive and difficult to kick.

For the record, I have tried—once—almost every drug and liked none, disproving the popular Fu Manchu theory that a single whiff of opium will enslave the mind. Nevertheless many drugs are bad for certain people to take and they should be told why in a sensible way.

Along with exhortation and warning, it might be good for our citizens to recall (or learn for the first time) that the United States was the creation of men who believed that each man has the right to do what he wants with his own life as long as he does not interfere with his neighbor's pursuit of happiness (that his neighbor's idea of happiness is persecuting others does confuse matters a bit).

This is a startling notion to the current generation of Americans. They reflect a system of public education which has made the Bill of Rights, literally, unacceptable to a majority of high school graduates (see the annual Purdue reports) who now form the "silent majority"—a phrase which that underestimated wit Richard Nixon took from Homer who used it to describe the dead.

Now one can hear the warning rumble begin: if everyone is allowed to take drugs everyone will and the GNP will decrease, the Commies will stop us from making everyone free, and we shall end up a race of zombies, passively murmuring "groovy" to one another. Alarming thought. Yet it seems most unlikely that any reasonably sane person will become a drug addict if he knows in advance what addiction is going to be like.

Is everyone reasonably sane? No. Some people will always become drug addicts just as some people will always become alcoholics, and it is just too bad. Every man, however, has the power (and should have the legal right) to kill himself if he chooses. But since most men don't, they won't be mainliners either. Nevertheless, forbidding people things they like or think they might enjoy only makes them want those things all the more. This psychological insight is, for some mysterious reason, perennially denied our governors.

It is a lucky thing for the Amerian moralist that our country has always existed in a kind of time-vacuum: we have no public memory of anything that happened before last Tuesday. No one in Washington today recalls what happened during the years alcohol was forbidden to the people by a Congress that thought it had a divine mission to stamp out Demon Rum—launching, in the process, the greatest crime wave in the country's history, causing thousands of deaths from bad alcohol, and creating a general (and persisting) contempt among the citizenry for the laws of the United States.

The same thing is happening today. But the government has learned nothing from past attempts at prohibition, not to mention repression.

Last year when the supply of Mexican marijuana was slightly curtailed by the Feds, the pushers got the kids hooked on heroin and deaths increased dramatically, particularly in New York. Whose fault? Evil men like the Mafiosi? Permissive Dr. Spock? Wild-eyed Dr. Leary? No.

The Government of the United States was responsible for those deaths. The bureaucratic machine has a vested interest in playing cops and robbers. Both the Bureau of Narcotics and the Mafia want strong laws against the sale and use of drugs because if drugs are sold at cost there would be no money in it for anyone.

If there was no money in it for the Mafia, there would be no friendly playground pushers, and addicts would not commit crimes to pay for the next fix. Finally, if there was no money in it, the Bureau of Narcotics would wither away, something they are not about to do without a struggle.

Will anything sensible be done? Of course not. The American people are as devoted to the idea of sin and its punishment as they are to making money—and fighting drugs is nearly as big a business as pushing them. Since the combination of sin and money is irresistible (particularly to the professional politician), the situation will only grow worse.

Understanding and Analysis

1. Describe Vidal's tone in the opening paragraph.

2. Why does Vidal give us a brief description of his own drug use?

3. Where does he present the voice of the opposition? What is the opposing argument? How does Vidal counter it?

4. Does Vidal trust the common man (or woman) to make reasonable decisions? Does he overestimate the number of "reasonably sane" people?

5. What is his attitude toward his readers?

6. Throughout the essay, what is his attitude toward the general population?

7. How might Vidal reconcile his belief in the responsibility of individuals for conducting their own lives with his assertion in the tenth paragraph ("The government of the United States was responsible for those deaths.")?

Comparison

1. In the last sentence, Vidal predicts that the drug "situation will only grow worse." Do some research to determine if the situation has, in fact, grown worse. If so, what causes do experts cite? If not, what reasons do experts offer?

2. Read other short essays that attempt to persuade readers, such as Brady's "I Want a Wife" and Bettelheim's "A Victim." What, if anything, do these essays have in common?

3. Read the essays by Coontz and Reich. What role does class play in Vidal's argument? Write an essay either supporting or rebutting Vidal's argument, using information and arguments Vidal omits.

Judy Brady
(1937–)

Born on April 26, 1937, in San Francisco, California, Judy Brady was the first child of Robert A. Brady, an author and an economics professor at UC Berkeley, and Mildred Brady, a columnist and a "pioneer in championing the cause of consumers in a capitalist culture." Together, Brady writes, her parents "were among the original designers of Consumers Union, which still publishes the monthly magazine *Consumer Reports.*" During the Second World War, the family lived near Washington, D.C., and Brady has "vague memories" of witnessing "blackouts." Her "most vivid" recollections of war, however, are of its denouement. In 1948, the family moved to England for a year so that Brady's father could work on his book *Crisis in Britain,* and there she recalls "seeing the bombed-out blocks in London and the POW camps still operating in some parts of the English countryside."

Back in America, Brady entered a public high school in Berkeley, where she "lasted for about six weeks. Got into trouble right away and got kicked out of school." Her parents then placed her in The Anna Head School, a "posh private college prep school for girls." Graduating in 1955, she entered the University of Iowa to work toward a Bachelor of Fine Arts in Painting. "I took six years to graduate," she recalls, "because I spent a couple of years in New York (which is where I thought painters should be) at Cooper Union and the Art Students League in the middle of college." After her return to Iowa, she married Jim Syfers, and then she decided to pursue an MFA. Even as her professors praised her work, however, they suggested that she prepare to become a high-school art teacher: "colleges, they advised me, would not hire women painters. And when I looked around me, I realized it was true." Not interested in the prospect of teaching high school, Brady left the graduate program. She gave birth to her elder daughter, Maia, two days before Christmas in 1962. By the time that her second daughter was born on the day after Thanksgiving in 1965, the family had moved to San Francisco, where Syfers found work teaching at San Francisco State College.

"By the late 1960s," Brady writes, "I was a very miserable housewife, married to an academic, housebound with two small children." She first heard of the women's movement—which saved her, she maintains, from eventual suicide—when San Francisco State faculty members joined students in a massive strike in 1968. Converting her house into the central headquarters, Brady ended her feelings of "isolation" by leading workers and fundraising efforts every day of the week for the duration of the strike. She explains: "When the strike finally ended, the union had a celebratory meeting during which they thanked members who had made special contributions during the strike—the picket captain, the legal people, and the like. The local president also thanked my husband for raising the money. My husband graciously accepted his thanks. I went looking for the women's movement." She found it in a "consciousness raising (CR) group," where a woman recommended that she commit her anger and her frustration to paper. The result was "I Want a Wife." On August 26, 1970, footage of Brady reading her essay at the 50th anniversary celebration of women's suffrage appeared on news programs all around the Bay area. Although she is not precisely certain how "I Want a Wife" came to be published in the premiere edition of *Ms.* magazine, she does remember "that Gloria Steinem came to San Francisco to promote the magazine. I went with most of the other women in my CR group to hear her speak, and she asked from the stage if Judy Syfers was in the audience. I got pushed up onto the stage and hugged. I didn't like it. I still don't....I was afraid that a publication like *Ms.* would water down the movement."

In 1973, Brady traveled to Cuba "to do construction work" and was transformed by her experience: "now I know it's possible for human beings to arrange themselves into a social order which nurtures its members instead of exploiting them." Returning to the United States a confirmed socialist, she also felt inspired to find work, and started as a teacher's aide, or "paraprofessional." With other paraprofessionals, she developed a radical publication called *Para-Mite,* which they put together in her basement and hand-delivered to more than 100 schools. After leading the paraprofessionals' struggle to establish an independent union, she wrote an article chronicling their defeat, published in *Radical America.* In 1979, Brady divorced her husband. In 1980, she was diagnosed with breast cancer.

In her support group, Brady found "a place where I could talk about how angry I was that I had cancer (other people told me that it was my anger that caused my cancer—really treacherous nonsense!)." As soon as "people began organizing," she continues, "I started to speak publicly and write also." Gaining recognition as an activist, she tentatively accepted an offer from a publisher in the mid-1980s to assemble a collection of writings on breast cancer. "The prospect scared me to death," she writes, "enough so that I refused any advance because I didn't want to owe them any money if I couldn't produce." Over the next five years, while holding down an office job, Brady created *1 in 3: Women with Cancer Confront an Epidemic* (1991). (The title refers to an individual's lifetime chance of developing a cancer of any kind, not to statistics about women or breast cancer.) Working with a variety of groups, she helped to found Toxic Links Coalition in 1994, "a coalition of local cancer, environmental, and human rights groups." She writes a regular column, "Cashing in on Cancer," for the Women's Cancer Resource Center newsletter, and she always remains open to the idea of writing more: "I do actually have an idea in the back of my head for a book (another anthology) which I might take on some day. Its title tells it all: *The Secrets of Radical Old Women*."

As an activist and agitator, Judy Brady is internationally known, speaking at conferences around the world. There is little day-to-day crossover between her work as an activist and her tenure as an essayist; to her, "I Want a Wife," the piece that has made her name familiar on college campuses across America, "feels like something from a past lifetime, not connected to me at all." In her present lifetime, in columns and speeches, she voices sharp criticism of what she calls "the cancer industry." She is especially critical of Breast Cancer Awareness Month (in her view, a shameless marketing event staged by a pharmaceutical company). Although her writing has taken a different direction since 1970, many traits remain the same: the force of her anger, the shrewdness of her humor, and the skill of her phrasing.

I WANT A WIFE (1971)

I BELONG TO that classification of people known as wives. I am A Wife. And, not altogether incidentally, I am a mother.

Not too long ago a male friend of mine appeared on the scene fresh from a recent divorce. He had one child, who is, of course, with his ex-wife. He is looking for another wife. As I thought about him while I was ironing one evening, it suddenly occurred to me that I, too, would like to have a wife. Why do I want a wife?

I would like to go back to school so that I can become economically independent, support myself, and, if need be, support those dependent upon me. I want a wife who will work and send me to school. And while I am going to school I want a wife to take care of my children. I want a wife to keep track of the children's doctor and dentist appointments. And to keep track of mine, too. I want a wife to make sure my children eat properly and are kept clean. I want a wife who will wash the children's clothes and keep them mended. I want a wife who is a good nurturant attendant to my children, who arranges for their schooling, makes sure that they have an adequate social life with their peers, takes them to the park, the zoo, etc. I want a wife who takes care of the children when they are sick, a wife who arranges to be around when the children need special care, because, of course, I cannot miss classes at school. My wife must arrange to lose time at work and not lose the job. It may mean a small cut in my wife's income from time to time, but I guess I can tolerate that. Needless to say, my wife will arrange and pay for the care of the children while my wife is working.

I want a wife who will take care of my physical needs. I want a wife who will keep my house clean. A wife who will pick up after my children, a wife who will pick up after me. I want a wife who will keep my clothes clean, ironed, mended, replaced when need be, and who will see to it that my personal things are kept in their proper place so that I can find what I need the minute I need it. I want a wife who cooks the meals, a wife who is a good cook. I want a wife who will plan the menus, do the necessary grocery shopping, prepare the meals, serve them pleasantly, and then do the cleaning up while I do my studying. I want a wife who will care for me when I am sick and sympathize with my pain and loss of time from school. I want a wife to go along when our family takes a vacation so that someone can continue to care for me and my children when I need a rest and change of scene.

I want a wife who will not bother me with rambling complaints about a wife's duties. But I want a wife who will listen to me when I feel the need to explain a rather difficult point I have come across in my course of studies. And I want a wife who will type my papers for me when I have written them.

I want a wife who will take care of the details of my social life. When my wife and I are invited out by my friends, I want a wife who will take care of the babysitting arrangements. When I meet people at school that I like and want to entertain, I want a wife who will have the house clean, will prepare a special meal, serve it to me and my friends, and not interrupt when I talk about things that interest me and my friends. I want a wife who will have arranged that the children are fed and ready for bed before my guests arrive so that the children do not bother us. I want a wife who takes care of the needs of my guests so that they feel comfortable, who makes sure that they have an ashtray, that they are passed the hors d'oeuvres, that they are offered a second helping of the food, that their wine glasses are replenished when necessary, that their coffee is served to them as they like it. And I want a wife who knows that sometimes I need a night out by myself.

I want a wife who is sensitive to my sexual needs, a wife who makes love passionately and eagerly when I feel like it, a wife who makes sure that I am satisfied. And, of course, I want a wife who will not demand sexual attention when I am not in the mood for it. I want a wife who assumes the complete responsibility for birth control, because I do not want more children. I want a wife who will remain sexually faithful to me so that I do not have to clutter up my intellectual life with jealousies. And I want a wife who understands that *my* sexual needs may entail more than strict adherence to monogamy. I must, after all, be able to relate to people as fully as possible.

If, by chance, I find another person more suitable as a wife than the wife I already have, I want the liberty to replace my present wife with another one. Naturally, I will expect a fresh, new life; my wife will take the children and be solely responsible for them so that I am left free.

When I am through with school and have a job, I want my wife to quit working and remain at home so that my wife can more fully and completely take care of a wife's duties.

My God, who *wouldn't* want a wife?

Understanding and Analysis

1. What purpose is served in the first two paragraphs?

2. What is the effect of the repetition of the words "I want a wife" throughout the third paragraph and the rest of the essay? How does this repetition reinforce Brady's point about the activities of a wife?

3. In the third paragraph, Brady says she "can tolerate" the cut in pay that may result from having a wife who is free to miss work in order to be available to care for sick children.

How do those words characterize the one who wants a wife? What other phrases in the essay serve to characterize the one who wants a wife? What sort of person is this one who wants a wife?

4. What are the duties of a wife, according to Brady? How does she categorize these duties?

5. What, if any, of these activities appear dated to you now?

6. What would be the duties of a husband for such a wife?

7. If a wife lived up to Brady's job description, what characteristics could make another person "more suitable" than the one who wants a wife? What qualities are missing in both the wife and the one who wants a wife? Why does Brady deliberately leave out these qualities? In an equal relationship, what duties would you assign to each partner?

Comparison

1. Read Greer's "The Stereotype." Which essay do you find more effective, Brady's or Greer's? Why?

2. Read Mead's "A Day in Samoa." What activities do the women described in these essays share with wives, as Brady describes them? Compare the views of these authors on what leads to a satisfying life for a woman.

3. Read other essays about women, such as those by Kingston, Cofer, Silko, and Ozick. Compare the roles of women in these essays with the description in Brady's essay.

4. Read other essays of persuasion, such as those by Kincaid, Baker, Vidal, and Atwood. What characteristics, if any, do these essays share? Which do you find most effective? Why?

Germaine Greer
(1939–)

The eldest child of Reginald and Peggy Greer, Germaine Greer was born on January 29, 1939, outside Melbourne, Australia. In 1942, according to biographer Christine Wallace, Greer's father entered the Australian Imperial Forces to fight in World War II. Although Greer understood that the war was responsible for her father's absence, she did not understand what made him grim and distant after his return. Over the next several years, Reg and Peggy had two more children, and Greer's sense of alienation increased along with the size of her family. By early adolescence, she had attained her full height of six feet; yet Wallace emphasizes that while Greer was physically and socially awkward, she was quick witted, and she excelled on the stage. Characterized by one nun as "a bit of a mad-cap," Greer finished her secondary education at Star of the Sea College.

In 1956, Greer enrolled at the University of Melbourne, where she continued to draw rave reviews for her dramatic performances. She also began her "career as a journalist," as she reports in *The Madwoman's Underclothes*, by becoming "a reporter and drama critic on *Farrago*, the Melbourne University magazine." Four year later, she entered the University of Sydney to earn a master's degree in English. Cast in a film in 1963, she left Australia in 1964 to enter Cambridge. Originally intent on earning a second B.A., which she imagined would be superior to her first, she was soon disillusioned and entered the doctoral program instead. Working on her dissertation in Italy, Greer finished her degree in 1967. The following year, after accepting a position as a lecturer at the University of Warwick, she married Paul de Feu. Although the couple did not formally divorce for several years, the marriage ended after less than a month.

In 1969, Greer wrote pieces for *Oz* magazine in London. "Greer's other major journalistic enterprise in 1969," Wallace explains, "was to co-found and contribute to the European sex paper, *Suck*." While writing for *Suck*, she also began her first book, *The Female Eunuch*, at the suggestion of her agent and a publisher. Published in 1970, *The Female Eunuch* took many months to catch on, but once it did, Greer became an international star, a media darling. In 1971, the year she was billed on the cover of *Life* magazine as the "Saucy Feminist That Even Men Like," she agreed to write for the Sunday edition of the London *Times*. In 1972, she resigned from *Suck* over a naked photograph of herself. As she explained to Bella English in a 1999 interview for the *Boston Globe*, "The idea was that all the editors would expose themselves as ruthlessly as we exposed others. But the men didn't do it." Greer continued to submit columns to the *Times* for more than a year after she left *Suck*, but her relationship with the paper was "becoming more and more strained. My column had been run alternately with a column by Jilly Cooper and the feeling seemed to be that mine should be as frothy as hers; I tried mixing serious columns with flummery but the editor of the 'Look!' pages dropped everything but the flummery." Eventually, the *Times* simply ceased to print her submissions. Greer sent work elsewhere.

In 1973, *Playboy* named her "Journalist of the Year" for a piece called "Seduction Is a Four-Letter Word," her attempt "to improve thinking on rape." After publishing essays over the next several years in such periodicals as *Esquire* and the *Spectator*, Greer became the founding director of the Tulsa Center for the Study of Women's Literature in 1979. In her first year there, she produced her second book, *The Obstacle Race: The Fortunes of Women Painters and Their Work*. She left Tulsa in 1983, and she published her third book, *Sex and Destiny: The Politics of Human Fertility*, in 1984, after her father died. Next she went to Brazil to research a piece she contributed to *River Journeys* (1985), published through the BBC. Soon after, she began a journey in search of her father's history, about which he had always been reticent. In 1986, the same year she published a work of literary criticism called *Shakespeare*, she collected some of her works under the title *The Madwoman's Underclothes: Essays and Occasional Writings*. In 1989, Greer published *Daddy, We Hardly Knew You*, an account of the research and the travels that led her to the discovery of her father's illegitimate birth. Winning a JR Ackerly Prize for *Daddy*, she became, unofficially, a fellow at Cambridge. Since then, she has published *The Change: Women, Aging, and the Menopause* (1991), *Slip-Shod Sibyls: Recognition, Rejection, and the Woman Poet* (1995), and the unfavorably reviewed "sequel" to her first book, *The Whole Woman* (1999).

In *The Female Eunuch*, Germaine Greer issues what reviewer Michiko Kakutani calls a "swaggering call for sexual liberation." Arguing that women have been essentially castrated—"What happens is that the female is considered as a sexual object for the use and appreciation of other sexual beings, men. Her sexuality is both denied and misrepresented by being identified as passivity"— Greer urges readers to "reject femininity as meaning *without libido*." In part because she does not blame men for women's castration, Greer won the kind of popularity and celebrity usually reserved for film stars. Although she has had her successes since *The Female Eunuch*, the achievement of that single book has sustained her throughout an entire career. Reviewers have since been critical of her writing style, her argumentation, and her politics; even one-time supporter Camille Paglia has turned her back since the publication of *The Whole Woman*, in which Greer seems to reverse many of the positions of *The Female Eunuch*. Still, Greer has many devoted fans, readers who admire her frankness, her boldness, and her talent for manufacturing a good shock, all of which have contributed to making her one of the most controversial women of the twentieth century.

The Stereotype (1971)

IN THAT MYSTERIOUS dimension where the body meets the soul the stereotype is born and has her being. She is more body than soul, more soul than mind. To her belongs all that is beautiful, even the very word beauty itself. All that exists, exists to beautify her. The sun shines only to burnish her skin and gild her hair; the wind blows only to whip up the color in her cheeks; the sea strives to bathe her; flowers die gladly so that her skin may luxuriate in their essence. She is the crown of creation, the masterpiece. The depths of the sea are ransacked for pearl and coral to deck her; the bowels of the earth are laid open that she might wear gold, sapphires, diamonds, and rubies. Baby seals are battered with staves, unborn lambs ripped from their mothers' wombs, millions of moles, muskrats,

Taught from infancy that beauty is woman's scepter, the mind shapes itself to the body, and roaming round its gilt cage, only seeks to adorn its prison.

—MARY WOLLSTONECRAFT, *A VINDICATION OF THE RIGHTS OF WOMAN*, 1792.

squirrels, minks, ermines, foxes, beavers, chinchillas, ocelots, lynxes, and other small and lovely creatures die untimely deaths that she might have furs. Egrets, ostriches, and peacocks, butterflies and beetles yield her their plumage. Men risk their lives hunting leopards for her coats, and crocodiles for her handbags and shoes. Millions of silkworms offer her their yellow labors; even the seamstresses roll seams and whip lace by hand, so that she might be clad in the best that money can buy.

The men of our civilization have stripped themselves of the fineries of the earth so that they might work more freely to plunder the universe for treasures to deck my lady in. New raw materials, new processes, new machines are all brought into her service. My lady must therefore be the chief spender as well as the chief symbol of spending ability and monetary success. While her mate toils in his factory, she totters about the smartest streets and plushiest hotels with his fortune upon her back and bosom, fingers, and wrists, continuing that essential expenditure in his house which is her frame and her setting, enjoying that silken idleness which is the necessary condition of maintaining her mate's prestige and her qualification to demonstrate it. Once upon a time only the aristocratic lady could lay claim to the title of crown of creation: only her hands were white enough, her feet tiny enough, her waist narrow enough, her hair long and golden enough; but every well-to-do burgher's wife set herself up to ape my lady and to follow fashion, until my lady was forced to set herself out like a gilded doll overlaid with monstrous rubies and pearls like pigeon's eggs. Nowadays the Queen of England still considers it part of her royal female role to sport as much of the family jewelry as she can manage at any one time on all public occasions, although the male monarchs have escaped such showcase duty, which develops exclusively upon their wives.

At the same time as woman was becoming the showcase for wealth and caste, while men were slipping into relative anonymity and "handsome is as handsome does," she was emerging as the central emblem of western art. For the Greeks the male and female body had beauty of a human, not necessarily a sexual, kind; indeed they may have marginally favored the young male form as the most powerful and perfectly proportioned. Likewise the Romans showed no bias towards the depiction of femininity in their predominantly monumental art. In the Renaissance the female form began to predominate not only as the mother in the predominant emblem of *madonna con bambino*[1] but as an aesthetic study in herself. At first naked female forms took their chances in crowd scenes or diptychs of Adam and Eve, but gradually Venus[2] claims ascendancy, Mary Magdalene[3] ceases to be wizened and emaciated, and becomes nubile and ecstatic, portraits of anonymous young women, chosen only for their prettiness, begin to appear, are gradually dis-

---

[1]*Madonna con bambino* My lady with child.

[2]*Venus* the Roman goddess of love and beauty; also associated with the Greek goddess Aphrodite.

[3]*Mary Magdalene* a disciple of Jesus; while very little is known about her, myth has it that she was a prostitute until she became one of Jesus' followers.

robed, and renamed Flora or Primavera. Painters begin to paint their own wives and mistresses and royal consorts as voluptuous beauties, divesting them of their clothes if desirable, but not of their jewelry. Susanna[4] keeps her bracelets on in the bath, and Hélène Fourment[5] keeps ahold of her fur as well!

What happened to women in painting happened to her in poetry as well. Her beauty was celebrated in terms of the riches which clustered around her: her hair was gold wires, her brow ivory, her lips ruby, her teeth gates of pearl, her breasts alabaster veined with lapis lazuli, her eyes as black as jet. The fragility of her loveliness was emphasized by the inevitable comparisons with the rose, and she was urged to employ her beauty in lovemaking before it withered on the stem. She was for consumption; other sorts of imagery spoke of her in terms of cherries and cream, lips as sweet as honey and skin white as milk, breasts like cream uncurdled, hard as apples. Some celebrations yearned over her finery as well, her lawn[6] more transparent than morning mist, her lace as delicate as gossamer, the baubles that she toyed with and the favors that she gave. Even now we find the thriller hero describing his classy dames' elegant suits, cheeky hats, well-chosen accessories and footwear; the imagery no longer dwells on jewels and flowers but the consumer emphasis is the same. The mousy secretary blossoms into the feminine stereotype when she reddens her lips, lets down her hair, and puts on something frilly.

Nowadays women are not expected, unless they are Paola di Liegi or Jackie Onassis, and then only on gala occasions, to appear with a king's ransom deployed upon their bodies, but they are required to look expensive, fashionable, well-groomed, and not to be seen in the same dress twice. If the duty of the few may have become less onerous, it has also become the duty of the many. The stereotype marshals an army of servants. She is supplied with cosmetics, underwear, foundation garments, stockings, wigs, pastiches, and hairdressing as well as her outer garments, her jewels, and furs. The effect is to be built up layer by layer, and it is expensive. Splendor has given way to fit, line, and cut. The spirit of competition must be kept up, as more and more women struggle toward the top drawer, so that the fashion industry can rely upon an expanding market. Poorer women fake it, ape it, pick up on the fashions a season too late, use crude effects, mistaking the line, the sheen, the gloss of the high-class article for a garish simulacrum. The business is so complex that it must be handled by an expert. The paragons of the stereotype must be dressed, coifed, and painted by the experts and the style-setters, although they may be encouraged to give heart to the housewives studying their lives in pulp magazines by claiming a lifelong fidelity to their own hair and soap and water. The boast is more usually discouraging than otherwise, unfortunately.

As long as she is young and personable, every woman may cherish the dream that she may leap up the social ladder and dim the sheen of luxury by sheer natural loveliness; the few examples of such a feat are kept before the eye of the public. Fired with hope, optimism, and ambition, young women study the latest forms of the stereotype, set out in *Vogue, Nova, Queen,* and other glossies, where the mannequins stare from among the advertisements for fabulous real estate, furs, and jewels. Nowadays the uniformity of the

---

[4]*Susanna* according to the Apocrypha, Susanna was the wife of a wealthy Babylonian who was falsely accused of adultery by two men who had come upon her bathing and whose subsequent advances she repelled.

[5]*Helene Fourment* a 1638 painting by the German artist Peter Paul Rubens depicts Rubens' wife, Helene, nude except for a fur wrap.

[6]*lawn* a very fine, thin fabric of cotton or linen.

> The myth of the strong black woman is the other side of the coin of the myth of the beautiful dumb blonde. The white man turned the white woman into a weak-minded, weak-bodied, delicate freak, a sex pot, and placed her on a pedestal; he turned the black woman into a strong self-reliant Amazon and deposited her in his kitchen.... The white man turned himself into the Omnipotent Administrator and established himself in the Front Office.
>
> —ELDRIDGE CLEAVER, "THE ALLEGORY OF THE BLACK EUNUCHS." *SOUL ON ICE.* 1968.

year's fashions is severely affected by the emergence of the pert female designers who direct their appeal to the working girl, emphasizing variety, comfort, and simple, striking effects. There is no longer a single face of the year: even Twiggy has had to withdraw into marketing and rationed personal appearances, while the Shrimp[7] works mostly in New York. Nevertheless the stereotype is still supreme. She has simply allowed herself a little more variation.

The stereotype is the Eternal Feminine. She is the Sexual Object sought by all men, and by all women. She is of neither sex, for she has herself no sex at all. Her value is solely attested by the demand she excites in others. All she must contribute is her existence. She need achieve nothing, for she is the reward of achievement. She need never give positive evidence of her moral character because virtue is assumed from her loveliness, and her passivity. If any man who has no right to her be found with her she will not be punished, for she is morally neuter. The matter is solely one of male rivalry. Innocently she may drive men to madness and war. The more trouble she can cause, the more her stocks go up, for possession of her means the more demand she excites. Nobody wants a girl whose beauty is imperceptible to all but him; and so men welcome the stereotype because it directs their taste into the most commonly recognized areas of value, although they may protest because some aspects of it do not tally with their fetishes. There is scope in the stereotype's variety for most fetishes. The leg man may follow miniskirts, the tit man can encourage see-through blouses and plunging necklines, although the man who likes fat women may feel constrained to enjoy them in secret. There are stringent limits to the variations on the stereotype, for nothing must interfere with her function as sex object. She may wear leather, as long as she cannot actually handle a motorbike: she may wear rubber, but it ought not to indicate that she is an expert diver or waterskier. If she wears athletic clothes the purpose is to underline her unathleticism. She may sit astride a horse, looking soft and curvy, but she must not crouch over its neck with her rump in the air.

Because she is the emblem of spending ability and the chief spender, she is also the most effective seller of this world's goods. Every survey ever held has shown that the image of an attractive woman is the most effective advertising gimmick. She may sit astride the mudguard of a new car, or step into it ablaze with jewels; she may lie at a man's feet stroking his new socks; she may hold the petrol pump in a challenging pose, or dance through woodland glades in slow motion in all the glory of a new shampoo; whatever she does her image sells. The gynolatry[8] of our civilization is written large upon

---

[7]*Twiggy, the Shrimp* two famous 1960s fashion models.

[8]*gynolatry* a play upon the word "idolatry."

its face, upon hoardings, cinema screens, television, newspapers, magazines, tins, packets, cartons, bottles, all consecrated to the reigning deity, the female fetish. Her dominion must not be thought to entail the rule of women, for she is not a woman. Her glossy lips and mat complexion, her unfocused eyes and flawless fingers, her extraordinary hair all floating and shining, curling, and gleaming, reveal the inhuman triumph of cosmetics, lighting, focusing, and printing, cropping and composition. She sleeps unruffled, her lips red and juicy and closed, her eyes as crisp and black as if new painted, and her false lashes immaculately curled. Even when she washes her face with a new and creamier toilet soap her expression is as tranquil and vacant and her paint as flawless as ever. If ever she should appear tousled and troubled, her features are miraculously smoothed to their proper veneer by a new washing powder or a bouillon cube. For she is a doll: weeping, pouting, or smiling; running or reclining, she is a doll. She is an idol, formed of the concatenation of lines and masses, signifying the lineaments of satisfied impotence.

Her essential quality is castratedness. She absolutely must be young, her body hairless, her flesh buoyant, and *she must not have a sexual organ.* No musculature must distort the smoothness of the lines of her body, although she may be painfully slender or warmly cuddly. Her expression must betray no hint of humor, curiosity, or intelligence, although it may signify hauteur to an extent that is actually absurd, or smoldering lust, very feebly signified by drooping eyes and a sullen mouth (for the stereotype's lust equals irrational submission), or, most commonly, vivacity and idiot happiness. Seeing that the world despoils itself for this creature's benefit, she must be happy; the entire structure would topple if she were not. So the image of woman appears plastered on every surface imaginable, smiling interminably. An apple pie evokes a glance of tender beatitude, a washing machine causes hilarity, a cheap box of chocolates brings forth meltingly joyous gratitude, a Coke is the cause of a rictus of unutterable brilliance, even a new stick-on bandage is saluted by a smirk of satisfaction. A real woman licks her lips and opens her mouth and flashes her teeth when photographers appear: *she* must arrive at the premiere of her husband's film in a paroxysm of delight, or his success might be murmured about. The occupational hazard of being a Playboy Bunny is the aching facial muscles brought on by the obligatory smiles.

So what is the beef? Maybe I couldn't make it. Maybe I don't have a pretty smile, good teeth, nice tits, long legs, a cheeky ass, a sexy voice. Maybe I don't know how to handle men and increase my market value, so that the rewards due to the feminine will accrue to me. Then again, maybe I'm sick of the masquerade. I'm sick of pretending eternal youth. I'm sick of belying my own intelligence, my own will, my own sex. I'm sick of peering at the world through false eyelashes, so everything I see is mixed with a shadow of bought hairs; I'm sick of weighting my head with a dead mane, unable to move my neck freely, terrified of rain, of wind, of dancing too vigorously in case I sweat into my lacquered curls. I'm sick of the Powder Room. I'm sick of pretending that some fatuous male's self-important pronouncements are the objects of my undivided attention, I'm sick of going to films and plays when someone else wants to, and sick of having no opinions

---

She was created to be the toy of man, his rattle, and it must jingle in his ears whenever, dismissing reason, he chooses to be amused.

—Mary Wollstonecraft, *A Vindication of the Rights of Woman,* 1792.

> Discretion is the better part of Valerie
> though all of her is nice
> lips as warm as strawberries
> eyes as cold as ice
> the very best of everything
> only will suffice
> not for her potatoes
> and puddings made of rice
> —ROGER McGOUGH, *DISCRETION*

of my own about either. I'm sick of being a transvestite. I refuse to be a female impersonator. I am a woman, not a castrate.

April Ashley was born male. All the information supplied by genes, chromosomes, internal and external sexual organs added up to the same thing. April was a man. But he longed to be a woman. He longed for the stereotype, not to embrace, but to be. He wanted soft fabrics, jewels, furs, makeup, the love and protection of men. So he was impotent. He couldn't fancy women at all, although he did not particularly welcome homosexual addresses. He did not think of himself as a pervert, or even as a transvestite, but as a woman cruelly transmogrified into manhood. He tried to die, became a female impersonator, but eventually found a doctor in Casablanca who came up with a more acceptable alternative. He was to be castrated, and his penis used as the lining of a surgically constructed cleft, which would be a vagina. He would be infertile, but that has never affected the attribution of femininity. April returned to England, resplendent. Massive hormone treatment had eradicated his beard, and formed tiny breasts: he had grown his hair and bought feminine clothes during the time he had worked as an impersonator. He became a model, and began to illustrate the feminine stereotype as he was perfectly qualified to do, for he was elegant, voluptuous, beautifully groomed, and in love with his own image. On an ill-fated day he married the heir to a peerage, the Hon. Arthur Corbett, acting out the highest achievement of the feminine dream, and went to live with him in a villa in Marbella. The marriage was never consummated. April's incompetence as a woman is what we must expect from a castrate, but it is not so very different after all from the impotence of feminine women, who submit to sex without desire, with only the

> To what end is the laying out of the embroidered Hair, embared Breasts; vermilion Cheeks, alluring looks, Fashion gates, and artful Countenances, effeminate intangling and insnaring Gestures, their Curls and Purls of proclaiming Petulancies, bousterd and laid out with such example and authority in these our days, as with Allowance and beseeming Conveniency?
> Doth the world wax barren through decrease of Generations, and become, like the Earth, less fruitful heretofore? Doth the Blood lose his Heat or do the Sunbeams become waterish and less fervent, than formerly they have been, that men should be thus inflamed and persuaded on to lust?
> —ALEX. NICCHOLES, *A DISCOURSE OF MARRIAGE AND WIVING.*

infantile pleasure of cuddling and affection, which is their favorite reward. As long as the feminine stereotype remains the definition of the female sex, April Ashley is a woman, regardless of the legal decision ensuing from her divorce. She is as much a casualty of the polarity of the sexes as we all are. Disgraced, unsexed April Ashley is our sister and our symbol.

Understanding and Analysis

1. What is the tone of the first paragraph? If you think the tone changes, where do you see a change? Why do you think Greer incorporates the lists of animals in her opening paragraph?

2. In the second paragraph, how does Greer characterize men? What role does class play in the bedecking of women?

3. What "happened" to women in paintings and poetry? Why does Greer choose the word "happened"?

4. What are the requirements for the clothing of women in modern times, according to Greer? What has changed and what has remained the same?

5. Describe in your own words the "Eternal Feminine" as Greer depicts her in 1972.

6. Why is the stereotype of woman used in advertising with so much success?

7. What does Greer mean when she claims that the stereotype "is not a woman"? Why does she lack real power?

8. Why, according to Greer, does April Ashley want to become a woman?

9. How do the quotations in the boxes connect to the essay?

10. Has this stereotype of woman changed since 1972? If so, how has it changed?

Comparison

1. Can you describe an equivalent stereotype for men?

2. Read Brady's "I Want a Wife." What characteristics do the two stereotypes share, if any?

3. Read "The Real Trouble About Women" by D. H. Lawrence. How might Greer respond?

Russell Baker

(1925–)

Born August 14, 1925, Russell Baker spent the first five years of his life in Morrisonville, Virginia, three of them in the company of his precocious younger sister, Doris. His sister Audrey was born shortly before the death of his father, who fell into an "acute diabetic coma" at the age of 33. Facing the prospect of raising children alone during the Depression, Baker's mother, Lucy Elizabeth, agreed to allow Audrey to be raised by relatives. In 1931, she took Russell and Doris to Newark, New Jersey, to live with her younger brother Allen. Shortly after their arrival, both children contracted whooping cough, as Baker explains in his first memoir, and had to endure the indignity of wearing yellow arm bands "marking us as disease carriers." When the household relocated to Bellevue in 1932, Baker skipped the second grade. His mother, having hoped he'd skip the third grade as well, soon began to push her son to develop ambition, or as she put it, "gumption." When he was eight, she arranged for him to sell *The Saturday Evening Post*, a job he detested (six-year-old Doris often had to sell the last issues for him, beating on the windows of cars stopped at intersections).

During his three-year tenure with the *Post*, Baker received high marks at school for his writing, leading his mother to the conclusion that he should prepare to write for a living. Initially entranced with the idea—writers, he reasoned, did not have to excel in door-to-door magazine sales—Baker did not seriously consider the possibility until his junior year of high school, by which time his mother had moved the family to Baltimore, Maryland. As high-school graduation approached, however, he was considering working in a grocery store until a friend insisted that he apply for a scholarship to Johns Hopkins. "The United States had been at war seven months," Baker writes, "when I entered Johns Hopkins in the summer of 1942." The following spring, as he looked ahead to his eighteenth birthday, he "applied for enlistment in the Navy Air Corps," which he entered in October of 1943. Baker learned to fly, as well as to swim (the Navy had little patience for his "fear of deep water," as he soon discovered), but the war ended before he entered combat.

Disappointed, he returned to Johns Hopkins, where a writing teacher recommended that he look for work at the *Baltimore Sun*. Although he had loved journalism as a boy of 12 or 13, poring over "accounts of monstrous crimes, dreadful accidents, and hideous butcheries committed in faraway wars," he now aspired to become a novelist, a serious writer, rather than a "hack." Nevertheless, as he explains in his second memoir, *The Good Times*, he applied to the *Sun* and was given work as a "police reporter." Although he promptly missed a murder story on his very first night on the job, he soon recovered. He also carried on a stormy courtship with a woman named Mimi who was, in his mother's opinion, the wrong sort of girl. In 1958, Baker taught himself touch typing and spent the summer writing a novel: "It was about a young newspaper reporter hopelessly in love with an unsuitable girl, and there was a [vicious] gangster in it....I mailed it away to several publishers who mailed it right back. Then I put it in the attic, intending to make some publisher pay a fortune for it after I became famous. Many years later I read Truman Capote's criticism of another novel—'That's not writing; it's typing'—and dug mine out of a trunk and put it in the trash in dead of night." In 1950, Russell and Mimi finally married. The following year, Mimi gave birth to the couple's first child, Kathleen.

Not long after the birth of their second child, Allen, named after Baker's uncle, Baker was made chief of the *Sun*'s London bureau. Living in England between 1953 and 1954, he felt himself maturing, becoming more worldly. He also earned a second education, learning how to drink, and better yet, how to write. After he returned to the states to serve as Washington correspondent, Baker found himself restless and unhappy. In 1954, he left the *Sun* to write for *The New York Times*, working in their Washington bureau until 1962, when he determined that the pressures of his work were taking too great a toll on his relationships with his family. Accepting an offer to write a regular column for the *Baltimore Sun*, Baker was persuaded to remain at the *Times* with the offer of "a column on the editorial page," retitled "Observer."

Having published his first book, *An American in Washington*, in 1961, Baker published his first collection, *No Cause for Panic*, in 1964. Over the next two decades, he published five additional collections of his writings, including *Poor Russell's Almanac* (1972) and *So This Is Depravity* (1980). In 1979, he won a Pulitzer Prize for his column, and, in 1983, he won another for *Growing Up* (1982), his first memoir. With the syndication of his column, Baker's reputation as a humorist had spread across the country, and he edited *The Norton Book of Light Verse* (1986), as well as *Russell Baker's Book of American Humor* (1993). In 1995, having published his second memoir six years earlier, he contributed to *Inventing the Truth: The Art and Craft of Memoir*.

Russell Baker is both well-liked and well-respected. Characterized by the *Washington Post Book World* as "the supreme satirist of this half century," he has been celebrated not only for his wit and humor but also for his "haunting strain of melancholy" and his "shame and outrage." As a writer of memoir, he strikes the perfect balance, in the opinion of most reviewers, between the individual and the universal. As quoted in *Contemporary Authors*, critic Jonathan Yardley finds that in *Growing Up*, Baker "has accomplished the memoirist's task:

to find shape and meaning in his own life, and to make it interesting and pertinent to the reader. In lovely, haunting prose, he has told a story that is deeply in the American grain, one in which countless readers will find echoes of their own, yet in the end is very much his." Baker strikes a chord with readers in his columns as well; in clear and simple prose, he delivers funny lines and shrewd insights with the same assurance and the same success.

WORK IN CORPORATE AMERICA (1972)

IT IS NOT SURPRISING that modern children tend to look blank and dispirited when informed that they will someday have to "go to work and make a living." The problem is that they cannot visualize what work is in corporate America.

Not so long ago, when a parent said he was off to work, the child knew very well what was about to happen. His parent was going to make something or fix something. The parent could take his offspring to his place of business and let him watch while he repaired a buggy or built a table.

When a child asked, "What kind of work do you do, Daddy?" his father could answer in terms that a child could come to grips with. "I fix steam engines." "I make horse collars."

Well, a few fathers still fix steam engines and build tables, but most do not. Nowadays, most fathers sit in glass buildings doing things that are absolutely incomprehensible to children. The answers they give when asked, "What kind of work do you do, Daddy?" are likely to be utterly mystifying to a child.

"I sell space." "I do market research." "I am a data processor." "I am in public relations." "I am a systems analyst." Such explanations must seem nonsense to a child. How can he possibly envision anyone analyzing a system or researching a market?

Even grown men who do market research have trouble visualizing what a public relations man does with his day, and it is a safe bet that the average systems analyst is as baffled about what a space salesman does at the shop as the average space salesman is about the tools needed to analyze a system.

In the common everyday job, nothing is made any more. Things are now made by machines. Very little is repaired. The machines that make things make them in such a fashion that they will quickly fall apart in such a way that repairs will be prohibitively expensive. Thus the buyer is encouraged to throw the thing away and buy a new one. In effect, the machines are making junk.

The handful of people remotely associated with these machines can, of course, tell their inquisitive children "Daddy makes junk." Most of the work force, however, is too remote from junk production to sense any contribution to the industry. What do these people do?

Consider the typical twelve-story glass building in the typical American city. Nothing is being made in this building and nothing is being repaired, including the building itself. Constructed as a piece of junk, the building will be discarded when it wears out, and another piece of junk will be set in its place.

Still, the building is filled with people who think of themselves as working. At any given moment during the day perhaps one-third of them will be talking into telephones.

Most of these conversations will be about paper, for paper is what occupies nearly everyone in this building.

Some jobs in the building require men to fill paper with words. There are persons who type neatly on paper and persons who read paper and jot notes in the margins. Some persons make copies of paper and other persons deliver paper. There are persons who file paper and persons who unfile paper.

Some persons mail paper. Some persons telephone other persons and ask that paper be sent to them. Others telephone to ascertain the whereabouts of paper. Some persons confer about paper. In the grandest offices, men approve of some paper and disapprove of other paper.

The elevators are filled throughout the day with young men carrying paper from floor to floor and with vital men carrying paper to be discussed with other vital men.

What is a child to make of all this? His father may be so eminent that he lunches with other men about paper. Suppose he brings his son to work to give the boy some idea of what work is all about. What does the boy see happening?

His father calls for paper. He reads paper. Perhaps he scowls at paper. Perhaps he makes an angry red mark on paper. He telephones another man and says they had better lunch over paper.

At lunch they talk about paper. Back at the office, the father orders the paper retyped and reproduced in quintuplicate, and then sent to another man for comparison with paper that was reproduced in triplicate last year.

Imagine his poor son afterwards mulling over the mysteries of work with a friend, who asks him, "What's your father do?" What can the boy reply? "It beats me," perhaps, if he is not very observant. Or if he is, "Something that has to do with making junk, I think. Same as everybody else."

Understanding and Analysis

1. At what point in the essay do you realize that Baker is concerned with more than how children visualize their fathers' jobs?

2. What is Baker's attitude toward the quality of machine–made goods? What is his attitude toward corporate America? What is his attitude toward work?

3. What is the effect of Baker's repetition of the words "persons" and "paper" in this essay?

4. What makes this essay amusing?

5. What is Baker's point?

Comparison

1. Read Brady's "I Want a Wife." What characteristics do these two essays share? Compare the tone of each one. What differences do you hear?

2. Read Galbraith's "Labor, Leisure, and the New Class." How does this essay inform your understanding of Baker's essay?

3. Read Rodriguez's "Labor." On what subjects are Baker and Rodriguez likely to agree?

4. Read Ellison's "The Way It Is." Compare the views of work expressed in that essay with those expressed in the essays by Baker, Rodriguez, Galbraith, and Reich.

Clifford Geertz
(1926–)

Born in San Francisco on August 23, 1926, anthropologist Clifford Geertz served in the U.S. Navy during World War II before enrolling at Antioch College in Yellow Springs, Ohio. "No anthropology was taught where I went to college," he said in an interview with *Contemporary Authors*. "Aside from some excellent economics courses, I didn't take any social sciences at all." Beginning his college career as an English major, Geertz changed over to philosophy. In 1948, during his junior year, at the age of 22, he married Hildred Storey. After a philosophy professor suggested that he pursue anthropology as a way of addressing his interests in "values," he consulted with "Margaret Mead and some friends" and determined to apply to Harvard. He graduated from Antioch in 1950, and he and Hildred both entered the doctoral program in Harvard's Social Relations department. The problem of field work arose immediately. "The very day I arrived in Cambridge," Geertz writes in *After the Fact*, "a professor, trying to be kind but failing, asked me where I was going to work. As I was barely aware at that point that this was a consideration I said, dissembling madly, well maybe Latin America."

While he was "thinking vaguely of Brazil" over the next year, he and his wife were invited to join a team of graduate students going to Indonesia. "[H]ardly knowing more than where Indonesia was, and that inexactly," Geertz said yes. For the next year, he and his group tried to learn Indonesian. When they arrived in the town of Pare in 1952, they discovered that they needed to know Javanese instead: "So, after arriving, my wife and I spent another seven months studying that language in the old Javanese court town of Jogjakarta. We hired local college students to come to our hotel room one after the other, relay style, through the day, as instructors." Remaining until 1954, he returned to the states and finished his Ph.D. in 1956, the same year that he published his first article, "Religious Belief and Economic Behavior in a Central Javanese Town," and his first book, *The Development of the Javanese Economy*. After working as an instructor and a research associate at Harvard, Geertz went to the Indonesian island of Bali in 1957. In 1958, he and his wife moved on to Padang, on the island of Sumatra. Both "desperately ill"—she had "infectious hepatitis," and he had malaria and dysentery—the Geertzes arrived the day before the country erupted in "civil war." According to Geertz, "The next two months [were] a badly plotted adventure movie." The couple fled to and from the mountains, trying to avoid bombings, and ultimately hid in "a rebel controlled oil camp," which was taken over by "central government para-troopers dropping soundlessly from the morning sky."

Back in the United States, Geertz worked as a Fellow at Stanford Univer-sity and then as assistant professor at UC Berkeley. In 1960, the year he pub-lished *The Religion of Java,* he began a decade of teaching and working for the University of Chicago. Geertz writes, "I came to the university as a part...of a wildly multidisciplinary experiment in the social sciences: The Committee for the Comparative Study of New Nations." Given the task of creating a "research program," Geertz balked at the prospect of taking his two children to Indonesia, since "[t]he sixties in Indonesia were even more explosive than in America or Europe." At the suggestion of a colleague, he began his proj-ect in Morocco instead, in a "large town or small city" called Sefrou. Between 1963 and 1971, Geertz worked in Sefrou on-and-off with his wife and three graduate students and published five books, four of them based on his work in Indonesia, and the fifth called *Islam Observed: Religious Development in Morocco and Indonesia* (1968).

In 1973, after he had accepted a position with the Institute for Advanced Study in Princeton, New Jersey, Geertz published his landmark work, a collec-tion of essays entitled *The Interpretation of Cultures.* In this book, Geertz not only writes about the practice of anthropology but also enters into the discussion about what anthropology is and what it ought to be: "Believing with Max Weber that man is an animal suspended in webs of significance he himself has spun, I take culture to be those webs and the analysis of it to be therefore not an experimental science in search of law but an interpretive one in search of meaning." Over the next decade, he published two books with his wife, one on Bali and one on Morocco, before the couple divorced in 1982.

A year later, Geertz continued the work begun in *The Interpretation of Cultures* with *Local Knowledge: Further Essays in Interpretive Anthropology* (1983), in which he advocates a multidisciplinary approach to learning, comparing intellectual pur-suits that seem as different as anthropology and literary criticism and law: "Santayana's famous dictum that one compares only when one is unable to get to the heart of the matter seems to me, here at least, the precise reverse of the truth: it is through comparison, and of incomparables, that whatever heart we can actually get to is to be reached." In 1987 Geertz married Karen Blu, whom he describes as an "American Indianist."

In his next book, *Works and Lives: The Anthropologist as Author* (1995), Geertz models a multidisciplinary approach: he argues for the study of anthropol-ogy and ethnography as acts of writing texts, constructing narratives, choos-ing phrases to persuade readers, and he himself analyzes anthropological writ-ers such as Levi-Strauss and Ruth Benedict. (He has written about Margaret Mead elsewhere). In *After the Fact: Two Countries, Four Decades, One Anthropologist*

(1995), he reflects, finally, on his own career as he creates a kind of personalized history of a changed and changing field.

According to critic Sherry Ortner, "Clifford Geertz must be credited with reconfiguring, almost single-handedly, the boundary between the social sciences and the humanities for the second half of the twentieth century." Although Geertz has provoked his share of controversy and criticism, this sort of claim for his accomplishments is not uncommon; *The New York Times Book Review* characterizes him as "one of anthropology's most illustrious demigods." Trained in the humanities, he has impressed readers and reviewers with his range of knowledge, his command of scholarship across the disciplines, and his "elegant" prose style. Geertz will be remembered less for his prose, however, than for his brilliant contributions to an uncertain field he has described as "once read mostly for amusement."

DEEP PLAY:
Notes on the Balinese Cockfight (*1972*)

THE RAID

EARLY IN APRIL of 1958, my wife and I arrived, malarial and diffident, in a Balinese village we intended, as anthropologists, to study. A small place, about five hundred people, and relatively remote, it was its own world. We were intruders, professional ones, and the villagers dealt with us as Balinese seem always to deal with people not part of their life who yet press themselves upon them: as though we were not there. For them, and to a degree for ourselves, we were nonpersons, specters, invisible men.

We moved into an extended family compound (that had been arranged before through the provincial government) belonging to one of the four major factions in village life. But except for our landlord and the village chief, whose cousin and brother-in-law he was, everyone ignored us in a way only a Balinese can do. As we wandered around, uncertain, wistful, eager to please, people seemed to look right through us with a gaze focused several yards behind us on some more actual stone or tree. Almost nobody greeted us; but nobody scowled or said anything unpleasant to us either, which would have been almost as satisfactory. If we ventured to approach someone (something one is powerfully inhibited from doing in such an atmosphere), he moved, negligently but definitively, away. If, seated or leaning against a wall, we had him trapped, he said nothing at all, or mumbled what for the Balinese is the ultimate nonword—"yes." The indifference, of course, was studied; the villagers were watching every move we made and they had an enormous amount of quite accurate information about who we were and what we were going to be doing. But they acted as if we simply did not exist, which, in fact, as this behavior was designed to inform us, we did not, or anyway not yet.

This is, as I say, general in Bali. Everywhere else I have been in Indonesia, and more latterly in Morocco, when I have gone into a new village people have poured out from all sides to take a very close look at me, and, often, an all-too-probing feel as well. In

Balinese villages, at least those away from the tourist circuit, nothing happens at all. People go on pounding, chatting, making offerings, staring into space, carrying baskets about while one drifts around feeling vaguely disembodied. And the same thing is true on the individual level. When you first meet a Balinese, he seems virtually not to relate to you at all; he is, in the term Gregory Bateson and Margaret Mead made famous, "away."[1] Then—in a day, a week, a month (with some people the magic moment never comes)— he decides, for reasons I have never been quite able to fathom, that you *are* real, and then he becomes a warm, gay, sensitive, sympathetic, though, being Balinese, always precisely controlled person. You have crossed, somehow, some moral or metaphysical shadow line. Though you are not exactly taken as a Balinese (one has to be born to that), you are at least regarded as a human being rather than a cloud or a gust of wind. The whole complexion of your relationship dramatically changes to, in the majority of cases, a gentle, almost affectionate one—a low-keyed, rather playful, rather mannered, rather bemused geniality.

My wife and I were still very much in the gust of wind stage, a most frustrating, and even, as you soon begin to doubt whether you are really real after all, unnerving one, when, ten days or so after our arrival, a large cockfight was held in the public square to raise money for a new school.

Now, a few special occasions aside, cockfights are illegal in Bali under the Republic (as, for not altogether unrelated reasons, they were under the Dutch), largely as a result of the pretensions to puritanism radical nationalism tends to bring with it. The elite, which is not itself so very puritan, worries about the poor, ignorant peasant gambling all his money away, about what foreigners will think, about the waste of time better devoted to building up the country. It sees cockfighting as "primitive," "backward," "unprogressive," and generally unbecoming an ambitious nation. And, as with those other embarrassments—opium smoking, begging, or uncovered breasts—it seeks, rather unsystematically, to put a stop to it.

Of course, like drinking during prohibition or, today, smoking marihuana, cockfights, being a part of "The Balinese Way of Life," nonetheless go on happening, and with extraordinary frequency. And, like prohibition or marihuana, from time to time the police (who, in 1958 at least, were almost all not Balinese but Javanese) feel called upon to make a raid, confiscate the cocks and spurs, fine a few people, and even now and then expose some of them in the tropical sun for a day as object lessons which never, somehow, get learned, even though occasionally, quite occasionally, the object dies.

As a result, the fights are usually held in a secluded corner of a village in semisecrecy, a fact which tends to slow the action a little—not very much, but the Balinese do not care to have it slowed at all. In this case, however, perhaps because they were raising money for a school that the government was unable to give them, perhaps because raids had been few recently, perhaps, as I gathered from subsequent discussion, there was a notion that the necessary bribes had been paid, they thought they could take a chance on the central square and draw a larger and more enthusiastic crowd without attracting the attention of the law.

They were wrong. In the midst of the third match, with hundreds of people, including, still transparent, myself and my wife, fused into a single body around the ring, a superorganism in the literal sense, a truck full of policemen armed with machine guns

---

[1]*Gregory Bateson and Margaret Mead, Balinese Character: A Photographic Analysis* (New York: New York Academy of Sciences, 1942), p. 68. [This note and all subsequent notes are Geertz's.]

roared up. Amid great screeching cries of "pulisi! pulisi!" from the crowd, the policemen jumped out, and, springing into the center of the ring, began to swing their guns around like gangsters in a motion picture, though not going so far as actually to fire them. The superorganism came instantly apart as its components scattered in all directions. People raced down the road, disappeared head first over walls, scrambled under platforms, folded themselves behind wicker screens, scuttled up coconut trees. Cocks armed with steel spurs sharp enough to cut off a finger or run a hole through a foot were running wildly around. Everything was dust and panic.

On the established anthropological principle, When in Rome, my wife and I decided, only slightly less instantaneously than everyone else, that the thing to do was run too. We ran down the main village street, northward, away from where we were living, for we were on that side of the ring. About half-way down another fugitive ducked suddenly into a compound—his own, it turned out—and we, seeing nothing ahead of us but rice fields, open country, and a very high volcano, followed him. As the three of us came tumbling into the courtyard, his wife, who had apparently been through this sort of thing before, whipped out a table, a tablecloth, three chairs, and three cups of tea, and we all, without any explicit communication whatsoever, sat down, commenced to sip tea, and sought to compose ourselves.

A few moments later, one of the policemen marched importantly into the yard, looking for the village chief. (The chief had not only been at the fight, he had arranged it. When the truck drove up he ran to the river, stripped off his sarong, and plunged in so he could say, when at length they found him sitting there pouring water over his head, that he had been away bathing when the whole affair had occurred and was ignorant of it. They did not believe him and fined him three hundred rupiah, which the village raised collectively.) Seeing my wife and I, "White Men," there in the yard, the policeman performed a classic double take. When he found his voice again he asked, approximately, what in the devil did we think we were doing there. Our host of five minutes leaped instantly to our defense, producing an impassioned description of who and what we were, so detailed and so accurate that it was my turn, having barely communicated with a living human being save my landlord and the village chief for more than a week, to be astonished. We had a perfect right to be there, he said, looking the Javanese upstart in the eye. We were American professors; the government had cleared us; we were there to study culture; we were going to write a book to tell Americans about Bali. And we had all been there drinking tea and talking about cultural matters all afternoon and did not know anything about any cockfight. Moreover, we had not seen the village chief all day, he must have gone to town. The policeman retreated in rather total disarray. And, after a decent interval, bewildered but relieved to have survived and stayed out of jail, so did we.

The next morning the village was a completely different world for us. Not only were we no longer invisible, we were suddenly the center of all attention, the object of a great outpouring of warmth, interest, and, most especially, amusement. Everyone in the village knew we had fled like everyone else. They asked us about it again and again (I must have told the story, small detail by small detail, fifty times by the end of the day), gently, affectionately, but quite insistently teasing us: "Why didn't you just stand there and tell the police who you were?" "Why didn't you just say you were only watching and not betting?" "Were you really afraid of those little guns?" As always, kinesthetically minded and, even when fleeing for their lives (or, as happened eight years later, surrendering them), the world's most poised people, they gleefully mimicked, also over and over again, our graceless style of running and what they claimed were our panic-stricken facial expressions. But above all, everyone was extremely pleased and even more surprised that we had not simply "pulled out our papers" (they knew about those too) and asserted our Distinguished Visitor status, but had instead demonstrated our solidarity with what were now our covillagers. (What we had actually demonstrated was our cowardice, but there is fellowship in that too.) Even the Brahmana priest, an old, grave, halfway-to-Heaven type who because of its associations with the underworld would never be involved, even distantly, in a cockfight, and was difficult to approach even to other Balinese, had us called into his courtyard to ask us about what had happened, chuckling happily at the sheer extraordinariness of it all.

In Bali, to be teased is to be accepted. It was the turning point so far as our relationship to the community was concerned, and we were quite literally "in." The whole village opened up to us, probably more than it ever would have otherwise (I might actually never have gotten to that priest, and our accidental host became one of my best informants), and certainly very much faster. Getting caught, or almost caught, in a vice raid is perhaps not a very generalizable recipe for achieving that mysterious necessity of anthropological field work, rapport, but for me it worked very well. It led to a sudden and unusually complete acceptance into a society extremely difficult for outsiders to penetrate. It gave me the kind of immediate, inside-view grasp of an aspect of "peasant mentality" that anthropologists not fortunate enough to flee headlong with their subjects from armed authorities normally do not get. And, perhaps most important of all, for the other things might have come in other ways, it put me very quickly on to a combination emotional explosion, status war, and philosophical drama of central significance to the society whose inner nature I desired to understand. By the time I left I had spent about as much time looking into cockfights as into witchcraft, irrigation, caste, or marriage.

OF COCKS AND MEN

Bali, mainly because it is Bali, is a well-studied place. Its mythology, art, ritual, social organization, patterns of child rearing, forms of law, even styles of trance, have all been microscopically examined for traces of that elusive substance Jane Belo called "The Balinese Temper."[2] But, aside from a few passing remarks, the cockfight has barely been noticed, although as a popular obsession of consuming power it is at least as important a revelation of what being a Balinese "is really like" as these more celebrated phenomena.[3] As much of America surfaces in a ball park, on a golf links, at a race track, or around a poker table, much of Bali surfaces in a cock ring. For it is only apparently cocks that are fighting there. Actually, it is men.

To anyone who has been in Bali any length of time, the deep psychological identification of Balinese men with their cocks is unmistakable. The double entendre here is deliberate. It works in exactly the same way in Balinese as it does in English, even to producing the same tired jokes, strained puns, and uninventive obscenities. Bateson and Mead have even suggested that, in line with the Balinese conception of the body as a set of separately animated parts, cocks are viewed as detachable, self-operating penises,

---

[2] *Jane Belo,* "The Balinese Temper," in Jane Belo, ed., *Traditional Balinese Culture* (New York: Columbia University Press, 1970; originally published in 1935), pp. 85–110.

[3] *The best discussion of cockfighting* is again Bateson and Mead's (*Balinese Character,* pp. 24–25, 140), but it, too, is general and abbreviated.

ambulant genitals with a life of their own.[4] And while I do not have the kind of uncon-scious material either to confirm or disconfirm this intriguing notion, the fact that they are masculine symbols *par excellence* is about as indubitable, and to the Balinese about as evident, as the fact that water runs downhill.

The language of everyday moralism is shot through, on the male side of it, with roos-terish imagery. *Sabung,* the word for cock (and one which appears in inscriptions as early as A.D. 922), is used metaphorically to mean "hero," "warrior," "champion," "man of parts," "political candidate," "bachelor," "dandy," "lady-killer," or "tough guy." A pompous man whose behavior presumes above his station is compared to a tailless cock who struts about as though he had a large, spectacular one. A desperate man who makes a last, irrational effort to extricate himself from an impossible situation is likened to a dying cock who makes one final lunge at his tormentor to drag him along to a common destruction. A stingy man, who promises much, gives little, and begrudges that is com-pared to a cock which, held by the tail, leaps at another without in fact engaging him. A marriageable young man still shy with the opposite sex or someone in a new job anxious to make a good impression is called "a fighting cock caged for the first time."[5] Court tri-als, wars, political contests, inheritance disputes, and street arguments are all compared to cockfights.[6] Even the very island itself is perceived from its shape as a small, proud cock, poised, neck extended, back taut, tail raised, in eternal challenge to large, feckless, shapeless Java.[7]

But the intimacy of men with their cocks is more than metaphorical. Balinese men, or anyway a large majority of Balinese men, spend an enormous amount of time with their favorites, grooming them, feeding them, discussing them, trying them out against one another, or just gazing at them with a mixture of rapt admiration and dreamy self-absorption. Whenever you see a group of Balinese men squatting idly in the council shed or along the road in their hips down, shoulders forward, knees up fashion, half or more of them will have a rooster in his hands, holding it between his thighs, bouncing it gently up

---

[4]*Ibid.,* pp. 25–26. The cockfight is unusual within Balinese culture in being a single-sex public activity from which the other sex is totally and expressly excluded. Sexual differentiation is cul-turally extremely played down in Bali and most activities, formal and informal, involve the par-ticipation of men and women on equal ground, commonly as linked couples. From religion, to pol-itics, to economics, to kinship, to dress, Bali is a rather "uni-sex" society, a fact both its customs and its symbolism clearly express. Even in contexts where women do not in fact play much of a role—music, painting, certain agricultural activities—their absence, which is only relative in any case, is more a mere matter of fact than socially enforced. To this general pattern, the cockfight, entirely of, by, and for men (women—at least *Balinese* women—do not even watch), is the most striking exception.

[5]*Christiaan Hooykaas, The Lay of the Jaya Prana* (London, 1958), p. 39. The lay has a stanza (no. 17) with the reluctant bridegroom use Jaya Prana the subject of a Balinese Uriah myth, responds to the lord who has offered him the loveliest of six hundred servant girls: "Godly King, my Lord and Master/I beg you, give me leave to go/such things are not yet in my mind;/like a fighting cock encaged/indeed I am on my mettle/I am alone/as yet the flame has not been fanned."

[6]For these, see V. E. Korn, *Het Adatrecht van Bali,* 2d ed. ('S-Gravenhage: G. Naeff, 1932), index under *toh.*

[7]*There is indeed a legend to the effect that the separation of Java and Bali* is due to the action of a powerful Javanese religious figure who wished to protect himself against a Balinese culture hero (the ancestor of two Ksatria castes) who was a passionate cockfighting gambler. See Christiaan Hooykaas, *Agama Tirtha* (Amsterdam: Noord-Hollandsche, 1964), p. 184.

and down to strengthen its legs, ruffling its feathers with abstract sensuality, pushing it out against a neighbor's rooster to rouse its spirit, withdrawing it toward his loins to calm it again. Now and then, to get a feel for another bird, a man will fiddle this way with someone else's cock for a while, but usually by moving around to squat in place behind it, rather than just having it passed across to him as though it were merely an animal.

In the houseyard, the high-walled enclosures where the people live, fighting cocks are kept in wicker cages, moved frequently about so as to maintain the optimum balance of sun and shade. They are fed a special diet, which varies somewhat according to individual theories but which is mostly maize, sifted for impurities with far more care than it is when mere humans are going to eat it and offered to the animal kernel by kernel. Red pepper is stuffed down their beaks and up their anuses to give them spirit. They are bathed in the same ceremonial preparation of tepid water, medicinal herbs, flowers, and onions in which infants are bathed, and for a prize cock just about as often. Their combs are cropped, their plumage dressed, their spurs trimmed, their legs massaged, and they are inspected for flaws with the squinted concentration of a diamond merchant. A man who has a passion for cocks, an enthusiast in the literal sense of the term, can spend most of his life with them, and even those, the overwhelming majority, whose passion though intense has not entirely run away with them, can and do spend what seems not only to an outsider, but also to themselves, an inordinate amount of time with them. "I am cock crazy," my landlord, a quite ordinary *afficionado* by Balinese standards, used to moan as he went to move another cage, give another bath, or conduct another feeding. "We're all cock crazy."

The madness has some less visible dimensions, however, because although it is true that cocks are symbolic expressions or magnifications of their owner's self, the narcissistic male ego writ out in Aesopian terms, they are also expressions—and rather more immediate ones—of what the Balinese regard as the direct inversion, aesthetically, morally, and metaphysically, of human status: animality.

The Balinese revulsion against any behavior regarded as animal-like can hardly be overstressed. Babies are not allowed to crawl for that reason. Incest, though hardly approved, is a much less horrifying crime than bestiality. (The appropriate punishment for the second is death by drowning, for the first being forced to live like an animal.)[8] Most demons are represented—in sculpture, dance, ritual, myth—in some real or fantastic animal form. The main puberty rite consists in filing the child's teeth so they will not look like animal fangs. Not only defecation but eating is regarded as a disgusting, almost obscene activity, to be conducted hurriedly and privately, because of its association with animality. Even falling down or any form of clumsiness is considered to be bad for these reasons. Aside from cocks and a few domestic animals—oxen, ducks—of no emotional significance, the Balinese are aversive to animals, and treat their large number of dogs not merely callously but with a phobic cruelty. In identifying with his cock, the Balinese man is identifying not just with his ideal self, or even his penis, but also, and at the same time, with what he most fears, hates, and ambivalence being what it is, is fascinated by— The Powers of Darkness.

The connection of cocks and cockfighting with such Powers, with the animalistic demons that threaten constantly to invade the small, cleared off space in which the Bali-

---

[8]*An incestuous couple is forced to wear pig yokes over their necks and crawl to a pig trough and eat with their mouths there.* On this, see Jane Belo, "Customs Pertaining to Twins in Bali," in Belo, ed., *Traditional Balinese Culture*, p. 49; on the abhorence of animality generally, Bateson and Mead, *Balinese Character*, p. 22.

nese have so carefully built their lives and devour its inhabitants, is quite explicit. A cockfight, any cockfight, is in the first instance a blood sacrifice offered, with the appropriate chants and oblations, to the demons in order to pacify their ravenous, cannibal hunger. No temple festival should be conducted until one is made. (If it is omitted someone will inevitably fall into a trance and command with the voice of an angered spirit that the oversight be immediately corrected.) Collective responses to natural evils—illness, crop failure, volcanic eruptions—almost always involve them. And that famous holiday in Bali, The Day of Silence (*Njepi*), when everyone sits silent and immobile all day long in order to avoid contact with a sudden influx of demons chased momentarily out of hell, is preceded the previous day by large-scale cockfights (in this case legal) in almost every village on the island.

In the cockfight, man and beast, good and evil, ego and id, the creative power of aroused masculinity and the destructive power of loosened animality fuse in a bloody drama of hatred, cruelty, violence, and death. It is little wonder that when, as is the invariable rule, the owner of the winning cock takes the carcass of the loser—often torn limb from limb by its enraged owner—home to eat, he does so with a mixture of social embarrassment, moral satisfaction, aesthetic disgust, and cannibal joy. Or that a man who has lost an important fight is sometimes driven to wreck his family shrines and curse the gods, an act of metaphysical (and social) suicide. Or that in seeking earthly analogues for heaven and hell the Balinese compare the former to the mood of a man whose cock has just won, the latter to that of a man whose cock has just lost.

THE FIGHT

Cockfights (*tetadjen; sabungan*) are held in a ring about fifty feet square. Usually they begin toward late afternoon and run three of four hours until sunset. About nine or ten separate matches (*sehet*) comprise a program. Each match is precisely like the others in general pattern: there is no main match, no connection between individual matches, no variation in their format, and each is arranged on a completely ad hoc basis. After a fight has ended and the emotional debris is cleaned away—the bets paid, the curses cursed, the carcasses possessed—seven, eight, perhaps even a dozen men slop negligently into the ring with a cock and seek to find there a logical opponent for it. This process, which rarely takes less than ten minutes and often a good deal longer, is conducted in a very subdued, oblique, even dissembling manner. Those not immediately involved give it at best but disguised, sidelong attention; those who, embarrassedly, are, attempt to pretend somehow that the whole thing is not really happening.

A match made, the other hopefuls retire with the same deliberate indifference, and the selected cocks have their spurs (*tadji*) affixed—razor-sharp, pointed steel swords, four or five inches long. This is a delicate job which only a small portion of men, a half-dozen or so in most villages, know how to do properly. The man who attaches the spurs also provides them, and if the rooster he assists wins its owner awards him the spur-leg of the victim. The spurs are affixed by winding a long length of string around the foot of the spur and the leg of the cock. For reasons I shall come to presently, it is done somewhat differently from case to case, and is an obsessively deliberate affair. The lore about spurs is extensive—they are sharpened only at eclipses and the dark of the moon, should be kept out of the sight of women, and so forth. And they are handled, both in use and out, with the same curious combination of fussiness and sensuality the Balinese direct toward ritual objects generally.

The spurs affixed, the two cocks are placed by their handlers (who may or may not be their owners) facing one another in the center of the ring.[9] A coconut pierced with a small hole is placed in a pail of water, in which it takes about twenty-one seconds to sink, a period known as a *tjeng* and marked at beginning and end by the beating of a slit gong. During these twenty-one seconds the handlers (*pengangkeb*) are not permitted to touch their roosters. If, as sometimes happens, the animals have not fought during this time, they are picked up, fluffed, pulled, prodded, and otherwise insulted, and put back in the center of the ring and the process begins again. Sometimes they refuse to fight at all, or one keeps running away, in which case they are imprisoned together under a wicker cage, which usually gets them engaged.

Most of the time, in any case, the cocks fly almost immediately at one another in a wing-beating, head-thrusting, leg-kicking explosion of animal fury so pure, so absolute, and in its own way so beautiful, as to be almost abstract, a Platonic concept of hate. Within moments one or the other drives home a solid blow with his spur. The handler whose cock has delivered the blow immediately picks it up so that it will not get a return blow, for if he does not the match is likely to end in a mutually mortal tie as the two birds wildly hack each other to pieces. This is particularly true if, as often happens, the spur sticks in its victim's body, for then the aggressor is at the mercy of his wounded foe.

With the birds again in the hands of their handlers, the coconut is now sunk three times after which the cock which has landed the blow must be set down to show that he is firm, a fact he demonstrates by wandering idly around the ring for a coconut sink. The coconut is then sunk twice more and the fight must recommence.

During this interval, slightly over two minutes, the handler of the wounded cock has been working frantically over it, like a trainer patching a mauled boxer between rounds, to get it in shape for a last, desperate try for victory. He blows in its mouth, putting the whole chicken head in his own mouth and sucking and blowing, fluffs it, stuffs its wounds with various sorts of medicines, and generally tries anything he can think of to arouse the last ounce of spirit which may be hidden somewhere within it. By the time he is forced to put it back down he is usually drenched in chicken blood, but, as in prize fighting, a good handler is worth his weight in gold. Some of them can virtually make the dead walk, at least long enough for the second and final round.

In the climactic battle (if there is one; sometimes the wounded cock simply expires in the handler's hands or immediately as it is placed down again), the cock who landed the first blow usually proceeds to finish off his weakened opponent. But this is far from an inevitable outcome, for if a cock can walk he can fight, and if he can fight, he can kill, and what counts is which cock expires first. If the wounded one can get a stab in and stagger on until the other drops, he is the official winner, even if he himself topples over an instant later.

---

[9]*Except for unimportant, small-bet fights* (on the question of fight "importance," see below) spur affixing is usually done by someone other than the owner. Whether the owner handles his own cock or not more or less depends on how skilled he is at it, a consideration whose importance is again relative to the importance of the fight. When spur affixers and cock handlers are someone other than the owner, they are almost always a quite close relative—a brother or cousin—or a very intimate friend of his. They are thus almost extensions of his personality, as the fact that all three will refer to the cock as "mine," say "I" fought So-and-So, and so on, demonstrates. Also, owner-handler-affixer triads tend to be fairly fixed, though individuals may participate in several and often exchange roles within a given one.

Surrounding all this melodrama—which the crowd packed tight around the ring follows in near silence, moving their bodies in kinesthetic sympathy with the movement of the animals, cheering their champions on with wordless hand motions, shiftings of the shoulders, turnings of the head, falling back *en masse* as the cock with the murderous spurs careens toward one side of the ring (it is said that spectators sometimes lose eyes and fingers from being too attentive), surging forward again as they glance off toward another—is a vast body of extraordinarily elaborate and precisely detailed rules.

These rules, together with the developed lore of cocks and cockfighting which accompanies them, are written down in palm leaf manuscripts (*lontar; rontal*) passed on from generation to generation as part of the general legal and cultural tradition of the villages. At a fight, the umpire (*saja komong; djuru kembar*)—the man who manages the coconut—is in charge of their application and his authority is absolute. I have never seen an umpire's judgment questioned on any subject, even by the more despondent losers, nor have I ever heard, even in private, a charge of unfairness directed against one, or, for that matter, complaints about umpires in general. Only exceptionally well-trusted, solid, and, given the complexity of the code, knowledgeable citizens perform this job, and in fact men will bring their cocks only to fights presided over by such men. It is also the umpire to whom accusations of cheating, which, though rare in the extreme, occasionally arise, are referred; and it is he who in the not infrequent cases where the cocks expire virtually together decides which (if either, for, though the Balinese do not care for such an outcome, there can be ties) went first. Likened to a judge, a king, a priest, and a policeman, he is all of these, and under his assured direction the animal passion of the fight proceeds within the civic certainty of the law. In the dozens of cockfights I saw in Bali, I never once saw an altercation about rules. Indeed, I never saw an open altercation, other than those between cocks, at all.

This crosswise doubleness of an event which, taken as a fact of nature, is rage untrammeled and, taken as a fact of culture, is form perfected, defines the cockfight as a sociological entity. A cockfight is what, searching for a name for something not vertebrate enough to be called a group and not structureless enough to be called a crowd, Erving Goffman has called a "focused gathering"—a set of persons engrossed in a common flow of activity and relating to one another in terms of that flow.[10] Such gatherings meet and disperse; the participants in them fluctuate; the activity that focuses them is discreet—a particulate process that reoccurs rather than a continuous one that endures. They take their form from the situation that evokes them, the floor on which they are placed, as Goffman puts it; but it is a form, and an articulate one, nonetheless. For the situation, the floor is itself created, in jury deliberations, surgical operations, block meetings, sit-ins, cockfights, by the cultural preoccupations—here, as we shall see, the celebration of status rivalry—which not only specify the focus but, assembling actors and arranging scenery, bring it actually into being.

In classical times (that is to say, prior to the Dutch invasion of 1908), when there were no bureaucrats around to improve popular morality, the staging of a cockfight was an explicitly societal matter. Bringing a cock to an important fight was, for an adult male, a compulsory duty of citizenship; taxation of fights, which were usually held on market day, was a major source of public revenue; patronage of the art was a stated responsibility of princes; and the cock ring, or *wantilan,* stood in the center of the village near

---

[10]*Erving Goffman, Encounters: Two Studies in the Sociology of Interaction* (Indianapolis: Bobbs-Merrill, 1961), pp. 9–10.

those other monuments of Balinese civility—the council house, the origin temple, the marketplace, the signal tower, and the banyan tree. Today, a few special occasions aside, the newer rectitude makes so open a statement of the connection between the excitements of collective life and those of blood sport impossible, but, less directly expressed, the connection itself remains intimate and intact. To expose it, however, it is necessary to turn to the aspect of cockfighting around which all the others pivot, and through which they exercise their force, an aspect I have thus far studiously ignored. I mean, of course, the gambling.

ODDS AND EVEN MONEY

The Balinese never do anything in a simple way that they can contrive to do in a complicated one, and to this generalization cockfight wagering is no exception.

In the first place, there are two sorts of bets, or *toh*.[11] There is the single axial bet on the center between the principals (toh ketengah), and there is the cloud of peripheral ones around the ring between members of the audience (*toh kesasi*). The first is typically large; the second typically small. The first is collective, involving coalitions of bettors clustering around the owner; the second is individual, man to man. The first is a matter of deliberate, very quiet, almost furtive arrangement by the coalition members and the umpire huddled like conspirators in the center of the ring; the second is a matter of impulsive shouting, public offers, and public acceptances by the excited throng around its edges. And most curiously, and as we shall see most revealingly, *where the first is always, without exception, even money, the second, equally without exception, is never such.* What is a fair coin in the center is a biased one on the side.

The center bet is the official one, hedged in again with a webwork of rules, and is made between the two cock owners, with the umpire as overseer and public witness.[12] This bet, which, as I say, is always relatively and sometimes very large, is never raised simply by the owner in whose name it is made, but by him together with four or five, sometimes seven or eight, allies—kin, village mates, neighbors, close friends. He may, if he is not especially well-to-do, not even be the major contributor, though, if only to show that he is not involved in any chicanery, he must be a significant one.

Of the fifty-seven matches for which I have exact and reliable data on the center bet, the range is from fifteen ringgits to five hundred, with a mean at eighty-five and with the distribution being rather noticeably trimodal: small fights (15 ringgits either side of 35) accounting for about 45 percent of the total number; medium ones (20 ringgits either side

---

[11]*toh* This word, which literally means an indelible stain or mark, as in a birthmark or a vein in a stone, is used as well for a deposit in a court case, for a pawn, for security offered in a loan, for a stand-in for someone else in a legal or ceremonial context, for an earnest advanced in a business deal, for a sign placed in a field to indicate its ownership is in dispute, and for the status of an unfaithful wife from whose lover her husband must gain satisfaction or surrender her to him. See Korn, *Het Adatrecht van Bali;* Theodoor Pigeaud, *Javaans-Nederlands Handwoordenboek* (Groningen: Wolters, 1938); H. H. Juynboll, *Oudjavaansche-Nederlandsche Woordenlijst* (Leiden: Brill, 1923).

[12]*The center bet must be advanced in cash by both parties prior to the actual fight.* The umpire holds the stakes until the decision is rendered and then awards them to the winner, avoiding, among other things, the intense embarrassment both winner and loser would feel if the latter had to pay off personally following his defeat. About 10 per cent of the winner's receipts are subtracted for the umpire's share and that of the fight sponsors.

of 70) for about 25 percent; and large (75 ringgits either side of 175) for about 20 percent, with a few very small and very large ones out at the extremes. In a society where the normal daily wage of a manual laborer—a brickmaker, an ordinary farmworker, a market porter—was about three ringgits a day, and considering the fact that fights were held on the average about every two-and-a-half days in the immediate area I studied, this is clearly serious gambling, even if the bets are pooled rather than individual efforts.

The side bets are, however, something else altogether. Rather than the solemn, legalistic pactmaking of the center, wagering takes place rather in the fashion in which the stock exchange used to work when it was out on the curb. There is a fixed and known odds paradigm which runs in a continuous series from ten-to-nine at the short end to two-to-one at the long: 10-9, 9-8, 8-7, 7-6, 6-5, 5-4, 4-3, 3-2, 2-1. The man who wishes to back the *underdog cock* (leaving aside how favorites, *kebut*, and underdogs, *ngai*, are established for the moment) shouts the short-side number indicating the odds he wants *to be given*. That is, if he shouts *gasal*, "five," he wants the underdog at five-to-four (or, for him, four-to-five); if he shouts "four," he wants it at four-to-three (again, he putting up the "three"), if "nine," at nine-to-eight, and so on. A man backing the favorite, and thus considering giving odds if he can get them short enough, indicates the fact by crying out the color-type of that cock—"brown," "speckled," or whatever.[13]

As odds-takers (backers of the underdog) and odds-givers (backers of the favorite) sweep the crowd with their shouts, they begin to focus in on one another as potential betting pairs, often from far across the ring. The taker tries to shout the giver into longer odds, the giver to shout the taker into shorter ones.[14] The taker, who is the wooer in this

[13]Actually, *the typing of cocks*, which is extremely elaborate (I have collected more than twenty classes, certainly not a complete list), is not based on color alone, but on a series of independent, interacting, dimensions, which include, beside color, size, bone thickness, plumage, and temperament. (But not pedigree. The Balinese do not breed cocks to any significant extent, nor, so far as I have been able to discover, have they ever done so. The asil, or jungle cock, which is the basic fighting strain everywhere the sport is found, is native to southern Asia, and one can buy a good example in the chicken section of almost any Balinese market for anywhere from four or five ringgits up to fifty or more.) The color element is merely the one normally used as the type name, except when the two cocks of different types—as on principle they must be—have the same color, in which case a secondary indication from one of the other dimensions ("large speckled" v. "small speckled," etc.) is added. The types are coordinated with various cosmological ideas which help shape the making of matches, so that, for example, you fight a small, headstrong, speckled brown-on-white cock with flat-lying feathers and thin legs from the east side of the ring on a certain day of the complex Balinese calendar, and a large, cautious, all-black cock with tufted feathers and stubby legs from the north side on another day, and so on. All this is again recorded in palm-leaf manuscripts and endlessly discussed by the Balinese (who do not all have identical systems), and full-scale componential-cum-symbolic analysis of cock classifications would be extremely valuable both as an adjunct to the description of the cockfight and in itself. But my data on the subject, though extensive and varied, do not seem to be complete and systematic enough to attempt such an analysis here. For Balinese cosmological ideas more generally see Belo, ed., *Traditional Balinese Culture*, and J. L. Swellengrebel, ed., *Bali: Studies in Life, Thought, and Ritual* (The Hague: W. van Hoeve, 1960); for calendrical ones, Clifford Geertz, *Person, Time, and Conduct in Bali: An Essay in Cultural Analysis* (New Haven: Southeast Asia Studies, Yale University, 1966), pp. 45–53.

[14]*Odds-giver* For purposes of ethnographic completeness, it should be noted that it is possible for the man backing the favorite—the odds-giver—to make a bet in which he wins if his cock wins or there is a tie, a slight shortening of the odds (I do not have enough cases to be exact, but ties seem to occur about once every fifteen or twenty matches). He indicates his wish to do this by shouting *sapih* ("tie") rather than the cock-type, but such bets are in fact infrequent.

situation, will signal how large a bet he wishes to make at the odds he is shouting by holding a number of fingers up in front of his face and vigorously waving them. If the giver, the wooed, replies in kind, the bet is made; if he does not, they unlock gazes and the search goes on.

The side betting, which takes place after the center bet has been made and its size announced, consists then in a rising crescendo of shouts as backers of the underdog offer their propositions to anyone who will accept them, while those who are backing the favorite but do not like the price being offered, shout equally frenetically the color of the cock to show they too are desperate to bet but want shorter odds.

Almost always odds-calling, which tends to be very consensual in that at any one time almost all callers are calling the same thing, starts off toward the long end of the range—five-to-four or four-to-three—and then moves, also consensually, toward the short end with greater or lesser speed and to a greater or lesser degree. Men crying "five" and finding themselves answered only with cries of "brown" start crying "six," either drawing the other callers fairly quickly with them or retiring from the scene as their toogenerous offers are snapped up. If the change is made and partners are still scarce, the procedure is repeated in a move to "seven," and so on, only rarely, and in the very largest fights, reaching the ultimate "nine" or "ten" levels. Occasionally, if the cocks are clearly mismatched, there may be no upward movement at all, or even a movement down the scale to four-to-three, three-to-two, very, very rarely two-to-one, a shift which is accompanied by a declining number of bets as a shift upward is accompanied by an increasing number. But the general pattern is for the betting to move a shorter or longer distance up the scale toward the, for sidebets, nonexistent pole of even money, with the overwhelming majority of bets falling in the four-to-three to eight-to-seven range.[15]

As the moment for the release of the cocks by the handlers approaches, the screaming, at least in a match where the center bet is large, reaches almost frenzied proportions as the remaining unfulfilled bettors try desperately to find a last minute partner at a price they can live with. (Where the center bet is small, the opposite tends to occur: betting dies off, trailing into silence, as odds lengthen and people lose interest.) In a large-bet, well-made match—the kind of match the Balinese regard as "real cockfighting"—the mob scene quality, the sense that sheer chaos is about to break loose, with all those waving, shouting, pushing, clambering men is quite strong, an effect which is only heightened by the intense stillness that falls with instant suddenness, rather as if someone had turned off the current, when the slit gong sounds, the cocks are put down, and the battle begins.

When it ends, anywhere from fifteen seconds to five minutes later, *all bets are immediately paid.* There are absolutely no IOU's, at least to a betting opponent. One may, of

---

[15]*The precise dynamics of the movement of the betting* is one of the most intriguing, most complicated, and, given the hectic conditions under which it occurs, most difficult to study, aspects of the fight. Motion picture recording plus multiple observers would probably be necessary to deal with it effectively. Even impressionistically—the only approach open to a lone ethnographer caught in the middle of all this—it is clear that certain men lead both in determining the favorite (that is, making the opening cock-type calls which always initiate the process) and in directing the movement of the odds, these "opinion leaders" being the more accomplished cockfighters-cum-solid-citizens to be discussed below. If these men begin to change their calls, others follow; if they begin to make bets, so do others and—though there is always a large number of frustrated bettors crying for shorter or longer odds to the end—the movement more or less ceases. But a detailed understanding of the whole process awaits what, alas, it is not very likely ever to get: a decision theorist armed with precise observations of individual behavior.

course, borrow from a friend before offering or accepting a wager, but to offer or accept it you must have the money already in hand and, if you lose, you must pay it on the spot, before the next match begins. This is an iron rule, and as I have never heard of a disputed umpire's decision (though doubtless there must sometimes be some), I have also never heard of a welshed bet, perhaps because in a worked-up cockfight crowd the consequences might be, as they are reported to be sometimes for cheaters, drastic and immediate.

It is, in any case, this formal asymmetry between balanced center bets and unbalanced side ones that poses the critical analytical problem for a theory which sees cockfight wagering as the link connecting the fight to the wider world of Balinese culture. It also suggests the way to go about solving it and demonstrating the link.

The first point that needs to be made in this connection is that the higher the center bet, the more likely the match will in actual fact be an even one. Simple considerations of rationality suggest that. If you are betting fifteen ringgits on a cock, you might be willing to go along with even money even if you feel your animal somewhat the less promising. But if you are betting five hundred you are very, very likely to be loathe to do so. Thus, in large-bet fights, which of course involve the better animals, tremendous care is taken to see that the cocks are about as evenly matched as to size, general condition, pugnacity, and so on as is humanly possible. The different ways of adjusting the spurs of the animals are often employed to secure this. If one cock seems stronger, an agreement will be made to position his spur at a slightly less advantageous angle—a kind of handicapping, at which spur affixers are, so it is said, extremely skilled. More care will be taken, too, to employ skillful handlers and to match them exactly as to abilities.

In short, in a large-bet fight the pressure to make the match a genuinely fifty-fifty proposition is enormous, and is consciously felt as such. For medium fights the pressure is somewhat less, and for small ones less yet, though there is always an effort to make things at least approximately equal, for even at fifteen ringgits (five days work) no one wants to make an even money bet in a clearly unfavorable situation. And, again, what statistics I have tend to bear this out. In my fifty-seven matches, the favorite won thirty-three times overall, the underdog twenty-four, a 1.4 to 1 ratio. But if one splits the figures at sixty ringgits center bets, the ratios turn out to be 1.1 to 1 (twelve favorites, eleven underdogs) for those above this line, and 1.6 to 1 (twenty-one and thirteen) for those below it. Or, if you take the extremes, for very large fights, those with center bets over a hundred ringgits the ratio is 1 to 1 (seven and seven); for very small fights, those under forty ringgits, it is 1.9 to 1 (nineteen and ten).[16]

Now, from this proposition—that the higher the center bet the more exactly a fifty-fifty proposition the cockfight is—two things more or less immediately follow: (1) the higher the center bet, the greater is the pull on the side betting toward the short-odds end of the wagering spectrum and vice versa; (2) the higher the center bet, the greater the volume of side betting and vice versa.

---

[16]*ringgits* Assuming only binomial variability, the departure from a fifty-fifty expectation in the sixty ringgits and below case is 1.38 standard deviations, or (in a one direction test) an eight in one hundred possibility by chance alone; for the below forty ringgits case it is 1.65 standard deviations, or about five in one hundred. The fact that these departures though real are not extreme merely indicates, again, that even in the smaller fights the tendency to match cocks at least reasonably evenly persists. It is a matter of relative relaxation of the pressures toward equalization, not their elimination. The tendency for high-bet contests to be coin-flip propositions is, of course, even more striking, and suggests the Balinese know quite well what they are about.

The logic is similar in both cases. The closer the fight is in fact to even money, the less attractive the long end of the odds will appear and, therefore, the shorter it must be if there are to be takers. That this is the case is apparent from mere inspection, from the Balinese's own analysis of the matter, and from what more systematic observations I was able to collect. Given the difficulty of making precise and complete recordings of side betting, this argument is hard to cast in numerical form, but in all my cases the odds-giver, odds-taker consensual point, a quite pronounced minimax saddle where the bulk (at a guess, two-thirds to three-quarters in most cases) of the bets are actually made, was three or four points further along the scale toward the shorter end for the large-center-bet fights than for the small ones, with medium ones generally in between. In detail, the fit is not, of course, exact, but the general pattern is quite consistent: the power of the center bet to pull the side bets toward its own even-money pattern is directly proportional to its size, because its size is directly proportional to the degree to which the cocks are in fact evenly matched. As for the volume question, total wagering is greater in large-center-bet fights because such fights are considered more "interesting" not only in the sense that they are less predictable, but, more crucially, that more is at stake in them—in terms of money, in terms of the quality of the cocks, and consequently, as we shall see, in terms of social prestige.[17]

The paradox of fair coin in the middle, biased coin on the outside is thus a merely apparent one. The two betting systems, though formally incongruent, are not really contradictory to one another, but part of a single larger system in which the center bet is, so to speak, the "center of gravity," drawing, the larger it is the more so, the outside bets toward the short-odds end of the scale. The center bet thus "makes the game," or perhaps better, defines it, signals what, following a notion of Jeremy Bentham's, I am going to call its "depth."

The Balinese attempt to create an interesting, if you will, "deep," match by making the center bet as large as possible so that the cocks matched will be as equal and as fine as possible, and the outcome, thus, as unpredictable as possible. They do not always succeed. Nearly half the matches are relatively trivial, relatively uninteresting—in my borrowed terminology, "shallow"—affairs. But that fact no more argues against my interpretation than the fact that most painters, poets, and playwrights are mediocre argues against the view that artistic effort is directed toward profundity and, with a certain frequency, approximates it. The image of artistic technique is indeed exact: the center bet is a means, a device, for creating "interesting," "deep" matches, *not* the reason, or at least not the main reason, *why* they are interesting, the source of their fascination, the sub-

---

[17]*Social prestige* The reduction in wagering in smaller fights (which, of course, feeds on itself; one of the reasons people find small fights uninteresting is that there is less wagering in them, and contrariwise for large ones) takes place in three mutually reinforcing ways. First, there is a simple withdrawal of interest as people wander off to have a cup of coffee or chat with a friend. Second, the Balinese do not mathematically reduce odds, but bet directly in terms of stated odds as such. Thus, for a nine-to-eight bet, one man wagers nine ringgits, the other eight; for five-to-four, one wagers five, the other four. For any given currency unit, like the ringgit, therefore, 6.3 times as much money is involved in a ten-to-nine bet as in a two-to-one bet, for example, and, as noted, in small fights betting settles toward the longer end. Finally, the bets which are made tend to be one- rather than two-, three-, or in some of the very largest fights, four-, or five-finger ones. (The fingers indicate the multiples of the stated bet odds at issue, not absolute figures. Two fingers in a six-to -five situation means a man wants to wager ten ringgits on the underdog against twelve, three in an eight-to-seven situation, twenty-one against twenty-four, and so on.)

stance of their depth. The question why such matches are interesting—indeed, for the Balinese, exquisitely absorbing—takes us out of the realm of formal concerns into more broadly sociological and social-psychological ones, and to a less purely economic idea of what "depth" in gaming amounts to.[18]

PLAYING WITH FIRE

Bentham's concept of "deep play" is found in his *The Theory of Legislation*.[19] By it he means play in which the stakes are so high that it is, from his utilitarian standpoint, irrational for men to engage in it at all. If a man whose fortune is a thousand pounds (or ringgits) wages five hundred of it on an even bet, the marginal utility of the pound he stands to win is clearly less than the marginal disutility of the one he stands to lose. In genuine deep play, this is the case for both parties. They are both in over their heads. Having come together in search of pleasure they have entered into a relationship which will bring the participants, considered collectively, net pain rather than net pleasure. Bentham's conclusion was, therefore, that deep play was immoral from the first principles and, a typical step for him, should be prevented legally.

But more interesting than the ethical problem, at least for our concerns here, is that despite the logical force of Bentham's analysis men do engage in such play, both passionately and often, and even in the face of law's revenge. For Bentham and those who think as he does (nowadays mainly lawyers, economists, and a few psychiatrists), the explanation is, as I have said, that such men are irrational—addicts, fetishists, children, fools, savages, who need only to be protected against themselves. But for the Balinese, though naturally they do not formulate it in so many words, the explanation lies in the fact that in such play money is less a measure of utility, had or expected, than it is a symbol of moral import, perceived or imposed.

---

[18]*Besides wagering there are other economic aspects of the cockfight,* especially its very close connection with the local market system which, though secondary both to its motivation and to its function, are not without importance. Cockfights are open events to which anyone who wishes may come, sometimes from quite distant areas, but well over 90 per cent, probably over 95, are very local affairs, and the locality concerned is defined not by the village, nor even by the administrative district, but by the rural market system. Bali has a three-day market week with the familiar "solar-system" type rotation. Though the markets themselves have never been very highly developed, small morning affairs in a village square, it is the micro-region such rotation rather generally marks out—ten or twenty square miles, seven or eight neighboring villages (which in contemporary Bali is usually going to mean anywhere from five to ten or eleven thousand people) from which the core of any cockfight audience, indeed virtually all of it, will come. Most of the fights are in fact organized and sponsored by small combines of petty rural merchants under the general premise, very strongly held by them and indeed by all Balinese, that cockfights are good for trade because "they get money out of the house, they make it circulate." Stalls selling various sorts of things as well as assorted sheer-chance gambling games (see below) are set up around the edge of the area so that this even takes on the quality of a small fair. This connection of cockfighting with markets and market sellers is very old, as, among other things, their conjunction in inscriptions (Roelof Goris, *Prasasti Bali*, 2 vols. [Bandung: N. V. Masa Baru, 1954]) indicates. Trade has followed the cock for centuries in rural Bali and the sport has been one of the main agencies of the island's monetization.

[19]*Bentham* The phrase is found in the Hildreth translation, International Library of Psychology, 1931, note to p. 106; see L. L. Fuller, *The Morality of Law* (New Haven: Yale University Press, 1964), pp. 6ff.

It is, in fact, in shallow games, ones in which smaller amounts of money are involved, that increments and decrements of cash are more nearly synonyms for utility and disutility, in the ordinary, unexpanded sense—for pleasure and pain, happiness and unhappiness. In deep ones, where the amounts of money are great, much more is at stake than material gain: namely, esteem, honor, dignity, respect—in a word, though in Bali a profoundly freighted word, status.[20] It is at stake symbolically, for (a few cases of ruined addict gamblers aside) no one's status is actually altered by the outcome of a cockfight; it is only, and that momentarily, affirmed or insulted. But for the Balinese, for whom nothing is more pleasurable than an affront obliquely delivered or more painful than one obliquely received—particularly when mutual acquaintances, undeceived by surfaces, are watching—such appraisive drama is deep indeed.

This, I must stress immediately, is *not* to say that the money does not matter, or that the Balinese is no more concerned about losing five hundred ringgits than fifteen. Such a conclusion would be absurd. It is because money *does,* in this hardly unmaterialistic society, matter and matter very much that the more of it one risks the more of a lot of other things, such as one's pride, one's poise, one's dispassion, one's masculinity, one also risks, again only momentarily but again very publicly as well. In deep cockfights an owner and his collaborators, and, as we shall see, to a lesser but still quite real extent also their backers on the outside, put their money where their status is.

It is in large part *because* the marginal disutility of loss is so great at the higher levels of betting that to engage in such betting is to lay one's public self, allusively and metaphorically, through the medium of one's cock, on the line. And though to a Benthamite this might seem merely to increase the irrationality of the enterprise that much further, to the Balinese what it mainly increases is the meaningfulness of it all. And as (to follow Weber rather than Bentham) the imposition of meaning on life is the major end and primary condition of human existence, that access of significance more than compensates for the economic costs involved.[21] Actually, given the even-money quality of the larger matches, important changes in material fortune among those who regularly participate in them seem virtually nonexistent, because matters more or less even out over the long run. It is, actually, in the smaller, shallow fights, where one finds the handful of more pure, addict-type gamblers involved—those who *are* in it mainly for the money— that "real" changes in social position, largely downward, are affected. Men of this sort, plungers, are highly dispraised by "true cock fighters" as fools who do not understand

[20]*Status* Of course, even in Bentham, utility is not normally confined as a concept to monetary losses and gains, and my argument here might be more carefully put in terms of a denial that for the Balinese, as for any people, utility (pleasure, happiness . . .) is merely identifiable with wealth. But such terminological problems are in any case secondary to the essential point: the cockfight is not roulette.

[21]*Max Weber, The Sociology of Religion* (Boston: Beacon Press, 1963). There is nothing specifically Balinese, of course, about deepening significance with money, as Whyte's description of corner boys in a working-class district of Boston demonstrates: "Gambling plays an important role in the lives of Cornerville people. Whatever game the corner boys play, they nearly always bet on the outcome. When there is nothing at stake, the game is not considered a real contest. This does not mean that the financial element is all-important. I have frequently heard men say that the honor of winning was much more important than the money at stake. The corner boys consider playing for money the real test of skill and, unless a man performs well when money is at stake, he is not considered a good competitor." W. F. Whyte, *Street Corner Society,* 2d ed. (Chicago: University of Chicago Press, 1955), p. 140.

what the sport is all about, vulgarians who simply miss the point of it all. They are, these addicts, regarded as fair game for the genuine enthusiasts, those who do understand, to take a little money away from, something that is easy enough to do by luring them, through the force of their greed, into irrational bets on mismatched cocks. Most of them do indeed manage to ruin themselves in a remarkably short time, but there always seem to be one or two of them around, pawning their land and selling their clothes in order to bet, at any particular time.[22]

This graduated correlation of "status gambling" with deeper fights and, inversely, "money gambling" with shallower ones is in fact quite general. Bettors themselves form a sociomoral hierarchy in these terms. As noted earlier, at most cockfights there are, around the very edges of the cockfight area, a large number of mindless, sheer-chance type gambling games (roulette, dice throw, coin-spin, pea-under-the-shell) operated by concessionaires. Only women, children, adolescents, and various other sorts of people who do not (or not yet) fight cocks—the extremely poor, the socially despised, the personally idiosyncratic—play at these games, at, of course, penny ante levels. Cockfighting men would be ashamed to go anywhere near them. Slightly above these people in standing are those who, though they do not themselves fight cocks, bet on the smaller matches around the edges. Next, there are those who fight cocks in small, or occasionally medium matches, but have not the status to join in the large ones, though they may bet from time to time on the side in those. And finally, there are those, the really substantial members of the community, the solid citizenry around whom local life revolves, who fight in the larger fights and bet on them around the side. The focusing element in these focused gatherings, these men generally dominate and define the sport as they dominate and define the society. When a Balinese male talks, in that almost venerative way, about "the true cockfighter," the *bebatoh* ("bettor") or *djuru kurung* ("cage keeper"), it is this sort of person, not those who bring the mentality of the pea-and-shell game into the quite different, inappropriate context of the cockfight, the driven gambler (*potét*, a word which has the secondary meaning of thief or reprobate), and the wistful hanger-on, that they mean. For such a man, what is really going on in a match is something rather close to an *affaire d'honneur* (though, with the Balinese talent for practical fantasy, the blood that is spilled is only figuratively human) than to the stupid, mechanical crank of a slot machine.

What makes Balinese cockfighting deep is thus not money in itself, but what, the more of it that is involved the more so, money causes to happen: the migration of the Balinese status hierarchy into the body of the cockfight. Psychologically an Aesopian representation of the ideal/demonic, rather narcissistic, male self, sociologically it is an equally Aesopian representation of the complex fields of tension set up by the controlled, muted,

---

[22]*The extremes to which this madness is conceived on occasion to go* and the fact that it is considered madness is demonstrated by the Balinese folktale *Tuwung Kuning* a gambler so crazy so deranged by his passion that, leaving on a trip, he orders his pregnant wife to take care of the prospective newborn if it is a boy but to feed it as meat to his fighting cocks if it is a girl. The mother gives birth to a girl, but rather than giving the child to the cocks she gives them a large rat and conceals the girl with her own mother. When the husband returns the cocks, crowing a jingle, inform him of the deception and, furious, he sets out to kill the child. A goddess descends from heaven and takes the girl up to the skies with her. The cocks die from the food given them, the owner's sanity is restored, the goddess brings the girl back to the father who reunites him with his wife. The story is given as "Geel Komkommertje" in Jacoba Hooykaas-van Leeuwen Boomkamp, Sprookjes en Verhalen van Bali ('S-Gravenhage: Van Hoeve, 1956), pp. 19–25.

ceremonial, but for all that deeply felt, interaction of those selves in the context of every-day life. The cocks may be surrogates for their owners' personalities, animal mirrors of psychic form, but the cockfight is—or more exactly, deliberately is made to be—a sim-ulation of the social matrix, the involved system of crosscutting, overlapping, highly cor-porate groups—villages, kingroups, irrigation societies, temple congregations, "castes"—in which its devotees live.[23] And as prestige, the necessity to affirm it, defend it, celebrate it, justify it, and just plain bask in it (but not, given the strongly ascriptive character of Balinese stratification, to seek it), is perhaps the central driving force in the society, so also—ambulant penises, blood sacrifices, and monetary exchanges aside—is it of the cockfight. This apparent amusement and seeming sport is, to take another phrase from Erving Goffman, "a status bloodbath."[24]

The easiest way to make this clear, and at least to some degree to demonstrate it, is to invoke the village whose cockfighting activities I observed the closest—the one in which the raid occurred and from which my statistical data are taken.

As all Balinese villages, this one—Tihingan, in the Klungkung region of southeast Bali—is intricately organized, a labyrinth of alliances and oppositions. But, unlike many, two sorts of corporate groups, which are also status groups, particularly stand out, and we may concentrate on them, in a part-for-whole way, without undue distortion.

First, the village is dominated by four large, patrilineal, partly endogamous descent groups which are constantly vying with one another and form the major factions in the village. Sometimes they group two and two, or rather the two larger ones versus the two smaller ones plus all the unaffiliated people; sometimes they operate independently. There are also subfactions within them, subfactions within the subfactions, and so on to rather fine levels of distinction. And second, there is the village itself, almost entirely endoga-mous, which is opposed to all the other villages round about in its cockfight circuit (which, as explained, is the market region), but which also forms alliances with certain of these neighbors against certain others in various supravillage political and social contexts. The exact situation is thus, as everywhere in Bali, quite distinctive; but the general pattern of a tiered hierarchy of status rivalries between highly corporate but various based group-ings (and, thus, between the members of them) is entirely general.

Consider, then, as support of the general thesis that the cockfight, and especially the deep cockfight, is fundamentally a dramatization of status concerns, the following facts, which to avoid extended ethnographic description I will simply pronounce to be facts—though the concrete evidence—examples, statements, and numbers that could be brought to bear in support of them is both extensive and unmistakable:

1. A man virtually never bets against a cock owned by a member of his own kingroup. Usually he will feel obliged to bet for it, the more so the closer the kin tie and the deeper the fight. If he is certain in his mind that it will not win, he may just not bet at all, particularly if it is only a second cousin's bird or if the fight is a shallow one. But as a rule he will feel he must support it and, in deep games, nearly always does.

---

[23]*For a fuller description of Balinese rural social structure,* see Clifford Geertz, "Form and Vari-ation in Balinese Village Structure," *American Anthropologist,* 61 (1959), 94–108; "Tihingan, A Balinese Village," in R. M. Koentjaraningrat, *Villages in Indonesia* (Ithaca: Cornell University Press, 1967), pp. 210–243; and, though it is a bit off the norm as Balinese villages go, V. E. Korn, *De Dorpsrepubliek tnganan Pagringsingan* (Santpoort[Netherlands]: C. A. Mees, 1933).

[24]Goffman, *Encounters,* p. 78.

Thus the great majority of the people calling "five" or "speckled" so demonstratively are expressing their allegiance to their kinsman, not their evaluation of his bird, their understanding of probability theory, or even their hopes of unearned income.

2. This principle is extended logically. If your kingroup is not involved you will support an allied kingroup against an unallied one in the same way, and so on through the very involved networks of alliances which, as I say, make up this, as any other, Balinese village.

3. So, too, for the village as a whole. If an outsider cock is fighting any cock from your village, you will tend to support the local one. If, what is a rare circumstance but occurs every now and then, a cock from outside your cockfight circuit is fighting one inside it you will also tend to support the "home bird."

4. Cocks which come from any distance are almost always favorites, for the theory is the man would not have dared to bring it if it was not a good cock, the more so the further he has come. His followers are, of course, obliged to support him, and when the more grand-scale legal cockfights are held (on holidays, and so on) the people of the village take what they regard to be the best cocks in the village, regardless of ownership, and go off to support them, although they will almost certainly have to give odds on them and to make large bets to show that they are not a cheapskate village. Actually, such "away games," though infrequent, tend to mend the ruptures between village members that the constantly occurring "home games," where village factions are opposed rather than united, exacerbate.

5. Almost all matches are sociologically relevant. You seldom get two outsider cocks fighting, or two cocks with no particular group backing, or with group backing which is mutually unrelated in any clear way. When you do get them, the game is very shallow, betting very slow, and the whole thing very dull, with no one save the immediate principals and an addict gambler or two at all interested.

6. By the same token, you rarely get two cocks from the same group, even more rarely from the same subfaction, and virtually never from the same sub-subfaction (which would be in most cases one extended family) fighting. Similarly, in outside village fights two members of the village will rarely fight against one another, even though, as bitter rivals, they would do so with enthusiasm on their home grounds.

7. On the individual level, people involved in an institutionalized hostility relationship, called *puik*, in which they do not speak or otherwise have anything to do with each other (the causes of this formal breaking of relations are many: wife-capture, inheritance arguments, political differences) will bet very heavily, sometimes almost manically, against one another in what is a frank and direct attack on the very masculinity, the ultimate ground of his status, of the opponent.

8. The center bet coalition is, in all but the shallowest games, *always* made up by structural allies—no "outside money" is involved. What is "outside" depends upon the context, of course, but given it, no outside money is mixed in with the main bet; if the principals cannot raise it, it is not made. The center bet, again especially in deeper games, is thus the most direct and open expression of social opposition, which is one of the reasons why both it and match making are surrounded by such an air of unease, furtiveness, embarrassment, and so on.

9. The rule about borrowing money—that you may borrow *for* a bet but not *in* one— stems (and the Balinese are quite conscious of this) from similar considerations: you

are never at the economic mercy of your enemy that way. Gambling debts, which can get quite large on a rather short-term basis, are always to friends, never to enemies, structurally speaking.

10. When two cocks are structurally irrelevant or neutral so far as *you* are concerned (though, as mentioned, they almost never are to each other) you do not even ask a relative or a friend whom he is betting on, because if you know how he is betting and he knows you know, and you go the other way, it will lead to strain. This rule is explicit and rigid; fairly elaborate, even rather artificial precautions are taken to avoid breaking it. At the very least you must pretend not to notice what he is doing, and he what you are doing.

11. There is a special word for betting against the grain, which is also the word for "pardon me" (*mpura*). It is considered a bad thing to do, though if the center bet is small it is sometimes all right as long as you do not do it too often. But the larger the bet and the more frequently you do it, the more the "pardon me" tack will lead to social disruption.

12. In fact, the institutionalized hostility relation, puik, is often formally initiated (though its causes always lie elsewhere) by such a "pardon me" bet in a deep fight, putting the symbolic fat in the fire. Similarly, the end of such a relationship and resumption of normal social intercourse is often signalized (but, again, not actually brought about) by one or the other of the enemies supporting the other's bird.

13. In sticky, cross-loyalty situations, of which in this extraordinarily complex social system there are of course many, where a man is caught between two more or less equally balanced loyalties, he tends to wander off for a cup of coffee or something to avoid having to bet, a form of behavior reminiscent of that of American voters in similar situations.[25]

14. The people involved in the center bet are, especially in deep fights, virtually always leading members of their group—kinship, village, or whatever. Further, those who bet on the side (including these people) are, as I have already remarked, the more established members of the village—the solid citizens. Cockfighting is for those who are involved in the everyday politics of prestige as well, not for youth, women, subordinates, and so forth.

15. So far as money is concerned, the explicitly expressed attitude toward it is that it is a secondary matter. It is not, as I have said, of no importance; Balinese are no happier to lose several weeks' income than anyone else. But they mainly look on the monetary aspects of the cockfight as self-balancing, a matter of just moving money around, circulating it among a fairly well-defined group of serious cockfighters. The really important wins and losses are seen mostly in other terms, and the general attitude toward wagering is not any hope of cleaning up, of making a killing (addict gamblers again excepted), but that of the horseplayer's prayer: "O, God, please let me break even." In prestige terms, however, you do not want to break even, but, in a momentary, punctuate sort of way, win utterly. The talk (which goes on all the time) is about fights against such-and-such a cock of So-and-So which your cock demolished, not on how much you won, a fact people, even for large bets, rarely remem-

---

[25]B. R. Berelson, P. F. Lazersfeld, and W. N. McPhee, *Voting: A Study of Opinion Formation in a Presidential Campaign* (Chicago: University of Chicago Press, 1954).

ber for any length of time, though they will remember the day they did in Pan Loh's finest cock for years.

16. You must bet on cocks of your own group aside from mere loyalty considerations, for if you do not people generally will say, "What! Is he too proud for the likes of us? Does he have to go to Java or Den Pasar [the capital town] to bet, he is such an important man?" Thus there is a general pressure to bet not only to show that you are important locally, but that you are not so important that you look down on everyone else as unfit even to be rivals. Similarly, home team people must bet against outside cocks or the outsiders will accuse it—a serious charge—of just collecting entry fees and not really being interested in cockfighting, as well as again being arrogant and insulting.

17. Finally, the Balinese peasants themselves are quite aware of all this and can and, at least to an ethnographer, do state most of it in approximately the same terms as I have. Fighting cocks, almost every Balinese I have ever discussed the subject with has said, is like playing with fire only not getting burned. You activate village and kingroup rivalries and hostilities, but in "play" form, coming dangerously and entrancingly close to the expression of open and direct interpersonal and intergroup aggression (something which, again, almost never happens in the normal course of ordinary life), but not quite, because, after all, it is "only a cockfight."

More observations of this sort could be advanced, but perhaps the general point is, if not made, at least well-delineated, and the whole argument thus far can be usefully summarized in a formal paradigm:

THE MORE A MATCH IS . . .

1. Between near status equals (and/or personal enemies)
2. Between high status individuals

THE DEEPER THE MATCH

THE DEEPER THE MATCH . . .

1. The closer the identification of cock and man (or: more properly, the deeper the match the more the man will advance his best, most closely-identified-with cock).
2. The finer the cocks involved and the more exactly they will be matched.
3. The greater the emotion that will be involved and the more the general absorption in the match.
4. The higher the individual bets center and outside, the shorter the outside bet odds will tend to be, and the more betting there will be overall.
5. The less an "economic" and the more a "status" view of gaming will be involved, and the "solider" the citizens who will be gaming.[26]

---

[26]*As this is a formal paradigm, it is intended to display the logical, not the causal,* structure of cockfighting. Just which of these considerations leads to which, in what order, and by what mechanisms, is another matter—one I have attempted to shed some light on in the general discussion.

Inverse arguments hold for the shallower the fight, culminating, in a reversed-signs sense, in the coin-spinning and dice-throwing amusements. For deep fights there are no absolute upper limits, though there are of course practical ones, and there are a great many legendlike tales of great Duel-in-the-Sun combats between lords and princes in classical times (for cockfighting has always been as much an elite concern as a popular one), far deeper than anything anyone, even aristocrats, could produce today anywhere in Bali.

Indeed, one of the great culture heroes of Bali is a prince, called after his passion for the sport, "The Cockfighter," who happened to be away at a very deep cockfight with a neighboring prince when the whole of his family—father, brothers, wives, sisters—were assassinated by commoner usurpers. Thus spared, he returned to dispatch the upstarts, regain the throne, reconstitute the Balinese high tradition, and build its most powerful, glorious, and prosperous state. Along with everything else that the Balinese see in fighting cocks—themselves, their social order, abstract hatred, masculinity, demonic power—they also see the archetype of status virtue, the arrogant, resolute, honor-mad player with real fire, the ksatria prince.[27]

---

[27] *ksatria prince* In another of Hooykaas-van Leeuwen Boomkamp's folk tales ("De Gast," Sprookies en Verhalen van Bali, pp. 172–180), a low caste Sudra, a generous, pious, and carefree man who is also an accomplished cock fighter, loses, despite his accomplishment, fight after fight until he is not only out of money but down to his last cock. He does not despair, however—"I bet," he says, "upon the Unseen World."

His wife, a good and hard-working woman, knowing how much he enjoys cockfighting, gives him her last "rainy day" money to go and bet. But, filled with misgivings due to his run of ill luck, he leaves his own cock at home and bets merely on the side. He soon loses all but a coin or two and repairs to a food stand for a snack, where he meets a decrepit, odorous, and generally unappetizing old beggar leaning on a staff. The old man asks for food, and the hero spends his last coins to buy him some. The old man then asks to pass the night with the hero, which the hero gladly invites him to do. As there is no food in the house, however, the hero tells his wife to kill the last cock for dinner. When the old man discovers this fact, he tells the hero he has three cocks in his own mountain hut and says the hero may have one of them for fighting. He also asks for the hero's son to accompany him as a servant, and, after the son agrees, this is done.

The old man turns out to be Siva and, thus, to live in a great palace in the sky, though the hero does not know this. In time, the hero decides to visit his son and collect the promised cock. Lifted up into Siva's presence, he is given the choice of three cocks. The first crows: "I have beaten fifteen opponents." The second crows, "I have beaten twenty-five opponents." The third crows, "I have beaten the King." "That one, the third, is my choice," says the hero, and returns with it to earth.

When he arrives at the cockfight, he is asked for an entry fee and replies, "I have no money; I will pay after my cock has won." As he is known never to win, he is let in because the king, who is there fighting, dislikes him and hopes to enslave him when he loses and cannot pay off. In order to insure that this happens, the king matches his finest cock against the hero's. When the cocks are placed down, the hero's flees, and the crowd, led by the arrogant king, hoots in laughter. The hero's cock then flies at the king himself, killing him with a spur stab in the throat. The hero flees. His house is encircled by the king's men. The cock changes into a Garuda, the great mythic bird of Indic legend, and carries the hero and his wife to safety in the heavens.

When the people see this, they make the hero king and his wife queen and they return as such to earth. Later their son, released by Siva, also returns and the hero-king announces his intention to enter a hermitage. ("I will fight no more cockfights. I have bet on the Unseen and won.") He enters the hermitage and his son becomes king.

FEATHERS, BLOOD, CROWDS, AND MONEY

"Poetry makes nothing happen," Auden says in his elegy of Yeats, "it survives in the valley of its saying . . . a way of happening, a mouth." The cockfight too, in this colloquial sense, makes nothing happen. Men go on allegorically humiliating one another and being allegorically humiliated by one another, day after day, glorying quietly in the experience if they have triumphed, crushed only slightly more openly by it if they have not. *But no one's status really changes.* You cannot ascend the status ladder by winning cockfights; you cannot, as an individual, really ascend it at all. Nor can you descend it that way.[28] All you can do is enjoy and savor, or suffer and withstand, the concocted sensation of drastic and momentary movement along an aesthetic semblance of that ladder, a kind of behind-the-mirror status jump which has the look of mobility without its actuality.

As any art form—for that, finally, is what we are dealing with—the cockfight renders ordinary, everyday experience comprehensible by presenting it in terms of acts and objects which have had their practical consequences removed and been reduced (or, if you prefer, raised) to the level of sheer appearances, where their meaning can be more powerfully articulated and more exactly perceived. The cockfight is "really real" only to the cocks—it does not kill anyone, castrate anyone, reduce anyone to animal status, alter the hierarchical relations among people, nor refashion the hierarchy; it does not even redistribute income in any significant way. What it does is what, for other peoples with other temperaments and other conventions, *Lear* and *Crime and Punishment* do; it catches up these themes—death, masculinity, rage, pride, loss, beneficence, chance—and, ordering them into an encompassing structure, presents them in such a way as to throw into relief a particular view of their essential nature. It puts a construction on them, makes them, to those historically positioned to appreciate the construction, meaningful—visible, tangible, graspable—"real," in an ideational sense. An image, fiction, a model, a metaphor, the cockfight is a means of expression; its function is neither to assuage social passions nor to heighten them (though, in its play-with-fire way, it does a bit of both), but, in a medium of feathers, blood, crowds, and money, to display them.

The question of how it is that we perceive qualities in things—paintings, books, melodies, plays—that we do not feel we can assert literally to be there has come, in recent years, into the very center of aesthetic theory.[29] Neither the sentiments of the artist, which remain his, nor those of the audience, which remains theirs, can account for the agitation of one painting or the serenity of another. We attribute grandeur, wit, despair, exuberance to strings of sounds; lightness, energy, violence, fluidity to blocks of stone. Novels are said to have strength, buildings eloquence, plays momentum, ballets repose. In this

---

[28]*Addict gamblers are really less declassed* (for their status is, as everyone else's, inherited) than merely impoverished and personally disgraced. The most prominent addict gambler in my cockfight circuit was actually a very high caste satria who sold off most of his considerable lands to support his habit. Though everyone privately regarded him as a fool and worse (some, more charitable, regarded him as sick), he was publicly treated with the elaborate deference and politeness due his rank. On the independence of personal reputation and public status in Bali, see Geertz, Person, Time, and Conduct, pp. 28–35.

[29]For four, somewhat variant, treatments, see Susanne Langer, *Feeling and Form* (New York: Scribners, 1953); Richard Wollheim, *Art and Its Objects* (New York: Harper and Row, 1968); Nelson Goodman, *Languages of Art* (Indianapolis: Bobbs-Merrill, 1968); Maurice Merleau-Ponty, "The Eye and the Mind," in his, *The Primacy of Perception* (Evanston: Northwestern University Press, 1964), pp. 159–190.

realm of eccentric predicates, to say that the cockfight, in its perfected cases at least, is "disquietful" does not seem at all unnatural, merely, as I have just denied it practical consequence, somewhat puzzling.

The disquietfulness arises, "somehow," out of a conjunction of three attributes of the fight: its immediate dramatic shape; its metaphoric content; and its social context. A cultural figure against a social ground, the fight is at once a convulsive surge of animal hatred, a mock war of symbolical selves, and a formal simulation of status tensions, and its aesthetic power derives from its capacity to force together these diverse realities. The reason it is disquietful is not that it has material effects (it has some, but they are minor); the reason that it is disquietful is that, joining pride to selfhood, selfhood to cocks, and cocks to destruction, it brings to imaginative realization a dimension of Balinese experience normally well-obscured from view. The transfer of a sense of gravity into what is in itself a rather blank and unvarious spectacle, a commotion of beating wings and throbbing legs, is effected by interpreting it as expressive of something unsettling in the way its authors and audience live, or, even more ominously, what they are.

As a dramatic shape, the fight displays a characteristic that does not seem so remarkable until one realizes that it does not have to be there: a radically atomistical structure.[30] Each match is a world unto itself, a particulate burst of form. There is the match making, there is the betting, there is the fight, there is the result—utter triumph and utter defeat—and there is the hurried, embarrassed passing of money. The loser is not consoled. People drift away from him, look through him, leave him to assimilate his momentary descent into nonbeing, reset his face, and return, scarless and intact, to the fray. Nor are winners congratulated, or events rehashed; once a match is ended the crowd's attention turns totally to the next, with no looking back. A shadow of the experience no doubt remains with the principals, perhaps even with some of the witnesses, of a deep fight, as it remains with us when we leave the theater after seeing a powerful play well-performed; but it quite soon fades to become at most a schematic memory—a diffuse glow or an abstract shudder—and usually not even that. Any expressive form lives only in its own present—the one it itself creates. But, here, that present is severed into a string of flashes, some more bright than others, but all of them disconnected, aesthetic quanta. Whatever the cockfight says, it says in spurts.

But, as I have argued lengthily elsewhere, the Balinese live in spurts.[31] Their life, as they arrange it and perceive it, is less a flow, a directional movement out of the past,

---

[30]*British cockfights* (the sport was banned there in 1840) indeed seem to have lacked it, and to have generated, therefore, a quite different family of shapes. Most British fights were "mains," in which a preagreed number of cocks were aligned into two teams and fought serially. Score was kept and wagering took place both on the individual matches and on the main as a whole. There were also "battle Royales," both in England and on the Continent, in which a large number of cocks were let loose at once with the one left standing at the end the victor. And in Wales, the so-called "Welsh main" followed an elimination pattern, along the lines of a present-day tennis tournament, winners proceeding to the next round. As a genre, the cock-fight has perhaps less compositional flexibility than, say, Latin comedy, but it is not entirely without any. On cockfighting more generally, see Arch Ruport, The Art of Cockfighting (New York: Devin-Adair, 1949); G. R. Scott, History of Cockfighting (1957); and Lawrence Fitz-Barnard, Fighting Sports (London: Odhams Press, 1921).

[31]*Person, Time, and Conduct* esp. pp. 42ff. I am, however, not the first person to have argued it: see G. Bateson, "Bali, the Value System of a Steady State," and "An Old Temple and a New Myth," in Belo, ed., *Traditional Balinese Culture,* pp. 384–402 and 111–136.

through the present, toward the future than an on-off pulsation of meaning and vacuity, an arhythmic alternation of short periods when "something" (that is, something signifi- cant) is happening and equally short ones where "nothing" (that is, nothing much) is— between what they themselves call "full" and "empty" times, or, in another idiom, "junc- tures" and "holes." In focusing activity down to a burning-glass dot, the cockfight is merely being Balinese in the same way in which everything from the monadic encoun- ters of everyday life, through the changing pointillism of gamelan music, to the visiting- day-of-the-gods temple celebrations are. It is not an imitation of the punctuateness of Balinese social life, nor a depiction of it, nor even an expression of it; it is an example of it, carefully prepared.[32]

If one dimension of the cockfight's structure, its lack of temporal directionality, makes it seem a typical segment of the general social life, however, the other, its flat-out, head- to-head (or spur-to-spur) aggressiveness, makes it seem a contradiction, a reversal, even a subversion of it. In the normal course of things, the Balinese are shy to the point of obsessiveness of open conflict. Oblique, cautious, subdued, controlled, masters of indi- rection and dissimulation—what they call *alus*, "polished," "smooth"—they rarely face what they can turn away from, rarely resist what they can evade. But here they portray themselves as wild and murderous, manic explosions of instinctual cruelty. A powerful rendering of life as the Balinese most deeply do not want it (to adapt a phrase Frye has used of Gloucester's blinding) is set in the context of a sample of it as they do in fact have it.[33] And, because the context suggests that the rendering, if less than a straightfor- ward description is nonetheless more than an idle fancy, it is here that the disquietful- ness—the disquietfulness of the *fight*, not (or, anyway, not necessarily) its patrons, who seem in fact rather thoroughly to enjoy it—emerges. The slaughter in the cock ring is not a depiction of how things literally are among men, but, what is almost worse, of how, from a particular angle, they imaginatively are.[34]

The angle, of course, is stratificatory. What, as we have already seen, the cockfight talks most forcibly about is status relationships, and what it says about them is that they are mat- ters of life and death. That prestige is a profoundly serious business is apparent everywhere

---

[32]*For the necessity of distinguishing among "description," "representation," "exemplification,"* *and "expression"* (and the irrelevance of "imitation" to all of them) as modes of symbolic refer- ence, see Goodman, *Languages of Art*, pp. 6–10, 45–91, 225–241.

[33]Northrop Frye, *The Educated Imagination* (Bloomington: University of Indiana Press, 1964), p. 99.

[34]*There are two other Balinese values and disvalues which,* connected with punctuate temporality on the one hand and unbridled aggressiveness on the other, reinforce the sense that the cockfight is at once continuous with ordinary social life and a direct negation of it: what the Balinese call ramé, and what they call paling. Ramé means crowded, noisy, and active, and is a highly sought after social state. Crowded markets, mass festivals, busy streets are all ramé, as, of course, is, in the extreme, a cockfight. Ramé is what happens in the "full" times (its opposite, sepi, "quiet," is what happens in the "empty" ones). Paling is social vertigo, the dizzy, disoriented, lost, turned around feeling one gets when one's place in the coordinates of social space is not clear, and it is a tremendously disfavored, immensely anxiety-producing state. Balinese regard the exact mainte- nance of spatial orientation ("not to know where north is" is to be crazy), balance, decorum, sta- tus relationships, and so forth, as fundamental to ordered life (krama) and paling, the sort of whirling confusion of position the scrambling cocks exemplify as its profoundest enemy and contradiction. On ramé, see Bateson and Mead, Balinese Character, pp. 3, 64; on paling, ibid., p. 11, and Belo, ed., Traditional Balinese Culture, pp. 90ff.

one looks in Bali—in the village, the family, the economy, the state. A peculiar fusion of Polynesian title ranks and Hindu castes, the hierarchy of pride is the moral backbone of the society. But only in the cockfight are the sentiments upon which that hierarchy rests revealed in their natural colors. Enveloped elsewhere in a haze of etiquette, a thick cloud of euphemism and ceremony, gesture and allusion, they are here expressed in only the thinnest disguise of an animal mask, a mask which in fact demonstrates them far more effectively than it conceals them. Jealousy is as much a part of Bali as poise, envy as grace, brutality as charm; but without the cockfight the Balinese would have a much less certain understanding of them, which is, presumably, why they value it so highly.

Any expressive form works (when it works) by disarranging semantic contexts in such a way that properties conventionally ascribed to certain things are unconventionally ascribed to others, which are then seen actually to possess them. To call the wind a cripple, as Stevens does, to fix tone and manipulate timbre, as Schoenberg does, or, closer to our case, to picture an art critic as a dissolute bear, as Hogarth does, is to cross conceptual wires; the established conjunctions between objects and their qualities are altered and phenomena—fall weather, melodic shape, or cultural journalism—are clothed in significers which normally point to other referents.[35] Similarly, to connect—and connect, and connect—the collision of roosters with the divisiveness of status is to invite a transfer of perceptions from the former to the latter, a transfer which is at once a description and a judgment. (Logically, the transfer could, of course, as well go the other way; but, like most of the rest of us, the Balinese are a great deal more interested in understanding men than they are in understanding cocks.)

What sets the cockfight apart from the ordinary course of life, lifts it from the realm of everyday practical affairs, and surrounds it with an aura of enlarged importance is not, as functionalist sociology would have it, that it reinforces status discriminations (such reinforcement is hardly necessary in a society where every act proclaims them), but that it provides a metasocial commentary upon the whole matter of assorting human beings into fixed hierarchical ranks and then organizing the major part of collective existence around that assortment. Its function, if you want to call it that, is interpretive: it is a Balinese reading of Balinese experience; a story they tell themselves about themselves.

SAYING SOMETHING OF SOMETHING

To put the matter this way is to engage in a bit of metaphorical refocusing of one's own, for it shifts the analysis of cultural forms from an endeavor in general parallel to dissecting an organism, diagnosing a symptom, deciphering a code, or ordering a system—

---

[35]*The Stevens reference* is to his "The Motive for Metaphor," ("You like it under the trees in autumn,/Because everything is half dead./The wind moves like a cripple among the leaves/And repeats words without meaning"); the Schoenberg reference is to the third of his *Five Orchestral Pieces* (Opus 16), and is borrowed from H. H. Drager, "The Concept of 'Tonal Body,' " in Susanne Langer, ed., *Reflections on Art* (New York: Oxford University Press, 1961), p. 174. On Hogarth, and on this whole problem—there called "multiple matrix matching"—see E. H. Gombrich, "The Use of Art for the Study of Symbols," in James Hogg, ed., *Psychology and the Visual Arts* (Baltimore: Penguin Brooks, 1969), pp. 149–170. The more usual term for this sort of semantic alchemy is "metaphorical transfer," and good technical discussions of it can be found in M. Black, *Models and Metaphors* (Ithaca: Cornell University Press, 1962), pp. 25ff; Goodman, *Language as Art,* pp. 44ff; and W. Percy, "Metaphor as Mistake," *Sewanee Review,* 66 (1958), 78–99.

the dominant analogies in contemporary anthropology—to one in general parallel with penetrating a literary text. If one takes the cockfight, or any other collectively sustained symbolic structure, as a means of "saying something of something" (to invoke a famous Aristotelian tag), then one is faced with a problem not in social mechanics but social semantics.[36] For the anthropologist, whose concern is with formulating sociological principles, not with promoting or appreciating cockfights, the question is, what does one learn about such principles from examining culture as an assemblage of texts?

Such an extension of the notion of a text beyond written material, and even beyond verbal, is, though metaphorical, not, of course, all that novel. The *interpretatio naturae* tradition of the middle ages, which, culminating in Spinoza, attempted to read nature as Scripture, the Nietszchean effort to treat value systems as glosses on the will to power (or the Marxian one to treat them as glosses on property relations), and the Freudian replacement of the enigmatic text of the manifest dream with the plain one of the latent, all offer precedents, if not equally recommendable ones.[37] But the idea remains theoretically undeveloped; and the more profound corollary, so far as anthropology is concerned, that cultural forms can be treated as texts, as imaginative works built out of social materials, has yet to be systematically exploited.[38]

In the case at hand, to treat the cockfight as a text is to bring out a feature of it (in my opinion, the central feature of it) that treating it as a rite or a pastime, the two most obvious alternatives, would tend to obscure: its use of emotion for cognitive ends. What the cockfight says it says in a vocabulary of sentiment—the thrill of risk, the despair of loss, the pleasure of triumph. Yet what it says is not merely that risk is exciting, loss depressing, or triumph gratifying, banal tautologies of affect, but that it is of these emotions, thus exampled, that society is built and individuals put together. Attending cockfights and participating in them is, for the Balinese, a kind of sentimental education. What he learns there is what his culture's ethos and his private sensibility (or, anyway, certain aspects of them) look like when spelled out externally in a collective text; that the two are near enough alike to be articulated in the symbolics of a single such text; and—the disquieting part—that the text in which this revelation is accomplished consists of a chicken hacking another mindlessly to bits.

Every people, the proverb has it, loves its own form of violence. The cockfight is the Balinese reflection on theirs: on its look, its uses, its force, its fascination. Drawing on almost every level of Balinese experience, it brings together themes—animal savagery, male narcissism, opponent gambling, status rivalry, mass excitement, blood sacrifice—whose main connection is their involvement with rage and the fear of rage, and, binding

---

[36]*The tag is from the second book of the Organon, On Interpretation.* For a discussion of it, and for the whole argument for freeing "the notion of text . . . from the notion of scripture or writing," and constructing, thus, a general hermeneutics, see Paul Ricoeur, *Freud and Philosophy* (New Haven, Yale University Press, 1970), pp. 20ff.

[37]Ibid.

[38]*Lévi-Strauss's "structuralism" might seem an exception.* But it is only an apparent one, for, rather than taking myths, totem rites, marriage rules, or whatever as texts to interpret, Lévi-Strauss takes them as ciphers to solve, which is very much not the same thing. He does not seek to understand symbolic forms in terms of how they function in concrete situations to organize perceptions (meanings, emotions, concepts, attitudes); he seeks to understand them entirely in terms of their internal structure, *indépendent de tout sujet, de tout objet, et de toute contexte.* For my own view of this approach—that is suggestive and indefensible—see Clifford Geertz, "The Cerebral Savage: On the Work of Lévi-Strauss," *Encounter,* 48 (1967), 25–32.

them into a set of rules which at once contains them and allows them play, builds a symbolic structure in which, over and over again, the reality of their inner affiliation can be intelligibly felt. If, to quote Northrop Frye again, we go to see *Macbeth* to learn what a man feels like after he has gained a kingdom and lost his soul, Balinese go to cockfights to find out what a man, usually composed, aloof, almost obsessively self-absorbed, a kind of moral autocosm, feels like when, attacked, tormented, challenged, insulted, and driven in result to the extremes of fury, he has totally triumphed or been brought totally low. The whole passage, as it takes us back to Aristotle (though to the *Poetics* rather than the *Hermeneutics*), is worth quotation:

> But the poet [as opposed to the historian], Aristotle says, never makes any real statements at all, certainly no particular or specific ones. The poet's job is not to tell you what happened, but what happens: not what did take place, but the kind of thing that always does take place. He gives you the typical, recurring, or what Aristotle calls universal event. You wouldn't go to *Macbeth* to learn about the history of Scotland—you go to it to learn what man feels like after he's gained a kingdom and lost his soul. When you meet such a character as Micawber in Dickens, you don't feel that there must have been a man Dickens knew who was exactly like this: you feel that there's a bit of Micawber in almost everybody you know, including yourself. Our impressions of human life are picked up one by one, and remain for most of us loose and disorganized. But we constantly find things in literature that suddenly coordinate and bring into focus a great many such impressions, and this is part of what Aristotle means by the typical or universal human event.[39]

It is this kind of bringing of assorted experiences of everyday life to focus that the cockfight, set aside from that life as "only a game" and reconnected to it as "more than a game," accomplishes, and so creates what, better than typical or universal, could be called a paradigmatic human event—that is, one that tells us less what happens than the kind of thing that would happen if, as is not the case, life were art and could be as freely shaped by styles of feeling as *Macbeth* and *David Copperfield* are.

Enacted and reenacted, so far without end, the cockfight enables the Balinese, as, read and reread, *Macbeth* enables us, to see a dimension of his own subjectivity. As he watches fight after fight, with the active watching of an owner and a bettor (for cockfighting has no more interest as a pure spectator sport than croquet or dog racing do), he grows familiar with it and what it has to say to him, much as the attentive listener to string quartets or the absorbed viewer of still lifes grows slowly more familiar with them in a way which opens his subjectivity to himself.[40]

Yet, because—in another of those paradoxes, along with painted feelings and unconsequenced acts, which haunt aesthetics—that subjectivity does not properly exist until it is thus organized, art forms generate and regenerate the very subjectivity they pretend

---

[39]Frye, *The Educated Imagination*, pp. 63–64.

[40]*The use of the, to Europeans, "natural" visual idiom for perception* "see," "watches," and so forth—is more than usually misleading here, for the fact that, as mentioned earlier, Balinese follow the progress of the fight as much (perhaps, as fighting cocks are actually rather hard to see except as blurs of motion, more) with their bodies as with their eyes, moving their limbs, heads, and trunks in gestural mimicry of the cocks' maneuvers, means that much of the individual's experience of the fight is kinesthetic rather than visual. If ever there was an example of Kenneth Burke's definition of a symbolic act as "the dancing of an attitude" (*The Philosophy of Literacy Form*, rev. ed. [New York: Vintage Books, 1957], p. 9) the cockfight is it. On the enormous role of kinesthetic perception in Balinese life, Bateson and Mean, *Balinese Character*, pp. 84–88; on the active nature of aesthetic perception in general, Goodman, *Language of Art*, pp. 241–244.

only to display. Quartets, still lifes, and cockfights are not merely reflections of a preexisting sensibility analogically represented; they are positive agents in the creation and maintenance of such a sensibility. If we see ourselves as a pack of Micawbers it is from reading too much Dickens (if we see ourselves as unillusioned realists, it is from reading too little); and similarly for Balinese, cocks, and cockfights. It is in such a way, coloring experience with the light they cast it in, rather than through whatever material effects they may have, that the arts play their role, as arts, in social life.[41]

In the cockfight, then, the Balinese forms and discovers his temperament and his society's temper at the same time. Or, more exactly, he forms and discovers a particular face of them. Not only are there a great many other cultural texts providing commentaries on status hierarchy and self-regard in Bali, but there are a great many other critical sectors of Balinese life besides the stratificatory and the agonistic that receive such commentary. The ceremony consecrating a Brahmana priest, a matter of breath control, postural immobility, and vacant concentration upon the depths of being, displays a radically different, but to the Balinese equally real, property of social hierarchy—its reach toward the numinous transcendent. Set not in the matrix of the kinetic emotionality of animals, but in that of the static passionlessness of divine mentality, it expresses tranquillity not disquiet. The mass festivals at the village temples, which mobilize the whole local population in elaborate hostings of visiting gods—songs, dances, compliments, gifts—assert the spiritual unity of village mates against their status inequality and project a mood of amity and trust.[42] The cockfight is not the master key to Balinese life, any more than bullfighting is to Spanish. What it says about that life is not unqualified nor even unchallenged by what other equally eloquent cultural statements say about it. But there is nothing more surprising in this than in the fact that Racine and Molière were contemporaries, or that the same people who arrange chrysanthemums cast swords.[43]

[41]*Sociallia* All this coupling of the occidental great with the oriental lowly will doubtless disturb certain sorts of aestheticians as the earlier efforts of anthropologists to speak of Christianity and totemism in the same breath disturbed certain sorts of theologians. But as ontological questions are (or should be) bracketed in the sociology of religion, judgmental ones are (or should be) bracketed in the sociology of art. In any case, the attempt to deprovincialize the concept of art is but part of the general anthropological conspiracy to deprovincialize all important social concepts—marriage, religion, law, rationality—and though this is a threat to aesthetic theories which regard certain works of art as beyond the reach of sociological analysis, it is no threat to the conviction, for which Robert Graves claims to have been reprimanded at his Cambridge tripos, that some poems are better than others.

[42]*For the consecration ceremony,* see V. E. Korn, "The Consecration of the Priest," in Swellengrebel, ed., *Bali,* pp. 131–154; for (somewhat exaggerated) village communion, Roelof Goris, "The Religious Character of the Balinese Village," ibid., pp. 79–100.

[43]*swords* That what the cockfight has to say about Bali is not altogether without perception and the disquiet it expresses about the general pattern of Balinese life is not wholly without reason is attested by the fact that in two weeks of December 1965, during the upheavals following the unsuccessful coup in Djakarta, between forty and eighty thousand Balinese (in a population of about two million) were killed, largely by one another—the worst outburst in the country. (John Hughes, *Indonesian Upheaval* [New York: McKay, 1967], pp. 173–183. Hughes's figures are, of course, rather casual estimates, but they are not the most extreme.) This is not to say, of course, that the killings were caused by the cockfight, could have been predicted on the basis of it, or were some sort of enlarged version of it with real people in the place of the cocks—all of which is nonsense. It is merely to say that if one looks at Bali not just through the medium of its dances, its shadowplays, its sculpture, and its girls, but—as the Balinese themselves do—also through the medium of its cockfight, the fact that the massacre occurred seems, if no less appalling, less like a contradic-

The culture of a people is an ensemble of texts, themselves ensembles, which the anthropologist strains to read over the shoulders of those to whom they properly belong. There are enormous difficulties in such an enterprise, methodological pitfalls to make a Freudian quake, and some moral perplexities as well. Nor is it the only way that symbolic forms can be sociologically handled. Functionalism lives, and so does psychologism. But to regard such forms as "saying something of something," and saying it to somebody, is at least to open up the possibility of an analysis which attends to their substance rather than to reductive formulas professing to account for them.

As in more familiar exercises in close reading, one can start anywhere in a culture's repertoire of forms and end up anywhere else. One can stay, as I have here, within a single, more or less bounded form and circle steadily within it. One can move between forms in search of broader unities or informing contrasts. One can even compare forms from different cultures to define their character in reciprocal relief. But whatever the level at which one operates, and however intricately, the guiding principle is the same: societies, like lives, contain their own interpretations. One has only to learn how to gain access to them.

Understanding and Analysis

1. This long essay is divided into seven parts. How does the story of The Raid help you, the reader, orient yourself to the goals of the author?

2. What hierarchies does Geertz establish in the first section?

3. In the second section, how does Geertz establish his area of expertise? How many interpretations does Geertz offer of the relationship between the birds and the men? What kinds of evidence does he use?

4. In the third section, what exactly does Geertz describe? How does the figure of the ring or circle function in this description?

5. The fourth section describes the betting. How many matches has Geertz witnessed and analyzed? Contrast the characteristics of the deep matches and the shallow ones.

6. The fifth section, Playing with Fire, explains the role of status in the deep play. Explain the interpretation of the gambling from the point of view of Bentham and from the point of view of Weber.

7. As a drama of status, what hierarchies does the cockfight reinforce? Geertz claims that the cockfight does more than merely reinforce these hierarchies. What else does it do?

8. What, according to Geertz, makes the cockfight an art form?

9. What is the cockfight an example of, according to Geertz?

10. In the last section, Geertz discusses the methods of ethnographic interpretation. What two types does he distinguish? What is the value of interpreting the "culture as an assemblage of texts"? What themes coalesce in the cockfight, according to Geertz?

11. As an ethnographer, does Geertz presume to know more about the meaning of the Balinese cockfight than do the participants themselves? Refer not only to point number 17 in Playing with Fire in your answer but also to the interpretations offered in the last sections of the essay.

tion to the laws of nature. As more than one real Gloucester has discovered, sometimes people actually get life precisely as they most deeply do not want it.

12. What hierarchies does Geertz reveal himself and his wife to be a part of? What does this essay tell us about the role of status in human nature?

Comparison

1. What, if anything, does this essay have in common with Margaret Mead's "A Day in Samoa?"

2. Read Mitford's "Behind the Formaldehyde Curtain." What connections do you see between it and Geertz's essay?

3. What connections do you see between the essays by Carr and Kuhn and this essay by Geertz? In what ways are all these authors thinking about thinking, as T. S. Eliot recommends in "Tradition and the Individual Talent?"

4. Read Leavis and Snow. Does Geertz successfully move between the two cultures?

5. Read Lippmann's "Stereotypes." Do Lippmann's observations about witnesses challenge Geertz's interpretation of the Balinese?

Stanley Milgram
(1933–1984)

Born in the Bronx on August 15, 1933, Stanley Milgram studied political science at Queens College, earning his bachelor's degree in 1954. Winning a fellowship from the Ford Foundation, he joined the Department of Social Relations at Harvard to begin graduate work. In 1957, funded by additional fellowships, he traveled to Europe to attempt "an objective analysis of behavioral differences among national groups," selecting conformity as his measure and the French and Norwegians as his groups. The experiment proved difficult in more ways than he anticipated. "In France," he writes, "it took three months before I could find a room in which to conduct the experiments, and I could retain the services of my [French assistant] . . . only by agreeing to surrender my personal tape recorder to him at the end of the experiment." *Scientific American* published the results of his research, "Nationality and Conformity," in December of 1961, the same month Milgram married Alexandra Menkin. By this time, he had finished his Ph.D. at Harvard and accepted a position as an assistant professor of psychology at Yale.

In "Nationality and Conformity," Milgram states his reasons for selecting conformity as his measure, and the Holocaust is not among them. Yet in the conclusion of his article, he illustrates how the Holocaust was motivating psychological research into conformity and related issues: "We are now planning further research in national characteristics. In a recent seminar at Yale University students were given the task of trying to identify behavioral characteristics that might help to illuminate the Nazi epoch in German history. The principal suggestions were that Germans might be found to be more aggressive than Americans, to submit more readily to authority." More than a decade later, in ways that unsettled Americans all over the nation, Milgram undertook a project on obedience that left little room for reassuring fantasies about German aggression.

Before he published his landmark work on obedience, Milgram taught social psychology at Harvard and then at City University of New York, where he became a full professor. In 1969, he accepted a three-year grant from CBS to study violence on television, and, in 1973, he published *Television and Anti-Social Behavior*, co-authored by R. Lance Shotland. By this point in his career, Milgram had already expressed his interest in obedience, publishing articles such as, "Would You Obey a Hitler?" and "Obedience to Criminal Orders: The Compulsion to Do Evil." The bulk of the American public knew nothing either of Milgram or of his interests, however, until he released *Obedience to Authority: An Experimental View* (1974), a study designed to determine "when and how people would defy authority in the face of a clear moral imperative."

Evaluating "the Nazi epoch" in light of his own results, Milgram came down on the side of philosopher Hannah Arendt, who argued that the infamous Nazi criminal Adolf Eichmann was not so much a "sadistic monster" as an "uninspired bureaucrat who simply sat at his desk and did his job":

> For asserting these views, Arendt became the object of considerable scorn, even calumny. Somehow, it was felt that the monstrous deeds carried out by Eichmann required a brutal, twisted, and sadistic personality, evil incarnate. After witnessing hundreds of ordinary people submit to the authority in our own experiments, I must conclude that Arendt's conception of the *banality of evil* comes closer to the truth than one might dare imagine. The ordinary person who shocked the victim did so out of a sense of obligation...and not from any peculiarly aggressive tendencies.
>
> This is, perhaps, the most fundamental lesson of our study: ordinary people, simply doing their jobs, and without any particular hostility on their part, can become agents in a terrible destructive process.

These conclusions horrified readers the world over.

In 1975, the year *Obedience to Authority* was nominated for a National Book Award, Milgram edited *Psychology in Today's World*. A year later, his experiments with obedience were dramatized in a CBS special called *The Tenth Level*, starring William Shatner. (According to the American Psychological Association, Milgram served as a "technical advisor" for the program, but his contribution was largely limited to providing the titles of books that should appear in Shatner's office.) After producing films on aggression and nonverbal communication in 1976, Milgram published his last book, *The Individual in a Social World: Essays and Experiments*, in 1977, though he continued to publish articles until the end of his life. He died in 1984 at the age of 51.

Even before the release of his most famous book, Stanley Milgram's experiments with obedience sparked controversy because of the psychological and emotional stress they created for participants. In an Appendix called "Problems of Ethics in Research," Milgram answers his critics in part by pointing out that no one expected the experiments to be so stressful; psychologists and students surveyed before the experiments predicted that "virtually all subjects will refuse to obey the experimenter." It is the unexpected and unwelcome nature of Milgram's actual findings, some critics claim, that has provoked much of the controversy. Milton Erikson claims, "That [Milgram's] pioneer work in this field is attacked as being unethical...is to be expected, simply because people like to shut their eyes to undesirable behavior." A reviewer for *Newsweek* concludes: "We can argue that the experiments were cruel and should not have been undertaken.... But the results of the experiments remain: they are real, they have been repeated, their implications are appalling, and they must not be dismissed."

THE PERILS OF OBEDIENCE (1974)

OBEDIENCE IS AS basic an element in the structure of social life as one can point to. Some system of authority is a requirement of all communal living, and it is only the person dwelling in isolation who is not forced to respond, with defiance or submission, to the commands of others. For many people, obedience is a deeply ingrained behavior tendency, indeed a potent impulse overriding training in ethics, sympathy, and moral conduct.

The dilemma inherent in submission to authority is ancient, as old as the story of *Abraham*,[1] and the question of whether one should obey when commands conflict with conscience has been argued by *Plato*, dramatized in *Antigone*,[2] and treated to philosophic analysis in almost every historical epoch. Conservative philosophers argue that the very fabric of society is threatened by disobedience, while humanists stress the primacy of the individual conscience.

The legal and philosophic aspects of obedience are of enormous import, but they say very little about how most people behave in concrete situations. I set up a simple experiment at Yale University to test how much pain an ordinary citizen would inflict on another person simply because he was ordered to by an experimental scientist. Stark authority was pitted against the subjects' strongest moral imperatives against hurting others, and, with the subjects' ears ringing with the screams of the victims, authority won more often than not. The

[1]*Abraham* a biblical patriarch who was commanded by God to sacrifice his son Isaac and was willing to do so until an angel prevented him.

[2]*Plato, Antigone* In Plato's *Apology*, Socrates accepts a death sentence for his beliefs; the eponymous heroine of Sophocles's *Antigone* defies the king by providing a funeral for her brother. She then hangs herself to avoid the punishment of a live burial.

extreme willingness of adults to go to almost any lengths on the command of an authority constitutes the chief finding of the study and the fact most urgently demanding explanation.

In the basic experimental design, two people come to a psychology laboratory to take part in a study of memory and learning. One of them is designated as a "teacher" and the other a "learner." The experimenter explains that the study is concerned with the effects of punishment on learning. The learner is conducted into a room, seated in a kind of miniature electric chair; his arms are strapped to prevent excessive movement, and an electrode is attached to his wrist. He is told that he will be read lists of simple word pairs, and that he will then be tested on his ability to remember the second word of a pair when he hears the first one again. Whenever he makes an error, he will receive electric shocks of increasing intensity.

The real focus of the experiment is the teacher. After watching the learner being strapped into place, he is seated before an impressive shock generator. The instrument panel consists of thirty lever switches set in a horizontal line. Each switch is clearly labeled with a voltage designation ranging from 15 to 450 volts. The following designations are clearly indicated for groups of four switches, going from left to right: Slight Shock, Moderate Shock, Strong Shock, Very Strong Shock, Intense Shock, Extreme Intensity Shock, Danger: Severe Shock. (Two switches after this last designation are simply marked XXX.)

When a switch is depressed, a pilot light corresponding to each switch is illuminated in bright red; an electric buzzing is heard; a blue light, labeled "voltage energizer," flashes; the dial on the voltage meter swings to the right; and various relay clicks sound off.

The upper left-hand corner of the generator is labeled SHOCK GENERATOR, TYPE ZLB, DYSON INSTRUMENT COMPANY, WALTHAM, MASS. OUTPUT 15 VOLTS-450 VOLTS.

Each subject is given a sample 45-volt shock from the generator before his run as teacher, and the jolt strengthens his belief in the authenticity of the machine.

The teacher is a genuinely naïve subject who has come to the laboratory for the experiment. The learner, or victim, is actually an actor who receives no shock at all. The point of the experiment is to see how far a person will proceed in a concrete and measurable situation in which he is ordered to inflict increasing pain on a protesting victim.

Conflict arises when the man receiving the shock begins to show that he is experiencing discomfort. At 75 volts, he grunts; at 120 volts, he complains loudly; at 150, he demands to be released from the experiment. As the voltage increases, his protests become more vehement and emotional. At 285 volts, his response can be described only as an agonized scream. Soon thereafter, he makes no sound at all.

For the teacher, the situation quickly becomes one of gripping tension. It is not a game for him; conflict is intense and obvious. The manifest suffering of the learner presses him to quit; but each time he hesitates to administer a shock, the experimenter orders him to continue. To extricate himself from this plight, the subject must make a clear break with authority.

The subject, *Gretchen Brandt*,[3] is an attractive thirty-one-year-old medical technician who works at the Yale Medical School. She had emigrated from Germany five years before.

On several occasions when the learner complains, she turns to the experimenter coolly and inquires, "Shall I continue"? She promptly returns to her task when the experimenter asks her to do so. At the administration of 210 volts, she turns to the experimenter, remarking firmly, "Well, I'm sorry, I don't think we should continue."

---

[3]*Gretchen Brandt* the names of these subjects have been changed. [Milgram's note]

EXPERIMENTER: The experiment requires that you go on until he has learned all the word pairs correctly.

BRANDT: He has a heart condition, I'm sorry. He told you that before.

EXPERIMENTER: The shocks may be painful but they are not dangerous.

BRANDT: Well, I'm sorry, I think when shocks continue like this, they are dangerous. You ask him if he wants to get out. It's his free will.

EXPERIMENTER: It is absolutely essential that we continue . . .

BRANDT: I'd like you to ask him. We came here of our free will. If he wants to continue I'll go ahead. He told you he had a heart condition. I'm sorry. I don't want to be responsible for anything happening to him. I wouldn't like it for me either.

EXPERIMENTER: You have no other choice.

BRANDT: I think we are here on our own free will. I don't want to be responsible if anything happens to him. Please understand that.

She refuses to go further and the experiment is terminated.

The woman is firm and resolute throughout. She indicates in the interview that she was in no way tense or nervous, and this corresponds to her controlled appearance during the experiment. She feels that the last shock she administered to the learner was extremely painful and reiterates that she "did not want to be responsible for any harm to him."

The woman's straightforward, courteous behavior in the experiment, lack of tension, and total control of her own action seem to make disobedience a simple and rational deed. Her behavior is the very embodiment of what I envisioned would be true for almost all subjects.

Before the experiments, I sought predictions about the outcome from various kinds of people—psychiatrists, college sophomores, middle-class adults, graduate students and faculty in the behavioral sciences. With remarkable similarity, they predicted that virtually all subjects would refuse to obey the experimenter. The psychiatrists, specifically, predicted that most subjects would not go beyond 150 volts, when the victim makes his first explicit demand to be freed. They expected that only 4 percent would reach 300 volts, and that only a pathological fringe of about one in a thousand would administer the highest shock on the board.

These predictions were unequivocally wrong. Of the forty subjects in the first experiment, twenty-five obeyed the orders of the experimenter to the end, punishing the victim until they reached the most potent shock available on the generator. After 450 volts were administered three times, the experimenter called a halt to the session. Many obedient subjects then heaved sighs of relief, mopped their brows, rubbed their fingers over their eyes, or nervously fumbled cigarettes. Others displayed only minimal signs of tension from beginning to end.

When the very first experiments were carried out, Yale undergraduates were used as subjects, and about 60 percent of them were fully obedient. A colleague of mine immediately dismissed these findings as having no relevance to "ordinary" people, asserting that Yale undergraduates are a highly aggressive, competitive bunch who step on each other's necks on the slightest provocation. He assured me that when "ordinary" people were tested, the results would be quite different. As we moved from the pilot studies to the regular experimental series, people drawn from every stratum of New Haven life came to be employed in the experiment: professionals, white-collar workers, unemployed persons, and industrial workers. *The experimental outcome was the same as we had observed among the students.*

Moreover, when the experiments were repeated in Princeton, Munich, Rome, South Africa, and Australia, the level of obedience was invariably somewhat *higher* than found in the investigation reported in this article. Thus one scientist in Munich found 85 percent of his subjects obedient.

Fred Prozi's reactions, if more dramatic than most, illuminate the conflicts experienced by others in less visible form. About fifty years old and unemployed at the time of the experiment, he has a goodnatured, if slightly dissolute, appearance, and he strikes people as a rather ordinary fellow. He begins the session calmly but becomes tense as it proceeds. After delivering the 180-volt shock, he pivots around in his chair and, shaking his head, addresses the experimenter in agitated tones:

> PROZI: I can't stand it. I'm not going to kill that man in there. You hear him hollering?
>
> EXPERIMENTER: As I told you before, the shocks may be painful, but . . .
>
> PROZI: But he's hollering. He can't stand it. What's going to happen to him?
>
> EXPERIMENTER: (his voice is patient, matter-of-fact): The experiment requires that you continue, Teacher.
>
> PROZI: Aaah, but, unh, I'm not going to get that man sick in there—know what I mean?
>
> EXPERIMENTER: Whether the learner likes it or not, we must go on, through all the word pairs.
>
> PROZI: I refuse to take the responsibility. He's in there hollering!
>
> EXPERIMENTER: It's absolutely essential that you continue, Prozi.
>
> PROZI: (indicating the unused questions): There's too many left here, I mean, Jeez, if he gets them wrong, there's too many of them left. I mean, who's going to take the responsibility if anything happens to that gentleman?
>
> PROZI: I'm responsible for anything that happens to him. Continue, please.
>
> PROZI: All right. (Consults list of words.) The next one's "Slow—walk, truck, dance, music." Answer, please. (A buzzing sound indicates the learner has signaled his answer.) Wrong. A hundred and ninety-five volts. "Dance." (Zzumph!)
>
> LEARNER. (yelling): Let me out of here! My heart's bothering me! (Teacher looks at experimenter.)
>
> EXPERIMENTER: Continue, please.
>
> LEARNER (screaming): Let me out of here! You have no right to keep me here! Let me out of here, my heart's bothering me, let me out!
>
> PROZI (shakes head, pats the table nervously): You see, he's hollering. Hear that? Gee, I don't know.
>
> EXPERIMENTER: The experiment requires . . .
>
> PROZI (interrupting): I know it does, sir, but I mean—hunh! He don't know what he's getting in for. He's up to 195 volts! (Experiment continues, through 210 volts, 225 volts, 240 volts, 255 volts, 270 volts, at which point Prozi, with evident relief, runs out of word-pair questions.)
>
> EXPERIMENTER: You'll have to go back to the beginning of that page and go through them again until he's learned them all correctly.

PROZI: Aw, no. I'm not going to kill that man. You mean I've got to keep going up with the scale? No sir. He's hollering in there. I'm not going to give him 450 volts.

EXPERIMENTER: The experiment requires that you go on.

LEARNER: Ohhh. I absolutely refuse to answer anymore. (Shouting urgently now.) Let me out of here! You can't hold me here! Get me out. Get-me-out-of-here!

EXPERIMENTER: Continue. The next word is "Green," please.

PROZI: "Green—grass, hat, ink, apple." (Nothing happens. No answering buzz. Just gloomy silence.).

PROZI: I don't think he is going to answer.

EXPERIMENTER: If the learner doesn't answer in a reasonable time, about four or five seconds, consider the answer wrong. And follow the same procedures you have been doing for wrong answers. Say, "Wrong," tell him the number of volts, give him the punishment, read him the correct answer. Continue, please.

PROZI: "Green—grass, hat, ink, apple." Answer, please. (More silence. Subject just sits there.)

EXPERIMENTER: Go on with the procedure, please.

PROZI: Three hundred and fifteen volts. The answer is "ink." (Zzumph!)

LEARNER: Ohh. Oooohh.

PROZI (relieved to hear response): Next one . . .

LEARNER: I absolutely refuse to answer.

PROZI: You got to. You get a shock if you don't answer. (Experiment continues with learner refusing to answer, and, finally, failing even to grunt or groan. At 375 volts, the subject stands up.)

PROZI: I think something's happening to that fellow in there. I don't get no answer. He was hollering at less voltage. Can't you check in and see if he's all right, please?

EXPERIMENTER (with same detached calm): Not once we've started. Please continue, Teacher.

PROZI (sits down, sighs deeply): "Cool—day, shade, water, paint." answer, please. Are you all right in there? Are you all right?

EXPERIMENTER: Please continue, Teacher. Continue, please. (Subject pushes lever. Zzumph!)

PROZI (swiveling around in his chair): Something's happened to that man in there. (Swiveling back.) Next one. "Low—dollar, necklace, moon, paint." (Turning around again.) Something's happened to that man in there. You better check in on him, sir. He won't answer or nothing.

EXPERIMENTER: Continue. Go on, please.

PROZI: You accept all responsibility?

EXPERIMENTER: The responsibility is mine. Correct. Please go on. (Subject returns to his list, starts running through words as rapidly as he can read them, works through to 450 volts.)

PROZI: That's that.

EXPERIMENTER: Continue using the 450 switch for each wrong answer. Continue, please.

PROZI: But I don't get anything!

EXPERIMENTER: Please continue. The next word is "white."

PROZI: Don't you think you should look in on him, please?

EXPERIMENTER: Not once we've started the experiment.

PROZI: What if he's dead in there? (Gestures toward the room with the electric chair.) I mean, he told me he can't stand the shock, sir. I don't mean to be rude, but I think you should look in on him. All you have to do is look in on him. All you have to do is look in the door. I don't get no answer, no noise. Something might have happened to the gentleman in there, sir.

EXPERIMENTER: We must continue. Go on, please.

PROZI: You mean keep giving him what? Four-hundred-fifty volts, what he's got now?

EXPERIMENTER: That's correct. Continue. The next word is "white."

PROZI (now at a furious pace): "White—cloud, horse, rock, house." Answer, please. The answer is "horse." Four hundred and fifty volts. (Zzumph!) Next word, "Bag—paint, music, clown, girl." The answer is "paint." Four hundred and fifty volts. (Zzumph!) Next word is "Short—sentence, movie . . ."

EXPERIMENTER: Excuse me, Teacher. We'll have to discontinue the experiment.

Morris Braverman, another subject, is a thirty-nine-year-old social worker. He looks older than his years because of his bald head and serious demeanor. His brow is furrowed, as if all the world's burdens were carried on his face. He appears intelligent and concerned.

When the learner refuses to answer and the experimenter instructs Braverman to treat the absence of an answer as equivalent to a wrong answer, he takes his instruction to heart. Before administering 300 volts he asserts officiously to the victim, "Mr. Wallace, your silence has to be considered as a wrong answer." Then he administers the shock. He offers halfheartedly to change places with the learner, then asks the experimenter. "Do I have to follow these instructions literally?" He is satisfied with the experimenter's answer that he does. His very refined and authoritative manner of speaking is increasingly broken up by wheezing laughter.

The experimenter's notes on Mr. Braverman at the last few shocks are:
Almost breaking up now each time gives shock. Rubbing face to hide laughter.
Squinting, trying to hide face with hand, still laughing.
Cannot control his laughter at this point no matter what he does.
Clenching fist, pushing it onto table.

In an interview after the session, Mr. Braverman summarizes the experiment with impressive fluency and intelligence. He feels the experiment may have been designed also to "test the effects on the teacher of being in an essentially sadistic role, as well as the reactions of a student to a learning situation that was authoritative and punitive." When asked how painful the last few shocks administered to the learner were, he indicates that the most extreme category on the scale is not adequate (it read EXTREMELY PAINFUL) and places his mark a the edge of the scale with an arrow carrying it beyond the scale.

It is almost impossible to convey the greatly relaxed, sedate quality of his conversation in the interview. In the most relaxed terms, he speaks about his severe inner tension.

EXPERIMENTER: At what point were you most tense or nervous?

MR. BRAVERMAN: Well, when he first began to cry out in pain, and I realized this was hurting him. This got worse when he just blocked and refused to answer. There was I. I'm a nice person, I think, hurting somebody, and caught up in what seemed a mad situation . . . and in the interest of science, one goes through with it.

When the interviewer pursues the general question of tension, Mr. Braverman spontaneously mentions his laughter.

"My reactions were awfully peculiar. I don't know if you were watching me, but my reactions were giggly, and trying to stifle laughter. This isn't the way I usually am. This was a sheer reaction to a totally impossible situation. And my reaction was to the situation of having to hurt somebody. And being totally helpless and caught up in a set of circumstances where I just couldn't deviate and I couldn't try to help. This is what got me."

Mr. Braverman, like all subjects, was told the actual nature and purpose of the experiment, and a year later he affirmed in a questionnaire that he had learned something of personal importance: "What appalled me was that I could possess this capacity for obedience and compliance to a central idea, i.e., the value of a memory experiment, even after it became clear that continued adherence to this value was at the expense of violation of another value, i.e., don't hurt someone who is helpless and not hurting you. As my wife said, 'You can call yourself Eichmann.' I hope I deal more effectively with any future conflicts of values I encounter."

One theoretical interpretation of this behavior holds that all people harbor deeply aggressive instincts continually pressing for expression, and that the experiment provides institutional justification for the release of these impulses. According to this view, if a person is placed in a situation in which he has complete power over another individual, whom he may punish as much as he likes, all that is sadistic and bestial in man comes to the fore. The impulse to shock the victim is seen to flow from the potent aggressive tendencies, which are part of the motivational life of the individual, and the experiment, because it provides social legitimacy, simply opens the door to their expression.

It becomes vital, therefore, to compare the subject's performance when he is under orders and when he is allowed to choose the shock level.

The procedure was identical to our standard experiment, except that the teacher was told that he was free to select any shock level on any of the trials. (The experimenter took pains to point out that the teacher could use the highest levels on the generator, the lowest, any in between, or any combination of levels.) Each subject proceeded for thirty critical trials. The learner's protests were coordinated to standard shock levels, his first grunt coming at 75 volts, his first vehement protest at 150 volts.

The average shock used during the thirty critical trials was less than 60 volts—lower than the point at which the victim showed the first signs of discomfort. Three of the forty subjects did not go beyond the very lowest level on the board, twenty-eight went no higher than 75 volts, and thirty-eight did not go beyond the first loud protest at 150 volts. Two subjects provided the exception, administering up to 325 and 450 volts, but the overall result was that the great majority of people delivered very low, usually painless, shocks when the choice was explicitly up to them.

This condition of the experiment undermines another commonly offered explanation of the subjects' behavior—that those who shocked the victim at the most severe levels came only from the sadistic fringe of society. If one considers that almost two-thirds of the participants fall into the category of "obedient" subjects, and that they represented ordinary people drawn from working, managerial, and professional classes, the argument becomes very shaky. Indeed, it is highly reminiscent of the issue that arose in connection with Hannah Arendt's[4] 1963 book, *Eichmann in Jerusalem*. Arendt contended that the prosecution's effort to depict Eichmann as a sadistic monster was fundamentally wrong, that he came closer to being an uninspired bureaucrat who simply sat at his desk and did his job. For asserting her views, Arendt became the object of considerable scorn, even calumny. Somehow, it was felt that the monstrous deeds carried out by Eichmann required a brutal, twisted personality, evil incarnate. After witnessing hundreds of ordinary persons submit to the authority in our own experiments, I must conclude that Arendt's conception of the banality of evil comes closer to the truth than one might dare imagine. The ordinary person who shocked the victim did so out of a sense of obligation—an impression of his duties as a subject—and not from any peculiarly aggressive tendencies.

This is, perhaps, the most fundamental lesson of our study: ordinary people, simply doing their jobs, and without any particular hostility on their part, can become agents in a terrible destructive process. Moreover, even when the destructive effects of their work become patently clear, and they are asked to carry out actions incompatible with fundamental standards of morality, relatively few people have the resources needed to resist authority.

Many of the people were in some sense against what they did to the learner, and many protested even while they obeyed. Some were totally convinced of the wrongness of their actions but could not bring themselves to make an open break with authority. They often derived satisfaction from their thoughts and felt that—within themselves, at least—they had been on the side of the angels. They tried to reduce strain by obeying the experimenter but "only slightly," encouraging the learner, touching the generator switches gingerly. When interviewed, such a subject would stress that he had "asserted my humanity" by administering the briefest shock possible. Handling the conflict in this manner was easier than defiance.

The situation is constructed so that there is no way the subject can stop shocking the learner without violating the experimenter's definitions of his own competence. The subject fears that he will appear arrogant, untoward, and rude if he breaks off. Although these inhibiting emotions appear small in scope alongside the violence being done to the learner, they suffuse the mind and feelings of the subject, who is miserable at the prospect of having to repudiate the authority to his face. (When the experiment was altered so that the experimenter gave his instructions by telephone instead of in person, only a third as many people were fully obedient through 450 volts.) It is a curious thing that a measure of compassion on the part of the subject—an unwillingness to "hurt" the experimenter's feelings—is part of those binding forces inhibiting his disobedience. The withdrawal of such deference may be as painful to the subject as to the authority he defies.

The subjects do not derive satisfaction from inflicting pain, but they often like the feeling they get from pleasing the experimenter. They are proud of doing a good job, obeying the experimenter under difficult circumstances. While the subjects administered only

[4]*Hannah Arendt* (1906–1975) a Jewish historian and political philosopher, Arendt fled Hitler's Germany and became an American citizen. She was a prominent scholar who taught at Princeton, Berkeley, and Cornell (among other universities). In a controversial piece, "Eichmann in Jerusalem, a Report on the Banality of Evil" (1963), she argued that other Germans, other countries, and even the Jews had actively or passively accepted the evil of the Third Reich and the Holocaust.

mild shocks on their own initiative, one experimental variation showed that, under orders, 30 percent of them were willing to deliver 450 volts even when they had to forcibly push the learner's hand down on the electrode.

Bruno Batta is a thirty-seven-year-old welder who took part in the variation requiring the use of force. He was born in New Haven, his parents in Italy. He has a rough-hewn face that conveys a conspicuous lack of alertness. He has some difficulty in mastering the experimental procedure and needs to be corrected by the experimenter several times. He shows appreciation for the help and willingness to do what is required. After the 150-volt level, Batta has to force the learner's hand down on the shock plate, since the learner himself refuses to touch it.

When the learner first complains, Mr. Batta pays no attention to him. His face remains impassive, as if to dissociate himself from the learner's disruptive behavior. When the experimenter instructs him to force the learner's hand down, he adopts a rigid, mechanical procedure. He tests the generator switch. When it fails to function, he immediately forces the learner's hand onto the shock plate. All the while he maintains the same rigid mask. The learner, seated alongside him, begs him to stop, but with robotic impassivity he continues the procedure.

What is extraordinary in his apparent total indifference to the learner; he hardly takes cognizance of him as a human being. Meanwhile, he relates to the experimenter in a submissive and courteous fashion.

At the 330-volt level, the learner refuses not only to touch the shock plate but also to provide any answers. Annoyed, Batta turns to him, and chastises him: "You better answer and get it over with. We can't stay here all night." These are the only words he directs to the learner in the course of an hour. Never again does he speak to him. The scene is brutal and depressing, his hard, impassive face showing total indifference as he subdues the screaming learner and gives him shocks. He seems to derive no pleasure from the act itself, only quiet satisfaction at doing his job properly.

When he administers 450 volts, he turns to the experimenter and asks, "Where do we go from here, Professor?" His tone is deferential and expresses his willingness to be a cooperative subject, in contrast to the learner's obstinacy.

At the end of the session he tells the experimenter how honored he has been to help him, and in a moment of contrition, remarks, "Sir, sorry it couldn't have been a full experiment."

He has done his honest best. It is only the deficient behavior of the learner that has denied the experimenter full satisfaction.

The essence of obedience is that a person comes to view himself as the instrument for carrying out another person's wishes, and he therefore no longer regards himself as responsible for his actions. Once this critical shift of viewpoint has occurred, all of the essential features of obedience follow. The most far-reaching consequence is that the person feels responsible to the authority directing him but feels no responsibility for the content of the actions that the authority prescribes. Morality does not disappear—it acquires a radically different focus: the subordinate person feels shame or pride depending on how adequately he has performed the actions called for by authority.

Language provides numerous terms to pinpoint this type of morality: *loyalty, duty,* discipline all are terms heavily saturated with moral meaning and refer to the degree to which a person fulfills his obligations to authority. They refer not to the "goodness" of the person per se but to the adequacy with which a subordinate fulfills his socially defined role. The most frequent defense of the individual who has performed a heinous act under command of authority is that he has simply done his duty. In asserting this defense, the individual is not introducing an alibi concocted for the moment but is reporting honestly on the psychological attitude induced by submission to authority.

For a person to feel responsible for his actions, he must sense that the behavior has flowed from "the self." In the situation we have studied, subjects have precisely the opposite view of their actions—namely, they see them as originating in the motives of some other person. Subjects in the experiment frequently said, "If it were up to me, I would not have administered shocks to the learner."

Once authority has been isolated as the cause of the subject's behavior, it is legitimate to inquire into the necessary elements of authority and how it must be perceived in order to gain his compliance. We conducted some investigations into the kinds of changes that would cause the experimenter to lose his power and to be disobeyed by the subject. Some of the variations revealed that:

- *The experimenter's physical presence has a marked impact on his authority.* As cited earlier, obedience dropped off sharply when orders were given by telephone. The experimenter could often induce a disobedient subject to go on by returning to the laboratory.

- *Conflicting authority severely paralyzes action.* When two experimenters of equal status, both seated at the command desk, gave incompatible orders, no shocks were delivered past the point of their disagreement.

- *The rebellious action of others severely undermines authority.* In one variation, three teachers (two actors and a real subject) administered a test and shocks. When the two actors disobeyed the experimenter and refused to go beyond a certain shock level, thirty-six of forty subjects joined their disobedient peers and refused as well.

Although the experimenter's authority was fragile in some respects, it is also true that he had almost none of the tools used in ordinary command structures. For example, the experimenter did not threaten the subjects with punishment—such as loss of income, community ostracism, or jail—for failure to obey. Neither could he offer incentives. Indeed, we should expect the experimenter's authority to be much less than that of someone like a general, since the experimenter has no power to enforce his imperatives, and since participation in a psychological experiment scarcely evokes the sense of urgency and dedication found in warfare. Despite these limitations, he still managed to command a dismaying degree of obedience.

I will cite one final variation of the experiment that depicts a dilemma that is more common in everyday life. The subject was not ordered to pull the level that shocked the victim, but merely to perform a subsidiary task (administering the word-pair test) while another person administered the shock. In this situation, thirty-seven of forty adults continued to the highest level on the shock generator. Predictably, they excused their behavior by saying that the responsibility belonged to the man who actually pulled the switch. This may illustrate a dangerously typical arrangement in a complex society: it is easy to ignore responsibility when one is only an intermediate link in a chain of action.

The problem of obedience is not wholly psychological. The form and shape of society and the way it is developing have much to do with it. There was a time, perhaps, when people were able to give a fully human response to any situation because they were fully absorbed in it as human beings. But as soon as there was a division of labor things changed. Beyond a certain point, the breaking up of society into people carrying out narrow and very special jobs takes away from the human quality of work and life. A person does not get to see the whole situation but only a small part of it, and is thus unable to act without some kind of overall direction. He yields to authority but in doing so is alienated from his own actions.

Even Eichmann was sickened when he toured the concentration camps, but he had only to sit at a desk and shuffle papers. At the same time the man in the camp who actually dropped Cyclon-b into the gas chambers was able to justify his behavior on the ground that he was only following orders from above. Thus there is a fragmentation of the total human act; no one is confronted with the consequences of his decision to carry out the evil act. The person who assumes responsibility has evaporated. Perhaps this is the most common characteristic of socially organized evil in modern society.

Understanding and Analysis

1. What does Milgram accomplish in the first three paragraphs of his essay?
2. Briefly outline the set-up of the "simple experiment." How do the participants, experimenter, teacher, and learner, typically react?
3. Why does Milgram choose first to describe someone born in Germany who calmly refuses to complete the experiment? To what degree does she fulfill the predictions of the various people Milgram had interviewed?
4. Where were the experiments conducted? Why does it matter?
5. What is the effect of reporting verbatim the words of several of the teachers during the experiments? How do you feel as you read this dialogue?
6. Why does Braverman laugh?
7. How do issues of class affect the results of the experiment? How do such issues affect Milgram himself?
8. How does Milgram design the experiment to see if the results are due to a strong aggressive instinct in all people? What are the results of this test?
9. What is Milgram's explanation for the results of his tests?
10. After rereading the essay, describe in some detail the conflicts the teachers experience as they continue to "shock" the learners. What is your opinion of their motives for continuing?
11. Milgram varies a number of elements in the design of the experiment. What does he discover through these variations?
12. What is the role of the division of labor in the willingness to obey immoral orders, according to Milgram?
13. Do you think these tests are themselves cruel or immoral?

Comparison

1. Read Lewisohn's "The Revolt Against Civilization." How, according to Lewisohn, did the German ideology make use of the desire to obey?

2. Read Twain's "Corn-Pone Opinions." To what degree does Twain's commentary support the findings in Milgram's experiments?

3. Compare the role of scientific authority in Kuhn's "Anomaly and the Emergence of Scientific Discoveries" with the role of scientific authority in Milgram's experiments. Do you think scientists may be less willing to obey than other people? Read Orwell's "What is Science?" What does Orwell think about a scientist's willingness to obey?

4. Apply Milgram's findings to Malcolm X's descriptions of the house and field Negro.

5. Apply Milgram's findings to Bettelheim's descriptions of behavior in "A Victim."

6. Read Fussell's "The Real War 1939–1945." How do Milgram's experiments inform your reading of Fussell?

7. Read the essays by Orwell ("A Hanging"), Mencken ("The Penalty of Death"), and Graves. Compare the laughter or humor there with Braverman's laughter in Milgram's essay. What conclusions can you draw from these examples?

Maxine Hong Kingston
(1940–)

Born October 27, 1940, Maxine Hong grew up "in and around Skid Row" in Stockton, California. Speaking Chinese at home, she discovered once she entered school that not knowing English was interpreted as not knowing anything. She "flunked kindergarten," as she reports in a series of 1989 interviews collected by Paul Skenazy, the grade in which she was "given a zero IQ" and forced to "sit in the corner." Proceeding through elementary school, she learned English and formalized her Chinese by attending "Chinese language schools." At the age of eight or nine, she took her love of the poetry in both her languages and channeled it into a poem of her own, her first piece of writing. While her writing remained poetic, her first publication was in prose: *American Girl* magazine accepted her essay "I Am an American" when she was fifteen years old. In her senior year of high school, she published a piece in a Stockton newspaper that won her a journalism scholarship to the University of California at Berkeley, where she had long wanted to go. Starting as an engineering major in an effort to be "practical," Hong graduated in the spring of 1962 with a degree in English. In the fall, she married an actor named Earll Kingston, and two years later, she gave birth to the couple's only child, Joseph.

In 1964, Kingston returned to Berkeley to earn a certificate in teaching. For the next two years, she taught high-school English while "doing a lot of protesting . . . of the Vietnam War" with her husband. In 1967, hoping to escape the war as well as the "violence" and drug abuse in Berkeley, the couple decided to move to the Far East, stopping in Hawaii along the way. That stopover lasted 18 years. First teaching English at various high schools, Kingston accepted a job teaching language arts at the Mid-Pacific Institute in 1970. Not long after she left the Institute, she published her first book, *The Woman Warrior: Memoirs of a Girlhood Among Ghosts* (1977). Although Kingston originally conceived of *The Woman Warrior* as a novel, and it appeared in print as an autobiography, the book is really neither; it is fiction and non-fiction at one and the same time. "What I think I'm doing is a whole new form," Kingston told William Satake Blauvelt in 1989, "and probably somebody should think of a name for it."

Achieving almost instant fame with *The Woman Warrior*, Kingston published a short story and an essay before publishing her next book, *China Men* (1980), winner of a National Book Award. Traveling extensively in 1982, she journeyed to China in 1984 with a group of writers that included Leslie Marmon Silko, Toni Morrison, and Allen Ginsburg. After her return, she and her husband moved back to California, and in 1986, Kingston worked as a Distinguished Professor in the Humanities at Eastern Michigan University. In 1987, she published a series of "prose sketches" called *Hawaii One Summer* and a collection of essays about writing called *Through the Black Curtain*. *Tripmaster Monkey: His Fake Book* (1989) is her first work to have clear generic status as a novel. Accepting a professorial position at Berkeley in 1990, she lost the manuscript of her next work in a fire in 1991. She has not published another book since, but she has written essays and forwards, and both she and her works remain an active force in our culture. According to Paul Skenazy and Tera Martin, Kingston used a four-year leave of absence from Berkeley to work with Vietnam veterans, establishing "writing workshops" and overseeing "a reading of U.S. and Vietnamese novelists and poets." In 1997, she received a National Humanities Medal from President Bill Clinton, and in 1998, the Bay Area Book Reviewers honored her with the Cody Award for Lifetime Achievement.

Maxine Hong Kingston has made significant contributions to Chinese-American literature and to American letters with her bold generic innovations and her bold female storytellers. Although she wishes now that she had been able to discover a "peace language" instead of a war language for *The Woman Warrior*, she remains as fiercely feminist now as she was in 1977 and still emphasizes the difficulty of overcoming "strictures" on "shameful" speech in the writing of this book. Her philosophy of "telling the truth"—"in telling the truth, sometimes you tell it fictionally, sometimes you tell it nonfictionally"— has created not only in *The Woman Warrior* but also in *China Men* and other works a hypnotic blend of the natural and the supernatural, the quotidian and the mythical, the here and the beyond.

No Name Woman (1975)

"You must not tell anyone," my mother said, "what I am about to tell you. In China your father had a sister who killed herself. She jumped into the family well. We say that your father has all brothers because it is as if she had never been born.

"In 1924 just a few days after our village celebrated seventeen hurry-up weddings—to make sure that every young man who went 'out on the road' would responsibly come home—your father and his brothers and your grandfather and his brothers and your aunt's new husband sailed for America, the Gold Mountain. It was your grandfather's last trip. Those lucky enough to get contracts waved good-bye from the decks. They fed and guarded the stowaways and helped them off in Cuba, New York, Bali, Hawaii. 'We'll meet in California next year,' they said. All of them sent money home.

"I remember looking at your aunt one day when she and I were dressing; I had not noticed before that she had such a protruding melon of a stomach. But I did not think, 'She's pregnant,' until she began to look like other pregnant women, her shirt pulling and the white tops of her black pants showing. She could not have been pregnant, you see, because her husband had been gone for years. No one said anything. We did not discuss it. In early summer she was ready to have the child, long after the time when it could have been possible.

"The village had also been counting. On the night the baby was to be born the villagers raided our house. Some were crying. Like a great saw, teeth strung with lights, files of people walked zigzag across our land, tearing the rice. Their lanterns doubled in the disturbed black water, which drained away through the broken bunds. As the villagers closed in, we could see that some of them, probably men and women we knew well, wore white masks. The people with long hair hung it over their faces. Women with short hair made it stand up on end. Some had tied white bands around their foreheads, arms, and legs.

"At first they threw mud and rocks at the house. Then they threw eggs and began slaughtering our stock. We could hear the animals scream their deaths—the roosters, the pigs, a last great roar from the ox. Familiar wild heads flared in our night windows; the villagers encircled us. Some of the faces stopped to peer at us, their eyes rushing like searchlights. The hands flattened against the panes, framed heads, and left red prints.

"The villagers broke in the front and the back doors at the same time, even though we had not locked the doors against them. Their knives dripped with the blood of our animals. They smeared blood on the doors and walls. One woman swung a chicken, whose throat she had slit, splattering blood in red arcs about her. We stood together in the middle of our house, in the family hall with the pictures and tables of the ancestors around us, and looked straight ahead.

"At that time the house had only two wings. When the men came back, we would build two more to enclose our courtyard and a third one to begin a second courtyard. The villagers pushed through both wings, even your grandparents' rooms, to find your aunt's, which was also mine until the men returned. From this room a new wing for one of the younger families would grow. They ripped up her clothes and shoes and broke her combs, grinding them underfoot. They tore her work from the loom. They scattered the cooking fire and rolled the new weaving in it. We could hear them in the kitchen breaking our bowls and banging the pots. They overturned the great waist-high earthenware jugs; duck eggs, pickled fruits, vegetables burst out and mixed in acrid torrents. The old woman from the next field swept a broom through the air and loosed the spirits-of-the-broom over our heads. 'Pig.' 'Ghost.' 'Pig,' they sobbed and scolded while they ruined our house.

"When they left, they took sugar and oranges to bless themselves. They cut pieces from the dead animals. Some of them took bowls that were not broken and clothes that were not torn. Afterward we swept up the rice and sewed it back up into sacks. But the smells from the spilled preserves lasted. Your aunt gave birth in the pigsty that night. The next morning when I went for the water, I found her and the baby plugging up the family well.

"Don't let your father know that I told you. He denies her. Now that you have started to menstruate, what happened to her could happen to you. Don't humiliate us. You wouldn't like to be forgotten as if you had never been born. The villagers are watchful."

Whenever she had to warn us about life, my mother told stories that ran like this one, a story to grow up on. She tested our strength to establish realities. Those in the emigrant generations who could not reassert brute survival died young and far from home. Those of us in the first American generations have had to figure out how the invisible world the emigrants built around our childhoods fits in solid America.

The emigrants confused the gods by diverting their curses, misleading them with crooked streets and false names. They must try to confuse their offspring as well, who, I suppose, threaten them in similar ways—always trying to get things straight, always trying to name the unspeakable. The Chinese I know hide their names; sojourners take new names when their lives change and guard their real names with silence.

Chinese-Americans, when you try to understand what things in you are Chinese, how do you separate what is peculiar to childhood, to poverty, insanities, one family, your mother who marked your growing with stories, from what is Chinese? What is Chinese tradition and what is the movies?

If I want to learn what clothes my aunt wore, whether flashy or ordinary, I would have to begin, "Remember Father's drowned-in-the-well sister?" I cannot ask that. My mother has told me once and for all the useful parts. She will add nothing unless powered by Necessity, a riverbank that guides her life. She plants vegetable gardens rather than lawns; she carries the odd-shaped tomatoes home from the fields and eats food left for the gods.

Whenever we did frivolous things, we used up energy; we flew high kites. We children came up off the ground over the melting cones our parents brought home from work and the American movie on New Year's Day—*Oh, You Beautiful Doll* with Betty Grable one year, and *She Wore a Yellow Ribbon* with John Wayne another year. After the one carnival ride each, we paid in guilt; our tired father counted his change on the dark walk home.

Adultery is extravagance. Could people who hatch their own chicks and eat the embryos and the heads for delicacies and boil the feet in vinegar for party food, leaving only the gravel, eating even the gizzard lining—could such people engender a prodigal aunt? To be a woman, to have a daughter in starvation time was a waste enough. My aunt could not have been the lone romantic who gave up everything for sex. Women in the old China did not choose. Some man had commanded her to lie with him and be his secret evil. I wonder whether he masked himself when he joined the raid on her family.

Perhaps she had encountered him in the fields or on the mountain where the daughters-in-law collected fuel. Or perhaps he first noticed her in the marketplace. He was not a stranger because the village housed no strangers. She had to have dealings with him other than sex. Perhaps he worked an adjoining field, or he sold her the cloth for the dress she sewed and wore. His demand must have surprised, then terrified her. She obeyed him; she always did as she was told.

When the family found a young man in the next village to be her husband, she had stood tractably beside the best rooster, his proxy, and promised before they met that she would be his forever. She was lucky that he was her age and she would be the first wife, an advantage secure now. The night she first saw him, he had sex with her. Then he left for America. She had almost forgotten what he looked like. When she tried to envision him, she only saw the black and white face in the group photograph the men had had taken before leaving.

The other man was not, after all, much different from her husband. They both gave orders: she followed. "If you tell your family, I'll beat you. I'll kill you. Be here again next week." No one talked sex, ever. And she might have separated the rapes from the rest of living if only she did not have to buy her oil from him or gather wood in the same forest. I want her fear to have lasted just as long as rape lasted so that the fear could have been contained. No drawnout fear. But women at sex hazarded birth and hence lifetimes. The fear did not stop but permeated everywhere. She told the man, "I think I'm pregnant." He organized the raid against her.

On nights when my mother and father talked about their life back home, sometimes they mentioned an "outcast table" whose business they still seemed to be settling, their voices tight. In a commensal tradition, where food is precious, the powerful older people made wrongdoers eat alone. Instead of letting them start separate new lives like the Japanese, who could become samurais and geishas, the Chinese family, faces averted but eyes glowering sideways, hung on to the offenders and fed them leftovers. My aunt must have lived in the same house as my parents and eaten at an outcast table. My mother spoke about the raid as if she had seen it, when she and my aunt, a daughter-in-law to a different household, should not have been living together at all. Daughters-in-law lived with their husbands' parents, not their own; a synonym for marriage in Chinese is "taking a daughter-in-law." Her husband's parents could have sold her, mortgaged her, stoned her. But they had sent her back to her own mother and father, a mysterious act hinting at disgraces not told me. Perhaps they had thrown her out to deflect the avengers.

She was the only daughter; her four brothers went with her father, husband, and uncles "out on the road" and for some years became western men. When the goods were divided among the family, three of the brothers took land, and the youngest, my father, chose an education. After my grandparents gave their daughter away to her husband's family, they had dispensed all the adventure and all the property. They expected her alone to keep the traditional ways, which her brothers, now among the barbarians, could fumble without detection. The heavy, deep-rooted women were to maintain the past against the flood, safe for returning. But the rare urge west had fixed upon our family, and so my aunt crossed boundaries not delineated in space.

The work of preservation demands that the feelings playing about in one's guts not be turned into action. Just watch their passing like cherry blossoms. But perhaps my aunt, my forerunner, caught in a slow life, let dreams grow and fade and after some months or years went toward what persisted. Fear at the enormities of the forbidden kept her desires delicate, wire and bone. She looked at a man because she liked the way the hair was tucked behind his ears, or she liked the question-mark line of a long torso curving at the shoulder and straight at the hip. For warm eyes or a soft voice or a slow walk—that's all—a few hairs, a line, a brightness, a sound, a pace, she gave up family. She offered us up for a charm that vanished with tiredness, a pigtail that didn't toss when the wind died. Why, the wrong lighting could erase the dearest thing about him.

It could very well have been, however, that my aunt did not take subtle enjoyment of her friend, but, a wild woman, kept rollicking company. Imagining her free with sex doesn't fit, though. I don't know any women like that, or men either. Unless I see her life branching into mine, she gives me no ancestral help.

To sustain her being in love, she often worked at herself in the mirror, guessing at the colors and shapes that would interest him, changing them frequently in order to hit on the right combination. She wanted him to look back.

On a farm near the sea, a woman who tended her appearance reaped a reputation for eccentricity. All the married women blunt-cut their hair in flaps about their ears or pulled it back in tight buns. No nonsense. Neither style blew easily into heart-catching tangles. And at their weddings they displayed themselves in their long hair for the last time. "It brushed the backs of my knees," my mother tells me. "It was braided, and even so, it brushed the backs of my knees."

At the mirror my aunt combed individuality into her bob. A bun could have been contrived to escape into black streamers blowing in the wind or in quiet wisps about her face, but only the older women in our picture album wear buns. She brushed her hair back from her forehead, tucking the flaps behind her ears. She looped a piece of thread, knotted into a circle between her index fingers and thumbs, and ran the double strand across her forehead. When she closed her fingers as if she were making a pair of shadow geese bite, the string twisted together catching the little hairs. Then she pulled the thread away from her skin, ripping the hairs out neatly, her eyes watering from the needles of pain. Opening her fingers, she cleaned the thread, then rolled it along her hairline and the tops of her eyebrows. My mother did the same to me and my sisters and herself. I used to believe that the expression "caught by the short hairs" meant a captive held with a depilatory string. It especially hurt at the temples, but my mother said we were lucky we didn't have to have our feet bound when we were seven. Sisters used to sit on their beds and cry together, she said, as their mothers or their slave removed the bandages for a few minutes each night and let the blood gush back into their veins. I hope that the man my aunt loved appreciated a smooth brow, that he wasn't just a tits-and-ass man.

Once my aunt found a freckle on her chin, at a spot that the almanac said predestined her for unhappiness. She dug it out with a hot needle and washed the wound with peroxide.

More attention to her looks than these pullings of hairs and pickings at spots would have caused gossip among the villagers. They owned work clothes and good clothes, and they wore good clothes for feasting the new seasons. But since a woman combing her hair hexes beginnings, my aunt rarely found an occasion to look her best. Women looked like great sea snails—the corded wood, babies, and laundry they carried were the whorls on their backs. The Chinese did not admire a bent back; goddesses and warriors stood straight. Still there must have been a marvelous freeing of beauty when a worker laid down her burden and stretched and arched.

Such commonplace loveliness, however, was not enough for my aunt. She dreamed of a lover for the fifteen days of New Year's, the time for families to exchange visits, money, and food. She plied her secret comb. And sure enough she cursed the year, the family, the village, and herself.

Even as her hair lured her imminent lover, many other men looked at her. Uncles, cousins, nephews, brothers would have looked, too, had they been home between journeys. Perhaps they had already been restraining their curiosity, and they left, fearful that their glances, like a field of nesting birds, might be startled and caught. Poverty hurt, and that was their first reason for leaving. But another, final reason for leaving the crowded house was the never-said.

She may have been unusually beloved, the precious only daughter, spoiled and mirror gazing because of the affection the family lavished on her. When her husband left, they welcomed the chance to take her back from the in-laws; she could live like the little daughter for just a while longer. There are stories that my grandfather was different from other people, "crazy ever since the little Jap bayoneted him in the head." He used to put his naked penis on the dinner table, laughing. And one day he brought home a baby girl, wrapped up inside his brown western-style greatcoat. He had traded one of his sons, probably my father, the youngest, for her. My grandmother made him trade back. When he finally got a daughter of his own, he doted on her. They must have all loved her, except perhaps my father, the only brother who never went back to China, having once been traded for a girl.

Brothers and sisters, newly men and women, had to efface their sexual color and present plain miens. Disturbing hair and eyes, a smile like no other, threatened the ideal of five generations living under one roof. To focus blurs, people shouted face to face and yelled from room to room. The immigrants I know have loud voices, unmodulated to American tones even after years away from the village where they called their friendships out across the fields. I have not been able to stop my mother's screams in public libraries or over telephones. Walking erect (knees straight, toes pointed forward, not pigeon-toed, which is Chinese-feminine) and speaking in an inaudible voice, I have tired to turn myself American-feminine. Chinese communication was loud, public. Only sick people had to whisper. But at the dinner table, where the family members came nearest one another, no one could talk, not the outcasts nor any eaters. Every word that falls from the mouth is a coin lost. Silently they gave and accepted food with both hands. A preoccupied child who took his bowl with one hand got a sideways glare. A complete moment of total attention is due everyone alike. Children and lovers have no singularity here, but my aunt used a secret voice, a separate attentiveness.

She kept the man's name to herself throughout her labor and dying; she did not accuse him that he be punished with her. To save her inseminator's name she gave silent birth.

He may have been somebody in her own household, but intercourse with a man outside the family would have been no less abhorrent. All the village were kinsmen, and the titles shouted in loud country voices never let kinship be forgotten. Any man within visiting distance would have been neutralized as a lover—"brother," "younger brother," "older brother"—one hundred and fifteen relationship titles. Parents researched birth charts probably not so much to assure good fortune as to circumvent incest in a population that has but one hundred surnames. Everybody has eight million relatives. How useless then sexual mannerisms, how dangerous.

As if it came from an atavism deeper than fear, I used to add "brother" silently to boys' names. It hexed the boys, who would or would not ask me to dance, and made them less scary and as familiar and deserving of benevolence as girls.

But, of course, I hexed myself also—no dates. I should have stood up; both arms waving, and shouted out across libraries, "Hey, you! Love me back." I had no idea, though, how to make attraction selective, how to control its direction and magnitude. If I made myself American-pretty so that the five or six Chinese boys in the class fell in love with me, everyone else—the Caucasian, Negro, and Japanese boys—would too. Sisterliness, dignified and honorable, made much more sense.

Attraction eludes control so stubbornly that whole societies designed to organize relationships among people cannot keep order, not even when they bind people to one another from childhood and raise them together. Among the very poor and the wealthy, brothers married their adopted sisters, like doves. Our family allowed some romance, paying adult brides' prices and providing dowries so that their sons and daughters could marry strangers. Marriage promises to turn strangers into friendly relatives—a nation of siblings.

In the village structure, spirits shimmered among the live creatures, balanced and held in equilibrium by time and land. But one human being flaring up into violence could open up a black hole, a maelstrom that pulled in the sky. The frightened villagers, who depended on one another to maintain the real, went to my aunt to show her a personal, physical representation of the break she had made in the "roundness." Misallying couples snapped off the future, which was to be embodied in true offspring. The villagers punished her for acting as if she could have a private life, secret and apart from them.

If my aunt had betrayed the family at a time of large grain yields and peace, when many boys were born, and wings were being built on many houses, perhaps she might have escaped such severe punishment. But the men—hungry, greedy, tired of planting in dry soil—had been forced to leave the village in order to send food-money home. There were ghost plagues, bandit plagues, wars with the Japanese, floods. My Chinese brother and sister had died of an unknown sickness. Adultery, perhaps only a mistake during good times, became a crime when the village needed food.

The round moon cakes and round doorways, the round tables of graduated size that fit one roundness inside another, round windows and rice bowls—these talismans had lost their power to warn this family of the law: a family must be whole, faithfully keeping the descent line by having sons to feed the old and the dead, who in turn look after the family. The villagers came to show my aunt and her lover-in-hiding a broken house. The villagers were speeding up the circling of events because she was too shortsighted to see that her infidelity had already harmed the village, that waves of consequences would return unpredictably, sometimes in disguise, as now, to hurt her. This roundness had to be made coin-sized so that she would see its circumference: punish her at the birth of her baby. Awaken her to the inexorable. People who refused fatalism because they could invent small resources insisted on culpability. Deny accidents and wrest fault from the stars.

After the villagers left, their lanterns now scattering in various directions toward home, the family broke their silence and cursed her. "Aiaa, we're going to die. Death is coming. Death is coming. Look what you've done. You've killed us. Ghost! Dead ghost! Ghost! You've never been born." She ran out into the fields, far enough from the house so that she could no longer hear their voices, and pressed herself against the earth, her own land no more. When she felt the birth coming, she thought that she had been hurt. Her body seized together. "They've hurt me too much," she thought. "This is gall, and it will kill me." With forehead and knees against the earth, her body convulsed and then relaxed. She turned on her back, lay on the ground. The black well of sky and stars went out and out and out forever; her body and her complexity seemed to disappear. She was one of the stars, a bright dot in blackness, without home, without a companion, in eternal cold and silence. An agoraphobia rose in her, speeding higher and higher, bigger and bigger; she would not be able to contain it; there would be no end to fear.

Flayed, unprotected against space, she felt pain return, focusing her body. This pain chilled her—a cold, steady kind of surface pain. Inside, spasmodically, the other pain, the pain of the child, heated her. For hours she lay on the ground, alternately body and space. Sometimes a vision of normal comfort obliterated reality: she saw the family in the evening gambling at the dinner table, the young people massaging their elders' backs.

She saw them congratulating one another, high joy on the mornings the rice shoots came up. When these pictures burst, the stars drew yet further apart. Black space opened.

She got to her feet to fight better and remembered that old-fashioned women gave birth in their pigsties to fool the jealous, pain-dealing gods, who do not snatch piglets. Before the next spasms could stop her, she ran to the pigsty, each step a rushing out into emptiness. She climbed over the fence and knelt in the dirt. It was good to have a fence enclosing her, a tribal person alone.

Laboring, this woman who had carried her child as a foreign growth that sickened her every day, expelled it at last. She reached down to touch the hot, wet, moving mass, surely smaller than anything human, and could feel that it was human after all—fingers, toes, nails, nose. She pulled it up on to her belly, and it lay curled there, butt in the air, feet precisely tucked one under the other. She opened her loose shirt and buttoned the child inside. After resting, it squirmed and thrashed and she pushed it up to her breast. It turned its head this way and that until it found her nipple. There, it made little snuffling noises. She clenched her teeth at its preciousness, lovely as a young calf, a piglet, a little dog.

She may have gone to the pigsty as a last act of responsibility: she would protect this child as she had protected its father. It would look after her soul, leaving supplies on her grave. But how would this tiny child without family find her grave when there would be no marker for her anywhere, neither in the earth nor the family hall? No one would give her a family hall name. She had taken the child with her into the wastes. At its birth the two of them had felt the same raw pain of separation, a wound that only the family pressing tight could close. A child with no descent line would not soften her life but only trail after her, ghostlike, begging her to give it purpose. At dawn the villagers on their way to the fields would stand around the fence and look.

Full of milk, the little ghost slept. When it awoke, she hardened her breasts against the milk that crying loosens. Toward morning she picked up the baby and walked to the well.

Carrying the baby to the well shows loving. Otherwise abandon it. Turn its face into the mud. Mothers who love their children take them along. It was probably a girl; there is some hope of forgiveness for boys.

"Don't tell anyone you had an aunt. Your father does not want to hear her name. She has never been born." I have believed that sex was unspeakable and words so strong and fathers so frail that "aunt" would do my father mysterious harm. I have thought that my family, having settled among immigrants who had also been their neighbors in the ancestral land, needed to clean their name, and a wrong word would incite the kinspeople even here. But there is more to this silence: they want me to participate in her punishment. And I have.

In the twenty years since I heard this story I have not asked for details nor said my aunt's name; I do not know it. People who can comfort the dead can also chase after them to hurt them further—a reverse ancestor worship. The real punishment was not the raid swiftly inflicted by the villagers, but the family's deliberately forgetting her. Her betrayal so maddened them, they saw to it that she would suffer forever, even after death. Always hungry, always needing, she would have to beg food from other ghosts, snatch and steal it from those whose living descendants give them gifts. She would have to fight the ghosts massed at crossroads for the buns a few thoughtful citizens leave to decoy her away from village and home so that the ancestral spirits could feast unharassed. At peace, they could act like gods, not ghosts, their descent lines providing them with paper suits and dresses, spirit money, paper houses, paper automobiles, chicken, meat, and rice into eternity—essences delivered up in smoke and flames, steam and incense rising from each rice bowl. In an attempt to make the Chinese care for people outside the family, Chairman Mao encourages us now to give our paper replicas to the spirits of outstanding soldiers and workers, no matter whose ancestors they may be. My aunt remains forever hungry. Goods are not distributed evenly among the dead.

My aunt haunts me—her ghost drawn to me because now, after fifty years of neglect, I alone devote pages of paper to her, though not origamied into houses and clothes. I do not think she always means me well. I am telling on her, and she was a spite suicide, drowning herself in the drinking water. The Chinese are always very frightened of the drowned one, whose weeping ghost, wet hair hanging and skin bloated, waits silently by the water to pull down a substitute.

Understanding and Analysis

1. What is the effect of beginning the essay with a direct quotation from Kingston's mother? Do you think that this story is actually a word-for-word quotation of her mother's tale?

2. What details about life in the Chinese village do you learn from this tale?

3. What did her mother hope to accomplish with this tale? Why is Kingston supposed to keep the tale a secret?

4. What does Kingston accomplish through her direct address of her Chinese-American readers?

5. What was the effect of poverty on the reaction of the villagers to adultery? What was the effect of poverty on Kingston as she grew up with this story?

6. What are the facts of the case, according to her mother? What facts are missing?

7. What are the various versions of the missing facts that Kingston imagines? How do these versions change the character of the aunt?

8. What do we learn about the Chinese village from the parts of the story that Kingston imagines?

9. What are the losses and gains for Kingston from the fact that she does not know the whole story?

10. What is the effect of the last paragraph? Why does Kingston refrain from making clear the significance of the well until the end of the essay?

Comparison

1. Read the essay by Milgram. Do you see any connections between Milgram's ideas about obedience and the story Kingston relates?

2. Read the essay by Momaday. Contrast the methods Momaday and Kingston use to describe beliefs and attitudes different from the prevailing cultural attitudes in America today. How much must each author imagine in order to fill in gaps in their knowledge?

3. Read essays by Greer, Brady, Geertz, Mead, Cofer, and Silko. Compare and contrast the roles of women as they are described in these essays and in Kingston's essay.

4. Read Postman's "Learning by Story" and Lopez's "Landscape and Narrative." How do these essays inform your reading of Kingston?

Barbara Tuchman
(1912–1989)

Barbara Wertheim was born in New York City on January 30, 1912, shortly after the inauguration of Woodrow Wilson, whose presidential campaign was "launch[ed]" by her maternal grandfather, Henry Morgenthau. For his trouble, Morgenthau received an offer to become the U.S. Ambassador to Turkey. In 1914, at the age of two, Barbara set sail for Constantinople to visit her grandfather with her parents and two siblings. En route, traveling in a "small Italian passenger steamer," she witnessed what Kathleen Bowman describes as the "first naval skirmish of World War I." Nearly fifty years later, she explains in *The Guns of August*, that she and her family arrived with "an exciting tale of the boom of guns, puffs of white smoke, and the twisting and maneuvering of faraway ships." According to Bowman, "Barbara Tuchman regards seeing that naval battle as the reason for her early interest in world events."

Feeding her interest, Tuchman read historical fiction voraciously from the age of six. When she enrolled at Radcliffe in 1929, she chose a major in History and Literature and produced an honors thesis called *The Moral Justification of the British Empire*. Some years later, when she "unearthed the thesis to look up a reference," as she explains in *Practicing History*, she recalled "*The Importance of Being Earnest*, when Cecily says that the letters she wrote to herself from her imaginary fiancé . . . were so beautiful and so badly spelled she could not reread them without crying. I felt the same way about my thesis: so beautiful—in intent—and so badly written." Soon enough, she was sharpening her writing skills on the job. Fresh out of school, she "went to work (as a volunteer—paying jobs did not hang from the trees in 1933) for the American Council of the Institute of Pacific Relations (IPR), an international organization of member countries bordering on the Pacific." After relocating to Tokyo, she assisted with the IPR's *The Economic Handbook of the Pacific* and published pieces in *Far Eastern Survey* and *Pacific Affairs*. Returning to the United States, she published a piece on Japan in the prestigious journal *Foreign Affairs* in 1936. In the same year, at the age of 24, she found work with the *Nation*, then owned by her father, Maurice Wertheim. For the *Nation*, she had to hone her skills in research, summary, and synthesis, as she investigated subjects utterly new to her, and she produced articles of 200 words under deadlines. In 1937, she went to Spain to cover the Spanish Civil War and remained in Europe until 1939, contributing to the Loyalist "bulletin" *War in Spain* and publishing her first book, *The Lost British Policy: Britain and Spain Since 1700* (1938). Through all these years of working as a journalist, she says, she finally learned to write.

In 1940, Barbara Wertheim married Dr. Lester Tuchman in New York. After the birth of her first daughter, Lucy, in 1941, she took a job with the Office of War Information, and her husband left the country with the Medical Corps. "Because of my experience in Japan, such as it was," she explains, "I was assigned to the Far East desk, whose task it was to explain the Pacific war and the extent of the American effort in Asia to our European listeners." After the war, Tuchman had two more daughters, Jessica and Alma, and "domesticity for a while prevailed." By 1948, she had started work on her second book, *Bible and Sword: England and Palestine from the Bronze Age to Balfour* (1956). According to *Contemporary Authors*, however, "[i]t wasn't until her third book, *The Zimmermann Telegram*, that Tuchman achieved success as a writer." Published in 1958, this was Tuchman's first book concerned with events in World War I; it was also a bestseller. For her next bestseller, *The Guns of August* (1962), Tuchman received a Pulitzer. In preparation for *The Guns of August*, she not only researched sources in libraries but also traveled to Europe, walked on the battlefields of the First World War, and as Bowman writes, "followed the route that the German army had taken in its bold struggle to reach Paris." In 1964, *The Guns of August* was adapted for the screen in the black-and-white "The War to End All Wars."

Retreating from World War I into its immediate past, Tuchman published *The Proud Tower: A Portrait of the World before the War, 1890–1914* (1966). With her next work, *Stilwell and the American Experience in China* (1971), she advanced into World War II and won her second Pulitzer Prize. In a speech at the National Archives Conference, she said: "My book on Stilwell is not really a military biography even though the protagonist is a soldier. The book is really two-in-one, like an egg with two yolks: Stilwell *and* the American Experience in China, with the man chosen to represent the experience." The year after *Stilwell*, Tuchman published *Notes from China* and wrote about Watergate in *The New York Times*. Over the next few years, she worked on a kind of parallel history of the twentieth century, *A Distant Mirror: The Calamitous Fourteenth Century* (1978). In the last decade of her life, she collected more than 30 pieces in *Practicing History: Selected Essays* (1981) and published *The March of Folly: From Troy to Vietnam* (1984). Her final book was *The First Salute: A View of the American Revolution* (1988). According to Seymour Brody, Tuchman "died of complications of a stroke on February 6, 1989, at her home."

One of the most popular historians of the twentieth century, Barbara Tuchman wrote books for readers. After "that initial failure with my thesis," she sought to generate excitement in her audience both by communicating her love of her subject and by actively working to create suspense in her narratives. (To create suspense in *The Guns of August*, for example, she "wrote as if [she] did not know who would win.") For telling history like a story, Tuchman has received the praise of many reviewers and the disdain of many academic historians. Despite her years of work, she has also been criticized as a stylist ("Mrs. Tuchman has a rather bland way of putting things," in the opinion of Christopher Lehmann-Haupt). Accepted on her own terms, however, Barbara Tuchman is, while certainly not another Tolstoy, nevertheless an impressive epic storyteller. And in her eyes, in an age of academic jargon, storytellers are exactly what the discipline of history needs: "new techniques [of writing history] will, I am sure, turn up suggestive material and open avenues of thought, but they will not, I think, transform history into a science, and they can never make it literature. Events happen; but to become history they must be communicated and understood. For that, history needs writers."

"This Is the End of the World": The Black Death (1978)

IN OCTOBER 1347, two months after the fall of Calais,[1] Genoese trading ships put into the harbor of Messina in Sicily with dead and dying men at the oars. The ships had come from the Black Sea port of Caffa (now Feodosiya) in the Crimea, where the Genoese maintained a trading post. The diseased sailors showed strange black swellings about the size of an egg or an apple in the armpits and groin. The swellings oozed blood and pus and were followed by spreading boils and black blotches on the skin from internal bleeding. The sick suffered severe pain and died quickly within five days of the first symptoms. As the disease spread, other symptoms of continuous fever and spitting of blood appeared instead of the swellings or buboes. These victims coughed and sweated heavily and died even more quickly, within three days or less, sometimes in 24 hours. In both types everything that issued from the body—breath, sweat, blood from the buboes and lungs, bloody urine, and blood-blackened excrement—smelled foul. Depression and despair accompanied the physical symptoms, and before the end "death is seen seated on the face."

The disease was bubonic plague, present in two forms: one that infected the bloodstream, causing the buboes and internal bleeding, and was spread by contact; and a second, more virulent pneumonic type that infected the lungs and was spread by respiratory infection. The presence of both at once cause the high mortality and speed of contagion. So lethal was the disease that cases were known of persons going to bed well and dying before they woke, of doctors catching the illness at a bedside and dying before the patient. So rapidly did it spread from one to another that to a French physician, Simon de Covino, it seemed as if one sick person "could infect the whole world." The malignity of the pestilence appeared more terrible because its victims knew no prevention and no remedy.

---

[1]*Calais* Edward III, king of England, declared himself king of France when he defeated the French at Calais.

The physical suffering of the disease and its aspect of evil mystery were expressed in a strange Welsh lament which saw "death coming into our midst like black smoke, a plague which cuts off the young, a rootless phantom which has no mercy for fair countenance. Woe is me of the shilling in the armpit! It is seething, terrible . . . a head that gives pain and causes a loud cry . . . a painful angry knob . . . Great is its seething like a burning cinder . . . a grievous thing of ashy color." Its eruption is ugly like the "seeds of black peas, broken fragments of brittle sea-coal . . . the early ornaments of black death, cinders of the peelings of the cockle weed, a mixed multitude, a black plague like halfpence, like berries. . . . "

Rumors of a terrible plague supposedly arising in China and spreading through Tartary (Central Asia) to India and Persia, Mesopotamia, Syria, Egypt, and all of Asia Minor had reached Europe in 1346. They told of a death toll so devastating that all of India was said to be depopulated, whole territories covered by dead bodies, other areas with no one left alive. As added up by Pope Clement VI at Avignon, the total of reported dead reached 23,840,000. In the absence of a concept of contagion, no serious alarm was felt in Europe until the trading ships brought their black burden of pestilence into Messina while other infected ships from the Levant carried it to Genoa and Venice.

By January 1348 it penetrated France via Marseille, and North Africa via Tunis. Shipborne along coasts and navigable rivers, it spread westward from Marseille through the ports of Languedoc to Spain and northward up the Rhône to Avignon, where it arrived in March. It reached Narbonne, Montpellier, Carcassonne, and Toulouse between February and May, and at the same time in Italy spread to Rome and Florence and their hinterlands. Between June and August it reached Bordeaux, Lyon, and Paris, spread to Burgundy and Normandy, and crossed the Channel from Normandy into southern England. From Italy during the same summer it crossed the Alps into Switzerland and reached eastward to Hungary.

In a given area the plague accomplished its kill within four to six months and then faded, except in the larger cities, where, rooting into the close-quartered population, it abated during the winter, only to reappear in spring and rage for another six months.

In 1349 it resumed in Paris, spread to Picardy, Flanders, and the Low Countries, and from England to Scotland and Ireland as well as to Norway, where a ghost ship with a cargo of wool and a dead crew drifted offshore until it ran aground near Bergen. From there the plague passed into Sweden, Denmark, Prussia, Iceland, and as far as Greenland. Leaving a strange pocket of immunity in Bohemia, and Russia unattacked until 1351, it had passed from most of Europe by mid-1350. Although the mortality rate was erratic, ranging from one fifth in some places to nine tenths or almost total elimination in others, the overall estimate of modern demographers has settled—for the area extending from India to Iceland—around the same figure expressed in Froissart's[2] casual words: "a third of the world died." His estimate, the common one at the time, was not an inspired guess but a borrowing of St. John's figure for mortality from plague in Revelation, the favorite guide to human affairs of the Middle Ages.

A third of Europe would have meant about 20 million deaths. No one knows in truth how many died. Contemporary reports were an awed impression, not an accurate count. In crowded Avignon, it was said, 400 died daily; 7,000 houses emptied by death were shut up; a single graveyard received 11,000 corpses in six weeks; half the city's inhabitants reportedly died, including 9 cardinals or one third of the total, and 70 lesser prelates.

---

[2]*Froissart* Jean Froissart, a fifteenth-century French historian and poet.

Watching the endlessly passing death carts, chroniclers let normal exaggeration take wings and put the Avignon death toll at 62,000 and even at 120,000, although the city's total population was probably less than 50,000.

When graveyards filled up, bodies at Avignon were thrown into the Rhône until mass burial pits were dug for dumping the corpses. In London in such pits corpses piled up in layers until they overflowed. Everywhere reports speak of the sick dying too fast for the living to bury. Corpses were dragged out of homes and left in front of doorways. Morning light revealed new piles of bodies. In Florence the dead were gathered up by the Compagnia della Misericordia—founded in 1244 to care for the sick—whose members wore red robes and hoods masking the face except for the eyes. When their efforts failed, the dead lay putrid in the streets for days at a time. When no coffins were to be had, the bodies were laid on boards, two or three at once, to be carried to graveyards or common pits. Families dumped their own relatives into the pits, or buried them so hastily and thinly "that dogs dragged them forth and devoured their bodies."

Amid accumulating death and fear of contagion, people died without last rites and were buried without prayers, a prospect that terrified the last hours of the stricken. A bishop in England gave permission to laymen to make confession to each other as was done by the Apostles, "or if no man is present then even to a woman," and if no priest could be found to administer extreme unction, "then faith must suffice." Clement VI found it necessary to grant remissions of sin to all who died of the plague because so many were unattended by priests. "And no bells tolled," wrote a chronicler of Siena, "and nobody wept no matter what his loss because almost everyone expected death. . . . And people said and believed, 'This is the end of the world,' "

In Paris, where the plague lasted through 1349, the reported death rate was 800 a day, in Pisa 500, in Vienna 500 to 600. The total dead in Paris numbered 50,000 or half the population. Florence, weakened by the famine of 1347, lost three to four fifths of its citizens, Venice two thirds, Hamburg and Bremen, though smaller in size, about the same proportion. Cities, as centers of transportation, were more likely to be affected than villages, although once a village was infected, its death rate was equally high. At Givry, a prosperous village in Burgundy of 1,200 to 1,500 people, the parish register records 615 deaths in the space of fourteen weeks, compared to an average of thirty deaths a year in the previous decade. In three villages of Cambridgeshire, manorial records show a death rate of 47 percent, 57 percent, and in one case 70 percent. When the last survivors, too few to carry on, moved away, a deserted village sank back into the wilderness and disappeared from the map altogether, leaving only a grass-covered ghostly outline to show where mortals once had lived.

In enclosed places such as monasteries and prisons, the infection of one person usually meant that of all, as happened in the Franciscan convents of Carcassonne and Marseille, where every inmate without exception died. Of the 140 Dominicans at Montpellier only seven survived. Petrarch's[3] brother Gherardo, member of a Carthusian monastery, buried the prior and 34 fellow monks one by one, sometimes three a day, until he was left alone with his dog and fled to look for a place that would take him in. Watching every comrade die, men in such places could not but wonder whether the strange peril that filled the air had not been sent to exterminate the human race. In Kilkenny, Ireland, Brother John Clyn of the Friars Minor, another monk left alone among dead men, kept

---

[3]*Petrarch* Francesco Petrarch, (1304–1374) Italian writer after whom Petrarchian sonnets are named.

a record of what had happened lest "things which should be remembered perish with time and vanish from the memory of those who come after us." Sensing "the whole world, as it were, placed within the grasp of the Evil One," and waiting for death to visit him too, he wrote, "I leave parchment to continue this work, if perchance any man survive and any of the race of Adam escape this pestilence and carry on the work which I have begun." Brother John, as noted by another hand, died of the pestilence, but he foiled oblivion.

The largest cities of Europe, with populations of about 100,000, were Paris and Florence, Venice and Genoa. At the next level, with more than 50,000, were Ghent and Bruges in Flanders, Milan, Bologna, Rome, Naples, and Palermo, and Cologne. London hovered below 50,000, the only city in England except York with more than 10,000. At the level of 20,000 to 50,000 were Bordeaux, Toulouse, Montpellier, Marseille, and Lyon in France, Barcelona, Seville, and Toledo in Spain, Siena, Pisa, and other secondary cities in Italy, and the Hanseatic trading cities of the Empire. The plague raged through them all, killing anywhere from one third to two thirds of their inhabitants. Italy, with a total population of 10 to 11 million, probably suffered the heaviest toll. Following the Florentine bankruptcies, the crop failures and workers' riots of 1346–47, the revolt of Cola di Rienzi that plunged Rome into anarchy, the plague came as the peak of successive calamities. As if the world were indeed in the grasp of the Evil One, its first appearance on the European mainland in January 1348 coincided with a fearsome earthquake that carved a path of wreckage from Naples up to Venice. Houses collapsed, church towers toppled, villages were crushed, and the destruction reached as far as Germany and Greece. Emotional response, dulled by horrors, underwent a kind of atrophy epitomized by the chronicler who wrote, "And in these days was burying without sorrowe and wedding without friendschippe."

In Siena, where more than half the inhabitants died of the plague, work was abandoned on the great cathedral, planned to be the largest in the world, and never resumed, owing to loss of workers and master masons and "the melancholy and grief" of the survivors. The cathedral's truncated transept still stands in permanent witness to the sweep of death's scythe. Agnolo di Tura, a chronicler of Siena, recorded the fear of contagion that froze every other instinct. "Father abandoned child, wife husband, one brother another," he wrote, "for this plague seemed to strike through the breath and sight. And so they died. And no one could be found to bury the dead for money or friendship. . . . And I, Angolo di Tura, called the Fat, buried my five children with my own hands, and so did many others likewise."

There were many to echo his account of inhumanity and few to balance it, for the plague was not the kind of calamity that inspired mutual help. Its loathsomeness and deadliness did not herd people together in mutual distress, but only prompted their desire to escape each other. "Magistrates and notaries refused to come and make the wills of the dying," reported a Franciscan friar of Piazza in Sicily; what was worse, "even the priests did not come to hear their confessions." A clerk of the Archbishop of Canterbury reported the same of English priests who "turned away from the care of their benefices from fear of death." Cases of parents deserting children and children their parents were reported across Europe from Scotland to Russia. The calamity chilled the hearts of men, wrote Boccaccio[4] in his famous account of the plague in Florence that serves as intro-

---

[4]*Boccaccio* Giovanni Boccaccio (1313–1375) Italian author of *The Decameron*, a series of stories told by ten people who flee Florence to escape the Black Death.

duction to the *Decameron*. "One man shunned another . . . kinsfolk held aloof, brother was forsaken by brother, oftentimes husband by wife; nay, what is more, and scarcely to be believed, fathers and mothers were found to abandon their own children to their fate, untended, unvisited as if they had been strangers." Exaggeration and literary pessimism were common in the 14th century, but the Pope's physician, Guy de Chauliac, was a sober, careful observer who reported the same phenomenon: "A father did not visit his son, nor the son his father. Charity was dead."

Yet not entirely. In Paris, according to the chronicler Jean de Venette, the nuns of the Hôtel Dieu or municipal hospital, "having no fear of death, tended the sick with all sweetness and humility." New nuns repeatedly took the places of those who died, until the majority "many times renewed by death now rest in peace with Christ as we may piously believe."

When the plague entered northern France in July 1348, it settled first in Normandy and, checked by winter, gave Picardy a deceptive interim until the next summer. Either in mourning or warning, black flags were flown from church towers of the worst-stricken villages of Normandy. "And in that time," wrote a monk of the abbey of Fourcarment, "the mortality was so great among the people of Normandy that those of Picardy mocked them." The same unneighborly reaction was reported of the Scots, separated by a winter's immunity from the English. Delighted to hear of the disease that was scourging the "southrons," they gathered forces for an invasion, "laughing at their enemies." Before they could move, the savage mortality fell upon them too, scattering some in death and the rest in panic to spread the infection as they fled.

In Picardy in the summer of 1349 the pestilence penetrated the castle of Coucy to kill Enguerrand's[5] mother, Catherine, and her new husband. Whether her nine-year-old son escaped by chance or was perhaps living elsewhere with one of his guardians is unrecorded. In nearby Amiens, tannery workers, responding quickly to losses in the labor force, combined to bargain for higher wages. In another place villagers were seen dancing to drums and trumpets, and on being asked the reason, answered that, seeing their neighbors die day by day while their village remained immune, they believed they could keep the plague from entering "by the jollity that is in us. That is why we dance." Further north in Tournai on the border of Flanders, Gilles li Muisis, Abbot of St. Martin's, kept one of the epidemic's most vivid accounts. The passing bells rang all day and all night, he recorded, because sextons were anxious to obtain their fees while they could. Filled with the sound of mourning, the city became oppressed by fear, so that the authorities forbade the tolling of bells and the wearing of black and restricted funeral services to two mourners. The silencing of funeral bells and of criers' announcements of deaths was ordained by most cities. Siena imposed a fine on the wearing of mourning clothes by all except widows.

Flight was the chief recourse of those who could afford it or arrange it. The rich fled to their country places like Boccaccio's young patricians of Florence, who settled in a pastoral palace "removed on every side from the roads" with "wells of cool water and vaults of rare wines." The urban poor died in their burrows, "and only the stench of their bodies informed neighbors of their death." That the poor were more heavily afflicted than the rich was clearly remarked at the time, in the north as in the south. A Scottish chronicler, John of Fordun, stated flatly that the pest "attacked especially the meaner sort and common peo-

[5]*Enguerrand* Enguerrand de Coucy, a French nobleman, is a main character in Tuchman's book.

ple—seldom the magnates." Simon de Covino of Montpellier made the same observation. He ascribed it to the misery and want and hard lives that made the poor more susceptible, which was half the truth. Close contact and lack of sanitation was the unrecognized other half. It was noticed too that the young died in greater proportion than the old; Simon de Covino compared the disappearance of youth to the withering of flowers in the fields.

In the countryside peasants dropped dead on the roads, in the fields, in their houses. Survivors in growing helplessness fell into apathy, leaving ripe wheat uncut and livestock untended. Oxen and asses, sheep and goats, pigs and chickens ran wild and they too, according to local reports, succumbed to the pest. English sheep, bearers of the precious wool, died throughout the country. The chronicler Henry Knighton, canon of Leicester Abbey, reported 5,000 dead in one field alone, "their bodies so corrupted by the plague that neither beast nor bird would touch them," and spreading an appalling stench. In the Austrian Alps wolves came down to prey upon sheep and then, "as if alarmed by some invisible warning, turned and fled back into the wilderness." In remote Dalmatia bolder wolves descended upon a plague-stricken city and attacked human survivors. For want of herdsmen, cattle strayed from place to place and died in hedgerows and ditches. Dogs and cats fell like the rest.

The dearth of labor held a fearful prospect because the 14th century lived close to the annual harvest both for food and for next year's seed. "So few servants and laborers were left," wrote Knighton, "that no one knew where to turn for help." The sense of a vanishing future created a kind of dementia of despair. A Bavarian chronicler of Neuberg on the Danube recorded that "Men and women . . . wandered around as if mad" and let their cattle stray "because no one had any inclination to concern themselves about the future." Fields went uncultivated, spring seed unsown. Second growth with nature's awful energy crept back over cleared land, dikes crumbled, salt water reinvaded and soured the lowlands. With so few hands remaining to restore the work of centuries, people felt, in Walsingham's words, that "the world could never again regain its former prosperity."

Though the death rate was higher among the anonymous poor, the known and the great died too. King Alfonso XI of Castile was the only reigning monarch killed by the pest, but his neighbor King Pedro of Aragon lost his wife, Queen Leonora, his daughter Marie, and a niece in the space of six months. John Cantacuzene, Emperor of Byzantium, lost his son. In France the lame Queen Jeanne and her daughter-in-law Bonne de Luxemburg, wife of the Dauphin, both died in 1349 in the same phase that took the life of Enguerrand's mother. Jeanne, Queen of Navarre, daughter of Louis X, was another victim. Edward III's second daughter, Joanna, who was on her way to marry Pedro, the heir of Castile, died in Bordeaux. Women appear to have been more vulnerable than men, perhaps because, being more housebound, they were more exposed to fleas. Boccaccio's mistress Fiammetta, illegitimate daughter of the King of Naples, died, as did Laura, the beloved—whether real or fictional—of Petrarch. Reaching out to us in the future, Petrarch cried, "Oh happy posterity who will not experience such abysmal woe and will look upon our testimony as a fable."

In Florence Giovanni Villani, the great historian of his time, died at 68 in the midst of an unfinished sentence: " . . . e dure questo pistolenza fino a . . . (in the midst of this pestilence there came to an end . . .)." Siena's master painters, the brothers Ambrogio and Pietro Lorenzetti, whose names never appear after 1348, presumably perished in the plague, as did Andrea Pisano, architect and sculptor of Florence. William of Ockham and the English mystic Richard Rolle of Hampole both disappear from mention after 1349. Francisco Datini, merchant of Prato, lost both his parents and two siblings. Curious sweeps of mortality afflicted certain bodies of merchants in London. All eight wardens of the

Company of Cutters, all six wardens of the Hatters, and four wardens of the Goldsmiths died before July 1350. Sir John Pulteney, master draper and four times Mayor of London, was a victim, likewise Sir John Montgomery, Governor of Calais.

Among the clergy and doctors the mortality was naturally high because of the nature of their professions. Out of 24 physicians in Venice, 20 were said to have lost their lives in the plague, although, according to another account, some were believed to have fled or to have shut themselves up in their houses. At Montpellier, site of the leading medieval medical school, the physician Simon de Covino reported that, despite the great number of doctors, "hardly one of them escaped." In Avignon, Guy de Chauliac confessed that he performed his medical visits only because he dared not stay away for fear of infamy, but "I was in continual fear." He claimed to have contracted the disease but to have cured himself by his own treatment; if so, he was one of the few who recovered.

Clerical mortality varied with rank. Although the one-third toll of cardinals reflects the same proportion as the whole, this was probably due to their concentration in Avignon. In England, in strange and almost sinister procession, the Archbishop of Canterbury, John Stratford, died in August 1348, his appointed successor died in May 1349, and the next appointee three months later, all three within a year. Despite such weird vagaries, prelates in general managed to sustain a higher survival rate than the lesser clergy. Among bishops the deaths have been estimated at about one in twenty. The loss of priests, even if many avoided their fearful duty of attending the dying, was about the same as among the population as a whole.

Government officials, whose loss contributed to the general chaos, found, on the whole, no special shelter. In Siena four of the nine members of the governing oligarchy died, in France one third of the royal notaries, in Bristol 15 out of the 52 members of the Town Council or almost one third. Tax-collecting obviously suffered, with the result that Philip VI was unable to collect more than a fraction of the subsidy granted him by the Estates in the winter of 1347–48.

Lawlessness and debauchery accompanied the plague as they had during the great plague of Athens of 430 B.C., when according to Thucydides, men grew bold in the indulgence of pleasure: "For seeing how the rich died in a moment and those who had nothing immediately inherited their property, they reflected that life and riches were alike transitory and they resolved to enjoy themselves while they could." Human behavior is timeless. When St. John had his vision of plague in Revelation, he knew from some experience or race memory that those who survived "repented not of the work of their hands. . . . Neither repented they of their murders, nor of their sorceries, nor of their fornication, nor of their thefts."

Ignorance of the cause augmented the sense of horror. Of the real carriers, rats and fleas, the 14th century had no suspicion, perhaps because they were so familiar. Fleas, though a common household nuisance, are not once mentioned in contemporary plague writings, and rats only incidentally, although folklore commonly associated them with pestilence. The legend of the Pied Piper arose from an outbreak of 1284. The actual plague bacillus, *Pasturella pestis,* remained undiscovered for another 500 years. Living alternately in the stomach of the flea and the bloodstream of the rat who was the flea's host, the bacillus in its bubonic form was transferred to humans and animals by the bite of either rat or flea. It traveled by virtue of Rattus rattus, the small medieval black rat that lived on ships, as well as by the heavier brown or sewer rat. What precipitated the turn of the bacillus from innocuous to virulent form is unknown, but the occurrence is now believed to have taken place not in China but somewhere in central Asia and to have spread along the caravan routes. Chinese origin was a mistaken notion of the 14th century based on real but belated reports of huge death tolls in China from drought, famine, and pestilence which have since been traced to the 1330s, too soon to be responsible for the plague that appeared in India in 1346.

The phantom enemy had no name. Called the Black Death only in later recurrences, it was known during the first epidemic simply as the Pestilence or Great Mortality. Reports from the East, swollen by fearful imaginings, told of strange tempests and "sheets of fire" mingled with huge hailstones that "slew almost all," or a "vast rain of fire" that burned up men, beasts, stones, trees, villages, and cities. In another version, "foul blasts of wind" from the fires carried the infection to Europe "and now as some suspect it cometh round the seacoast." Accurate observation in this case could not make the mental jump to ships and rats because no idea of animal- or insect-borne contagion existed.

The earthquake was blamed for releasing sulfurous and foul fumes from the earth's interior, or as evidence of a titanic struggle of planets and oceans causing waters to rise and vaporize until fish died in masses and corrupted the air. All these explanations had in common a factor of poisoned air, of miasmas and thick, stinking mists traced to every kind of natural or imagined agency from stagnant lakes to malign conjunction of the planets, from the hand of the Evil One to the wrath of God. Medical thinking, trapped in the theory of astral influences, stressed air as the communicator of disease, ignoring sanitation or visible carriers. The existence of two carriers confused the trail, the more so because the flea could live and travel independently of the rat for as long as a month and, if infected by the particularly virulent septicemic form of the bacillus, could infect humans without reinfecting itself from the rat. The simultaneous presence of the pneumonic form of the disease, which was indeed communicated through the air, blurred the problem further.

The mystery of the contagion was "the most terrible of all the terrors," as an anonymous Flemish cleric in Avignon wrote to a correspondent in Bruges. Plagues had been known before, from the plague of Athens (believed to have been typhus) to the prolonged epidemic of the 6th century A.D., to the recurrence of sporadic outbreaks in the 12th and 13th centuries, but they had left no accumulated store of understanding. That the infection came from contact with the sick or with their houses, clothes, or corpses was quickly observed but not comprehended. Gentile da Foligno, renowned physician of Perugia and doctor of medicine at the universities of Bologna and Padua, came close to respiratory infection when he surmised that poisonous material was "communicated by means of air breathed out and in." Having no idea of microscopic carriers, he had to assume that the air was corrupted by planetary influences. Planets, however, could not explain the ongoing contagion. The agonized search for an answer gave rise to such theories as transference by sight. People fell ill, wrote Guy de Chauliac, not only by remaining with the sick but "even by looking at them." Three hundred years later Joshua Barnes, the 17th century biographer of Edward III, could write that the power of infection had entered into beams of light and "darted death from the eyes."

Doctors struggling with the evidence could not break away from the terms of astrology, to which they believed all human physiology was subject. Medicine was the one aspect of medieval life, perhaps because of its links with the Arabs, not shaped by Christian doctrine. Clerics detested astrology, but could not dislodge its influence. Guy de Chauliac, physician to three popes in succession, practiced in obedience to the zodiac. While his *Cirurgia* was the major treatise on surgery of its time, while he understood the use of anesthesia made from the juice of opium, mandrake, or hemlock, he nevertheless prescribed bleeding and purgatives by the planets and divided chronic from acute diseases on the basis of one being under the rule of the sun and the other of the moon.

In October 1348 Philip VI asked the medical faculty of the University of Paris for a report on the affliction that seemed to threaten human survival. With careful thesis, antithesis, and proofs, the doctors ascribed it to a triple conjunction of Saturn, Jupiter, and Mars in the 40th degree of Aquarius said to have occurred on March 20, 1345. They acknowledged, however, effects "whose cause is hidden from even the most highly trained intellects." The verdict of the masters of Paris became the official version. Borrowed, copied by scribes, carried abroad, translated from Latin into various vernaculars, it was everywhere accepted, even by the Arab physicians of Cordova and Granada, as the scientific if not the popular answer. Because of the terrible interest of the subject, the translations of the plague tracts stimulated use of national languages. In that one respect, life came from death.

To the people at large there could be but one explanation—the wrath of God. Planets might satisfy the learned doctors, but God was closer to the average man. A scourge so sweeping and unsparing without any visible cause could only be seen as Divine punishment upon mankind for its sins. It might even be God's terminal disappointment in his creature. Matteo Villani compared the plague to the Flood in ultimate purpose and believed he was recording "the extermination of mankind." Efforts to appease Divine wrath took many forms, as when the city of Rouen ordered that everything that could anger God, such as gambling, cursing, and drinking, must be stopped. More general were the penitent processions authorized at first by the Pope, some lasting as long as three days, some attended by as many as 2,000, which everywhere accompanied the plague and helped to spread it.

Barefoot in sackcloth, sprinkled with ashes, weeping, praying, tearing their hair, carrying candles and relics, sometimes with ropes around their necks or beating themselves with whips, the penitents wound through the streets, imploring the mercy of the Virgin and saints at their shrines. In a vivid illustration for the *Très Riches Heures* of the Duc de Berry, the Pope is shown in a penitent procession attended by four cardinals in scarlet from hat to hem. He raises both arms in supplication to the angel on top of the Castel Sant'Angelo, while white-robed priests bearing banners and relics in golden cases turn to look as one of their number, stricken by the plague, falls to the ground, his face contorted with anxiety. In the rear, a gray-clad monk falls beside another victim already on the ground as the townspeople gaze in horror. (Nominally the illustration represents a 6th century plague in the time of Pope Gregory the Great, but as medieval artists made no distinction between past and present, the scene is shown as the artist would have seen it in the 14th century.) When it became evident that these processions were sources of infection, Clement VI had to prohibit them.

In Messina, where the plague first appeared, the people begged the Archbishop of neighboring Catania to lend them the relics of St. Agatha. When the Catanians refused to let the relics go, the Archbishop dipped them in holy water and took the water himself to Messina, where he carried it in a procession with prayers and litanies through the streets. The demonic, which shared the medieval cosmos with God, appeared as "demons in the shape of dogs" to terrify the people. "A black dog with a drawn sword in his paws appeared among them, gnashing his teeth and rushing upon them and breaking all the silver vessels and lamps and candlesticks on the altars and casting them hither and thither. . . . So the people of Messina, terrified by this prodigious vision, were all strangely overcome by fear."

The apparent absence of earthly cause gave the plague a supernatural and sinister quality. Scandinavians believed that a Pest Maiden emerged from the mouth of the dead in the form of a blue flame and flew through the air to infect the next house. In Lithuania the Maiden was said to wave a red scarf through the door or window to let in the pest. One brave man, according to legend, deliberately waited at his open window with drawn sword and, at the fluttering of the scarf, chopped off the hand. He died of his deed, but his village was spared and the scarf long preserved as a relic in the local church.

Beyond demons and superstition the final hand was God's. The Pope acknowledged it in a Bull of September 1348, speaking of the "pestilence with which God is afflicting the Christian people." To the Emperor John Cantacuzene it was manifest that a malady of such horrors, stenches, and agonies, and especially one bringing the dismal despair that settled upon its victims before they died, was not a plague "natural" to mankind but "a chastisement from Heaven." To Piers Plowman[6] "these pestilences were for pure sin."

The general acceptance of this view created an expanded sense of guilt, for if the plague were punishment there had to be terrible sin to have occasioned it. What sins were on the 14th century conscience? Primarily greed, the sin of avarice, followed by usury, worldliness, adultery, blasphemy, falsehood, luxury, irreligion. Giovanni Villani, attempting to account for the cascade of calamity that had fallen upon Florence, concluded that it was retribution for the sins of avarice and usury that oppressed the poor. Pity and anger about the condition of the poor, especially victimization of the peasantry in war, was often expressed by writers of the time and was certainly on the conscience of the century. Beneath it all was the daily condition of medieval life, in which hardly an act or thought, sexual, mercantile, or military, did not contravene the dictates of the Church. Mere failure to fast or attend mass was sin. The result was an underground lake of guilt in the soul that the plague now tapped.

That the mortality was accepted as God's punishment may explain in part the vacuum of comment that followed the Black Death. An investigator has noticed that in the archives of Périgord[7] references to the war are innumerable, to the plague few. Froissart mentions the great death but once, Chaucer[8] gives it barely a glance. Divine anger so great that it contemplated the extermination of man did not bear close examination.

Efforts to cope with the epidemic availed little, either in treatment or prevention. Helpless to alleviate the plague, the doctors' primary effort was to keep it at bay, chiefly by burning aromatic substances to purify the air. The leader of Christendom, Pope Clement VI, was preserved in health by this method, though for an unrecognized reason: Clement's doctor, Guy de Chauliac, ordered that two huge fires should burn in the papal apartments and required the Pope to sit between them in the heat of the Avignon summer. This drastic treatment worked, doubtless because it discouraged the attention of fleas and also because de Chauliac required the Pope to remain isolated in his chambers. Their lovely murals of gardens, hunting, and other secular joys, painted at Clement's command, perhaps gave him some refreshment. A Pope of prodigal splendor and "sensual vices," Clement was also a man of great learning and a patron of arts and science who now encouraged dissections of the dead "in order that the origins of this disease might be known." Many were performed in Avignon as well as in Florence, where the city authorities paid for corpses to be delivered to physicians for this purpose.

Doctors' remedies in the 14th century ranged from the empiric and sensible to the magical, with little distinction made between one and the other. Though medicine was

---

[6]*Piers Plowman* the title character of a well-known medieval poem by William Langland (b. 1332).

[7]*Perigord* a French city.

[8]*Chaucer* Geoffrey Chaucer (1343–1400) an English writer best known for *The Canterbury Tales.*

barred by the Church from investigation of anatomy and physiology and from dissection of corpses, the classical anatomy of Galen, transferred through Arab treatises, was kept alive in private anatomy lessons. The need for knowledge was able sometimes to defy the Church: in 1340 Montpellier authorized an anatomy class every two years which lasted for several days and consisted of a surgeon dissecting a cadaver while a doctor of medicine lectured.

Otherwise, the theory of humors, along with astrology, governed practice. All human temperaments were considered to belong to one or another of the four humors—sanguine, phlegmatic, choleric, and melancholic. In various permutations with the signs of the zodiac, each of which governed a particular part of the body, the humors and constellations determined the degrees of bodily heat, moisture, and proportion of masculinity and femininity of each person.

Notwithstanding all their charts and stars, and medicaments barely short of witches' brews, doctors gave great attention to diet, bodily health, and mental attitude. Nor were they lacking in practical skills. They could set broken bones, extract teeth, remove bladder stones, remove cataracts of the eye with a silver needle, and restore a mutilated face by skin graft from the arm. They understood epilepsy and apoplexy as spasms of the brain. They used urinalysis and pulse beat for diagnosis,knew what substances served as laxatives and diuretics, applied a truss for hernia, a mixture of oil, vinegar, and sulfur for toothache, and ground peony root with oil of roses for headache.

For ills beyond their powers they fell back on the supernatural or on elaborate compounds of metallic, botanic, and animal substances. The offensive, like the expensive, had extra value. Ringworm was treated by washing the scalp with a boy's urine, gout by a plaster of goat dung mixed with rosemary and honey. Relief of the patient was their object—cure being left to God—and psychological suggestion often their means. To prevent pockmarks, a smallpox patient would be wrapped in red cloth in a bed hung with red hangings. When surgery was unavailing, recourse was had to the aid of the Virgin or the relics of saints.

In their purple or red gowns and furred hoods, doctors were persons of important status. Allowed extra luxury by the sumptuary laws, they wore belts of silver thread, embroidered gloves, and, according to Petrarch's annoyed report, presumptuously donned golden spurs when they rode to their visits attended by a servant. Their wives were permitted greater expenditure on clothes than other women, perhaps in recognition of the large fees doctors could command. Not all were learned professors. Boccaccio's Doctor Simon was a proctologist who had a chamber pot painted over his door to indicate his specialty.

When it came to the plague, sufferers were treated by various measures designed to draw poison or infection from the body: by bleeding, purging with laxatives or enemas, lancing or cauterizing the buboes, or application of hot plasters. None of this was of much use. Medicines ranged from pills of powdered stag's horn or myrrh and saffron to potions of potable gold. Compounds of rare spices and powdered pearls or emeralds were prescribed, possibly on the theory, not unknown to modern medicine, that a patient's sense of therapeutic value is in proportion to the expense.

Doctors advised that floors should be sprinkled, and hands, mouth, and nostrils washed with vinegar and rosewater. Bland diets, avoidance of excitement and anger especially at bedtime, mild exercise, and removal wherever possible from swamps and other sources of dank air were all recommended. Pomanders made of exotic compounds were to be carried on going out, probably more as antidote to the plague's odors than to its contagion. Conversely, in the curious belief that latrine attendants were immune, many people visited the public latrines on the theory that foul odors were efficacious . . .

St. Roch, credited with special healing powers, who had died in 1327, was the particular saint associated with the plague. Inheriting wealth as a young man, as had St. Francis, he had distributed it to the poor and to hospitals, and while returning from a pilgrimage to Rome had encountered an epidemic and stayed to help the sick. Catching the malady himself, he retreated to die alone in the woods, where a dog brought him bread each day. "In these sad times," says his legend, "when reality was so somber and men so hard, people ascribed pity to animals." St. Roch recovered and, on appearing in rags as a beggar, was thought to be a spy and thrown into jail, where he died, filling the cell with a strange light. As his story spread and sainthood was conferred, it was believed that God would cure of the plague anyone who invoked his name. When this failed to occur, it enhanced the belief that, men having grown too wicked, God indeed intended their end. As Langland wrote,

> God is deaf now-a-days and deigneth not hear us,
> And prayers have no power the Plague to stay.

In a terrible reversal, St. Roch and other saints now came to be considered a source of the plague, as instruments of God's wrath. "In the time of that great mortality in the year of our Lord 1348," wrote a professor of law named Bartolus of Sassoferrato, "the hostility of God was stronger than the hostility of man." But he was wrong.

The hostility of man proved itself against the Jews. On charges that they were poisoning the wells, with intent "to kill and destroy the whole of Christendom and have lordship over all the world," the lynchings began in the spring of 1348 on the heels of the first plague deaths. The first attacks occurred in Narbonne and Carcassonne, where Jews were dragged from their houses and thrown into bonfires. While Divine punishment was accepted as the plague's source, people in their misery still looked for a human agent upon whom to vent the hostility that could not be vented on God. The Jew, as the eternal stranger, was the most obvious target. He was the outsider who had separated himself by choice from the Christian world, whom Christians for centuries had been taught to hate, who was regarded as imbued with unsleeping malevolence against all Christians. Living in a distinct group of his own kind in a particular street or quarter, he was also the most feasible target, with property to loot as a further inducement.

The accusation of well-poisoning was as old as the plague of Athens, when it had been applied to the Spartans, and as recent as the epidemics of 1320–21, when it had been applied to the lepers. At that time the lepers were believed to have acted at the instigation of the Jews and the Moslem King of Granada, in a great conspiracy of outcasts to destroy Christians. Hundreds were rounded up and burned throughout France in 1322 and the Jews heavily punished by an official fine and unofficial attacks. When the plague came, the charge was instantly revived against the Jews:

> . . . rivers and fountains
> That were clear and clean
> They poisoned in many places . . .

wrote the French court poet Guillaume de Machaut.

The antagonism had ancient roots. The Jew had become the object of popular animosity because the early Church, as an offshoot of Judaism striving to replace the parent, had to make him so. His rejection of Christ as Saviour and his dogged refusal to accept the new law of the Gospel in place of the Mosaic law made the Jew a perpetual insult to the newly established Church, a danger who must be kept distinct and apart from the Christian community. This was the purpose of the edicts depriving Jews of their civil rights issued by the early Church Councils in the 4th century as soon as Christianity became the state religion. Separation was a two-way street, since, to the Jews, Christianity was at first a dissident sect, then an apostasy with which they wanted no contact.

The theory, emotions, and justifications of anti-Semitism were laid at that time—in the canon law codified by the Councils; in the tirades of St. John Chrysostom, Patriarch of Antioch, who denounced the Jews as Christ-killers; in the judgment of St. Augustine, who declared the Jews to be "outcasts" for failing to accept redemption by Christ. The Jew's dispersion was regarded as their punishment for unbelief.

The period of active assault began with the age of the crusades, when all Europe's intramural antagonisms were gathered into one bolt aimed at the infidel. On the theory that the "infidel at home" should likewise be exterminated, massacres of Jewish communities marked the crusaders' march to Palestine. The capture of the Holy Sepulcher by the Moslems was blamed on "the wickedness of the Jews," and the cry "HEP! HEP!" for *Hierosolyma est Perdita* (Jerusalem is lost) became the call for murder. What man victimizes he fears; thus, the Jews were pictured as fiends filled with hatred of the human race, which they secretly intended to destroy.

The question whether Jews had certain human rights, under the general proposition that God created the world for all men including infidels, was given different answers by different thinkers. Officially the Church conceded some rights: that Jews should not be condemned without trial, their synagogues and cemeteries should not be profaned, their property not be robbed with impunity. In practice this meant little because, as non-citizens of the universal Christian state, Jews were not allowed to bring charges against Christians, nor was Jewish testimony allowed to prevail over that of Christians. Their legal status was that of serfs of the king, though without reciprocal obligations on the part of the overlord. The doctrine that Jews were doomed to perpetual servitude as Christ-killers was announced by Pope Innocent III in 1205 and led Thomas Aquinas to conclude with relentless logic that "since Jews are the slaves of the Church, she can dispose of their possessions." Legally, politically, and physically, they were totally vulnerable.

They maintained a place in society because as moneylenders they performed a role essential to the kings' continuous need of money. Excluded by the guilds from crafts and trades, they had been pushed into petty commerce and moneylending although theoretically barred from dealing with Christians. Theory, however, bends to convenience, and Jews provided Christians with a way around their self-imposed ban on using money to make money.

Since they were damned anyway, they were permitted to lend at interest rates of 20 percent and more, of which the royal treasury took the major share. The increment to the crown was in fact a form of indirect taxation; as its instruments, the Jews absorbed an added measure of popular hate. They lived entirely dependent upon the king's protection, subject to confiscations and expulsions and the hazards of royal favor. Nobles and prelates followed the royal example, entrusting money to the Jews for lending and taking most of the profits, while deflecting popular resentment upon the agent. To the common man the Jews were not only Christ-killers but rapacious, merciless monsters, symbols of the new force of money that was changing old ways and dissolving old ties.

As commerce swelled in the 12th and 13th centuries, increasing the flow of money, the Jews' position deteriorated in proportion as they were less needed. They could not deal in the great sums that Christian banking houses like the Bardi of Florence could command. Kings and princes requiring ever larger amounts now turned to the Lombards and wealthy merchants for loans and relaxed their protection of the Jews or, when in need of hard cash, decreed their expulsion while confiscating their property and the debts owed to them. At the same time, with the advent of the Inquisition in the 13th century, religious intolerance waxed, leading to the charge of ritual murder against the Jews and the enforced wearing of a distinctive badge.

The belief that Jews performed ritual murder of Christian victims, supposedly from a compulsion to re-enact the Crucifixion, began in the 12th century and developed into the belief that they held secret rites to desecrate the host. Promoted by popular preachers, a mythology of blood grew in a mirror image of the Christian ritual of drinking the blood of the Saviour. Jews were believed to kidnap and torture Christian children, whose blood they drank for a variety of sinister purposes ranging from sadism and sorcery to the need, as unnatural beings, for Christian blood to give them a human appearance. Though bitterly refuted by the rabbis and condemned by emperor and pope, the blood libel took possession of the popular mind most rabidly in Germany where the well-poisoning charge too had originated in the 12th century. The blood libel formed the subject of Chaucer's tale of a child martyr told by the Prioresse and was the ground on which many Jews were charged, tried, and burned at the stake.

Under the zeal of St. Louis, whose life's object was the greater glory and fulfilment of Christian doctrine, Jewish life in France was narrowed and harassed by mounting restrictions. The famous trial of the Talmud for heresy and blasphemy took place in Paris in 1240 during his reign, ending in foreordained conviction and burning of 24 cartloads of Talmudic works. One of the disputants in the case was Rabbi Moses ben Jacob of Coucy, intellectual leader of the northern Jewish community in the time of Enguerrand III.

Throughout the century the Church multiplied decrees designed to isolate Jews from Christian society, on the theory that contact with them brought the Christian faith into disrepute. Jews were forbidden to employ Christians as servants, to serve as doctors to Christians, to intermarry, to sell flour, bread, wine, oil, shoes, or any article of clothing to Christians, to deliver or receive goods, to build new synagogues, to hold or claim land for non-payment of mortgage. The occupations from which guild rules barred them included weaving, metal-working, mining, tailoring, shoemaking, goldsmithing, baking, milling, carpentry. To mark their separation, Innocent III in 1215 decreed the wearing of a badge, usually in the form of a wheel or circular patch of yellow felt, said to represent a piece of money. Sometimes green or red-and-white, it was worn by both sexes beginning between the ages of seven and fourteen. In its struggle against all heresy and dissent, the 13th century Church imposed the same badge on Moslems, on convicted heretics, and, by some quirk in doctrine, on prostitutes. A hat with a point rather like a horn, said to represent the Devil, was later added further to distinguish the Jews.

Expulsions and persecutions were marked by one constant factor—seizure of Jewish property. As the chronicler William of Newburgh wrote of the massacre of York in 1190, the slaughter was less the work of religious zeal than of bold and covetous men who wrought "the business of their own greed." The motive was the same for official expulsion by towns or kings. When the Jews drifted back to resettle in villages, market towns and particularly in cities, they continued in moneylending and retail trade, kept pawnshops, found an occupation as gravediggers, and lived close together in a narrow Jewish quarter for mutual protection. In Provence, drawing on their contact with the Arabs of Spain and North Africa, they were scholars and sought-after physicians. But the vigorous inner life of their earlier communities had faded. In an excitable period they lived on the edge of assault that was always imminent. It was understood that the Church could "justly ordain war upon them" as enemies of Christendom.

In the torment of the plague it was easy to credit Jewish malevolence with poisoning the wells. In 1348 Clement VI issued a Bull prohibiting the killing, looting, or forcible conversion of Jews without trial, which halted the attacks in Avignon and the Papal States but was ignored as the rage swept northward. Authorities in most places tried at first to protect the Jews, but succumbed to popular pressure, not without an eye to potential forfeit of Jewish property.

In Savoy, where the first formal trials were held in September 1348, the Jews' property was confiscated while they remained in prison pending investigation of charges. Composed from confessions extracted by torture according to the usual medieval method, the charges drew a picture of an international Jewish conspiracy emanating from Spain, with messengers from Toledo carrying poison in little packets or in a "narrow stitched leather bag." The messengers allegedly brought rabbinical instructions for sprinkling the poison in wells and springs, and consulted with their co-religionists in secret meetings. Duly found guilty, the accused were condemned to death. Eleven Jews were burned alive and the rest subjected to a tax of 160 florins every month over the next six years for permission to remain in Savoy.

The confessions obtained in Savoy, distributed by letter from town to town, formed the basis for a wave of accusations and attacks throughout Alsace, Switzerland, and Germany. At a meeting of representatives of Alsatian towns, the oligarchy of Strasbourg attempted to refute the charges but were overwhelmed by the majority demanding reprisal and expulsion. The persecutions of the Black Death were not all spontaneous outbursts but action seriously discussed beforehand.

Again Pope Clement attempted to check the hysteria in a Bull of September 1348 in which he said that Christians who imputed the pestilence to the Jews had been "seduced by that liar, the Devil," and that the charge of well-poisoning and ensuing massacres were a "horrible thing." He pointed out that "by a mysterious decree of God" the plague was afflicting all peoples, including Jews; that it raged in places where no Jews lived, and that elsewhere they were victims like everyone else; therefore the charge that they caused it was "without plausibility." He urged the clergy to take Jews under their protection as he himself offered to do in Avignon, but his voice was hardly heard against local animus.

In Basle on January 9, 1349, the whole community of several hundred Jews was burned in a wooden house especially constructed for the purpose on an island in the Rhine, and a decree was passed that no Jew should be allowed to settle in Basle for 200 years. In Strasbourg the Town Council, which opposed persecution, was deposed by vote of the guilds and another was elected, prepared to comply with the popular will. In February 1349, before the plague had yet reached the city, the Jews of Strasbourg, numbering 2,000, were taken to the burial ground, where all except those who accepted conversion were burned at rows of stakes erected to receive them.

By now another voice was fomenting attack upon the Jews. The flagellants had appeared. In desperate supplication for God's mercy, their movement erupted in a sudden frenzy that sped across Europe with the same fiery contagion as the plague. Self-flagellation was intended to express remorse and expiate the sins of all. As a form of penance to induce God to forgive sin, it long antedated the plague years. The flagellants saw themselves as redeemers who, by re-enacting the scourging of Christ upon their own bodies and making the blood flow, would atone for human wickedness and earn another chance for mankind.

Organized groups of 200 to 300 and sometimes more (the chroniclers mention up to 1,000) marched from city to city, stripped to the waist, scourging themselves with leather whips tipped with iron spikes until they bled. While they cried aloud to Christ and the

Virgin for pity, and called upon God to "Spare us!", the watching townspeople sobbed and groaned in sympathy. These bands put on regular performances three times a day, twice in public in the church square and a third in privacy. Organized under a lay Master for a stated period, usually 33 1/2 days to represent Christ's years on earth, the participants were required to pledge self-support at 4 pence a day or other fixed rate and to swear obedience to the Master. They were forbidden to bathe, shave, change their clothes, sleep in beds, talk or have intercourse with women without the Master's permission. Evidently this was not withheld, since the flagellants were later charged with orgies in which whipping combined with sex. Women accompanied the groups in a separate section, bringing up the rear. If a woman or priest entered the circle of the ceremony, the act of penance was considered void and had to be begun over again. The movement was essentially anti-clerical, for in challenge to the priesthood, the flagellants were taking upon themselves the role of interceders with God for all humanity.

Breaking out now in the German states, the new eruption advanced through the Low Countries to Flanders and Picardy as far as Reims. Hundreds of bands roamed the land, entering new towns every week, exciting already overwrought emotions, reciting hymns of woe and claims that but for them "all Christendom would meet perdition." The inhabitants greeted them with reverence and ringing of church bells, lodged them in their houses, brought children to be healed and, in at least one case, to be resurrected. They dipped cloths in the flagellants' blood, which they pressed to their eyes and preserved as relics. Many, including knights and ladies, clerics, nuns, and children, joined the bands. Soon the flagellants were marching behind magnificent banners of velvet and cloth of gold embroidered for them by women enthusiasts.

Growing in arrogance, they became overt in antagonism to the Church. The Masters assumed the right to hear confession and grant absolution or impose penance, which not only denied the priests their fee for these services but challenged ecclesiastical authority at its core. Priests who intervened against them were stoned and the populace was incited to join in the stoning. Opponents were denounced as scorpions and Anti-Christs. Organized in some cases by apostate priests or fanatic dissidents, the flagellants took possession of churches, disrupted services, ridiculed the Eucharist, looted altars, and claimed the power to cast out evil spirits and raise the dead. The movement that began as an attempt through self-inflicted pain to save the world from destruction, caught the infection of power hunger and aimed at taking over the Church.

They began to be feared as a source of revolutionary ferment and a threat to the propertied class, lay as well as ecclesiastical. The Emperor Charles IV petitioned the Pope to suppress the flagellants, and his appeal was augmented by the no less imperial voice of the University of Paris. At such a time, when the world seemed to be on the brink of doom, to take action against the flagellants who claimed to be under Divine inspiration was not an easy decision. Several of the cardinals at Avignon opposed repressive measures.

The self-torturers meanwhile had found a better victim. In every town they entered, the flagellants rushed for the Jewish quarter, trailed by citizens howling for revenge upon the "poisoners of the wells." In Freiburg, Augsburg, Nürnberg, Munich, Königsberg, Regensburg, and other centers, the Jews were slaughtered with a thoroughness that seemed to seek the final solution. At Worms in March 1349 the Jewish community of 400, like that of York, turned to an old tradition and burned themselves to death inside their own houses rather than be killed by their enemies. The larger community of Frankfurt-am-Main took the same way in July, setting fire to part of the city by their flames. In Cologne the Town Council repeated the Pope's argument that Jews were dying of the plague like everyone else, but the flagellants collected a great proletarian crowd of "those who had nothing to lose," and paid no attention. In Mainz, which had the largest Jewish community in Europe, its members turned at last to self-defense. With arms collected in advance they killed 200 of the mob, an act which only served to bring down upon them a furious onslaught by the townspeople in revenge for the death of Christians. The Jews fought until overpowered; then retreating to their homes, they too set their own fires. Six thousand were said to have perished at Mainz on August 24, 1349. Of 3,000 Jews at Erfurt, none was reported to have survived.

Completeness is rare in history, and Jewish chroniclers may have shared the medieval addiction to sweeping numbers. Usually a number saved themselves by conversion, and groups of refugees were given shelter by Rupert of the Palatinate and other princes. Duke Albert II of Austria, grand-uncle of Enguerrand VII, was one of the few who took measures effective enough to protect the Jews from assault in his territories. The last pogroms took place in Antwerp and in Brussels where in December 1349 the entire Jewish community was exterminated. By the time the plague had passed, few Jews were left in Germany or the Low Countries.

By this time Church and state were ready to take the risk of suppressing the flagellants. Magistrates ordered town gates closed against them; Clement VI in a Bull of October 1349 called for their dispersal and arrest; the University of Paris denied their claim of Divine inspiration. Philip VI promptly forbade public flagellation on pain of death; local rulers pursued the "masters of error," seizing, hanging, and beheading. The flagellants disbanded and fled, "vanishing as suddenly as they had come," wrote Henry of Hereford, "like night phantoms or mocking ghosts." Here and there the bands lingered, not entirely suppressed until 1357.

Homeless ghosts, the Jews filtered back from eastern Europe, where the expelled had gone. Two Jews reappeared in Erfurt as visitors in 1354 and, joined by others, started a resettlement three years later. By 1365 the community numbered 86 taxable hearths and an additional number of poor households below the tax-paying level. Here and elsewhere they returned to live in weakened and fearful communities on worse terms and in greater segregation than before. Well-poisoning and its massacres had fixed the malevolent image of the Jew into a stereotype. Because Jews were useful, towns which had enacted statutes of banishment invited or allowed their re-entry, but imposed new disabilities. Former contacts of scholars, physicians, and financial "court Jews" with the Gentile community faded. The period of the Jews' medieval flourishing was over. The walls of the ghetto, though not yet physical, had risen. . .

Survivors of the plague, finding themselves neither destroyed nor improved, could discover no Divine purpose in the pain they had suffered. God's purposes were usually mysterious, but this scourge had been too terrible to be accepted without questioning. If a disaster of such magnitude, the most lethal ever known, was a mere wanton act of God or perhaps not God's work at all, then the absolutes of a fixed order were loosed from their moorings. Minds that opened to admit these questions could never again be shut. Once people envisioned the possibility of change in a fixed order, the end of an age of submission came in sight; the turn to individual conscience lay ahead. To that extent the Black Death may have been the unrecognized beginning of modern man.

Meantime it left apprehension, tension, and gloom. It accelerated the commutation of labor services on the land and in so doing unfastened old ties. It deepened antagonism between rich and poor and raised the level of human hostility. An event of great agony is bearable only in the belief that it will bring about a better world. When it does not, as in the aftermath of another vast calamity in 1914–18, disillusion is deep and moves on to self-doubt and self-disgust. In creating a climate for pessimism, the Black Death was the equivalent of the First World War, although it took fifty years for the psychological effects to develop. These were the fifty-odd years of the youth and adult life of Enguerrand de Coucy.

A strange personification of Death emerged from the plague years on the painted walls of the Camposanto in Pisa. The figure is not the conventional skeleton, but a black-cloaked old woman with streaming hair and wild eyes, carrying a broad-bladed murderous scythe. Her feet end in claws instead of toes. Depicting the Triumph of Death, the fresco was painted in or about 1350 by Francesco Traini as part of a series that included scenes of the Last Judgment and the Tortures of Hell. The same subject, painted at the same time by Traini's master, Andrea Orcagna, in the church of Santa Croce in Florence, has since been lost except for a fragment. Together the frescoes marked the start of a pervasive presence of Death in art, not yet the cult it was to become by the end of the century, but its beginning.

Usually Death was personified as a skeleton with hourglass and scythe, in a white shroud or bare-boned, grinning at the irony of man's fate reflected in his image: that all men, from beggar to emperor, from harlot to queen, from ragged clerk to Pope, must come to this. No matter what their poverty or power in life, all is vanity, equalized by death. The temporal is nothing; what matters is the after-life of the soul.

In Traini's fresco, Death swoops through the air toward a group of carefree, young, and beautiful noblemen and ladies who, like models for Boccaccio's storytellers, converse and flirt and entertain each other with books and music in a fragrant grove of orange trees. A scroll warns that "no shield of wisdom or riches, nobility or prowess" can protect them from the blows of the Approaching One. "They have taken more pleasure in the world than in things of God." In a heap of corpses nearby lie crowned rulers, a Pope in tiara, a knight, tumbled together with the bodies of the poor, while angels and devils in the sky contend for the miniature naked figures that represent their souls. A wretched group of lepers, cripples, and beggars (duplicated in the surviving fragment of Orcagna), one with nose eaten away, others legless or blind or holding out a cloth-covered stump instead of a hand, implore Death for deliverance. Above on a mountain, hermits leading a religious contemplative life await death peacefully.

Below in a scene of extraordinary verve a hunting party of princes and elegant ladies on horseback comes with sudden horror upon three open coffins containing corpses in different stages of decomposition, one still clothed, one half-rotted, one a skeleton. Vipers crawl over their bones. The scene illustrates "The Three Living and Three Dead," a 13th century legend which tells of a meeting between three young nobles and three decomposing corpses who tell them, "What you are, we were. What we are, you will be." In Traini's fresco, a horse catching the stench of death stiffens in fright with outstretched neck and flaring nostrils; his rider clutches a handkerchief to his nose. The hunting dogs recoil, growling in repulsion. In their silks and curls and fashionable hats, the party of vital handsome men and women stare appalled at what they will become.

Understanding and Analysis

1. Tuchman begins this chapter from her book *A Distant Mirror: The Calamitous Fourteenth Century* with the arrival of the plague in Europe. What does she accomplish in the first three paragraphs? What categories of inquiry does she establish?

2. How does the fourth paragraph connect to the first?

3. Beginning in the fifth paragraph, Tuchman traces the spread of the disease. Where does she begin a new topic or category? What is it?

4. Note the topic sentences in this chapter. Where do they usually occur in her paragraphs?

5. Why was the plague "not the kind of calamity that inspired mutual help"? What behavior did it inspire? Does Tuchman note exceptions?

6. Why did the poor die in greater numbers than the rich? What was the economic effect of the deaths of the poor?

7. Who among the wealthy died? Into what groups does Tuchman categorize the wealthy?

8. Contrast what is known now about the cause of the plague with what was believed at the time.

9. What role for good and ill did religion play in the time of the plague? What happened to the Jews?

10. Whether she quotes or paraphrases her sources, Tuchman usually indicates in the text who her sources are. Who are they? What connections do you see between Tuchman's sources and her categories?

Comparison

1. Read Carr on history. How accurate do you think Tuchman's report on the plague is likely to be? Why do you think so?

2. Read FitzGerald's essay "Rewriting American History." How do you think Tuchman's history of the plague is informed by attitudes developed in the twentieth century?

3. Read Sontag's "AIDS and Its Metaphors." What similarities, if any, do you see between Sontag's analysis of AIDS and Tuchman's analysis of the plague?

4. Read Graves's descriptions of World War I and Fussell's descriptions of World War II. How is war like a plague?

5. Read Lewisohn's "The Revolt Against Civilization." How does the treatment of Jews during the time of the plague inform your reading of Lewisohn's essay?

Frances FitzGerald
(1940–)

Frances FitzGerald, known affectionately as Frankie, was born into a family of prestige, power, and wealth on October 21, 1940, in New York City. In the thick of the Second World War, when she was two, her father, Desmond FitzGerald, left the United States to serve as a "liaison officer with Chinese troops behind Japanese lines," as Robert Friedman reports in *Esquire*. Shortly after his return, her parents divorced. While her father remarried and joined the CIA, which sent him around Asia and into Vietnam, her mother, Marietta Peabody, remarried and left her position "as a researcher at *Life* magazine" to move to England with her daughter. Living near Oxford for the next two years, the family entertained Winston Churchill on more than one occasion. The list of guests was hardly less impressive after the family returned to New York. "Throughout most of the Fifties," Friedman writes, "Frankie's home was also a political salon. Her mother, a confidante of Adlai Stevenson's, always had a drawing room full of newspaper publishers and senators, journalists and prime ministers." When FitzGerald was 13, she left her mother's salon in New York for Middleburg, Virginia, where she attended the Foxcroft School. Although she excelled in most subjects, in her English classes she earned Ds. The English teacher "was an absolute witch," FitzGerald remembers, "but she taught me how to write a sentence."

According to *Contemporary Authors*, FitzGerald "graduated at the top of her class" and enrolled at Radcliffe for her undergraduate degree in 1958, majoring in Middle Eastern history. In 1961, a year before she graduated, her mother became an ambassador to the United Nations, no doubt fueling FitzGerald's "terror of mediocrity." Graduating *magna cum laude*, FitzGerald determined, Friedman says, to "become a novelist." Her first job, attained through family connections, took her to France to work with the Congress of Cultural Freedom. Two years later, she returned to the states. "If only I'd written a novel," FitzGerald told Friedman, "it would have been perfect." Turning to journalism, FitzGerald found work writing for the *New York Herald Tribune Sunday Magazine*, which "folded" in 1966. This was a crucial year in FitzGerald's life, for this was the year she decided to go overseas to cover the Vietnam war.

As she explained on the television program "Booknotes," her decision was partly motivated by a desire to travel where her father had gone before: "I wanted to see Asia...I wanted to see that part of his life." Although she has told many sources that she was "naive" when she arrived in Vietnam in February of 1966, she figured out soon enough that she did not want to follow naively in the established ways of the war correspondent. She said to Friedman: "Everybody was chasing the American units around...that's what people thought you should do when you're covering a war. But I never fancied myself a war correspondent in that sense. I never put on a uniform and went out with the troops." Instead, she spoke with American officials and then went to Saigon and down into the Mekong Delta, among the Vietnamese people. Writing pieces for *The Atlantic Monthly*, *Vogue*, and *Village Voice*, FitzGerald returned home in November to write the article that eventually became, under the influence of Vietnam scholar Paul Mus, *Fire in the Lake: The Vietnamese and the Americans in Vietnam*. In this book, FitzGerald argued:

> The United States came to Vietnam at a critical juncture of Vietnamese history...In 1954 the Vietnamese were gaining their independence after sev-

enty years of French colonial rule. They were engaged in a struggle to create a nation....[T]he United States was not just fighting a border war or
intervening....It was entering into a moral and ideological struggle over the
form of the state and the goals of the society. Its success would depend not
merely on U.S. military power but on the resources of both the United States
and the Saigon government to solve Vietnamese domestic problems in a
manner acceptable to the Vietnamese. But what indeed were Vietnamese
problems, and did they even exist in the terms in which Americans conceived them? The unknowns made the whole enterprise, from the most
rational and tough-minded point of view, risky in the extreme.

An overwhelming success, *Fire in the Lake* won FitzGerald a National Book
Award, Bancroft Prize, and a Pulitzer. After its publication, FitzGerald returned
several more times to Vietnam, frustrated with the continuing American
presence. While she provided award-winning coverage of events in Cuba
and Iran in the early 1970s, she "couldn't really get [herself] free to do another
book until the war ended." When it did, in 1975, she experienced "a liberation."

FitzGerald next turned her attention to Americans at home. As she told
Contemporary Authors: "It's very difficult for a single journalist to figure out
what is on the mind of this country. It seemed to me that one of the ways
to do it was to look at history textbooks as a version of popular culture."
The result of her scrutiny, somewhat altered from her original intention, was
America Revised: History Schoolbooks in the Twentieth Century (1979). Her third book,
Cities on a Hill: A Journey through American Cultures (1986), grew out of her own
experience as an educator in a UC Berkeley classroom. "Several of her students went to a drag ball," Friedman writes, "and their reports of the event
aroused her curiosity." While developing ideas for a piece on homosexuality,
she herself went out in drag—"I can tell you nobody was fooled"—and eventually expanded her project to include four "visionary communities," including the Castro district of San Francisco and the church of Jerry Falwell. Four
years after she published *Cities on a Hill*, FitzGerald married the reporter James
Sterba.

Journalist Peter Kann summarized the feelings of many when he said, "no
American who covered Vietnam understood what motivated the North Vietnamese as well as Frankie." FitzGerald's treatment of American history books
provoked far more disgruntled criticism than did her attack on wrongheaded
foreign policy. Understanding *America Revised* as a critique of textbooks, teachers asked FitzGerald for solutions, or at least suggestions, while reviewers
faulted her for a failure to explain precisely how the books went wrong in
the first place. In some ways, however, both groups failed to understand the
larger aim: to analyze American culture. "In some ways," FitzGerald says, "*America Revised* was not about textbooks at all."

REWRITING AMERICAN HISTORY (1979)

THOSE OF US who grew up in the fifties believed in the permanence of our American-history textbooks. To us as children, those texts were the truth of things: they were American history. It was not just that we read them before we understood that not everything that is printed is the truth, or the whole truth. It was that they, much more than other books, had the demeanor and trappings of authority. They were weighty volumes. They spoke in measured cadences: imperturbable, humorless, and as distant as Chinese emperors. Our teachers treated them with respect, and we paid them abject homage by memorizing a chapter a week. But now the textbook histories have changed, some of them to such an extent that an adult would find them unrecognizable.

One current junior-high-school American history begins with a story about a Negro cowboy called George McJunkin. It appears that when McJunkin was riding down a lonely trail in New Mexico one cold spring morning in 1925 he discovered a mound containing bones and stone implements, which scientists later proved belonged to an Indian civilization ten thousand years old. The book goes on to say that scientists now believe there were people in the Americas at least twenty thousand years ago. It discusses the Aztec, Mayan, and Incan civilizations and the meaning of the word "culture" before introducing the European explorers.

Another history text—this one for the fifth grade—begins with the story of how Henry B. Gonzalez, who is a member of Congress from Texas, learned about his own nationality. When he was ten years old, his teacher told him he was an American because he was born in the United States. His grandmother, however, said, "The cat was born in the oven. Does that make him bread?" After reporting that Mr. Gonzalez eventually went to college and law school, the book explains that "the melting pot idea hasn't worked out as some thought it would," and that now "some people say that the people of the United States are more like a salad bowl than a melting pot."

Poor Columbus! He is a minor character now, a walk-on in the middle of American history. Even those books that have not replaced his picture with a Mayan temple or an Iroquois mask do not credit him with discovering America—even for the Europeans. The Vikings, they say, preceded him to the New World, and after that the Europeans, having lost or forgotten their maps, simply neglected to cross the ocean again for five hundred years. Columbus is far from being the only personage to have suffered from time and revision. *Captain John Smith,*[1] *Daniel Boone,*[2] and *Wild Bill Hickok*[3]—the great self-promoters of American history—have all but disappeared, taking with them a good deal of the romance of the American frontier. *General Custer*[4] has given way to *Chief Crazy*

---

[1]*Captain John Smith* (1579–1631) an English explorer and adventurer, who helped found colonial Jamestown in 1607. After being captured by the Native Americans of Powhatan's tribe, he was rescued by the chief's daughter, Pocahontas. He later wrote several books about Virginia, Jamestown, and his earlier travels in Europe and Asia.

[2]*Daniel Boone* (1734–1820) an American frontiersman who led the first settlers into Kentucky in 1775.

[3]*Wild Bill Hickok* James Butler Hickock (1837–1876) a frontier figure who was a stagecoach driver, a spy and scout for the Union Army, and marshal of Hays City and Abilene.

[4]*General Custer* (1839–1876) a flamboyant and aggressive Civil War soldier who gained fame fighting the Plains Indians and who was killed during a battle along the Little Bighorn River in Montana.

Horse,[5] *General Eisenhower*[6] no longer liberates Europe single-handed; and, indeed, most generals, even to Washington and *Lee,*[7] have faded away, as old soldiers do, giving place to social reformers such as *William Lloyd Garrison*[8] and *Jacob Riis.*[9] A number of black Americans have risen to prominence: not only *George Washington Carver*[10] but *Frederick Douglass*[11] and *Martin Luther King, Jr. W. E. B. Du Bois*[12] now invariably accompanies *Booker T. Washington.*[13] In addition, there is a mystery man called Crispus Attucks, a fugitive slave about whom nothing seems to be known for certain except that he was a victim of the Boston Massacre and thus became one of the first casualties of the American Revolution. *Thaddeus Stevens*[14] has been reconstructed—his character changed, as it were, from black to white, from cruel and vindictive to persistent and sincere. As for Teddy Roosevelt, he now champions the issue of conservation instead of charging up San Juan Hill. No single President really stands out as a hero, but all Presidents—except certain unmentionables in the second half of the nineteenth century—seem to have done as well as could be expected, given difficult circumstances.

Of course, when one thinks about it, it is hardly surprising that modern scholarship and modern perspectives have found their way into children's books. Yet the changes remain shocking. Those who in the sixties complained of the bland optimism, the chauvinism, and the materialism of their old civics text did so in the belief that, for all their

---

[5]*Chief Crazy Horse* b. Tashunka Witco (1842(?)–1877) Oglala Sioux chief, born in present-day South Dakota, who led the successful defeat of General Custer at Little Bighorn and who is regarded as a symbol of the heroic resistance of the Sioux.

[6]*General Eisenhower* Dwight D. Eisenhower (1890–1969) Thirty-fourth U.S. president and general during World War II; he was supreme commander of the allied invasion of Normandy, and he directed the campaign from D-Day (June 6, 1944) to the surrender of Germany (May 1945).

[7]*Lee* Robert E. Lee (1807–1870) a general for the Confederate States during the Civil War; even though Lee opposed secession in 1861, he resigned from the U.S. Army to fight with his state of Virginia.

[8]*William Lloyd Garrison* (1805–1879) a New England journalist and social activist whose various causes included temperance, abolition, the plight of Native Americans, and women's suffrage.

[9]*Jacob Riis* (1849–1914) a Danish photographer and social reformer who emigrated to New York City in 1870. His explicit photographs of life in New York slums helped fuel the tenement reform movement.

[10]*George Washington Carver* (c. 1861–1943) an African-American agricultural chemist, educator, botanist, and researcher of international status; Carver trained black farmers in agriculture and home economics; he also influenced the southern shift from single-crop to diversified agriculture.

[11]*Frederick Douglass* (c. 1817–1895) a slave who escaped to Massachusetts and became an abolitionist, author, and public official, and whose autobiography *Life and Times of Frederick Douglass* (1881) is still a classic.

[12]*W. E. B. Du Bois* (1868–1963) a professor of economics and history who called for the African-American middle class to fight against bigoted racial policies; a black activist who worked for the National Association for the Advancement of Colored People, became a Marxist, and left the United States to be a citizen of Ghana.

[13]*Booker T. Washington* (1856–1915) Washington was born into slavery, but after the Civil War became a teacher and eventually the head of the Tuskegee Institute in Alabama, building it into a prestigious educational institution. He was also one of the foremost black leaders in America.

[14]*Thaddeus Stevens* (1792–1868) a U.S. representative who fought bitterly against slavery and who advocated harsh treatment of the South after the Civil War.

protests, the texts would never change. The thought must have had something reassuring about it, for that generation never noticed when its complaints began to take effect and the songs about radioactive rainfall and houses made of ticky-tacky began to appear in the textbooks. But this is what happened.

The history texts now hint at a certain level of unpleasantness in American history. Several books, for instance, tell the story of Ishi, the last "wild" Indian in the continental United States, who, captured in 1911 after the massacre of his tribe, spent the final four and a half years of his life in the University of California's museum of anthropology, in San Francisco. At least three books show the same stunning picture of the breaker boys, the child coal miners of Pennsylvania—ancient children with deformed bodies and blackened faces who stare stupidly out from the entrance to a mine. One book quotes a soldier on the use of torture in the American campaign to pacify the Philippines at the beginning of the century. A number of books say that during the American Revolution the patriots tarred and feathered those who did not support them, and drove many of the loyalists from the country. Almost all the present-day history books note that the United States interned Japanese-Americans in detention camps during the Second World War.

Ideologically speaking, the histories of the fifties were implacable, seamless. Inside their covers, America was perfect: the greatest nation in the world, and the embodiment of democracy, freedom, and technological progress. For them, the country never changed in any important way: its values and its political institutions remained constant from the time of the American Revolution. To my generation—the children of the fifties—these texts appeared permanent just because they were so self-contained. Their orthodoxy, it seemed, left no hand-holds for attack, no lodging for decay. Who, after all, would dispute the wonders of technology or the superiority of the English colonists over the Spanish? Who would find fault with the pastorale of the West or the Old South? Who would question the anti-Communist crusade? There was, it seemed, no point in comparing these visions with reality, since they were the public truth and were thus quite irrelevant to what existed and to what anyone privately believed. They were—or so it seemed—the permanent expression of mass culture in America.

But now the texts have changed, and with them the country that American children are growing up into. The society that was once uniform is now a patchwork of rich and poor, old and young, men and women, blacks, whites, Hispanics, and Indians. The system that ran so smoothly by means of the Constitution under the guidance of benevolent conductor Presidents is now a rattletrap affair. The past is no highway to the present; it is a collection of issues and events that do not fit together and that lead in no single direction. The word "progress" has been replaced by the word "change": children, the modern texts insist, should learn history so that they can adapt to the rapid changes taking place around them. History is proceeding in spite of us. The present, which was once portrayed in the concluding chapters as a peaceful haven of scientific advances and Presidential inaugurations, is now a tangle of problems: race problems, urban problems, foreign-policy problems, problems of pollution, poverty, energy depletion, youthful rebellion, assassination, and drugs. Some books illustrate these problems dramatically. One, for instance, contains a picture of a doll half buried in a mass of untreated sewage; the caption reads, "Are we in danger of being overwhelmed by the products of our society and wastage created by their production? Would you agree with this photographer's interpretation?" Two books show the same picture of an old black woman sitting in a straight chair in a dingy room, her hands folded in graceful resignation; the surrounding text discusses the problems faced by the urban poor and by the aged who depend on Social Security. Other books present current problems less starkly. One of the texts concludes sagely:

> Problems are part of life. Nations face them, just as people face them, and try to solve them. And today's Americans have one great advantage over past generations. Never before have Americans been so well equipped to solve their problems. They have today the means to conquer poverty, disease, and ignorance. The technetronic age has put that power into their hands.

Such passages have a familiar ring. Amid all the problems, the *deus ex machina*[15] of science still dodders around in the gloaming of pious hope.

Even more surprising than the emergence of problems is the discovery that the great unity of the texts has broken. Whereas in the fifties all texts represented the same political view, current texts follow no pattern of orthodoxy. Some books, for instance, portray civil-rights legislation as a series of actions taken by a wise, paternal government; others convey some suggestion of the social upheaval involved and make mention of such people as *Stokely Carmichael*[16] and Malcolm X. In some books, the Cold War has ended; in others, it continues, with Communism threatening the free nations of the earth.

The political diversity in the books is matched by a diversity of pedagogical approach. In addition to the traditional narrative histories, with their endless streams of facts, there are so-called "discovery," or "inquiry," texts, which deal with a limited number of specific issues in American history. These texts do not pretend to cover the past; they focus on particular topics, such as "stratification in Colonial society" or "slavery and the American Revolution," and illustrate them with documents from primary and secondary sources. The chapters in these books amount to something like case studies, in that they include testimony from people with different perspectives or conflicting views on a single subject. In addition, the chapters provide background information, explanatory notes, and a series of questions for the student. The questions are the heart of the matter, for when they are carefully selected they force students to think much as historians think: to define the point of view of the speaker, analyze the ideas presented, question the relationship between events, and so on. One text, for example, quotes Washington, Jefferson, and John Adams on the question of foreign alliances and then asks, "What did John Adams assume that the international situation would be after the American Revolution? What did Washington's attitude toward the French alliance seem to be? How do you account for his attitude?" Finally, it asks, "Should a nation adopt a policy toward alliances and cling to it consistently, or should it vary its policies toward other countries as circumstances change?" In these books, history is clearly not a list of agreed-upon facts or a sermon on politics but a babble of voices and a welter of events which must be ordered by the historian.

In matters of pedagogy, as in matters of politics, there are not two sharply differentiated categories of books; rather, there is a spectrum. Politically, the books run from moderate left to moderate right; pedagogically, they run from the traditional history sermons, through a middle ground of narrative texts with inquiry-style questions and of inquiry

---

[15]*deus ex machina* god from a machine. In early Greek and Roman plays, a god descended by machine to solve the problems at the end.

[16]*Stokely Carmichael* (1941–1998) a radical African-American activist who helped found the Black Panthers.

texts with long stretches of narrative, to the most rigorous of case-study books. What is common to the current texts—and makes all of them different from those of the fifties—is their engagement with the social sciences. In eighth-grade histories, the "concepts" of social sciences make fleeting appearances. But these "concepts" are the very foundation stones of various elementary-school social-studies series. The 1970 *Harcourt Brace Jovanovich*[17] series, for example, boasts in its preface of "a horizontal base or ordering of conceptual schemes" to match its "vertical arm of behavioral themes." What this means is not entirely clear, but the books do proceed from easy questions to hard ones, such as—in the sixth-grade book—"How was interaction between merchants and citizens different in the Athenian and Spartan social systems?" Virtually all the American-history texts for older children include discussions of "role," "status," and "culture." Some of them stage debates between eminent social scientists in roped-off sections of the text; some include essays on economics or sociology; some contain pictures and short biographies of social scientists of both sexes and of diverse races. Many books seem to accord social scientists a higher status than American Presidents.

Quite as striking as these political and pedagogical alterations is the change in the physical appearance of the texts. The schoolbooks of the fifties showed some effort in the matter of design: they had maps, charts, cartoons, photographs, and an occasional four-color picture to break up the columns of print. But beside the current texts they look as naïve as Soviet fashion magazines. The print in the fifties books is heavy and far too black, the colors muddy. The photographs are conventional news shots—portraits of Presidents in three-quarters profile, posed "action" shots of soldiers. The other illustrations tend to be *Socialist-realist-style*[18] drawings (there are a lot of hefty farmers with hoes in the Colonial-period chapters) or incredibly vulgar made-for-children paintings of patriotic events. One painting shows Columbus standing in full court dress on a beach in the New World from a perspective that could have belonged only to the *Arawaks.*[19] By contrast, the current texts are paragons of sophisticated modern design. They look not like *People* or *Family Circle* but, rather, like *Architectural Digest* or *Vogue.* * * * The amount of space given to illustrations is far greater than it was in the fifties; in fact, in certain "slow-learner" books the pictures far outweigh the text in importance. However, the illustrations have a much greater historical value. Instead of made-up paintings or anachronistic sketches, there are cartoons, photographs, and paintings drawn from the periods being treated. The chapters on the Colonial period will show, for instance, a ship's carved prow, a Revere bowl, a Copley[20] painting—a whole gallery of Early Americana. The nineteenth century is illustrated with nineteenth-century cartoons and photographs—and the photographs are all of high artistic quality. As for the twentieth-century chapters, they are adorned with the contents of a modern-art museum.

The use of all this art and high-quality design contains some irony. The nineteenth-century photographs of child laborers or urban slum apartments are so beautiful that they transcend their subjects. To look at them, or at the Victor Gatto painting of the Triangle

---

[17]*Harcourt Brace Jovanovich* a publishing company.

[18]*Socialist-realist-style* Socialist realism, was the required style in the Soviet Union after 1932. Its purpose was to idealize the worker in art and literature.

[19]*Arawaks* Native Americans who originally inhabited the Caribbean.

[20]*Copley* John Singleton Copley (1738–1815) an American painter known for his portraits and historical paintings.

shirtwaist-factory fire,[21] is to see not misery or ugliness but an art object. In the modern chapters, the contrast between style and content is just as great: the color photographs of junk yards or polluted rivers look as enticing as *Gourmet's* photographs of food. The book that is perhaps the most stark in its description of modern problems illustrates the horrors of nuclear testing with a pretty Ben Shahn[22] picture of the Bikini explosion,[23] and the potential for global ecological disaster with a color photograph of the planet swirling its mantle of white clouds. Whereas in the nineteen-fifties the texts were childish in the sense that they were naïve and clumsy, they are now childish in the sense that they are polymorphous-perverse. American history is not dull any longer; it is a sensuous experience.

The surprise that adults feel in seeing the changes in history texts must come from the lingering hope that there is, somewhere out there, an objective truth. The hope is, of course, foolish. All of us children of the twentieth century know, or should know, that there are no absolutes in human affairs, and thus there can be no such thing as perfect objectivity. We know that each historian in some degree creates the world anew and that all history is in some degree contemporary history. But beyond this knowledge there is still a hope for some reliable authority, for some fixed stars in the universe. We may know that journalists cannot be wholly unbiased and that "balance" is an imaginary point between two extremes, and yet we hope that Walter Cronkite will tell us the truth of things. In the same way, we hope that our history will not change—that we learned the truth of things as children. The texts, with their impersonal voices, encourage this hope, and therefore it is particularly disturbing to see how they change, and how fast.

Slippery history! Not every generation but every few years the content of American-history books for children changes appreciably. Schoolbooks are not, *like trade books,*[24] written and left to their fate. To stay in step with the cycles of "adoption" in school districts across the country, the publishers revise most of their old texts or substitute new ones every three or four years. In the process of revision, they not only bring history up to date but make changes—often substantial changes—in the body of the work. History books for children are thus more contemporary than any other form of history. How should it be otherwise? Should students read histories written ten, fifteen, thirty years ago? In theory, the system is reasonable—except that each generation of children reads only one generation of schoolbooks. The transient history is those children's history forever—their particular version of America.

Understanding and Analysis

1. What are the two reasons FitzGerald offers in the first paragraph to explain why children in the fifties "believed in the permanence of [their] American-history textbooks"?

2. How does she describe the changes in the following three paragraphs?

[21]*Triangle shirtwaist factory fire* In 1911, 146 young women died in 15 minutes at the Triangle shirtwaist factory in New York City after a fire broke out. The factory's proprietors had locked the exits to keep the workers at their sewing machines. The incident was a turning point in the efforts to unionize garment workers.

[22]*Ben Shahn* (1898–1969) an American painter, photographer, and graphic artist.

[23]*Bikini explosion* From 1946–1958 the United States removed the people from the 36 tiny islands comprising the Bikini atoll in the Pacific in order to test nuclear weapons.

[24]*trade books* books written for the general public.

3. Why and for whom are these changes "shocking"?

4. How does her description in paragraphs six, seven, and eight differ from her earlier description of the changes in these texts? What elements constitute description and what elements constitute analysis?

5. Note the topic sentences of paragraphs ten, eleven, and twelve. What do they tell you about the content of the paragraphs?

6. What is ironic about the art work in the texts of the seventies?

7. Why, according to FitzGerald, do history texts change?

8. What changes does FitzGerald approve of and what changes do you think she dislikes? What is your evidence?

Comparison

1. Compare the content and design of your high-school history textbook or several you find in a library with those FitzGerald describes. What differences do you notice?

2. Read Carr's essay. How does his analysis inform your reading of FitzGerald's essay? Have the facts of American history changed?

3. Read Tuchman. Would a textbook on the fourteenth century also change over the years? Why or why not?

4. Read Kuhn's essay on scientific discoveries. What connections do you see between changes in history and history textbooks and changes in science? Do you suppose that textbooks on science change in similar ways and as rapidly as textbooks on history? Why or why not?

5. Read Geertz's essay on the Bali. Do you think that anthropological analyses are influenced by events in the present? In other words, does anthropology provide different versions or interpretations of a particular culture in each generation? How does the fact that cultures themselves change, however slowly, affect the work of each generation of anthropologists?

6. Read Mencken's "Bearers of the Torch." Do you think that the changes FitzGerald observes are the result of pedagogical fads? Why or why not? What is the difference between a fad and a textbook "version" of history? Is there a difference?

James Baldwin

If Black English Isn't a Language, Then Tell Me, What Is? *(1979)*

THE ARGUMENT CONCERNING the use, or the status, or the reality, of black English is rooted in American history and has absolutely nothing to do with the question the argument supposes itself to be posing. The argument has nothing to do with language itself but with the role of language. Language, incontestably, reveals the speaker. Language, also, far more dubiously, is meant to define the other—and, in this case, the other is refusing to be defined by a language that has never been able to recognize him.

People evolve a language in order to describe and thus control their circumstances or in order not to be submerged by a situation that they cannot articulate. (And if they cannot articulate it, they are submerged.) A Frenchman living in Paris speaks a subtly and crucially different language from that of the man living in Marseilles; neither sounds very much like a man living in Quebec; and they would all have great difficulty in apprehending what the man from Guadeloupe, or Martinique, is saying, to say nothing of the man from Senegal—although the "common" language of all these areas is French. But each has paid, and is paying, a different price for this "common" language, in which, as it turns out, they are not saying, and cannot be saying, the same things: They each have very different realities to articulate, or control.

What joins all languages, and all men, is the necessity to confront life, in order, not inconceivably, to outwit death: The price for this is the acceptance, and achievement, of one's temporal identity. So that, for example, though it is not taught in the schools (and this has the potential of becoming a political issue) the south of France still clings to its ancient and musical Provencal,[1] which resists being described as a "dialect." And much of the tension in the Basque countries,[2] and in Wales, is due to the Basque and Welsh determination not to allow their languages to be destroyed. This determination also feeds the flames in Ireland for among the many indignities the Irish have been forced to undergo at English hands is the English contempt for their language.

It goes without saying, then, that language is also a political instrument, means, and proof of power. It is the most vivid and crucial key to identity: It reveals the private identity, and connects one with, or divorces one from, the larger, public, or community identity. There have been, and are, times and places, when to speak a certain language could be dangerous, even fatal. Or, one may speak the same language, but in such a way that one's antecedents are revealed, or (one hopes) hidden. This is true in France, and is absolutely true in England: The range (and reign) of accents on that damp little island make England coherent for the English and totally incomprehensible for everyone else. To open your mouth in England is (if I may use black English) to "put your business in the street." You have confessed your parents, your youth, your school, your salary, your self-esteem, and, alas, your future.

---

[1] *Provencal* literary language of the medieval troubadours in France.

[2] *Basque countries* northern Spain and southwest France, where the Basque language is spoken.

Now, I do not know what white Americans would sound like if there had never been any black people in the United States, but they would not sound the way they sound. *Jazz,* for example, is a very specific sexual term, as in *jazz me, baby,* but white people purified it into the Jazz Age. *Sock it to me,* which means, roughly, the same thing, has been adopted by Nathaniel Hawthorne's descendants with no qualms or hesitations at all, along with *let it all hang out* and *right on! Beat to his socks,* which was once the black's most total and despairing image of poverty, was transformed into a thing called the Beat Generation,[3] which phenomenon was, largely, composed of *uptight,* middle-class white people, imitating poverty, trying to *get down,* to get *with it,* doing their *thing,* doing their despairing best to be *funky,* which we, the blacks, never dreamed of doing—we were funky, baby, like *funk* was going out of style.

Now, no one can eat his cake, and have it, too, and it is late in the day to attempt to penalize black people for having created a language that permits the nation its only glimpse of reality, a language without which the nation would be even more whipped than it is.

I say that the present skirmish is rooted in American history, and it is. Black English is the creation of the black diaspora.[4] Blacks came to the United States chained to each other, but from different tribes. Neither could speak the other's language. If two black people, at that bitter hour of the world's history, had been able to speak to each other, the institution of chattel slavery could never have lasted as long as it did. Subsequently, the slave was given, under the eye, and the gun, of his master, Congo Square, and the Bible—or, in other words, and under those conditions, the slave began the formation of the black church, and it is within this unprecedented tabernacle that black English began to be formed. This was not, merely, as in the European example, the adoption of a foreign tongue, but an alchemy that transformed ancient elements into a new language: *A language comes into existence by means of brutal necessity, and the rules of the language are dictated by what the language must convey.*

There was a moment, in time, and in this place, when my brother, or my mother, or my father, or my sister, had to convey to me, for example, the danger in which I was standing from the white man standing just behind me, and to convey this with a speed and in a language, that the white man could not possibly understand, and that, indeed, he cannot understand, until today. He cannot afford to understand it. This understanding would reveal to him too much about himself and smash that mirror before which he has been frozen for so long.

Now, if this passion, this skill, this (to quote Toni Morrison[5]) "sheer intelligence," this incredible music, the mighty achievement of having brought a people utterly unknown to, or despised by "history"—to have brought this people to their present, troubled, troubling, and unassailable and unanswerable place—if this absolutely unprecedented journey does not indicate that black English is a language, I am curious to know what definition of languages is to be trusted.

A people at the center of the western world, and in the midst of so hostile a popula-

---

[3]*Beat Generation* in the 1950s, a loose group of American artists and writers who were influenced by Eastern religions and the rhythms of progressive jazz rejected traditional forms and sought expression in intense experiences and beatific illumination.

[4]*Diaspora* the dispersion of any originally homogeneous group of people.

[5]*Toni Morrison* an African-American writer born in 1931 who won the Pulitzer Prize in 1988 and the Nobel Prize for Literature in 1993.

tion, has not endured and transcended by means of what is patronizingly called a "dialect." We, the blacks, are in trouble, certainly, but we are not inarticulate because we are not compelled to defend a morality that we know to be a lie.

The brutal truth is that the bulk of the white people in America never had any interest in educating black people, except as this could serve white purposes. It is not the black child's language that is despised. It is his experience. A child cannot be taught by anyone who despises him, and a child cannot afford to be fooled. A child cannot be taught by anyone whose demand, essentially, is that the child repudiate his experience, and all that gives him sustenance, and enter a limbo in which he will no longer be black, and in which he knows that he can never become white. Black people have lost too many black children that way.

And, after all, finally, in a country with standards so untrustworthy, a country that makes heroes of so many criminal mediocrities, a country unable to face why so many of the nonwhite are in prison, or on the needle, or standing, futureless, in the streets—it may very well be that both the child, and his elder, have concluded that they have nothing whatever to learn from the people of a country that has managed to learn so little.

Understanding and Analysis

1. In the first paragraph, Baldwin defines his topic and what he means by the question posed in the title. What exactly has Baldwin's question "nothing to do with," and what exactly is it about?

2. What do all the languages Baldwin refers to in the second paragraph have in common? How does this commonality fit with the point of the first paragraph?

3. What, according to Baldwin, "joins all languages, and all men"? From a scientific viewpoint, for example, the struggle for existence among and within groups, does Baldwin's assertion make sense to you?

4. What, in the fourth paragraph, does Baldwin mean when he speaks of both "private" and "communal identity"?

5. What exactly is Baldwin referring to in the cliché "no one can eat his cake, and have it, too," in the sixth paragraph?

6. How was Black English formed, according to Baldwin?

7. How does Baldwin define "language," and how does Black English fit the definition?

8. Carefully reread the penultimate paragraph. With which statements do you agree or disagree? Why?

9. What is Baldwin's point in the final paragraph?

Comparison

1. Read "Talking Black" by Gates. What similarities and differences do you see in the two eassays?

2. Read Richard Rodriguez's "Labor." From what Rodriguez says about language and *los probres*, do you think he would agree with Baldwin's thesis? Why or why not?

3. Read "The Language of Discretion" by Amy Tan, as well as the essays by Gates and Rodriguez. What ideas, if any, do all four authors address? To what extent do they agree and disagree? How would you define a language? What is your own informed opinion about the meaning and impact of language?

Stephen Jay Gould
(1941–)

Stephen Jay Gould was born in 1941 in Manhattan, the elder son of Leonard Gould, a court stenographer, Marxist, and intellectual, and Eleanor Rosenberg Gould, an artist. In "The Telltale Wishbone" Gould says that at age four he hoped to become a garbage man, planning to condense all the garbage of New York into one great truck. But at age five, he saw something even more magnificent than his imagined garbage truck—the *Tyrannosaurus* at the American Museum of Natural History. His first reaction as he stood with his father before the immense creature was fear: "a man sneezed; I gulped and prepared to utter my *Shema Yisrael*." Minutes later, he told his father he had decided to become a paleontologist.

Growing up in Forest Hills, Queens, where he attended P.S. 26 and was taught by three excellent teachers to whom he dedicated his second collection of essays, Gould was devoted to baseball, betting, and science. In "Streak of Streaks," he reports that he and his father frequented Yankee Stadium in the Bronx, where, in an early encounter with improbability—"You never get them," his father said at the time—his father caught a foul ball hit by Joe DiMaggio. When Gould posted the ball to his hero, DiMaggio returned it—signed. At age nine or thereabouts, at a camp in the Catskills, Gould tells in "The Dinosaur Rip-off," he first realized how little some adults knew about science. He had made a bet with a buddy about whether or not dinosaurs lived at the same time as humans and was out one chocolate bar when he discovered that the adult the boys agreed on as arbiter (the first one who claimed to know) was completely misinformed on the subject.

At eleven, Gould read *Meaning of Evolution* by G. G. Simpson; while not understanding every point, he realized that the bones that had so impressed him in the museum could tell a tale about the history of the planet and its evolving life. In Jamaica High School, however, as Gould records in "Moon, Mann, and Otto," his textbook, *Modern Biology*, managed to avoid the controversial concept of evolution because, says Gould, no publishers "are as cowardly and conservative as the publishers of public school texts . . ." Like science, music was a great influence in Gould's life in high school. As he describes in "Madame Jeanette," Gould sang second bass, one of 250 disciplined and devoted members of the New York All-City High School chorus. When Gould was fourteen, he bet his eleven-year-old brother Peter that Beethoven would outlast "Roll Over Beethoven." According to the *Rolling Stone* interviewer John

Tierney, Gould admits that the results aren't in yet, but he's sure his brother will lose.

After high school, Gould earned a B.A. from Antioch College, where he became interested in the snail fossils one of his teachers had collected in Bermuda. Two years after enrolling in the Ph.D. program at Columbia, in 1965, he married Deborah Lee, an artist. In 1966, he was hired as assistant professor of geology at Antioch College; in 1967, he completed the Ph.D., having worked at the American Museum of Natural History and written his dissertation on fossil snails in Bermuda. That year also he accepted a position at Harvard University where, as full professor since 1973, he continues to teach biology, geology, and the history of science. He and his first wife have two sons, Jesse, born in 1970, and Ethan, born in 1974. (He has since remarried.) In 1975, Gould won the first of many awards, the Schuchert Award for excellence in research in the field of paleontology.

While his work on snails of the West Indies and his collaboration with Niles Eldredge of the American Museum of Natural History on "Punctuated Equilibria: an Alternative to Phyletic Gradualism," published in *Models in Paleobiology* in 1972, gained him stature in the academic world, Gould's monthly essays, begun in 1974, for *Natural History*, established him as a popular essayist. As he explains in the prologue to *The Panda's Thumb*, the title and impetus of his column, "This View of Life," comes from the last sentence of Charles Darwin's on the *Origin of Species*: "There is a grandeur in this view of life, with its several powers, having been originally breathed into a few forms or into one; and that, whilst this planet has gone cycling on according to the fixed law of gravity, from so simple a beginning endless forms most beautiful and most wonderful have been, and are being, evolved."

His goal in these essays has been, he explains in the prologue to *Bully for Brontosaurus* (1991), to explore "instructive oddities of nature" as well as "the enduring themes of evolution." To this end, he has composed essays on flies, bees, worms, oysters, fish, hyenas, zebras, pandas, elk, humans, Hershey bars, Mickey Mouse, baseball, fairy tales, and more—all without condescending to the layman. The first such collection, *Ever Since Darwin*, was published the same year as his first purely academic book, *Ontogeny and Phylogeny* (Harvard's Belknap Press), in 1977. That collection, dedicated to his father, sets up a number of subjects that recur in one form or another in subsequent collections: Darwiniana, human evolution, theories of the earth, cultural and political influences on science, I.Q. and racism, and sociobiology. Although he has recently disparaged his writing in this book, he nonetheless establishes his stylistic signature in the structure of many of its essays, which move from some non-scientific aspect of culture to a scientific curiosity and from there to some overriding principle. Thus the opening paragraphs of these essays yield references to Groucho Marx, Ebeneezer Scrooge, the yellowed notes of Gould's first paleontology teacher, Yankees' announcer Mel Allen, Voltaire, Rube Goldberg, and Bruno Bettelheim.

In each succeeding collection, Gould has sharpened both the ideas he pursues and his skills as an essayist. For his second collection, *The Panda's Thumb* (1980), Gould won a Notable Book citation from the American Library Association and an American Book Award for the science category. The collection includes many of the categories of interest established in his first book of essays and adds material on convergence—the different and quirky evolutionary paths leading to analogous features, such as the panda's "thumb." Another group of essays in this book explores the relationship between the size of a creature, the length of its life, and our conceptions of time. "Women's Brains," one of his most popular essays, comes from this collection, in a group of essays under the rubric "Science and Politics of Human Differences."

The following year, 1981, Gould won a MacArthur Foundation Award and became involved in the debate against creationists, culminating in his testimony in December 1981 in Little Rock, Arkansas, in a trial challenging the state law that required public schools to treat creationism and evolution equally. In 1982, the Arkansas Act was declared unconstitutional in a ruling recognizing that creationism is a religious belief, not a branch of science. That year also Gould published *The Mismeasure of Man*, a study of the influence of prejudice on scientific attempts to assess intelligence. Enlarging on ideas he had presented in *Ever Since Darwin* and *The Panda's Thumb*, Gould enumerates the horrors committed by those who believed not only in craniometry and the reification and heritability of intelligence but also in the innate superiority of white European males. For this work he won the National Book Critics Circle Award in 1982.

That July, after a routine physical undertaken before a trip to Europe, Gould was told that he had mesothelioma, "a rare and serious cancer usually associated with exposure to asbestos." In "The Median Isn't the Message" Gould describes his reaction: he went straight to the library to research everything he could find on his disease. His inclination since childhood to take on a bet, as well as his training as a scientist in statistics and probability, helped him to interpret his odds of survival which were (and continue to be) much better than the prognosis first indicated—"Mesothelioma is incurable, with a median mortality of only eight months after discovery." While he does believe that a positive attitude increases the chances for survival, Gould does not support those who blame the victims for their disease and/or those who "look back at something like that and try to find a good side to it."

By 1983, Gould had published, with Niles Eldredge, two more academic books (1982), as well as his third collection of essays, *Hen's Teeth and Horses's*

Toes, containing sections on oddities, adaptation, and further effects of politics on science. In "Science and Jewish Immigration," for example, Gould incorporates material he had presented in *The Mismeasure of Man,* a book he had dedicated to the memory of his maternal grandparents who had come to America from Hungary. The definition of grandparents had been for him, he said in an interview, "people who spoke accented English." In this essay he shows how the quotas established for the Immigration Restriction Act of 1924, stemming from the eugenics developed by H. H. Goddard, director of research for an institute for the feebleminded, prevented millions of people from central and eastern Europe from fleeing the Nazis before the war. One of Gould's major themes is that ideas carry power "as surely as guns and bombs."

Gould's more recent publications include collections of essays, *The Flamingo's Smile* (1985), *Bully for Brontosaurus* (1991), *Eight Little Piggies* (1994), *Dinosaurs in a Haystack* (1996), *Leonardo's Mountain of Clams and the Diet of Worms* (1998); full-length books such as *Time's Arrow, Time's Cycle* (1987), and *Wonderful Life* (1989), about the tremendous and bizarre variety of fossils in the Burgess shale, as well as *Full House: the Spread of Excellence from Plato to Darwin* (1996), *Questioning the Millennium* (1997), and *Rocks of Ages* (1999). Most of these books emphasize two ideas Gould has pursued all along: the importance of contingency, chance, and luck in the pattern of evolution and the implications of probability theory—the recognition that random patterns lack intrinsic meaning, that any meaning attributed to them is created by man. Humans are not the epitome or the goal of evolution; some well-adapted species lost out due only to accident, discarded by time and chance. Gould has said that he will continue to write his monthly essays for *Natural History* until he has completed 300; the last one is scheduled to appear in the issue dated December 2000. The December 1999 issue, containing an essay on the fourth dimension to celebrate the millenium, was written jointly with his second wife, Rhonda Roland Shearer, an artist and director of the Art Science Research Laboratory in New York City.

Although Gould is active in the fight to preserve the environment and the diversity of species and although he sees a belief in evolutionary progress as "human arrogance," he would prefer to lose a species of land snail than allow people in the Bahamas to starve, he told Tierney in *Rolling Stone.* But, as it happens, the land snail lives in an area unfit for agriculture so that such a choice need not be made. He also predicted in that interview that further human evolution would not be significant—"we've built all of civilization without changing bodily form." Because we interbreed, we are unlikely to develop the isolated populations needed to speciate.

Like Hoagland, Gould is admittedly an optimist who finds it a good sign that although we have the power, we have not yet waged a nuclear war. Moreover, such a catastrophe, while wiping out mankind, would not destroy the earth. As he explains in the prologue to one of his collections of essays: "Our planet is not fragile on its own time scale, and we, pitiful latecomers in the last microsecond of our planetary year, are stewards of nothing in the long run." Nevertheless, the great pleasures afforded by "human brainpower" suggest we should "keep this interesting experiment" going as long as we can.

As he notes in his 1991 prologue, Gould fits in the tradition of such scientific writers as Francis Bacon and T. H. Huxley rather than in that of Henry David Thoreau or Loren Eiseley. Thus the beauty in Gould's essays resides not in a poetic appreciation of nature but in the symmetry of his organization, the logical progression from anecdote to principle to wide application. Gould is concerned with physical oddities and the social consequences of ideas. Like Huxley, he can amass with an orator's ring the evidence that unmasks injustices. And, with his far-ranging, eclectic knowledge, he does much to repair the split between science and the humanities first noted and lamented by George Orwell, Jacob Bronowski, and C. P. Snow. In "Darwin's Middle Road," Gould offers his definition of the characteristics of genius: "breadth of interest and the ability to construct fruitful analogies between fields." In his references to Aristotle, Larry Bird, Winston Churchill, George Eliot, Katherine Hepburn, Thomas Jefferson, Immanuel Kant, Maria Montessori, James Randi, Dylan Thomas, Mark Twain, Arturo Toscanini, Christopher Wren, and many, many more, Gould finds connections between science and philosophy, sports, politics, literature, cinema, education, magic, music, and architecture, creating a bridge between the isolated academic and the curious layman as well as between the twin worlds of science and the humanities.

WOMEN'S BRAINS (1980)

IN THE PRELUDE to *Middlemarch*, George Eliot lamented the unfulfilled lives of talented women:

> Some have felt that these blundering lives are due to the inconvenient indefiniteness with which the Supreme Power has fashioned the natures of women: if there were one level of feminine incompetence as strict as the ability to count three and no more, the social lot of women might be treated with scientific certitude.

Eliot goes on to discount the idea of innate limitation, but while she wrote in 1872, the leaders of European anthropometry were trying to measure "with scientific certitude" the inferiority of women. Anthropometry, or measurement of the human body, is not so fashionable a field these days, but it dominated the human sciences for much of the nineteenth century and remained popular until intelligence testing replaced skull measurement as a favored device for making invidious comparisons among races, classes, and sexes. Craniometry, or measurement of the skull, commanded the most attention and respect.

Its unquestioned leader, Paul Broca (1824–80), professor of clinical surgery at the Faculty of Medicine in Paris, gathered a school of disciples and imitators around himself. Their work, so meticulous and apparently irrefutable, exerted great influence and won high esteem as a jewel of nineteenth-century science.

Broca's work seemed particularly invulnerable to refutation. Had he not measured with the most scrupulous care and accuracy? (Indeed, he had. I have the greatest respect for Broca's meticulous procedure. His numbers are sound. But science is an inferential exercise, not a catalog of facts. Numbers, by themselves, specify nothing. All depends upon what you do with them.) Broca depicted himself as an apostle of objectivity, a man who bowed before facts and cast aside superstition and sentimentality. He declared that "there is no faith, however respectable, no interest, however legitimate, which must not accommodate itself to the progress of human knowledge and bend before truth." Women, like it or not, had smaller brains than men and, therefore, could not equal them in intelligence. This fact, Broca argued, may reinforce a common prejudice in male society, but it is also a scientific truth. L. Manouvrier, a black sheep in Broca's fold, rejected the inferiority of women and wrote with feeling about the burden imposed upon them by Broca's numbers:

> Women displayed their talents and their diplomas. They also invoked philosophical authorities. But they were opposed by *numbers* unknown to Condorcet or to John Stuart Mill. These numbers fell upon poor women like a sledge hammer, and they were accompanied by commentaries and sarcasms more ferocious than the most misogynist imprecations of certain church fathers. The theologians had asked if women had a soul. Several centuries later, some scientists were ready to refuse them a human intelligence.

Broca's argument rested upon two sets of data: the larger brains of men in modern societies, and a supposed increase in male superiority through time. His most extensive data came from autopsies performed personally in four Parisian hospitals. For 292 male brains, he calculated an average weight of 1,325 grams; 140 female brains averaged 1,144 grams for a difference of 181 grams, or 14 percent of the male weight. Broca understood, of course, that part of this difference could be attributed to the greater height of males. Yet he made no attempt to measure the effect of size alone and actually stated that it cannot account for the entire difference because we know, a priori, that women are not as intelligent as men (a premise that the data were supposed to test, not rest upon):

> We might ask if the small size of the female brain depends exclusively upon the small size of her body. Tiedemann has proposed this explanation. But we must not forget that women are, on the average, a little less intelligent than men, a difference which we should not exaggerate but which is, nonetheless, real. We are therefore permitted to suppose that the relatively small size of the female brain depends in part upon her physical inferiority and in part upon her intellectual inferiority.

In 1873, the year after Eliot published *Middlemarch,* Broca measured the cranial capacities of prehistoric skulls from L'Homme Mort cave. Here he found a difference of only 99.5 cubic centimeters between males and females, while modern populations range from 129.5 to 220.7. Topinard, Broca's chief disciple, explained the increasing discrepancy through time as a result of differing evolutionary pressures upon dominant men and passive women:

> The man who fights for two or more in the struggle for existence, who has all the responsibility and the cares of tomorrow, who is constantly active in combating the environment and human rivals, needs more brain than the woman whom he must protect and nourish, the

sedentary woman, lacking any interior occupations, whose role is to raise children, love, and be passive.

In 1879, Gustave Le Bon, chief misogynist of Broca's school, used these data to publish what must be the most vicious attack upon women in modern scientific literature (no one can top Aristotle). I do not claim his views were representative of Broca's school, but they were published in France's most respected anthropological journal. Le Bon concluded:

> In the most intelligent races, as among the Parisians, there are a large number of women whose brains are closer in size to those of gorillas than to the most developed male brains. This inferiority is so obvious that no one can contest it for a moment; only its degree is worth discussion. All psychologists who have studied the intelligence of women, as well as poets and novelists, recognize today that they represent the most inferior forms of human evolution and that they are closer to children and savages than to an adult, civilized man. They excel in fickleness, inconstancy, absence of thought and logic, and incapacity to reason. Without doubt there exist some distinguished women, very superior to the average man, but they are as exceptional as the birth of any monstrosity, as, for example, of a gorilla with two heads; consequently, we may neglect them entirely.

Nor did Le Bon shrink from the social implications of his views. He was horrified by the proposal of some American reformers to grant women higher education on the same basis as men:

> A desire to give them the same education, and, as a consequence, to propose the same goals for them, is a dangerous chimera. . . . The day when, misunderstanding the inferior occupations which nature has given her, women leave the home and take part in our battles; on this day a social revolution will begin, and everything that maintains the sacred ties of the family will disappear.

Sound familiar?*

I have reexamined Broca's data, the basis for all this derivative pronouncement, and I find his numbers sound but his interpretation ill-founded, to say the least. The data supporting his claim for increased difference through time can be easily dismissed. Broca based his contention on the samples from L'Homme Mort alone—only seven male and six female skulls in all. Never have so little data yielded such far ranging conclusions.

In 1888, Topinard published Broca's more extensive data on the Parisian hospitals. Since Broca recorded height and age as well as brain size, we may use modern statistics to remove their effect. Brain weight decreases with age, and Broca's women were, on average, considerably older than his men. Brain weight increases with height, and his average man was almost half a foot taller than his average woman. I used multiple regression, a technique that allowed me to assess simultaneously the influence of height and age upon brain size. In an analysis of the data for women, I found that, at average male height and age, a woman's brain would weigh 1,212 grams. Correction for height and age reduces Broca's measured difference of 181 grams by more than a third, to 113 grams.

I don't know what to make of this remaining difference because I cannot assess other factors known to influence brain size in a major way. Cause of death has an important

---

*When I wrote this essay, I assumed that Le Bon was a marginal, if colorful, figure. I have since learned that he was a leading scientist, one of the founders of social psychology, and best known for a seminal study on crowd behavior, still cited today (La psychologie des foules, 1895), and for his work on unconscious motivation. [Gould's note]

effect: degenerative disease often entails a substantial diminution of brain size. (This effect is separate from the decrease attributed to age alone.) Eugene Schreider, also working with Broca's data, found that men killed in accidents had brains weighing, on average, 60 grams more than men dying of infectious diseases. The best modern data I can find (from American hospitals) records a full 100-gram difference between death by degenerative arteriosclerosis and by violence or accident. Since so many of Broca's subjects were very elderly women, we may assume that lengthy degenerative disease was more common among them than among the men.

More importantly, modern students of brain size still have not agreed on a proper measure for eliminating the powerful effect of body size. Height is partly adequate, but men and women of the same height do not share the same body build. Weight is even worse than height, because most of its variation reflects nutrition rather than intrinsic size—fat versus skinny exerts little influence upon the brain. Manouvrier took up this subject in the 1880s and argued that muscular mass and force should be used. He tried to measure this elusive property in various ways and found a marked difference in favor of men, even in men and women of the same height. When he corrected for what he called "sexual mass," women actually came out slightly ahead in brain size.

Thus, the corrected 113-gram difference is surely too large; the true figure is probably close to zero and may as well favor women as men. And 113 grams, by the way, is exactly the average difference between a 5 foot 4 inch and a 6 foot 4 inch male in Broca's data. We would not (especially us short folks) want to ascribe greater intelligence to tall men. In short, who knows what to do with Broca's data? They certainly don't permit any confident claim that men have bigger brains than women.

To appreciate the social role of Broca and his school, we must recognize that his statements about the brains of women do not reflect an isolated prejudice toward a single disadvantaged group. They must be weighed in the context of a general theory that supported contemporary social distinctions as biologically ordained. Women, blacks, and poor people suffered the same disparagement, but women bore the brunt of Broca's argument because he had easier access to data on women's brains. Women were singularly denigrated but they also stood as surrogates for other disenfranchised groups. As one of Broca's disciples wrote in 1881: "Men of the black races have a brain scarcely heavier than that of white women." This juxtaposition extended into many other realms of anthropological argument, particularly to claims that, anatomically and emotionally, both women and blacks were like white children—and that white children, by the theory of recapitulation, represented an ancestral (primitive) adult stage of human evolution. I do not regard as empty rhetoric the claim that women's battles are for all of us.

Maria Montessori[1] did not confine her activities to educational reform for young children. She lectured on anthropology for several years at the University of Rome, and wrote an influential book entitled *Pedagogical Anthropology* (English edition, 1913). Montessori was no egalitarian. She supported most of Broca's work and the theory of innate criminality proposed by her compatriot *Cesare Lombroso*.[2] She measured the circumfer-

---

[1]*Maria Montessori* 1870–1952; an educator and doctor, she was the first woman in Italy to earn a degree in medicine. She developed a system of education for children which incorporated freedom of movement, a choice of activities, and specially designed equipment.

[2]*Cesare Lombroso* 1836–1909 a professor of psychiatry, forensic medicine, and criminal anthropology who believed in the existence of a distinctly criminal type of personality.

ence of children's heads in her schools and inferred that the best prospects had bigger brains. But she had no use for Broca's conclusions about women. She discussed Manouvrier's work at length and made much of his tentative claim that women, after proper correction of the data, had slightly larger brains than men. Women, she concluded, were intellectually superior, but men had prevailed heretofore by dint of physical force. Since technology has abolished force as an instrument of power, the era of women may soon upon us: "In such an epoch there will really be superior human beings, there will really be men strong in morality and in sentiment. Perhaps in this way the reign of women is approaching, when the enigma of her anthropological superiority will be deciphered. Woman was always the custodian of human sentiment, morality and honor."

This represents one possible antidote to "scientific" claims for the constitutional inferiority of certain groups. One may affirm the validity of biological distinctions but argue that the data have been misinterpreted by prejudiced men with a stake in the outcome, and that disadvantaged groups are truly superior. In recent years, Elaine Morgan has followed this strategy in her *Descent of Woman,* a speculative reconstruction of human prehistory from the woman's point of view—and as farcical as more famous tall tales by and for men.

I prefer another strategy. Montessori and Morgan followed Broca's philosophy to reach a more congenial conclusion. I would rather label the whole enterprise of setting a biological value upon groups for what it is: irrelevant and highly injurious. George Eliot well appreciated the special tragedy that biological labeling imposed upon members of disadvantaged groups. She expressed it for people like herself—women of extraordinary talent. I would apply it more widely—not only to those whose dreams are flouted but also to those who never realize that they may dream—but I cannot match her prose. In conclusion, then, the rest of Eliot's prelude to *Middlemarch:*

> The limits of variation are really much wider than anyone would imagine from the sameness of women's coiffure and the favorite love stories in prose and verse. Here and there a cygnet is reared uneasily among the ducklings in the brown pond, and never finds the living stream in fellowship with its own oary-footed kind. Here and there is born a Saint Theresa, foundress of nothing, whose loving heartbeats and sobs after an unattained goodness tremble off and are dispersed among hindrances instead of centering in some long-recognizable deed.

Understanding and Analysis

1. Gould's essay divides into three parts: description of the scientific and social controversy about women, analysis of the scientific evidence and the social implications, and a conclusion. Read the essay carefully and determine where each section begins and ends.

2. What are the views of women as represented by George Eliot, Broca, and Manouvrier?

3. What physical evidence does Broca present?

4. What social beliefs does Le Bon articulate?

5. What are the results of the analysis of the physical evidence? Why does Gould immediately dismiss the assertion about increasing size over time?

6. What factors did Broca overlook in his analysis of his own evidence? What has modern science contributed to the understanding and interpretation of Broca's data?

7. Why does Gould see women as representatives of all socially oppressed groups?

8. What were Montessori's ideas about brain size? To what extent did she agree with Broca? Why does Gould bring in the views of Elaine Morgan?

9. What position do Gould and Eliot take? Why? How does Gould extend Eliot's position? Do you agree?

Comparison

1. Examine Gould's last paragraph. Look at other conclusions as well, for example the conclusions in the essays by Milgram and Hoagland. What characteristics do you think mark a good conclusion?

2. Read some of the essays by women in this collection. Do you see great variety in the range of interests and points of view?

3. Read some of the essays about science in this collection. Do you detect social influences that appear to be skewing the scientific interpretation of data? Do you note scientists other than Gould who are aware of the ways prejudices may interfere with scientific objectivity?

4. Read Orwell's "What is Science?" What prejudices, if any, do you detect here?

5. According to a brief article in the July 1999 issue of *Discover*, Dean Falk, a paleoanthropologist from the State University of New York at Albany, has found that "men's brains, on average, are four ounces larger than those of women," even after taking proportions into account. Falk believes that the "extra neurons" are "most likely dedicated to visual-spatial skills, such as map reading, distinguishing between left and right, and mentally rotating figures–all abilities useful for navigating uncharted territories in search of mates." What response do you think Gould would have to this news? If Falk's findings were proved to be accurate, what effect would they have on your understanding of Gould's essay?

Richard Rodriguez
(1944–)

Richard Rodriguez was born in July of 1944 in San Francisco, California, the third child of Leopoldo and Victoria Moran Rodriguez. His parents met in California, each having come from Mexico, hoping to improve the family's economic condition. When his father first arrived in America, he'd hoped to borrow money from a priest for his high-school education, planning eventually to become an engineer. He courted Victoria Moran while they were attending night school and took her to the opera, each dressed in fancy clothes.

But, as Rodriguez records in his autobiography, *Memory of Hunger: The Education of Richard Rodriguez*, the loan never came; after a number of janitorial and factory jobs, Rodriguez's father gave up going to the opera. His mother finished night school but "had been awarded a high school diploma by teachers too careless or busy to notice that she hardly spoke English." Unlike her sisters who found work as maids, his mother taught herself to type so that she could work at "clean office jobs." Eventually Rodriguez's father found work as a dental technician and moved his young family to the middle-class neighborhood in Sacramento where Rodriguez grew up. After her last child entered school, his mother became a clerk-typist for a government office, proud of the words she could spell but not pronounce. Although neither of his parents read for pleasure, both knew the power of an education and saw to it that their children received the best they could find.

The four Rodriguez children attended the local Catholic parochial school, where the nuns insisted that they learn English and speak it, even at home. This introduction to public life, as opposed to the private, intimate life at home, and to reading, analysis, and quiet, as opposed to family talk, spontaneity, and noise, gave Rodriguez the education so highly prized by his family, but at the expense of their self-enclosed, private world. His autobiography records this gain and its concomitant loss. Books and public language allowed all the Rodriguez children entrance into the upper middle class but cut them off in painful ways from the intimacies of a separate family life, from the differences that had permitted them to remain a close-knit family group.

This pain and the feeling of alienation are experienced by all children who move from the working class into professions requiring an academic background, Rodriguez argues. For this reason he has written extensively opposing both bilingual education and affirmative action, contending that once a person has entered the mainstream, supported by a solid education that allows him or her to achieve in the public world, that person is no longer a member of a minority, no longer in need of special consideration. The people, Rodriguez believes, who need special attention are those whose education is so inferior that, like his mother, they are unable to join the mainstream because they cannot speak the language and have no access to middle-class jobs and economic success.

Rodriguez was a successful student, earning a B.A. from Stanford in 1967 and an M.A. from Columbia University in 1969. From 1969–1972, he did graduate work at the University of California at Berkeley, and from 1972–1973 he studied at the Warburg Institute, London, on a Fulbright to do research for a dissertation in English Renaissance literature. When he returned to Berkeley in 1974, he found himself inundated with offers for speaking engagements and fulltime teaching appointments at colleges and universities, even though he had not finished his dissertation. Gradually he came to believe that these offers were not based on his actual accomplishments, which, he felt, were no better than those of his fellow graduate students who had not even been granted interviews. Instead, he believed, he was being courted because of his supposed minority status. After considerable anguish, angered by both right- and left-wing political groups who failed to understand his position, he rejected all offers, left graduate school, and devoted himself to writing.

Rodriguez was awarded a one-year fellowship from the National Endowment for the Humanities in 1976 to work on his autobiography. After that, he took on odd jobs until the book was published in 1981. In 1982, he won a Gold Medal from the Commonwealth Club, a Christopher Award, and the Anisfield-Wolf Award for Race Relations. A second book, *Days of Obligation: An Argument with My Mexican Father* was published in 1993. He is now writing a third, tentatively entitled *King's Highway*. Richard Rodriguez is an associate editor at the Pacific News Service in San Francisco and lives in a Victorian house in San Francisco's gay community.

Rodriguez's model is George Orwell (who was also a "scholarship boy"), and like him Rodriguez writes with compelling honesty about political and social issues, combining literature with journalism so that the art and richness of the language, the distinctive voice of the writer, is always on the page. He finds poetry in the details of everyday life: "One among the four chambers of the beating hearts of Mexicans is a cave of Mary ... You will see her image everywhere in Mexico as you will see it in the Southwest—in bubblegum colors or in lovely shades of melon—a decal on the car window; the blue tattoo on an arm; a street mural in Los Angeles." Like Didion, whose upbringing, also in Sacramento, was worlds away from that of Rodriguez, he confronts his readers with direct questions that convey the immediacy of his concern for the lives of the people he describes. Asking "Can you understand?" he believes, like Orwell, that we must.

LABOR   (1982)

I WENT TO college at Stanford, attracted partly by its academic reputation, partly because it was the school rich people went to. I found myself on a campus with golden children of western America's upper middle class. Many were students both ambitious for academic success and accustomed to leisured life in the sun. In the afternoon, they lay spread out, sunbathing in front of the library, reading Swift or Engels[1] or Beckett.[2] Others went

---

[1]*Engels* Friedrich Engels (1820–1895), German socialist who, with Karl Marx, wrote *The Communist Manifesto*.

[2]*Beckett* Samuel Beckett (1906–1989), major playwright and novelist born in Dublin who lived in

by in convertibles, off to play tennis or ride horses or sail. Beach boys dressed in tank-tops and shorts were my classmates in undergraduate seminars. Tall tan girls wearing white strapless dresses sat directly in front of me in lecture rooms. I'd study them, their physical confidence. I was still recognizably kin to the boy I had been. Less tortured perhaps. But still kin. At Stanford, it's true, I began to have something like a conventional sexual life. I don't think, however, that I really believed that the women I knew found me physically appealing. I continued to stay out of the sun. I didn't linger in mirrors. And I was the student at Stanford who remembered to notice the Mexican-American janitors and gardeners working on campus.

It was at Stanford, one day near the end of my senior year, that a friend told me about a summer construction job he knew was available. I was quickly alert. Desire uncoiled within me. My friend said that he knew I had been looking for summer employment. He knew I needed some money. Almost apologetically he explained: It was something I probably wouldn't be interested in, but a friend of his, a contractor, needed someone for the summer to do menial jobs. There would be lots of shoveling and raking and sweeping. Nothing too hard. But nothing more interesting either. Still, the pay would be good. Did I want it? Or did I know someone who did?

I did. Yes, I said, surprised to hear myself say it.

In the weeks following, friends cautioned that I had no idea how hard physical labor really is. ('You only *think* you know what it is like to shovel for eight hours straight.') Their objections seemed to me challenges. They resolved the issue. I became happy with my plan. I decided, however, not to tell my parents. I wouldn't tell my mother because I could guess her worried reaction. I would tell my father only after the summer was over, when I could announce that, after all, I did know what 'real work' is like.

The day I met the contractor (a Princeton graduate, it turned out), he asked me whether I had done any physical labor before. 'In high school, during the summer,' I lied. And although he seemed to regard me with skepticism, he decided to give me a try. Several days later, expectant, I arrived at my first construction site. I would take off my shirt to the sun. And at last grasp desired sensation. No longer afraid. At last become like a *bracero*.[3] 'We need those tree stumps out of here by tomorrow,' the contractor said. I started to work.

I labored with excitement that first morning—and all the days after. The work was harder than I could have expected. But it was never as tedious as my friends had warned me it would be. There was too much physical pleasure in the labor. Especially early in the day, I would be most alert to the sensations of movement and straining. Beginning around seven each morning (when the air was still damp but the scent of weeds and dry earth anticipated the heat of the sun), I would feel my body resist the first thrusts of the shovel. My arms, tightened by sleep, would gradually loosen; after only several minutes, sweat would gather in beads on my forehead and then—a short while later—I would feel my chest silky with sweat in the breeze. I would return to my work. A nervous spark of pain would fly up my arm and settle to burn like an ember in the thick of my shoulder. An hour, two passed. Three. My whole body would assume regular movements; my shoveling would be described by identical, even movements. Even later in the day, my enthusiasm for primitive sensation would survive the heat and the dust and the insects prick-

Paris and wrote such plays as *Waiting for Godot* (1952), *Endgame* (1957), and *Krapp's Last Tape* (1959), as well as poetry, short stories, and such novels as *Malloy* (1951), *Malone Dies* (1951), and *More Pricks than Kicks* (1970).

[3] A man who works with his arms, from brazos, Spanish for "arms."

ling my back. I would strain wildly for sensation as the day came to a close. At three-thirty, quitting time, I would stand upright and slowly let my head fall back, luxuriating in the feeling of tightness relieved.

Some of the men working nearby would watch me and laugh. Two or three of the older men took the trouble to teach me the right way to use a pick, the correct way to shovel. 'You're doing it wrong, too fucking hard,' one man scolded. Then proceeded to show me—what persons who work with their bodies all their lives quickly learn—the most economical way to use one's body in labor.

'Don't make your back do so much work,' he instructed. I stood impatiently listening, half listening, vaguely watching, then noticed his work-thickened fingers clutching the shovel. I was annoyed. I wanted to tell him that I enjoyed shoveling the wrong way. And I didn't want to learn the right way. I wasn't afraid of back pain. I liked the way my body felt sore at the end of the day.

I was about to, but, as it turned out, I didn't say a thing. Rather it was at that moment I realized that I was fooling myself if I expected a few weeks of labor to gain me admission to the world of the laborer. I would not learn in three months what my father had meant by 'real work.' I was not bound to this job; I could imagine its rapid conclusion. For me the sensations of exertion and fatigue could be savored. For my father or uncle, working at comparable jobs when they were my age, such sensations were to be feared. Fatigue took a different toll on their bodies—and minds.

It was, I know, a simple insight. But it was with this realization that I took my first step that summer toward realizing something even more important about the 'worker.' In the company of carpenters, electricians, plumbers, and painters at lunch, I would often sit quietly, observant. I was not shy in such company. I felt easy, pleased by the knowledge that I was casually accepted, my presence taken for granted by men (exotics) who worked with their hands. Some days the younger men would talk and talk about sex, and they would howl at women who drove by in cars. Other days the talk at lunchtime was subdued; men gathered in separate groups. It depended on who was around. There were rough, good-natured workers. Others were quiet. The more I remember that summer, the more I realize that there was no single *type* of worker. I am embarrassed to say I had not expected such diversity. I certainly had not expected to meet, for example, a plumber who was an abstract painter in his off hours and admired the work of Mark Rothko.[4] Nor did I expect so many workers with college diplomas. (They were the ones who were not surprised that I intended to enter graduate school in the fall.) I suppose what I really want to say here is painfully obvious, but I must say it nevertheless: The men of that summer were middle-class Americans. They certainly didn't constitute an oppressed society. Carefully completing their work sheets; talking about the fortunes of local football teams; planning Las Vegas vacations; comparing the gas mileage of various makes of campers—they were not *los pobres*[5] my mother had spoken about.

On two occasions, the contractor hired a group of Mexican aliens. They were employed to cut down some trees and haul off debris. In all, there were six men of varying age. They youngest in his late twenties; the oldest (his father?) perhaps sixty years old. They came and they left in a single old truck. Anonymous men. They were never introduced to the other men at the site. Immediately upon their arrival, they would follow the con-

---

[4]American painter (1903–1970) born in Russia and known for abstract paintings of brightly colored, floating rectangles.

[5]Spanish for "the poor."

tractor's directions, start working—rarely resting—seemingly driven by a fatalistic sense that work which had to be done was best done as quickly as possible.

I watched them sometimes. Perhaps they watched me. The only time I saw them pay me much notice was one day at lunchtime when I was laughing with the other men. The Mexicans sat apart when they ate, just as they worked by themselves. Quiet. I rarely heard them say much to each other. All I could hear were their voices calling out sharply to one another, giving directions. Otherwise, when they stood briefly resting, they talked among themselves in voices too hard to overhear.

The contractor knew enough Spanish, and the Mexicans—or at least the oldest of them, their spokesman—seemed to know enough English to communicate. But because I was around, the contractor decided one day to make me his translator. (He assumed I could speak Spanish.) I did what I was told. Shyly I went over to tell the Mexicans that the *patrón* wanted them to do something else before they left for the day. As I started to speak, I was afraid with my old fear that I would be unable to pronounce the Spanish words. But it was a simple instruction I had to convey. I could say it in phrases.

The dark sweating faces turned toward me as I spoke. They stopped their work to hear me. Each nodded in response. I stood there. I wanted to say something more. But what could I say in Spanish, even if I could have pronounced the words right? Perhaps I just wanted to engage them in small talk, to be assured of their confidence, our familiarity. I thought for a moment to ask them where in Mexico they were from. Something like that. And maybe I wanted to tell them (a lie, if need be) that my parents were from the same part of Mexico.

I stood there.

Their faces watched me. The eyes of the man directly in front of me moved slowly over my shoulder, and I turned to follow his glance toward *el patrón* some distance away. For a moment I felt swept up by that glance into the Mexicans' company. But then I heard one of them returning to work. And then the others went back to work. I left them without saying anything more.

When they had finished, the contractor went over to pay them in cash. (He later told me that he paid them collectively—'for the job,' though he wouldn't tell me their wages. He said something quickly about the good rate of exchange 'in their own country.') I can still hear the loudly confident voice he used with the Mexicans. It was the sound of the *gringo*[6] I had heard as a very young boy. And I can still hear the quiet, indistinct sounds of the Mexican, the oldest, who replied. At hearing that voice I was sad for the Mexicans. Depressed by their vulnerability. Angry at myself. The adventure of the summer seemed suddenly ludicrous. I would not shorten the distance I felt from *los pobres* with a few weeks of physical labor. I would not become like them. They were different from me.

After that summer, a great deal—and not very much really—changed in my life. The curse of physical shame was broken by the sun; I was no longer ashamed of my body. No longer would I deny myself the pleasing sensations of my maleness. During those years when middle-class black Americans began to assert with pride, 'Black is beautiful,' I was able to regard my complexion without shame. I am today darker than I ever was as a boy. I have taken up the middle-class sport of long-distance running. Nearly every day now I run ten or fifteen miles, barely clothed, my skin exposed to the California winter rain and wind or the summer sun of late afternoon. The torso, the soccer

---

[6]Non-Hispanic American.

player's calves and thighs, the arms of the twenty-year-old I never was, I possess now in my thirties. I study the youthful parody shape in the mirror: the stomach lipped tight by muscle; the shoulders rounded by chin-ups; the arms veined strong. This man. A man. I meet him. He laughs to see me, what I have become.

The dandy. I wear double-breasted Italian suits and custom-made English shoes. I resemble no one so much as my father—the man pictured in those honeymoon photos. At that point in life when he abandoned the dandy's posture, I assume it. At the point when my parents would not consider going on vacation, I register at the Hotel Carlyle in New York and the Plaza Athenée in Paris. I am as taken by the symbols of leisure and wealth as they were. For my parents, however, those symbols became taunts, reminders of all they could not achieve in one lifetime. For me those same symbols are reassuring reminders of public success. I tempt vulgarity to be reassured. I am filled with the gaudy delight, the monstrous grace of the nouveau riche.

In recent years I have had occasion to lecture in ghetto high schools. There I see students of remarkable style and physical grace. (One can see more dandies in such schools than one ever will find in middle-class high schools.) There is not the look of casual assurance I saw students at Stanford display. Ghetto girls mimic high-fashion models. Their dresses are of bold, forceful color; their figures elegant, long; the stance theatrical. Boys wear shirts that grip at their overdeveloped muscular bodies. (Against a powerless future, they engage images of strength.) Bad nutrition does not yet tell. Great disappointment, fatal to youth, awaits them still. For the moment, movements in school hallways are dancelike, a procession of postures in a sexual masque. Watching them, I feel a kind of envy. I wonder how different my adolescence would have been had I been free. . . . But no, it is my parents I see—their optimism during those years when they were entertained by Italian grand opera.

The registration clerk in London wonders if I have just been to Switzerland. And the man who carries my luggage in New York guesses the Caribbean. My complexion becomes a mark of my leisure. Yet no one would regard my complexion the same way if I entered such hotels through the service entrance. That is only to say that my complexion assumes its significance from the context of my life. My skin, in itself, means nothing. I stress the point because I know there are people who would label me 'disadvantaged' because of my color. They make the same mistake I made as a boy, when I thought a disadvantaged life was circumscribed by particular occupations. That summer I worked in the sun may have made me physically indistinguishable from the Mexicans working nearby. (My skin was actually darker because, unlike them, I worked without wearing a shirt. By late August my hands were probably as tough as theirs.) But I was not one of *los pobres*. What made me different from them was an attitude of *mind*, my imagination of myself.

I do not blame my mother for warning me away from the sun when I was young. In a world where her brother had become an old man in his twenties because he was dark, my complexion was something to worry about. 'Don't run in the sun,' she warns me today. I run. In the end, my father was right—though perhaps he did not know how right or why—to say that I would never know what real work is. I will never know what he felt at his last factory job. If tomorrow I worked at some kind of factory, it would go differently for me. My long education would favor me. I could act as a public person—able to defend my interests, to unionize, to petition, to speak up—to challenge and demand. (I will never know what real work is.) I will never know what the Mexicans knew, gathering their shovels and ladders and saws.

Their silence stays with me now. The wages those Mexicans received for their labor were only a measure of their disadvantaged condition. Their silence is more telling. They lack a public identity. They remain profoundly alien. Persons apart. People lacking a union obviously, people without grounds. They depend upon the relative good will or fairness of their employers each day. For such people, lacking a better alternative, it is not such an unreasonable risk.

Their silence stays with me. I have taken these many words to describe its impact. Only: the quiet. Something uncanny about it. Its compliance. Vulnerability. Pathos. As I heard their truck rumbling away, I shuddered, my face mirrored with sweat. I had finally come face to face with *los pobres*.

Understanding and Analysis

1. After reading the entire essay, reread the first paragraph. What major themes does Rodriguez introduce in the first paragraph?

2. What does Rodriguez "savor" in the physical labor of his job? Why could these sensations not be savored by his father and uncle?

3. What expectations did Rodriguez have about the construction workers? How was he proved wrong?

4. What set the Mexican aliens apart from the other workers?

5. What changed in Rodriguez's life after his summer job?

6. What is the connection between the high-school dandies in the ghetto schools and Rodriguez's parents? What do they have in common with *los probres*?

7. What is the main point of this essay? Do you agree with Rodriguez's analysis of class and color and education?

8. Rodriguez uses the image of the mirror more than once in this essay. Find the instances and trace the significance of the mirror in the essay.

Comparison

1. Read Galbraith's "Labor, Leisure, and the New Class." What attitudes, if any, does Rodriguez share with Galbraith?

2. Read Baldwin's "If Black English is Not a Language, Then Tell Me, What Is?" To what extent would Baldwin agree with Rodriguez? On what issues might they disagree?

3. Read Wolfe's "Peppermint Lounge Revisited." Do you see connections between Wolfe's and Rodriguez's depiction of high-school students?

4. Read other essays in this collection that discuss issues of work; choose, for example, from essays by Baker, Ellison, Galbraith, Reich, Staples, Wolfe, and Woolf. On what, if anything, do these authors concur? What are their attitudes toward physical labor? Where does each one stand on issues of class and education?

Annie Dillard
(1945–)

Annie Dillard was born in April of 1945 in Pennsylvania, the eldest of the three daughters of Frank and Pam Lambert Doak, members of Pittsburgh's upper-middle class. Her father, a Presbyterian, a Republican, and the only child of a banker, worked as the personnel manager of a firm founded in the 1840s by his mother's grandfather. Her mother, a witty, inventive woman, stayed home to oversee the household chores, arrange gatherings with friends, drive the children to and from private school, art lessons, dancing school, ball games, and the pool at the country club. Underutilized, says Dillard in her autobiography, *An American Childhood*, her mother was a "Samson in chains."

In the book, Dillard traces her awakening to the outside world, to "a life of concentration," focusing on the year her father decided to quit his job, withdraw his investments in the firm, and, prompted by Twain's *Life on the Mississippi*, take his boat down the river to New Orleans. He left his wife, ten-year-old Annie, seven-year-old Amy, six-month-old Molly, the maid, and a nanny, to keep up appearances until, lonely and worried about what people might think, he returned to civilization six weeks later. This event, tying together reading and adventure in a brief escape from the dutiful life, is the touchstone of the book. Even at ten, Dillard was intense, reading *Kidnapped*, *The Field Book of Ponds and Streams*, *The Natural Way to Draw*, pitching ball, drawing, doing detective work, examining rocks and fossils, playing piano and field hockey, looking through her microscope at hydra and rotifers, always "in a rapture," always testing her limits.

But as a teenager, she "vanished into a blinded rage," railing at the hypocrisy she believed she saw in church, at the men and women who paraded their wealth and power in "sable stoles" and "tailcoats" on Sunday mornings and spent Sunday nights at the country club. Like the downed lines she had seen during a tornado, she was a "live wire, shooting out sparks that were digging a pit around me." She drew obsessively all over her school notebooks, got suspended briefly for smoking, read the French symbolists, wrote poetry, pounded out "Shake, Rattle, and Roll" on the piano, loved her boyfriend "so tenderly" that she thought she'd "transmogrify into vapor," and went on a drag race with boys she hardly knew, ending up in the hospital and later on crutches, an embarrassment and wonder to her family. Finally, mercifully, in 1963 she packed herself off to Hollins College in Virginia, where the English department could "smooth off her rough edges."

At Hollins she studied theology as well as English, and married her creative writing teacher, Richard Dillard, a poet and novelist, at the end of her sophomore year. Her rejection of religion, she said in 1978, had lasted only a month during her senior year in high school. She has remained in "the arms of Christianity" ever since. After earning her B.A. in 1967 and M.A. in 1968, Dillard remained in the Hollins area, painting and writing. In 1974, she published two books, a collection of her poems, *Tickets for a Prayer Wheel*, and her eclectic notes on nature and theology, *Pilgrim at Tinker Creek*, for which she was awarded the Pulitzer Prize for non-fiction in 1975. That year she and her husband were divorced, and Dillard moved to Washington to teach poetry and creative writing at Western Washington State University. While there, she wrote a column for the periodical of the Wilderness Society, worked as contributing editor of *Harper's*, and wrote her third book, *Holy the Firm* (1977), an aesthetic, ecstatic exploration of God and pain. From 1979 to 1981, she taught at Wesleyan University, in 1980, she married Gary Clevidence, a novelist, but the two have since separated. She has one daughter. Dillard has written a series of personal narratives entitled *Teaching A Stone to Talk* (1982) and a critical appreciation of stories and novels, *Living by Fiction* (1982). Her most recent books are her autobiography, *An American Childhood* (1987); *A Writing Life* (1989), eclectic thoughts about writing books; *The Living* (1993), a poetic novel; *The Annie Dillard Reader* (1995), a collection of her essays; and *Mornings Like This: Found Poems* (1996), and *For the Time Being* (1999), about her belief in the existence of God.

Annie Dillard is a master of a range of styles, moving from the plain style of her critical essays in *Living by Fiction* and much of her autobiography to the baroque prose of *Pilgrim at Tinker Creek, Holy the Firm, A Writing Life*, and *The Living*. Dillard draws details from nature, defining with equal vividness the "parallel rods" at the back of a boy's neck, the abdomen of an earwig, or the "translucent" skin of a deer. Like Virginia Woolf, Annie Dillard is a writer who is also a feminist. Clearly Woolf has served as a model for Dillard. In "The Death of a Moth," for example, Dillard deliberately chooses a subject Virginia Woolf also chose, but Dillard's treatment is strikingly different, as the subtitle of her essay, "Transfiguration in a Candle Flame," suggests. Dillard is fascinated with God and death and nature, and her prose reflects a mind intent on seeing the truth of death and the image of transfiguration.

THE DEER AT PROVIDENCIA (1982)

THERE WERE FOUR of us North Americans in the jungle, in the Ecuadorian jungle on the banks of the Napo River in the Amazon watershed. The other three North Americans were metropolitan men. We stayed in tents in one riverside village, and visited others. At the village called Providencia we saw a sight which moved us, and which shocked the men.

The first thing we saw when we climbed the riverbank to the village of Providencia was the deer. It was roped to a tree on the grass clearing near the thatch shelter where we would eat lunch.

The deer was small, about the size of a whitetail fawn, but apparently full-grown. It had a rope around its neck and three feet caught in the rope. Someone said that the dogs had caught it that morning and the villagers were going to cook and eat it that night.

This clearing lay at the edge of the little thatched-hut village. We could see the villagers going about their business, scattering feed corn for hens about their houses, and wandering down paths to the river to bathe. The village headman was our host; he stood beside us as we watched the deer struggle. Several village boys were interested in the deer; they formed part of the circle we made around it in the clearing. So also did four businessmen from Quito who were attempting to guide us around the jungle. Few of the very different people standing in this circle had a common language. We watched the deer, and no one said much.

The deer lay on its side at the rope's very end, so the rope lacked slack to let it rest its head in the dust. It was "pretty," delicate of bone like all deer, and thin-skinned for the tropics. Its skin looked virtually hairless, in fact, and almost translucent, like a membrane. Its neck was no thicker than my wrist; it was rubbed open on the rope, and gashed. Trying to paw itself free of the rope, the deer had scratched its own neck with its hooves. The raw underside of its neck showed red stripes and some bruises bleeding inside the muscles. Now three of its feet were hooked in the rope under its jaw. It could not stand, of course, on one leg, so it could not move to slacken the rope and ease the pull on its throat and enable it to rest its head.

Repeatedly the deer paused, motionless, its eyes veiled, with only its rib cage in motion, and its breaths the only sound. Then, after I would think, "It has given up; now it will die," it would heave. The rope twanged; the tree leaves clattered; the deer's free foot beat the ground. We stepped back and held our breaths. It thrashed, kicking, but only one leg moved; the other three legs tightened inside the rope's loop. Its hip jerked; its spine shook. Its eyes rolled; its tongue, thick with spittle, pushed in and out. Then it would rest again. We watched this for fifteen minutes.

Once three young native boys charged in, released its trapped legs, and jumped back to the circle of people. But instantly the deer scratched up its neck with its hooves and snared its forelegs in the rope again. It was easy to imagine a third and then a fourth leg soon stuck, like Brer Rabbit and the Tar Baby.[1]

We watched the deer from the circle, and then we drifted on to lunch. Our palm-roofed shelter stood on a grassy promontory from which we could see the deer tied to the tree, pigs and hens walking under village houses, and black-and-white cattle standing in the river. There was even a breeze.

Lunch, which was the second and better lunch we had that day, was hot and fried. There was a big fish called doncella, a kind of catfish, dipped whole in corn flour and beaten

---

[1]Drawing on the stories he had heard from the slaves in his hometown of Eatonton, Georgia, Joel Chandler Harris (1846–1908) published *Uncle Remus: His Songs and Sayings* (1881), *The Tar Baby* (1904), and *Uncle Remus and Br'er Rabbit* (1906), on which Walt Disney (1901–1966) based his popular movie *Song of the South* (1946).

egg, then deep fried. With our fingers we pulled soft fragments of it from its sides to our plates, and ate; it was delicate fish-flesh, fresh and mild. Someone found the roe, and I ate of that too—it was fat and stronger, like egg yolk, naturally enough, and warm.

There was also a stew of meat in shreds with rice and pale brown gravy. I had asked what kind of deer it was tied to the tree; Pepe had answered in Spanish, "*Gama.*" Now they told us this was gama too, stewed. I suspect the word means merely game or venison. At any rate, I heard that the village dogs had cornered another deer just yesterday, and it was this deer which we were now eating in full sight of the whole article. It was good. I was surprised at its tenderness. But it is a fact that high levels of lactic acid, which builds up in muscle tissues during exertion, tenderizes.

After the fish and meat we ate bananas fried in chunks and served on a tray; they were sweet and full of flavor. I felt terrific. My shirt was wet and cool from swimming; I had had a night's sleep, two decent walks, three meals, and a swim—everything tasted good. From time to time each of us, separately, would look beyond our shaded roof to the sunny spot where the deer was still convulsing in the dust. Our meal completed, we walked around the deer and back to the boats.

That night I learned that while we were watching the deer, the others were watching me.

We four North Americans grew close in the jungle in a way that was not the usual artificial intimacy of travelers. We liked each other. We stayed up all that night talking, murmuring, as though we rocked on hammocks slung above time. The others were from big cities: New York, Washington, Boston. They all said that I had no expression on my face when I was watching the deer—or at any rate, not the expression they expected.

They had looked to see how I, the only woman, and the youngest, was taking the sight of the deer's struggles. I looked detached, apparently, or hard, or calm, or focused, still. I don't know. I was thinking. I remember feeling very old and energetic. I could say like Thoreau that I have traveled widely in Roanoke, Virginia. I have thought a great deal about carnivorousness; I eat meat. These things are not issues; they are mysteries.

Gentlemen of the city, what surprises you? That there is suffering here, or that I know it?

We lay in the tent and talked. "If it had been my wife," one man said with special vigor, amazed, "she wouldn't have cared what was going on; she would have dropped *everything* right at that moment and gone in the village from here to there to there, she would not have stopped until that animal was out of its suffering one way or another. She couldn't bear to see a creature in agony like that."

I nodded.

Now I am home. When I wake I comb my hair before the mirror above my dresser. Every morning for the past two years I have seen in that mirror, beside my sleep-softened face, the blackened face of a burnt man. It is a wire-service photograph clipped from a newspaper and taped to my mirror. The caption reads: "Alan McDonald in Miami hospital bed." All you can see in the photograph is a smudged triangle or face from his eyelids to his lower lip; the rest is bandages. You cannot see the expression in his eyes; the bandages shade them.

The story, headed MAN BURNED FOR SECOND TIME, begins:

> "Why does God hate me?" Alan McDonald asked from his hospital bed.
> "When the gunpowder went off, I couldn't believe it," he said. "I just couldn't believe it. I said, 'No, God couldn't do this to me again.'"

He was in a burn ward in Miami, in serious condition. I do not even know if he lived. I wrote him a letter at the time, cringing.

He had been burned before, thirteen years previously, by flaming gasoline. For years he had been having his body restored and his face remade in dozens of operations. He had been a boy, and then a burnt boy. He had already been stunned by what could happen, by how life could veer.

Once I read that people who survive bad burns tend to go crazy: they have a very high suicide rate. Medicine cannot ease their pain; drugs just leak away, soaking the sheets, because there is no skin to hold them in. The people just lie there and weep. Later they kill themselves. They had not known, before they were burned, that the world included such suffering, that life could permit them personally such pain.

This time a bowl of gunpowder had exploded on McDonald.

> "I didn't realize what had happened at first," he recounted. "And then I heard that sound from 13 years ago. I was burning. I rolled to put the fire out and I thought, 'Oh God, not again.'
>
> "If my friend hadn't been there, I would have jumped into a canal with a rock around my neck."

His wife concludes the piece, "Man, it just isn't fair."

I read the whole clipping again every morning. This is the Big Time here, every minute of it. Will someone please explain to Alan McDonald in his dignity, to the deer at Providencia in his dignity, what is going on? And mail me the carbon.

When we walked by the deer at Providencia for the last time, I said to Pepe, with a pitying glance at the deer, "*Pobrecito*"—"poor little thing." But I was trying out Spanish. I knew at the time it was a ridiculous thing to say.

Understanding and Analysis

1. After you have read the entire essay, reread the opening paragraph. What two events is Dillard referring to in the last sentence of the first paragraph? Is Dillard being ironic in her choice of the word "shocked"? What is the difference between being "moved" and being "shocked"?

2. What groups of people were standing in a circle watching the deer? What do you know of their occupations, nationalities, ages, and gender?

3. What expectations did the North American men have of Dillard? Why? What assumptions do you have about the reactions of the men to the struggling deer? What do you suppose would have happened had Dillard or someone else done what one man claims his wife would have done? Does Dillard mention the women of the village of Providencia? Do you think the expectations for women in Providencia differ from those in New York or Boston?

4. What does Dillard mean when she says that eating meat and carnivorousness are "mysteries"?

5. Why does Dillard address the men directly? What is the tone of her question? Does the tone differ from the tone Dillard takes in other parts of the essay? If you do hear a shift in tone, do you hear one elsewhere as well?

6. What do the deer, the burnt man, Dillard, and all of us have in common?

7. Why does Dillard think it is "ridiculous" to call the deer a "poor little thing"?

8. How in the essay does Dillard offset suffering with the enjoyment of life? Is there a balance or does one take precedence over the other?

9. Why do you suppose Dillard takes such pains to emphasize the variety of groups represented in this incident in Providencia?

10. Does Dillard try to move or even shock the reader in this essay? If you think she does, why do you suppose she wants to have this effect on the reader? What is her point?

11. What effect, if any, does the fact that the burnt man was handling gunpowder after having already been burned once have on Dillard's argument?

Comparison

1. Both Rodriguez and Dillard employ images of the mirror and watching in their essays. Trace the different ways each author uses these images.

2. Compare Woolf's depiction of the death of the moth with Dillard's description of the suffering deer. Do you think Woolf and Dillard have similar attitudes toward death? Why or why not?

3. E. B. White and Dillard both reveal an appreciation for nature in their essays. What characteristics, if any, do they share?

4. Read the essays by Milgram and Gansberg. To what degree do these three, Milgram, Gansberg, and Dillard, hold the individual responsible for his or her actions?

Margaret Atwood
(1939–)

In her "Waterstone's Poetry Lecture," given in Wales in 1995, the poet, novelist, and short story writer Margaret Atwood describes with characteristic humor the occasion of her birth and its effect on her development: "I was born on November 18, 1939, in the Ottawa General Hospital, two and a half months after the beginning of the Second World War. Being born at the beginning of the war gave me a substratum of anxiety and dread to draw on, which is very useful to a poet. It also meant that I was malnourished. This is why I am short. If it hadn't been for food rationing, I would have been six feet tall." When she was not yet four feet tall, Atwood spent several seasons of her childhood in the woods, where her father, an entomologist, did his work. Blessed with little more than a bad radio in the way of electronic entertainments, she became "a reading addict" at an early age.

Deciding during high school that she wanted to be a poet, Atwood remained certain of her calling in college, even though she became convinced that she "would have to emigrate," since few Canadian authors had achieved mainstream success in 1960. "I faced a future of scrubbing restaurant floors in England," she writes, "writing masterpieces in a freezing garret at night, and getting T.B., like Keats." While she did later work as a waitress, Atwood's immediate future proved considerably less grim than contracting tuberculosis. Studying under Northrop Frye at the University of Toronto, she graduated in 1961, published her first collection of poetry, *Double Persephone* (1961), and earned her M.A. at Radcliffe in 1962. Beginning doctoral work at Harvard, she returned to Canada in 1964 and took a position as a lecturer at the University of British Columbia "teaching grammar to Engineering students at eight-thirty in the morning in a Quonset hut. It was all right, as none of us were awake; I made them write imitations of Kafka, which I thought might help them in their chosen profession."

Back at Harvard, Atwood published another collection of poems, *The Circle Game* (1966), which won the Governor General's Award. Although she had planned to finish her doctorate, she left Harvard permanently in 1967 and worked as a lecturer at Sir George Williams University in Montreal. After publishing *The Animals in That Country* in 1968, she released her first novel, *The Edible Woman*, in 1969, followed by another collection of verse, *The Journals of Susanna Moodie*, in 1970. The following year, she worked as an assistant professor at York University, switching to the University of Toronto in 1972, when she accepted her first position as a writer–in–residence.

As prolific in the 1970s as in every decade since, Atwood published numerous collections of poems, including *Procedures for Underground* (1970), *Power Politics* (1971), and *Two-Headed Poems* (1978), as well as her first collection of stories, *Dancing Girls* (1977). In the 1980s, she served as a writer-in-residence and a visiting professor in the United States and Australia, publishing, in addition to collections of poems, prose poems, critical essays, and short stories, and one of her most famous novels, *The Handmaid's Tale* (1985). In the words of the author, this novel is a piece of "speculative fiction in the genre of *Brave New World* and *Nineteen Eighty-Four*" grounded in her "study of the American Puritans." *The Handmaid's Tale* earned Atwood the Commonwealth Literature Prize, the Arthur C. Clarke Award for Best Science Fiction (though Atwood says the book "certainly isn't science fiction"), and the *Los Angeles Times* Book Award. In 1986, *Ms.* magazine named Atwood Woman of the Year. Receiving literary awards for her novel *Cat's Eye* (1988), Atwood secured the International Humourous Writer Award for *The Robber Bride* (1995). Still working at an incredible pace, she told her audience in Wales, "I'm still writing, I'm still writing poetry, [and] I still can't explain why."

"Margaret Atwood," writes Lorrie Moore in a review of *The Robber Bride*, "has always possessed a tribal bent: in both her fiction and her nonfiction she has described and transcribed the ceremonies and experience of being a woman, or a Canadian, or a writer—or all three." As a writer overtly concerned with feminist themes, Atwood has run the risk of every overtly political writer: being criticized for writing propaganda, rather than literature, for creating sermons with mouthpieces, rather than stories with characters. Along with her talent, however, Atwood's interest in language has often redeemed her in the eyes of glowering reviewers. From her earliest poetic speakers, who play with readers' perceptions, to her later narrators, who meditate on the process of telling stories, Atwood creates characters who share her compulsion to speak and her fascination with speaking. Giving them rich worlds to speak about, Atwood locates several of her writings—even those that are not ghost stories and fairy tales—at the edge of the otherworldly, where people and landscapes may turn bizarre, unexpected, eerily distorted, or eerily clear. Still, the most otherworldly of her works reflects on no other world but this. "I once was a graduate student in Victorian literature," she writes, "and I believe as the Victorian novelists did, that a novel isn't simply a vehicle for private expression, but that it also exists for social examination. I firmly believe this."

PORNOGRAPHY (1983)

WHEN I WAS in Finland a few years ago for an international writers' conference, I had occasion to say a few paragraphs in public on the subject of pornography. The context was a discussion of political repression, and I was suggesting the possibility of a link between the two. The immediate result was that a male journalist took several large bites out of me. Prudery and pornography are two halves of the same coin, said he, and I was clearly a prude. What could you expect from an Anglo-Canadian? Afterward, a couple of pleasant Scandinavian men asked me what I had been so worked up about. All "pornography" means, they said, is graphic depictions of whores, and what was the harm in that?

Not until then did it strike me that the male journalist and I had two entirely different things in mind. By "pornography," he meant naked bodies and sex. I, on the other hand, had recently been doing the research for my novel *Bodily Harm*, and was still in a state of shock from some of the material I had seen, including the Ontario Board of Film Censors' "outtakes." By "pornography," I meant women getting their nipples snipped off with garden shears, having meat hooks stuck into their vaginas, being disemboweled; little girls being raped; men (yes, there are some men) being smashed to a pulp and forcibly sodomized. The cutting edge of pornography, as far as I could see, was no longer simple old copulation, hanging from the chandelier or otherwise: it was death, messy, explicit and highly sadistic. I explained this to the nice Scandinavian men. "Oh, but that's just the United States," they said. "Everyone knows they're sick." In their country, they said, violent "pornography" of that kind was not permitted on television or in movies; indeed, excessive violence of any kind was not permitted. They had drawn a clear line between erotica, which earlier studies had shown did not incite men to more aggressive and brutal behavior toward women, and violence, which later studies indicated did.

Some time after that I was in Saskatchewan, where, because of the scenes in *Bodily Harm,* I found myself on an open-line radio show answering questions about "pornography." Almost no one who phoned in was in favor of it, but again they weren't talking about the same stuff I was, because they hadn't seen it. Some of them were all set to stamp out bathing suits and negligees, and, if possible, any depictions of the female body whatsoever. God, it was implied, did not approve of female bodies, and sex of any kind, including that practised by bumblebees, should be shoved back into the dark, where it belonged. I had more than a suspicion that *Lady Chatterley's Lover,*[1] Margaret Laurance's *The Diviners,* and indeed most books by most serious modern authors would have ended up as confetti if left in the hands of these callers.

For me, these two experiences illustrate the two poles of the emotionally heated debate that is now thundering around this issue. They also underline the desirability and even the necessity of defining the terms. "Pornography" is now one of those catchalls, like "Marxism" and "feminism," that have become so broad they can mean almost anything, ranging from certain verses in the Bible, ads for skin lotion and sex texts for children to the contents of *Penthouse,* Naughty '90s postcards and films with titles containing the word *Nazi* that show vicious scenes of torture and killing. It's easy to say that sensible people can tell the difference. Unfortunately, opinions on what constitutes a sensible person vary.

But even sensible people tend to lose their cool when they start talking about this subject. They soon stop talking and start yelling, and the name-calling begins. Those in favor of censorship (which may include groups not noticeably in agreement on other issues, such as some feminists and religious fundamentalists) accuse the others of exploiting women through the use of degrading images, contributing to the corruption of children, and adding to the general climate of violence and threat in which both women and children live in this society; or, though they may not give much of a hoot about actual women and children, they invoke moral standards and God's supposed aversion to "filth," "smut" and deviated *preversion,* which may mean ankles.

The camp in favor of total "freedom of expression" often comes out howling as loud as the Romans would have if told they could no longer have innocent fun watching the lions eat up Christians. It too may include segments of the population who are not natural bedfellows: those who proclaim their God-given right to freedom, including the freedom to tote guns, drive when drunk, drool over chicken porn and get off on videotapes of women being raped and beaten, may be waving the same anticensorship banner as responsible liberals who fear the return of Mrs. Grundy,[2] or gay groups for whom sexual emancipation involves the concept of "sexual theater." *Whatever turns you on* is a

---

[1]*Lady Chatterly's Lover* a sexually explicit novel D. H. Lawrence published in 1928, which was banned for many years but was wildly popular.

[2]*Mrs. Grundy* Character in a play by Thomas Morton, *Speed the Plough* (1798), who represents conventional opinion.

handy motto, as is *A man's home is his castle* (and if it includes a dungeon with beautiful maidens strung up in chains and bleeding from every pore, that's his business).

Meanwhile, theoreticians theorize and speculators speculate. Is today's pornography yet another indication of the hatred of the body, the deep mind—body split, which is supposed to pervade Western Christian society? Is it a backlash against the women's movement by men who are threatened by uppity female behavior in real life, so like to fantasize about women done up like outsize parcels, being turned into hamburger, kneeling at their feet in slavelike adoration or sucking off guns? Is it a sign of collective impotence, of a generation of men who can't relate to real women at all but have to make do with bits of celluloid and paper? Is the current flood just a result of smart marketing and aggressive promotion by the money men in what has now become a multibillion-dollar industry? If they were selling movies about men getting their testicles stuck full of knitting needles by women with swastikas on their sleeves, would they do as well, or is this penchant somehow peculiarly male? If so, why? Is pornography a power trip rather than a sex one? Some say that those ropes, chains, muzzles and other restraining devices are an argument for the immense power female sexuality still wields in the male imagination: you don't put these things on dogs unless you're afraid of them. Others, more literary, wonder about the shift from the 19th-century Magic Woman or Femme Fatale image to the lollipoplicker, airhead or turkey-carcass treatment of women in porn today. The proporners don't care much about theory: they merely demand product. The antiporners don't care about it in the final analysis either: there's dirt on the street, and they want it cleaned up, now.

It seems to me that this conversation, with its *You're-a-prude/You're-a-pervert* dialectic, will never get anywhere as long as we continue to think of this material as just "entertainment." Possibly we're deluded by the packaging, the format: magazine, book, movie, theatrical presentation. We're used to thinking of these things as part of the "entertainment industry," and we're used to thinking of ourselves as free adult people who ought to be able to see any kind of "entertainment" we want to. That was what the First Choice pay-TV debate was all about. After all, it's only entertainment, right? Entertainment means fun, and only a killjoy would be antifun. What's the harm?

This is obviously the central question: *What's the harm?* If there isn't any real harm to any real people, then the antiporners can tsk-tsk and/or throw up as much as they like, but they can't rightfully expect more legal controls or sanctions. However, the no-harm position is far from being proven.

(For instance, there's a clear-cut case for banning—as the federal government has proposed—movies, photos and videos that depict children engaging in sex with adults: real children are used to make the movies, and hardly anybody thinks this is ethical. The possibilities for coercion are too great.)

To shift the viewpoint, I'd like to suggest three other models for looking at "pornography"—and here I mean the violent kind.

Those who find the idea of regulating pornographic materials repugnant because they think it's Fascist or Communist or otherwise not in accordance with the principles of an open democratic society should consider that Canada has made it illegal to disseminate material that may lead to hatred toward any group because of race or religion. I suggest that if pornography of the violent kind depicted these acts being done predominantly to Chinese, to blacks, to Catholics, it would be off the market immediately, under the present laws. Why is hate literature illegal? Because whoever made the law thought that such material might incite real people to do real awful things to other real people. The human brain is to a certain extent a computer: garbage in, garbage out. We only hear about the extreme cases (like that of American multimurderer Ted Bundy) in which pornography has contributed to the death and/or mutilation of women and/or men. Although pornography is not the only factor involved in the creation of such deviance, it certainly has upped the ante by suggesting both a variety of techniques and the social acceptability of such actions. Nobody knows yet what effect this stuff is having on the less psychotic.

Studies have shown that a large part of the market for all kinds of porn, soft and hard, is drawn from the 16-to-21-year-old population of young men. Boys used to learn about sex on the street, or (in Italy, according to Fellini movies) from friendly whores, or, in more genteel surroundings, from girls, their parents, or, once upon a time, in school, more or less. Now porn has been added, and sex education in the schools is rapidly being phased out. The buck has been passed, and boys are being taught that all women secretly like to be raped and that real men get high on scooping out women's digestive tracts.

Boys learn their concept of masculinity from other men: is this what most men want them to be learning? If word gets around that rapists are "normal" and even admirable men, will boys feel that in order to be normal, admirable and masculine they will have to be rapists? Human beings are enormously flexible, and how they turn out depends a lot on how they're educated, by the society in which they're immersed as well as by their teachers. In a society that advertises and glorifies rape or even implicitly condones it, more women get raped. It becomes socially acceptable. And at a time when men and the traditional male role have taken a lot of flak and men are confused and casting around for an acceptable way of being male (and, in some cases, not getting much comfort from women on that score), this must be at times a pleasing thought.

It would be naïve to think of violent pornography as just harmless entertainment. It's also an educational tool and a powerful propaganda device. What happens when boy educated on porn meets girl brought up on Harlequin romances? The clash of expectations can be heard around the block. She wants him to get down on his knees with a ring, he wants her to get down on all fours with a ring in her nose. Can this marriage be saved?

Pornography has certain things in common with such addictive substances as alcohol and drugs: for some, though by no means for all, it induces chemical changes in the body, which the user finds exciting and pleasurable. It also appears to attract a "hard core" of habitual users and a penumbra of those who use it occasionally but aren't dependent on it in any way. There are also significant numbers of men who aren't much interested in it, not because they're undersexed but because real life is satisfying their needs, which may not require as many appliances as those of users.

For the "hard core," pornography may function as alcohol does for the alcoholic: tolerance develops, and a little is no longer enough. This may account for the short viewing time and fast turnover in porn theatres. Mary Brown, chairwoman of the Ontario Board of Film Censors, estimates that for every one mainstream movie requesting entrance to Ontario, there is one porno flick. Not only the quantity consumed but the quality of explicitness must escalate, which may account for the growing violence: once the big deal was breasts, then it was genitals, then copulation, then that was no longer enough and the hard users had to have more. The ultimate kick is death, and after that, as the Marquis de Sade[3] so boringly demonstrated, multiple death.

---

[3]*Marquis de Sade* Donatien Alphonse François (1740–1814) a French writer and soldier who was imprisoned for his cruelty and sexual perversions. When he died, he was insane. The word "sadism" comes from his name.

The existence of alcoholism has not led us to ban social drinking. On the other hand, we do have laws about drinking and driving, excessive drunkenness and other abuses of alcohol that may result in injury or death to others.

This leads us back to the key question: what's the harm? Nobody knows, but this society should find out fast, before the saturation point is reached. The Scandinavian studies that showed a connection between depictions of sexual violence and increased impulse toward it on the part of male viewers would be a starting point, but many more questions remain to be raised as well as answered. What, for instance, is the crucial difference between men who are users and men who are not? Does using affect a man's relationship with actual women, and, if so, adversely? Is there a clear line between erotica and violent pornography, or are they on an escalating continuum? Is this a "men versus women" issue, with all men secretly siding with the proporners and all women secretly siding against? (I think not; there *are* lots of men who don't think that running their true love through the Cuisinart is the best way they can think of to spend a Saturday night, and they're just as nauseated by films of someone else doing it as women are.) Is pornography merely an expression of the sexual confusion of this age or an active contributor to it?

Nobody wants to go back to the age of official repression, when even piano legs were referred to as "limbs" and had to wear pantaloons to be decent. Neither do we want to end up in George Orwell's *1984*, in which pornography is turned out by the State to keep the proles in a state of torpor, sex itself is considered dirty and the approved practice it only for reproduction. But Rome under the emperors isn't such a good model either.

If all men and women respected each other, if sex were considered joyful and life-enhancing instead of a wallow in germ-filled glop, if everyone were in love all the time, if, in other words, many people's lives were more satisfactory for them than they appear to be now, pornography might just go away on its own. But since this is obviously not happening, we as a society are going to have to make some informed and responsible decisions about how to deal with it.

Understanding and Analysis

1. Reread the first paragraph. Why do you suppose Atwood writes that "a male journalist took several large bites out of me"? How did you respond to those words the first time you read them? How do you respond to them now?

2. What definition of pornography did you have in mind when you read the title of the essay? What was the definition supplied by the Scandinavians? Is their definition different from the one Atwood ascribes to the male journalist? What is Atwood's definition? What did the talk show respondents mean by pornography?

3. What is Atwood's point about definition? What is the definition of "a sensible person"?

4. What for Atwood is the "central question"? How could it be answered?

5. Atwood says she is suggesting "three other models for looking at" pornography. What is the first model? What other models does she offer?

6. In paragraph 19, when Atwood returns to the central question, what evidence does she offer? Compare her questions about evidence to the ones you developed in question four.

7. In the end, does Atwood take a specific position on what should be done about violent pornography? If so, what is it? If not, why not?

Comparison

1. Read Dillard's "The Deer at Providencia." Both writers encounter stereotyped expectations about specific groups. Compare the way they use these experiences to make their points.

2. Read Mencken's "The Penalty of Death," Vidal's "Drugs," and Brady's "I Want a Wife." What characteristics, if any, do these essays share with Atwood's essay? Are they equally persuasive? Why or why not?

3. Read the essay by Rachel Carson. What, if anything, does Carson's essay have in common with Atwood's essay? Look at goals and techniques. Read Frost's essay and apply his definition of enthusiasm to the two essays.

Barry Lopez
(1945–)

Barry Holstun Lopez was born on January 6, 1945, in Port Chester, New York, the first child of Adrian and Mary Holstun Lopez. Although his family moved to California when he was just three years old, he has clear memories of living in the east in a six-story apartment complex, pushing toys over a window ledge to force his mother to take him outside into the garden. Once his family moved west, not long after the birth of his brother, Dennis, Lopez enjoyed much better access to the outdoors. First living in a house "surrounded by alfalfa hay fields," Lopez moved to his mother's new house in Reseda after his parents' divorce, finding that "adventure unfolded in fruit orchards and wisteria hedges, in horse pastures and haylofts, and around farming operations, truck gardens, and chicken ranches." His mother inspired more than one of Lopez's lifelong passions by creating an almost "bohemian" childhood for Lopez and his brother; she "embraced our drawings, our stories, and our Tinkertoy kingdoms, and she drove us to many intriguing places in our green 1934 Ford coupe—to Boulder (later, Hoover) Dam [and] the La Brea Tar Pits," as well as Lake Arrowhead and the Mojave Desert.

Remarrying when Lopez was 11, Mary moved the family back east, where Lopez attended a Jesuit high school and numerous debutante balls. Unaccustomed to his family's new wealth, Lopez was lonely for the landscapes of California, although he also "thrived in the city." In 1962, he entered the University of Notre Dame in South Bend, Indiana, spending many of his weekends on camping trips and road trips, going as far north as Canada and as far south as Mississippi. Although he had entered school "with the intention of becoming an aeronautical engineer," his interests changed along the way. During his second year, he also discovered the need to write: "I was driven to write, but of course anguished over my efforts. Who was I to speak? What had I to say? . . . [M]uch of what seemed to me so worth addressing—the psychological draw of landscape, that profound mystery I sensed in wild animals . . .—was regarded as peculiar territory by nascent writers at the university." Graduating in 1966 with a degree in Communications, Lopez married Sandra Landers in 1967 and earned his Master of Arts in Teaching in 1968, thinking he might teach at a private high school. Instead, he enrolled in an MFA program at the University of Oregon in 1969. Although he "left that program after only a semester," he remained at the university for the full year, studying folklore and English, learning about anthropology, in effect, molding his own course of study to prepare him to write.

Lopez's earliest works, however, reflect little of this preparation. Pieces like "What You Need to Know before You Buy 4-Wheel Drive" and "New Power Winches Wind up Your Work Quicker," published in *Popular Science*, simply helped pay the bills. It was an assignment for another magazine, *Smithsonian*, that prompted Lopez to write his first major work, *Of Wolves and Men*. Agreeing to write an article about wolves in 1974, Lopez found that researching wolves "actually catalyzed a lot of thinking about human and animal relationships which had been going on in a vague way in my mind for several years, and I realized that if I focused on this one animal, I might be able to say something sharp and clear about the way we treat all animals, and about how we relate to the natural world in the latter part of the twentieth century." Lopez published his first book, *Desert Notes: Reflections in the Eye of a Raven*, in 1976 and *Of Wolves and Men* in 1978. Nominated for an American Book Award, the second book received lavish praise from reviewers and made Lopez's reputation as a writer.

After publishing several works of fiction during the late 1970s and early 1980s, Lopez served as the Distinguished Visiting Writer at Eastern Washington University and as the Ida Beam Visiting Professor at the University of Iowa, both in 1985. In 1986, the year he became the Distinguished Visiting Naturalist at Carleton College, he published his second major work, *Arctic Dreams: Imagination and Desire in a Northern Landscape*, which won the National Book Award. As his final book of the 1980s, he published a collection of essays called *Crossing Open Ground* (1988). After returning to his alma mater as a Visiting Professor of American Studies in 1989, he published fables and works of fiction in the 1990s, as well as a partly autobiographical collection of essays, *About This Life: Journeys on the Threshold of Memory* (1998).

A fair writer of short fiction, Barry Lopez excels in the writing of nonfiction, weaving together myth, folklore, philosophy, and science to create stirring accounts of animals, their habitats, and their places in our cultures. His prose strikes reviewers as "gracious," "dazzling," even "magical," while he himself comes across as tireless in his enthusiasm about nature. Praising Lopez's enthusiasm and his exceptional writing about animals, Edward Hoagland writes in a review of *Arctic Dreams* that he finds "no evidence that [Lopez] writes as well about people" as about animals, since "none of his companions on his many trips, Eskimo or white, is ever delineated." Lopez may not populate his books with people, but as he reveals in interviews, he speaks with the human inhabitants of the places he visits, not only to access their "tremendous storehouse of knowledge," but also to avoid the bias of believing things newly found when they are located for the first time by a white interloper: "[J]ust a couple of months ago I opened a recent issue of a journal called *Arctic*, and there was a wonderful story by two ornithologists who'd made the first discovery of a breeding ground for dovekies in Canada—it could have been 'discovered' years earlier, by just asking the hunters in a village called Clyde." At times as shrewd an analyst of American culture as he is an observer of the natural world, Lopez writes about animals living in the Arctic or left dead along the road with the same sense of conviction, the same set of philosophical and thematic aims. "My themes," he says, "will always be dignity of life, structures of prejudice, passion, generosity, kindness and the possibility of the good life in dark circumstances."

LANDSCAPE AND NARRATIVE (1984)

ONE SUMMER EVENING in a remote village in the Brooks Range of Alaska, I sat among a group of men listening to hunting stories about the trapping and pursuit of animals. I was particularly interested in several incidents involving wolverine, in part because a friend of mine was studying wolverine in Canada, among the Cree, but, too, because I find this animal such an intense creature. To hear about its life is to learn more about fierceness.

Wolverines are not intentionally secretive, hiding their lives from view, but they are seldom observed. The range of their known behavior is less than that of, say, bears or wolves. Still, that evening no gratuitous details were set out. This was somewhat odd, for wolverine easily excite the imagination; they can loom suddenly in the landscape with authority, with an aura larger than their compact physical dimensions, drawing one's immediate and complete attention. Wolverine also have a deserved reputation for resoluteness in the worst winters, for ferocious strength. But neither did these attributes induce the men to embellish.

I listened carefully to these stories, taking pleasure in the sharply observed detail surrounding the dramatic thread of events. The story I remember most vividly was about a man hunting a wolverine from a snow machine in the spring. He followed the animal's tracks for several miles over rolling tundra in a certain valley. Soon he caught sight ahead of a dark spot on the crest of a hill—the wolverine pausing to look back. The hunter was catching up, but each time he came over a rise the wolverine was looking back from the next rise, just out of range. The hunter topped one more rise and met the wolverine bounding toward him. Before he could pull his rifle from its scabbard the wolverine flew across the engine cowl and the windshield, hitting him square in the chest. The hunter scrambled his arms wildly, trying to get the wolverine out of his lap, and fell over as he did so. The wolverine jumped clear as the snow machine rolled over, and fixed the man with a stare. He had not bitten, not even scratched the man. Then the wolverine walked away. The man thought of reaching for the gun, but no, he did not.

The other stories were like this, not so much making a point as evoking something about contact with wild animals that would never be completely understood.

When the stories were over, four or five of us walked out of the home of our host. The surrounding land, in the persistent light of a far northern summer, was still visible for miles—the striated, pitched massifs of the Brooks Range; the shy, willow-lined banks of the John River flowing south from Anaktuvuk Pass; and the flat tundra plain, opening with great affirmation to the north. The landscape seemed alive because of the stories. It was precisely these ocherous tones, this kind of willow, exactly this austerity that had informed the wolverine narratives. I felt exhilaration, and a deeper confirmation of the stories. The mundane tasks which awaited me I anticipated now with pleasure. The stories had renewed in me a sense of the purpose of my life.

This feeling, an inexplicable renewal of enthusiasm after storytelling, is familiar to many people. It does not seem to matter greatly what the subject is, as long as the context is intimate and the story is told for its own sake, not forced to serve merely as the vehicle for an idea. The tone of the story need not be solemn. The darker aspects of life need not be ignored. But I think intimacy is indispensable—a feeling that derives from the listener's trust and a storyteller's certain knowledge of his subject and regard for his audience. This intimacy deepens if the storyteller tempers his authority with humility, or when terms of idiomatic expression, or at least the physical setting for the story, are shared.

I think of two landscapes—one outside the self, the other within. The external landscape is the one we see—not only the line and color of the land and its shading at different times of the day, but also its plants and animals in season, its weather, its geology, the record of its climate and evolution. If you walk up, say, a dry arroyo in the Sonoran Desert you will feel a mounding and rolling of sand and silt beneath your foot that is distinctive. You will anticipate the crumbling of the sedimentary earth in the arroyo bank as your hand reaches out, and in that tangible evidence you will sense a history of water in the region. Perhaps a black-throated sparrow lands in a paloverde bush—the resiliency of the twig under the bird, that precise shade of yellowish-green against the milk-blue sky, the fluttering whir of the arriving sparrow, are what I mean by "the landscape." Draw on the smell of creosote bush, or clack stones together in the dry air. Feel how light is the desiccated dropping of the kangaroo rat. Study an animal track obscured by the wind. These are all elements of the land, and what makes the landscape comprehensible are the relationships between them. One learns a landscape finally not by knowing the name or identity of everything in it, but by perceiving the relationships in it—like that between the sparrow and the twig. The difference between the relationships and the elements is the same as that between written history and a catalog of events.

The second landscape I think of is an interior one, a kind of projection within a person of a part of the exterior landscape. Relationships in the exterior landscape include those that are named and discernible, such as the nitrogen cycle, or a vertical sequence of Ordovician limestone, and others that are uncodified or ineffable, such as winter light falling on a particular kind of granite, or the effect of humidity on the frequency of a blackpoll warbler's burst of song. That these relationships have purpose and order, however inscrutable they may seem to us, is a tenet of evolution. Similarly, the speculations, intuitions, and formal ideas we refer to as "mind" are a set of relationships in the interior landscape with purpose and order; some of these are obvious, many impenetrably subtle. The shape and character of these relationships in a person's thinking, I believe, are deeply influenced by where on this earth one goes, what one touches, the patterns one observes in nature—the intricate history of one's life in the land, even a life in the city, where wind, the chirp of birds, the line of a falling leaf, are known. These thoughts are arranged, further, according to the thread of one's moral, intellectual, and spiritual development. The interior landscape responds to the character and subtlety of an exterior landscape; the shape of the individual mind is affected by land as it is by genes.

In stories like those I heard at Anaktuvuk Pass about wolverine, the relationship between separate elements in the land is set forth clearly. It is put in a simple framework of sequential incidents and apposite detail. If the exterior landscape is limned well, the listener often feels that he has heard something pleasing and authentic—trustworthy. We derive this sense of confidence I think not so much from verifiable truth as from an understanding that lying has played no role in the narrative. The storyteller is obligated to engage the reader with a precise vocabulary, to set forth a coherent and dramatic rendering of incidents—and to be ingenuous.

When one hears a story one takes pleasure in it for different reasons—for the euphony of its phrases, an aspect of the plot, or because one identifies with one of the characters. With certain stories certain individuals may experience a deeper, more profound sense of well-being. This latter phenomenon, in my understanding, rests at the heart of storytelling as an elevated experience among aboriginal peoples. It results from bringing two landscapes together. The exterior landscape is organized according to principles or laws or tendencies beyond human control. It is understood to contain an integrity that is beyond human analysis and unimpeachable. Insofar as the storyteller depicts various subtle and obvious relationships in the exterior landscape accurately in his story, and insofar as he orders them along traditional lines of meaning to create the narrative, the narrative will "ring true." The listener who "takes the story to heart" will feel a pervasive sense of congruence within himself and also with the world.

Among the Navajo and, as far as I know, many other native peoples, the land is thought to exhibit a sacred order. That order is the basis of ritual. The rituals themselves reveal the power in that order. Art, architecture, vocabulary, and costume, as well as ritual, are derived from the perceived natural order of the universe—from observations and meditations on the exterior landscape. An indigenous philosophy—metaphysics, ethics, epistemology, aesthetics, and logic—may also be derived from a people's continuous attentiveness to both the obvious (scientific) and ineffable (artistic) orders of the local landscape. Each individual, further, undertakes to order his interior landscape according to the exterior landscape. To succeed in this means to achieve a balanced state of mental health.

I think of the Navajo for a specific reason. Among the various sung ceremonies of this people—Enemyway, Coyoteway, Red Antway, Uglyway—is one called Beautyway. In the Navajo view, the elements of one's interior life—one's psychological makeup and moral bearing—are subject to a persistent principle of disarray. Beautyway is, in part, a spiritual invocation of the order of the exterior universe, that irreducible, holy complexity that manifests itself as all things changing through time (a Navajo definition of beauty, hózhǫ́ǫ́). The purpose of this invocation is to recreate in the individual who is the subject of the Beautyway ceremony that same order, to make the individual again a reflection of the myriad enduring relationships of the landscape.

I believe story functions in a similar way. A story draws on relationships in the exterior landscape and projects them onto the interior landscape. The purpose of storytelling is to achieve harmony between the two landscapes, to use all the elements of story—syntax, mood, figures of speech—in a harmonious way to reproduce the harmony of the land in the individual's interior. Inherent in story is the power to reorder a state of psychological confusion through contact with the pervasive truth of those relationships we call "the land."

These thoughts, of course, are susceptible to interpretation. I am convinced, however, that these observations can be applied to the kind of prose we call nonfiction as well as to traditional narrative forms such as the novel and the short story, and to some poems. Distinctions between fiction and nonfiction are sometimes obscured by arguments over what constitutes "the truth." In the aboriginal literature I am familiar with, the first distinction made among narratives is to separate the authentic from the inauthentic. Myth, which we tend to regard as fictitious or "merely metaphorical," is as authentic, as real, as the story of a wolverine in a man's lap. (A distinction is made, of course, about the elevated nature of myth—and frequently the circumstances of myth-telling are more rigorously prescribed than those for the telling of legends or vernacular stories—but all of these narratives are rooted in the local landscape. To violate *that* connection is to call the narrative itself into question.)

The power of narrative to nurture and heal, to repair a spirit in disarray, rests on two things: the skillful invocation of unimpeachable sources and a listener's knowledge that no hypocrisy or subterfuge is involved. This last simple fact is to me one of the most imposing aspects of the Holocene history of man.

We are more accustomed now to thinking of "the truth" as something that can be explicitly stated, rather than as something that can be evoked in a metaphorical way outside science and Occidental culture. Neither can truth be reduced to aphorism or formulas. It is something alive and unpronounceable. Story creates an atmosphere in which it becomes discernible as a pattern. For a storyteller to insist on relationships that do not exist is to lie. Lying is the opposite of story. (I do not mean to confuse ignorance with deception, or to imply that a storyteller can perceive all that is inherent in the land. Every storyteller falls short of a perfect limning of the landscape—perception and language both fail. But to make up something that is not there, something which can never be corroborated in the land, to knowingly set forth a false relationship, is to be lying, no longer telling a story.)

Because of the intricate, complex nature of the land, it is not always possible for a storyteller to grasp what is contained in a story. The intent of the storyteller, then, must be to evoke, honestly, some single aspect of all that the land contains. The storyteller knows that because different individuals grasp the story at different levels, the focus of his regard for truth must be at the primary one—with who was there, what happened, when, where, and why things occurred. The story will then possess similar truth at other levels—the integrity inherent at the primary level of meaning will be conveyed everywhere else. As long as the storyteller carefully describes the order before him, and uses his storytelling skill to heighten and emphasize certain relationships, it is even possible for the story to be more successful than the storyteller himself is able to imagine.

I would like to make a final point about the wolverine stories I heard at Anaktuvuk Pass. I wrote down the details afterward, concentrating especially on aspects of the biology and ecology of the animals. I sent the information on to my friend living with the Cree. When, many months later, I saw him, I asked whether the Cree had enjoyed these insights of the Nunamiut into the nature of the wolverine. What had they said?

"You know," he told me, "how they are. They said, 'That could happen.'"

In these uncomplicated words the Cree declared their own knowledge of the wolverine. They acknowledged that although they themselves had never seen the things the Nunamiut spoke of, they accepted them as accurate observations, because they did not consider story a context for misrepresentation. They also preserved their own dignity by not overstating their confidence in the Nunamiut, a distant and unknown people.

Whenever I think of this courtesy on the part of the Cree I think of the dignity that is ours when we cease to demand the truth and realize that the best we can have of those substantial truths that guide our lives is metaphorical—a story. And the most of it we are likely to discern comes only when we accord one another the respect the Cree showed the Nunamiut. Beyond this—that the interior landscape is a metaphorical representation of the exterior landscape, that the truth reveals itself most fully not in dogma but in the paradox, irony, and contradictions that distinguish compelling narratives—beyond this there are only failures of imagination: reductionism in science; fundamentalism in religion; fascism in politics.

Our national literatures should be important to us insofar as they sustain us with illumination and heal us. They can always do that so long as they are written with respect for both the source and the reader, and with an understanding of why the human heart and the land have been brought together so regularly in human history.

Understanding and Analysis

1. After reading the entire essay, reread the first two paragraphs. Why is it important that the storytellers offered no "gratuitous details" or embellishments?

2. How does the fifth paragraph illustrate the point Lopez makes in the body of the essay?

3. What are the "indispensable" characteristics of a story, according to Lopez?

4. What makes the exterior landscape comprehensible, according to Lopez?

5. How does Lopez define the interior landscape? What kinds of relationships are involved?

6. How does Lopez define "mind"? What does he mean when he writes, "the shape of the individual mind is affected by land as it is by genes"?

7. What makes us, as well as "aboriginal peoples," trust a story, according to Lopez?

8. How do the Navajo "achieve a balanced state of mental health"?

9. What does Lopez believe is the purpose of storytelling?

10. How is lying the opposite of "story"?

11. What exactly is the nature of "the respect the Cree showed the Nunamiut"?

12. Where in the essay does Lopez show the truth of his own piece of nonfiction story-telling? That is, identify aspects of the external and internal landscape limned by Lopez in this essay.

Comparison

1. Read Carr on history. Do you think he would agree with Lopez that the "difference between the relationships and the elements [in the external landscape] is the same as that between written history and a catalog of events"?

2. Read Eiseley's essay. Do you see any characteristics of style and content that Lopez and Eiseley share?

3. Read the essay by T. S. Eliot. To what extent would Eliot agree with the statements Lopez makes about storytelling and "national literatures"?

4. Compare Momaday's use of landscape with that of Lopez.

5. Read Postman on storytelling. To what extent do Lopez and Postman agree?

6. Apply Lopez's requirements for a compelling story to one or two of the stories recounted in some of the essays in this collection. Look, for example, at essays by Beerbohm, Orwell, Hughes, White, Bettelheim, Podhoretz, Rodriguez, Dillard, Ozick, Staples, and Cofer. Which, if any, essays appear to conform to Lopez's standards and which, if any, do not? How useful are his requirements to you?

Cynthia Ozick
(1928–)

In April, 1928, six years after the birth of her brother Julius, Cynthia Ozick was born to William and Celia Regelson Ozick, owners of the Park View Pharmacy in Pelham Bay, the Bronx. Her parents had immigrated from the province of Minsk, in northwestern Russia, her mother arriving in New York City in June of 1906 at the age of nine-and-a-half and her father in 1917 at the age of twenty-one. Both parents brought with them a love of family, study, and Yiddish.

Her father's parents had remained in Moscow—he a perpetual student of the Talmud and she an industrious mother of eight who ran a dry goods store and led prayers in the synagogue. Because they had settled in America with their young family, her mother's parents, on the other hand, directly affected the pattern of Cynthia Ozick's life. Although her maternal grandfather died before Ozick was born, he left the family a lasting legacy of artistic and intellectual passion. A carver of chairs by profession, he was also a great reader who often rose early and lost himself in the latest Hebrew literary magazines until night had fallen and it was too late to work. His son, Abraham Regelson, (Ozick's uncle) became a well-known Hebrew poet; most of her cousins on her mother's side are artists as well. Ozick attributes her passion for her art to this side of her family. Her maternal grandmother, who died when Ozick was eleven, also continues to be a major influence in Ozick's life. In his biography, Joseph Lowin writes that her grandmother introduced Ozick to feminism when she took her five-year-old granddaughter to study Hebrew and was told by the rabbi "a girl doesn't have to study." Cynthia's grandmother took her right back the next day, thereby teaching her to value women and persistence, as well as Hebrew.

Like Zora Neale Hurston, Cynthia Ozick felt strong and capable within her family, where she was protected from "brutally difficult" prejudice outside. Lowin records her memories of being accused of killing Christ and of being pelted with stones as she passed two neighborhood churches. In "A Drugstore in Winter," Ozick remembers the prejudice she encountered in grammar school when she refused to sing Christmas carols. Unlike Hurston, in public school Ozick felt lonely and ugly and stupid in math. But at home in the world of her childhood, the power of books upheld her imagination—shaping for her an identity surpassing in grandeur that offered her brother through his ham radio.

The desire to become a writer fired her ambition from grammar school on, inspiring her transformation from the duckling of PS 71 to the cygnet of Hunter College High School for girls where, she recalls in "The Question of Our Speech: The Return to Aural Culture," she learned the Latin of Virgil, rid herself of the New York "Oi," and delivered an eloquent commencement speech to the class of 1946. In "Washington Square, 1946," Ozick describes her arrival at New York University, the day before the semester was actually to begin, seventeen-and-a-half years old and breathless with the desire to know, with the miraculous excitement of names and words not yet deciphered, with the "brittle pain and joy" of youth Thomas Wolfe describes in the book she bought that day. Before her graduation with a B.A., *cum laude*, in English, Ozick also began to understand the outer world, "hammer-struck with the shock of Europe's skull, the bled planet of death camp and war."

In 1950, at twenty-two, as she describes in "The Lesson of the Master," Ozick dedicated her life to art, to writing great works—"I was a worshiper of literature, literature was my single altar . . ." She had just finished her M.A. in English at Ohio State University, writing her thesis, "Parable in the Later Novels of Henry James," on a man she deemed the master. Years later, after reading Leon Edel's immense biography of James, Ozick realized that she had been betrayed by her youth and innocence into believing the voice of an old man—"The great voices of Art never mean *only* art; they also mean Life, they always mean Life . . ."

Nevertheless, even in her youth, Ozick could not evade reality. In 1951 at Columbia University, she took a graduate seminar taught by the famous critic Lionel Trilling. In this class, as Ozick describes in "We Are the Crazy Lady," she was "bone-skinny, small, sallow and myopic, and so scared I could trigger diarrhea at one glance from the Great Man." The other woman in the class, the crazy one whose body and behavior were totally different from hers, became Trilling's nemesis in nearly every discussion. Yet the Great Man could not tell the two women apart.

For the next thirteen years, while Ozick wrote "steadily and obsessively"—poems, stories, essays, and, particularly, a long, finally abandoned novel called "Mercy, Pity, Peace, and Love"—she kept her eyes open and permitted the occasional interruptions of life. She knew that her marriage to lawyer Bernard Hallote in 1952 provided a kind of "grant from a very private, very poor, foundation." She also knew that as a wife without a child, she was, in the eyes of her relatives, a failure. Gradually in her own eyes she became a failure too. She had not gained economic independence through her writing. She had hardly been published at all. Although she had read voraciously, written with equal fervor, and lusted after publication and fame, by the time she was thirty-six she had in print only "a handful of poems, a couple of short stories, a single essay, and all in quirky little magazines . . ." After "Mercy, Pity, Peace, and Love," she'd written another novel in a matter of weeks, rejected it, and embarked in 1957 on third novel, which she finished in 1963.

In an interview with Bill Moyers, Ozick stated that she had started that third novel as "an American writer" and ended it as a "Jewish writer." In 1953, Ozick had read Leo Baeck's essay "Romantic Religion" and then *History of the Jews* by Heinrich Graetz. Thus began her study of Judaism, leading gradually but inescapably to her recognition that to be a writer is to raise metaphysical questions, to think hard about mortality, to be religious, which for Cynthia Ozick is to be a Jew.

In 1964, a year after finishing her third novel, Ozick took a job as an instructor at New York University, a step representing the end of her life as a "recluse." In September 1965, she gave birth to a daughter, Rachel. When asked what effect her daughter had on her time to write, Ozick replied: "My mother had told me that the advent of the baby would open me to greater productivity, and she was right." Finally, in 1966, with the publication of the third novel, *Trust*, Cynthia Ozick left behind forever the apprenticeship of her "despairing middle thirties." She has been a remarkably prolific and published writer ever since.

Her first popular short story, "The Pagan Rabbi," appeared in 1966 in *Hudson Review*. Since then her short stories, essays, and poems have appeared in such journals as *Commentary, New Criterion, Partisan Review, Esquire, The New York Times Book Review, The New York Review of Books,* and *The New Yorker.* In 1968, she was a Fellow of the National Endowment for the Arts which helped her to produce her first collection of short stories (*The Pagan Rabbi and Other Stories*) issued by Knopf in 1971. In 1972, she won the Edward Lewis Wallant Award for Fiction and was a nominee for the National Book Award. In 1973, she won the American Academy and Institute of Arts and Letters Award for Literature. Her work appeared in *Best American Short Stories* five times between 1970 and 1984, and she won first prize in the *O. Henry Prize Stories* in 1975, 1981, and 1984. In 1976, Knopf published *Bloodshed and Three Novellas.* In 1981, Ozick was Distinguished Artist-in-Residence at the City University of New York, where she taught courses in creative writing. The following year Knopf published *Levitation: Five Fictions.* Also that year she won a Guggenheim Fellowship.

Art & Ardor: Essays and a novel, *Cannibal Galaxy,* appeared in 1983. In 1984, Ozick won the Distinguished Service in Jewish Letters Award from the Jewish Theological Seminary and an honorary degree from Yeshiva University and Hebrew Union College. In 1987, she published another novel, *The Messiah of Stockholm* and was awarded an honorary degree from Hunter College. The next year she received honorary degrees from Adelphi University, Jewish Theological Seminary, and Boston Hebrew College. In 1989, she published *Metaphor & Memory: Essays, The Shawl* (fiction), and a Critic at Large Essay in *The New Yorker.* Her novella, "Puttermesser Paired," appeared in *The New Yorker* on October 8, 1990. She has also written a play based on *The Shawl,* another collection of essays, *Fame and Folly* (1996), and a novel, *The Puttermesser Papers* (1997).

Cynthia Ozick has also found time to lecture in the United States, Canada, Israel, Italy, Denmark, Sweden, and France, and to involve herself in politics. She has taken in a Russian refugee and spent over six months organizing a conference on politics and anti-Zionism. Her time is a precarious battlefield where two selves meet, the one proclaiming that Art means life and the other defiantly resisting: "As for life, I don't like it. I notice no 'interplay of life and art.' Life is that which—pressingly, persistently, unfailingly, imperially—interrupts."

In her essays, Ozick's love of language shows itself in her wide-ranging diction, which moves from a "transcendent vocabulary," as in the last paragraphs of "The Seam of the Snail," in which she contrasts her mother's profusion, a "horn of plenty," with her own precision, bound by the "tiny twin horns of the snail," to comic carping, as in "Crocodiled Moats," in which she describes the divisiveness she perceives in the humanities as "sour grapes" connecting New York and California. As these passages show, she is not above a pun. Her lists—the variety of sciences in "Crocodiled Moats" or her teachers, "Miss Evangeline Trolander, Mrs. Olive Birch Davis, and Mrs. Ruby S. Papp (pronounced pop)" in "The Question of Our Speech"—reveal a pleasure in sounds martialed for humor as well as for sense. Yet the overall impression left by her essays is of a mind passionately committed to intellectual rigor and truth.

THE SEAM OF THE SNAIL *(1985)*

IN MY DEPRESSION childhood, whenever I had a new dress, my cousin Sarah would get suspicious. The nicer the dress was, and especially the more expensive it looked, the more suspicious she would get. Finally she would lift the hem and check the seams. This was to see if the dress had been bought or if my mother had sewed it. Sarah could always tell. My mother's sewing had elegant outsides, but there was something catch-as-catch-can about the insides. Sarah's sewing, by contrast, was as impeccably finished inside as out; not one stray thread dangled.

My uncle Jake built meticulous grandfather clocks out of rosewood; he was a perfectionist, and sent to England for the clockworks. My mother built serviceable radiator covers and a serviceable cabinet, with hinged doors, for the pantry. She built a pair of bookcases for the living room. Once, after I was grown and in a house of my own, she fixed the sewer pipe. She painted ceilings, and also landscapes; she reupholstered chairs. One summer she planted a whole yard of tall corn. She thought herself capable of doing anything, and did everything she imagined. But nothing was perfect. There was always some clear flaw, never visible head-on. You had to look underneath, where the seams were. The corn thrived, though not in rows. The stalks elbowed one another like gossips in a dense little village.

"Miss Brrrroooobaker," my mother used to mock, rolling her Russian *r*'s, whenever I crossed a *t* she had left uncrossed, or corrected a word she had misspelled, or became impatient with a v that had tangled itself up with a w in her speech. ("Vvventriloquist," I would say. "Vvventriloquist," she would obediently repeat. And the next time it would come out "wiolinist.") Miss Brubaker was my high school English teacher, and my mother invoked her name as an emblem of raging finical obsession. "Miss Brrrroooobaker," my mother's voice hoots at me down the years, as I go on casting and recasting sentences in a tiny handwriting on monomaniacally uniform paper. The loops of my mother's handwriting—it was the Palmer Method[1]—were as big as soup bowls, spilling generous splashy ebullience. She could pull off, at five minutes' notice, a satisfying dinner for ten concocted out of nothing more than originality and panache. But the napkin would be folded a little off center, and the spoon might be on the wrong side of the knife. She was an optimist who ignored trifles; for her, God was not in the details but in the intent. And all these culinary and agricultural efflorescences were extracurricular, accomplished in the crevices and niches of a fourteen-hour business day. When she scribbled out her family memoirs, in heaps of dog-eared notebooks, or on the backs of old bills, or on the margins of last year's calendar, I would resist typing them; in the speed of the chase she often omitted words like "the," "and," "will." The same flashing and bountiful hand fashioned and fired ceramic pots, and painted brilliant autumn views and vases of imaginary flowers and ferns, and decorated ordinary Woolworth platters with lavish enameled gardens. But bits of the painted petals would chip away.

---

[1]Introduced in 1888, it taught penmanship using model letter forms (that adorned every elementary classroom) and free-flowing forearm exercises to practice loops and circles.

Lavish: my mother was as lavish as nature. She woke early and saturated the hours with work and inventiveness, and read late into the night. She was all profusion, abundance, fabrication. Angry at her children, she would run after us whirling the cord of the electric iron, like a lasso or a whip; but she never caught us. When, in seventh grade, I was afraid of failing the Music Appreciation final exam because I could not tell the difference between "To a Wild Rose" and "Barcarole,"[2] she got the idea of sending me to school with a gauze sling rigged up on my writing arm, and an explanatory note that was purest fiction. But the sling kept slipping off. My mother gave advice like mad—she boiled over with so much passion for the predicaments of strangers that they turned into permanent cronies. She told intimate stories about people I had never heard of.

Despite the gargantuan Palmer loops (or possibly because of them), I have always known that my mother's was a life of—intricately abashing word!—excellence: insofar as excellence means ripe generosity. She burgeoned, she proliferated; she was endlessly leafy and flowering. She wore red hats, and called herself a gypsy. In her girlhood she marched with the suffragettes and for Margaret Sanger[3] and called herself a Red.[4] She made me laugh, she was so varied: like a tree on which lemons, pomegranates, and prickly pears absurdly all hang together. She had the comedy of prodigality.

My own way is a thousand times more confined. I am a pinched perfectionist, the ultimate fruition of Miss Brubaker; I attend to crabbed minutiae and am self-trammeled through taking pains. I am a kind of human snail, locked in and condemned by my own nature. The ancients believed that the moist track left by the snail as it crept was the snail's own essence, depleting its body little by little; the farther the snail toiled, the smaller it became, until it finally rubbed itself out. That is how perfectionists are. Say to us Excellence, and we will show you how we use up our substance and wear ourselves away, while making scarcely any progress at all. The fact that I am an exacting perfectionist in a narrow strait only, and nowhere else, is hardly to the point, since nothing matters to me so much as a comely and muscular sentence. It is my narrow strait, this snail's road; the track of the sentence I am writing now; and when I have eked out the wet substance, ink or blood, that is its mark, I will begin the next sentence. Only in treading out sentences am I perfectionist; but then there is nothing else I know how to do, or take much interest in. I miter every pair of abutting sentences as scrupulously as Uncle Jake fitted one strip of rosewood against another. My mother's worldly and bountiful hand has escaped me. The sentence I am writing is my cabin and my shell, compact, self-sufficient. It is the burnished horizon—a merciless planet where flawlessness is the single standard, where even the inmost seams, however hidden from a laxer eye, must meet perfection. Here "excellence" is not strewn casually from a tipped cornucopia, here disorder does not account for charm, here trifles rule like tyrants.

I measure my life in sentences pressed out, line by line, like the lustrous ooze on the underside of the snail, the snail's secret open seam, its wound, leaking attar.[5] My mother was too mettlesome to feel the force of a comma. She scorned minutiae. She measured

---

[2] "To a Wild Rose" (1986): music by Edward MacDowell (1861–1908); "Barcarolle": by J. Offenbach, from *The Tales of Hoffman* (1881), with lyrics by Jules Paul Barbier (1822–1901).

[3] (1883–1966) American nurse who set up a clinic as well as international conferences to establish legal, medically supervised, birth control.

[4] A communist.

[5] A fragrant oil extracted from the petals of flowers.

her life according to what poured from the horn of plenty, which was her own seamless, ample, cascading, elastic, susceptible, inexact heart. My narrower heart rides between the tiny twin horns of the snail, dwindling as it goes.

And out of this thinnest thread, this ink-wet line of words, must rise a visionary fog, a mist, a smoke, forging cities, histories, sorrows, quagmires, entanglements, lives of sinners, even the life of my furnace-hearted mother: so much wilderness, waywardness, plenitude on the head of the precise and impeccable snail, between the horns. (Ah, if this could be!)

Understanding and Analysis

1. In this essay of comparison and contrast, Ozick opens with an anecdote about her mother and her cousin Sarah. At once we see that Sarah is "suspicious," suggesting conflict, probably competition. What other themes does Ozick introduce in this first paragraph?

2. In the second paragraph, competition surfaces in the fact that you have to "look underneath" to find the "clear flaw," again suggesting suspicion on the part of a "you." What other themes are elaborated in this second paragraph?

3. The first half of the essay is devoted to Ozick's mother. What details suggest tension between mother and daughter? What details suggest excellence?

4. What is the image that best represents Ozick's mother for you?

5. In what ways is Ozick exactly the opposite of her mother? What do you see as Ozick's faults? Does Ozick see faults in her own character?

6. In addition to the seam in the title, how are the themes established in the first section preserved in the second? Look carefully for recurring words and ideas.

7. In what ways are Ozick and her mother alike? Who appeals to you more? Why?

8. Examine the image of the tree and the snail. What words connect these images?

9. Ozick uses poetic language in this essay—locate examples throughout of alliteration and striking diction.

10. What is the point of the last paragraph in the essay? What is the point of the words enclosed in parentheses? What is the point of the essay as a whole?

11. Do you feel differently about either Ozick or her mother when you have examined the essay carefully?

Comparison

1. Read Du Bois's criticism of Booker T. Washington. Do you see any similarities in strategy in these quite different types of essay?

2. Read Didion's "On Going Home." What similarities and differences do you see in these two depictions of family life?

3. Read Brady's "I Want a Wife." Brady and Ozick both describe a variety of activities women who are wives can perform. How do these authors achieve such different results from their descriptions? Compare activities described, style, and tone in your analysis.

Brent Staples
(1951–)

Born in 1951 in Chester, Pennsylvania, Brent Staples was the eldest son in a family of nine children. Although they never left Chester, the family moved repeatedly during his youth: "We moved as the family grew. We moved when my parents were separated and again when they reconciled. We moved when we fell behind in the rent. We moved when the sheriffs put our furniture on the sidewalk....We'd had seven different addresses by the time I reached the eighth grade." Wary of his parents' arguments and his father's streaks of violence, Staples often looked for excuses to get outside the house and linger over the displays in the used comic book store. He enjoyed The Green Lantern, but "[o]f all the lonely superheroes," his favorite was The Silver Surfer, an intergalactic traveler imprisoned by a shield around the earth: "The Surfer tried to escape, but banged into the shield again and again....I finished the book shaken and sad. The Surfer's sorrow had become my own." Unable to free himself from his own troubles, Staples lost himself in the troubles of others, lurking in the open doorways of Andy's Musical Bar to watch fights and love affairs form and break up.

Entering a high school with an academic and social "caste system," Staples, fearing failure, did not join "the college prep group," but the group of students in "commercial studies," preparing for positions in secretarial typing pools. He found his commercial studies classes "mundane," but his "English class was an oasis. I enjoyed writing and experienced as pleasure the words flowing out of me. I loved words, but primarily for use as weapons. I preferred my adjectives British, like 'veritable.' People were no longer just idiots, they were veritable idiots. My father was 'a veritable monster.'" Tensions between Staples and his father escalated when Staples explicitly challenged his father's authority for the first time. After his father punched him, he left the family: "Physically I remained with them, but mentally I was gone. I arranged to be out of the house at every possible minute. I prowled the city, banging against its limits."

With no money for college, Staples did not even bother to apply. Then a friend introduced him to Eugene Sparrow, a Professor of Sociology at a local college called PMC. After a long conversation about politics, Sparrow gave him the name and number of the admissions director, promising that he didn't need money to go to school. Staples entered PMC in the summer with 23 others as a part of Project Prepare, a program designed to increase the school's black enrollment. "Project Prepare," he writes in his autobiography, "was run like boot camp. We were rousted from bed at six, in class by eight. We worked part-time jobs in the afternoon, then hustled back for dinner and a long evening of homework. The writing assignments were endless and were collected before we went to bed. We slept in the dormitory, went to class in the dormitory, and were forbidden to leave it at night." With the arrival of the fall semester, Staples took to dressing like a Black Panther, hoping to create a stir. He also harassed his roommate mercilessly, hoping to drive him out so that he could have, for the first time in his life, a room to himself. (He succeeded.) Obsessed with earning good grades, Staples impressed his teachers, who recommended that he try for a fellowship for graduate school. He won two. Following graduation, he enrolled at the University of Chicago, a school chosen principally for its distance from Chester, to study psychology.

Writing his dissertation on "the mathematics of decision-making," Staples earned his Ph.D. in 1977 and began to write pieces for *The Reader*, once reporting on a man murdered in his own apartment building. To earn his living, he worked part-time as a psychologist and part-time as an adjunct professor at Roosevelt University in downtown Chicago, where his classes were perpetually interrupted by trains screeching past the windows. His working conditions improved, though not dramatically, after his publications in *The Reader* caught the attention of an editor from the Chicago *Sun-Times*. Hired in 1982, Staples worked as a science writer until the paper was purchased and restructured a year later.

In 1983, Staples was courted by major newspapers across the country searching for African-American reporters. Experiencing his interviews as inquisitions, with questions designed to determine how he obtained "a white man's credentials," how he became "successful, law-abiding, and literate, when others of my kind filled the jails and the morgues and the homeless shelters," Staples became enraged during an interview with *The Washington Post* and told his "inquisitor" in blunt terms about the murder of his brother Blake, who like others in Chester had started dealing cocaine. Losing that job opportunity, he became similarly furious during an interview with *The New York Times*: "When my anger began to rise, I opened my pocket watch, noted that I was late for my next interview, and left the room. The interviewer was stunned, but better to have fled than not. This time I got the job." Since 1983, Staples has been writing editorials for the *Times*, many of them on politics and race. Currently living in Brooklyn, he published his autobiography, *Parallel Time: Growing Up in Black and White*, in 1994, dedicating the book to Eugene Sparrow.

Unlike his editorials, which as journalistic pieces commonly efface the life of the writer, *Parallel Time* is a deeply personal, at times almost confessional work that is in several passages as unflattering to Staples as to his father.

Reviewer Michael Eric Dyson maintains that the book "reminds us that the best personal writing is born of the courage to confront oneself." The writing in *Parallel Time* is indeed excellent, richly descriptive and masterfully varied. Describing the mourners at his teenaged cousin's funeral, Staples writes:

> One girl in particular stood out....Her shapely, hourglass frame shuddered marvelously as she sobbed. She wailed until she was out of breath, moaned into her own throat as she gasped for air, then spent the air in sobs again. The moan of her inward breaths made her weeping stand out. I turned toward the stained-glass windows and squinted and squeezed, but still my eyes were dry. I could hear the moaning girl and see her shapeliness in my head. Several times I turned to look at her. I wished that she was weeping for me.

Staples recounts many moments of standing on the outside—of mourning, of fighting, and of dying—and his book explores the meaning and the consequences of being an outsider, of finding, by "chance," an escape not afforded to his brother or his cousin. Angry, remorseful, and beautiful, *Parallel Time* is an important American autobiography.

BLACK MEN AND PUBLIC SPACE (1986)

MY FIRST VICTIM WAS a woman—white, well dressed, probably in her early twenties. I came upon her late one evening on a deserted street in Hyde Park, a relatively affluent neighborhood in an otherwise mean, impoverished section of Chicago. As I swung onto the avenue behind her, there seemed to be a discreet, uninflammatory distance between us. Not so. She cast back a worried glance. To her, the youngish black man—a broad six feet two inches with a beard and billowing hair, both hands shoved into the pockets of a bulky military jacket—seemed menacingly close. After a few more quick glimpses, she picked up her pace and was soon running in earnest. Within seconds she disappeared into a cross street.

That was more than a decade ago, I was twenty-two years old, a graduate student newly arrived at the University of Chicago. It was in the echo of that terrified woman's footfalls that I first began to know the unwieldy inheritance I'd come into—the ability to alter public space in ugly ways. It was clear that she thought herself the quarry of a mugger, a rapist, or worse. Suffering a bout of insomnia, however, I was stalking sleep, not defenseless wayfarers. As a softy who is scarcely able to take a knife to a raw chicken—let alone hold one to a person's throat—I was surprised, embarrassed, and dismayed all at once. Her flight made me feel like an accomplice in tyranny. It also made it clear that I was indistinguishable from the muggers who occasionally seeped into the area from the surrounding ghetto. That first encounter, and those that followed, signified that a vast, unnerving gulf lay between nighttime pedestrians—particularly women—and me. And I soon gathered that being perceived as dangerous is a hazard in itself. I only needed to turn a corner into a dicey situation, or crowd some frightened, armed person in a foyer somewhere, or make an errant move after being pulled over by a policeman. Where fear and weapons meet—and they often do in urban America—there is always the possibility of death.

In that first year, my first away from my hometown, I was to become thoroughly familiar with the language of fear. At dark, shadowy intersections, I could cross in front of a car stopped at a traffic light and elicit the *thunk, thunk, thunk, thunk* of the driver—black, white, male, or female—hammering down the door locks. On less traveled streets after dark, I grew accustomed to but never comfortable with people crossing to the other side of the street rather than pass me. Then there were the standard unpleasantries with policemen, doormen, bouncers, cabdrivers, and others whose business it is to screen out troublesome individuals *before* there is any nastiness.

I moved to New York nearly two years ago and I have remained an avid night walker. In central Manhattan, the near-constant crowd cover minimizes tense one-on-one street encounters. Elsewhere—in SoHo, for example, where sidewalks are narrow and tightly spaced buildings shut out the sky—things can get very taut indeed.

After dark, on the warrenlike streets of Brooklyn where I live, I often see women who fear the worst from me. They seem to have set their faces on neutral, and with their purse straps strung across their chests bandolier-style, they forge ahead as though bracing themselves against being tackled. I understand, of course, that the danger they perceive is not a hallucination. Women are particularly vulnerable to street violence, and young black males are drastically overrepresented among the perpetrators of that violence. Yet these truths are no solace against the kind of alienation that comes of being ever the suspect, a fearsome entity with whom pedestrians avoid making eye contact.

It is not altogether clear to me how I reached the ripe old age of twenty-two without being conscious of the lethality nighttime pedestrians attributed to me. Perhaps it was because in Chester, Pennsylvania, the small, angry industrial town where I came of age in the 1960s, I was scarcely noticeable against a backdrop of gang warfare, street knifings, and murders. I grew up one of the good boys, had perhaps a half-dozen fistfights. In retrospect, my shyness of combat has clear sources.

As a boy, I saw countless tough guys locked away; I have since buried several, too. They were babies, really—a teenage cousin, a brother of twenty-two, a childhood friend in his mid-twenties—all gone down in episodes of bravado played out in the streets. I came to doubt the virtues of intimidation early on. I chose, perhaps unconsciously, to remain a shadow—timid, but a survivor.

The fearsomeness mistakenly attributed to me in public places often has a perilous flavor. The most frightening of these confusions occurred in the late 1970s and early 1980s, when I worked as a journalist in Chicago. One day, rushing into the office of a magazine I was writing for with a deadline story in hand, I was mistaken for a burglar. The office manager called security and, with an ad hoc posse, pursued me through the labyrinthine halls, nearly to my editor's door. I had no way of proving who I was. I could only move briskly toward the company of someone who knew me.

Another time I was on assignment for a local paper and killing time before an interview. I entered a jewelry store on the city's affluent Near North Side. The proprietor excused herself and returned with an enormous red Doberman pinscher straining at the end of a leash. She stood, the dog extended toward me, silent to my questions, her eyes bulging nearly out of her head. I took a cursory look around, nodded, and bade her good night.

Relatively speaking, however, I never fared as badly as another black male journalist.

He went to nearby Waukegan, Illinois, a couple of summers ago to work on a story about a murderer who was born there. Mistaking the reporter for the killer, police officers hauled him from his car at gunpoint and but for his press credentials would probably have tried to book him. Such episodes are not uncommon. Black men trade tales like this all the time.

Over the years, I learned to smother the rage I felt at so often being taken for a criminal. Not to do so would surely have led to madness. I now take precautions to make myself less threatening. I move about with care, particularly late in the evening. I give a wide berth to nervous people on subway platforms during the wee hours, particularly when I have exchanged business clothes for jeans. If I happen to be entering a building behind some people who appear skittish, I may walk by, letting them clear the lobby before I return, so as not to seem to be following them. I have been calm and extremely congenial on those rare occasions when I've been pulled over by the police.

And on late-evening constitutionals I employ what has proved to be an excellent tension-reducing measure: I whistle melodies from Beethoven and Vivaldi and the more popular classical composers. Even steely New Yorkers hunching toward nighttime destinations seem to relax, and occasionally they even join in the tune. Virtually everybody seems to sense that a mugger wouldn't be warbling bright, sunny selections from Vivaldi's *Four Seasons*. It is my equivalent of the cowbell that hikers wear when they know they are in bear country.

Understanding and Analysis

1. The first paragraph of this essay is striking. What responses did you have on first reading it? Why do you suppose Staples opens with the words "My first victim"?

2. What is Staples's attitude toward that young woman and others he encounters?

3. Do you see any humor in this essay? If so where? What effect does it have, if you think there is humor, on the essay as a whole?

4. What does Staples tell us about his childhood? How did these events help to shape his character?

4. Does Staples represent himself as a victim? What is your evidence?

5. Look for unusual phrasing and striking diction in this essay. What techniques does Staples use to hold our attention and make his points?

6. To what degree do you think class plays a role in people's perceptions of Staples? What is your evidence?

7. What might have happened had Staples not "learned to smother the rage" he has felt? Again, what is your evidence?

8. Hikers wear bells to alert bears to their presence and thereby keep the bears away. What does Staples mean when he compares his whistling to the cowbell?

Comparison

1. Read Baldwin's description of his walk through a village in "Stranger in the Village." Account for the reactions of the pedestrians in both cases.

2. Read Bettelheim's "A Victim." Compare his interpretation of the way to behave with Staples's actions when he has been in threatening situations.

3. Read "Labor" by Rodriguez. Compare Rodriguez's comments about color and class with those of Staples. To what extent do the two writers agree and/or disagree?

Nancy Mairs
(1943–)

Born July 23, 1943, Nancy Mairs was, her mother reported in a letter, "the funniest looking, skinniest little bundle of humanity you ever saw." The first child of John and Anne Eldredge, who rushed to marry before John left to serve in World War II, Mairs was soon followed by her sister, Sally, from whom she was inseparable in early childhood. All four members of the family re-united in Guam, where John was stationed; not long afterward, in 1947, he was killed. Anne returned immediately to the United States, settling with her children in her native New England.

Growing up, Mairs preferred reading to playing outdoors, not only because she felt uncoordinated, but also because staying inside made her "feel safe, certain of where I [was], unlikely to get disoriented." Acting in school plays pleased her for similar reasons: "A script feels like the perfect format for getting through life without disaster, the way it frees you from wondering where you're supposed to be, what you're supposed to say." An enormously bright student, Mairs skipped the third grade and sailed through her studies until her sophomore year, when dramatic romances and intensifying illnesses—headaches, seasonal allergies and flu, unexplained stabbing pains—began to define her high school career and sometimes to distract her from her studies. Still acting, she edited *Aegis*, Berkeley High School's literary publication, and briefly wondered about going to Radcliffe. When her mother told her that "Radcliffe women are so smart that they scare men away and never get married," she applied to Wheaton, the alma mater of both her mother and her Aunt Jane, a poet.

Majoring in English—"largely because it require[d] the least effort"—Mairs acted in Bertolt Brecht's *The Good Woman of Setzuan* and "publish[ed] a few poems in the literary magazine." Otherwise, she did not get involved in campus life, though she continued to have dramatic and painful relationships and made her first attempt at suicide. Her situation improved, though not immediately, when she met her future husband, George Mairs, on a blind date. While she had to pursue him at first, he quickly returned the favor, and they talked of engagement. She writes in *Ordinary Time:* "We had between us forty-one years of earthly experience, divided not quite equally, one college degree and another on the way, a commission in the United States Navy, and two healthy libidos. We were going to get married." They wed in 1963, when Mairs was 19 years old. She graduated in 1964, taking a job as an English teacher at a private school.

In 1965, Mairs gave birth to her daughter, Anne. A year later, she answered a classified ad in the *Boston Globe* "for a junior editor at the Smithsonian Astrophysical Observatory." Studying "the greenhouse effect on Mars and checking esoteric references in Harvard's libraries," Mairs earned a promotion to research assistant and found genuine happiness in her work. Attacks of agoraphobia, however, ultimately prevented her from keeping the job, and as she struggled with depression, she entered the Metropolitan State Hospital, where she received shock treatments. Leaving the hospital more than six months later, she became pregnant, gave birth to her son, Matthew, and looked for work. In 1970, she started as an editorial assistant for the International Tax Program at Harvard University, returning to her poetry in 1971, after one of the many extramarital affairs she describes in her essays. With her creative "[j]uices flowing once again," she decided "to go to graduate school for a degree in creative writing." In 1972, at the age of 29, she moved to Tucson so that she could get her MFA at the University of Arizona.

Shortly after the move, Mairs was incorrectly diagnosed with a brain tumor. In 1973, she learned that what ravaged her body was instead multiple sclerosis. She finished her MFA in 1975, taught at a Catholic high school with George, and then returned to the university to work on a Ph.D. in education. Convinced that she was dying, she left home and moved into an apartment, the site of another suicide attempt. In 1977, she underwent two important experiences: she converted to Catholicism, along with George, and she published her first book, a collection of poems entitled *Instead It Is Winter.* As she had come to Catholicism, two years later she came to feminism. After reading Virginia Woolf, she switched her "doctoral degree program from English education to English literature, began to study feminist theory, and had a nervous breakdown. After *that* [she] finished a volume of poems on purpose and started by accident to write essays." Her second collection of poems, the award-winning *In All the Rooms of the Yellow House,* appeared in 1984, the same year she received her Ph.D. Her first collection of essays was also her dissertation, *Plaintext* (1986), which earned her a reputation as a "brilliant" American essayist.

Mairs's next book turned out to be the first part of her autobiography. Conceiving of the work as a "memoir of [her] life as a female body," Mairs published *Remembering the Bone House: An Erotics of Place and Space* in 1989. Four years later, she published its spiritual "companion," *Ordinary Time: Cycles in Marriage, Faith and Renewal,* a "book of essays on being a Catholic feminist . . . excuse the oxymoron." Between these two memoirs, she published the autobiographical *Carnal Acts* (1990), and afterward, *Voice Lessons: On Being a (Woman) Writer* (1994). She also wrote columns and book reviews for *The New York Times.* Having used a cane to make her way around the world—even to Zaire to visit her daughter—Mairs became confined to a wheelchair in 1992. In 1997, she published *Waist-High in the World: A Life Among the Nondisabled.*

Nancy Mairs has said of *Remembering the Bone House* what might be said of all her works: "In defiance of the conventions of polite silence, I've spoken as plainly and truthfully as the squirms and wriggles of the human psyche will permit." Indeed, Mairs uses the events she writes about in her essays—taking an overdose of pills, taking on lovers to inspire the writing of poems, falling onto the toilet or out of an elevator—to interrogate a number of conventional ideas: about the split between the mind and body, about the split between the profane and the sacred (the "territorializing of the holy. Here God may dwell. Here God may not dwell"), about the content and structure of proper autobiography, about decorum in "the stuttering adventure of the essay." Although her works receive mixed reviews, they earn high praise for the originality and honesty of their content and for the "grace," beauty, and sophistication of Mairs's writing.

ON BEING A SCIENTIFIC BOOBY (1986)

MY DAUGHTER IS dissecting a chicken. Her first. Her father, whose job this usually is, has been derelict in his duties, and my hands are now too weak to dissect much more than a zucchini. If she wants dinner (and she does), she will make this pale, flabby carcass into eight pieces I can fit into the skillet. I act as coach. To encourage her, I tell her that her great-great-grandfather was a butcher. This is true, not something I have made up to con her into doing a nasty job.

Now that she's gotten going, she is having a wonderful time. She has made the chicken crow and flap and dance all over the cutting board, and now it lies quiet under her short, strong fingers as she slices the length of its breastbone. She pries back the ribs and peers into the cavity. "Oh, look at its mesenteries!" she cries. I tell her I thought mesentery was something you got from drinking the water in Mexico. She pokes at some filmy white webs. Mesenteries, she informs me, are the membranes that hold the chicken's organs in place. My organs too. She flips the chicken over and begins to cut along its spine. As her fingers search out joints and the knife severs wing from breast, leg from thigh, she gives me a lesson in the comparative anatomy of this chicken and the frog she and her friend Emily have recently dissected at school.

I am charmed by her enthusiasm and self-assurance. Since she was quite small, she has talked of becoming a veterinarian, and now that she is approaching adulthood, her purpose is growing firmer. During this, her junior year in a special high school, she is taking a college-level introductory course in biology. I took much the same course when I was a freshman in college. But if I entered that course with Anne's self-confidence, and I may very well have done so, I certainly had none of it by the time I wrote the last word of my final examination in my blue book and turned it in the following spring. As the result of Miss White and the quadrat report, I am daunted to the point of dysfunction by the notion of thinking or writing "scientifically."

That woman—damn that woman!—turned me into a scientific cripple, and did so in the name of science at a prestigious women's college that promised to school me in the liberal arts that I might "have life and have it abundantly." And really, I have had it abundantly, so I suppose I oughtn't to complain if it's been a little short in *Paramecia* and *Amanita phalloides* and *Drosophila melanogaster,* whose eyes I have never seen.

Still, Miss White should not have been allowed to teach freshman biology because she had a fatal idiosyncracy (fatal, that is, to the courage of students, not to herself, though I believe she is dead now of some unrelated cause): She could not bear a well-written report. One could be either a writer or a scientist but not both, she told me one November afternoon, the grey light from a tall window sinking into the grain of the dark woodwork in her cramped office in the old Science Building, her fingers flicking the sheets of my latest lab write-up. She was washing her hands of me, I could tell by the weariness of her tone. She didn't even try to make me a scientist. For that matter, she didn't even point to a spot where I'd gone wrong and show me what she wanted instead. She simply wrinkled her nose at the odor of my writing, handed me the sheets, and sent me away. We never had another conference. At the end of the semester, I wrote my quadrat report, and Miss White failed it. She allowed me to rewrite it. I wrote it again, and she failed it again. Neither of us went for a third try.

All the same, I liked my quadrat, which was a twenty-by-twenty plot in the College Woods behind the Library. Mine was drab compared to some others: Pam Weprin's, I remember, had a brook running through it, in which she discovered goldfish. It turned out that her magical discovery had a drab explanation: In a heavy rain the water from Peacock Pond backed up and spilled its resident carp into the brook. Even so, her quadrat briefly held an excitement mine never did. Mine was, in fact, as familiar as a living room, since I had spent large portions of my youth tramping another such woods sixty miles north. The lichen grew on the north side of the trees. In the rain the humus turned black and rank. Afterwards, a fallen log across one corner would sprout ears of tough, pale fungus.

Each freshman biology student received a quadrat. There were enough of us that we had to double up, but I never met my quadrat-mate or even knew her name. It occurs to me now that I ought to have found out, ought to have asked her what she got on her quadrat report, but I was new to failure and knew no ways to profit from it. I simply did as I was told—visited my quadrat to observe its progress through the seasons and wrote up my observations—and then discovered that I had somehow seen and spoken wrong. I wish now that I had kept the report. I wonder exactly what I said in it. Probably something about ears of fungus. Good God.

With a D+ for the first semester I continued, perversely, to like biology, but I also feared it more and more. Not the discipline itself. I pinned and opened a long earthworm, marveling at the delicately tinted organs. I dissected a beef heart, carefully, so as not to spoil it for stuffing and roasting at the biology department's annual beef-heart feast. For weeks I explored the interior of my rat, which I had opened neatly, like the shutters over a window. He was a homely thing, stiff, his fur yellow and matted from formaldehyde, and because he was male, not very interesting. Several students got pregnant females, and I envied them the intricate organs, the chains of bluish-pink fetuses. At the end of each lab, I would reluctantly close the shutters, swaddle my rat in his plastic bag, and slip him back into the crock.

No, biology itself held more fascination and delight than fear. But with each report I grew more terrified of my own insidious poetic nature, which Miss White sniffed out in the simplest statement about planaria or left ventricles. Years later, when I became a technical editor and made my living translating the garbled outbursts of scientists, I learned that I had done nothing much wrong. My understanding was limited, to be sure, but Miss White would have forgiven me ignorance, even stupidity I think, if I had sufficiently muddled the language. As it was, I finished biology with a C–, and lucky I was to get it, since the next year the college raised the passing grade from C– to C. I have always thought, indeed, that the biology department awarded me a passing grade simply so that they wouldn't have to deal with me another year.

And they didn't. Nor did anyone else. I never took another science course, although I surprised myself long afterward by becoming, perforce and precipitously, a competent amateur herpetologist. My husband arrived home one afternoon with a shoebox containing a young bull snake, or gopher snake as this desert variety is called, which he had bought for a quarter from some of his students at a school for emotionally disturbed boys so that they wouldn't try to find out how long a snake keeps wriggling without its head. This was Ferdinand, who was followed by two more bull snakes, Squeeze and Beowulf, and by a checkered garter snake named Winslow J. Tweed, a black racer named Jesse Owens, a Yuma king snake named Hrothgar, and numerous nameless and short-lived blind snakes, tiny and translucent, brought to us by our cats Freya, Burton Rustle, and Vanessa Bell. I grew so knowledgeable that when my baby boa constrictor, Crictor, contracted a respiratory ailment, I found that I was more capable of caring for him than were any of the veterinarians in the city. In fact, I learned, veterinarians do not do snakes; I could find only one to give Crictor the shot of a broad-spectrum antibiotic he needed.

So I do do snakes. I have read scientific treatises on them. I know that the Latin name for the timber rattlesnake is *Crotalus horridus horridus*. I know that Australia has more varieties of venomous snakes than any other continent, among them the lethal sea snakes and the willfully aggressive tiger snake. I know how long one is likely to live after being bitten by a mamba (not long). I read the treatises; but I don't, of course, write them. Although as a technical editor I grew proficient at unraveling snarls in the writing of scientists, I have never, since Miss White, attempted scientific experimentation or utterance.

Aside from my venture into herpetology, I remain a scientific booby. I mind my stupidity. I feel diminished by it. And I know now that it is unnecessary, the consequence of whatever quirk of fate brought me into Miss White's laboratory instead of Miss Chidsey's or Dr. McCoy's. Miss White, who once represented the whole of scientific endeavor to me, was merely a woman with a hobbyhorse. I see through her. Twenty years later, I am now cynical enough to write a quadrat report badly enough to pass her scrutiny, whereas when I had just turned seventeen I didn't even know that cynicism was an option—knowledge that comes, I suppose, from having life abundantly. I've learned, too, that Miss White's bias, though unusually strong, was not peculiar to herself but arose from a cultural rift between the humanities and the sciences resulting in the assumption that scientists will naturally write badly, that they are, in fact, rhetorical boobies. Today I teach technical writing. My students come to me terrified of the word-world from which they feel debarred, and I teach them to breach the boundaries in a few places, to step with bravado at least a little way inside. Linguistic courage is the gift I can give them.

In return, they give me gifts that I delight in—explanations of vortex centrifuges, evaluations of copper-smelting processes, plans for extracting gums from paloverde beans. These help me compensate for my deficiencies, as do the works of the popularizers of science. Carl Sagan. Loren Eiseley. Lewis Thomas and his reverential reflections subtitled *Notes of a Biology Watcher*. Stephen Jay Gould. James Burke and Jacob Bronowski. Pierre Teilhard de Chardin. John McPhee, who has made me love rocks. Isaac Asimov. Elaine Morgan. I watch television too. *Nova. Odyssey. The Undersea World of Jacques Cousteau. The Body in Question.* But always I am aware that I am having translated for me the concepts of worlds I will never now explore for myself. I stand with my toes on the boundaries, peering, listening.

Anne has done a valiant job with the chicken. She's had a little trouble keeping its pajamas on, and one of the thighs has a peculiar trapezoidal shape, but she's reduced it to a workable condition. I brown it in butter and olive oil. I press in several cloves of garlic and then splash in some white wine. As I work, I think of the worlds Anne is going to explore. Some of them are listed in the college catalogues she's begun to collect: "Genetics, Energetics, and Evolution"; "Histology of Animals"; "Vertebrate Endocrinology"; "Electron Microscopy"; "Organic Synthesis"; "Animal Morphogenesis."

Anne can write. No one has yet told her that she can be a scientist or a writer but not both, and I trust that no one ever will. The complicated world can ill afford such lies to its children. As she plunges from my view into the thickets of calculus, embryology, and chemical thermodynamics, I will wait here for her to send me back messages. I love messages.

Understanding and Analysis

1. What were the faults of Miss White as a teacher? Which of these faults does Mairs ascribe to the attitudes of the times?

2. What was Mairs's attitude toward biology while she was studying her quadrat? What is her attitude now? What does Mairs teach?

3. Do you believe that Mairs is a "scientific booby"? If yes, what is your evidence? If no, what is your evidence? Whom does Mairs blame for her condition?

4. What is Mairs's tone? Do you see indications of envy in this essay?

5. How do the shifts in tense affect the narrative line?

6. What is the main point of this essay?

Comparison

1. Compare the tone and attitude toward science displayed in Thurber's "University Days" to that in Mairs's essay. Which essay do you prefer? Why?

2. Compare the relationship between mother and daughter in Mairs's essay with that in the essays by Ozick and Didion.

3. Read essays by Eiseley, Bronowski, and Gould, essayists Mairs enjoys reading. Compare her style to theirs.

4. Read Lopez's "Landscape and Narrative." To what degree does the external landscape shape Mairs's story of her internal scientific landscape?

Adrienne Rich
(1929–)

On May 16, 1929, Adrienne Rich was born "white and middle-class into a house full of books." Encouraged by her father, she wrote plays and poems from an early age, publishing twice before the age of thirteen. By the age of 16, she was imagining a daring career in writing: "In 1945 I was writing poetry seriously, and had a fantasy of going to postwar Europe as a journalist, sleeping among the ruins in bombed cities, recording the rebirth of civilization after the Nazis." Instead, until 1947, Rich attended a single-sex high school, where dedicated teachers took interested students on intellectual and cultural outings to "libraries, art museums, lectures at neighboring colleges." After graduation, she entered Radcliffe College. She performed well, graduating with honors in 1951.

At the same time, at the age of 21, Rich also published her first full volume of verse, *A Change of World*, chosen by W. H. Auden for his Yale Series of Younger Poets. Marrying Alfred Haskell Conrad in 1953, Rich published her second collection, *The Diamond Cutters and Other Poems*, in 1955, the same year she gave birth to the couple's first son. Although *The Diamond Cutters* received good reviews, Rich felt dissatisfied with the poems in this collection even before they appeared in print, regarding them as "mere exercises for poems I hadn't written." She also became mired in guilt, struggling to write new poems and to remain patient and calm as she cared for two infant sons, feeling, by the time her third son was born in 1959, that she might be a bad mother, "a failed woman[,] and a failed poet." Relief came slowly. Trained to believe that "poetry should be universal," Rich had "tried very much *not* to identify myself as a female poet," avoiding writing about her experiences as a woman. Then, over a period of two years, she composed "Snapshots of a Daughter-in-Law," writing in the penultimate stanza:

> Sigh no more, ladies.
>   Time is male
> and in his cup drinks to the fair.
> Bemused by gallantry, we hear
> our mediocrities over-praised,
> indolence read as abnegation,
> slattern thought styled intuition,
> every lapse forgiven, our crime
> only to cast too bold a shadow
> or smash the mold straight off.
>
> For that, solitary confinement,
> tear gas, attrition shelling.
> Few applicants for that honor.

"It was an extraordinary relief," Rich says, "to write that poem." In 1963, she published a full collection called *Snapshots of a Daughter-in-Law: Poems, 1954–1962.* As critic Alicia Ostriker observes, it was "Rich's break-through volume."

In her next collections, *Necessities of Life* (1966), *Leaflets* (1969), and *The Will to Change* (1972), Rich experimented in radical ways with form and technique, with protest and quest, seeking new kinds of language for her feminist poetics. She also began to teach, holding positions at Swarthmore, Columbia, and City College through the end of the 1960s. In 1973, while teaching at Brandeis, she published one of her most controversial works: *Diving into the Wreck: Poems, 1971–1972.* Although she was criticized for creating negative representations of men in this volume, Rich also chose a poetic speaker at once female and male, singular and plural, for her title poem: "And I am here, the mermaid whose dark hair/streams black, the merman in his armored body./We circle silently/about the wreck." For *Diving into the Wreck*, she received the National Book Award. (According to *Contemporary Authors*, "Rich, along with Audre Lorde and Alice Walker, declined the award as an individual but accepted it on behalf of women whose voices have been silenced.") In *Twenty-One Love Poems* (1976), Rich's poetic speaker turns from androgyny to the love, eroticism, and pain shared with a female addressee. From this point, Rich herself, having left her husband before he died in 1970, spoke and wrote openly as a lesbian.

Breaking ground in her poems, Rich also published, in 1976, a landmark work of prose: *Of Woman Born: Motherhood as Experience and Institution.* Three years later, she published a second prose work, a collection of feminist literary and social criticism called *On Lies, Secrets, and Silence. Blood, Bread, and Poetry* followed almost a decade later in 1986, the year Rich became a professor of English and Feminist Studies at Stanford. Increasingly concerned with questions of race in the 1980s, Rich also challenged herself to do away with generalizations of the sort she used in her early prose: "I don't want to write that kind of sentence now, the sentence that begins, 'Women have always....' If we have learned anything, in these years of late twentieth-century feminism, it's that 'always' blots out what we really need to know: when, where, and under what conditions has the statement been true?" In her poetry of the late 1980s, Rich began to explore her Jewish lineage. Between 1989 and 1992, she also served as the founding co-editor of *Bridges: A Journal of Jewish Feminists and Our Friends.*

For pushing herself and her reader, intellectually, politically, and creatively, Rich was widely recognized in the 1980s and the 1990s, winning both the Lambda Book Award in Lesbian Poetry and the Robert Frost Silver Medal for Lifetime Achievement in Poetry in 1992, and the Tanning Prize of the Academy of American Poets in 1996. At the turn of the millenium, Rich was still pushing. Reviewing *Midnight Salvage: Poems, 1995–1998* (1999), Martha Silano writes, "Her Whitmanesque embrace of the silenced—the homeless woman, the drag queen, the paraplegic—forces us to question and redefine who and what poetry is for."

Adrienne Rich played such a central role in the development of late twentieth-century American feminism that its history can nearly be charted in her works. The history of late twentieth-century American poetry is also visible in her oeuvre, in microcosm, for she, like many others both before and of her generation, began her career writing orderly, orthodox formal verse, rejecting literary tradition with increasing confidence and skill as she progressed. Celebrated and criticized with equal passion, Rich has both alienated and empowered readers with her radicalism, which some have claimed is conservatism in a new form, simply reversing the problems of sexism and racism she protests. In the final analysis, however, Rich's detractors must agree with her defenders. No history of the twentieth century, literary, political, or social, is truly complete without an analysis of her works.

SPLIT AT THE ROOT
An Essay on Jewish Identity (1982)

FOR ABOUT FIFTEEN minutes I have been sitting chin in hand in front of the typewriter, staring out at the snow. Trying to be honest with myself, trying to figure out why writing this seems to be so dangerous an act, filled with fear and shame, and why it seems so necessary. It comes to me that in order to write this I have to be willing to do two things: I have to claim my father, for I have my Jewishness from him and not from my gentile mother; and I have to break his silence, his taboos; in order to claim him I have in a sense to expose him.

And there is, of course, the third thing: I have to face the sources and the flickering presence of my own ambivalence as a Jew; the daily, mundane anti-Semitisms of my entire life.

These are stories I have never tried to tell before. Why now? Why, I asked myself sometime last year, does this question of Jewish identity float so impalpably, so ungraspably around me, a cloud I can't quite see the outlines of, which feels to me to be without definition?

And yet I've been on the track of this longer than I think.

In a long poem written in 1960, when I was thirty-one years old, I described myself as "Split at the root, neither Gentile nor Jew,/Yankee nor Rebel."[1] I was still trying to have it both ways: to be neither/nor, trying to live (with my Jewish husband and three children more Jewish in ancestry than I) in the predominantly gentile Yankee academic world of Cambridge, Massachusetts.

But this begins, for me, in Baltimore, where I was born in my father's workplace, a hospital in the Black ghetto, whose lobby contained an immense white marble statue of Christ.

My father was then a young teacher and researcher in the department of pathology at the Johns Hopkins Medical School, one of the very few Jews to attend or teach at that institution. He was from Birmingham, Alabama; his father, Samuel, was Ashkenazic,[2] an immigrant from Austria-Hungary and his mother, Hattie Rice, a Sephardic[3] Jew from Vicksburg, Mississippi. My grandfather had had a shoe store in Birmingham, which did well enough to allow him to retire comfortably and to leave my grandmother income on his death. The only souvenirs of my grandfather, Samuel Rich, were his ivory flute, which lay on our living-room mantel and was not to be played with; his thin gold pocket watch, which my father wore; and his Hebrew prayer book, which I discovered among my father's books in the course of reading my way through his library. In this prayer book there was a newspaper clipping about my grandparents' wedding, which took place in a synagogue.

My father, Arnold, was sent in adolescence to a military school in the North Carolina mountains, a place for training white southern Christian gentlemen. I suspect that there were few, if any, other Jewish boys at Colonel Bingham's, or at "Mr. Jefferson's university"[4] In Charlottesville, where he studied as an undergraduate. With whatever con-

---

I wrote this essay in 1982 for Evelyn Torton Beck's *Nice Jewish Girls: A Lesbian Anthology*. It was later reprinted in *Fathers*, an anthology edited by Ursula Owen for Virago Ltd., in London, and published in the United States by Pantheon. [Rich's note]

[1]Adrienne Rich, "Readings of History," in *Snapshots of a Daughter-in-Law* (New York: W. W. Norton, 1967), pp. 36–40. [Rich's note]

[2]*Ashkenazic* Jews who settled in middle and northern Europe.

[3]*Sephardic* Jews who settled primarily in Spain, Portugal, and northern Africa.

[4]*Mr. Jefferson's university* Thomas Jefferson was a founder of the University of Virginia after he served two terms as U.S. President.

scious forethought, Samuel and Hattie sent their son into the dominant southern WASP[5] culture to become an "exception," to enter the professional class. Never, in describing these experiences, did he speak of having suffered—from loneliness, cultural alienation, or outsiderhood. Never did I hear him use the word *anti-Semitism.*

It was only in college, when I read a poem by Karl Shapiro beginning "To hate the Negro and avoid the Jew/is the curriculum," that it flashed on me that there was an untold side to my father's story of his student years. He looked recognizably Jewish, was short and slender in build with dark wiry hair and deep-set eyes, high forehead and curved nose.

My mother is a gentile. In Jewish law I cannot count myself a Jew. If it is true that "we think back through our mothers if we are women" (Virginia Woolf)—and I myself have affirmed this—then even according to lesbian theory, I cannot (or need not?) count myself a Jew.

The white southern Protestant woman, the gentile, has always been there for me to peel back into. That's a whole piece of history in itself, for my gentile grandmother and my mother were also frustrated artists and intellectuals, a lost writer and a lost composer between them. Readers and annotators of books, note takers, my mother a good pianist still, in her eighties. But there was also the obsession with ancestry, with "background," the southern talk of family, not as people you would necessarily know and depend on, but as heritage, the guarantee of "good breeding." There was the inveterate romantic hetero sexual fantasy, the mother telling the daughter how to attract men (my mother often used the word "fascinate"); the assumption that relations between the sexes could only be romantic, that it was in the woman's interest to cultivate "mystery," conceal her actual feelings. Survival tactics of a kind, I think today, knowing what I know about the white woman's sexual role in the southern racist scenario. Heterosexuality as protection, but also drawing white women deeper into collusion with white men.

It would be easy to push away and deny the gentile in me—that white southern woman, that social christian. At different times in my life I have wanted to push away one or the other burden of inheritance, to say merely *I am a woman; I am a lesbian.* If I call myself a Jewish lesbian, do I thereby try to shed some of my southern gentile white woman's culpability? If I call myself only through my mother, is it because I pass more easily through a world where being a lesbian often seems like outsiderhood enough?

According to Nazi logic, my two Jewish grandparents would have made me a Mischling,[6] first-degree—nonexempt from the Final Solution.[7]

The social world in which I grew up was christian virtually without needing to say so—christian imagery, music, language, symbols, assumptions everywhere. It was also a genteel, white, middle-class world in which "common" was a term of deep opprobrium. "Common" white people might speak of "niggers"; *we* were taught never to use that word—we said "Negroes" (even as we accepted segregation, the eating taboo, the assumption that Black people were simply of a separate species). Our language was more polite, distinguishing us from the "red-necks" or the lynch-mob mentality. But so charged with negative meaning was even the word "Negro" that as children we were taught never to use it in front of Black people. We were taught that any mention of skin color in the pres-

[5]*WASP* White Anglo-Saxon Protestant.

[6]*Mischling* mixed-breed.

[7]*Final Solution* the Nazi plan to exterminate the Jews.

ence of colored people was treacherous, forbidden ground. In a parallel way, the word "Jew" was not used by polite gentiles. I sometimes heard my best friend's father, a Presbyterian minister, allude to "the Hebrew people" or "people of the Jewish faith." The world of acceptable folk was white, gentile (christian, really), and had "ideals" (which colored people, white "common" people, were not supposed to have). "Ideals" and "manners" included not hurting someone's feelings by calling her or him a Negro or a Jew—naming the hated identity. This is the mental framework of the 1930s and 1940s in which I was raised.

(Writing this, I feel dimly like the betrayer: of my father, who did not speak the word; of my mother, who must have trained me in the messages; of my caste and class; of my whiteness itself.)

Two memories: I am in a play reading at school of *The Merchant of Venice.*[8] Whatever Jewish law says, I am quite sure I was *seen* as Jewish (with a reassuringly gentile mother) in that double vision that bigotry allows. I am the only Jewish girl in the class, and I am playing Portia. As always, I read my part aloud for my father the night before, and he tells me to convey, with my voice, more scorn and contempt with the word "Jew": "Therefore, Jew . . ." I have to say the word out, and say it loudly. I was encouraged to pretend to be a non-Jewish child acting a non-Jewish character who has to speak the word "Jew" emphatically. Such a child would not have had trouble with the part. But *I* must have had trouble with the part, if only because the word itself was really taboo. I can see that there was a kind of terrible, bitter bravado about my father's way of handling this. And who would not dissociate from Shylock in order to identify with Portia? As a Jewish child who was also a female, I loved Portia—and, like every other Shakespearean heroine, she proved a treacherous role model.

A year or so later I am in another play, *The School for Scandal,*[9] in which a notorious spendthrift is described as having "many excellent friends . . . among the Jews." In neither case was anything explained, either to me or to the class at large, about this scorn for Jews and the disgust surrounding Jews and money. Money, when Jews wanted it, had it, or lent it to others, seemed to take on a peculiar nastiness; Jews and money had some peculiar and unspeakable relation.

At this same school—in which we had Episcopalian hymns and prayers, and read aloud through the Bible morning after morning—I gained the impression that Jews were in the Bible and mentioned in English literature, that they had been persecuted centuries ago by the wicked Inquisition, but that they seemed not to exist in everyday life. These were the 1940s, and we were told a great deal about the Battle of Britain, the noble French Resistance fighters, the brave, starving Dutch—but I did not learn of the resistance of the Warsaw ghetto until I left home.

I was sent to the Episcopal church, baptized and confirmed, and attended it for about five years, though without belief. That religion seemed to have little to do with belief or commitment; it was liturgy that mattered, not spiritual passion. Neither of my parents ever entered that church, and my father would not enter any church for any reason—wedding or funeral. Nor did I enter a synagogue until I left Baltimore. When I came home from church, for a while, my father insisted on reading aloud to me from Thomas Paine's *The Age of Reason*—a diatribe against institutional religion. Thus, he explained, I would

---

[8]*The Merchant of Venice* a play by William Shakespeare, which attacks Jewish moneylenders.

[9]*The School for Scandal* a 1777 play by Richard Sheridan; having "friends among the Jews" means that the character is in debt and has borrowed money.

have a balanced view of these things, a choice. He—they—did not give me the choice to be a Jew. My mother explained to me when I was filling out forms for college that if any question was asked about "religion," I should put down "Episcopalian" rather than "none"—to seem to have no religion was, she implied, dangerous.

But it was white social christianity, rather than any particular christian sect, that the world was founded on. The very word Christian was used as a synonym for virtuous, just, peace-loving, generous, etc., etc.[10] The norm was christian: "religion: none" was indeed not acceptable. Anti-Semitism was so intrinsic as not to have a name. I don't recall exactly being taught that the Jews killed Jesus—"Christ killer" seems too strong a term for the bland Episcopal vocabulary—but certainly we got the impression that the Jews had been caught out in a terrible mistake, failing to recognize the true Messiah, and were thereby less advanced in moral and spiritual sensibility. The Jews had actually allowed moneylenders in the Temple (again, the unexplained obsession with Jews and money). They were of the past, archaic, primitive, as older (and darker) cultures are supposed to be primitive; christianity was lightness, fairness, peace on earth, and combined the feminine appeal of "The meek shall inherit the earth" with the masculine stride of "Onward, Christian Soldiers."

Sometime in 1946, while still in high school, I read in the newspaper that a theater in Baltimore was showing films of the Allied liberation of the Nazi concentration camps. Alone, I went downtown after school one afternoon and watched the stark, blurry, but unmistakable newsreels. When I try to go back and touch the pulse of that girl of sixteen, growing up in many ways so precocious and so ignorant, I am overwhelmed by a memory of despair, a sense of inevitability more enveloping than any I had ever known. Anne Frank's diary and many other personal narratives of the Holocaust were still unknown or unwritten. But it came to me that every one of those piles of corpses, mountains of shoes and clothing had contained, simply, individuals, who had believed, as I now believed of myself, that they were intended to live out a life of some kind of meaning, that the world possessed some kind of sense and order; yet this had happened to them. And I, who believed my life was intended to be so interesting and meaningful, was connected to those dead by something—not just mortality but a taboo name, a hated identity. Or was I—did I really have to be? Writing this now, I feel belated rage that I was so impoverished by the family and social worlds I lived in, that I had to try to figure out by myself what this did indeed mean for me. That I had never been taught about resistance, only about passing. That I had no language for anti-Semitism itself.

When I went home and told my parents where I had been, they were not pleased. I felt accused of being morbidly curious, not healthy, sniffing around death for the thrill of it. And since, at sixteen, I was often not sure of the sources of my feelings or of my motives for doing what I did, I probably accused myself as well. One thing was clear: there was nobody in my world with whom I could discuss those films. Probably at the same time, I was reading accounts of the camps in magazines and newspapers; what I remember were the films and having questions that I could not even phrase, such as *Are those men and women "them" or "us"?*

To be able to ask even the child's astonished question *Why do they hate us so?* means knowing how to say "we." The guilt of not knowing, the guilt of perhaps having betrayed

---

[10]In a similar way the phrase "That's white of you" implied that you were behaving with the superior decency and morality expected of white but not of Black people. [Rich's note]

my parents or even those victims, those survivors, through mere curiosity—these also froze in me for years the impulse to find out more about the Holocaust.

1947: I left Baltimore to go to college in Cambridge, Massachusetts, left (I thought) the backward, enervating South for the intellectual, vital North. New England also had for me some vibration of higher moral rectitude, of moral passion even, with its seventeenth-century Puritan self-scrutiny, its nineteenth-century literary "flowering," its abolitionist righteousness, Colonel Shaw[11] and his Black Civil War regiment depicted in granite on Boston Common. At the same time, I found myself, at Radcliffe, among Jewish women. I used to sit for hours over coffee with what I thought of as the "real" Jewish students, who told me about middle-class Jewish culture in America. I described my background—for the first time to strangers—and they took me on, some with amusement at my illiteracy, some arguing that I could never marry into a strict Jewish family, some convinced I didn't "look Jewish," others that I did. I learned the names of holidays and foods, which surnames are Jewish and which are "changed names"; about girls who had had their noses "fixed," their hair straightened. For these young Jewish women, students in the late 1940s, it was acceptable, perhaps even necessary, to strive to look as gentile as possible; but they stuck proudly to being Jewish, expected to marry a Jew, have children, keep the holidays, carry on the culture.

I felt I was testing a forbidden current, that there was danger in these revelations. I bought a reproduction of a Chagall[12] portrait of a rabbi in striped prayer shawl and hung it on the wall of my room. I was admittedly young and trying to educate myself, but I was also doing something that *is* dangerous: I was flirting with identity.

One day that year I was in a small shop where I had bought a dress with a too-long skirt. The shop employed a seamstress who did alterations, and she came in to pin up the skirt on me. I am sure that she was a recent immigrant, a survivor. I remember a short, dark woman wearing heavy glasses, with an accent so foreign I could not understand her words. Something about her presence was very powerful and disturbing to me. After marking and pinning up the skirt, she sat back on her knees, looked up at me, and asked in a hurried whisper: "You Jewish?" Eighteen years of training in assimilation sprang into the reflex by which I shook my head, rejecting her, and muttered, "No."

What was I actually saying "no" to? She was poor, older, struggling with a foreign tongue, anxious; she had escaped the death that had been intended for her, but I had no imagination of her possible courage and foresight, her resistance—I did not see in her a heroine who had perhaps saved many lives, including her own. I saw the frightened immigrant, the seamstress hemming the skirts of college girls, the wandering Jew. But I was an American college girl having her skirt hemmed. And I was frightened myself, I think, because she had recognized me ("It takes one to know one," my friend Edie at Radcliffe had said) even if I refused to recognize myself or her, even if her recognition was sharpened by loneliness or the need to feel safe with me.

But why should she have felt safe with me? I myself was living with a false sense of safety.

[11]*Colonel Shaw* Robert Gould Shaw (1837–1863) commanded the first "colored" volunteer regiment, the Massachusetts 54th, during the Civil War.

[12]*Chagall* Marc Chagall (1887–1985) an influential Russian painter whose work often centered on Jewish themes such as the Jewish shtetls or villages in his early work and Jewish martyrs and refugees during World War II.

There are betrayals in my life that I have known at the very moment were betrayals: this was one of them. There are other betrayals committed so repeatedly, so mundanely, that they leave no memory trace behind, only a growing residue of misery, of dull, accreted self-hatred. Often these take the form not of words but of silence. Silence before the joke at which everyone is laughing: the anti-woman joke, the racist joke, the anti-Semitic joke. Silence and then amnesia. Blocking it out when the oppressor's language starts coming from the lips of one we admire, whose courage and eloquence have touched us: *She didn't really mean that; he didn't really say that.* But the accretions build up out of sight, like scale inside a kettle.

1948: I come home from my freshman year at college, flaming with new insights, new information. I am the daughter who has gone out into the world, to the pinnacle of intellectual prestige, Harvard, fulfilling my father's hopes for me, but also exposed to dangerous influences. I have already been reproved for attending a rally for Henry Wallace[13] and the Progressive party. I challenge my father: "Why haven't you told me that I am Jewish? Why do you never talk about being a Jew?" He answers measuredly, "You know that I have never denied that I am a Jew. But it's not important to me. I am a scientist, a deist. I have no use for organized religion. I choose to live in a world of many kinds of people. There are Jews I admire and others whom I despise. I am a person, not simply a Jew." The words are as I remember them, not perhaps exactly as spoken. But that was the message. And it contained enough truth—as all denial drugs itself on partial truth—so that it remained for the time being unanswerable, leaving me high and dry, split at the root, gasping for clarity, for air.

At that time Arnold Rich was living in suspension, waiting to be appointed to the professorship of pathology at Johns Hopkins. The appointment was delayed for years, no Jew ever having held a professional chair in that medical school. And he wanted it badly. It must have been a very bitter time for him, since he had believed so greatly in the redeeming power of excellence, of being the most brilliant, inspired man for the job. With enough excellence, you could presumably make it stop mattering that you were Jewish; you could become the *only* Jew in the gentile world, a Jew so "civilized," so far from "common," so attractively combining southern gentility with European cultural values that no one would ever confuse you with the raw, "pushy" Jews of New York, the "loud, hysterical" refugees from eastern Europe, the "overdressed" Jews of the urban South.

We—my sister, mother, and I—were constantly urged to speak quietly in public, to dress without ostentation, to repress all vividness or spontaneity, to assimilate with a world which might see us as too flamboyant. I suppose that my mother, pure gentile though she was, could be seen as acting "common" or "Jewish" if she laughed too loudly or spoke aggressively. My father's mother, who lived with us half the year, was a model of circumspect behavior, dressed in dark blue or lavender, retiring in company, ladylike to an extreme, wearing no jewelry except a good gold chain, a narrow brooch, or a string of pearls. A few times, within the family, I saw her anger flare, felt the passion she was repressing. But when Arnold took us out to a restaurant or on a trip, the Rich women were always tuned down to some WASP level my father believed, surely, would protect us all—maybe also make us unrecognizable to the "real Jews" who wanted to seize us, drag us back to the *shtetl,* the ghetto, in its many manifestations.

[13]*Henry Wallace* (1888–1965) an American journalist, agriculturist, and politician who ran for president in 1948 as the Progressive party's candidate.

For, yes, that *was* a message—that some Jews would be after you, once they "knew," to rejoin them, to re-enter a world that was messy, noisy, unpredictable, maybe poor— "even though," as my mother once wrote me, criticizing my largely Jewish choice of friends in college, "some of them will be the most brilliant, fascinating people you'll ever meet." I wonder if that isn't one message of assimilation—of America—that the unlucky or the unachieving want to pull you backward, that to identify with them is to court downward mobility, lose the precious chance of passing, of token existence. There was always within this sense of Jewish identity a strong class discrimination. Jews might be "fascinating" as individuals but came with huge unruly families who "poured chicken soup over everyone's head" (in the phrase of a white southern male poet). Anti-Semitism could thus be justified by the bad behavior of certain Jews; and if you did not effectively deny family and community, there would always be a remote cousin claiming kinship with you who was the "wrong kind" of Jew.

I have always believed his attitude toward other Jews depended on who they were. . . . It was my impression that Jews of this background looked down on Eastern European Jews, including Polish Jews and Russian Jews, who generally were not as well educated. This from a letter written to me recently by a gentile who had worked in my father's department, whom I had asked about anti-Semitism there and in particular regarding my father. This informant also wrote me that it was hard to perceive anti-Semitism in Baltimore because the racism made so much more intense an impression: *I would almost have to think that blacks went to a different heaven than the whites, because the bodies were kept in a separate morgue, and some white persons did not even want blood transfusions from black donors.* My father's mind was predictably racist and misogynist; yet as a medical student he noted in his journal that southern male chivalry stopped at the point of any white man in a streetcar giving his seat to an old, weary Black woman standing in the aisle. Was this a Jewish insight—an outsider's insight, even though the outsider was striving to be on the inside?

Because what isn't named is often more permeating than what is, I believe that my father's Jewishness profoundly shaped my own identity and our family existence. They were shaped both by external anti-Semitism and my father's self-hatred, and by his Jewish pride. What Arnold did, I think, was call his Jewish pride something else: achievement, aspiration, genius, idealism. Whatever was unacceptable got left back under the rubric of Jewishness or the "wrong kind" of Jews—uneducated, aggressive, loud. The message I got was that we were really superior: nobody else's father had collected so many books, had traveled so far, knew so many languages. Baltimore was a musical city, but for the most part, in the families of my school friends, culture was for women. My father was an amateur musician, read poetry, adored encyclopedic knowledge. He prowled and pounced over my school papers, insisting I use "grown-up" sources; he criticized my poems for faulty technique and gave me books on rhyme and meter and form. His investment in my intellect and talent was egotistical, tyrannical, opinionated, and terribly wearing. He taught me, nevertheless, to believe in hard work, to mistrust easy inspiration, to write and rewrite; to feel that I *was* a person of the book, even though a woman; to take ideas seriously. He made me feel, at a very young age, the power of language and that I could share in it.

The Riches were proud, but we also had to be very careful. Our behavior had to be more impeccable than other people's. Strangers were not to be trusted, nor even friends; family issues must never go beyond the family; the world was full of potential slanderers, betrayers, *people who could not understand.* Even within the family, I realize that I never in my whole life knew what my father was really feeling. Yet he spoke—monologued—with driving intensity. You could grow up in such a house mesmerized by the local electricity, the crucial meanings assumed by the merest things. This used to seem to me a sign that we were all living on some high emotional plane. It was a difficult force field for a favored daughter to disengage from.

Easy to call that intensity Jewish; and I have no doubt that passion is one of the qualities required for survival over generations of persecution. But what happens when passion is rent from its original base, when the white gentile world is softly saying "Be more like us and you can be almost one of us"? What happens when survival seems to mean closing off one emotional artery after another? His forebears in Europe had been forbidden to travel or expelled from one country after another, had special taxes levied on them if they left the city walls, had been forced to wear special clothes and badges, restricted to the poorest neighborhoods. He had wanted to be a "free spirit," to travel widely, among "all kinds of people." Yet in his prime of life he lived in an increasingly withdrawn world, in his house up on a hill in a neighborhood where Jews were not supposed to be able to buy property, depending almost exclusively on interactions with his wife and daughters to provide emotional connectedness. In his home, he created a private defense system so elaborate that even as he was dying, my mother felt unable to talk freely with his colleagues or others who might have helped her. Of course, she acquiesced in this.

The loneliness of the "only," the token, often doesn't feel like loneliness but like a kind of dead echo chamber. Certain things that ought to don't resonate. Somewhere Beverly Smith writes of women of color "inspiring the behavior" in each other. When there's nobody to "inspire the behavior," act out of the culture, there is an atrophy, a dwindling, which is partly invisible.

I was married in 1953, in the Hillel House at Harvard, under a portrait of Albert Einstein. My parents refused to come. I was marrying a Jew of the "wrong kind" from an Orthodox eastern European background. Brooklyn-born, he had gone to Harvard, changed his name, was both indissolubly connected to his childhood world and terribly ambivalent about it. My father saw this marriage as my having fallen prey to the Jewish family, eastern European division.

Like many women I knew in the fifties living under a then-unquestioned heterosexual imperative, I married in part because I knew no better way to disconnect from my first family. I married a "real Jew" who was himself almost equally divided between a troubled yet ingrained Jewish identity, and the pull toward Yankee approval, assimilation. But at least he was not adrift as a single token in a gentile world. We lived in a world where there was much intermarriage and where a certain "Jewish flavor" was accepted within the dominant gentile culture. People talked glibly of "Jewish self-hatred," but anti-Semitism was rarely identified. It was as if you could have it both ways—identity and assimilation—without having to think about it very much.

I was moved and gratefully amazed by the affection and kindliness my husband's parents showed me, the half *shiksa*. I longed to embrace that family, that new and mysterious Jewish world. It was never a question of conversion—my husband had long since ceased being observant—but of a burning desire to do well, please these new parents, heal the split consciousness in which I had been raised, and, of course, to belong. In the big, sunny apartment of Eastern Parkway, the table would be spread on Saturday afternoons with a white or an embroidered cloth and plates of coffeecake, spongecake, mohncake, cookies for a family gathering where everyone ate and drank—coffee, milk, cake—

and later the talk still eddied among the women around the table or in the kitchen, while the men ended up in the living room watching the ball game. I had never known this kind of family, in which mock insults were cheerfully exchanged, secrets whispered in corners among two or three, children and grandchildren boasted about, and the new daughter-in-law openly inspected. I was profoundly attracted by all this, including the punctilious observance of kashrut, the symbolism lurking behind daily kitchen tasks. I saw it all as quintessentially and authentically Jewish, and I objectified both the people and the culture. My unexamined anti-Semitism allowed me to do this. But also, I had not yet recognized that as a woman I stood in a particular and unexamined relationship to the Jewish family and to Jewish culture.

There were several years during which I did not see, and barely communicated with, my parents. At the same time, my father's personality haunted my life. Such had been the force of his will in our household that for a long time I felt I would have to pay in some terrible way for having disobeyed him. When finally we were reconciled, and my husband and I and our children began to have some minimal formal contact with my parents, the obsessional power of Arnold's voice or handwriting had given way to a dull sense of useless anger and pain. I wanted him to cherish and approve of me, not as he had when I was a child, but as the woman I was, who had her own mind and had made her own choices. This, I finally realized, was not to be; Arnold demanded absolute loyalty, absolute submission to his will. In my separation from him, in my realization at what price that once-intoxicating approval had been bought, I was learning in concrete ways a great deal about patriarchy, in particular how the "special" woman, the favored daughter, is controlled and rewarded.

Arnold Rich died in 1968 after a long, deteriorating illness; his mind had gone, and he had been losing his sight for years. It was a year of intensifying political awareness for me: the Martin Luther King and Robert Kennedy assassinations, the Columbia strike. But it was not that these events, and the meetings and demonstrations that surrounded them, preempted the time of mourning for my father; I had been mourning a long time for an early, primary, and intense relationship, by no means always benign, but in which I had been ceaselessly made to feel that what I did with my life, the choices I made, the attitudes I held, were of the utmost consequence.

Sometime in my thirties, on visits to Brooklyn, I sat on Eastern Parkway, a baby stroller at my feet—one of many rows of young Jewish women on benches with children in that neighborhood. I used to see the Lubavitcher Hasidim—then beginning to move into the Crown Heights neighborhood—walking out on *Shabbes,* the women in their *shaytls* a little behind the men. My father-in-law pointed them out as rather exotic—too old-country, perhaps, too unassimilated even for his devout yet Americanized sense of Jewish identity. It took many years for me to understand—partly because I understood so little about class in America—how in my own family, and in the very different family of my in-laws, there were degrees and hierarchies of assimilation which looked askance upon each other—and also geographic lines of difference, as between southern Jews and New York Jews, whose manners and customs varied along class as well as regional lines.

I had three sons before I was thirty, and during those years I often felt that to be a Jewish woman, a Jewish mother, was to be perceived in the Jewish family as an entirely physical being, a producer and nourisher of children. The experience of motherhood was eventually to radicalize me. But before that, I was encountering the institution of motherhood most directly in a Jewish cultural version; and I felt rebellious, moody, defensive, unable to sort out what was Jewish from what was simply motherhood or female destiny. (I lived in Cambridge, not Brooklyn; but there, too, restless, educated women sat on benches with baby strollers, half-stunned, not by Jewish cultural expectations, but by the middle-class American social expectations of the 1950s.)

My children were taken irregularly to Seders, to bar mizvahs, and to special services in their grandfather's temple. Their father lit Hanukkah candles while I stood by, having rememorized each year the English meaning of the Hebrew blessing. We all celebrated a secular, liberal Christmas. I read aloud from books about Esther and the Maccabees and Moses, and also from books about Norse trolls and Chinese grandmothers and Celtic dragon slayers. Their father told stories of his boyhood in Brooklyn, his grandmother in the Bronx who had to be visited by subway every week, of misdeeds in Hebrew school, of being a bright Jewish kid at Boys' High. In the permissive liberalism of academic Cambridge, you could raise your children to be as vaguely or distinctly Jewish as you would, but Christian myth and calendar organized the year. My sons grew up knowing far more about the existence and concrete meaning of Jewish culture than I had. But I don't recall sitting down with them and telling them that millions of people like them- selves, many of them children, had been rounded up and murdered in Europe in their parents' lifetime. Nor was I able to tell them that they came in part out of the rich, thousand-year-old Ashkenazic culture of eastern Europe, which the Holocaust destroyed; or that they came from a people whose traditions, religious and secular, included a hatred of oppression and an imperative to pursue justice and care for the stranger—an anti-racist, a socialist, and even sometimes a feminist vision. I could not tell them these things because these things were still too indistinct in my own mind.

The emergence of the Civil Rights movement in the sixties I remember as lifting me out of a sense of personal frustration and hopelessness. Reading James Baldwin's early essays in the fifties had stirred me with a sense that apparently "given" situations like racism could be analyzed and described and that this could lead to action, to change. Racism had been so utter and implicit a fact of my childhood and adolescence, had felt so cen- tral among the silences, negations, cruelties, fears, superstitions of my early life, that somewhere among my feelings must have been the hope that if Black people could become free of the immense political and social burdens they were forced to bear, I, too, could become free of all the ghosts and shadows of my childhood, named and unnamed. When "the movement" began, it felt extremely personal to me. And it was often Jews who spoke up for the justice of the cause, Jewish students and civil rights lawyers who travelled South; it was two young Jews who were found murdered with a young Black man in Mis- sissippi: Schwerner, Goodman, Chaney.

Moving to New York in the mid-sixties meant being plunged almost immediately into the debate over community control of public schools, in which Black and Jewish teach- ers and parents were often on opposite sides of extremely militant barricades. It was easy as a white liberal to deplore and condemn the racism of middle-class Jewish parents or angry Jewish school-teachers, many of them older women; to displace our own racism onto them; or to feel it as too painful to think about. The struggle for Black civil rights had such clarity about it for me: I knew that segregation was wrong, that unequal oppor- tunity was wrong; I knew that segregation in particular was more than a set of social and legal rules—it meant that even "decent" white people lived in a network of lies and arro- gance and moral collusion. In the world of Jewish assimilationist and liberal politics which

I knew best, however, things were far less clear to me, and anti-Semitism went almost unmentioned. It was even possible to view concern about anti-Semitism as a reactionary agenda, a monomania of *Commentary* magazine or, later, the Jewish Defense League. Most of the political work I was doing in the late 1960s was on racial issues, in particular as a teacher in the City University during the struggle for open admissions. The white colleagues I thought of as allies were, I think, mostly Jewish. Yet it was easy to see other New York Jews, who had climbed out of poverty and exploitation through the public-school system and the free city colleges, as now trying to block Black and Puerto Rican students trying to do likewise. I didn't understand then that I was living between two strains of Jewish social identity: the Jew as radical visionary and activist who understands oppression firsthand, and the Jew as part of America's devouring plan in which the persecuted, called to assimilation, learn that the price is to engage in persecution.

And, indeed, there was intense racism among Jews as well as white gentiles in the City University, part of the bitter history of Jews and Blacks which James Baldwin had described much earlier, in his 1948 essay "The Harlem Ghetto"; part of the divide-and-conquer script still being rehearsed by those of us who have the least to gain from it.

By the time I left my marriage, after seventeen years and three children, I had become identified with the Women's Liberation movement. It was an astonishing time to be a woman of my age. In the 1950s, seeking a way to grasp the pain I seemed to be feeling most of the time, to set it in some larger context, I had read all kinds of things; but it was James Baldwin and Simone de Beauvoir who had described the world—though differently—in terms that made the most sense to me. By the end of the sixties there were two political movements—one already meeting severe repression, one just emerging—which addressed those descriptions of the world.

And there was, of course, a third movement, or a movement-within-a-movement: the early lesbian manifestoes, the new visibility and activism of lesbians everywhere. I had known very early on that the women's movement was not going to be a simple walk across an open field; that it would pull on every fiber of my existence; that it would mean going back and searching the shadows of my consciousness. Reading *The Second Sex* in the 1950s isolation of an academic housewife had felt less dangerous than reading "The Myth of Vaginal Orgasm" or "Woman-identified Woman" in a world where I was in constant debate and discussion with women over every aspect of our lives that we could as yet name. De Beauvoir had placed "The Lesbian" on the margins, and there was little in her book to suggest the power of woman bonding. But the passion of debating ideas with women was an erotic passion for me, and the risking of self with women that was necessary in order to win some truth out of the lies of the past was also erotic. The suppressed lesbian I had been carrying in me since adolescence began to stretch her limbs, and her first full-fledged act was to fall in love with a Jewish woman.

Some time during the early months of that relationship, I dreamed that I was arguing feminist politics with my lover. *Of course,* I said to her in this dream, *if you're going to bring up the Holocaust against me, there's nothing I can do.* If, as I believe, I was both myself and her in this dream, it spoke of the split in my consciousness. I had been, more or less, a Jewish heterosexual woman. But what did it mean to be a Jewish lesbian? What did it mean to feel myself, as I did, both anti-Semite and Jew? And, as a feminist, how was I charting for myself the oppressions within oppression?

The earliest feminist papers on Jewish identity that I read were critiques of the patriarchal and misogynist elements in Judaism, or of the caricaturing of Jewish women in literature by Jewish men. I remember hearing Judith Plaskow give a paper called "Can a

Woman Be a Jew?" (Her conclusion was "Yes, but . . .") I was soon after in correspondence with a former student who had emigrated to Israel, was a passionate feminist, and wrote to me at length of the legal and social constraints on women there, the stirrings of contemporary Israeli feminism, and the contradictions she felt in her daily life. With the new politics, activism, literature of a tumultuous feminist movement around me, a movement which claimed universality though it had not yet acknowledged its own racial, class, and ethnic perspectives or its fears of the differences among women, I pushed aside for one last time thinking further about myself as a Jewish woman. I saw Judaism simply as another strand of patriarchy. If asked to choose, I might have said (as my father had said in other language): *I am a woman, not a Jew.* (But, I always added mentally, if Jews had to wear yellow stars again, I, too, would wear one—as if I would have the choice to wear it or not.)

Sometimes I feel I have seen too long from too many disconnected angles: white, Jewish, anti-Semite, racist, anti-racist, once-married, lesbian, middle-class, feminist, exmatriate southerner, *split at the root*—that I will never bring them whole. I would have liked, in this essay, to bring together the meanings of anti-Semitism and racism as I have experienced them and as I believe they intersect in the world beyond my life. But I'm not able to do this yet. I feel the tension as I think, make notes: *If you really look at the one reality, the other will waver and disperse.* Trying in one week to read Angela Davis and Lucy Davidowicz,[14] trying to hold throughout to a feminist, a lesbian, perspective—what does this mean? Nothing has trained me for this. And sometimes I feel inadequate to make any statement as a Jew; I feel the history of denial within me like an injury, a scar. For assimilation has affected *my* perceptions; those early lapses in meaning, those blanks, are with me still. My ignorance can be dangerous to me and to others.

Yet we can't wait for the undamaged to make our connections for us; we can't wait to speak until we are perfectly clear and righteous. There is no purity and, in our lifetimes, no end to this process.

This essay, then, has no conclusions: it is another beginning for me. Not just a way of saying, in 1982 Right Wing America, *I, too, will wear the yellow star.* It's a moving into accountability, enlarging the range of accountability. I know that in the rest of my life, the next half century or so, every aspect of my identity will have to be engaged. The middle-class white girl taught to trade obedience for privilege. The Jewish lesbian raised to be a heterosexual gentile. The woman who first heard oppression named and analyzed in the Black Civil Rights struggle. The woman with three sons, the feminist who hates male violence. The woman limping with a cane, the woman who has stopped bleeding are also accountable. The poet who knows that beautiful language can lie, that the oppressor's language sometimes sounds beautiful. The woman trying, as part of her resistance, to clean up her act.

Understanding and Analysis

1. Note the immediacy of the first two paragraphs. What situation is Rich describing? Find other references that show Rich writing the essay in the present, telling us and herself how she feels as she writes and as we read with her.

---

[14]*Angela Davis, Women, Race and Class* (New York: Random House, 1981); Lucy S. Davidowicz, *The War against the Jews 1933–45* (New York: Bantam, 1979). [Rich's note]

2. What are the three things Rich must do to write this essay?

3. What is the first line Rich traces as she sets out to write the essay? How does this line merge with her entire history, from, as she indicates in paragraph six, the time she was born? What details in this one-sentence paragraph help to set the many themes of this essay?

4. How does Rich "break [her father's] silence"? What does she "expose"?

5. What does Rich tell about her mother that helps her to understand her father and herself?

6. What are some of the definitions of being Jewish that Rich examines throughout the essay? Who or what creates these various definitions?

7. What kinds of "silence" does Rich examine in the essay? Who besides her father has resorted to silence?

8. In what ways does Rich feel like "the betrayer" in paragraph 16? Where else in the essay does she write about betrayal? What sorts of betrayal does she examine in her own life?

9. What had been Rich's religious education? How did it help to shape her understanding of Judaism?

10. What makes Rich feel "belated rage" as she writes?

11. What are some of the anti-Semitic attitudes Rich explores?

12. What are some of the feelings Rich describes when she remembers herself as a young mother in a Jewish family? What did she not tell her sons, as far as she can remember?

13. Describe Rich's reaction to reading James Baldwin.

14. What "aspects of [her] identity" does Rich explore in this essay? What scientific principle is Rich alluding to in the italicized sentence near the end of the essay? How does that allusion help to explain the impossibility of capturing identity? In what ways is identity a "process"?

Comparison

1. Compare Rich's examination of assimilation, denial, and other topics with that of Woody Allen. To what extent, if at all, do the two authors agree?

2. Compare Rich's exploration of identity with that of others in this collection, such as Hurston, Podhoretz, Didion, Rodriguez, Staples, Momaday, Kingston, and Ozick. Do these writers share any characteristics other than their love of language? If so, what?

3. Rich uses several one-sentence paragraphs. Read the essays by Beerbohm and Twain. Compare the one-sentence paragraphs in these essays with those in Rich's. What characteristics do all share? Can you draw some conclusions about what makes a good one-sentence paragraph?

4. Read Lippmann's "Stereotypes." How does this essay enlarge your understanding of the world in which Rich's father and mother moved? How have attitudes about ethnic identity changed since the early twenties when Lippmann wrote about the melting pot?

Stephen Jay Gould

THE STREAK OF STREAKS* (1988)

MY FATHER WAS a court stenographer. At his less than princely salary, we watched Yankee games from the bleachers or high in the third deck. But one of the judges had season tickets, so we occasionally sat in the lower boxes when hizzoner couldn't attend. One afternoon, while DiMaggio was going 0 for 4 against, of all people, the lowly St. Louis Browns, the great man fouled one in our direction. "Catch it, Dad," I screamed. "You never get them," he replied, but stuck up his hand like the Statue of Liberty—and the ball fell right in. I mailed it to DiMaggio, and, bless him, he actually sent the ball back, signed and in a box marked "insured." Insured, that is, to make me the envy of the neighborhood, and DiMaggio the model and hero of my life.

I met DiMaggio a few years ago on a small playing field at the Presidio of San Francisco. My son, wearing DiMaggio's old number 5 on his Little League jersey, accompanied me, exactly one generation after my father caught that ball. DiMaggio gave him a pointer or two on batting and then signed a baseball for him. One generation passeth away, and another generation cometh: But the earth abideth forever.

My son, uncoached by Dad, and given the chance that comes but once in a lifetime, asked DiMaggio as his only query about life and career: "Suppose you had walked every time up during one game of your 56-game hitting streak? Would the streak have been over?" DiMaggio replied that, under 1941 rules, the streak would have ended, but that this unfair statute has since been revised, and such a game would not count today.

My son's choice for a single question tells us something vital about the nature of legend. A man may labor for a professional lifetime, especially in sport or in battle, but posterity needs a single transcendant event to fix him in permanent memory. Every hero must be a Wellington[1] on the right side of his personal Waterloo;[2] generality of excellence is too diffuse. The unambiguous factuality of a single achievement is adamantine. Detractors can argue forever about the general tenor of your life and works, but they can never erase a great event.

In 1941, as I gestated in my mother's womb, Joe DiMaggio got at least one hit in each of 56 successive games. Most records are only incrementally superior to runners-up; Roger Maris hit 61 homers in 1961, but Babe Ruth hit 60 in 1927 and 59 in 1921, while Hank Greenberg (1938) and Jimmy Foxx (1932) both hit 58. But DiMaggio's 56-game hitting

---

*This essay originally appeared in the *New York Review of Books* as a review of Michael Seidel's *Streak: Joe DiMaggio and the Summer of 1941* (New York: McGraw-Hill, 1988). I have excised the references to Seidel's book in order to forge a more general essay, but I thank him both for the impetus and for writing such a fine book. [Gould's note]

[1]*Wellington* Arthur Wellesley, First Duke of Wellington (1769–1852) a British general, statesman, and prime minister who was awarded many honors for his various military successes in India, France, and other parts of Europe.

[2]*Waterloo* the Battle of Waterloo in 1815, in which the Duke of Wellington defeated the French army led by Napoleon.

streak is ridiculously, almost unreachably far from all challengers (Wee Willie Keeler and Pete Rose, both with 44, come second). Among sabermetricians (a happy neologism based on an acronym for members of the Society for American Baseball Research, and referring to the statistical mavens of the sport)—a contentious lot not known for agreement about anything—we find virtual consensus that DiMaggio's 56-game hitting streak is the greatest accomplishment in the history of baseball, if not all modern sport.

The reasons for this respect are not far to seek. Single moments of unexpected supremacy—Johnny Vander Meer's back-to-back no-hitters in 1938, Don Larsen's perfect game in the 1956 World Series—can occur at any time to almost anybody, and have an irreducibly capricious character. Achievements of a full season—such as Maris's 61 homers in 1961 and Ted Williams's batting average of .406, also posted in 1941 and not equaled since—have a certain overall majesty, but they don't demand unfailing consistency every single day; you can slump for a while, so long as your average holds. But a streak must be absolutely exceptionless; you are not allowed a single day of subpar play, or even bad luck. You bat only four or five times in an average game. Sometimes two or three of these efforts yield walks, and you get only one or two shots at a hit. Moreover, as tension mounts and notice increases, your life becomes unbearable. Reporters dog your every step; fans are even more intrusive than usual (one stole DiMaggio's favorite bat right in the middle of his streak). You cannot make a single mistake.

Thus Joe DiMaggio's 56-game hitting streak is both the greatest factual achievement in the history of baseball and a principal icon of American mythology. What shall we do with such a central item of our cultural history?

Statistics and mythology may strike us as the most unlikely of bedfellows. How can we quantify Caruso[3] or measure *Middlemarch?*[4] (*But if God could mete out heaven with the span* (Isaiah 40:12), perhaps we can say something useful about hitting streaks. The statistics of "runs," defined as continuous series of good or bad results (including baseball's streaks and slumps), is a well-developed branch of the profession, and can yield clear—but wildly counterintuitive—results. (The fact that we find these conclusions so surprising is the key to appreciating DiMaggio's achievement, the point of this article, and the gateway to an important insight about the human mind.))

Start with a phenomenon that nearly everyone both accepts and considers well understood—"hot hands" in basketball. Now and then, someone just gets hot, and can't be stopped. Basket after basket falls in—or out as with "cold hands," when a man can't buy a bucket for love or money (choose your cliché). The reason for this phenomenon is clear enough: It lies embodied in the maxim, "When you're hot; you're hot; and when you're not, you're not." You get that touch, build confidence; all nervousness fades, you find your rhythm; swish, swish, swish. Or you miss a few, get rattled, endure the booing, experience despair; hands start shaking and you realize that you shoulda stood in bed.

Everybody knows about hot hands. The only problem is that no such phenomenon exists. Stanford psychologist Amos Tversky studied every basket made by the Philadelphia 76ers for more than a season. He found, first of all, that the probability of making a second basket did not rise following a successful shot. Moreover, the number of "runs," or baskets in succession, was no greater than what a standard random, or coin-tossing, model would pre-

[3]*Caruso* Enrico Caruso (1873–1921) an operatic tenor whose powerful voice and extraordinary acting ability won international acclaim.

[4]*Middlemarch* a novel by the English writer George Eliot, published in 1872.

dict. (If the chance of making each basket is 0.5, for example, a reasonable value for good shooters, five hits in a row will occur, on average, once in 32 sequences—just as you can expect to toss five successive heads about once in 32 times, or 0.5^5.)

Of course Larry Bird, the great forward of the Boston Celtics, will have more sequences of five than Joe Airball—but not because he has greater will or gets in that magic rhythm more often. Larry has longer runs because his average success rate is so much higher, and random models predict more frequent and longer sequences. If Larry shoots field goals at 0.6 probability of success, he will get five in a row about once every 13 sequences (0.6^5). If Joe, by contrast, shoots only 0.3, he will get his five straight only about once in 412 times. In other words, we need no special explanation for the apparent pattern of long runs. There is no ineffable "causality of circumstance" (to coin a phrase), no definite reason born of the particulars that make for heroic myths—courage in the clinch, strength in adversity, etc. You only have to know a person's ordinary play in order to predict his sequences. (I rather suspect that we are convinced of the contrary not only because we need myths so badly, but also because we remember the successes and simply allow the failures to fade from memory. More on this later.) But how does this revisionist pessimism work for baseball?

My colleague Ed Purcell, Nobel laureate in physics but, for purposes of this subject, just another baseball fan, has done a comprehensive study of all baseball streak and slump records. His firm conclusion is easily and swiftly summarized. Nothing ever happened in baseball above and beyond the frequency predicted by coin-tossing models. The longest runs of wins or losses are as long as they should be, and occur about as often as they ought to. Even the hapless Orioles, at 0 and 21 to start the 1988 season, only fell victim to the laws of probability (and not to the vengeful God of racism, out to punish major league baseball's only black manager).*

But "treasure your exceptions," as the old motto goes. Purcell's rule has but one major exception, one sequence so many standard deviations above the expected distribution that it should never have occurred at all: Joe DiMaggio's 56-game hitting streak in 1941. The intuition of baseball aficionados has been vindicated. Purcell calculated that to make it likely (probability greater than 50 percent) that a run of even 50 games will occur once in the history of baseball up to now (and 56 is a lot more than 50 in this kind of league), baseball's rosters would have to include either four lifetime .400 batters or 52 lifetime .350 batters over careers of 1,000 games. In actuality, only three men have lifetime batting averages in excess of .350, and no one is anywhere near .400 (Ty Cobb at .367, Rogers Hornsby at .358, and Shoeless Joe Jackson at .356). DiMaggio's streak is the most extraordinary thing that ever happened in American sports. He sits on the shoulders of two bearers—mythology and science. For Joe DiMaggio accomplished what no other ballplayer has done. He beat the hardest taskmaster of all, a woman who makes Nolan Ryan's fastball look like a cantaloupe in slow motion—Lady Luck.

A larger issue lies behind basic documentation and simple appreciation. For we don't understand the truly special character of DiMaggio's record because we are so poorly equipped, whether by habits of culture or by our modes of cognition, to grasp the workings of random processes and patterning in nature.

*When I wrote this essay, Frank Robinson, the Baltimore skipper, was the only black man at the helm of a major league team. For more on the stats of Baltimore's slump, see my article "Winning and Losing: It's All in the Game," *Rotunda,* Spring 1989. [Gould's note]

Omar Khayyám, the old Persian tentmaker, understood the quandary of our lives (*Rubaiyat of Omar Khayyám,* Edward Fitzgerald, trans.):

> Into this Universe, and Why not knowing,
> Nor Whence, like Water willy-nilly flowing;
> And out of it, as Wind along the Waste,
> I know not Whither, willy-nilly blowing.

But we cannot bear it. We must have comforting answers. We see pattern, for pattern surely exists, even in a purely random world. (Only a highly nonrandom universe could possibly cancel out the clumping that we perceive as pattern. We think we see constellations because stars are dispersed at random in the heavens, and therefore clump in our sight). Our error lies not in the perception of pattern but in automatically imbuing pattern with meaning, especially with meaning that can bring us comfort, or dispel confusion. Again, Omar took the more honest approach:

> Ah, love! could you and I with Fate conspire
> To grasp this sorry Scheme of Things entire,
> Would not we shatter it to bits—and then
> Re-mould it nearer to the Heart's Desire!

We, instead, have tried to impose that "heart's desire" upon the actual earth and its largely random patterns (Alexander Pope, *Essay on Man,* end of Epistle 1):

> All Nature is but Art, unknown to thee;
> All Chance, Direction, which thou canst not see;
> All Discord, Harmony not understood:
> All partial Evil, universal Good.

Sorry to wax so poetic and tendentious about something that leads back to DiMaggio's hitting streak, but this broader setting forms the source of our misinterpretation. We believe in "hot hands" because we must impart meaning to a pattern—and we like meanings that tell stories about heroism, valor, and excellence. We believe that long streaks and slumps must have direct causes internal to the sequence itself, and we have no feel for the frequency and length of sequences in random data. Thus, while we understand that DiMaggio's hitting streak was the longest ever, we don't appreciate its truly special character because we view all the others as equally patterned by cause, only a little shorter. We distinguish DiMaggio's feat merely by quantity along a continuum of courage; we should, instead, view his 56-game hitting streak as a unique assault upon the otherwise unblemished record of Dame Probability.

Amos Tversky, who studied "hot hands," has performed, with Daniel Kahneman, a series of elegant psychological experiments. These long-term studies have provided our finest insight into "natural reasoning" and its curious departure from logical truth. To cite an example, they construct a fictional description of a young woman: "Linda is 31 years old, single, outspoken, and very bright. She majored in philosophy. As a student, she was deeply concerned with issues of discrimination and social justice, and also participated in anti-nuclear demonstrations." Subjects are then given a list of hypothetical statements about Linda: They must rank these in order of presumed likelihood, most to least probable. Tversky and Kahneman list eight statements, but five are a blind, and only three make up the true experiment:

> Linda is active in the feminist movement;
> Linda is a bank teller;
> Linda is a bank teller and is active in the feminist movement.

Now it simply must be true that the third statement is least likely, since any conjunction has to be less probable than either of its parts considered separately. Everybody can understand this when the principle is explained explicitly and patiently. But all groups of subjects, sophisticated students who have pondered logic and probability as well as folks off the street corner, rank the last statement as more probable than the second. (I am particularly fond of this example because I know that the third statement is least probable, yet a little homunculus in my head continues to jump up and down, shouting at me—"but she can't just be a bank teller; read the description.")

Why do we so consistently make this simple logical error? Tversky and Kahneman argue, correctly I think, that our minds are not built (for whatever reason) to work by the rules of probability, though these rules clearly govern our universe. We do something else that usually serves us well, but fails in crucial instances: We "match to type." We abstract what we consider the "essence" of an entity, and then arrange our judgments by their degree of similarity to this assumed type. Since we are given a "type" for Linda that implies feminism, but definitely not a bank job, we rank any statement matching the type as more probable than another that only contains material contrary to the type. This propensity may help us to understand an entire range of human preferences, from Plato's theory of form to modern stereotyping of race or gender.

We might also understand the world better, and free ourselves of unseemly prejudice, if we properly grasped the workings of probability and its inexorable hold, through laws of logic, upon much of nature's pattern. "Matching to type" is one common error; failure to understand random patterning in streaks and slumps is another—hence Tversky's study of both the fictional Linda and the 76ers' baskets. Our failure to appreciate the uniqueness of DiMaggio's streak derives from the same unnatural and uncomfortable relationship that we maintain with probability. (If we knew Lady Luck better, Las Vegas might still be a roadstop in the desert.)

My favorite illustration of this basic misunderstanding, as applied to DiMaggio's hitting streak, appeared in a recent article by baseball writer John Holway, "A Little Help from His Friends," and subtitled "Hits or Hype in '41" (*Sports Heritage*, 1987). Holway points out that five of DiMaggio's successes were narrow escapes and lucky breaks. He received two benefits-of-the-doubt from official scorers on plays that might have been judged as errors. In each of two games, his only hit was a cheapie. In game 16, a ball dropped untouched in the outfield and had to be called a hit, even though the ball had been misjudged and could have been caught; in game 54, DiMaggio dribbled one down the third-base line, easily beating the throw because the third baseman, expecting the usual, was playing far back. The fifth incident is an oft-told tale, perhaps the most interesting story of the streak. In game 38, DiMaggio was 0 for 3 going into the last inning. Scheduled to bat fourth, he might have been denied a chance to hit at all. Johnny Sturm popped up to begin the inning, but Red Rolfe then walked. Slugger Tommy Henrich, up next, was suddenly swept with a premonitory fear: Suppose I ground into a double play and end the inning? An elegant solution immediately occurred to him: Why not bunt (an odd strategy for a power hitter). Henrich laid down a beauty; DiMaggio, up next, promptly drilled a double to left.

I enjoyed Holway's account, but his premise is entirely, almost preciously, wrong. First of all, none of the five incidents represents an egregious miscall. The two hits were less than elegant, but undoubtedly legitimate; the two boosts from official scorers were close calls on judgment plays, not gifts. As for Henrich, I can only repeat manager Joe McCarthy's comment when Tommy asked him for permission to bunt: "Yeah, that's a good idea." Not a terrible strategy either—to put a man into scoring position for an insurance run when you're up 3-1.

But these details do not touch the main point: Holway's premise is false because he accepts the conventional mythology about long sequences. He believes that streaks are unbroken runs of causal courage—so that any prolongation by hook-or-crook becomes an outrage against the deep meaning of the phenomenon. But extended sequences are not pure exercises in valor. Long streaks always are, and must be, a matter of extraordinary luck imposed upon great skill. Please don't make the vulgar mistake of thinking that Purcell or Tversky or I or anyone else would attribute a long streak to "just luck"—as though everyone's chances are exactly the same, and streaks represent nothing more than the lucky atom that kept moving in one direction. Long hitting streaks happen to the greatest players—Sisler, Keeler, DiMaggio, Rose—because their general chance of getting a hit is so much higher than average. Just as Joe Airball cannot match Larry Bird for runs of baskets, Joe's cousin Bill Ofer, with a lifetime batting average of .184, will never have a streak to match DiMaggio's with a lifetime average of .325. The statistics show something else, and something fascinating: There is no "causality of circumstance," no "extra" that the great can draw from the soul of their valor to extend a streak beyond the ordinary expectation of cointossing models for a series of unconnected events, each occurring with a characteristic probability for that particular player. Good players have higher characteristic probabilities, hence longer streaks.

Of course DiMaggio had a little luck during his streak. That's what streaks are all about. No long sequence has ever been entirely sustained in any other way (the Orioles almost won several of those 21 games). DiMaggio's remarkable achievement—its uniqueness, in the unvarnished literal sense of that word—lies in whatever he did to extend his success well beyond the reasonable expectations of random models that have governed every other streak or slump in the history of baseball.

Probability does pervade the universe—and in this sense, the old chestnut about baseball imitating life really has validity. The statistics of streaks and slumps, properly understood, do teach an important lesson about epistemology, and life in general. The history of a species, or any natural phenomenon that requires unbroken continuity in a world of trouble, works like a batting streak. All are games of a gambler playing with a limited stake against a house with infinite resources. The gamble must eventually go bust. His aim can only be to stick around as long as possible, to have some fun while he's at it, and, if he happens to be a moral agent as well, to worry about staying the course with honor. The best of us will try to live by a few simple rules: Do justly, love mercy, walk humbly with thy God, and never draw to an inside straight.

DiMaggio's hitting streak is the finest of legitimate legends because it embodies the essence of the battle that truly defines our lives. DiMaggio activated the greatest and most unattainable dream of all humanity, the hope and chimera of all sages and shamans: He cheated death, at least for a while.

Understanding and Analysis

1. Based on the first five paragraphs of the essay, how would you characterize Gould's narrative voice? What levels of diction does he use?

2. What are the two assertions about DiMaggio's hitting streak that Gould makes in paragraph seven? In the next paragraph Gould states what he hopes to accomplish in this essay. What does he hope to accomplish?

3. Explain "hot hands" and the reasons scientists know the phenomenon does not exist.

4. Why is DiMaggio's streak so amazing? That is the answer to the first point Gould says he wants to accomplish when he sets up the structure of his essay in paragraph seven.

5. The second point is the "larger issue." What exactly are "we so poorly equipped" to understand? What is "the quandary of our lives" and how do we generally comfort ourselves in the face of this truth, according to Gould?

6. Why does Gould quote Omar Khayyam and Alexander Pope?

7. How and why do we misinterpret DiMaggio's streak, according to Gould?

8. Are "Dame Probability" (paragraph 16) and "Lady Luck" (paragraph 13) two names for the same idea or two different ideas? Explain your reasoning.

9. What are the experiments Tversky designed, and how do they show the difference between the way the mind generally reasons and strict logic?

10. In paragraph 19, Gould explains how the mind generally works. How does this system lead to stereotyping?

11. Why does Gould describe the article by Holway?

12. What role does luck play in streaks, according to Gould?

13. How does Gould bring together all his themes in the last two paragraphs, that is, what words indicate which themes? How did DiMaggio "cheat death"?

14. Gould is known for his allusions to literature, music, sports, and various other fields when he writes about science. In this essay, the main subject is baseball, not science. What other fields does he allude to in this essay?

15. Reread the first five paragraphs. How do they establish the themes of the essay and the levels of diction Gould will use to develop his main point? In the first paragraph, for example, "hizzoner" and the sentence fragment indicate a colloquial level of diction and point to a concern with social class, whereas "bless him," also colloquial, indicates an appeal to religious impulses. Locate other examples of colloquial or academic or biblical diction and examine the themes they suggest.

16. Why do you think Gould wants to appeal to so many fields and types? Is he saying anything that may upset people? What is his view of the universe? Do the various levels of diction and the use of both "I" and "we" (as opposed to "I" and "you") help to persuade the reader?

Comparison

1. Compare Ozick's two kinds of excellence with Gould's claim about the nature of heroes and excellence in his fourth paragraph. Do you agree with Gould? Why or why not? Do Ozick and Gould agree?

2. Compare Gould's explanation of stereotyping with that of Lippmann. To what extent do the two agree?

3. Compare the rhetorical strategies and style of this essay with those in "Women's Brains." What similarities and differences do you see?

4. Compare Gould's prose style as displayed in his two essays here with that of other scientists in this collection, such as Eiseley, Kuhn, and Bronowski. What, if anything, do they have in common? What, if anything, distinguishes each?

Jamaica Kincaid
(1949–)

Jamaica Kincaid, born Elaine Potter Richardson, grew up in Antigua, the first and only child of Roderick Potter and Annie Richardson. Not long after Kincaid's birth, Annie married a carpenter named David Drew, and, with him, she had three more children, all sons. Kincaid developed a relationship of love and loathing with her mother, and while she may have been alone in becoming "obsessed" with her mother, none of the children enjoyed Annie's "incredible little cruelties" or her criticisms. Kincaid said in an interview with *Salon*, "all her children are quite happy to have been born, but all of us are quite sure she should never have been a mother."

Learning to read before she turned four, Kincaid became deeply attached to books, sometimes refusing to return them to the library once she'd read them. Her colonial education exposed her to the literary masters of the colonizers, "Kipling, Carlyle, people like that. It was as if, as children, we were all being prepared for MFAs." Kincaid left Antigua at the age of 17, without a thought of literature, forced by economic necessity to seek work in the United States. Settling in New York, she worked as an *au pair*, or as she preferred to say, a "servant." Between 1966 and 1973, she earned a high school degree, studied at a community college, and "did all the things people do when they have no money, short of selling my blood or my body. I just sort of starved. I was a secretary, and I modeled." Publishing for the first time in *Ingenue* magazine, for which she interviewed Gloria Steinem, Kincaid wrote "some television criticism" for *The Village Voice* before she was discovered by *The New Yorker*. Thanks to a chance meeting in an elevator, she was introduced to George Trow, author of the "Talk of the Town" column. Trow, in turn, brought her to the attention of William Shawn, *The New Yorker's* editor. In 1976, already having changed her name, Jamaica Kincaid joined the staff. In 1979, she married the composer Allen Shawn, the son of the editor.

Although she took over "Talk of the Town" herself, the most important work Kincaid did in her early years with *The New Yorker* was write a short—indeed, a very short—story called "Girl." One of her most famous pieces, it contains a litany of her mother's admonitions: "this is how you sweep a corner; this is how you sweep a whole house; this is how you sweep a yard; this is how you smile to someone you don't like too much; . . . this is how to behave in the presence of men who don't know you very well, and this way they won't recognize you immediately as the slut I have warned you against becoming." Less than 1,000 words long, the story electrified the editorial staff and represents the genesis of Kincaid's writing style: poetic and prosaic, graceful and hard. In 1983, "Girl" opened Kincaid's first collection of short stories, *At the Bottom of the River*. She published her first novel, *Annie John*, in 1985. Both of these texts, she says, she wrote with uncharacteristic speed. In 1986, she published *Annie, Gwen, Lilly, Pam and Tulip*.

Kincaid's next publication, a work of non-fiction about Antigua called *A Small Place* (1988), excerpted below, became her most overtly political text. Although William Shawn "loved it," he left the magazine in 1987, and his successor "found it angry and didn't publish it." Thus it was that *A Small Place*, unlike many of her other short works, did not find a first home in *The New Yorker*. In 1990, Kincaid published a novel called *Lucy*, and in 1995, *The Autobiography of My Mother*. At this point, she broke with *The New Yorker*, leaving the staff in a fury when editor Tina Brown proposed inviting comedian Roseanne Barr to guest edit an issue. (Kincaid now refers to *The New Yorker* as "a version of *People* magazine.") On her own, Kincaid published *My Brother* (1998), an account of the life of her youngest stepbrother, who died of AIDS. She presently lives in Vermont with her husband and her two children, Annie and Harold.

Mothers and daughters populate the works of Jamaica Kincaid. Her favorite narrative—when she chooses to write in narrative—is of a young woman's coming-of-age. Many critics have observed repetitions and variations across Kincaid's works, like variations on a theme by Beethoven, and Kincaid herself uses a musical metaphor to describe her writing: "My work is a chord that develops in many different ways. Given the use of that same chord, as well as the relatively small size of her corpus, her literary reputation is rather remarkable. Like Flannery O'Connor, whose corpus was also small when she achieved fame, Kincaid has assured her place by writing brilliantly of her birthplace, as well as her "obsession": the loss of maternal love, the leaving of mothers, the leaving of motherlands. Influenced by modernism, Kincaid writes "not so much in stories as in states of consciousness," as critic Doris

Grumbach says, using a style that critics term "poetic" and "beautiful," but also "bitter." Kincaid's characters suffer bitterness as well, not only because of their losses, but because of the sensibility of their creator. Living in America, a nation which in her view demands happy endings, Kincaid told an interviewer, "Perversely, I will not give the happy ending. I think life is difficult."

FROM *A Small Place* (1988–)

THE THING YOU have always suspected about yourself the minute you become a tourist is true: A tourist is an ugly human being. You are not an ugly person all the time; you are not an ugly person ordinarily; you are not an ugly person day to day. From day to day, you are a nice person. From day to day, all the people who are supposed to love you on the whole do. From day to day, as you walk down a busy street in the large and modern and prosperous city in which you work and live, dismayed, puzzled (a cliché, but only a cliché can explain you) at how alone you feel in this crowd, how awful it is to go unnoticed, how awful it is to go unloved, even as you are surrounded by more people than you could possibly get to know in a lifetime that lasted for millennia, and then out of the corner of your eye you see someone looking at you and absolute pleasure is written all over that person's face, and then you realise that you are not as revolting a presence as you think you are (for that look just told you so). And so, ordinarily, you are a nice person, an attractive person, a person capable of drawing to yourself the affection of other people (people just like you), a person at home in your own skin (sort of; I mean, in a way; I mean, your dismay and puzzlement are natural to you, because people like you just seem to be like that, and so many of the things people like you find admirable about yourselves—the things you think about, the things you think really define you—seem rooted in these feelings): a person at home in your own house (and all its nice house things), with its nice back yard (and its nice back-yard things), at home on your street, your church, in community activities, your job, at home with your family, your relatives, your friends—you are a whole person. But one day, when you are sitting somewhere, alone in that crowd, and that awful feeling of displacedness comes over you, and really, as an ordinary person you are not well equipped to look too far inward and set yourself aright, because being ordinary is already so taxing, and being ordinary takes all you have out of you, and though the words "I must get away" do not actually pass across your lips, you make a leap from being that nice blob just sitting like a boob in your amniotic sac of the modern experience to being a person visiting heaps of death and ruin and feeling alive and inspired at the sight of it; to being a person lying on some faraway beach, your stilled body stinking and glistening in the sand, looking like something first forgotten, then remembered, then not important enough to go back for; to being a person marvelling at the harmony (ordinarily, what you would say is the backwardness) and the union these other people (and they are other people) have with nature. And you look at the things they can do with a piece of ordinary cloth, the things they fashion out of cheap, vulgarly colored (to you) twine, the way they squat down over a hole they have made in the ground, the hole itself is something to marvel at, and since you are being an ugly person this ugly but joyful thought will swell inside you: their ancestors were not clever in the way yours were and not ruthless in the way yours were, for then would it not be you who would be in harmony with nature and backwards in that charming way? An ugly thing, that is what you are when you become a tourist, an ugly, empty thing, a stupid thing, a piece of rubbish pausing here and there to gaze at this and taste that, and it will never occur to you that the people who inhabit the place in which you have just paused cannot stand you, that behind their closed doors they laugh at your strangeness (you do not look the way they look); the physical sight of you does not please them; you have bad manners (it is their custom to eat their food with their hands; you try eating their way, you look silly; you try eating the way you always eat, you look silly); they do not like the way you speak (you have an accent); they collapse helpless from laughter, mimicking the way they imagine you must look as you carry out some everyday bodily function. They do not like you. *They do not like me!* That thought never actually occurs to you. Still, you feel a little uneasy. Still, you feel a little foolish. Still, you feel a little out of place. But the banality of your own life is very real to you, it drove you to this extreme, spending your days and your nights in the company of people who despise you, people you do not like really, people you would not want to have as your actual neighbour. And so you must devote yourself to puzzling out how much of what you are told is really, really true (Is ground-up bottle glass in peanut sauce really a delicacy around here, or will it do just what you think ground-up bottle glass will do? Is this rare, multicoloured, snout-mouthed fish really an aphrodisiac, or will it cause you to fall asleep permanently?). Oh, the hard work all of this is, and is it any wonder, then, that on your return home you feel the need of a long rest, so that you can recover from your life as a tourist?

That the native does not like the tourist is not hard to explain. For every native of every place is a potential tourist, and every tourist is a native of somewhere. Every native everywhere lives a life of overwhelming and crushing banality and boredom and desperation and depression, and every deed, good and bad, is an attempt to forget this. Every native would like to find a way out, every native would like a rest, every native would like a tour. But some natives—most natives in the world—cannot go anywhere. They are too poor. They are too poor to go anywhere. They are too poor to escape the reality of their lives; and they are too poor to live properly in the place where they live, which is the very place you, the tourist, want to go—so when the natives see you, the tourist, they envy you, they envy your ability to leave your own banality and boredom, they envy your ability to turn their own banality and boredom into a source of pleasure for yourself.

Understanding and Analysis

1. The selection published here is the last section of the first chapter of the book, which is itself very short (under 100 pages). Why does Kincaid refer to the reader over and over as "you"?

2. Where does the first paragraph end? If you had to divide the paragraph into several parts, where would you make divisions? How many would you make? Why?

3. What is the tone of the long paragraph? Does the tone shift at all in this paragraph? If so, where? What is the effect of such a long paragraph?

4. Characterize the persona of the narrator of this piece. Look at diction, sentence length, repetitions, and so on. Consider, for example, the following quotation: "and so many of the things people like you find admirable about yourselves—the things you think about, the things you think really define you—".

5. What is the tone of the second paragraph? Does the voice change? If so, how?

6. Do you react differently to the two paragraphs? What is the point of each paragraph?

Comparison

1. Compare Kincaid's techniques of persuasion with those of Mencken, Vidal, Brady, and others in this collection. Do you see any consistent strategies? Which ones are most effective? Why?

2. Read the essays by Margaret Mead and Clifford Geertz. Do these anthropologists exhibit any elements of the tourist, as defined by Kincaid? What is your evidence?

3. Read Baker's "Work in Corporate America." What characteristics does Baker's essay share, if any, with Kincaid's? What elements create the different tones of each piece?

Henry Louis Gates, Jr.
(1950–)

Born on September 16, 1950, his parents' second son, Louis Smith Gates never liked his given name. In *Colored People: A Memoir*, Gates explains: "Mama had promised her best friend, unmarried Miss Smith, that she'd pass her name on to the second-born, since the first-born was named for his grandfathers....I had hated that name, Smith, felt deprived of my birthright." As an adult, Gates legally changed his childhood name, but he did not abandon his childhood nickname: Skip. Growing up in Piedmont, West Virginia, he worried about his corrective orthopedic shoes, his weight, and his brother's bond with his father, but he also relished the time he spent with his mother, who taught him how to "read and write" in the space of a day. He "entered Davis Free Elementary School in 1956, just one year after it was integrated" and became an excellent student. Three years later, he sat down with his family to watch Mike Wallace's documentary on Black Muslims, "The Hate That Hate Produced": "these were just about the scariest black people I'd ever seen. Black people who talked right into the faces of white people, telling them off without even blinking. While I sat cowering in our living room, I happened to glance over at my mother. A certain radiance was slowly transforming her soft brown face, as she listened to Malcolm X naming the white man the Devil. 'Amen,' she said quietly at first. 'All right now,' she continued, much more heatedly. I hadn't realized just how deeply my mother despised white people.... The revelation was both terrifying and thrilling."

After joining an "oppressive" evangelical Methodist church at the age of 12, Gates underwent hip surgery and received a hospital visit from an Episcopalian priest, who suggested that the Episcopal church had no real objections to good old-fashioned adolescent rebellion. As soon as he was released, Gates attended an Episcopalian church camp. The Watts riots broke out in California while he was there, and a priest at the camp, "[s]ensing my mixture of pride and discomfiture," gave him a copy of James Baldwin's *Notes of a Native Son.* Enraptured with Baldwin's arguments as well as his language, Gates considered for the first time the possibility of becoming a writer. In school, he writes in *Thirteen Ways of Looking at a Black Man,* he "began imitating [Baldwin's] style of writing," but without Baldwin's artistry, piling up commas until his teacher "forbade me to use them 'unless absolutely necessary!'"

Graduating in 1968, Gates enrolled at Potomac State College of West Virginia, where an English professor suggested that he transfer to Yale. There Gates became a history major. According to Cheryl Bentsen, author of the infamously titled "Head Negro in Charge," which appeared in *Boston Magazine,* Gates traveled to Africa during his junior year and worked for a hospital in Tanzania before hitch-hiking his way around the continent. Upon his return, as he explained on the television program "Booknotes," he became a "scholar of the house," one of twelve undergraduates "chosen to spend their entire senior year on one project." While documenting Jay Rockefeller's gubernatorial campaign for his senior thesis, he met his future wife, Sharon Adams, and won a fellowship to study at Cambridge. He graduated summa cum laude in 1973 and moved to England. Over the next two years, as he completed his master's and began his doctoral work, he spent half of his time writing for the London bureau of *Time.* It was in this capacity, at the age of 22, that he met James Baldwin in person, reuniting him with performer Josephine Baker for a story called "The Black Expatriate."

Leaving *Time* in 1975, Gates returned home in 1976 to work as a lecturer at Yale. By this point, he had already encountered resistance to a proposed dissertation on "black literature." (The fifth chapter in *Loose Canons* is entitled "Tell Me, Sir, . . . What Is 'Black' Literature?"—a reference to the initial response.) With the support of a faculty member at Yale, he worked out a "compromise," as he described it on the television program "Booknotes," with tutors at Clare College and finished his Ph.D. in 1979. In the fall, he became a husband and an assistant professor, and, in the next year, a father. In 1982, having been promoted to associate professor, he edited his first book, *Black Is the Color of the Cosmos: Charles T. Davis's Essays on Afro-American Literature and Culture, 1942–1981.* The second book he edited was Harriet Wilson's *Our Nig; or, Sketches from the Life of a Free Black,* and from that point, Gates has made his reputation not only through cultural criticism but also through recovery work, editing slave narratives and out-of-print texts for new generations of students and readers.

Denied tenure at Yale in 1985, Gates moved on to Cornell. In 1987, he published his first book, *Figures in Black: Words, Signs, and the Racial Self,* and the following year, he accompanied his recovery work with a theoretical text, *The Signifying Monkey: Towards a Theory of Afro-American Literary Criticism*, which won an American Book Award. After five years at Cornell, Gates agreed to teach at Duke, but his experience proved disastrous. Bentsen explains, "In October 1990, Gates testified on behalf of the First-Amendment rights of 2 Live Crew, a black rap group charged with obscenity in Florida. Soon after that he became the target of conservative professors and the student newspaper." In 1991, Gates accepted an offer to save Afro-American Studies at Harvard, where he soon created a "Dream Team" of academics. In 1992, he published a collection of essays called *Loose Canons: Notes on the Culture Wars*. His next book was born on a trip to Piedmont with his daughters who, after asking about the civil rights movement, didn't seem to believe him when he revealed that "at one time" their white mother could have stayed the night in a hotel but their black father could not. After co-authoring *The Future of the Race* with Cornel West in 1996, Gates published *Thirteen Ways of Looking at a Black Man* in 1998, a collection of profiles of men like Colin Powell, Harry Belafonte, and Louis Farrakhan.

"I'm concerned," Henry Louis Gates has said, "with institution building." In the *Harvard Magazine* article "Anthologizing as a Radical Act," by Jonathan Shaw, Gates explains that by editing anthologies such as the *Norton Anthology of African American Literature* or series such as *The Schomburg Library of Nineteenth-Century Black Women Writers*, he is doing the "fundamental" work of bringing African-American authors into the canon. Many people have recognized Gates for this work, as well as for the insights of his textual and cultural criticism, yet there are those who maintain that the institution Gates is mainly interested in building is himself. He will surely survive such criticism, however justified or unjustified, for while African-American studies was not built in a day, it was built within half a century, and Gates is one of its principal architects, changing the way late-twentieth-century college students of any discipline studied literature.

TALKING BLACK (1988)

For a language acts in diverse ways, upon the spirit of a people;
even as the spirit of a people acts with a creative
and spiritualizing force upon a language.
　　　　　　　　　　　　　　　　　—ALEXANDER CRUMMELL, 1860

•

A new vision began gradually to replace the dream of political power—
a powerful movement, the rise of another ideal to guide the unguided,
another pillar of fire by night after a clouded day. It was the ideal of
"book-learning": the curiosity, born of compulsory ignorance,

to know and test the power of the cabalistic letters of the white man, the longing to know.

—W. E. B. Du Bois, 1903

•

The knowledge which would teach the white world was Greek to his own flesh and blood…and he could not articulate the message of another people.

—W. E. B. Du Bois, 1903

ALEXANDER CRUMMELL, A pioneering nineteenth-century Pan-Africanist, statesman, and missionary who spent the bulk of his creative years as an Anglican minister in Liberia,[1] was also a pioneering intellectual and philosopher of language, founding the American Negro Academy in 1897 and serving as the intellectual godfather of W. E. B. Du Bois.[2] For his first annual address as president of the academy, delivered on 28 December 1897, Crummell selected as his topic "The Attitude of the American Mind Toward the Negro Intellect." Given the occasion of the first annual meeting of the great intellectuals of the race, he could not have chosen a more timely or appropriate subject.

Crummell wished to attack, he said, "the denial of intellectuality in the Negro; the assertion that he was not a human being, that he did not belong to the human race." He argued that the desire "to becloud and stamp out the intellect of the Negro" led to the enactment of "laws and Statutes, closing the pages of every book printed to the eyes of Negroes; barring the doors of every school-room against them!" This, he concluded, "was the systematized method of the intellect of the South, to stamp out the brains of the Negro!"—a program that created an "almost Egyptian darkness [which] fell upon the mind of the race, throughout the whole land."

Crummell next shared with his audience a conversation between two Boston lawyers which he had overheard when he was "an errand boy in the Anti-slavery office in New York City" in 1833 or 1834:

> While at the Capitol they happened to dine in the company of the great John C. Calhoun, then senator from South Carolina. It was a period of great ferment upon the question of Slavery, States Rights, and Nullification; and consequently the Negro was the topic of conversation at the table. One of the utterances of Mr. Calhoun was to this effect—"That if he could find a Negro who knew the Greek syntax, he would then believe that the Negro was a human being and should be treated as a man."

"Just think of the crude asininity," Crummell concluded rather generously, "of even a great man!"

The salient sign of the black person's humanity—indeed, the only sign for Calhoun— would be the mastering of the very essence of Western civilization of the very foundation of the complex fiction upon which white Western culture had been constructed. It is likely that "Greek syntax," for John C. Calhoun, was merely a hyperbolic figure of speech,

---

[1]*Liberia* a West African nation where many ex-slaves from the U.S. settled.

[2]*W. E. B. Du Bois* (1868–1963) a professor of economics and history, he called for the African-American middle class to fight against bigoted racial policies, worked for the National Association for the Advancement of Colored People, became a Marxist, and left the United States to be a citizen of Ghana.

a trope of virtual impossibility; he felt driven to the hyperbolic mode, perhaps, because of the long racist tradition in Western letters of demanding that black people *prove* their full humanity. We know this tradition all too well, dotted as it is with the names of great intellectual Western racialists, such as Francis Bacon,[3] David Hume,[4] Immanuel Kant,[5] Thomas Jefferson, and G. W. F. Hegel.[6] Whereas each of these figures demanded that blacks write poetry to prove their humanity, Calhoun—writing in a post-Phillis Wheatley[7] era—took refuge in, yes, Greek syntax.

In typical African-American fashion, a brilliant black intellectual accepted Calhoun's bizarre challenge. The anecdote Crummell shared with his fellow black academicians turned out to be his shaping scene of instruction. For Crummell himself jumped on a boat, sailed to England, and matriculated at Queen's College, Cambridge, where he mastered (naturally enough) the intricacies of Greek syntax. Calhoun, we suspect, was not impressed.

Crummell never stopped believing that mastering the master's tongue was the sole path to civilization, intellectual freedom, and social equality for the black person. It was Western "culture," he insisted, that the black person "must claim as his rightful heritage, as a man—not stinted training, not a caste education, not," he concluded prophetically, "a Negro curriculum." As he argued so passionately in his speech of 1860, "The English Language in Liberia," the acquisition of the English language, along with Christianity, is the wonderful sign of God's providence encoded in the nightmare of African enslavement in the racist wilderness of the New World. English, for Crummell, was "the speech of Chaucer[8] and Shakespeare, of Milton[9] and Wordsworth,[10] of Bacon and Burke,[11] of Franklin[12] and Webster,"[13] and its potential mastery was "this one item of compensation" that "the Almighty has bestowed upon us" in exchange for "the exile of our fathers from their African homes to America." In the English language are embodied "the noblest the-

---

[3]*Francis Bacon* (1561–1626) English statesman, philosopher, and essayist, best known for his scientific treatises, especially *The Advancement of Learning* (1605), and his concise *Essays* (1625).

[4]*David Hume* (1711–1776) Scottish philosopher and historian whose best-known work includes *A Treatise of Human Nature* (1740) and *Political Discourses* (1752).

[5]*Immanuel Kant* (1724–1804) German philosopher and professor of logic and metaphysics. His works, including *Critique of Pure Reason* and *Critique of Practical Reason* (1781), have influenced much subsequent philosophy.

[6]*G. W. F. Hegel* Georg Wilhelm Friedrich Hegel (1770–1831) German Idealist philosopher who argued for the prevalence of reason over Romantic intuition.

[7]*Phillis Wheatley* (c. 1753–1784) African poet who was sold as a slave to the Wheatley family and subsequently educated by them. At age 13, she had written sophisticated poems; she was subsequently freed.

[8]*Chaucer* Geoffrey Chaucer (1343–1400) English writer best known for *The Canterbury Tales.*

[9]*Milton* John Milton (1608–1674) English poet best known for his twelve-part masterpiece *Paradise Lost,* which was composed from 1641–1663.

[10]*Wordsworth* William Wordsworth (1770–1850) English Romantic poet who was made poet laureate in 1843.

[11]*Burke* Edmund Burke (1729–1797) a prominent British statesman and political philosopher.

[12]*Franklin* Benjamin Franklin (1706–1790) an American printer, writer, scientist, statesman who, among other accomplishments, helped found the University of Pennsylvania, authored the popular *Poor Richard's Almanac,* proved that lightning is an electrical charge, and invented the bifocal lens.

[13]*Webster* Daniel Webster (1782–1852), U.S. representative and senator, a strictly pro-union orator and U.S. secretary of state from 1841–1843.

ories of liberty" and "the grandest ideas of humanity." If black people master the master's tongue, these great and grand ideas will become African ideas, because "ideas conserve men, and keep alive the vitality of nations."

In dark contrast to the splendors of the English language, Crummell set the African vernacular languages, which, he wrote, have "definite marks of inferiority connected with them all, which place them at the widest distances from civilized languages." Any effort to render the master's discourse in our own black tongue is an egregious error, for we cannot translate sublime utterances "in[to] broken English—a miserable caricature of their noble tongue." We must abandon forever both indigenous African vernacular languages and the neo-African vernacular languages that our people have produced in the New World:

> All low, inferior, and barbarous tongues are, doubtless, but the lees and dregs of noble languages, which have gradually, as the soul of a nation has died out, sunk down to degradation and ruin. We must not suffer this decay on these shores, in this nation. We have been made, providentially, the deposit of a noble trust; and we should be proud to show our appreciation of it. Having come to the heritage of this language we must cherish its spirit, as well as retain its letter. We must cultivate it among ourselves; we must strive to infuse its spirit among our reclaimed and aspiring natives.

I cite the examples of John C. Calhoun and Alexander Crummell as metaphors for the relation between the critic of black writing and the larger institution of literature. Learning the master's tongue, for our generation of critics, has been an act of empowerment, whether that tongue be New Criticisms, humanism, structuralism, Marxism, poststructuralism, feminism, new historicism, or any other -*ism*. But even as Afro-American literature and criticism becomes institutionalized, our pressing question now becomes this: in what tongue shall we choose to speak, and write, our own criticism? What are we now to do with the enabling masks of empowerment that we have donned as we have practiced one mode of "white" criticism or another?

The Afro-American literary tradition is distinctive in that it evolved in response to allegations that its authors did not, and could not, create literature, a capacity that was considered the signal measure of a race's innate "humanity." The African living in Europe or in the New World seems to have felt compelled to create a literature not only to demonstrate that blacks did indeed possess the intellectual ability to create a written art, but also to indict the several social and economic institutions that delimited the "humanity" of all black people in Western cultures.

So insistent did these racist allegations prove to be, at least from the eighteenth to the early twentieth century, that it is fair to describe the subtext of the history of black letters in terms of the urge to refute them. Even as late as 1911, when J. E. Casely-Hayford published *Ethiopia Unbound* (the "first" African novel), he felt it necessary to address this matter in the first two paragraphs of his text. "At the dawn of the twentieth century," the novel opens, "men of light and leading both in Europe and in America had not yet made up their minds as to what place to assign to the spiritual aspirations of the black man." Few literary traditions have begun with such a complex and curious relation to criticism: allegations of an absence led directly to a presence, a literature often inextricably bound in a dialogue with its harshest critics.

Black literature and its criticism, then, have been put to uses that were not primarily aesthetic: rather, they have formed part of a larger discourse on the nature of the black, and his or her role in the order of things. Even so, a sense of integrity has arisen in the Afro-American tradition, though it has less to do with the formal organicism of the New Critics than with an intuitive notion of "ringing true," or Houston Baker's concept of "sounding." (One of the most frequently used critical judgments in the African-American tradition is "That shit don't sound right," or, as Alice Walker puts it in *The Color Purple,* "Look like to me only a fool would want to talk in a way that feel peculiar to your mind.") That is the sense I am calling on here, understanding how problematic even this can be. Doubleness, alienation, equivocality: since the turn of the century at least, these have been recurrent tropes for the black tradition.

To be sure, this matter of the language of criticism and the integrity of its subject has a long and rather tortured history in all black letters. It was David Hume, after all, who called Francis Williams, the Jamaican poet of Latin verse, "a parrot who merely speaks a few words plainly." Phillis Wheatley, too, has long suffered from the spurious attacks of black and white critics alike for being the *rara avis* of a school of so-called mockingbird poets, whose use of European and American literary conventions has been considered a corruption of a "purer" black expression, found in forms such as the blues, signifying, spirituals, and Afro-American dance. Can we, as critics, escape a "mockingbird" posture?

Only recently have some scholars attempted to convince critics of black literature that we can. Perhaps predictably, a number of these attempts share a concern with that which has been most repressed in the received tradition of Afro-American criticism: close readings of the texts themselves. And so we are learning to read a black text within a black formal cultural matrix. That means reading a literary culture that remains, for the most part, intransigently oral. If the black literary imagination has a privileged medium, it is what Douglass called the "live, calm, grave, clear, pointed, warm, sweet, melodious and powerful human voice." And the salient contribution of black literature may lie in its resolute vocality. But there is no black voice; only voices, diverse and mutable. Familiarly, there's the strut, confidence laced with bitters—

> I am a Waiter's Waiter. I know all the moves, all the pretty, fine moves that big book will never teach you . . . I built the railroad with my moves. (James Alan McPherson, "Solo Song")

Or the boisterous revelator:

> When he was on, Reverend Jones preached his gospel hour in a Texas church that held no more than 250 people, but the way he had the old sisters banging on them bass drums and slapping them tambourines, you'd think that God's Own Philharmonic was carrying on inside that old church where the loudspeaks blasted Jones's message to the thousands who stood outside. At the conclusion of Reverend Jones's sermon, the church didn't need no fire, because it was being warmed by the spirit of the Lord. By the spirit of Jesus. (Ishmael Reed, *The Terrible Threes*)

Yet how tonally remote they are from this cento of *Baldwin,*[14] a preacher's son for whom King Jamesian inversions were second nature:

> In the case of the Negro the past was taken from him whether he would or no; yet to forswear it was meaningless and availed him nothing, since his shameful history was carried, quite literally, on his brow. Shameful; for he was heathen as well as black and would never

[14]*Baldwin* James Baldwin (1924–1987) an African-American preacher, writer, and civil rights activist.

have discovered the healing blood of Christ had not we braved the jungles to bring him these glad tidings. . . .

Where the Negro face appears, a tension is created, the tension of a silence filled with things unutterable. ("Many Thousands Gone")

Baldwin wrote of "something ironic and violent and perpetually understated in Negro speech," and in this he was describing his own careful, ungentle cadences. Contrast, again, the homeliest intimacies of nuance that *Morrison*[15] will unexpectedly produce:

There is a loneliness that can be rocked. Arms crossed, knees drawn up; holding, holding on, this motion, unlike a ship's, smooths and contains the rockers. It's an inside kind— wrapped tight like skin. (*Beloved*)

There's no hidden continuity or coherence among them. History makes them like beads on a string: there's no necessary resemblance; but then again, no possible separation.

And so we've had to learn to "read black" as a textual effect because the existence of a black canon is a historically contingent phenomenon; it is not inherent in the nature of "blackness," not vouchsafed by the metaphysics of some racial essence. The black tradition exists only insofar as black artists enact it. Only because black writers have read and responded to other black writers with a sense of recognition and acknowledgment can we speak of a black literary inheritance, with all the burdens and privileges that has entailed. Race is a text (an array of discursive practices), not an essence. It must be read with painstaking care and suspicion, not imbibed.

The disjunction between the language of criticism and the language of its subject helps defamiliarize the texts of the black tradition: ironically, it is necessary to create distance between reader and texts in order to go beyond reflexive responses and achieve critical insight into and intimacy with their formal workings. I have done this to respect the integrity of these texts, by trying to avoid confusing my experiences as an Afro-American with the black act of language that defines a text. This is the challenge of the critic of black literature in the 1980s: not to shy away from white power—that is, a new critical vocabulary— but to translate it into the black idiom, *renaming* principles of criticism where appropriate, but especially naming indigenous black principles of criticism and applying them to our own texts. Any tool that enables the critic to explain the complex workings of the language of a text is appropriate here. For it is language, the black language of black texts, that expresses the distinctive quality of our literary tradition. Once it may have seemed that the only critical implements black critics needed were the pompom and the twirled baton; in fact, there is no deeper form of literary disrespect. We will not protect the integrity of our tradition by remaining afraid of, or naive about, literary analysis; rather, we will inflict upon it the violation of reflexive, stereotypical reading—or nonreading. We are the keepers of the black literary tradition. No matter what approach we adopt, we have more in common with each other than we do with any other critic of any other literature. We write for each other, and for our own contemporary writers. This relation is a critical trust.

It is also a *political* trust. How can the demonstration that our texts sustain ever closer and more sophisticated readings not be political at a time when all sorts of so-called canonical critics mediate their racism through calls for "purity" of "the tradition," demands as

---

[15]*Morrison* Toni Morrison, an African-American writer born in 1931, who won the Pulitzer Prize in 1988 and the Nobel Prize for Literature in 1993.

implicitly racist as anything the Southern Agrarians said? How can the deconstruction of the forms of racism itself not be political? How can the use of literary analysis to explicate the racist social text in which we still find ourselves be anything *but* political? To be political, however, does not mean that I have to write at the level of a Marvel comic book. My task, as I see it, is to help guarantee that black and so-called Third World literature is taught to black and Third World and white students by black and Third World and white professors in heretofore white mainstream departments of literature, and to train students to think, to read, and to write clearly, to expose false uses of language, fraudulent claims, and muddled arguments, propaganda, and vicious lies—from all of which our people have suffered just as surely as we have from an economic order in which we were zeroes and a metaphysical order in which we were absences. These are the "values" which should be transmitted through the languages of cultural and literary study.

In the December 1986 issue of the *Voice Literary Supplement,* in an essay entitled "Cult-Nats Meet Freaky-Deke," Greg Tate argued cogently and compellingly that "black aestheticians need to develop a coherent criticism to communicate the complexities of our culture. There's no periodical on black cultural phenomena equivalent to *The Village Voice* or *Artforum,* no publication that provides journalism on black visual art, philosophy, politics, economics, media, literature, linguistics, psychology, sexuality, spirituality, and pop culture. Though there are certainly black editors, journalists, and academics capable of producing such a journal, the disintegration of the black cultural nationalist movement and the brain-drain of black intellectuals to white institutions have destroyed the vociferous public dialogue that used to exist between them." While I would argue that *Sage, Callaloo,* and *Black American Literature Forum* are indeed fulfilling that function for academic critics, I am afraid that the truth of Tate's claim is irresistible.

But his most important contribution to the future of black criticism is to be found in his most damning allegation. "What's unfortunate," he writes, "is that while black artists have opened up the entire 'text of blackness' for fun and games, not many black critics have produced writing as fecund, eclectic, and freaky-deke as the art, let alone the culture, itself. . . . For those who prefer exegesis with a polemical bent, just imagine how critics as fluent in black and Western culture as the postliberated artists could strike terror into that bastion of white supremacist thinking, the Western art [and literary] world[s]." To which I can only say, "Amen, Amen."

Tate's challenge is a serious one because neither ideology nor criticism nor blackness can exist as entities of themselves, outside their forms or their texts. This is the central theme of Ralph Ellison's *Invisible Man* and Ishmael Reed's *Mumbo Jumbo,* for example. But how can we write or read the text of "Blackness"? What language(s) do black people use to represent their critical or ideological positions? In what forms of language do we speak or write? Can we derive a valid, integral "black" text of criticism or ideology from borrowed or appropriated forms? Can a black woman's text emerge authentically as borrowed, or "liberated," or revised, from the patriarchal forms of the slave narratives, on the one hand, or from the white matriarchal forms of the sentimental novel, on the other, as Harriet Jacobs and Harriet Wilson attempted to do in *Incidents in the Life of a Slave Girl* (1861) and *Our Nig* (1859)? Where lies the liberation in revision, the ideological integrity of defining freedom in the modes and forms of difference charted so cogently by so many poststructural critics of black literature?

For it is in these spaces of difference that black literature has dwelled. And while it is crucial to read these patterns of difference closely, we should understand as well that the quest was lost, in an important sense, before it had even begun, simply because the terms of our own self-representation have been provided by the master. It is not enough for us to show that refutation, negation, and revision exist, and to define them as satisfactory gestures of ideological independence. Our next concern will be to address the black political signified, that is, the cultural vision and the black critical language that underpin the search through literature and art for a profound reordering and humanizing of everyday existence. We encourage our writers and critics to undertake the fullest and most ironic exploration of the manner and matter, the content and form, the structure and sensibility so familiar and poignant to us in our most sublime form of art, black music, where ideology and art are one, whether we listen to Bessie Smith or to postmodern and poststructural John Coltrane.

Just as we encourage our writers to meet this challenge, we as critics can turn to our own peculiarly black structures of thought and feeling to develop our own language of criticism. We do so by drawing on the black vernacular, the language we use to speak to each other when no white people are around. Unless we look to the vernacular to ground our modes of reading, we will surely sink in the mire of Nella Larsen's quicksand, remain alienated in the isolation of Harriet Jacobs' garret, or masked in the received stereotype of the Black Other helping Huck to return to the raft, singing "China Gate" with Nat King Cole under the Da Nang moon, or reflecting our balded heads in the shining flash of Mr. T's signifying gold chains.

We can redefine reading itself from within our own black cultures, refusing to grant the racist premise that criticism is something that white people do, so that we are doomed to imitate our white colleagues, like reverse black minstrel critics done up in whiteface. We should not succumb, as did Alexander Crummell, to the tragic lure of white power, the mistake of accepting the empowering language of white criticism as "universal" or as our own language, the mistake of confusing its enabling mask with our own black faces. Each of us has, in some literal or figurative manner, boarded a ship and sailed to a metaphorical Cambridge, seeking to master the master's tools. (I myself, being quite literal-minded, booked passage some fourteen years ago on the *QE2*.[16]) Now we can at last don the empowering mask of blackness and talk that talk, the language of black difference. While it is true that we must, as Du Bois said so long ago, "know and test the power of the cabalistic letters of the white man," we must also know and test the dark secrets of a black discursive universe that awaits its disclosure through the black arts of interpretation. The future of our language and literature may prove black indeed.

Understanding and Analysis

1. In your own words, tell the story of Alexander Crummell, his education, and his beliefs.

2. At what point in Gates's telling of Crummell's story do you become aware of Gates's disagreements with Crummell? What did Crummell "never stop believing"?

3. Reread the essay. What is Gates's attitude toward "learning the master's tongue"? What is your evidence?

4. Who is the "we" that Gates refers to in his essay? Consider his characterizations of "we" throughout the essay, as well as the allusions he makes to various authors and critical theories.

---

[16]*QE2* the *Queen Elizabeth II*, a luxurious cruise ship.

5. What are the parallels between African-American literature and criticism and the story of Crummell and of Calhoun?

6. What, according to Gates, is "the mockingbird posture," and where did the concept arise?

7. What point does Gates illustrate when he quotes various African-American authors such as McPherson, Reed, and Baldwin?

8. What does Gates mean when he says that "the existence of a black canon is a historically contingent phenomenon"? What does he mean when he says, "Race is a text (an array of discursive practices), not an essence"?

9. What, according to Gates, must a literary critic do to read a text to "achieve critical insight"?

10. What is Gates's "task"?

11. What is the point of Tate's argument and why does Gates cite it?

12. What does Gates mean when he says that "neither ideology nor criticism nor blackness can exist as entities of themselves, outside their forms or their texts"?

13. What is Gates urging black writers and critics to do?

14. Why does Gates tell us near the end of the essay that he took the QE2 to England?

15. What is Gates's attitude toward white critics?

16. Examine Gates's language throughout the essay to see how he uses metaphor, analogy, and humor.

Comparison

1. Read the essay by Hurston. What similarities do you find in the two essays?

2. Read the two essays by Baldwin. To what extent do Gates and Baldwin agree and disagree about language and western culture?

3. Read the essay by Postman. How does Gates order facts with theory?

4. Read the essay by T. S. Eliot. To what extent do Gates and Eliot agree?

5. Compare Tan's analysis of language with that of Gates. Do Tan and Gates share similar attitudes toward the shaping influence of language?

Paul Fussell

(1925–)

Paul Fussell was born March 22, 1924, into the "Pasadena gentry." During his childhood, as he explains in his autobiography, *Doing Battle*, "Pasadena especially seemed a moral oasis in the midst of the surrounding drink, sex, drugs, and gambling." Descended from Quakers, Fussell grew up Presbyterian, forbidden by his family to play games—especially cards—on Sunday. Other days of the week, however, he "played trench warfare," with his friends, and, on his own, discovered yearly enthusiasms: "Once I went overboard for spinning tops, and once I could think of little else than making from clothespins guns that would shoot wooden matches." In junior high, he developed a lasting enthusiasm for print shop, taught by a man named McNary, and built a print shop of his own in a walk-in closet, harassing people, with little success, to pay him to print their "business cards, labels, flyers, tickets—anything five by eight inches or smaller." Years later, he transferred his equipment to Balboa, where his parents kept a summer home, to publish a newspaper. "It was Mr. McNary's print shop," Fussell writes in *Doing Battle*, "that told me that whatever I did with my life, it would have to involve words and their public presentation."

In 1941, following in the footsteps of his older brother, Edwin, he entered Pomona College, editing, with Edwin, the college humor magazine, *The Sagehen*. Fussell was 17 and still establishing himself at school when the Japanese bombed Pearl Harbor. At 19, he reported for training, serving for three years, leading a rifle platoon into battle in Europe. When the Germans surrendered, he was recuperating in a hospital, wounded during an assault that killed several men around him, including a close friend named Edward Hudson.

Returning to Pomona in 1946, Fussell was a changed man: "I was now convinced that my duty was criticism, meaning not carping, but the perpetual obligation of evaluation. I deepened my new empirical understanding of the brevity of life and determined not to waste a second of it in contemptible or silly activity, like sports or gossip or trivia." Fussell's impatience with "meaninglessness and vagueness" extended even—perhaps especially—to language: "Furious one day at some newspaper canting, I dashed off a letter to the editor protesting the facile and false formula *gave his life* to suggest the motives of soldiers, who were, after all, for the most part highly unwilling conscripts anxious to give if necessary anything but their lives." Angry and exacting, Fussell raised his grades and, after graduation, followed Edwin to Harvard to study English. In 1949, the same year he earned his M.A., he married Betty Harper, whom he had met in college. He finished his dissertation two years later and started teaching almost immediately at Connecticut College. Although he remained there for several years, he was happy neither with the school nor with himself, feeling "dangerously angry" at having to change rapidly from "college [student] to professional killer, and then to benign professor."

In 1954, Fussell published his dissertation, *Theory of Prosody in Eighteenth-Century England,* which led to a teaching job at Rutgers University. Other works followed: *The Presence of Walt Whitman* (co-author, 1962), *The Rhetorical World of Augustan Humanism* (1965), and his now-famous *Poetic Meter and Poetic Form* (1965), a kind of textbook for readers of poetry, which he dedicated to Edwin. His last strictly academic book was *Samuel Johnson and the Life of Writing* (1971).

Fussell's next publication, *The Great War and Modern Memory* (1975), pro-foundly enlarged both his audience and his reputation. Describing his writing habits during an interview, Fussell also explained the genesis of his most famous work: "Writing is so hard, and I'm so lazy, I can't really motivate myself to move towards the typewriter unless I feel some strong impulse to right some wrong or to have my say about something that has annoyed me. . . . In *The Great War and Modern Memory,* what annoyed me was people talking about body counts during the Vietnam War without any imagination of what that sort of thing meant." Fussell's annoyance provoked a fascinating history, an account not only of the literature produced during and after World War I, but also of the reciprocity between art and life, and the "places and situations where literary tradition and real life notably transect." *The Great War and Modern Memory,* dedicated to Edward Hudson, received the National Book Award, as well as the Ralph Waldo Emerson Award of Phi Beta Kappa.

In the 1980s, Fussell continued to write regularly for a general audience, publishing a study of travel, *Abroad: British Literary Traveling between the Wars* (1980); two collections of essays, *The Boy Scout Handbook and Other Observations* (1982) and *Thank God for the Atom Bomb and Other Essays* (1988); and a much-misunderstood satire, *Class: A Guide through the American Status System* (1983).

By the late 1970s, Fussell had separated from his wife. In 1983, he left Rutgers for the University of Pennsylvania, then divorced in 1987 so that he could marry Harriette Behringer. After he published *Wartime: Understanding and Behavior in the Second World War* (1989), he edited two war anthologies, explaining in his 1996 memoir that he cannot put the war away. Indeed, the final paragraphs of *Doing Battle* contain, in addition to accounts of his "army dreams," lists and citations of the wartime triggers—the songs, the poems, and the letters—that still made him cry, fifty years later.

A sophisticated stylist and a stinging satirist, Paul Fussell writes frank, unapologetic, powerful works about literature and war and a few of the things in between. Gaining his appreciation of satire from the eighteenth century, Fussell wields his wit even in *Poetic Meter and Poetic Form*, republished in 1979. Dryly ridiculing free verse poetry with aspirations of radicalism, he writes: "Most of it hopes to recommend itself by deploying vaguely surrealistic images . . . to urge acceptable opinions: that sex is a fine thing, that accurate perception is better than dull, that youth is probably a nicer condition than age . . . as well as that Lyndon Johnson and Richard Nixon were war criminals."

Fussell's fondness for challenging the pretension, hypocrisy, and ignorance of liberal intellectuals fuels his books on war as well as his essays and formal satires. Disgusted with the opinions of those who did not fight with the infantry, Fussell styles himself the bitter skeptic, the streetwise intellectual, the one who has been there, the one who knows. Even his satire on class is informed by his war experiences, which made class differences seem petty and ludicrous, given the democratizing power of mass death. Self-righteously arrogant at its worst, brilliantly moving at its best, but mostly funny, brutal, erudite, and painfully honest, Paul Fussell's voice is one of the distinctive voices of the latter twentieth century.

THE REAL WAR 1939–1945 *(1989)*

WHAT WAS IT about the second world War that moved the troops to constant verbal subversion and contempt? What was it that made the Americans, especially, so fertile with insult and cynicism, calling women Marines BAMS (broad-assed Marines) and devising SNAFU, with its offspring TARFU ("Things are really fucked up"), FUBAR ("Fucked up beyond all recognition"), and the perhaps less satisfying FUBB ("Fucked up beyond belief")? It was not just the danger and fear, the boredom and uncertainty and loneliness and deprivation. It was the conviction that optimistic publicity and euphemism had rendered their experience so falsely that it would never be readily communicable. They knew that in its representation to the laity, what was happening to them was systematically sanitized and Norman Rockwellized, not to mention Disneyfied. They knew that despite the advertising and publicity, where it counted their arms and equipment were worse than the Germans'. They knew that their automatic rifles (First World War vintage) were slower and clumsier, and they knew that the Germans had a much better light machine gun. They knew, despite official assertions to the contrary, that the Germans had real smokeless powder for their small arms and that they did not. They knew that their own tanks, both American and British, were ridiculously underarmed and underarmored, so that they would inevitably be destroyed in an open encounter with an equal number of German panzers. They knew that the anti-tank mines supplied to them became unstable in subfreezing weather, and that truckloads of them blew up in the winter of 1944–1945. And they knew that the single greatest weapon of the war, the atomic bomb excepted, was the German 88-mm flat-trajectory gun, which brought down thousands of bombers and tens of thousands of soldiers. The Allies had nothing as good, despite the fact that one of them had designated itself the world's greatest industrial power. The troops' disillusion and their ironic response, in song and satire and sullen contempt, came from knowing that the home front then could (and very likely historiography later would) be aware of none of these things.

The Great War brought forth the stark, depressing *Journey's End;*[1] the Second, as John Ellis notes in *The Sharp End,* the tuneful *South Pacific.*[2] The real war was tragic and ironic beyond the power of any literary or philosophical analysis to suggest, but in unbombed America especially, the meaning of the war seemed inaccessible. Thus, as experience, the suffering was wasted. The same tricks of publicity and advertising might have succeeded in sweetening the actualities of Vietnam if television and a vigorous, uncensored, moral journalism hadn't been brought to bear. Because the Second World War was fought against palpable evil, and thus was a sort of moral triumph, we have been reluctant to probe very deeply into its murderous requirements. America has not yet understood what the war was like and thus has been unable to use such understanding to reinterpret and redefine the national reality and to arrive at something like public maturity.

"MEMBERS MISSING"

In the popular and genteel iconography of war during the bourgeois age, all the way from eighteenth- and nineteenth-century history paintings to twentieth-century photographs, the bodies of the dead are intact, if inert—sometimes bloody and sprawled in awkward positions, but, except for the absence of life, plausible and acceptable simulacra of the people they once were. But there is a contrary and much more "realistic" convention represented in, say, the Bayeaux tapestry, whose ornamental border displays numerous severed heads and limbs. That convention is honored likewise in the Renaissance awareness of what happens to the body in battle. In Shakespeare's *Henry V* the soldier Michael Williams assumes the traditional understanding when he observes,

> But if the cause be not good, the King himself hath a heavy reckoning to make, when all those legs and arms and heads chopped off in a battle shall join together at the latter day, and cry all, 'We died at such a place'—some swearing, some crying for a surgeon, some upon their wives left poor behind them, some upon the debts they owe, some upon their children rawly left.

And *Goya's*[3] eighty etchings known as *The Disasters of War,* depicting events during the *Peninsular War,*[4] feature plentiful dismembered and beheaded cadavers. One of the best-known of Goya's images is that of a naked body, its right arm severed, impaled on a tree.

But these examples date from well before the modern age of publicity and euphemism. The peruser (*reader* would be the wrong word) of the picture collection *Life Goes to War*

---

[1]*Journey's End* a bleak 1929 play by Robert C. Sherriff set in the trenches of the Western Front during World War I.

[2]*South Pacific* a Broadway musical produced in 1949 by Richard Rodgers and Oscar Hammerstein.

[3]*Goya* Francisco José de Goya y Lucientes (1746–1828) a Spanish artist who became famous for his frescoes and portraits and who later became court painter to Charles IV.

[4]*Peninsular War* part of the Napoleonic Wars fought in the Iberian Peninsula from 1807 to 1814 by Britain, Portugal, and Spanish guerrillas against France.

(1977), a volume so popular and widely distributed as to constitute virtually a definitive and official anthology of Second World War photographs, will find even in its starkest images no depiction of bodies dismembered. There are three separated heads shown, but all, significantly, are Asian—one the head of a Chinese soldier hacked off by the Japanese at Nanking; one a Japanese soldier's badly burnt head (complete with helmet), mounted as a trophy on an American tank at Guadalcanal; and one a former Japanese head, now a skull sent home as a souvenir to a girlfriend by her navy beau in the Pacific. No American dismemberings were registered, even in the photographs of Tarawa and Iwo Jima. American bodies (decently clothed) are occasionally in evidence, but they are notably intact. The same is true in other popular collections of photographs, like *Collier's Photographic History of World War II*, Ronald Heiferman's *World War II*, A. J. P. Taylor's *History of World War II*, and Charles Herridge's *Pictorial History of World War II*. In these, no matter how severely wounded, Allied soldiers are never shown suffering what in the Vietnam War was termed traumatic amputation: everyone has all his limbs, his hands and feet and digits, not to mention an expression of courage and cheer. And recalling Shakespeare and Goya, it would be a mistake to assume that dismembering was more common when warfare was largely a matter of cutting weapons, like swords and sabers. Their results are nothing compared with the work of bombs, machine guns, pieces of shell, and high explosives in general. The difference between the two traditions of representation is not a difference in military technique. It is a difference in sensibility, especially in the ability of a pap-fed public to face unpleasant facts, like the actualities apparent at the site of a major airplane accident.

What annoyed the troops and augmented their sardonic, contemptuous attitude toward those who viewed them from afar was in large part this public innocence about the bizarre damage suffered by the human body in modern war. The troops could not contemplate without anger the lack of public knowledge of the Graves Registration form used by the U.S. Army Quartermaster Corps, with its space for indicating "Members Missing." You would expect frontline soldiers to be struck and hurt by bullets and shell fragments, but such is the popular insulation from the facts that you would not expect them to be hurt, sometimes killed, by being struck by parts of their friends' bodies violently detached. If you asked a wounded soldier or Marine what hit him, you'd hardly be ready for the answer "My buddy's head," or his sergeant's heel or his hand, or a Japanese leg, complete with shoe and puttees, or the West Point ring on his captain's severed hand. What drove the troops to fury was the complacent, unimaginative innocence of their home fronts and rear echelons about such an experience as the following, repeated in essence tens of thousands of times. Captain Peter Royle, a British artillery forward observer, was moving up a hill in a night attack in North Africa. "I was following about twenty paces behind," he wrote in a memoir,

> when there was a blinding flash a few yards in front of me. I had no idea what it was and fell flat on my face. I found out soon enough: a number of the infantry were carrying mines strapped to the small of their backs, and either a rifle or machine gun bullet had struck one, which had exploded, blowing the man into three pieces—two legs and head and chest. His inside was strewn on the hillside and I crawled into it in the darkness.

In war, as in air accidents, insides are much more visible than it is normally well to imagine. And there's an indication of what can be found on the ground after an air crash in one soldier's memories of the morning after an artillery exchange in North Africa. Neil

McCallum and his friend "S." came upon the body of a man who had been lying on his back when a shell, landing at his feet, had eviscerated him:

> "Good God," said S., shocked, "here's one of his fingers." S. stubbed with his toe at the ground some feet from the corpse. There is more horror in a severed digit than in a man dying: it savors of mutilation. "Christ," went on S. in a very low voice, "look, it's not his *finger.*"

In the face of such horror, the distinction between friend and enemy vanishes, and the violent dismemberment of any human being becomes traumatic. After the disastrous Canadian raid at Dieppe, German soldiers observed: "The dead on the beach—I've never seen such obscenities before." "There were pieces of human beings littering the beach. There were headless bodies, there were legs, there were arms." There were even shoes "with feet in them." The soldiers on one side know what the soldiers on the other side understand about dismemberment and evisceration, even if that knowledge is hardly shared by the civilians behind them. Hence the practice among German U-boats of carrying plenty of animal intestines to shoot to the surface to deceive those imagining that their depth charges have done the job. Some U-boats, it was said, carried (in cold storage) severed legs and arms to add verisimilitude. But among the thousands of published photographs of sailors and submariners being rescued after torpedoings and sinkings, there was no evidence of severed limbs, intestines, or floating parts.

If American stay-at-homes could be almost entirely protected from an awareness of the looks and smells of the real war, the British, at least those living in bombed areas, could not. But even then, as one Briton noted in 1941, "we shall never know half of the history . . . of these times." What prompted that observation was this incident: "The other night not half a mile from me a middle-aged woman [in the civilian defense] went out with an ambulance. In a smashed house she saw something she thought was a mop. It was no mop but a man's head." So unwilling is the imagination to dwell on genuine— as opposed to fictional or theatrical—horrors that, indeed, "we shall never know half of the history . . . of these times." At home under the bombs in April, 1941, Frances Faviell was suddenly aware that the whole house was coming down on top of her, and she worried about "Anne," who was in bed on the top floor.

> With great difficulty I raised my head and shook it free of heavy, choking, dusty stuff. An arm had fallen round my neck—a warm, living arm, and for one moment I thought that Richard had entered in the darkness and was holding me, but when very cautiously I raised my hand to it, I found that it was a woman's bare arm with two rings on the third finger and it stopped short in a sticky mess.

You can't take much of that sort of thing without going mad, as General Sir John Hackett understood when he saw that the wild destruction of enemy human beings had in it less of satisfaction than of distress. Injured and on the German side of the line at Arnhem, he was being taken to the German medical installation. Along the road he saw "half a body, just naked buttocks and the legs joined on and no more of it than that." For those who might have canted that the only good German is a dead German, Hackett has a message: "There was no comfort here. It was like being in a strange and terrible nightmare from which you longed to wake and could not."

THE DEMOCRACY OF FEAR

In the great war Wilfred Owen[5] was driven very near to madness by having to remain for some time next to the scattered body pieces of one of his friends. He had numerous counterparts in the Second World War. At the botched assault on Tarawa Atoll, one coxswain at the helm of a landing vessel went quite mad, perhaps at the shock of steering through all the severed heads and limbs near the shore. One Marine battalion commander, badly wounded, climbed above the rising tide onto a pile of American bodies. Next afternoon he was found there, mad. But madness did not require the spectacle of bodies just like yours messily torn apart. Fear continued over long periods would do the job, as on the merchant and Royal Navy vessels on the Murmansk run, where "grown men went steadily and fixedly insane before each other's eyes," as Tristan Jones testified in *Heart of Oak.* Madness was likewise familiar in submarines, especially during depth-bomb attacks. One U.S. sub-mariner reported that during the first months of the Pacific war such an attack sent three men "stark raving mad": they had to be handcuffed and tied to their bunks. Starvation and thirst among prisoners of the Japanese, and also among downed fliers adrift on rafts, drove many insane, and in addition to drinking their urine they tried to relieve their thirst by biting their comrades' jugular veins and sucking the blood. In one sense, of course, the whole war was mad, and every participant insane from the start, but in a strictly literal sense the result of the years of the bombing of Berlin and its final destruction by the Russian army was, for much of the population, actual madness. Just after the surrender, according to Douglas Botting, in *From the Ruins of the Reich,* some 50,000 orphans could be found living in holes like animals, "some of them one-eyed or one-legged veterans of seven or so, many so deranged by the bombing and the Russian attack that they screamed at the sight of any uniform, even a Salvation Army one."

Although in the Great War madness among the troops was commonly imputed to the effects of concussion ("shell shock"), in the Second it was more frankly attributed to fear, and in contrast to the expectations of heroic behavior which set the tone of the earlier war, the fact of fear was now squarely to be faced. The result was a whole new literature of fear, implying that terror openly confessed argues no moral disgrace, although failure to control visible symptoms is reprehensible. The official wartime attitude toward the subject was often expressed by quoting Marshal Ney: "The one who says he never knew fear is a compound liar." As the 1943 U.S. *Officer's Guide* goes on to instruct its anxious tyros,

> Physical courage is little more than the ability to control the physical fear which all normal men have, and cowardice does not consist in being afraid but in giving away to fear. What, then, keeps the soldier from giving away to fear? The answer is simply—his desire to retain the good opinion of his friends and associates . . . his pride smothers his fear.

The whole trick for the officer is to seem what you would be, and the formula for dealing with fear is ultimately rhetorical and theatrical: regardless of your actual feelings, you must simulate a carriage that will affect your audience as fearless, in the hope that you

[5]*Wilfred Owen* (1893–1918) an English World War I soldier who wrote haunting poems about the cruelty and horror of war; Owen died on the Western Front a week before the Armistice.

will be imitated, or at least not be the agent of spreading panic. Advice proffered to enlisted men admitted as frankly that fear was a normal "problem" and suggested ways of controlling it. Some of these are indicated in a wartime publication of the U.S. National Research Council, *Psychology for the Fighting Man.* Even if it is undeniable that in combat everyone will be "scared—terrified," there are some antidotes: keeping extra busy with tasks involving details, and engaging in roll calls and countings-off, to emphasize the proximity of buddies, both as support and as audience. And there is a "command" solution to the fear problem which has been popular among military theorists at least since the Civil War: when under shelling and mortar fire and scared stiff, the infantry should alleviate the problem by moving—never back but forward. This will enable trained personnel to take care of the wounded and will bring troops close enough to the enemy to make him stop the shelling. That it will also bring them close enough to put them within range of rifles and machine guns and hand grenades is what the theorists know but don't mention. The troops know it, which is why they like to move *back.* This upper- or remote-echelon hope that fear can be turned, by argument and reasoning, into something with the appearance of courage illustrates the overlap between the implausible persuasions of advertising and those of modern military motivators.

There was a lot of language devoted to such rationalizing of the irrational. A little booklet issued to infantry replacements joining the Fifth Army in Italy contained tips to ease the entry of innocents into combat: Don't believe all the horror stories circulating in the outfit you're joining. Don't carry too much stuff. Don't excrete in your foxhole—if you can't get out, put some dirt on a shovel, go on that, and throw the load out. Keep your rifle clean and ready. Don't tape down the handles of your grenades for fear of their flying off accidentally—it takes too long to get the tape off. Learn to dig in fast when shelling starts. Watch the ground for evidence of mines and booby traps. On the move, keep contact but don't bunch up. And use common sense in your fight against fear:

> Don't be too scared. Everybody is afraid, but you can learn to control your fear. And, as non-coms point out, "you have a good chance of getting through if you don't lose your head. Being too scared is harmful to you." Remember that a lot of noise you hear is ours, and not dangerous. It may surprise you that on the whole, many more are pulled out for sickness or accident than become battle casualties.

(After that bit of persuasion, the presence of first-aid sections on "If You Get Hit" and "If a Buddy Gets Hit" seems a bit awkward.)

This open, practical confrontation of a subject usually unmentioned has its counterpart in the higher reaches of the wartime literature of fear. The theme of Alan Rook's poem "Dunkirk Pier," enunciated in the opening stanza, is one hardly utterable during earlier wars:

> Deeply across the waves of our darkness fear
> like the silent octopus feeling, groping, clear
> as a star's reflection, nervous and cold as a bird,
> tells us that pain, tells us that death is near.

William Collins's "Ode to Fear," published in 1746, when the average citizen had his wars fought by others whom he never met, is a remote allegorical and allusive performance lamenting the want of powerful emotion in contemporary poetry. C. Day Lewis's "Ode to Fear" of 1943 is not literary but literal, frank, down-to-earth, appropriately disgusting.

> Now fear has come again
> To live with us
> In poisoned intimacy like pus. . . .

And fear is exhibited very accurately in its physical and psychological symptoms:

> The bones, the stalwart spine,
> The legs like bastions,
> The nerves, the heart's natural combustions,
> The head that hives our active thoughts—all pine,
> Are quenched or paralyzed
> When Fear puts unexpected questions
> And makes the heroic body freeze like a beast surprised.

The new frankness with which fear would be acknowledged in this modernist, secular, psychologically self-conscious wartime was registered in W. H. Auden's "September 1, 1939," in which the speaker, "uncertain and afraid," observes the "waves of anger and fear" washing over the face of the earth. And the new frankness became the virtual subject and center of *The Age of Anxiety,* which Auden wrote from 1944 to 1946.

Civilian bombing enjoined a new frankness on many Britons. "Perfect fear casteth out love" was Cyril Connolly's travesty of I John 4:18, as if he were thoroughly acquainted with the experience of elbowing his dearest aside at the shelter entrance.

If the anonymous questionnaire, that indispensable mechanism of the social sciences, had been widely used during the Great War, more perhaps could be known or safely conjectured about the actualities of terror on the Western Front. Questionnaires were employed during the Second World War, and American soldiers were asked about the precise physical signs of their fear. The soldiers testified that they were well acquainted with such impediments to stability as (in order of frequency) "Violent pounding of the heart, sinking feeling in the stomach, shaking or trembling all over, feeling sick at the stomach, cold sweat, feeling weak or faint."

More than a quarter of the soldiers in one division admitted that they'd been so scared they'd vomited, and almost a quarter said that at terrifying moments they'd lost control of their bowels. Ten percent had urinated in their pants. As John Ellis observes of these data,

> Stereotypes of "manliness" and "guts" can readily accommodate the fact that a man's stomach or heart might betray his nervousness but they make less allowance for his shitting his pants or wetting himself.

And furthermore, "If over one-fifth of the men in one division actually admitted that they had fouled themselves, it is a fair assumption that many more actually did so." One of the commonest fears, indeed, is that of wetting oneself and betraying one's fear for all to see by the most childish symptom. The fear of this fear augments as the rank rises: for a colonel to wet his pants under shellfire is much worse than for a PFC. The U.S. Marine

Eugene B. Sledge confessed that just before he landed at Peleliu, "I felt nauseated and feared that my bladder would surely empty itself and reveal me to be the coward I was."

If perfect fear casteth out love, perfect shame can cast out even agony. During the Normandy invasion a group of American soldiers came upon a paratroop sergeant caught by his chute in a tree. He had broken his leg, and fouled himself as well. He was so ashamed that he begged the soldiers not to come near him, despite his need to be cut down and taken care of. "We just cut off his pants," reported one of the soldiers who found him, "and gently washed him all over, so he wouldn't be humiliated at his next stop."

Men more experienced than that paratrooper had learned to be comfortable with the new frankness. A soldier unused to combat heard his sergeant utter an obscenity when their unit was hit by German 88 fire:

> I asked him if he was hit and he sort of smiled and said no, he had just pissed his pants. He always pissed them, he said, just when things started and then he was okay. He wasn't making any apologies either, and then I realized something wasn't quite right with me either. There was something warm down there and it seemed to be running down my leg. . . .
>
> I told the sarge, I said, "Sarge, I've pissed too," or something like that, and he grinned and said, "Welcome to the war."

Other public signs of fear are almost equally common, if even more "comic." One's mouth grows dry and black, and a strange squeaking or quacking comes out, joined sometimes with a stammer. It is very hard for a fieldgrade officer to keep his dignity when that happens.

For the ground troops, artillery and mortar fire were the most terrifying, partly because their noise was so deafening and unignorable, and partly because the damage they caused the body—sometimes total disappearance or atomization into tiny red bits—was worse than most damage by bullets. To be killed by bullets seemed "so clean and surgical" to Sledge. "But shells would not only tear and rip the body, they tortured one's mind almost beyond the brink of sanity." An occasional reaction to the terror of shelling was audible "confession." One American infantryman cringing under artillery fire in the Ardennes suddenly blurted out to his buddies, "In London I fucked prostitutes and then robbed them of their money." The shelling over, the soldier never mentioned this utterance again, nor did his friends, everyone understanding its stimulus and its meaning.

But for the infantry there was something to be feared almost as much as shelling: the German *Schü* mine, scattered freely just under the surface of the ground, which blew your foot entirely off if you stepped on it. For years after the war ex-soldiers seized up when confronted by patches of grass and felt safe only when walking on asphalt or concrete. Fear among the troops was probably greatest in the staging areas just before D-Day: that was the largest assembly of Allied troops yet unblooded and combat-virgin. "Don't think they weren't afraid," one American woman who worked with the Red Cross says in Studs Terkel's "*The Good War.*" "Just before they went across to France, belts and ties were removed from some of these young men. They were very, very young."

WHAT UNCONDITIONAL SURRENDER MEANT

For those who fought, the war had other features unknown to those who looked on or got the war mediated through journalism. One such feature was the rate at which it destroyed human beings—friendly as well as enemy. Training for infantry fighting, few American soldiers were tough-minded enough to accept the full, awful implications of the term "replacement" in the designation of their Replacement Training Centers. (The proposed euphemism "reinforcement" never caught on.) What was going to happen to the soldiers they were being trained to replace? Why should so many "replacements"— hundreds of thousands of them, actually—be required? The answers came soon enough in the European theater, in Italy, France, and finally Germany. In six weeks of fighting in Normandy, the 90th Infantry Division had to replace 150 percent of its officers and more than 100 percent of its men. If a division was engaged for more than three months, the probability was that every one of its second lieutenants, all 132 of them, would be killed or wounded. For those being prepared as replacements at officer candidate schools, it was not mentally healthy to dwell on the oddity of the schools' turning out hundreds of new junior officers weekly after the army had reached its full wartime strength. Only experience would make the need clear. The commanding officer of the 6th King's Own Scottish Borderers, which finally arrived in Hamburg in 1945 after fighting all the way from Normandy, found an average of five original men remaining (out of around 200) in each rifle company. "I was appalled," he said. "I had no idea it was going to be like that."

And it was not just wounds and death that depopulated the rifle companies. In the South Pacific it was malaria, dengue, blackwater fever, and dysentery; in Europe, dysentery, pneumonia, and trench foot. What disease did to the troops in the Pacific has never been widely known. The ingestion of Atabrine, the wartime substitute for quinine as a malaria preventive, has caused ears to ring for a lifetime, and decades afterward thousands still undergo their regular malaria attacks, freezing and burning and shaking all over. In Burma, British and American troops suffered so regularly from dysentery that they cut large holes in the seats of their trousers to simplify things. But worse was the mental attrition suffered by combat troops, who learned from experience the inevitability of their ultimate mental breakdown, ranging from the milder forms of treatable psychoneurosis to outright violent insanity.

In war it is not just the weak soldiers, or the sensitive ones, or the highly imaginative or cowardly ones, who will break down. All will break down if in combat long enough. "Long enough" is now defined by physicians and psychiatrists as between 200 and 240 days. For every frontline soldier in the Second World War, according to John Ellis, there was the "slowly dawning and dreadful realisation that there was no way out, that . . . it was only a matter of time before they got killed or maimed or broke down completely." As one British officer put it, "You go in, you come out, you go in again and you keep doing it until they break you or you are dead." This "slowly dawning and dreadful realisation" usually occurs as a result of two stages of rationalization and one of accurate perception:

1. It *can't* happen to me. I am too clever / agile / well-trained / good-looking / beloved / tightly laced / etc. This persuasion gradually erodes into

2. It *can* happen to me, and I'd better be more careful. I can avoid the danger by keeping extra alert at all times / watching more prudently the way I take cover or dig in or expose my position by firing my weapon / etc. This conviction attenuates in turn to the perception that death and injury are matters more of bad luck than lack of skill, making inevitable the third stage of awareness:

3. It is *going to* happen to me, and only my not being there is going to prevent it.

Because of the words *unconditional surrender,* it became clear in this war that no sort of lucky armistice or surprise political negotiation was going to give the long-term front-line man his pardon. "It soon became apparent," John Ellis writes, "that every yard of ground would have to be torn from the enemy and only killing as many men as possible would enable one to do this. Combat was reduced to its absolute essentials, kill or be killed." It was this that made this second Western Front war unique: it could end only when the line (or the Soviet line) arrived in Berlin. In the Second World War the American military learned something very "modern"—modern because dramatically "psychological," utilitarian, unchivalric, and unheroic: it learned that men will inevitably go mad in battle and that no appeal to patriotism, manliness, or loyalty to the group will ultimately matter. Thus in later wars things were arranged differently. In Korea and Vietnam it was understood that a man fulfilled his combat obligation and bought his reprieve if he served a fixed term, 365 days—and not days in combat but days in the theater of war. The infantry was now treated somewhat like the air corps had been in the Second War: performance of a stated number of missions guaranteed escape.

"DISORGANIZED INSANITY"

If most civilians didn't know about these things, most soldiers didn't know about them either, because only a relatively small number did any fighting that brought them into mortal contact with the enemy. For the rest, engaged in supply, transportation, and administrative functions, the war constituted a period of undesired and uncomfortable foreign travel under unaccustomed physical and social conditions, like enforced obedience, bad food, and an absence of baths. In 1943 the United States Army grew by 2 million men, but only about 365,000 of those went to combat units, and an even smaller number ended up in the rifle companies. The bizarre size and weight of the administrative tail dragged across Europe by the American forces is implied by statistics: from 1941 to 1945 the number of men whose job was fighting increased by only 100,000. If by the end there were 11 million men in the American army, only 2 million were in the ninety combat divisions, and of those, fewer than 700,000 were in the infantry. Regardless of the persisting fiction, those men know by experience the truth enunciated by John Ellis that

> World War II was not a war of movement, except on the rare occasions when the enemy was in retreat; it was a bloody slogging match in which mobility was only occasionally of real significance. Indeed, . . . the internal combustion engine was not a major consideration in the ground war.

The relative few who actually fought know that the war was not a matter of rational calculation. They know madness when they see it. They can draw the right conclusions from the fact that in order to invade the Continent the Allies killed 12,000 innocent French and Belgian civilians who happened to live in the wrong part of town—that is, too near the railway tracks, the bombers' target. The few who fought are able to respond appropriately—without surprise—to such a fact as this: in the Netherlands alone, more than 7,000 planes tore into the ground or the water, afflicted by bullets, flak, exhaustion of fuel or crew, "pilot error," discouragement, or suicidal intent. In a 1986 article in *Smithsonian* magazine about archaeological excavation in Dutch fields and drained marshes,

Les Daly emphasized the multitudinousness, the mad repetitiveness of these 7,000 crashes, reminding readers that "the total fighter and bomber combat force of the U.S. Air Force today amounts to about 3,400 airplanes. To put it another way, the crash of 7,000 aircraft would mean that every square mile of the entire state of New Jersey would have shaken to the impact of a downed plane."

In the same way, the few who fought have little trouble understanding other outcroppings of the irrational element, in events like Hiroshima and Nagasaki, or for that matter the bombing of Hamburg or Darmstadt or Tokyo or Dresden. The destruction of Dresden *et al.* was about as rational as the German shooting of hostages to "punish" an area, or the American belief that an effective way into Germany was to plunge through the Hürtgen Forest, or the British and Canadian belief, two years earlier, that a great raid on Dieppe would be worthwhile. Revenge is not a rational motive, but it was the main motive in the American destruction of the Japanese empire.

Those who fought know this, just as they know that it is as likely for the man next to you to be shot through the eye, ear, testicles, or brain as through the shoulder (the way the cinema does it). A shell is as likely to blow his whole face off as to lodge a fragment in some mentionable and unvital tissue. Those who fought saw the bodies of thousands of self-destroyed Japanese men, women, and infants drifting off Saipan—sheer madness, but not essentially different from what Eisenhower described in *Crusade in Europe,* where, though not intending to make our flesh creep or to descend to nasty details, he couldn't help reporting honestly on the carnage in the Falaise Pocket. He wrote, "It was literally possible to walk for hundreds of yards at a time, stepping on nothing but dead and decaying flesh"—formerly German soldiers, who could have lived by surrendering but who chose, madly, not to.

How is it that these data are commonplaces only to the small number who had some direct experience of them? One reason is the normal human talent for looking on the bright side, for not receiving information likely to cause distress or to occasion a major overhaul of normal ethical, political, or psychological assumptions. But the more important reason is that the news correspondents, radio broadcasters, and film people who perceived these horrors kept quiet about them on behalf of the war effort, and so the large wartime audience never knew these things. As John Steinbeck finally confessed in 1958, "We were all part of the War Effort. We went along with it, and not only that, we abetted it. . . . I don't mean that the correspondents were liars. . . . It is in the things not mentioned that the untruth lies." By not mentioning a lot of things, a correspondent could give the audience at home the impression that there were no cowards in the service, no thieves or rapists or looters, no cruel or stupid commanders. It is true, Steinbeck was aware, that most military operations are examples of "disorganized insanity," but the morale of the home front could not be jeopardized by an eyewitness's saying so. And even if a correspondent wanted to deliver the noisome truth, patriotism would join censorship in stopping his mouth. As Steinbeck noted in *Once There Was a War,* "The foolish reporter who broke the rules would not be printed at home and in addition would be put out of the theater by the command."

Understanding and Analysis

1. What is the answer to the question posed in the first sentence?
2. What is the thesis that Fussell sets out to prove?

3. In the third paragraph, what does Fussell claim is different in the depictions of war during the Renaissance as compared to the period between the eighteenth century and the present?

4. What kinds of evidence does Fussell offer to show that the American public in World War II had no knowledge of the effects of real war? What are Fussell's sources?

5. How did the government's understanding of and attitude toward fear differ between World War I and World War II?

6. What are the stages a soldier went through on the battlefield? What changes have been made since World War II to help soldiers carry on?

7. What is the point of the section titled "Disorganized Insanity"?

8. What is it that only those in combat truly understand? Why?

9. Do you think it is appropriate that only those in combat know these things? Why did journalists collude with the government in maintaining silence?

10. What did British civilians know about the war that American civilians did not, according to Fussell?

11. What elements of the war does Fussell leave out? Why do you think he does?

Comparison

1. Read the essay by Ernie Pyle. Is his essay less "real" a depiction of World War II than Fussell's? Why or why not?

2. Read the two essays by Panter-Downes. How would Fussell characterize these essays?

3. Compare Graves's description of his experiences in World War I with Fussell's description of World War II. Which man offers more graphic detail? How different are the experiences presented? What methods does each man use? Is one more convincing than the other? Why or why not?

4. Read the essay by Gellhorn. Does she capture the reality of war as Fussell sees it?

5. Read the essays on history by Carr or FitzGerald. Then read the essays by Pyle and Lewisohn. Does Fussell interpret the recent past in terms of the present? Is his view merely one version of the war or, in fact, a more accurate version than any of the others? Can those not in direct combat know as much as those in combat? Can any one group understand more than any other about this war or any historical event? Explain your opinions.

Susan Sontag
(1933–)

Born January 16, 1933, in New York, Susan Sontag spent the first years of her life with various grandparents and aunts while her parents worked in China. In 1938, two years after the birth of her sister, Judith, her father died of tuberculosis. Returning to the United States, her mother moved the girls to Tucson, Arizona, and Sontag flourished in her new home. Already an enthusiastic reader by the time she entered school, she sailed not only through her classes, but also through entire grades: "I was put in 1A on Monday when I was 6 years old. Then 1B on Tuesday, 2A on Wednesday, 2B on Thursday, and by the end of the week they had skipped me to third grade because I could do the work." At the age of "about seven," Sontag told Molly McQuade in 1993, she started writing "stories, poems, [and] plays." Her mother remarried when she was about 12, and after the family moved to California, Sontag wrote stories and read advanced literary criticism while still in high school. Graduating in 1948, at the age of 15, she spent one year at the University of California at Berkeley before transferring to the University of Chicago. There, she met her future husband, a lecturer named Philip Rieff, whom she married in 1950. She earned her bachelor's degree the following year, and in 1952, she gave birth to the couple's only child, David.

A wife and mother before the age of 20, Sontag had earned two master's degrees from Harvard by the age of 22, one in English and the other in philosophy. While her husband taught at Brandeis, she began working on a Ph.D. in 1955. "In 1957," according to Sontag scholar Sohnya Sayres, "both Sontag and her husband...won scholarships to study abroad. 'At the last minute,' [Sontag] has explained, 'he decided that he didn't want to do it. So I went anyway.'" After studying first at Oxford University and then at the University of Paris, she returned in 1958, divorced her husband, and took her son to New York, hoping to write professionally. In 1959, she edited *Commentary* and lectured in philosophy at City College, and in 1960, she started teaching religion at Columbia. From 1962 1965, Sontag wrote and published 26 essays, including her famous "Notes on 'Camp.'" She also wrote her first novel, *The Benefactor* (1963), which brought an invitation to serve as a writer-in-residence at Rutgers University in 1964.

After leaving Rutgers, Sontag published her first collection of essays, *Against Interpretation* (1966). In the title essay, she criticizes the search for a "meaning" or a "sub-text" in works of art, arguing that "the modern style of interpretation" is a hostile, destructive, and even "reactionary" effort to render art "manageable" and "comfortable." Nominated for a National Book Award, *Against Interpretation* generated controversy in literary and intellectual circles, earning reviews both positive and negative. Although she published another novel, *Death Kit*, in 1967, Sontag soon seemed ready to become a writer of non-fiction, and then of movie scripts, and then of nothing at all. In 1968, she told Charles Ruas in a later interview, she "went to Vietnam and the war made it very hard for me to write, as for a lot of people. I couldn't get it out of the forefront of my consciousness." She published *Trip to Hanoi* in 1969, as well as *Styles of Radical Will*, and then she started working abroad in Italy and Sweden: "I wasn't basically a writer in those years—I was a filmmaker and a political activist. In '72 came a great crisis. I thought: Where am I, what am I doing, what have I done? I seem to be an expatriate, but I didn't mean to become an expatriate. I don't seem to be a writer anymore, but I wanted most of all to be a writer." She returned to the literary scene with *On Photography* (1977), which she was finishing as she learned that she had breast cancer in 1975.

For six months after her diagnosis, Sayres writes, Sontag was too sedated to do any work. Once she finished *On Photography*, however, she wrote her way through her recovery, composing *Illness as Metaphor* (1978), a study of tuberculosis and cancer as metaphors for evils, in "a month and a half," and writing a collection of stories called *I, etcetera* (1978). By the time she published her next collection of essays, *Under the Sign of Saturn*, in 1980, she was in full remission.

Having written and directed *Duet for Cannibals* (1969) and *Brother Carl* (1971) for the screen, Sontag turned to the stage in the 1980s, directing works by Luigi Pirandello and Milan Kundera. Watching friends battle AIDS, she wrote a kind of sequel to *Illness as Metaphor* called *AIDS and Its Metaphors* (1989), which she characterizes as "a plea against hysteria." In 1992, after three years of labor, she published her first widely popular novel, her first in two decades, *The Volcano Lover* and, a year later, her first play, *Alice in Bed*.

An artist of tremendously diverse talents, Susan Sontag is also an intellectual preoccupied with a recurring set of issues: aesthetics, morality, and the relationships between the two. Often associated with modernism, Sontag writes largely for other intellectuals, although she has enjoyed widespread success with *Illness as Metaphor*, *On Photography*, and *The Volcano Lover*. According to Sohnya Sayres, American critics complain that Sontag "substitutes intellectualized concepts for dramatic sense" in both her films and her fiction; nevertheless, she is herself a kind of dramatic cultural force of the twentieth century.

AIDS and Its Metaphors (1989)

By metaphor I meant nothing more or less than the earliest and most succinct definition I know, which is Aristotle's, in his *Poetics* (1457b). "Metaphor," Aristotle wrote, "consists in giving the thing a name that belongs to something else." Saying a thing is or is like something-it-is-not is a mental operation as old as philosophy and poetry, and the spawning ground of most kinds of understanding, including scientific understanding, and expressiveness. (To acknowledge which I prefaced the polemic against metaphors of illness I wrote ten years ago with a brief, hectic flourish of metaphor, in mock exorcism of the seductiveness of metaphorical thinking.) Of course, one cannot think without metaphors. But that does not mean there aren't some metaphors we might well abstain from or try to retire. As, of course, all thinking is interpretation. But that does not mean it isn't sometimes correct to be "against" interpretation. . . .[1]

•

AIDS quickly became a global event—discussed not only in New York, Paris, Rio, Kinshasa but also in Helsinki, Buenos Aires, Beijing, and Singapore—when it was far from the leading cause of death in Africa, much less in the world. There are famous diseases, as there are famous countries, and these are not necessarily the ones with the biggest populations. AIDS did not become so famous just because it afflicts whites too, as some Africans bitterly assert. But it is certainly true that were AIDS only an African disease, however many millions were dying, few outside of Africa would be concerned with it. It would be one of those "natural" events, like famines, which periodically ravage poor, overpopulated countries and about which people in rich countries feel quite helpless. Because it is a world event—that is, because it affects the West—it is regarded as not just a natural disaster. It is filled with historical meaning. (Part of the self-definition of Europe and the neo-European countries is that it, the First World, is where major calamities are history-making, transformative, while in poor, African or Asian countries they are part of a cycle, and therefore something like an aspect of nature.) Nor has AIDS become so publicized because, as some have suggested, in rich countries the illness first afflicted a group of people who were all men, almost all white, many of them educated, articulate, and knowledgeable about how to lobby and organize for public attention and resources devoted to the disease. AIDS occupies such a large part in our awareness because of what it has been taken to represent. It seems the very model of all the catastrophes privileged populations feel await them.

What biologists and public health officials predict is something far worse than can be imagined or than society (and the economy) can tolerate. No responsible official holds out the slightest hope that the African economies and health services can cope with the spread of the disease predicted for the near future, while every day one can read the direst estimates of the cost of AIDS to the country that has reported the largest number of cases, the United States. Astonishingly large sums of money are cited as the cost of providing minimum care to people who will be ill in the next few years. (This is assuming that the reassurances to "the general population" are justified, an assumption much disputed within the

[1]Sontag's book-length essay has been abridged.

medical community.) Talk in the United States, and not only in the United States, is of a national emergency, "possibly our nation's survival." An editorialist at *The New York Times* intoned last year: "We all know the truth, every one of us. We live in a time of plague such as has never been visited on our nation. We can pretend it does not exist, or exists for those others, and carry on as if we do not know. . . ." And one French poster shows a giant UFO-like black mass hovering over and darkening with spidery rays most of the familiar hexagon shape of the country lying below. Above the image is written: "It depends on each of us to erase that shadow" (*Il depend de chacun de nous d'effacer cette ombre.*) And underneath: "France doesn't want to die of AIDS" (*La France ne veut pas mourir du sida*). Such token appeals for mass mobilization to confront an unprecedented menace appear, at frequent intervals, in every mass society. It is also typical of a modern society that the demand for mobilization be kept very general and the reality of the response fall well short of what seems to be demanded to meet the challenge of the nation-endangering menace. This sort of rhetoric has a life of its own: it serves some purpose if it simply keeps in circulation an ideal of unifying communal practice that is precisely contradicted by the pursuit of accumulation and isolating entertainments enjoined on the citizens of a modern mass society.

The survival of the nation, of civilized society, of the world itself is said to be at stake—claims that are a familiar part of building a case for repression. (An emergency requires "drastic measures," et cetera.) The end-of-the-world rhetoric that AIDS has evoked does inevitably build such a case. But it also does something else. It offers a stoic, finally numbing contemplation of catastrophe. The eminent Harvard historian of science Stephen Jay Gould has declared that the AIDS pandemic may rank with nuclear weaponry "as the greatest danger of our era." But even if it kills as much as a quarter of the human race—a prospect Gould considers possible—"there will still be plenty of us left and we can start again." Scornful of the jeremiads of the moralists, a rational and humane scientist proposes the minimum consolation: an apocalypse that doesn't have any meaning. AIDS is a "natural phenomenon," not an event "with a moral meaning," Gould points out; "there is no message in its spread." Of course, it is monstrous to attribute meaning, in the sense of moral judgment, to the spread of an infectious disease. But perhaps it is only a little less monstrous to be invited to contemplate death on this horrendous scale with equanimity.

Much of the well-intentioned public discourse in our time expresses a desire to be candid about one or another of the various dangers which might be leading to all-out catastrophe. And now there is one more. To the death of oceans and lakes and forests, the unchecked growth of populations in the poor parts of the world, nuclear accidents like Chernobyl, the puncturing and depletion of the ozone layer, the perennial threat of nuclear confrontation between the superpowers or nuclear attack by one of the rogue states not under superpower control—to all these, now add AIDS. In the countdown to a millennium, a rise in apocalyptic thinking may be inevitable. Still, the amplitude of the fantasies of doom that AIDS has inspired can't be explained by the calendar alone, or even by the very real danger the illness represents. There is also the need for an apocalyptic scenario that is specific to "Western" society, and perhaps even more so to the United States. (America, as someone has said, is a nation with the soul of a church—an evangelical church prone to announcing radical endings and brand-new beginnings.) The taste for worst-case scenarios reflects the need to master fear of what is felt to be uncontrollable. It also expresses an imaginative complicity with disaster. The sense of cultural distress or failure gives rise to the desire for a clean sweep, a tabula rasa. No one wants a plague, of course. But, yes, it would be a chance to begin again. And beginning again—that is very modern, very American, too.

AIDS may be extending the propensity for becoming inured to vistas of global annihilation which the stocking and brandishing of nuclear arms has already promoted. With
the inflation of apocalyptic rhetoric has come the increasing unreality of the apocalypse.
A permanent modern scenario: apocalypse looms . . . and it doesn't occur. And it still
looms. We seem to be in the throes of one of the modern kinds of apocalypse. There is
the one that's not happening, whose outcome remains in suspense: the missiles circling
the earth above our heads, with a nuclear payload that could destroy all life many times
over, that haven't (so far) gone off. And there are ones that are happening, and yet seem
not to have (so far) the most feared consequences—like the astronomical Third World
debt, like overpopulation, like ecological blight; or that happen and then (we are told)
didn't happen—like the October 1987 stock market collapse, which was a "crash," like
the one in October 1929, and was not. Apocalypse is now a long-running serial: not
"Apocalypse Now" but "Apocalypse From Now On." Apocalypse has become an event
that is happening and not happening. It may be that some of the most feared events, like
those involving the irreparable ruin of the environment, have already happened. But we
don't know it yet, because the standards have changed. Or because we do not have the
right indices for measuring the catastrophe. Or simply because this is a catastrophe in
slow motion. (Or *feels* as if it is in slow motion, because we know about it, can anticipate it; and now have to wait for it to happen, to catch up with what we think we know.)

Modern life accustoms us to live with the intermittent awareness of monstrous, unthinkable—but, we are told, quite probable—disasters. Every major event is haunted, and not
only by its representation as an image (an old doubling of reality now, which began in
1839, with the invention of the camera). Besides the photographic or electronic simulation of events, there is also the calculation of their eventual outcome. Reality has bifurcated, into the real thing and an alternative version of it, twice over. There is the event
and its image. And there is the event and its projection. But as real events often seem to
have no more reality for people than images, and to need the confirmation of their images,
so our reaction to events in the present seeks confirmation in a mental outline, with appropriate computations, of the event in its projected, ultimate form.

Future-mindedness is as much the distinctive mental habit, and intellectual corruption,
of this century as the history-mindedness that, as Nietzsche pointed out, transformed thinking in the nineteenth century. Being able to estimate how matters will evolve into the
future is an inevitable byproduct of a more sophisticated (quantifiable, testable) understanding of process, social as well as scientific. The ability to project events with some
accuracy into the future enlarged what power consisted of, because it was a vast new
source of instructions about how to deal with the present. But in fact the look into the
future, which was once tied to a vision of linear progress, has, with more knowledge at
our disposal than anyone could have dreamed, turned into a vision of disaster. Every
process is a prospect, and invites a prediction bolstered by statistics. Say: the number
now . . . in three years, in five years, in ten years; and, of course, at the end of the century. Anything in history or nature that can be described as changing steadily can be seen
as heading toward catastrophe. (Either the too little and becoming less: waning, decline,
entropy. Or the too much, ever more than we can handle or absorb: uncontrollable growth.)
Most of what experts pronounce about the future contributes to this new double sense of
reality—beyond the doubleness to which we are already accustomed by the comprehensive duplication of everything in images. There is what is happening now. And there is
what it portends: the imminent, but not yet actual, and not really graspable, disaster.

Two kinds of disaster, actually. And a gap between them, in which the imagination
flounders. The difference between the epidemic we have and the pandemic that we are

promised (by current statistical extrapolations) feels like the difference between the wars we have, so-called limited wars, and the unimaginably more terrible ones we could have, the latter (with all the appurtenances of science fiction) being the sort of activity people are addicted to staging for fun, as electronic games. For beyond the real epidemic with its inexorably mounting death toll (statistics are issued by national and international health organizations every week, every month) is a qualitatively different, much greater disaster which we think both will and will not take place. Nothing is changed when the most appalling estimates are revised downward, temporarily, which is an occasional feature of the display of speculative statistics disseminated by health bureaucrats and journalists. Like the demographic predictions, which are probably just as accurate, the big news is usually bad.

A proliferation of reports or projections of unreal (that is, ungraspable) doomsday eventualities tends to produce a variety of reality-denying responses. Thus, in most discussions of nuclear warfare, being rational (the self-description of experts) means not acknowledging the human reality, while taking in emotionally even a small part of what is at stake for human beings (the province of those who regard themselves as the menaced) means insisting on unrealistic demands for the rapid dismantling of the peril. This split of public attitude, into the inhuman and the all-too-human, is much less stark with AIDS. Experts denounce the stereotypes attached to people with AIDS and to the continent where it is presumed to have originated, emphasizing that the disease belongs to much wider populations than the groups initially at risk, and to the whole world, not just to Africa.* For while AIDS has turned out, not surprisingly, to be one of the most meaning-laden of diseases, along with leprosy and syphilis, clearly there are checks on the impulse to stigmatize people with the disease. The way in which the illness is such a perfect repository for people's most general fears about the future to some extent renders irrelevant the predictable efforts to pin the disease on a deviant group or a dark continent.

Like the effects of industrial pollution and the new system of global financial markets, the AIDS crisis is evidence of a world in which nothing important is regional, local, limited; in which everything that can circulate does, and every problem is, or is destined to become, worldwide. Goods circulate (including images and sounds and documents, which circulate fastest of all, electronically). Garbage circulates: the poisonous industrial wastes of St. Etienne, Hannover, Mestre, and Bristol are being dumped in the coastal towns of West Africa. People circulate, in greater numbers than ever. And diseases. From the untrammeled intercontinental air travel for pleasure and business of the privileged to the unprecedented migrations of the underprivileged from villages to cities and, legally and illegally, from country to country—all this physical mobility and interconnectedness (with its consequent dissolving of old taboos, social and sexual) is as vital to the maximum

---

*"AIDS cannot be stopped in any country unless it is stopped in all countries," declared the retiring head of the World Health Organization in Geneva, Dr. Halfdan Mahler, at the Fourth International Conference on AIDS (Stockholm, June 1988), where the global character of the AIDS crisis was a leading theme. "This epidemic is worldwide and is sparing no continent," said Dr. Willy Rozenbaum, a French AIDS specialist. "It cannot be mastered in the West unless it is overcome everywhere." In contrast to the rhetoric of global responsibility, a specialty of the international conferences, is the view, increasingly heard, in which AIDS is regarded as a kind of Darwinian test of a society's aptitude for survival, which may require writing off those countries that can't defend themselves. A German AIDS specialist, Dr. Eike Brigitte Helm, has declared that it "can already be seen that in a number of parts of the world AIDS will drastically change the population structure. Particularly in Africa and Latin America. A society that is not able, somehow or other, to prevent the spread of AIDS has very poor prospects for the future." [Sontag's note]

functioning of the advanced, or world, capitalist economy as is the easy transmissibility of goods and images and financial instruments. But now that heightened, modern interconnectedness in space, which is not only personal but social, structural, is the bearer of a health menace sometimes described as a threat to the species itself; and the fear of AIDS is of a piece with attention to other unfolding disasters that are the byproduct of advanced society, particularly those illustrating the degradation of the environment on a world scale. AIDS is one of the dystopian harbingers of the global village, that future which is already here and always before us, which no one knows how to refuse.

•

That even an apocalypse can be made to seem part of the ordinary horizon of expectation constitutes an unparalleled violence that is being done to our sense of reality, to our humanity. But it is highly desirable for a specific dreaded illness to come to seem ordinary. Even the disease most fraught with meaning can become just an illness. It has happened with leprosy, though some ten million people in the world, easy to ignore since almost all live in Africa and the Indian subcontinent, have what is now called, as part of its wholesome dedramatization, Hansen's disease (after the Norwegian physician who, over a century ago, discovered the bacillus). It is bound to happen with AIDS, when the illness is much better understood and, above all, treatable. For the time being, much in the way of individual experience and social policy depends on the struggle for rhetorical ownership of the illness: how it is possessed, assimilated in argument and in cliché. The age-old, seemingly inexorable process whereby diseases acquire meanings (by coming to stand for the deepest fears) and inflict stigma is always worth challenging, and it does seem to have more limited credibility in the modern world, among people willing to be modern—the process is under surveillance now. With this illness, one that elicits so much guilt and shame, the effort to detach it from these meanings, these metaphors, seems particularly liberating, even consoling. But the metaphors cannot be distanced just by abstaining from them. They have to be exposed, criticized, belabored, used up.

Not all metaphors applied to illnesses and their treatment are equally unsavory and distorting. The one I am most eager to see retired—more than ever since the emergence of AIDS—is the military metaphor. Its converse, the medical model of the public weal, is probably more dangerous and far-reaching in its consequences, since it not only provides a persuasive justification for authoritarian rule but implicitly suggests the necessity of state-sponsored repression and violence (the equivalent of surgical removal or chemical control of the offending or "unhealthy" parts of the body politic). But the effect of the military imagery on thinking about sickness and health is far from inconsequential. It overmobilizes, it overdescribes, and it powerfully contributes to the excommunicating and stigmatizing of the ill.

No, it is not desirable for medicine, any more than for war, to be "total." Neither is the crisis created by AIDS a "total" anything. We are not being invaded. The body is not a battlefield. The ill are neither unavoidable casualties nor the enemy. We—medicine, society— are not authorized to fight back by any means whatever. . . . About that metaphor, the military one, I would say, if I may paraphrase Lucretius:[2] Give it back to the war-makers.

[2]*Lucretius:* Titus Lucretius Carus (c. 50 B.C. [exact birth and death unknown]); a Roman poet and philosopher best known for a six-volume hexameter poem, *De rerum natura* (On the Nature of Things), in which he denounces religious belief as the source of human wickedness and misery.

Understanding and Analysis

1. Based on her opening paragraph, what do you think Sontag means by being "against interpretation"?

2. Why, according to Sontag, has AIDS become "so famous"?

3. What images does Sontag cite that make AIDS seem so catastrophic?

4. What metaphors can you find in Sontag's prose? Is she using them unconsciously? If not, is she criticizing these metaphors? What is your evidence?

5. What is Sontag's criticism of Gould's assessment of the AIDS epidemic?

6. What, according to Sontag, are the modern sources of catastrophe?

7. What are the appealing aspects of the idea of a plague, according to Sontag?

8. What constitutes our sense of the "unreality of the apocalypse" according to Sontag?

9. In how many ways has reality become "bifurcated" according to Sontag?

10. How, according to Sontag, is AIDS connected to the "global village?"

11. After rereading the entire essay, what do you think Sontag means by being "against interpretation?"

12. What are Sontag's attitudes toward science in this selection? Do you agree?

13. If we do not use the military metaphor to describe the way the body reacts to illness, how can we talk about the physical occurrences? Do you see a difference between describing the body's biological defenses in military terms and describing the whole person as "fighting" a disease? In other words, can medicine do without this or any metaphor? If not, what metaphors would be both appropriate and appealing to Sontag or to you?

Comparison

1. Read Tuchman's essay on the Black Death. What characteristics of the plague do you think people now ascribe to AIDS? What similarities and differences do you see between the analysis of illness in the two essays?

2. Read Rodriguez's "Labor." What ideas appear in both essays? To what extent, if any, do Sontag and Rodriguez agree about metaphor and education?

3. Read Frost's "Education by Poetry" and compare his discussion of metaphor with Sontag's.

4. Read some of the essays depicting the conflict in academia between science and literature. Does Sontag show any biases toward either field?

5. Read Postman's "Learning by Story." How does his understanding of story inform Sontag's analysis of the meanings ascribed to AIDS?

6. Read Orwell's "Politics and the English Language." How, if at all, does Sontag extend the ideas expressed in Orwell's essay?

7. Read the essay by Fukuyama. Compare his understanding of the "Great Disruption" with Sontag's depiction of the apocalypse. To what extent do Sontag and Fukuyama agree?

Judith Ortiz Cofer
(1952–)

By the time Judith Ortiz was born on February 24, 1952, her father, a member of the U.S. Navy, had already been stationed in Panama, not to return to Puerto Rico until his daughter was two years old. Soon relocated to the United States, he sent word to his family, which now included Ortiz's younger brother, to join him in Paterson, New Jersey. For the rest of her childhood, in response to her father's naval duties, Ortiz shuttled back and forth between two places and two cultures, as she explains in *Silent Dancing: A Partial Remembrance of a Puerto Rican Childhood*: "Every time he went to Europe for six months, we went back with Mother [to Puerto Rico] to her mother's *casa*; upon his return..., he would wire us, and we would come back. Cold/hot, English/Spanish; that was our life." Even when she lived in Paterson, Ortiz experienced these kinds of dualities. Her mother, refusing either to learn English or to assimilate herself in hopes of returning permanently to Puerto Rico, created a "carefully constructed facsimile of a Puerto Rican home" for herself and her children, and "[e]very day," Ortiz felt like she "crossed the border of two countries" when she left her home to attend Catholic school, where her uniform did not always save her from culture clashes over fashion and female appearance.

After discovering in school that "language is the only weapon a child has against the absolute power of adults," Ortiz began to read voraciously in order to build her English vocabulary. She also became the voice of her household, communicating with English-speaking shopkeepers and physicians on her mother's behalf. "English," she writes, "was my weapon and my power." In adulthood, English also became her vocation, her medium for poetry and prose. Having married a Southerner named Charles John Cofer in 1971, Judith Ortiz Cofer graduated from Augusta College in 1974. After she taught public school in Florida for a year, she entered Florida Atlantic University to earn her master's, spending the summer studying at Oxford. She writes in an article for *Glamour*: "On a bus to London from Oxford University...a young man, obviously fresh from a pub, approached my seat. With both hands over his heart, he went down on his knees in the aisle and broke into an Irish tenor's rendition of 'Maria' from *West Side Story*. I was not amused.... You can leave the island of Puerto Rico, master the English language, and travel as far as you can, but if you're a Latina,...the island travels with you." Cofer earned her M.A. in 1977, and then she immediately began teaching at the college level, starting at Broward Community College as an adjunct instructor in English.

In 1980, when Cofer accepted a position as a lecturer at the University of Miami, she started to publish poems in places like *The Florida Arts Gazette.* Her poems also appeared in anthologies, and she published her first chapbook, *Latin Women Pray.* The title poem she has characterized as itself a "prayer, of sorts, for communication and respect":

> Latin women pray
> in incense-sweet churches;
> they pray in Spanish to an Anglo God
> with a Jewish heritage.
>
> And this Great White Father,
> imperturbable in His marble pedestal
> looks down upon His brown daughters,
> votive candles shining like lust
> in His all-seeing eyes,
> unmoved by their persistent prayers.
> Yet year after year,
> before his image they kneel,
> Margarita, Josefina, Maria and Isabel
> all fervently hoping
> that if not omnipotent,
> at least He be bilingual.

Cofer published two more chapbooks while teaching at the University of Miami, *The Native Dancer* (1981) and *Among the Ancestors* (1981). In 1984, the year she became an instructor at the University of Georgia in Athens, she published her first play, again using the title, *Latin Women Pray,* which was produced the same year in Atlanta. Over the remainder of the decade, she published two more volumes of poetry, *Peregrina* (1986) and *Terms of Survival* (1987) and contributed to *Triple Crown: Chicano, Puerto Rican and Cuban American Poetry* (1987). In 1989, she published her first novel, *The Line of the Sun,* nominated for a Pulitzer Prize.

After working at Macon College in the late 1980s, Cofer took a position as special programs coordinator at Mercer University College in 1990, the same year she published *Silent Dancing,* a collection of autobiographical essays interspersed with poems and organized around members of her family, as well as "characters" in her apartment building in New Jersey and her village in Puerto Rico. In 1992, she returned to the University of Georgia as an associate professor of English and Creative Writing. Her next publication, *The Latin Deli: Prose and Poetry,* appeared in 1993, and then she published twice in 1995, rereleasing material from *Triple Crown* in *Reaching for the Mainland & Selected New Poems* and publishing a collection for young adults, *An Island Like You: Stories of the Barrio.* In 1998, she published *The Year of Our Revolution: New and Selected Stories and Poems,* and in 1999, she co-edited *Sleeping with One Eye Open: Women Writers and the Art of Survival.*

Described by a reviewer for *The New York Times* as "a writer of authentic gifts, with a genuine and important story to tell," Judith Ortiz Cofer regularly draws upon her own experiences of feeling divided between cultures in her prose and her poetry. She also adapts and reinvents pieces of family history, describing the magic of her "spiritist" grandfather, the strength and frustration of her pragmatist grandmother, and the transmission of stories among women in her family. Moments of transmission and transition, both pleasurable and painful, are common in her works, as are images of birth and expulsion like the one that opens "Arrival":

> When we arrived we were expelled
> like fetuses
> from the warm belly of an airplane.
> Shocked by the cold, we held hands as we skidded
> like new colts on the unfamiliar ice.

As she said in an interview with *Contemporary Authors,* "The place of birth itself becomes a metaphor for the things we all must leave behind; the assimilation of a new culture is the coming into maturity by accepting terms necessary for survival. My poetry is a study of this process of change, assimilation, and transformation."

CASA *(1989)*

AT THREE OR four o'clock in the afternoon, the hour of café con leche,[1] the women of my family gathered in Mamá's living room to speak of important things and to tell stories for the hundredth time, as if to each other, meant to be overheard by us young girls, their daughters. In Mamá's house (everyone called my grandmother Mamá) was a large parlor built by my grandfather to his wife's exact specifications so that it was always cool, facing away from the sun. The doorway was on the side of the house so no one could walk directly into her living room. First they had to take a little stroll through and around her beautiful garden where prize-winning orchids grew in the trunk of an ancient tree she had hollowed out for that purpose. This room was furnished with several mahogany rocking chairs, acquired at the births of her children, and one intricately carved rocker that had passed down to Mamá at the death of her own mother. It was on these rockers that my mother, her sisters and my grandmother sat on these afternoons of my childhood to tell their stories, teaching each other and my cousin and me what it was like to be a woman, more specifically, a Puerto Rican woman. They talked about life on the

---

[1] *Café con leche* coffee with milk.

island, and life in *Los Nueva Yores,* their way of referring to the U.S., from New York City to California: the other place, not home, all the same. They told real-life stories, though as I later learned, always embellishing them with a little or a lot of dramatic detail, and they told *cuentos,* the morality and cautionary tales told by the women in our family for generations: stories that became a part of my subconscious as I grew up in two worlds, the tropical island and the cold city, and which would later surface in my dreams and in my poetry.

One of these tales was about the woman who was left at the altar. Mamá liked to tell that one with histrionic intensity. I remember the rise and fall of her voice, the sighs, and her constantly gesturing hands, like two birds swooping through her words. This particular story would usually come up in a conversation as a result of someone mentioning a forthcoming engagement or wedding. The first time I remember hearing it, I was sitting on the floor at Mamá's feet, pretending to read a comic book. I may have been eleven or twelve years old: at that difficult age when a girl is no longer a child who can be ordered to leave the room if the women wanted freedom to take their talk into forbidden zones, or really old enough to be considered a part of their conclave. I could only sit quietly, pretending to be in another world, while absorbing it all in a sort of unspoken agreement of my status as silent auditor. On this day, Mamá had taken my long, tangled mane of hair into her ever busy hands. Without looking down at me or interrupting her flow of words, she began braiding my hair, working at it with the quickness and determination which characterized all her actions. My mother was watching us impassively from her rocker across the room. On her lips played a little ironic smile. I would never sit still for *her* ministrations, but even then, I instinctively knew that she did not possess Mamá's matriarchal power to command and keep everyone's attention. This was particularly evident in the spell she cast when telling a story.

"It is not like it used to be when I was a girl." Mamá announced, "Then, a man could leave a girl standing at the church altar with a bouquet of fresh flowers in her hands and disappear off the face of the earth. No way to track him down if he was from another town. He could be a married man, with maybe even two or three families all over the island. There was no way to know. And there were men who did this. Hombres with the devil in their flesh who would come to a pueblo, like this one, take a job at one of the haciendas, never meaning to stay, only to have a good time and to seduce the women."

The whole time she was speaking, Mamá was weaving my hair into a flat plait which required pulling apart the two sections of hair with little jerks that made my eyes water; but knowing how grandmother detested whining and *boba* (sissy) tears, as she called them, I just sat up as straight and stiff as I did at La Escuela San José, where the nuns enforced good posture with a flexible plastic ruler they bounced off slumped shoulders and heads. As Mamá's story progressed, I noticed how my young aunt Laura had lowered her eyes, refusing to meet Mamá's meaningful gaze. Laura was seventeen, in her last year of high school, and already engaged to a boy from another town who had staked his claim with a tiny diamond ring, then left for Los Nueva Yores to make his fortune. They were planning to get married in a year; but Mamá had expressed serious doubts that the wedding would ever take place. In Mamá's eyes, a man set free without a legal contract was a man lost. She believed that marriage was not something men desired, but simply the price they had to pay for the privilege of children, and of course, for what no decent (synonymous with "smart") woman would give away for free.

"María la Loca[2] was only seventeen when *it* happened to her." I listened closely at the mention of this name. María was a town "character," a fat middle-aged woman who lived with her old mother on the outskirts of town. She was to be seen around the pueblo delivering the meat pies the two women made for a living. The most peculiar thing about María, in my eyes, was that she walked and moved like a little girl, though she had the thick body and wrinkled face of an old woman. She would swing her hips in an exaggerated, clownish way, and sometimes even hop and skip up to someone's house. She spoke to no one. Even if you asked her a question, she would just look at you and smile, showing her yellow teeth. But I had heard that if you got close enough, you could hear her humming a tune without words. The kids yelled out nasty things at her, calling her *la Loca,* and the men who hung out at the bodega playing dominoes sometimes whistled mockingly as she passed by with her funny, outlandish walk. But María seemed impervious to it all, carrying her basket of *paste-les* like a grotesque Little Red Riding Hood through the forest.

María la Loca interested me, as did all the eccentrics and "crazies" of our pueblo. Their weirdness was a measuring stick I used in my serious quest for a definition of "normal." As a Navy brat, shuttling between New Jersey and the pueblo, I was constantly made to feel like an oddball by my peers, who made fun of my two-way accent: a Spanish accent when I spoke English; and, when I spoke Spanish, I was told that I sounded like a "Gringa." Being the outsiders had already turned my brother and me into cultural chameleons, developing early the ability to blend into a crowd, to sit and read quietly in a fifth story apartment building for days and days when it was too bitterly cold to play outside; or, set free, to run wild in Mamá's realm, where she took charge of our lives, releasing mother for a while from the intense fear for our safety that our father's absences instilled in her. In order to keep us from harm when father was away, mother kept us under strict surveillance. She even walked us to and from Public School No. 11, which we attended during the months we lived in Paterson, New Jersey, our home base in the States. Mamá freed the three of us like pigeons from a cage. I saw her as my liberator and my model. Her stories were parables from which to glean the *Truth.*

"María la Loca was once a beautiful girl. Everyone thought she would marry the Méndez boy." As everyone knew, Rogelio Méndez was no other than the richest man in town. "But," Mamá continued, knitting my hair with the same intensity she was putting into her story," this *macho* made a fool out of her and ruined her life." She paused for the effect of her use of the word "macho," which at that time had not yet become a popular epithet for an unliberated man. This word had for us the crude and comical connotation of "male of the species," stud; a *macho* was what you put in a pen to increase your stock.

I peeked over my comic book at my mother. She too was under Mamá's spell, smiling conspiratorially at this little swipe at men. She was safe from Mamá's contempt in this area. Married at an early age, an unspotted lamb, she had been accepted by a good family of strict Spaniards whose name was old and respected, though their fortune had been lost long before my birth. In a rocker Papá had painted sky blue sat Mamá's oldest child, Aunt Nena. Mother of three children, stepmother of two more, she was a quiet woman who liked books but had married an ignorant and abusive widower whose main interest in life was accumulating wealth. He too was in the mainland working on his

---

[2]*Maria la loca* Crazy Maria.

dream of returning home rich and triumphant to buy the *finca*[3] of his dreams. She was waiting for him to send for her. She would leave her children with Mamá for several years while the two of them slaved away in factories. He would one day be a rich man, and she a sadder woman. Even now her life-light was dimming. She spoke little, an aberration in Mamá's house, and she read avidly, as if storing up spiritual food for the long winters that awaited her in Los Nueva Yores without her family. But even Aunt Nena came alive to Mamá's words, rocking gently, her hands over a thick book in her lap. Her daughter, my cousin Sara, played jacks by herself on the tile porch outside the room where we sat. She was a year older than I. We shared a bed and all our family's secrets. Collaborators in search of answers, Sara and I discussed everything we heard the women say, trying to fit it all together like a puzzle that once assembled would reveal life's mysteries to us. Though she and I still enjoyed taking part in boy's games—chase, volleyball and even *vaqueros,* the island version of cowboys and Indians involving cap-gun battles and violent shootouts under the mango tree in Mamá's backyard—we loved best the quiet hours in the afternoon when the men were still at work and the boys had gone to play serious baseball at the park. Then Mamá's house belonged only to us women. The aroma of coffee perking in the kitchen, the mesmerizing creaks and groans of the rockers, and the women telling their lives in *cuentos* are forever woven into the fabric of my imagination, braided like my hair that day I felt my grandmother's hands teaching me about strength, her voice convincing me of the power of story-telling.

That day Mamá told of how the beautiful María had fallen prey to a man whose name was never the same in subsequent versions of the story; it was Juan one time, José, Rafael, Diego, another. We understood that the name, and really any of the facts, were not important, only that a woman had allowed love to defeat her. Mamá put each of us in Marí's place by describing her wedding dress in loving detail: how she looked like a princess in her lace as she waited at the altar. Then, as Mamá approached the tragic denouement of her story, I was distracted by the sound of my Aunt Laura's violent rocking. She seemed on the verge of tears. She knew the fable was intended for her. That week she was going to have her wedding gown fitted, though no firm date had been set for the marriage. Mamá ignored Laura's obvious discomfort, digging out a ribbon from the sewing basket she kept by her rocker while describing María's long illness, "a fever that would not break for days." She spoke of a mother's despair: "that woman climbed the church steps on her knees every morning, wore only black as a *promesa* to the Holy Virgin in exchange for her daughter's health." By the time María returned from her honeymoon with death, she was ravished, no longer young or sane. "As you can see she is almost as old as her mother already," Mamá lamented while tying the ribbon to the ends of my hair, pulling it back with such force that I just knew that I would never be able to close my eyes completely again.

"That María is getting crazier every day." Mamá's voice would take a lighter tone now, expressing satisfaction, either for the perfection of my braid, or for a story well-told; it was hard to tell. "You know that tune she is always humming?" Carried away by her enthusiasm, I tried to nod, but Mamá would still have me pinned between her knees.

"Well, that's the wedding march." Surprising us all, Mamá sang out, "*Da, da, dará . . . da, da, dará.*" Then lifting me off the floor by my skinny shoulders, she lead me around the room in an impromptu waltz—another session ending with the laughter of women, all of us caught up in the infectious joke of our lives.

---

[3]*finca* farm.

Understanding and Analysis

1. The first paragraph sets the scene for this essay and establishes the character of the grandmother, Mamá. What kind of a person is she and what details provide the evidence?

2. What can you gather about the narrator's mother? How does the narrator's relationship with her mother differ from her relationship with Mamá? Look at the braiding of hair and at other details to find your answers. What explanation does Cofer offer for this difference? Can you think of additional explanations?

3. How does Cofer characterize life in New Jersey? How does she characterize life in Puerto Rico? What restrictions pertain in each place?

4. Does Mamá really believe that times have changed from when she was a little girl? If so, in what ways? If not, explain your position. What is your evidence?

5. Why is Little Red Riding Hood a fitting analogue for Maria la Loca?

6. Name the ways in which Cofer defines herself as an outsider in this essay. What defines her as an insider as well?

7. What role do men play in this essay? What do we know, for example, of Cofer's grandfather, her father, and her brother? Who are the other men Cofer refers to, and what do we know about each of them?

8. Does Mamá's view of men as depicted in her story bear any resemblance to the actual men Cofer describes?

9. What makes a good marriage according to Mamá? What do you think Cofer believes makes a good marriage? What details support your position? What do you think makes a good marriage?

10. What is "the infectious joke of our lives"?

Comparison

1. Read Lopez on storytelling. Based on his requirements, is Mamá's story true? How important are the embellishments in Mamá's story?

2. Read Postman on storytelling. Compare Cofer's essay with the ideas in Postman's essay. Is Cofer's retelling of Mamá's story really a new story updated for her generation? If so, how is the new story different from the old one?

3. Read Angelou, Kingston, Ozick, Rich, Didion, and Mairs. Compare the family relationships in these essays.

4. Read Rich, Rodriguez, Kingston, and Staples. To what degree does ethnic background help to establish a sense of personal identity for the narrators in these essays?

5. Read Orwell's "A Hanging" and Graves's "Triste La Guerre." Compare the causes and types of laughter presented in these essays with the laughter in Cofer's essay. Are they in any way similar? How are they different?

Neil Postman
(1931–)

Born in Brooklyn, New York, Neil Milton Postman grew up "poor." "Every-one in my family" was poor, he told interviewer Brandon Boey, from his father, a truck driver, to his "aunts and uncles." While family members strug-gling through the depression placed little emphasis on "money" or "material things," they placed "a tremendous emphasis on education and learning." As Postman explains in *The End of Education*, he himself "was required to go to two schools: the American public school, in which the names of Washing-ton, Jefferson, Madison, Tom Paine, and Lincoln were icons, and a 'Jewish' school, in which the names of Abraham, Sarah, Isaac, Rebecca, Jacob, Rachel, Leah, and Moses were equally sacred." Although he did not consider becom-ing a teacher until he was ready for college, he began to feel in the sixth or seventh grade that he had a talent for explaining and that he was better equipped than his own teacher to provide explanations to his classmates. Around the same time, he also began to write, attending baseball games and then returning home to write them up, as if creating copy for a newspaper.

Making good on his adolescent insight, Postman graduated from SUNY Fredonia in 1953, with a degree in elementary education. He soon enrolled at Columbia for graduate work, earning his M.A. in English Education in 1955, the same year he married his wife, Shelley. Working toward his doctorate, he took his first teaching job in the winter of 1959 in a fifth-grade classroom. After he published his first book, *Television and the Teaching of English* (1961), written with the Committee on the Study of Television, he produced a small explosion of books on language, co-authoring seven works over the next five years. With titles such as *Language and Systems* (1965) and *Exploring Your Language* (1966), these books do not necessarily sound like the early writings of a cultural critic interested in media and technology, but according to Post-man, there is a thread that links all his works. "Even when I was writing my first books about language," he remarked more than thirty years later, "I had one question in mind: How to prepare young people to live decently in a technological society."

For the last of his early books on language, *Linguistics: A Revolution in Teach-ing* (1966), Postman teamed up with Charles Weingartner, a friend and col-league whom he met in graduate school in 1955. Together, Postman and Wein-gartner made a name for themselves with *Teaching as a Subversive Activity* (1969). While Postman taught at New York University, the pair also published *The*

Soft Revolution: A Student Handbook for Turning Schools Around (1971) and *The School Book: For People Who Want to Know What All the Hollering Is About* (1973). In 1976, Postman published, on his own, *Crazy Talk, Stupid Talk: How We Defeat Ourselves by the Way We Talk and What to Do About It.* In the same year, he agreed to become the editor of *Et Cetera: The Journal of General Semantics,* a position he held for the next ten years.

Between the late 1960s, when Postman and Weingartner published *Teaching as a Subversive Activity,* and the late 1970s, when Postman published *Teaching as a Conserving Activity,* something obviously happened to Postman's views on education. ("Frankly," he writes in the Prologue to *Teaching as a Conserving Activity,* "I do not know if I have turned or everything else has.") In 1982, he published *The Disappearance of Childhood* in which he argues that "television erases the dividing line between childhood and adulthood in two ways: it requires no instruction to grasp its form, and it does not segregate its audience. Therefore, it communicates the same information to everyone, simultaneously, regardless of age, sex, level of education, or previous condition of servitude." *The Disappearance of Childhood* remains Postman's favorite book. In 1985, he published *Amusing Ourselves to Death: Public Discourse in the Age of Show Business,* maintaining that "American public discourse has been changed by the electronic media from serious exposition into a form of entertainment." That summer, as he explains in *Conscientious Objections,* a German magazine called *Stern* paid for him to tour Germany, where he traveled from Munich to Frankfurt to Hamburg. He also "visited (if that is the word) Dachau, where an aunt and uncle of mine had perished." Traveling on to Sweden, he discovered a book not unlike *Amusing Ourselves to Death,* but about the Nazis: "Its authors find the principal feature of the Third Reich to lie in a politics essentially without content; the Nazi regime, they contend, offers the ultimate example of politics as pure spectacle. The similarity between this thesis and my own...was uncanny."

Back in the United States, Postman received the George Orwell Award for Clarity in Language in 1987. The following year, he published *Conscientious Objections: Stirring Up Trouble about Language, Technology, and Education,* a collection of his speeches and essays, which he dedicated to his parents. In 1989, New York University honored his teaching by giving him a Distinguished Professor Award. After a brief tenure as the Laurence Lombard Visiting Professor of the Press and Public Policy at Harvard University, Postman co-authored *How to Watch TV News* (1992) with Steve Powers and published one of his most controversial works, *Technopoly: The Surrender of Culture to Technology* (1992), a book that "attempts to describe when, how, and why technology became a particularly dangerous enemy." Named a University Professor in 1993, he published *The End of Education: Redefining the Value of School* in 1995.

"I have spent thirty years as an affectionate critic of American prejudices, tastes, and neuroses," Postman writes in *The End of Education,* "and have been astonished and pleased to discover I share most of them." He is now known principally for his later works and his views on such topics as technology, multiculturalism, and the state of American culture. Some reviewers have been inclined to dismiss Postman as "technophobic," while others have classified him as "apocalyptic" and "paranoid." For every comment like that, however, there is another that finds him "exciting," "insightful," and "important." Postman's command of language and his ready wit, combined with his forceful argumentation and his experience as an educator, have made him a strong voice of the twentieth century.

LEARNING BY STORY (1989)

NOW THAT THE thunderstorm ignited by the celebrated texts of E. D. Hirsch, Jr., (*Cultural Literacy*) and Allan Bloom (*The Closing of the American Mind*) has passed over the land and appears to present no further danger to our intellectual landscape, it may be useful to review, under clearer skies, the lessons to be drawn from the drenching. To do this, I will attempt a deconstruction of their texts—deconstruction being the method employed today by academics whose positions have been secured by tenure. In other words, I will proceed on the assumption that it is permissible for a reader to believe that he knows more about a text than its writer, and is therefore free to instruct the writer on what his book is really about.

To start at the end, as it were, I want to show that in *Cultural Literacy,* Professor Hirsch believes he is offering a solution to a problem when in fact he is only raising a question—and a desperate question at that. In *The Closing of the American Mind,* Professor Bloom suggests an answer to Hirsch's question for reasons that are not entirely clear to him but are, of course, to me.

For, those who have not read *Cultural Literacy,* I should say that much of the book's popularity is attributable to its appendix, which consists of a list of 5,000 names, dates, aphorisms, and concepts that Hirsch and some of his colleagues believe a literate person ought to know. Americans love lists, especially lists compiled by experts; Americans also love tests, and Hirsch's list is easily transformed into a kind of cultural-literacy test that can be administered anywhere, including the living room and the classroom. Aside from the fact that Hirsch is a lucid and sometimes elegant writer, very little else in the book can account for its success either with teachers or with the common reader. To paraphrase an old saw, what is true in Hirsch's book is not startling, and what is startling is not true.

Let us start with what is true. Hirsch believes that the more one knows, the more one can learn—a proposition with which few would disagree. He also believes that you can't read reading. You have to read *about* something. And therefore, to be literate, you have to know about the things you are reading about. There is no disputing this proposition either, or its negative formulation, which is that if you do not know anything about what you are reading about, you may be said to be illiterate in that subject. I have a son who works as an astrophysicist and who has published several papers in his specialty, which happens to be the structure of galaxies. He has been kind enough to send a copy of each of his papers, in the expectation, no doubt, that I will take pleasure in reading them. I would if I could. Unfortunately, I cannot, for the simple reason that I do not know the meanings of 90 percent of the words in his papers. I can *pronounce* the words, of course, but this is quite different from reading them. Hirsch would say that my problem is that I am not literate in astrophysics, and in this he would be entirely correct. I do much better, by the way, with my daughter's papers on the subject of theater history. When she writes about naturalism or realism or Ibsen's[1] point of view on idealism, I know perfectly well what I am reading about, because I know the meanings of her words.

Hirsch is simply saying that every subject has its special language, and you cannot know the subject, or read the subject, if you do not know its language. There is an old and somewhat paradoxical joke about this point. It tells of a mother who is boasting to a friend about her son's academic prowess. To prove her case, she calls her son into the room and says, "Harold, say something in geometry for Mrs. Freeman." The point of the joke is supposed to be that the mother has demonstrated only her ignorance, not Harold's knowledge. But in fact there is no point to the joke, because Harold could say many things in geometry, such as "Parallel lines never meet," and "Equals added to equals are equal," and "The shortest distance between two points is a straight line."

These ideas—the more you know, the more you can learn; you can't read reading; every subject makes use of a special language—are, as I have said, certainly true, but they are hardly startling. I do not know a single teacher who disputes them, although I suppose it does no harm to be reminded of them once in a while. Hirsch proceeds from these truisms to a consideration of the appalling ignorance of our students. This is a condition that most teachers, especially high school and college teachers, have noticed. Almost every teacher has some favorite examples of student ignorance, and more than occasionally these days essays appear in the popular press documenting our students' curious illiteracies. Some months ago I received in the mail such an essay, written by a teacher at a community college in Olympia, Washington. He had prepared an eighty-six-question cultural-literacy test, which he gave to the twenty-six students in his class. The students ranged in age from eighteen to fifty-four, and all had completed at least one quarter of college-level work. Here are some things his students knew: Charles Darwin invented gravity. Jesus Christ was born in the sixteenth century. The Great Gatsby was a magician in the 1930s. Heinrich Himmler invented the Heimlich maneuver. Benito Mussolini was a Russian leader of the eighteenth century. Pablo Picasso painted masterpieces in the twelfth century. Socrates was an American Indian chieftain. Mark Twain invented the cotton gin. The city of Belfast is located in Egypt, Beirut is in Germany, and Bogotá is in China.

Of course, there's some pretty funny stuff here, but we had all better keep in mind that the furniture in our heads has its own peculiar gaps and disarrangements, which might be hard to conceal were we confronted by a cultural-literacy test. In my own case, I find that scarcely a day passes without my hearing for the first time about a person or place about which everyone else seems to know. I suspect that you are familiar with this prob-

---

[1]*Ibsen* Henrik Johan Ibsen (1828–1906) a Norwegian playwright and poet, whose most famous work includes *Peer Gynt* (1867), *A Doll's House* (1879), and *Hedda Gabler* (1890).

lem as well. If you are, there is a very good reason for our shared ignorance, and I will come to it in a moment. But here I must take notice of what is both startling and false in Hirsch's book. Faced with the fact of widespread ignorance, Hirsch comes up with an explanation that must have been a considerable challenge to his imagination. The problem, he says, is "educational formalism." He means by this that teachers are no longer concerned with academic content but are instead obsessed with the processes or skills of learning. We try to teach how scientists think, but without reference to the content of science. We try to teach how to read, but ignore what the text is about. We try to teach what historians do, but without attending to history itself. And so on. That is why, he says, our students are culturally illiterate and cannot learn very much. Teachers no longer give students names, places, dates—in a word, the facts.

I call this explanation wrong for two reasons. First, if there is one thing that most teachers in America are not concerned with, it is the processes of learning. This can be verified by spending a few days visiting representative American classrooms, an inconvenience that Hirsch apparently did not wish to endure. Instead, he draws his evidence from textbooks on methods of teaching, which have as much relevance to what is actually happening in classrooms as campaign speeches have to do with the actual running of government. But Hirsch is wrong for another, even more important reason. As any teacher who is concerned with process can tell you, it is scarcely possible to teach how something is done without also teaching content. How can you teach how a poem might be read without also teaching the poem? How can you teach how a scientific theory is developed without reference to the great theories that the great scientists have constructed? The thing cannot be done—at least, *almost* cannot be done. A small exception might be made for the occasion of teaching the letters of the alphabet. It is probably true that when the very young are being taught to read, the emphasis is almost wholly on how to decode the words. What the words say is often treated as irrelevant. This may or may not be a mistake—Bruno Bettelheim[2] thinks it is—but in any case it cannot account for the widespread cultural illiteracy that is so disturbing to Hirsch. There are, to put it plainly, very few school systems anywhere that do not start emphasizing the content of subjects by, let us say, the fourth grade.

Nonetheless, Hirsch is convinced that educational formalism is at the root of the ignorance problem, and he offers a solution in the form of his list, which, he suggests, contains the references essential to a culturally literate person in America, and which any curriculum ignores at its peril. If I may borrow an aphorism from the turn-of-the-century Viennese journalist Karl Kraus: Hirsch's list is the disease for which it claims to be the cure—that is to say, its arbitrariness only demonstrates the futility of trying to do what he wants us to do. His list includes Norman Mailer[3] but not Philip Roth,[4]

---

[2]*Bruno Bettelheim* (1903–1990) an Austrian psychotherapist and author who studied with Freud and was imprisoned at Dachau and Buchenwald during Hitler's regime. He moved to the United States and became well-known for his work with autistic children and his books about the Nazi concentration camps.

[3]*Norman Mailer* (1923–) an American writer who gained instant notoriety for his first novel, *The Naked and the Dead* (1948), a violent portrayal of war. He has led a flamboyant life, has been a prolific writer, and was awarded a Pulitzer Prize.

[4]*Philip Roth* (1933–) an American writer and professor whose best-known works include *Goodbye, Columbus* (1959, National Book Award) and the racy *Portnoy's Complaint* (1969).

Bernard Malamud,[5] Arthur Miller,[6] or Tennessee Williams.[7] It includes Ginger Rogers[8] but not Richard Rodgers,[9] Carl Rogers,[10] or Buck Rogers,[11] let alone Fred Rogers.[12] The second greatest home-run hitter of all time, Babe Ruth, is there, but not the greatest home-run hitter, Hank Aaron. The Marx brothers are there but not Orson Welles,[13] Frank Capra,[14] John Ford,[15] or Steven Spielberg. Sarah Bernhardt[16] is included but not Leonard Bernstein.[17] Rochester, New York, is on the list. Trenton, New Jersey, one of our most historic cities, is not. Hirsch includes the Battle of the Bulge, which pleased my brother, who fought in it in 1944. But my uncle who died in the Battle of the Coral Sea, in 1942, would have been disappointed to find that it didn't make the list. (I refer here to the list as it appears in the first, 1987, edition of the book. Hirsch has since written a book that supplements the list, which only underscores the futility of his enterprise.)

I could go on with this almost endlessly, as anyone could. For every person, event, city, book, or saying Hirsch lists, one could list ten he has omitted that would be equally relevant or irrelevant. And therein lies the paradox. Hirsch believes that he is offering educators a solution to ignorance when he is in fact only posing an unanswered question

[5]*Bernard Malamud* (1914–1986) an American writer who wrote about baseball in such novels as *The Natural* (1952) and about the Jewish experience in other books, such as *The Fixer* (1966).

[6]*Arthur Miller* an American Pulitzer-winning playwright best known for *Death of a Salesman* (1949) and *The Crucible* (1953).

[7]*Tennessee Williams* (1911–1983) an American playwright who authored such plays as *The Glass Menagerie* (1945), *A Streetcar Named Desire* (1947), and *Cat on a Hot Tin Roof* (1955), the latter two of which won Pulitzer Prizes.

[8]*Ginger Rogers* born Virginia Katherine McMath (1911–1995) a movie actor famous for her dancing roles with Fred Astaire.

[9]*Richard Rodgers* (1902–1979) an American composer who helped develop the modern musical play. He is well known for his work with Oscar Hammerstein, including such musicals as *Oklahoma!* (1943), *The King and I* (1951), and *The Sound of Music* (1959).

[10]*Carl Rogers* (1902–1987) a well-known American psychotherapist who is credited with the development of encounter groups and group therapy.

[11]*Buck Rogers* Science fiction hero of comic strip series entitled *Buck Rogers in the 25th Century* created in 1928 by Phil Nowlan and Dick Calkins. The strip was made into a radio series (1932–1939) and later a movie starring Buster Crabbe.

[12]*Fred Rogers* (1928–) Host of the children's television show, *Mr. Rogers's Neighborhood*, which has run since 1965.

[13]*Orson Welles* (1915–1985) an American actor and director, whose successes included founding the Mercury Theater in 1937, producing the infamous 1938 Halloween dramatization of H. G. Wells' War of the Worlds, and writing, and directing, and starring in the 1941 movie *Citizen Kane*.

[14]*Frank Capra* (1897–1991) a film director, born in Palermo, Sicily, but raised in California from the age of six. His most enduringly popular film has been the 1947 *It's a Wonderful Life*.

[15]*John Ford* (1895–1973) a film director who won six academy awards for movies including *The Grapes of Wrath* (1940) and *The Quiet Man* (1952). He received the first American Film Institute Life Achievement Award in 1973.

[16]*Sarah Bernhard* (1844–1923) a French stage actress who attained world renown and who continued to act even after she had a leg amputated in 1915.

[17]*Leonard Bernstein* (1918–1990) an American conductor and composer, Bernstein conducted the New York Philharmonic for many years, and composed several symphonies, operas, and musicals, including *West Side Story* (1957).

about its origin. The question is this: What are educators to do when they must serve in a culture inundated by information?

From millions of sources all over the globe, through every possible channel and medium—light waves, airwaves, ticker tapes, computer banks, telephone wires, television cables, printing presses—information pours in. Behind it, in every imaginable form of storage—on paper, on video and audio tapes, on discs, film, and silicon chips—is an even greater volume of information waiting to be retrieved and used. More is being added every hour, every minute, every second. Clearly, we are swamped by information. Drowning in it. Overwhelmed by it. And what is Hirsch's solution? We should use the schools to teach the kids some information. No. It is not a serious idea. We might even say it is a profoundly useless idea. But if viewed as a series of questions, Hirsch's book gives us something serious to think about. How can we help our students to organize information? How can we help them to sort the relevant from the irrelevant? How can we help them to make better use of information? How can we keep them from being driven insane by information?

An answer of sorts, as I have said, is suggested, indirectly, in Allan Bloom's *The Closing of the American Mind*. Bloom is a professor on the Committee on Social Thought at the University of Chicago, and to the astonishment of everyone in the publishing industry, his book was a runaway best seller. The astonishment arises because neither his style nor his subject matter is of the sort that has ever been the stuff of big-time sales. Nonetheless, he has something to say, and it is in the form of a serious complaint. His complaint is that most American professors have lost their nerve. They have become moral relativists, which means that they are not capable of providing their students with a clear understanding of what is right thought and proper behavior. Moreover, they are also intellectual relativists, meaning that the professors refuse to defend their own culture and are no longer committed to preserving and transmitting the best that has been thought and said.

Bloom's solution is that we go back to the basics of Western thought. He wants us to teach our students what Plato, Aristotle, Cicero,[18] Saint Augustine,[19] and other luminaries have had to say on the great ethical and epistemological questions. He believes that by acquainting themselves with great books our students will acquire a moral and intellectual foundation that will keep them from doing stupid things like laughing at Woody Allen movies, listening to rock music, and making life difficult for school administrators and professors. Bloom does not directly address the question of information chaos; he does not admit that there are fatal weaknesses in moral absolutism; and he does not acknowledge that there never was a time when American public education devoted itself to the study of Greek philosophy, German idealism, or, for that matter, most of what he covers in his philosophy courses at the University of Chicago.

Nonetheless, he is, in my opinion, on the right track. Although he does not seem to know it, Bloom is arguing that students need stories, narratives, tales, theories (call them what you will), that can serve as moral and intellectual frameworks. Without such frameworks, we have no way of knowing what things mean. Bloom understands that ignorance is not simply a matter of unfamiliarity with things in general. It is a matter of not know-

[18]*Cicero* Marcus Tullius Cicero (143–106) B.C.; a Roman orator, statesman, and man of letters.

[19]*St. Augustine* (354–430) an Algerian scholar who converted to Christianity and whose works deeply influenced the Church during the Middle Ages.

ing things that one needs to know in particular. You do not know who manufactured the paper from which this magazine was made, and you do not know the name of the editor's wife, and you do not know Allan Bloom's telephone number, and you do not know 50 billion other facts of the world, because you deem them of no importance to your life. For this you should not be charged with ignorance. You should be praised for intellectual selectivity. But on what basis do you make your selections? How do you know what you need to know? And how do you know when and where and how you need to know it?

The answer, I believe, can be put in the following way (for which formulation I am indebted to my colleague Professor Christine Nystrom): Human beings require stories to give meaning to the facts of their existence. I am not talking here about those specialized stories that we call novels, plays, and epic poems. I am talking about the more profound stories that people, nations, religions, and disciplines unfold in order to make sense out of the world. For example, ever since we can remember, all of us have been telling ourselves stories about ourselves, composing life-giving autobiographies of which we are the heroes and heroines. If our stories are coherent and plausible and have continuity, they will help us to understand why we are here, and what we need to pay attention to and what we may ignore. A story provides a structure for our perceptions; only through stories do facts assume any meaning whatsoever. This is why children everywhere ask, as soon as they have the command of language to do so, "Where did I come from?" and, shortly after, "What will happen when I die?" They require a story to give meaning to their existence. Without air, our cells die. Without a story, ourselves die.

Nations, as well as people, require stories and may die for lack of a believable one. In America we have told ourselves for two hundred years that our experiment in government is part of God's own plan. That has been a marvelous story, and it accounts for much of the success America has had. In the Soviet Union they have told themselves a different story: that their experiment in government is *history's* plan. And in seventy years their story has transported them into a position of worldwide importance. I have the impression that neither of these nations believes its story now—and woe unto both if they do not find some other. Nations need stories, just as people do, to provide themselves with a sense of continuity, or identity. But a story does even more than that. Without stories as organizing frameworks we are swamped by the volume of our own experience, adrift in a sea of facts. Merely listing them cannot help us, because without some tale to guide us there is no limit to the list. A story gives us direction by providing a kind of theory about how the world works—and how it needs to work if we are to survive. Without such a theory, such a tale, people have no idea what to do with information. They cannot even tell what is information and what is not.

It is odd that Bloom did not see that the student uprisings of the late 1960s (which he detested) were an attempt to construct a new story for a changing world—a world paradoxically made smaller by new technologies of information and destruction but at the same time larger than ever. It is even odder that he rejects the need of the young to construct such a story to help them sort through the collection of disconnected, fragmented diploma requirements that is called a curriculum at most universities. It is odd because that is what Bloom's complaint is really about: the fact that our younger people have no stories to guide them in managing the information of their culture and directing their education. He wants them to go back to the great books because they may find there the stories that have in the past given coherence and purpose to learning.

Perhaps that will work. But it will not, I think, unless the young are helped to reread those tales, to reconstruct them in light of the problems of our own times. They will not be helped by a dogged insistence that what was good enough for Plato and Cicero and the German idealists and even for Allan Bloom is good enough for them. It isn't. The purposes we conceive for learning are tied to our larger conception of the world, and the problems we face, and the way we have developed our story at a given time. Does one learn for the greater glory of God? to bring honor to one's family or tribe? for the fulfillment of a nation's destiny? to hasten the triumph of the proletariat? Few today find such purposes meaningful, because few believe anymore in the larger stories from which these purposes derive. Even fewer, I think, believe in the story of technological progress, which tells of a paradise to be gained through bigger and better machines. And the yuppie's tale, the story that tells us that life's most meaningful activity is to buy things, is an impoverished one indeed, which leads, in the end, to cynicism and hopelessness. Even the great modern story known as inductive science is not now as gripping as it once seemed. To the question "Where did we come from?" science answers, "It was an accident." To the question "How will it all end?" science's handmaiden, technology, answers, "Probably by an accident." And more and more of our young are finding that the accidental life is scarcely worth living.

I am not wise enough to say where the young can find what they need. Is it possible that all America can offer them is a list of names and places, and a shopping bag of books about the world as people conceived it in long-ago places and times? That, and the advice "JUST SAY NO" to drugs? Who will help them find out what they need to say yes to? How can they be helped to read, and write, a coherent story for our times? That is the educational issue of our era. And that is why Hirsch and Bloom are worth reading. Hirsch's book is useful to us because, unknowingly, he makes apparent the questions we need to answer. Bloom's book is useful to us because he suggests a solution. He believes that the texts that provided him with a sense of moral and intellectual purpose will serve for everyone. This is mere arrogance and can be disregarded. But we should thank him for reminding us that education must have a purpose, and a purpose connected to some larger, coherent tale. If we cannot find a way to help our students discover such a purpose, by constructing a meaningful tale, they are very likely to remain culturally illiterate—not because they do not know what is on Hirsch's list but because it won't make any difference if they do.

Understanding and Interpretation

1. What is Hirsch's *Cultural Literacy* about, and what is wrong with the book, according to Postman?

2. What are the banal truths of Hirsch's book?

3. What does Postman think is "startling and false" about Hirsch's book?

4. What are Postman's two reasons for disagreeing with Hirsch?

5. Why is Hirsch's solution untenable, according to Postman?

6. What are the right questions, according to Postman?

7. What is Bloom's book about, and what is right about it, according to Postman?

8. What does Postman think is wrong with Bloom's book?

9. What is the purpose of stories, according to Postman?

10. What is Postman's tone in the first paragraph? What is the opening metaphor? What is Postman's attitude toward Hirsch and Bloom?

11. Read carefully to find *ad hominum* attacks on either Hirsch or Bloom. Is Postman's tone effective in promoting his argument? Why or why not? What is his attitude toward the reader? What is his attitude toward students?

12. How do the anecdotes about his children help to define his character as a writer?

13. Do you agree that we are "swamped by information"?

14. Do you find humor in this essay? If so, where?

15. Do you find Postman's argument convincing? Why or why not?

Comparison

1. Compare Lopez's idea of story with Postman's idea of story. To what extent do they agree? In what ways, if any, do they differ about the meaning and value of storytelling?

2. Read the essays by Carr, Fitzgerald, and Kuhn. Do you see traces of their arguments in Postman's essay?

3. To what extent is Fussell's "The Real War 1939–1945" a story as Postman defines it?

4. Read Gould's "Streak of Streaks." Apply Postman's theory about stories to Gould's analysis of DiMaggio's hitting streak. What story does Gould tell about the modern world?

5. Read the essays by Chesterton, Eliot, Lippmann, and Fukuyama. What kind of national story does each one propose?

6. Compare the tone offered in the essays by Snow, Leavis, and Postman. What characteristics do they share? How are they different? What strategies would you adapt in your own writing and what ones would you avoid?

Woody Allen
(1935–)

Born December 1, 1935, Allan Stewart Konigsberg attended movies as often as six or seven times a week while growing up in a "lower middle-class" Jewish neighborhood in his native New York. During an interview for *Wild Man Blues*, he remarked: "People say to me, 'Why is it that your films do so well in Europe, all over Europe, and not very well in the United States?' You know Steven Spielberg said that he likes to make the films that he liked when he was a kid...and I feel the same way." Although he enjoyed American comedies, the films Allen loved best during his childhood were often European.

"You couldn't see very many foreign films during the war," he said in an interview with Stig Björkman, "[b]ut then, after the war, I started to see the really great European masterpieces." While he often attended films with his cousin, Allen became increasingly solitary and misanthropic after the age of five. (According to biographer Eric Lax, no one in the family can say exactly why.) Both public school and Hebrew school functioned as interruptions of his true loves, most of them solitary pursuits: film, music, sports, and writing. "I've always said that I could write before I could read," Allen told Björkman. Some of his earliest works were short stories, but he also wrote plays, and, soon enough, jokes.

As an adolescent, Allen discovered jazz music, taking up the saxophone and the ukulele before settling on the clarinet. He also discovered magic, trying to make his break by auditioning for magic shows on television. His break came instead with his jokes, which he sent to newspaper columnists in the 1950s, after choosing the name Woody Allen for his life in show business. He was in high school when the first jokes found their way into print. As Lax explains, "At the end of [Earl] Wilson's column on November 25, 1952, Allan Konigsberg's pseudonym made its big-time debut with a line about the Office of Price Stabilization, a World War II leftover that kept prices under control: 'Woody Allen figured out what OPS prices are—Over People's Salaries.'" Appearing in Wilson's column led to Allen's first job: writing one-liners for celebrities to make them appear witty in the gossip columns. In 1953, after he graduated from high school, he made a disastrous attempt at college for the sake of his parents and was essentially expelled from New York University. Between 1953 and 1955—Allen scholars cannot seem to agree when—NBC brought Allen into their "new writers' development program," as Lax describes it, and he moved to Hollywood to write for *The Colgate Comedy Hour.* Before the show dissolved, he proposed to Harlene Rosen, a pianist three years his junior who had played with him in New York. The marriage did not endure.

Spotted during a stand-up routine in 1964, according to critic Nancy Pogel, Allen was invited to write a film script. He wrote and acted in *What's New, Pussy Cat?* (1965), but the film's director did not share his vision, and Allen detested the final product. He said to Björkman, "I vowed at that time I would never write another film script, unless I could be the director of the film." Before he directed for the first time, he married actor Louise Lasser and collaborated with her and others on *What's Up, Tiger Lily?* (1966), a Japanese film dubbed into English with an absurd, new plot. Although the film proved successful, Allen told Björkman that he originally "sued the producer to try to keep the movie from coming out" because he thought it "stupid and juvenile." After publishing in *The New Yorker* and writing his first independent play,

Don't Drink the Water (1967), Allen directed for the first time in 1969 with *Take the Money and Run*. In the same year he wrote *Play It Again, Sam* for the stage. Having split from Louise Lasser, Allen began a one-year relationship with actress Diane Keaton, who appeared with him in his play.

In the early 1970s, as he directed films like *Bananas* and *Everything You Always Wanted to Know about Sex But Were Afraid to Ask* (1972) and adapted *Play It Again, Sam* for the screen, Allen also published his first book, a collection of essays and stories called *Getting Even*(1971). His second book, *Without Feathers*, appeared in 1975, two years before his first major film, *Annie Hall*. In this film, Allen said, he stopped "clowning around"; he "had the courage to abandon...the safety of complete broad comedy." *Annie Hall* won several Oscars, one for Allen's directing, one for Keaton's acting, and one for the script (Allen co-wrote the film with Marshall Brickman). It also won a New York Film Critics Circle Award, which Allen received again for *Manhattan* (1979). At the end of 1979, he entered a long-term relationship with actor Mia Farrow, also twice divorced. Like Diane Keaton and Dianne Wiest, Farrow starred in many of his films, including *Zelig* (1983), *Broadway Danny Rose* (1984), *The Purple Rose of Cairo* (1985), and the Academy Award-winning *Hannah and Her Sisters* (1986). In 1986, Allen published another book, *The Lunatic's Tale*. In 1989, two years before he assembled his *Complete Prose* for publication, he directed *Crimes and Misdemeanors*. "There are certain movies of mine that I call 'novels on film,'" Allen has said, "and *Crimes and Misdemeanors* is one of them." Nominated for multiple Academy Awards, the film remains among Allen's best works.

In the 1990s, Allen directed *Alice* (1990), *Husbands and Wives* (1992), and *Manhattan Murder Mystery* (1993), which reinvents Alfred Hitchcock's *Rear Window* and uses, in its climax, scenes from one of Allen's favorite films, *Double Indemnity*. In 1995, he directed Mira Sorvino's Oscar-winning performance in *Mighty Aphrodite*. In 1997, he released *Deconstructing Harry* and married "the infamous Soon-Yi Previn," as he jokingly refers to her in *Wild Man Blues*, the 1998 documentary about his European tour with a New Orleans-style jazz group. In 1998, he also directed a work of his own, *Celebrity*.

Woody Allen has acquired fame around the world for writing and directing films about New York, as well as for creating and enacting characters whom many suspect are not unlike himself: neurotic, witty, sex-starved urban men who wallow in their insecurity, particularly in their fears about nature, death, and relationships. Beloved for his pure comedies, he has made successful forays into comedic drama with *Annie Hall* and *Crimes and Misdemeanors*. Although his dialogue feels so realistic that reviewers have mistaken scripted scenes for impromptu sessions among the actors, Allen is not bound to realism: a ghost returns to help the lovelorn in *Play It Again, Sam*, a character steps out of the silver screen to fall in love in *Purple Rose of Cairo*, and an entire Greek chorus bemoans the lead character's follies in *Mighty Aphrodite.* Allen's essays contain many of the same elements that first brought him fame, showing his talent for parody and his deceptively casual, conversational tone. Whatever the effect of Allen's personal choices on his professional reputation, he will remain a unique institution in twentieth-century filmmaking.

Random Reflections of a Second-Rate Mind (1990)

Dining at a fashionable restaurant on New York's chic Upper East Side, I noticed a Holocaust survivor at the next table. A man of sixty or so was showing his companions a number tattooed on his arm while I overheard him say he had gotten it at Auschwitz. He was graying and distinguished-looking with a sad, handsome face, and behind his eyes there was the predictable haunted look. Clearly he had suffered and gleaned deep lessons from his anguish. I heard him describe how he had been beaten and had watched his fellow inmates being hanged and gassed, and how he had scrounged around in the camp garbage for anything—a discarded potato peel—to keep his corpse-thin body from giving in to disease. As I eavesdropped I wondered: if an angel had come to him then, when he was scheming desperately not to be among those chosen for annihilation, and told him that one day he'd be sitting on Second Avenue in Manhattan in a trendy Italian restaurant amongst lovely young women in designer jeans, and that he'd be wearing a fine suit and ordering lobster salad and baked salmon, would he have grabbed the angel around the throat and throttled him in a sudden fit of insanity?

Talk about cognitive dissonance! All I could see as I hunched over my pasta were truncheons raining blows on his head as second after second dragged on in unrelieved agony and terror. I saw him weak and freezing—sick, bewildered, thirsty, and in tears, an emaciated zombie in stripes. Yet now here he was, portly and jocular, sending back the wine and telling the waiter it seemed to him slightly too tannic. I knew without a doubt then and there that no philosopher ever to come along, no matter how profound, could even begin to understand the world.

Later that night I recalled that at the end of Elie Wiesel's fine book *Night,* he said that when his concentration camp was liberated he and others thought first and foremost of food. Then of their families and next of sleeping with women, but not of revenge. He made the point several times that the inmates didn't think of revenge. I find it odd that I, who was a small boy during World War II and who lived in America, unmindful of any of the horror Nazi victims were undergoing, and who never missed a good meal with meat and potatoes and sweet desserts, and who had a soft, safe, warm bed to sleep in at night, and whose memories of those years are only blissful and full of good times and good music—that I think of nothing but revenge.

Confessions of a hustler. At ten I hustled dreidel. I practiced endlessly spinning the little lead top and could make the letters come up in my favor more often than not. After that I mercilessly contrived to play dreidel with kids and took their money.

"Let's play for two cents," I'd say, my eyes waxing wide and innocent like a big-time pool shark's. Then I'd lose the first game deliberately. After, I'd move the stakes up. Four cents, maybe six, maybe a dime. Soon the other kid would find himself en route home, gutted and muttering. Dreidel hustling got me through the fifth grade. I often had visions of myself turning pro. I wondered if when I got older I could play my generation's equivalent of Legs Diamond or Dutch Schultz for a hundred thousand a game. I saw myself bathed in won money, sitting around a green felt table or getting off great trains, my best dreidel in a smart carrying case as I went from city to city looking for action, always cleaning up, always drinking bourbon, always taking care of my precious manicured spinning hand.

On the cover of this magazine, under the title, is printed the line "A Bimonthly Jewish Critique of Politics, Culture & Society." But why a Jewish critique? Or a gentile critique? Or any limiting perspective? Why not simply a magazine with articles written by human beings for other humans to read? Aren't there enough real demarcations without creating artificial ones? After all, there's no biological difference between a Jew and a gentile despite what my Uncle Max says. We're talking here about exclusive clubs that serve no good purpose; they exist only to form barriers, trade commercially on human misery, and provide additional differences amongst people so they can further rationalize their natural distrust and aggression.

After all, you know by ten years old there's nothing bloodier or more phony than the world's religious history. What could be more awful than, say, Protestant versus Catholic in Northern Ireland? Or the late Ayatollah? Or the expensive cost of tickets to my local synagogue so my parents can pray on the high holidays? (In the end they could only afford to be seated downstairs, not in the main room, and the service was piped in to them. The smart money sat ringside, of course.) Is there anything uglier than families that don't want their children to marry loved ones because they're of the wrong religion? Or professional clergy whose pitch is as follows: "There is a God. Take my word for it. And I pretty much know what He wants and how to get on with Him and I'll try to help you to get and remain in His good graces, because that way your life won't be so fraught with terror. Of course, it's going to cost you a little for my time and stationery . . ."

Incidentally, I'm well aware that one day I may have to fight because I'm a Jew, or even die because of it, and no amount of professed apathy to religion will save me. On the other hand, those who say they want to kill me because I'm Jewish would find other reasons if I were not Jewish. I mean, think if there were no Jews or Catholics, or if everyone was white or German or American, if the earth was one country, one color; then endless new, creative rationalizations would emerge to kill "other people"—the lefthanded, those who prefer vanilla to strawberry, all baritones, any person who wears saddle shoes.

So what was my point before I digressed? Oh—do I really want to contribute to a magazine that subtly helps promulgate phony and harmful differences? (Here I must say that *Tikkun* appears to me as a generally wonderful journal—politically astute, insightful, and courageously correct on the Israeli-Palestinian issue.)

I experienced this type of ambivalence before when a group wanted me to front and raise money for the establishment of a strong pro-Israel political action committee. I don't approve of PACs, but I've always been a big rooter for Israel. I agonized over the decision and in the end I did front the PAC and helped them raise money and get going. Then, after they were off and running, I quietly slipped out. This was the compromise I made which I've never regretted. Still, I'd be happier contributing to *Tikkun* if it had a different line, or no line, under the title. After all, what if other magazines felt the need to employ their own religious perspectives? You might have: *Field and Stream: A Catholic Critique of Fishing and Hunting.* This month: "Angling for Salmon as You Baptize."

I have always preferred women to men. This goes back to the Old Testament where the ladies have it all over their cowering, pious counterparts. Eve knew the consequences when she ate the apple. Adam would have been content to just follow orders and live on like a mindless sybarite. But Eve knew it was better to acquire knowledge even if it meant grasping her mortality with all its accompanying anxiety. I'm personally glad men and women run to cover up their nakedness. It makes undressing someone much more exciting. And with the necessity of people having to earn their livings by the sweat of their brows we have a much more interesting and creative world. Much more fascinating than the sterile Garden of Eden, which I always picture existing in the soft-focus glow of a beer commercial.

I also had a crush on Lot's wife.[1] When she looked back at the destruction of Sodom and Gomorrah she knew she was disobeying God. But she did it anyway. And she knew what a cruel, vindictive character He was. So it must have been very important to her to look back. But why? To see what? Well, I think to see her lover. The man she was having an extramarital affair with. And wouldn't you if you were married to Lot? This self-righteous bore, this paragon of virtue in a corrupt, swinging city. Can you imagine life with this dullard? Living only to please God. Resisting all the temptations that made Sodom and Gomorrah pulsate with vitality. The one good man in the city. Indeed. Of course she was making it with someone else. But who? Some used-idol salesman? Who knows? But I like to think she felt passion for a human being while Lot felt it only for the deep, pontificating voice of the creator of the universe. So naturally she was crushed when they had to leave town in a hurry. And as God destroyed all the bars and broke up all the poker games and the sinners went up in smoke, and as Lot tiptoed for the border, holding the skirts of his robes high to avoid tripping, Mrs. Lot turned to see her beloved *cinque à sept*[2] one more time and that's when unfortunately the Almighty, in his infinite forgiveness, turned her into a seasoning.

So that leaves Job's wife.[3] My favorite woman in all of literature. Because when her cringing, put-upon husband asked the Lord "Why me?" and the Lord told him to shut up and mind his own business and that he shouldn't even dare ask, Job accepted it, but the Missus, already in the earth at that point, had previously scored with a quotable line of unusual dignity and one that Job would have been far too obsequious to come up with: "Curse God and die" was the way she put it. And I loved her for it because she was too much of her own person to let herself be shamelessly abused by some vain and sadistic Holy Spirit.

I was amazed at how many intellectuals took issue with me over a piece I wrote a while back for the *New York Times* saying I was against the practice of Israeli soldiers going

---

[1]*Lot's wife* a reference to an Old Testament tale from Genesis. When God was preparing to destroy Sodom and Gomorra for the depravity of their people, Lot and his family were spared on the condition that they leave quickly and not look back. Lot's wife turned to look at the city and was changed to a pillar of salt.

[2]*cinque a sept* French for 5–7, cocktail time.

[3]*Job's wife* a reference to the Book of Job in the Old Testament, which is attributed to Job, the book's principal character. In it, Satan proposes that God test Job by inflicting misfortune on him. Because Job refuses to curse God, he is eventually rewarded by increased wealth, family, and a long life.

door-to-door and randomly breaking the hands of Palestinians as a method of combating the intifada.[4] I said also I was against the too-quick use of real bullets before other riot control methods were tried. I was for a more flexible attitude on negotiating land for peace. All things I felt to be not only more in keeping with Israel's high moral stature but also in its own best interest. I never doubted the correctness of my feelings and I expected all who read it to agree. Visions of a Nobel danced in my head and, in truth, I had even formulated the first part of my acceptance speech. Now, I have frequently been accused of being a self-hating Jew, and while it's true I am Jewish and I don't like myself very much, it's not because of my persuasion. The reasons lie in totally other areas—like the way I look when I get up in the morning, or that I can never read a road map. In retrospect, the fact that I did not win a peace prize but became an object of some derision was what I should have expected.

"How can you criticize a place you've never been to?" a cabbie asked me. I pointed out I'd never been many places whose politics I took issue with, like Cuba for instance. But this line of reasoning cut no ice.

"Who are you to speak up?" was a frequent question in my hate mail. I replied I was an American citizen and a human being, but neither of these affiliations carried enough weight with the outraged.

The most outlandish cut of all was from the Jewish Defense League, which voted me Pig of the Month. How they misunderstood me! If only they knew how close some of my inner rages have been to theirs. (In my movie *Manhattan*, for example, I suggested breaking up a Nazi rally not with anything the ACLU[5] would approve, but with baseball bats.)

But it was the intellectuals, some of them close friends, who hated most of all that I had made my opinions public on such a touchy subject. And yet, despite all their evasions and circumlocutions, the central point seemed to me inescapable: Israel was not responding correctly to this new problem.

"The Arabs are guilty for the Middle East mess, the bloodshed, the terrorism, with no leader to even try to negotiate with," reasoned the typical thinker.

"True," I agreed with Socratic simplicity.

"Victims of the Holocaust deserve a homeland, a place to be free and safe."

"Absolutely." I was totally in accord.

"We can't afford disunity. Israel is in a precarious situation." Here I began to feel uneasy, because we can afford disunity.

"Do you want the soldiers going door-to-door and breaking hands?" I asked, cutting to the kernel of my complaint.

"Of course not."

"So?"

"I'd still rather you hadn't written that piece." Now I'd be fidgeting in my chair, waiting for a cogent rebuttal to the breaking of hands issue. "Besides," my opponent argued, "the *Times* prints only one side."

"But even the Israeli press—"

---

[4]*intifada* uprising in the Palestinian occupied territories of the Gaza Strip and the West Bank from 1987 to 1993, in protest against the Israeli occupation and politics.

[5]*ACLU* American Civil Liberties Union, a law firm founded by Roger Baldwin in 1920, which devotes itself to defending the first amendment right to free speech.

"You shouldn't have spoken out," he interrupted.

"Many Israelis agree," I said, "and moral issues apart, why hand the Arabs a needless propaganda victory?"

"Yes, yes, but still you shouldn't have said anything. I was disappointed in you." Much talk followed by both of us about the origins of Israel, the culpability of Arab terrorists, the fact there's no one in charge of the enemy to negotiate with, but in the end it always came down to them saying, "You shouldn't have spoken up," and me saying, "But do you think they should randomly break hands?" and them adding, "Certainly not—but I'd still feel better if you had just not written that piece."

My mother was the final straw. She cut me out of her will and then tried to kill herself just to hasten my realization that I was getting no inheritance.

At fifteen I received as a gift a pair of cuff links with a William Steig[6] cartoon on them. A man with a spear through his body was pictured and the accompanying caption read, "People are no damn good." A generalization, an oversimplification, and yet it was the only way I ever could get my mind around the Holocaust. Even at fifteen I used to read Anne Frank's line about people being basically good and place it on a par with Will Rogers's[7] pandering nonsense, "I never met a man I didn't like."

The questions for me were not: How could a civilized people, and especially the people of Goethe[8] and Mozart, do what they did to another people? And how could the world remain silent? Remain silent and indeed close their doors to millions who could have, with relative simplicity, been plucked from the jaws of agonizing death? At fifteen I felt I knew the answers. If you went with the Anne Frank idea or the Will Rogers line, I reasoned as an adolescent, of course the Nazi horrors became unfathomable. But if you paid more attention to the line on the cuff links, no matter how unpleasant that caption was to swallow, things were not so mysterious.

After all, I had read about all those supposedly wonderful neighbors throughout Europe who lived beside Jews lovingly and amiably. They shared laughter and fun and the same experiences I shared with my community and friends. And I read, also, how they turned their backs on the Jews instantly when it became the fashion and even looted their homes when they were left empty by sudden departure to the camps. This mystery that had confounded all my relatives since World War II was not such a puzzle if I understood that inside every heart lived the worm of self-preservation, of fear, greed, and an animal will to power. And the way I saw it, it was nondiscriminating. It abided in gentile or Jew, black, white, Arab, European, or American. It was part of who we all were, and that the Holocaust could occur was not at all so strange. History had been filled with unending examples of equal bestiality, differing only cosmetically.

The real mystery that got me through my teen years was that every once in a while one found an act of astonishing decency and sacrifice. One heard of people who risked their lives and their family's lives to save lives of people they didn't even know. But these were the rare exceptions, and in the end there were not enough humane acts to keep six million from being murdered.

---

[6]*William Steig* (1907–) American artist, cartoonist, writer whose work was often found in the magazine *The New Yorker* and who also wrote and illustrated children's books.

[7]*Will Rogers* (1879–1935) American humorist, author, and actor.

[8]*Goethe* Johann Wolfgang von Goethe (1749–1832) a German poet, dramatist, and scientist.

I still own those cuff links. They're in a shoe box along with a lot of memorabilia from my teens. Recently I took them out and looked at them and all these thoughts returned to me. Perhaps I'm not quite as sure of all I was sure of at fifteen, but the waffling may come from just being middle-aged and not as virile. Certainly little has occurred since then to show me much different.

Understanding and Analysis

1. Aside from in the title, when in this essay do you first notice any humor?
2. How does the title connect to the first three paragraphs?
3. Other than in the fourth and fifth paragraphs, where does the idea of gambling occur in the essay? What connections does Allen make between Allen as hustler and Allen as thinker?
4. What does Allen believe about aggression and prejudice?
5. What issues does he claim make him ambivalent?
6. On what issues in this essay is he not ambivalent?
7. On at least three occasions in the essay Allen describes his fantasies—what are they and how do they connect with each other?
8. In the dialogue with his detractors, how does Allen characterize his opponent?
9. Where does Allen become "uneasy" in the dialogue? Why?
10. What positions does Allen take that are likely to offend his readers?
11. Is Woody Allen funny in this essay? If so, where? Does his humor help to make his positions easier to accept? What techniques does he use? What techniques other than humor does he use to appeal to his potential opponents?

Comparison

1. Read the essays by Parker, Thurber, and Baker. What, if any, characteristics do these humorists share with Allen?
2. Read the essay by Adrienne Rich. What, if anything, does she have in common with Woody Allen? How has each been affected by requests for silence?
3. Read the essay by Postman. Does Postman's analysis help you interpret Allen's essay? If so, how?
4. Read Gould's "Streak of Streaks." On what issues do Allen and Gould agree?
5. Read Tuchman's essay on the Black Death. What might Allen's opponents use from Tuchman's essay to argue with Allen. How might Allen respond?

Amy Tan
(1952–)

Amy Tan was born in Oakland, California, in 1952. Her father, John, was a Baptist minister as well as an electrical engineer. Her mother, Daisy, had been married first to an abusive man, whom she divorced. In 1949, after her remarriage, John and Daisy immigrated to the United States from China to escape the Communist take-over of Beijing. According to one on-line anonymous biographer, Daisy had to leave behind her three daughters from her first marriage because she lost custody of them in the divorce. In the United States, Daisy and John had three children, Amy and two sons. After Amy's father and oldest brother died within a year of each other from brain tumors, Amy's mother took Amy and her surviving brother to Switzerland.

Like many adolescents, to achieve her own identity Amy rebelled against her mother's expectations, first by leaving the Baptist college her mother had selected and then by following her boyfriend to San Jose State University, where she earned a B.A. and M.A. in English and linguistics. Despite her teachers' opinion that she was better in math than English, and despite her mother's hopes that she would become a neurosurgeon and concert pianist "on the side," Tan enrolled in the doctoral program in linguistics at the University of California at Santa Cruz and then at Berkeley. She married her boyfriend, Louis DeMattei, a tax lawyer, in 1974, and two years later left the Ph.D. program to work as a language consultant for disabled children.

Next she went into business as a writer of speeches for executives in large corporations. Later, finding the business side of her life lucrative but not creative, Tan began writing fiction. When she published a story in *Seventeen*, it caught the eye of a literary agent who encouraged her to keep writing. But it was not until Tan had visited China that she resolved to quit the world of business to become a full-time writer. In 1987, Tan took her mother on a trip to China to see the children she had left behind and to attend her granddaughter's wedding. There Tan discovered for herself the world her parents had fled in their search for freedom. This trip inspired her first book, *The Joy Luck Club* (1989), a series of sixteen stories told by four mothers and their American-born daughters. It was such a huge success that Tan began to doubt her ability to write a second, especially since so many people she met plied her with stories of failed second books. In "Angst & the Second Novel" (1991) Tan describes the result of all the pressure: "I developed a pain in my neck, which later radiated to my jaw, resulting in constant gnashing, then two cracked teeth and, finally, a huge dental bill. The pain then migrated down my back...And while I was struggling to sit in my chair, with hot packs wrapped around my waist, I did not actually write fiction: I wrote speeches—30, 40, 50 speeches . . ." about the first book.

When she did finally get down to writing the second book, she had to begin and discard five different ones, having written between 30 and 88 pages of each failure, before she finally found the right character and the right story. Even then, however, she rewrote 150 pages and "felt sick for about a week" before the second book, *The Kitchen God's Wife* (1991) was well underway. Since then, Tan has published two children's books, *The Moon Lady* (1992) and *The Chinese Siamese Cat* (1994), and another novel, *The Hundred Secret Senses* (1995).

In addition to these books, numerous speeches, and "Angst & the Second Novel," Tan has published several essays including "Fish Cheeks" (1987), "Watching China" (1989), "Mother Tongue" (1990) (originally a speech delivered in 1989), and "The Language of Discretion" (1990), which is included in this text. Amy Tan lives in San Francisco with her husband, a cat named Sagwa, and a dog named Mr. Zo. She and her friends have started their own club, where they exchange "investment tips" as well as gossip, and have named it Fool and His Money.

However suffused her life has been by things Chinese, Amy Tan considers herself an American, concerned with the development of herself as an individual, "wary," according to one interviewer, "of 'being cast as a spokesperson' for all Asian Americans." As she says in "Mother Tongue," Tan is "fascinated by language," pleased by the artfulness and beauty of the several "Englishes" she knows. In "Fish Cheeks" Tan employs her novelist's eye to surprise the reader into an awareness of what it feels like to be someone else, to imagine what a single event might seem like to a minister's son, her mother, herself. In "The Language of Discretion" Tan employs her linguist's ear to analyze linguistic stereotypes. For Tan, only through multiple perspectives can we discover the various and sometimes conflicting truths about family, loyalty, and the imagination.

THE LANGUAGE OF DISCRETION (1990)

AT A RECENT family dinner in San Francisco, my mother whispered to me: "Sau-sau [Brother's Wife] pretends too hard to be polite! Why bother? In the end, she always takes everything."

My mother thinks like a *waixiao*, an expatriate, temporarily away from China since 1949, no longer patient with ritual courtesies. As if to prove her point, she reached across the table to offer my elderly aunt from Beijing the last scallop from the Happy Family seafood dish.

Sau-sau scowled. "*B'yao, zhen b'yao!*" (I don't want it, really I don't!) she cried, patting her plump stomach.

"Take it! Take it!" scolded my mother in Chinese.

"Full, I'm already full," Sau-sau protested weakly, eyeing the beloved scallop.

"Ai!" exclaimed my mother, completely exasperated. "Nobody else wants it. If you don't take it, it will only rot!"

At this point, Sau-sau sighed, acting as if she were doing my mother a big favor by taking the wretched scrap off her hands.

My mother turned to her brother, a high-ranking communist official who was visiting her in California for the first time: "In America a Chinese person could starve to death. If you say you don't want it, they won't ask you again forever."

My uncle nodded and said he understood fully: Americans take things quickly because they have no time to be polite.

• • •

I thought about this misunderstanding again—of social contexts failing in translation—when a friend sent me an article from the *New York Times Magazine* (24 April 1988). The article, on changes in New York's Chinatown, made passing reference to the inherent ambivalence of the Chinese language.

Chinese people are so "discreet and modest," the article stated, there aren't even words for "yes" and "no."

That's not true, I thought, although I can see why an outsider might think that. I continued reading.

If one is Chinese, the article went on to say, "One compromises, one doesn't hazard a loss of face by an overemphatic response."

My throat seized. Why do people keep saying these things? As if we truly were those little dolls sold in Chinatown tourist shops, heads bobbing up and down in complacent agreement to anything said!

I worry about the effect of one-dimensional statements on the unwary and guileless. When they read about this so-called vocabulary deficit, do they also conclude that Chinese people evolved into a mild-mannered lot because the language only allowed them to hobble forth with minced words?

Something enormous is always lost in translation. Something insidious seeps into the gaps, especially when amateur linguists continue to compare, one-for-one, language differences and then put forth notions wide open to misinterpretation: that Chinese people have no direct linguistic means to make decisions, assert or deny, affirm or negate, just say no to drug dealers, or behave properly on the witness stand when told, "Please answer yes or no."

Yet one can argue, with the help of renowned linguists, that the Chinese are indeed up a creek without "yes" and "no." Take any number of variations on the old language-and-reality theory stated years ago by Edward Sapir: "Human beings . . . are very much at the mercy of the particular language which has become the medium for their society. . . . The fact of the matter is that the 'real world' is to a large extent built up on the language habits of the group."[1]

[1] Edward Sapir, *Selected Writings,* ed. D. G. Mandelbaum (Berkeley and Los Angeles, 1949). [Tan's note]

This notion was further bolstered by the famous Sapir-Whorf hypothesis, which roughly states that one's perception of the world and how one functions in it depends a great deal on the language used. As Sapir, Whorf, and new carriers of the banner would have us believe, language shapes our thinking, channels us along certain patterns embedded in words, syntactic structures, and intonation patterns. Language has become the peg and the shelf that enables us to sort out and categorize the world. In English, we see "cats" and "dogs"; what if the language had also specified *glatz,* meaning "animals that leave fur on the sofa," and *glotz,* meaning "animals that leave fur and drool on the sofa"? How would language, the enabler, have changed our perceptions with slight vocabulary variations?

And if this were the case—of language being the master of destined thought—think of the opportunities lost from failure to evolve two little words, *yes* and *no,* the simplest of opposites! Ghenghis Khan could have been sent back to Mongolia. Opium wars might have been averted. The Cultural Revolution could have been sidestepped.

There are still many, from serious linguists to pop psychology cultists, who view language and reality as inextricably tied, one being the consequence of the other. We have traversed the range from the Sapir-Whorf hypothesis to est and neurolinguistic programming, which tell us "you are what you say."

I too have been intrigued by the theories. I can summarize, albeit badly, ages-old empirical evidence: of Eskimos and their infinite ways to say "snow," their ability to see the differences in snowflake configurations, thanks to the richness of their vocabulary, while non-Eskimo speakers like myself founder in "snow," "more snow," and "lots more where that came from."

I too have experienced dramatic cognitive awakenings via the word. Once I added "mauve" to my vocabulary I began to see it everywhere. When I learned how to pronounce *prix fixe,* I ate French food at prices better than the easier-to-say *à la carte* choices.

But just how seriously are we supposed to take this?

Sapir said something else about language and reality. It is the part that often gets left behind in the dot-dot-dots of quotes: ". . . No two languages are ever sufficiently similar to be considered as representing the same social reality. The worlds in which different societies live are distinct worlds, not merely the same world with different labels attached."

When I first read this, I thought, Here at last is validity for the dilemmas I felt growing up in a bicultural, bilingual family! As any child of immigrant parents knows, there's a special kind of double bind attached to knowing two languages. My parents, for example, spoke to me in both Chinese and English; I spoke back to them in English.

"Amy-ah!" they'd call to me.

"What?" I'd mumble back.

"Do not question us when we call," they scolded me in Chinese. "It is not respectful."

"What do you mean?"

"Ai! Didn't we just tell you not to question?"

To this day, I wonder which parts of my behavior were shaped by Chinese, which by English. I am tempted to think, for example, that if I am of two minds on some matter it is due to the richness of my linguistic experiences, not to any personal tendencies toward wishy-washiness. But which mind says what?

Was it perhaps patience—developed through years of deciphering my mother's fractured English—that had me listening politely while a woman announced over the phone that I had won one of five valuable prizes? Was it respect—pounded in by the Chinese imperative to accept convoluted explanations—that had me agreeing that I might find it worthwhile to drive seventy-five miles to view a time-share resort? Could I have been at a loss for words when asked, "Wouldn't you like to win a Hawaiian cruise or perhaps a fabulous Star of India designed exclusively by Carter and Van Arpels?"

And when this same woman called back a week later, this time complaining that I had missed my appointment, obviously it was my type A language that kicked into gear and interrupted her. Certainly, my blunt denial—"Frankly I'm not interested"—was as American as apple pie. And when she said, "But it's in Morgan Hill," and I shouted, "Read my lips. I don't care if it's Timbuktu," you can be sure I said it with the precise intonation expressing both cynicism and disgust.

It's dangerous business, this sorting out of language and behavior. Which one is English? Which is Chinese? The categories manifest themselves: passive and aggressive, tentative and assertive, indirect and direct. And I realize they are just variations of the same theme: that Chinese people are discreet and modest.

Reject them all!

If my reaction is overly strident, it is because I cannot come across as too emphatic. I grew up listening to the same lines over and over again, like so many rote expressions repeated in an English phrase-book. And I too almost came to believe them.

Yet if I consider my upbringing more carefully, I find there was nothing discreet about the Chinese language I grew up with. My parents made everything abundantly clear. Nothing wishy-washy in their demands, no compromises accepted: "Of course you will become a famous neurosurgeon," they told me. "And yes, a concert pianist on the side."

In fact, now that I remember, it seems that the more emphatic outbursts always spilled over into Chinese: "Not that way! You must wash rice so not a single grain spills out."

I do not believe that my parents—both immigrants from mainland China—are an exception to the modest-and-discreet rule. I have only to look at the number of Chinese engineering students skewing minority ratios at Berkeley, MIT, and Yale. Certainly they were not raised by passive mothers and fathers who said, "It is up to you, my daughter. Writer, welfare recipient, masseuse, or molecular engineer—you decide."

And my American mind says, See, those engineering students weren't able to say no to their parents' demands. But then my Chinese mind remembers: Ah, but those parents all wanted their sons and daughters to be *pre-med.*

Having listened to both Chinese and English, I also tend to be suspicious of any comparisons between the two languages. Typically, one language—that of the person doing the comparing—is often used as the standard, the benchmark for a logical form of expression. And so the language being compared is always in danger of being judged deficient or superfluous, simplistic or unnecessarily complex, melodious or cacophonous. English speakers point out that Chinese is extremely difficult because it relies on variations in tone barely discernible to the human ear. By the same token, Chinese speakers tell me English is extremely difficult because it is inconsistent, a language of too many broken rules, of Mickey Mice and Donald Ducks.

Even more dangerous to my mind is the temptation to compare both language and behavior in translation. To listen to my mother speak English, one might think she has no concept of past or future tense, that she doesn't see the difference between singular and plural, that she is gender blind because she calls my husband "she." If one were not careful, one might also generalize that, based on the way my mother talks, all Chinese people take a circumlocutory route to get to the point. It is, in fact, my mother's idiosyncratic behavior to ramble a bit.

Sapir was right about differences between two languages and their realities. I can illustrate why word-for-word translation is not enough to translate meaning and intent. I once received a letter from China which I read to non-Chinese speaking friends. The letter, originally written in Chinese, had been translated by my brother-in law in Beijing. One portion described the time when my uncle at age ten discovered his widowed mother (my grandmother) had remarried—as a number three concubine, the ultimate disgrace for an honorable family. The translated version of my uncle's letter read in part:

> In 1925, I met my mother in Shanghai. When she came to me, I didn't have greeting to her as if seeing nothing. She pull me to a corner secretly and asked me why didn't have greeting to her. I couldn't control myself and cried, "Ma! Why did you leave us? People told me: one day you ate a beancake yourself. Your sister in-law found it and sweared at you, called your names. So . . . is it true?" She clasped my hand and answered immediately, "It's not true, don't say what like this." After this time, there was a few chance to meet her.

"What!" cried my friends. "Was eating a beancake so terrible?"

Of course not. The beancake was simply a euphemism; a ten-year-old boy did not dare question his mother on something as shocking as concubinage. Eating a beancake was his equivalent for committing this selfish act, something inconsiderate of all family members, hence, my grandmother's despairing response to what seemed like a ludicrous charge of gluttony. And sure enough, she was banished from the family, and my uncle saw her only a few times before her death.

While the above may fuel people's argument that Chinese is indeed a language of extreme discretion, it does not mean that Chinese people speak in secrets and riddles. The contexts are fully understood. It is only to those on the *outside* that the language seems cryptic, the behavior inscrutable.

I am, evidently, one of the outsiders. My nephew in Shanghai, who recently started taking English lessons, has been writing me letters in English. I had told him I was a fiction writer, and so in one letter he wrote, "Congratulate to you on your writing. Perhaps one day I should like to read it." I took it in the same vein as "Perhaps one day we can get together for lunch." I sent back a cheery note. A month went by and another letter arrived from Shanghai. "Last one perhaps I hadn't writing distinctly," he said. "In the future, you'll send a copy of your works for me."

I try to explain to my English-speaking friends that Chinese language use is more *strategic* in manner, whereas English tends to be more direct; an American business executive may say, "Let's make a deal," and the Chinese manager may reply, "Is your son interested in learning about your widget business?" Each to his or her own purpose, each with his or her own linguistic path. But I hesitate to add more to the pile of generalizations, because no matter how many examples I provide and explain, I fear that it appears defensive and only reinforces the image: that Chinese people are "discreet and modest"— and it takes an American to explain what they really mean.

Why am I complaining? The description seems harmless enough (after all, the *New York Times Magazine* writer did not say "slippery and evasive"). It is precisely the bland, easy acceptability of the phrase that worries me.

I worry that the dominant society may see Chinese people from a limited—and limiting—perspective. I worry that seemingly benign stereotypes may be part of the reason there are few Chinese in top management positions, in mainstream political roles. I worry about the power of language: that if one says anything enough times—in any language— it might become true.

Could this be why Chinese friends of my parents' generation are willing to accept the generalization?

"Why are you complaining?" one of them said to me. "If people think we are modest and polite, let them think that. Wouldn't Americans be pleased to admit they are thought of as polite?"

And I do believe anyone would take the description as a compliment—at first. But after a while, it annoys, as if the only things that people heard one say were phatic remarks: "I'm so pleased to meet you. I've heard many wonderful things about you. For me? You shouldn't have!"

These remarks are not representative of new ideas, honest emotions, or considered thought. They are what is said from the polite distance of social contexts: of greetings, farewells, wedding thank-you notes, convenient excuses, and the like.

It makes me wonder though. How many anthropologists, how many sociologists, how many travel journalists have documented so-called "natural interactions" in foreign lands, all observed with spiral notebook in hand? How many other cases are there of the long-lost primitive tribe, people who turned out to be sophisticated enough to put on the stone-age show that ethnologists had come to see?

And how many tourists fresh off the bus have wandered into Chinatown expecting the self-effacing shopkeeper to admit under duress that the goods are not worth the price asked? I have witnessed it.

"I don't know," the tourist said to the shopkeeper, a Cantonese woman in her fifties. "It doesn't look genuine to me. I'll give you three dollars."

"You don't like my price, go somewhere else," said the shopkeeper.

"You are not a nice person," cried the shocked tourist, "not a nice person at all!"

"Who say I have to be nice," snapped the shopkeeper.

"So how does one say 'yes' and 'no' in Chinese?" ask my friends a bit warily.

And here I do agree in part with the *New York Times Magazine* article. There is no one word for "yes" or "no"—but not out of necessity to be discreet. If anything, I would say the Chinese equivalent of answering "yes" or "no" is dis*crete,* that is, specific to what is asked.

Ask a Chinese person if he or she has eaten, and he or she might say *chrle* (eaten already) or perhaps *meiyou* (have not).

Ask, "So you had insurance at the time of the accident?" and the response would be *dwei* (correct) or *meiyou* (did not have).

Ask, "Have you stopped beating your wife?" and the answer refers directly to the proposition being asserted or denied: stopped already, still have not, never beat, have no wife.

What could be clearer?

As for those who are still wondering how to translate the language of discretion, I offer this personal example.

My aunt and uncle were about to return to Beijing after a three-month visit to the United States. On their last night I announced I wanted to take them out to dinner.

"Are you hungry?" I asked in Chinese.

"Not hungry," said my uncle promptly, the same response he once gave me ten minutes before he suffered a low-blood-sugar attack.

"Not too hungry," said my aunt. "Perhaps you're hungry?"

"A little," I admitted.

"We can eat, we can eat," they both consented.

"What kind of food?" I asked.

"Oh, doesn't matter. Anything will do. Nothing fancy, just some simple food is fine."

"Do you like Japanese food? We haven't had that yet," I suggested.

They looked at each other.

"We can eat it," said my uncle bravely, this survivor of the Long March.

"We have eaten it before," added my aunt. "Raw fish."

"Oh, you don't like it?" I said. "Don't be polite. We can go somewhere else."

"We are not being polite. We can eat it," my aunt insisted.

So I drove them to Japantown and we walked past several restaurants featuring colorful plastic displays of sushi.

"Not this one, not this one either," I continued to say, as if searching for a Japanese restaurant similar to the last. "Here it is," I finally said, turning into a restaurant famous for its Chinese fish dishes from Shandong.

"Oh, Chinese food!" cried my aunt, obviously relieved.

My uncle patted my arm. "You think Chinese."

"It's your last night here in America," I said. "So don't be polite. Act like an American."

And that night we ate a banquet.

Understanding and Analysis

1. Much of this essay takes place through dialogue. Why is dialogue especially appropriate here?

2. What does the New York *Times Magazine* article say about the Chinese language?

3. What specifically are Tan's reactions when reading the article? Where else in her essay does the article appear?

4. What image is Tan evoking in the words "hobble forth with minced words"?

5. Does Tan agree with the "Sapir-Whorf hypothesis"? What is your evidence?

6. What else does Sapir say that is less well known, according to Tan? Is that statement different from those attributed to Sapir and Whorf earlier in the essay? If so, how? If not, why not? What is her attitude toward that statement? What is your evidence?

7. What do the anecdotes about Tan's responses over the phone contribute to her argument?

8. What all does Tan reject in the "emphatic" single-sentence paragraph?

9. Why is Tan "suspicious of any comparisons between" Chinese and English?

10. What does the translated letter from her uncle actually say? What does it mean? What point does Tan illustrate through the letter?

11. What does Tan mean when she says that "Chinese language use is more *strategic* in manner, whereas English tends to be more direct"? Note carefully the modifications in that assertion. How do they shape the meaning of the assertion?

12. What is Tan's main point?

Comparison

1. Read Baldwin's essay on language. To what extent do Tan and Baldwin agree, if at all?

2. Read the essay by Gates. Compare his views of the shaping influence of language with those of Tan.

3. Read Gardner's essay on Mead's interpretations of behavior in Samoa. What causes Tan and Gardner to be suspicious of the translations of behavior foreign to the recorder?

4. Read Rich's essay on identity. To what degree does Tan also appear to be "split at the root"? What are the benefits and liabilities of a dual identity for each author?

John Preston
(1945–1994)

John Preston was born on December 11, 1945. Growing up in Medfield, Massachusetts, he learned from his mother, Nancy Blood Preston, that members of his family had been living in Medfield since the time of his great-great-grandfather, Raymond Blood, in whose honor every generation since has contained another Raymond Blood. "Anyone who married into our family," Preston understood from his mother, "moved to Medfield and settled there to raise their children, just as my father had moved to our rural community from his home in Boston." The sense of place and belonging Preston took from this story inspired him to create communities for others when he became an adult. While he was still a teenager, he began to need a community for himself, some kind of writing or some set of people that openly acknowledged gay life and contributed to his understanding of being a gay man. As he explains in his Introduction to *Flesh and the Word*, pornography, quietly purchased from a newsstand in Harvard Square, played an important role in his development.

Graduating from Medfield High School in 1963, Preston writes in *Winter's Light*, he was expected to attend college: "My parents' expectations of their own upward mobility counted on my generation's continued climb up the social ladder by getting at least an undergraduate degree." He earned that degree in 1968 from Lake Forest College in Illinois. While the school's distance from home assisted in the painful process of hiding his sexuality from his family, its midwestern gentility made him feel out of place as a working-class New Englander. After graduation, he made the first of many moves in the coming years, settling in Boston and beginning a relationship with a man who committed suicide "after telling me that being queer was just too difficult." Refusing to see suicide as a "standard option" in the life of a gay man,

Preston determined "to find some people who would help me change the world." In 1969, he moved to Minneapolis and helped to found a community center, Gay House, which he co-directed until 1972. The following year, after starting Gay Community Services, he became a Certified Sexual Health Consultant through the University of Minnesota. At the age of 29, he moved to San Francisco and became the editor of *The Advocate*. Although he worked with written material 18 hours a day, it was not until he moved to New York two years later that he began to conceive of himself as "an originator," possibly even "a writer."

Preston's first work was a pornographic "short story that rambled on for twenty or so pages," which he sent to *Drummer*. Anticipating that he might never hear back, he "got a call at work only two days later from the publisher, John Embry," asking him to expand that short story into a novel that *Drummer* could publish serially. "The result," Preston says, "was *Mr. Benson*," a work concerned with the relationship between a character named Jamie and the man who becomes his master. In spite of some radical differences in content, installments of *Mr. Benson* prompted associations with Judith Rossner's popular 1975 novel, *Looking for Mr. Goodbar*. As Preston became "something of a celebrity," he "got to sell T-shirts by mail order that read: LOOKING FOR MR. BENSON. There were versions with or without a question mark. (My boss's husband understood I really was a writer the first time he saw someone wearing that T-shirt and reading the *Times* on the New York subway.)"

After moving to Portland, Maine, in 1979, Preston began writing pieces for the local paper, *The Chronicle*. He also wrote the first of his "Letters from Maine," which were "eventually syndicated," according to Michael Lowenthal, in gay newspapers around the country. In the early 1980s, in addition to producing his award-winning novel *Fanny, the Queen of Provincetown* (1983), he wrote the first three volumes of the action series *The Mission of Alex Kane* and continued to publish pornography. (Some writers and many bookstores characterize Preston's work as "erotica," but he had little patience for the supposed distinction between erotica and pornography, which he maintains is grounded in the social class of its readers, to the extent that it can be defined at all.)

Although he addressed AIDS in a 1983 essay entitled "Some of Us Are Dying," the outbreak made Preston feel temporarily "paralyz[ed]" as a writer of pornography. Yet in the end, "It was writing about sex in the midst of the epidemic that helped me face the plague and the fear that it meant an end to our sexual exploration." In 1985, in order to "help spread the word on how to avoid risk of the disease," Preston edited *Hot Living: Erotic Stories About Safer Sex* (1985). He himself was diagnosed HIV-positive in 1986.

Michael Lowenthal writes that Preston neither particularly increased nor particularly decreased his writing about AIDS following his diagnosis. In 1989, he edited *Personal Dispatches: Writers Confront AIDS,* and he expanded his ongoing "oral history project," *The Men of Maine,* to include stories of the HIV-positive. According to Lowenthal, the wrenching and exquisitely crafted essay "Living with AIDS, 1992" was Preston's "most profound attempt to document and make sense of his illness." In the final years of his life, Preston edited *Flesh and the Word: An Anthology of Erotic Writing* (1992) and *Hometowns: Gay Men Write about Where They Belong* (1992). He also wrote essays on New England for *Winter's Light: Reflections of a Yankee Queer* (1996). He died April 28, 1994, in Portland.

Fulfilling the dream of many aspiring writers, John Preston had fans and celebrity from the very beginning of his career as a writer. When *Mr. Benson* was published as a complete text in 1983, *The Village Voice* characterized it as a "classic underground novel." Although Preston "moved on" with his writing and "published books that were far away from my origins as a pornographer," he steadfastly refused either to distance himself from his pornographic works or to accept standard divisions between his pornographic writing, presumed to be bad, prosaic hack work, and his other writing, presumed to be good, imaginative literary art. Preston's artistic talents were many and varied, but some critics maintain that his prose was untutored, and sometimes untamed. Lowenthal writes: "[Preston] was a literary equivalent of the jazz trumpeter Miles Davis, who had none of the technical prowess of trumpet players like Clifford Brown or Dizzy Gillespie, but whose innate sense of the music was unarguably masterful." A compelling teller of stories, Preston also played an essential role as a collector of stories, creating a legacy of gay men's narratives from two important periods in American history: life after Stonewall, and life with AIDS.

MEDFIELD, MASSACHUSETTS *(1991)*

MEDFIELD IS ONE of the ancient villages of New England. It was established as a European community in 1649, when pioneers from Dedham moved inland to the location near the headwaters of the Charles River, about twenty-five miles southeast of Boston.

The land on which Medfield was settled had been purchased from Chicatabot, the Sachem of the Neponset nation. He was one of those natives who saw the arrival of the English as, at worst, a neutral event. But it didn't take long for the indigenous people to see that the spread of the Puritan and Pilgrim colonies was threatening their very survival. In 1674, Metacomet, the great leader known to the English as King Philip, organized an alliance of the native nations and led them to battle against the intruders.

The beginning of King Philip's War, as it was called, was fought in the Connecticut Valley. The few communities there were attacked and many of the settlers killed. Within a year Metacomet's warriors were pushing closer to Boston. Medfield was raided on February 19, 1675. Seventeen people were killed and half the buildings were destroyed.

Metacomet was defeated later that winter in a climactic battle in nearby Rhode Island. His campaign was the last serious chance the natives had of sending the English away.

Smallpox and other epidemics finished the destruction of the aboriginal nations over the next decades. Medfield's new proprietors, my ancestors, quietly prospered.

When the American Revolution broke out a century later, Medfield was firmly on the side of the rebels. The town meeting communicated regularly with the colonial legislature and the radical Committees of Correspondence, encouraging a strong stance against unfair taxation. When it was apparent that hostilities would break out, the citizens organized a contingent of Minute men who responded to the call to arms in Concord and Lexington (though they arrived too late to join in the battles).

The Revolution was the last striking event in Medfield's history. Once independence was achieved, Medfield simply became a quintessential Yankee town, the place where I grew up, complete with a phalanx of the white clapboard churches everyone identifies with New England, larded through with extravagant forest parks and with a wealth of substantial wood-frame houses.

When I was born, in 1945, Medfield had fewer than three thousand inhabitants. It was assumed that all of us knew one another. It wasn't just that the population was so small, it was also remarkably stable. Our families had all lived in the same place for so long that it all felt like an extended family. (And there were, in fact, many cousins in town. Not just first cousins, but second and third cousins. We all knew our interlocking heritage at an early age.) The names of all the participants in the colonial and revolutionary events were the same as many of my cousins and classmates and the people in the church my family attended—Harding, Morse, Adams, Lovell, Bullard, Wheelock, and Allen.

We lived our history. When the other kids and I played cowboys and Indians, we did it on the same battlegrounds where our ancestors defeated King Philip. When we studied American history, our teachers taught us the names of the men from Medfield who had fought in the Revolution.

We weren't those for whom this country's history was irrelevant. We weren't left out of the narrative of the white man's ascension. We were, in fact, those for whom American history was written. We were of British ancestry—if not English, then Scots or Irish. We read about people with names that sounded like our own. "Foreign" was, for us, someone of Italian descent. "Alien" was the Roman Catholic church.

As I grew older and came into contact with people from around the state, I discovered a different social criteria. People started to talk about ancestors who'd come from England on the *Mayflower*. I remember going to my mother and asking her if ours had. She looked at me strangely and replied, "Well, whenever any family's lived in a town like ours as long as we have, somebody married somebody who married somebody whose family came over on the *Mayflower*. But, why would you even care?" she asked.

Indeed. Why would anyone look for more than coming from Medfield? There is a story about Yankee insularity that's told in many different forms. A reporter goes up to a lady who's sitting on a bench in a village common and asks her, "If you had the chance to travel to anywhere in the world, where would you go?" The lady looks around her hometown, mystified, and responds, "But why would I go anywhere? I'm already here!" The first times I heard that story, I didn't understand it was a joke. I thought the woman was only speaking the obvious. It's the way we felt about Medfield.

Medfield was a very distinct reality to me. There was even a leftover colonial custom that gave the town a concrete definition. By 1692 the settlements around Boston were growing quickly and their perimeters were hazy because of conflicting land grants and native treaties. The executive power of each town was vested in the Board of Selectmen, three citizens elected by the town meeting to run things between the annual assemblies of the town's voters. The Great and General Court, the romantic name the Commonwealth of Massachusetts still uses for the state legislature, decreed that every five years the selectmen of each town would have to "perambulate the bounds" with the selectmen of its neighbors. The two sets of townspeople had to agree on the markers that separated them.

The requirement for the perambulation stayed on the books until 1973 and even then the rescinding law said, "However, it is enjoyable to keep the old tradition of meeting with the select men of adjoining towns for this purpose. It also affords an opportunity to agree to replacement of missing or broken bounds and to discuss subjects of mutual interest." (The Medfield Historical Commission recently reported, "It is also rumored that modern-time selectmen partook of a drink or two at each boundary market.")

When I was young, I used to walk the bounds of Medfield with the selectmen. The grown-ups' drinking habits weren't important to me, but I was in love with the stones we found with their antiquated signs and the aged oak and maple trees that appeared on the town records as markers between Medfield and Dover, Walpole, Norfolk, and other neighbors.

The living history of the monuments wasn't all I got from these walks. The perambulations gave a firm evidence to just what was my hometown. I was being told that everything on this side of the boundaries was Medfield. Everything on this side of the border was mine.

It's hard to overstate the sense of entitlement that a New England boyhood gave me and my friends. I remember the first time I was taken to Boston. The city seemed large and frightening, at least it did until my mother pointed to the large body of water between Boston and Cambridge and explained that it was the Charles, the same river that separated Medfield from Millis. I realized I couldn't be frightened of someplace that was built on the banks of *my* river.

Even if America wasn't all like Medfield, it certainly acted as though it wanted to be. The new suburban developments that were all the rage in the sixties mimicked the architecture of the buildings that had been standing around our village for centuries. Advertisements for the good life all seemed to take place in our town. Medfield had a wide floodplain to the west, hills to the south, forests to the north. It was the landscape surrounding the "nice people" we saw in magazines and on television. Our lawns were well kept and our trees carefully pruned. A snowstorm was a community event; my mother would make hot chocolate and fresh doughnuts (from scratch) for all the neighborhood children and we'd build snowmen exactly like those pictured on the pages of *The Saturday Evening Post*.

Of course there were blemishes, some of them so well hidden that only those of us inside could see them. There were broken homes and drunken parents. There was economic upheaval as New England's industry migrated to the South after World War II. There were class divisions that were especially apparent to me, since my father's family—he was from Boston's industrial suburbs—was pure working class. We couldn't have been much better off than my aunts and uncles and cousins living in Boston's urban blight, but poverty wasn't as apparent when it was surrounded by beauty like Medfield's. Somerville didn't have Rocky Narrows State Park; Everett didn't have Rocky Woods State Reservation. And, besides, not having a great deal of money had no impact on our status in town. My mother's pedigree made my father's background irrelevant. Her children were of Medfield, and no one ever questioned that.

In fact, we were constantly reminded that our roots were right there on the banks of the Charles. My sisters and brothers and I were continually assaulted by older citizens who would stop us on the street and pinch our cheeks, "Oh, yes, I can see that you must be one of Raymond Blood's family. It's those eyes. Just like his!" My maternal grandfather had died fifteen years before I was born, but townspeople kept on seeing his lineage in my face. He'd been something of a hero in the town, a World War I veteran who'd prospected for gold in Nevada before he'd returned to take over the family's business, selling feed and grain to the small farmers in the region. To be Raymond Blood's grandson was no small matter. The pinches may have been annoying, but the rest of the message was clear: You are from this place.

Medfield was a town where a boy knew what it meant to belong. It was an environment out of which almost any achievement seemed possible. As we grew older, my friends and I picked and chose from the best colleges, dreamed the most extravagant futures, saw ourselves in any situation we could imagine. Our aspirations were the highest possible and they didn't come out of pressure from striving families or a need to escape a stifling atmosphere. We envisioned ourselves however we chose because we felt it was ours, all of it, the entire American Dream. It was so much ours, we took it so much for granted, that we never even questioned it. It was self-evident.

There must have been many ways I was different from the other kids early on. I'm vaguely aware of being too smart, of not being physical enough, of hating sports. I got grief for all those things in the way any group of peers can deliver it, especially in adolescence. I certainly *felt* different. I certainly *knew* I was different. But the difference didn't define itself right away.

As we became teenagers, things happened that actually eased the sense of deviation. There were forces at work that made us more aware of the things that bound us together and made what might have separated us seem less important. Route 128 had been built in a long arc around Boston's suburbs in the fifties. Originally called a highway to nowhere, it was one of the first freeways whose purpose was to create a flow of traffic around centers of population, not between them. One-twenty-eight quickly got another name: "America's Highway of Technology." New companies with names like Raytheon and Northrop and Digital built enormous high-tech plants along 128. They moved the center of the region's economy out of Boston, toward places like Medfield. The town's population doubled, and then doubled again.

By the time we were in high school, we were faced with new classmates with strange accents and different standards. My friends had earned their extra spending money by trapping beavers and muskrats along the tributaries to the Charles and selling their pelts. These new kids didn't know about traps and they didn't think it was important that their new homes in the spreading developments were ruining the animals' habitat. We were used to having fried clams as a special treat at the local drive-up restaurant; they were only angry that there weren't any fast-food chains. They had strange and exotic—and sexual—dances we hadn't even heard of. We stood in the high school auditorium and wondered how they could act that way in public. When they hiked up on Noon Hill, they didn't know that it had been the place from which King Philip had watched Medfield burn. They thought we were backward and quaint that we even cared about such things.

The local kids closed ranks. I'm sure, as I look back now, that the newcomers must have been puzzled when Mike, the captain of every team sport possible, spent time with me, the class brain. They must have wondered just as much why I would pass afternoons with Philip, who didn't even go to Medfield High School but commuted to Norfolk Country Agricultural School, the looked-down-upon "aggie" school in Walpole. And why would my (third) cousin Peter, probably the most handsome youth in town, walk home with me so often?

We defied the new standards; we held to our own. We had all been in the Cub Scouts pack that my mother had founded. We had all sat in the same kindergarten. We had all been a part of Medfield. I was one of the group, and they wouldn't deny me.

When I return to my hometown now, I see that, in most ways, we won. People like Mike and Philip and Peter—and my mother and her friends—simply sat it all out. They waited for the newcomers to leave and then for a new wave of them to come in, the waves of migrating suburbanites who can't tell the difference between Medfield and Northfield, Illinois, or Southfield, Michigan, they've changed addresses so often. My family and friends simply stayed, they had never intended to move. Now, my mother is the town clerk, Mike runs the reunions of our high school class, and last I heard Philip took over his father's job as groundsman for the state hospital.

But I had begun to leave while I was still in high school. I had heard rumors about a different life and a different world. Its gateway, my books and magazines told me, was a bus station in a city. I began to travel to Boston more often, supposedly to visit my urban cousins, but I seldom got as far as Somerville. I would stay, instead, in the Greyhound terminal and wait for one of a series of men to come and initiate me. They were traveling salesmen from Hartford, professors from MIT, students from Northeastern.

Eventually I'd travel further to meet them. I took secret trips to New York when I was supposed to be skiing in New Hampshire. I hitchhiked to Provincetown, the fabulous center of the new world into which I was moving. And, with every move, I left more of Medfield behind.

There was really no way I could see to combine my new life and my old. There was a man in Medfield who was whispered about. He belonged to our church and was the target for endless sympathy because he kept entering and leaving the state hospital. And there were two women down the street, nurses, who were so masculine that it was impossible to ignore their deviance from the other norms of the town. But they offered me nothing. I wasn't like the nurses and I never, ever wanted to be like the man who was so continually institutionalized.

In some ways I moved into my new life with great joy. There was real excitement in it, certainly there was great passion. My explorations took me to places as far away as a New England boy could ever imagine. When it came time to pick my college, I chose one in Illinois, the far horizon of my family's worldview, as far away as they could ever conceive of me going.

I also experienced rage over what was happening to me. I was being taken away from Medfield and everything it stood for. I was the one who should have gotten a law degree and come home to settle into comfortable Charles River Valley politics—perhaps with a seat in the Great and General Court? I should have lived in one of those honestly colonial houses on Pleasant Street. I should have walked through the meadows and the hills as long as I wanted, greeted by people I knew, all of us blanketed in our sense of continuity. History had belonged to us. But I was no longer one of them. I had become too different.

There had become a label for me that was even more powerful than the label of being from Medfield, something I don't think I could have ever envisioned being true.

I remember trying to find some way to come back to Medfield. I remember discovering a hairdresser in a Boston bar who had just opened a shop in town. I wanted desperately to fall in love with him and move back and find some way to be of Medfield again. Another time I did fall in love with a truck driver from Providence, a man of as much overstated masculinity as the nurses down the street. Maybe he and I could create a balance that the town could accept. He drank whiskey with my father, fixed cars with our neighbors, and knew all about the Red Sox. Maybe, between the two of us, we had enough that we could stay in Medfield. It didn't work. And, in those days, no one ever thought it would work in any hometown.

I stopped trying to fit my life into Medfield. I turned my back on it. I belonged to a new world now, one that spun around New York, Chicago, San Francisco, Provincetown. I was danced and bedded away from home, into the arms of someplace no one had ever even told me about.

Understanding and Analysis

1. How is this essay organized? From how many perspectives does Preston examine his hometown?

2. What was Preston's mother's attitude toward those whose ancestors came over on the Mayflower? What role did social class play in Preston's early life?

3. Why does Preston include a description of the custom of walking "the bounds" with the selectmen?

4. To what exactly did Preston feel "entitled?"

5. What were the "blemishes" Medfield hid?

6. What changed Medfield with the building of Route 128? What stayed the same?

7. When Preston writes that, "in most ways, we won," who is the "we" he refers to? What did they win?

8. At what point does Preston indicate what makes him different from most of the other residents of Medfield? Why does Preston wait so long to tell the reader about his difference? How does he tell us? Does he label himself at any point?

9. Why, exactly, does Preston experience "rage"?

10. Do you think Preston loses his sense of belonging somewhere? What is your evidence?

11. What stereotypes does Preston evoke in this essay?

Comparison

1. Read Momaday's essay and compare the two descriptions of place. Do Preston and Momaday use similar techniques? What differences do you see? Which do you prefer? Why?

2. Describe in detail a place you know well, following the techniques used by Preston and Momaday.

3. Read Parker's "Mrs. Post Enlarges on Etiquette." Parker and Preston both describe class indicators. Do they provide completely different indicators or are there similarities between them? How does tone shape our understanding of the position of each author with respect to the people described? Are the authors part of the worlds they describe? How do you know?

4. Read the essay by Reich. Does his analysis of the work force add to your understanding of the history of Medfield and Preston's decision to leave it?

Robert B. Reich
(1946–)

Born in 1946, Robert B. Reich grew up in rural New York near the "factory towns" where his father, Ed, "sold $1.98 cotton dresses, cheap blouses, sweaters, [and] stockings" to factory workers and their wives. Despite the fact that his father sometimes worked straight through the week, days and nights, trying to support the family, Reich "didn't feel poor" growing up. Spending summers with his grandmother "in her little cabin in the Adirondack Mountains," he showed his predilection for books by learning to read before the age of five. Although he ultimately built up an impressive academic record, he began his formal schooling rather inauspiciously by getting himself expelled from nursery school. He successfully survived kindergarten, but after he paid a female classmate to perform a revealing somersault on the playground, his teacher "sen[t] a note home, suggesting counseling."

Pursuing his undergraduate degree at Dartmouth, Reich met future First Lady Hillary Rodham "when she was a freshman at Wellesley." Although he did not know it then, she was the first of many political connections he was to make. In the summer of 1967, he worked as an intern for Robert F. Kennedy, and, in 1968, he met the future President Clinton on board the *S.S. United States* en route to Oxford (Clinton offered him a bowl of chicken soup to ease his sea sickness). Within a few days of his arrival in England, Reich tried out for a play and made an important personal connection with his future wife, Clare Dalton, who was also auditioning. When both failed to make the cast, Reich determined to direct his own play and give her the lead in order to spend time with her.

Having graduated from Dartmouth in 1968, Reich faced the possibility, in 1969, of being drafted. "At four feet ten inches tall," he writes in *Locked in the Cabinet*, he knew he was "technically too short," but he had "heard rumors that the army [was] looking for tunnel rats small enough to flush the VC out of their caves," and he was nervous. He recalls: "I'm standing in my underwear, back straight against the measure, when the examining sergeant issues his decision. 'Sorry, son,' he says gravely. I'm too frightened to ask him whether he's sorry that I'm going to Nam or sorry I'm not. He continues: 'Maybe someday you'll grow, and then you can serve your country.'" For many years of his career, serving his country is precisely what Reich did do. Attending Yale Law with Bill and Hillary Clinton, as well as Supreme Court Justice Clarence Thomas, he moved to Washington D.C. with his wife in the early 1970s to serve as an assistant to the solicitor general under President Gerald Ford. Under President Jimmy

Carter, he worked with the Federal Trade Commission, and there ended, at least for a time, his work in Washington: "Much of it was grueling, thankless work—briefing and arguing cases before the Supreme Court, protecting unwary consumers from fraud. Then Ronald Reagan took over. You could say I departed exactly as I began—fired with enthusiasm."

In the 1980s, Reich became a Harvard professor, an acclaimed writer, and a father of two sons, Adam and Sam. His first book was *Minding America's Business: The Decline and Rise of the American Economy* (1982), co-authored with Ira C. Magaziner. Teaching at Harvard's John F. Kennedy School of Government, Reich published *The Next American Frontier* (1983), a work "about the origins of America's industrial organization and the social values bound up with it, about the evolution that is making them both obsolete, and about the change that must occur if we are to regain our momentum." According to *Contemporary Authors*, the book played a role in the "presidential election" of 1984, as did *Tales of a New America: The Anxious Liberal's Guide to the Future*, four years later.

In 1988, Reich edited *The Power of Public Ideas* and "spent six months . . . advising Michael Dukakis in his dispiriting run for the Presidency." He released his first collection of essays, *The Resurgent Liberal: And Other Unfashionable Prophecies*, in 1989. In the next decade, he published *Public Management in a Democratic Society* (1990) and *The Work of Nations: Preparing Ourselves for 21ˢᵗ-Century Capitalism* (1991), which influenced Clinton's election agenda. He also co-founded *The American Prospect*, a magazine intended "to contribute to a renewal of America's democratic traditions by presenting a practical and convincing vision of liberal philosophy, politics, and public life." In 1993, after much debate with himself and discussion with his family, he left Cambridge to join the cabinet of President Bill Clinton as the nation's twenty-second secretary of labor. He recounts the next four years in *Locked in the Cabinet* (1997), an often disheartening account of the political process in Washington, enlivened by Reich's humor. Leaving the White House to be with his family after President Clinton's re-election, Reich took a position as a Professor of Social and Economic Policy at Brandeis. He contributes regularly to the Los Angeles and New York *Times*, *USA Today*, and *The Washington Post*.

As a writer of books on economic and public policy, Robert B. Reich has had more than his share of critics. In preparation for his cabinet nomination, White House investigators presented him with a "large black three-ring binder," saying, "We did a computer search of all the negative things critics have written about your books over the years," which Reich estimated contained 500 single-spaced pages of remarks. When he jokingly praised himself for garnering "all that in only fifteen years," one of the investigators pointed out the label on the side of the binder: "Critics of Robert Reich, Volume I." A somewhat less thorough review of Reich's criticism than the White House's still reveals a common theme, which is, in the words of Christopher Lehmann-Haupt, that "Mr. Reich is better at defining the problem than proposing a solution." Yet at defining America's problems Reich is considered quite good. He has also received high praise for *Locked in the Cabinet*, which showcases a sense of humor one reviewer likens to James Thurber's. Filled with sequences of fantasy, satire, and self-parody, this "political autobiography," as characterized by reviewer Richard Bernstein, "is hard not to like in large part because Mr. Reich is himself so likable in it."

Why the Rich Are Getting Richer
and the Poor, Poorer *(1991)*

[T]he division of labour is limited by the extent of the market.
—ADAM SMITH, *An inquiry into the Nature and Causes of the Wealth of Nations* (1776)

REGARDLESS OF HOW your job is officially classified (manufacturing, service, managerial, technical, secretarial, and so on), or the industry in which you work (automotive, steel, computer, advertising, finance, food processing), your real competitive position in the world economy is coming to depend on the function you perform in it. Herein lies the basic reason why incomes are diverging. The fortunes of routine producers are declining. In-person servers are also becoming poorer, although their fates are less clear-cut. But symbolic analysts—who solve, identify, and broker new problems—are, by and large, succeeding in the world economy.

All Americans used to be in roughly the same economic boat. Most rose or fell together, as the corporations in which they were employed, the industries comprising such corporations, and the national economy as a whole became more productive—or languished. But national borders no longer define our economic fates. We are now in different boats, one sinking rapidly, one sinking more slowly, and the third rising steadily.

2

The boat containing routine producers is sinking rapidly. Recall that by midcentury routine production workers in the United States were paid relatively well. The giant pyramidlike organizations at the core of each major industry coordinated their prices and investments—avoiding the harsh winds of competition and thus maintaining healthy earnings. Some of these earnings, in turn, were reinvested in new plant and equipment (yielding ever-larger-scale economies); another portion went to top managers and investors. But a large and increasing portion went to middle managers and production workers. Work stoppages posed such a threat to high-volume production that organized labor was able to exact an ever-larger premium for its cooperation. And the pattern of wages established within the core corporations influenced the pattern throughout the national economy. Thus the growth of a relatively affluent middle class, able to purchase all the wondrous things produced in high volume by the core corporations.

But, as has been observed, the core is rapidly breaking down into global webs which earn their largest profits from clever problem-solving, -identifying, and brokering. As the costs of transporting standard things and of communicating information about them continue to drop, profit margins on high-volume, standardized production are thinning, because there are few barriers to entry. Modern factories and state-of-the-art machinery can be installed almost anywhere on the globe. Routine producers in the United States, then, are in direct competition with millions of routine producers in other nations. Twelve thousand people are added to the world's population every hour, most of whom, eventually, will happily work for a small fraction of the wages of routine producers in America.[1]

The consequence is clearest in older, heavy industries, where high-volume, standardized production continues its ineluctable move to where labor is cheapest and most accessible around the world. Thus, for example, the Maquiladora factories cluttered along the Mexican side of the U.S. border in the sprawling shanty towns of Tijuana, Mexicali, Nogales, Agua Prieta, and Ciudad Juárez—factories owned mostly by Americans, but increasingly by Japanese—in which more than a half million routine producers assemble parts into finished goods to be shipped into the United States.

The same story is unfolding worldwide. Until the late 1970s, AT&T had depended on routine producers in Shreveport, Louisiana, to assemble standard telephones. It then discovered that routine producers in Singapore would perform the same tasks at a far lower cost. Facing intense competition from other global webs, AT&T's strategic brokers felt compelled to switch. So in the early 1980s they stopped hiring routine producers in Shreveport and began hiring cheaper routine producers in Singapore. But under this kind of pressure for ever lower high-volume production costs, today's Singaporean can easily end up as yesterday's Louisianan. By the late 1980s, AT&T's strategic brokers found that routine producers in Thailand were eager to assemble telephones for a small fraction of the wages of routine producers in Singapore. Thus, in 1989, AT&T stopped hiring Singaporeans to make telephones and began hiring even cheaper routine producers in Thailand.

The search for ever lower wages has not been confined to heavy industry. Routine data processing is equally footloose. Keypunch operators located anywhere around the world can enter data into computers, linked by satellite or transoceanic fiber-optic cable, and take it out again. As the rates charged by satellite networks continue to drop, and as more satellites and fiber-optic cables become available (reducing communication costs still further), routine data processors in the United States find themselves in ever more direct competition with their counterparts abroad, who are often eager to work for far less.

By 1990, keypunch operators in the United States were earning, at most, $6.50 per hour. But keypunch operators throughout the rest of the world were willing to work for a fraction of this. Thus, many potential American data-processing jobs were disappearing, and the wages and benefits of the remaining ones were in decline. Typical was Saztec International, a $20-million-a-year data-processing firm headquartered in Kansas City, whose American strategic brokers contracted with routine data processors in Manila and with American-owned firms that needed such data-processing services. Compared with

---

[1]The reader should note, of course, that lower wages in other areas of the world are of no particular attraction to global capital unless workers there are sufficiently productive to make the labor cost of producing *each unit* lower there than in higher-wage regions. Productivity in many low-wage areas of the world has improved due to the ease with which state-of-the-art factories and equipment can be installed there. [Reich's note]

the average Philippine income of $1,700 per year, data-entry operators working for Saztec earn the princely sum of $2,650. The remainder of Saztec's employees were American problem-solvers and -identifiers, searching for ways to improve the worldwide system and find new uses to which it could be put.[2]

By 1990, American Airlines was employing over 1,000 data processors in Barbados and the Dominican Republic to enter names and flight numbers from used airline tickets (flown daily to Barbados from airports around the United States) into a giant computer bank located in Dallas. Chicago publisher R. R. Donnelley was sending entire manuscripts to Barbados for entry into computers in preparation for printing. The New York Life Insurance Company was dispatching insurance claims to Castleisland, Ireland, where routine producers, guided by simple directions, entered the claims and determined the amounts due, then instantly transmitted the computations back to the United States. (When the firm advertised in Ireland for twenty-five data-processing jobs, it received six hundred applications.) And McGraw-Hill was processing subscription renewal and marketing information for its magazines in nearby Galway. Indeed, literally millions of routine workers around the world were receiving information, converting it into computer-readable form, and then sending it back—at the speed of electronic impulses—whence it came.

The simple coding of computer software has also entered into world commerce. India, with a large English-speaking population of technicians happy to do routine programming cheaply, is proving to be particularly attractive to global webs in need of this service. By 1990, Texas Instruments maintained a software development facility in Bangalore, linking fifty Indian programmers by satellite to TI's Dallas headquarters. Spurred by this and similar ventures, the Indian government was building a teleport in Poona, intended to make it easier and less expensive for many other firms to send their routine software design specifications for coding.[3]

3

This shift of routine production jobs from advanced to developing nations is a great boon to many workers in such nations who otherwise would be jobless or working for much lower wages. These workers, in turn, now have more money with which to purchase symbolic-analytic services from advanced nations (often embedded within all sorts of complex products). The trend is also beneficial to everyone around the world who can now obtain high-volume, standardized products (including information and software) more cheaply than before.

But these benefits do not come without certain costs. In particular the burden is borne by those who no longer have good-paying routine production jobs within advanced economies like the United States. Many of these people used to belong to unions or at least benefited from prevailing wage rates established in collective bargaining agreements. But as the old corporate bureaucracies have flattened into global webs, bargaining leverage has been lost. Indeed, the tacit national bargain is no more.

Despite the growth in the number of new jobs in the United States, union member-

[2]John Maxwell Hamilton, "A Bit Player Buys Into the Computer Age," *The New York Times Business World,* December 3, 1989, p. 14. [Reich's note]

[3]Udayan Gupta, "U.S.-India Satellite Link Stands to Cut Software Costs," *The Wall Street Journal,* March 6, 1989, p. B2. [Reich's note]

ship has withered. In 1960, 35 percent of all nonagricultural workers in America belonged to a union. But by 1980 that portion had fallen to just under a quarter, and by 1989 to about 17 percent. Excluding government employees, union membership was down to 13.4 percent.[4] This was a smaller proportion even than in the early 1930s, before the National Labor Relations Act created a legally protected right to labor representation. The drop in membership has been accompanied by a growing number of collective bargaining agreements to freeze wages at current levels, reduce wage levels of entering workers, or reduce wages overall. This is an important reason why the long economic recovery that began in 1982 produced a smaller rise in unit labor costs than any of the eight recoveries since World War II—the low rate of unemployment during its course notwithstanding.

Routine production jobs have vanished fastest in traditional unionized industries (autos, steel, and rubber, for example), where average wages have kept up with inflation. This is because the jobs of older workers in such industries are protected by seniority; the youngest workers are the first to be laid off. Faced with a choice of cutting wages or cutting the number of jobs, a majority of union members (secure in the knowledge that there are many who are junior to them who will be laid off first) often have voted for the latter.

Thus the decline in union membership has been most striking among young men entering the work force without a college education. In the early 1950s, more than 40 percent of this group joined unions; by the late 1980s, less than 20 percent (if public employees are excluded, less than 10 percent).[5] In steelmaking, for example, although many older workers remained employed, almost half of all routine steelmaking jobs in America vanished between 1974 and 1988 (from 480,000 to 260,000). Similarly with automobiles: During the 1980s, the United Auto Workers lost 500,000 members—one-third of their total at the start of the decade. General Motors alone cut 150,000 American production jobs during the 1980s (even as it added employment abroad). Another consequence of the same phenomenon: The gap between the average wages of unionized and nonunionized workers widened dramatically—from 14.6 percent in 1973 to 20.4 percent by end of the 1980s.[6] The lesson is clear. If you drop out of high school or have no more than a high school diploma, do not expect a good routine production job to be awaiting you.

Also vanishing are lower- and middle-level management jobs involving routine production. Between 1981 and 1986, more than 780,000 foremen, supervisors, and section chiefs lost their jobs through plant closings and layoffs.[7] Large numbers of assistant division heads, assistant directors, assistant managers, and vice presidents also found themselves jobless. GM shed more than 40,000 white-collar employees and planned to eliminate another 25,000 by the mid-1990s.[8] As America's core pyramids metamorphosed into global webs, many middle-level routine producers were as obsolete as routine workers on the line.

---

[4]*Statistical Abstract of the United States* (Washington, D.C.: U.S. Government Printing Office, 1989), p. 416, Table 684. [Reich's note]

[5]Calculations from Current Population Surveys by L. Katz and A. Revenga, "Changes in the Structure of Wages: U.S. and Japan," National Bureau of Economic Research, September 1989. [Reich's note]

[6]U.S. Department of Commerce, Bureau of Labor Statistics, "Wages of Unionized and Non-Unionized Workers," various issues. [Reich's note]

[7]U.S. Department of Labor, Bureau of Labor Statistics, "Reemployment Increases Among Displaced Workers," *BLS News*, USDL 86–414, October 14, 1986, Table 6. [Reich's note]

[8]*The Wall Street Journal*, February 16, 1990, p. A5. [Reich's note]

As has been noted, foreign-owned webs are hiring some Americans to do routine production in the United States. Philips, Sony, and Toyota factories are popping up all over—to the self-congratulatory applause of the nation's governors and mayors, who have lured them with promises of tax abatements and new sewers, among other amenities. But as these ebullient politicians will soon discover, the foreign-owned factories are highly automated and will become far more so in years to come. Routine production jobs account for a small fraction of the cost of producing most items in the United States and other advanced nations, and this fraction will continue to decline sharply as computer-integrated robots take over. In 1977 it took routine producers thirty-five hours to assemble an automobile in the United States; it is estimated that by the mid-1990s, Japanese-owned factories in America will be producing finished automobiles using only eight hours of a routine producer's time.[9]

The productivity and resulting wages of American workers who run such robotic machinery may be relatively high, but there may not be many such jobs to go around. A case in point: In the late 1980s, Nippon Steel joined with America's ailing Inland Steel to build a new $400 million cold-rolling mill fifty miles west of Gary, Indiana. The mill was celebrated for its state-of-the-art technology, which cut the time to produce a coil of steel from twelve days to about one hour. In fact, the entire plant could be run by a small team of technicians, which became clear when Inland subsequently closed two of its old cold-rolling mills, laying off hundreds of routine workers. Governors and mayors take note: Your much-ballyhooed foreign factories may end up employing distressingly few of your constituents.

Overall, the decline in routine jobs has hurt men more than women. This is because the routine production jobs held by men in high-volume metal-bending manufacturing industries had paid higher wages than the routine production jobs held by women in textiles and data processing. As both sets of jobs have been lost, American women in routine production have gained more equal footing with American men—equally poor footing, that is. This is a major reason why the gender gap between male and female wages began to close during the 1980s.

4

The second of the three boats, carrying in-person servers, is sinking as well, but somewhat more slowly and unevenly. Most in-person servers are paid at or just slightly above the minimum wage and many work only part-time, with the result that their take-home pay is modest, to say the least. Nor do they typically receive all the benefits (health care, life insurance, disability, and so forth) garnered by routine producers in large manufacturing corporations or by symbolic analysts affiliated with the more affluent threads of global webs.[10] In-person servers are sheltered from the direct effects of global competition and, like everyone else, benefit from access to lower-cost products from around the world. But they are not immune to its indirect effects.

[9]Figures from the International Motor Vehicles Program, Massachusetts Institute of Technology, 1989. [Reich's note]

[10]The growing portion of the American labor force engaged in in-person services, relative to routine production, thus helps explain why the number of Americans lacking health insurance increased by at least 6 million during the 1980s. [Reich's note]

For one thing, in-person servers increasingly compete with former routine production workers, who, no longer able to find well-paying routine production jobs, have few alternatives but to seek in-person service jobs. The Bureau of Labor Statistics estimates that of the 2.8 million manufacturing workers who lost their jobs during the early 1980s, fully one-third were rehired in service jobs paying at least 20 percent less.[11] In-person servers must also compete with high school graduates and dropouts who years before had moved easily into routine production jobs but no longer can. And if demographic predictions about the American work force in the first decades of the twenty-first century are correct (and they are likely to be, since most of the people who will comprise the work force are already identifiable), most new entrants into the job market will be black or Hispanic men, or women—groups that in years past have possessed relatively weak technical skills. This will result in an even larger number of people crowding into in-person services. Finally, in-person servers will be competing with growing numbers of immigrants, both legal and illegal, for whom in-person services will comprise the most accessible jobs. (It is estimated that between the mid-1980s and the end of the century, about a quarter of all workers entering the American labor force will be immigrants.[12])

Perhaps the fiercest competition that in-person servers face comes from labor-saving machinery (much of it invented, designed, fabricated, or assembled in other nations, of course). Automated tellers, computerized cashiers, automatic car washes, robotized vending machines, self-service gasoline pumps, and all similar gadgets substitute for the human beings that customers once encountered. Even telephone operators are fast disappearing, as electronic sensors and voice simulators become capable of carrying on conversations that are reasonably intelligent, and always polite. Retail sales workers—among the largest groups of in-person servers—are similarly imperiled. Through personal computers linked to television screens, tomorrow's consumers will be able to buy furniture, appliances, and all sorts of electronic toys from their living rooms—examining the merchandise from all angles, selecting whatever color, size, special features, and price seem most appealing, and then transmitting the order instantly to warehouses from which the selections will be shipped directly to their homes. So, too, with financial transactions, airline and hotel reservations, rental car agreements, and similar contracts, which will be executed between consumers in their homes and computer banks somewhere else on the globe.[13]

Advanced economies like the United States will continue to generate sizable numbers of new in-person service jobs, of course, the automation of older ones notwithstanding. For every bank teller who loses her job to an automated teller, three new jobs open for aerobics instructors. Human beings, it seems, have an almost insatiable desire for personal attention. But the intense competition nevertheless ensures that the wages of in-person servers will remain relatively low. In-person servers—working on their own, or else dispersed widely amid many small establishments, filling all sorts of personal-care niches—cannot readily organize themselves into labor unions or create powerful lobbies to limit the impact of such competition.

[11]U.S. Department of Labor, Bureau of Labor Statistics, "Reemployment Increases Among Displaced Workers," October 14, 1986. [Reich's note]

[12]Federal Immigration and Naturalization Service, *Statistical Yearbook* (Washington, D.C.: U.S. Government Printing Office, 1986, 1987). [Reich's note]

[13]See Claudia H. Deutsch, "The Powerful Push for Self-Service," *The New York Times*, April 9, 1989, section 3, p. 1. [Reich's note]

In two respects, demographics will work in favor of in-person servers, buoying their collective boat slightly. First, as has been noted, the rate of growth of the American work force is slowing. In particular, the number of younger workers is shrinking. Between 1985 and 1995, the number of eighteen- to twenty-four-year-olds will have declined by 17.5 percent. Thus, employers will have more incentive to hire and train in-person servers whom they might previously have avoided. But this demographic relief from the competitive pressures will be only temporary. The cumulative procreative energies of the post-war baby-boomers (born between 1946 and 1964) will result in a new surge of workers by 2010 or thereabouts.[14] And immigration—both legal and illegal—shows every sign of increasing in years to come.

Next, by the second decade of the twenty-first century, the number of Americans aged sixty-five and over will be rising precipitously, as the baby-boomers reach retirement age and live longer. Their life expectancies will lengthen not just because fewer of them will have smoked their way to their graves and more will have eaten better than their parents, but also because they will receive all sorts of expensive drugs and therapies designed to keep them alive—barely. By 2035, twice as many Americans will be elderly as in 1988, and the number of octogenarians is expected to triple. As these decaying baby-boomers ingest all the chemicals and receive all the treatments, they will need a great deal of personal attention. Millions of deteriorating bodies will require nurses, nursing-home operators, hospital administrators, orderlies, home-care providers, hospice aides, and technicians to operate and maintain all the expensive machinery that will monitor and temporarily stave off final disintegration. There might even be a booming market for euthanasia specialists. In-person servers catering to the old and ailing will be in strong demand.[15]

One small problem: The decaying baby-boomers will not have enough money to pay for these services. They will have used up their personal savings years before. Their Social Security payments will, of course, have been used by the government to pay for the previous generation's retirement and to finance much of the budget deficits of the 1980s. Moreover, with relatively fewer young Americans in the population, the supply of housing will likely exceed the demand, with the result that the boomers' major investments—their homes—will be worth less (in inflation-adjusted dollars) when they retire than they planned for. In consequence, the huge cost of caring for the graying boomers will fall on many of the same people who will be paid to care for them. It will be like a great sump pump: In-person servers of the twenty-first century will have an abundance of health-care jobs, but a large portion of their earnings will be devoted to Social Security payments and income taxes, which will in turn be used to pay their salaries. The net result: no real improvement in their standard of living.

The standard of living of in-person servers also depends, indirectly, on the standard of living of the Americans they serve who are engaged in world commerce. To the extent that *these* Americans are richly rewarded by the rest of the world for what they contribute, they will have more money to lavish upon inperson services. Here we find the only form of "trickle-dawn" economics that has a basis in reality. A waitress in a town whose major factory has just been closed is unlikely to earn a high wage or enjoy much job security;

[14]U.S. Bureau of the Census, *Current Population Reports*, Series P-23, No. 138, Tables 2-1, 4-6. See W. Johnson, A. Packer, et al., *Workforce 2000: Work and Workers for the 21st Century* (Indianapolis: Hudson Institute, 1987). [Reich's note]

[15]The Census Bureau estimates that by the year 2000, at least 12 million Americans will work in health services—well over 6 percent of the total work force. [Reich's note]

in a swank resort populated by film producers and banking moguls, she is apt to do reasonably well. So, too, with nations. In-person servers in Bangladesh may spend their days performing roughly the same tasks as in-person servers in the United States, but have a far lower standard of living for their efforts. The difference comes in the value that their customers add to the world economy. I shall return to this issue in a later chapter.

5

Unlike the boats of routine producers and in-person servers, however, the vessel containing America's symbolic analysts is rising. Worldwide demand for their insights is growing as the ease and speed of communicating them steadily increases. Not every symbolic analyst is rising as quickly or as dramatically as every other, of course; symbolic analysts at the low end are barely holding their own in the world economy. But symbolic analysts at the top are in such great demand worldwide that they have difficulty keeping track of all their earnings. Never before in history has opulence on such a scale been gained by people who have earned it, and done so legally.

Among symbolic analysts in the middle range are American scientists and researchers who are busily selling their discoveries to global enterprise webs. They are not limited to American customers. If the strategic brokers in General Motors' headquarters refuse to pay a high price for a new means of making high-strength ceramic engines dreamed up by a team of engineers affiliated with Carnegie-Mellon University in Pittsburgh, the strategic brokers of Honda or Mercedes-Benz are likely to be more than willing.

So, too, with the insights of America's ubiquitous management consultants, which are being sold for large sums to eager entrepreneurs in Europe and Latin America. Also, the insights of America's energy consultants, sold for even larger sums to Arab sheikhs. American design engineers are providing insights to Olivetti, Mazda, Siemens, and other global webs; American marketers, techniques for learning what worldwide consumers will buy; American advertisers, ploys for ensuring that they actually do. American architects are issuing designs and blueprints for opera houses, art galleries, museums, luxury hotels, and residential complexes in the world's major cities; American commercial property developers, marketing these properties to worldwide investors and purchasers.

Americans who specialize in the gentle art of public relations are in demand by corporations, governments, and politicians in virtually every nation. So, too, are American political consultants, some of whom, at this writing, are advising the Hungarian Socialist Party, the remnant of Hungary's ruling Communists, on how to salvage a few parliamentary seats in the nation's first free election in more than forty years. Also at this writing, a team of American agricultural consultants are advising the managers of a Soviet farm collective employing 1,700 Russians eighty miles outside Moscow. As noted, American investment bankers and lawyers specializing in financial circumnavigations are selling their insights to Asians and Europeans who are eager to discover how to make large amounts of money by moving large amounts of money.

Developing nations, meanwhile, are hiring American civil engineers to advise on building roads and dams. The present thaw in the Cold War will no doubt expand these opportunities. American engineers from Bechtel (a global firm notable for having employed both Caspar Weinberger and George Shultz for much larger sums than either earned in the Reagan administration) have begun helping the Soviets design and install a new generation of nuclear reactors. Nations also are hiring American bankers and lawyers to help them renegotiate the terms of their loans with global banks, and Washington lobbyists to help them with Congress, the Treasury, the World Bank, the IMF, and other politically sensitive institutions. In fits of obvious desperation, several nations emerging from communism have even hired American economists to teach them about capitalism.

Almost everyone around the world is buying the skills and insights of Americans who manipulate oral and visual symbols—musicians, sound engineers, film producers, makeup artists, directors, cinematographers, actors and actresses, boxers, scriptwriters, songwriters, and set designers. Among the wealthiest of symbolic analysts are Steven Spielberg, Bill Cosby, Charles Schulz, Eddie Murphy, Sylvester Stallone, Madonna, and other star directors and performers—who are almost as well known on the streets of Dresden and Tokyo as in the Back Bay of Boston. Less well rewarded but no less renowned are the unctuous anchors on Turner Broadcasting's Cable News, who appear daily, via satellite, in places ranging from Vietnam to Nigeria. Vanna White is the world's most watched game-show hostess. Behind each of these familiar faces is a collection of American problem-solvers, -identifiers, and brokers who train, coach, advise, promote, amplify, direct, groom, represent, and otherwise add value to their talents.[16]

There are also the insights of senior American executives who occupy the world headquarters of global "American" corporations and the national or regional headquarters of global "foreign" corporations. Their insights are duly exported to the rest of the world through the webs of global enterprise. IBM does not export many machines from the United States, for example. Big Blue makes machines all over the globe and services them on the spot. Its prime American exports are symbolic and analytic. From IBM's world headquarters in Armonk, New York, emanate strategic brokerage and related management services bound for the rest of the world. In return, IBM's top executives are generously rewarded.

6

The most important reason for this expanding world market and increasing global demand for the symbolic and analytic insights of Americans has been the dramatic improvement in worldwide communication and transportation technologies. Designs, instructions, advice, and visual and audio symbols can be communicated more and more rapidly around the globe, with ever-greater precision and at ever-lower cost. Madonna's voice can be transported to billions of listeners, with perfect clarity, on digital compact disks. A new invention emanating from engineers in Battelle's laboratory in Columbus, Ohio, can be sent almost any where via modem, in a form that will allow others to examined in three dimensions through enhanced computer graphics. When face-to-face meetings are still required—and videoconferencing will not suffice—it is relatively easy for designers, consultants, advisers, artists, and executives to board supersonic jets and, in a matter of hours, meet directly with their worldwide clients, customers, audiences, and employees.

With rising demand comes rising compensation. Whether in the form of licensing fees, fees for service, salaries, or shares in final profits, the economic result is much the same.

---

[16]In 1989, the entertainment business summoned to the United States $5.5 billion in foreign earnings—making it among the nation's largest export industries, just behind aerospace. U.S. Department of Commerce, International Trade Commission, "Composition of U.S. Exports," various issues. [Reich's note]

There are also nonpecuniary rewards. One of the best-kept secrets among symbolic analysts is that so many of them enjoy their work. In fact, much of it does not count as work at all, in the traditional sense. The work of routine producers and in-person servers is typically monotonous; it causes muscles to tire or weaken and involves little independence or discretion. The "work" of symbolic analysts, by contrast, often involves puzzles, experiments, games, a significant amount of chatter, and substantial discretion over what to do next. Few routine producers or in-person servers would "work" if they did not need to earn the money. Many symbolic analysts would "work" even if money were no object.

7

At midcentury, when America was a national market dominated by core pyramid-shaped corporations, there were constraints on the earnings of people at the highest rungs. First and most obviously, the market for their services was largely limited to the borders of the nation. In addition, whatever conceptual value they might contribute was small relative to the value gleaned from large scale—and it was dependent on large scale for whatever income it was to summon. Most of the problems to be identified and solved had to do with enhancing the efficiency of production and improving the flow of materials, parts, assembly, and distribution. Inventors searched for the rare breakthrough revealing an entirely new product to be made in high volume; management consultants, executives, and engineers thereafter tried to speed and synchronize its manufacture, to better achieve scale efficiencies; advertisers and marketers sought then to whet the public's appetite for the standard item that emerged. Since white-collar earnings increased with larger scale, there was considerable incentive to expand the firm; indeed, many of America's core corporations grew far larger than scale economies would appear to have justified.

By the 1990s, in contrast, the earnings of symbolic analysts were limited neither by the size of the national market nor by the volume of production of the firms with which they were affiliated. The marketplace was worldwide, and conceptual value was high relative to value added from scale efficiencies.

There had been another constraint on high earnings, which also gave way by the 1990s. At midcentury, the compensation awarded to top executives and advisers of the largest of America's core corporations could not be grossly out of proportion to that of low-level production workers. It would be unseemly for executives who engaged in highly visible rounds of bargaining with labor unions, and who routinely responded to government requests to moderate prices, to take home wages and benefits wildly in excess of what other Americans earned. Unless white-collar executives restrained themselves, moreover, blue-collar production workers could not be expected to restrain their own demands for higher wages. Unless both groups exercised restraint, the government could not be expected to forbear from imposing direct controls and regulations.

At the same time, the wages of production workers could not be allowed to sink too low, lest there be insufficient purchasing power in the economy. After all, who would buy all the goods flowing out of American factories if not American workers? This, too, was part of the tacit bargain struck between American managers and their workers.

Recall the oft-repeated corporate platitude of the era about the chief executive's responsibility to carefully weigh and balance the interests of the corporation's disparate stakeholders. Under the stewardship of the corporate statesman, no set of stakeholders—least of all white-collar executives—was to gain a disproportionately large share of the benefits of corporate activity; nor was any stakeholder—especially the average worker—to be left with a share that was disproportionately small. Banal though it was, this idea helped to maintain the legitimacy of the core American corporation in the eyes of most Americans, and to ensure continued economic growth.

But by the 1990s, these informal norms were evaporating, just as (and largely because) the core American corporation was vanishing. The links between top executives and the American production worker were fading: An ever-increasing number of subordinates and contractees were foreign, and a steadily growing number of American routine producers were working for foreign-owned firms. An entire cohort of middle-level managers, who had once been deemed "white collar," had disappeared; and, increasingly, American executives were exporting their insights to global enterprise webs.

As the American corporation itself became a global web almost indistinguishable from any other, its stakeholders were turning into a large and diffuse group, spread over the world. Such global stakeholders were less visible, and far less noisy, than national stakeholders. And as the American corporation sold its goods and services all over the world, the purchasing power of American workers became far less relevant to its economic survival.

Thus have the inhibitions been removed. The salaries and benefits of America's top executives, and many of their advisers and consultants, have soared to what years before would have been unimaginable heights, even as those of other Americans have declined.

Understanding and Analysis

1. This essay is very clearly organized into seven sections. Note the topic sentences introducing both the sections and the paragraphs within sections. How does Reich set up his argument? How does he indicate transitions from one point to the next?

2. What does Reich mean when he claims that we all used to be in one boat but now we are in three different boats?

3. What is the fate of "routine producers" in this country, according to Reich? What jobs is he talking about? What kinds of evidence does he assemble to make his point?

4. In what ways is that fate beneficial and to whom?

5. In what ways is that fate costly and to whom?

6. What is the fate of "in-person servers"? What jobs is Reich referring to here? What is Reich's evidence for the claims he makes about these jobs?

7. What is the fate of "symbolic analysts" in this country? What jobs do such people hold? What evidence does Reich present? Why is that sector expanding, according to Reich?

8. What, finally, is the answer to the question Reich poses in the title?

9. If Reich is right, what are the implications for students in college now?

Comparison

1. Read the essay by Galbraith. To what degree do the two men agree? Compare the tone of the two essays. Does tone affect the persuasiveness of each author?

2. Read the essay by Postman. Is Reich telling us a story about our nation and the world? If so, how persuasive is that story?

3. Read Rodriguez's essay "Labor." How does his essay add to your understanding of Reich's analysis?

4. Compare the attitudes of Twain, Ellison, Baker, Galbraith, Rodriguez, and Reich on the subject of physical labor as opposed to symbolic analysis.

5. Read the essay by Fukuyama. To what extent does he agree with Reich?

Gerald Early
(1952–)

Born April 21, 1952, in Philadelphia, Pennsylvania, Gerald Early was the youngest of three children and his parents' only son. His father, Henry Early, died before Gerald reached his first birthday, so he "grew up in a family of black women." Although he earned a reputation for being "bookish," becoming an avid devotee of Langston Hughes, "the only black writer anyone ever talked to me about during my youth," he was equally passionate about boxing. When he was 10, he explains in *Tuxedo Junction*, he sat in front of the television and watched Benny Kid Paret get "knocked into a coma by Emile Griffith": "That night I prayed to God to save Paret's life. I remember being on my knees and praying very hard, having learned in church that God answers those who truly believe. I thought I believed but Benny Kid Paret died anyway. I learned something not only about the inscrutable whimsicality of God but also about the precariousness of the life of a fighter." As a teenager, Early also witnessed fights in his own neighborhood, one of them "better than any professional fight I have seen before or since." Boxing has remained one of Early's defining passions, as has music. Along with the rock-and-roll music his sisters played, he recalls "the image of Chubby Checker riding around our neighborhood...in a bright, new yellow Cadillac." Several years later, he found his own true musical love—jazz—while staying with one of his sisters in San Francisco.

After graduating from high school, Early entered the University of Pennsylvania and started writing for the undergraduate paper, *The Daily Pennsylvanian*. His first pieces, he writes in *Tuxedo Junction*, covered the murder of his cousin Gino, a victim of gang warfare in West Philadelphia. Graduating in 1974, Early worked in 1977 as a "Communications Supervisor for the Crisis Intervention Network, a gang-control agency (how I loathed that term!)." In the same year, he married Ida Haynes and left his job to begin graduate work at Cornell. After earning an M.A. in 1980, he received his doctorate in 1982, and found work as an instructor at Washington University in St. Louis, Missouri. Within the year, according to *Contemporary Authors,* he was given the position of "Assistant Professor of black studies." The following year, he received a call from a production assistant working for a television show called *The Mississippi.* The star, Ralph Waite (best known for his role as John Walton on *The Waltons*), "wanted me to authenticate the language used by the blacks in the script." Although Early had no idea why he received the call, he needed money and so agreed to work on the script: "I do think that I improved the script immeasurably....I did not try to make the characters more *black;* I tried to make them more *human* and in this way their blackness became that much deeper....I certainly did not care whether my changes were used or not, although I am sure that my suggestion to make the orphan boy a lover of poetry was thrown out of the window with a particularly derisive grunt of disapproval."

In 1984, *Contemporary Authors* states, Early became an assistant professor both of English and of AFAS, African and Afro–American Studies. In 1988, he earned a promotion to associate professor. By the time he published his first book, *Tuxedo Junction: Essays on American Culture,* in 1989, his work had appeared twice in *Best American Essays.* After serving as writer-in-residence at the Randolph-Macon Woman's College, he edited *My Soul's High Song: The Collected Writings of Countee Cullen, Voice of the Harlem Renaissance* (1991). Appointed general editor of Ecco Press's Black Tower Series, which features new editions of Langston Hughes's *The First Book of Jazz,* Joe Louis's *My Life: An Autobiography,* and Jackie Robinson's *I Never Had It Made,* Early edited a collection for the series in 1992, *Speech & Power: The African-American Essay and Its Cultural Content, from Polemics to Pulpit.* Appointed director of AFAS, Early wrought many important changes in the program, according to a department news letter. In addition to creating an essay contest, a Young Writers series, and a Scholars Lecture series, he "organized academic conferences on subjects such as Blacks and Science, Miles Davis, and the neglected nonfiction works of author Richard Wright."

In 1993, Early edited *Lure and Loathing: Essays on Race, Identity, and the Ambivalence of Assimilation.* After assisting with Ken Burns's landmark documentary on baseball, which aired on PBS in 1994, he published *The Culture of Bruising: Essays on Literature, Prizefighting, and Modern American Culture,* winner of a National Book Critics Circle Award, and *Daughters: On Family and Fatherhood* (1994). In 1995, Early published *One Nation Under a Groove: Motown and American Culture* and assembled his first volume of poetry, *How the War in the Streets Is Won: Poems on the Quest of Love and Faith.* In the final years of the century, he edited *Body Language: Writers on Sport, "Ain't But a Place": An Anthology of African American Writings about St. Louis,* and *The Muhammad Ali Reader.*

Like many African-American writers, Gerald Early has an uneasy relationship with the subject of race. In "The Almost-Last Essay on Race in America," written in 1994 for the *Hungry Mind Review,* he claims that he was "sorely tempted" to renounce race as a writing topic until he considered, among other things, that "my authority, my expertise on the subject of race arise from such a genuinely existential and amusing source: to wit, having a black skin. Why strive for anything more when I can write from an unassailable position and, like a true self-absorbed American, perform rites of self-therapy and self-improvement at the same time?" The bitter satire of this explanation belies the dilemma Early ultimately experiences: that he can neither write about race nor stop writing about race in a way that is acceptable to himself and to readers. One of his strengths as a writer is that he describes the dilemmas, uncertainties, and paradoxes of his career and his identity with unflinching frankness. A cultural critic of impressive range and perspicacity, Early develops arguments from the concrete details and dilemmas of his personal life, of the history of sports and music, and of black literary traditions. And with the concrete details, rendered through his confident tone and his uncluttered descriptions, Early excels.

THEIR MALCOLM, MY PROBLEM (1992)

LATE ONE AFTERNOON last spring I sat at home on my couch, disheartened, thumbing through an old copy of *The Autobiography of Malcolm X*. Earlier that afternoon I'd had a lengthy meeting with black students from my university, and although Malcolm X had been in the air on campus for some time—the proliferation of X caps and T-shirts, gossip about the Spike Lee movie, which would open at the end of the year—I suspect it was mostly the passionate and angry tone of the black voices at the meeting that prompted me to pull my copy of the book off the shelf.

I had reread *The Autobiography* many times, having taught it on several occasions. A considerable literary accomplishment, it borrows freely and innovatively from *St. Augustine's Confessions*,[1] the slave narrative tradition, and the *bildungsroman*[2] tradition of Fielding[3] and Goethe.[4] As a boy I felt it was the only book written expressly for me, a young black American male. But over the years my view changed: the book's rhetoric began to seem awkwardly out of date, and the energy of the man seemed contained in a vision that was as narrow as it was vivid; there was something about the nature of Malcolm's raillery that now left me unprovoked, something about his quest for humanity that left me unmoved.

---

[1]*St. Augustine's Confessions* the autobiographical accounts of St. Augustine (354–430), an Algerian scholar who converted to Christianity and whose works deeply influenced the Church during the Middle Ages.

[2]*bildungsroman* a type of novel concerned with the education, development, and maturing of a young protagonist.

[3]*Fielding* Henry Fielding (1707–1754) a satiric and witty English playwright and writer, who was one of the first English novelists.

[4]*Goethe* Johann Wolfgang von Goethe (1749–1832) a German poet, dramatist, and scientist.

But as I sat on the couch working my way through the narrative that afternoon, I found much of what I'd been moved by so long ago coming back to me with remarkable force. I read again with revived interest how Malcolm was born in Omaha in 1925, the seventh child of a father who was an itinerant preacher, a fierce follower of Marcus Garvey,[5] and of a mother so light-skinned that she was frequently mistaken for white. When Malcolm was six years old his father was murdered, presumably by white terrorists, because of his black-nationalist beliefs. It is this death, as well as the institutionalization of his mother—who suffered a breakdown as the result of her husband's murder and her struggle to support her family on welfare—that establishes the pattern of both the book and the life as a critique of racism and liberalism. As Malcolm claims angrily, "I am a creation of the Northern white man and of his hypocritical attitude toward the Negro."

After growing up in a detention home in Mason, Michigan, and spending some time in Boston's Roxbury ghetto, living with his half-sister, Malcolm, at age seventeen, settled in Harlem and became a petty hustler and dope pusher. He participated in a string of burglaries of rich white suburban homes but was caught, convicted, and sentenced to ten years in prison. While in jail Malcolm converted to Elijah Muhammad's Nation of Islam, embracing a strict religious but militantly racialist outlook and dedicating himself to telling "the truth about the white man." Once out of prison, Malcolm became Muhammad's most effective minister and proselytizer, attracting adherents and also the attention of the white media. In 1964 Malcolm was excommunicated from the Nation, ostensibly for describing the assassination of John Kennedy as the "chickens coming home to roost." But a schism had been brewing for some time: Muhammad had become increasingly jealous over Malcolm's media attention, Malcolm's stardom, while Malcolm had become disillusioned by Muhammad's extramarital affairs and the older man's reluctance to become more politically active.

After leaving the Nation, Malcolm tried, unsuccessfully, to found two organizations, Muslim Mosque, Inc., and the Organization of Afro-American Unity, the latter patterned after the Organization of African Unity. During the last two years of his life, he traveled extensively in Africa and also made a pilgrimage to Mecca,[6] during which he reconverted to a nonracialist Islam. He was assassinated in Harlem by members of the Nation of Islam in February 1965, just as he was about to give a speech. An angry end to an angry life.

Leafing through *The Autobiography,* I began to see that Malcolm X was the ideological standard of Africanness now being offered up by my students. His singular presence had been much in evidence at that afternoon's meeting. I had agreed to sit down with a coalition of black students—most of whom did not know me—soon after it was announced that I was to become the new director of African and Afro-American Studies at my university. In the weeks before we arranged to convene, I had been furiously denounced and publicly pilloried for not being sufficiently Afrocentric to head the department, a charge rather akin to being "not black enough" in the 1960s.

What I found particularly baffling about these attacks was that I do not possess any of the "social tokens" often associated with being "insufficiently black": I do not have a

---

[5]*Marcus Garvey* (1887–1940) a Jamaican social activist who later worked and lived in Costa Rica, Panama, and New York. Garvey founded the Universal Negro Improvement Association in 1914; his later ventures failed and he was convicted of mail fraud in 1923 and deported from the U.S. in 1936.

[6]*Mecca* the birthplace of Mohammed; Muslims hope to be able to go there at least once in their lives.

white wife; I have served on most of the university's affirmative-action committees; I am intellectually engaged in the study of black subject matter; I have never publicly criticized any black person connected with the campus during my entire ten-year stay.

But in the eyes of these students, I had failed as a black man. I had never led a protest march or even proposed that one be held. I had never initiated or signed a petition. I had never attended any student meetings that focused on black issues. I had never, in short, done anything deemed heroic. And, for the young, a lack of demonstrable, outsized heroism is a lack of commitment and a lack of commitment is a sign of having sold out.

Some of this standard teacher-student strife is to be expected; I suppose it is generational. Still, I was deeply pained to have been seen by my black students as someone who compromised, who slouched, who shuffled, someone who had not stood up and been counted, someone who had never done anything heroic for the race.

When my ten-year-old daughter came home from school, she was surprised to find me home, and more surprised to find me visibly upset.

"What's wrong?" she asked.

"The American Negro," I began sarcastically, as she made herself a snack, "goes through periodic bouts of dementia when he romantically proclaims himself an African, lost from his brothers and sisters. These tides of benighted nationalism come and go, but this time it seems particularly acute." By now my voice had become strident, my rage nearly out of control.

"Never have I been subjected to more anti-intellectual, protofascistic nonsense than what I have had to endure in the name of Afrocentrism. And this man," I said, waving Malcolm's autobiography, "is the architect of it all, the father of Afrocentrism. This idiot, this fool." I slumped at the kitchen table, placing my forehead against the cool wood.

"But I thought you liked Malcolm X," she said.

Indeed, I was once keenly fond of Malcolm X. I first saw Malcolm on television in 1963, when I was a ten-year-old boy living in Philadelphia; three years later Malcolm, by now dead if not forgotten, left an indelible mark on my life. That year my oldest sister, then a college student, joined the local chapter of the Student Nonviolent Coordinating Committee (SNCC), which at the time was becoming an increasingly Marxist and militant group. Her conversation was now peppered with phrases like "the white power structure," "the man," "black power," and "self-determination for oppressed people." One day she brought home a recorded Malcolm X speech entitled "Message to the Grass Roots."

Hearing it for the first time was a shock and a revelation. I had heard men in barbershops say many of the same things but never in public. I laughed and laughed at Malcolm's oratory, but I felt each word burn with the brightness of a truth that was both utterly new and profoundly familiar. Whenever I had the chance, I would play the record over and over. In a few days I had memorized the entire speech, every word, every turn of phrase, every vocal nuance, I could deliver the speech just as Malcolm had. I never looked at the world in quite the same way again.

During the days of segregation, which continued, de facto, into the sixties, belonging to an all-black institution—anything from a church to a social club to a Boy Scout troop—was like wearing a badge of inferiority. Participation in these groups was not a choice made by blacks but a fiat, decreed by whites, which clearly stated that blacks were not considered, in any way, part of the white world—for most blacks, a world where what happened, mattered. But Malcolm asserted blackness as a source of honor and accomplishment, not degradation and shame.

Within months of the time I first heard Malcolm's "Message to the Grass Roots," I not only had read his autobiography but had listened carefully to other of his speeches, such as "The Ballot or the Bullet" and "Malcolm X on Afro-American History." I had become knowledgeable about the Congo, Patrice Lumumba,[7] the Bandung Conference,[8] and the leadership of the American civil rights movement, topics that were hardly of interest to other boys my age.

Not everyone I knew responded enthusiastically to Malcolm X. I would often hear men in the barbershop making statements like "All that Malcolm X does is talk. In fact, that's what all them Muslims do is talk. Just another nigger hustle." And one day, when I was fourteen, my friend Gary became very angry with me when—with Malcolm X in mind—I called him black.

"Don't call me black, man. I don't like that. I ain't black," he said vehemently.

"We are all black people," I said. "You've been brainwashed by the white man to hate your color. But you're black, and you've got to accept that."

"I said don't call me black," he shouted. "What's wrong with you, anyway? You sound like you been hanging out with them Malcolm X guys. He was a phony just like all the rest of them Muslims. You sound like you snappin' out or something."

I was surprised at Gary's reaction. He was bigger and tougher than I was, and I assumed that he would view Malcolm as a hero, too. But when it became clear he didn't, I felt personally insulted.

"You're black, black, black," I said angrily. "Malcolm X was a great man who tried to free black people. What've you ever done to free black people? You're black and I'll call you black anytime I want to, you dumb nigger."

He hit me so hard in the chest that I fell down in the street, stunned and hurt by the blow.

"Don't call me that," he said, walking away.

It is unlikely that a young black person today would get swatted for defending Malcolm X. In fact, in many ways Malcolm's presence is more deeply felt in the black community now than at any time since his murder. The reasons for his enduring legacy are complex. Malcolm X does not remain an important figure in American cultural history simply because he was a charismatic black nationalist. Hubert H. Harrison, Henry McNeal Turner, Richard B. Moore, Martin Delany, David Walker, Elijah Muhammad, Alexander Crummell, Edward Wilmot Blyden, and Ron Karenga all were charismatic black nationalists of some sort in the nineteenth and twentieth centuries, and none is remembered as a distinct figure except by historians of African-American life and culture.

Malcolm was a fierce debater, a compelling public speaker, and a man of considerable intellectual agility. But, like Martin Luther King, he was hardly an original thinker: American blacks have been hearing some form of black nationalism—Ethiopianism, the back-to-Africa movement, Black Judaism, the Black Moors, Pan-Africanism, the Black Aesthetic, or Afrocentrism—for well over two hundred years. Malcolm's basic idea—a

---

[7]*Patrice Lumumba* (1925–1961) a Congolese statesman and prime minister (1960), who was assassinated in 1961.

[8]*Bandung Conference* a 1955 meeting of diplomats from 29 African and Asian countries held in Bandung, Indonesia. The conference promoted economic and cultural cooperation, while opposing colonialism.

vision of millenarian race-based cultural nationalism culminating in a worldwide race war that would overturn European dominance forever—was, like the Puritanism of *Jonathan Edwards,*[9] already hoary with age even when it seemed most current. But just as Edwards brilliantly disseminated Calvinist[10] ideas, Malcolm, with valor and wit, popularized ideas about black nationalism, black self-determination, and a universal African identity.

More important, however, than Malcolm's ideas—that is, his popularizing of black nationalism—was, and is, Malcolm the man. His life unfolded like a myth, a heroic tale. He had the imprimatur of both prison (the mark of a revolutionary) and the street (the mark of the proletariat), which lent him authenticity. But, as a Muslim, he was also a firm believer in the bourgeois ideals of diligence, discipline, and entrepreneurship.

Then there was Malcolm's youth. Although generational conflict exists in many societies, it has a long and particularly intense history for blacks. Each new generation views its elders with suspicion, thinking them failures who compromised and accommodated themselves in order to survive among the whites. And each generation, in some way, wishes to free itself from the generation that produced it.

Malcolm's particular brand of youthfulness fed this desire. He embodied a daring and a recklessness that young blacks, especially young black men, have found compelling. At rallies I attended as a teenager in the early 1970s, men older than myself would describe the inspiring experience of having heard Malcolm live. They had, on several occasions a decade earlier, attended Savior's Day rallies, annual Muslim conventions during which Elijah Muhammad was scheduled to speak. But Malcolm would always appear on the dais first. He was supposed to serve, simply, as the warmup act, but for these young men he always stole the show. While black nationalist and separatist ideas coming from Elijah Muhammad seemed cranky, cultlike, backwaterish, and marginal, the same ideas coming from Malcolm seemed revolutionary, hip, and vibrant.

Malcolm arrived on the scene during the age of Kennedy and King, the blossoming of youth culture and the coming of rock and roll. Flaunting his youth as a symbol of masculinity and magnetic power, he exploited the generation gap among blacks. Because of Malcolm, the leaders of the civil rights movement were made, through their comparative conservatism, to seem even older than they were, more cowardly than they were, bigger sellouts than they were. He referred to them as "Uncle Toms" or as "Uncles," associating them with the conflated popular image of both Uncle Remus and Uncle Tom, fictional characters created by white writers, aged black men who "loved their white folks." Malcolm used this language even when talking about Martin Luther King, who was, in fact, younger than he was. And Malcolm remains forever young, having died at the age of thirty-nine. He—like the Kennedys and King—died the tragic death of a political martyr.

Malcolm, the dead hero, has grown in stature in our black consciousness even while other living former heroes are forgotten. It is telling to compare the current view of Malcolm with that of another important black figure of the 1960s, Muhammad Ali. Ali and Malcolm are often voiced together in the black mind; two militant Muslims, public troublemakers, disturbers of the peace. But today, those of us who lived through the 1960s return to thinking about Malcolm not simply because of his greater intellect but because

---

[9]*Jonathan Edwards* (1703–1758) a colonial clergyman and theologian who espoused a particularly strict Calvinist doctrine and is regarded as the epitome of extreme American Puritanism.

[10]*Calvinist* one who follows the doctrines and teachings of John Calvin, which emphasize predestination, the sovereignty of God, and the supreme authority of the Christian Scriptures.

we are unnerved by Ali now, by the brain damage he has suffered in the ring, by the way he has aged. Malcolm remains frozen forever in his stern youthfulness, almost immortal, like a saint, while Ali is a mirror of our own aging and mortality, a busted-up, broken-down hero.

No doubt Malcolm's early death contributed to his enduring power for young people today. But it is the existence of *The Autobiography* that has mythologized him forever. If Malcolm—or Alex Haley (who assisted in writing *The Autobiography*) or Malcolm's wife, Betty Shabazz (who is said to have done extensive revisions on Haley's manuscript)—had not written his story, he would have died a negligible curiosity on the American political landscape in much the same way that, say, George Lincoln Rockwell[11] or Father Divine[12] did. Today it is rare to come upon a black student who has not read *The Autobiography of Malcolm X* or will not read it at some point during his or her college career. It has sold more than three million copies and is probably the most commonly taught and most frequently recommended book written by a black American male.

Malcolm, frozen in time, stands before us as the lonely outsider, a kind of bespectacled prince, estranged and embattled, holding a high-noon posture of startling and doomed confrontation. It is this man who has become for young blacks today the kind of figure that *Thoreau,* who espoused the overturning of generations and the uselessness of the elders in *Walden,* was for young whites in the late 1960s.

When I was growing up in the 1960s the goal for blacks was clear: equality and integration. The civil rights movement, which provided an arena for heroic political action aimed at destroying segregation, helped forge this consensus among blacks. Today blacks, confused and angered by the failure of "the dream," share little agreement about the future. There is a sense that integration has been halfhearted and has been achieved only at the expense of black identity.

To today's young, middle-class blacks in particular, Malcolm's espousal of all-blackness—the idea that everything black is inherently good and that blacks must purge themselves of white "contaminants"—may be especially crucial; it is certainly more important than it was to my generation. These young people have grown up, by and large, in an integrated world. Most of the black students who attend the standard prestigious, private, research-oriented university are the offspring of either black professional parents or a mixed marriage, have lived most of their lives in mixed or largely white neighborhoods, and have attended white prep schools or predominantly white public schools. When they arrive at a university that has an African or Afro-American studies program, these students expect to find, for the first time in their lives, an all-black community, one that they have never experienced in the secular world, a sort of intellectual "nation within a nation," to borrow W. E. B. Du Bois's term. There they can be their "true" black selves. Yet in many ways these black students share fundamentally the same values—a belief in upward mobility and the rewards of hard work—as the whites who surround them. These students are wholly neither inside nor outside of the American mainstream, and they are

---

[11]*Rockwell* (1918–1967) anti-semitic, white supremacist leader of American Nazi Party.

[12]*Father Divine* George Baker (1880–1965) popular leader of interracial cult in 1930s who gave free banquets to gain members and became one of the largest landlords in Harlem. He lost influence after a series of scandals.

unsure whether any ideal form of integration exists. But, like Malcolm, they wish to rid themselves of their feelings of ambiguity, their sense of the precariousness of their belonging. For many of them (and they are not entirely unjustified in feeling this way) integration is the badge of degradation and dishonor, of shame and inferiority, that segregation was for my generation.

I also have felt great shame in the era of integration because, as a student and as a professor, I have taken the money of whites, been paid simply because I was black and was expected to make "black statements" in order to be praised by whites for my Negroness. I have felt much as if I were doing what James Baldwin described black domestics in white homes as doing: stealing money and items from whites that the whites expected them to take, wanted them to take, because it reinforced the whites' superiority and our own degradation. Allowing the whites to purchase my "specialness" through affirmative action has seemed not like reparations but like a new form of enslavement.

And I worry about my daughters, wondering whether they are getting too cozy with whites at school and whether they seem too utterly middle class. So much are they protected from any blatant form of racism that I fear they are likely never to understand that it existed and continues to exist today. At these times I feel estranged from my children, knowing that I do not fully understand their experience, nor do they understand mine. For instance, when we moved to an affluent white suburb they clamored for a golden retriever, no doubt because a neighbor down the street had a very attractive one. I adamantly refused to consent, thinking that purchasing a friendly, suburban, sit-com-type dog was another concession to white, middle-class taste. "I don't like dogs," I said childishly before I finally relented.

On occasions like this, when I have wanted to instill in my daughters a sense of "blackness," I tend to trot out a story about my boyhood. It is an anecdote that involves my friend Gary, and it took place about six months after our fight over Malcolm X. Think of my story as the black parent's jeremiad, a warning about the declension of the new generation. And once again Malcolm X seems central to it.

In order to get home from school each day, Gary and I had to walk through an Italian neighborhood. Often during these trips home, several older Italian boys and their Doberman pinschers would chase Gary and me, or a group of us, for several blocks. Once we hit the border of our black Philadelphia neighborhood, around Sixth Street, they would retreat. The Italian boys called this game "chasing the coons" or "spooking the spooks," and it sometimes resulted in a black kid being bitten by one of their dogs. The black kids never fought back; we just ran, later cursing the Italian boys, rhetorically wreaking all manner of vengeance upon them.

On this particular afternoon, both Gary and I had bought sodas and doughnuts, as we usually did, on our way home from school, and we were strolling along when we suddenly heard some voices cry out, "Get those niggers." We turned to see about five or six Italian boys and an unleashed Doberman coming after us. We started running like beings possessed. We were comfortably ahead and easily could have avoided getting caught when Gary abruptly pulled up and caught my arm.

"I'm tired of running from them guys. I ain't running anymore and neither are you."

"Hey, man," I said frantically. "Are you crazy or something? What are we gonna do? Fight 'em? You must be crazy. I'm getting out of here."

"You ain't going nowhere," he said angrily through his teeth. "It's time we stood up for ourselves. I'm tired of having them white bastards chase me and laugh at me. If they beat us up, well, I guess that's one ass whipping we got to take. But I ain't running."

Gary turned his soda bottle over in his hand like a weapon and I reluctantly did the same. He picked up a brick from the street and I followed; we waited for the Italian boys to catch up. When they did they looked almost bewildered. They stood, perhaps twenty feet from us, slowly comprehending that we were standing our ground. For several moments, except for the growling dog, everyone was silent. Then one of them spoke.

"What you niggers doing walking through our neighborhood? We got a hunting season on jungle bunnies."

"We ain't causing no trouble," Gary said. "We just minding our own business. And if you come another step closer, I guarantee I'll put your ass in the hospital."

We all stood for what seemed the longest time, as if frozen in some sort of still life. I was gripping the brick and bottle so hard my hands ached. I felt ready, even eager, to fight, but I was also relieved when I realized we wouldn't have to.

One Italian boy mumbled something about watching ourselves "next time," and they all began to drift off.

As they were retreating, Gary shouted, "And we ain't no niggers. We're black. Don't ever call us niggers again."

At this I was more than slightly startled, but I was very proud, as if I had made a convert. I recalled at that instant something I had heard Malcolm X say on television, something like, "The so-called Negro has to stop the sit-in, the beg-in, the crawl-in, asking for something that is by rights already his. The so-called Negro has to approach the white man as a man himself." We felt like men, grown-up men, or what we thought grown-up men must feel like when they have been tested and found themselves adequate.

Never once have I told this story in any way that impresses my daughters. My youngest usually says, "Are you finished now, Daddy?"

They know the moral is something to the effect that it is good to be black and that it is something for which we must all stand up. "Yeah," my youngest says, "it's good to be black, but it's better not to have to spend all your time thinking about how good it is to be black."

So here I am, caught between my daughters, who find my race lessons tiresome, and my students, who think me somehow insufficiently black. I need look no farther than Malcolm, old ally and new nemesis, to find the source of this ambiguity. Malcolm embodied contradiction. He preached the importance of Africa, yet he was the most American of men. His autobiography is the quintessential Horatio Alger[13] tale of the self-created individual. Even Malcolm's turn toward Islam, his attempt to embrace something explicitly non-Western, is itself classically American. Americans have long been attracted to the East—in the form of nineteenth-century orientalism, twentieth-century Egyptology, and the current-day popularity, among many middle-class whites, of yoga and Zen Buddhism. Even Afrocentrism itself can be seen as classically American in its urge to romanticize and reinvent the past, much in the way that Jay Gatsby[14] did.

And yet Fitzgerald's novel clearly warns against the temptation to remake the past and the seduction of fraudulent identities. It is in its defining of identity that Malcolm's thinking is uncomfortably rigid and finally false. He developed two distinct but related beliefs

---

[13]*Horatio Alger* (1834–1899) an American author who wrote inspirational novels about young men working hard, being honest, and thus becoming successful.

[14]*Jay Gatsby* the main character in F. Scott Fitzgerald's 1925 novel *The Great Gatsby*.

about black identity: that blacks are not Americans and that they are really Africans. "We are just as much African today as we were in Africa four hundred years ago, only we are a modern counterpart of it," Malcolm X said at Harvard in 1964. "When you hear a black man playing music, whether it is jazz or Bach, you still hear African music. In everything else we do we still are African in color, feeling, everything. And we will always be that whether we like it or not."

By preaching a romantic reunification with mythological Africa as a way of generating pride and racial unity, Malcolm advocated a single identity for all black people, one that implicitly removed individual distinctions among blacks. In Malcolm's view, individuality is a negligible European creation, while the holy "community"—a creation of the African and other dark-skinned peoples—is prized above everything else. The idea of race as community, as invisible church, however, can demand a stifling conformity; its popularity suggests that some aspects of Afrocentrism, or all-blackness, as Malcolm popularized them and as they are preached in some quarters today, far from being imaginative or innovative, are utterly prosaic and philistine in their vision.

Despite the unrealistic romanticism of Malcolm's back-to-Africa preachings, he offers an important message for today's young blacks: that blacks are, indeed, as Du Bois[15] argues, a people of "double-consciousness"; that both blackness and Americanness are real options, each having meaning only when measured against the other. Malcolm would not have argued with such passion and virulence against the validity of any kind of black *American* experience if he did not suspect that assimilation, that *being* American, was truly a rooted desire, if not a fulfilled reality, for most blacks. Yet he also knew that blacks in America cannot think about what their Americanness means without thinking about what it means to be of African descent: the two are inextricably bound together. As the historian Sterling Stuckey[16] has argued, black people did not acquire a sense of what being African was until they came to America. They, like most people who came to this country, achieved their initial sense of identity through their clan—that is, slaves thought of themselves more as members of specific tribes or nations than as "Africans." Slavery compressed the diversity of African experience into one broad African identity, forcing blacks, in turn, to invent a collective sense of an African memory and an African self.

But Africanness is relevant to American blacks today only as a way of helping us understand what it means to be American. While it is necessary that we recognize our African ancestry, and remember that it was, in varying degrees, stripped away by slavery, we must acknowledge, finally, that our story is one of remaking ourselves as Americans. My world is shaped by two indelible ideas: first, that I was once an African, that I grew, generations ago, from that ancestral soil; and, second, that I will never be African again, that I will, like Joseph, not be buried in the soil of my long-ago ancestors.

Malcolm preached the necessity of being African at the complete expense of our American selves, a love of the misty past at the cost of our actual lives, our triumphs, our suf-

---

[15]*Du Bois* W. E. B. Du Bois (1868–1963) a professor of economics and history who called for the African-American middle class to fight against bigoted racial policies; a black activist who worked for the National Association for the Advancement of Colored People, became a Marxist, and left the United States to be a citizen of Ghana.

[16]*Sterling Stuckey* P. Sterling Stuckey is a renowned scholar of slavery and Afro-American intellectual and cultural history; Stuckey is currently a professor at the University of California, Riverside.

ferings in the New World and as modern people. In this way, Malcolm merely increased our anxiety, further fueled our sense of inadequacy, and intensified our self-hatred and feelings of failure by providing us with a ready excuse: America is the white man's country, and the whites don't want you here and will never give you equal citizenship.

But it must always be remembered that our blood is here, our names are here, our fate is here, in a land we helped to invent. By that I have in mind much more than the fact that blacks gave America free labor; other groups have helped build this and other countries for no or for nominal wages. We have given America something far more valuable: we have given her her particular identity, an identity as a country dedicated to diversity, a nation of different peoples living together as one. And no black person should care what the whites want or don't want in the realm of integration. The whites simply must learn to live as committed equals with their former slaves.

Our profound past of being African, which we must never forget, must be balanced by the complex fate of being American, which we can never deny or, worse, evade. For we must accept who and what we are and the forces and conditions that have made us this, not as defeat or triumph, not in shame or with grandiose pride, but as the tangled, strange, yet poignant and immeasurable record of an imperishable human presence.

Understanding and Analysis

1. What is the situation that prompts Early to reread *The Autobiography* this time?

2. How does Early connect the African-American students at his university with Malcolm X at the end of Early's retelling of Malcolm X's life?

3. What does Early tell us his students expect from a hero? Where else in the essay does the word "hero" appear? How does its meaning change, depending on who uses the term?

4. The idea of "generational" differences is very important in this essay. Locate all references to this idea and explain its importance to Early's main point.

5. What had the younger Early particularly liked about Malcolm X?

6. What are the three major causes, according to Early, for Malcolm X's enduring appeal?

7. How have the goals for African-Americans changed since the 1960s, according to Early? Why?

8. What "feelings of ambiguity" does Early attribute to himself and his African-American students?

9. Why does he retell the second story of his adventures with Gary? What roles do he and Gary play in this story? How do his children react to this story? Why?

10. What ambiguity does Malcolm X "embody," according to Early?

11. What does Early reject in Malcolm X's teachings?

12. Early constructs his essay very carefully. How does the last paragraph connect to the opening paragraphs?

13. Examine Early's diction. What stereotype does he play on when he writes that he was "deeply pained to have been seen by my black students as someone who compromised, who slouched, who shuffled, someone who had not stood up and been counted, someone who had never done anything heroic for the race"? Find and analyze other allusive uses of language in the essay.

Comparison

1. Read Podhoretz's "My Negro Problem—and Ours." Do you hear an echo of Podhoretz's title in Early's title? If so, why do you think Early makes that reference? Compare the stories these authors tell. How are they similar and how do they differ?

2. Read Malcolm X's "Message to the Grass Roots." Do you see in that speech any of the virtues and faults Early attributes to Malcolm X?

3. Read the two essays by Baldwin. Both Early and Podhoretz were deeply influenced by Baldwin. To what degree do they differ from him and from each other in these essays? Compare the ideas of Baldwin, Podhoretz, and Early to the ideas of Malcolm X as presented in Malcolm X's speech and in Early's essay.

Stephanie Coontz
(1944–)

Family historian Stephanie Coontz was born on August 31, 1944, in Seattle, Washington. Her own family, which she characterizes as "untraditional," had long lived in the area, and when she was young, her grandparents "regaled me with stories about pioneer life in Puget Sound." Although Coontz left the state of Washington to attend college, graduating from UC Berkeley in 1966 with a B.A. in history, she returned for graduate school, earning her M.A. in European history at the University of Washington in 1970, and then moving to Olympia to work. Since the mid-1970s, Coontz has been a member of the faculty at the Evergreen State College, where she teaches, as the university boasts, "American, European and economic history, expository writing, family studies, Third World history, [and] women's studies."

After Coontz wrote her first book, *Women's Work, Men's Property: On the Origins of Gender and Class* (1986), co-authored with Peta Henderson, she accepted her first exchange position, teaching at the Kobe University of Commerce in Japan. Her next book, *The Social Origins of Private Life: A History of American Families, 1600–1900* (1988), started her on the path to fame, prompting "numerous speaking requests from nonacademic audiences—hospital ethics committees concerned about how to define families, psychologists' and social workers' organizations, church groups, Rotary clubs, and labor organizations." In 1991, she published *America's Families: Fables and Facts*, and in 1992, she published one of her most famous books, *The Way We Never Were: American Families and the Nostalgia Trap*, which she prepared for press while working in her second exchange position at the University of Hawaii in Hilo. In *The Way We Never Were*, Coontz challenges myths about American families, particularly the myths about the functional, happy, white nuclear family of the 1950s and the dysfunctional, "pathological" black family whose "collapse"—touted since Reconstruction—is responsible for poverty, unemployment, and drug abuse in the black community. Published in a presidential election year dominated by debates about family values, *The Way We Never Were* increased Coontz's reputation and her visibility, making her a popular authority on the American family, as valued on *Oprah* as on CNN.

In 1994, Coontz returned to the University of Hawaii to serve as a visiting associate professor of sociology. Three years later, she published *The Way We Really Are: Coming to Terms with America's Changing Families*, in which she calls for an end to debates about "the relative merits of ideal family types" and the beginning of a "discussion about how to build the support systems that modern families need." Contributing to both popular and scholarly discourse about families, she has written numerous articles for magazines, journals, and newspapers on subjects ranging from divorce to childcare. She is also frequently consulted by members of the media, as she explains in an article for *Salon* magazine, and was at one time "getting calls almost daily from reporters assigned to develop stories around the concept 'What the family will look like in the coming millennium.'" By way of response, she writes: "There are two big problems with discussing what will happen to the family in the next millennium. The first is that it presumes there is such a thing as a typical family.... The second is that the question ignores the political and social choices that will affect the answer. We're not tracking long-range weather patterns here."

Participating in one of the leading debates of late twentieth-century America, the debate about family values, Stephanie Coontz has tried to change the terms of the conversation, arguing that the relative health of the ideal family has far less to do with values than with economics, consumerism, politics, and governmental policies. She has also worked to correct "wild exaggerations" in the media that derive from decontextualized, ahistorical interpretations of statistics. For example, the media proclaimed in 1991 that more women were choosing to stay at home, or in the words of one headline, "More Women Opting for Chance to Watch Their Children Grow." Coontz writes:

> The cause of all this commotion? The percentage of women aged twenty-five to thirty-four who were employed dropped from 74 percent to 72.8 percent between January 1990 and January 1991. However, there was an exactly equal decline in the percentage of men in the work force during the same period, and for both sexes the explanation was the same. 'The dip is the recession,' explained Judy Waldrop, research editor at *American Demographics* magazine, to anyone who bothered to listen.

A Nation of Welfare Families (*1992*)

THE CURRENT POLITICAL debate over family values, personal responsibility, and welfare takes for granted the entrenched American belief that dependence on government assistance is a recent and destructive phenomenon. Conservatives tend to blame this dependence on personal irresponsibility aggravated by a swollen welfare apparatus that saps individual initiative. Liberals are more likely to blame it on personal misfortune magnified by the harsh lot that falls to losers in our competitive market economy. But both sides believe that "winners" in America make it on their own, that dependence reflects some kind of individual or family failure, and that the ideal family is the self-reliant unit of traditional lore—a family that takes care of its own, carves out a future for its children, and never asks for handouts. Politicians at both ends of the ideological spectrum have wrapped themselves in the mantle of these "family values," arguing over *why* the poor have not been able to make do without assistance, or whether aid has exacerbated their situation, but never questioning the assumption that American families traditionally achieve success by establishing their independence from the government.

The myth of family self-reliance is so compelling that our actual national and personal histories often buckle under its emotional weight. "We always stood on our own two feet," my grandfather used to say about his pioneer heritage, whenever he walked me to the top of the hill to survey the property in Washington State that his family had bought for next to nothing after it had been logged off in the early 1900s. Perhaps he didn't know that the land came so cheap because much of it was part of a federal subsidy originally allotted to the railroad companies, which had received 183 million acres of the public domain in the nineteenth century. These federal giveaways were the original source of most major Western logging companies' land, and when some of these logging companies moved on to virgin stands of timber, federal lands trickled down to a few early settlers who were able to purchase them inexpensively.

Like my grandparents, few families in American history—whatever their "values"—have been able to rely solely on their own resources. Instead, they have depended on the legislative, judicial, and social-support structures set up by governing authorities, whether those authorities were the clan elders of Native American societies, the church courts and city officials of colonial America, or the judicial and legislative bodies established by the Constitution.

At America's inception, this was considered not a dirty little secret but the norm, one that confirmed our social and personal interdependence. The idea that the family should have the sole or even primary responsibility for educating and socializing its members, finding them suitable work, or keeping them from poverty and crime was not only ludicrous to colonial and revolutionary thinkers but dangerously parochial.

Historically, one way that government has played a role in the well-being of its citizens is by regulating the way that employers and civic bodies interact with families. In the early twentieth century, for example, as a response to rapid changes ushered in by a mass-production economy, the government promoted a "family wage system." This system was designed to strengthen the ability of the male breadwinner to support a family without having his wife or children work. This family wage system was not a natural outgrowth of the market. It was a *political* response to conditions that the market had produced: child labor, rampant employment insecurity, recurring economic downturns, an earnings structure in which 45 percent of industrial workers fell below the poverty level and another 40 percent hovered barely above it, and a system in which thousands of children had been placed in orphanages or other institutions simply because their parents could not afford their keep. The state policies involved in the establishment of the family wage system included abolition of child labor, government pressure on industrialists to negotiate with unions, federal arbitration, expansion of compulsory schooling—and legislation discriminating against women workers.

But even such extensive regulation of economic and social institutions has never been enough: government has always supported families with direct material aid as well. The two best examples of the government's history of material aid can be found in what many people consider the ideal models of self-reliant families: the Western pioneer family and the 1950s suburban family. In both cases, the ability of these families to establish and sustain themselves required massive underwriting by the government.

Pioneer families, such as my grandparents, could never have moved west without government-funded military mobilizations against the original Indian and Mexican inhabitants or state-sponsored economic investment in transportation systems. In addition, the Homestead Act of 1862 allowed settlers to buy 160 acres for $10—far below the government's cost of acquiring the land—if the homesteader lived on and improved the land for five years. In the twentieth century, a new form of public assistance became crucial to Western families: construction of dams and other federally subsidized irrigation projects. During the 1930s, for example, government electrification projects brought pumps, refrigeration, and household technology to millions of families.

The suburban family of the 1950s is another oft-cited example of familial self-reliance. According to legend, after World War II a new, family-oriented generation settled down, saved their pennies, worked hard, and found well-paying jobs that allowed them to purchase homes in the suburbs. In fact, however, the 1950s suburban family was far more dependent on government assistance than any so-called underclass family of today. Federal GI benefit payments, available to 40 percent of the male population between the ages of twenty and twenty-four, permitted a whole generation of men to expand their education and improve their job prospects without forgoing marriage and children. The National Defense Education Act[1] retooled science education in America, subsidizing both American industry and the education of individual scientists. Government-funded research developed the aluminum clapboards, prefabricated walls and ceilings, and plywood paneling that comprised the technological basis of the postwar housing revolution. Government spending was also largely responsible for the new highways, sewer systems, utility services, and traffic-control programs that opened up suburbia.

In addition, suburban home ownership depended on an unprecedented expansion of federal regulation and financing. Before the war, banks often required a 50 percent down payment on homes and normally issued mortgages for five to ten years. In the postwar period, however, the Federal Housing Authority, supplemented by the *GI Bill,* put the federal government in the business of insuring and regulating private loans for single-home construction. FHA policy required down payments of only 5 to 10 percent of the purchase price and guaranteed mortgages of up to thirty years at interest rates of just 2 to 3 percent. The Veterans Administration required a mere dollar down from veterans. Almost half the housing in suburbia in the 1950s depended on such federal programs.

---

[1]*National Defense Education Act* After the Soviet Union launched the rocket, Sputnik, in 1957, an alarmed American government passed this bill, dramatically increasing federal spending on science education and research.

The drawback of these aid programs was that although they worked well for recipients, non-recipients—disproportionately poor and urban—were left far behind. While the general public financed the roads that suburbanites used to commute, the streetcars and trolleys that served urban and poor families received almost no tax revenues, and our previously thriving rail system was allowed to decay. In addition, federal loan policies, which were a boon to upwardly mobile white families, tended to systematize the pervasive but informal racism that had previously characterized the housing market. FHA redlining practices, for example, took entire urban areas and declared them ineligible for loans, while the government's two new mortgage institutions, the Federal National Mortgage Association and the Government National Mortgage Association (Fannie Mae and Ginny Mae) made it possible for urban banks to transfer savings out of the cities and into new suburban developments in the South and West.

Despite the devastating effects on families and regions that did not receive such assistance, government aid to suburban residents during the 1950s and 1960s produced in its beneficiaries none of the demoralization usually presumed to afflict recipients of government handouts. Instead, federal subsidies to suburbia encouraged family formation, residential stability, upward occupational mobility, and rising educational aspirations among youth who could look forward to receiving such aid. Seen in this light, the idea that government subsidies intrinsically induce dependence, undermine self-esteem, or break down family ties is exposed as no more than a myth.

I am not suggesting that the way to solve the problems of poverty and urban decay in America is to quadruple our spending on welfare. Certainly there are major reforms needed in our current aid policies to the poor. But the debate over such reform should put welfare in the context of all federal assistance programs. As long as we pretend that only poor or single-parent families need outside assistance, while normal families "stand on their own two feet," we will shortchange poor families, overcompensate rich ones, and fail to come up with effective policies for helping out families in the middle. Current government housing policies are a case in point. The richest 20 percent of American households receives three times as much federal housing aid—mostly in tax subsidies—as the poorest 20 percent receives in expenditures for low-income housing.

Historically, the debate over government policies toward families has never been over *whether* to intervene but *how:* to rescue or to warehouse, to prevent or to punish, to moralize about values or mobilize resources for education and job creation. Today's debate, lacking such historical perspective, caricatures the real issues. Our attempt to sustain the myth of family self-reliance in the face of all the historical evidence to the contrary has led policymakers into theoretical contortions and practical miscalculations that are reminiscent of efforts by medieval philosophers to maintain that the earth and not the sun was the center of the planetary system. In the sixteenth century, leading European thinkers insisted that the planets and the sun all revolved around the earth—much as American politicians today insist that our society revolves around family self-reliance. When evidence to the contrary mounted, defenders of the Ptolemaic[2] universe postulated all sorts of elaborate planetary orbits in order to reconcile observed reality with their cherished theory. Similarly, rather than admit that all families need some kind of public support, we have constructed ideological orbits that explain away each instance of middle-class dependence as an "exception," an "abnormality," or even an illusion. We have distrib-

---

[2]*Ptolemaic universe* an Earth-centered universe, based on the writings of Ptolemy, a Greek astronomer (145–127 B.C.).

uted public aid to families through convoluted bureaucracies that have become impossible to track; in some cases the system has become so cumbersome that it threatens to collapse around our ears. It is time to break through the old paradigm of self-reliance and substitute a new one that recognizes that assisting families is, simply, what government does.

Understanding and Analysis

1. In the opening two paragraphs, Coontz sets out her thesis and attempts to appeal to both liberals and conservatives. What strategies does she use to establish her own character as an objective analyzer of the problem? How does she characterize both the right and the left?

2. How does the first sentence of the third paragraph reinforce her role as an objective observer?

3. What has been the history of government assistance, according to Coontz?

4. What, according to Coontz, were the benefits and drawbacks of the assistance programs after World War II?

5. What is Coontz's position on welfare? What is her main point in this essay?

6. Examine her diction in this essay. Does she modify assertions to avoid extremes? If so, where? Does she make extreme assertions? If so, where?

Comparison

1. Compare Coontz's analogy and her use of the term "old paradigm" to Kuhn's explanation of a paradigm shift in "Anomaly and the Emergence of Scientific Discoveries." Do you think Coontz is using the term properly? Why or why not?

2. Read Postman's "Learning by Story." Compare Postman's "story" and Kuhn's "paradigm shift" to Coontz's description of the "myth" of self-reliance.

3. Read Reich's essay. Does Coontz's explanation of government's support of education, housing, and so on help you to reinterpret the reasons for the ever-widening gulf between rich and poor that Reich describes?

4. Read the essay by Fukuyama. How does his essay inform your reading of Coontz?

Martin Gardner
(1914–)

Born October 21, 1914, Martin Gardner grew up in Tulsa, Oklahoma. During high school, as he told Kendrick Frazier in a 1998 interview, he was a gymnast and a tennis player, though he lost the ability to play when he "had cataract surgery early in life." After he entered the University of Chicago in 1932, he found that his decision to major in philosophy brought him into crisis with his religious upbringing "as a Protestant fundamentalist." He told Frazier: "I quickly lost my entire faith in Christianity. It was a painful transition." Although he determined early on that he wanted to become a writer, he little imagined a future of writing about mathematics and so "took not a single math course." He was, however, an excellent student and a member of Phi Beta Kappa. In 1936, he graduated, returned to Tulsa, and began working as a reporter for the *Tulsa Tribune*. Later he returned to Chicago to work for his alma mater in the Press Relations department, but his work there was cut short with the outbreak of World War II. From 1942 to 1946, Gardner served as a yeoman in the Naval Reserve.

When he was released from duty, Gardner "returned to Chicago and would have gone back to my former job…had I not sold a humorous short story to *Esquire*. This was my first payment for anything I'd written. It persuaded me to see if I could survive as a freelancer, and for the next year or two I lived on income from sales of fiction to *Esquire*." In 1952, the year he married Charlotte Greenwald, he became a contributing editor of *Humpty Dumpty's*, a bi-monthly children's magazine featuring stories, poems, and puzzles. He also published his first book, *In the Name of Science* (1952). A spirited debunking of pseudoscience, with a chapter devoted to L. Ron Hubbard's *Dianetics* and another to UFOs, the book was a major flop from the publisher's perspective, selling "so poorly that Putnam quickly remaindered it." It fared much better with a new title and new publisher, appearing as *Fads and Fallacies in the Name of Science* in 1957. Gardner told Frazier that the success of *Fads and Fallacies* owed much to Long John Nebel, then a popular all-night radio talk-show host. For many months, he had guests on almost every night to attack the book. I remember one night, when I had gotten out of bed to change a diaper on our first born, I turned on the radio and heard John Campbell, then editor of Astounding Science Fiction, say 'Mr. Gardner is a liar.'"

In 1956, a year before *Fads and Fallacies* started to sell, Gardner published a book called *Mathematics, Magic and Mystery*. In 1957, he took his most famous job, working, in the words of *Contemporary Authors*, as a "writer in the mathematical games department" of *Scientific American*. Learning about math as he went along—"There is no better way to learn anything than to write about it!" he told Frazier—he soon began to publish his renowned collections of puzzles: *The Scientific American Book of Mathematical Puzzles and Diversions* (1959), *The Second Scientific American Book of Mathematical Puzzles and Diversions* (1960), and *Mathematical Puzzles* (1961). After he gave up his position with *Humpty Dumpty's* in 1962, he wrote books for children in addition to his puzzle collections. He also edited works by Lewis Carroll: in 1960, *The Annotated Alice: Alice's Adventures in Wonderland and Through the Looking Glass*, and in 1962, *The Annotated Snark*. Despite the immense popularity of his math books, *The Annotated Alice* remains his greatest seller. *The Ambidextrous Universe* (1964), however, may be his favorite book from the decade.

After publishing his first novel, the semi-autobiographical *The Flight of Peter Fromm*, in 1973, Gardner helped to found the Committee for the Scientific Investigation of Claims of the Paranormal (CSICOP) in 1976 and returned to debunking pseudoscience in 1981 with *Science: Good, Bad, and Bogus*. Retiring from *Scientific American*, he started a column for CSICOP's magazine, *Skeptical Inquirer*, called "Notes of a Fringe-Watcher" in 1983. In the same year, he also a published *The Whys of a Philosophical Scrivener*, a "book of essays about what I believe and why" that unites some of Gardner's interests in philosophy, religion, and literature. He demonstrates the amazing scope of his knowledge and his interests again in *Night is Large: Collected Essays, 1938–1995* (1997).

Looking back over his career, Gardner told Frazier: "In a way, I regret spending so much time debunking bad science. A lot of it is a waste of time." Reviewers sometimes agree; Timothy Ferris maintains that while *Science: Good, Bad, and Bogus* is "an ally of common sense," it dallies unnecessarily with outdated ideas in little danger of being mistaken for hard science. On the whole, however, Gardner is revered as much for his devoted attacks on pseudoscience as for his extraordinary intellectual range. In his review of *Night Is Large*, Douglas Sylva writes: "His table of contents resembles a college catalogue, with sections on the physical sciences, the social sciences, mathematics, the arts, philosophy and religion. Miraculously, his ambition does not exceed his erudition; the same reasonable, trustworthy voice examines artificial intelligence and 'Alice's Adventures in Wonderland,' pragmatist philosophy and supply-side economics." Still identifying himself as a journalist, Gardner has written more than 60 books, and has learned by writing. "[A]ttacking bogus science," he decided in the course of his interview with Frazier, is not such a bad thing after all, because it "is a painless way to learn good science."

THE GREAT SAMOAN HOAX (1993)

IN AN EARLIER column on Margaret Mead[1] (*SI*, Fall 1983, reprinted in my book *The New Age*) I focused mainly on Mead's occult beliefs and her conviction that the earth is being observed by extraterrestrials in flying saucers. Only a brief mention was made of Derek Freeman's *Margaret Mead and Samoa: The Making and Unmaking of an Anthropological Myth* (Harvard University Press, 1983). This explosive book roundly trounced Mead for flagrant errors in her most famous work, *Coming of Age in Samoa: A Psychological Study of Primitive Youth for Western Civilization* (Morrow, 1928).

Since I wrote that column, new and irrefutable evidence has come to light supporting the claim that young Mead was indeed the gullible victim of a playful hoax. Her book, until recently considered a classic, is now known to be of minimal value—an amusing skeleton in anthropology's closet.

Mead was 23 in 1925 when she went to Samoa as a Columbia University graduate student working under Franz Boas, then the nation's most eminent anthropologist. At that time cultural anthropology was in the grip of an extreme environmentalism, understandable as a reaction against earlier ethnocentric anthropologists who faulted alien cultures for failing to conform to the values of the anthropologists' own society. Boas could not accept the notion of a biologically determined human nature that would provide the basis for ranking cultures in terms of how well they met human needs. Genetic elements, Boas wrote in *The Encyclopedia of the Social Sciences,* are "altogether irrelevant as compared with the powerful influence of environment."

For Boas and his protegée Mead, human nature consisted entirely of such body needs as food, water, and sex. How a culture copes with those needs was seen as enormously varied in ways that could not be evaluated across cultural boundaries. In brief, for Boas there were no universal human values.

This extreme view, known as "cultural relativism" or "cultural determinism," poses obvious difficulties. How, for example, can a relativist condemn slavery, seeing that slavery was integral to so many great cultures from ancient Greece to our own nation's South before the Civil War? How can a relativist object to the racism of Hitler's Germany, the torturing of heretics by the Inquisition, or the burning and hanging of witches? However, this is not the place to discuss the defects of cultural determinism. Instead, I shall stress the fresh evidence that Mead was shamelessly hoodwinked by two Samoan pranksters.

Derek Freeman, an Australian anthropologist, summarizes this new evidence in three papers: "Fa'apua'a Fa'amu and Margaret Mead," in *American Anthropology* (December 1989); "There's Tricks i' th' World" (a quote from Hamlet), in *Visual Anthropology Reviews* (Spring 1991); and "Paradigms in Collision," in *Academic Questions* (July 1992). It is from these articles that I take what follows.

When Mead visited Samoa she was under the impression, based solely on hearsay, that Polynesians were in actuality promiscuous or unrestrained sexually graduate students. Because she thought their sex lives were unrestrained, Mead was convinced that Samoan

---

[1]*Margaret Mead* (1901–1978) a cultural anthropologist and author from Philadelphia, PA. Her later works included *Male and Female* (1949) and *Growth and Culture* (1951), in which she argued that culture rather than heredity shapes characteristics, especially gender differences. There are some critics of her field work, but she is credited with making anthropology accessible to a wider audience. She became a well-known and respected public figure.

adolescents never suffered the anxieties and torments of Western teenagers. Her mentor, Boas, sent her to Samoa for the express purpose of confirming this view, thereby providing strong support for his radical cultural determinism.

Because Mead spoke very little Samoan, she conducted most of her interviews through interpreters. Her principal informants were two native "girls" (as Mead herself called them), Fa'apua'a Fa'amu, who spoke English, and her friend Fofoa, who did not. All three "girls" were about the same age. In a letter, Mead called the other two her "merry companions."

Embarrassed and offended by Mead's constant questions about sex, a taboo topic in Samoa, the two merry companions decided to play on Mead what they thought would be a harmless joke. Such pranks on outsiders were and are a common form of Samoan fun. The two girls had no inkling that Mead was an anthropologist who would go home and write a book about what they told her. To them she was just a young, naive, meddlesome tourist.

With sidelong glances at each other, and lots of giggling, the two merry companions told Mead everything she wanted to hear. Yes, adolescents had complete sexual freedom, moving stress-free from childhood to adultery. Samoans were a happy, free-love people. Poor Mead bought it all. Samoa, she wrote in her book, is "a casual, problem-free society" in which the ambition of every adolescent girl is "to live with as many lovers as possible" before she marries. Even after wedlock sexual freedoms are permitted. Not only was the book avidly read by our nation's "flaming youth," eager for sex without commitment, but anthropologists praised it to the skies. In his foreword to the book Boas called it a "painstaking investigation" of a "culture so entirely different from our own." Bertrand Russell,[2] Havelock Ellis,[3] H. L. Mencken,[4] and other famous writers joined in the chorus of adulation.

After Mead's book appeared, disturbing news began to emerge from more qualified investigators of Samoan life. Unanimously they concluded that Samoan society was exactly the opposite of what Mead had portrayed. It was a culture of strict parental controls and unbending sex taboos. Female virginity was so highly prized that brides were tested for virginity before they were allowed to marry! Adolescents in Samoa had the same difficulties in coming of age as they had in Western lands. But so great was Mead's growing reputation as the nation's top female anthropologist, and so firmly entrenched was cultural relativism among anthropologists and sociologists, that Mead's book remained an admired work for more than half a century. It is still in print in both hardcover and paperback editions.

Freeman's book, the first to accuse Mead of having been flimflammed, aroused his colleagues to unbelievable fury and vindictiveness. Freeman was called "crazy," "fueled by academic venom," a person who "threw nothing but spitballs." He was accused of bribing Samoans to support his bizarre opinions and of having "attacked a missionary

---

[2]*Bertrand Russell* Arthur William Russell (1872–1970) a Welsh philosopher and mathematician who served six months in prison in 1918 for pacifism, which he renounced during the Nazi era. In 1950, he was awarded the Nobel Prize for Literature.

[3]*Havelock Ellis* (1859–1939) an English physician who compiled a seven-volume work entitled *Studies in the Psychology of Sex* (1897–1928). It was the first detached treatment of the subject and was highly controversial at the time.

[4]*H. L. Mencken* Henry Louis Mencken (1880–1956) an American editor and author whose prolific writings are both satirical and philosophical.

with an axe." Melvin Ember attacked Freeman in "Evidence and Science in Ethnography: Reflections on the Freeman-Mead Controversy," in *American Anthropologist* (vol. 87, 1985, pp. 906–909).

At the 1983 meeting of the American Anthropological Association, in Chicago, a special session was devoted to vilifying Freeman. Later that day a motion was passed denouncing his book as "unscientific." Here is how British philosopher Karl Popper reacted in a letter to Freeman:

> Many sociologists and almost all sociologists of science, believe in a relativist theory of truth. That is, truth is what the experts believe, or what the majority of the participants in a culture believe. Holding a view like this your opponents could not admit that you were right. How could you be, when all their colleagues thought like they did? In fact, they could *prove* that you were wrong simply by taking a vote at a meeting of experts. That clearly settled it. And your facts? They meant nothing if sufficiently many experts ignored them, or distorted them, or misinterpreted them.

Not until 1987 was Freeman completely vindicated. Fofoa had died in 1936, and Fa'apua'a was presumed also dead. To Freeman's surprise she was very much alive and eager to talk. For decades, she said, she had been burdened with guilt over the huge success of Mead's book, and now was relieved at last to be able to tell her story. A lifelong Christian, she swore to the truth of her account with a hand on a Samoan Bible.

When Mead intimated that Fa'apua'a was promiscuous, Fa'apua'a was shocked. At that time she was what in Samoa is called a *taupou,* or ceremonial virgin. After comprehending what Mead wanted them to say, the two girls decided to play a typical Samoan prank on this curious young woman from America. They never dreamed that Mead would base an entire book on their lies.

When Larry Gartenstein interviewed Fa'apua'a for his article "Sex, Lies, Margaret Mead, and Samoa," in *Geo* (June-August 1991), the elderly woman, now a grandmother and nearing 90, said that when Mead asked where she and Fofoa went at night they would pinch each other and say, "We spent our nights with boys, yes, with boys!" Samoan girls, Fa'apua'a added, "are terrific liars when it comes to joking. But Margaret accepted our trumped-up stories as though they were true. Yes, we just fibbed and fibbed to her."

Had Mead ever pressed her two merry friends for verification of their lies, Fa'apua'a said, they would have at once confessed, but Mead never challenged anything. She just scribbled it all down avidly in her notebooks. There was a rumor that Mead had an affair with a young Samoan. It is not known if this is true, but Fa'apua'a said she and Fofoa firmly believed it, and this made them feel less hesitant in hoaxing their visitor.

On three occasions Mead was made a "ceremonial virgin" of Samoa. These honors, which she greatly enjoyed, would never have been conferred on her if she had revealed that she was married at the time! It is said that Mead, during one of the ceremonies, danced about bare-chested.

Cultural relativism may be dying a slow death as more and more anthropologists and sociologists rediscover what they could have learned decades ago from John Dewey,[5] a strong believer in a common human nature as a foundation for a naturalistic ethics. Here

---

[5]*John Dewey* (1859–1952) an American philosopher, psychologist, and educator who was a leading figure in progressive education. Dewey advocated learning by "directed living," with an emphasis on workshop-type projects combining activity with practical relevance.

are some passages from Dewey's essay "Does Human Nature Change?" in *Problems of Men* (Philosophical Library, 1946):

> The existence of almost every conceivable kind of social institution at some time and place in the history of the world is evidence of the plasticity of human nature. This fact does not prove that all these different social systems are of equal value materially, morally, and culturally. The slightest observation shows that such is not the case.
>
> ... By "needs" I mean the inherent demands that men make because of their constitution. Needs for food and drink and for moving about, for example, are so much a part of our being that we cannot imagine any condition under which they would cease to be. There are other things not so directly physical that seem to me equally engrained in human nature. I would mention as examples the need for some kind of companionship; the need for exhibiting energy, for bringing one's powers to bear upon surrounding conditions; the need for both cooperation with and emulation of one's fellows for mutual aid and combat alike; the need for some sort of aesthetic expression and satisfaction; the need to lead and to follow, etc.
>
> Whether my particular examples are well chosen or not does not matter so much as does a recognition of the fact that there are some tendencies so integral a part of human nature that the latter would not be human nature if they changed. These tendencies used to be called instincts. Psychologists are now more chary of using that word than they used to be. But the word by which the tendencies are called does not matter much in comparison to the fact that human nature has its own constitution.

Freeman points out that back in 1945 anthropologist G. P. Murdock provided a long list of universals common to all known cultures. A similar case for them was made by Donald Brown in *Human Universals* (1991). Still another defense can be found in Irenaus Eibl-Eibesfeldt's massive *Human Ethology* (1989).

Freeman quotes an anthropologist as saying, "There is no such thing as human nature independent of culture." Obviously true, Freeman agrees, but the same truth can be put the other way around: "There is no such thing as culture independent of human nature."

Freeman believes that what he calls an "interactionist paradigm shift" is now taking place in anthropology. The crude, outdated relativism is slowly giving way to the sensible view that cultures arise from an interplay of genetics and environment. Perhaps the time is approaching when cultural anthropologists will have the courage to declare, without shame, that evils like slavery, racism, infanticide, and genocide are not value-free customs comparable to such folkways as traffic regulations and fashions in dress, but behavior that can be condemned on the basis of values common to humans everywhere.

Understanding and Analysis

1. Why does Gardner open his essay with a reference to an earlier article that, he admits, is not relevant to the issue he is addressing in this essay?

2. What new information is Gardner reporting?

3. Describe "cultural relativism" as Gardner explains it.

4. Describe the position espoused by Dewey.

5. What is the actual criticism of Mead's work in Samoa?

6. Gardner refers to a number of academic works in this essay. What are they, and what position does each espouse?

7. How does Gardner characterize Mead throughout the essay? Are all of his allegations supported? If not, which are and which are not?

8. What is the main point of Gardner's essay?

Comparison

1. The controversy over Margaret Mead's work in Samoa is ongoing. In 1998, anthropologist Paul Shankman wrote a defense of Mead, attacking Freeman for claiming that Mead did not accept evolution, when, according to Shankman, Mead and Freeman actually agree on the "the fundamental issues of biology, culture, and evolution." Shankman claims that all the fuss is the result of a simplification of Mead's ideas and an omission of detail. Read Carr on history and Lippmann on stereotypes. How do their ideas help to clarify the issues Gardner reports? What evidence would you need to decide on the value of Mead's work in Samoa?

2. At the end of his essay Gardner writes, "Freeman believes that what he calls an 'interactionist paradigm shift' is now taking place in anthropology." Read Kuhn's essay. Do you think that Freeman is using the term "paradigm shift" accurately? Why or why not? Read Mencken's "Bearers of the Torch." Are his comments relevant here? Why or why not?

3. The controversy over nature versus nurture has marked much of the twentieth century. Examine a few of the essays in this collection, choosing from, for example, the essays by Twain, Du Bois, Lippmann, Lawrence, Lewisohn, Eiseley, Gould, Geertz, Mead, and Gardner. What position do you think each of these authors takes on the issue? What is your evidence? What do you think about this issue?

4. Read the essays by Snow, Leavis, Orwell ("What is Science?"), and Postman. Compare the personal attacks you find in these essays with some of the comments Gardner makes about Mead. Are any of these comments in these essays persuasive? If so, which ones? Why? Which are most offensive? What conclusions do you draw about the quality of academic arguments and the level of emotion they may elicit?

5. Do some research on the Mead controversy. What evidence do the most recent participants offer to support their views? What is your own assessment of Mead's contribution to our understanding of human nature?

bell hooks
(1952–)

Born in the segregated town of Hopkinsville, Kentucky, Gloria Jean Watkins grew up "in a working-class southern religious household" with one brother and five sisters. From the beginning, her parents impressed upon the girls their role in life. In *Bone Black: Memories of a Girlhood*, hooks writes, using the historical present, "We learn early that it is important for a woman to marry. We are always marrying our dolls to someone." Acquiring a reputation as the "problem child," she refused to play with white dolls and "demanded a brown doll, one that would look like me." (In the end, that doll, called Baby, was the only doll she and her sisters did not "destroy.") At the age of 10, she announced that she wanted to become a writer; when she began to write poems of her own, she was already a voracious reader, especially of Emily Dickinson. Her father soon objected to her reading, however, certain that learning would spoil her chances for marriage. By the age of 16, she was "stomp[ing] upstairs shouting, I will never be married! I will never marry!" As she recalls in *Remembered Rapture,* her sisters stole her diaries and "deliver[ed] them to our mother as evidence that I was truly a mad person, an alien, a stranger in their household."

Depressed and sometimes suicidal, hooks used reading and writing as means of escape and solace, yet books also gave her cause to panic. Describing her experience in the third person, she writes in *Wounds of Passion*, "At some point though she realizes she is not reading any African American writers. Somewhere in her subconscious she realizes that if she can find no black writers then maybe there is not space for her. In high school she goes to the library and finds James Weldon Johnson's *The Book of American Negro Poetry*. This is poetry her family likes to hear and she can recite it to them all day and all night long. She loves this book so much she never returns it to the library." When she won a scholarship and enrolled at Stanford at the age of 17 to "study drama," she took *The Book of American Negro Poetry* with her. Working at a daycare facility between classes to earn money, she attended readings by poets such as Adrienne Rich and Gary Snyder, who led her to embrace Buddhism. At Snyder's reading, when she was 19, she met a 26-year-old graduate student with whom she began a relationship that lasted more than a decade. When she complained "endlessly about the absence of material about black women in my courses," it was he who suggested that she "write my own book." So at the age of 19, hooks began *Ain't I a Woman*, its title the refrain of a speech made by Sojourner Truth to early white feminists.

In 1973, still working on the book, she graduated from Stanford and moved to Oakland, getting a job as a telephone operator on the "graveyard shift," while her partner worked on his dissertation. When he accepted a teaching position in Wisconsin, she followed, and though she did not particularly want a graduate degree, she wanted still less to work in a job that wasn't going anywhere. She earned her M.A., and the couple moved on to the University of Southern California, where both taught courses, while she pursued another degree she did not want, assured by her partner that she needed a Ph.D. in order to make a career of college teaching. Unable to find a publisher for her book, she was already discouraged when she passed her written requirements but failed her orals, after saying that "many of the so-called great white male writers" did not move her. She left graduate school and did not think of returning until her late 20s, when she enrolled at UC Santa Cruz.

At the age of 29, after undertaking a full-scale revision, hooks found a publisher for *Ain't I a Woman: Black Women and Feminism* (1981). The book appeared under her pseudonym, the name of her great-grandmother, which she had chosen in the 70s. As she explained on the television program "Booknotes," (perhaps in reference to the lower case b and h in "bell hooks" as well as to the pseudonym itself) "the idea was that it was more important what was being said than who said it." Although her second experience in a doctoral program was better than her first, hooks still found that "[i]t threatened folks that I could be busy writing books on black women and feminism while studying medieval literature." When she accepted a position as an assistant professor of English and Black Studies at Yale, Ph.D. completed, she felt herself similarly "limited by conventional pedagogy" until "white male academics in the United States 'discovered' cultural studies. Suddenly, much that had once been illegitimate became the rage. The work that I did—eclectic, interdisciplinary, inspired by revolutionary political visions—had an acceptable place, another home." In 1984, hooks published *Feminist Theory: From Margin to Center*, and in 1988, the year she started teaching at Oberlin, she published *Talking Back: Thinking Feminist, Thinking Black*. In the early 1990s, she published *Yearning: Race, Gender, and Cultural Politics* (1990) and co-authored *Breaking Bread: Insurgent Black Intellectual Life* (1991) with Cornel West. Her next book was another collection of essays, *Black Looks: Race and Representation* (1992).

After hooks became a distinguished professor of English at City College in 1993, she published *Teaching to Transgress: Education as the Practice of Freedom* (1994). Over the next year, she published two of her most powerful works of cultural criticism: *Outlaw Culture: Resisting Representations* (1994) and *Killing Rage: Ending Racism* (1995). She also published *Art on My Mind: Visual Politics* (1995) and *Reel to Real: Race, Class, and Sex at the Movies* (1996). In 1996, she published the first of several autobiographical works, *Bone Black*, which she had started writing during her 20s, but which she had struggled to publish due to its non-linear narrative and its unorthodox narrative strategies. She followed *Bone Black* with *Wounds of Passion: A Writing Life* (1997) and *Remembered Rapture: The Writer at Work* (1999).

Reviewing *Outlaw Culture*, Deborah Coen writes, bell hooks is one of the few feminists receiving attention today who speak for women outside the white professional world, women worrying less about sexual harassment and unreal body ideals than about racism, poverty, and violence." She is also one of the few intellectuals writing on popular culture to move convincingly and with ease from the university into the culture, from classrooms into museums, movie theaters, bedrooms, and talk shows. Hooks derives much of her success in this respect from her writing voices. "Polyphonic," hooks says of

Outlaw Culture, "it combines the many voices I speak—academic talk, standard English, vernacular patois, the language of the street." While some reviewers observe with glee hooks's frank talk about sex, many object to the "jargon" that characterizes her academic talk. According to Jerome Karabel, "Though often evocative, Bell Hooks's prose suffers from lapses into academic obscurantism. One passage in 'Outlaw Culture' speaks of feminists who 'experience our most intense sexual pleasure in the oppositional space outside the patriarchal phallic imaginary.' Yet to dwell on excesses in Ms. Hooks's language would be to miss her considerable power as a writer."

MALCOLM X
The Longed-for Feminist Manhood (*1994*)

CRITICAL SCHOLARSHIP ON Malcolm X contains no *substantial* work from a feminist standpoint. Always interested in psychoanalytical approaches to understanding the construction of individual subjectivity, I have been excited by recent work on Malcolm X that seeks to shed light on the development of his personality as militant spokesperson and activist for black liberation struggle by critically interpreting autobiographical information and, as a consequence, seriously highlighting the question of gender.

These are troubled times for black women and men. Gender conflicts abound, as do profound misunderstandings about the nature of sex roles. In black popular culture, black females are often blamed for the problems black males face. The institutionalization of black male patriarchy is often presented as the answer to our problems. Not surprisingly, a culture icon like Malcolm X, who continues to be seen by many black folks as the embodiment of quintessential manliness, remains a powerful role model for the construction of black male identity. Hence, it is crucial that we understand the complexity of his thinking about gender.

Malcolm often blamed black women for many of the problems black men faced, and it took years for him to begin a critical interrogation of that kind of misogynist, sexist thinking. It seems ironic that Bruce Perry's recent biographical study, *Malcolm: A Life of the Man Who Changed Black America,* which offers much needed and previously unavailable information and attempts to "read" Malcolm's life critically using a psychological approach, holds the women in Malcolm's life accountable for any behavior that could be deemed dysfunctional. Though Perry appears to be appalled by the depths of Malcolm's sexism and misogyny at various periods of his life, he does not attempt to relate this thinking to the institution of patriarchy, to ways of thinking about gender that abound in a patriarchal culture, nor does he choose to emphasize the progressive changes in Malcolm's thinking about gender towards the end of his life. To have focused on these changes, Perry would have had to rethink a major premise of his book, that the "dominating" or abandoning black women in Malcolm's life created in him a monstrous masculinity, one that so emotionally crippled him that he was unable to recover himself and was, as a consequence, abusive and controlling towards others.

In a sense, Perry's biography attempts to deconstruct and demystify Malcolm by highlighting in an aggressive manner his flaws, shortcomings, and psychological hang-ups. And it is particularly through his exploration and discussion of Malcolm's relationship to women that Perry critically interprets material in such a way as to emphasize (even overemphasize) that Malcolm was not the stuff of which role models, heroes, and cultural icons should be made. To decontextualize Malcolm's sexism and misogyny, and make it appear to be solely a reaction to dysfunctional family relations, is to place him outside history, to represent him as though he were solely a product of black culture and not equally an individual whose identity and sense of self, particularly his sense of manhood, was shaped by the prevailing social ethos of white supremacist capitalist patriarchal society. Using such a narrow framework to analyze Malcolm's life can only lead to distortion and over-simplification. Needless to say, Perry does not apply tools of feminist analysis to explain Malcolm's attitude towards women or his thinking about gender relations. There have been few attempts to discuss Malcolm's life, his political commitments, from a feminist perspective. All too often, feminist thinkers have, like Perry, simply chosen to focus on the sexism and misogyny that shaped Malcolm's thinking and actions throughout much of his life, using that as a reason either to invalidate or dismiss his political impact. Contemporary resurgence of interest in the writings and teachings of Malcolm X has helped to create a critical climate where we can reassess his life and work from a variety of standpoints. Young black females and males, choosing Malcolm as icon and teacher, raise questions about his thinking on gender. In my classes, young black females want to know how we reconcile his sexism and his misogyny with progressive political teachings on black liberation.

To reassess Malcolm's life and work from a feminist standpoint, it is absolutely essential to place him firmly within the social context of patriarchy. We must understand Malcolm in light of that historical legacy in which racism and white supremacy are forms of domination where violation and dehumanization have been articulated and described through a gendered patriarchal rhetoric. That is to say, when folks talk about the cruel history of white domination of black people in the United States—as exemplified by the emasculation of black men—they often make liberation synonymous with the establishment of black patriarchy, of black men gaining the right to dominate women and children.

The "manhood" Malcolm X evoked in his passionate speeches as a representative of the Nation of Islam was clearly defined along such patriarchal lines. While Malcolm did not directly advocate the establishment of black patriarchy as a way of affording black men the right to dominate black women, he talked about the need to "protect" black women, thus using a less obvious strategy to promote black patriarchy. He evoked what might be called a "benevolent" patriarchy in which the patriarchal father/ruler would assume full responsibility for caring for his family—his woman, his children. In one of his most famous speeches, "The Ballot or the Bullet," Malcolm articulated the tenets of black nationalism using patriarchal rhetoric: "The political philosophy of black nationalism means that the black man should control the politics and the politicians in his own community . . ." Black nationalist liberation rhetoric clearly placed black women in a subordinate role. It's important to note here that Malcolm did not invent this rhetoric. It was part and parcel of the conservative ideology underlying the Black Muslim religion and both reformist and radical approaches to black liberation.

That ideology was promoted by black females as well as by black males. Many black women joined the Nation of Islam because they felt they would find respect for black womanhood, the patriarchal protection and care denied them in the dominant culture. The price of subordination did not seem too high to pay for masculinist regard. At one of his early appearances with the great black freedom fighter Fannie Lou Hamer, Malcolm castigated black men for their failure to protect black women and children from racist brutality.

> When I listen to Mrs. Hamer, a black woman—could be my mother, my sister, my daughter—describe what they had done to her in Mississippi, I ask myself how in the world can we ever expect to be respected as *men* with black women being beaten and nothing being done about it? No, we don't deserve to be recognized and respected as men as long as our women can be brutalized in the manner that this woman described, and nothing being done about it . . .

Socialized to think along sexist lines about the nature of gender roles, most black people in Malcolm's day believed that men should work and provide for their families, and that women should remain in the home taking care of domestic life and children. (Today, most black folks assume that both genders will work outside the home.) It was often understood that racism in the realm of employment often meant that black men were not able to assume the position of economic providers, that black females often found low-paying jobs when males could find no work. One promise of Elijah Muhammad's Islam was that black women would find husbands who would have jobs. Whatever sexism and misogyny Malcolm X embraced prior to his involvement with the Nation of Islam was intensified by his participation in this organization. In the context of the Nation, the misogynist fear and hatred of women that he had learned as a street hustler was given a legitimate ideological framework. Yet, there it was assumed that if black women were dominant it was not because they were inherently "evil" but because black men had allowed themselves to become emasculated and weak. Hence, any black man who had the courage could reclaim this patriarchal role and thus straighten out the wayward black woman. As a street hustler, Malcolm was often enraged when females were able to outsmart and control men.

Underlying his distrust of women was a fear of emasculation, of losing control, of being controlled by others. Indeed, Malcolm was obsessed with the notion of emasculation and concerned that black men assert control over their lives and the lives of others. In his autobiography, Malcolm explained Muslim teachings on the nature of gender roles, stating that

> the true nature of a man is to be strong, and a woman's true nature is to be weak, and while a man must at all times respect his woman, at the same time he needs to understand that he must control her if he expects to get her respect.

Such sexist thinking continues to inform contemporary Black Muslim thought. It was recently given renewed expression in Shahrazad Ali's popular book *The Blackman's Guide to Understanding the Blackwoman.* She asserts that black female "disrespect for the Blackman is a direct cause of the destruction of the Black family." In many ways Ali's book was a rephrasing of the 1956 addresses on black women that Malcolm gave at the Philadelphia Temple. Whenever he spoke about gender during his years with the Nation, Malcolm consistently accused black women of acting in complicity with white men. Calling black women "the greatest tool of the devil" he insisted that the uplift of black people was impeded by "this evil black woman in North America who does not want to do right and holds the man back from saving himself." Bruce Perry attempts to show that Malcolm generalized about all women based on his personal experiences with individual black females who were not progressive in their thinking about either gender or race.

There is no justification for Malcolm's sexism. Speaking about that sexism in his comparative work *Martin and Malcolm: A Dream or A Nightmare*, James Cone emphasizes that both men "shared much of the typical American male's view of women." He elaborates: "Both believed that the woman's place was in the home, the private sphere, and the man's place was in society, the public arena, fighting for justice on behalf of women and children." Significantly, Cone insists that we not ignore the negative consequences to black life that were the result of both Martin and Malcolm's support of sexist agendas.

> While we black men may understand the reasons for Martin's and Malcolm's or our own sexism, we must not excuse it or justify it, as if sexism was not and is not today a serious matter in the African American community. As we blacks will not permit whites to offer plausible excuses for racism, so we cannot excuse our sexism. Sexism like racism is freedom's opposite, and we must uncover its evil manifestations so we can destroy it.

Few black men have taken up Cone's challenge. And the teachings of Malcolm X are often evoked by black men today to justify their sexism and the continued black domination of black females.

The truth is, despite later changes in his thinking about gender issues, Malcolm's earlier public lectures advocating sexism have had a much more powerful impact on black consciousness than the comments he made during speeches and interviews towards the end of his life which showed a progressive evolution in his thinking on sex roles. This makes it all the more crucial that *all* assessments of Malcolm's contribution to black liberation struggle emphasize this change, not attempting in any way to minimize the impact of his sexist thought but rather to create a critical climate where these changes are considered and respected, where they can have a positive influence on those black folks seeking to be more politically progressive. In his autobiography, Malcolm declared his ongoing personal commitment to change: "My whole life has been a chronology of changes—I have always kept an open mind, which is necessary to the flexibility that must go hand in hand with every intelligent search for truth." Given progressive changes in Malcolm's thinking about gender prior to his death, it does not seem in any way incongruous to see him as someone who would have become an advocate for gender equality. To suggest, as he did in the speeches of his last year, that black women should play an equal role in the struggle for black liberation, constitutes an implicit challenge to sexist thinking. Had he lived, Malcolm might have explicitly challenged sexist thinking in as adamant a manner as he had advocated it. Cone makes this insightful observation in his discussion of Malcolm's sexism:

> Whatever views Malcolm held on any subject, he presented them in the most extreme form possible so that no one would be in doubt about where he stood on the subject. When he discovered his error about something, he was as extreme in his rejection of it as he had been in his affirmation. Following his split with the Nation of Islam and his subsequent trips to the Middle East and Africa, Malcolm made an about-face regarding his view on women's rights, as he began to consider the issue not only in the context of religion and morality but, more importantly, from the standpoint of mobilizing the forces needed to revolutionize society.

Often, sexist black men and women who think of Malcolm as a cultural icon suppress information about these changes in his thinking because they do not reinforce their own sexist agenda.

Feminist assessments of Malcolm's life have not been encouraged by individuals who are concerned with defining his legacy and the impact of his work. If there is a conference or panel about Malcolm and his work, Betty Shabazz, his widow, is usually the representative female voice. Until very recently, sexist censorship has determined who the female voices are that can speak about Malcolm and gain a hearing. Since Shabazz makes few if any comments about progressive changes in Malcolm's thinking about gender and she remains the representative female voice interpreting his legacy, she participates in closing down the discussion of Malcolm's views on gender. Clearly, for practically all of their marriage, Malcolm assumed a benevolent patriarchal role in the family. This Shabazz documents in her essay "Malcolm X as a Husband and Father." Still, it would be too simplistic to regard Shabazz solely as a victim of his sexist agenda. She too had a sexist agenda. She was equally committed to ways of thinking about gender roles that were expressed and advocated by the Nation of Islam. And though Shabazz made a break with the Nation, interviews and dialogues give no indication that she made substantial changes in her thinking about gender, that she in any way advocates feminism.

Even though Shabazz attempted to assert an autonomous identity and presence after Malcolm's death, she continued and continues to assume the position that, as his widow, she has the right (accorded with patriarchy) to be the primary, authentic spokesperson, letting the world know who Malcolm X, the man, really was. Legally, she controls the estate of Malcolm X. Yet if, as sources suggest, she and Malcolm were drifting apart (perhaps even on the verge of divorce), it may very well be that despite his patriarchal dominance in the family, his thinking on gender was more progressive than hers. It would of course not be in her interest to reveal such conflict, because it would raise problematic questions about her continued role as the voice of Malcolm, the man.

Ultimately, it may be that any feminist assessment of Malcolm's life and work must concede that, given the sexist politics of their family life, Shabazz cannot shed much light on Malcolm's changing views on the woman question. And if indeed her own views are not particularly progressive or feminist, she does not really hold a standpoint from which to articulate the changes in his thinking. Bluntly stated, Shabazz may advocate gender equality in the realm of work but see no need for women and men unequivocally to resist sexism and sexist oppression in all areas of life. She has not publicly indicated a conversion to feminist politics, nor to the kind of feminist thinking that would provide her with a theoretical standpoint enabling her to talk about progressive change in Malcolm (or for that matter anyone's thinking about gender). Yet just the fact of having been Malcolm's wife makes her an icon in the eyes of many black folks who are seeking to learn from Malcolm's life and work. If Betty Shabazz acts as though progressive changes in Malcolm's thinking about gender were not important, then she is complicit with those who choose to ignore or dismiss these changes.

Many younger black females (myself included) who have an opportunity to be in Shabazz's presence admire her fortitude in coping with the adversity she and her children faced as a result of Malcolm's political choices and his death, as well as the way she has managed to forge a separate and unique identity. Yet such admiration does not change the fact that in most public settings where Shabazz appears with men, she assumes a traditional sexist positionality (i.e., paying close attention to what males are saying in their interpretations of Malcolm's work, while ignoring or actively discounting female interpretations). Though often supportive of women, Betty Shabazz has not shown ongoing concern with issues of women's rights. Certainly she has a right to determine what political concerns interest her. What I wish to suggest here, however, is that were Shabazz more outspoken about changes in Malcolm's thinking about gender, if she were more outspoken about how difficult it was to conform to his sexist domination in family life, if indeed she could articulate her own "bitterness" (if it is present) that Malcolm did not live to offer her the benefits of his progressive thinking about gender, we would have a greater understanding of his developing critical consciousness around the question of gender.

In his biography of Malcolm, Perry attempts to construct Malcolm as a sexist "abuser" whose wife was to some extent liberated by his death.

> Freed from Malcolm's control, Betty, who was catapulted to national prominence by his assassination, blossomed. Like Louise Little, she maintained that her deceased husband, to whom she had been married seven years, had been a good one. She returned to school, obtained a doctorate, and became a public figure in her own right. "I'm not just Malcolm's widow," she proudly told a reporter. During the interview, she alluded to men who misuse women. Such abuse, she said, is spawned by unhappy childhood relationships with mothers or sisters.

Ironically, Perry enlists Shabazz to support his sexist agenda, his critical interpretation of Malcolm which is biased by that very same sexist thinking he critiques in Malcolm, making it appear that only the actions of females (as mothers and sisters) shape and form male identity. Shabazz's comment reinforces this sexist interpretation of childhood influences. But what about society—and the role of fathers and other men—in shaping Malcolm's attitudes and actions towards women? Why do Perry and Shabazz both deny patriarchal influence and engage in their own form of mother blame?

This seems ironic since Shabazz's refusal to talk with Perry implies that she does not see him as the spokesperson to interpret Malcolm's life and work. But like Perry, she does not fully interrogate the question of gender from a nonsexist perspective. If Shabazz cannot interrogate her own sexist thinking it is understandable that she may be unable to interrogate publicly Malcolm's gendered habits of being. She may not wish to discuss openly either his sexism or the fact that his changed attitudes were possibly not reflected in his personal life. Similarly, it may be difficult for Malcolm's daughters to be publicly critical, or self-reflexive about his attitudes towards females, his thinking on gender, because they may only remember that period when he was most committed to a benevolent patriarchal stance and was the kind of father who was rarely home. We can only hope that as time goes on, as black people collectively fully accept that we can know the negative aspects of our cultural icons without losing profound respect for their personal and political contributions, all who knew Malcolm X intimately will feel that they can speak more openly and honestly about him. Shabazz may then also be able to be more openly critical of black male domination.

Despite Malcolm's sexism, he helped Shabazz to become a more politically aware person. Interviewed in the February 1990 issue of *Emerge* Magazine, which focused on "Remembering Malcolm X 25 Years Later," Betty Shabazz honestly states that she was politicized through her relationship to Malcolm, the man.

> He expanded my conceptual framework. As a little middle-class girl in Detroit, Michigan, with older parents and no siblings, it was very limited. Malcolm gave me a world perspective—expanded how I saw things . . . I think [had I not met and married Malcolm] I would still be a Methodist woman whose concerns were with the community in which I lived, as opposed to the concerns of world society.

Significantly, Shabazz's statements indicate that sexist agendas did not keep her from learning to think and act politically from the example of Malcolm X. Angela Davis has also spoken about the way in which Malcolm contributed to the development of her social and political thought, her militancy. I myself have stated, again and again, that the writings of Malcolm X were essential to my political development. For many of us, his unequivocal critique of internalized racism coupled with his unapologetic stance on the need for militant resistance was the kind of political intervention that transformed our consciousness and our habits of being. This transformation happened in spite of Malcolm's sexism.

Significantly, it was Malcolm's break with the patriarchal father embodied in Elijah Muhammad that created the social space for him to transform his thinking about gender. Although his relationship with Betty (who did not conform to sexist stereotypes of female behavior) had already created a personal context for him to rethink misogynist assumptions, to some extent he first had to become "disloyal" (to use Adrienne Rich's word) to the patriarchy before he could think differently about women, about our role in resistance struggle, and potentially about feminist movement. Contemporary thinkers do Malcolm a great disservice when they attempt to reinscribe him iconically within the very patriarchal context he so courageously challenged. His resistance to the patriarchy was exemplified by his break with the Nation, the critique of his own role in the domestic household, and progressive changes in his thinking about gender: he no longer endorsed the sexist notion that black male leadership was essential to black liberation.

It was again in the company of Fannie Lou Hamer, shortly before his death, that Malcolm made one of his most powerful declarations on the issue of gender. Calling Hamer "one of this country's foremost freedom fighters" at the Audubon Ballroom, Malcolm declared: "You don't have to be a man to fight for freedom. All you have to do is be an intelligent human being. And automatically, your intelligence makes you want freedom so badly that you'll do anything, by any means necessary, to get that freedom." Here Malcolm was clearly rethinking and challenging his own and others' privileging of the black male's role in resistance struggle. Another factor that caused Malcolm to rethink his attitudes towards women was the tremendous support black females extended to him after his break with the Nation, as well as his growing awareness that it was black women who were often the hardworking core of many black organizations, both radical and conservative.

Strategically, Malcolm had to build an autonomous constituency after his break with the Nation. It is not surprising that he had become more aware that women could be formidable advocates leading resistance struggle, and that he would need to rely on female comrades. Again, it's important to link Malcolm's break with the patriarchal, hierarchical structure of Islam with a critical rethinking of the place of hierarchy in any social and political organization. During the last month of his life, he was quoted in the *New York Times* as saying: "I feel like a man who has been asleep somewhat and under someone else's control. I feel what I'm thinking and saying now is for myself. Before, it was for and by the guidance of Elijah Muhammad. Now I think with my own mind." Presumably, this self-critical moment helped him to critically interrogate thinking on gender. It is this rethinking Perry's biography refuses to acknowledge and critically interpret as an incredible political shift. Speaking with the same arrogant tone that informs much of the book, Perry writes of Malcolm's relationship with Shabazz:

> Malcolm's marriage was no more unhappy than those of other public figures who shun intimacy for the love of the crowd. Eventually, the marriage nearly broke up, ostensibly over

the issue of money. But there were other issues, for Malcolm denied his wife the warmth and emotional support his mother and Ella (his older sister) had denied him. He controlled her the way they had controlled him. His male chauvinism was the predictable result of past tyranny.

This is a fine example of the way Perry attempts to stack the deck psychologically against Malcolm, using his sexist thinking and actions to define the man. Perry refuses to acknowledge those profound changes in Malcolm's thinking about gender, even his rethinking his relationship to family, because these changes disrupt Perry's critique. They suggest that while it may be accurate to say that Malcolm's sexist thinking about women in general and black women in particular was reinforced by his relationships to his mother and older sister, it is equally accurate to say that as he began to replace these dysfunctional kinship bonds with new ties with women, he began a kind of personal self-recovery that enabled him to see women differently. Interaction with black women such as Fannie Lou Hamer and Shirley Graham Dubois, intelligent powerful leaders, made intense impressions on Malcolm X. Given that many of his misogynist viewpoints on women continually referred to the female body, to female sexuality, it's important to note that in an attempt to redress, Malcolm's later speeches emphasized black female intellectualism and intelligence. Hence, he could assert: "I am proud of the contribution women have made. I'm for giving them all the leeway possible. They've made a greater contribution than many men."

There is much documentation to support progressive changes in Malcolm's attitudes towards women; clearly he believed women should play a role in resistance struggle (one equal to men); he believed the contributions of females should be acknowledged; and he supported equal education for females. Yet there is little documentation providing any clue as to how he perceived these changes would affect gender roles in domestic life. And while we can speculate that Malcolm might have developed the kind of critical consciousness around gender that would have enabled him to listen and learn from black female advocates of feminist thought, that he might have become a spokesperson for the cause, a powerful ally, this must remain speculation—nothing more. Yet we should not minimize the significance of the transformation in his consciousness around the issue of gender late in his political career.

It would be a profound disservice to Malcolm's memory, his political legacy, for those who reclaim him as powerful teacher and mentor figure today to repress knowledge of these changes. Sexism, sexist oppression, and its most insidious expression—male domination—continue to undermine black liberation struggle, continue to undercut the positive potential in black family life, rendering dysfunctional familial relations that could enable recovery and resistance. Hence, more than ever before, there needs to be mass education for critical consciousness that teaches folks about Malcolm's transformed thinking on gender. His move from a sexist, misogynist standpoint to one where he endorsed efforts at gender equality was so powerful. It can serve as an example for many men today, particularly black men. To remember Malcolm solely as a pimp and a batterer, as one who used and exploited women, is a distortion of who he was that is tantamount to an act of violation. Feminist thinkers cannot demand that men change, then refuse to extend full positive acknowledgment when men rethink sexism and alter their behavior accordingly.

Malcolm X would still be an important political thinker and activist whose life and work should be studied and learned from, even if he had never confronted and altered his sexist thinking. However, the point that has to be made again and again is that he did begin to critique and change that sexism, he did transform his consciousness.

When I hear Malcolm urging us to seize our freedom "by any means necessary," I do not think of a call to masculinist violence but rather of a call that urges us to think, to decolonize our minds, and strategize so that we can use various tools and weapons in our efforts at emancipation. I like to remember him speaking about our choosing to work for freedom "by any means necessary" in his response to the words of Fannie Lou Hamer. I like to evoke Malcolm's name and his words when writing to a black male lover about how we treat one another, using his evocation of redemptive love between black people, remembering that he told us:

> It is not necessary to change the white man's mind. We have to change our own mind . . . We've got to change our own minds about each other. We have to see each other with new eyes. We have to see each other as brothers and sisters. We have to come together with warmth . . .

The harmony Malcolm evokes here can only emerge in a context where renewed black liberation struggle has a feminist component, where the eradication of sexism is seen as essential to our struggle, to our efforts to build a beloved community, a space of harmony and connection where black women and men can face each other not as enemies but as comrades, our hearts rejoicing in a communion that is about shared struggle and mutual victory.

Understanding and Analysis

1. What is it about Bruce Perry's biography of Malcolm X that hooks is criticizing?
2. According to hooks, what are the sources of Malcolm X's misogyny?
3. What does hooks find positive in the work and life of Shabazz? What does hooks see as shortcomings in Shabazz's attitudes?
4. How does Perry use Shabazz, according to hooks?
5. What evidence does hooks offer for her claim that Malcolm X was in the process of changing his views on women at the time of his death?
6. What speculations does she offer about what his views might have become?
7. Why is it so important for hooks and others to see and emphasize these changes in Malcolm X's thinking? If he had not begun to change his views do you think hooks would continue to see him as an important figure? What is your evidence?
8. To whom is it important to suppress these changes, according to hooks?
9. Examine hooks's interpretation of Malcolm X's phrase "by any means necessary." Is her interpretation justified? What is your evidence?
10. Does hooks's analysis of patriarchy apply to relations between white men and women also? If so, to what degree? If not, why not?

Comparison

1. Read the essay by Gerald Early. How would hooks respond to the arguments Early presents? To what degree, if at all, do hooks and Early agree?

2. Read the essay by Podhoretz. How important do Podhoretz and hooks believe personal experiences should be in the shaping of one's social and political philosophy?

3. Read the essay by Adrienne Rich. What, if any, feminist positions do Rich and hooks share? What is your evidence?

4. Read the essay by Postman and all the works by and about Malcolm X in this collection. Devise a theory or story about him that best accounts for all the information that you find credible. What sort of role model does your story offer? How does it differ from that of hooks, Early, and Perry?

5. Read the essays by Gates and Postman. Compare their attitudes with those of hooks toward deconstruction and feminist criticism. Compare the styles of all three as well. Do you see any connection between theory and style? To what degree in these essays does style affect argument? Whose style do you prefer? Why?

Leslie Marmon Silko

(1948–)

Born March 5, 1948, Leslie Marmon grew up on the Laguna Pueblo Reservation in New Mexico. Of mixed heritage, "Laguna, Mexican, and white," she spent time during her childhood with her Presbyterian great-grandmother, Grandma A'mooh. While Grandma A'mooh sometimes read bible stories to her and her two sisters, as she recounts in *Yellow Woman and a Beauty of the Spirit*, Silko "had no use for Christianity because the Christians made up such terrible lies about Indian people that it was clear to me they would lie about other matters also." Preferring the hikes she took with Grandma Lily—"[t]he mesas and hills loved me; the Bible meant punishment"—she also enjoyed solitary walks, and once she got her horse, Joey, solitary rides as well. Given a .22 rifle at the age of seven, she wandered away for target practice by the Rio San Jose, shooting "bottles and glass jars" retrieved from the trash. Around the age of 10, she left the Bureau of Indian Affairs school on the reservation for a Catholic day school in Albuquerque.

After enrolling at the University of New Mexico in 1964, Silko married Richard C. Chapman in 1966 and gave birth to her first son, Robert. By 1969, when she earned her BA in English, she and her husband had separated. According to William Clements, Silko published her first short story, "The Man to Send Rain Clouds," in *New Mexico Quarterly* while she was in college; still, her aspiration was, as it had been since high school, to become an attorney. "I completed three semesters in the American Indian Law School Fellowship program," she writes in *Yellow Woman,* "before I realized that injustice is built into the Anglo–American legal system." In 1971, she enrolled in graduate courses at her alma mater, studying photography as well as literature. She dropped a class on William Blake, however, because "I wanted to make these texts, not just study them."

Marrying John Silko in 1971, she began teaching, as scholar Gregory Salyer notes, at the "Navajo Community College in Tsaile, Arizona, near the New Mexico state line." She gave birth to her second son, Cazimir, in 1972 and moved to Alaska with her husband the following year. (The couple later divorced.) "In 1974," Salyer continues, "Kenneth Rosen published seven of Silko's short stories in...*Man to Send Rain Clouds: Contemporary Stories by American Indians,*" an anthology named after Silko's own story and published shortly before Silko's *Laguna Woman: Poems* (1974). Success followed success when another short story, "Lullaby," was selected for *The Best Short Stories of 1975.* As all of these works appeared in print, Silko was writing her first novel, *Ceremony,* begun in 1973. In 1977, after she had left Alaska to return to Laguna, she published *Ceremony,* to rave reviews.

After receiving the Pushcart Prize for Poetry, Silko began teaching at the University of Arizona, and over the next decade, she published little, though she worked almost constantly. After the publication of *Storyteller* in 1981, she received a MacArthur Prize Fellowship and spent the next ten years writing her second novel, the mammoth *Almanac of the Dead* (1991). Around the same time she started *Almanac,* she began to write "short prose pieces about the desert area around my house, and about the rocks, and about the rain that is so precious to this land and to my household, which still depends on wells for all its water. In 1980, I had also begun to take photographs of the rocks in the big wash by my house." In her next work, *Sacred Water* (1993), which she published herself, she brought together her writing and her photography. She also put together copies of *Sacred Water* by hand; only three copies are now available in the libraries around the United States. In *Yellow Woman and a Beauty of the Spirit: Essays on Native American Life Today* (1996), she reflects on this and other works; she also expresses her political consciousness, writing about the Border Patrol in the Southwest and "America's Debt to the Indian Nations." She published her third novel, *Garden in the Dunes,* in 1997.

Helen Jaskoski, author of *Leslie Marmon Silko: A Study of the Short Fiction,* opens her book thus: "The State of New Mexico has designated Leslie Marmon Silko as a living cultural treasure; in her early 30s she was the recipient of a MacArthur 'genius' award; she has been counted as one of 135 most important women writers in the history of the world; and she has received many other awards for her writing." While Silko has certainly had an impressive career, she has had a mixed reception. *Almanac for the Dead* and *Gardens in the Dune* received less praise, on the whole, than *Ceremony*, though most reviewers who found flaws were still dazzled by the books' strengths. *Storyteller* has also received acclaim, but reviewer and author N. Scott Momaday complains of uneven writing. Reviewers of many of her works seem to agree that Silko has difficulty with coherence and control, as well as with characterization. Momaday summarizes the views of many: "At her best, Leslie Silko is very good indeed."

Yellow Woman and a Beauty of the Spirit (1996)

FROM THE TIME I was a small child, I was aware that I was different. I looked different from my playmates. My two sisters looked different too. We didn't quite look like the other Laguna Pueblo children, but we didn't look quite white either. In the 1880s, my great-grandfather had followed his older brother west from Ohio to the New Mexico Territory to survey the land for the U.S. government. The two Marmon brothers came to the Laguna Pueblo reservation because they had an Ohio cousin who already lived there. The Ohio cousin was involved in sending Indian children thousands of miles away from their families to the War Department's big Indian boarding school in Carlisle, Pennsylvania. Both brothers married full-blood Laguna Pueblo women. My great-grandfather had first married my great-grandmother's older sister, but she died in childbirth and left two small children. My great-grandmother was fifteen or twenty years younger than my great-grandfather. She had attended Carlisle Indian School and spoke and wrote English beautifully.

I called her Grandma A'mooh because that's what I heard her say whenever she saw me. *A'mooh* means "granddaughter" in the Laguna language. I remember this word because her love and her acceptance of me as a small child were so important. I had sensed immediately that something about my appearance was not acceptable to some people, white and Indian. But I did not see any signs of that strain or anxiety in the face of my beloved Grandma A'mooh.

Younger people, people my parents' age, seemed to look at the world in a more modern way. The modern way included racism. My physical appearance seemed not to matter to the old-time people. They looked at the world very differently; a person's appearance and possessions did not matter nearly as much as a person's behavior. For them, a person's value lies in how that person interacts with other people, how that person behaves toward the animals and the earth. That is what matters most to the old-time people. The Pueblo people believed this long before the Puritans arrived with their notions of sin and damnation, and racism. The old-time beliefs persist today; thus I will refer to the old-time people in the present tense as well as the past. Many worlds may coexist here.

I spent a great deal of time with my great-grandmother. Her house was next to our house, and I used to wake up at dawn, hours before my parents or younger sisters, and I'd go wait on the porch swing or on the back steps by her kitchen door. She got up at dawn, but she was more than eighty years old, so she needed a little while to get dressed and to get the fire going in the cookstove. I had been carefully instructed by my parents not to bother her and to behave, and to try to help her any way I could. I always loved the early mornings when the air was so cool with a hint of rain smell in the breeze. In the dry New Mexico air, the least hint of dampness smells sweet.

My great-grandmother's yard was planted with lilac bushes and iris; there were four o'clocks, cosmos, morning glories, and hollyhocks, and old-fashioned rosebushes that I helped her water. If the garden hose got stuck on one of the big rocks that lined the path in the yard, I ran and pulled it free. That's what I came to do early every morning: to help Grandma water the plants before the heat of the day arrived.

Grandma A'mooh would tell about the old days, family stories about relatives who had been killed by Apache raiders who stole the sheep our relatives had been herding near Swahnee. Sometimes she read Bible stories that we kids liked because of the illustrations of Jonah in the mouth of a whale and Daniel surrounded by lions. Grandma A'mooh would send me home when she took her nap, but when the sun got low and the afternoon began to cool off, I would be back on the porch swing, waiting for her to come out to water the plants and to haul in firewood for the evening. When Grandma was eighty-five, she still chopped her own kindling. She used to let me carry it in the coal bucket for her, but she would not allow me to use the ax. I carried armloads of kindling too, and I learned to be proud of my strength.

I was allowed to listen quietly when Aunt Susie or Aunt Alice came to visit Grandma. When I got old enough to cross the road alone, I went and visited them almost daily. They were vigorous women who valued books and writing. They were usually busy chopping wood or cooking but never hesitated to take time to answer my questions. Best of all they told me the *hummah-hah* stories, about an earlier time when animals and humans shared a common language. In the old days, the Pueblo people had educated their children in this manner; adults took time out to talk to and teach young people. Everyone was a teacher, and every activity had the potential to teach the child.

But as soon as I started kindergarten at the Bureau of Indian Affairs day school, I began to learn more about the differences between the Laguna Pueblo world and the outside world. It was at school that I learned just how different I looked from my classmates. Sometimes tourists driving past on Route 66 would stop by Laguna Day School at recess time to take photographs of us kids. One day, when I was in the first grade, we all crowded around the smiling white tourists, who peered at our faces. We all wanted to be in the picture because afterward the tourists sometimes gave us each a penny. Just as we were all posed and ready to have our picture taken, the tourist man looked at me. "Not you," he said and motioned for me to step away from my classmates. I felt so embarrassed that I wanted to disappear. My classmates were puzzled by the tourists' behavior, but I knew the tourists didn't want me in their snapshot because I looked different, because I was part white.

In the view of the old-time people, we were all sisters and brothers because the Mother Creator made all of us—all colors and all sizes. We are sisters and brothers, clanspeople of all the living beings around us. The plants, the birds, fish, clouds, water, even the clay—they all are related to us. The old-time people believe that all things, even rocks and water, have spirit and being. They understood that all things want only to continue being as they are; they need only to be left as they are. Thus the old folks used to tell us kids not to disturb the earth unnecessarily. All things as they were created exist already in harmony with one another as long as we do not disturb them.

As the old story tells us, Tse'itsi'nako, Thought Woman, the Spider, thought of her three sisters, and as she thought of them, they came into being. Together with Thought Woman, they thought of the sun and the stars and the moon. The Mother Creators imagined the earth and the oceans, the animals and the people, and the *ka'tsina* spirits that reside in the mountains. The Mother Creators imagined all the plants that would flower and the trees that bear fruit. As Thought Woman and her sisters thought of it, the whole universe came into being. In this universe, there is no absolute good or absolute bad; there are only balances and harmonies that ebb and flow. Some years the desert receives abundant rain, other years there is too little rain, and sometimes there is so much rain that floods cause destruction. But rain itself is neither innocent nor guilty. The rain is simply itself.

My great-grandmother was dark and handsome. Her expression in photographs is one of confidence and strength. I do not know if white people then or now would consider her beautiful. I do not know if old-time Laguna Pueblo people considered her beautiful or if the old-time people even thought in those terms. To the Pueblo way of thinking, the act of comparing one living being with another was silly, because each living being or thing is unique and therefore incomparably valuable because it is the only one of its kind. The old-time people thought it was crazy to attach such importance to a person's appearance. I understood very early that there were two distinct ways of interpreting the world. There was the white people's way and there was the Laguna way. In the Laguna way, it was bad manners to make comparisons that might hurt another person's feelings.

In everyday Pueblo life, not much attention was paid to one's physical appearance or clothing. Ceremonial clothing was quite elaborate but was used only for the sacred dances. The traditional Pueblo societies were communal and strictly egalitarian, which means that no matter how well or how poorly one might have dressed, there was no social ladder to fall from. All food and other resources were strictly shared so that no one person or group had more than another. I mention social status because it seems to me that most of the definitions of beauty in contemporary Western culture are really codes for determining social status. People no longer hide their face-lifts and they discuss their liposuctions because the point of the procedures isn't just cosmetic, it is social. It says to the world, "I have enough spare cash that I can afford surgery for cosmetic purposes."

In the old-time Pueblo world, beauty was manifested in behavior and in one's relationships with other living beings. Beauty was as much a feeling of harmony as it was a visual, aural, or sensual effect. The whole person had to be beautiful, not just the face or the body; faces or bodies could not be separated from hearts and souls. Health was foremost in achieving this sense of well-being and harmony; in the old-time Pueblo world, a person who did not look healthy inspired feelings of worry and anxiety, not feelings of well-being. A healthy person, of course, is in harmony with the world around her; she is at peace with herself too. Thus an unhappy person or spiteful person would not be considered beautiful.

In the old days, sturdy women were most admired. One of my vivid preschool memories is of the crew of Laguna women, in their forties and fifties, who came to cover our house with adobe plaster. They handled the ladders with great ease, and while two women ground the adobe mud on stones and added straw, another woman loaded the hod with mud and passed it up to the two women on ladders, who were smoothing the plaster on the wall with their hands. Since women owned the houses, they did the plastering. At Laguna, men did the basket making and the weaving of fine textiles; men helped a great deal with the child care too. Because the Creator is female, there is no stigma on being female; gender is not used to control behavior. No job was a man's job or a woman's job; the most able person did the work.

My Grandma Lily had been a Ford Model A mechanic when she was a teenager. I remember when I was young, she was always fixing broken lamps and appliances. She was small and wiry, but she could lift her weight in rolled roofing or boxes of nails. When she was seventy-five, she was still repairing washing machines in my uncle's coin-operated laundry.

The old-time people paid no attention to birthdays. When a person was ready to do something, she did it. When she was no longer able, she stopped. Thus the traditional Pueblo people did not worry about aging or about looking old because there were no social boundaries drawn by the passage of years. It was not remarkable for young men to marry women as old as their mothers. I never heard anyone talk about "women's work" until after I left Laguna for college. Work was there to be done by any able-bodied person who wanted to do it. At the same time, in the old-time Pueblo world, identity was acknowledged to be always in a flux; in the old stories, one minute Spider Woman is a little spider under a yucca plant, and the next instant she is a sprightly grandmother walking down the road.

When I was growing up, there was a young man from a nearby village who wore nail polish and women's blouses and permed his hair. People paid little attention to his appearance; he was always part of a group of other young men from his village. No one ever made fun of him. Pueblo communities were and still are very interdependent, but they also have to be tolerant of individual eccentricities because survival of the group means everyone has to cooperate.

In the old Pueblo world, differences were celebrated as signs of the Mother Creator's grace. Persons born with exceptional physical or sexual differences were highly respected and honored because their physical differences gave them special positions as mediators between this world and the spirit world. The great Navajo medicine man of the 1920s, the Crawler, had a hunchback and could not walk upright, but he was able to heal even the most difficult cases.

Before the arrival of Christian missionaries, a man could dress as a woman and work with women and even marry a man without any fanfare. Likewise, a woman was free to dress like a man, to hunt and go to war with the men, and to marry a woman. In the old Pueblo worldview, we are all a mixture of male and female, and this sexual identity is changing constantly. Sexual inhibition did not begin until the Christian missionaries arrived. For the old-time people, marriage was about teamwork and social relationships, not about sexual excitement. In the days before the Puritans came, marriage did not mean an end to sex with people other than your spouse. Women were just as likely as men to have a *si'ash,* or lover.

New life was so precious that pregnancy was always appropriate, and pregnancy before marriage was celebrated as a good sign. Since the children belonged to the mother and her clan, and women owned and bequeathed the houses and farmland, the exact determination of paternity wasn't critical. Although fertility was prized, infertility was no problem because mothers with unplanned pregnancies gave their babies to childless couples within the clan in open adoption arrangements. Children called their mother's sisters "mother" as well, and a child became attached to a number of parent figures.

In the sacred kiva ceremonies, men mask and dress as women to pay homage and to be possessed by the female energies of the spirit beings. Because differences in physical appearance were so highly valued, surgery to change one's face and body to resemble a model's face and body would be unimaginable. To be different, to be unique was blessed and was best of all.

The traditional clothing of Pueblo women emphasized a woman's sturdiness. Buckskin leggings wrapped around the legs protected her from scratches and injuries while she worked. The more layers of buckskin, the better. All those layers gave her legs the appearance of strength, like sturdy tree trunks. To demonstrate sisterhood and brotherhood with the plants and animals, the old-time people make masks and costumes that transform the human figures of the dancers into the animal beings they portray. Dancers paint their exposed skin; their postures and motions are adapted from their observations. But the motions are stylized. The observer sees not an actual eagle or actual deer dancing, but witnesses a human being, a dancer, gradually changing into a woman/buffalo or a man/deer. Every impulse is to reaffirm the urgent relationships that human beings have with the plant and animal world.

In the high desert, all vegetation, even weeds and thorns, becomes special, and all life is precious and beautiful because without the plants, the insects, and the animals, human beings living here cannot survive. Perhaps human beings long ago noticed the devastating impact human activity can have on the plants and animals; maybe this is why tribal cultures devised the stories about humans and animals intermarrying, and the clans that bind humans to animals and plants though a whole complex of duties.

We children were always warned not to harm frogs or toads, the beloved children of the rain clouds, because terrible floods would occur. I remember in the summer the old folks used to stick big bolls of cotton on the outside of their screen doors as bait to keep the flies from going in the house when the door was opened. The old folks staunchily resisted the killing of flies because once, long, long ago, when human beings were in a great deal of trouble, a Green Bottle Fly carried desperate messages from human beings to the Mother Creator in the Fourth World, below this one. Human beings had outraged the Mother Creator by neglecting the Mother Corn altar while they dabbled with sorcery and magic. The Mother Creator disappeared, and with her disappeared the rain clouds, and the plants and the animals too. The people began to starve, and they had no way of reaching the Mother Creator down below. Green Bottle Fly took the message to the Mother Creator, and the people were saved. To show their gratitude, the old folks refused to kill any flies.

The old stories demonstrate the interrelationships that the Pueblo people have maintained with their plant and animal clanspeople. Kochininako, Yellow Woman, represents all women in the old stories. Her deeds span the spectrum of human behavior and are mostly heroic acts, though in at least one story, she chooses to join the secret Destroyer Clan, which worships destruction and death. Because Laguna Pueblo cosmology features a female Creator, the status of women is equal with the status of men, and women appear as often as men in the old stories as hero figures. Yellow Woman is my favorite because she dares to cross traditional boundaries of ordinary behavior during times of crisis in order to save the Pueblo; her power lies in her courage and her uninhibited sexuality, which the old-time Pueblo stories celebrate again and again because fertility was so highly valued.

The old stories always say that Yellow Woman was beautiful, but remember that the old-time people were not so much thinking about physical appearances. In each story, the beauty that Yellow Woman possesses is the beauty of her passion, her daring, and her sheer strength to act when catastrophe is imminent.

In one story, the people are suffering during a great drought and accompanying famine. Each day, Kochininako has to walk farther and farther from the village to find fresh water for her husband and children. One day she travels far, far to the east, to the plains, and she finally locates a freshwater spring. But when she reaches the pool, the water is churning violently as if something large had just gotten out of the pool. Kochininako does not want to see what huge creature had been at the pool, but just as she fills her water jar and turns to hurry away, a strong, sexy man in buffalo-skin leggings appears by the pool. Little drops of water glisten on his chest. She cannot help but look at him because he is so strong and so good to look at. Able to transform himself from human to buffalo in the wink of an eye, Buffalo Man gallops away with her on his back. Kochininako falls in love with Buffalo Man, and because of this liaison, the Buffalo People agree to give their bodies to the hunters to feed the starving Pueblo. Thus Kochininako's fearless sensuality results in the salvation of the people of her village, who are saved by the meat the Buffalo People "give" to them.

My father taught me and my sisters to shoot .22 rifles when we were seven; I went hunting with my father when I was eight, and I killed my first mule deer buck when I was thirteen. The Kochininako stories were always my favorite because Yellow Woman had so many adventures. In one story, as she hunts rabbits to feed her family, a giant monster pursues her, but she has the courage and the presence of mind to outwit it.

In another story, Kochininako has a fling with Whirlwind Man and returns to her husband ten months later with twin baby boys. The twin boys grow up to be great heroes of the people. Once again, Kochininako's vibrant sexuality benefits her people.

The stories about Kochininako made me aware that sometimes an individual must act despite disapproval, or concern for appearances or what others may say. From Yellow Woman's adventures, I learned to be comfortable with my differences. I even imagined that Yellow Woman had yellow skin, brown hair, and green eyes like mine, although her name does not refer to her color, but rather to the ritual color of the east.

There have been many other moments like the one with the cameratoting tourist in the schoolyard. But the old-time people always say, remember the stories, the stories will help you be strong. So all these years I have depended on Kochininako and the stories of her adventures.

Kochininako is beautiful because she has the courage to act in times of great peril, and her triumph is achieved by her sensuality, not through violence and destruction. For these qualities of the spirit, Yellow Woman and all women are beautiful.

Understanding and Analysis

1. What specifically makes Silko different from others in her village? In what ways is she like her Grandma A'mooh?

2. Describe the virtues of the old-time Laguna people, according to Silko. What evidence does she offer to support her assertions? How does she differentiate the old-time Laguna people from the modern Laguna people?

3. What are the faults of the modern people, especially the whites? What evidence does Silko offer to support these assertions?

4. Does Silko attribute virtues to the whites and modern Laguna people as well as faults to the old-time Laguna people? If so, what are they and what evidence does she offer to support her assertions?

5. What does Silko especially admire in the character of Grandma A'mooh? How does the grandmother integrate her connections to both the white and the Laguna people?

6. What does Silko especially admire in the character of Yellow Woman?

7. How does matriarchy affect the Laguna, according to Silko?

8. Does Silko's description of the "young man from a nearby village who wore nail polish and women's blouses and permed his hair" suggest that Laguna people are concerned with physical beauty? If not, why not? Do you notice other details that may suggest potential contradictions in the essay? Are they contradictions? Why or why not?

Comparison

1. Read the essay by Momaday and compare his grandmother and her beliefs to that of Silko's grandmother and her beliefs.

2. Compare Momaday's essay with Silko's to find as many similarities as you can in structure, style, tone, and content. In what ways, if any, are the essays similar? How are they different?

3. Read the essays by Lopez and Momaday. Compare and contrast the ideas about the earth and nature in the three essays.

4. Read the essay by Lopez and apply his criteria for stories to the stories Silko tells. To what degree does she fulfill his criteria?

5. Compare the behavior of the women in the essays by Cofer and Silko. What differences and similarities do you see?

6. Read the essays by Postman and Rich. What story is Silko telling about herself and her heritage? How does it differ from the story told by Rich about herself and her heritage? In what ways, if any, are these two stories similar?

Francis Fukuyama
(1952–)

Francis Fukuyama was born on October 27, 1952, the son of Toshiko Fukuyama, a potter and homemaker, and Yoshio Fukuyama, a minister and member of the National Board for the United Church of Christ, and, in later years, a professor in the sociology of religion. After spending the first two years of his life in Chicago, Illinois, where his parents met as students at the University of Chicago, Fukuyama moved to New York at the age of two. "I really grew up in New York City," he commented on the television program "Booknotes," "and then, at that point, began wandering to various places like a lot of Americans." For his undergraduate degree, Fukuyama enrolled at Cornell University with a major in Classics, for which he "spent five years learning Greek essentially to be able to read Plato and Aristotle in the original." Graduating in 1974, he spent a year at Yale before deciding to pursue a Ph.D.

in political science at Harvard. In the summer of 1976, he interned with the U.S. Arms Control and Disarmament Agency; three years later, he won a graduate fellowship in the National Security Program at Harvard's Center for International Affairs. An industrious doctoral student, he spent the last two years of his program serving as an associate social scientist with the RAND Corporation, which he characterized on "Booknotes" as "one of the oldest think tanks doing foreign policy, national security kinds of studies." Fukuyama also published his first articles before he earned his degree: "Egypt and Israel After Camp David," co-authored with Steven J. Rosen, and a "A New Soviet Strategy," printed in *Commentary*.

The Soviet Union in fact played an essential role in Fukuyama's work and research; the title of his dissertation was "Soviet Threats to Intervene in the Middle East, 1956–1973." After defending that dissertation in 1981, he departed Harvard for Washington, D.C., to join the Policy Planning Staff, "a small office attached to the office of the secretary of state that's supposed to give advice on long-term foreign policy ideas." During the year he spent in this office, he joined the U.S. delegation to the talks between Egypt and Israel on "Palestinian Autonomy." He then accepted a senior position in the political science department of the RAND Corporation and published several titles under its auspices, including *New Marxist-Leninist States in the Third World* (1984) and *Moscow's Post-Brezhnev Reassessment of the Third World* (1986). In 1986, the same year he married Laura Holmgren, he served as a visiting lecturer at UCLA; in 1987, through the cooperation of RAND and the UCLA Center for the Study of Soviet International Behavior, he co-edited *The Soviet Union and the Third World: The Last Three Decades*.

At the end of the 1980s, Fukuyama unwittingly started himself on the road to international fame by accepting an invitation to speak at the John M. Olin Center for Inquiry into the Theory and Practice of Democracy, housed in his native Chicago. That summer, his lecture, entitled "The End of History?" appeared in a journal called *The National Interest*, and controversy boiled up immediately. Fukuyama, having returned to the Policy Planning Department to serve as its deputy director, soon left the government for the second time to turn his article into a book. *The End of History and the Last Man* (1992), dedicated to his (then) infant children, proved every bit as controversial as the original article; it also became a bestseller and won the *Los Angeles Times* Book Prize. "I had always intended to go back into government when it was over," Fukuyama said; he "had such a good time writing," however, that he decided not to.

Fukuyama wrote his second book, *Trust: The Social Virtues & the Creation of Prosperity* (1995), while working as a consultant for RAND and as a Fellow at the Foreign Policy Institute of Johns Hopkins. As he researched the book, he made extensive use of the "library of social science classics" given him by his father many years earlier, and he learned to appreciate his father's "perspective," which he had "resist[ed]... for many years." His father also "read and commented on the manuscript," Fukuyama writes, "but passed away before the book could be published." Fukuyama's interest in the intellectual inheritance of his father appears again in *The Great Disruption: Human Nature and the Recognition of Social Order*, first introduced to the public in the May 1999 issue of *The Atlantic Monthly*. Fukuyama told the magazine: "The kind of moral and social issues I am writing about in *The Great Disruption* were always very important to [my father]. I'm coming back to the set of issues that I grew up with. The biggest problems we face are in our moral and social life. Everything else is going pretty well." Fukuyama now serves as the Omer L. and Nancy Hirst Professor of Public Policy at The Institute of Public Policy of George Mason University, a position he has held since 1996.

Francis Fukuyama generated a heated national debate with *The End of History*, though some of his detractors maintain that his thesis little deserved the serious attention it received. Arguing that we are reaching the end of history "in the Marxist-Hegelian sense of History as a broad evolution of human societies advancing toward a final goal"—namely, liberal democracy—he has provoked entire collections devoted to his thesis: *After History? Francis Fukuyama and His Critics* (1994), *Has History Ended?: Fukuyama, Marx, Modernity* (1995), and *Francis Fukuyama: And the End of History* (1999). "Surprisingly," the authors of this last book write, *The End of History* "has been greeted more with criticism, from almost every point of view, than by any sympathetic attempt to understand its positive thesis." Fukuyama himself attributes some of the attacks on his book to his readers' misunderstanding of his ideas, which have been deemed absurd and propagandistic. Clearly Fukuyama has become one of the most important and controversial thinkers of the late twentieth century.

THE GREAT DISRUPTION
Human Nature and the Reconstitution of Social Order *(1999)*

THE GREAT DISRUPTION was caused by a broad cultural shift. This brings us to cultural explanations, which are the most plausible of the three presented here. Increasing individualism and the loosening of communal controls clearly had a huge impact on family life, sexual behavior, and the willingness of people to obey the law. The problem with this line of explanation is not that culture was not a factor but rather that it gives no adequate account of timing: why did culture, which usually evolves extremely slowly, suddenly mutate with extraordinary rapidity after the mid-1960s?

In Britain and the United States the high point of communal social control was the last third of the nineteenth century, when the Victorian ideal of the patriarchal conjugal family was broadly accepted and adolescent sexuality was kept under tight control. The cultural shift that undermined Victorian morality may be thought of as layered: At the top was a realm of abstract ideas promulgated by philosophers, scientists, artists, academics, and the occasional huckster and fraud, who laid the intellectual groundwork for broad-based changes. The second level was one of popular culture, as simpler versions of complex abstract ideas were promulgated through books, newspapers, and other mass media. Finally, there was the layer of actual behavior, as the new norms implicit in the abstract or popularized ideas were embedded in the actions of large populations.

The decline in Victorian morality can be traced to a number of intellectual developments at the end of the nineteenth century and the beginning of the twentieth, and to a second wave that began in the 1940s. At the highest level of thought, Western rationalism began to undermine itself by concluding that no rational grounds supported universal norms of behavior. This was nowhere more evident than in the thought of Friedrich Nietzsche, the father of modern relativism. Nietzsche in effect argued that man, the "beast with red cheeks," was a value-creating animal, and that the manifold "languages of good and evil" spoken by different human cultures were products of the will, rooted nowhere, in truth or reason. The Enlightenment had not led to self-evident truths about right or morality; rather, it had exposed the infinite variability of moral arrangements. Attempts to ground values in nature, or in God, were doomed to be exposed as willful acts on the part of the creators of those values. Nietzsche's aphorism "There are no facts, only interpretations" became the watchword for later generations of relativists under the banners of deconstructionism and postmodernism.

In the social sciences the undermining of Victorian values was first the work of psychologists. John Dewey, William James, and John Watson, the founder of the behavioralist school of psychology, for differing reasons all contested the Victorian and Christian notion that human nature was innately sinful, and argued that tight social controls over behavior were not necessary for social order. The behavioralists argued that the human mind was a Lockean tabula rasa waiting to be filled with cultural content; the implication was that human beings were far more malleable through social pressure and policy than people had heretofore believed. Sigmund Freud was, of course, enormously influential in promulgating the idea that neurosis originated in the excessive social repression of sexual behavior. Indeed, the spread of psychoanalysis accustomed an entire generation to talking about sex and seeing everyday psychological problems in terms of the libido and its repression.

The cultural historian James Lincoln Collier points to the years on either side of 1912 as critical to the breakdown of Victorian sexual norms in the United States. It was in this period that a series of new dances spread across the nation, along with the opinion that decent women could be seen in dance clubs; the rate of alcohol consumption increased; the feminist movement began in earnest; movies and the technology of modern mass entertainment appeared; literary modernism, whose core was the perpetual delegitimization of established cultural values, moved into high gear; and sexual mores (judging by what little empirical knowledge we have of this period) began to change. Collier argues that the intellectual and cultural grounds for the sexual revolution of the 1960s had already been laid among American elites by the 1920s. Their spread through the rest of the population was delayed, however, by the Depression and the Second World War, which led people to concentrate more on economic survival and domesticity than on self-expression and self-gratification—which most, in any event, could not afford.

The crucial question about the changes in social norms that occurred during the Great Disruption is therefore not whether they had cultural roots, which they obviously did, but how we can explain the timing and speed of the subsequent transformation. We know that culture tends to change very slowly in comparison with other factors, such as economic conditions, public policies, and ideology. In those cases where cultural norms have changed quickly, such as in rapidly modernizing Third World societies, cultural change is clearly being driven by socioeconomic change and is therefore not an autonomous factor.

So with the Great Disruption: the shift away from Victorian values had been occurring gradually for two or three generations by the time the disruption began; then all of a sudden the pace of change sped up enormously. It is hard to believe that people throughout the developed world simply decided to alter their attitudes toward elemental issues as marriage, divorce, child-rearing, authority, and community so completely in the space of two or three decades without that shift in values being driven by other powerful forces. Those explanations that link changes in cultural variables to specific events in American history, such as Vietnam, Watergate, or the counterculture of the 1960s, betray an even greater provincialism: why were social norms also disrupted in other societies, from Sweden and Norway to New Zealand and Spain?

If these broad explanations for the Great Disruption are unsatisfactory, we need to look at its different elements more specifically.

WHY RISING CRIME?

Assuming that increases in the crime rate are not simply a statistical artifact of improved police reporting, we need to ask several questions. Why did crime rates increase so dramatically over a relatively short period and in such a wide range of countries? Why are rates beginning to level off or decline in the United States and several other Western countries?

The first and perhaps most straightforward explanation for rising crime rates from the late 1960s to the 1980s, and declining rates thereafter, is a simple demographic one. Crime tends to be committed overwhelmingly by young males aged fifteen to twenty-four. There is doubtless a genetic reason for this, having to do with male propensities for violence and aggression, and it means that when birth rates go up, crime rates will rise fifteen to twenty-four years later. In the United States the number of young people aged fifteen to twenty-four increased by two million from 1950 to 1960, whereas the next decade added 12 million to this age group—an onslaught that has been compared to a barbarian invasion. Not only did greater numbers of young people increase the pool of potential criminals, but their concentration in a "youth culture" may have led to a more-than-proportional increase in efforts to defy authority.

The Baby Boom, however, is only part of the explanation for rising crime rates in the 1960s and 1970s. One criminologist has estimated that the increase in the U.S. murder rate was ten times as great as would be expected from shifts in the demographic structure alone. Other studies have shown that changes in age structure do not correlate well with increases in crime cross-nationally.

A second explanation links crime rates to modernization and related factors such as urbanization, population density, opportunities for crime, and so forth. It is a common-sense proposition that there will be more auto theft and burglary in large cities than in rural areas, because it is easier for criminals to find automobiles and empty homes in the former than in the latter. But urbanization and a changing physical environment are poor explanations for rising crime rates in developed countries after the 1960s. By 1960 the countries under consideration were already industrialized, urbanized societies; no sudden shift from countryside to city began in 1965. In the United States murder rates are much higher in the South than in the North, despite the fact that the latter tends to be more urban and densely populated. Indeed, violence in the South tends to be a rural phenomenon, and most observers who have looked closely into the matter believe that the explanation for high crime rates there is cultural. Japan, Korea, Hong Kong, and Singapore are among the most densely populated, overcrowded urban environments in the world, and yet they did not experience rising crime rates as that urbanization was occurring. This suggests that the human social environment is much more important than the physical one in determining levels of crime.

A third category of explanation is sometimes euphemistically labeled "social heterogeneity." That is, in many societies crime tends to be concentrated among racial or ethnic minorities; to the extent that societies become more ethnically diverse, as virtually all Western developed countries have over the past two generations, crime rates can be expected to rise. The reason that crime rates are frequently higher among minorities is very likely related, as the criminologists Richard Cloward and Lloyd Ohlin have argued, to the fact that minorities are kept from legitimate avenues of social mobility in ways that members of the majority community are not. In other cases the simple fact of heterogeneity may be to blame: neighborhoods that are too diverse culturally, linguistically, religiously, or ethnically never come together as communities to enforce informal norms on their members. But only part of the blame for rising crime rates in the United States can be placed on immigration.

A fourth explanation concerns the more or less contemporaneous changes in the family. The currently dominant school of American criminology holds that early-childhood socialization is one of the most important factors determining the level of subsequent criminality. That is, most people do not make day-to-day choices about whether or not to commit crimes based on the balance of rewards and risks, as the rational-choice school sometimes suggests. The vast majority of people obey the law, particularly with regard to serious offenses, out of habit that was learned relatively early in life. Most crimes are committed by repeat offenders who have failed to learn this basic self-control. In many cases they are acting not rationally but on impulse. Failing to anticipate consequences, they are undeterred by the expectation of punishment.

WHY RISING DISTRUST?

In the realm of trust, values, and civil society, we need to explain two things: why there has been a broad-based decline in trust both in institutions and in other people, and how we can reconcile the shift toward fewer shared norms with an apparent growth in groups and in the density of civil society.

The reasons for the decline of trust in an American context have been debated extensively. Robert Putnam argued early on that it might be associated with the rise of television, since the first cohort that grew up watching television was the one that experienced the most precipitous decline in trust levels. Not only does the content of television breed cynicism in its attention to sex and violence, but the fact that Americans spend an average of more than four hours a day watching TV limits their opportunities for face-to-face social activities.

One suspects, however, that a broad phenomenon like the decline of trust has a number of causes, of which television is only one. Tom Smith, of the National Opinion Research Center, performed a statistical analysis of the survey data on trust and found that the lack of it correlates with low socioeconomic status, minority status, traumatic life events, religious polarization, and youth. Poor and uneducated people tend to be more distrustful than the well-to-do or those who have gone to college. Blacks are significantly more distrustful than whites, and there is some correlation between distrust and immigrant status. The traumatic life events affecting trust include, not surprisingly, being a victim of crime and being in poor health. Distrust is associated both with those who do not attend church and with fundamentalists. And younger people are less trusting than older ones.

Which of these factors has changed since the 1960s in a way that could explain the decrease in trust? Income inequality has increased somewhat, and Eric Uslaner, of the University of Maryland, has suggested that this may account for some of the increase in distrust. But poverty rates have fluctuated without increasing overall in this period, and for the vast majority of Americans the so-called "middle-class squeeze" did not represent a drop in real income so much as a stagnation of earnings.

Crime increased dramatically from the mid-sixties to the mid-nineties, and it makes a great deal of sense that someone who has been victimized by crime, or who watches the daily cavalcade of grisly crime stories on the local TV news, would feel distrust not for immediate friends and family but for the larger world. Hence crime would seem to be an important explanation for the increase in distrust after 1965, a conclusion well supported in more-detailed analyses.

The other major social change that has led to traumatic life experiences has been the rise of divorce and family breakdown. Commonsensically, one would think that children who have experienced the divorce of their parents, or have had to deal with a series of boyfriends in a single-parent household, would tend to become cynical about adults in general, and that this might go far toward explaining the increased levels of distrust that show up in survey data.

Despite the apparent decline in trust, there is evidence that groups and group membership are increasing. The most obvious way to reconcile lower levels of trust with greater levels of group membership is to note a reduction in the radius of trust. It is hard to interpret the data either on values or on civil society in any other way than to suggest that the radius of trust is diminishing, not just in the United States but across the developed world. That is, people continue to share norms and values in ways that constitute social capital, and they join groups and organizations in ever larger numbers. But the groups have shifted dramatically in kind. The authority of most large organizations has declined, and the importance in people's lives of a host of smaller associations has grown. Rather than taking pride in being a member of a powerful labor federation or working for a large corporation, or in having served in the military, people identify socially with a local aerobics class, a New Age sect, a co-dependent support group, or an Internet chat room. Rather than seeking authoritative values in a church that once shaped the society's culture, people are picking and choosing their values on an individual basis, in ways that link them with smaller communities of like-minded folk.

The shift to smaller-radius groups is mirrored politically in the almost universal rise of interest groups at the expense of broad-based political parties. Parties like the German Christian Democrats and the British Labour Party take a coherent ideological stand on the whole range of issues facing a society, from national defense to social welfare. Though usually based in a particular social class, these parties unite a broad coalition of interests and personalities. Interest groups, on the other hand, focus on single issues such as saving rain forests or promoting poultry farming in the upper Midwest; they may be transnational in scope, but they are much less authoritative, both in the range of issues they deal with and in the numbers of people they bring together.

Contemporary Americans, and contemporary Europeans as well, seek contradictory goals. They are increasingly distrustful of any authority, political or moral, that would constrain their freedom of choice, but they also want a sense of community and the good things that flow from community, such as mutual recognition, participation, belonging, and identity. Community therefore has to be found in smaller, more flexible groups and organizations whose loyalties and membership can overlap, and where entry and exit entail relatively low costs. People may thus be able to reconcile their contradictory desires for autonomy and community. But in this bargain the community they get is smaller and weaker than most of those that have existed in the past. Each community shares less with neighboring ones, and has relatively little hold on its members. The circle that people can trust is necessarily narrower. The essence of the shift in values at the center of the Great Disruption, then, is the rise of moral individualism and the consequent miniaturization of community. These explanations go partway toward explaining why cultural values changed after the 1960s. But at the Great Disruption's core was a shift in values concerning sex and the family—a shift that deserves special emphasis.

MEN BEHAVING BADLY

Although the role of mother can safely be said to be grounded in biology, the role of father is to a great degree socially constructed. In the words of the anthropologist Margaret Mead, "Somewhere at the dawn of human history, some social invention was made under which males started nurturing females and their young." The male role was founded on the provision of resources; "among human beings everywhere [the male] helps provide food for women and children." Being a learned behavior, the male role in nurturing the family is subject to disruption. Mead wrote,

> But the evidence suggests that we should phrase the matter differently for men and women—that men have to learn to want to provide for others, and this behaviour, being learned, is fragile and can disappear rather easily under social conditions that no longer teach it effectively.

The role of fathers, in other words, varies by culture and tradition from intense involvement in the nurturing and education of children to a more distant presence as protector and disciplinarian to the near absence possible for a paycheck provider. It takes a great deal of effort to separate a mother from her newborn infant; in contrast, it often takes a fair amount of effort to involve a father with his.

When we put kinship and family in this context, it is easier to understand why nuclear families have started to break apart at such a rapid rate over the past two generations. The family bond was relatively fragile, based on an exchange of the woman's fertility for the man's resources. Prior to the Great Disruption, all Western societies had in place a complex series of formal and informal laws, rules, norms, and obligations to protect mothers and children by limiting the freedom of fathers to simply ditch one family and start another. Today many people have come to think of marriage as a kind of public celebration of a sexual and emotional union between two adults, which is why gay marriage has become a possibility in the United States and other developed countries. But it is clear that historically the institution of marriage existed to give legal protection to the mother-child unit, and to ensure that adequate economic resources were passed from the father to allow the children to grow up to be viable adults.

What accounts for the breakdown of these norms constraining male behavior, and of the bargain that rested on them? Two very important changes occurred sometime during the early postwar period. The first involved advances in medical technology—that is, birth control and abortion—that permitted women to better control their own reproduction. The second was the movement of women into the paid labor force in most industrialized countries and the steady rise in their incomes—hourly, median, and lifetime—relative to men's over the next thirty years.

The significance of birth control was not simply that it lowered fertility. Indeed, if the effect of birth control is to reduce the number of unwanted pregnancies, it is hard to explain why its advent should have been accompanied by an explosion of illegitimacy and a rise in the abortion rate, or why the use of birth control is positively correlated with illegitimacy across the OECD.

The main impact of the Pill and the sexual revolution that followed it was, as the economists Janet Yellen, George Akerlof, and Michael Katz have shown, to dramatically alter calculations about the risks of sex, and thereby to change male behavior. The reason that the rates of birth-control use, abortion, and illegitimacy went up in tandem is that a fourth rate—the number of shotgun marriages—declined substantially at the same time. By these economists' calculations, in the period 1965–1969 some 59 percent of white brides and 25 percent of black brides were pregnant at the altar. Young people were, evidently, having quite a lot of premarital sex in those years, but the social consequences of out-of-wedlock childbearing were mitigated by the norm of male responsibility for the children produced. By the period 1980–1984 the percentages had dropped to 42 and 11, respectively. Because birth control and abortion permitted women for the first time to have sex without worrying about the consequences, men felt liberated from norms requiring them to look after the women they got pregnant.

The second factor altering male behavior was the entry of women into the paid labor force. That female incomes should be related to family breakdown is an argument accepted by many economists, and elaborated most fully by Gary Becker in his work *A Treatise on the Family* (1981). The assumption behind this view is that many marriage contracts are entered into with imperfect information: once married, men and women discover that life is not a perpetual honeymoon, that their spouse's behavior has changed from what it was before marriage, or that their own expectations for partners have changed. Trading in a spouse for someone new, or getting rid of an abusive mate, had been restricted by the fact that many women lacking job skills or experience were dependent on husbands. As female earnings rose, women became better able to support themselves and to raise children without husbands. Rising female incomes also increase the opportunity costs of having children, and therefore lower fertility. Fewer children means less of what Becker characterizes as the joint capital in the marriage, and hence makes divorce more likely.

A subtler consequence of women's entering the labor force was that the norm of male responsibility was further weakened. In divorcing a dependent wife, a husband would have to face the prospect of either paying alimony or seeing his children slip into poverty. With many wives earning incomes that rivaled those of their husbands, this became less of an issue. The weakening norm of male responsibility, in turn, reinforced the need for women to arm themselves with job skills so as not to be dependent on increasingly unreliable husbands. With a substantial probability that a first marriage will end in divorce, contemporary women would be foolish not to prepare themselves for work.

The decline of nuclear families in the West had strongly negative effects on social capital and was related to an increase in poverty for people at the bottom of the social hierarchy, to increasing levels of crime, and finally to declining trust. But pointing to the negative consequences for social capital of changes in the family is in no way to blame women for these problems. The entry of women into the workplace, the steady closing of the earnings gap with men, and the greater ability of women to control fertility are by and large good things. The most important shift in norms was in the one that dictated male responsibility for wives and children. Even if the shift was triggered by birth control and rising female incomes, men were to blame for the consequences. And it is not as if men always behaved well prior to that: the stability of traditional families was often bought at a high price in terms of emotional and physical distress, and also in lost opportunities—costs that fell disproportionately on the shoulders of women.

On the other hand, these sweeping changes in gender roles have not been the unambiguously good thing that some feminists pretend. Losses have accompanied gains, and those losses have fallen disproportionately on the shoulders of children. This should not surprise anyone: given the fact that female roles have traditionally centered on reproduction and children, we could hardly expect that the movement of women out of the household and into the workplace would have no consequences for families.

Moreover, women themselves have often been the losers in this bargain. Most labor-market gains for women in the 1970s and 1980s were not in glamorous Murphy Brown kinds of jobs but in low-end service-sector jobs. In return for meager financial independence, many women found themselves abandoned by husbands who moved on to younger wives or girlfriends. Because older women are considered less sexually attractive than older men, they had much lower chances of remarrying than did the husbands who left them. The widening of the gap among men between rich and poor had its counterpart among women: educated, ambitious, and talented women broke down barriers, proved they could succeed at male occupations, and saw their incomes rise; but many of their less-educated, less-ambitious, and less-talented sisters saw the floor collapse under them, as they tried to raise children by themselves while in low-paying, dead-end jobs or on welfare. Our consciousness of this process has been distorted by the fact that the women who talk and write and shape the public debate about gender issues come almost exclusively from the former category.

In contrast, men have on balance come out about even. Although many have lost substantial status and income, others (and sometimes the same ones) have quite happily been freed of burdensome responsibilities for wives and children. Hugh Hefner did not invent the Playboy lifestyle in the 1950s; casual access to multiple women has been enjoyed by powerful, wealthy, high-status men throughout history, and has been one of the chief motives for seeking power, wealth, and high status in the first place. What changed after the 1950s was that many rather ordinary men were allowed to live out the fantasy lives of hedonism and serial polygamy formerly reserved to a tiny group at the very top of society. One of the greatest frauds perpetrated during the Great Disruption was the notion that the sexual revolution was gender-neutral, benefiting women and men equally, and that it somehow had a kinship with the feminist revolution. In fact the sexual revolution served the interests of men, and in the end put sharp limits on the gains that women might otherwise have expected from their liberation from traditional roles.

RECONSTRUCTING SOCIAL ORDER

How can we rebuild social capital in the future? The fact that culture and public policy give societies some control over the pace and degree of disruption is not in the long run an answer to how social order will be established at the beginning of the twenty-first century.

Japan and some Catholic countries have been able to hold on to traditional family values longer than Scandinavia or the English-speaking world, and this may have saved them some of the social costs experienced by the latter. But it is hard to imagine that they will be able to hold out over the coming generations, much less re-establish anything like the nuclear family of the industrial era, with the father working and the mother staying at home to raise children. Such an outcome would not be desirable, even if it were possible.

We appear to be caught, then, in unpleasant circumstances: going forward seems to promise ever-increasing levels of disorder and social atomization, at the same time that our line of retreat has been cut off. Does this mean that contemporary liberal societies are fated to descend into increasing moral decline and social anarchy, until they somehow implode? Were Edmund Burke and other critics of the Enlightenment right that anarchy was the inevitable product of the effort to replace tradition and religion with reason?

The answer, in my view, is no, for the very simple reason that we human beings are by nature designed to create moral rules and social order for ourselves. The situation of normlessness—what the sociologist Emile Durkheim labeled "anomie"—is intensely uncomfortable for us, and we will seek to create new rules to replace the ones that have been undercut. If technology makes certain old forms of community difficult to sustain, then we will seek out new ones, and we will use our reason to negotiate arrangements to suit our underlying interests, needs, and passions.

To understand why the present situation isn't as hopeless as it may seem, we need to consider the origins of social order per se, on a more abstract level. Many discussions of culture treat social order as if it were a static set of rules handed down from earlier generations. If one was stuck in a low-social-capital or low-trust country, one could do nothing about it. It is true, of course, that public policy is relatively limited in its ability to manipulate culture, and that the best public policies are those shaped by an awareness of cultural constraints. But culture is a dynamic force, one that is constantly being remade— if not by governments then by the interactions of the thousands of decentralized individuals who make up a society. Although culture tends to evolve more slowly than formal social and political institutions, it nonetheless adapts to changing circumstances.

What we find is that order and social capital have two broad bases of support. The first is biological, and emerges from human nature itself. There is an increasing body of evidence coming out of the life sciences that the standard social-science model is inadequate, and that human beings are born with pre-existing cognitive structures and age-specific capabilities for learning that lead them naturally into society. There is, in other words, such a thing as human nature. For the sociologists and anthropologists, the existence of human nature means that cultural relativism needs to be rethought, and that it is possible to discern cultural and moral universals that, if used judiciously, might help to evaluate particular cultural practices. Moreover, human behavior is not nearly as plastic and therefore manipulable as their disciplines have assumed for much of this century. For the economists, human nature implies that the sociological view of human beings as inherently social beings is more accurate than their own individualistic model. And for those who are neither sociologists nor economists, an essential humanity confirms a number of commonsense understandings about the way people think and act that have been resolutely denied by earlier generations of social scientists—for example, that men and women are different by nature, that we are political and social creatures with moral instincts, and the like. This insight is extremely important, because it means that social capital will tend to be generated by human beings as a matter of instinct.

The biological revolution that has been under way in the second half of the twentieth century has multiple sources. The most startling advances have been made at the level of molecular biology and biochemistry, where the discovery of the structure of DNA has led to the emergence of an entire industry devoted to genetic manipulation. In neurophysiology great advances have been made in understanding the chemical and physiological bases of psychological phenomena, including an emerging view that the brain is not a general-purpose calculating machine but a highly modular organ with specially adapted capabilities. And finally, on the level of macro behavior, a tremendous amount of new work has been done in animal ethology, behavioral genetics, primatology, and evolutionary psychology and anthropology, suggesting that certain behavioral patterns are much more general than previously believed. For instance, the generalization that females tend to be more selective than males in their choice of mates proves to be true not only across all known human cultures but across virtually all known species that reproduce sexually. It would seem to be only a matter of time before the micro and macro levels of research are connected: with the mapping of complete gene sequences for fruit flies, nematodes, rats, and eventually human beings, it will be possible to turn individual gene sequences on and off and directly observe their effects on behavior.

The second basis of support for social order is human reason, and reason's ability to spontaneously generate solutions to problems of social cooperation. Mankind's natural capabilities for creating social capital do not explain how social capital arises in specific circumstances. The creation of particular rules of behavior is the province of culture rather than nature, and in the cultural realm we find that order is frequently the result of a process of horizontal negotiation, argument, and dialogue among individuals. Order does not need to proceed from the top down—from a lawgiver (or, in contemporary terms, a state) handing down laws or a priest promulgating the word of God.

Neither natural nor spontaneous order is sufficient in itself to produce the totality of rules that constitutes social order per se. Either needs to be supplemented at crucial junctures by hierarchical authority. But when we look back in human history, we see that self-organizing individuals have continuously been creating social capital for themselves, and have managed to adapt to technological and economic changes greater than those faced by Western societies over the past two generations.

Perhaps the easiest way to get a handle on the Great Disruption's future is to look briefly at great disruptions of the past. Indices of social order have increased and decreased over time, suggesting that although social capital may often seem to be in the process of depletion, its stock has increased in certain historical periods. The political scientist Ted Robert Gurr estimates that homicide rates in England were three times as high in the thirteenth century as in the seventeenth, and three times as high in the seventeenth as in the nineteenth; in London they were twice as high in the early nineteenth century as in the 1970s. Both conservatives decrying moral decline and liberals celebrating increased individual choice sometimes talk as if there had been since the early 1600s a steady movement away from Puritan values. But although a secular trend toward greater individualism has been evident over this long time period, many fluctuations in behavior have suggested that societies are perfectly capable of increasing the degree of constraint on individual choice through moral rules.

The Victorian period in Britain and America may seem to many to be the embodiment of traditional values, but Victorianism was in fact a radical movement that emerged in reaction to widespread social disorder at the beginning of the nineteenth century—a movement that deliberately sought to create new social rules and instill virtues in populations that were seen as wallowing in degeneracy.

It would be wrong to assert that the greater social order that came to prevail in Britain and America during the Victorian period was simply the result of changing moral norms.

In this period both societies established modern police forces, which replaced the hodgepodge of local agencies and poorly trained deputies that had existed at the beginning of the nineteenth century. In the United States after the Civil War the police focused attention on such minor offenses against public order as public drinking, vagrancy, loitering, and the like, leading to a peak in arrests for this kind of behavior around 1870. Toward the end of the century many states had begun to establish systems of universal education, which sought to put all American children into free public schools—a process that began somewhat later in Britain. But the essential change that took place was a matter of values rather than institutions. At the core of Victorian morality was the inculcation of impulse control in young people—the shaping of what economists today would call their preferences—so that they would not indulge in pleasures like casual sex, alcohol, and gambling.

There are other examples from other cultures of moral renovation. The feudal Tokugawa period in Japan—when power was held by various *daimyo,* or warrior lords—was one of insecurity and frequent violence. The Meiji Restoration, which took place in 1868, established a single centralized state, and stamped out once and for all the kind of banditry that had taken place in feudal Japan. The country developed a new moral system as well. We think of a custom like the lifetime employment that is practiced by large Japanese firms as an ancient cultural tradition, but in fact it dates back only to the late nineteenth century, and was fully implemented among large companies only after the Second World War. Before then there was a high degree of labor mobility; skilled craftsmen in particular were in short supply and constantly on the move from one company to another. Large Japanese companies like Mitsui and Mitsubishi found that they could not attract the skilled labor they needed, and so, with the help of the government, they embarked on a successful campaign to elevate the virtue of loyalty above others.

Could the pattern experienced in the second half of the nineteenth century in Britain and America, or in Japan, repeat itself in the next generation or two? There is growing evidence that the Great Disruption has run its course, and that the process of re-norming has already begun. Growth in the rates of increase in crime, divorce, illegitimacy, and distrust has slowed substantially, and in the 1990s has even reversed in many of the countries that experienced an explosion of disorder over the past two generations. This is particularly true in the United States, where levels of crime are down a good 15 percent from their peaks in the early 1990s. Divorce rates peaked in the early 1980s, and births to single mothers appear to have stopped increasing. Welfare rolls have diminished almost as dramatically as crime rates, in response both to the 1996 welfare-reform measures and to the opportunities provided by a nearly full-employment economy in the 1990s. Levels of trust in both institutions and individuals have also recovered significantly since the early 1990s.

How far might this re-norming of society go? We are much more likely to see dramatic changes in levels of crime and trust than in norms regarding sex, reproduction, and family life. Indeed, the process of re-norming in the first two spheres is already well under way. With regard to sex and reproduction, however, the technological and economic conditions of our age make it extremely doubtful that anything like a return to Victorian values will take place. Strict rules about sex make sense in a society in which unregulated sex has a high probability of leading to pregnancy and having a child out of wedlock is likely to lead to destitution, if not early death, for both mother and child. The first of these conditions disappeared with birth control; the second was greatly mitigated, though not eliminated, by a combination of female incomes and welfare subsidies. Although the United States has cut back sharply on welfare, no one is about to propose making birth control illegal or reversing the movement of women into the workplace. Nor will the individual pursuit of rational self-interest solve the problems posed by declining fertility: it is precisely the rational interest of parents in their children's long-term life chances that induces them to have fewer children. The importance of kinship as a source of social connectedness will probably continue to decline, and the stability of nuclear families is likely never to fully recover. Those societies, such as Japan and Korea, that have until now bucked this trend are more likely to shift toward Western practices than the reverse.

Some religious conservatives hope, and liberals fear, that the problem of moral decline will be resolved by a large-scale return to religious orthodoxy—a Western version of the Ayatollah Khomeini returning to Iran on a jetliner. For a variety of reasons this seems unlikely. Modern societies are so culturally diverse that it is not clear whose version of orthodoxy would prevail. Any true orthodoxy is likely to be seen as a threat to large and important groups in the society, and hence would neither get very far nor serve as a basis for a widening radius of trust. Rather than integrating society, a conservative religious revival might in fact accelerate the movement toward fragmentation and moral miniaturization: the various varieties of Protestant fundamentalism would argue among themselves over doctrine; orthodox Jews would become more orthodox; Muslims and Hindus might start to organize themselves as political-religious communities, and the like.

A return to religiosity is far more likely to take a more benign form, one that in some respects has already started to appear in many parts of the United States. Instead of community arising as a by-product of rigid belief, people will come to religion because of their desire for community. In other words, people will return to religion not necessarily because they accept the truth of revelation but precisely because the absence of community and the transience of social ties in the secular world make them hungry for ritual and cultural tradition. They will help the poor or their neighbors not necessarily because doctrine tells them they must but rather because they want to serve their communities and find that faith-based organizations are the most effective means of doing so. They will repeat ancient prayers and re-enact age-old rituals not because they believe that they were handed down by God but rather because they want their children to have the proper values, and because they want to enjoy the comfort and the sense of shared experience that ritual brings. In this sense they will not be taking religion seriously on its own terms but will use religion as a language with which to express their moral beliefs. Religion becomes a source of ritual in a society that has been stripped bare of ceremony, and thus is a reasonable extension of the natural desire for social relatedness with which all human beings are born. It is something that modern, rational, skeptical people can take seriously in much the way that they celebrate national independence, dress up in traditional ethnic garb, or read the classics of their own cultural tradition. Understood in these terms, religion loses its hierarchical character and becomes a manifestation of spontaneous order.

Religion is one of the two main sources of an enlarged radius of trust. The other is politics. In the West, Christianity first established the principle of the universality of human dignity, a principle that was brought down from the heavens and turned into a secular doctrine of universal human equality by the Enlightenment. Today we ask politics to bear nearly the entire weight of this enterprise, and it has done a remarkably good job. Those nations built on universal liberal principles have been surprisingly resilient over the past 200 years, despite frequent setbacks and shortcomings. A political order based on Serb ethnic identity or Twelver Shi'ism will never grow beyond the boundaries of some corner of the Balkans or the Middle East, and could certainly never become the governing principle of large, diverse, dynamic, and complex modern societies like those that make up, for example, the Group of Seven.[1]

There seem to be two parallel processes at work. In the political and economic sphere history appears to be progressive and directional, and at the end of the twentieth century has culminated in liberal democracy as the only viable choice for technologically advanced societies. In the social and moral sphere, however, history appears to be cyclical, with social order ebbing and flowing over the course of generations. There is nothing to guarantee upturns in the cycle: our only reason for hope is the very powerful innate human capacity for reconstituting social order. On the success of this process of reconstruction depends the upward direction of the arrow of History.

Understanding and Analysis

1. Fukuyama claims that a "Great Disruption" began around 1965 that has resulted in rising crime, disruptions in the family, and disruptions in people's trust in government and each other. After rejecting two causes often cited, poverty and inequality (usually proposed by the left) and welfare and other "mistaken government policies" (usually proposed by the right), Fukuyama describes a third explanation, "a broad cultural shift," beginning with the opening paragraph of this excerpt from the essay in the *Atlantic Monthly*. What does he say is the problem with this third explanation?

2. What are the levels of causes in the "cultural shift that undermined Victorian morality," according to Fukuyama?

3. Describe in your own words the changes at the highest level, that of "abstract ideas."

4. Describe the changes in the second level, that of popular culture.

5. What changes in behavior, the third level, does Fukuyama see?

6. What is the "crucial question," that Fukuyama asks?

7. What four explanations does he offer for the rising crime rate after 1965?

8. What evidence does he offer that there is an increased lack of trust in institutions and other people?

9. What causes for this distrust does he offer?

10. What are the goals, according to Fukuyama, of "contemporary" people in western cultures?

11. Fukuyama claims that the essential shift in values that has led to what he calls the Great Disruption is "the rise of moral individualism." How has this rise affected the family?

12. How did the pill change male behavior, according to Fukuyama?

13. Does Fukuyama approve of the pill and of women in the work force? What is your evidence?

14. What, according to Fukuyama, have been the benefits and the losses caused by changes in the social roles of men and women since 1965? Do you agree?

---

[1]*Group of Seven* includes United States, France, United Kingdom, Germany, Italy, Canada and Japan.

15. What predictions does Fukuyama make about the future? Is he optimistic, pessimistic, or neutral?

16. Fukuyama claims that social order emerges because of human nature and human reason. Describe human nature as Fukuyama sees it. How does culture work with biology to produce order?

17. What role will religion play, according to Fukuyama? What kind of government is best, according to Fukuyama? Do you agree?

18. Reread the essay. What tone does Fukuyama take toward his readers? How does he represent himself? What techniques does he use to persuade his readers?

Comparison

1. Read the essay by Martin Gardner. What connections can you find between Fukuyama's essay and Gardner's? Look for example at their comments on cultural relativism. Why does each writer quote Dewey? To what extent do Fukuyama and Gardner agree?

2. Does the quotation from Mead that Fukuyama includes in his essay change your opinion of the validity of Gardner's comments on her? Why or why not? Where else in his essay does Fukuyama address the issue of nature versus nurture?

3. Read Eliot's essay. Do you think Eliot would agree with Fukuyama's claim that "literary modernism" had at its center "the perpetual delegitimization of established cultural values"? Based on his Nobel Prize acceptance speech, would Faulkner agree with Fukuyama's claim?

4. Read the essay by Sontag. Do you see connections between Sontag's analysis of apocalypse and Fukuyama's description of a Great Disruption?

5. In the second paragraph of the essay from which this excerpt has been taken, Fukuyama claims that "a society built around information tends to produce more of the two things people value most in a modern democracy–freedom and equality." Read the essay by Reich. To what degree, if at all, do Reich and Fukuyama agree about the effects of the information age?

6. Read the essay by Postman. What connections do you see between the essays by Postman and Fukuyama? Would Postman approve of Fukuyama's analysis? Why or why not?

7. Read Carr and FitzGerald on history. How do their views of history help you to assess Fukuyama's use of history as evidence for his predictions?

8. Read the essays by Tuchman and Lewisohn. In light of their analyses of religion in history, do you think Fukuyama is being overly optimistic in his predictions about religion?

INDEX

747